ENCYCLOPAEDIA OF
ADMINISTRATIVE LAW

ENCYCLOPAEDIA
OF
ADMINISTRATIVE LAW

Vol. 1

An Introduction to Administrative Law

Edited by

S.R. Sharma

ANMOL PUBLICATIONS PVT. LTD.
NEW DELHI - 110 002 (INDIA)

ANMOL PUBLICATIONS PVT. LTD.
4374/4B, Ansari Road, Daryaganj
New Delhi - 110 002
Ph.: 23261597, 23278000
Visit us at: www.anmolpublications.com

Encyclopaedia of Administrative Law

First Edition, 2003

ISBN 81-261-1478-9 (Set)

PRINTED IN INDIA

Published by J.L. Kumar for Anmol Publications Pvt. Ltd., New Delhi - 110 002 and Printed at Mehra Offset Press, Delhi.

Contents

Preface

In the modern political era administrative law has taken on a preeminent role in regulating relations between the machinery of government and the individual citizen. At its core is the control of power specifically the review by the judiciary of the way in which executive power has been used. Consequently the subject embraces a huge range of issues, some of them highly politicized. In recent years these have included the legality of a ban on blood sports, whether the courts can order a minister to suspend the operation of a primary Act of Parliament, whether a minister can ban certain types of interview from being broadcast, the powers of local authorities to spend public money, or to refuse to do so, the scope of the discretion vested in the police officers to determine policing policy, the scope of the powers vested in the Home Secretary regarding parole for prisoners convicted of murder, whether the courts could declare invalid an exercise of prerogative power, and the availability of damages in respect of unlawful action by public bodies. It will be seen that it is largely the product of judicial activity, although its existence is increasingly recognised in statutory provisions.

The growth in administrative law has to a large extent mirrored the increase in the level of state involvement in many aspects of every day life during the twentieth century, generating the need for a coherent and effective body of rules to govern relations between individuals and the state. Students of constitutional law will readily recognise that administrative law is in reality an out growth of the doctrine of the separation of powers. It is evidence of the judiciary acting as a check on the powers of the executive, and perhaps even the legislature, in some respects. It should not be assumed, however, that any such coherent and effective body of rules actually exists yet. Administrative law is a constantly evolving subject.

In view of the above consideration in mind about the administrative law, that a comprehensive encyclopaedia has been prepared which focuses on the comparative dimensions of administrative law.

The editor is extremely grateful to the British Council Library in New Delhi, the American Information Centre, New Delhi, and the Central Secretariat Library, New Delhi for their valuable assistance in preparing the encyclopaedia. The editor is equally beholden to Shri J.L. Kumar, Managing Director, Anmol Publications Pvt. Ltd., New Delhi for publishing the encyclopaedia in a very short time.

—Dr. S.R. Sharma

I

Constitutional and Pure Juristic Theory

A Clear line of distinction divides a doctrine of constitutional law from one of pure jurisprudential theory. The first is special in its application and relates to a particular system of constitutional law; the second relates to the very nature of public law, and is, therefore, general in character, and applies to the State, whatever may be its particular type of governmental organization or its special system of constitutional jurisprudence. Sovereignty we have found to be an essential attribute of the State. Its nature and qualities are determined by pure political or jurisprudential theory. Its modes of exercise in any given State are, however, determined by the system of government and of constitutional law which that State has established for itself. The determination in each particular case of these modes is, therefore, a matter of constitutional law, the discussion of which might be omitted in such a treatise as the present one. However, it seems proper that a certain amount of space should be devoted to this matter if only for the purpose of making more plain the distinction between sovereignty as a purely juristic concept, and the same term when employed to indicate the ultimate source whence the ethic right of a given government to exist is drawn, or the actual forces which, in fact, determine the policies of that government, or, finally, the organ or organs which, under the given system of constitutional law, may be said to have the final or supreme legal right to express the will of the State.

Constitutional Theory of Pure Monarchy. As a matter of pure political or juristic theory, the State remains the same whatever may be its form of government or constitutional jurisprudence. That jurisprudence may start with the premise that the original and continuing fountain of all legal authority is the Crown. Deductions from this premise are: that by the will of the ruling monarch all other organs of government have been created and continue to exist; that from that will such legal powers as they possess have been derived; and that by that will they may, at any time, be curtailed or wholly withdrawn; and that, if a written constitution exists, its legal force is dependent upon that will. These are the constitutional doctrines upon which a system of pure monarchy is founded.

Secondly, the constitutional jurisprudence of the State may take as its logical basis or starting point, the principle that certain organs of government other than the Crown, such as elected legislative chambers or an electorate having referendal legislative powers, shall divide with the Crown, upon a basis of full legal or constitutional equality, the various or certain powers of government, that is, in such a way that these several organs may act independently of each other as to the specific powers constitutionally vested in them, or that they may be legally obliged to co-operate with one another.

In such a constitutional system it is obvious that all its provisions derive their legal force from some single source. If these provisions are to be found in a written Constitution or fundamental instruments of government, the original and continuing fountain of all legality, corresponding to the legal autocracy of the absolute monarch, is the particular organ or complexus of organs of government, or electorate or determinate group of individuals acting *ad hoc* as an organ of government, which is recognized to have the legal right to change the terms of the written Constitution, which Constitution, therefore, however it may have been originally adopted, is to be regarded as continuing to have force of law only because the constitutional organ or complexus of organs so wills it. This is the constitutional situation which now exits in practically all of its States of the world.

A third constitutional or governmental possibility is that exhibited by Great Britain which has a King, and does not possess a formal written Constitution or instrument of government, but has, nevertheless, built for itself a complicated and yet definite system of government and a body of constitutional principles according to which that plenitude of constitutional power, which, in a pure monarchy, is vested in the Crown , is vested in the Crown and a Parliament, the members of one House of which sit, for the most part, by hereditary right, and the members of the other House by selection by an electorate which has been broadened from time to time until now it includes nearly all adults citizens.

Consent of the Governed. A fourth constitutional doctrine, often asserted, but never actually put into force, and, in fact, practically impossible of operation, is that which declares that all governmental powers are validated by the consent of all the governed. Regarded as an ethical proposition, this assertion will be examined in the volume on Ethical Political Philosophy, referred to in the preface. Regarded as a legal or constitutional principle it is easy enough to show that it has never been adopted by any State, and that, as a practical proposition, it cannot be.

The Statement of the American Declaration of Independence that "Governments derive their just powers from the consent of the governed," considered as an absolute one that applies to all States is, of course, an ethical proposition, the validity of which is not of concern to the analytical jurist. If it be advanced as a constitutional principle the term "governed" becomes synonymous with the People or citizen body of the State, and it then becomes necessary to ask if this aggregate of individuals is to be viewed distributively, or collectively as a corporate unit. If in former sense, all valid legal or political authority is at once rendered impossible and the State destroyed. By this doctrine, as Bluntschli says, " the State is resolved into its atoms, and supreme power ascribed to the unorganized mass or to the majority of these individuals. This extreme radical opinion contradicts the very essence of the State, which is the basis of sovereignty."[1] If the latter view is taken, and the governed regarded as a corporate unit, it is necessary to determine, who are to be regarded as the constituent members of this composite political body, and the modes in which it can make its legal will authentically manifest.

As regards this matter of membership, but two alternatives are possible: either the People, thus viewed as the sole source of positive law, as the legally supreme organs of the Government, must be conceived of as including every citizen or subject of the State, children and infants of the tenderest years as well as adults, the wholly uneducated as well as the educated, the feeble minded as well as those of sane intelligence, and each of them given a right to participate in determining the laws and policies of the State,—a result so obviously absurd, from a practical point of view, that no politically organized body of individuals has ever attempted it; or the other alternative accepted that the "active citizens," to use Rousseau's phrase, are to be limited to certain classes of individuals who are to participate directly in the operation of the government, or, indirectly, as an electorate either for the purpose of selecting representatives who will act for them, or by way of the initiative to propose laws, or the referendum to pass final judgement upon laws which their elected representatives draft, or which they themselves have initiated.

If, then, we take this second view as to constitutional meaning of "consent of the governed," the way is at once opened to all forms of government, except possibly that of autocratic or pure monarchy as described above. If the step is once taken of conceding that a portion of the governed, less than the whole, may arrogate to itself the legal right to act for the whole People and to claim obedience to its commands upon the part of those citizens who are excluded from this "active citizenship," there is no logical limit to the process. Such a small portion of the whole citizen body may claim the right to act for the whole that, instead of being what is ordinarily known as democratic or popular in character, the Government become highly aristocratic or oligarchic. It may even assume a monarch form with extensive discretionary powers vested in the ruler, provided only that it is understood that this monarchic rules not by reason of any inherent personal right of his own but as an agent of the body of active citizens, small or large as that body may chance to be. Furthermore, this electorate, in every constitutionally organized State, can act legally only according to predetermined forms, in conventions or assemblies, or by registering their will at prescribed times and in the modes already fixed by law. And, even when so acting, it is necessary that there should be definite laws as to what proportion of the votes cast shall be deemed to express the will of the entire electorate, and as such, to bind the entire citizen body.

It is plain, then, that, as a constitutional proposition, the doctrine of popular sovereignty, or sovereignty of the people, carries with it little more than the negation of the doctrine that supports absolute or pure monarchy. Indeed, it is barely possible to hold that it does not do even this,—that, in other words, the autocratic monarch can declare himself to be the agent or representative of his entire people in exactly, and in as logical, a sense as that in which a portion of the entire People arrogate to itself the legal right to speak and act for the whole.

The value, then, of constitutional government is not that it places Sovereignty in the hands of the people, but that it prescribes definite ways in which this sovereign power shall be exercised by the State. The value of popular government is that it provides the means through which the wishes of the people may be known and felt, and that thus the conduct of a State may be brought into conformity thereto. Constitutional government thus perfects the citizen from arbitrary action on the part of the State: popular government secures to him the probability that his wishes and interests will be considered.

Public Opinion. Sharply distinguishable from the doctrine of popular sovereignty according to which, as an ethical proposition, the just powers of government are declared to be necessarily based upon the consent of the governed, as well as from the constitutional doctrine that the legal powers of all the organs of government are to be traced back, in the last resort, to grants from an electorate or other constituent body which is assumed to represent and speak for the entire body of citizens, is the doctrine, or rather the assertion of the fact, that, in all States, whether autocratically or democratically organized, the actual dominance of power lies with the governed, and that, therefore, their will may not be opposed, except to a limited extent, by those who occupy the official or legal seats of power.

The facts is, as must be apparent to all, that there are limits to the endurance of any people, however patient, unenlightened, and submissive, and, that, when oppressed beyond this limit, they will prefer the evils of open resistance to those of submission; and, if this oppression be carried so far as to excite the opposition of the entire people or a large portion of them, the ruling powers will be overthrown. These are facts that are necessarily recognized by every ruler. As Hume well says, "As force is always on the side of the governed, the governors have nothing to support them but opinion. It is therefore on opinion only that government is founded, and this maxim extends to the most despotic military governments as well as to the most free and most popular."[2]

In fact, Austin himself expressly and repeatedly affirms that the legal sovereign is actually controlled in the exercise of power by the wishes of the community. In this very definition he says, "If a determinate human superior not in a habit of obedience to a like superior receive *habitual* obedience," etc., the word "habitual" thus indicating the possibility of the sovereign will being opposed. Again he says, "If perfect or complete independence be of the essence of sovereign power, there is not in fact the human power to which it will apply. Every government, let it be ever so powerful, renders occasional obedience to the commands of other governments. And every government defers habitually to the opinions and sentiments of its sovereign subjects."[3] And, also, "To an indefinite though limited extent, the monarch is superior to the governed, his power being commonly sufficient to secure compliance with his will. But the governed, collectively or in mass, are also the superior of the monarch who is checked in the abuse of his might by fear of exciting their anger and of arousing to active resistance the might which slumbers in the multitudes."[4]

It is plain that, when dealing with this popular ultimately conditioning force, which exists in all politics societies, we are not dealing with a legal factor. It may be, as Lieber describes it, the sense and sentiment of the community which gives meaning to the letter and life to the law, and without which the written law is a mere husk,[5] but it is, nevertheless, not a legal force, but, a Woodrow Wilson has defined it, "a catalogue of influences."[6]

As has been already several times said, sovereignty a legal force or element can be exercised only through the organs of the constitutionally established Government.[7]

Those doctrinaires who emphasize this factor of "popular sovereignty," and make it include a right of revolution, are not always careful to explain that this "right", so far as it is anything more than mere might, is either rather than legal in character. By the mere fact of people putting themselves in a revolutionary attitude toward their government, that is, by attempting the enforcement of their demands in ways other than those provided by law, they are placed outside of the State so far as such acts are concerned. However proper their conduct from a moral standpoint, from a legal standpoint they are then acting not as a body politic, but as a mob. They have, in fact, expressly repudiated State agencies. This, then, cannot be an act of Sovereignty, for Sovereignty, as expressly defined and conceded by all, is of the State and is possessed by a political community, and not by an uncivic aggregate of men. Until a people become politically organized there is no Sovereignty.[8]

If it be necessary to make this point still more conclusive, the circumstances may be pointed out that in all cases the actions of States are, as a matter of fact, largely determined and limited by the claims of other States, and thus their independence is practically governed by influences identical in character with those exercised by the public opinion of their own citizens. The legal, or rather non-legal, nature of both are the same. No greater validity can be predicated of the one than of the other, yet even Lieber and Jameson would not hold that Sovereignty rests, not with the individual States, but in a Community of States.

"Political" Sovereignty. Professor Ritchie, in an article upon this subject[9] distinguishes between this power of the people exercised by public opinion, which he terms "the ultimate *political Sovereignty,*" and the highest political power of the State as exercised through its legally established organs, which he designates as "legal Sovereignty." It is undoubtedly correct thus to make this distinction, but, to the writer, it seems unfortunate that the same term, "Sovereignty," should be applied to two forces so radically different, even though distinguishing adjectives be prefixed. It is not better to term such extra-legal force simply "Public Opinion" or "General Will," and to limit the word "Sovereignty" to its purely legal application?

In thus distinguishing between Sovereignty and General Will or Public Opinion, between legal absolutism of the State and its powers as absolutely limited by political exigencies, we are, in fact, but stating a result that correlates with the position which we shall assume in regard to the relation of custom to law.[10] That is to say, we shall deny to the people a capacity for legislation except through State organs. It is the essential office of representative or public government to make an approximately correct formulation of Public Opinion, and to secure political action in conformity thereto,[11] but this is not to place the exercise of Sovereignty in the unorganized community.

In conclusion, then, of this point, it may be said that, though legally absolute, Sovereignty is to be considered in reference to the institutions, the character of the people governed, and other objective conditions. While force is and always must be an incident of Sovereignty, the highest ideal of statesmanship is to render the actual exercise of such force as seldom necessary as possible, and the extent to which this aim is attained will depend largely upon the degree in which State action corresponds with the desires of Public Opinion or the General Will. As T. H. Green says, "If once the coercive power which must always be an incident of Sovereignty becomes the characteristics thing about it in its relation to the people governed, this must indicate one of two things; either that the general interest in the maintenance of equal rights has lost its hold upon the people, or that the Sovereignty no longer adequately fulfils the function of maintaining such rights, and thus has lost the support derived from the general sense of interest in supporting it… It is certain that when the idea of coercive force is that predominantly associated with the law-enforcing power, either a disruption of the State or a change in the sources of Sovereignty must sooner or later take place."[12]

Souveraineté Nationale. A constitutional doctrine superficially resembling and often confused with that of "popular sovereignty" is that known as "Souveraineté Nationale," which the French, since the time of the Revolution, have, except for a single exception—the Charter of 1814—

adopted as the fundamental principle of their constitutional jurisprudence. Article 3 of the Declaration of the Rights of Man and the Citizen of 1789 declared that "all sovereignty resides essentially in the Nation. No body, no individual may exercise any authority which has not expressly emanated from it." The Constitution of 1791 declared that "The sovereignty is one, indivisible, inalienable and imprescriptible. It belongs to the Nation." A similar declaration occurred in the Constitution of the Year III. It was impliedly affirmed by plebiscites under the Constitution of the Year VIII, and the Empire. It was again explicitly declared in the Constitutions of 1848 and 1852, in the Resolution of February 17, 1871, and in the Preamble of the Constitutional Law of August 31, 1871.

This principle, as Malberg so well shows in his analysis of it[13] is best interpreted in the light of the historical conditions under which it was first enunciated, and, as thus interpreted, is shown to have the negative purpose of denying, once for all, the fundamental constitutional principle of the former French Monarchy that all constitutional power found its source in the King, and that he had as inherent divine or patrimonial right of rulership. As opposed to this royal doctrine, the doctrine of Souveraineté Nationale asserts that no person has such a personal or inherent right to exercise political power. Such a right can only be a delegated or constitutional one —one that has been created and sanctioned by the French Nation.

This constitutional premise that the ultimate constituent power is vested in the Nation has meant that sovereignty, as a legal concept, resides, not distributively in each of the individuals that compose the Nation, but in the citizen body as an individual and indivisible whole. In the Constitution of 1791 sovereignty is expressly declared to be one and indivisible. It is thus clear that, from the beginning, the doctrine was essentially different from the popular sovereignty of Rousseau. Indeed, the first constitution, that of 1791, made no attempt to provide a legislative body the members of which would be elected by a direct and universal suffrage. And later constitutions, without abandoning the doctrine of Souveraineté Nationale, limited the suffrage to holders of landed property, and, in the Charter of 1830, established even a monarchy—of course a constitutionally limited one.

In result, then, according to this doctrine, the Nation is declared to have that exclusive right to exercise the sovereign or constitutional powers, which, prior to 1789, had been claimed by the King.

It might at first be thought that this investment of sovereignty in the Nation, conceived of as an indivisible political whole or corporate unit, amounts to practically the same thing as the ascription of sovereignty to the State, as assumed in the present treatise. The two doctrines are not, however, the same. Souveraineté Nationale is a special constitutional doctrine. It permits indeed, the establishment and maintenance of a great variety of governments, its only requirement being that they and their several organs and officials shall be deemed to have only such legal powers of rulership as they may have obtained by way of delegation by the Nation, that is, by those constituent bodies that are assumed to speak for the Nation. The doctrine therefore renders constitutionally impossible all forms of government which are founded upon, or which involves, the recognition of a right of rulership inhering as a personal underived right, in particular persons or groups of individuals. The doctrine of the sovereignty of the State, upon the otherhand, as developed in the present treatise, is one of pure political or juristic theory. It is wholly indifferent to and, therefore, is compatible with, any form of government, whether autocratic or democratic.[14] In other words, the concepts of Nation (or People) and the State are not to be confused. The vesting of sovereignty in the Nation or people is, as has been said, a constitutional doctrine and not one of pure political theory.

Austin's Theory as to the Determinateness of the Situs of Sovereignty in the Body-Politic. As is well-known, in his definitions of law and of the State Austin emphasized the idea that a law is a command that emanates from a *determinate* source, and that, as a prerequisite to the existence of a State, there must exist a determinate individual or a determinate group of individuals who possess the sovereign right of declaring law, and who, in addition, are able to secure, if not the uniform, at the least the habitual, obedience to this law upon the part of the bulk of the community to which it is addressed.

Austin says: "If a determinate human superior, not in a habit of obedience to a like superior, receive habitual obedience from the bulk of a given society, that determinate superior is sovereign in that society, and that society (including the superior) is a society political and independent."[15] This determinate human superior, Austin elsewhere says, may be a single individual definitely marked out, or a body of individuals the members of which may be determined by some definite ascertainable quality or characteristic.

It is especially to be observed in this definition that Austin vests the sovereignty, not in the State, but in this determinate individual or body of individuals. There is no question as to this for he goes on to say: "It is only through an ellipsis that the society is termed independent. The part truly independent (independent, that is to say, of a determinate human superior) is not the society, but the sovereign portion of that society." And again he says: "An independent political society is divisible into two portions, namely, the portion of its members which is sovereign and superior, and the portion of its members which is merely subject... When the sovereign portion consists of a single member, the supreme government is properly termed a monarchy, or the sovereign is properly termed a monarch."

At the point the doctrine developed in the present treatise depart from those of Austin. Austin, it is clear, does not make that distinction between the State and its Government, between pure political theory and constitutional doctrine, which the author has continued to emphasize. It may be granted to Austin that a command or positive law must issue from a determinate source, but, in political theory, that determinate source is always the particular State that is under examination.

Legislative Power. Bearing in mind what has gone before, it is evident that the search for the determinate sovereign governmental organ of a State is an enquiry that has to be separately performed for each State, and the answer obtained from the special system of constitutional jurisprudence which such State possesses. This much, however, may be declared in general terms: that sovereignty being the omnicompetent legal will of the State, its operation is especially manifested when the policies of the State are declared. These policies are for the most part embodied in the laws of the State, but may also, as, for example, in international affairs, be decided upon or made known either in the form of treaties or by other executives declarations or action. In a very true sense, however, every act of every organs of government, if justified by existing constitutional and statute law, is an act of sovereignty. In a more special sense, however, the State's sovereignty is manifested in the enactment of the laws which determine what the various organs of government shall be legally competent to do. There is thus some force in the statement of Locke that, "In all cases whilst the Government subsists the legislative is the supreme power. For what can give laws to another must needs be superior to him, and since the legislative is no otherwise legislative of the society but by the right it has to make laws for all parts, and every member of the society prescribing rules to their actions, and giving power of execution where they are transgressed, the legislative must needs to supreme, and all other powers in any members of the parts of the society derived from and subordinate to it."[16]

It has already been pointed out that the electorate of a State is to be distinguished from the People or entire citizen body. There are instances in which the electorate acts as a legislative organ. This happens whenever there exists a constitutional provision or practice according to which law may be created by a *referendum* or other plebiscital method. When so called upon for its vote, the electorate is to be considered *ad hoc* a legislative body. Of course, in those cases where a vote of the people is had merely for the purpose of discovering what the public sentiment is upon a given proposal, and without the power of such a vote itself to give a legal validity or non-validity to the proposal, we do not have the electorate exercising the law-making power.

Understanding now by Sovereignty a power which is capable of exercise only through existing governmental agencies, it necessarily follows that this supreme power is exhibited whenever the will of the State is expressed. In fact, it is almost correct to say that the sovereign will is the State, that the State exists only as a supreme controlling will, and that its life is only displayed in the declaration of binding commands, the enforcement of which is left to mere executive agents. These executive agents, while acting as such, have no will of their own, and are but implements for the performance of that will which gives to them a political and legal authority.

This, then, locates the exercise of Sovereignty in the law-making bodies. By whomsoever, or whatsoever body, therefore, the will of the State is expressed, and the law created, there we have Sovereignty exercised. If we distinguish between executive, judicial and legislative departments of the State, it is in this last-named department that the exercise of Sovereignty rests. The only point that we must remember is that the term "legislative" must not be so narrowly construed as to limit its application to those bodies by which formal statutory enactments are made. Insofar as the chief executive of the State has the ordinance power, he, may express the sovereign will and therefore exercise Sovereignty. As we know, this power was, in former times, very extensive in England, and still persists to a considerable degree in all modern States. The entire constitutional history of England is in fact but little more than a record of the manner in which this royal power of law-making has been curtailed, and the legislative power of Parliament taken its place. Again, constitutional conventions, insofar as they have the direct power of creating constitutional law, exercise this sovereign power. Finally, insofar as courts are the organs of the State for the creation of law, they express the will of the State and hence exercise Sovereignty.

It may be said that courts are able to legislate only be the acquiescence of the legislative body which may negative by statute the principles which they have declared; and hence that they act but as agents of the legislature proper. In the same way, it may also be said that, in many States, the ordinary legislature exercises its powers only by right of constitutional law, and therefore that it, in turn, but voices the will of those who establish this fundamental law. This is certainly true, and therefore, in any given State, it may be said, in one sense, that the organ possesses the final sovereign power which creates those laws that organize the Government, and distribute powers among its several governmental agents. In a measure we have already discussed this point in our consideration of the nature of constitutional provisions as compared with that of other forms of law. In a country like England, such a supreme body is the Parliament, but is those countries where government rest upon written constitutions, it is organs that have the legal right to modify the terms of such instruments.

By some jurists it is asserted that courts create law not merely by reason of the fact that they established and apply rules that have previously had no legal—or even customary—existence, but because in them lies the authority to determine the meaning to be given to the laws as enacted by the formal legislative organs of the government. Thus Gray, after defining the law of a State as "composed of the rules which the courts, that is the judicial organs of that body, lay down for the determination of legal rights and duties,"[17] in a later section[18] says:

"The true view, as I submit, is that the Law is what the judges declare; that statutes, precedents, the opinions of experts, customs, and morality are the sources of the Law; that back of everything lie the opinions of the ruling spirits of the community; who have the power to close any of the sources; but that so long they do not interfere, the judges, in establishing Law, have resource to there sources."

Earlier in his volume, Professor Gray had made his position upon this point still more emphatic in the following words: "It has been sometimes said that the Law is composed of two parts,—legislative law and judge-made law, but, in truth, all law is judge-made law. The shape in which a statute is imposed on the community as a guide for conduct is that statute as interpreted by the courts. The courts put life into the dead words of the statute."[19]

It cannot be denied that there is considerable force in the foregoing views; and the extent that it is accepted it increases the part played by the courts as the legislative or will-expressing organs of the State. But so long as the courts, in fact, make no claim of right and in fact exercise no right to construe statutes in a wholly arbitrary manner, according to their own opinions as to the justice or expediency of the rules of conduct embodied in the enactments of the legislature, but limit their function to the interpretation or construction of the language of these statutes, the doctrine which denies a real law-making function to the legislature seems a forced one. In any case, however, the will that is declared and enforced is that of the Sovereign State.

Austin's Error. It might have been thought that Austin, in his search for the determinate superior in a given politically organized society, would have been satisfied when he had found the supreme law-making organ of government. But this he was not content to do, and, by continuing his search, overstepped the bounds of the jurisprudence for the determination of the limits of which his lectures were denoted, and wandered confusedly in the realms of political or social forces.

Thus, Austin located sovereignty in Great Britain in the Kings, Lords, and Commons. But by Commons he was not content to mean the lower branch of Parliament, but designated thereby the electors of the lower house. "Speaking accurately," he says, "the members of the commons' house are merely trustees for the body by which they are elected and appointed; and consequently the Sovereignty always resides in the Kings and the peers, with the electoral body of the commons."[20] Here, as Professor Ritchic has pointed out, he no longer speaks as a lawyer. "For a lawyer *qua* lawyer a law is good law though it were passed by a Parliament which had abolished the Septennial Act and had gone on sitting as long as the Long Parliament, quite as much as if the law were passed by a newly summoned Parliament of the elected part of which, an overwhelming majority, had been returned expressly pledged to vote for this very law. With the wishes or feelings of the electors the lawyer as lawyer has nothing whatever to do, however much they may affect him as a politician or as a reasonable man."[21] To the same effect is the dictum of Professor Dicey, that nothing is more certain than that no English judge ever conceded, or under the present constitution can concede that Parliament is in any legal sense a trustee for the electors: a dictum that is conclusively verified by the power of Parliament, several times exercised, to lengthen its own existence without any reference to the voters by whom its members had been elected for a shorter period.[22]

In like manner, in the case of the United States, Austin does not discover legal Sovereignty in the legislature bodies of the individual Commonwealths, or in the federal Congress, or in both combined. He sees the legal competence of these bodies apparently limited by written constitutions, and therefore places Sovereignty in the electorates that select the bodies by which these written instruments may be amended. "I believe," says he, "that the Sovereignty of each of the States, and also of the larger State arising from the federal union, resides in the State's government, not its ordinary legislature, but the body of its citizens which appoint its ordinary legislature, and which, the union apart, is properly sovereign therein."[23]

The same criticism is here valid that was applied to Austin's location of Sovereignty in the English electorate. His doctrines are unsatisfactory, not only to the jurist but to those who, when they speak of sovereignty, refer to the ultimate force of Public Opinion, for those who take this latter view make the electorate but an organ of the whole body of citizens, by whom it is influenced and in many ways controlled.

Professor John Dewey makes also the criticism that this electorate is not even determinate. His argument is as follows: If the electorate be the Sovereign, then each voter is a sharer in the Sovereignty. But what of the voters who prove to be in the minority? "If we say he (*i.e.,* one of the minority) did share in Sovereignty because he had a right to vote, we say Sovereignty may be exercised apart from the utterance of commands, indeed, even in opposing the fundamental command. But if we say that, since not participating in the expression of the supreme command, he is not sovereign, the question arises by what right he voted at all."[24]

This reasoning of Professor Dewey is unsatisfactory. It is just as applicable to a legislative body as to a popular gathering. What of the members of the minority in the English Parliament? The fact is, that when Austin or any other writer refers to an electorate as exercising Sovereignty, he, or they, refer to such an electorate as a collective body of which each member possesses an indivisible portion of the Sovereignty of the whole. That is, that the citizen shares in the Sovereignty not as an individual but as a member of the whole. Each citizen holds, as lawyers say, *per tout* only, and not *per my*, as Professor Dewey would seem to think. Rousseau makes this distinction very plain by expressly distinguishing between the "will of all" and the "General Will."[25] The distinction between Sovereignty as a juristic conception and the ultimate conditioning power of popular opinion, was, however, one that was never reached by Rousseau, who completely identifies Sovereignty with the "General Will." It is in consequence of this assumption, that, in searching for the manner in which this sovereign power may be legally exercised, he was forced to hold that "laws being but authentic acts of the General Will, the sovereign cannot act except when the People is assembled."[26] And again, that "Sovereignty cannot be represented for the same reason that it cannot be alienated; it consists essentially of the General Will, and the will cannot be represented; it is the same or it is different; there is no mean. The deputies of the people then are not, and cannot be its representatives, they are only its commissioners; they can conclude nothing definitely. Any law which the people in person has not ratified is null; it is not a law."[27] Thus the position is taken that all authority exercised other than by warranty of the general assembly of the people is illegal, and a government thus acting has only a *de facto* and not a *de jure* existence—a position according to which there was not at the time of Rousseau's writing, nor has there been since, a State in Europe in which rebellion would have been an illegal act.

Comparing these views with those held by Hobbes and Locke, we find that, according to the former of these writers, a sovereign organ, be it a monarch or a popular assembly, is made practically identical with the sovereign State itself, and, as such, incapable of legal limitation. Thus, in all truthfulness, the absolute ruler might say that *l'état, c'est moi.* The agent is identified with the principal, government is confused with the State, the machine absorbs the power that moves it. Apart, however, from this confusion between State and Government Hobbes developed a substantially correct theory of law and Sovereignty, though he needlessly based it upon an illogical fiction.

Locke, though founding his system on the same fictional contract, came much nearer the comprehension of the true nature of government in his declaration of its limited delegated character, and the essentially representative capacity, of all political agents. It would also seem that at times he perceived the distinction between the actual ultimate power of the people to condition political action, and the legal or sovereign action of the State. Thus he declares "the community may be said in this respect to be always the supreme power but not as considered under any form of government, because this power of the people can never take place till the government be dissolved."[28] But his preconceived ideas of natural rights and of sovereignty as resting upon a contract make him speak in general of this ultimate right of the people as something more than a mere moral right, or as power founded upon mere might. For the same reason he does not always sufficiently recognize that the State may be so organized as to permit sovereign action greatly opposed to public will and to public interest, and yet strictly constitutional and legal. Thus, in considering what is to be done in case an executive, to whom has been entrusted the power of calling together the legislative branch, should refuse to exercise such power, to the detriment of the people, he describes such action as "contrary to the trust put in him that does so," and as "a state of war with the people who have a right to reinstate their legislative in the exercise of their power."[29]

Here the theory of a contract between governed and governing again crops out. The juristic fact is, however, that government agents exercise a power delegated or granted to them by the State, and not one created by a joining of their wills with those of the subjects. The only will concerned is that of the State. Public officials are, in other words, agents of the State, not of the People. They have no legal relation to the people as such, and, therefore, there can be no breach of contract with them in whatever manner they may exercise their power. If they exceed their legal competence, or are in any way guilty of non-feasance or malfeasance of office, they are punishable only by the State. Therefore, any action of theirs, however oppressive, does not, as Locke would say, *ipso facto* deprive them of political power, and place them in a state of war with their former subjects. Such action is not even illegal if within their competence, and is as fully valid as would be the most beneficent measure. If *ultra vires*, however, the action is of course illegal and not an act of the State, but of the official as a private individual, and one for which he is personally responsible. But such illegality extends only to the particular act itself. It has no influence over the general public or sovereign *status* of such official. Rousseau is thus perfectly correct in denying that a Government is established by a contract.

References

1. *Theory of the State*, trans. 2d ed., p. 497.
2. *Collected Essays*, pt. I, No. 4.
3. *Lectures on Jurisprudence*, ed. 1867, Vol. I, p. 242.
4. *The Province of Jurisprudence Determined*, p. 14 (ed. 1861). So also, *idem*, note to p. 192, and p. 272; Professor Dewey, in the *Political Science Quarterly* for March, 1894, shows the tendency of the, Maine and others to treat Austin's system as if it ignored this ultimate conditions power of popular approval.
5. *Political Ethics*, sec. 65.
6. *An Old Master and Other Essays*, p. 78.
7. *Cf.* the argument of Daniel Webster in the case of *Luther* v. *Border* 7 How. 1.
8. Thus says Bluntschli in his *Staatswörterbuch*: "Es giebt keine Souveränetät der Gesells. Keine Souveränetät vor oder über dem State. Die Souveränetät

als ein staalicher zunächst ein staatrechtlicher Begriff ist durch die Existenz und durch die Verfassung des Staates bedingt."

To the same effect says Cooley (*Constitutional Limitations,* 3d ed., p. 598): "The voice of the people in their sovereign capacity can only be a legal force when expressed at the times and under the conditions which they themselves have prescribed and pointed out by the constitution, ... and if by any portion of the people, however large, as attempt should be made to interfere with the regular working of the agencies of government at any other time, or on any other mode than as allowed by existing law, either constitutional or statutory, it would be revolutionary."

According to Judge Jameson, sovereignty resides in a society only as a body politic; "in the corporate unit resulting from the organization of many into one, and not in the individuals constituting such unit, nor in any number of them as such, nor even in all of them, except as organized into a body politic and *acting as such.*" (*The Constitutional*, p. 21) However, though assuming this correct position, he proceeds to declare that Sovereignty may be exercised in an extra-governmental or revolutionary manner. Its characteristics as a legal power is thus explicitly abandoned. "Sovereignty," says he, "manifests itself in two ways: first, *indirectly* through individuals acting as agents or representatives of the sovereign, and constituting the civil government; and, secondly, *directly* by organic movements of the political society itself, without the ministry of agents; the movements referred to exhibiting themselves either in those social agitations, of which the resultant is known as *public opinion*, that *vis a tergo* in all free commonwealths, by which the machinery of government is put and kept in orderly motion; or in manifestations of *original power* by which political or social changes are achieved irregularly, under the operation of forces wielded by the body politic itself immediately." (*Idem*, p. 23 Citation is made of Lieber's *Political Ethics*, vol. I, p. 256). But what the tests are by which "organic movements" of society are to be distinguished; how Sovereignty, as necessarily inhering in a social body only as a political body, and exercised *as such*, can likewise be discovered in mere opinion or in "irregular" acts for the achievement of social as well as political changes; what valuable distinction there is between revolutionary and legal conduct—a distinction emphasized throughout the work;—these are questions that Judge Jameson does not attempt to answer. (*Cf.* his article entitled "National Sovereignty," in the *Pol. Sci. Quar.*, vol. V, p. 193)

9. "On the Conception of Sovereignty," *Annals of the Amer. Acad. Pol. and Soc. Science,* January, 1891.
10. See chapter, "The Nature of Positive Law."
11. See the remarks of Dicey (*Law of the Constitution*, pp. 73-76), according to which the function of representative government is to produce a coincidence between what he terms the "external limits" to Sovereignty, arising from the possibility of resistance on the part of the people, and the

"internal limits," depending upon the wishes of those who wield the Sovereign power.

12. Green, *Philosophical Works,* vol. II, p. 410. To many persons it will seem that these remarks of Green have a pertinency to present conditions in the United States with reference to the enforcement of the Eighteenth Amendment to the Federal Constitution.
13. *Contribution à la Théorie Générale de l'État,* vol. II, pp. 167-187.
14. Malberg is, therefore, not quite correct when, contrasting the constitutional doctrine of the pure monarchy with that of Souveraineté Nationale, he says: "Dans le premier, l'État ne personnifie que lui mêmela, nation n'étant que l'un des facteurs dont la réunion a pour effet de former l'établissement public État; dans le second, la nation n'estpe seulement l'un des éléments qui concourent à constituter l'État, maiseb s'identifie avec lui et il ne personnifie qu'elle. Dans le premier système encore, l'État devient une personne par le fait qu'il a un organe prope le monarque; dans le second, la personne État, étant identique avech personne nation, existe par le fait que la nation elle-même se trous organisée. Enfin et par suite de ses différences initiales, dans le premise système, le monarque a puissance sur la nation considérée comm élément subalterne de l'État; dans le second c'est, au contraire, la nation qui a puissance sur le monarque envisagé comme organe national' *Op. cit.,* II, p. 189.
15. *Province of Jurisprudence Determined*, chap. VI.
16. *Two Treatises of Government*, bk. II, chap. 13.
17. *The Nature and Source of Law*, sec. 191.
18. *Idem,* sec. 602.
19. *Op. cit.,* sec. 276. Professor Gray quotes with approval the words of Bishop Hoadly: "Nay, whoever hath an absolute authority to interpret any written or spoken laws, it is He who is truly the law-giver, to all intents and purposes, and not the person who first wrote and spoke them."
20. *The Province of Jurisprudence Determined,* ed. 1861, p. 201.
21. *Annals of the Am. Acad. of Pol. and Soc. Science,* January, 1891, p. 392.
22. *Law of the Constitution,* 4th ed., pp. 69-71. We may profitably quote the following paragraphs as not only showing this point, but as illustrating the distinction that we have emphasized between Sovereignty as a purely legal conception, and as the ultimate conditioning force of public opinion: "It should, however, be carefully noted," says Dicey, "that the term 'Sovereignty,' as long as it accurately employed in the sense in which Austin sometimes uses it, is a merely legal conception, and means simply the power of law-making, unrestricted by any legal limit. If the term 'Sovereignty' be thus used, the sovereign power under the English constitution is clearly 'Parliament.' But the word 'Sovereignty' is sometimes employed in a political, rather than in a strictly legal sense. That body is

'politically' sovereign or supreme in a State the will of which is ultimately obeyed by the citizens of the State. In this sense of the word, the electors of Great Britain may be said to be, together with the Crown and the Lords, or perhaps, in strict accuracy, independently of the King and the Peers, the body in which sovereign power is vested...But this is a political and not a legal fact. The elector can in the long run always enforce their will. But the courts will take no notice of the will of the electors. The judges know nothing about any will of the people except in so far as that will is expressed by an Act of Parliament, and would never suffer the validity of a statute to be questioned on the ground of its being passed to kept alive in opposition to the wishes of the electors."

23. *The Province of Jurisprudence Determined,* ed. 1861, p. 222.
24. "Austin's Theory of Sovereignty," *Pol. Sci. Quar.,* March 1894.
25. *The Social Contract,* bk. II, chap. III.
26. *Idem,* bk. III, chap. XII.
27. *Two Treatises of Government,* bk. III, chap. XV.
28. *Two Treatises of Government,* bk. II, p. 149.
29. *Two Treatises of Government,* bk. II, p. 155.

II

The Nature of Positive Law

The ascription of Sovereignty to the State, and the definition of Sovereignty as legal omnicompetence have made it necessary to view the State as the sole source of law in a positive or strictly juristic sense. This is a proposition which many have found the most difficult to accept of all the assertions of analytical jurisprudence and it will therefore be necessary to consider it with some degree of care, and especially is this so because of the varying meanings which are commonly attached to the word "Law."

As opposed to the description of Law as the sequences of events in the physical universe—sequences that occur without reference to and beyond the control of men's wills—the jurist uses the word as declaring a rule or principle for the governance of human action. Its characteristics in this sense is that it is capable of being expressed as a distinct proposition to rational beings in the form and character of a command. As thus conceived, a law implies that he who issues it has, or claims to have some sort of legal authority over the persons whose actions are to be controlled; that, in other words, as between him and them there is a relation of jural superiority and inferiority. Out of this relation also arises the idea of legal obligation upon the part of those to whom the commands are directed, and of legal right upon the part of those who will be beneficially interested in having these obligations fulfilled.

Laws, as Austin says, are rules laid down for the guidance of intelligent beings by intelligent beings having authority over them. As thus defined, they include commands set by God to men, and those set by men to men. With the former, jurisprudence is not concerned. But, even with regard to the laws set by men to men, the analytical jurist is concerned only with those which are issued by men who claim a political superiority over those men whose actions are to be controlled by them. Laws, thus set, are spoken of as positive in character.

Rules of conduct not in the form of commands from a superior to an inferior, Austin continues, are rules of morality, and, though often spoken of as laws, are not properly so-called, or at least, are not properly so-called if the term law be used in its sense of a command emanating from a determinate political source. Such are the so-called laws of honor or of fashion, and other rules of conduct supported by public opinion. These become "positive" rules, though still not positive laws, when they assume the form of commands from determinate human beings but not as based upon a claim of political superiority. They become positive laws, or laws properly so-called only when there is this relationship of political superiority and political inferiority.

Thus, with reference to the recognized rules of conduct regulating the relations between States, Austin says, "These are not laws properly so-called. But one supreme government may doubtless command another to forber from a kind of conduct which the [so-called] law of nations condemns. And, though it is fashioned on law which is law improperly so called, this command is law in the proper sense of the term [but no a 'positive' law]. Speaking precisely, the command is a rule of positive morality set by a determinate author. For, as a supreme government is in a state of subjection to another the command, though fashioned on the law of nation would not amount to a positive law. Nor does the government which gives the command act as the executor of a command proceeding from the uncertain body—the collective family or aggregate of nations. That government may, however, act as the executor of a command proceeding from a definite number of sovereign States allied under a treaty. In that case there would be a command issuing from the allied States collectively, and enforced by the one government as their minister. This would be still a rule of positive morality and not positive law, because the government of State which is to be coerced would not (on the hypothesis) be in state of subjection either to the allied governments collectively, or to the government which has for the occasion acted as their minister."

Austin, as we have seen, classifies also constitutional laws as rules of positive morality rather than as positive laws properly so-called. His error in this respect has already been examined.

We are thus prepared for the statement of Austin that: "Every positive law or every law simply and strictly so-called, is set by a sovereign person, or a sovereign body of persons, to a member or members of the independent political society wherein that person or body is sovereign or supreme."

In another place Austin somewhat expands the statement which we have quoted by saying that every positive law is set directly or circuitously by the sovereign, and, therefore, that laws may be declared by private persons in pursuance of legal rights.

The foregoing are declarations of fact, and the question is whether they may be squared with other well known facts, and especially with the fact that the judicial tribunals of all governments, in the settlement of controversies coming before them, apply principles or rules of conduct which have not found previous explicit and definite statement as commands of the State of which these tribunals are the governmental agents.

If, in a given State, one wishes to determine concretely what are the law of that State, it is certainly correct to say that they are the rules or principles which the judicial tribunals of the State will apply in the cases adjudicated by them. Thus says Salmond: "Law consists of the rules recognized and acted on in courts of justice"[1]; or; as Gray declares: "The Law of the State or of any organized body of men is composed of the rules which the courts that is, the judicial organs of that body, lay down for the determination of legal rights and duties."[2]

It was of course obvious to Austin, as it has been to all those who have accepted his proposition that the States will is to be viewed as the creative source of all positive law, that the rules or substantive principles of conduct embodied in the decisions of courts have been, in considerable measure, the product of popular custom or of the practice of the courts themselves. Hence it has been contended by many that the Austinian doctrine is not in accordance with obvious and incontestable facts. In other words, it is argued that the large body of legal principles commonly called customary law, which the courts apply and the State enforces, arises independently of State enactment. Especially has this criticism of the orthodox analytical jurist been advanced by writers of what is termed the Historical School of Jurisprudence, and by those who will cling to doctrines of Natural Law.

The contention of Natural Law adherents that the State is not to be viewed as the sole creator of law, is sufficiently disposed of by pointing out that, granting all that is claimed, the only result is to show, as an ethical proposition, those in possession of political power should be guided by certain fundamental and absolute principles of justice and moral right when determining the positive laws which they will cause to be enforced by political power. The argument of the Historical School of Jurists requires, however, a more detailed examination. In England this school is headed by the name of Sir Henry Maine, and, upon the Continent by Savigny and Puchta. In general American writers are also of this school.

"Positive Law," says Savigny, "springs from that general spirit which animates all the members of the Nation, and the unity of the law is revealed necessarily to their consciences and is by no means the effect of chance."[3] The growth of custom he compares to that of language, and continues: "Law which lives in the common consciousness of the people is not composed of abstract rules. It exists rather in the actual perception of a legal institute in its organic connection, and the rule is appears in its logical form so soon as the need for it is felt; it is then singled out from connection, and is translated in an artificial manner."[4] In other words, according to Savigny law exists as law independently of the State. It is the creation of the national consciousness or spirit of a people and is evidenced by their customary habits. Even formal statutory enactments, according to this view, are able to secure recognition and enforcement only insofar as they conform in their provisions to the "Spirit" of the people. When, therefore, they are formally enunciated by the courts or legislatures, the function of the State is rather that of realizing and enforcing the law than of creating it.

While the above quotations from Savigny serve to show what has undoubtedly been the dominant attitude of German jurists during the last century, certain of their number show a tendency to turn to a position more similar to that of the analytical jurists of England. Especially is this apparent in Ihering's *Zweck im Recht,* and Lasson's *System der Rechtsphilosophie.*

In England, on the other hand, the high authority of the Austinian School has been considered as greatly shaken by the historical method introduced into the study of law by Sir Henry Maine. This writer is supposed to have pointed out that, throughout the greater portion of the world's history, law was created otherwise than according to the Austinian theory, and, therefore, that, if his conception of the source of law be applicable at all, it is applicable only to highly developed States. The following quotation from Maine sufficiently indicates his position. Referring to an Indian despot, he says: "At first sight there could be no more perfect embodiment than Runjett Singh of sovereignty as conceived by Austin. He was absolutely despotic. Except occasionally on his wild frontier he kept the most perfect order. He could have commanded anything: the smallest disobedience to his commands would have been followed by death or mutilation, and this was perfectly well-known to the enormous majority of his subjects. Yet I doubt whether once in all his life he issued a command which Austin would call a law... He had all material of power and he exercised it in various ways. But he never made law."[5]

It is to be observed that Maine admits the verbal truth of Austin's theory, for he adds: "I do not for a moment assert that the existence of such a state of political society falsifies Austin's theory. The maxim by which objections to it are disposed of is, as I have so often said before, that what the sovereign permits, he commands." The position which is taken, however, in the present work is that there is more than a verbal truth in the thesis that all law, as law, emanates from the sovereign; and that when a customary rule is declared by a court of justice to be one which the State will enforce, such rule becomes specifically distinct from what it had before been.

A characteristic American argument against the Austinian view is that contained in the opening chapters of Wharton's *Commentaries on American Law.* This author writes as follows: "By whom were existing English statutes winnowed in the colonies of Massachusetts and Pennsylvania, for instance, so as to retain such as suited the temper and met the wants of the people, and to set aside all others? This was not done by the colonial assemblies; had such a process of radical revision been attempted by these assemblies it would have been promptly vetoed by the king in Council. It was not done by the British Parliament, though the British Parliament assumed to be the sole supreme legislature by whose laws these colonies were controlled. It was done by popular assent produced by national conscience and national need. It is true that when the colonies became independent sovereigns they passed laws by which the process of selection and rejection thus carried out was approved. But it was never pretended that the process of selection and rejection derived its authority from such legislation. On the contrary, when the colonies became sovereigns, what their court said was, 'the law of the land, in this respect, was not imposed by the sovereign on the people, but was adopted by the people and afterwards accepted by the sovereign.' The same may be said of the rulings of our courts as to international and interstate law, and the law regulating Indian tribes."[6] And again he says: "That custom makes the law and not law custom, is shown by the fact just noticed, that when a custom is recognized by the courts as existing, the recognition operates retrospectively, the custom being regarded as law before it was judicially recognized."[7]

In considering now these criticisms that are made upon the Austinian position as to the nature of law, it is to be observed that much the greater part of these objections are in fact examples of *ignoratio elenchi,* the confusion arising, as Holland correctly points out, from the ambiguous sense in which the term "source of law" may be used.[8] This expression may be used either to denote the mode in which, or the person through whom, have been formulated those rules which have acquired the force of law; or, to denote the authority which gives them that force.

Now, so far as it is used in the first sense, there is no denial made by the Analytical School that custom is, in very large measure, the source of law; that is, that, through this medium, have arisen the principles of social conduct that have been subsequently embodied in law. Furthermore, it is not asserted that, as an actual fact, the exigencies of public life have not at all times demanded that the sovereign power should found the expression of its will upon these rules. What the analytical jurist does maintain is, that these customary rules do not become law in a strictly legal or positive sense, until they are accepted by the political power. As Austin says, "There can be no law without a judicial sanction, and until custom has been adopted as law by courts of justice it is always uncertain whether it will be sustained by that sanction or not."[9] And, again, "The description, completion, and correction of positive morality are as much an end for which political government is wanted, as the obtaining by its establishment of a more cogent sanction. But the sovereign makes it law, not by the mere description, but by the sanction with which he clothes it."[10]

It is obvious that the objections that have been founded on the historical evidences quoted by Wharton and Maine are applicable solely to the question of the origination of the principles embodied in the law,—a question with which the Austinians are not concerned. Thus, when Maine says that the Indian despot never made a law, he can only mean that he never arbitrarily established a general rule of conduct. What he did do, however, was to accept such rules of conduct as rules of the State, and thereby, as the Analytical School claims, elevate such principles into legal rules. It is no answer to say that, in the case of many of the earlier monarchies, they were simply tax-collecting empires, and that there was no attempt, or even desire, on the part of their rulers to interfere with the domestic rules that obtained in the various portions of their kingdoms. The point is, that the very least important of the customary rules that obtained acceptance in those countries by the lowest courts or judicial officers, thereby obtained a sanction that was ultimately supported by the entire strength of the sovereign political authority.

Again, it is no answer to the assertion that the State is the sole creator of law to show that no State can maintain its control that does not in general accept as its will those principles of justice and utility that are evolved by the customary habit of its people; that, in other words, the attempt on its part to establish arbitrary rules of conduct not based on the needs and capacities of the people, as evidenced by their customary habits of life, would lead inevitably to revolt and revolution. This would only show that, as a principle of political expediency (i.e., of caution and prudence), a general acceptance of customary rule is necessary. The fact that legislative commands or judicially declared principles of conduct are not enforced, or, possibly, cannot be enforced because of the active or passive resistance upon the part of the people that an attempt to put them into effect would arouse, does not deprive these state-sanctioned orders of their right to be entitled laws; for it is not the actual enforcement of a rule by the State which transmutes it into a positive law, but the authentic manifestation by the State that it accepts or declares that rule to be an expression of its sovereign will.

Finally, it is not a refutation of the position which is here defended, to point to the fact that a court of justice, in accepting a custom as law, does not declare that henceforth such principle shall obtain as law, but holds it to have been the law at the time of the accruing of the cause of action whose merits are then decided.

The position of Holland, who is possibly the best exponent of Austin's system today, differs from that of Austin upon this point, and is an attempt, it would seem, to avoid the objection rather than to answer it. Holland says: "The Courts have, therefore, long ago established as a fundamental principle of law, subject of course in each case to many restrictions and qualifications, that, in the absence of a specific rule of written law, regard is to be had in looking for the rule which governs a given set of circumstances, not only to equity and to previous decision, but also to custom. Binding authority has thus been conceded to custom, provided it fulfils certain requirements, the nature of which has also long since been settled, and provided it is not superseded by law of a higher authority. When, therefore, a given set of circumstances is brought into Court, and the Court decides upon them by bringing them within the operation of a custom, the Court appeals to that custom as it might to any other pre-existent law. It does not *proprio motu* then for the first time make that custom a law; it merely decides as a fact that there exists a legal custom, about which there might up to that moment have been some question, as there might about the interpretation of an Act of Parliament. It then applies the custom to the circumstances just as it might have applied an Act of Parliament to them. A good custom or an intelligible Act of Parliament either exists or does not exist objectively, before the case comes into Court; although it is from the decision of the Court in the particular case that a subjective knowledge is first possible for the people of the existence or non-existence of the alleged custom, or that this or that is the meaning of the Act of Parliament."[11]

It would certainly seem that Holland admits the very point against which he contends, when he says that the court does not for the first time make a custom a law by its adjudication, but "merely decides as a fact that there exists a legal custom about which there might up to that moment have been some question, as there might about the interpretation of an Act of Parliament." This certainly limits the action of the court to one of interpretation. And, as one of his critics has properly said, "To say that customs are regarded as laws by virtue of a tacit law to effect, is simply to beg the whole question. It is to say that custom is law is virtue of custom."[12]

The proper position upon this point would seem to be to admit frankly that judicial legislation is *ex post facto* legislation. But what has this to do with the question as to the effect of such decisions of the courts upon custom? It is, to be sure, a general principle of legislation that laws should not be retroactive in their effect, but this is a principle dictated by general consideration of justice, and not of necessity. There is no more inherent difficulty in the State establishing retroactive law than there is in its creating law that shall be of only prospective application. That this is the case, is seen in the necessity of explicitly providing in our own written constitutions that neither Congress nor the State legislatures shall pass *ex post facto* enactments. In the case of legislatures not thus arbitrarily limited, as, for example, the British Parliament, no court would hold a retroactive act invalid if passed according to due forms and procedure. Laws established by means of formal statutory enactments are, as a rule, created without reference to particular cases, and therefore injustice would necessarily result had such enactments a retroactive character. When, however, we come to judicial legislation, we come to a field where this *ex post facto* principle is not recognized,—not recognized because from the very nature of the case no necessity of justice demands it. By the recognition of a custom as law, no arbitrary or novel doctrines of right are established by the court. Principles only are declared as enforcible that already obtain in practice among the people. Hence, no possible injustice is done by declaring such customer then and there to be laws, and at the same time applying them to the causes of action that have previously accrued. There is no need to predicate a tacit law to the effect that such customs shall be law, but simply to admit that judicial legislation is *ex post facto* legislation and to defend it as such; in fine, to make the action of the court not simply interpretative, but actually creative of law.

We may, then, accept as valid the reasoning of Austin when he says:[13]

"At its origin, a custom is a rule of conduct which the governed observe spontaneously or not in pursuance of a law set by a political superior. The custom is transmuted into positive law when it is adopted as such, either by being expressly embodied in statutes promulgated by the sovereign authority, or implicitly by decisions of the courts of justice which are enforced by the power of the State.

"For a legal rule introduced by a judicial decision (whether suggested by custom or not) is in effect legislation by the sovereign. A subordinate or subject judge is merely a minister. The rules which he makes derive their legal force from authority given by the State; an authority which the State may confer expressly, but which it commonly imparts by way of acquiescence. For, since the State may reverse the rules which he makes, and yet permits him to enforce them by the power of the political community, its sovereign will that the rules shall obtain as law, is clearly evinced by its conduct though not by its express declaration...Like other significations of desire, a command is express or tacit. If the desire be signified by words (written or spoken) the command is express. If the desire is signified by conduct (or by any signs of desire which are not words) the command is tacit. Now when customs are turned into legal rules by decisions of subject judges, the legal rules which emerge from the customs are tacit commands of the sovereign legislature. The State which is able to abolish, permits its members to express them; and it therefore signifies its pleasure by its voluntary acquiescence, that they shall serve as a law to the governed."

A little reflection shows how indefinite would be the term "law" if applied to custom and civil rules alike. So long as customary rules retain their purely customary form, that which gives to them force and efficiency for regulation is not the threat of coercion, or the imposition of penalties by a superior power in case of their violation. Their force is solely derived from the pressure of public opinion, of religious sanction, of individual sense of right, or the possibility of personal retaliation on the part of those persons injured by such violation. Such influences as these are of the most variable character, and personal in the highest degree. Their force depends almost wholly upon the subjective condition of the individual, upon his own peculiar temperament of the mind, his sense of justice, his religious reverence, his regard for the traditional, his power of self-restraint, and his sensitiveness to the goodwill of the community. Such principles, then, possess no force of their own, no compelling power; obedience to them is secured only by the voluntary consent of the individual, such consent being based upon the dictates of reason, expediency, and right that dwell within his own breast.

When, therefore, it is asked so to broaden the connotation of the term "law" as to include such elements as these, it may be answered that logical exactness and scientific accuracy demand that a more definite meaning be given to this word. Definitions are valuable only insofar as they give a precision of meaning to words and expressions. Their sole utility consists in the demarcation of a definite field within which the word or phrase is applicable, and it will be apparent that to include within the meaning of law elements that differ so widely as the purely customary principles of which we have been speaking, and the rigid rules of conduct, formally enunciated by the State and enforcible by its sovereign right, is to create a signification for the word that cannot be sufficiently definite to serve as a basis upon which to found a formal science of jurisprudence and politics. What decisive and universally applicable definition shall we give to law, if custom is to share with the State the power of its creation? When shall we know at any one time what is and what is not the law? What but confusion must necessarily result from conceiving two co-ordinate law-making authorities, each having the right to create law independently of the other, or to abrogate and overrule each other's creations?

In result, then, we are justified in defining law, in the strict positive or juristic sense, as those rules of conduct that courts of justice apply in the exercise of their jurisdictions. As distinguished from all other rules of conduct that obtain more or less general recognition in a community of men, they are such as have for their validity the sanction of the State. The scientific value of such a definite connotation of the term "law" is obviously great. By it alone is rendered possible a definite and exact knowledge of the facts to which this department of knowledge relates, and a sound basis afforded upon which to rest the conception of the Sovereignty of the State.[14]

The sense in which the courts rather than the formal law-making or legislative branches of a government may be said to be organs through which the State creates its law has been examined in the preceding chapter in which the location of sovereignty in the body-politic was considered. The matter of the recognition and application of international law principles by municipal courts is discussed in the chapter entitled "International Law."[15] The argument there stated applies as well to the recognition and enforcement by one State of the municipal law of another State.

Permissive Laws. The objection to viewing laws as "commands" of the State, based upon the fact that many laws are permissive rather than mandatory or declaratory in character, is sufficiently answered by pointing out that in all cases where this is so there are created or recognized rights which have a legal force and which are protected by laws which are mandatory in character. Of permissive and merely declaratory laws, it can always be claimed that they are to be considered not as complete legal provisions but as integral parts of the mandatory laws which support them.

Considerable discussion has centered around the point whether the term law, in a positive or any other sense, should be limited in its application to those expressions of the States' will which state a general rule. To the writer, however, it seems clear that any order, or decree, or administrative ordinance, even though it relate to the performance of but a single act by a particular individual, is a law; that is, it expresses the sovereign will of the State if it is one which has the support of some more general law or is declared in pursuance of a legally delegated governmental power.[16]

Actual Enforcement Not an Essential Element in the Concept of Positive Law. A more difficult question is whether it is necessary that a rule should be actually enforced in order that it may properly be termed a law in a strictly positive sense.

It is the opinion of the writer that this is not necessary. In discussing the nature of the State's sovereignty it was pointed out that the ascription to the State of legal omnicompetence carries with it no implication that the States, or rather those who control their governmental agencies, have the actual power to carry into effect any policies that they may desire or see fit to adopt. So, in determining what is positive law, the only criterion is whether the rules or act commanded by it is an authentic expression of the State's will as determined by existing constitutional law,—is, in other words, a rule of conduct or a command which the constituted courts will, if resorted to, order obeyed.

Such a court order may, in fact, be not obeyed either because the executive branch of the government refuses to lend its assistance, or because there is such popular resistance that the executive, though willing, finds itself unable to enforce it, or deems it inexpedient to do so. In such cases all that can be said is that there has been a violation of law which, however, no more destroys the law, as law, than is the criminal law destroyed when crime is committed.[17]

Sanction. Austin and those who follow him emphasize in the concept of law, the element of sanction, by which they mean the penalty or evil threatened to be inflicted upon those legal inferiors who fail to obey the commands of their legal superiors. Thus, in his *Province of Jurisprudence Determined,*[18] Austin says, "A command is distinguished from other significations of desire, not by the style in which the desire is signified, but by the power and the purpose of the party commanding to inflict an evil or pain in case the desire is disregarded. If you cannot or will not harm me in case I comply not with your wish, the expression of your wish is not a command, although you utter your wish in imperative phrase."

Austin does not go to the extent of declaring that an unenforced command ceases to be command, and is not, therefore, a law. He is content to assert that, in order that an expressed desire may be classified as a command, there should be some likelihood, however small, that some sort of evil or pain, however slight, will be inflicted by the one expressing the desire upon those to whom it is addressed who do not conform to it. Thus he says: "The magnitude of the eventual evil, and the magnitude of the chance of incurring it, are foriegn to the matter in question. The greater the evil, and the greater the chance of incurring it, the greater is the efficiency of the command, and the greater is the strength of the obligation. But when there is the smallest chance of incurring the smallest evil the expression of a wish amounts to a command, and, therefore imposes a duty."

Austin here attenuates his own distinction between a command and a wish to an extent that makes it a worthless one. In place of the idea thus rejected, the writer would emphasize the circumstance that a positive law, as distinguished from either a wish or a command has the official imprimatur of the State, and that this should be the essential fact connoted by the term Sanction. A law thus becomes an order or command issued by some one who claims a right upon his own part to the obedience of those whom he addresses, and, therefore, of a genuine obligation upon their part to obey. In the case of a divine law or command, this right and correlative obligation is based upon the fatherhood or other conceived status of superiority which the Divine Being has as compared with that of the individuals whose conduct is sought to be regulated and controlled. In the case of a positive law, such as we are concerned with in the present treatise, the superiority to the law-giver is a political or legal one. This plainly appears when we have to deal with the distinction between *de jure* and *de facto* governments. When a person is directed to do a certain thing by a government which he does not recognize as having legal right to control his actions, he cannot deny that the direction amounts to a command, for he may know that serious evil or pain will almost surely be inflicted upon him in case he does not conform, in his conduct to the direction he has received. But, even if he obeys, he does not admit that he has fulfilled a legal obligation. Upon the contrary, as to him, the matter has been nothing more than one of illegal force or power. Of course, if the Government that issues the order does so in pursuance of a claim upon its part that it has a legal right to require the obedience of those to whom the order is addressed, the order is a positive law when regarded from the point of view of that Government.

The true sanction of a positive law consists, then, in the fact that the authority issuing it claims to be politically superior to the persons to whom it is directed; or, looking at the law from the point of view of the ones commanded, that they recognize the law-issuing authority as having a legal right to regulate their conduct in the premises.[19]

References

1. *Jurisprudence.*
2. *The Nature and Sources of Law,* sec. 191.
3. *System des heutigen romischen Rechts,* sec. 7.
4. *Idem,* sec. 7.
5. *Early History of Institutions*, p. 380.
6. *Commentaries on American Law,* sec. 2.
7. *Idem*, sec. 15, note.
8. *Elements of Jurisprudence,* 6th ed., p. 49.
9. *Lectures on Jurisprudence,* sec. II, p. 564.
10. *Idem,* sec. II, p. 567.
11. *Elements of Jurisprudence,* 6th ed., pp. 54–55.
12. Prof. John Dewey in *Pol. Sci. Quar.*, March, 1894, p. 47.
13. *Province of Jurisprudence Determined,* Lecture I.
14. Regarding the value of Austin's conception of law and Sovereignty, Mr. Justice Markby (*Elements of Law*, 2d ed., p. 4) speaks as follows: "Austin, by establishing the distinction between law and morals, not only laid the foundation for a science of law, but cleared the conception of law and of sovereignty of a number of pernicious consequences to which, in the hands of his predecessors, it had been supposed to lead. Laws, as Austin has shown, must be legally binding; and yet a law may be unjust. Resistance to authority cannot be a legal right, and yet it may be a virtue."

15. See chap. VI.
16. A by-law of a corporation, or a rule established by any other society or body which has not a public character, that is, which is not a part of the governmental organization of the State, is a *fact* rather than a law—a fact to which, as in the case of other facts, the courts will attach significance in determining the law to be applied in controversies involving such fact or facts.
17. *Cf. Gray, Nature and Sources of Law,* sec. 234 ff. Gray, discussing the situation presented when juries fail to convict persons violating in established law, as for example, a law forbidding the sale of wine, says: "This statute, being followed by the courts is an element of the law in the State, but it is not the whole law. It is also doubtless law in the State that no one shall be punished for crime except after being found guilty by a jury. The whole law must be taken together. We say the law is that a man selling, wine shall be punished, but in truth the law is, that a man selling wine and convicted thereof by a jury shall be punished. If there has been no conviction by a jury, one of the elements which the law declares necessary for the infliction of punishment does not exist."

    In a later section (§260) Gray discusses the situation presented when two or more courts of coördinate power render divergent decisions as to what is the law, and says that it must then be said that, as to the matter involved, there is no established law. This conclusion is not wholly satisfactory. For the judgements or decrees of the courts in each case constitute the law for the parties to such cases. They are legally bound by them. The result is, not that there is no law upon the subject involved, but that—unfortunate though it may be—it is a different one in the different jurisdictions of the courts which have passed upon it, and that, as a result, there is probably uncertainty as to what the law will be declared to be in still other jurisdictions of the State.
18. Lecture I
19. Austin's emphasis upon the idea of force or compulsion, that is, upon the matter of obtaining, in fact, obedience to the directions contained in laws, appears also in his definition of sovereignty and of sovereign bodies-politic. There he says, "If a determinate human superior. not in a habit of obedience to a like superior, receive habitual obedience from the bulk of a given society, that determinate superior is sovereign in that society and that society (including the superior) is a society political and independent." *The Province of Jurisprudence Determined,* chap. IV.

III

The Birth and Death of State: A Juristical Consideration

The juristic birth of a particular State occurs when the political organization that is involved first assumes, or becomes endowed with, the attribute of sovereignty. In order, then, that this genesis may be determined, if it has occurred within a period concerning which authentic historical records exist, it is first necessary that some conclusions be reached as to the tests by which the existence of the quality of sovereignty in a given body-politic may be certainly recognised, and some agreement be reached as to the processes by which this juristic attribute may be created. It will conduce to clearness of thought if we separate the discussion of the tests by which the existence of sovereignty may be determined, from the juristic processes by which sovereignty may be brought into being. And first as to the processes.

One Sovereignty Cannot Create Another Sovereignty. It would seem to be a necessary logical conclusion from the nature of sovereignty that legal authority cannot, by its own will or act, create another authority legally superior or even equal to itself. The created cannot, be the equal and much less the superior of its creator: it necessarily remains but the agent for the exercise of the authority of the political being that brings it into being. When, therefore this juristically created entity functions volitionally, it can do more than express what, in the last analysis, is the legal will of its legal progenitor.

Sovereignty Cannot Be Created by a Union of Sovereignties. The Same reasoning applies to the attempt of a number of severally sovereign political entities to create, by a joint action or common agreement among themselves, an authority legally superior to themselves. A general or public will, in other words, cannot be created by a mere union of individual or private wills. Thus, a numbers of severally sovereign States may create for themselves organs of government which each of them will severally regard as their own governmental organs for the purposes specified, and through which they will be able to maintain concerted and unified action. But they cannot create above and over themselves a sovereign body-public. As a result, sovereign States may enter into agreements or compacts with one another by which they or their peoples become morally or politically or internationally obligated, but they cannot conceivably be legally bound by the terms of the treaty or compact into which they have entered or, by that treaty or compact, create a legal superior which, for the future, can legally control them by its commands.

John C. Calhoun, in his *Discourse on the Constitution and Government of the United States*, expounded the logic of this proposition in a manner that has since permitted no successful denial. His argument is so cogent that it may profitably be quoted at length. Starting with the premise that the Constitution of the United States of America was, in its essential character, a product of the concurring wills of the original thirteen severally sovereign American Commonwealths, he says of its National instrument of government:

"They (the States) stand (to it) in the relation of superior to subordinate—the creator to the created. The people of the several States called it into existence, and conferred by it on the Government, whatever power or authority it possesses. Regarded simply as a constitution, it is as subordinate to them as are their respective State Constitutions, and it imposes no more restrictions on the exercise of any of their sovereign rights than they do."

Such, says Calhoun, remains the relation of the States to their common agent, the National Government. As between themselves, the States having ratified and adopted the constitution, "they stand to it in the relation of parties to a constitutional compact, and of course, it is binding between them as a *compact*, and not on or over them as a *Constitution*. But, as solemn and sacred as it is, and as high as the obligations may be which it imposes, still it is but a *compact* and not a *Constitution,* regarded in reference to the people of the several State in their sovereign capacity... Hence, a State, acting in the same manner in which it ratified and adopted the constitution, may be guilty of violating it *as a compact*, but cannot be guilty of violating it as a *law*. The case is the reverse as to the action of its citizens, regarding them in their individual capacity. To them it is a law, —

the supreme law within its sphere. They may be guilty of violating it *as a law*, or of violating the laws and treaties made in pursuance of, or under its authority, regarded as laws or treaties, but cannot be guilty of violating it as a *compact*. The constitution was established *over them* by their respective States, to whom they owed allegiance, and they are under the same obligation to respect and obey its authority, within its respective sphere, as they are to respect and obey their respective State constitutions; and for the same reasons, namely: that the State to which they owe allegiance, commanded it in both cases."[1]

Sovereignty Cannot Be Transferred. It follows from what has been already determined, that one sovereign State can no more obtain its sovereignty by a transfer from one another sovereign State already in being, than it can create *de novo*, a sovereignty over and above itself.

As a matter of fact, of course, it often happens that one State extends its jurisdiction over the citizen body and lands of another State, and, not infrequently, this extension is marked and evidenced by the formal consent of the governing authorities of the State whose lands and citizen are thus absorbed. But, juristically viewed, the change is due to a unilateral act upon the part of the annexing State, which, exercising its sovereign authority, asserts its legal control over the annexed lands and their inhabitants. In other words, the political jurisdiction thus obtained owes its juristic validity in no wise to any consenting act of the State previously having jurisdiction over the lands and peoples that have come under the new sovereignty. This is true even when the transfer of sovereignty is provided for by a treaty between the two States concerned. In such a case the treaty acknowledges rather than accomplishes the transfer."[2]

Juristically viewed the same result is obtained when we have to deal with the recognition by a State of the independence of a colony or province which has withdrawn from beneath the sovereignty under which it has formerly lived. In such a case the existence of the new State dates from the time of the withdrawal, and not from the time when its independence is conceded by the parent State; and the existence of its sovereignty is founded upon the fact that it no longer recognizes allegiance or renders obedience to the old sovereignty, and not upon the fact that the old sovereignty has by a treaty or other form of declaration indicated that it no longer claims its allegiance. So, similarly, the sovereignty of any new State which is recognized by other States as such and admitted into the "Family of Nations" is not created by or founded upon, such international recognition. That recognition is extended by each state when it sees fit, and, when accorded, is nothing more than an acknowledgment of an accomplished fact. There is no claim that the recognition is a creative act; and this fact is shown, if indeed any demonstration is needed, that it frequently happens that recognition of a new sovereignty is denied by one or more States for years after its existence has been conceded by the other States. If, then, a creative character were assigned to "Recognition" the absurd result would be reached that the new State both existed and did not exist, its status being determined not by any real fact of independent existence, but, in each case, by what night fortuitously happen to be the state of mind of other bodies-politic.

Applying the foregoing reasoning, by way of illustration, to the United States of America, it is seen that the colonies formerly in allegiance to Great Britain acquired their sovereignties when they organized themselves as Independent communities. Their autonomous condition did not date from the promulgation of the treaty of peace with the mother country, but, if any precise date can be assigned to it, from the signing of the Declaration of Independence. This doctrine was accepted by the Supreme Court of the United States in the case of *McIlvaine v. Coxe's Lessee*[3] in the opinion in which case it is said: "The several States which compose this Union, so far at least as regards their municipal regulations, became entitled, from the time when they declared themselves independent, to all the rights and powers of sovereign States, and they did not derive them from concessions made by the British King. The treaty of peace contains a recognition of their independence, not a grant of it."

A somewhat different proposition is presented when a new State emerges from the Union of two or more sovereign States. The juristic interpretation of this political transaction will receive full consideration in the chapter dealing with the so-called Composite State. It is sufficient here to say that where there is such a merger of formerly sovereign States and the creation of a single new sovereign body, the original States must be conceived to have gone out of existence, and the bodies-politic which continue to bear their name and apparently continue their existence, must be regarded as new bodies-politic of an essentially different nature. They are non-sovereign bodies,[4] which, in contemplation of constitutional law, are the creations of the new sovereignty, and have a status only insofar as they are conceived of as products of its will. The original sovereignties cease to exist; and the new sovereignty rests upon its own basis and is not the product of their union. Their agreement to unite, as evidenced in a treaty or other instrument, is thus of no juristic significance. Its importance is purely thus of no juristic significance. Its importance is purely political, marking, as it does, merely the acquiescence of the peoples of the original

States, or, at least, of their governing bodies, in their dissolution as independent bodies-politic, and their willingness to live under the new sovereignty which is to come into being.

Where a portion of the lands and the citizens of one State are transferred from beneath one sovereignty and brought under the jurisdiction of another sovereignty, there is clearly no transfer of its sovereignty by the one State to the other. Both States remain in existence with their several sovereignties unimpaired.[5]

To the historian it may be convenient to date the origin of a new State from the adoption of a constitution, as, for example, to date the birth of the United States from 1789; but, to the jurist, the Constitution must be viewed as a Law,—as the product of the legislative will of a State already in existence, and as providing an outline for its governmental machinery. The State itself must be conceived of as the product of the desire and will of a people of maintain a political existence as a group, as a sovereign legal person, acknowledging no legal control arising outside of its own will. Synchronously with the establishment of this political unity is the establishment, more or less spontaneously and informally, of new instrumentalities for the expression of the State's will or the adoption as its own for the same purpose of old governmental organs already in existence. Thus, if we conceive that a sovereign national state existed in 1789, we must view that State as accepting *ad hoc*, as its own organs the conventions in the several States which ratified the Constitution.

Non-Juristic Origin of Sovereignty. In result, then, we may say that, strictly speaking, a juristic origin cannot be ascribed to sovereignty. Legally, each sovereign State starts, as it were, *de novo*, and cannot have any legal bonds that unite it to any previously existing political body. Juristically a new State can take its origin only by the entire withdrawal of the people organized under it from the civic bonds under which they may have been living, and the establishment by them of a new body-politic. Not until the old State has been destroyed, either peaceably or by force, can the new State take its rise. It cannot derive its vitality from the old, for, as we have seen, the transference of sovereignty is a legal impossibility.

A State Cannot Commit Juristic Felo de Se. It has been earlier pointed out that the sovereign State may, through it constitutional law, fix the manner in which and the governmental organs through which, its sovereignty is to be exercised, but that these self-set constitutional limitations are necessarily repealable by the State, acting in pursuance of that same sovereign authority which enabled it to establish them in the first place, and that thus the State's sovereignty is neither destroyed nor impaired. It has also been shown that a change in form of the governmental organization of a State does not mean that the existence of the State has been destroyed and a new sovereignty created.

Dicey in his *Law of the Constitution* [6] says: "The impossibility of placing a limit on the exercise of sovereignty, does not in any way prohibit either logically or a matter of fact, the abdication of sovereignty. This is worth observation because a strange dogma is sometimes put forth that a sovereign power, such as the Parliament of the United Kingdom, can never by its own act dives itself of sovereignty. The position, however, is clearly untenable. An autocrat, such as the Russian Czar, can undoubtedly abdicate; but sovereignty, or the possession of a supreme power in a State, whether it be in the hands of a Czar or of a Parliament, is always one and the same quality. If the Czar can abdicate, so can Parliament. To argue or imply that because sovereignty is not limitable (which is true) it cannot be surrendered (which is palpably untrue) involves the confusion of two district ideas. It is like arguing that because no man can, while he lives, give up, do what he will, his freedom of volition, so no man can commit suicide. A sovereign power can divest itself of authority in two ways, and (it is submitted) in two ways only. It may simply put an end to its own existence. Parliament could extinguish itself by legally dissolving itself and leaving no means whereby a subsequent Parliament could be legally summoned. It sovereign, again, may transfer sovereign authority to another person or body of persons."

Here it is clear that Dicey is confusing the existence of the sovereign State with the continuance of the governmental machinery through which its sovereignty is exercised. The abdication of an absolute monarch on the surrender of power by a legal omnipotent legislation body does not operate to destroy the State which stands back of those governmental agencies.[7]

The Annexation of the Hawaiian Islands by the United States Juristically Analyzed. Instances have occurred, however, in which one State, by its own official act, has consented to its own absorption into another State and thus to a cessation of its own independent existence. An illustration of this was exhibited in 1897-1898, when the Hawaiian Islands were incorporated into and became an integral part of the territory of the United States. Article XXXII of the Constitution of the Republic of Hawaii, adopted in 1894, expressly authorized the President, with the approval of his Cabinet and ratification of the Senate, to make a treaty of political union between the Republic and the United States of America. The power thus granted was exercised in 1897, a treaty providing for union with the United States being negotiated by the President with the approval of his Cabinet and ratified by the Hawaiian Senate. This treaty was not, however, ratified by the treaty-making organ of the United States– the President and Senate. Instead, a Joint Resolution was adopted on July 7, 1898, by the two Houses of the American Congress, which read, in part as follows:

"Whereas, the Government of the Republic of Hawaii having in due form signified its consent, in the manner provided by its Constitution, to cede absolutely and without reserve to the United States the absolute fee and ownership of all public Government or crown lands, public buildings or edifices, ports, harbors, military equipment, and all other public property of every kind and description belonging to the Government of the Hawaiian Islands together with every right and appurtenance thereto appertaining; therefore be it.

"Resolved, that said cession is accepted, ratified and confirmed and that the said Hawaiian Islands and their dependencies be, and they are hereby annexed as a part of the territory of the United States, and are subject to the sovereign dominion thereof, and that all and singular the property and rights hereinbefore mentioned are vested in the United States of America."

Later, on August 12, 1898, upon the occasion of the formal raising of the American flag over the Hawaiian Islands, Mr. Dole, who until then had been the President of the Hawaiian Republic, addressing the American representative, said:

"A treaty of political union having been made, and the cession formally consented to by the Republic of Hawaii having been accepted by the Union States of America, I now in the interest of the Hawaiian body-politic, and with full confidence in the honor, justice and friendship of the American people, yield out to you as the representative of the Government of the United States, the sovereignty and public property of the Hawaiian Islands."

Analyzing the foregoing steps by means of which the absorption of Hawaii into the United States, and its consequent disappearance as a sovereign entity was effected, it is clear that, so far as the United States was concerned, no more than a moral or political significance was attached to the fact that the Hawaiian Government, presumably voicing the wishes of the Hawaiian people, had given its assent to the annexation. As a legal proposition, the extension of American sovereignty over the Islands resulted from the act of the American Government as manifested in the Joint Resolution. As to the legal effect, if any, which the action of the Hawaiian Government had as towards the Hawaiian people or State, it can be said that it was not an illegal act since it was one authorized by the Hawaiian constitution; and yet it cannot be said to have operated, *ipso facto*, to terminate the juristic life of the Hawaiian State. That did not occur until the American sovereignty was extended over the Islands and their inhabitants. It is correct, therefore, to say that, even in this case, in which express constitutional authority was given to the Government to agree to union with the United States, the annihilating stroke to the Hawaiian sovereignty was the act of the American State.

Summary. In result then, we are justified in saying that, as regards the termination of sovereignty, the situation is the reverse of that of its birth or creation. In other words, every State derives its sovereignty from itself. Sovereignty is a spontaneous or self-generated status and is never derived from an outside source. Upon the other hand, the juristic death of a sovereign State necessarily results from the act of another State, except perhaps in the conceivable case of the disappearance of every vestige of political authority over a people brought about by the acts of that people and without acceptance by them of the sovereignty of or the assertion of such sovereignty by another State.

As contrasted with the birth of a sovereign body-politic, the creation of a non-sovereign bodies always due to the juristic act of some other sovereign State. But sovereign and non-sovereign entities are alike as regards their death or destruction. In both cases this is brought about by the act of another State.

Tests for the Determination of the Existence of Sovereignty. As has been above pointed out, the question as to the manner in which, from a juristic point of view, a sovereignty may be created or terminated, is distinct from the enquiry as to the tests by which the existence of a sovereign body-politic may be determined.

The conclusion that we have reached that each sovereignty begins *de navo*, and is not the juristic product of another sovereign will, leads necessarily to the proposition that the existence or non-existence of sovereignty is, strictly speaking, a matter of fact rather than a law. This fact is whether or not the political organization in question is regarded as having complete juristic competence to determine its own legal powers.

The phrase "recognized as having" is used advisedly since it points to the fact that if sovereignty, in its strict juristic sense, be divorced from the ideas of physical power, of ethical rights, or of political expediency, the question whether or not a given political organization is an agency of a legal sovereignty depends upon the point of view from which it is regarded. It is not only conceivable, but often the actual case, that a given government is regarded by certain of the individuals of a community as legally entitled to declare and enforce the will of the sovereign State, whereas other persons of that same community assert that the Government in question has no legal basis and therefore that it is not qualified, in their opinion, to express and enforce the sovereign will to which they conceive themselves to be subject, and, consequently, that such actual powers of coercion over them as it is able to exercise are matters of mere superiority of might and not of legal right. Thus arises the important distinction between Governments *de facto* merely, and those which are *de jure*.

De Facto and De Jure Governments Distinguished. As an abstract to detached proposition, it cannot be said that any given governments *de jure* or *de facto,* for the application of the terms necessarily depends upon the points of views of those who employ them. Thus a government is *de jure* as well as *de facto* when it is recognized as such by the individuals over whom its control is extended. It is *de facto* but not *de jure* as to any particular individual when, though actually in existence and able to exercise a certain amount of power, its legal character is denied by him. Thus, in the case of an attempted revolution, from the standpoint of those who have repudiated their allegiance to the old State, who refuse obedience to its government, and have organized for themselves a new political machinery, the old government has only an actual and not a legal existence, the new government being the only one which, in their eyes, possesses a legal basis. Upon the other hand, from the point of view of those who still support the old State, the newly established government has but a *de facto* existence, the old government being regarded as the only legal organization. Thus, during the American Civil War, the existence of the Southern Confederacy as a State, through regarded as *de jure* by its adherents, was never recognized by the United States nor by Foreign Powers. The existence of a *de facto* Confederate Government was, however, recognized by the United States for belligerent purposes. The continued allegiance of its supporters to the United States was, however, always asserted by the United States, and no legal force of any sort was ever ascribed, then, or after the end of the war, to any of the acts of the Southern Confederacy. No formal treaty of peace was entered into between the United States and the Southern Confederacy, the surrender of its armies being received simply as military acts, and its Government permitted to go out of actual existence without any formal action to mark its demise.

Thus, also, in 1660, when the Stuarts were restored to rule in England, the beginning of the reign of King Charles II was dated from the death of his father, Charles I, in 1649, for, from the standpoint of the Stuarts, the Commonwealth Government, though in actual control for more than a decade, had never had more than a *de facto* existence. So, also, when the Bourbons again ascended the French throne, the first ruler took the title of Louis the Eighteenth, although the legitimate successor of Louis the Sixteenth never, in fact, for a moment held the reins of government. If he had done so, however, he would have been styled Louis the Seventeenth. During the time that the Commonwealth Government was in existence in England and the period of revolutionary rule in France, the governments that existed were, of course, *de jure*, regarded from the points of view of their supporters.

No government which is regarded as *de facto* can be said to evolve by mere effluxion of time into a *de jure* government. Therefore Bryce is not correct when he says: "Sovereignty *de facto*, when it has lasted for a certain time and shown itself stable, ripens into sovereignty *de jure*."[8] What really happens in such a case is that the persons who at first deny a legal character to the *de facto* government abandon this point of view, accept the situation of fact, and give their allegiance to the existence government.

Final Test of Sovereignty. In the chapter which follows, dealing with the Federal State, we shall have occasion to apply, in the case of the United States, the distinction that has been made between governments *de facto* merely, and those which are *de jure*, and also to examine the juristic tests by means of which it is possible to determine whether, in the American Union, the sovereignty resides in the National body or is retained by each of the constituent States. The general proposition may here be laid down, however, that the presence or absence of sovereignty in a given political entity depends upon whether or not that entity has such complete control over its own legal competence that it cannot, against its own legal will, be legally bound in any way whatsoever by the legal will of another political body. This is the one and final test of sovereignty. The sovereign state may, in other words, bind itself to any extent by its own will, in the form of constitutional limitations laid upon the powers of its own governmental agencies, or, by treaties it may give its undertaking to other States not to exercise certain of its powers, or to exercise them only in certain ways, but these self-set limitations it may legally—if not morally—escape from by an exercise of that same sovereign will in pursuance of which they were created. Its sovereignty is not, therefore, impaired. If, then, we find a political entity so united to, or so associated with, another political entity that it cannot escape from that union or association without a breach of law, as distinguished from a violation of international or moral obligation, it is not a sovereign State. If, upon the other hand, it can escape without its secession being an illegal act, it remains sovereign. Having this right, it may, while still retaining its sovereignty, enter into comprehensive agreements as to conforming its actions to those of other States with which it may associate itself, or as to accepting as its own the acts of a common governing agency which it, or those other States, may have agreed to establish and maintain.

The foregoing reasoning applies to cases in which a new sovereignty is created in derogation of one or more pre-existing sovereignties. When this is not the case, whatever political changes may occur relate only to alterations in governmental structure. No new State is created and no State goes out of existence. This is true, as has been earlier adverted to in the chapter dealing with Government, even when the changes in political organization have been brought about by means not sanctioned by pre-existing constitutional law. In this latter case it is perhaps possible to conceive of the State, as organized in its older Government, as going out of existence and a new State as being born with a new Government. But such an interpretation hardly seems necessitated by juristic logic. It would mean that, with the demise of the older sovereignty, all the existing legal rights and duties, public and private, would have to be regarded as destroyed, because the legal basis upon which they had rested would have been removed, and they would then have to be conceived of as impliedly recreated by the new sovereignty. It seems simpler and sufficiently logical to regard the original State as maintaining a continued existence and as having merely given to itself, by an original and direct constitutive act, a new governmental organization.

References

1. *Works of Calhoun*, vol. I, p. 275. The italics are in the original.
2. Upon this point may be quoted the following from Brownson's *The American Republic*, chap. IX: "An independent State, a nation, may with or without its consent, lose its sovereignty, but only by being merged in, or subjected to, another. Independent sovereign States cannot, by convention

or mutual agreement, from themselves into a single sovereign State or nation. The compact or agreement is made by the sovereign States, and binds by virtue of the sovereign power of each of the contracting parties. To destroy that sovereign power would be to annul the compact, and render void the agreement. The agreement can be valid and binding only on condition that each of the contracting parties retains the sovereignty that rendered it competent to enter into the compact; and States that retain severally their sovereignty do not form a single State or Nation. The States in convention cannot become a new and single sovereign State unless they lose their several sovereignty and merge it in the new sovereignty; but this they cannot do by agreement, because the moment the parties to the agreement cease to be sovereign, the agreement on which alone depends the new sovereign State is vacated in like manner as a contract is vacated by the death of the parties. The convention either of sovereign States or of sovereign individuals, with the best will in the world, can form only a compact, whatever its terms or conditions—is only an alliance, a league or a confederation, which no one can pretend is a sovereign State or republic."

3. 2 Cranch 280.
4. Whether or not they may properly be termed States will be later considered.
5. It is, of course, possible for a state to relinquish and consent to the incorporation into another State, of a portion of its own territory without at the same time surrendering, or the annexing State claiming, the primary allegiance of the inhabitants of the territories which are concerned. Where such allegiance is not altered, these inhabitants, by the transfer of the territory which they occupy, become resident aliens in their relation to the annexing State. It may, indeed, be said that it is now the practice of civilized States, when territories are transferred from one to another sovereignty, to provide that their inhabitants may have the option whether or not they will become citizens of the annexing State. See, for example, the treaty by which the jurisdiction of Spain over the Philippines and Porto Rico was surrendered and the jurisdiction of the United States over these islands asserted.
6. Fourth ed., p. 65.
7. Westlake in his *International Law*, p. 63, is thus correct when he says, "It is impossible that the extinction of a State, or even its union with another State on terms involving the loss of its separate existence as a State of International Law, can ever be effected by voluntary arrangement in a constitutional manner. This is so, even when the extinction or union is voted by a parliament which, for all purposes comprised in carrying on the State as it exists, is regarded as omnipotent."
8. *Studies in History and Jurisprudence;* chapter: "The Nature of Sovereignty."

IV

The Federal State

The facts that seem that to make especially difficult the application of the principles that have been evolved with reference to the subject of Sovereignty, are those presented by the various types of so-called Composite or Federal States. To many publicists, these political forms exhibit examples of States with divided or limited sovereignty, of non-sovereign political bodies but yet entitled to be termed States, and of sovereign States juristically created by the joint action of other States.

Associations of States. The problem of properly classifying and designating the various associations into which the States of the world have at different times entered, is one that has especially attracted the attention of German publicists. The most important work in this field is, perhaps, that of Jellinek, entitled "*Die Lehre von de Staatenverbindungen,*" which we have already had occasion to cite. Other works are those of Brie, Western-kamp, and Waitz. This subject is also, of course, considered by all writers dealing particularly with the public law of the German Empire. The work of Laband[1] is especially valuable in this respect. Those American writers who have dealt with the constitutional character of their own States, have generally limited themselves to a consideration of the differences between a "Federal State" and a "Confederacy".[2]

Jellinek, in his classification of associations, make the first division into *Unorganized* and *Organized* Unions.[3] These names serve to indicate the distinction that is made between the two classes. In the first class are included instances in which more or less permanent relations between States have been entered into for the regulation of certain mutual interests, but in which no central organization has been created. Such common action as is necessary in these unions is had through one or more of the governmental organs of the individual States. Of course there is not created in any of such cases what would be called a Composite State even by those publicists who use the term "non-sovereign State." Within this category fall such types as "Alliances" for offence or defence, and for the guarantee of particular rights or status, as, for example, the perpetual neutrality of particular territories.

Within this class Jellinek also places that type which he terms the *Staatenstaat*, or that form of union in which there is a superior and an inferior State or States, the latter receiving the orders from the former as from a Foreign Power, and the citizens of the inferior States owing allegiance only to their own States. The most conspicuous historical examples of this type have been the feudal States of the Middle Ages, and the mediaeval German Empire. Of this nature, also have been the relations between the Ottoman Porte and some of its Christian Provinces, as well as the relation between the United States and some of the Indian tribes. Of this order was the relation of Egypt and Turkey, and of Nicaragua and the Mosquito Indians.

All of the above unions Jellinek designates as unorganized unions of a juristic character (*Nichtorganisirte Verbindungen mit juristischem Charakter*). We may properly ask ourselves, however, whether these "Alliances" constitute in any proper sense of the word "unions" of States. Every international treaty provides for the regulation of certain interests in common, and according to conditions mutually agreed upon. In the above-mentioned instances there is not the first beginning made or step taken toward the fusion of the contracting States. Certainly, at any rate, they cannot be designated as unions of a juristic character, for, as analysis will later show, treaty relations are not of this character.[4]

Coming now to "Organized Unions" we find in them, as their name imports, permanent central organs. They admit of segregation into the four following classes: (1) International Administrative Unions, (2) The Realunion and Personalunion, (3) The Staatenbund (Confederacy), and (4) The Bundesstaat (Federal State).

Examples of the first sub-class are combinations of States for the common regulation of particular interests wherein permanent administrative authorities are created. Of this kind are the commissions for the regulation of navigation upon the rivers Po and Danube, and the international Postal and Telegraph Unions. There is the same objection to considering these types of unions of States that we have made to the whole of the class of unorganized unions above considered.

By the term "*Realunion*" is indicated by German publicists that composite type of State life in which there is an intimate and lasting union entered into between two or more sovereign States, according to which there is a common ruler, but a preservation of the territorial divisions, and a recognition and protection of the constitutional rights of each of the uniting States. Thus, it is "that form which arises when two or more independent States unite for common protection, according to which one and the same physical person appears as the representative of the States' authority and according to which the extending of this union to other functions is not forbidden."[5] In other words, the essential element of the Realunion is that it is provided by the constitution of each member State that the representative of its Sovereignty (*Repräsentationshoheit*) shall be in one and the same physical person, and that this connection shall obtain irrespective of who the prescribed qualifications happen to determine this common ruler shall be. The most conspicuous example of this form of union is that formerly exhibited by Austria and Hungary, and Norway and Sweden. And, it may be added, the relation between Great Britain and its "Dominions" is tending toward, if it has not already reached, this type of political association.

It will be seen that that which distinguishes a Realunion from a simple sovereign State whose organization provides for distinct governmental agencies in different portions of its domain is that the members of the union are true sovereign States and that though the powers of the Crown of all of them are vested in the same individual, that individual is constitutionally viewed as having as many distinct official or public personalities as there are State over which he rules. Thus it is possible that, as to one of the States he may be constitutionally regarded as the original and subsisting source of all legal authority, while, as to another of the States he may be viewed as possessing only such powers as have been delegated to him by the citizen body from whose will it is assumed that all legal legitimacy is derived.

A type of union much resembling the Realunion, and, in fact, juristically of the same class, is the so-called Personal union. The distinction between the two consists merely in the fact that the associated States come to have the same ruler only by reason of the casual circumstance that their rules of royal descent, as fixed by their several systems of constitutional law, happen to call to their thrones the same person. In such cases the union of course lasts only during the reigns of such monarchs. Of this character were the relations for a time between England and Hanover, Denmark and Schleswig-Holstein, Prussia and Neuenburg; and such was the relation that once existed between Holland and Luxemburg. In these cases the ruler is to be considered as possessing as many political personalities as there are States under his rule. It is thus proper to consider each of the members of a Personalunion as well of the Realunion as having its own ruling head. The Sovereignty of each of the individual States is preserved.[6]

Federal States (Bundesstaaten) and Confederacies (Staatenbunden). The two main types of the composite State are the Confederacy (*Staatenbund*) and the Federal State (*Bundesstaat*), and a critical examination of the nature of these two forms will serve to bring out the general principles that the applicable in determining the juristic form of ail kinds of political unions. The necessity of this examination is amply testified to by the great diversity that exists in the views held by different publicists upon the various points involved. Thus, Waitz, Bluntschli, Ruttiman, de Tocqueville, and many American writers, maintain the doctrine of divided sovereignty in a Federal State. As regards the nature of our own union, Wheaton and Halleck and other international law writers declare that the international sovereignty of the individual State is destroyed, but domestic sovereignty retained, though it is apparent that in taking this view a conception of sovereignty is taken that makes of it a mere collection of powers so loosely related that they may be separated without loss of real sovereignty to the possessor of any part. According to Twiss, the members of our union though not "independent" are yet "all sovereign States."[7] According to Calhoun and his school, they are completely sovereign; while by the opponents of that school they are held as entirely devoid of this character. As opposed to complete sovereignty, either of the individual States or of the national government, Brownson holds that, "while the sovereignty is and must be in the States, it is in the States united and not in the States severally." "The organic American people do not exist as a consolidated people or State, they exist only as organized into distinct but inseparable States."[8]

Treitschke did not attempt a rigorous juristic analysis of the Federal State, but he evidently had a conception of it peculiar to himself, for he maintained that, in the German Empire, Prussia remained sovereign, although the sovereignties of all the other member States had been swallowed up in that of the Empire.[9]

LeFur says that the peculiar characteristic of the Federal State is the joint participation of the several subordinate states collectively, and their citizen individually, in the formation of the sovereign will : "Un seul caractère peut être considéré comme appartenant en propre à l'Etat fédéral, c'est l'existence dans cette forme l'Etats, entre l'Etat lui-même et les citoyens, d'un neaveau facteur coopérant comme les derniers à la formation de la volonté souveraine. Ce nouveau facteur, cesont les Etats particuliers, qui participent à la souverainti sous une double forme, tantôt indirectement par l'intermédiaire de leur representants, tantôt directement, surtout en matière de revision constitutionnelle, grâce a l'existence d'un véritable referendum d'Etats, semblable à celui qui existe au profit des citoyens dans les républiques démocratiques. Cette participation de certain collectivitiés publiques à la formation de la volonté souveraine existe, on l'a vu, dans tout Etat fédéral; et a l'inverse elle n'existe que la."[10]

Von Mohl declares that the sovereignty is divided between the collective state and its members: "Also Bundesstaat bezeichnet man aber bekanntlich die jenige Vereinigung von Staaten, uber welcher eine gemeinschaftliche Regierung mit allen dazu nothwendigen Rechten und Organen besteht, so dass die Selbständigkeit und namentlich die volkerrechtliche Souveränität der einzelnen theilnehemenden Staaten sehr geschmalert ist, und eine durchgehende Theilung der Regierungsrechts zwischen ihnen und der oberen Gesammtgewalt staatfindet."[11]

Borel, who has given us one of the best discussions of the subject, defines a Federal State as: "un Etat souverain, dont les membres ne sont pas souverains… L'Etat fédératif est done l'Etat dans lequel une certaine participation a l'exercice du pouvoir souverain est accordee à des collectivitiés inférieures, soit qu'on les adjoigne à l'organe souverain pour la formation de lavolonté nationale, soit que, prises dans leur totalité elles forment elles-même cet organe souverain."[12]

This diversity of opinions could be further multiplied if it would serve any good purpose. The point has, however, been made sufficiently plain that, upon this most important topic of public law, an almost chaos of thought reigns. The explanation for this must be that there has not been a proper analysis of the problem as a purely juristic one. We shall therefore be justified if we consider this question with some degree of particularity.

Preliminary Propositions. As an introduction to this examination it will be well to repeat certain of the propositions which have been already established and which will furnish the premises of our argument. These are:

1. That sovereignty signifies the legal competence of the State to determine its own legal rights and obligations as well as those of all persons, natural and artificial, over whom it claims jurisdiction.
2. That sovereignty, thus denoting the legally omnipotent will of the State, is indivisible and inalienable.
3. That two or more States, each possessing this sovereignty or legal omnipotence, cannot enter into relations with one another which are of a strictly legal character. This is a topic which will be more fully discussed in a later chapter, but it is sufficient here to say that inasmuch as a law, *in sensu strictiore*, imports a command from a legal superior to a legal inferior, it cannot apply to relations between two or more sovereign states which stand towards one another as equals. They can enter into agreements that create moral or political but not legal obligations.
4. From this third proposition it follows, that a sovereign State cannot be created through the joint action of two or more previously existing sovereign States. In other words, sovereignty cannot be the product of a treaty.

These principles being established, it is clear that, when dealing with political groups composed of two or more bodies-politic terming themselves States,[13] but two possible juristic alternatives are presented. Either the central or so-called federal body possesses the sovereignty, in which case the federated units are wholly without sovereignty; or these federated units are severally sovereign in which case the central body is wholly without this attribute. If, then, we give the name Federation or Federal Union or Federal State (*Bundesstaat*) to the first of these forms, and to the second the name Confederation or Confederacy (*Staatenbund*), we find that these two political types stand almost poles apart from one another. They are not different species of the same genus, but are juristically antithetical to each other.

Confederacies. In a Confederation the member States retain their full sovereignty and legal independence and strictly speaking, no central State is created. There is a common or central governement but no central sovereignty. The central government is thus nothing more than the common organ or complexus of organs which the severally sovereign States establish and maintain for the carrying out of purposes with reference to which these States have agreed to act as a unit. This central government may thus be viewed as, in effect, a branch of the government of each of the associated States, and all the authority that it exercises as obtained by delegation from these States. The instrument which defines the power of the central government and the corresponding obligation of the States may be known as a Constitution, but accurately speaking, it is nothing more than a treaty to compact between the States, and derives its validity from their consent to it.

This being the juristic nature of a confederacy any member State may withdraw from it without being chargeable with the commission of an illegal act, and this is so even though the articles of confederation may provide for a perpetual union. Such a withdrawal by one or more States may be a violation of international good faith and furnish serious grounds for complaint upon the part of the States remaining within the confederation, but it cannot be properly asserted by them that the secession is an illegal or unconstitutional act.

Distinct from the right of secession is the claim sometimes put forth that, in a confederacy, each member State retains the right to determine whether or not it will permit the enforcement within its limits of those orders of the central government which, in the opinion of such State, are not authorized by the constitution or articles of union. This is known as the doctrine of Nullification. Here again it may be said that, inasmuch as each State is admitted to be legally sovereign, it cannot be held to act illegally if it refuse obedience to orders of which it disapproves. But such a disobedience, unless expressly recognized by the articles of union, is necessarily a breach of those articles; and, furthermore, the assertion of the right is, in itself, and unreasonable one, for, if exercised, the effect is, to allow a State to remain in the confederation and obtain all the advantages flowing from it while at the same time refusing to abide by such special commands as happen to be onerous or otherwise objectionable to itself. The claim of a right of nullification is thus, some ways, a more extreme claim than is the assertion of a right of secession from the Union.[14]

Among the more important examples of confederacies may be mentioned the old German Union which lasted from 1815 to 1866, the Swiss Confederacy under the Part of 1815 (1815 to 1840), and the Union of the former American Colonies from 1781 to 1789 under the Articles of Confederation.

Federal States. As distinguished from a confederacy a federal State (Bundesstaat) connotes the existence of a true central sovereign State, composed of constituent States which are not themselves severally sovereign. There are some jurists who deny that these constituent bodies-politic may be properly termed States, but is common speech they are usually spoken of as such, and the question whether or not this is technically correct from a juristic standpoint, will, for the present, be postponed.

The central government of a federal State, being conceived of as the organ of a true central State, is not to be regarded as the common organ through which the member States of the Union realize certain of their individual ends. Rather, the reverse is the case, for the central State, being admittedly sovereign, and the member States not sovereign, their governments may properly be regarded as organs through which the central State exercises its sovereign will in the several areas of the sovereign member States.

The federal State is thus to be viewed as deriving it authority from its own inherent sovereignty and not by way of delegation from the member States. It may, indeed, be the historical fact that the Union was established at the common desire and by the joint cooperation of these States, but, if it be conceded that a national sovereignty exists, it is irrelevant, legally speaking, how this was brought about. The constitutional result is that the member States may no longer be viewed as themselves sovereign and upon a constitutional level with the National State.

Federal States and Confederacies Distinguished. In the Federal State, then, a true central State is created, its several units are legally and constitutionally united, and sovereignty–the power of ultimately determining one's own legal competence–resides in the federal body. In the Confederacy, on the other hand, the individual States retain their character as States, and their relations to each other are of an international or treaty character. Consequently no central State is created, and sovereignty lies wholly within such individual political units. What union there is in the Confederacy is the creation of the wills of the individual States. In a Federal State, on the other hand, its foundation rests in itself. It is created by the people as a whole, and the individual States are creations of its will. In the case of a Federal State, historically founded upon a union of previously existing sovereign States, one is to consider the citizens of the Federal State as first divesting themselves of their old State Sovereignties, and then, as a People, establishing a national Federal State. These two volitional acts may be synchronous and made apparent by a single outward act, viz, the establishment of a federal control, but they are distinct acts from a political standpoint. The apparent continued existence in the Federal States of what were formerly independent political bodies, is not real. Those bodies-politic are destroyed when their citizens transfer their allegiance to the central power. They are recreated as bodies-politic by the federal constitution. They are thus creations of the Federal State, and, as Lincoln said in his first message to Congress, "The States have their status in the Union and they have no other legal status. The Union is older than any of the States, and in fact created them as States."[15]

Thus, if we take the position that a national State was created by the American people in 1789, we must consider them to have become a psychologically united People before that time and to have destroyed their former individual States when they established the present Federal States. This being so, the fact that the constitution was adopted by conventions convened in what had formerly been the several States, must be interpreted as meaning merely that a united People saw fit, for the sake of convenience and expediency, to utilize existing governments machinery and territorial divisions for the formal adoption of its new constitution. And that therefore such conventions were, in fact, Federal and not State organs.

Austin states so concisely the distinctions between federal States and Confederacies, his words deserve quotation. He says:

"A composite (federal) state, and a system of confederated states, are broadly distinguished by the following differences. In the case of a composite state, the several united societies are one indpendent society, or are severally subject to one sovereign body; which through its minister, the general government, and through its members and ministers the several united governments, is habitually and generally obeyed in each of the united societies, and also in the larger society arising from the union of all. In the case of a system of confederate states, the several compacted societies are not one society, and are not subject to a common sovereign; or (changing the phrase) each of the several societies is an independent and political society, and each of their several governments is properly sovereign or supreme. Though the aggregate of the several governments was the framer of the federal compact, and may subsequently pass resolutions concerning the entire confederacy, neither the terms of that compact, nor such subsequent resolutions, are enforced in any of the societies by the authority of that aggregate body. To each of the confederated governments, these terms and resolutions are merely articles of agreement which it spontaneously adopts; and they owe their legal effect, in its own political society, to laws and other commands which it makes or fashions upon them, and which, of its own authority, it addressed to its own subjects. In short, a system of confederated states is not essentially different from a number of independent governments connected by an ordinary alliance. And where independent governments are connected by an ordinary alliances, none of the allied governments is subject to the allied governments considered as an aggregate body; though each of the allied governments adopts the terms of the alliance, and commonly enforces those terms, by laws and commands of its own, in its own independent community. Indeed, a system of confederated states, and a number of independent governments connected by an ordinary alliance, cannot be distinguished precisely through general or abstract expressions. So long as we abide in general expressions, we can only affirm, generally and vaguely, that the compact of the former is intended to be temporary; and that the ends or purposes which are embraced by the compact are commonly more numerous, and are commonly more complicated, than those which the alliance contemplates."[16]

Distinctions Improperly Made. The analysis of the Federal State as thus far conducted enables us, by way of negative criticism, to point out the invalidity of the following *criteria* that have at times been applied in distinguishing the *Staatenbund* and *Bundesstaat*.

First, the distinction does not lie in the amount of powers actually vested in the central government as compared with those retained by the individual States. As long as the governments of the individual members of the union are considered as parts of the central government, no essential distinction can arise regarding the distribution and actual exercise of its powers. Sovereignty consists not so much in the actual and immediate exercise of functions as in the power potentially possessed to draw to oneself those particular powers that may be seen fit. Federal States may be conceived in which but very few functions are centrally exercised; and, on the other hand, Confederacies imagined, in which the powers of the central government are most ample. But in neither case is the political character of the union thus determined.

Secondly, the distinction between these two political types does not consist in the fact that in the Federal State the operation of federal law is in all cases, directly upon individuals, while, in the Confederacy, the acts of the central power apply to the States as such and through them to their citizens. It is true that the Federal State must not be dependent upon the acquiescence of the individual States for the execution of its laws, bit it is entirely possible that the Federal State may, in some instances at least, operate through the individual States as such.

Also, vice versa, in the Confederation law may operate in some instances directly upon the individual. Thus, while Americans have been accustomed to distinguish the present Union from that maintained under the Articles of Confederation upon this ground, as a matter of fact this rule does not hold good in all cases. As Madison points out in the Federalist.[17] "In some instances, as has been shown, the powers of the new government will act on the States in their collective characters. In some instances also, those of the existing government act immediately on individuals. In cases of capture; of piracy; of the postoffice; or coins; weights, and measures; or trade with the Indians; of claims under grants of land, by different States; and above all, in the case of trials by courts-martial in the army and navy, by which death may be inflicted without the intervention of a jury, or even of a civil magistrate; in all these cases the powers of the confederation operate immediately on the persons and interests of individual citizens."

In fact, then, provided the Federal State has the direct or primary allegiance of the governed, the exact means through which laws are executed is not juristically significant. The essential point is as to whose will is embodies in them. Political expediency demands that the greater and more important functions of the Federal State should be performed through its own central organs rather than through those political bodies in which there rest historical traditions of complete Sovereignty and national autonomy, and a jealousy of over control by the central power. If the Federal State trusts too much to such particular organs there is the danger of its commands being less faithfully performed than they would be by its own agents. This had been the consideration that has caused the United States to create its own courts and marshals and other officials for the determination and execution of matters of federal or interstate interest. In cases where there is even a remote danger of rebellion on the part of the States, the necessity that the central power should keep well within its own hands not only the formulation but the execution of its own orders is proportionately enhanced. The same principles require that, in Confederacies, where there is danger that the central power may usurp the Sovereignty, the States should limit to the smallest amount the functions actually exercised by their common and central organs.

Thirdly, the absence of a requirement for unanimous consent of the States for purposes of amendment of the instrument of union is not decisive as to the non-confederate character of such union. For example, the constitution of the Confederate States of 1861-65, though avowedly creating but a *Staatenbund*, did not require such unanimity. In this case the express provision that each State was to continue individually sovereign, and with the right at any time to withdraw from the union, saved the union from being a federal one. Without this express sovereign provision, the power of a fraction of the individual States to amend the constitution, against the will of the remaining fraction, would necessarily have resulted in creating a *Bundesstaat*. For, under such a condition, it would have been theoretically possible at any time for any particular State to be subjected to a legal control against its own will,—a condition incompatible with its Sovereignty.[18]

On the other hand, where there is this requirement of unanimity of vote for purposes of constitutional amendment, a Confederacy is not necessarily created, any more than the absence of such a provision denotes the existence of a Federal State. To be sure, under such a condition, no individual State can be further deprived of any of its powers without its own consent, yet, on the other hand, it may not legally escape from the obligations already imposed upon it by the constitution, or withdraw from the union. Where there is not this power on the part of a State of avoiding obligations already created the Sovereignty must be held to rest with the central authority. The fact that the unanimous vote of the federated States is necessary means only that the federal State has made the act of altering its actual competence extremely difficult. In other words, no one individual State has the legal power to alter its actual legal competence, and hence is not sovereign. The central State alone has the power of constitutional amendment, though it is a power subject to extreme formal limitation. But the fact that it is so formally limited does not mean that the power does not exist, any more than it can be claimed that the old Polish assembly did not have legislative power because of the existence of the *liberum veto.* Practically, of course, in any State of developing civilization, such a condition as this in which the individual State has not the power of secession, and, at the same time, the central power cannot change its governmental powers except under conditions that in the great majority of cases could not be obtained, would soon prove unworkable and would precipitate a revolution either by way of succession on the part of the individual States, or by an unconstitutional enlargement of central powers.

Fourthly, and finally, the distinction between a Federal and a Confederate State is not one of enumerated or un-enumerated powers. It is not a question, as has been already said, of the amount of powers actually exercised at any one time by the central government. Even Westerkamp, who holds the distinction between these two types of union to be a quantitative rather than a qualitative one, does not place any weight upon this feature.[19]

The True Test. The final test in all cases is, as has been so many times said, the power or lack of power of the individual State to determine the extent of its own obligations under the articles of union, and, in the last resort, if their view be not acquiesced in by the general government, to withdraw from the union. Where it is constitutionally provided that, in case of alleged conflict between federal and state law, such conflict shall be considered by a federal tribunal whose decrees are enforceable by the federal executive, then, in such case, a *Bundesstaat* certainly exists. If, on the other hand, it be held that a dissatisfied State has the right of secession, there is only a provisional right of federal enforcement, namely, provisional upon the consent of the State to remain in the union.

Nullification. The doctrine of nullification which grants to the individual members of the union the right to refuse obedience to any general law that it deems inconsistent with the articles of union is of course applicable only to a Confederacy. But even there it cannot be termed a legal "right" of nullification. Each member of the union, being completely sovereign, may govern its action by its own will, and no other member may legally say nay. But, as practical proposition, it is inconceivable that the assertion of such a power on the part of a particular State would not lead to disruption of the union. For it can scarcely be imagined that the other members would consent to the avoidance by such State of the execution of a part of the general law while they held themselves bound to it. Such a condition of affairs would, in fact, result, *ipso facto,* in a destruction of the union to that extent, its sole purpose being to secure a concert of action in matters of general interest. It would, indeed, be a just *casus belli* against the State so refusing obedience to the agreement in which it bound itself to common action. Jefferson, the author of the Kentucky Resolutions, himself asserted the propriety of even a confederate government coercing a State when he wrote to Cartwright advising the Congress of the old Confederacy to send a frigate and compel a State to pay its quota of taxes.

American and German Federations Contrasted. The foregoing has had reference to the essential juristic distinction between Confederacies and Federal States. It has been seen that the difference is not a quantitative one as to the number or importance of the powers which are exercised by the central government. With reference to most of the functions of government it is a matter of policy rather than of constitutional or juristic necessity as to which of them shall be exercised by organs and agencies of the central government or by the member States through their several governmental organizations. Thus the United States and the German Republic are both types of Federal States, but they differ widely in this respect. The United States is legislatively decentralized; that is, the great body of the private law is furnished by each State of the union for its own citizens. The subjects of legislation that are placed within the control of the national congress, though very important, are not many in number. From the governmental point of view, however, the United States is a highly developed Federal Union, for there exists a complete central governmental machinery–executive and judicial as well as legislative–through which all the federal powers are exercised. Only in a very few instances are federal laws enforced through the agencies of the individual State.

As contrasted with the United States, the German Republic is legislatively highly centralized. The entire body of the private law and judicial procedure, civil and criminal, is within the control of the national Parliament, the States retaining legislative powers only with reference to their own public law and local police. When, however, it comes to the interpretation and execution of the law thus federally determined, the governments of the States are relied upon. Thus the executive branch of the national government includes only those bureaus or departments which have to deal with certain national matters the execution of which it is impossible to concede to the States, and there is no complete judicial system such as is found in the United States.

It does not need to be pointed out that it is an element of weakness for the Federal State to be obliged to resort to the authorities of the member States for the enforcement of its commands. In Germany, however, this weakness under the Empire was rendered negligible by reason of the fact that one State–Prussia–had a prestige and military power that made futile any attempt upon the part of the other States to resist its will, and that the king of this State was *ex officio* Emperor of the Union and constitutionally vested with the duty of bringing back into obedience to federal authority such States as might be declared by the *Bundesrath* to be derelict in the performance of their imperial duties. In such cases the imperial coercion was to be applied directly to the States concerned.

In the United States the existence of complete executive and judicial departments makes possible the vindication of national supremacy by applying compulsion to the individuals who resist the national authority. If, in justification of this resistance, these individuals appeal to laws or executive orders which their respective States have issued, the reply is that, insofar as those laws or orders are in violation of the Federal Constitution or laws, they are without legal force and therefore furnish no legal defence for any actions taken in pursuance of them. Thus, in constitutional theory, the American Civil War of 1861-1865 was contest carried on by the United States against the citizens of the eleven Southern States which had sought to withdraw from the union, rather than against those States themselves.

Citizenship in Federal States. In all federally organized States the aim is to harmonize the continued existence of the member States with the maintenance of national unity and strength. Thus we find alongside of national citizenship the recognition of a State citizenship which has no real analogue in the most autonomous local government areas of unitary States.

In the United States there was for many years a dispute as to the constitutional nexus or relation between federal and state citizenship–whether the former depended upon or arose out of the latter or vice versa–and this controversy was not finally settled until the adoption, in 1868, of the Fourteenth Amendment to the Federal Constitution. This made it certain that federal citizenship was to be held paramount to State citizenship, for, upon the one hand, the States were permitted to play no part in determining who should be deemed citizens of the United States, and upon the other hand, they were not henceforth to be able to control their own citizenship since it was provided that any person enjoying national citizenship should, by mere residence within a State (which that State could not constitutionally prevent), become one of its own citizens. As regards both federal and State citizenship the Fourteenth Amendment declared in absolute terms that "All persons born or naturalized in the United States, and subject to the jurisdiction thereof, are citizens of the United States and of the State wherein they reside."

Though thus placed upon a subordinate plane, the effect of this amendment was not in any way to destroy or to merge State citizenship in the national citizenship. To each citizenship are still attached distinctive and important appurtenant rights, the enumeration or specific description of which would, however, carry us too far into the special constitutional jurisprudence of the United States.

Under the German Imperial Constitution prior to 1918 every citizen of a constituent State was, *ipso facto* a citizen of the Empire but there could also be an imperial citizenship without state citizenship, as for example, of one living in a German colony (*Schutzgebiete)* or accepting an Imperial office.[20] The constitution of the recently established German Republic gives to the National Government exclusive jurisdiction to determine all matters of citizenship (Article 6) and declares (Article 110) that citizenship in the Republic and in the States shall be acquired or lost in accordance with the provisions of national laws passed in pursuance of this national authority. It is, however, specifically declared that every citizen of a State shall be at the same time a citizen of the Republic.

In the constitution of the Swiss Republic it is declared that "every citizen of a canton is a Swiss citizen."

Territories and Dependencies of a Federal State. There is nothing in the nature and form of a federally organized State to make impossible the extension of its sovereignty over areas which are not included within the limits of the member States. Thus, since the beginnings of its existence, the United States has possessed what are called "Territories" which are not States, which occupy a different constitutional status, and have only such autonomous powers and rights of self government as Congress sees fit to grant to them. Some of these areas, known as "Unorganized Territories," have had almost no self-government, while to others, known as "Organized Territories," Congress has given complete governmental structures, including locally elected legislatures. The governors and judges of these organized Territories have, however, been appointed by the President of the United States and the acts of the legislatures have been subject to annulment by Congress,–a right which Congress has, however, very seldom exercised. Since the Spanish-American War the United States has possessed the Philippine and Hawaiian Islands, Porto Rico and other less important islands, which are termed Insular Dependencies but which are, in all but name, colonies pure and simple. In a number of decisions defining the constitutional status of these islands the federal Supreme Court has introduced what is practically a new classification of Territories, dividing them into two groups according to whether or not they have been "incorporated" into the United States. By these decisions it is held that certain constitutional guarantees do not apply to those Territories which have not been "incorporated" but do apply to those which have been accorded this status. Thus, for example, the constitutional provision that all indirect taxes shall be "uniform throughout the United States," has been held not necessarily applicable to "unincorporated" areas. It lies within the discretion of Congress to determine when incorporation shall take place; but, whether incorporated or not, the form of government which a Territory is to enjoy is a matter with regard to which Congress can act as it sees fit.

Constitutional provision is made for the admission of new States into the American Union and thirty-five have been admitted, all of them, with the exception of Texas, being created out of areas previously under the sovereignty of the United States. Texas seceded from Mexico, its independence was recognized by the United States, and it was then admitted to the Union as a State without passing through the Territorial status.

The German Empire, from 1871 to 1919, possessed the Imperial Territories of Alsace and Lorraine. These two provinces, taken from France were, step by step, accorded greater rights of self-government, and a higher constitutional status until, shortly before the outbreak of the Great War, they enjoyed most of the rights possessed by the States of the Empire. In the Dominion of Canada and in the Commonwealth of Australia considerable areas exist which are not accorded the full rights of federal membership. To New Zealand and Australia have been given by the League of Nations "mandates" over certain of the South Pacific islands formerly belonging to Germany.

Equality of States. It is not essential to the federal form of government that the member States should all stand in exactly the same relation to the federal government as regards their respective autonomous power or of their citizens to participate in the control and management of the general government.

In the United States, however, the doctrine of State equality prevails. It is true that different States have a different voting power in the election of the President and Vice-President, and send different quotas of representatives to the lower house of Congress. But these differences arise out of differences of population and are determined by a rule which is uniform in its application to all of the States, so that, even here, it cannot be said that the States are constitutionally unequal.

In Canada the Provinces, and in Australia the States, have equal constitutional rights, and the same is substantially true in Switzerland, where, however, certain of the cantons are known as "half-cantons," which send only one member to the Council of States, whereas the other cantons send two, and have but half a vote when constitutional amendments are being passed upon.

In the old German Empire, however, there were substantial differences in constitutional power of the different States. These are too numerous to enumerate but as illustrations of them it may be mentioned that Prussia's King was *ex officio* the German Emperor, and that to Bavaria, Würtemburg and Baden special rights were accorded with reference to the control of the posts and telegraphs and taxes upon brandy and beer.

Residual Power. In the United States the federal government possesses only those powers specifically given to it by the constitution and such as are "necessary and proper" for the carrying into effect of these specifically granted powers. The State governments, are thus the residual claimants to all powers not granted to the federal government or specifically denied to them by the National Constitution. In the Canadian Federation a greater attempt is made to enumerate just what powers shall be possessed by the Provinces as well as by the Dominion Government, but, from the nature of the case, such enumeration could not be exhaustive and, though the language of the British North American Act of 1867 which serves as the Canadian Constitution is not very plain, it has been established by judicial interpretation that the residual or unenumerated powers belong to the Central Government. In the Australian Commonwealth, in Switzerland, and in Germany the General Government possess only those powers specifically, or by necessary implication, granted to it. The fact, however, that in Switzerland and Germany the constitutionality of a federal statute may not be questioned in the courts, makes it, of course, possible for the federal legislature to construe its own powers as liberally as it may please.

Federal Supervision of the States. In all federally organized states the general government is given certain rights of supervision over the States in order to see that they faithfully execute not only to seeing that the national supremacy is maintained and the free and efficient exercise of its powers in no way interfered with, but to making it certain that the member States do not violate certain personal and property rights which are specially recognized and guaranteed in the Federal Constitution. It may, however, be remarked that in the United States, until the adoption in 1868 of the Fourteenth Amendment to the Federal Constitution, this federal guarantee of protection to the individual against oppressive action upon the part of his own individual State extended only to a few specific matters such as the impairment of the obligation of contracts and protection against penal laws of an *ex post facto* character. Since the adoption of the Fourteenth Amendment, however, the private rights of the individual have to a considerable extent been brought under the protecting power of the National Government by the operation of the provision of that Amendment that no State "shall deprive any person of life, liberty or property, without due process of law; nor deny to any person within its jurisdiction the equal protection of the laws." The requirement of "due process of law" has been given a very broad construction so that it includes not only matters of procedure but substantive rights, irrespective of the procedure by which they may be affected. Thus, in all their dealings with their own citizens or with those who happen to be within their borders, including corporations, the Federal Government sees to it that private rights of life, liberty and property shall not be abridged except upon good grounds, and that, in every case, the procedure by which they are affected shall be such as furnishes the individual affected an opportunity to present before an impartial tribunal such arguments or evidence as he may have, showing why he or his rights should not be brought within the control of a given State law.

Coercion of its Member Commonwealths by a Federal State. In a Confederacy which is, as we have seen, a league of severing States, it is quite appropriate that where one or more of these States may refuse obedience to the commands of the central government coercion should be applied directly upon these States as such. When this becomes necessary a state of public war immediately ensues.

In a Federal State the possibility of enforcing national authority by proceeding directly against the recalcitrant commonwealth is not excluded. Indeed, express provision was made for this in the constitution of the German Empire, Article 19 of which declared that: "If the States of the Confederation do not fulfil their constitutional duties, they may be compelled to do so by execution. This execution shall be decided upon by the *Bundesrath*, and carried out by the Emperor." It is quite logical that this provision for commonwealth coercion should have been made in view of the fact that, in general, in Germany, federal laws were carried into execution through the governmental agencies of the member commonwealths.

In the United States, with but few and unimportant exceptions, federal laws are executed through Federal Governmental agencies and federal officials. It has thus resulted that the constitutional principle has become fixed that the supremacy of the national will is to be maintained, not by direct action against the member States, but by proceedings against individuals, anything in the Constitution or laws of any State to the contrary notwithstanding, and irrespective of what may be the opinions of those exercising the political powers of those States.[21]

The individual States, having a political status only as members of the Union, have not the legal power to place themselves, as political bodies, in opposition to the national will. Their legislatures, their courts, or their executive officials may attempt acts unwarranted by the federal Constitution or federal law, and they may even command that their citizens generally shall refuse obedience to some specified federal laws or to federal authorities generally, but in all such cases such acts are, legally viewed, simply void, and all individuals obeying them subject to punishment as offenders against national law. The fact that their respective States have directed them to refuse obedience or to offer resistance to the execution of the federal laws can afford them no immunity from punishment, for no one can shelter himself behind as unconstitutional law, such a law being, in truth, as we have seen, not a law at all, but only an unsuccessful attempt at a law.

Thus, President Lincoln, in his first inaugural message assumed a correct constitutional position when he declared that the Federal Government could not wage public war against a State, not, however, because of a lack of constitutional authority to maintain in every respect federal supremacy, but because, from the very nature of the Union, there could not be public war between the Union and its member States. After an argument tending to show the sovereign character of the Union, and that it was intended to be perpetual, he declared: "It follows from these views that no State upon its own mere motion can lawfully get out of the Union; that resolves and ordinances to that effect are legally void, and that sets of violence within any State or States against the authority of the United States are in surrectionary or revolutionary, according to circumstances. I therefore consider that, in view of the Constitution and the laws, the Union is unbroken, and to the extent of my ability I shall take care, as the Constitution itself expressly enjoins upon me, that the laws of the Union be faithfully executed in all the States... In doing this there needs to be no bloodshed or violence, and there shall be none unless it be forced upon the national authority. The power conferred upon me will be used to hold occupy and possess the property and places belonging to the Government and to collect the duty and imposts; but beyond what may be necessary for these objects, there will be no invasions, no using of force against or among the people anywhere."

In taking this position Lincoln had to treat the war that had begun as merely an insurrection in which the coercion and punishments were to be applied to individuals. Thus he began his Proclamation of April 15, 1861, in which he called for seventy-five thousand of the militia of the States, by saying: "Whereas the laws of the United States have been for some time past and now are opposed and the execution thereof obstructed in the States of South Carolina, Georgia, Alabama, Florida, Mississippi, Louisiana and Texas, by combinations too powerful to be suppressed by the ordinary course of judicial proceeding;" and closed by commanding "the persons composing the combinations aforesaid to disperse and retire peaceably to their respective abodes within twenty days from this date."

As further showing the theory as to the nature of the contest that was held by the National Government is the fact that Congress did not "declare war" against the South or, when the struggle was over, enter into a treaty of peace with the Southern Confederacy. The United States did not recognize that the Confederacy had or could have a standing as a political power with which it might deal as with a foreign State. One after another, the surrender of his forces by each Confederate general was accepted as an act of war and thus the Confederacy left to collapse and disappear without any formal, official act to mark its demise.

The possession by the Federal Government of full power to protect any right and enforce any law of its own at any time, and at any place within its territorial limits, any resistance of private individuals, or state officials, acting with or without the authority of state law to the contrary notwithstanding, has been uniformly asserted by the Supreme Court whenever such an assertion has been necessary.[22]

Powers Necessarily Possessed by a Federal Government. Although it is not possible to distinguish a sovereign Federal State from a Confederacy upon a purely quantitative comparison of the functions exercised in each by the central government, there are certain powers which, as a practical proposition, the central government of a Federal State must possess and directly exercise.

It has already been seen that the National Government must have the right to determine finally and conclusively the extent of its own legal powers as well as those of the member States, and there must also exist legal processes by means of which these final decisions as to constitutional competency may be enforced. Negatively stated, this means that the member States shall not have a legal right, under any circumstances, to "nullify" a federal law. Together with this legal right of final determination of conflicts of jurisdiction between national and State government must go the possession by the Federal Government of an adequate military force to enforce its decisions.

It is practically imperative that, in a federal State, the control of foreign affairs should be in the hands of the central government. In some federal States the member States are permitted to have intercourse with foreign

States and even to enter into treaties with them with regard to certain local purposes, but in no case are these individual States allowed to have direct relations with foreign States with regard to matters of general political importance, and in all cases the National State is held responsible by foreign States for any breaches of international right or treaty obligations which the individual States may have authorized or which have been committed within their several borders. In the United States this international responsibility of the Federal Government has at times given rise to very serious embarrassments upon its part, for upon these occasions it has found itself internationally responsible for conditions which it was legally unable to control. This legal incompetence has been due, however, rather to the failure of Congress to enact the necessary legislation than to an absolute lack of constitutional authority in the Central Government.

As the sole representative of the Nation in its international dealings it is of course necessary that a Federal Government should possess adequate military forces for purposes of both offense and defense–or at least it should possess the constitutional authority to provide for and maintain an adequate army and navy when the occasion for their use arises.

As a practical proposition it is also necessary that the Federal Government should be constitutionally empowered to raise an adequate income, either by taxes or loans or both. It is, of course, possible to provide that that financial needs of the general government shall be met by assessments levied upon the States as such, and apportioned among them according to their size, wealth, population or any other principle that seems just and politically expedient. This, in part, was the plan pursued in the German Empire. In Germany there were special reasons why "matricular" contributions of the States, as they are called, were provided for, but, in general, it may be said that it is expedient that the National Government should be able to provide itself with funds without needing in any way the cooperation or acquiescence of the federal States. So important is this principle felt to be in the United States that the individual States are not permitted to levy the smallest tax upon the bonds or other evidences of indebtedness of the National, or upon the income derived from them.

Though perhaps not indispensable, experience has shown that it is highly desirable that, in a Federal State, the General Government should be authorized to regulate trade and commerce among the States, including, if found expedient, the construction, ownership and direct operation of inter-state railways and steamship lines, the telegraph, telephone, wireless and other means of communication. An opinion, is indeed, widely held that this authority should include as well as those instrumentalities of trade and communication which operate wholly within State lines, for , in the present day, so intimate are inter-State and intra-State commercial relations, a severance of the two, placing the regulation of the one in the hands of the General Government and of the other in the hands of the several State Governments, is often impossible and, where possible, not desirable.

It is also very desirable, though not absolutely necessary, that, in a Federal State, the control of the currency should be subject to the regulation, if not exclusively vested in the hands, of the National Government. The reasons for this require no elaboration.

One other power which it is highly important that a Federal Government should possess is the right to require that the citizens of each State in the Union shall be accorded in all the other States of the Union those civil rights of residence, ownership and use of property, freedom of contact, guarantees of rights of speech and press, due process of law, etc., which those States accord to their own citizens. In fact, no State should be permitted to discriminate in any way, except as to political rights, between its own citizens and those of the other States. And even as to these political rights provisions should exist whereby, without onerous restrictions, the citizens of one State may obtain citizenship in another State and thereby become entitled to the political rights which appertain to that status.

In all the federal States which now exist care in taken to provide for this inter-state comity. Thus, in the United States, it is constitutionally established that a State cannot forbid the citizens of other States of the Union from establishing their residence within its borders and thereby becoming its citizens; and it specifically provided that no State shall "deny to any person within its jurisdiction the equal protection of the laws," and furthermore, that "full faith and credit shall be given in each State to the public acts, records and judicial proceedings of every other State"; and that "the citizens of each State shall be entitled to all privileges and immunities of citizens in the several States." With reference to this last requirement we have the statement of the Federal Supreme Court that "It has been justly said that no provision of the Constitution has tended as strongly to constitute the citizens of the United States one people as this. Indeed, without some provision of the kind, removing from the citizens of each State the disabilities of alienage in the others, and giving the equality of privilege with citizens of those States, the Republic would have constituted little more than a league of States; it would not have constituted the Union which now exists."[23]

Disadvantages of the Federal System of Government. The disadvantages of the federal system of government are obvious. It necessarily means, to a considerable extent, a duplication of governmental machinery, and this is especially so in a federation of the American type in which practically all the national functions are exercised through national agencies.

A federal government is thus a complicated as well as an expensive method of political rule. In addition, it is politically and administratively weak. It is politically weak because authority is divided, and there is ever the danger that the member States will refuse to fulfil the constitutional duties or, at least, will be negligent and lax in so doing. In the United States, as is well-known there were numberless conflicts between federal and State authorities which aroused bitter feelings and finally into the bloody four years' Civil War of 1861-65. And, he has been earlier adverted to, there have been not a few occasions upon which the federal government has been greatly embarrassed in its dealings with foreign nations by the failure or open refusal of the States to give full recognition within their borders to the international rights of resident aliens. And there are pending at this time questions of this sort for which no fully satisfactory solution has been found.

Administratively viewed the federal system is an unsatisfactory one because State borders constitute jurisdictional lines which State authorities cannot cross. This greatly hinders the administration of justice, making difficult and often impossible the serving of that notice upon defendants of the beginning of judicial proceedings which must be had in order that jurisdiction may be obtained to proceed against them; the attendance of unwilling witnesses in another State cannot be obtained; property removed from one State to another in order to escape taxation or liability for seizure in payment of a debt or legal judgment is difficult to reach; when a personal judgement obtained in one State it cannot be enforced in another State except by instituting a new suit upon it in the State in which its enforcement is sought; and, finally troublesome extradition proceedings must be gone through with before fugitives from the justice of one State can be apprehended in a State to which they may have fled.

When, as in the United States, each States determines for itself the private laws, civil and criminal, which are to have validity within its limits, the practical disadvantages of the federal system are multiplied. To mention but a few of the disadvantages thus arising: legal instruments, including wills, deeds and all sorts of commercial contracts may be valid in some States while inoperative in others; common law principles receive different international in the different States; statutory laws are alike in no two States; a child may be legitimate in one State and illegitimate in another, and a man may be deemed married or unmarried according to the State he is in,–he may even be regarded as married to one woman in one State and the husband of another woman in another State; a corporation having a legal existence in the jurisdiction of its birth has no right to do business in another State without its consent unless it happens to be engaged in interstate commerce which activity, fortunately, is placed within the regulating control of the General Government. In the United States the attempt is made to overcome some of this diversity of State law by the drafting of model acts dealing with some of the more important subjects, such as negotiable instruments, marriage and divorce, and securing their adoption in identical terms by the several States. This, however, is a very tedious and slow process, and even when uniformity has been thus secured, it is impossible to maintain it, for there is no constitutional way of guaranteeing that the statutes thus adopted will receive the same interpretation by the courts of the different States. The only real solution of this evil is, therefore, to transfer the control or regulation of these matters to the legislative power of the central government whose laws will have validity throughout the Union. And, in this connection, it may be remarked that, in all the Federal Unions of the world, the tendency has been to extend the scope of the federal power.

To make more nearly complete the enumeration of the disadvantages inherent in the federal system, the fact needs to be pointed out that federalism necessarily leads to innumerable technical controversies between the States themselves, and between them and the Union as to their respective spheres of authority. As Dicey has said, "federalism means legalism. "that is, the settlement by juristic interpretations of disputes which, in other States, are disposed of upon a basis of equity, compromise and political expediency. It is certain, therefore, that, irrespective of any other considerations, the federal system is not suited to a people who are not habituated to the rule of law, trained in an appreciation of legal distinctions, and disposed to acquiesce in judicial determinations even with reference to matters of the greatest political importance.

Advantages of the Federal Form. The special advantage of the federal form consists in the fact that it permits the satisfaction in fuller form than is possible under any ordinary system of local government of the desire that may be felt by the citizens of the individual States to preserve their rights of self-government while at the same time yielding obedience, as to certain matters, to a common political authority.

It is, however, to be observed, that legitimate though this desire may be, it is one which is founded upon sentimental grounds rather than upon considerations of governmental efficiency. And this is shown by the significant fact that the federal system has seldom been adopted save as a means of securing cooperation between bodies-politic which were previously independent of one another, and around which have grown feeling of loyalty and affection which have made their citizens unwilling to purchase national unity and strength if that was to mean a total destruction of their several States as distinct political entities. This has been the case with the United States, Germany, Switzerland, Canada and Australia. With reference to all of these, the federal form was thus adopted, not willingly as the best possible form of political rule, but more or less unwillingly as a means of securing the amount of national strength and unity that circumstances made indispensable, while preserving, as far as possible, the independence of the several States to which their citizens had become historically attached. Thus it has been said of the American Union that it was "wrung from the grinding necessities of a reluctant people"; and as we know, the feeling that their primary and truest allegiance belonged to their individual States rather than to the National Government persisted in the minds of many long after the national constitution was adopted, and seventy years later was strong enough to lead the citizens of eleven of the States to secede from the Union and attempt, at an enormous sacrifice of human lives and property, to maintain their independence.

References

1. *Das Staatsrecht des Deutschen Reiches.*
2. Professor A. B. Hart is the author of a monograph entitled "As Introduction to the Study of Federal Government" (*Harvard Univ. Historical Monographs,* No. 2), which is rich in bibliographical matter. The work is, however, descriptive, and comparative, rather than theoretical. The work of the English historian Freemanm entitled *Federal Government*, is limited to an historical examiation of the Grecian types.
3. Here, again, it is more accurate to speak of associations rather than of unions of States, for, as has been earlier pointed out. States cannot form juristic unions. It is belived, however, that no confusion of thought will be caused by confirming to the general usage of terms.

4. Upon this point, compare Gareis *Allgemeines Staatsrecht,* pp. 103-105.
5. Jellinek, *Die Lehre von den Staatenverbindungen,* p. 215.
6. Thus says Jellinek (*op. cit.,* p. 212), "Die Personalunion ensteit durch Momente, welche keine Willenseingung der Staaten voraussetan und zur Folge haben, die Realunion hingegen beruht auf dem uberenstimmenden, geeinigten Willen der Staaten, welche die Fülle der Staatsgewalt, die Entscheidung üsber die wichtigsten Angelegenheiten or Staaten Einer natürlichen Persönlichkeit zuweisen." In his latest, work *Allgemeine Staatslehre*, Dritte Auflage, p. 751, Jellinek, as to the dictinction between Personalunion and Realunion, says "Die ursprünglic. Unterscheidung beider Typen, je nachdem bloss die Person des Morarchen order überdies staatliche Angelegenheiten den einzelnen Staatergemeinsam seien, die noch in der ausserdeutschen Leteratur und in on Sprache der Tagesprese angetroffen wird, ist auf rein äusserliched Merkmalen basiert und rechtlich belanglos."
7. The *Law of Nations Considered as Independent Political Communications* vol. I. p. 23.
8. *The American Republic*, pp. 221, 245.
9. Politics, chapter XXII.
10. *État fédéral et confederation d'États*, p. 673.
11. *Staatsuissenschaften,* vol. I, p. 560. (Ed. 1855)
12. *La Souveraineté et l'État Fédératif*, pp. 74, 172.
13. Whether or not properly so terming themselves will be later considered.
14. In 1861, at the time of the secession of the Southern States from American Union, a number of their leading spokesmen took pains if say that they repudiated the doctrine that the States, while remaining in the Union, might "nullify" for their own citizens such acts of the Union as they might disapprove.
15. Bearing upon this point, as well as upon the comparison which we have before made of our individual Commonwealths with their own subdivisions, may be cited the following quotation from an address by Lincoln to the Legislature, at Indianapolis, February 12, 1861. "In what consists the special sacredness of a State? I speak not of the position assigned to a State in the Union by the Constitutions; for that, by the bond, we all recognize. That position, however, a State cannot carry out of the Union with it. I speak of that assumed primary right of a State to rule all which is *less* than itself, and ruin all which is larger than itself. If a State and a country in a given case should be equal in extent and territory, and equal in number of inhabitants, in what, as a matter of principle, is the State better than the country? Would an exchange of names be an exchange of *rights* upon principle? On what rightful principle may a State, being no more than one-fiftieth part of the nation in soil and population, break up the nation and then, cover a proportionately larger subdivision of itself in the most arbitrary way. What mysterious right to play tyrant is conferred on

a district a county, with its people, by merely calling it a State?" From what he been said in this chapter, it would follow that ascription of "limited sovereignty" to the members of our Union by American courts and Congress is, strictly speaking, incorrect. A more proper phrase work be that of "limited legal competence."

16. *The Province of Jurisprudence Determined*, ed. 1861, pp. 223-224.
17. No. 40. See also Westerkamp, *Staatenbund und Bundesstaat.*
18. "Granting the correctness of the theory that the several States were once political sovereignties, and that each surrendered a portion of its inherent powers to the general government, such surrender would go no further than the express provisions of the constitution; as to all other matters not reached by that instrument, their sovereignty would remain intact. By this theory, then, it is entirely impossible that three-fourths of the States can compel the remaining one-fourth to give up a further portion of their attributes contrary to their will." Pomeroy, *Constitutional Law*, p. 111.
19. *Staatenbund und Bundesstaat*, p. 45.
20. See the Imperial Law of June 1, 1879.
21. A possible exception to the generally of the foregoing statement would be with reference to suits in the Supreme Court of the United States by the United States or by a State of the Union against another State of the Union.
22. See the chapter immediately following and the author's *Constitutional Law of the United States*, vol I. Chap IV. "The Supremacy of Federal Authority."
23. *Paul* v. *Virginia,* 8 Wallace 168

V

Non-Sovereign Bodies-Politic

The discussion of the juristic nature of the federally organized State has raised the important question whether it is proper to designate its members as "States." And the same query may be raised with reference to those bodies-politic such as the Dominion of Canada, the Commonwealth of Australia, New Zealand, or the South African Union, which, though falling within the general category of dependencies or colonies, nevertheless possess very wide autonomous powers.

In Switzerland the federated units are known as Cantons; in Canada and the Argentine they are known as Provinces, but in Mexico, Australia, Germany and the United States they are termed States. Upon the other hand it is universally conceded that the administrative subdivisions of a sovereign State are not entitled to be designated as States, notwithstanding the fact that they may exercise a wide measure of self-governing, discretionary powers. In order, then, to concede the title of States to the units of a Federal Union and deny it to all other subdivisions of a sovereign State, it becomes necessary, if the term is to be used with scientific strictness, to find some juristic attribute or attributes which distinguish the constituent members of a *Bundesstaat* from other non-sovereign bodies. If such an attribute or attributes can be found it will be possible to draft a definition of the term State from which the concept of sovereignty is excluded, with the result that it will be proper to speak of non-sovereign as well as of sovereign States. If, however, it to be found that, having once jettisoned the attribute of sovereignty, it is impossible to distinguish juristically such bodies as the members of a Federal State, or autonomous colonies, from other and less important non-sovereign units, then we shall be forced, in order to preserve any sort of exact meaning to the term "State," to deny its applicability to any but sovereign bodies-politic.

Brie and Rosin. Those writers who have sought to designate as "States" certain non-sovereign bodies have not agreed upon the criteria which are to be regarded as distinguishing those bodies from other politically inferior political units to which they do not concede this title. Thus, to give but a few examples, Brie and Rosin find the essential characteristic of a State, whether sovereign or non-sovereign, in its aim or end. Brie describes this state aim as a national as distinguished from a local one; while Rosin speaks of it as universal as distinguished from particular. Rosin writes: " The Commune (*Gemeinde*) is the organism of the local community; the State is the organization of the Nation.... Whereas the satisfaction of common interests resulting from the fact of a union of individuals in the same place and in adjoining places is the aim of the commune, the State has for its aim the task of realizing the genuine national interests of a people united in its quality as a national collectivity."

The unsatisfactory character of attempts such as these to find the essential mark of statehood in the aim or purpose of the group is at once evident. Not only is a juristic distinction thus based upon a quality that is without juristic connotation, but the attribute itself is one that may not be certainly or precisely determined. What are the marks which indubitably differentiate national from local aims? Are such political units as the Australian Commonwealth or the Dominion of Canada without national aspirations? Can these great political bodies be said to be without national aims when such diminutive States as San Marino or Monaco are said to possess them? Rosin himself admits that, in a State composed of States, there are national interests super imposed upon national interests. If so, how distinguish the one from the other?

Brie criticizes Rosin's doctrine of national aims as too vague, but his substitution of universality of purpose is hardly an improvement. He writes: "Die allseitige ergänzende Natur des Staatzweckes its das für den Bergriff des Staats principale Moment, wodurch sich ins besondere auch seine Eigenart gegenüber allen anderen menschlichem Gemeinwesen bestimmt." And, as he goes on to assert, to this universality of aim is necessarily added a corresponding legal competency. But this, it would seem if logically pursued, again brings in the attribute of sovereignty as the distinguishing criterion of statehood—the very position he has been seeking to avoid.

Laband. The leading commentator upon the German imperial constitution, Laband, argues that the members of the Empire might properly be termed States because they possessed rights of their own. "Own rights" he defines as those which originate in the subjects who exercise them; and, that the members of the Empire were thus endowed, he deduces from the fact that they existed as sovereign and independent States before the Union was formed.

The conclusions which we have earlier reached in this treatise are sufficient to show the invalidity of Laband's reasoning. Aside from the fact, which logic has forced upon us, that, in a Federal State, the constituent members must be juristically regarded as deriving their existence as well as their powers from the sovereignty of the Federal State, Laband's position is unsatisfactory because the attribute which he predicates of the constituent members of the Empire is one that, in many cases, may also be ascribed to certain portions of unitary States—portions which originally existed as independent and sovereign bodies-politic. Furthermore, Laband's doctrine would make it necessary to hold that, whereas, in certain Federal States, the members units may be termed States, in other Federal States they may not. Thus, for example, it could not be maintained that the "States" of the Mexican Union enjoy rights of their own, since they never were independent and sovereign political entities. And, what is still more unsatisfactory from the standpoint of juristic, analysis, one would be obliged to assert that, in the American Union, the original thirteen States together with Texas, alone, among the forty-eight members of the American Union, are entitled to the term States, since they alone ever enjoyed that original sovereignty and independence from which the possession of "own rights" may be deduced. In other words, the theory of Laband leads to the result, not simply that juristic analysis of *Bundesstaaten* leads, in different instances, to different conclusions, but that, as applied to unions such as the United States, certain of the members have a juristic status different from that of the others, although constitutional doctrine and uniform practice recognize that they all have the same legal status.

The objectives, as above outlined, to Laband's definition of the non-sovereign State, as originally advanced by him, led him, in later editions of his work, to modify them somewhat,—not, however, by way of wholly abandoning his criterion of "own right," but by rendering it somewhat less important. Thus, in these later editions, he says that the essential characteristics of the State is its own right of domination. Domination thus becomes the essential characteristic of statehood, and this attribute he defines as an original legal superiority of the dominating political person over the dominated persons, coupled with the power to coerce those to whom its command are addressed. The fact, says Laband, that, within this sphere of dominance, the non-sovereign State is controlled by certain prescriptions or limitations imposed upon it by a superior State is not destructive of the statehood of the inferior State. It still remains a State and generically distinct from a mere administrative subdivision of a State by reason of the fact that it has, by its own right, the faculty or power, which the administrative subdivisions does not have, to constrain the persons to whom its commands are addressed, that is, to exercise this power without appealing to any other political authority for its permission or sanction.[1]

Laband's attempted distinction between non-sovereign bodies and mere administrative subdivisions os sovereign States so closely resembles that of Jellinek, we may postpone our criticism of it until we have stated Jellinek's position and argument.

Jellinek saw the error of Laband's original doctrine that purely historical facts can play a decisive part in a matter of juristic status. He agreed, however, with Laband that there might be non-sovereign States, that the constituent members of a *Bundesstaat* fall within this class, and that the attribute which distinguishes non-sovereign political bodies is the possession by them of "own rights."

In order to detect this distinguishing quality is non-sovereign bodies, Jellinek in his earlier work says: " It is not essential to the conception of one's own right that it should have arisen in the person of its possessor; furthermore it is not necessary that it should be such as cannot be again withdrawn against its own will.... The essence of one's own right consists neither in its originality, nor in the impossibility of its being withdrawn. Its specific characteristic is solely and entirely that the one to whom it belongs is legally unanswerable for its exercise."[2]

In his later work, *Das Recht des Modernen Staates*, in which he says that he has definitely summed up his political philosophy, Jellinek returned to this subject, but did not substantially modify the views previously expressed, although he developed them somewhat.

The essential characteristics of a State, Jellinek says is the possession of a power to command which is not derived from any other source—the authority to command by reason of its own power, and, as a consequence according to its own right. The content of this power is not a matter of significance. Whenever there is a community which is able to exercise its dominion according to an order which is valid by reason of an original authority and also by original means of restraint, that community is a State.

The existence if this decisive political power, he says is manifested by the existence of an independent organ charged with the exercise of this power. An organization of its own and the enjoyment of this power which is tie to it is, then, the prime characteristic which distinguishing a State from a group which is not a State. Whenever therefore, a political body receives its constitution from another power in such manner that this constitution rests not upon the will of that political body but upon a law emanating from a foreign power, we have an example not of a State, but of a constituent part of a State. Consequently, the members of the German Empire was States, since their were able to organize themselves according to constitutions which were based exclusively upon their own wills, and these constitutions were they own laws and not those of the Empire. Likewise, the constitutions of the Cantons of Switzerland and of the several States of the American Union are State Constitutions properly so-called since they rest exclusively upon the laws of the States and not upon the will of the Federal State which is superimposed upon them.

The fact that it is required by the American and Swiss Federal Constitutions that the member States shall maintain governments republican in form, Jellinek declares, is not inconsistent with the assertion that the constitutions of the member States rest exclusively upon their own will. The same is true when wholly foreign States have joined in the establishment of a constitution for another community. This Community, he asserts, remains a State if its constitution is considered, *pro futuro*, as exclusively an original act of its will, so that it may be able to alert it without obtaining any external consent.

Turning now to political units which may not properly be termed States, Jellinek holds that these groups receive their organization from a superior legal source. Thus, Lorraine, while it remained a part of the German empire, was not a State, nor are the English dominions of Canada and Australia, notwithstanding the very considerable autonomous powers with which they are endowed. For their constitutions are acts of the parliament of Great Britain. So, also, the kingdom and countries of the former Austrian Empire possessed constitutions which had been proclaimed as fundamental laws of the State, but these had been given by the Emperor and by the chief authority of each of the States themselves, and, for their amendment, there was required the imperial consent. These communities, therefore, lacked to character of statehood.

Further elaborating his position, Jellinek says that, in order to attribute statehood to a political group, it is essential that its highest organ of government—that which assures its perpetuity—should be independent. This organ may not coincide with the organ of another State. Thus, before 1918, Croatia, by its relation to Hungary, and Finland, by its relation to Russia, were not States, since the King of Croatia was juridically the King of Hungary, and the Prince of Finland was juridically the Tsar of Russia.

The first quality of the independent authority which characterizes the State, says Jellinek, is the right to create for itself all the organs materially essential to the laws which the State provides. It is therefore necessary that a veritable State should be so organized that it may be placed within a definite class as regards its governmental organization. Thus Würtemberg and Baden were monarchies; Hamburg, Berne and Pennsylvania were republics. Furthermore, non-sovereign bodies, in order to be entitled to be termed States, must be so completely organized governmentally that they will be able to stand forth as sovereign and completely organized States immediately upon the disappearance of the sovereign authority to which they have been subjected. This is not true of autonomous bodies which have not the character of States. These autonomous bodies, morever, though able to issue orders with penalties prescribed for their violation, have the authority to enforce them only by reason of power delegated to them by the superior political State, and it is this lack of power to command in an absolute manner, and with a legally irresistible right of coercion that denotes their non-statehood. Thus, as distinguished from Laband, Jelllinek emphasizes not so much the idea that the legal powers of the non-state entities are granted or delegated to them by political entities which are entitled to be termed States, as that these non-state bodies have no original coercive authority to execute such orders as they are conceded to have the legal right issue. In short, the non-sovereign body which is entitled to be termed a State, as distinguished from the non-sovereign body, which is not entitled, has, according to Jellinek, an original legal right of its own to provide for itself a complete governmental organization, with executive legislative and judicial powers. It thus has, of its own right, authority to enforce, as well as to create, legal obligations and rights. It is distinguished from the sovereign State only by reason of the fact that its sphere of legal authority is a limited one—limited by the authority of the sovereign State to which it is subordinated.

In order that we may have clearly before us Jellinek's doctrine, as stated in his last published work, the following is quoted from his *Allgemeine Staatslehre:*

"Wo ein Gemeinwesen aus ursprünglicher Macht und mit ursprünglichen Zwangsmitteln Herrschaft über seine Glieder und sein Gebiet gemäss einer ihm eigenthümlichen Ordnung zu üben vermag, da ist ein Staat vorhanden. Das Dasein einer Staatsgewalt aüssert sich zunächst in dem Dasein einer selbständiger, sie versehender Organe. Eigene Organisation und die mit ihr verknüpfte Machtverteilung ist das erste Merkmal, um den Staat vom nichtstaatlichen Verbande zu trennen. Wo immer daher ein gemeinwesen seine Verfassung von einer andern Macht erhält, so dass sie nicht auf seinem Willen, sondern dauernd auf dem Gesetze dieser Macht ruht, da ist kein Staat, sondern nur das Glied eines Staates vorhanden. Daher sind die deutschen Gliedstaaten Staaten, denn sie können sich durch ihre eigenen, ausschliesslich auf ihrem Willen beruhenden Verfassungen organisieren, die ihre Gesetze, nicht die des Reiches sind. Ebenso sind die Verfassungen der schweizerischen Kantone, der Einzelstaaten der amerikanischen Union Staatsverfassungen, denn sie beruhen ausschliesslich auf ihren eigenen Gesetzen, nicht auf dem Willen des übergeordneten Bundesstaates. Es können Schranken in den bundesstaatlichen Gesetzen für die Verfassungen der Gliedstaaten gezogen sein (z. B. Verbot einer anderen als der republikanischen Staatsform, wie in der Schweiz und in den Vereinigten Staaten): sie bleiben trotzdem ausschliesslich Gesetze der Gliedstaaten. Selbst wenn ein Gemeinwesen unter der Mitwirkung fremder Staaten sein Verfassung empfangen hat, so ist es Staat, wena diese Verfassung pro futuro ausschliesslich als sein originäler Willensakt auzusehen ist, so dass sie von ihm ohne weitere Ermächtigung abgeändert werden kann.

"Wo hingegen ein Herrschergewalt übender Verband seine Organisation von einem über ihm stehenden Staate als dessen Gesetz empfangen hat, da ist kein Staat vorhanden. So vor allem bei den Kommunen, deren Verfassung stets auf Staatsgesetzen ruht, die höchstens in untergeordneten Dingen eine begrenzte Organisationsbefugniss zugestehen.... Daher ist Elsass-Lothringes kein Staat,...daher sind die mit weitestgehender Autonomie ausgerüsteten englischen Charterkolonien, wie Kanada, die Südafrikanische Union, Australien, keine Staaten, denn ihre Verfassungen sind in englischen Gesetze enthalten, in Parlamentsakten Grossbritanniens, die rechtlich jederzeit vom Parlament wieder geändert werden können, ohne dass der betreffenden Kolonie ein gesetzliches Mitwirkungsrecht an solcher Verfassungsanderung zustände."[3]

As regards the status of the constituent units of a Bundesstaat, Jellinek, in another place, declares that they are to be viewed as States with respect to certain of their functions, and as mere organs of the superior sovereign State as to other of their activities. He says: "Die Glieder des Bundesstaates sind als solche, soweit sie an der Herrschaft des Bundes teilnehmen, nicht Staaten, sondern Organe des Bundesstaates und, soweit sie unterworfen sind und überhaupt noch einen selbständigen,Willen aüssern können, nichtstatliche Verbände, und nur die physische Identität dieses Verbandes mit dem Gliedstaate führt zu der ungenauen Vorstellung, dass der Gliedstaat als solcher dem Bundestaate unterworfen sei. Daher hat der Gliedstaat nur nach zwei Richtungen hin staatlichen Charakter : als Gemeinwesen, das von der Bunderstaatsgewalt frei ist und als Träger von öffentlichrechtlichen Ansprüchen an den Bundesstaat gemäss dessen Verfassung."[4]

Criticism of Laband and Jellinek. It will have been seen that both Laband and Jellinek seek to invest the non-sovereign State with at least a certain sphere of legal authority that may truly be spoken of as, legally if not historically, underived from and uncontrolled by the superior State under whose sovereignty it exists, and that it is the possession of this authority that distinguishes it from the mere administrative agency of a sovereign State. It would seem,however, that the attempt to draw this distinction is an unsuccessful one. Unless one is willing to concede that sovereignty is divisible, which Laband and Jellinek are willing to do, and which, if admitted, would mean that the notion of sovereignty must be given a juristic meaning quite different from that which is attached to it by practically all publicists, it is futile to speak of a political entity as possessing original powers or rights of its own when these powers may be exercised only within a limited sphere of political control, and when the extent of this sphere is legally determined, and may be further curtailed or even wholly destroyed, by an exercise of the legal will of another political body. If this is the case, then it is not correct to say that certain subordinate or non-sovereign political bodies can express independent wills of their own as to any matter whatsoever. Therefore, the threefold division of political bodies into those which can exercise an independent legal will as to all matters (sovereign States) ; those which can exercise it as to some matters (non-sovereign States); and those which can exercise it as to no matters (non-States) is logically an impossible one. If the body that is termed a non-sovereign State retains such powers as it has only by the legal sufferance of the sovereign State whose sovereignty it recognizes, its legal powers are as much dependent upon the will of the sovereign State as are those of the lowest administrative agency of that State. To both of them may be granted by that State a discretion as to how or when the rights vested in them are to be exercised, but this does not alter the fact that the legal will that is exercised is, when traced back to its ultimate source, that of the sovereign State.

If it be declared that the activities of the non-sovereign State, when acting within its constitutionally determined sphere of authority, are not subject to the control of the sovereign State, whereas the activities agency or local governing body are or may be constantly controlled, and that this constitutes an essential distinction, the answer is that, in fact, the right of the sovereign State to control exists in both cases, and the only difference is as to the manner in which under the law as it exists at any given time, it may be legally exercised. So long as an administrative agency keeps within the field of discretionary action granted by law, its act are legal, whatever they may be. But as a rule, this discretionary authority may be readily abridged or destroyed by an ordinary statute or order of an administrative superior. In the case of the so-called non-sovereign State, existing law may provide that its legal competency may be changed only by the more difficult process of amending existing constitutional provisions, but that this is a difference which does not create an essential juristic distinction, our earlier discussion of the nature of constitutional law as compared with ordinary law, must have made plain. In both cases the legal competency of the inferior is determined by the will of the superior body, although, in the one case, a greater degree of formality surrounds the alteration of such competence than it does in the other.

If it were true that, in the operation of a sovereign upon a non-sovereign entity, the sovereign entity had only the power of preventing the non-sovereign entity from exceeding its constitutional powers, there might be warrant for claiming as essential distinction between such a non-sovereign political being and a mere administrative district. But, as a matter of fact, the sovereign State always and necessarily possesses, in addition to this negative and prohibitory power, the ability to alter at will the legal competence of the subordinate body, even to the extent of utterly destroying it. As Jellinek himself says in another work, "The sovereignty of the superior State as contrasted with the non-sovereign State, appears in three ways: first, in a negative control by it of the activities of the latter; second, in the power of the sovereign State to use the non-sovereign State for its own ends, be it as the direct object of its will or as a relatively independent member of a federal union ; thirdly, the sovereign State has at all times the right to draw to itself is a constitutional manner the highest rights belonging to the non-sovereign State. The existence of the non-sovereign state as a State is therefore itself determined by the sovereign will of the supreme State, to an extent to which no formal *a priori* legal limit can be set."[5]

Woodrow Wilson, who accepts Jellinek's reasoning upon this point, says, "In the federal State, self-determination with the respect to their law as a whole, has been lost by the member States. They cannot extend, they cannot even determine, their own powers conclusively without appeal to the federal authorities." But, he continues, "They are still States because their powers are original and inherent, not derivative; because their political rights are not also legal duties; and because they can apply to their commands the full imperative sanctions of law. But their sphere is limited by the presiding and sovereign powers of a State superordinated to them, the extent of whose authority is determined under constitutional forms and guarantees, by itself."[6]

"Their powers are original," Wilson says. But, are they? If the States have their status as political bodies only in the Union, as Lincoln declared, in what sense can their power be said to be original, except in an historical sense, as related to the time when they were independent States, if ever they were? Juristically viewed, the legal competence of the members of the composite State is derived from the federal Constitution.[7] Secondly, Wilson says, they are States, "because their political rights are not also legal duties." If the writer correctly understand this, it is meant that, to a very great extent, the exercise or non-exercise, or the manner of exercise of their powers is left to their own discretion. But is not this true as well, to a considerable extent atleast, of such bodies as cities and countries, which all would concede to be merely administrative units. Finally, Wilson says, these non-sovereign bodies are States because, "they can apply the full imperative sanctions of law." In other words, that all rules of conduct promulagted by them within their legal competence are valid as laws. But this is no less true of all administrative bodies.

It thus appears that, from a juristic standpoint, no fundamental distinction can be drawn between no-sovereign members of a federal State and their administrative units. What difference there is, aside from historical associations, in one of degree, that is, as to the scope and powers and the ease with which the superordinated power may alter this competence. As a matter of fact, in several of the so-called States of the American Union, various of their urban districts are protected in their administrative competences by provisions in the constitutions of their respective Commonwealths. This is true in more than twenty States.[8] But we do not, for this reason, consider such protective districts any less purely administrative units, or to be distinguished in specific character from other less favoured towns and counties.

A question which remain to be answered is: What effect should the conclusion that has been reached have upon political terminology? In other words, does it becomes necessary rigorously to confine the use of the word "State" to those bodies-politic or political persons that may properly be said to possess sovereignty? If the term State is to be regarded as a technical one, scientific accuracy would seem to demand that this be done, for, as has been seen, if it be employed in a sense that is in anywise broader, it becomes impossible to refuse to apply it to political units or organizations which political scientists in the past have never so dignified. Upon the other hand, if only those political entities are to be designated as States which are sovereign in character, common usage will be equally violated by excluding from in application many political units which have been almost universally so denominated. The only escape from these two alternatives, both of them highly objectionable would seem to be for the analytical jurist to abandon the effort to give scientific precision to the term State and to obtain accuracy of expression by qualifying it, when necessary, with such adjective as sovereign, non-sovereign and the like. If one were starting with a clear sheet, or essaying to formulate a scientifically exact terminology for the analytical jurist their can be little doubts that it would be wise to refuse to designate as State those political entities in which sovereignty does not inhere, but, as it is, with a wider but less precise usage practical universal, such a restriction is not practicable. This conclusion the present author has been reluctantly compelled to accept.[9]

Federal Government and Local Government as Distinguished in Practice. The description which has been given of a federal system is sufficient to show that, in such a scheme of government, the member States occupy a position which resembles that of the local government areas of unitary States to which considerable autonomous powers are given. One is therefore justified in asking what precisely are the characteristics which distinguish a federally organized government from a unitary government in which wide discretionary powers and liberal rights of self-government have been granted to local areas? Or, to state the question in another form, in just what respects do the member States of a federally organized State differ from the autonomous administrative areas of the unitary State?

The difference is considerable, but, as has been already pointed out, the distinction does not lie in the possession by the member States of any part of a sovereignty which is not possessed by the local governing areas. Both the member States and the local areas derive such powers as they possess from the sovereign State of which they are constituent parts. The governments of both are local agencies for the purposes of the central government. Their political powers are emanations from the sovereignty of the National State. They have a legal status only as parts of the Government of that State, and no status independently of it. In these juristic aspects they are alike. As a matter of practical fact, however, there are important differences between the members of a Federal Union and the autonomous administration districts of the unitary State.

In the first place, though not recognized as sovereign entities, the members of a federal State so far resemble sovereign States that, except as qualified by federal obligations, they usually stand towards each other as independent and foreign powers. This means that each member body constitutes a jurisdiction outside of which none of its act,—executive, legislative or judicial,—have any force. Thus, a law enacted by one of the federal units or a writ issued by one of its courts, has no operative force outside of its own territorial limits, and no one of its officials can exercise any official authority beyond such borders. This is the general principle which applies between sovereign States, and it applies to the members of a federated union subject only to such provisions as may exist in the national Constitution with regard in inter-member relations. Thus, in the United States, notwithstanding the constitutional provisions which have been cited with regard to interstate comity, and to the giving of full faith and credit by each State to the public acts of the other States, it still remains true that the States are without the legal power to issue a judicial writ upon which the presence of a witness who is in another State may be obtained, and a notice of the beginning of a suit against a non-resident does not give jurisdiction to the courts of a State except in those cases which are known as actions *in rem*. And a judgement obtained in the courts of one State will not, as such, be executed by another State. A suit must first be brought upon that judgement, as one would upon a promissory note, in the State in which enforcement is sought.[10]

Nor can one State compel another State to return to it fugitives from its justice.[11]

A further respect in which the members of a federal State are distinguished from local government areas, and in which they resemble sovereign States, is that they have, as has been earlier pointed out, a citizenship of their own. And this citizenship imports such an allegiance upon the part of the citizens that a breach of it may probably be punished as high treason.

As distinguished from local government areas, the States of a federal union usually hold such self-governing powers as they have in firmer legal possession. This is due to the fact that these rights are enumerated and guaranteed in the written constitution upon which the Federal Union is itself based. Thus the Supreme Court of the United States has declared that the United States is an "indestructible union composed of indestructible States." This is possibly a somewhat exaggerated statement, since, by amendment of the federal Constitution, it is conceivably possible, by strictly legal means, to deprive the States of any or all of the self-governing powers which they possess, and this could be done against the will of any particular State, since the unanimous approval of the States to amendments of the federal Constitution is not required.[12] But, even if this be juristically possible, it still remains true that, as a practical proposition, the units of a Federation have a firmer possession of their several jurisdictions than have the local governing bodies of administrative areas.

This constitutional security of the members of a federal union is, in most cases, rendered still more firm by reason of the fact that, before the establishment of the Union, that were independent States, and were, in historical fact, if not in juristic interpretation, the creators of the Union. They thus have back of them a political sentiment in support of their self-governing status to which local government areas can seldom lay claim. Not in all cases, however, have the member States of federal unions originally been independent States. Thus, in the United States, only fourteen of the present members can be said to have been originally sovereign bodies-politic; and, in the Dominion of Canada, only Ontario, Quebec, Nova Scotia, Prince Edward Island, and New Brunswick were originally separate colonies; and none of the present States of Mexico, Argentine and Brazil can lay claim to having had an independent existence prior to the establishment of the Union of which they are the constituent parts.

Another and most important distinction which places the member States of a federal union upon a plane of dignity and importance far above the most autonomous local government areas is that, subject to few restrictions each federated body is able to determine for itself the form of its own government,––a right which includes also the authority to establish fro itself such local government agencies as it sees fit. Thus, each State of Germany or of the United States, or of Australia, and each Canton of

Switzerland or Province of Canada, has its own distinct body of constitutional law which determines not only its form of government, but the principles in accordance with which it is to be operated. In sharp contrast with this is the principle that the local subdivisions of unitary States have their forms of government determined for them by national law.

A further respect in which the member States of such federations as the United States, Canada, and Australia occupy a more independent existence than do the local government areas of any unitary States is that legislative authority is given to each federated States to determine for its own inhabitants the great body of the law, civil and criminal, substantive and procedural, which regulate their private relations, whereas local government agencies have no opinion but to enforce the laws which they receive from the central government. In Germany and Switzerland the entire body of the private law is placed within the legislative competency of the central government, and, in this respect, therefore, the Swiss Cantons and the individual German States resemble the local governments of unitary States. But, upon the other hand, as has been earlier pointed out, these nationally created laws are interpreted and enforced almost wholly through the governmental agencies of the States which thus gain in executive importance what they have lost legislatively as compared with States of Australia and of the United States, or the Provinces of Canada.

In this connection it may be said generally, although the principle cannot be laid down in precise terms, that local governments, however autonomous, are conceived of as primarily the agents to carry out, within their respective areas, the will of the external government. It may be that they are permitted in large measure to select for themselves the public officials by whom they are to be locally governed, and with regard to purely local matters they may be given discretionary authority as to what regulations shall be issued and enforced, but it remains true that several governing agencies are conceived of as acting, *ad hoc*, as mere agencies of the central government.

As thus regarded, the operations of local governments are commonly subject to greater supervision and control by the central authorities than are the activities of the member States of a federal union. Oridinarily the acts of federated States, if falling within the constitutional fields marked out for them by the national constitution are not subject to censure or annulment by the central government. It is only when some prohibition of the national constitution is violated, or some national right invaded, that a cause for national intervention arises. With regard to local governments, however, the central government usually exercises a continuous and comprehensive supervision.

For the most part it is within the discretion of the federated States to determine whether or not their constitutional powers shall be exercised. For local governments there is usually no such option. To them their duties are more often mandatory in character, and, when there is a failure upon their part to carry out the orders which they have received, the correction usually comes in a more direct and summary manner than is the case when the States of a federal union are derelict in the fulfilment of their federal obligations.

Because of the wide range of their autonomous powers, the member States of all federated unions are equipped with practically complete frameworks of government,—executive, legislative, and judicial,—so complete, in fact, that, should the central government be destroyed, then States would be practically ready at once to exercise through their existing governments the function previously performed by the general government, and then to stand forth as fully organized bodies-politic. Strongly contrasted with this completeness of organization are the governmental agencies of the most autonomous and self-governing administrative areas. In very many cases, indeed, local governments possess no real legislative bodies, but only executive officials who have ordinance-making powers. Thus, in the entire United States, there is not a single local government, if we except the cities, which is provided with a legislative body, distinct from the executive agents, and composed of elected representatives of the people; although there are in the "Towns" brief annual meetings of the citizens or taxpayers. In England, since 1888, there have been locally-elected "County Councils" and, since 1894, "District Councils," but these have had administrative rather than legislative powers and they operate almost wholly through committees.

References

1. Laband, *Deutsches Reichstaatsrecht*, published in 1907, p. 11.
2. *Die lehre von den Staatenverbindungen,* pp. 41-42.
3. *Allgemeine Staatslehre* (ed. 1922), p. 490. See also Jellinek's short treatise, published in 1896, entitled *Ueber Staatsfragmente,* pp. 11-17.
4. *Allgemeine Staatslehre* (1922), p.773.
5. *Gesetz und Verordnung*, p. 203.

6. *An Old Master and Other Essays,* chapter on "Political Sovereignty", pp. 93-94.
7. In what sense, it may be asked, can those present members of our Union, which have been admitted since 1789, be said to have possessed, "original" powers?
8. Commenting upon this fact, Professor Burgess says: "This is a most various question. It demonstrated the fact that the government of the Commonwealth has ceased to be, in many respects, the natural local government." Article "The American Commonwealth," in *Pol. Sci. Quar.* vol. I, No. 1.
9. Professor Burgess has suggested that the units of a sovereign federally organized State might be known as "commonwealths," and thus the necessity of designating them as States avoided. Reviews Laband's *Deutsches Reichsstaatsrecht* in the *Pol. Sci. Quar.* (vol. III, p. 128), he says: "The learned author betrays much anxiety to preserve to the separate States the character of real States, while he denies to them the possession of any sovereign power. The jurist come again to the front, and rescues the State from the category of organizations having only derived powers by the proposition that the distinguishing characteristic of the State in general is not sovereignty, but the power to command and compel obedience to its commands from the free subjects of the State. It seems to me that his distinction will not hold. If this power to command and to compel obedience be underived and independent, then it is sovereignty pure and simple. If on other hand, it be in any sense derivative, then the criterion of distinction which Dr. Laband sets up between the relation of the State to the Union and that of the municipal divisions of the State to the State largely breaks down, since these municipal divisions have also the power to command and compel obedience to their commands from the free subjects of the State, and in their case this is clearly a vested power. If sovereignty in the federal system be exclusively in the Union, then it seems to me that this makes the Union the only real State, and that the only distinction which remains between the separate States and the municipalities lies in the fact that, while the municipalities derive their authority from the States in a positive and definite manner, the States derive their power from the Union in a permissive and general manner. To be completely scientific, then, in our nomenclature and emancipate ourselves completely from the power of customary phrases, we should give the name State only to the Union and find some other term to designate its members. In America we have already the suitable title Commonwealth.'"

   This is an interesting suggestion, but for the reasons indicated above, not a practicable one.
10. The clause of the federal constitution which decrees that full flesh and credit shall be given to the public acts of the other States that applies so

that in the suit thus instituted, the judgement may not be attacked upon its merits.

11. Interstate extradition is provided for by the federal Constitution, but it has been held by the Supreme Court that, though mandatory in turns, there is no constitutional means by which the States may be compiled to fulfil the obligations thus laid upon them.
12. Possible exceptions to the above statement are exhibited in the constitutional provisions that no State shall be deprived of its right to equal representations in the Senate, and that new States shall not be carried out of parts of the original States or by the union of two or more of them, without the consent of the States thus concerned. It is, however, arguable that even these inhibitions can be overcome by first deleting them from the Constitution by the ordinary process of constitutional amendement.

VI

Law and Sovereignty in the Light of International Law

Thus, far, in considering the sovereign State as a concept of public law, we have been dealing with it in its national aspect, and have found it to be conceived of as a legal person possessing a legally supreme will, and its commands as having the force of positive law. We come now to consider in what sense and to what extent a similar conception is applicable when the State is regarded not in its relations to those individuals who are within the control of its municipal law, but as vis-à-vis to other States which are similarly sovereign with regard to their respective citizens or subjects.

From what has been already said, it will have appeared first of all, that in International Law, the State is envisaged as a "person." It is an entity viewed as possessing a will, and as the subject of rights and obligations. This personality is similar in its conceptual character to that of the State of municipal law, and, in the great majority of cases, the sovereign municipal person has also an international personality. The two personalities are, however, distinct, and only error can result from confusing or identifying them. The rights and obligations which are connoted by international personality are different, both in essential nature and in contest, from those which spring from municipal personality and they are created, applied and enforced by different means.

Based upon its predicated sovereignty, the State of national or municipal law asserts that there are no limits to its will, and that the expressions of that will operate as commands to all those over whom it chooses to claim authority. The State, municipally considered, is not the creation of law, but lives and has its being in the realm of law, for, at the same time that it is the sole and ultimate source of all law it is, by its very nature, compelled to operate according to the rules thus laid down. It is able to act only through its Government, and an act unauthorized by law, even though committed by a government official, is not an act of the Government or of the State of which it is the agent.

As contrasted with this municipal conception of the State, the State of International Law asserts that it has *de facto* power or control over a given territory, and that it will not tolerate within its limits the exercise of any political authority save such as it consents to. Reciprocally, it holds itself responsible to other States for the manner in which, in the exercise of such exclusive jurisdiction, it may affect the rights or interests of other States.

This may be said to be the central conception of International Law, and, if all States were content with their existing territories, if boundaries were certain and undisputed, and if each State held itself unconcerned with whatever action might be taken by other States within their several limits, no opportunity for international discard would be presented. But, in fact, territorial boundaries have not been certainly and finally fixed, and, until the present, there have been vast areas of lands in Asia and Africa and elsewhere which have had no governments the rights of which have been recognized by the greater States of the world, and there has been a context struggle between these greater States to bring within their respective controls the areas which by practically common consent have been considered as appropriate for annexation. Also, there have been the high seas, which are treated as subject to no sovereign control and as therefore open to free and common use by the citizens of all the States. These waters, however, have not been neutralized in the sense that in time of war belligerent operations upon them may not be conducted.

Furthermore, although each State claims exclusively jurisdiction over its own territories, it does not hold itself indifferent to what other States may do within their respective territories. Over those persons whom, according to its own municipal law, it claims as its own citizens and as owing primary allegiance to itself, each State asserts a right to exercise a certain amount of guardianship wherever they may be. And, in addition to this, it is urged as a matter of international comity, if not of strict right, that, subject to reasonable police restrictions, other State should permit these citizens to travel and reside and carry on business within their several jurisdictions. Thus it has come about, especially during recent years when the means of transportation and communication have been highly developed, that every great State has a considerable number of its citizens traveling or residing in the other States of the world. And, even when its citizens are not thus abroad, they have many commercial relations with the citizens of other States or directly with those States themselves.

In all these cases, each State asserts the right to see that the persons and property of its respectively citizens are reasonably protected against violence or unduly discriminative treatment. Finally, all the States of the world have entered into many special treaty relations with one another whereby their general international rights and responsibilities have been modified. Thus it has come about that international relations have become highly complicated and furnish many opportunities for inter-state friction and discord. In order to reduce this friction and possibility of strife to a minimum the statesmen and publicists of all nations have sought to render as definite, and, in their operation, as reciprocally beneficial, as possible the rules and principles that are to be commonly recognized as determining the rights and duties arising out of the inter-relations into which, in modern times, the different States of the world and their citizens are brought.

When disputes have arisen, the effort has been to provide orderly and equitable modes for the settlement; and, finally, when these have failed and war, the *ultima ratio*, has been resorted to, the attempt has been made to establish rules for the conduct of warfare which will limit its horrors to the combatants, and to minimize its devastating effects upon non-combatants. In almost all wars the interests of neutral States become necessarily involved, and, for the determination of the reciprocal rights and responsibilities thus created, another large body of rules and principles had been evolved.

The total result thus is that, though starting from an essentially individualistic doctrine of State exclusiveness and independence, a great and complicated corpus of technical international principles had come into being. It still remains true, however, that the doctrines of exclusive territorial jurisdiction which have been outlined, and of the State as an international entity or person which is the bearer or "subject" of certain rights and corresponding duties, are the fundamental concepts, from which, by logical deduction, are explained and justified the special rules which regulate international relations. The more complicated and technical these provisions of international law, the more important it becomes that the basic ideas upon which they rest should be searched out and clarified.

Municipal and International Jurisprudential Concepts Distinguished. Leaving the domain of municipal life, and entering the field of international law, one finds the principles which regulate the relations of States *inter se* approximately as definite and as formalistic in character as are those which constitute the body of municipal law. Moreover, they are, in general amenable to much the same analysis as that applicable to municipal law. Furthermore, the concepts that they connote, such as rights, obligations and the like, seem much the same. When, however, we subject these ideas to careful scrutiny, we find, in fact, that we have to deal with principles and concepts which have only a superficial or analogous resemblance to those of municipal law,—that, fundamentally, there is a difference between these two fields of jurisprudence which makes necessary the formation of new definitions of law, of legal rights, and of legal obligations, and a new conception of the State as the subject and object of these rights and obligations.

When we forsake the field of constitutional or municipal law and enter that of international relation we no longer have to deal with legal superiors and legal inferiors. Here we find no supreme will, but legally speaking, a collection of equal wills, and the conflict, or at least the interplay, of independent powers. This is the fundamental premise of those who attempt the systematic statement of the principles which govern the relations of States to one another. It is true that the more developed and civilized States of the world are spoken of as forming a "Family of Nations," and that from this fact it is quite proper to argue that *ubi societas, ibi jus est*. But the *jus* which is thus brought into being has not the same essential character as has that of municipal life. Especially is this shown in the origin of International Law, although the manner in which it is determined and enforced is not without significance.

As regards their origin, the laws governing international relations do not find their birth in the mandatory utterances of supreme wills declaring to inferior persons what for them shall be deemed legally right and legally wrong. Instead, they derive their force from the fact that they have been accepted by those political persons–the States–whose actions they regulate. This acceptance may, indeed, be one which, for the most part, the States may not find it practicable to avoid, even should they so desire, and thus, in fact the rules of international intercourse may, *arguendo*, be admitted to be as definite, and, in general, as uniformly conformed to as are the provisions of the municipal law of the most orderly State. This, however, does not change the essential character of those international laws as rules which obtain between equals rather than as commands addressed by a superior legislative will to persons who are conceived of as subject to its control.

It would plainly appear, then, that the idea of Sovereignty, as it is found in constitutional law, can find no proper place among international conceptions. The word is, indeed, generally used in the literature of international jurisprudence, but, when thus employed, it has a meaning which is so different from that which it has in the municipal field that it is most unfortunate that it should ever have obtained this currency. It would have been far better if some such term as Independency had been employed. This word, far better than Sovereignty, would indicate the fact that, regarded from the point of view of positive law, complete individualism prevails in the international field. Socially, economically and morally there may be a family of nations, – a *societas maxima*,–but, looked at from the point of view of the constitutional jurist, international life is atomistic, noncivic, individualistic. Thus regarded, nations are, as individuals, in that "state of nature" in which Hobbes, Locke, Rousseau, and the other natural law writers placed primitive man. Even when, by formal treaties, independent States have established rules by which, with reference to the matter specified, their future dealings with one another are to be regulated, there has been no creation of law in a positive or Austinian sense, for, as to those matters, the contracting parties remain subject only to their own wills and not to that of an outside or foreign power. As Jellinek briefly puts it: "Der Staatenvertrag bindet aber er unterwirft nicht."[1]

The Relation Between International Law and Municipal Law. So independent and inherently diverse in character are international and municipal laws, it is not possible for the one to be created by the other; international law cannot be created by municipal law, and municipal law cannot owe its origin to international law. The two systems are, however, often brought into such close factual relations that the absence of this causal nexus is not always evident, and it is therefore necessary to justify somewhat more fully the truth of the proposition that has been stated.

Municipal Law Cannot Create International Law. That no one State can, by its own legislative fiat or judicial decree create international rules that are to bind the actions of other States is generally admitted. That such municipal acts may often have a strongly persuasive international force is granted, but that they may be determinative of the rights of other States is never conceded. It may, indeed, be pointed out that, were the doctrine once established that municipal law could create international law, the doom of international law as a fixed and generally binding body of principles would be at once pronounced. For not only would it thus be within the recognized right of each State to escape from the application of previously acknowledge rules of international law, but that law itself would lose its generality and have a content that would vary for each State.

So appropriate upon this point is the language of the Supreme Court of the United States in the case of *The Scotia*[2] that, though it may be superogatory, it will be quoted. Mr. Justice Swayne, who rendered the decision, was speaking of the maritime law, but the doctrine is applicable to general international law. "Undoubtedly," he says, "no single nation can change the law of the sea. That law is of universal obligation, and no statute of one or two nations can create obligations for the world. Like all laws of nature, it rests upon the common consent of civilized communities. It is of force, not because it was prescribed by any superior power, but because it has been generally accepted as a rule of conduct."

International Law Cannot Create Municipal Law. That international law cannot create municipal law is not so generally admitted. Indeed, probably the greater number of writers assert that it has this force. In support of this contention attention is called to the many declarations of the national courts of almost all civilized States that international law is a part of the municipal law which they are called upon to apply when the rights of litigants before them are therein involved.

It is true that courts adopt and apply established principles of international law, but in so applying and enforcing them, they consider them as having been first impliedly adopted by the State as a portion of its own municipal law. Thus though the principles which international laws embody are the product of international usage and agreement, their legal force, as rules controlling the administration of justice between litigants, is derived from the sanction of the State whose courts administer them, and by whose laws the courts themselves are created.

The adoption and modes of ascertainment of international laws by the courts are analogous to the manner in which the courts of Great Britain and the United States determine and enforce non-statutory common law principles. Just as the private common law may be modified by statute (though this must usually be by express declaration and not by implication), so a national legislature has full power to bind the courts by statutes which modify the generally accepted principles of international conduct. In the very early case of *The Charming Betsy*[3] decided in 1804, it seems to have been accepted as a principle not needing argument that the court would be bound by an act of Congress providing a rule different from that laid down by international law, the only observation made being that "an act of Congress ought never to be construed to violate the law of nations if any other possible construction remains." In *The Nereide*[4] Marshall again declared: "Till an act [of Congress] be passed the court is bound by the law of nations, which is a part of the law of the land". In *Hilton v. Guyot*[5] the court said:

International law in its widest and most comprehensive sense– including not only question of right between nations, governed by what has been appropriately called the law of nations, but also questions arising under what is usually called private international law or the conflict of laws, and concerning the rights of persons within the territory and dominion of one nation, by reason of acts, private or public, done within the dominion of another nation – is part of our law, and must be ascertained and administered by the courts of justice, as often as such questions are presented in litigation between man and man, duly submitted to their determination. The most certain guide, no doubt, for the decision of such questions is a treaty or a statute of this country. But when, as is the case here, there is no written law upon the subject, the duty still rests upon the judicial tribunals of ascertaining and declaring what the law is whenever it becomes necessary to do so in order to determine the rights of parties to suits regularly brought before them. In doing this, the courts must obtain such aid as they can from judicial decisions, from the works of jurists and commentators, and from the sets and usages of civilized nations.

In the case of *The Lottawanna,* sub nominee *Rodd v. Heartt*[6] is set out in the clearest possible manner the extent to which, and the manner in which, any body of law, not originally municipal may, by adoption, become such. That case had reference to the adoption by the United States of the general principles of maritime law, but, as is pointed out in the argument, the principle is the same with reference to international law. Mr. Justice Bradley, speaking for the court, said:

The ground on which we are asked to overrule the judgment in the case of *The General Smith* is that by the general maritime law those who furnish necessary materials, repairs, and supplies to a used have a lien on such a vessel therefore, as well when furnished in her home port as when furnished in a foreign port, and that the courts of admiralty are bound to give effect to that lien.

The proposition affirms that the general maritime law governs the case, and is binding on the courts of the United States. But it is hardly necessary to argue that the general maritime law is only so far operative as law in any country as it is adopted by the laws and usages of that country. In this respect it is like international law or the laws of war, which have the effect of law in no country further than they are accepted and received as such; or, like the case of the civil law, which forms the basis of most European laws, but which has the force of law in each State only so far as it is adopted therein, and with such modifications as are deemed expedient. The adoption of the common law by the several States of this Union also presents an analogous case. It is the basis of all the State laws, but is modified as each sees fit. Perhaps the maritime law is more uniformly followed by commercial nations than the civil and common law by those who use them. But, like those laws, however fixed, definite and beneficial the theoretical code of maritime a law may be, it can have only so far the effect of law in any country as it is permitted to have. But the actual maritime law can hardly be said to have a fixed and definite form as to all the subjects which may be embraced within its scope. Whilst it is true that the great mass of maritime law is the same in all commercial countries, yet in each country peculiarities exist either as to some of the rules or in the mode of enforcing them. Especially is this the case on the outside boundaries of the law, where it comes in contact with or shades off into the local or municipal law of the particular country and effects only its own merchants or people in their relations to each other; whereas, in matters affecting the stranger or foreigner the commonly received law of the whole commercial world is more assiduously observed–as, in justice, it should be. No one doubts that every nation may adopt its own maritime code. France may adopt one; England another; the United States a third; still, the convenience of the commercial world, bound together, as it is, by mutual relation of trade and intercourse, demand that in all essential things wherein those relations bring them in contact, there should be uniform law founded on natural reason and justice. Hence, the adoption by all commercial nations (our own included) of the general maritime law as the basis and groundwork of all their maritime regulations. But no nation regards itself as precluded from making occasional modification suited to its locality and the genius of its own people and institutions, especially in matters that are of merely local and municipal consequence, and do not affect other nations. It will be found, therefore, that the maritime codes of France, England, Sweden, and other countries are not one and the same in every particular; but that, while there is a great correspondence between them, arising from the fact that each adopts the general principles and the great mass of the general maritime law as the basis of its system, there are varying shades of difference corresponding to the respective territories, climate, and genius of the people of each country respectively. Each state adopts the maritime law, not as a code having any independent or inherent force, *proprio vigore*, but as its own law, with such modifications and qualilfications as it sees fit. Thus adopted, and thus qualified in each case, it becomes the maritime law of the particular nation which adopts it. And without such voluntary adoption it would not be law. And thus it happens that, from the general practice of commercial nations in making the same general law the basis and groundwork of their respective maritime systems, the great mass of maritime law which is thus received by these nations in common to be the common maritime law of the world.

The same principle which guides our courts in the adoption and enforcement of principles of international law is accepted by courts of Great Britain, namely, the presumption that the State whose laws they apply has, by the fact of its existence as a member of the Family of Nations, accepted for its guidance in international matters the generally recognized rules of international law of procedure. When, however, as the State has by treaty or statute, or otherwise, shown that it does not accept a given international law principle, such principle does not receive judicial recognition.

A leading and often-cited English case upon this point is *The Queen v. Keyn,*[7] decided in 1876. The essential question involved in this case was whether, by the operation of the general principle of international law which treats the marginal waters of a country as territorial, the municipal court might, in the absence of any express statutory grant of power, exercise jurisdiction with reference to an act committed upon such waters. The court of last resort in its decision denied that the international law, however well established, could operate, *ex proprio vigore,* to extend the jurisdiction of a municipal court. In some way, it was declared, the assent of the State whose law the court is applying must be shown. International usage, participated in by the State in question, may show this assent; but it is the assent of the State and not the international usage which erects the principle into a law recognizable and enforceable by the courts.

"To be binding," said Cockburn, C.J., "the law must have received the assent of the nations who are to be bound by it. This assent may be expressed, as by treaty or the acknowledged concurrence of governments, or may be implied from established usage–an instance of which is to be found in the fact that merchant vessels on the high seas are held to be subject to the law of the nation under whose flag they sail, while in the ports of a foreign state they are subject to the local law as well as to that of their own country. In the absence of proof of assent, as derived from one or other of these sources, no unanimity on the part of theoretical writers would warrant the judicial application of the law on the sole authority of their views or statements. Nor, in my opinion, would the cleared proof of unanimous assent on the part of other nations be sufficient to authorize the tribunals of this country to apply, without an act of Parliament, what would practically amount to a new law. In so doing we should be unjustifiably usurping the province of the legislature. The assent of nations of doubtless sufficient to give the power of parliamentary legislation in a matter otherwise within the sphere of international law, but it would be powerless to confer without such legislation a jurisdiction beyond and unknown to the law."[8]

By a law passed in 1878,[9] Parliament granted the jurisdiction which, in *Queen* v. *Keyn*, the court held itself to be without. The statement is sometimes made that the enactment of this law was equivalent to a parliamentary declaration of the erroneousness of the court's decision. This, of course, it was not. The preamble of that act does indeed declare that "the rightful jurisdiction of Her Majesty, her heirs and successors, extends and has always extended over the open seas adjacent to the coasts of the United Kingdom," but this legislative declaration necessarily extended only to a denial of the fact upon which the court had founded its judgment, and not to an assertion of the fallacy of the *ratio decidendi* employed by the court. Indeed, it does not need to be said that it is not within the power of a legislature, whatever the extent of its law-making powers, to control processes of judicial reasoning. It may lay down laws by which the courts will in the future be bound, and it may even provide principles of statutory construction which shall henceforth be followed, but it cannot be any declaration render erroneous the process of reasoning which a court has employed. It may, for the future, with reference to specified matters, render inapplicable that reasoning, but cannot render it erroneous as applied in the past.

As a matter of fact the English courts have continued to the present day to assert the doctrine declared in *Queen* v. *Keyn.* In the very recent case of the West Rand *Central Gold Mining Co.* v. *King.*,[10] the Lord Chief Justice, in his opinion, said:

The second proposition urged, that international law forms part of the law of England, requires a word of explanation and comment. It is quite true that whatever has received the common consent of civilized nations must have received the assent of our country, and that to which we have assented along with other nations in general may properly be called international law, and as such will be acknowledged and applied by our municipal tribunals when legitimate occasion arises for those tribunals to decide questions to which doctrines of international law may be relevant. But any doctrine as invoked must be one really accepted as binding between nations, and the international law sought to be applied must, like anything else, be proved by satisfactory evidence, which must show either that the particular proposition put forward has been recognized and acted upon by our country, or that it is of such a nature, and has been so widely and generally accepted, that it can hardly be supposed that civilized state would repudiate it. The mere opinions of jurists, however eminent or learned, that it ought to be so recognized, are not in themselves sufficient. They must have received the express sanction of international agreement, or gradually have grown to be part of international law by their frequent practical recognition in dealings between various nations. We adopt the language used by Lord Russell of Killoween in his address at Saratoga in 1896 on the subject of International Law and Arbitration: 'What then, is international law? I know no better definition of it than it is the sum of the rules or usages which civilized states have agreed shall be binding on them in their dealings with one another.' In our judgment, the second proposition for which Lord Robert Cecil contended in his argument before us ought to be treated as correct only if the term 'international law' is understood in the sense, and subject to the limitations of application, which we have explained. The authorities which he cited in support of the proposition are entirely in accord with and, indeed, well illustrate our judgment upon this branch of the arguments advanced on behalf of the suppliants. For instance, *Barbuit's Case,* Cas. Tal. 281; *Triquet* v. *Bath,* 3 Burr 1478; and *Heathfield* v. *Chilton*, 4 Burr. 2016, are cases in which the courts of law have recognized and have given effect to the privilege of ambassadors as established by international law. But the expressions used by Lord Mansfield, when dealing with the particular and recognized rule of international law on this subject, that the law of nations forms part of the law of England ought not to be construed so as to include as part of the law of England opinions of textwriters upon a question as to which there is no evidence that Great Britain has ever assented, and a *fortiori* if they are contrary to the principles of her laws as declared by her courts. The cases of *Wolff* v. *Oxholm*, 6 M. & S. 92; 18 R.R. 313, and *Rex* v. *Keyn*, 2 Ex. D. 63, are only illustrations of the same rule–namely, that questions of international law may arise, and may have to be considered in connection with the administration of municipal law.

In *Mortensen* v. *Peters*,[11] decided in 1906, the High Court of Justiciary of Scotland said:

It is a trite observation that there is no such thing as a standard of international law, extraneous to the domestic law of a kingdom, to which appeal may be made. International law, so far as this court is concerned, is the body of doctrine regarding the international rights and duties of states which has been adopted and made part of the law of Scotland.

The comparatively recent case of *The Zamora*,[12] decided by the Judicial Committee of the Privy Council, is fully consistent with the position here taken. In that case the central question was whether the British prize courts were to hold themselves bound by certain rules issued by the King in Council in exercise of his prerogative powers, that is, without express authorization so to do by act of Parliament. It was held that the court was not so bound. The Judicial Committee in the course of its opinion pointed out that, under the Act of Parliament, the Prize Court was obligated to enforce generally accepted rules of international law except insofar as these might be modified by the municipal law of Great Britain; that this law could not be determined by executive order; and that, therefore, except when otherwise provided by Parliament, the court was compelled to find its rules in the accepted doctrines of international law. "If," said the Judicial Committee, "an Order in Council were binding on the Prize Court, such court would be compelled to act contrary to the express terms of the commission from which it derived its jurisdiction." And, before this, the Judicial Committee had said: "Of course, the Prize Court was a municipal court and its decrees and orders owed their validity to municipal law. The law which it enforced might, therefore, in one sense, be considered a branch of municipal law."

In support of the position that international law is a part of municipal law the recent American case of *Paquete Habana*[13] decided by the Supreme Court in 1899 has been cited.[14] This case involved the question whether, in the absence of municipal law, the principle that fishing smacks belonging to an enemy are not subject to seizure had become so well recognized in international law as to warrant the courts in declaring illegal a capture made by the United States naval forces. In its opinion the court said:

International law is part of our law, and must be ascertained and administered by the courts of justice of appropriate jurisdiction as often as questions of right depending upon it are duly presented for their determination. For this purpose, where there is no treaty, and no controlling executive or legislative act or judicial decision, resort must be had to the customs and usages of civilized nations, and, as evidence of these, to the work of jurists and commentators, who by years of labour, research, and experience have made themselves peculiarly well acquainted with the subjects of which they treat. Such works are resorted to by judicial tribunals, not for the speculations of their authors concerning what the law ought to be, but for trustworthy evidence of what the law really is.

In a dissenting opinion by the Chief Justice, Justices Harlan and McKenna concurring, the argument is not so much a denial that the exemption of fishing smacks from capture in time of war was a practice generally sanctioned by modern practice and by the opinions of international law writers, as that it lay within the discretion of the executive power to determine the rigors of war, and that, in the proclamation and directions which, in the exercise of that discretion had been issued, no such exemption had been expressly or impliedly authorized.

In this case we undoubtedly have the acceptance by our courts of an international usage as law, and that, too, a usage in whose favour neither universal and long-continued acceptance by nations nor unanimous advocacy by scientific commentators could be successfully urged. But this was by no means a repudiation of the principle declared by the Supreme Court in *The Lottawana.* The Federal Constitution provides that Congress shall have the power to define and punish offenses against the law of nations, and to make rules concerning captures on land and water. Furthermore, it is declared that treaties made under the authority of the United States shall be the supreme law of the land. The courts have repeatedly held that effect of these clauses, which recognize the existence of a body of international laws and grant to Congress the power to punish offenses against them, is to adopt these laws into our municipal law *en bloc* except where Congress or the treaty-making power has expressly changed them. Furthermore, it is held that the commonly accepted principles of international law, insofar as they had been embodied in the English common law, have been adopted into American law with the acceptance, substantially *en bloc*, of that common law. When, then, Congress has not acted, the courts properly hold that it is its intention that the generally recognized principles of international conduct should be applied. In exactly the same way it has been held that, with reference to the regulation of interstate commerce, the silence of Congress is deemed equivalent to an expression of its will that commerce shall be free from control by the States of the Union. There was, therefore, in this Paquete Habana Case that acceptance by the State which the courts have consistently declared is required for the transmutation of an international rule into a municipal command.

When the doctrine is declared that municipal law may not be altered or determined by international law, no distinction is made between the general principles of international law and the special obligations which, by treaties, States see fit to impose upon themselves. It is true that treaties entered into by the United States become a part of its own municipal law, but this is the result of an express constitutional provision.[15] Where there is no such express provision in a State's own laws or constitution, it is universally held that the municipal law may not be altered by a treaty. This, for example, is emphatically asserted in *Walker* v. *Baird*[16] by the Judicial Committee of the Privy Council, affirming on appeal a judgment of the Supreme Court of Newfoundland, Commenting on this case, Cobbett points out that "it serves to show that international agreements to which this country [Great Britain] may be a party, and obligation arising therefrom, will not be regarded as a part of the ordinary law of the land, except insofar as they may have received the assent of the Legislature. Hence, in English law, treaties which affect private rights must have a legislative sanction. Thus, extradition treaties are carried into effect by Orders in Council, made under the Extradition Acts, 1870 to 1906; international copyright arrangements are carried out by Orders in Council under the International Copyright Acts, 1844 to 1866; whilst even commercial treaties are sometimes given effect to by act of Parliament."

And, in a subsequent note, Cobbett so excellently summarizes the true English doctrine that its quotation, in *extenso,* is justified. He says:

The true relation may perhaps be expressed in the following propositions: English Law recognizes the Existence of International Law as a body of rules capable of being ascertained, and when ascertained as binding upon States either by immemorial usage[17] or by virtue of agreement. When once a rule of International Law is shown to have received the assent of civilized States, it will also be deemed to have received the assent of the country, and will in that character be applied by English courts in cases coming before them to which such rule may be relevant. But there are certain rights and obligations arising out of international relations, or purporting to rest upon international law, which will not be deemed to be within the competence of municipal courts.[18] So in *Cook* v. *Sprigg* (1899 A. C. 572) it was held that annexation was an act of State, and that obligation arising under a treaty to that effect were not of a kind which a municipal court could enforce. Moreover, the courts in interpreting and applying municipal law, whilst they will always seek to adopt such a construction as will not bring it into conflict with the law of nations, cannot of course give effect to its rules however clear, or to rights or obligations deducible therefrom, in cases where those rules derogate from or are inconsistent with the positive regulations of municipal law. With respect to treaties, in particular, the Crown or executive cannot claim, in virtue of any obligations arising out of a treaty not sanctioned by Statute, to modify or interfere with rights arising under the ordinary laws of the land. At the same time the inability of the courts to give effect to international obligations as against subjects will not, of course, have the effect of freeing a State from its international responsibility for their non-fulfilment. English law embraces a variety of Statutes which have been passed from time to time for the purpose of enabling the Crown and the executive to carry out more effectively it international obligations, and more especially to enter into and carry out particular treaty arrangements concluded with other States, and to this extent international law, and the obligations arising thereunder, will constitute a part of the law of the land to which the courts will in a proper case give full effect.[19]

Is International Law "Positive" in Character? In the preceding sections it has been shown that international law may not be assimilated to municipal law,–that it does not become positive municipal law until it has passed through the transmuting process of acceptance by the States whose courts enforce it. We have now to consider whether, without regard to its relation to municipal law, it may properly be termed "positive" in character, that is, law in the strict Austinian or analytical sense.

Clearly it cannot be so regarded for it lacks the essential quality of embodying commands issued by political superiors to political inferiors. This, however, does not mean, as has been previously suggested, that the title "laws" should not be given to these international rules if it be borne in mind that the term, when so employed, has a meaning different from that which it has when used by the analytical jurist when speaking of municipal laws.

In order that the position taken in this treatise with regard to the juristic nature of International Law may be given its proper setting, it will be worth while to present and comment upon the typical arguments of publicists who have stated the contrary doctrine.

In his essay entitled "Methods of Jurisprudence," Pollock says:[20]

International Law is a true branch of jurisprudence, nothwithstanding what may be said about its want of sovereign power and a tribunal. You may define it as 'positive international morality' not having the nature of law [as does Austin] but if you do the facts are against you. For what are the facts?

(1) The doctrines of international law are founded on legal not simply on ethical ideas. They are not merely prevalent opinions as to what is morally right and proper, but something as closely analogous to civil laws as the nature of the case will admit. They purport to be rules of strict justice, not counsels of perfection.[21]

(2) Since they have assumed a coherent shape they have been the special study of men of law, and have been discussed by the methods appropriate to jurisprudence, and not by those of moral philosophy.

(3) There is a practical test and a conclusive one. If international law were only a kind of morality, the framers of state papers concerning foreign policy would throw all their strength on moral argument. But, as a matter of fact, this is not what they do. They appeal not to the general feeling of moral rightness, but to precedents, and to opinions of specialists. They assume the existence among statesmen and publicists of a series of legal as distinct from moral obligation in the affairs of nations.

(4) Further, there is actually an international morality, distinct from, and incompatible with international law in the usual sense. As a citizen among citizens, so a nation among nations may do things which are discourteous, high-handed, savoring of sharp practice or otherwise invidious and disliked, and yet within its admitted right and giving no formal ground of complaint. There is a margin of discretionary behaviour which is the province not of claims and dispatches but of "friendly representations" and "good offices."

These facts, thus stated by Pollock, may be at once and fully admitted, and the conclusion conceded that there is a body of international principles that may fairly be said to constitute a system of jurisprudence as distinguished from one of morality, and that Austin's designation of international law as nothing more than positive morality is therefore misleading, if not absolutely erroneous, but it is none the less true that these juristic principles do not come within the ordinary accepted definition of civil or municipal law. If the two bodies of law are to be brought under a single rubric it is necessary that a broader definition be given to municipal law than is ordinarily given it.

This is what T. J. Lawrence, Oppenheim, and many other publicists do. Thus, after defining International Law as composed of "the rules which determine the conduct of the general body of civilized States in their mutual dealings," and pointing out that by thus using the term "rules" instead of "laws" he is able to discard altogether the phrase "rights and obligations," Lawrence says: "If we are content with the definitions of

Richard Hooker, the great Elizabethan divine, who spoke of the law as 'any rule of canon whereby actions are framed,' we may apply the term to those regulations concerning international conduct which meet with general acceptance of civilized communities."[22]

Oppenheim defines law as "a body of rules for human conduct within a community which by common consent of this community shall be enforced by external power."[23] By this definition, as he points out, three essential conditions of the existence of law are posited–a community, a body of rules for human conduct within the community, and a common consent to their enforcement by external power as distinguished from their enforcement by the internal conscience. These three essentials, he declares, are to be found in the rules which regulate the relations of States with each other: the civilised States do constitute a veritable community; they are definite rules that are accepted by common consent; and they are enforced by external authority.

The Development of International Law. If we date the rise of the science of international jurisprudence from the beginning of the seventeenth century, we find that, in the earlier phases, International Law was closely allied with if not assimilated to, the moral of "natural" laws and that, during that period its rules presented a corresponding indefiniteness, their ethical sanction was *in for interno,* and their actual observance was far from general or uniform. Indeed, at that time, the effort of such informers as Grotius and his immediate followers was to escape from the international practices that prevailed by appealing to principles founded in the very nature of reason and morality. The uninterrupted tendency since that time has, however, been to substitute the rules manifested in actual practices for abstract principles, and this tendency has been hastened by the increasing habit of nations to provide by treaties conventional rules for the guidance of their international affairs. These treaties have, of course, served to create rules only for the States parties to them, but where the same or substantially similar provisions have found a place in a number of treaties, and especially where a considerable number of nations have been parties to the treaties the effect has been to cause these provisions to be regarded as voicing the deliberate judgment of the international world. Thus, whereas, in earlier times, treaties were but seldom entered into except at the termination of armed struggles, and were limited in scope to the settlement of the dynastic, territorial or other disputes, the modern world has seen treaties employed for the purpose of establishing general rules for the future guidance of international life. At first this wider and legislative function of treaties was resorted to only when, upon the termination of some general war, the nations found themselves convened for the purpose of fixing the conditions of peace; but the present age has witnessed the assembling of Conferences embracing all or many of the members of the family of nations for the sole purpose of the creating rules for the regulation of international relations. Thus the general will of the international world has shown an increasing tendency to become articulate and legislative. Furthermore, as is well known, the attempt has been made, and with no small degree of success, to establish tribunals more or less judicial in character[24] for the settlement of international disputes. And finally, projects have been seriously discussed by publicists which would involve, if realized, the establishment of an international executive force for compelling obedience upon the part of recalcitrant nations to the generally recognized principles of international law. However, even were such an aim fully realized, it could hardly be said that international law would be thereby transmuted into positive law, unless the international judicial tribunals were given a general jurisdiction over international disputes, and unless, also, and what is still more important, the international legislative body, similar to the Hague Conferences should have ascribed to them unlimited law-making powers, and, of course, its declarations given an immediate and not merely an *ad referendum* character. When and only when, such conditions are met, will it be proper to say that a *civitas maxima* has been established with a territorial jurisdiction including the *orbem terrarum* and the utterances of its will entitled to be termed "positive" laws.

It none the less remains true, however, that, at the present time, there exists a body of rules regulating international relations which, though supported by the strongest feeling of morality and expediency, find their source no longer in abstract and vague doctrines of natural law, but in precedent and convention; which are sufficiently definite and susceptible of classification and logical arrangement; which for the most part may be referred back to, and supported by, fundamental propositions regarding the nature of the State as an international person, and with rights and obligations attaching to it as such; and which international rules are therefore susceptible of being brought together into a systematic and scientific whole. In short, the analytical political philosopher is provided with the material for a science of international law in as true a sense as he is when concerned with the construction of a philosophy of the State as nationally or municipally viewed.

It is further to be observed that what, in a comprehensive sense, is known as International Law is made up of several fairly distinct bodies of principles which vary as regards the obligatory and absolute force ascribed to them. Thus, just as in the field of national life there are many rules which Austin describes as rules of "positive morality," the justice and expediency of which are generally recognized, and which in fact are very generally conformed to, but which have not back of them the authority and sanction of the State; so, in the international field, there are many rules of what is known as international morality, or comity, the violation of which by one State is looked upon with disfavour by other States but not as illegal in a strict sense of the word. Thus, for example, principles of international comity provide that one State shall not refuse to have commercial or other dealings with other States, and that, subject to reasonable police regulations, it shall permit the nationals of those other States to travel or become domiciled and carry on business within its borders. Furthermore, this same comity demands that, in the privileges which one State extends to the subjects of other States, arbitrary distinctions shall not be made either between different classes of the subjects of the same State, or, generally between the nationals of different States. Thus, at the present time, Japan has shown dissatisfaction because the United States has denied to her subject certain rights of immigration, naturalization land-holding, and school privileges which are conceded to the citizens of other States. At the same time Japan recognizes that international law, in *sensu stricttiore*, grants to each State a comprehensive right to exercise its full discretion with regard to these matters and that, therefore, strictly speaking, she has no legal claim to redress. Many instances, similar to this, could be cited in which international comity is recognized as creating what may be called moral rights, or obligations of friendship or respect as distinguished from those which international law, properly speaking, supports.

Another phase of international relations which deserves at least mention is the bearing which "national policies" have upon the rights of other nations as established by international law. Not infrequently the effect of these policies is to infringe the rights which, in principle, every independent State is conceded by international law to possess. A most conspicuous instance of this is furnished by the Monroe Doctrine as declared by the United States. Although it is conceded that every independent State has the right, as such, to acquire or dispose of territory as a result of a war, or by way of purchase and sale, and Doctrine amounts to a declaration that the United States will not permit other States to acquire additional territory or political control in the Western Hemisphere, by any means, or under any circumstances. The same general result follows in all those cases in which particular States lay claim to what are known as

"Spheres of Influence." It is seen also in the notice recently (March 15, 1922) served upon the other Powers by Great Britain that, though it regards Egypt as now constituting a sovereign and independent State, "the welfare and integrity of Egypt are necessary to the peace and safety of the British Empire, which will therefore always maintain as an essential British interest the special relations between itself and Egypt long recognized by other Governments," and that, as so declared, the British Government "will not admit them to be questioned or discussed by any other Power." "In pursuance of this principle," the notice continues, "they [the British Government] will regard as an unfriendly act any attempt at interference in the affairs of Egypt by another Power, and they will consider any aggression against the territory of Egypt as an act to be repelled with all the means at their command." This declaration, it is to be observed, was a unilateral act upon the part of Great Britain and not one founded upon an agreement between itself and Egypt.

This general aspect of international life has recently been dwelt upon by Professor Jesse Reeves in a luminous paper in which he points out that, until this factor is taken into account, and the assertions of national policies brought into conformity with the general principles of international law, it is vain to hope that all international controversies may be brought within the jurisdiction of judicial as distinguished from arbitral tribunals. These national policies, he says, furnish the dynamic factors of international policies, he says, furnish the dynamic factors of international life, and, furthermore, "have to do not only with the relations of State with each other, a subject to which international law in the past has confined itself, but with the larger relations of groups to groups both within and without States, of individual to individuals, of world-movements of population, of earth-hunger and its appeasement, and of the strivings of international commercial competition. These things must be reduced to the regime of law, to an acceptance of a universal *status quo*; and in the past this has never come about except under a universal imperial dominion, or World-State. Slowly and painfully must the edifice be reconstructed, from foundation to superstructure. The basis of a regime of law among States must be those really juristic principles recognized by the members of the world-society as not repugnant to the realization of national ideals on the one hand, and, on the other as fitting in with the generally accepted ideals of justice and of fair dealing on the part of peoples within a State."

"Finally," Professor Reeves points out, "there must be recognized what may be called the sphere of an international law of crime. It is possible that in combating Austin's doctrine that international law is not true law, we are in danger of neglecting what he claimed for it, a positive international morality... Acts which shock the most obvious claims of humanity come to be looked at, not as international crimes, but as international torts, to be adjusted through diplomatic apology and assuaged by money payment. Anything whether in the form of certain kinds of propaganda or in the smugly polished phrases of utterance, which glosses over the essentially anti-social and therefore criminal nature of certain international acts may contribute to a fatal confusion of ideas."[25]

References

1. *Gesetz und Verordnung,* p. 205.
2. 14 Wallace 170 (1871).
3. 2 Cr. 64.
4. 9 Cr. 388.
5. 159 U. S. 113.
6. 21 Wall 558.
7. In the instant case it was held that Parliament had given to the court only the jurisdiction formerly exercises by the Admiral which of not cover the case at bar.
8. 41 and 42 Vict., chap. 73.
9. L.R. (1905), 2 K.B. 391.
10. *Law Reports, 2 Exchequer Division*, 68.
11. 14 Scots, L. T. R. 227.
12. L. R. (1916), 2 A. C. 77.
13. 175 U. S. 677.
14. See, for example, the article by Dr. J. B. Scott in the *American Journal of International Law*, October, 1907, "The Legal Nature of International Law."
15. Art. VI, Sec. 2: "This Constitution and the laws of the United States which shall be made in pursuance thereof; and all treaties made, or which shall be made, under authority of the United States, shall be the supreme law of the land."
16. A.C. 491 (1892). Cf. Cobbett, *Cases and Opinions on International Law*, p. 19.
17. Which, of course, indicates assent.
18. Citing *West Rand Central Gold Mining Co.* v. *The King*, 2 K. B. 391.
19. *Op. cit.*, p. 21 Cobbett, in footnotes, gives references to authorities supporting each of these propositions.
20. In his volume entitled *Oxford Lecturees*.
21. This is an important point. Many writers appear to think that if international

rules are denied the title laws in the positive or analytical sense, they are thereby declared to be nothing more than rules of morality. Austin is responsible for this mistake. International rules or principles are entitled to be termed laws, even though they may not properly be spoken of as laws in the sense in which that term is employed in municipal jurisprudence.

22. *International Law*, sec. 9.
23. *International Law*, 3d ed., sec. 5.
24. It is not necessary here to consider the distinction between "arbitration and the "Judicial settlement" of international controversies. It may be said, however, that while both methods have their special advantages and disadvantages the establishment of "judicial tribunals," as distinguished from courts or "boards of arbitration" would cause international more closely to approximate to municipal law as regards the mode of determination and its application to specific controversies.
25. *American Political Science Review,* February, 1916 (vol. X, p. 70). "The Justiciability of International Disputes.

VII

Territorial Jurisdiction

In this chapter the leading cases in American and English courts will be examined in order to show the extent to which, and the manner in which, judicial application has been made of the doctrines which, in the Part One of this treatise, have been deductively obtained from the conceptions which Public Law employs. This examination will demonstrate the correctness of the assertion, made at the outset that the doctrines of international and constitutional jurisprudence stand in such logical relations to one another, and to certain fundamental assumptions regarding the nature of the State and its legal competence, as to create bodies of coherent juristic thought.

The predication to it of Sovereignty necessarily implies that, from a standpoint of mere legal competence, the State has the power to determine, in every respect, what legal rights and obligations it will recognize with respect to itself. This means that it is legally qualified to claim either concurrent or exclusive jurisdiction over such persons and portions of the earth's surface, or the space above it as it may see fit. Each sovereign State thus has, *ex hypothesi*, the potential legal authority to subject to its legal control the entire surface of the globe and all those who dwell upon it. In other words, it is obligatory upon the judicial and executive officials of every sovereign State to recognize the validity of, and to the extent of their several actual powers, to give effect to, all declaration of policy of their respective governments, irrespective of what effect the carrying out of these policies may have upon the foreign relations of their respective States. Of course, in many cases there may arise questions as to the legal competence of the particular governmental organs or officials to issue the orders, or to enact or declare the policies involved, but these are matters wholly of constitutional limitations which the States have themselves laid upon their own governmental agencies, and do not disturb the postulate that there inheres in sovereign States the legal competence to remove these limitations if they so see fit, and thus to qualify their policy-forming or law-determining organs to assert, in behalf of themselves, whatever character or scope of jurisdiction, personal or territorial, they may deem desirable.[1]

This being the legal situation, it follows that, as long as there are a number of States, each with this unlimited potential jurisdictional competence, opportunity is provided for inter-State conflicts by reason of two or more States claiming exclusive or conflicting legal control over the same persons or the same areas. The adjustment or prevention of these conflicts is the task of international law, but the fact the necessities of international life compel each sovereign State to refrain from the exercise, in certain respects, of a jurisdiction over persons and territory which it might, if it saw fit, bring within the scope of its legal will, does not in any wise, or to any degree, derogate from that legal omnipotency, which , from the municipal point of view, it possesses.

That the courts of a country are bound to follow the determinations of their respective governments with respect to the territorial extent of the jurisdiction claimed by them is an accepted principle of the public law of all States.

In *Foster* v. *Neilson,*[1a] the Supreme Court of the United States, speaking of the exercise of territorial jurisdiction, said: "A question like this is, as has been truly said, more a political than a legal question, and, in its discussion, the courts of every country must respect the pronounced will of the legislature." In *Ex parte Cooper*[2], the same court considered itself bound by the action of the political departments of the government in claiming jurisdiction to an extent of fifty-nine miles from the shores of Alaska. Most emphatic of all is the statement of the court in *Jones v. United States.*[3] In that case, speaking for a unanimous court, Mr. Justice Gray said:

> Who is the Sovereign, *de jure* or *de facto*, of a territory is not a judicial, but a political question, the determination of which by the legislative and executive departments of any government conclusively binds the judges as well as all other officers, citizens and subjects of that government. This principle has always been upheld by this court and has been affirmed under a great variety of circumstances... All

courts of justice are bound to take judicial notice of the territorial extent of the jurisdiction exercised by the Government whose laws they administer or of its recognition or denial of the sovereignty of a foreign power, as appearing from the public acts of the legislature and executive, although those acts are not formally put in evidence, nor accord with the pleadings.

Effect of Annexation on Laws of Annexed Territory. It necessarily follows from the general principles of sovereignty that, after annexation, the laws previously obtaining in a given territory no longer are able tc draw legal vitality from the former sovereignty, and that, insofar as they are to continue to have legal power, they must look to the will of the new sovereign. This will may be expressed tacitly, or by affirmative expression, and as a matter of enlightened political practice, annexing States generally follow the rule that these laws, so far as they are not contrary to their own public policies, shall continue in force until expressly altered or repealed. Thus in the case of *Chicago, Rock Island and Pacific Railway Co.* v. *McGlinn*[4], the Supreme Court of the United States said:

> The contention of the Railroad Company is that the Act of Kansas became inoperative within the Reservation upon the cession to the United States of exclusive jurisdiction over it. We are clear that this contention cannot be maintained. It is a general rule of public law, recognized and acted upon by the United States, that whenever political jurisdiction and legislative power over any territory are transferred from one nation or sovereignty to another, the municipal laws of the country, that is, laws which are intended for the protection of private rights, continue in force until abrogated or changed by the new government or sovereign. By the cession public property passes from one government to the other, but private property remains as before, and with it those municipal laws which are designed to secure its peaceful use and enjoyment. As a matter of course, all laws, ordinances, and regulations in conflict with the political character, institutions and Constitution of the new government, are at once displaced. Thus, upon a cession of political jurisdiction and legislative power—and the latter is involved in the former—to the United States, the laws of the country in support of an established religion or abridging the freedom of the press, or authorizing cruel and unusual punishments, and the like, would at once cease to be of obligatory force without any declaration to that effect;[5] and the laws of the country on other subjects would

necessarily be superseded by existing laws of the new government upon the same matters.

In the case of the *United States* v. *Percheman,*[6] the Supreme Court was called upon to examine the validity of certain land grants of the Spanish governor of Florida issued prior to the annexation of that territory by the United States. In the opinion rendered by the Court Chief Justice Marshall said:

> It is very unusual, even in cases of conquest, for the conqueror to do more than displace the sovereign and assume dominion over the country. The modern usage of nations, which has become law, would be violated; that sense of justice and of right which is acknowledged and felt by the whole civilized world would be outraged, if private property should be generally confiscated, or private right annulled. The people change their allegiance; their relation to their ancient sovereign is dissolved; but their relations to each other, and their rights of property, remain undisturbed. If this be the modern rule even in cases of conquest, who can doubt its application to the case of an amicable cession of territory.

This is strong language, but there is no suggestion that it does not lie within the legal power of the new government (subject, of course, to the limitations of its own constitutional laws) to act as it might seem fit with regard to the private as well as to the public rights of the inhabitants of annexed territories.

State Succession. In Part One of this volume the general principles governing the transfer of the obligations of State whose territory is annexed in whole or in part by another State, have been stated and do not need to be here repeated. It will, however, be worth while to refer to the holding of the British court of King's Bench in the case of *West Rand Central Gold Mining Co.* v. *Rex*, decided in 1905.[7] This case is an interesting one not only as regards the matter of State Succession, but as exhibiting the nature of an "Act of State" as conceived of in English law (a topic later to be discussed) and also as illustrating the relation of international law to the law of England. In this case, by a petition of right, the plaintiff sought to recover certain amounts of gold which, prior to the war between Great Britain and the South African Republic, had been seized by that government. The claim was that, by annexation of the Republic to Great Britain, the liability in the matter had been shifted from the former to the latter. On demurrer is was held that the petition disclosed no right which could be enforced against the King in any municipal court.

The court not only denied that there was any certainly established rule of international law requiring the assumption by a conquering and annexing State of the liabilities of an annexed State, but that, so far as such a rule could be said to be favoured by international law writers, it was inconsistent with the law as recognized for many years by the English courts.

The case involved an alleged contractual liability. In the latter part of his opinion the Lord Chief Justice implied that had the interest been one based upon perfected title, especially to land, and therefore, an interest for the divesting of which affirmative state action would be required, the doctrine might have been a different one. He said: "It must not be forgotten that the obligations of conquering States with regard to private property of private individuals, particularly land as to which the title had already been perfected before the conquest or annexation, are altogether different from the obligations which arise in respect of personal rights by contract. As is said in more cases than one, cession of territory does not mean the confiscation of the property of individuals in that territory. If a particular piece of property has been conveyed to a private owner or has been pledged, or a lien has been created upon it, considerations arise which are different from those which have to be considered when the question is whether the contractual obligation of the conquered State towards individuals is to be undertaken by the conquering State."

As to the American cases[8] cited by counsel for the West Rand Co., the Chief Justice observed that they all related to landed property in annexed areas, and that, in all of them, the treaties of cession or subsequent statutes of the United States had declared that the rights of private property were to be respected, and that no question had been involved of the duty of the United Sates to fulfil the obligation of the former sovereignties.

Recognition of States. The same sovereign power which enables each sovereign State to determine for itself the extent of its territorial dominion, enables it to determine, in a manner conclusively binding upon its own courts, what other States it will recognize as sovereign, and the extent of their several territorial dominions. Those legally conclusive determinations are reached by the so-called political departments of government, namely, those having constitutional authority to deal with the relations of the State to other States. Furthermore, international law and practice, in agreement with national or municipal law, declares that such sovereign

State must, and of a right should, determine for itself, in each particular case, whether or not recognition shall be accorded.[9]

In *Williams* v. *Insurance Co.* [10] the Supreme Court of the United States said:

Can there be any doubt that when the executive branch of the government which is charged with our foreign relations, shall, in its correspondence with a foreign nation, assume a fact in regard to the sovereignty of any island or country, it is conclusive on the judicial department? And in this view it is not material to inquire, nor is it in the province of the court to determine, whether the executive be right or wrong. It is enough to know that, in the exercise of his constitutional functions, he had decided the question. Having done this under the responsibilities which belong to him, it is obligatory on the people and government of the Union.

Earlier than this, in the case of the *Cherokee Nation* v. *Georgia*[11] the same court had said: "It is a rule which has been repeatedly sanctioned by this court, that the judicial department is to consider as sovereign and independent States or Nations those powers that are recognized as such by the executive and legislative departments of the government, they being more particularly entrusted with our foreign relations."

The English doctrine as to the conclusiveness, so far as the courts are concerned, of the determination of the political departments of the government is the same as that of the United States. In the case of *The Charkieh*[12] Sir Robert Fillimore took a different view, but he was expressly overruled in 1894 by the Court of Appeal in the case of *Mighell* v. *The Sultan of Johore*, Lord Esher, in that case, saying: "When there is an authoritative certificate of the Queen through her Minister of State as to the status of another sovereign, that, in the courts of this country, is conclusive."[13]

Recognition of Government. The matter of the recognition of Government or heads of States a distinct from the recognition of the States themselves will be discussed later on.[14]

Determination of Extent of Territorial Jurisdiction. Equally conclusive upon the courts are the determinations of the political department as to the territorial extent of the British dominion itself.

In *Regina* v. *Keyn*,[15] decided in 1876 one of the questions was as to the territorial jurisdiction of Great Britain over waters within three miles of her coasts. In the course of his opinion Chief Justice Cockburn said: "That such legislation [asserting jurisdiction], whether consistent with the general law of nations or not, would be binding on the tribunals of this country—leaving the question of its consistency with international law to be determined between the governments of the respective nations–can of course admit of no doubt."

In the same case Justice Brett, in a dissenting opinion–his dissent being based upon the denial of the position assumed by the majority that an affirmative act of Parliament asserting the jurisdiction and vesting in the court authority to adjudicate cases of the instant class was needed–said: "The question what is or what is not a part of the realm, is in my opinion not in general a question for a judge to decide...? What are the limits of the realm should in general be declared by Parliament."

So, also, the Judicial Committee of the Privy Council, the next year, in the case of *Direct United States Cable Co.* v. *Anglo-American Telegraph Co.*[16] said, with reference to the political status of the Bay of Conception: "Moreover, [a circumstance] which, in a British tribunal, is conclusive, the British Legislature has by act of Parliament declared it to be a part of the British territory."

Finally, by Section 4 the Foreign Jurisdiction Act of 1891, the British Parliament expressly declared that whenever, in any civil or criminal proceedings, a question should be raised as to the existence of British jurisdiction, the decision of the Secretary of State should be taken as final by all tribunals.

Neutral or Belligerent Status. It has been seen that the courts of States are bound by the declarations of the so-called political departments of their own governments as to the extent of territorial jurisdiction claimed respectively by these States, and as to what foreign States are to be recognized as having sovereignty over particular foreign areas. Similarly, in times of war, all courts hold themselves bound by the decisions of their respective political departments as to whether given territories are to be regarded as having a neutral or belligerent status. The existence of a state of war between foreign States or with thir own State is also a matter upon which the courts hold themselves conclusively bound by the determinations of the constitutionally competent political departments of their own governments.

Exclusiveness of Territorial Jurisdiction. That, within the area which it claims as peculiarly its own, a sovereign State will not permit, except with its own consent, the exercise of legal jurisdiction by any other State, is a principle of public law so universally advanced that it is scarcely necessary to vouch authorities in its support. It will be sufficient to give the classic statement of it by Chief Justice Marshall in the case of the Exchange.[17]

The jurisdiction of the nation within its own territory is necessarily exclusive and absolute. It is susceptible of no limitation not imposed by itself. Any restriction upon it, deriving validity from an external source, would imply a diminution of its sovereignty to the extent of the restriction, and an investment of that sovereignty to the same extent in the power which would impose such restriction. All exceptions, therefore, to the full and complete owner of a nation within its own territories, must be traced up to the consent of the nation itself. They can flow from no other legitimate source. This consent may be either express or implied.

From this principle it follows that all those instances of what is termed extraterritorial jurisdiction which are commonly recognized by modern States, such as that pertaining to the persons of foreign sovereigns, to foreign ships of war in the ports or territorial waters of other States, the immunity of foreign diplomatic officials from local jurisdiction, etc., as well as those instances in which, in certain countries of the Levant and Eastern Asia, foreigners are suable only in the consular or other courts of their own countries and have applied to them only the laws of their own countries, are all to be deemed authorized by the express or implied consent of the local territorial sovereign.[18]

It would seem, then, that there is no necessity for the faction, so often employed, that the public ship of a nation is to be deemed a part of the territory of the State of which it belongs, or that the residence of a diplomatic official is to be similarly viewed.[19]

Correlative Complete Responsibility. It scarcely needs to be said that the correlative to the claim of exclusiveness of jurisdiction is the strict accountability to which a State may be held by other States for the equitable and reasonable manner in which this jurisdiction is exercised over their own respective nationals and their property, or, indeed, with regard to any matters in which they conceive their just interests to be involved. Stated in other words, this doctrine is that no State is conceded by other States the right to plead either a *de facto* or constitutional *non possumus* as an excuse for failure to fulfil the obligations imposed upon it by generally recognized international law. From such a plea it is prevented by its claim of right to deny to all other States the exercise of jurisdiction within its own limits.

The United States has, at times, been greatly embarrassed by, but has not been able to escape from, the application of this principle, by reason of its peculiar constitutional system. Under this system it is with the National Government alone that foreign States have relations and to it alone they look for the fulfilment of international obligations, an yet, in fact, that Government has not, in all cases, had the constitutional or statutory power to protect or give adequate relief to resident aliens who have been injured by reason of the failure of state authorities to give them proper protection or, after injury, properly to punish those who have been guilty of the wrongs complained of.

Space will not permit even a brief account of the international controversies to which the United States has been a party, arising out of injuries received by aliens at the hands of mobs or in time of riots,[20] or even to discuss the embarrassing situation which arose by reason of the inability of the National Government to secure the release from the custody of the State of New York of one McLeod who was being criminally prosecuted for an act the responsibility for which had been assumed by the Government of Great Britain[21]. We may, however, quote the following from a communication of the British Foreign Office to the American Secretary of State, Daniel Webster: "Neither can Her Majesty's Government admit for a moment the validity of the doctrine… that the Federal Government of the United States has no power to interface in the, matter in question, and that the decision thereof must rest solely and entirely with the State of New York. With the particulars of the internal compact which may exist between the several States that compose the Union, foreign Powers have nothing to do; the relations of foreign Powers are with the aggregate Union, that Union is to them represented by the Federal Government, and of that Union the Federal Government is to them the only organ. Therefore, when a foreign State has redress to demand for a wrong done to it by any State of the Union, it is to the Federal Government, and not to the separate State that such Power must look for redress for that wrong. And such foreign Power cannot admit the plea that the separate State is an independent body over which the Federal Government has no control. It is obvious that such a doctrine, if admitted, would at once go to a dissolution of the Union so far as its relations with foreign Powers are concerned; and that Foreign Powers, in such case, instead of accrediting diplomatic agents to the Federal Government, would send such agents not to that Government, but to the Government of each separate State."[22]

It is seen, then, that when one Government is notified by another Government that it assumes responsibility for an act, the notified Government, as a matter of policy as well as of proper international procedure, will not attempt to hold personally responsible in its courts the individual who has committed the act is to be made, instead, if any issue growing out of that act is to be made, will consider the matter one to be dealt with directly between the two Governments. In other words, it is deemed a matter of comity, or of due respect to the dignity of a Government, that the propriety of acts which it has ordered or assumed responsibility for, should not be questioned in municipal courts. In the McLeod case the United States was so unfortunately circumstanced by its peculiar constitutional system it did not have the legal means of compelling the courts of one of the States of the Union to obey this direction of discontinuance. But that, as a matter of international comity, the judicial proceedings against McLeod should have been discontinued, the foreign office of the United States fully recognized. The American Secretary of State, Mr. Webster, said: "The Government of the United States entertains no doubt that after this avowal of the transaction as a public transaction authorized and undertaken by the British authorities, individuals concerned in it ought not by the principles of public law and the general usage of civilized States to be holden personally responsible in the civilized tribunals of law for their participation in it."

Mutual Respect of States for Each Others' Sovereignty. A mutual respect by States of each other's sovereignty has led to the doctrine that the determinations of the courts of one State, when acting with regard to persons or property over whom they have obtained jurisdiction will not be judicially questioned by the courts of other States.[23] If those other States feel themselves aggrieved by the acts of another States, whether executive or judicial, their only resources is to diplomatic protest, and if this fails, to force.

In *Dobree et als.* v. *Napier et al.,*[24] the British court held that, notwithstanding the provisions of a British Act of Parliament with regard to foreign enlistments, and action would not lie against a British citizen who, in the service of a foreign State, at peace with Great Britain, had captured upon the high seas a British vessel for breaking a blockade, and which was thereupon condemned by a prize court of the capturing State. The court said: "The sentence of a foreign court of competent jurisdiction, condemning a neutral vessel taken in war, as prize, is binding and conclusive on all the world; and no English court of law can call in question the propriety, or the grounds, of such condemnation."

This case is authority for the doctrine that acts upon the high seas done or authorized by a foreign sovereignty, and held legitimate by its courts cannot furnish ground for suits in the British courts.

In *Regina* v. *Lesley,*[25] decided in 1860, the Court for Crown Cases Reserved, upon the authority of *Dobree* v. *Napier*, held that a trespass committed on a British ship, under contract with a foreign State, while in the territorial waters of that State, and authorized by that State, could not furnish ground for an action in British courts against the trespasser; but that, upon the high seas, acts done in a British ship were to be regarded as governed by British law, and the authority of no foreign State could extend to them so as to make them non-justiciable.

In this case it is clear thatt he doctrine was asserted that a State could not throw the mantle of its authorization over acts committed outside its own territorial jurisdiction. It would appear, however, that the doctrine does not apply to acts which involve more than private interests and rise to the dignity of matters of high policy, that is, where they concern questions which are normally determined by direct international dealing of States with one another, as, for example, was the fact in the McLeod Case.[26]

It is of course clear that one State has no legal authority directly to control proceedings in the courts of another State, and that, therefore, in case it desires them discontinued or otherwise controlled, it must task the Foreign Office of the other State to cause the necessary direction to be transmitted to its judicial tribunals. It might be proper for the Government of one State to ask leave of the court of another State to intervene in a suit in order to file its statement that it assumed responsibility for an act upon which the instant proceedings were predicated, but, ordinarily, in this statement would be filed by the defendant by way of defense. In the United States the President has the authority to direct the Attorney General to cause a *nolle prosequi* to be entered in judicial proceedings, civil or criminal, instituted by the United States, but no such order of discontinuance could be issued to authorities of the States of the Union; nor, in most of the Sates, has the States executive such a power. In those cases, then, in which a foreign sovereign has assumed responsibility for an act, and in which the executive, federal or state, has not the legal power to control the judicial proceedings, it remains for the courts themselves to take appropriate action.

Quite different from the situation that has just been discussed is that presented when the civil liability that is sought by the plaintiff to be imposed upon the defendant is one that depends, for its existence, upon foreign law. In such a case the court has a discretionary right, the exercise of which is guided by principles of policy and international comity, as to whether or not it will recognize and enforce the liability thus accruing. Having this discretionary right, the refusal of a court to recognize and enforce the liability cannot be held to deny to the plaintiff a right to which, by law, he is entitled. It is not, therefore, a denial to him of due process of law.

It cannot, then, be contended that the obligation upon the part of one Government, at the request or demand of another Government, to discontinue judicial proceedings in its own courts against individuals who have violated its laws, has a basis of legal necessity, for, as has been said, there is no nexus between one State and the law of another State which will make it possible, legally speaking, for the first State either to control the governmental agencies of another State or to determine the legality of its acts as tested by the municipal law of that other State. It is, however, always within the political or international right of one State to protest to another State, and, in case that protest is not heeded, to take whatever action it sees fit, if the judicial tribunals or other governmental agencies of another State have taken or are about to take action which the protesting State deems prejudicial to its own interests or dignity, or to the legitimate interest or dignity of its own citizens. In such cases the point at issue is not the legality, *in sensu strictiore*, of the action in question, but the propriety of the exercise by the State of its sovereign rights,—a propriety that is to be determined by principles of international comity and usual international practice. Therefore, viewed simply as a principle of municipal law, as a question of strict legal right divorced from considerations of policy and comity, the New York State court was correct when, in the McLeod case, it said; "England… could legally impart no protection to her subjects concerned in the destruction of the *Caroline*, either as a party to any war, to any act of public jurisdiction exercised by way of defence, or sending her servants into a territory at peace." And, later on in the opinion: "Whatever obligation his [the accused's] nation may be under to save him harmless, this can be done only on the condition that he confine himself within her territory."[27]

The McLeod case illustrate the class of cases in which the act involved is committed within the territorial jurisdiction of the State whose courts are asked to take cognizance of it. A quite different question is presented when the act is committed abroad and responsibility for it assumed by the local sovereign. Here it is quite plain that, in proceedings instituted in tribunals of another State the *lex loci actus* should govern, and that the formal approval of the local sovereign of an act should be deemed conclusive of its legality as tested by the local law, and, if the subjects of other States are injured by such act they should be remitted to the political departments of their respective government for them to take such action as they may deem appropriate or feasible in the premises.

It is well established that this doctrine applies as well to acts ordered or approved by *de facto* governments as to those sanctioned by political establishments regarding whose legal status there is no question. A leading American case upon this point is *Underhill* v. *Hernandez,*[28] decided by the United States Supreme Court in 1897.

This case was an action brought by Underhill, as American citizen, against one Hernandez, who, while military commander, deriving his authority from a *de facto* government in Venezuela, had ordered Underhill's detention and confinement. The inferior court dismissed the action upon the ground that the act complained of had been that of the Venezuela Government, and the Supreme Court, affirming this degree, and speaking through Chief Justice Fuller, said:

> Every sovereign State is bound to respect the independence of every other sovereign State, and the courts of one country will not sit in judgement on the acts of the Government of another State done within its own territory. Redress of grievances by reason of such acts must be obtained through the means open to be availed of by sovereign powers as between themselves. Nor can the principie be confined to lawful or recognized Governments, or to cases where redress can manifestly be had through public channels. The immunity of individuals from suits brought in foreign tribunals for acts done within their own States, in the exercise of governmental authority, whether as civil officers or as military commanders, must necessarily extend to the agents of Governments ruling by paramount force as a matter of fact...If the party seeking to dislodge the existing Government succeed, and the independence of the Government it has set up is recognized, then the acts of such Government from the commencement of its existence are regarded as those of as independent nation. If the revolt fails of success, still, if actual war has been waged, acts of legitimate warfare cannot be made the basis of individual liability.[29]

This matter of the non-justiciability in municipal courts of acts of foreign sovereignties was again discussed by the United States Supreme Court in the case of *American Banana Co.* v. *United Fruit Co.,*[30] decided in 1909.

This was an action to recover damages provided for by the so-called Sherman Anti-Trust Act of 1890, and was based upon the claim that the defendant corporation had corruptly instigated the Government of Costa

Rica to take action whereby the plaintiffs' properties were injured. Dismissing the complaint, the court said: "Not only were the acts of the defendant in Panama or Costa Rica not within the Sherman Act, but they were not torts of the place, and therefore were not torts at all, however contrary to the ethical and economic postulates of that statute. The substance of the complaint is that, the plantation being within the *de facto* jurisdiction of Costa Rica, that State took and Keeps possession of it by virtue of its sovereign power. But a seizure by a State is not a thing that can be complained of elsewhere in the courts (*Underhill* v. *Hernandez*). The fact, if it be a fact, that *de jure* the estate is in Panama, does not matter in the least; sovereignty is pure fact. The fact has been recognized by the United States, and, by the implication of the bill, is assented to by Panama. The fundamental reason why persuading a sovereign power to do this or that cannot be a tort is not that the sovereign cannot be joined as defendant or because it must be assumed to be acting lawfully... The fundamental reason is that it is a contradiction in terms to say that, within its jurisdiction, it is unlawful to persuade a sovereign power to bring about a result that it declares by its conduct to be desirable and proper. It does not, and foreign courts cannot, admit that the influences were improper or the result bad. It makes the persuasion lawful by its own act. The very meaning of sovereignty is that the decree of the sovereign makes law. See *Kawananakoa* v. *Polyblank*, 205 U. S. 349... The acts of the soldiers and officials of Costa Rica are not alleged to have been without the consent of the Government, and must taken to have been done by its order. It ratified them, at all events, and adopted and keeps the possession taken by them."[31]

In *Oetjen* v. *Central Leather Co.*,[32] the Supreme Court of the United States was called upon to consider the effect to be given in American courts to acts committed in Mexico under the authority of a Government which, at the time, had not been recognized as either *de facto* or *de jure* by the American Government, but which had later been so recognized. After referring to the principle that, in matter of recognition of foreign Governments the courts are conclusively bound by the determinations of the political departments of their own Government, and that recognition, when accorded, has a retroactive effect so far as concerns the acts of that Government, the Court said: "The principle that the conduct of one independent Government cannot be successfully questioned in the courts of another is as applicable to a case involving the title to property brought within the custody of a court, such as we have here, as it was held to be in the cases cited[33] in which claims for damages were based upon acts done in a foreign country, for it rests at last upon the highest considerations of international comity and expediency. To permit the validity of the acts of one friendly State to be re-examined and perhaps condemned by the courts of another would very certainly imperil the amicable relation between Governments and vex the peace of nations."

Aerial Jurisdiction. With the development of the art of navigating the air the extent to which it will be internationally, as well as nationally, expedient that a State should have jurisdiction over the air above its land area is a matter which as yet has not received clear determination. It does not appear, however, that the introduction of this new element into the political problem will make it necessary to change accepted fundamental notions of the State's jurisdictional powers. Before the Great War international conferences assembled at Paris and Verona with a view to seeing if all the States of the world, or a major part of them, might not come to some general agreement upon this subject and thus avoid occasion for dispute. The matter was also considered at various meetings of the Institute of International Law. At the Paris Peace Conference, in 1919, aerial jurisdiction was discussed and a convention drawn up and signed, October 13, 1919, to which the five principal Allied Powers were named as parties. The rules of this agreement apply only in times of peace, and therefore, do not restrain the action of the parties to it in times of war either as neutrals or belligerents. But the convention does explicitly recognize, as a fundamental proposition, that each State has complete and exclusive jurisdiction over the air space above its land area and territorial waters.[34]

Garner[35] classified as follows the various international law writers as regards the doctrines recommended by them for adoption by the nations of the world:

1. "Those who assert that the air is or should be absolutely free for purposes of aerial navigation by aviators of all countries."
2. "Those who assert the general principle of the freedom of the air subject to a certain right of control by the subjacent State over the superincumbent atmosphere up to a certain height. This area they call the 'territorial zone'."
3. "Those who advocate the general principle of the freedom of the air but allow the underlying State to exercise control over it up to an indefinite height for purposes of self-protection and preservation."
4. "Those who content for the absolute sovereignty of the underlying State for any and all purposes over the aerial domain above the territory."

5. "Those who contend for the principle of absolute sovereignty subject to the right of free passage... This is the view embodied in the convention relating to international air navigation, agreed to by the representatives of the Allied and Associated Powers at the Peace Conference in 1919."[36]

The rule adopted by the Institute of International Law in 1906 declares the air domain to be free in war as in peace, subject only to the right of underlying States to take appropriate measures to protect persons and property upon their respective soils.

Radio. The rapid development of radio communication throughout the world has rendered still more necessary an agreement of the nations upon some generally binding rules as to the use of the air for purposes of wireless operations, whether in times of peace or of war.[37]

References

1. See the very valuable article by Professor Ernest Lorenzen, "Territoriality, Public Policy and the Conflict of Laws," in the *Yale Law Journal*, May, 1924, in which is pointed out the error of attempting to found systems of municipal law upon the promise that the jurisdiction of States is wholly territorial in character.

1a. 2 Peters 253.

2. 143 U. S. 472.
3. 137 U. S. 202.
4. 114 U. S. 542. This case involved the cession to the United States by one of its own member-States of exclusive federal jurisdiction. The principles declared are, however, drawn from international jurisprudence.
5. Laws of these kinds are forbidden by the United States Constitution.
6. 7 Pet. 51.
7. 2 K. B. 391.
8. *United States* v. *Percheman*, 7 Pet. 51; *Mitchell* v. *United States*, 9 Pet. 711; *Smith v. United States*, 10 Pet. 326; *Strother* v. *Lucas*, 12 Pet. 410.
9. "No new State has by International Law a right to demand recognition, although practically such recognition cannot in the long run be withheld, because without it there is no possibility of entering into intercourse with new State...History nevertheless records many cases of deferred recognition, and, apart from other proof, it becomes thereby apparent that the granting or denial of recognition is not a matter of International Law but of international practice." Oppenheim, *International Law*, vol. I, sec. 72 (2d ed.).

10. 13 Pet. 415.
11. 5 Pet. 1.
12. 1873, 4 A. & E. 39.
13. L. R. 1894, 1 Q. B. 149
14. Post, chap. XX.
15. Law Reports, 2 Ex. Div. 63. This case is often cited as *The Franconia.*
16. 1877, 2 A. C. 394.
17. 7 Cranch. 116.
18. The juristic competency of a State to exercise extraterritorial authority will be later examined. See *post,* chap. XXII.
19. W. E. Hall stands preëminent among English and American jurists as regard the attempt to found accepted rules of International Law upon basic juristic principles. In Chapter IV of his *International Law,* entitled "Sovereignty in Relation to the territory of the State," with regard to the ordinarily recognized immunities which go under the name of extraterritoriality, he says: "The relation created by these immunities is usually indicated by the metaphorical term extraterritoriality, the persons and things in enjoyment of them being regarded as detached portions of the State to which they belong, moving about on the surface of foreign territory and remaining separate from it. The term is picturesque; it brings vividly before the mind one aspect at least of the relation in which an exempted person or thing stands to a foreign State; but it may be doubted whether its picturesqueness has not enabled it to seize too strongly upon the imagination. Extraterritoriality has been transformed from a metaphor into a legal fact. Persons and things which are more or less exempted from local jurisdiction are said to be in law outside the State in which they are. In this form there is evidently a danger lest the significance of the conception should be exaggerated. If extraterritoriality is taken, not merely as a rough way of describing the effect of certain immunities, but as a principle of law, it becomes, or at any rate it is ready to become, an independent source of legal rule, displacing the principle of the exclusiveness of territorial sovereignty within the range of its possible operation in all cases in which practice is unsettled or contested. This course is conceivably its actual position. But the exclusiveness of territorial sovereignty is so important to international law and lies so near its root, that no doctrine which rests upon a mere fiction can be lightly assumed to have been accepted as controlling it."

    After discussing the various grounds of expediency and courtesy which have led to the granting of these immunities, Hall says: "if the view that has been presented of the extent and nature of the immunities which have been hitherto discussed be correct, it is clear that the fiction of extraterritoriality is not needed to explain them, and even that its use is inconvenient...The fiction is...inconvenient, because it gives a false notion of identity between immunities which are really distinct both in object and extent, and because no set of immunities fully corresponds with what is implied in the doctrine. Nothing in any case is gained by introducing the complexity of fiction when a practice can be sufficiently explained by reference to requirements of national life which have given rise to it; where the fiction fails even to correspond with usage, its adoption is indefensible."

The author of the present volume heartily concurs with these views. In connection with this subject it may be said that exactness of terminology would require the use of the expression "exterritoriality" when immunity from local jurisdiction is referred to; and that "extraterritoriality" is the proper word when reference is had to the operation of municipal law outside of the territorial limits of the State creating it. In fact, however, this preciseness of terminology has not been generally attempted by International Law writers.

20. For instance, the New Orleans Spanish Riots of 1851, the Denver Chinese Riot of 1880, the Chinese Riots of 1885 at Rock Springs in the Territory of Wyoming, the Chinese Riots of the same year in Seattle, the lynching of Italians in 1891 at New Orleans. In these cases the United States was not willing to acknowledge in explicit language, its full international responsibility, but, in fact, in most instances at least, granted, *ex gratia,* pecuniary damages to the persons injured or to their families.
21. As to this important case, see *British and Foreign State Papers*, vols. XXIX and XXX, and Moore, *Digest of International Law,* vol. II, p. 25, and authorities there cited.
22. The American Government did not, in this case, seek to controvert the doctrine thus stated, but tried to shift the issue to a somewhat different ground. In the Cutting Case, arising in 1886, the United States took towards Mexico quite the same position that England had taken in the McLeod Case. In a careful document entitled *Repord on Extraterritorial Crime and the Cutting Case*, Dr. John Bassett Moore, then Third Assistant Secretary of State, said (p. 19): "It is not proposed to discuss the extent of the control of the Federal Executive of Mexico over the authorities of the States which compose that Republic. This is a question of municipal law, which, in accordance with the rule that the authorities of a nation are the proper interpreters of its municipal regulations, may be left to the Mexican Government. But it should not be forgotten that, while a domestic difficulty may be accepted as a plea for delay, it cannot be set up as a bar to the ultimate performance of international obligations, and cannot, therefore, be held to prevent a demand upon a Government for the fulfilment of those obligations. To hold otherwise would be to assert the supremacy of municipal regulations, and permit each nation to prescribe the measure of its international duty."
23. For a fuller discussion of this topic see *post*, chap. XVIII.
24. 2 Bingham's New Cases 781.

25. 29 L. J. M. 97.
26. Moore, in his *Act of the State in English Law*, p. 125, says: "Lesley's Case probably means no more than: that the mere authority of the foreign sovereign, irrespective of the subject-matter and the other facts of the case, does not constitute a justification, or put the matter out of court. There is, in fact, a distinction to be drawn between acts done or purporting to be done in the ordinary course of the country's law which is limited by the sovereignty of that country; and, on the other hand, acts to which we apply the term 'State' or 'high policy' or 'sovereign' which are recognizable as referable to the relations of States *inter se*, and as to which it is immaterial what is the attitude of the law of either of the countries concerned. Of the first class, the facts in Lesley's case are an illustration...Illustrations of the second class may be found in such an avowed invasion of territory as the Jameson Raid. If in that case the British authorities had avowed and adopted the acts of Dr. Jameson and his associates, then, though a national act of invasion in the circumstances might have been treacherous and disgraceful to a civilized Power, the actual actors would not upon principle have been punishable in any court of the injured State. The Classical case upon this subject is McLeod's Case."
27. *People* v. *McLeod*, 1 Hill, 377, and 25 Wenddell, 433; 37 *Amrican Decisions*, 328.
28. 168 U. S. 250.
29. Citing *U. S.* v. *Rice*, 4 Wheaton, 246; *Fleming* v. *Page*, 9 Howard, 603; *Thorington* v. *Smith*, 8 Wallace, 1; *Williams* v. *Bruffy*, 96 U. S. 176; *Ford* v. *Surget*, 97 U. S. 594; *Daw* v. *Johnson*, 100 U. S. 158.
30. 213 U. S. 347.
31. For a discussion of this case with reference to the possible extraterritorial force of the Sherman Act, see *post*, p. 408.
32. 246 U. S. 297.
33. *Williams* v. *Bruffy*, 96 U. S. 176; *Underhill* v. *Hernandez*, 168 U. S. 150.
34. For a reference to the leading discussions of this topic see the third edition (1920) of Oppenheim's *International Law*, vol. I, p. 352 et sec. Also see the article of professor G. G. Wilson, "Aerial Jurisdiction" in the *American Political Science Review*, vol. V, p. 71 (May, 1911); G. G. Bogret, "Problems in Aviation Law" in the *Cornell Law Quarterly*, vol. VI, p. 271; and Garner, *International Law and the World War*, vol. I, p. 478 and numerous authorities there cited.
35. *Op. cit.*, vol. I, p. 479.
36. Garner lists the names of writers giving, respectively, their adherence to the enumerated doctrines.
37. See the testimony of O. D. Young, of the Radio Corporation of America, before the committee on Interstate Commerce of the United States Senate, 66th Congress, third session. (U. S. Government Printing Office, 1921).

VIII

Personal Jurisdiction

Citizenship. The juristic conception of the State which has been outlined emphasizes the fact that citizenship is a status imposed by the State upon such individuals as it desires to draw beneath its authority, and is not in any sense a status created by or dependent upon the consent of the citizens themselves. From this it logically follows that each State is universally recognized to have the power of determining for itself who shall be deemed its subjects—whether according to the rule of *jus soli* or *jus sanguinis*, or both; who may become its naturalized citizens, and under what conditions; what rights shall be granted to aliens, domiciled or undomiciled; who may enter or remain within its territorial borders; and whether or not the right of expatriation shall be recognized, and, if recognized, upon what conditions.

It has already been seen that it is a premise of public law that a sovereign political power has the legal authority to extend its political control over such territory and such individuals as it may see fit, and that it would thus be conceivably possible for any given State to extend its jurisdiction over all persons whomsoever. As a matter of practical fact, however, no State attempts to exercise this *plenitudo potestatis* and hence arises a distinction between those who are regarded as owing an allegiance to a given territory and those who do not. Those who are deemed to owe this allegiance are divisible into two classes. The first of these classes includes those who are deemed citizens or subjects, and who have obtained or have had imposed upon them their status as such by reason of the nationality of their parents or birth within the territorial jurisdiction of the State, or have been formally assimilated to these by adoption by the State by a process that is called "naturalization." Ordinarily, of course, this process of naturalization is one which is initiated and desired by the one thus seeking a new citizenship, but not infrequently this new citizenship is imposed without the desire or consent of the persons affected, as for example, when, by treaty or statute, the inhabitants of an annexed district are naturalized *en bloc.*

Never is it the case that one may claim citizenship as a legal right, nor may it be surrendered or in any way gotten rid of, save with the consent of the State to which it is due. This is a doctrine of public law enforced by all sovereign States.

The allegiance of citizens or subjects is thus, so far as the control over it by themselves is concerned, permanent in character, and independent of the place where they may happen to be. This legal control which a State may exercise over its own citizens whether within or without its own territorial limits has already been adverted to.

Furthermore, it is within the legal power and discretion of every State to group its own citizens into various classes and to award to the members of each special class such special public and private rights and duties as it may judge best. This, however, is a detail of a State's constitutional jurisprudence which has no bearing upon the essential nature of citizenship or allegiance. And equally immaterial upon this point is the question whether a State founds the status of citizenship upon the place of birth (*jus soli*) or the nationality of the parent or parents (*jus sanguinis*) or upon both. Also without significance are the special conditions, if any, upon which a State permits either naturalization of the renunciation of citizenship (*expatriation*).

Resident Aliens. The second class of persons who owe obedience to a State is made up of those persons who, though citizens of other States, are for the time being within the territorial limits of the State in question. These persons are universally held to be in genuine allegiance to this State, although it is an allegiance which lasts only so long as they remain within the borders of this State, and is somewhat qualified, in practice at least, by the rule that the local sovereignty will not compel aliens to bear arms except for the purpose of maintaining domestic order, in the benefits of which they themselves partake, or, possibly, to prevent invasion, but in no case are they required to fight against the countries of their natural allegiance.

It is, then, proper to hold that the *civitas*, or body-politic, of a State includes all persons who are within its territorial limits, as well as those of its own citizens who are beyond its borders.

The status of liens with regard to their allegiance to the local sovereignty is not influenced by the fact whether or not they are domiciled.[1] Domiciliation, according to all developed systems of law, carries with it certain changes in the legal rights and responsibilities of the persons affected by it, but it does not increase or alter the allegiance which the alien owes to the territorial sovereign. Nor is the existence of this allegiance placed in doubt by reason of the fact that, as a matter of international comity and expediency, a resident alien is not ordinarily called upon to perform certain military services which are, or may be, exacted of the citizen. The allegiance to the territorial sovereign which is imposed upon the resident alien finds its ethical or practical basis in the maxim *protectio trahit subjectionem et subjectio protectionem*. Thus Webster, when Secretary of State, in his report in Thrasher's case in 1851, declared:

> Independently of a residence with intention to continue such a residence; independently of any domiciliation; independently of the taking of any oath of allegiance, or renouncing any former allegiance, it is well-known that by the public law an alien, or a stranger born, for so long a time as he continues with in the dominions of a foreign government, owes obedience to the laws of that government, and may be punished for treason or for such other causes as a native-born subject might be, unless his case is varied by some treaty stipulation.[2]

Double Citizenship. The ascription to resident aliens of allegiance to the local sovereign does not, of course, carry with it annulment or even a temporary suspension of the allegiance due by those aliens to the States of which they may be citizen, although, as we have already seen, their native States are, as a practical fact, not able to exercise any jurisdiction over them, save with the consent of the local State.

Not simply a double allegiance, but a double primary citizenship is created when the citizens of a State which does not recognize the right of expatriation is naturalized by another State. In certain cases there may even be a triple citizenship, as, for example of a child born in England of American parents and residing later in France. And it may be possible to imagine cases, under the operation of varying municipal laws, in which the allegiance of an individual may be claimed by four or more States. It is possible for a person to be without any citizenship and thus to be an alien in whatever State he may happen to be. An illustration of this condition of Statelessness is given in the *International Law Notes* for February, 1916, where it is said:

An illegitimate child born in Russia of an English mother is actually destitute of nationality because the English Common Law regards him as an alien and there is no statute to help him, while, according to Russian law, he does not acquire Russian nationality. Again, all individuals who have absolutely and finally lost their original nationality, without acquiring another, are, in fact, destitute of nationality. In Austria, for instance, one emigrating without permission of the State loses his nationality and so is destitute of nationality until he acquires another.

In practice the point is usually of little consequence, since such individual are in most States treated in much the same way as subjects. Hall suggests the adoption of an International rule ascribing a nationality of domicile to such persons.[3]

To some writers this multiple citizenship has seemed abnormal and as indicating that the definition of citizenship has broken down. In truth, however, there is nothing that is confusing or that is logically inconsistent in this phenomenon of public law. When we revert to the fact that sovereignty, the relation of a political superior to a political inferior, is personal in character, that it is a purely legal concept, and that, as a concept, it is applicable only in the field of municipal law, and, especially, when we clearly apprehend the nature of that legal omnipotence which that legal theory predicates of the State, and distinguish this claim from exclusiveness of territorial jurisdiction asserted in international law,—when these principles and premises are borne in mind, the difficulties conceived to surround the subject of citizenship and allegiance wholly disappear.[4]

In what has been already said, it has appeared that the essential status of the resident alien is not greatly different from that of the citizen. Such differences of rights and obligations as do exits are the creations of municipal law and are often no greater than those which exist between different classes of citizens. Thus, from the board constitutional standpoint, the inhabitants of the Philippines, tribal Indians upon their reservations, the inhabitants of incorporated territories of the States of the Union, are all citizens or subjects of the United Sates. The differences in political and civil rights, however, which by the constitution and by statute separate them into distinct classes are certainly no greater or even as great as those which, in many of the States, mark off the domiciled alien from the general citizen body. And, in this connection, it may be remarked that there has been in modern times a marked and unbroken tendency among all civilized States to minimize the distinctions which municipal law creates between the citizen and the domiciled or even the undomiciled alien. Thus in England today the civil and political disqualifications of the alien, in times of peace at least, are very few and relatively unimportant; and, in a number of the States of the American Union, even the suffrage is granted to the aliens who have taken out what are called their "first papers," that is, have indicated that it is their intention to seek naturalization when their length of residence within the country, will, under federal statute, permit them to do so.

Rights with Respect to Aliens. It is but reasonable that States, when they concede to other States the right to exercise jurisdiction over such of their own national as are within the territorial limits of such other States, should insist that those States should provide systems of law and of courts, and, in actual practice, so administer them, as to furnish substantial legal justice to alien residents. This does not mean that a State must or should extent to aliens within its borders all the civil, or, mush less, all the political rights or privileges which it grants to its own citizens; but it does mean that aliens must or should be given adequate opportunity to have such legal rights as are granted to them by the local law impartially and judicially determined, and, when thus determined, protected.

Enlightened international practice during recent years has led States to grant to resident aliens most of the civil rights that are granted to their own citizens, but this has been the result of humanity and international comity, and not of a conceded juristic necessity. In other words, each sovereign State has a discretionary right to determine what, if any, civil and political rights aliens within borders are to possess, and, indeed, whether, upon any term, they are to be permitted to enter or remain within its borders. Thus, throughout the world, instances abound in which, for special reasons, aliens in general, or aliens of particular countries, are denied the enjoyment of specific legal rights, privileges, or immunities which the citizens of the countries in which they are freely enjoy. For instance, in the United States, the nationals of certain other countries are not allowed to enter at all. So, also, in addition to the specific civil disabilities suffered by all aliens, certain classes of aliens are not permitted to seek naturalization as American citizens, although this privilege is granted to all other resident aliens.

It is not surprising that the States whose nationals are thus selected out and denied the rights or privileges which are granted to the nationals of other States should feel aggrieved, and seek to have this inequality of treatment corrected. But, unless they are able to point to undertaking, in treaty form or otherwise, upon the part of the discriminating State, that such discrimination will not be made, the protesting States have no legal basis for complaint. There may, indeed, be a question whether they have even an ethical or economic ground of grievance. In other words, Constitutional Law recognizes the right of every sovereign State to determine not only who shall be deemed or permitted to become its own citizens, but to decide as a matter of discretionary policy what aliens, if any shall cross its borders, and what legal rights, if any, shall be conceded to those who are tolerated within its territorial limits. And this unlimited constitutional doctrines that have been described. Publicists are therefore pretty well agreed that, prior to the Boer War, Great Britain had no legal ground of the complaint against the Transvaal because of the severe restrictions laid by that Republic upon the right of British and other aliens to obtain naturalization as its citizens. Whatever other ground for complaint Great Britain may have had, she had a legal a case only insofar as she could point to pertinent provisions of subsisting treaties between herself and the Transvaal.

In those countries which have not developed bodies of law and systems of courts which command the confidence of the other Powers, those other Powers, when possible obtain by treaties the right to maintain their own courts for the trial of cases in which their own nationals are parties defendant. Where this extraterritorial jurisdiction does not exist, all States assert the right to take action, through their political departments, in cases in which they believe that their nationals have not been given full and fair hearing of their cases in foreign tribunals or have not had their rights determined in accordance with the *lex föri*, or where, as in the Cutting Case, later to be referred to,[5] it is held that the foreign courts have improperly asserted a jurisdiction over the nationals of the complaining State.[6]

It does not need to be said that the Government of one State will not, through its foreign office, make complaint to another State in all cases in which its nationals assert that the courts of that State have not properly weighed the evidence in the cases in which they have been parties, or have not correctly construed their own municipal law. It is only when it appears that there has been a gross miscarriage of justice, due to what strongly appears to be the incompetence, dishonesty, or partiality of the courts, that the Governments of the aggrieved nationals feel themselves warranted in making protest to foreign Governments because of action which their courts have taken.

"The regularity and legality of a court's practice and procedure are to be judged by the local law, which need not, however, manifest the liberal principles of Anglo-American law. For example, in countries in which the inquisitorial system of criminal law prevails, a fair application of the law to aliens and citizens alike removes all ground of complaint on the part of foreign countries, even of those adopting the accusatory system. Provided the system of law conforms to a reasonable standard of civilized justice and provided it is fairly administered, aliens have no cause for complaint.

"The personal acts of judges either in their private capacity or so grossly violative of their judicial functions that they may be held to be personal acts, do not entail any liability of the Government. For their private acts they are liable as other individuals."[7]

Some writers attempt to make a distinction between judgement of municipal courts which, though deemed unjust, have been reached without violation or misapplication of municipal or international law, and those which have involved violations or misapplication of law with a result that there has been a substantial denial of justice. This distinction would seem to be of value as a guiding principle, and to suggest that, as a rule, governments should confine their protests to the latter class of cases, but practically all Governments have, upon occasion, asserted the right to interpose in behalf of their nationals in extreme cases of the former class. Upon this general point, Borchard says:[8]

"While, on principle, the erroneous or merely unjust decision of a court involving no unlawfulness or irregularity in procedure should not involve the State in responsibility, the failure of the higher courts to disapprove violations of national or international law by minor officials or other authorities fixes an international responsibility upon the State, and a flagrant or notorious injustice is not easily distinguishable from a denial of justice. Similarly, the judgement of a court in violation of a treaty or in international law serves to render the State responsible.

"It is fundamental principle that the acts of inferior judges or courts do not render the State internationally liable when the claimant has failed to exhaust his local means of redress by judicial appeal or otherwise, for only the highest court to which a case is appealable may be considered an authority involving the responsibility of the State."

Effect of Military Occupation upon Allegiance. To what extent mere military occupation of a territory by the forces of a State, which does not claim to have permanently annexed such area to its own territory, operates to bring the persons within such occupied area under allegiance to the occupying State, deserves, perhaps, a word of discussion.

It is a doctrine of American constitutional law that mere conquest or military occupation of a territory of another State does not operate to annex such territory to the occupying State, but that the inhabitants of the occupied district, no longer receiving the protection of their native State, for the time being owe no allegiance to it, and, beingunder the control and protection of the victorious power, owe to that power fealty and obedience. As Chancellor Kent observes:

> If a portion of the country be taken and held by conquest in war, the conqueror acquires the right of the conquered as to its dominion and government, and children born in the armies of a state, while abroad, and occupying a foreign country, are deemed to be born in the allegiance of the sovereign to whom the army belongs. It is equally the doctrine of the English common law that during such hostile occupation of a territory, and the parents adhering to the enemy as subject *de facto*, their children, born such a temporary dominion, are not born under the ligeance of the conquered.

And he adds that there is no reason why the same principle should not apply to the United States.[9]

In the quite early case of *United States* v. *Rice*[10] the effect of military possession was discussed with reference to the port of Castine, in Maine, which, for a time during the War of 1812, was in the possession of the British military forces, but, after the restoration of peace, was restored to the United States. In that case the court said:

> It appears, by the pleading, that on the first day of September, 1814, Castine was captured by the enemy, and remained in his exclusive possession, under the command and control of his military and naval force, until after the ratification of the treaty of peace in February, 1815... By the conquest and military occupation of Castine, the enemy acquired that firm possession which enabled him to exercise the fullest rights of sovereignty over that place. The sovereignty of the United States could no longer be rightfully enforced there, or be obligatory upon the inhabitants who remained and submitted to the conquerors. By the surrender the inhabitants passed under a temporary allegiance, to the British government, and weer bound by such laws, and such only, as it chose to recognize and impose. From the nature of the case, no other laws could be obligatory upon them for where there is no protection or allegiance or sovereignty, there can be no claim to obedience. Castine was, therefore , during this period, so far as respected our revenue laws, to be deemed a foreign port; and goods imported into it by the inhabitants, were subject to such duties only as the British government chose to require. Such goods were in no correct sense imported into the United States. The

subsequent evacuation by the enemy, and resumption of authority by the United States, did not, and could not, change the character of the previous transactions.

In *Fleming* v. *Page* [11] the question arose whether duties levied upon goods entering the port of Tampico, Mexico, at the time it was in the military possession of the United States, were properly levied under the act of Congress laying duties goods imported from a foreign country. Chief Justice Taney, who rendered the opinion of the court, said:

It is true, that, when Tampico had been captured, and the State of Tamaulipas subjugated, other nations were bound to regard the country, while our possession continued, as the territory of the United States, and to respect it as such. For, by the laws and usage of nations, conquest is a valid title, while the victor maintains the exclusive possession of the captured country. The citizens of no other nation, therefore, had a right to enter it without the permission of the American authorities, nor to hold intercourse with its inhabitants, not to trade with them. As regarded all other nations, it was a part of the United States, and belonged to them exclusively, as the territory included in our established boundaries.

But yet it was not a part of this Union. For every nation which acquires territory by treaty or conquest, holds it according to its own institutions and laws. And the relation in which the port of Tampico stood to the United States while it was occupied by their arms did not depend upon the laws of nation, but upon our own Constitution and acts of Congress. The power of the President under which Tampico and the State of Tamaulipas were conquered and held in subjection was simply that of a military commander prosecuting a war waged against a public enemy by the authority of his government. And the country from which these goods were imported was invaded and subdued, and occupied as the territory of a foreign hostile nation, as a portion of Mexico, and was held in possession in order to distress and harass the enemy. While it was occupied by our troops, they were in an enemy's country, and not in their own; the inhabitants were still foreigners and enemies, and owed to the United States nothing more than the submission and obedience, sometimes called temporary allegiance, which is done from a conquered enemy, when he surrenders to a force which he is unable to resist. But the boundaries of the United States, as they existed when war was declared against Mexico, were not extended by the conquest; nor could they be regulated by the varying incidents of war, and be enlarged or diminished as the armies on either side advanced or retreated. They remained unchanged. And every place which was out of limits of the United States, as previously established by the political authorities of the government, was still foreign; nor did our laws extend over it. Tampico was therefore, a foreign port when this shipment was made.

Upon first thought it may appear that the doctrine declared in *Fleming* v. *Page* is not in harmony with that uttered in *United States* v. *Rice*, for, in the former case, it was held that mere military occupation was not sufficient to annex the territory occupied to the United States, whereas, in the latter case, it was declared that military occupation by the forces of another State did not operate to render the port foreign to the United States. If these two decisions had been given by an international tribunal, and had reference to the status of the territories viewed internationally, they undoubtedly would have been inharmonious. Looked at from the international side, a country belongs to that power which is in effective control of it. Thus viewed, therefore, Castine belonged to Great Britain while its military forces were in paramount control of it. In like manner, Tampico, viewed internationally, was a port of the United States, and other States would have held the United States responsible for anything that might have occurred there while it was in possession. But when, as was the case both in *United States* v. *Rice* and *Fleming* v. *Page,* the question was purely one of domestic municipal law, it was within the province of the Supreme Court to determine in each case the status of the territory concerned according to the peculiar municipal or constitutional law which it was interpreting and applying. In other words, in the Fleming v. Page case the Supreme Court would not have been justified in declaring that Tampico did not, during American occupancy, belong to the United States in an international sense; whereas it was justified in holding that, from the viewpoint of American constitutional law, it was not a part of the United States, any more than, for example, was Cuba during the time of its administration by American authorities.[12]

During the Great War the armed forced of Germany were in occupation of all the territories of Serbia and Montenegro. The question may be asked as to what international status these States had during this period of occupation. The answer is that, remembering that it lies within the right of each International State to determine the other States which it will recognize as co-equals with itself in the family of nations, it is certain that as long as Serbia and Montenegro were in the complete military occupation of Germany, that country would not admit that these countries were international States *in esse*; although, if there was no intention of ultimate annexation, Germany might have admitted that they were international persons *in posse*. Certainly, however, the allies of Serbia and Montenegro would have continued to recognize their international existence. But this would have been not because they asserted that an international State could exist without territory but because they regarded Serbia and Montenegro as still entitled to the territories of which the Germans were in *de facto* but not in *de jure* occupation. In the case under consideration, the view of the allies would have been that the *de facto* military occupation by the Germans was a temporary and tentative one.

References

1. "In its ordinary acceptation, a person's domicile is the place where he lives or has his home. In a strict and legal sense, that is properly the domicile of a person, where he has his true, fixed permanent home and principal establishment, and to which, whenever he is absent, he has the intention of returning." *Anderson*, 42 Vt. Reports, 350. No term of actual residence is necessarily required in order to establish a domicile. It may be created the moment a person comes to a place *animo manendi.*
2. Webster's Works 6, 526. For approvals of this doctrine by the United States Supreme Court, see *United States* v. *Carlisle*, 16 Wall 147; and *United States* v. *Wong Kim Ark.*, 169 U. S., 649.
3. For other instances of "statelessness," see *Yale Law Journal*, vol. XXVII, p. 840.
4. Under the Aliens Restriction Act of 1914, in England, this point has been important in several cases where persons have attempted to prove that they have lost their original nationality.
5. *Post,* p. 413.
6. Daniel Webster, Secretary of State, writing to the Minister of Spain, in 1843, said: "Nations are bound to maintain respectable tribunals to which the subjects of States at peace may have recourse for the redress of injuries and the maintenance of their rights. If the character of these tribunals be respectable, impartial, and independent, their decisions are to be regarded as conclusive...If the tribunal be competent, if it be free from unjust influence, if it be impartial and independent, and if it have heard the case fully and fairly, its judgement is to stand as decisive of the matters before it. This principle governs in regard to the decisions of courts of common law, courts of equity, and especially courts of admiralty, whose proceedings so often affect the rights and interests of citizens of foreign States and Governments." Quoted by Moore, *Digest of International Law,* vol. II, p. 5. See also the statements of the American Secretary of the State in the Cutting Case, Later to be quoted, p. 414.

7. Borchard, *Diplomatic Protection of Citizens Abroad,* p. 198. If the Government in question should accept the responsibility for such acts of its judges, or if there are not available to the aggrieved parties adequate judicial proceedings against judges, the matter becomes one which the Governments of the aggrieved parties can properly take cognizance of.
8. *Diplomatic Protection of Citizens Abroad,* p. 197.
9. *Commentaries on American Law,* 6th ed., vol. II, p. 42.
10. 4 Wheaton 246.
11. 9 Howard 603.
12. For further discussion by the United States Supreme Court of the cases referred to in the text see *De Lima* v. *Bidwell*, 182 U. S. 1. In *Neeley* v. *Henkel* (180 U. S. 109), with reference to the status of Cuba during American occupation, the Supreme Court said: "Cuba is none the less foreign territory, within the meaning of the act of Congress, because it is under a military governor appointed by and representing the President in the Work of assisting the inhabitants of that island to establish a government of their own, under which, as a free and independent people, they may control their own affairs without interference by other nations. The occupancy of the island by the troops of the United States was the necessary result of the war. That result could not have been avoided by the United States consistently with the principles of international law or with its obligations to the people of Cuba.

    "It is true that as between Spain and the United States—indeed, as between the United States and all foreign nations—Cuba, upon the cessation of hostilities with Spain and after the treaty of Paris, was to be treated as if it were conquered territory. But as between the United States and Cuba that island is territory held in trust for the inhabitants of Cuba, to whom it rightfully belongs, and to whose exclusive control it will be surrendered when a stable government shall have been established by their voluntary action."

    In *Dooley* v. *United States* (182 U. S. 222), one of the "Insular Cases" decided in 1901, the doctrine of *Fleming* v. *Page* was applied in fixing the status of Proto Rico while under the military government of the United States, but prior to the ratification of the treaty of peace ceding the island to the United States. The court said: "[During this period] and the United States and Porto Rico were still foreign countries with respect to each other, and the same right which authorized us to exact duties upon merchandise imported from Porto Rico to the United States authorized the military commander in Porto Rico to exact duties upon goods imported into that island from the United States. The fact that, notwithstanding the military occupation of the United States, Porto Rico remained a foreign country within the revenue laws, is established by the case of *Fleming* v. *Page.*"

IX

De Facto and De Jure Governments

Distinct from the question of the recognition by one State of another body-politic as a sovereign and independent State, is the question as to recognition of a given political organization as the Government of that independent entity. Here, as in the case of the recognition of the State itself, the matter is one for the determination of the political departments of the recognizing or non-recognizing Governments, according to their judgement as to what the facts warrant or their own public policies dictate.

The question as to the *locus standi* of foreign Governments is raised in the courts of other Governments when they are called upon to consider the right of the foreign Governments to sue, or their liability to be sued, and when the legal effect to be given to their acts is in question.

De Facto and De Jure Governments. The distinction between *de facto* and *de jure* Governments was discussed from the standpoint of municipal law, and the point emphasized that a given Government may be regarded as merely *de facto* if looked at from the point of view of those who deny its legal legitimacy, while it may be properly be declared to be *de jure* in character when considered from the point of view of those who support it. When, then, a Government is spoken of as *de facto* merely, it is always to be understood, in municipal law, that it is viewed from the standpoint of those who give their adherence to another Government as the only political organization entitled, as of legal right, to exercise authority over the territories and persons concerned. In the present chapter we shall examine more carefully the legal deductions to be drawn from this distinction between *de facto* and *de jure* Governments, and also consider the significance of this distinction within the realm of international relations.

Varieties of De Facto Governments Municipally Viewed. The questions that arise in national or municipal law as to the legal effect to be attached to Governments which have maintained for a time, or in particular areas, a *de facto* political control in opposition to the *de jure* Government are illustrated in the two cases of *Thorington* v. *Smith* [2] and *Williams* v. *Bruffy*,[3] decided by the Supreme Court of the United States, and from whose opinion quotations of considerable length are justified.

In *Thorington* v. *Smith* the chief question before the court was as to whether a contract for the payment of Confederate notes, made during the Civil War, between private parties residing within the Confederate States, should be enforced in the courts of the United States. In the course of its opinion the court said:

> There are several degree of what is called *de facto* government. Such a government, in its highest degree, assumes a character very closely resembling that of a lawful government. This is when the usurping government expels the regular authorities from their customary seats and functions, and establishes itself in their place, and so becomes the actual government of a country. The distinguishing characteristic of such a government is, that adherents to it in war against the government *de jure* do not incur the penalties of treason; and under certain limitations, obligations assumed by it in behalf of the country, or otherwise, will, in general, be respected by the government *de jure* when restored. It is very certain that the Confederate Government was never acknowledged by the United States as a *de facto* government in this sense. Nor was it acknowledged as such by other powers. No treaty was made with it by any civilized States. No obligations of a national character were created by it, binding after its dissolution, on the States which it represented, or on the National Government. From a very early period of the Civil War to its close, it was regarded as simply the military representative of the insurrection against the authority of the United States.
>
> But there is another description of government, called also by publicists a government *de facto*, but which might, perhaps, be more aptly denominated a government of paramount force. Its distinguishing characteristics are (1) that its existence is maintained by active military power within the Territories, and against the rightful authority of an established and lawful government; and (2) that while it exist, it must

necessarily be obeyed in civil matters by private citizens who, by acts of obedience, rendered in submission to such force, do not become responsible, as wrongdoers, for those acts, though not warranted by the laws of the rightful government. Actual governments of this sort are established over districts differing greatly in extent and conditions. They are usually administered directly by military authority, but they may be administered civil authority, supported more or less directly by military force. One example of this sort of government is found in the case of Castine, in Maine, reduced to British possession during the war of 1812... A like example is found in the case of Tampico, occupied during the war with Mexico by the troops of the United States. It was determined by this court, in *Fleming* v. *Page* (9 How. 603; 13 L. ed. 276), that although Tampico did not become a part of the United States in consequence of that occupation, still, having come together with the whole State of Tamaulipas, of which it was part, into the exclusive possession of the national forces, it must be regarded and respected by other nation as the territory of the United States. These were cases of temporary possession of territory by lawful and regular governments at war with the country of which the territory so possessed was part. The central government established for the insurgent States differed from the temporary governments at Castine and Tampico in the circumstance that its authority did not originate in lawful acts of regular war, but it was not, on that account, less actual or less supreme. And we think that it must be classed among the governments of which these are examples. It is to be observed that the rights and obligations of a belligerent were conceded to it, in its military character, very soon after the war began, from motives of humanity and expediency by the United States. The whole territory controlled by it was thereafter held to be enemies' territory, and the inhabitants of that territory were held, in most respects, for enemies. To the extent, then, of actual supremacy, however unlawfully gained, in all matters of government within its military line, the power of the insurgent government cannot be questioned. That supremacy did not justify acts of hostility to the United States. How far it should excuse them must be left to the lawful government upon the re-establishment of its authority. But it made obedience to its authority, in civil and local matters, not only a necessity but a duty. Without such obedience, civil order was impossible.

After describing the Confederate Government established, and the actual control exercised by, the insurgent States, the court said:

> It was by this Government, exercising its power throughout an immense territory, that the Confederate notes were issued early in the war, and these notes in a short time became almost exclusively the currency of the insurgent States. As contracts in themselves, except in the contingency of successful revolution, these notes were nullities, for, except in that event, there could be no payer... While the war lasted, however, they had a certain contingent value, and were used as money in nearly all the business transactions of millions of people. They must be regarded, therefore, as a currency imposed on the community by irresistible force... Contracts stipulating for payment in this currency...have no necessary relation to the hostile Government...They are transactions in the ordinary course of civil society, and, though they may indirectly and remotely promote the ends of unlawful Government, are without blame, except when proved to have been entered into with actual intent to further invasion or insurrection. We cannot doubt that such contract should be enforced in the courts of the United States, after the restoration of peace, to the extent of their just obligation.

In the case of *Williams* v. *Bruffy*,[4] the Court was called upon to consider the legal effect to be given to a sequestration during the Civil War, by the Confederate Government of a debt. Speaking of a *de facto* Government the court said that they are of two kinds:

> One 'of them is such as exist after it has expelled the regularly constituted authorities from the seats of power and the public offices, and established its own functionaries in their places, so as to represent in fact the sovereignty of the Nation. Such was the Government of England under the Commonwealth established upon the execution of the King and the overthrow of the Loyalists. As far as other nations are concerned, such a Government is treated as, in most respects, possessing rightful authority; its contracts and treaties are usually enforced; its acquisitions are retained; its legislation is in general recognised; and the rights acquired under it are, with few execptations, respected after the restiration of teh authorities which were expelled... But the Confederate Government was not of this kind. It never represented the nation, it never entered into any treaties, nor was it ever recognized as that of an independent power. It collected an immense military force and temporarily expelled the authorities of the

> United States from the territory over which it exercised an usurped dominion: but in that expulsion the United States never acquiesced; on the contrary, they immediately resorted to similar force to regain possession of that territory and re-establish their authority, and they continued to use such force until they succeeded...
>
> The other kind of *de facto* governments... is such as exists where a portion of the inhabitants of a country have separated themselves from the parents States and established an independent Government. The validity of its acts, both against the parent State and its citizens or subjects, depends entirely upon its ultimate success. If it fail to establish itself permanently, all such acts perish with it. It succeeded, and became recognized, its acts from the commencement of its existence are upheld as those of an independent nation. Such was the case of the State Governments under the old Confederation on their separation from the British Crown—no case has been cited in argument, and we think none can be found, in which the acts of a portion of a State unsuccessfully attempting to establish a separate revolutionary government have been sustained as a matter of legal right.

Referring to its holding in *Thorington* v. *Smith*,[5] the court said that all that had been held in that case was that, while the Confederate Government exercised actual supremacy of force in a given territory, obedience to its authority by the inhabitants of that territory was a matter of necessity, and, in the interest of order, a duty; but that no concession was made by the court as to the rightfulness of the authority exercised. So, also, in the *Prize Cases*,[6] all that had been recognized was that the Confederate forces should be treated as belligerents, and that a state of war existed such as warranted the treatment of the territory of the States in secession as enemy territory and its inhabitants as enemies, and their property on the high seas as subject to capture.

In *The Lilla*,[7] a District Court of the United States, sitting in admiralty, refused, in 1862, to admit that the Confederates in the American Civil War had established a Government to whose acts the United States Court could be called upon to attach a legal validity. It is true, said Judge Sprague, the Confederates were treated in some respects as belligerents, and therefore, their Government recognized as a *de facto* one for belligerent purposes, but, as held in the case of *The Amy Warwick*,[8] third did not import an abandonment by the United States of its claim of continued sovereignty over the areas and the inhabitants of the States which had attempted to secede from the Union. "Most assuredly," he said, "I shall not recognize the Southern Confederate as a nation or as having a government competent to establish prize courts. No proceedings of any such supposed tribunals can have any validity here, and a sale under them would convey no title to the purchaser, nor would it confer upon him any right to give a title to others."

Status of Conquered Domestic Territory. In *New Orleans* v. *New York Mail Steamship Co.*[9] was considered the status of territory of the Southern Confederacy which had been conquered by the federal forces. The court held that the federal forces in possession might exercise the same absolute authority as in the case of territory conquered from a foreign State. The court said:

"Although the city of New Orleans was conquered or taken possession of in a civil war waged on the part of the United States to put down an insurrection and restore the supremacy of the National Government in the Confederate States, that Government had the same power and rights in territory held by conquest as if the territory had belonged to a foreign country, and had been subjugated in a foreign war. The *Prize Cases*, 2 Black 635; *Mrs. Alexender's Cotton*, 2 Wall. 404; *Mauren* v. *Ins. Co.*, 6 Wall. 1. In such cases the conquering power has a right to displace the pre-existing authority, and to assume, to such extent as it may deem proper, the exercise by itself of all powers and functions of government. It may appoint all the necessary officers and clothe them with designated powers, larger or smaller, according to its pleasure. It may prescribe the revenues to be paid, and apply them to its own use or otherwise. It may do anything necessary to strengthen itself and weaken the enemy. There is no limit to the powers that may be exerted in such cases, save those which are found in the laws and usages of war. These principles have the sanction of all publicists who have considered the subject. They have been repeatedly recognized and applied by this court. *Cross* v. *Harrison*, 16 How. 164; *Leitensdoefer* v. *Webb*, 20 How. 176; *The Grapeshot*, 9 Wall. 129. In the case last cited the President had, by Proclamation, established in New Orleans a Provisional Court for the State of Louisiana, and defined its jurisdiction. This court held the Proclamation a rightful exercise of the power of the Executive, the court valid, and its decrees binding upon the parties brought before it. In such cases the laws of war take the place of the Constitution and laws of the United States as applied in time of peace."

De Facto and De Jure Governments Internationally Viewed. We have now to consider the significance in international relations of the distinction between *de facto* and *de jure* Governments.

Though often referred to, and without doubt of considerable political significance, it seems clear that, in municipal courts, the question whether another Government has been recognized by their own Government as *de jure*, as distinguished from *de facto*, is juristically unimportant. Indeed there is some difficulty in determining just what significance it attached to the distinction by the departments of government which control the foreign relations of States. Certain it is that when a Government "recognizes" another Government as either *de facto* or *de jure*, there is no pronouncement upon its part as to the legality of the steps by means of which that Government may have come into existence. Thus, as Oppenheim says: "Recognition of as new head of a State by no means implies the recognition of such head as the legitimate head of the State. Recognition is, in fact, nothing else than declaration of other States that they are ready to deal with a certain individual as the highest organ of a particular State, without prejudice to the question whether such individual is, or is not, to be considered as the legitimate head of that State."[10]

The writer has not succeeded in finding an official or even quasi-official statement of just what is held to be the nature or political importance of the distinction between the recognition by one Government as *de facto* or *de jure* in character, but it would appear that, from the point of view of another Government, a Government is regarded as *de jure* when it is given full and, presumably, permanent recognition as the organization qualified to speak and act for the territory and people over whom it claims jurisdiction, and especially when a particular individual if formally recognized as the titular head of that Government. Thus it has been officially held that the then existing Government of Mexico was recognized by the United States, October 19, 1915, as *de facto* in character, and, on August 31, 1917, as *de jure* when Carranza was recognized as its President.[11]

However, there have often occurred cases in which one Government, in order to show its displeasure with regard to something done by another Government, has withdrawn for a time its diplomatic representatives from the capital or court of that other Government, without thereby indicating, or intending to indicate, that it no longer recognized that Government as the *de jure* Government of the State in question.

When a Government has come into existence by the forcible or illegal overthrow of a former Government, and, for a time, maintain its authority, but is later overthrown by the former Government which re-establishes its authority, the first Government is spoken of in municipal law, as we have seen, as having had only a *de facto* existence, but, whatever sort of recognition it may have had from other Governments, those other Governments, as we shall presently see, will hold the re-established Government or, indeed, any other future Government of the State in question, responsible for the acts of the *de facto* Government. This results from the fundamental doctrine that a sovereign State is internationally responsible for what occurs within its own territory, and for acts of those who, in fact, exercise the dominant political control. In other words, a recognized Government in being is internationally liable not only for its own acts but for those of the Governments which it has overthrown or which have preceded it. And this principle applies equally to treatise or other agreements or undertakings into which the former Governments have entered. In domestic or municipal law, however, the doctrine is a very different one, the acts of *de facto* Governments which do not attain a *de jure* status, being held wholly illegal, and, therefore not such as to furnish a basis for the claim of legal rights.

Recognition. It would appear, then, that, in international relations the distinction between *de facto* and *de jure* Governments is of little, if any, legal significance. In either case, the recognition of the Government by the political department of another Government has substantially the same effect in and upon the courts of the recognizing State. The following are some of the cases which illustrate this.

Lurther v. *Sago & Co.,*[12] decided in 1921, was an action brought to establish the plaintiff's title to certain goods imported into England from Russia by the defendant who had bought them from the Republican Government of Russia which, in 1919, had forcibly taken the goods from the plaintiff. The plaintiff contended that the Republican Government had no legal existence as the Government of Russia, and had not been recognized as such by the British Government. As an alternative plea, he contended that the decree of the Republican Government which had ordered the confiscation of his goods was not one which, upon moral grounds, should be given legal effect to by the British courts.

When this case came on for trial, in 1920, in the Court of King's Bench, the court was informed by the British Foreign Office that the British Government had not recognized the Soviet Government as the Government of Russian Federative Republic or of any sovereign power or State. Mr. Justice Roche, thereupon, speaking for the court, said: "I am therefore unable to recognize it, or to hold that it has sovereignty, or is able by decree to deprive the plaintiffs of their property." However, by the time the case came on for a hearing in the Court of Appeal it appeared that the British Government had altered its position with regard to the Soviet Government. In a letter from the Foreign Office it was declared that the British Government had recognized the Soviet Government as the *de facto* Government of Russia, and, also that the "Provisional Government," which came into power in March, 1917, and remained in authority until December of the same year, had been similarly recognized. The Court of Appeal thereupon, while holding that the decision of the lower Court had been a correct one in the light of the facts as they then stood, reversed its holding and held that the Soviet Government was one the legal validity of whose acts should be judicially recognized.

Attempt was made by the counsel for the respondents to draw a distinction, at least as to its retroactive effect, between the recognition of a Government as *de jure* and its recognition as *de facto* only. In his opinion Lord Justice Banks said:

"For some purpose no doubt a distinction can be drawn between the effect of the recognition by a sovereign State of one form of Government or of the other, but for the present purpose, in my opinion, no distinction can be drawn. The Government of this country having...recognized the Soviet Government as the Government really in possession of the powers of sovereignty in Russia, the acts of that Government must be treated by the courts of this country with all the respect due to the acts of a duly recognized foreign sovereign State."

As to the allegation that the decree of confiscation was so immoral as not to furnish a basis for rights that the courts of a foreign State could be called upon to give effect to, the Lord Justice said:

"The question before the court is not one in which the assistance of the court is asked to enforce the law of some foreign country to which legitimate objection might be taken, as in *Hope v. Hope*, 8 De Gex. Mac. and G. 731, and *Kaufman* v. *Gerson*, 20 Times L. R. 277 (1904), 1 K. B. 591. The question before the court is as to the title to goods lying in a foreign country [at the time of sale] which a subject of that country, being the owner of them by the law of that country, has sold under a f.o.b. contract for export to this country. The court is asked to ignore the law of the foreign country under which the vendor acquired his title, and to lend its assistance to prevent the purchaser from dealing with the goods. I do not think that any authority can be produced to support the contention."

In support of his judgement, the Lord Justice then quoted the following from the opinion of Mr. Justice Blackburn in *Santos* v. *Illidge* (8 C.B., N.S. 876):

"Assuming the taking to have been prohibited by a British Act, still the taking having been of property locally situated in a foreign country in a manner lawful according to the laws of that country, I apprehend that the property actually passed by the sale and vested in the purchasers, though they committed a felony according to our law by taking it... Though the vendors were British subjects, the validity of the transfer must, on every principle of law, depend upon the local law of Brazil and not upon that of the country of the purchaser."

In *Republic of Peru* v. *Peruvian Guano Co.*[13] Justice Chitty said:

> One of the principal grounds relied on by the plaintiffs is that the agreement of compromise was made on behalf of the *de facto* Government of the Republic which was not the *de jure* Government. But the court is bound to take cognizance of the recognition of a *de facto* Government by the Government of this country, and it was admitted by plaintiff's counsel at the bar that the *de facto* Government was duly recognized by the Queen. So soon as it has been shown that a *de facto* Government of a foreign State has been recognized by the Government of this country, no further inquiry is permitted in a court of justice here. The court declines to investigate, and indeed has no proper means of investigating, the title of the actual Government of a foreign State which has been thus recognized. This attempted distinction between the *de facto* and the *de jure* Government which runs through the statement of claim is untenable.

In *Ricaud* v. *American Metal Co.*[14] the Supreme Court of the United States, answering questions certified to it by a Circuit Court of Appeals, declared that the seizure, condemnation and sale of personal property in Mexico by agents of the Carranza Government, which was then seeking to overthrow the older Huerta Government, and which later was recognized by the United States as the *de facto*, and, still later, as the *de jure* Government of Mexico, operated to divest the title of an American citizen not in or a resident of Mexico when the seizure and condemnation occurred. If entitled to any redress, this citizen, it was declared, would have to seek it either in the courts of Mexico or through the political departments of the American Government. The court, speaking through Mr. Justice Clarke, said:

> The revolution inaugurated by General Carranza against General Huerta proved successful, and the Government established by him has been recognized by the political department of our Government as the *de facto* and later as the *de jure* Government of Mexico, which decision binds the judges as well as all other officers and citizens of the Government... This recognition is retroactive in effect and validates all the actions of the Carranza Government from the commencement of its existence...It is settled that the courts will take judicial notice of such recognition as we have here, of the Carranza Government by the political department of our Government... and that the courts of one independent Government will not sit in judgement on the validity of the acts of another, done within its own territory... This rule, however, does not deprive the courts of jurisdiction once acquired over a case. It requires only that when it is made to appear that the foreign Government has acted in a given way on the subject matter of the litigation, the details of such action or the merit of the result cannot be questioned, but must be accepted by our courts as a rule for their decision.

Local and General De Facto Governments. The international doctrine as to *de facto* Governments becomes one especially difficult to apply in the case of political organizations which, in opposition to the *de jure* governments, are able to maintain a *de facto* control over only a portion of the territory of the State concerned. In such cases they are spoken of as Local to distinguish them from General *de facto* Governments. Professor Borchard, in an able article[15] has dealt with this topic and from that article we quote the following:

> A General Government *de facto*, having completely taken the place of the regularly constituted authorities in the State, binds the Nation. So far as international obligations are concerned, it represents the State. It succeeds to the debts of the regular Government it has displaced, and transmits its own obligations to succeeding titular Governments. Its loans and contracts bind the State, and the State is responsible for the governmental acts of the *de facto* authorities. In general its treaties are valid obligations of the State. It may alienate the national territory, and the judgements of the courts are admitted to be effective after its authority has ceased. An exception to these rules has occasionally been noted in the practice of some of the States of Latin America, which declare null and void the acts of a usurping *de facto* intermediary Government when the regular

Government it has displaced succeeds in restoring its control. Nevertheless, acts validly undertaken in the name of the State and having an international character cannot lightly be repudiated and foreign Governments generally insists on their bending force...

The responsibility of a State for the acts of a local *de facto* Government involves more delicate questions... The power of such a *de facto* Government to involve the responsibility of the State depends largely upon its ultimate success, so that most of its international acts, e.g., treaties, etc., are affected with a suspensive condition. Nevertheless, even if it fails, definite executed reslts follow from its merely temporary possession of administrative control within a defined area.

Thus, as Professor Borchard goes on to show, foreigners, as a matter of necessity, must submit to the jurisdiction thus exercised, and cannot be later punished or penalized by the *de jure* Government for so doing, and taxes thus paid cannot rightfully again be collected. As a general rule, however, a succeeding *de jure* Government is not liable for the debts contracted by the *de facto* Government which has been overthrown,— persons contracting with such a Government do so at their peril.

It is well established as a doctrine of International law that when a *de jure* Government has been recognized as a belligerent by those who are in arms against it, it is thereby released from its liability to its own citizens for the act of those in rebellion against its authority. However, it cannot thereby release itself from all responsibility to other Power or to their citizens, for the acts of the belligerent authorities.

References

1. P. 178.
2. 8 Wall. 1.
3. 96 U. S. 176.
4. 96 U. S. 176.
5. 8 Wall 1.
6. 2 Beacks 635.
7. 2 Spr. 177, Fed. Cas. no. 8348.
8. 2 Spr. 123, Fed. Cas. no. 341.
9. 20 wall. 387; 22 L. ed. 354.
10. *International Law*, 3d ed., vol. I, p.528. Oppenheim here speaks of a head of a State, but as to the point under discussion there is no distinction between recognition of him and that of the Government he represents.

11. On October 19, 1915, the American Secretary of State, in a letter to the representative of the Mexican Government, said:

"My Dear Mr. Arredondo: It is my pleasure to inform you that the President of the United States takes this opportunity of extending recognition to the *de facto* government of Mexico, of which Gen. Venustiano Carranza is the Chief Executive."

"The Government of the United States will be pleased to receive formally in Washington a diplomatic representative of the *de facto* government as soon as it shall please Gen. Carranza to designate and appoint such representative; and, reciprocally, the Government of the United States will accredit to the *de facto* government a diplomatic representative as soon as the President has had opportunity to designate such representative."

On August 31, 1917, the President of the United States, communicating directly with General Carranza, and addressing him as President of the United Mexican States, said:

"Great and Good Friend:

"I have received the letter of the Ist of May last, in which Your Excellency announced your assumption of the Presidency of the Republic and your entrance upon the duties of the office.

"I cordially reciprocate the sentiments you express for the continuance of the friendly relations which have heretofore existed between the United States of America and the United Mexican States, and I assure Your Excellency of my best wishes for your personal welfare and for the prosperity of the Republic over which you have been called to preside."

12. 37 T. H. R. 777.
13. L. R. 36 Ch. D. 489 (1887).
14. 246 U. S. 304. See also *Oetjen* v. *Central Leather* Co., 246 U. S. 297.
15. "International Pecuniary Claims Against Mexico" in the *Yale Law Journal,* March, 1917 (vol. XXVI, p. 339). In footnotes, Professor Borchard cites authorities supporting his propositions.

X

Jurisdiction Over Property

Of the complete jurisdiction of a sovereign State over all property within its territorial limits, whether for purposes of taxation, of eminent domain, or the regulation of its use in private hands, there is no dispute. Controversies as to jurisdiction, therefore, seldom if ever arise with regard to corporeal things. It is only with reference to incorporeal hereditaments or intangible personality that questions as to *situs* for purpose of legal regulation or control occur.

Many of these questions are solved by applying the principle that *mobilia sequuntur personam*, but no State permits this general doctrine or fiction to defeat its jurisdiction if there are any substantial grounds for holding that the personality or incorporeal hereditament has a *situs* within its borders independently of the place of residence or domicil of its owner. Thus, States have not hesitated, under certain circumstances, to exercise jurisdiction over intangible personality, even when owned by non-resident aliens, when the evidences of ownership— the bonds, promissory writings, mortgage instruments, or other evidences of credits—are, in fact, situated within their respective limits. In other cases, as will presently be seen, States base their rights of legal control, especially for purposes of taxation, upon the fact that the credits taxed are in the form of profits arising out of corporate or other business undertaking carried on within its borders, or that the mortgages or other liens are upon property similarity situated. An examination of some of the decisions of the Supreme Court of the United States with reference to the exercise of Jurisdiction of this kind will disclose the general doctrines declared by American courts, and the reasoning upon which they have been based.

Special Considerations Applicable to States of the American Union. A considerable number of the cases which will be examined relate to the taxing powers of the individual States of the American Union. Because of the fact that these States have their powers curtailed by certain express or implied limitations in the Federal Constitution with reference, for example, to the impairing the obligation of contracts, to the taking of property without due process of law, to interference with interstate or foreign commerce, and to the denial to citizens of the other States of the Union of privileges and immunities enjoyed by their own citizens, the validity of their tax laws as well as other laws comes before the Federal Supreme Court for final determination. These States, as between themselves, are foreign governments and their jurisdiction are strictly territorial in character, and therefore, as between themselves, the Federal Supreme Court applies the same principles of public law that govern the relations of sovereign States to one another, and, for that reason we may quote the decisions of that eminent tribunal as to its conception of these general jurisprudential principles so far as concern the facts upon which municipal legal control may be predicated. In so far, however, as the decisions of the Supreme Court turn upon specific provision sof the American Constitution or arise out of any special constitutional characteristics of the American Union, they are, of course, without determining or interpretative force in the field of general publi law.

Two further facts with regard to the jurisdictional powers of the States of the American Union are to be observed. Because their exists above them the sovereign National Government and its supreme judicial tribunal, the Supreme Court of the United States, all questions of jurisdiction are judicially determined, and resort cannot be had to the political modes of protesting or redressing wrongs claimed to be suffered by one State because of a wrongful or oppressive exercise of jurisdiction by another State of the Union. In the second place, because of the non-sovereign status of these States, and the fact that they have no dealings, as independent political persons, with foreign States, they are wholly incapacitated fromk exercising jurisdiction over their own citizens who have obtained a foreign domicil. Thus, as is elsewhere pointed out, while it is a generally accepted principle of public law that a soverign State may assert whatever jurisdiction it pleases over its own citizens wherever they may be, holding them responsible in its courts for breaches of its own laws both civilly and criminally, for acts committed by them while in foreign countries, the same is not true of the member States of the American Union. They can take no cognizance of acts committed outside their own territorial limits upon the ground that the accused or tort feasors are its own citizens. And, of course, these States have no jurisdiction upon the high seas such as sovereign States possess. Furthermore, as a matter of express provision of the Federal Constitution, each of them is compelled to give full faith and credit to the public acts, records and judicial proceedings of the other States of the Union,—an obligation which, as between sovereign States, is voluntary in character and discretionary in extent.

In the case of *United States* v. *Bennett*,[1] decided in 1914, the Supreme Court, dwelling upon the principles to be applied in determining the jurisdictional powers of the individual States as distinct from those applicable in the case of the Union, pointed out that while the attempt of one of these States to tax property outside its territorial limits would be in violation of the provision of the Federal Constitution which prohibits it from taking property without due process of law, the same was not true of the United States itself. The Court said: "the application to the States of the rule of due process relied upon [by counsel in the case] comes from the fact that their spheres of activity are enforced and protected by the Constitution and therefore it is impossible for one State [of the Union] to reach out and tax property in another without violating the Constitution, for where the power of the one ends the authority of the other begins. But this has no application to the Government of the United States so far as its admitted taxing power is concerned. It is coextensive with the limits of the United States; it knows no restriction except where one is expressed in or arises from the Constitution, and therefore embraces all the attributes which pertain to sovereignty in the fullest sense...Because the limitations of the Constitution are barriers bordering the States and preventing them from transcending the limits of their authority, and thus destroying the rights of other States [of the Union], and at the same time saving their rights from destruction by the other States, in other words, of maintaining and preserving the rights of all the States, affords no ground for constructing an imaginary constitutional boundary around the exterior confines of the United States for the purpose of shutting that Government off from the exertion of powers which inherently belong to it by virtue of its sovereignty."

Territorial Jurisdiction of the British "Dominions." As regards the strictly territorial extent of their several jurisdictions, the British Dominions have a status similar to that of the individual States of the American Union. A discussion of the doctrines developed with reference to this matter of Dominion jurisdiction is the subject of a separate chapter in Keith's standard treatise on *Responsible Government in The Dominions.*[1a]

That the legislative or other jurisdictional powers vested by the British Parliament in the several colonies or Dominions of the British Empire, unless expressely otherwise provided by Act of Parliament, may be exercised by them only within their respective limits, or, at the most, with reference to violations of their respective municipal laws committed outside those limits by persons domiciled within them, has been repeatedly declared by the courts and by the Imperial Government. Thus, for example, special Acts of the British Parliament have been needed in order to provide for the extradition of fugitives from the justice of one colony or Dominion found in another possession of the British Crown. Some of the questions regarding the *situs* of personal property for purposes of taxation by the Dominions have resembled very much those have arisen in the States of the American Union.

Taxation. The decision of the Supreme Court in the case known by the descriptive title "State Tax on Foreign-Held Bonds,"[2] decided in 1873, has been one of the most discussed of the decisions of that court, and the doctrine there in declared, if not repudiated by later decisions, has at least been held down to practically the precise point then decided, namely, that bonds are property in the hands of their holders, and that, when these holders are no-residents of the States in which the company issuing them is incorporated or doing business, they are beyond the jurisdiction of that State.

With regard to the general powers of taxation which a State possesses, Justice Field, rendering the opinion for a unanimous court, said:

"The power of taxation, however vast in its character and searching in its extent, is necessarily limited to subjects within the jurisdiction of the State. These subjects are persons, property and business which last is, of course, also kind of property. Whatever form taxation may assume, whether as duties, imposts, excises or licenses, it must relate to one of these subjects. It is not possible to conceive of any other, though, as applied to them, the taxation may be exercised in a great variety of ways. It may touch property in every shape, in its natural condition, in its manufactured form, and in its various transmutation. And the amount of the taxation may be determined by the value of the property, or its use, or its capacity, or its productiveness. Unless restrained by provisions of the Federal Constitution, the power of the State as to the mode, form and extent of taxation is unlimited, where the subjects to which it applies are within her jurisdiction."

To this description of the State's taxing power may be added the statement, which has been earlier discussed, that sovereign States retain jurisdiction over their own citizens or subjects wherever they may be, whether for taxation or other purposes.[3]

In this Foreign-Held Bonds case the State law was held invalid because, as applied to the bonds, it was in violation of the provision of the Federal Constitution that no State of the Union shall pass a law impairing the obligation of contracts.[4] The obligation impaired was that between the corporations which were ordered to pay the tax and their non-resident bond-holders.

In *Hayes* v. *Pacific Steamship Co.*,[5] it was held that a State might not tax as property a ship of a foreign registry which was only temporarily in a port of the State,—which was, as it were, *in transitu*. Substantially the same was held in *Morgan* v. *Parham*.[6] So, also, in *St. Louis* v. *Wiggins Ferry Co.*,[7] it was held that the State of Missouri could not tax ferry-boats belonging to an Illinois company which boats were laid up on the Illinois shore when not in use. The Court said: "Where there is jurisdiction neither as to person nor property, the imposition of a tax would be *ultra vires* and void. If the legislature of State should enact that the citizens or property of another State or country should be taxed in the same manner as the persons and property within it sown limits and subject to its authority, or in any manner whatsoever, such a law would be as much a nullity as if in conflict with the most explicit constitutional inhibition, Jurisdiction is an necessary to valid legislative as to valid judicial action."

In *Ogden* v. *Saunders*,[8] the Supreme Court held that a State of the Union could not give an extraterritorial effect to its insolvency laws.

Due Process of Law. In the immediately foregoing cases the Supreme Court of the United States held that State laws invalid simply as *ultra vires* from the standpoint of territorial jurisdiction, and without reference to any specific inhibition laid upon the States by the Federal Constitution. However, in the later cases of *Louisville, etc., Ferry Co.* v. *Kentucky*,[9] decided in 1903, and *Delaware, L. & W. R.R. Co.* v. *Pennsylvania*,[10] decided in 1905, the Federal Supreme Court declared that an attempt of a State to tax property which did not have its situs within the State was in violation of the express prohibition laid upon the States by the Federal Constitution that they should deprive no person of property without due process of law.[11]

In the first of these cases was in validated the attempt of the State of Kentucky to include, for the purpose of taxation, the value of a franchise granted by the State of Indiana to a Kentucky ferry company. "There is, in our judgement," Said the court, no escape from the conclusion that Kentucky thus asserts its authority to tax a property right, an incorporeal hereditament,[12] which has its situs in Indiana...The taxation of that franchise or incorporeal hereditament by Kentucky is, in our opinion, a deprivation by that State of the property of the ferry company without due process of law in violation of the Fourteenth Amendment of the Constitution of the United States; as much so as if the State taxed the real-estate owned by that company in Indiana."

In *Delaware L. & W. R.R. Co.* v. *Pennsylvania*, the court, upon the same constitutional ground, held that a State of the Union could not, for purposes of taxation, include in the appraisement of the capital stock of a domestic corporation the value of coal mined by its within the State, but situated within other States, and there awaiting sale when the appraisement was made.

In *Union Refrigerator Transit Co.* v. *Kentucky,*[13] decided in 1905, the court similarly held that due process of law denied a corporation of Kentucky by a tax of that State assessed upon its rolling stock permanently located in other States and there used for carrying on the company's business. The court said: "The arguments in favour of the taxation of intangible property at the domicil of the owner have application to tangible property. The fact that such property is visible, easily found, and difficult to conceal, and the tax readily collectible, is so cogent an argument for its taxation at its situs, that of of late there is general consensus of opinion that it is taxable in the State where it is permanently located and employed, and where it receives its entire protection, irrespective of the domicil of the owner." (Citing numerous cases)

In *Maguire* v. *Trefry,*[14] decided in 1920, the court held valid the law of the State of Massachusetts taxing the income of a resident of the State from a trust, administered under the laws of another State, in securities in the possession of the trustee in such other State. "It is true," said the court, "that the legal title of the property is held by the trustee in Pennsylvania. But it is so held for the beneficiary of the trust, and such beneficiary has an equitable right, title, and interest distinct from its legal ownership... It is this property right belonging to the beneficiary, realized in the shape of income which is the subject matter of the tax under the statute of Massachusetts."

In *Savings and Loan Society* v. *Multnomah County,*[15] the court expressly overruled the dictum in the State tax on Foreign-Held Bonds case that a non-resident mortgagee's equitable interest in land may not be taxed to him in the State where the land is situated.

In *Corry* v. *Baltimore,*[16] the court held that prior adjudications had conclusively settled the doctrine that the State could fix, for purposes of taxation, the situs of stock in a domestic corporation, whether held by resident or non-residents.

Inheritance Taxes. Some questions regarding the *situs* of property have been raised in connection with inheritance taxes. In general, however, with reference to the estates of non-resident decedents it has been held that, as to property within the States, the tax may be upheld as upon the right of succession or as a transfer of title tax. Thus, in *Blackstone v. Miller*,[17] the court upheld a tax upon the transfer, under the will of a non-resident, of debts due the decedent by citizens of the taxing State. The court said: "No one doubts that succession to a tangible chattel may be taxed wherever the property is found, and note the less that the law of the situs accepts its rule of succession from the law of the domicil, or that by the law of the domicil the chattel is a part of a *universitas* and is taken into account again in the succession tax there...The question, then, is narrowed to whether a distinction is to be taken between tangible chattels and the deposit in this case...If the transfer of the deposit necessarily depends upon and involves the law of New York [the taxing State in the instant case] for its exercise, or, in other words, if the transfer is subject to the power of the State of New York, then New York may subject the transfer to a tax... It is plain that the transfer does depend upon the law of New York, not because of any theoretical speculation concerning the whereabouts of the debt, but because of the practical fact of its power over the person of the debtor."[18]

Taxation of Foreign Shareholders of Domestic Corporations. In *Michigan Central R. R. Co.* v. *Slack*,[19] the Supreme Court, interpreting and applying a provision of the Federal Internal Revenue law as amended by the law of 1886, upheld as an excise tax a percentum tax on interest due by an American corporation, doing business in America, on its bonds issued before the revenue law was enacted and held at the time by non-resident foreigners. The law in question levied a general tax on corporations, such as was the plaintiff company, to be paid by them out of their earnings, income and profits, and provided that the amounts payable should be deducted by the companies from their dividends, interest or funded debt, etc. and paid over to the revenue agents of the American Government.

In the course of its opinion the Court said: "Whether Congress, having the power to enforce the law, has the authority to levy such a tax on the interest due by a citizen of the United States to one who is not domiciled within our limits, and who owes the Government no allegiance, is a question which we do not think necessary to the decision of this case. The tax, in our opinion, is essentially an excise on the business of the class of corporations mentioned in the statute." In other words, the tax was not, in truth, upon the non-resident holders of the bonds, although it was deducted from and paid out of the interest due them as such holders, but upon the corporations which paid the interest. However, the court went on to say: "It is true that the Act went further, and declared that, except when the company has contracted otherwise, it might deducted this tax from the amount due the bondholders. And where the bondholder was subject to congressional legislation by reason of citizenship, residence or situs of the property taxed, it was within the lawful power of Congress to do so. Whether, as a question of international law, this declaration would relieve the corporation from the obligation to pay its foreign bondholder the full sum for which it contracted, we need not discuss; for this court, on all such subjects is bound by the legislative and political departments of its own Government."

In *United States* v. *Erie R. R. Co.*,[20] decided in 1882, which was an action to recover taxes paid under protest, levied under the same revenue provision as that involved in the case just considered, Chief Justice Waite declared that the authority of that case should govern. Justice Bradley and Harlan concurred in the judgement rendered, but not for the reasons stated in the earlier case. Justice Bradley, speaking for Justice Harlan as well as himself, said that he had always been of the opinion that the tax in question was on the incomes *pro tanto* of the holders of the bonds or stocks of the companies concerned. "The objection," he said, "that Congress had no power to tax non-resident aliens, is met by the fact that the tax was not assessed against them personally but against the *rem*, the credit, the debt due *to* them. Congress has the right to tax all property within the jurisdiction of the United States with certain exceptions not necessary to be noted. The money due to non-resident bondholders in this case was in the United States,—in the hands of the company—before it could be transmitted to London, or other place where the bondholders resided. While here it was liable to taxation."

Continuing, Justice Bradley went on to define the general jurisdictional powers of a government in the following significant, even if *obiter*, words: "Whether taxation thus imposed would be respected by foreign Governments if the creditor could bring before their courts the debtor company or its property, does not concern us in considering the question now presented. There is nothing in the Constitution [nor, he might have added, in the nature of any sovereign State] which authorizes this court, or any other court, to disaffirm the power of Congress to lay the tax. Congress is its own judge of the propriety or expediency of laying it.

Indeed, insofar as the power of Congress is concerned, regarded in reference to any power the courts have to limit or restrain it, I see no reason why Congress may not lay a tax upon any property on which the Government can lay its hands, whether within or without the jurisdiction of the United States. If, in imitation of the dues lived by Denmark upon vessels passing through the Cattegat Sound, Congress should levy a duty upon all vessels passing through the Strait of Florida, I do not know of any power which the courts possess to prevent it. It might create complications with foreign Governments, it is true, and involve the country in war, but Congress has the power, if it chooses to take the responsibility, of creating, or giving occasion to such complications. The responsibility rest upon it alone."

Justice Field, in a dissenting opinion rendered in this case, took the position that the tax involved was upon the income of non-resident aliens and nothing else. Upon this point he was in agreement with Justices Bradley and Harlan, but, differing from them, he declared that, from the very nature of political authority, a sovereign State is without legal right to tax the incomes of persons over whom it has no jurisdiction either by way of citizenship or residence. "The foreign owner of these bonds," he said, quoting the language the lower court had used, "was not in nay respect subject to the jurisdiction of the United States, neither was this portion of his income. His debtor [the company] was, and so was the money of his debtor, but the money of his debtor did not become a part of his income until it was paid to him, and in this case the payment was outside of the United States in accordance with the obligations of the contract which he held." "There are,'' continued Justice Field, "limitations upon the powers of all governments, without any express designation of them in their organic law; limitations which inhere in their very nature and structure, and this is one of them—that no rightful authority can be exercised by them over alien subjects, or citizen abroad or over their property there situated."

Here it is clear that Justice Field fell back upon a doctrine of what may be termed natural or inherent limitations—limitations derived from no legal source, but imposed by the very nature of things, and as a matter of absolute ethical obligation.

It is, indeed, surprising that this Justice should have been willing to give his support to a theory that, long before his time, had been thoroughly discredited, and in support of which he could adduce no judicial precendents. He did, indeed, assert that the courts in England had considered the doctrine to be so obligatory upon them that, where general terms used in Acts of Parliament seemed to contravene it, they had narrowed the construction so as to avoid that result. But, admitting this to be true, this is far from a declaration by the English courts that in cases where, because of the explicit language used, it was not possible to escape by means of construction from the force of parliamentary commands, they would in this or an other case, refuse to recognize the validity of such commands.[21]

Income Taxes. The question of the situs of property for the purposes of taxation is an especially acute one with reference to income taxes. Both in England and the United States such taxes have been imposed upon persons, whether citizens or not, and whether resident or not, with respect to profits derived from business enterprises carried on within their respective territories.

In the United States the Acts of 1861 and 1864 confined the tax to residents and to citizens residing abroad, but the Act of 1866 added the provision: "And a like tax shall be levied, collected, and paid annually upon the gains, profits, and income of every business trade, or profession carried on in the United States by persons residing without the United States, not citizens thereof"; and this same or a similar provisions was embodied in the Acts of 1870, 1894, and 1913. Similar provisions are also to be found in the income tax laws of some of the States of the American Union, and, in the case of *Shaffer* v. *Carter,*[22] decided in 1920, the constitutionality of these acts was examined by the Supreme Court of the United States.

In this case of *Shaffer* v. *Carter* one of the questions involved was as to the constitutionality of a tax levied by the State of Oklahoma upon net incomes derived by non-residents from property owned by them within the State and from business or professions carried on by them within its borders. The law was upheld, the court saying:

"We deem it clear, upon principle as well as on authority, that just as a State may impose general income taxes upon its own citizens and residents whose persons are subject to its control, it may, as a necessary consequence, levy a duty of like character, and not more onerous in its effect, upon income accruing to non-residents from their property or business within the State, or their occupations carried on therein; enforcing payment, so far as it can, by the exercise of a just control over persons and property within its borders.[23]...The very fact that a citizen of one state has the right to hold property or carry on an occupation or business in another is a very reasonable ground for subjecting such non-resident, although not personally, yet to the extent of his property held or his occupation or business carried on therein, to a duty to pay taxes not more onerous in effect than those imposed under like circumstances upon citizens of the latter State."

This last qualification as to equality of treatment between residents and non-residents being one specially imposed upon the States of the American Union by the Federal Constitution, would not apply to the Federal Government in its dealings with non-residents in foreign States.

To the contention that the income tax in question was, in its very nature, a personal one, or a "subjective tax imposing personal liability upon the recipient of the income," and, therefore, as to a non-resident, beyond the jurisdictional power of the State, the court replied that the essential point was as to its practical operation and effect,—"the personal element cannot, by any fiction, oust the jurisdiction of the State within which the income actually arises and whose authority over it operates *in rem.*"

In the case of *De Ganay* v. *Lederer*,[24] decided in 1919, the Supreme Court of the United States upheld the federal income tax law as to the income from stocks and bonds of corporations organized under laws of the United States, and from bonds and mortgages secured upon property in the United States, owned by a non-resident alien, which income was collected and transmitted to such alien by an agent domiciled in the United States who had physical possession of the securities under a power of attorney which gave him authority to sell, assign or transfer any of them and to invest or reinvest the proceeds from such sales. These being the circumstances, the court declared that the securities constituted property which had its situs in the United States. To the contention of counsel that certificates of stock, bonds and mortgages are not themselves property but merely evidences of ownership of property, the court replied that, in general parlance and usage, they are so considered, and that the words of the Congressional statute are to be constructed in the light of such usage. As to the situs of this property, the court said that the maxim *mobilia sequuntur personam* declares what, in many cases, is but a fiction which has to yield when the facts and circumstances of cases require it, and that there is abundant judicial authority (citing cases) that notes, bonds and mortgages may acquire a situs at a place other than the domicil of their owners and be there reached by the taxing power.[25]

In *Buck* v. *Beach,*[26] the Supreme Court held that the here presence of promissory notes within the State was not sufficient to create a situs, for purpose of taxation by that State, of the tangible personalty represented by such instruments, and that it was immaterial that these instruments had been sent into the State by their owner in order to avoid taxation upon them by the State of his residence. The court said: "The debts here in question were not property within the State of Indiana, nor were the promissory notes themselves, which were only evidence of such debts. The rule giving jurisdiction where the speciality may be found has no application to a promissory note."

Upon the other hand, in *Metropolitan Life Insurance Co.* v. *New Orleans*,[27] the court held that a company could not escape taxation by sending the evidences of credits outside of the State, when there were other reasons why the company should be taxed upon them. In this case the plaintiff, a foreign corporation, was doing business within the State and the court said: "The State undertook to tax the capital employed in the business precisely as it taxed the capital of its own citizens in like situation. For the purpose of arriving at the amount of capital actually employed it caused the credit arising out of the business to be assessed. We think the State had the power to do this, and that the foreigner doing business cannot escape taxation upon his capital by removing temporarily from the State evidences of credits in the form of notes. Under such circumstances they have a taxable situs in the State of their origin."[28]

A careful examination of the cases which have been reviewed shows that not yet has the Supreme Court of the United States found it necessary to pass squarely upon the jurisdictional power of the United States to tax non-resident aliens upon intangible personality which cannot be construed to be actually or physically within the United States, or to be of the nature of a licence or excise or franchise tax upon business carried on within, or special corporate rights granted by, the United States.[29]

The present federal income tax law requires the payment by non-resident aliens of a tax assessed upon incomes derived by them from all property owned or from any business or profession carried on in the United States. This tax, it is to be observed, is collected in many cases by the United States, not directly from the recipients of the income but from the corporations or concerns which earn it, and before it is paid over to those to whom it is due. It yet remains to be seen whether the Supreme Court will find itself able to hold that such income is property within the United States, even though the instruments evidencing the ownership of the property from which the income is derived are not physically within the United States, and the owners are non-resident aliens and have no agents in the United States from the collection, or collection and reinvestment, of the incomes due them. If, however, one may judge by the general trend of the cases that have been reviewed, it is more than likely that the Supreme Court, when the question is presented to it, will uphold the federal law in this respect. If it should do so, it would of course be within the right of foreign Governments to hold that such income cannot properly be deemed to be property within the United States, and, therefore, to complain that the United States, taking advantage of the fact that it has within its actual control the property or businesses from which such income is derived, is improperly withholding property from the citizens of the complaining States, who are not residing and have no domicil in, and own no property located within, the United States. In other words, they might admit, as, of course, they would be compelled to admit, that the United States may tax business carried on or property located within its borders or the income of non-resident aliens merely by reason of the fact that such income is derived from the earning of such businesses or property: that the payments due to their own citizens remain the property of the concerns earning them until they are paid over to the persons to whom they are due, and that only when so paid to and received by these creditors do they become income, by which time, in the case of non-resident aliens they will have passed beyond the jurisdiction of the United States.

Such an argument as this would of course be valid only as a matter of international right are as a rule sanctioned by generally accepted international law. It would have no force in municipal courts. For them, as has been so often reiterated, the only question would be as to what the municipal law provided. If, in bald terms, the statute should declare that a tax should be levied personally upon non-resident aliens, who owned no property within the State, who derived no income from property located or business carried on within the State, or that a tax should be levied upon alien-owned property located outside of the State, the courts of the enacting State would be bound to recognize the validity of such a law. The courts, when called upon to issue a decree in enforcement of such taxes might not be able to find any property within its jurisdiction against which a judgement *in rem* could be entered and enforced, but, if the municipal law so provided, it might enter a judgement *in personam* in default against the defendant, which might be satisfied out of property within the jurisdiction of the court which, at some later time, the defendant might come into possession of. It scarcely need to be said that if the attempt were made to institute proceedings in a foreign jurisdiction to collect this judgement out of property there located and owned by the defendant, the courts of that

State would be justified in refusing to give force to the judgement decrees, which, as to itself, would be foreign ones.[30]

A possible constitutional difficulty peculiar to the United States with reference to income taxation and not related to the implications of its sovereignty, is that raised by the powers of Congress under the Federal Constitution to levy direct taxes. Should it take the position which has been indicated, the court would have to hold that the tax thus collected was an income tax even though the jurisdiction to levy it was founded upon the proposition that the interest of the non-resident aliens in the earnings of the property or business represented by the stock, bonds or mortgages held by them, constituted property within the jurisdiction of the United States. For if the tax were not still regarded as upon incomes it would be a direct tax not covered by the Seventeenth Amendment to the Federal Constitution, and would therefore have to be apportioned among the States of the Union according to their respective populations.[31]

Addendum. Since the preceding pages were in type the Supreme Court of the United States, in the case of *Cook* v. *Tait*,[32] has decided that the United States might impose a tax on income received by an American citizen who, at the time the income was received, was permanently resident and domiciled in a foreign country; the income being derived from property located in that country. The scope and the power of a sovereign State to tax, it was declared, "is based on the presumption that the government by its very nature benefits the citizen and his property wherever found." This doctrine, it was asserted, was implicit in the holding of the court in *United States* v. *Bennett*,[33] which, in effect, held that "the basis of the power to tax was not and cannot be made dependent upon the situs of the property in all cases, it being in or out of the United States nor was not and cannot be made dependent upon the domicil of the citizen, that being in or out of the United States, but upon the relation of the latter to him as citizen."

References

1. 232 U. S. 299.

1a. Vol. I, part III, chap. II, "the Territorial Limitation on Dominion Legislation." See also Keith's *Imperial Unity and the Dominions* (pp. 132 *et seq.*), which is in a manner, a supplement to his earlier three-volume work.

2. *Cleveland, etc., R. R. Co. v. Pennsylvania,* 15 Wall. 300.

3. As to the situs of the property involved in this case, the court said: "Corporations may be taxed, like natural persons, upon their property and business. But debts owings by corporations, like debts owing by

individuals, are not property of the debtors in any sense; they are obligations of the debtors, and only possess value in the hands of the creditors. With them they are property, and in their hands they may be taxed. To call debts property of the debtors is simply to misuse terms. All the property there can be, in the nature of things, in debts of corporations, belongs to the creditors, to whom they are payable, and follows their domicil, wherever that may be. Their debts can have no locality separate from the parties to whom they are due."

In other cases the Supreme Court of the United States has held that the right of foreign corporation or non-resident to do business within a State may be subjected to what is in the nature of a license or excise tax. It has also been held that where foreign-held evidences of ownership or of credits are placed in the hands of resident agents for the purpose of collecting the interests, rents, etc., and of reinvesting the proceeds, that are to be deemed to have their situs within the State and therefore taxable by the State.

4. Article I, section 10.
5. 17 Howard 596.
6. 16 Wallace 471.
7. 11 Wallace 423.
8. 12 Wheaton 214.
9. 188 U. S. 385.
10. 198 U. S. 341.
11. Fourteenth Amendment. As to this shifting of ground by the Federal Supreme Court, see the article by Dr. F. J. Goodnow, "Congressional Regulation of State Taxation," in the *Pol. Sci. Quar.*, vol. XXVIII (1913), p. 405.
12. An incorporeal hereditament is ordinarily distinguished from intangible personalty by being a right attached to land.
13. 199 U. S. 194.
14. 253 U. S. 12.
15. 169 U. S. 421.
16. 196 U. S. 466.
17. 188 U. S. 189.
18. See also *Keeney* v. *New York*, 222 U. S. 525.
19. 100 U. S. (10 Otto), 595.
20. 106 U. S. (16 Otto), 327.
21. Justice Field also cites the case of *The Apollon* (9 Wheaton 362), which has been earlier discussed, and which, it has been shown, does not support, except possibly in an *obiter* manner, the doctrine in whose behalf Justice field adduces it.
22. 252 U. S. 37. See also *Travis v. Yale and Towne Manufacturing Co.*, 252 U. S. 60.

23. The court, in this statement, introduced the qualification that the tax upon non-resident should not be more onerous than upon residents, because of the express provision of the Federal Constitution that "the citizens of each State shall be entitled to all privileges and immunities of citizens in the several States" (Art. IV, Sec. 2).
24. 250 U. S. 376.
25. Quoting a decision of a state court (*Jefferson* v. *Smith,* 88 N. Y. 576), the Supreme Court said: "It is clear from the statutes referred to and the authorities cited and from the understanding of business men in commercial transactions, as well as of jurists and legislators, that mortgages, bonds, bill and notes have for many purposes come to be regarded as property, and not as the mere evidences of debts, and that they may thus have a situs at the place where they are found, like other visible tangible chattels,"

    As to the conformity of the doctrine of the instant case with that of the case of State Tax on Foreign Held Bonds (15 Wallace, 300), the court said: "The taxation in that case was on the interest on bonds held out of the State. Bonds and negotiable instruments are more than mere evidences of debt. The debt is inseparable from the paper which declares and constitutes it, by a tradition which comes down from more archaic conditions."
26. 206 U. S. 392.
27. 205 U. S. 395.
28. Justices Day and Brewer dissented.
29. In *R, R.* v. *Jackson,* 7 Wallace 262, the court held that Congress had not intended, by its Income Tax Law of 1864, to tax incomes of non-resident aliens.
30. For an interesting discussion of movements that have been made to obtain an international agreement and harmony of practice with regard to the taxation of intangible personal property especially with reference to incomes, see the articles by G. G. Cobaugh, "International Comity in Taxation" in the *Journal of Political Economy* for April, 1923, vol. XXXI, p. 262.
31. Article I, section 9, paragraph 4, of the Federal Constitution provides: "No capitation, or other direct tax shall be laid, unless in proportion to the census or enumeration hereinbefore directed to be taken."

    The Seventeenth Amendement provides: "The Congress shall have power to lay and collect taxes on incomes, from whatever sources derived, without apportionment among the several States, and without regard to any census or enumeration."
32. 44 Supreme Court Reporter, 444.
33. 232 U. S. 299.

XI

The Origin of the State Historically and Psychologically Considered

Analytical jurisprudence is concerned not so much with the evolution of political institutions as with the juristic analysis of these institutions as they exits at any given time. Nevertheless, the determination of the historical processes by which distinctively political life has grown out of non-political, social life is not without importance since light is thus thrown upon the nature of political as distinguishes from other types or kinds of communal existence of men. Furthermore, as to any given legally sovereign organization, it is important to determine the manner in which its juristic birth may be interpreted, and, if possible, to fix the moment in time of that birth. So, similarly, as will be discussed in the chapter which is to follow, it is important to determine the modes in which is to follow, it is important to determine the modes in which the juristic life of a State may be terminated and the juristic consequences which flow from such a dissolution. First, then, we will speak, in general terms, of the historical origin of political life among men.[1]

Historical Origins. The study of origing is always an attractive one, and the work of many anthropologists has thrown a vast amount of light upon the early history of social and political institutions. The parts played by consanguinity by religion (especially by the worship of ancestors) , by the communal ownership of land and other economic interests, and above all by the influence of the family upon the development of social and political life , have all been carefully considered . The significance of totem worship, of endogamy and exogamy, of polygamy of polyandry, and of patriarchal life has been discussed in the light of the facts presented by the earliest literary and archaeological records and interpreted by analogy with the present customs of races now in the lowest stages of civilization. All of these facts have been compared and exhaustively studied, but the absolute origin of civic life has not been historically determined. The fact is that the first subjection of man to public authority of some sort or other must have been practically coaeval with the beginning of his social life, and this carries us back to periods of human development interiors to those that furnish historical records.

Furthermore, even after we reach periods regarding which we have authentic historical information, we are often without exact knowledge as to the manner in which the men of those times viewed their own institutions. However, reasoning back from such later records as we have, and judging from analogy with the thoughts and customs of peoples of whose primitive institutions we have knowledge, we can, after all, form a fairly confident opinion as to the character of the ideas held concerning social and political institutions during their very early stages of development, if not at the time of their original institution.

One thing we know with practical certainty, and this that, from the time when any sense whatever of social or political obligation came to be recognized by men, the ideas of religious sanction, of customary obligation, and of legal authority, were so intermixed that they were not distinguished even in thought. Law, in a juristic sense, was not distinguished from what Austin would term "positive morality," and this morality was deemed to derive its obligatory force from super-human sources. A divine sanction or prohibition was attached to nearly every act of which the social group took any direct cognizance. The family group had its gods and its divinely ordered rules of conduct, as did the larger social groups of which the families were the constituents units. A "consciousness of kind" and common material interest may, in reality, have furnished the cement that kept the groups together, but all the historical evidence that we have indicates that, to the individuals themselves, the uniting bond was conceived to be a religious one, and community of worship the one objective evidence of their unity. Thus, whatever may have been the actual origin or utilitarian basis of any recognized rule of conduct or principle of authority, the source was conceived to be in the will of the gods, and its compelling force derived from the evil which it was believed the gods would inflict upon those who should fail to confirm to it.

Regarding the probable historical steps by which political as distinguished from merely social institutions arose among men, and by which a corresponding distinction in thought between a political, a social or religious sense of obligation was created, varying theories or conclusions have been reached by anthropologists and other scholars.

The Patriarchal Theory. According to the so-called Patriarchal theory, to which Sir Henry Maine and Herbert Spencer have given the support of their names, the primitive type of society among all early peoples, or at any rate, among the Aryans and Semites, was one in which all individuals were grouped into families or households, united by bonds of kinship (real or fictitious), marriage, or domestic service, and ruled over in a practically absolute manner by the chief male or patriarch. As long as this stage persisted, the family, according to this theory, remained the sole social unit and the *patria potestas* the only political authority. By a natural process of growth, as this theory goes on to hold, these families or households grew into clans, clan into tribes, and the tribes, by conquests and alliances, into nations. At the same time, corresponding to this increase in communal life, the political powers of the heads of the families developed into those of the chiefs of the clans, and these, in turn, into the authority of then King of the tribe or of the nation.

The simplicity and apparent reasonableness of this explanation of early social and political development immediately secured for it a wide acceptance. Later years, however, witnessed a destructive criticism of it, especially by such writers as L. H. Morgan[2], and J. F. McClennan.[3] According to these critics, social life in its earliest forms, exhibited a horde condition in which there was an almost complete promiscuity in sexual relations, and out of which, only as a later historical development, did patriarchal or family life, headed by the male, emerge.

Whether or not the patriarchal type of family life was the original form of social organization, either generally or for particular races, is, after all, not a matter of considerable importance to the political scientist. But what is of importance to him is the fact that a better reading of history shows that the patriarch's authority was not the germ out of which developed, by a natural process of growth, first the power of the chiefs of the clans and tribes, and then those of the State. In addition, and what is still more significance to the political scientist, is the fact that a careful analysis of patriarchal power shows that it is so different, in its very nature, from political authority, that, as an *a priori* proposition, it is difficult to see how it could have developed into that authority.

The Tribes. Viewed historically, it is probably true that, founded as it is upon the physical facts of parentage, there existed among all races of men some sort of family life before any other social units were formed. But it is equally probable, that, before the family grew into patriarchal form, a grouping into tribes had taken place. In truth, aside from the temporary association of mother and child, which the helpless condition of the latter necessitates, the tribal form of association is the simplest conceivable type of social and political organization. For its establishment and maintenance nothing more is needed than a slight feeling of friendship between its constituent members, and a recognition of its offensive or defensive value in war—a recognition which stern experience must, at a very early time, have almost universally brought about. For the maintenance of tribal authority, no more elaborate form of government is needed than a chieftain whose right to direct and command is founded upon a personal prowess, and whose sphere of authority, in war, is that of a military commander, and, in peace, that of an arbitrator of private disputes. As savagery gave way by degrees to civilization, a double development undoubtedly went on. Upon the one hand, the authority of the tribe increased and is sphere of authority over its individual members widened; while, upon the other hand, within the tribe, family life increased in its integrity and control until it assumed, in many communities at least, the patriarchal form. Thus, instead of the family developing into the tribe, the likelihood is that there was a synchronous or parallel development of both social units.

The Clan. The historical relation of the clan, gens, or sept to the family upon the one side, and to the tribe or nation upon the other side, has been a point even more disputed than that of the family to the tribe. As stated above, a once generally accepted theory was that the clans were originally formed from families,—that several families united to form a clan, or that single families ultimately became so large as, in themselves, to constitute clans. Modern scholars, however, are now disposed to deny that this was the probable course of development. Morgan bases this denial upon the view that, in primitive societies, exogamy is the general rule.

It is not necessary, however, to rest the denial of a genetic relationship between the clan and the family upon the more or less uncertain matter of exogamy. A better proof is that which proceeds from the fact that the aims, functions, and basis of membership of the clan are different from those of the family. The family is founded upon kinship, actual or assumed, and in it, the degree of relationship is fundamental. Its head is, as a rule, determined by birth and not be voluntary selection on the part of its members, and he rules rather as owner of the persona subject to his authority than as a leader or judge over them. In the clan, upon the other hand, although a certain degree of community of blood is usually present or assumed, degrees of relationship are not recognized, or, if recognized, are not deemed important. The real bond of unions is a religious one. The clan possesses a certain amount of common property, it exercises certain important functions in the way of settlement of disputes between its members, and in furnishing mutual aid and protection; but its one essential, avowed end is the maintenance of a common worship.

In membership the clan resembles the tribe. That is to say, its constituent units are the individuals themselves and not groups of them. Its members are, of course, grouped into families, just as are the citizens of the modern State, but the elementary cells are individuals, and whatever authority the clan possesses is exercised directly upon them.[4]

As to the historical relationship of the clan to the tribe there is a dispute among scholars, some maintaining the tribe results from a union of clans, others asserting that the tribe comes first in point of time, and later exhibits a differentiation into clans. It is not unlikely that, in some instances, clans united to form a tribe; in other cases, that the tribal relationship was first established and the clans a later development.[5]

The question as to which came first in point of time, the clan or the tribe, is of importance to the historian. To the political scientist the significant point is that these two types of human groupings were generally alike as regards both their form of organization and their units of membership. Both were associations of individuals having common interests, and were ruled over by chiefs whose rights or rulership were based upon their personal qualifications. The trice thus differed from the clan rather in size and scope of functions than in essential nature. There were, however, the following differences: the fact of a general kinship was more emphasized in the clan than in the tribe, and the maintenance of a common worship was deemed more essential. The tribe had its gods and spiritual religious rites, just as had the clan, but community of religion was rather one of the outward symbols of tribal unity than the basis upon which it was founded. Primarily the tribe existed for the purpose of offence and defence against other tribes, and assistance in the performance of this duty was supported to be obtained from the gods of the tribe. Upon the other hand, in the clan the maintenance of a particular worship was the chief aim sought, the elements of mutual help and common ownership of property being secondary.

Origin of Political Authority. As regards the genesis of political as distinct from social authority over men, it would seem to be clear that its beginning is to be traced to the tribe, or to clan in those cases in which the tribe was a product of the growth of a clan or of the union of two or more clans. In other words, political authority cannot be properly regarded as having developed out of the patriarchal authority found in the early family. Even if it be held that some sort of family life must have existed before the formation of gentile or tribal associations, the groups of such individuals thus formed cannot be said to have exhibited distinctively political characteristics: they were purely social units founded upon the facts of parentage. Their members were limited to specific determinate individuals. The bond of union was a temporary one, and the status of the members was that of virtual slaves or chattels of the family's head, and not that of citizens. It is true that, in early times, the control of many matters, now regulated by the commands of the State, was in the hands of the head of the family but its interests and authority were essentially private in character. It never was, and never became a subject of public law.[6]

As contrasted with that of the family, the authority of the tribe must have been, from the beginning, purely political in character. Its chief derived his right to rule from the actual agreement or acquiescence of his subjects. No absolute limits were fixed to the membership of the tribe, nor to the duration of its existence; no degrees of citizenship were recognized; and, so far as its sphere of control extended, it was sovereign and self-sufficient. It was not one of a number of groups of equal status and co-ordinate power which composed a larger social unit.

It is of course true that, in the earliest times, the form of governmental organization that obtained was simple in the extreme, and that the extent to which the attempt was made to control the acts of its individual members, was comparatively slight, but, once established, the tribe and its authority furnished a beginning out of which the modern political State could develop by a mere process of elaborating its governmental organization and extending its control over additional human interests and activities. Thus, once established, an event which must have occurred very early in the history of every people, the tribe was able to grow, by conquest or natural increase, into the nation, its government into that of the modern State, and the authentic expressions of its will into the great systems of jurisprudence which the complicated character of present day life makes necessary. Beginning with a jurisdiction that extended little beyond that of direction in times of war, and judgement in a comparatively few matters in times of peace, the tribe had but to stretch out gradually its control, first by way of increase of its executive and judicial functions, an then, finally, by the exercise of direct legislative authority, in order to develop into the sovereign body-politic of today which practically monopolizes the legal right to employ physical coercion.

In this process of development, political authority has not changed its essential character, whatever may have been the varying importance of the family or other social groupings within the body-politic. From the very beginning, as Hearn correctly says, "the State is not composed of other social organism. Its member may be members of other social organisms, and the activities of these other social organisms may or may not clash, or tend to clash, with the activities of the State. But the organization of the State is complete within itself, and its power, within its own sphere and over its own members, is supreme. It has its own worship, its own property, it sown functions, its own claim upon its members, its own duties towards them. It respects the right and duties of the other associations which it includes, and does not, at least in its earlier stages, seek to interface with the relations of its members to any of those other associations."[7]

Psychological Origin of Political Authority. Just as it is an idea or sentimental that transmutes an aggregate of individuals into a nation, so it is a desire for political unity that provides a psychological basis for the State. As the eminent Austrian publicist, Jellinek, has put it, "The inner ground of the origin of the State is the fact that an aggregate of persons has a conscious feeling of its unity, and gives expression to this unity by organizing itself as a volitional and active subject."[8]

It may be correct to say this desire for political union is, in many cases at least, the moving force that brings about the establishment of the State, but the mere existence of this psychological condition, granting, in a particular instance, that it exists, is not sufficient ground for asserting that a body-politic has been created. A State is not born until this subjective condition leads to the existence, in objective fact, of a ruling political organization. Other conditions favouring, or at least not hindering, this objective realization will result from the subjective inclination. But, except in rare cases, there is not this absence of hindrance. The political *status quo ante* has always to be considered. Existing political institutions and methods have the support of tradition, backed by the natural indisposition of men to change their habits and manner of life, especially when they cannot foresee with absolute precision the results that will follow from a change. And, most of all, an existing political authority is always supported by an enormous weight of selfish interest. To the desire to rule, which is almost universal in the human breast, are added the material and social interests and honors that are bound up in an existing political régime, thus making those in power reluctant to consent to even a change in administration, much less to the establishment of a new body-politic. It thus frequently happens that there exists in the minds of a community of people a desire for a political unity of particular sort, and that this desire would be of sufficient strength to maintain the unity of a State, were it once established and organized, but that objective conditions prevent for many years the realization of such an end. It is only when this pent-up flood of feeling rises to sufficient height and Strength to burst the existing political barriers that hold it in, that a new State is created.

As has been said, the natural tendency of the feeling of ethnic or cultural unity is to find expression in political unity. The two sentiments, then, that lie at the basis of the Nation and of the State are largely similar. The same conditions that tend to create the feeling of Nationality tend also, in most cases, to demand the establishment of the State. Absolute identity of these two sentiments, however, cannot be affirmed. It is possible, in other words, for a well developed feeling of Nationality to exist with but slight desire for political unity. On the other hand, we find instances in which the establishment of political unity is clearly demanded by a People, among whom there is no other claim of Nationality. The factors that create the feeling of Nationality are community of race, language, historical tradition, mutuality of economic interests, and like degree of civilization. That which calls for the establishment of political control over a definite territory and community may be nothing more than political expediency,—the necessity for self-defensive or offensive strength. Certainly the feelings of American and British Nationality were very strong at the time of the severance of the American colonies from their mother country, yet independent political organization was nevertheless demanded and obtained by the Americans. Strong feelings of common Nationality were frequently displayed by the Greeks, especially when combating a common foe, yet at no time during the height of Grecian prosperity was political unity called for. At the present that we see three distinct Nationalities organized under the Swiss Government with no demand for separate political existence.

To those who would say that a national feeling does not truly exists unless there be a demand for political unity,—that, in other words, the desire for such unity is a necessary consequence of the feeling of Nationality, it is to be replied, that this gives a more intensive and exacting definition to the sentiment of Nationality than is usually ascribed to it. It is an obvious fact that we often have instances of political unions in which there is an absence of such elements as community of the race, language, custom, and historical tradition. It is, therefore, impossible to identify the desire for political unity, even before it obtains realization, with the sentiment of Nationality, unless we assume the position that only political expediency is able to create the feeling of Nationality. But to do this is not only to go counter to all accepted usage of terms, but, in fact, entirely to destroy the very idea of Nationality, which is supposed to rest upon other than political foundations. Though intimately connected, it seems best, then, to distinguish from each other the feelings of National and Political unity; in fine, to recognize that though the desire for political unity does, as a rule, arise from and out of a sentiment of Nationality, it may arise independently of it.

An attempt to argue the existence of a State and of political sovereignty from the mere fact of a condition of mind which has not found outward objective expression is seen in the argument of Professor Burgess in support of his contention that a National State existed in America during the period from the time of the outbreak of the Revolution of the American colonies against their mother country, that is, before the adoption, in 1789, of the Federal Constitution. During the years when the former colonies were associated under the Articles of Confederation—from 1781 to 1789—he is forced to admit that the thirteen former colonies were severally sovereign, for the Articles incontestably constituted only a League and not a constitutional Union, but this sovereignty, thus enjoyed by the States he speaks of as "unsurped."[9] In thus speaking, however, it is clear that he is led to take positions that are logically absurd, for it must appear that, if there had been a real will upon the part of the people during those years to create a National State, one would have come into being. And equally we must hold that the existence of the Thirteen States as several sovereign bodies must have been due to a will to that effect upon the part of those who constituted their citizen bodies.

There has been inclination on the part of many publicists to refuse the designation of State to the earlier type of political life, especially to those undeveloped groups within have not obtained for themselves a settled abode. Those taking this ground must be considered as governed by a special conception of the State. According to the conception adopted in the present work designation of State cannot be refused to any independent society of men that its politically organized.[10] In other words, low order of development does not deprive an institution of its generic name. A society is politically organized if it have established within it and over it a public authority for the control of those interest that are connected with its orderly existence, and the enforcement of its jural ideal, however crude and limited that ideal may be. Thus organized, a society of men is properly embraced within the scope of the *Staatsidee* and is as truly a State as when in its more developed form.

To make this point clear, we can, for this particular purpose, liken the term "State" as used in Political Science to the term "living being" as employed in Biological Science. The biologist does not refuse to recognize a living beings the lowest orders of life, even through they be but mere splotched of protoplasm, so structureless and homogenous in composition that different individuals can be scarcely distinguished, and in each of which the most powerful microscope in barely able to discover differentiation of parts. The point that is conclusive to him is that such beings have crossed the line from the inorganic to the organic, from the inert to the living, and that with them is contained a possible growth, potential development. Likewise, for purposes of illustration, we may compare, though not identify, the growth of the living being toward a higher life. With the development of political institutions. In both there appear an increasing differentiation of parts, and growth in variety of their needs. As the higher forms are assumed, the organism becomes more definitely and delicately constructed; its activities become increasingly self-directive, until finally the self-conscious individual appears. At the same time that this elaboration of structure has proceeded, varying influences and conditions of life have caused individuals to differ from one another until the number of classes, genera, and species becomes almost beyond estimate.

The development of political society is characterized by these same features. With the advance of civilization come augmented social needs and activities. The governmental organization of the State becomes a more complex structure, and is endowed with wider, and, at the same time, more definite power, and the exercise of these powers becomes more intelligently controlled, and in a sense self-directed, that is, dictated rather by the interest of the governed than by the personal interest of the individuals in whom the exercise of the State's powers happens to be entrusted. Likewise, from substantial similarity of governmental organization, in the early stages, States, in the course of their development, assume diverging forms. Geographic, ethnic, economic, and moral conditions, all have their influence in determining the direction in which the development of political forms proceeds. Distinctions arise as to the number of interests to be regulated by the State, as to the extent to which the people generally shall participate, either activity or by way of popular control, in the administration of their public affairs, and as to the manner in which the powers of the State shall be distributed among its several departments. Thus arise all those varieties of governments running from the despotic Oriental State to the democracy of the Swiss communes. Later arise such forms as the Feudal State, and the so-called national State. Within each of these classes are also to be found the members distinguished from each other by the greatest variety of internal organizations. The manner and order in which these various forms have historically appeared, belong, however, rather to historical and descriptive Political Science, than to Political Philosophy.

There has been some speculation upon the part of political theorists as to the minimum number of individuals required in order to constitute a State. It would seem that no such minimum can be logically fixed. As our argument proceeds, it will appear that all of the essential juristic elements of the State are such as can be predicated as well as of a small as of a large body of individuals. Aristotle fixes a limit below which the number of citizens should not go, but this is based not so much upon logical grounds as upon the non-juristic principle that when a community is so small that there is not the possibility of a varied life the true ethical aim of the State cannot be attained. Austin denies the possibility of a State being constituted from a single family upon the ground of its absurdity, and quotes Montesquies as taking the same positions.[11] After admitting that a single family living in total estrangement from every other community might exhibits all the traits of an Independent political society, Austin, however, says: "But, since the number of its members is extremely minute, it would, I believe, be esteemed a society in a state of nature; that is, a society consisting of persons not in a state of subjection. Without an application of the terms, which would somewhat smack of the ridiculous, we could hardly style the society, a society *political* and independent, the imperative father and chief a *monarch* or *sovereign*, or the obedient mother and children *subjects*."[12] As to this Clark says:[13] "In this *dominion* so-called (ownership) of the original patriarch, *law* is *possible*. He *may*, that is, govern by *general rules*. It is not, however, *probable*, because he would have little interest in setting, or at least in adhering to, such rules. He would be more likely to govern by means of *occasional commands*." In other words, though it is entirely improbable that a single, isolated family should ever become *politically* organized, it is not logically impossible. It is not the size but the lack of that element of possible perpetuity of dominion that prevents the family from becoming, *as such*, a State.[14]

References

1. In the paragraphs which immediately follow, the author has drawn liberally from the first chapter of his *Political Theories of the Ancient World*, a work published in 1903.
2. *Ancient Society*, 1907.
3. *Studies in Ancient History*, 1874; second series 1896.
4. F. Hearn, *The Aryan Household*, p. 138. Speaking of the Roman gentes Hearn says: "There were many *familiae* of the Claudii and of the Cornelii, but there were Claudii and Cornelii before any of the *familiae* come into existence. On the other hand there were *gentes* such as the Mantii and the Marii who never seemed to have branched into any *familiae*." However, Fustel de Coulange (*Ancient City*, book II, chap. X, p. 3) says: "The Gens was not an association of families... it was a family itself. It might comprise only a single line, or produce several branches, it was always but one family."
5. Jenks, *History of Politics*, p. 19.
6. Cf. Bentham, *A Fragment on Government*, sec. XIII, note C.
7. *The Aryan Household*, p. 318. For an excellent popular discussion of the development of the modern State from its primitive form in Edward Jenks, *The State and the Nation*, published in 1919.
8. *Die Lehre von den Staatenverbindungen*, p. 157.
9. *Pol. Sci. Quar.*, vol. I, p. 9, "The American Commonwealth."
10. "The moment of the organisation of every society," says Pulsrky, "in which it presents itself as independent, dominant, and capable of asserting its own conditions of life *by force*, forms always a distinct phase in the process of association; and whenever any particular society assumes this form it appears as the State. The State is properly a law-creating and law-maintaining society which proclaims and asserts the conditions of its existence in connection with its own conduct and that of its subjects, through commanding, permissive, and prohibitory rules." *Theory of Law and Civil Society*, p. 216.
11. *Spirit of Laws*, book I, chap. III.
12. *Province of Jurisprudence Determined*, 2d ed. 1861, Lect. VI, p. 183.
13. *Practical Jurisprudence*, p. 147.
14. Italics in the original. For a comment upon the logical value of the argument based upon the ridiculous see Maine, *Early History of Institutions*, p. 379.

Index

C

D

E

F

W

ENCYCLOPAEDIA OF ADMINISTRATIVE LAW

ENCYCLOPAEDIA
OF
ADMINISTRATIVE LAW

Vol. 3

The British Administrative Law

Edited by

S.R. Sharma

ANMOL PUBLICATIONS PVT. LTD.
NEW DELHI - 110 002 (INDIA)

ANMOL PUBLICATIONS PVT. LTD.
4374/4B, Ansari Road, Daryaganj
New Delhi - 110 002
Ph.: 23261597, 23278000
Visit us at: www.anmolpublications.com

Encyclopaedia of Administrative Law

First Edition, 2003

ISBN 81-261-1478-9 (Set)

PRINTED IN INDIA

Published by J.L. Kumar for Anmol Publications Pvt. Ltd., New Delhi - 110 002 and Printed at Mehra Offset Press, Delhi.

CONTENTS

Preface

In the modern political era administrative law has taken on a preeminent role in regulating relations between the machinery of government and the individual citizen. At its core is the control of power specifically the review by the judiciary of the way in which executive power has been used. Consequently the subject embraces a huge range of issues, some of them highly politicized. In recent years these have included the legality of a ban on blood sports, whether the courts can order a minister to suspend the operation of a primary Act of Parliament, whether a minister can ban certain types of interview from being broadcast, the powers of local authorities to spend public money, or to refuse to do so, the scope of the discretion vested in the police officers to determine policing policy, the scope of the powers vested in the Home Secretary regarding parole for prisoners convicted of murder, whether the courts could declare invalid an exercise of prerogative power, and the availability of damages in respect of unlawful action by public bodies. It will be seen that it is largely the product of judicial activity, although its existence is increasingly recognised in statutory provisions.

The growth in administrative law has to a large extent mirrored the increase in the level of state involvement in many aspects of every day life during the twentieth century, generating the need for a coherent and effective body of rules to govern relations between individuals and the state. Students of constitutional law will readily recognise that administrative law is in reality an out growth of the doctrine of the separation of powers. It is evidence of the judiciary acting as a check on the powers of the executive, and perhaps even the legislature, in some respects. It should not be assumed, however, that any such coherent and effective body of rules actually exists yet. Administrative law is a constantly evolving subject.

In view of the above consideration in mind about the administrative law, that a comprehensive encyclopaedia has been prepared which focuses on the comparative dimensions of administrative law.

The editor is extremely grateful to the British Council Library in New Delhi, the American Information Centre, New Delhi, and the Central Secretariat Library, New Delhi for their valuable assistance in preparing the encyclopaedia. The editor is equally beholden to Shri J.L. Kumar, Managing Director, Anmol Publications Pvt. Ltd., New Delhi for publishing the encyclopaedia in a very short time.

—Dr. S.R. Sharma

1

THE REQUIREMENT OF LOCUS STANDI

THE TESTS APPLIED AT THE LEAVE AND AT THE SUBSTANTIVE STAGES ARE NOT THE SAME

R v Inland Revenue Commissioners ex p National Federation of Self-Employed and Small Businesses Ltd (1982) HL

In order to avoid tax, casual workers in the newspaper industry had been in the habit of giving false names when drawing their pay. The Inland Revenue Commissioners (IRC) decided to offer them an amnesty in respect of past tax avoidance in return for their co-operation in the future. The federation sought a declaration that the IRC's decision to grant the amnesty was unlawful, and mandamus to compel the IRC to assess and collect all arrears of tax. The IRC opposed the application on the ground, *inter alia,* that the federation did not have sufficient interest within the terms of RSC Ord 53 r 3(5). The rule provided that The court shall not grant leave unless it considers that the applicant has a sufficient interest in the matter to which the application relates'. Leave to apply for judicial review was refused on these grounds by the Divisional Court but granted by a majority in the Court of Appeal. The IRC appealed to the House of Lords.

Held, allowing the appeal, that the rule required the applicant to show a sufficient interest *in the matter to which the application relates.* In all but the simplest cases, it was therefore necessary first to determine the nature of the matter in question at the substantive hearing and only then to judge the sufficiency of the applicant's interest in it. Where a favourable view of the applicant's *locus standi* had been taken at the leave stage, it might still alter as a result of the substantive hearing. *Per* Lord Diplock:

My Lords, at the threshold stage, for the federation to make out a *prima facie* case of reasonable suspicion that the Board in showing a discriminatory leniency to a substantial class of taxpayers had done so for ulterior reasons extraneous to good management, and thereby deprived the national exchequer of considerable sums of money, constituted what was, in my view, reason enough for the Divisional Court to consider that the federation, or, for that matter, any taxpayer, had a sufficient interest to apply to have the question whether the Board were acting *ultra vires* reviewed by the court. The whole purpose of requiring that leave should first be obtained to make the application for judicial review would be defeated if the court were to go into the matter in any depth at that stage. If, on a quick perusal of the material then available, the court thinks that it discloses what might on further consideration turn nut to be an arguable case in favour of granting to the applicant the relief claimed, it ought, in the exercise of a judicial discretion, to give him leave to apply for that relief. The discretion which the court is exercising at this stage is not the same as that which it is called on to exercise when all the evidence is in and the matter has been fully argued at the hearing of the application.

The federation had no sufficient interest in the confidential affairs of another taxpayer (*per* Lord Wilberforce) and had failed to show any conduct that was *ultra vires* or unlawful (*per* Lord Diplock). Had it made out a case to the effect that the Inland Revenue had abused its managerial discretion, Lord Scarman would have held that it had shown a sufficient interest for the grant of leave to proceed further with its application.

Per Lord Wilberforce:

... the standing requirement may vary in strictness according to the remedy sought.

Q Do you agree that the words of r 3(5) discourage the treatment of sufficient interest as a preliminary point?

THE TEST FOR *LOCUS STANDI* MAY VARY ACCORDING TO THE REMEDY SOUGHT

R v Felixstowe Justices ex p Leigh (1987)

The applicant was a journalist who wanted to know the names of the individuals who had sat on the bench of a magistrates' court. He had not been involved in any capacity in the trial which he was seeking to report, nor had he been present at the proceedings. He sought a declaration that the justices had improperly decided that they should not disclose their names, and mandamus to compel them to disclose their names.

Held that magistrates should not seek to carry out their functions anonymously. In view of the seriousness of this matter, the applicant did have sufficient standing to obtain the declaration. However, he did not have sufficient standing to obtain mandamus to compel the magistrates on this bench to disclose their names.

RECENT DECISIONS ON *LOCUS STANDI*

R v Secretary of State for the Environment ex p Rose Theatre Trust Co (1990)

The remains of the Rose Theatre, which had seen the first performances of works by Shakespeare and Marlowe, were discovered during redevelopment works in the London Borough of Southwark. The applicant, whose members included distinguished archaeologists and actors, was formed in order to campaign for the protection of the remains. The applicant applied to the Secretary of State to protect the remains by scheduling them pursuant to powers granted to him by the Ancient Monuments and Archaeological Areas Act 1979. He refused. The applicant sought judicial review.

Held that the applicant did not have a sufficient interest to apply for judicial review. Where individuals did not have sufficient interest, they did not obtain it by incorporating themselves into an association. Although the Secretary of State had corresponded with the applicant, that could not and should not afford the applicant sufficient interest to challenge the decision.

R v Secretary of State for Social Services *ex* p Child Poverty Action Group (1990) CA

The applicant contended that the provisions of ss 98 and 99 of the Social Security Act 1975 had been wrongly interpreted by the respondent, and that in accordance claims for supplementary benefit had not been handled in accordance with the intentions of the legislature. In view of the importance of the issue, the respondent did not dispute the applicant's *locus standi* in the Divisional Court, although it reserved its right to argue the point in analogous cases in the future. Counsel for the respondent wished to adopt the same approach before the Court of Appeal.

Held that the applicant would be not be granted declaratory relief, and that the question of *locus standi* therefore did not arise. However, the respondent's reservation of its position on *locus standi* was inappropriate. *Locus standi* went to the jurisdiction of the court. The parties might not by agreement confer on the court a jurisdiction which it did not otherwise have.

Q What other reasons, besides the importance of the case, may discourage a respondent from contesting an application on *locus standi*?

R v Secretary of State for Foreign and Commonwealth Affairs ex p Rees-Mogg (1994)

The applicant sought a declaration that the UK could not lawfully ratify the Treaty of European Union signed at Maastricht on 7 February 1992.

Held that the application for judicial review, assuming it to relate to a justiciable issue, would be dismissed on the merits. There was no dispute as to the applicant's *locus standi,* and therefore it was not appropriate to say anything more about it. The court did, however, accept 'without question that Lord Rees-Mogg brings the proceedings because of his sincere concern for constitutional issues'.

Q What are the consequences (if any) of this decision: (a) for the law relating to *locus standi*; and (b) for the principle that all are equal under the law?

R v HM Inspectorate of Pollution ex p Greenpeace (1994)

British Nuclear Fuels plc proposed to test its new thermal oxide reprocessing plant (THORP) in Cumbria before it became fully operational. To this end, a variation of existing authorisations was obtained from the respondent. The applicant, an environmental protection organisation of international standing, was concerned about levels of radioactive emission from THORP. It sought an order of certiorari to quash the respondent's decision to vary the authorisations, and an injunction to stay the implementation of the authorisations and to prevent the testing. The respondent denied that the applicant had a sufficient interest in the matter.

Held, dismissing the substantive application, that the decision to vary the authorisations had been properly made. The applicant did have a sufficient interest. In deciding on *locus standi*, a court was to take into account the nature of the applicant, the extent of its interest in the issues raised, the remedy sought to be obtained, and the nature of the relief sought to be achieved. Here, the applicant was an entirely responsible and respected body with a genuine concern for the environment. It had 2,500 members in the Cumbria region. If the applicant were denied *locus standi*, those it represented might not have an effective way to bring issues of concern to them before the court. *Per* Otton J:

Consequently, a less well informed challenge might be mounted which would stretch unnecessarily the court's resources and which would not afford the court the assistance it requires to do justice between the parties. Further, if the unsuccessful applicant had the benefit of legal aid, it might leave the respondent and BNFL without an effective remedy in costs.

The applicant was enabled by its expertise to mount a carefully selected, focused, relevant and well argued challenge. The applicant was seeking certiorari, not mandamus: less stringent *locus standi* principles applied to the former remedy. The applicant had been treated as one of the consultees during the consultation process. However:

> ... it must not be assumed that Greenpeace (or any other interest group) will automatically be afforded

standing in any subsequent application for judicial review ... This will have to be considered on a case by case basis at the leave stage and if the threshold is crossed again at the substantive hearing as a matter of discretion.

R V Secretary of State for Foreign Affairs ex p World Development Movement Ltd (1995)

The applicant sought judicial review of the Secretary of State's decision to make a grant to Malaysia under s 1(1) of the Overseas Development and Co-operation Act 1980. The grant was to be used for the funding of the Pergau Dam project. Section 1(1) confined the use of the power to the promoting of development. The applicant submitted that only sound development projects could lawfully be funded. The Secretary of State had received advice that the Pergau Dam project was not economically sound, had been motivated for purposes not permitted by the Act, and had taken into account irrelevant considerations in making his decision.

Held that the funding was not directed towards the promotion of development, and that it was therefore *ultra vires* the Act. On the issue of the applicant's *locus standi,* the court considered that there was nothing in *Ex p National Federation of Self-Employed* to deny standing. Further, an increasingly liberal approach to standing had been taken during the 12 years since that decision. The merits of the application were an important, if not a dominant factor when considering standing. Here, the issue raised was of importance, the rule of law required to be vindicated, there was unlikely to be any other responsible challenger, and the court further took into account the nature of the breach of duty alleged against the Secretary of State, and the prominence of the applicants in their field. If the court had been able to accept in *Ex p Rees-Mogg* that the applicant there had standing in the light of his sincere concerns for constitutional issues', then *a fortiori* the present applicant had the expertise and interest to be granted standing.

Q Did the court in *Ex p Rees-Mogg* accept that the applicant had standing *in the light of his* sincere concerns for constitutional issues? Must it now be taken to have done so?

R v Somerset County Council ex p Dixon (1997)

The applicant sought leave to challenge the county council's decision to permit the expansion of limestone quarrying. He was resident in the area affected, a parish councillor, and a member of more than one body concerned with the environment. It was argued against him that he had no personal right or interest which was threatened by the proposed quarrying activities.

Held that he had sufficient *locus standi* for leave to be granted, though it was in fact refused on other grounds. Sedley J rejected the argument that the applicant's interest needed to be superior to that of the general public, expressly disapproving *Rose Theatre Trust Co* (above) on this point. At the leave stage, the test for *locus standi* was designed only to prevent abuse of the court by busybodies and troublemakers. To attempt to raise the threshold above that level was misconceived. At the substantive stage, the question of the applicant's standing was one factor to be weighed with others in the decision whether or not to grant a remedy. The real question was whether the applicant could argue that some substantial default or abuse had been committed by the respondent, and not whether his personal rights or interests were involved. Sedley J added that doctrinal distinctions between standing for the different remedies had been supplanted by the practical question of the application's substantive merit.

2

THE NATURE OF JUDICIAL REVIEW

THE JURISDICTION

Judicial review is essentially a procedure whereby the courts are able to determine the lawfulness of the exercise of executive power. It is concerned with the legality of the decision-making process as opposed to the merits of the actual decision. The courts have traditionally rejected suggestions, at least since 1688, that they may review the lawfulness of an Act of Parliament. The same cannot be said of delegated legislation. It is beyond doubt that such legislation is subject to the supervisory jurisdiction of the courts. In this sense, therefore, judicial review entails the courts upholding the principle of the legislative supremacy of Parliament where the power to make legislation does not derive from the prerogative.

Parliament confers a power on a minister or a public body to make delegated legislation by inserting an appropriately worded section or subsection into an Act, the enabling or parent Act. Thus, for example, a minister may be given the power to make such regulations as he thinks fit in order to give effect to the purposes of the Act. If he chooses to exercise that power, he must ensure that he does not exceed its scope. In other words, he must ensure that he acts intra vires. Where, however, it is argued that he has acted beyond his powers (ultra vires), the courts may intervene following an application for judicial review and grant one of the remedies if they find that he has indeed acted ultra vires. Judicial review is therefore an important mechanism for ensuring that power is not abused. It may be argued, as Professor Jowell has done, that it amounts to the practical application of the Rule of Law (para 3.28).

In order for the judiciary to carry out this important task, it is essential that they are separate from and independent of the executive. Judges who could be appointed and dismissed at the whim of politicians may, in the words of Lord Atkin in *Liversidge v Anderson* (1942), become 'more executive minded than the executive'. If this were to happen, an application for judicial review would have little chance of success and the procedure would be an ineffective bulwark against the abuse of power. Thus the effective operation of the judicial review jurisdiction is dependent upon there being a degree of separation of powers within the UK constitution.

An unfettered discretion?

The power conferred upon a minister to make delegated legislation may be extremely wide. Similarly, it may appear that he has wide and unfettered discretion as to related matters, such as who to consult prior to exercising his law-making power. Where a statutory discretion is very wide, it may take on the appearance of being without limits. However, unlimited discretionary power has the potential to be abused and accordingly when it has been claimed to exist, the courts have shown themselves willing to identify certain limits within which it must be exercised.

Podfield v Minister of Agriculture, Fisheries and Food (1968). The Agricultural Marketing Act 1958 regulated the marketing of various agricultural products, such as milk. By virtue of s 19(3)(b), a committee of investigation could consider and report to the minister as to the operation of any scheme in respect of which he had received a complaint, if he so directed. A dairy farmers' association complained to the minister about the operation of a price fixing scheme operated by the Milk Marketing Board. The minister refused to refer the complaint to a committee of investigation and the farmers accordingly sought an order of mandamus to compel him to do so. HL held: that the order would be granted. Parliament must have conferred the discretion with the intention that it should be used to promote the policy and objects of the Act. These were to be determined by the court by construing the Act as a whole. The minister had misdirected himself in law as to the intention of the Act which imposed a duty upon him to have complaints investigated where they were substantial, genuine and indicated that the board had acted contrary to the public interest.

Padfield thus demonstrates that in identifying the scope of delegated powers, the courts are required to construe the relevant statute so as to identify Parliament's intention. Where the words in the statute are vague or ambiguous, it is now possible for the courts to use Hansard, the official report of Parliament's proceedings, as an aid to interpretation following the decision of the HL in *Pepper* v *Hart* (1993). The use of Hansard is limited, however, to ministerial statements or those of the promoter of the Bill.

The postscript to the decision in *Padfield* also illustrates an important practical feature of judicial review proceedings: a successful challenge may not result in the desired outcome. The effect of the HL decision was that the minister had to refer the dairy farmers' complaint to a committee of investigation. He did this but subsequently declined to follow the advice which they gave him, as he was entitled to do. Having thus acted lawfully, his decision could not be the subject of further judicial review proceedings.

Review not *appeal*

It is clear from the foregoing that the judicial review jurisdiction operates within distinct limits. It is a supervisory rather than an appellate jurisdiction. Accordingly, the role of the court is to supervise the exercise of discretionary power in order to ensure that it has been exercised lawfully. In *R v Secretary of State for the Environment, ex p Hammersmith & Fulham London Borough Council* (1991), Lord Donaldson MR likened the role of the judge in judicial review proceedings to that of a referee in a football match. He remarked that:

> 'In football ... the moves made by the players and the tactics employed by the teams are matters entirely for them. The referee is only involved when it appears

> that some player has acted in breach of the rules. The referee may then stop the play and take some remedial action, but, tempting though it may be, it is not for him to express any view on the skill of the players or, how he would have acted in their position. Still less, following a breach of the rules does he take over one of the positions of the players. So too with the judiciary...'

A court must not consider the merits of the particular decision, whether it was right or wrong, when hearing a judicial review application. To substitute its own view for that of the decision-maker would, in the words of Lord Ackner in *R v Secretary of State for the Home Department*, ex *p Brind* (1991), amount to 'a wrongful usurpation of power by the judiciary'. Nevertheless, we shall see when we come to consider the grounds for review in the next chapter that there may be a case for arguing that some of these actually blur the distinction between the legality and the merits of a decision.

It is by no means uncommon for a statute to create an appeal system for dealing with disputes relating to decisions made under the Act. A right of appeal is conferred upon specified categories of persons, and the appeal itself may be heard by a variety of different bodies which include courts, tribunals, inquiries, ministers or inspectors. Where such an appeals system exists, it is likely that the courts will require this remedy to be exhausted before allowing a judicial review application to proceed. This was described as a 'cardinal principle' by Purchase LJ in *R v Epping and Harlow General Comrs*, ex *p Goldstraw* (1983). Nevertheless, in exceptional circumstances, a court may allow an application for judicial review to proceed even where an alternative remedy is available. In exercising this discretion, a court may take into account a number of factors as described in *Ex p Waldron* (1986). These may include: the extent to which the alternative statutory remedy can deal with the matter fully, the comparative speed with which the alternative remedies can determine the matter; and, the extent to which the matter requires the specialist knowledge or expertise possessed by the appellate body in order to be determined.

Procedural reform

Prior to the reforms made to the Rules of the Supreme Court (RSC) Order 53 in 1977, an applicant seeking one of the prerogative orders was, to use the words of Lord Diplock in *O'Reilly Mackman* (1983), at a 'considerable procedural disadvantage' as compared with the tribunal or body whose decision the applicant was seeking to challenge. The key disadvantages in the pre-1977 procedure were that:

- no provision was made for discovery;
- evidence was required to be on affidavit, but there was no express provision for cross-examination of deponents;
- a claim for damages for breach of a private law right arising out of a public law decision could not be included in an Order 53 application - damages could only be claimed in a separate action begun by writ; and
- declarations or injunctions were not available in proceedings under Order 53 - they could only be obtained in actions begun by writ or originating summons.

The reforms which were made to Order 53 in 1977 in large part addressed these issues. As a quid pro quo, however, the time limit for challenging a decision was reduced from six to three months. Although a single procedure known as an application for judicial review had been created whereby an applicant could seek to obtain every type of remedy for the protection of his rights in public law, Order 53 did not expressly provide that it was an exclusive procedure. Neither did s 3 1 of the Superme Court Act 1981 (SCA 1981). Thus it became necessary for the courts to consider whether an applicant seeking a declaration or an injunction was still entitled to do so by way of writ or originating summons, or whether he must now apply for judicial review.

The rule in *O'Reilly v Mackman*

The landmark decision on the question of the correct procedure to follow was handed down by the HL several years after the procedural reforms took effect.

O'Reilly v Mackman (1983). Four prisoners took part in riots at Hull prison. Each was charged with an offence against prison discipline contrary to the Prison Rules 1964. An inquiry into each case was held by the board of prison visitors. The board upheld the charges in each case and imposed various penalties, including loss of remission. All four prisoners commenced actions against the board, either by writ or originating summons, seeking declarations that the board's finding and penalties were null and void due its failure to observe the principles of natural justice. The board sought to have the proceedings struck out as an abuse of the process of the court. It claimed that the prisoners ought to have proceeded by way of judicial review under RSC Order 53. Peter Pain J took the view that the law offered the prisoners a choice and that they had not therefore abused the process of the court by opting for ordinary actions rather than judicial review. The board's appeal to the CA was upheld. HL held: dismissing the prisoners' appeal against the CA's decision, that now that the disadvantages to applicants under the old procedure had been removed by the reforms of 1977, it would as a general rule be contrary to public policy, and an abuse of the process of the court, to allow an applicant to seek to enforce public law rights by way of ordinary action rather than by way of judicial review.

The general rule established by the HL in *O'Reilly v Mackman* is, therefore, that public law decisions ought to be challenged by way of an application for judicial review, whereas private law matters are to be dealt with by ordinary action. In other words, despite the silence of Order 53 and s 31 of the SCA 1981 on this matter, the effect of the HL ruling in *O'Reilly* is that procedural exclusivity is a by-product of the 1977 reforms. In the years that have followed, therefore, it has been necessary for the courts to attempt to make a distinction between public law and private law matters. Moreover, given that Lord Diplock stressed in *O'Reilly* that the effect of the HL decision was to establish a 'general rule' to which 'there may be exceptions', arguments have subsequently been advanced that a particular situation does indeed amount to an exception to the general rule.

Cocks *v Thanet District Council* (1983). C instituted proceedings against TDC in the county court. He claimed that both he and his family were homeless and in priority need, and that the council were therefore under a duty to provide either temporary or permanent accommodation under the Housing (Homeless Persons) Act 1977. The issue on appeal was whether the proceedings were properly brought by action, or whether they could only be brought by application for judicial review. HL held: that housing authorities functions under the 1977 Act were essentially public law functions. Whether or not they had a duty to house a person under the Act was a matter for them to decide following appropriate inquiries. If they did reach a decision that they were under a duty to house a person, that decision gave rise to rights and obligations in private law. In the present case, the housing authority had not decided the public law question in favour of C. He therefore did not have any private law rights to enforce. In the light of the principles expounded in *O'Reilly v Mackman* (1983), it would be an abuse of the process of the court to allow C to seek relief in respect of his claim otherwise than by an application for judicial review.

Roy v Kensington and Chelsea and Westminster Family Practitioner Committee (1992). Dr R was a GP carrying out work for the NHS. The remuneration for his services was provided for under regulations. These provided that a GP was not eligible for the full rate of the basic practice allowance unless the FPC considered that he was devoting a substantial amount of time to his NHS work. The FPC took the view that Dr R was not and therefore reduced his practice allowance by 20%. Dr R brought an action against the FPC claiming, amongst other things, that the committee was in breach of contract. The FPC applied to strike out his claim as an abuse of process. It claimed that he ought to have challenged their decision by way of an application for judicial review. Before the QBD, Dr R's claim was struck out. On appeal, the CA allowed the claim to stand. The FPC appealed. HL held: that an issue which was concerned exclusively with a public right should be determined in judicial review proceedings.

However, where a litigant was asserting a private law right, which incidentally involved the examination of a public law issue (the FPC's decision), he was not debarred from seeking to establish that right by ordinary action. Dr R had a bundle of private law rights, including the right to be paid for work done, which entitled him to sue for their alleged breach. It was not an abuse of the process of the court to proceed as Dr R had done.

Mercury Communications Ltd v Director General of Telecommunications (1996). In 1984, two companies, BT and M, were granted licences to operate telecommunications systems under the Telecommunications Act 1984. In 1986, they entered into an agreement for the provision of services pursuant to a condition in BT's licence. A clause in that agreement provided for the review of the agreement after five years if either party believed that a fundamental change in circumstances had occurred. Disagreements as to terms were to be referred to the Director General (DG) for determination. An issue was referred to the DG and he made a determination. M challenged that determination and issued an originating summons. The DG and BT claimed that this was an abuse of process because the DG's determination was a public law matter which could only be challenged by judicial review. Longmore J dismissed their summonses. The CA upheld their appeal. M appealed. HL held: in deciding whether an action was property brought by way of private law or public law, the key question was whether the proceedings constituted an abuse of the process of the court. On the facts, the dispute related to the terms of the contract between the two parties, even though the office of DG was created by statute and the DG did have public law duties The originating summons procedure was at least as well suited and possibly better suited to the determination of the issues. M's proceedings had not been an abuse of process.

The decisions in these three appeals demonstrate different aspects of the rule in *O'Reilly v Mackman*. Whereas *Cocks* is a good illustration of the application of that rule where the sole issue was a public law matter, *Roy* is an example of an exception to the general rule where both private law and public law matters were involved. Although the HL stopped short of describing the relationship between Dr Roy and the FPC as a contract (as the CA had done), they nevertheless felt that he did have private law rights against the committee which were capable of being enforced by ordinary action. Moreover, attention was drawn to the fact that the remedy which Dr Roy wanted, an order for the full payment of the practice allowance, could not be obtained directly in judicial review proceedings. Even if his application were successful, he would have had to institute further proceedings to obtain the money.

In giving judgment in *Roy*, Lord Lowry referred to an argument which had been put to their Lordships by counsel for Dr Roy. This considered that two approaches could be taken to the rule in *O'Reilly v Mackman*. A 'broad approach' would mean that the rule:

> '... did not apply generally against bringing actions to vindicate private rights in all circumstances in which those actions involved a challenge to a public law act or decision, but that it merely required the aggrieved person to proceed by judicial review only when private rights were not at stake.'

Conversely, the 'narrow approach' assumed:

> 'that the rule applied generally to *all* proceedings in which public law acts or decisions were challenged, subject to some exceptions when private law rights were involved.'

Although Lord Lowry expressed a preference for the 'broad approach', because it was 'traditionally orthodox' and would 'have the practical merit of getting rid of a procedural minefield', the case was actually decided in Dr Roy's favour on the basis of the 'narrow approach'. The broad approach would have the effect of limiting the rule in *O'Reilly* in that it would only require an individual to proceed by way of judicial review if there were no private law rights in issue. Where there were private law rights in issue, an action could be commenced even if public law matters were also involved. The narrow approach would actually widen the scope of the rule since it would require any case which involved public law matters to proceed by way of an application for judicial review, even though private law rights may also be at issue.

The decision in *Mercury Communications* illustrates the HL taking a relaxed approach to the rule in *O'Reilly* and recognising that there needs to be some measure of procedural flexibility. Rather than compartmentalising cases as either public law or private law matters which, in any event, is a difficult distinction to draw (see below), the HL placed greater emphasis on the need to avoid an abuse of the process. Thus as Professor Craig has noted, whereas *O'Reilly* assumes that to proceed by a means other than judicial review would be an abuse of process, *Mercury Communications* allows for flexibility in the choice of proceedings provided that they do not amount to an abuse of process.

The public law/private law distinction

Distinguishing between public law and private law matters has an increased importance given that the practical effect of *O'Reilly v Mackman* is procedural exclusivity. However, working out this distinction is by no means an easy matter.

Traditionally, the starting point has been to ascertain whether the decision-maker is a public or private body since judicial review only operates in respect of the decisions of public bodies. A public body will, generally speaking, derive its power from statute, delegated legislation made under statute, or from a non-statutory source such as the prerogative. Thus local councils are clearly public bodies in that they are established under statute and many of the powers which they exercise are conferred on them by statute. Private bodies, however, derive their power or authority not from statute, but from the agreement of those who are subject to their jurisdiction.

R v Disciplinary Committee of the Jockey Club, ex p Aga Khan (1993). The Aga Khan owned a racehorse which won the 1989 Oaks, a classic race for fillies, at Epsom racecourse. The horse was subsequently disqualified after traces of a banned substance were found in a urine sample. The Aga Khan sought to challenge the decision of the committee by way of an application for judicial review. The QBD held on a preliminary issue that the committee's decision was not susceptible to judicial review. The Aga Khan appealed. CA held: despite the fact that the Jockey Club regulated a significant national activity and had wide powers to do so, it was not in its origin, history, constitution or membership a public body. It was barely mentioned in statute and it had not been woven into a system of governmental control. The powers which it had over those who agreed to be bound by the Rules of Racing derived from the agreement of the parties. It was therefore a private body and as such was not susceptible to judicial review.

As is often the case, it is a relatively straightforward task to identify that which occupies either end of the spectrum. Bodies which are patently public at one end, and those which are equally patently private at the other eg companies. Difficulties arise, however, the nearer we get to the middle of the spectrum. Whilst the source of a body's power will often provide the answer to the question 'Is it a public body?' this is by no means always the case.

R v Panel on Take-overs and Mergers, ex p Datafin plc (1987). The panel was a body established by the City of London to regulate takeovers and mergers. Its powers were derived from neither statute nor the common law, although it did operate within a statutory framework. D sought judicial review of the panel's decision to reject a complaint which it had made. Hodgson J refused D leave to apply on the ground that the court had no jurisdiction to hear the application. D appealed. CA held: in deciding whether or not a body is subject to judicial review, although the source of its power would normally decide the issue, it was not the sole test. A court was also entitled to look at the nature of the power which the body exercised. Having regard to the wide ranging powers of the panel and the importance of the task that it performed, it was a body which was susceptible to judicial review. However, application for leave was refused on the facts because none of the grounds for review were present.

The decision in *Datafin* is significant in that it recognises that a body may rightly be described as a 'public body' because of the nature of the functions which it performs. It is also significant because the CA accepted the argument that had the City not established the panel for its own regulation, the government would have been likely to set up a public body to perform the same function. In *R v Chief Rabbi of the United Hebrew Congregation* of *GB and the Commonwealth, ex p Wachmann* (1993), Simon Brown J rejected the submission that in the exercise of his disciplinary functions, the Chief Rabbi was subject to judicial review. In so doing, he observed that:

> To say of decisions of a given body that they are public law decisions with public law consequences means something more than that they are decisions which may be of great interest or concern to the public or, indeed, which may have consequences for the public. To attract the court's supervisory jurisdiction there must be not merely a public but potentially a governmental interest in the decision-making power in question ... where non-governmental bodies have hitherto been held to be reviewable, they have generally been operating as an integral part of a regulatory system which, although itself non-statutory, is nevertheless supported by statutory powers and penalties clearly indicative of government concern...it is a feature of all these cases that, were there no self-regulatory body in existence, Parliament would almost inevitably intervene to control the activity in question'.

In a number of subsequent cases, counsel have argued this latter point. It has to be noted, however, that even where they have succeeded, it has not necessarily affected the decision. Thus in *ex p Aga Khan*, although Sir Thomas Bingham MR was 'willing to accept that if the Jockey Club did not regulate this activity the government would probably be driven to create a public body to do so', as we have seen, the application for leave was defeated on the ground that the Jockey Club was a private body. Moreover, in *R v Football Association Ltd, ex p Football League* (1993), Rose LJ responded to the argument that if the FA did not run football, the government would create a public body to do so with the observation that:

> 'On the contrary, the evidence of commercial interest in the professional game is such as to suggest that a far more likely intervener to run football would be a

> television or similar company rooted in the entertainment business or a commercial company....'

Collateral challenge

The decision in *O'Reilly v Mackman* has thus placed great emphasis upon the distinction between public law and private law matters. Moreover, *O'Reilly* has raised a further issue: whether the existence of the rule prevents a person from challenging the validity of a public law decision in proceedings brought against them. In short, can a public law matter be used as a shield not a sword, or does the rule require that in those circumstances, an application for judicial review should be brought?

This issue clearly gives rise to important practical considerations and to wider considerations of justice and fairness. Is it right that an individual should be denied a defence in proceedings brought against them merely because they ought to have instituted proceedings themselves? Should a person be convicted under a law that would have been held to be invalid had it been challenged in judicial review proceedings? The unfairness may be greater in the event of a criminal prosecution, but the injustice would still exist in civil proceedings.

Wandsworth London Borough Council v Winder (1984). The local authority pursuant to its powers under the Housing Act 1957 resolved to increase rents generally. W, a council tenant, refused to pay the increased element of the rent. The local authority sued him in the county court for rent arrears and possession of the property. As a defence to those proceedings, W claimed that the resolutions and notices of increase were ultra vires. The local authority sought to strike out the defence as an abuse of the process of the court. It claimed that W ought to have proceeded by way of judicial review. HL held: that the reforms made to RSC Order 53 were procedural in nature. They did not prevent W from challenging the validity of the authority's decision as a defence in proceedings brought against him by the authority. W had not abused the process of the court.

The decision in *Winder* thus demonstrates that a defence alleging the invalidity of a public law decision may still be raised in civil law proceedings, despite *O'Reilly v Mackman*. Is the same true where the proceedings involve the alleged commission of a criminal offence?

R v Crown Court at Reading, ex p Hutchinson (1988). The defendants were protesters at the Greenham Common Air Base. They were convicted by magistrates of an offence contrary to the Royal Air Force Greenham Common Byelaws 1985. This prohibited entering, passing or remaining in or over the protected area without permission. They appealed against their conviction on the basis that the byelaws were invalid. The Crown Court felt that it was unable to rule on this question. The defendants therefore sought an order of mandamus to compel them to do so. QBD held: where a defendant wishes to challenge the validity of a byelaw as a defence to summary proceedings brought against them, a magistrates' court or a Crown Court (on appeal) could hear such a defence. Neither s 31 of the SCA nor RSC Order 53 had removed the jurisdiction to do so. It was neither necessary nor appropriate for summary proceedings to be adjourned so that the validity of a byelaw could be determined by the HCt in judicial review proceedings.

Bugg v DPP (1993). The defendants were convicted by magistrates of entering a protected area contrary to byelaws made under the Military Lands Act 1892. An appeal to the Crown Court was dismissed. They appealed to the DC contending, amongst other things, that the byelaws were invalid because the protected area to which they related had not been sufficiently identified. DC held: that byelaws could be either substantively invalid ie beyond the power under which they were made or patently unreasonable, or procedurally invalid i.e. a procedural requirement in their making had not been complied with eg a failure to consult.

The principle which therefore emerges from these two decisions is that where D is being prosecuted for the breach of a byelaw, it is permissible to question the validity of that byelaw as a defence. In *Bugg* the DC sought to qualify the application of this general principle by making a distinction between substantive invalidity and procedural invalidity. The significance of the distinction lay in the fact that in criminal proceedings for contravention of the byelaw, the court had the jurisdiction to determine the issue of substantive invalidity but did not have the jurisdiction to determine whether or not the byelaw was procedurally invalid.

Several reasons were advanced in support of this distinction. It was noted, for example, that to argue that a byelaw was substantively invalid did not require evidence: it could be determined by reference to the byelaw and the authority under which it was made. To argue, however, that a byelaw was procedurally invalid did require evidence which would not be available in criminal proceedings because the maker of the byelaw would not be party to those proceedings. Moreover, allowing argument relating to procedural invalidity to be advanced during criminal proceedings was seen as a way of circumventing the safeguards in the judicial review procedure eg the time limit, which are designed to protect public authorities from inappropriate applications.

The distinction between substantive and procedural invalidity was subsequently doubted by the HL in *R v Wicks* (1998), a case concerned with D's non-compliance with an enforcement notice issued is under the town and country planning legislation. However, in a later decision of the same court, *Bugg v DPP* was overruled.

Boddington v British Transport Police (1999). B was convicted by a stipendiary magistrate of the offence of smoking in a railway carriage contrary to a byelaw made under the Transport Act 1962, as amended. That conferred, inter alia, a power to make byelaws '(c) with respect to the smoking of tobacco in railway carriages and elsewhere and that prevention of nuisances'. B appealed against his conviction. HL held that D may raise as a defence to a criminal charge the contention that a byelaw or an administrative decision made pursuant to powers conferred by it is ultra vires. The observations in *Bugg* were contrary to authority and principle. It was inappropriate to distinguish between substantive and procedural invalidity. The byelaw in the present case was valid since it fell within the scope of the authority under which it had been made.

In giving judgment in *Boddington,* Lord Steyn observed that a practical consequence of the decision in *Bugg* was that a defendant may be convicted under a byelaw which was in fact invalid. In his opinion, this was 'an unacceptable consequence in a democracy based on the rule of law'. Whilst Lord Steyn recognised that *Bugg* allowed for the possibility of challenge by way of judicial review, he felt that there were a number of factors which limited the effectiveness of such a challenge:

> The defendant may, however, be out of time before he becomes aware of the existence of the byelaw. He may lack the resources to defend his interest in two courts. He may not be able to obtain legal aid for an application for leave to apply for judicial review. Leave to apply for judicial review may be refused. At a substantive hearing the scope for demanding examination of witnesses in the Divisional Court may be restricted. He may be denied a remedy on a discretionary basis. The possibility of judicial review will, therefore, in no way compensate him for the loss of the right to defend himself by a defensive challenge to the byelaw in cases where the invalidity of the byelaw might afford him with a defence to the charge.'

Exclusion of Judicial review

Given the importance of the court's supervisory jurisdiction over the exercise of executive power, it is not surprising that Parliament has attempted on occasion to prevent that jurisdiction from being exercised. The mechanism for doing this has been to insert a provision to that effect in the relevant Act. Such provisions may take one of a variety of different forms.

Ouster clauses

Ouster clauses may take one of several forms. Finality clauses, as their name implies, attempt to render the decision of the relevant body or tribunal final and hence beyond the control of the QBD. Other examples of ouster clauses include 'no certiorari clauses' and 'shall not be questioned' clauses. The fact that a number of different alternatives have been used in statutes is symptomatic of the reluctance of the judiciary to accept restrictions on their ability to intervene. Nowhere was this more apparent than in the leading case of *Anisminic*.

Anisminic v Foreign Compensation Commission (1969). A were the owners of property in Egypt which was sequestrated by the Egyptian government in 1956 and subsequently sold to an Egyptian organisation. Under a Treaty between the United Arab Republic and the UK, compensation was paid for property which had been confiscated. This was to be distributed by the FCC which had been established under the Foreign Compensation Act 1950. A sought to challenge the FCC's decision that it was not entitled to compensation by applying for a declaration. However, s 4(4) of the 1950 Act provided that any determination by the FCC 'shall not be called into question in any court of law'. The case therefore turned on the effect of this provision HL held: that it was a well-established principle that statutory provisions seeking to oust the ordinary jurisdiction of the court should be interpreted restrictively. Where they were reasonably capable of bearing two meanings, the meaning which preserved the jurisdiction of the court would be preferred. Section 4(4) only protected those determinations of the FCC that were not a nullity. The decision in respect of A was not a determination because the FCC had acted outside its jurisdiction. Thus it was not protected from challenge in the courts.

Section 4(4) of the Foreign Compensation Act 1950 amounted to a complete ouster clause and yet the HL interpreted it in such a way as to preserve the court's supervisory jurisdiction. It was able to do this by asserting that this is what Parliament must have intended in enacting the provision. Nevertheless, it might be argued that in the case of complete ouster clauses, their effect is determined not by the words used but by judicial attitudes towards them. This gives rise to an inherent constitutional danger. A court which seeks to interpret ouster clauses in such a way as to preserve its jurisdiction runs the risk of acting contrary to the will of Parliament. Unchallengeable decision-making powers have the potential to be abused and therefore the courts are reluctant to stand back from them. However, where this may lead to a conflict with Parliament, the courts must tread carefully, ever mindful of the constitutional limits of the judicial role.

Time limit clauses

Unlike complete ouster clauses, time limit clauses do not seek to preclude legal challenge per se. Instead, they are partial ouster clauses in that they provide for the possibility of legal challenge within a prescribed time limit. In the planning legislation, the most commonly prescribed time limit is six weeks from the date of the relevant decision. Time limit clauses are therefore less iniquitous than complete ouster clauses. This helps to explain why they have been treated more favourably by the courts.

Smith v East Elloe RDC (1956). Under the Acquisition of Land (Authorisation Procedure) Act 1946, an aggrieved person had the right to challenge the validity of a compulsory purchase order within six weeks of the date of the confirmation or making of the order. Subject to this right, a compulsory purchase order was not to be challenged in any legal proceedings whatsoever. Property owned by S was the subject of such an order. Its validity was challenged six years after it had been made. HL held: by a majority, that the validity of the compulsory purchase order could not be impugned. It was the duty of the court to give the words of the statute their proper meaning.

The decision in *Smith* illustrates the HL approaching the task of statutory interpretation as we would expect: giving effect to the plain meaning of the words used by Parliament. It should be noted, however, that *Smith* predates *Anisminic*. Thus, it later became necessary to consider whether *Smith* remained a binding authority.

R v Secretary of State for the Environment, ex p Ostler (1977). Under the Highways Act 1959, a person aggrieved by the making of a compulsory purchase order could challenge its validity, within six weeks of the date on which notice of its publication had been given, by applying to the HCt. Subject to this, the order was not to be questioned in any legal proceedings whatsoever. O sought to challenge an order when he became aware that an objection to a relief road had been withdrawn as a consequence of a secret assurance which would have had a detrimental impact on his own business. His challenge took place some months after the expiry of the six weeks CA held: his complaint could not be considered because he had not commenced proceedings within the time limit.

The decision in *Ostler* thus confirms that Smith remains a binding authority despite *Anisminic*. Lord Denning MR sought to distinguish *Smith* and *Anisminic* on a number of grounds. One such ground related to the now defunct distinction between judicial and administrative decisions (see *Ridge v Baldwin* (1964), paras 12.36-12.37). Of the remaining grounds, the most compelling appears to relate to public policy. In short, the six-week time limit is adhered to for reasons of certainty. It enables the authority to act upon the relevant decision, in the case of a compulsory purchase order by acquiring the relevant property and demolishing it etc, without fear of the order being challenged at some later and doubtless inconvenient date.

The procedure for judicial review

The procedure for making an application for judicial review essentially involves two stages: a leave stage which, if successful, is followed by a hearing of the substantive issues raised by the case.

Leave stage

A person wishing to challenge a public law decision must first seek and obtain the leave of the HCt to apply for judicial review: s 31 (3) of the SCA 1981. The mechanics of seeking leave are laid down in rule 3 of RSC Order 53.

An application for leave is made before a judge ex parte ie in the absence of the respondent. It is made on Form 86A which is filed with the Crown Office. The form contains a statement of a number of particulars, which include the name and description of the applicant, the grounds for the application and the relief sought. It is accompanied by an affidavit verifying the facts relied on. The application itself may be determined with or without a hearing, and may take place either in the judge's chambers or in open court. Where an application is refused by a judge, the applicant may renew it by applying to a single judge sitting in open court or to a DC of the QBD. This must be done within 10 days of receiving the judge's notice of refusal.

In deciding whether or not to grant leave, a judge has a considerable measure of discretion. The rationale for the leave stage is that it is a means by which unmeritorious claims can be filtered out in order to prevent them wasting the time of the court. An unmeritorious claim may be one in which there is clearly no public law element, or where the time limit for making an application has expired and there is no good reason for extending it (see below). Alternatively, it may be where the applicant does not have a sufficient interest in the matter complained of (see below). If the judge has formed this latter opinion, he must not grant leave.

Where leave has been granted, this does not act as a bar to reopening leave stage matters at a substantive hearing. Thus, for example, a respondent may question whether the applicant has a sufficient interest in the matter at a substantive hearing even though this was decided in the applicant's favour at the leave stage. Since the respondent was not present at that stage, the substantive hearing provides the first real opportunity to raise such an argument.

Furthermore, where leave has been granted, it does not necessarily follow that the case will proceed to a substantive hearing. Post-leave withdrawals may occur for a variety of different reasons. The examples given by Bridges et al suggest that the impetus for withdrawal may come from either party. Thus an applicant may be advised not to proceed further when the full extent of the respondent's case becomes apparent at the post-leave stage. Alternatively, a respondent may accept the force of an applicant's case and therefore seek a settlement.

Locus Standi

On receipt of an application for leave to apply for judicial review, a court must consider whether or not the applicant has standing. The existence of the locus standi requirement means that in effect, some applicants will obtain the assistance of the courts in enforcing their rights whereas others will not. Standing will initially be determined at the leave stage, but it may also feature prominently in the substantive hearing for the reason referred to above. Since the decision involves the exercise of discretion on the part of the judge (albeit based on fact and law), it is not surprising that there is some variation in the case law on this aspect of judicial review.

Sir Konrad Schiemann has argued that the label exercise of discretion' 'conceals more than it reveals and prevents challenge, improvement and systemisation'. He has made the case for developing a set of clear principles on which locus standi decisions would be based. These would 'emerge with the aid of appellate courts and academic writers'. Are there any clear principles that emerge from the following cases?

IRC v National Federation of Self-Employed and Small Businesses Ltd (1982). Casual workers in the printing industry (the 'Fleet Street Casuals'); had avoided paying income tax on their earnings. This practice had come to the attention of the Inland Revenue. An agreement was; reached whereby the workers would register in respect of their casuals. employment and pay income tax in the normal way. Investigations as to unpaid tax in previous years were not to be made. The NFSESB sought an order of mandamus to compel the Commissioners to assess and collect the arrears of tax. HL held: in cases other than simple cases where it is clear that the applicant does not have a sufficient interest, the question of sufficient interest cannot be considered as an isolated point; it must be considered together with the legal and factual context. Having regard to the duties of the Revenue and the operation of the tax system itself, as a general principle, no one taxpayer has a sufficient interest in the tax affairs of another. The principle applies especially to groups of taxpayers: an aggregate of individuals each of which had no interest cannot of itself have an interest.

R v Secretary of State for the Environment, ex p Rose Theatre Trust Co (1990). The remains of the Rose Theatre were discovered in the process of developing a site for office accommodation. A group of persons, including archaeologists, formed a trust company as part of a campaign to preserve the site. The trust applied to the SoS to schedule the site under the Ancient Monuments and Archaeolog Areas Act 1979 so as to protect it from development without his consent. He declined to do so and the trust sought judicial review of that decision. QBD held: the application would be dismissed since the SoS had not taken irrelevant matters into account in making his decision. On the question of standing, the trust could have no greater claim to a sufficient interest than its members had before it was formed. Since no individual member of the Trust had standing, it followed that the trust created by those individuals did not have standing either.

R v HM Inspectorate of Pollution, ex p Greenpeace (No 2) (1994). The Inspectorate granted applications by British Nuclear Fuels for variations of authorisations to discharge liquid and gaseous radioactive waste from its premises at Sellafield so as to include its thermal oxide reprocessing plant. The original authorisations had been granted pursuant to s 6(1) of the Radioactive Substances Act 1960. Greenpeace (G) applied for judicial review of the inspectorate's decision. QBD held: although the court could not find for the applicant on the merits of the case, approaching the locus standi question as primarily one of discretion, the court concluded that G did have standing. G was an eminently respectable organisation with a genuine interest in the issues raised by the application. It had a significant national and international membership, but more importantly, 2,500 of its members lived in Cumbria. With its access to scientific and legal expertise, G was in a position to mount a focused, relevant and well-argued challenge on behalf of those who might not otherwise have an effective way to bring the issues before the court.

In neither *Rose Theatre* nor *Greenpeace* was the decision on locus standi central to the determination of the case. Nevertheless, the views expressed on this point illustrate the variation in judicial opinion referred to above. Clearly the question of standing has to be determined on a case-by-case basis and it follows, therefore, that an individual or organisation may have a sufficient interest in respect of one application but not in respect of another. However, it is possible to argue that since *Rose Theatre*, the judiciary have adopted a more liberal approach to standing.

Thus in *R v Secretary of State for Foreign Affairs,* ex *p World Development Movement Ltd* (1995), the applicant was held to have locus standi to challenge the government's decision to contribute financial aid to the Pergau Dam scheme in Malaysia. In reaching this conclusion, the court took into account a number of factors. These included: the importance of vindicating the rule of law; the importance of the issue raised; the likely absence of any other responsible challenger; and the national and international expertise of the applicants coupled with their interest in promoting and protecting aid to underdeveloped countries. The liberal approach to standing is even more apparent in *R v Secretary of State for Foreign and Commonwealth Affairs, ex p Rees-Mogg* (1994), where the applicant was held to have a sufficient interest to challenge the decision to ratify the Maastricht Treaty on the basis of his 'sincere concern for constitutional issues'. Might it have been possible for all students of public law to have advanced a similar argument?

Reform of locus standi

In Administrative *Law: Judicial Review and Statutory Appeals* (I994), the Law Commission has proposed that a 'two-track system' of standing ought to be adopted (para 5.20). The first track would relate to those who had been personally adversely affected by the decision which they are seeking to challenge. Thus where a person had their legal rights or; legitimate expectations adversely affected, they 'should normally be given standing as a matter of course'. The second track would be discretionary and would cover cases where there is a sufficient public interest in the matter being litigated.

Cane has argued that the phrase 'adversely affected' is not really much of an improvement on 'sufficiently interested'. He offers the alternative of 'sufficiently personally interested' to emphasise the personal nature of the standing. More important, however, are Cane's criticisms of the second track. He has argued that in the law on standing, an important distinction must be made between 'personal standing' ie on the basis of an applicant's own personal interests, and 'representational standing'. It is this second type of standing which he further divides into three categories:

- 'associational standing';
- 'public interest standing'; and
- 'surrogate standing'.

'Associational standing' occurs where an unincorporated group or corporation acts on behalf of its members, whereas 'public interest standing' occurs where an individual or group seeks to challenge a decision in the public interest rather than directly on behalf of others. Surrogate standing' involves an individual acting as a nominal applicant on behalf of another individual who is the real applicant. In order for there to be genuine associational standing, Cane argues that 'the represented must have some degree of control over or some "democratic stake" ... in the conduct of the representative'. He further argues that there is no need for a 'democratic stake' where an application is made in the public interest. Although Cane recognises that the courts have not made the distinction between associational and public interest standing, he nevertheless argues that it is a distinction which the law ought to recognise.

Time limit

In addition to the limitations on judicial review which have already been considered, it must be noted that the procedure is subject to a time limit. The rationale for this appears to be administrative certainty. In short, in order to allow administrative decisions to be acted upon, it is necessary that there is a point in time beyond which they can no longer be subject to challenge.

Where the QBD considers that there has been undue delay in making an application for judicial review, it may refuse to grant leave or any relief sought (s 31(6) of the SCA 1981). This provision must be read in the light of rule 4 of RSC Order 53. This provides that:

> 'An application for leave to apply for judicial review shall be made promptly and in any event within three months from the date when the grounds for the application first arose unless the Court considers that there is good reason for extending the period within which the application shall be made'.

In the light of rule 4, it is possible, therefore, that an application for leave to apply for judicial review may be made within three months and yet still be refused on the basis that it has not been made sufficiently promptly. This is what happened in *R v Independent Television Commission, exp TV NI Ltd* (1991) where the CA dismissed a renewed application for Judicial review where the applicants sought to challenge decisions made by the Commission relating to the grant of broadcasting licences to television companies. In giving judgment, Lord Donaldson MR stated the position thus:

> 'I saw it reported in the press that all the applicants had until 16 January, that is to say three months from 16 October, in which to apply for judicial review. That just is not correct. In these matters people must act with the utmost promptitude because so many third parties are affected by the decision and are entitled to act on it unless they have clear and prompt notice that the decision is challenged'.

The fact that both s 32 of the SCA 1981 and RSC Order 53 make provision for time limits is unfortunate, especially when it is borne in mind that there is inconsistency between the two. For example, s 31 is concerned with delay in respect of applications for leave and substantive relief, whereas rule 4 is only concerned with the former. Moreover, in deciding whether or not to permit an extension to the time limit, s 31 considers its effect upon the rights of any person or whether it would be detrimental to good administration, whereas rule 4 looks at the question from the viewpoint of the applicant and whether or not there is a good reason for the delay. The position is further complicated by the fact that both the rule and the section are stated to be without prejudice to a statutory provision or a rule respectively.

In the leading case *Caswell v Dairy Produce Quota Tribunal for England and Wales* (1990), the HL sought to reconcile these two provisions and came to the conclusion that a failure to apply for judicial review promptly in accordance with rule 4 amounted to undue delay for the purposes of s 31 (6) of the 1981 Act. A solution to this unfortunate overlap would be to repeal one of the provisions. This was attempted in the Administration of Justice Bill 1985, but the relevant clause fell along with all the other provisions when the Bill was abandoned. The Law Commission has taken the view that time limits should be dealt with in the RSC rather than in primary legislation (para 5.25). Accordingly in a draft Order 53 attached to its report, it proposed that the three-month time limit should be retained.

JUDICIAL REVIEW IN PRACTICE

Subject-matter of applications

The procedural aspects of judicial review have thus been described. However, in order to better understand judicial review, several practical points need to be noted. The first of these relates to the subject-matter of applications. Empirical research undertaken by the Public Law Project has revealed that applications for leave occur across a wide array of subject areas. Thus between 1987-89 and the first quarter of 1991, applications for leave were brought in respect of tax, education, transport, agriculture and environment matters, to name but a few. However, the proportion of each as a percentage of the total number of applications made during this period was relatively small. The major subject areas were:

- crime;
- immigration; and
- housing.

Collectively these three areas accounted for more than half of all the applications for leave in each of the relevant years. If the last two subject areas are further broken down into types, it is apparent from the research that immigration applications were made in respect of decisions relating to, inter alia:

- asylum;
- entry clearance;
- leave to enter:
- illegal entry; and
- deportation.

Housing applications concerned decisions in respect of, inter alia:

- homeless persons;
- housing benefits;
- compulsory purchase orders;
- rates; and
- repairs.

Despite the breadth of subject areas revealed by the research, there are some which account for a tiny proportion of the numbers of applications made. Perhaps the most surprising of these are welfare benefits because, as the authors note, millions of decisions as to individual entitlement are made on an annual basis.

Parties to the proceedings

A second practical point to note about judicial review concerns the parties to the proceedings. The research conducted to date reveals that the overwhelming majority of applications are made by individuals, although the statistics can be slightly misleading on this point in that they do not reveal the capacity in which the individual is acting. As the authors note, it is quite possible that an individual may be acting on behalf of a wider group of persons or an organisation. The proportion of non-individual applicants for judicial review is therefore statistically small. It consists of:

- companies;
- non-governmental organisations such as environmental pressure groups;
- central government;
- local authorities; and
- non-departmental public bodies such as the DPP and the CPS.

The geographical spread of these applicants is somewhat limited. Figures for the first quarter of 1991 revealed that more than half of the applications for leave made during this period emanated from London. This is not so very surprising given that applications must be both lodged and heard in the High Court which is situated in the capita!. Indeed, as the authors note, that figure may be misleading in that regional applicants may opt to instruct London solicitors rather than those in their own areas. Nevertheless, there is clearly an element of centralisation in the judicial review process which has the potential to discourage individuals, bodies or organisations from making applications.

Statistically the respondents to judicial review applications fall into three main categories:

- central government;
- local government; and
- courts and tribunals.

Given the high incidence of applications relating to immigration matters, it is hardly surprising that the Home Office is the most frequently challenged government department. In respect of local government, the decisions most frequently challenged relate to homelessness, other housing matters, town and country planning, licensing, education and family matters.

Judicial discretion in leave applications

One final point to note concerns the impact of judicial discretion on leave decisions. Given that the whole of the judicial review procedure involves the exercise of considerable discretion on the part of the judiciary, it is perhaps inevitable that there should be some degree of variation between individual judges in terms of the decisions that they make. However, the Public Law Project has found that quite wide discrepancies exist in the leave grant rates of individual judges. Patently this is a cause for concern. If judicial decision-making in this area is believed to be arbitrary by the wider public, the process of judicial review will thereby be devalued.

FURTHER READING

Bridges, Meszaros and Sunkin *Judicial Review in Perspective* (1995).

P Cane 'Standing up for the Public' [1995] PL 276.

P P Craig *Administrative Law* (4th edn, 1999).

Law Commission *Administrative Law: Judicial Review and Statutory Appeals* (1994) (Law Com No 226).

Sir Konrad Schiemann 'Locus Standi' [1990] PL 342.

A Tanney 'Procedural Exclusivity in Administrative Law' [1994] PL. 51.

SELF-TEST QUESTIONS

1. Why have the courts been unwilling to accept the discretion may be limitless?
2. How can a review be distinguished from an appeal?
3. What rule was established by the HL in *O'Reilly v Mackman?* Can it be argued that in the later decided cases, the courts0 have taken a pragmatic approach to the scope of this rule?
4. Does the decision of the HL in *Boddington* represent a welcome clarification of the position with regard to collateral challenge?
5. In the words of Sir Konrad Schiemann, 'does locus standi matter or are the courts becoming so liberal that we can forget it?'
6. An alternative to the present arrangements on standing would be to allow anyone to seek judicial review of any decision which they wished to challenge. What would be the advantages and disadvantages of such a system?
7. Applying Cane's distinction between associational and public interest standing to the *Fleet Street Casuals* case, the *Rose Theatre* case and the *Greenpeace* case, which type of standing, associational or public interest, describes the status of the applicant?

3

THE GROUNDS FOR JUDICIAL REVIEW

INTRODUCTION

In considering the grounds for judicial review, two cases are of central importance: *Associated Provincial Picture Houses Ltd v Wednesbury Corpn* (1948) - the *Wednesbury* case - and *Council of Civil Service Unions v Minister for the Civil Service* (1985) - the *GCHQ* case. In neither case did the courts establish new or novel grounds for review. Their importance lies not in innovation but in their distillation of the various principles on which the decision-making process may be subject to legal challenge before the courts.

The actual decision in the *Wednesbury* case is not really that important. It concerned a challenge to a decision by the corporation to attach a condition to a cinema licence whereby children under the age of 15 were not permitted into a cinema on a Sunday. It was argued by the plaintiff that such a condition was unreasonable and that it was therefore beyond the powers of the corporation to have imposed it. The CA concluded that the condition was in fact reasonable, although it is at least open to argument whether the same conclusion would be reached on the facts were the case to be decided in the modern day. However, the significance of the case lies in the judgment of Lord Greene MR. In that judgment, in which he stressed the supervisory as opposed to the appellate nature of the jurisdiction. Lord Greene identified a number of principles which could form the basis of a challenge to the exercise of executive discretion. These principles, which have come to be known as the 'Wednesbury principles', can be stated thus:

- the exercise of a discretion must be a real exercise of the discretion;
- in exercising a discretion, the decision-maker must have regard to relevant matters and must disregard irrelevant matters;
- a discretion must not be exercised for reasons of bad faith or dishonesty;
- a discretion must be exercised for the purpose for which it was intended.

In addition to these principles, Lord Greene noted that as a general proposition, a discretion must be exercised 'reasonably'. If a discretion were exercised contrary to any one of the principles stated above, it would be possible to conclude that the decision-maker had acted unreasonably. However, in the years since the *Wednesbury* case was decided, 'Wednesbury unreasonableness' has been accorded a rather narrower meaning. Nowhere is this more apparent than in the other leading case on the grounds for review, the *GCHQ* case.

The facts of the *GCHQ* case have been stated elsewhere and will not therefore be repeated here. It will be remembered that in that case, the HL established the general principle that the exercise of prerogative power could be subject to review by the courts. Whether or not a particular exercise of the prerogative was subject to review would depend upon whether it was a justiciable issue. In delivering his judgment in *GCHQ*, Lord Diplock expressed the view that judicial review had reached a stage of development whereby 'one can conveniently classify under three heads the grounds upon which administrative action is subject to control...' Those three heads are: illegality; irrationality and procedural impropriety.

These three heads are convenient terms which encapsulate a number of different principles upon which the exercise of discretionary power may be subject to review. Moreover, the heads and the principles are not mutually exclusive. A decision will often be challenged on the basis of several different review principles, and it may be that more than one such argument is upheld by the court. Thus, for example, where a decision is based on an irrelevant consideration, that irrelevant consideration may reflect an improper purpose on the part of the decision-maker.

Illegality

In *GCHQ*, Lord Diplock observed that: 'By "illegality" as a ground for judicial review I mean that the decision-maker must understand correctly the law that regulates his decision-making power and must give effect to it'. In truth, this definition sheds little real light on the principles which fall under this head. These will be considered below.

Relevant/irrelevant considerations

In exercising a discretion, a decision-maker must have regard to relevant matters and must disregard irrelevant matters. Lord Irvine has argued that there are in fact three categories of consideration. In addition to the two already mentioned, he argues that there are considerations which 'may, in the decision maker's discretion, be taken into account'. In support of this view, Lord Irvine refers to a case in which the legality of a ban on stag hunting was considered.

R v Somerset County Council, ex p Fewings (1995). The local authority owned common land. Its environment committee met to consider stag hunting and resolved that it should be allowed to continue on the land. At a full local authority meeting, however, a resolution was passed banning stag hunting. Most of those who voted in favour of a ban were influenced by the argument that hunting was unacceptably and unnecessarily cruel. The applicants, who regularly hunted on the land, sought judicial review. Laws J held that the resolution was an unlawful exercise of its power under s 120 (1) (b) of the Local Government Act 1972, to acquire and manage land for the 'benefit, improvement or development of their area'. In his judgment, hunting could only be banned if it were decided that there were better ways of managing the deer herd or because it was necessary to preserve or enhance the amenity of the area. The argument that hunting was morally repulsive was an irrelevant consideration. The council appealed. CA held: dismissing the appeal, that the council had not exercised its power for the object prescribed in s 120 (l) (b) of the 1972 Act. It had wrongly equated itself with the position of a private landowner. It had not considered what benefit a ban would have on the area, or conversely, what detriment an absence of a ban would cause. Animal welfare and social considerations were relevant matters to take into account. Moral arguments were not necessarily irrelevant considerations contrary to what Laws J had decided.

In Lord Irvine's opinion, by deciding in *Fewings* that moral considerations were not necessarily irrelevant, Sir Thomas Bingham MR was 'regarding such considerations as in the third category' ie as considerations which a decision-maker may, exercising his discretion, take into account.

Frequently statute will afford some indication as to the nature of relevant considerations when conferring a discretionary power upon a decision-maker. Thus, for example, in deciding whether or not to grant panning permission, the Town and Country Planning Act 1990 requires a local authority to 'have regard to the provisions of the development plan, so far as material to the application, and to any other material considerations' (s 70(2)). Where, however, no such guidance is provided by the statute, the task of identifying relevant/irrelevant considerations is more difficult. This will require the courts to construe the statute. Where the purpose for which a discretion has been conferred is clear, relevant considerations will be those which aim to achieve that purpose. In carrying out this interpretative role, a court must be careful to avoid substituting its own view as to the appropriateness of considerations.

R v Port Talbot Borough Council, ex p Jones (1988). K, a local councillor, applied for housing accommodation. She was accorded priority status and was subsequently granted the tenancy of a three-bedroomed council house despite the fact that she lived alone. The chairman of the housing tenancy committee justified the decision on the basis that: in order to carry out her council work, K needed a house in which to receive visits from members of the public; there was no prospect of a two-bedroomed house becoming available; a reasonable period of time had passed (18 months) between the decision to re-house and the grant of a tenancy; and, K needed to live in the ward (Aberavon) which she represented. DC held: the council's policy was to provide suitable accommodation for those on the waiting list. The decision to grant K a tenancy in order that she could better fight an election, without regard to the needs of others on the waiting list and contrary to the opinions of the council's officers, was a clear case of a decision based on irrelevant considerations.

Roberts v Hopwood (1925). Poplar Borough Council had the power to pay their employees 'such salaries and wages as they may think fit'. In exercising that power, the council paid uniform wages to its employees which greatly exceeded the general wages level at the time. Moreover, the council paid equal wages to male and female employees, contrary to normal practice. When the cost of living fell, the council maintained its wage levels, despite the fact that comparable wages in the private sector were lower. The district auditor objected to the payments and accordingly surcharged those councillors who had voted for them. HL held: the councillors had taken account of irrelevant considerations - socialist philanthropy and feminist ambition - and had disregarded relevant considerations - the wage levels in the labour market and the burden which would be placed on the ratepayers as a consequence of their decision.

R v Secretary of State for the Home Department, ex p Asif Khan (1985). The SoS issued a circular setting out the criteria he would apply in admitting children into the UK for adoption. The applicant sought judicial review of a refusal to admit a relative's child which he wished to adopt. He argued that the criteria had not been followed. CA held: the circular amounted to the SoS making his own rules. He had in effect stated those matters which he regarded as relevant in making a decision. Since the criteria said nothing about the natural parent's ability to care for the child - the basis of the decision by the SoS - and there was no general sweeping up clause, it followed that the decision was based on an irrelevant consideration.

Although the principle of relevant considerations requires that relevant matters are taken into account in the decision-making process, it does not prescribe how much weight is to be given to competing relevant considerations: that is a matter for the decision-maker, not the courts: see *Tesco Stores Ltd v Secretary of State for the*

Environment (1995). Where a decision has been reached and both relevant and irrelevant considerations have featured in the decision-making process, the decision is not necessarily unlawful. Whether or not it is will depend upon the extent to which irrelevant considerations have influenced the decision. If the decision would have been the same in the absence of irrelevant considerations, it will not be unlawful. If, however, irrelevant considerations have so influenced the final decision as to make it something other than it would have been had they not been considered, the decision is unlawful.

R v Broadcasting Complaints Commission, ex p Owen (1985). The applicant was the leader of the Social Democratic Party. He wrote to the BCC complaining that the broadcasting organisations were paying considerably more attention to the views of the Labour Party in their news and current affairs broadcasts than they were to his party, despite the fact that there was little between the parties in terms of the percentage of votes cast at the 1983 General Election. The BCC responded by saying that it had no jurisdiction to hear the complaint under s 54 of the Broadcasting Act 1981. Moreover, even if it had jurisdiction, it would not have upheld the complaint for a variety of stated reasons. Held: the BCC was wrong to think that it did not have jurisdiction to hear the complaint. Of the five reasons which it gave for not upholding the compliant, four were valid in law. The fact that one was bad in law would not, however, cause the court to intervene by way of judicial review provided that it was satisfied that precisely the same decision would have been reached on the other valid reasons.

In exercising a discretion, there are clearly certain matters which a local authority will be entitled to take into account. Thus for the individual councillor, a manifesto commitment, a political policy or pledge, a party whip or the views and opinions of political colleagues are all relevant considerations in the decision-making process, provided that they do not amount to a fetter on discretion (see below). Similarly, in performing its various tasks and functions, it is a relevant consideration for a local authority to have regard to its duty under the Race Relations Act 1976 to promote good race relations in its area: see *Wheeler v Leicester City*

Council (1985) and *R v Lewisham London Borough Council, ex p Shell UK Ltd* (1988). In a number of cases, the courts have taken the view that in exercising a discretion, local authorities should have regard to the fiduciary duty which they owe to ratepayers.

Fiduciary duty

Local authorities are responsible for the collection and spending of vasts sums of money at the local level. Money, principally in the form of council tax, is collected so as to enable a local authority to fulfil its statutory duties and provide essential services such as education, housing, rubbish collection and the maintenance of the highways. A local authority owes a fiduciary duty to those from whom it collects this money that it will not be spent thriftlessly, but that it will be used to provide these services in a way which benefits the community as a whole. Where it is shown that this fiduciary duty has been breached, the courts will be quick to intervene.

Prescott v Birmingham Corpn (1955). The Corporation operated trams and buses in Birmingham. It resolved to put a scheme into operation which would give free travel to women over 64 and men over 69 on six days of the week. The scheme operated for about a year before P, a local ratepayer, sought a declaration that it was illegal. Vaisey J held: the subsidising of particular classes of society was a matter for Parliament, not the Corporation. The Corporation had no inherent power to provide such benefits to the elderly which were based on discrimination and favouritism towards a section of society, and which therefore offended against the principle of equality.

Bromley London Borough Council v Greater London Council (1983). Under s 1 of the Transport (London) Act 1969, the GLC was under a general duty to develop policies and encourage measures which promoted 'the provision of integrated, efficient and economic transport facilities and services for Greater London'. Section 4 of the Act placed the responsibility for implementing the policies on the London Transport Executive (LTE). In July 1981, the GLC passed a resolution implementing a commitment by the majority group on the council in an election manifesto to reduce fares charged by the LTE by 25%. To finance this policy (at a cost of £69m), the GLC required all the London Boroughs to pay a supplementary rate. Bromley sought judicial review in the form of an order of certiorari to quash the rate DC refused their application. CA reversed that decision and granted the order. GLC and LTE appealed. HL held: dismissing the appeal, that both the LTE and GLC had acted ultra vires by arbitrarily reducing fares in a way which had no regard for business principles. The decision to reduce fares was a thriftless use of ratepayers' money and was in breach of the fiduciary duty that the GLC owed to its ratepayers.

The breach of the council's fiduciary duty in both of these cases was enough to entitle the courts to hold that they had acted unlawfully. However, in *Bromley,* three of the five Law Lords who heard the appeal considered that the GLC had acted unlawfully for another reason: they had not properly exercised their discretion by considering themselves bound by the majority group's commitment in their election manifesto to implement the fare reduction scheme. In short, the GLC had fettered its discretion.

Fettering of a discretion

Decision-makers are clearly put in a position where they have a large measure of discretion as to the decision which they reach in a particular case. In exercising that discretion, they will inevitably take account of a variety of different factors. As we have already noted, they must take care to ensure that they have regard to relevant considerations and disregard irrelevant considerations. Moreover, even where a decision is based on relevant considerations, a decision-maker must ensure that such considerations have not fettered their discretion. In other words, they must not allow those considerations to so influence their thinking that they cannot be said to have exercised a discretion in the decision-making process.

R v Secretary of State for the Environment, ex p *Brent London Borough Council* (1982). The Local Government Act 1974 introduced a system for the payment by the SoS of an annual rate support grant to local authorities to aid their general expenditure. A different government was elected in 1979 and it decided to alter the system. Pending the introduction of amending legislation, the government encouraged local authorities to reduce their expenditure in accordance with government targets. The SoS was not happy with some of the budgets that he received from local authorities. He announced that when transitional arrangements in the amending legislation (Local Government, Planning and Land Act 1980) came into effect, he would use them against local authorities which had disregarded the government's targets unless they could show that they had made exceptional efforts to reduce expenditure. The relevant local authorities to which this applied were informed of the last day on which they could secure exemption from the transitional arrangements. The local authorities' association wrote to the SoS asking for a meeting. He replied that he did not believe a meeting would have any practical effect. The SoS subsequently exercised his discretion under the new legislation to reduce the amount of rate support grant payable to the relevant local authorities. They sought an order of certiorari to quash his decision. DC held: granting the order, that the SoS had a duty not to fetter his discretion when making a decision under the new legislation. However, he had breached that duty by refusing to meet the applicant's representatives and seeing whether they had any new suggestions to make about his policy to use the transitional arrangements against them.

R v Waltham Forest London Borough Council, ex p Baxter (1988). A local authority resolved by vote at a council meeting to increase the general rate for the borough. At a meeting of the majority group on the council held prior to the council meeting, a number of councillors voted against the proposed rate increase. At the council meeting, however, they all voted for the increase in accordance with their party whip. Members of a ratepayer's group who opposed the increase sought judicial review of the resolution. They claimed that certain councillors had taken an irrelevant factor into account (the party whip) in voting for the increase, and that they had fettered their discretion by obeying the party whip. DC dismissed their application. They appealed. CA held: dismissing their appeal, that a councillor was under a duty to make up his own mind as to how to vote on a resolution. He must not vote blindly in support of a party policy since this would amount to fettering his discretion. On the facts, however, the councillors who voted initially against but then for the resolution had exercised a free choice.

The legal position of an elected representative when exercising a discretion was conveniently summarised in the judgments in *ex p Baxter*. In the words of Sir John Donaldson MR, the duty of a councillor:

> '... is to make up his own mind on how to vote, giving such weight as he thinks appropriate to the views of other councillors and to the policy of the group of which he is a member. It is only if he abdicates his personal responsibility that questions can arise as to the validity of his vote. The distinction between giving great weight to the views of colleagues and to party policy, on the one hand, and voting blindly in support of party policy may on occasion be a fine one, but it is nevertheless very real.'

Moreover, in the same case, Russell LJ observed that:

> 'Party loyalty, party unanimity, party policy were all relevant considerations for the individual councillor. The vote becomes unlawful only when the councillor allows these considerations or any other outside influences so to dominate as to exclude other considerations which are required for a balanced judgment. If, by blindly toeing the party line, the councillor deprives himself of any real choice or the exercise of any real discretion, then his vote can be impugned and any resolution supported by his vote potentially flawed.'

Improper purpose

Where Parliament confers a power on a decision-maker, it does so intending that the power should be used for a particular purpose or purposes. In many cases, the purpose for which the power was conferred will be expressly stated in the statute. Alternatively, it may be determined by necessary implication. Provided that a decision-maker acts in accordance with the statutory purpose or purposes, he will have acted lawfully. If, however, he acts for an improper purpose, the courts will be prepared to intervene.

Congreve v Home Office (1976). An announcement was made that as from 1 April, the cost of a TV licence would be increased from £12 to L18. C and several thousand others took out a new licence before this date (at the old price) despite the fact that their exiting licence would not expire until after 1 April. The Home Office wrote to the holders of these overlapping licences and demanded the additional fee of £6. If they refused to pay, they were threatened with the revocation of the licence. Subsequently the Home Office altered its stance and proposed that the licence would be revoked at the end of eight months. C refused to pay the £6. He sought a declaration that the revocation of his licence would be unlawful. HCt refused to grant him the declaration. CA held: the minister had no power to revoke the licences which had been granted lawfully, save where the licensee had done something wrong eg paid by a cheque which later 'bounced'. A revocation in the present circumstances would amount to a misuse of the power conferred on him by Parliament. The demand for the £6 was also unlawful because it represented an attempt to levy a charge without the authority of Parliament.

Wheeler v Leicester City Council (1985). Three members of the Leicester Rugby Club were invited to tour South Africa with the England rugby team. The City Council was opposed to the apartheid regime in South Africa and it supported the policy of not maintaining sporting links with that country. It asked the club to condemn the tour and to put pressure on its players not to participate. Moreover, it put four questions to the club, each of which it wanted answered in the affirmative. Although the club sympathised with the council's stance, it was not entitled to prevent its members from going on the tour. The players went on the tour and the council subsequently passed a resolution banning the club from using a recreation ground which the council controlled for a period of 12 months. The club sought an order of certiorari to quash the council's decision. Forbes J dismissed their application. The club's appeal to the CA was dismissed. It further appealed. HL held: the ban on the use of the recreation ground was unreasonable, unfair and amounted to procedural impropriety. Moreover, it amounted to the use of a statutory power (in the management of its property) for an improper purpose because the council were seeking to punish the club when the club had done nothing wrong.

In *R v Lewisham London Borough Council, ex p Shell UK Ltd* (1988), the DC held that the council's decision to boycott Shell's products because of that company's trading links with South Africa was not unreasonable. However, it did declare that the council's decision and campaign to persuade other councils not to use Shell products was unlawful because it was done for a purpose other than to satisfy public opinion or race relations ie to put pressure on the company to sever trading links with South Africa. For a further example of the use of power for an improper purpose, see *R v Ealing London Borough, ex p Times Newspapers* (1986).

Bad faith

In the *Wednesbury* case, Lord Greene noted that a decision could be quashed on the basis of having been made in bad faith or dishonestly. Subsequently in *Connock Chose District Council v Kelly* (1978), Megaw LJ observed that:

> '... bad faith or, as it is sometimes put, 'lack of good faith', means dishonesty; not necessarily for a financial motive, but still dishonesty. It always involves a grave charge. It must not be treated as a synonym for an honest, although mistaken, taking into consideration of a factor which is in law irrelevant...'

Since bad faith involves 'a grave charge' against a public authority, only the most compelling evidence will justify a court making a finding in favour of the applicant.

R v Derbyshire County Council, ex p Times Supplements (1990). Under s 38 of the Education (No 2) Act 1986, local education authorities were under a duty to advertise vacancies 'in a manner likely....to bring it to the notice of persons.. .who are qualified to fill the post', Articles published in *The Sunday Time* were critical of individuals and the education authority itself. The council decided to stop advertising vacancies in The *Times Educational*

Supplement and any other publication owned by Rupert Murdoch, despite the fact that these publications were read by the greatest number of potential applicants for the posts. The papers sought judicial review. DC held: the council's decisions had been made in bad faith. They had not been taken on educational grounds. Instead, they were motivated by vindictiveness towards the papers.

Thus where a decision-maker has acted dishonestly by claiming to have acted for a particular motive when in reality the decision was taken with another motive in mind, he may be said to have acted in bad faith. If, for the example, a council made tree preservation order under the planning legislation merely to justify its refusal to grant a developer planning permission, then it could be said to have acted in bad faith: sew *J.H. Smith (Hale) Ltd v Macclesfiled Borough Council* (1998), were Laws J rejected a 'serious charge' of this nature on the basis that it was not supported by the evidence.

Irrationality

In *GCHQ*, Lord Dilpock implied that irrationality and 'Wednesbury unreasonableness' in its narrow sense were effectively the same thing. Irrationality applied to 'a decision which is so outrageous in its defiance of logic or of accepted moral standards that no sensible person who had applied his mind to the question to be decided would have arrived at it'. In *Wednesbury* itself, Lord Greene spoke of a decision being 'so unreasonable that no reasonable authority could ever have come to it'. Similarly in *Nottinghamshire County Council v Secretary of State for the Environment* (1986), Lord Scarman referred to an action as being 'so unreasonable as to be verging on an absurdity'. Occasionally the courts have referred to a decision which is 'perverse' or 'totally unreasonable'. Whatever the description, it is apparent that an irrational 'decision clearly involves the misuse of power.

In order to succeed under the ground of irrationality, an applicant must overcome a high threshold of proof. It is not enough to establish that the impugned decision is one which a reasonable person would not have reached. Rather, it is necessary to show that the decision would not have been reached by any reasonable person. In *R v Secretary of State for the Home Department, ex p Brind* (1991), Lord Ackner noted that the test for irrationality has sometimes been criticised for being too high. However, in his opinion, this was necessary in order to underline the fact that judicial review is a supervisory rather than an appellate jurisdiction. This observation highlights the constitutional dangers inherent in the judiciary declaring decisions to be irrational. If a decision is described as being 'absurd', or 'outrageous in its defiance of logic', the merits of that decision are clearly being questioned. In effect, it could be argued that the decision has been held to be wrong. Accordingly, arguments involving irrationality have rarely succeeded before the courts, unless that is, the decision can be said to have been totally unreasonable. *Backhouse v Lambeth London Borough Council* (1972). The council was under a statutory duty to increase the average rents charged for its dwellings by a specified amount. In purported compliance with that duty, the council achieved the average increase per dwelling by increasing the rent of one unoccupied dwelling by £18,000 per week. Held: the decision was totally unreasonable.

Hall & Co Ltd v Shoreham-by-Sea UDC (1964). Under the relevant planning legislation, local authorities had the power to grant planning permission subject to such conditions as the council 'think fit'. H was granted planning permission subject to the condition that an access road should be constructed over the entire frontage of their site at their own expense. Moreover, the public was to have a right of way over it. CA held: it was not enough to say that the condition was unreasonable or unduly onerous. In order to justify a declaration that the condition was ultra vires, it must be shown that it was so unreasonable that no reasonable council could have imposed it. The condition was utterly unreasonable in that it sought to transfer the public burden of constructing a road onto the private shoulders of the developer. Parliament could not have intended such a result.

R v Ministry of Defence, ex p Smith (1996). The Ministry of Defence policy regarding homosexuality was that it was incompatible with service in the armed forces. Service personnel who were known to be homosexual or who engaged in homosexual activity were discharged from the forces. The four appellants, three men and a woman, had been discharged on this basis. None of them had committed any offence or engaged in homosexual acts on service premises. They challenged the lawfulness of their discharge on the basis that it was in accordance with a policy which was irrational. CA held: the greater the policy content of a decision, and the more remote the subject-matter of a decision from ordinary judicial experience, the more hesitant a court should be in holding a decision to be irrational. The existing policy could not be described as irrational at the time when the appellants were discharged. It was supported by both Houses of Parliament and by those to whom the ministry looked for professional advice. Moreover although in some countries there had been a relaxation of the ban on homosexuals in their armed forces, such changes were too recent to yield much valuable experience.

The last of these cases, *ex p Smith,* demonstrates that the threshold of irrationality is a high one and that it had not been crossed in that case. If irrationality succeeds so rarely as a ground for review, why is it argued so regularly before the courts? The answer lies in the practicalities of the judicial review procedure itself. In the early stages of an application, especially at the leave stage, an applicant may have a relatively limited amount of information available to him. From this information, it may not be possible to construct an argument that a decision-maker has, for example, acted for an improper purpose or that he has taken irrelevant factors into account in the process of making a decision. As the proceedings progress, however, further information may become available which justifies such arguments. Until that point in time has been reached, arguments as to irrationality may sustain the application because they can be based on the decision alone. It is possible to assert that a decision is so unreasonable that no reasonable decision-maker could have reached it in the absence of evidence to that effect. It is not possible to sustain a contention that a decision was based on an irrelevant matter where the nature of that irrelevant matter cannot be identified in support of the claim.

It has been argued by Walker that there are a number of difficulties with the label 'irrationality'. In his opinion, three such difficulties may be identified: the label wrongly suggests that the test is logicality; the label ignores the important role of morals; and the label may be unnecessarily rude. These criticisms are certainly thought-provoking and they may not be without foundation, if we were to dispense with 'irrationality' and opt for an alternative label which properly describes this ground of review, what do you think that label should be? 'Unreasonableness'? 'Outside the limits of reason'? 'Illogicality'? 'Immorality'? 'Proportionality'?

Proportionality

In *GCHQ*, Lord Diplock acknowledged that in the future, there may be additions to the three heads which he had identified. One particular ground which he had in mind was proportionality. Proportionality is a well established principle in the administrative law of a number of EC member states, and it is a principle which is recognised in EC law. It is also a principle which is reflected in the jurisprudence of the European Court of Human Rights.

Proportionality is sometimes explained by the expression 'taking a sledgehammer to crack a nut'. This rather graphic description does, however, convey the essence of the 'ground'. To argue that a decision or a course of action is disproportionate does not amount to an attack on the objective itself. Rather, it constitutes an attack on the means by which such an objective is to be achieved. In other words, it is an argument that the same objective could have been achieved by some more proportionate means. Once again, therefore, there are constitutional dangers with this argument. For a court to hold that a decision or a course of action was disproportionate would be for it to come very close to substituting its own view for that of the decision-maker. In effect, the court would be saying to the decision-maker that he had chosen the wrong option. With these constitutional dangers in mind, it is not surprising that the English courts have generally tended to approach proportionality with care. An exception occurred, however, in *R v Barnsley Metropolitan Borough Council, ex p Hook* (1976).

The facts of *ex p Hook* are not really important. Suffice it to say that the case concerned a challenge to a decision to revoke a market trader's licence on the ground that bias had been present in the decision-making process. Strictly speaking, the case was decided in the applicant's favour on that basis alone. However, both Lord Denning MR and Sir John Pennycuick agreed that 'there are old cases which show that the court can interfere by certiorari if a punishment is altogether excessive and out of proportion to the occasion'. Had it been necessary to do so, they would have quashed the council's decision on that basis alone. The third judge to hear the appeal, Scarman LJ (as he then was), made no mention of proportionality in his judgment.

In the later case of *Rv Secretary of State for the Home Department, ex p Brind* (1991), directives issued by the Home Secretary to the BBC and the IBA prohibiting the direct broadcasting of the statements of terrorists and supporters of terrorism were challenged by journalists. It was argued, amongst other things, that the Home Secretary had acted beyond his power by acting disproportionately and in a manner which was contrary to art 10 of the European Convention on Human Rights. In response to this argument, the HL noted that a decision which suffers from a lack of proportionality is also therefore an irrational decision. In other words, it is a decision which no reasonable decision-maker could have made. However, to accept proportionality as a ground for review in its own right would, in the opinion of the HL, unavoidably lead to an enquiry into the merits of a decision. In the words of Lord Ackner:

> 'Unless and until Parliament incorporates the convention into domestic law ... there appears to me to be at present no basis upon which the proportionality doctrine applied by the European Court can be followed by the courts of this country...'

Now that incorporation has taken place in the form of the Human Rights Act 1998 (much of which is yet to come into force), it follows that the courts in this country will have to grapple with the principle of proportionality when considering alleged breaches of the convention rights. This point has been made quite forcefully by the Lord Chancellor. Speaking extra-judicially, Lord Irvine has observed that when considering the exceptions to the convention rights:

> "... the courts will in this area have to apply the Convention principle of proportionality. This means the court will be looking *substantively* at that question. It will not be limited to a secondary review of the decision making process but at the primary question of the decision itself.'

However, the current orthodoxy with regard to the position of the doctrine of proportionality in domestic administrative law was recently reaffirmed in *R v Secretary of State for the Home Department, ex p Al-Fayed* (1999). In that case, Ognall J rejected an invitation to extend the ambit of the doctrine into domestic law where a fundamental human right, the right to citizenship, was at stake. He did so on the basis that the HL in both *GCHQ* and *Brind* had taken the view that the doctrine did not form part of domestic law.

Procedural impropriety

Procedural impropriety was the third ground of challenge which Lord Diplock acknowledged in *GCHQ*. The phrase was chosen deliberately so as to encompass two areas: a failure to observe procedural rules laid down in statute; and a failure to observe the basic common law rules of natural justice.

Procedural ultra vires

Where a public body acting in reliance upon statutory powers has failed to comply with the procedures laid down in the relevant Act, it can be said to have acted ultra vires. Such procedures may take a variety of different forms. A common procedural requirement in an enabling Act is consultation. Thus, for example, a minister may be under a statutory duty to consult certain specified organisations or such organisations as he thinks fit prior to making a decision. Where the requirement to consult is mandatory, a failure to comply with it ensures that the procedure is thereby ultra vires.

Agricultural, Horticultural and Forestry Industry Training Board v Aylesbury Mushrooms (1972). The Industrial Training Act 1964 made provision for the establishment of industrial training boards. Under s 1 (4), prior to creating such a board, a minister was required to consult any organisation or association of organisations which appeared to him to be representative of people working in the relevant industry. The minister was minded to set up the plaintiff board and consulted the National Farmers Union. He did not, however, consult a subsidiary body of the NFU, the Mushroom Growers Association. QBD held: under the terms of s 1(4), some consultation by the minister was mandatory. Whether any particular organisation had to be consulted depended upon a subjective test ie the minister's own belief. Consultation amounted to the communication of a genuine invitation, extended with a receptive mind, to give advice. Since there had not been communication and the opportunity of responding, there had been no consultation.

It is clear from the *Aylesbury Mushrooms* case that consultation involves affording a consultee a proper opportunity to make representations. It also requires that any representations that are made are genuinely considered. It does not mean, however, that the decision-maker is bound to follow the advice which he receives. As long as the obligation to consult has been complied with, the decision-maker will not have acted in a procedurally improper manner even if his decision is in direct conflict with the advice given. Where a mandatory requirement to consult has not been complied with, the party which was not consulted will not be bound by the relevant decision. Thus in *Aylesbury Mushrooms*, the Mushroom Growers Association were not bound by the order, although the order remained effective as against those who were consulted or did not need to be consulted.

A further example of a statutory procedural requirement is the obligation to give reasons for a decision. Ministers and certain specified tribunals are under a general duty to give a statement of the reasons for a decision which they have made by virtue of s 10 of the Tribunals and Inquiries Act 1992. This general duty does not apply, however, where a specific enactment has already made provision for the giving of reasons. Under the common law, there is no general duty to give reasons. However, as we shall see, it is possible to argue that the courts are currently moving in the direction of imposing such a duty on decision-makers.

Natural justice

The common law rules or principles of natural justice which are imposed by the courts comprise two elements: *audi alteram partem* (hear both sides); and *nemo judex in causa sua* (there should be an absence of bias with no person being a judge in their own cause). These two Latin maxims thus signify the standards which are to be met in the decision-making process. They seek to ensure that an individual is given a proper opportunity to present his side of the case prior to a decision being reached, and that the decision itself is reached in an objective manner by an independent and impartial decision-maker. In truth, there are certain linguistic difficulties with the principles of natural justice. Whilst the manner in which they are expressed is appropriate where adjudicative functions are being performed, such as in the courtroom, they seem less suitable in respect of purely administrative decisions. A minister or panel charged with the responsibility of granting licences may not find them very helpful when they turn their minds to the question of the standards to be met in the decision-making process. Accordingly, in more recent times, it has become commonplace to talk in terms of 'fairness' or a 'duty to act fairly'. This term has the advantage of being sufficiently wide to embrace all manner of decisions, from those which are judicial in nature to those which are rightly classed as administrative.

The Decision in Ridge v Baldwin

Historically, the courts have not always been prepared to imply the principles of natural justice in all types of decision-making process. Thus despite cases such as *Cooper v Wandsworth Board of Works* (1863), where it was held that C ought to have been heard by the Board before it exercised its statutory power to demolish a house which had been built in breach of planning laws, a distinction emerged in the law between judicial or quasi-judicial decisions on the one hand, and administrative decisions on the other. The distinction was important in the present context because the principles of natural justice were held to apply to judicial (or quasi-judicial decisions) but not to administrative decisions.

Franklin v Minister of Town and Country Planning (1948). In order to relieve London's population density, it was proposed that several new towns should be constructed close to the capital. Stevenage was proposed as a new town by the minister, although many objections were received from the local population. Nevertheless, a draft order designating Stevenage as a new town was publicised in accordance with the New Towns Act 1946. A public local inquiry was held, but despite continued objections, the minister decided to make the order. The appellants who owned houses and land in the area sought to challenge the decision. They argued, amongst other things, that the minister was biased in that he had stated that he would make the order before considering any of the objections. Henn Collins J held for the appellants on the basis that the minister had not complied with his duty to act judicially. His decision was reversed by the CA. The appellants appealed. HL held: in agreement with the CA, that the appellants had not shown that the Minister was biased. He had not been acting in a judicial or quasi-judicial capacity at the material time. Rather, his duties under the 1946 Act were purely administrative.

The distinction between judicial and administrative decisions was, in the words of Lord Denning MR in *R v Gaming Board for Great Britain, ex p Benaim and Khaida* (1970) a 'heresy' that 'was scotched in *Ridge* v *Baldwin*'.

Ridge v Baldwin (1964). R, the chief constable of Brighton, was indicted along with other officers for conspiracy to obstruct the course of justice. He was acquitted but the other officers were convicted. In passing sentence, the trial judge was critical of R, remarking that he had not set a good example to his officers and that he did not have the leadership skills necessary for office. Similar comments were made a week or so later by the judge in respect of a further charge of corruption for which no evidence was adduced. The following day, R was dismissed by the Watch Committee under a power conferred by s 191 (4) of the Municipal Corporations Act 1882. He was not given any notice of the meeting, and neither was he afforded an opportunity to make representations to the committee. A subsequent appeal to the Home Secretary under the Police (Appeals) Act 1927 was dismissed. R sought a declaration from the HCt that his dismissal was illegal and contrary to the principles of natural justice. Streatfield J held that the Watch Committee had acted in accordance with natural justice. CA held that the principles did not need to be followed because the committee had acted in an administrative rather than a judicial capacity. R appealed. HL held: after reviewing the authorities, that although they had sometimes proved to be difficult to reconcile, this was because insufficient attention had been paid to the fact that there was a great difference between the kinds of cases in which the principles of natural justice had been sought to be applied. There was an unbroken line of authority to the effect that an officer cannot be lawfully dismissed without first telling him what is alleged against him and hearing his defence or explanation (Lord Reid).

For R, the outcome was important because if his dismissal were upheld, he would loose his pension rights. If he were required to resign, however, he would not. Nevertheless, from a wider perspective, *Ridge v Baldwin* is a landmark decision in that it sweeps away the distinction between judicial and administrative decisions and instead focuses attention on what effect the decision will have on the individual. The greater the effect in terms of an individual's rights, the more likely the courts will be to require that the standards of natural justice have been complied with. However, it must be borne in mind that the principles of natural justice are not a hard and fast set of rules. What fairness requires will depend upon the particular circumstances. In the words of Lord Bridge in *Lloyd v McMahon* (1987):

> '... the so-called rules of natural justice are not engraved on tablets of stone. To use the phrase which better expresses the underlying concept, what the requirements of fairness demand when any body, domestic, administrative or judicial, has to make a

> decision which will affect the rights of individuals depends on the character of the decision-making body, the kind of decision it has to make and the statutory or other framework in which it operates.'

Legitimate expectations

The phrase 'legitimate expectation' was first coined by Lord Denning MR in *Schmidt v Secretary of State for Home Affairs* (1969) to denote something less than a right which may nevertheless be protected by the principles of natural justice. In essence, a legitimate expectation amounts to an expectation of receiving some benefit or privilege to which the individual has no right. However, the phrase has been used by the courts in a number of different contexts with the result that 'there are many semantic confusions which have bedevilled this area of our law' (per Simon Brown LJ in *R v Devon County Council, ex p Baker (*1995)).

A body or person may have a legitimate expectation to be heard on the basis of a past practice which can reasonably be expected to continue. Thus in the *GCHQ* case, the HL ruled that but for the overriding interests of national security, the court would have upheld the appellants' legitimate expectation to be consulted prior to their conditions of service being altered, since this had been the practice ever since GCHQ was established in 1947. A legitimate expectation may also be created by way of an express undertaking or promise given on behalf of a public authority by a person authorised to do so.

*R v Liverpool Corpn, ex p Liverpool Taxi Fleet Operators' Association (*1972). Under s 37 of the Town Clauses Act 1847, a city council had the power to license such number of hackney carriages in its area as it thought fit. The applicants, who represented 300 existing licence holders, were concerned that new licences would adversely affect the interests of their members. They were given a written assurance by the town clerk that they would be consulted if any change in the number of licences was contemplated. However, the council subsequently passed a resolution to increase the number of licences;" CA held: when considering applications for licences, the council was under a duty to act fairly. It was not at liberty to disregard its undertaking without notice to and representations from the applicants. The council had acted unfairly. A prohibition order was granted to prevent the council acting on its resolutions.

The undertaking which the council had given in the above case was not binding upon them. If it were so, this would have constituted a fetter on its discretion which would have been unlawful under the 'Wednesbury principles'. Nevertheless, if the council wished to depart from its undertaking, it could only do so after it had properly considered the representations from all interested parties.

A legitimate expectation may also be created by an established policy. Thus in the previously mentioned case of *R v Secretary of State for the Home Department, ex p Asif Khan* (1985), the Home Office circular which the Khans received created a legitimate expectation that their case would be decided upon the basis of the published criteria. When the Secretary of State decided their application on the basis of a criterion not mentioned in the circular, he had taken account of an irrelevant consideration. He had also acted unfairly and unreasonably. The justification for the decisions in both *ex p Liverpool Taxi Fleet Operators' Association* and *ex p Khan* is that it would be contrary to the interests of good administration to allow public authorities to resile from promises or undertakings given as to procedures to be followed. Provided that such undertakings or policies do not interfere with a statutory duty, fairness requires that they are complied with. Moreover, if they are to be altered, fairness also requires that those affected by the changes are given an opportunity to be heard.

Thus in the words of Taylor J in *R v Secretary of State for the Home Department, ex p Ruddock* (1987), 'the doctrine of legitimate expectation in essence imposes a duty to act fairly'. This duty to act fairly applies in the context of legitimate procedural expectations as demonstrated by *ex p Liverpool Taxi Fleet Operators' Association*. It also applies where there is a legitimate expectation of a substantive benefit. In *ex p Ruddock*, that substantive benefit was that individuals not falling within the government's published criteria for telephone tapping would not have their telephone calls intercepted by the security services.

One of the most common examples of a legitimate expectation of a substantive benefit occurs in the realm of licensing. The licence itself represents the substantive benefit. The legitimate expectation to receive that benefit may arise by way of an undertaking, a policy or a practice. Those who are responsible for issuing or granting licences are under a general duty to act fairly. However, what the duty requires in terms of the standards of fairness to be applied in a particular case depends upon whether a person is an applicant for a licence, whether they have a legitimate expectation of receiving the licence, or whether they already hold a licence.

McInnes v Onslow Fane (1978). The plaintiff had held a licence to promote boxing bouts as well as a trainer's licence and a master of ceremonies licence. These licences were all withdrawn by the British Boxing Board of Control following an incident at a boxing match. Subsequently the plaintiff applied to the Board for a manager's licence. His applications were refused on six separate occasions. In respect of the last occasion, he sought a declaration that the Board had acted unfairly in that it had not informed him of the case against him and because it had not granted him an oral hearing. Sir Robert Megarry V-C held: dismissing the plaintiffs claims, that where the court is entitled to require that natural justice be observed, three types of decision could be identified: forfeiture cases; expectation cases; and application cases. The requirements of natural justice were different with regard to each. In the present case, since the plaintiff was merely an applicant, the duty to act fairly required that that the Board act honestly and without bias or caprice.

The decision in McInnes is important for several different reasons. First and foremost amongst these is what it tells us about natural justice or fairness. Patently this is a flexible concept according to the type of decision made. In the forfeiture cases, where an existing right has been taken away, Sir Robert Megarry V-C felt that three features of natural justice were apt: the right to an unbiased tribunal; the right to notice of the charges; and the right to be heard in answer to the charges. At the other end of the spectrum, the mere applicant was entitled to very little, as *McInnes* itself demonstrates. What Sir Robert Megarry V-C termed the 'intermediate category', the expectation cases, arose where the applicant had a legitimate expectation, based on what had previously happened, that his application would be granted. Thus, for example, a person seeking the renewal of a licence would have a legitimate expectation that it would be granted. Sir Robert Megarry V-C considered that these cases were more akin to the forfeiture rather than the application cases. Accordingly, at the very least, natural justice required that the individual should be informed as to why he was no longer considered to be suitable for the licence which he had previously held.

The decision in *Mclnnes* is also of interest in that it presages a tendency amongst the judiciary, apparent in subsequent judicial review cases (see, for example, *R v Disciplnary Committee of the Jockey Club, ex p Aga Khan* (1993) and *R v Football Association Ltd, ex p Football League* (1993)), towards a reluctance to interfere with the decisions made by sports governing bodies. Towards the end of his judgment, Sir Robert Megarry V-C made the point unequivocally:

> The concepts of natural justice and the duty to be fair must not be allowed to discredit themselves by making unreasonable requirements and imposing undue burdens.'

The right to a fair hearing

The right to a fair hearing is a core feature of the principles of natural justice or the duty to act fairly. Traditionally it has been expressed in the Latin maxim *'audi alteram portem'* (hear both sides). In truth, the right to a fair hearing is a broad concept which means something more than simply allowing the parties to put their side of the case. It is implicit in the principle that a person should be given sufficient notice of a hearing in order that they can prepare their case. Moreover, to be able to do this in an effective manner, it is imperative that they are properly informed of the case against them. However, there may be circumstances where the requirements of fairness are overridden by other interests.

Thus in *R v Secretary of State for the Home Department, ex p Hosenball* (1977), a case involving a challenge to the Secretary of

State's decision to deport H on the ground that his continued presence in the UK was not conducive to the public good, it was accepted by the CA that H knew nothing and had been told nothing of the nature of the confidential information which formed the basis of the decision. He had not been given the opportunity of correcting or contradicting any of the information, or of testing it by cross-examination. Moreover, he had not been given sufficient information as to the charges against him so as to be able to respond to them. Nevertheless, in the words of Lord Denning MR, this was:

> '... a case in which national security is involved, and our history shows that, when the state itself is endangered, our cherished freedoms may have to take second place. Even natural justice itself may suffer a setback ... The rules of natural justice have to be modified in regard to foreigners here who prove themselves unwelcome and ought to be deported.'

It is difficult to be precise as to what form a 'hearing' will take. The right to a fair hearing need not entail an oral hearing. It may be that the decision-maker is of the opinion that cases can be dealt with on the basis of written submissions. This may be a particularly attractive option where, for example, the decision-maker is a licensing body dealing with a great many applications. Provided that this has meant that a person has had a reasonable opportunity to put their case, fairness is unlikely to make further demands of the decision-making procedure. Where, however, a decision could have profound consequences for an individual in terms of their liberty or livelihood, it is likely that fairness will require a decision-making process which entails an oral hearing. At the hearing itself, fairness will require that individuals have the opportunity to contest the evidence adduced against them. Where that evidence takes the form of witness statements, fairness may require that an opportunity is afforded to cross-examine the witnesses. However, this is not an absolute right. Whether or not cross-examination is permitted will fall to be determined according to the circumstances of the particular case.

A right to legal representation?

Where an oral hearing is held, it might be assumed that the parties have a right to be legally represented. However, this is not the case. Thus in *R v Board of Visitors* of *HM Prison, The Maze, ex p Hone* (1988), where the appellants alleged that the Board's decisions not to allow them to be legally represented during disciplinary proceeding amounted to a breach of natural justice, Lord Goff observed that:

> 'I am unable to accept ... that any person charged with a crime (or the equivalent thereof) and liable to punishment is entitled as a matter of natural justice to legal representation. No doubt it is true that a charged with a crime before a criminal court is entitled to legal representation ... No doubt it is also correct that a board of visitors is bound to give effect to the rules of natural justice. But it does not follow that, simply because a charge before a disciplinary tribunal such as a board of visitors relates to facts which in law constitute a crime, the rules of natural justice require the tribunal to grant legal representation'.

Whether or not legal representation will be allowed is initially a matter for the decision-maker to determine. In exercising its discretion, it may take a number of factors into account. For example, if a complex point of law is at issue, it may be that the decision-maker would allow legal representation. Similarly, if the individual does not have the capacity to present his own case, fairness may require that legal representation be allowed. Thus in *Pett v Greyhound Racing Association* (1969), where P faced the prospect of loosing his livelihood if allegations of doping greyhounds were made out against him, Lord Denning MR remarked that:

> 'It is not every man who has the ability to defend himself on his own. He cannot bring out the point in his own favour or the weakness in the other side. He may be tongue-tied or nervous, confused or wanting in intelligence. He cannot examine or cross-examine witnesses... [in a court] if justice is to be done, he ought

> to have the help of someone to speak for him; and who better than a lawyer who has been trained for the task? I should have thought, therefore, that when a man's reputation or livelihood is at stake, he not only has the right to speak by his own mouth. He also has a right to speak by counsel or solicitor.'

Reasons

We have already seen that on occasion, a statutory provision may require a decision-maker to give reasons for a decision. Few would deny as a matter of principle that this is a reasonable and appropriate aspect of procedural fairness. It seems only right that a person ought to be informed of the reasons why a decision has gone against them. Nevertheless, at common law, there is no duty on the decision-maker to give reasons.

R v Gaming Board for Great Britain, ex *p Benaim and Khaida* (1970). By virtue of the Gaming Act 1968, gaming could only take place in premises licensed by magistrates. However, prior to applying for a licence, it was necessary to obtain a certificate of consent from the Gaming Board (set up under the 1968 Act). The applicants were denied a certificate and the Board refused to give reasons for its decision. They sought an order of certiorari to quash the Board's refusal and an order of mandamus to compel the Board to inform them of the case against them. CA held: the Board was bound to observe the rules of natural justice. It ought to be able to give an applicant a sufficient indication of the objections raised against him so as to enable him to answer them. However, it was not bound to give the reasons for its decision.

Similarly in *McInnes* v *Onslow Fane* (1978), Sir Robert Megarry V-C observed that: 'there is no general obligation to give reasons for a decision'. Where, for example, a board, panel or local authority is dealing with a great many applications for licences, the fact that it is not under a duty to give reasons for its decisions may serve to ease the administrative burden which has been placed upon it. In such circumstances, a failure to give reasons may be due to entirely genuine considerations. However, difficulties arise where no reasons have been given for a decision and there do not appear to be any to justify the conclusion reached. In these circumstances, a court may be at liberty to infer that there was no good reason for the decision: see Lord Upjohn in *Padfield v Minister of Agriculture, Food and Fisheries* (1968).

Since the *Gaming Board* case was decided, it has become possible to discern an increasing willingness on the part of the judiciary to rule in a given situation that the duty to act fairly required that reasons be given for a decision. Thus in *R v Civil Service Appeal Board, ex p Cunningham* (1991), the CA held that natural justice required that the Board should give reasons for its decision relating to an unfair dismissal claim. In reaching such a conclusion, the CA was influenced by factors such as: there was no appeal from the board's determination; in making a determination it was carrying out a judicial function; the board was susceptible to judicial review; it was not a case where the giving of reasons would be harmful to the public interest.

In a later case, the HL was also required to consider the legal position vis-a-vis the giving of reasons.

R v Secretary of State for the Home Department, ex p Doody (1994). The applicants were serving mandatory life sentences for murder. Parole could only be considered by the Parole Board following the expiration of a prescribed period. This period was set by the Home Secretary (HS) following recommendations by the trial judges. In the present case, the HS decided not to follow those recommendations and set lengthier prescribed periods. The applicants claimed that he had acted unlawfully by failing to give reasons for his decisions. HL held: the procedure was unfair. Although the law does not recognise a general duty to give reasons for an administrative decision, such a duty may in appropriate circumstances be implied. It was contrary to the public interest not to give reasons in the present case. Moreover, since the decision of the HS was susceptible to judicial review, an effective attack on it could only be mounted if his reasoning was disclosed.

The decision in *Doody* demonstrates, therefore, that where an individual's liberty is at issue, a duty to give reasons for his continued incarceration arises. The proposition that there is no general duty to give reasons nevertheless remains valid, and accordingly, whether or not reasons should have been given will be decided on a case-by-case basis.

R v Higher Education Funding Council, ex p Institute of Dental Surgery (1994). The institute sought to challenge by way of judicial review a decision made by the Funding Council as to the institute's research rating. It argued that the council was under a duty to give reasons for its decision, and that the absence of reasons indicated that its decision was irrational. DC held: this was an example of a decision in respect of which fairness did not demand that reasons be given.

In *ex p Institute of Dental Surgery*, the DC acknowledged that there are a number of factors in favour of requiring reasons to be given for a decision. These included:

- concentrating the decision-maker's mind on the right questions;
- demonstrating to the recipient of the decision that this was so;
- showing that the issues have been properly addressed and how the decision has been reached; or
- alerting the recipient to a justiciable flaw in the process.

Conversely, there were other factors in favour of not requiring reasons to be given. These included:

- that it may place an undue burden on the decision-maker;
- that it would demand the appearance of unanimity where there is diversity;
- that it would call for the articulation of value judgments which were sometimes inexpressible; and
- it would encourage people to examine the reasons looking for previously unsuspected grounds of challenge.

For a helpful summary of the principles which have emerged from *Cunningham*, *Doody* and *ex p Institute of Dental Surgery*, see the judgment of Hooper J in *R v Ministry of Defence*, ex *p Murray* (1998). In that case, which involved the judicial review of decisions by a District Court-Martial to imprison M for six months, to reduce him to the ranks and to dismiss him from the army, in holding that reasons should be given for those decisions, Lord Bingham CJ observed that:

> 'An unreasoned decision, followed by unreasoned rejections of applications for review, leaves an uneasy suspicion (which reasons might dispel) that justice may not have been done.'

The rule against bias

It is self-evident that in order for a decision-making process to be fair, there should be an absence of bias. What amounts to bias is, however, a rather more difficult and practically important matter, especially when it is borne in mind that 'bias is an insidious thing that, even though a person may in good faith believe that he was acting impartially, his mind may unconsciously be affected by bias' (per Lord Goff in *R v Gough* (1993)).

Until recently, the authorities revealed that the English courts had developed two tests for identifying bias: reasonable suspicion of bias; and real likelihood of bias. Thus in *R v Altrincham Justices, ex p Pennington* (1975), Lord Widgery favoured the former test, whereas in *R v Metropolitan London Rent Assessment Panel Committee, ex p Properties Co (FGC) Ltd* (1969), Lord Denning spoke in terms of the real likelihood of bias test. Although the distinction between bodies performing a judicial and an administrative function is no longer important in terms of the application of the principles of natural justice (see *Ridge v Baldwin* (1964), there was a school of thought that it did still have an influence on which of the tests for bias should apply. Thus in *Steeples v Derbyshire County Council* (1984), Webster J cautiously advocated the stricter standard (reasonable suspicion of bias) being applied to bodies with judicial functions and the less strict standard (real likelihood of bias), being applied to administrative bodies. Such distinctions have been rendered unnecessary by a recent decision of the HL.

R v Gough (1993). G was tried for conspiring with his brother to rob a betting shop. Proceedings against his brother had been dropped at the committal stage. Nevertheless, during the trial, a photograph of the brother was shown to the jury and his name was mentioned. At the end of the trial, G was convicted and sentenced to 15 years' imprisonment. His brother protested from the public gallery and at this point, one of the jurors realised that the brother was her neighbour. G appealed against his conviction on the basis that this amounted to a serious irregularity in the conduct of the trial. His appeal was rejected by the CA. HL held: dismissing his appeal, that it was both possible and desirable that the same test should be applicable in all cases of apparent bias. That test was a real danger of bias. Real danger was preferable to real likelihood so as to encourage the courts to think in terms of the possibility rather than the probability of bias. Applying that test to the facts of the case, there was no ground for disturbing the jury's verdict.

Subsequently the 'real danger of bias' test has been held to apply to statements made by a coroner: *R v Inner West London Coroner, ex p Dallaglio* (1994). Its general application to decisions of a judicial or administrative nature was confirmed in *R v Secretary of State for the Environment, ex p Kirkstall Valley Campaign* (1996). However, in *R v Local Comr for Administration in North and North East England, ex p Liverpool City Council* (1999), Hooper J held that although the 'real danger of bias' test might be applicable on an application for judicial review of a planning decision, the commissioner was entitled to apply a more stringent test set out in the National Code of Local Government Conduct. This was the test by which councillors had agreed to be bound. Interestingly, as Professor Craig has noted, the *Gough* test has either not been used or has been modified in some Commonwealth jurisdictions. Thus in *Gascor v Ellicott* (1997), Tadgell JA in the Supreme Court of Victoria observed that:

'Although the criterion of apprehension of partiality of prejudice is possibility, not likelihood, a reasonable apprehension is to be established to the court's satisfaction: it is a reasonable and not a fanciful or fantastic apprehension that is to be established; and the apprehension is to be attributed to an observer who is "fair minded" - which means "reasonable".'

Pecuniary interest *bias*

Occasions may arise where a person scheduled to sit in a judicial capacity would have a pecuniary interest in the outcome of the proceedings. In these circumstances, the appropriate course of action would be to declare the interest and stand down from the case since as Blackburn J observed in *R v Rand* (1866): 'any direct pecuniary interest, however small, in the subject of inquiry, does disqualify a person from acting as judge in the matter'. Where this has not been done, the courts will be quick to set aside a decision even though there is no actual evidence of bias. Their reason for so acting is that public confidence in the administration of justice would be undermined if the decision were allowed to stand. In the words of Lord Hewart CJ in *R v Sussex Justices*, ex *p McCarthy* (1924), it is of 'fundamental importance that justice should not only be done, but should manifestly be seen to be done'. Two cases serve to illustrate the point.

Grand Junction Canal Co v Dimes (1852). Lord Cottenham LC owned a substantial shareholding in the defendant canal company. He heard an appeal and affirmed an earlier decision in favour of the company. There was an appeal to the HL on the grounds that the LC was disqualified by reason of his pecuniary interest in the case. HL held: the LC was disqualified from hearing the case. The principle that no man should be a judge in his own cause was not confined to a case in which he was a party. It also applied to a cause in which he has an interest.

R v Bow Street Metropoliton Stipendiary Magistrate Court, ex *p Pinochet Legarte (No 2)* (1999). P was the former Head of State of Chile. Whilst in the UK his extradition was sought by the government of Spain which wanted him to stand trial for crimes against humanity alleged to have been committed whilst he was Head of State. Warrants for his arrest were issued by the magistrates. The HL was required to consider the extent and scope of the immunity of a former Head of State from arrest and extradition proceedings. Before the appeal was heard, a committee of three Law Lords granted Amnesty International (AI) and several other interested parties leave to intervene in the appeal. AI therefore made written submissions and were represented by counsel. The HL decided by a majority of 3:2 that P was not entitled to immunity. Subsequently it became apparent that one of the Law Lords in the majority was a director and chairperson of Amnesty International Ltd, the charitable arm of AI. P's lawyers therefore appealed. HL held: where the decision of a judge would lead to the promotion of a cause with which he was involved together with one of the parties, he would be automatically excluded from hearing the matter even though he had no pecuniary interest in the outcome of the case. On the facts of the present case, Lord Hoffmann was automatically disqualified from hearing the appeal. The matter would therefore be referred to another committee of the HL for rehearing.

It must be appreciated that in neither of these two cases was it alleged that either judge was in fact biased. However, the nature of their relationships with a canal company on the one hand and AI on the other were sufficient to disqualify them. The decision in *ex p Pinochet* (No 2) is therefore novel in that, hitherto, a pecuniary or proprietary interest had been the basis of automatic disqualification. Lord Hoffmann had neither kind of interest.

The 'real danger of bias' test was at issue in a number of appeals recently heard by the CA. Whilst the majority of these were rejected by the court, in *Timmins v Gormley* (2000), the appeal was allowed on the grounds of bias. The CA concluded that although there was no evidence of actual bias, the views expressed by a recorder in his writings on personal injuries claims indicated that he had strong pro-claimant and anti-insurer views. Applying a broad common sense approach, the CA concluded, not without misgiving, that there was a real danger that a person with such views might unconsciously lean in favour of the claimant and against the defendant when determining the issues between them.

FURTHER READING

P P Craig 'Legitimate Expectations: A Conceptual Analysis' (1992) 107 LQR 79.

4

THE DOCTRINE OF LEGITIMATE EXPECTATIONS

THE EMERGENCE OF THE DOCTRINE IN ENGLISH ADMINISTRATIVE LAW

Schmidt v Secretary of State for Home Affairs (1969) CA

The plaintiffs were Scientology students who had applied for an extension to their leave to remain in the UK. Their application was rejected. They sought a declaration that the refusal was *ultra vires,* on the grounds that they had not been given an opportunity to be heard.

Held, *per* Lord Denning MR, that the question whether a hearing was required depended on whether the applicants had some right, interest or legitimate expectation of which it would not be fair to deprive them without hearing what they had to say. In respect of their entitlement to remain for the period originally limited, they had; in respect of an extension to that period, they had not.

LEGITIMATE EXPECTATION AS A MEANS OF ESTABLISHING *LOCUS STANDI*

O'Reilly v Mackman (1983) HL

Per Lord Diplock:

> ... all that each applicant had was a legitimate expectation, based on his knowledge of what is the general practice, that he would be granted the

> maximum remission ... of one-third of his sentence if by that time no disciplinary award of forfeiture of remission had been made against him ... such legitimate expectation gave to each appellant a sufficient interest to challenge the legality of the adverse disciplinary award made against him by the board.

THE RECOGNITION OF LEGITIMATE EXPECTATIONS

Findlay v Secretary of State for the Home Department (1984) HL

In October 1983, the Home Secretary announced his intention to abolish the joint Home Office/Parole Board committee which had formerly recommended when a life prisoner should first be considered by a local review committee for parole, and to determine that date himself in consultation with the judiciary. He further announced that prisoners sentenced for certain classes of offence would in future normally serve at least 20 years of their sentences. The appellants, who were affected by the changes in policy, sought, *inter alia*, an order of prohibition to prevent the Home Secretary from applying the new policy to them, arguing that the policy constituted a fettering of the Home Secretary's discretion and that they had a legitimate expectation of release at the date that would have been set under the previous policy.

Held, dismissing the appeals, that the adoption of the policy did not amount to a fettering of discretion since it did not preclude the consideration of individual cases, and that the expectation contended for by the appellants did not arise. *Per* Lord Scarman:

> They had good reason under the practice which had prevailed before the adoption of the new policy to expect release much earlier than became likely after its adoption ... It is said that the refusal to except them from the new policy was an unlawful act on the part of the Secretary of State in that his decision frustrated their expectation. But what was their *legitimate* expectation? Given the substance and purpose of the legislative provisions governing parole, the most that

> a convicted prisoner can legitimately expect is that his case will be examined individually in the light of whatever policy the Secretary of State sees fit to adopt, provided always that the adopted policy is a lawful exercise of the discretion conferred upon him by the statute.

R v Board of Inland Revenue ex p MFK Underwriting Agencies (1990)

With a view to offering an improved investment opportunity to the Lloyds market, certain US banks proposed to issue index-linked US or Canadian dollar securities for the investment of US or Canadian premium income. The banks and their advisors approached the Revenue independently for confirmation that the index-linked element payable on redemption of the securities would be taxed as a capital gain, and not as income. The responses of Revenue officials indicated that they considered the index-linked element would be taxable as capital gain rather than income. The applicants purchased index-linked bonds, on the basis that they would be so taxed. In fact, the Revenue later decided to tax the index-linked element as income. The applicants sought judicial review of the Revenue's decision, contending that it breached their legitimate expectations, and was therefore unfair and amounted to an abuse of power.

Held, dismissing the application, that, although the Revenue had informally promulgated guidelines and indicated its likely approach to the taxation question, several factors required to be proved before its responses could fetter performance of its public duty to collect taxes payable on a proper construction of the relevant law. The taxpayer would have had to have provided full details of the matter on which he sought the Revenue's ruling. He would have had to have made plain that a fully considered ruling was sought and to have specified the use to which he intended to put that ruling. The Revenue would be bound only by a ruling or statement which was clear, unambiguous and devoid of relevant qualification. In the judgment of Bingham LJ, it was one thing to ask an official of the Revenue whether he shared the taxpayer's view of a legislative provision, but quite another to ask whether the Revenue would forgo a claim to tax on any other basis.

***R v Inland Revenue Commissioners ex p Unilever plc* (1996) CA**

By s 393 of the Income and Corporation Taxes Act 1988, a taxpayer might make a claim for trading loss relief within two years from the end of the accounting period in which the loss was sustained or within such further period as the Board may allow'. For many years, it had been the applicant's practice to offset trading loss against profits when submitting preliminary accounts. However, the offsetting of trading loss was expressly notified only after the finalisation of each year's accounts. As a result of the complexity of the applicant's tax affairs, this notification had fallen outside the statutory time period on 30 occasions. In respect of three recent accounting periods, the Revenue refused to allow the applicant loss relief on the ground that its claim was late. The applicant argued: (a) that the preliminary accounts constituted notification of claim within the period; or (b) that in fairness the Revenue's past acquiescence debarred it from reversing its practice; and (c) that the Revenue should have exercised its statutory discretion in the applicant's favour. At first instance, the application succeeded on grounds (b) and (c).

Held, upholding the decision at first instance, that the claims had not been made within the two year period. However, the Revenue's rejection of the applicant's claims without advance notice was so unfair as to amount to an abuse of power. It was true that the Revenue had made no dear, unambiguous and unqualified representation that it would accept late claims, nor could it be said to have acquiesced in or waived a non-compliance of which it had simply been unaware. However, the facts of the present case were unique. The entitlement to claim trading loss was a fundamental one. There was no useful purpose to be achieved by an insistence on the merely regulatory statutory time limit. The error with regard to the time limit was common to both parties, and the Revenue would presumably have alerted the applicant to its prejudicial consequences had it realised it. The tax now claimed was to be regarded as an adventitious windfall accruing to the Revenue through the mistake of an honest and compliant taxpayer. In the circumstances, that claim was so unfair as to amount to an abuse of power. Equally (and, in the judgment of the Master of the Rolls, this and the preceding point were substantially the same), the Revenue's failure to exercise its statutory discretion to extend the time limit was so unreasonable as to satisfy the public law test of irrationality.

R v Swale Borough Council and Medway Ports Authority ex p The Royal Society for the Protection of Birds (1991)

The applicant, a conservation charity with over half a million members, sought to challenge the grant of planning permission by the Council to the Authority for the 'land reclamation' of 125 acres of Lappel Bank, a site of recognised environmental importance under domestic and international law. The applicant argued, *inter alia,* that its officer, Dr Clarke, had received an assurance in the course of correspondence that he would be consulted on any application received, and that this legitimate expectation had been breached. The respondents contended that the assurance of consultation had been given only in the context of development proposals already received. It could not reasonably have been taken to extend to any application in the relevant location, and the absence of any immediate protest by the applicants when Dr Clarke was not consulted suggested further that he had, in fact, had no legitimate expectation of consultation.

Simon Brown J noted that Dr Clarke was as convinced that he had been entitled to be consulted as the respondent was that no such entitlement had arisen. The approach to such a misunderstanding being free from authority in public law, Simon Brown J adopted a contractual test; only if the reasonable bystander would regard the promise as being made in the sense contended for by the applicant would his expectation be regarded as not merely reasonable but legitimate also. On the application of this test to the facts, the applicants' contention was to be preferred. However, since they had unduly delayed so that the grant of relief would now be likely to cause substantial prejudice to third parties, their challenge was dismissed.

R v Secretary of State for the Home Department ex p Hargreaves (1996) CA

LEGITIMATE EXPECTATION AS A MEANS OF SECURING PROCEDURAL RIGHTS

Attorney General for Hong Kong v Ng Yuen Shiu (1983) PC

The government of Hong Kong announced that it was terminating its policy of not repatriating illegal immigrants from China who had reached the urban area of Hong Kong. The applicant and others, illegal immigrants of Chinese origin from Macau, sought to clarify their position. They were told by the Secretary for Security that they would be interviewed, and that each case would be treated on its own merits. A removal order was made against the applicant.

Held that the removal order would be quashed. Although the applicant, as an illegal immigrant, had no general right to a fair hearing before a removal order was made against him, he had a legitimate expectation of a fair hearing based on what he had been told by the Secretary for Security. When a public authority had promised to follow a certain procedure, it was in the interest of good administration that it should act fairly and should implement its promise, so long as implementation did not interfere with its statutory duty. The quashing of the removal order was, however, entirely without prejudice to the making of a new order once the applicant had been heard.

LEGITIMATE EXPECTATION AS A MEANS OF SECURING SUBSTANTIVE RIGHTS

R v Secretary of State for the Home Department ex p Khan (1984) CA

The applicant wished to adopt the child of a relative, living with its natural mother in Pakistan. Although the Immigration Rules did not permit a child's entry for these purposes, a Home Office circular stated that, in exceptional circumstances, the Secretary of State would permit entry if specified criteria were met. The criteria appeared to be satisfied in Khan's case, but the Secretary of State applied different criteria and refused entry leave to the child. The applicant sought an order of certiorari.

Held, granting the order, that the Home Office circular gave the applicant a legitimate expectation that entry would be granted if the specified criteria were met. The Secretary of State was at liberty to change his policy, but before he did so vis a vis a recipient of the circular, he would be obliged to give full and serious consideration whether some overriding public interest justified the change.

R v Secretary of State for the Home Department ex p Ruddock (1987)

The applicant alleged that the Secretary of State had authorised the interception of her telephone calls in order to gain party political advantage. The criteria governing the issue of interception warrants had been published six times between 1952 and I982, and adopted by the Secretary of State. The applicant argued that she had a legitimate expectation that the Secretary of State would abide by the criteria when deciding whether to intercept her calls, and that in her case, the criteria were not met. Counsel for the Secretary of State contended that the doctrine of legitimate expectation related only to cases where an applicant's expectation was of being consulted or given the opportunity to make representations before a decision adverse to the applicant was taken. It had no relevance in the present circumstances, where the efficacy of the interception depended on the maintenance of secrecy.

Held, dismissing the application, that the applicant's evidence did not establish that the Secretary of State had acted for an improper purpose. However, the applicant did have a legitimate expectation. Although most of the cases on legitimate expectation were concerned with a right to be heard, the doctrine was not so confined. *Per* Taylor J: 'In a case where, *ex hypothesi,* there is no right to be heard, it may be thought the more important to fair dealing that a promise or undertaking given by a Minister as to how he will proceed should be kept.' Here, the expectation arose both from an express promise given on behalf of a public authority, and from the existence of a regular practice which the applicant could reasonably expect to continue. The Secretary of State had adduced evidence that all decisions within his purview had been made in accordance with the criteria, and therefore the applicant's expectation had not been disappointed.

R v Ministry of Agriculture, Fisheries and Food ex p Hamble (Offshore) Fisheries Ltd (1995)

Arguing against the substantive legitimate expectation claimed by the applicant, counsel for the respondent relied on a passage from the judgment of Laws J in *R v Secretary of State for Transport ex p Richmond upon Thames London Borough Council* (1994) to establish that neither precedent nor principle permitted the vindication of substantive legitimate expectations. Disagreeing, Sedley J noted that *Ruddock* and *Findlay (obiter)* had recognised the possibility of substantive legitimate expectations, and continued:

> In my respectful view, principle as well as precedent points to these conclusions ... It is difficult to see why it is any less unfair to frustrate a legitimate expectation that something will or will not be done by the decision maker than it is to frustrate a legitimate expectation that the applicant will be listened to before the decision maker decides whether to take a particular step. Such a doctrine does not risk fettering a public body in the discharge of public duties because no individual can legitimately expect the discharge of public duties to stand still or to be distorted because of that individual's peculiar position.

CONSIDERATIONS OVERRIDING LEGITIMATE EXPECTATIONS

National security

Council of Civil Service Unions v Minister for the Civil Service (1985) HL

The Government Communications Headquarters (GCHQ) was responsible for the provision of intelligence to the government, and for the security of military and official communications. Since the establishment of GCHQ in 1947, its staff had been permitted to belong to civil service trade unions, and GCHQ management had regularly consulted with the unions. Following industrial action at GCHQ, the Prime Minister (in her capacity as Minister for the Civil Service) sought to curtail staff rights of trade union membership by an instruction issued under prerogative powers for controlling the Civil Service. The CCSU sought a declaration that the Minister had acted unfairly in removing staff rights of trade union membership without consultation. The Minister argued that consultation would have provoked the very disruption and endangering of national security which her instruction was intended to terminate.

Held, proceeding on the basis that the exercise of delegated prerogative powers was justifiable, that, although the staff had no legal right to prior consultation, they had a legitimate expectation to it. Such expectation might arise either from an express promise given by a public authority or, as here, from a regular practice of consultation which the applicant could reasonably expect to continue. In the absence of evidence that an issue of national security was involved, it would have been proper to grant the declaration sought.

The need to preserve freedom of administrative action

R v Secretary of State for Health ex p United States Tobacco (1992)

The applicant manufactured oral snuff. In 1985, when the government was already aware of a link between oral snuff and cancer, the applicant received a government grant. At the same time, the government obtained the applicant's agreement to place a health warning on its product, and not to market it to those aged less than 18 years. In 1988, the Department of Health announced that it intended to ban the manufacture of oral snuff. The applicant sought judicial review on two grounds: first, that the Secretary of State was in breach of a statutory duty to consult it as an affected party, and, secondly, that it had a legitimate expectation that it would be permitted to continue to manufacture snuff as long as it kept to its agreement regarding marketing and the health warning.

Held that the applicant would succeed on the first ground and fail on the second. The applicant had no legitimate expectation. *Per* Taylor LJ, the Secretary of State's discretion to change his policy could not be fettered by moral obligations to the applicant deriving from the earlier favourable treatment of them'. *Per* Morland J, the applicant 'must have been aware that their expectations could never fetter the Secretary of State's public duty to promote and safeguard the health of the public'.

> Q Instead of holding that the applicant's legitimate expectation is overridden here by the public interest in continuing governmental freedom of action, the court denies that a legitimate expectation arises in the first place. Is the distinction of any importance?

R v Ministry of Agriculture, Fisheries and Food ex p Hamble (Offshore) Fisheries (1995)

The applicant's arguments based on legitimate expectation failed. Legitimacy, in the sense in which it applied to expectations in public law, was not absolute. Its presence was to be gauged by balancing the expectations induced by government and the policy considerations which militated against their fulfilment. Sedley J continued:

> The balance must in the first instance be for the policy maker to strike; but if the outcome is challenged by way of judicial review, *I do not consider that the court's criterion* is *the bare rationality of the policy maker's conclusion.* While policy is for the policy maker alone, the fairness of his or her decision not to accommodate reasonable expectations which the policy will thwart remains the court's concern (as of course does the lawfulness of the policy). To postulate this is not to place the judge in the seat of the Minister ... it is the court's task to recognise the constitutional importance of ministerial freedom to formulate and to reformulate policy; but it is equally the court's duty to protect the interests of those individuals whose expectation of different treatment has a legitimacy which *in fairness* outtops the policy choice which threatens to frustrate it ... legitimate expectation is now in effect a term of art, reserved for expectations which are not only reasonable but which will be sustained by the court in the face of changes of policy ... whether this point has been reached is determined by the court, whether on the grounds of rationality, of legality *or of fairness*, of all of which the court, not the decision maker, is the arbiter. [Emphasis supplied.]

R v Secretary of State for the Home Department ex p Hargreaves (1996) CA

The applicants were three prisoners serving sentences at HMP Risley. Pursuant to rules made by the Secretary of State and in force at the beginning of their sentences, they would have been eligible to apply for periods of home leave after serving one-third of their terms of imprisonment. These rules were communicated to prisoners in the form of a notice and 'compact', setting out responsibilities undertaken by the prison, and requiring signed commitments to norms of good behaviour by the prisoners. In response to perceived public concern, the Secretary of State amended the rules by statutory instrument in 1995 with the result that eligibility to home leave accrued only on the completion of half the sentence to be served by a prisoner. The applicants claimed that the change denied them a legitimate expectation on the terms of the original rules. The Divisional Court dismissed the applications on the grounds: (a) that no clear and unambiguous representations had been established, and (b) that the correct test by which to judge the Secretary of State's change of policy was not the balance of fairness and proportionality, but the public law test of irrationality.

Held, upholding the judgment of the Divisional Court, that the principle in *Findlay* disposed of the present case. Although it was to be regretted that the compact and notice had insufficiently stressed the dependence of entitlement to home leave and other privileges upon the regime currently in force, those documents nevertheless suggested that this was the position, and certainly contained no contrary indications. Where procedural irregularity was alleged against a Minister, it was appropriate to inquire into the fairness of the procedure adopted by him, but where, as in the present case, a substantive defect was alleged, it fell to be judged by the far stricter irrationality test. The contrary suggestion by Sedley J in *Hamble* was inconsistent with authority and heretical.

Q Is a frustration of a legitimate expectation as to procedure *prima facie* to be regarded as a 'procedural irregularity' or as a 'substantive defect'?

5

THE DUTY TO GIVE REASONS

THE CONSEQUENCES OF FAILURE TO GIVE REASONS

Padfield v Minister for Agriculture, Fisheries and Food (1968) HL

Per Lord Pearce:

> It all the *prima facie* reasons seem to point in favour of [the Minister] taking a certain course to carry out the intention of Parliament in respect of a power which it has given to him in that regard, and he gives no reason whatever for taking a contary court, the course may infer that he has no good reason and that he is not using the power given by Parliament to carry out its intentions.

R v Secretary of State for Trade and Industry ex p Lonrho pic (1989) HL

Lonrho sought judicial review of, *inter alia,* the refusal of the Secretary of State to refer a rival company's acquisition of shares in House of Fraser to the Monopolies and Mergers Commission. Lonrho alleged that the refusal to refer was irrational, and submitted that the Secretary of State's failure to give reasons for his decision should lead to the conclusion that he had no proper reason for it.

Held, dismissing Lonrho's appeal on these and other grounds, that Lonrho had failed to establish that the Secretary of State had acted irrationally. *Per* Lord Keith:

> The absence ot reasons for a decision where there is no duty to give them cannot of itself provide any support for the suggested irrationality of the decision. The only significance of the absence of reasons is that if all the other known facts and circumstances appear to point overwhelmingly in favour or a different decision, the decision maker who has given no reasons cannot complain if the court draws the inference that he had no rational reason for his decision.

CIRCUMSTANCES IN WHICH THE COMMON LAW IMPOSES A DUTY TO GIVE REASONS

R v Civil Service Appeal Board ex p Cunningham (1991) CA

The applicant, a prisoner officer, was dismissed after accusations against him that he had assaulted a prisoner. As a civil servant, he had to seek compensation for unfair dismissal from the Civil Service Appeal Board, rather than from an industrial tribunal. The board awarded him approximately one-third of the sum he could have expected to receive from an industrial tribunal, and gave no reasons for its decision.

Held that, in the circumstances, the board was under a duty to give reasons for its decision. Leggatt LJ considered it obvious that, for reasons of fairness, the applicant should be entitled to know the reasons for the award, so that in the event of error he would be in a position to apply to court for judicial review to challenge it. He had 'a legitimate grievance, because it looks as though his compensation is less than it should be, and yet he has not been told the basis of the assessment'. The absence of reasons did not by itself entitle the court to hold that the award was not supportable. But the unexplained meagreness of the award did compel that inference.

In the view of McCowan LJ, not only had justice not been seen to be done, but there was no way, in the absence of reasons from the board, in which it could be judged whether in fact it had been done. McCowan LJ stated that he was influenced by the following factors:

(1) There is no appeal from the board's determination of the amount of compensation.

(2) In making that determination, the board is carrying out a judicial function.

(3) The board is susceptible to judicial review.

(4) The procedure provided for by the code, that is to say, the provision of a recommendation without reasons is insufficient to achieve justice.

(5) There is no statute which requires the courts to tolerate that unfairness.

(6) The giving of short reasons would not frustrate the apparent purpose of the code.

(7) It is not a case where the giving of reasons would be harmful to the public interest.

Lord Donaldson MR considered that the board was a judicial body carrying out functions akin to those of an industrial tribunal. Fairness demanded that, just as an industrial tribunal would be under a duty to give reasons by virtue of the Tribunals and Inquiries Act 1958, so the board should give sufficient reasons for its decision to enable the parties to know the issues to which it addressed its mind and that it acted lawfully.

Doody v Secretary of State for the Home Department (1993) HL

Mandatory life sentences consisted of two periods of time - a fixed penal period, reflecting the requirements of retribution and deterrence, and the remaining 'risk period', at some time during which the prisoner might be released on licence. There were two inputs into the fixing of the penal period; recommendations made after trial by the trial judge, and a decision by the Home Secretary. The applicant argued that he was entitled to be told by the Home Secretary what penal period had been recommended by the judiciary and any departure by the Home Secretary from it. He further claimed that he should be told the reasons both for the judiciary's and the Home Secretary's views. In the Court of Appeal, he succeeded in all but the last of his claims.

Held that he should succeed in the final part of his claim as well. Lord Mustill began by reiterating the fact that the present law recognises no general duty to give reasons for an administrative decision, but added that in appropriate circumstances a duty might be implied. He explained the two approaches which led him to impose a duty in the present case. First, a refusal to give reasons was not fair to the prisoner. It was a matter of unparalleled importance to him. In the case of any other sentence, the prisoner would as a matter of course be told the reasons for it at the time of sentencing:

> Contrast this with the position of the prisoner sentenced for murder. He never sees the Home Secretary; he cannot fathom how his mind is working ... I therefore simply ask, is it fair that the mandatory life prisoner should be wholly deprived of the information which all other prisoners receive as a matter of course. I am clearly of opinion that it is not.

Lord Mustill added that he could have arrived at the same conclusion by the route taken in *Ex p Cunningham* (above):

> I think it important that there should be an effective means of detecting the kind of error which would entitle the court to intervene, and in practice I regard it as necessary for this purpose that the reasoning of the Home Secretary should be disclosed.

R v Mayor, Commonalty and Citizens of London ex p Matson (1996) CA

The applicant sought to be elected an alderman of the Corporation of the City of London. The election process consisted of two stages. At the first, the common councilmen of a ward, meeting in a wardmote, voted whether or not to confirm a candidate as an alderman elect. The applicant received a substantial majority of the votes cast at this stage. At the second stage, the candidate was asked to complete a questionnaire, and was then interviewed in private by the court of aldermen. At this stage, the applicant's candidacy was rejected by an overwhelming majority. The applicant initially sought either an order of certiorari to quash the decision of the court of aldermen, or an order directing that court to reconsider its decision and reach a decision in accordance with the findings of the High Court or the Court of Appeal. On appeal from the rejection of his application by the High Court, the Court of Appeal found that the decision against the applicant could not in itself be impugned on the grounds either of irrationality or procedural unfairness.

Held that the applicant's remaining submission that the court of aldermen was under a duty to give reasons for its decision was correct. The decision was not on its face aberrant, but fairness and natural justice required the giving of reasons. This was so because (amongst other considerations) it had been suggested to the applicant in the course of his interview that he had in the past acted in an inappropriate manner and he had been invited to explain himself; in the absence of reasons, he had no way of knowing if the refusal of his candidacy arose despite the acceptance of his explanation or because of its rejection. Nor could he know whether to stand for election again and, if so, what further information to supply to the court of aldermen. In the circumstances, his rejection cast a shadow on his reputation. The giving of short reasons would not impede the working of the court of aldermen, but would enable it to ensure that its decisions in every case were sound and manifestly just and in the interests of the City.

R v Secretary of State for the Home Department ex p Al Fayed (1997) CA

Section 44(2) of the British Nationality Act 1981 provides:

> The Secretary of State ... shall not be required to assign any reason for the grant or referral of any application under this Act the decision on which is at his discretion; and the discretion of the Secretary of State ... on any such application shall not be subject to appeal to, or review in, any court.

The applicants sought judicial review of the decision of the Secretary of State to reject their applications for naturalisation. The respondent accepted that s 44(2) did not oust the jurisdiction of the court to review a decision of the Secretary of State under any of the usual heads of judicial review.

Held, by a majority, that, in the absence of s 44(2), a duty of fairness was owed to the applicants. The consequences of an adverse decision on naturalisation were of an importance which would give rise to a right to be informed of concerns which might lead to the refusal of the application, and a right to be heard in answer to such concerns. Properly understood, s 44(2) did not negate that duty which, in the instant case, would be met by requiring the Secretary of State to give the applicants sufficient information as to the subject matter of his decision to enable them to make such submissions as they wished. Were it not for s 44(2), the present case was such that reasons for the Secretary of State's refusal should have been given.

RATIONALES FOR THE IMPOSITION OF A DUTY TO GIVE REASONS

R v Higher Education Funding Council ex p Institute of Dental Surgery (1994)

The Council had power to make grants for research to universities. Grant was awarded according to a rating system administered by the Council. The applicant institute, a university college, had previously been rated three on a scale out of five. In 1992, it was rated two out of five. Its grant was accordingly cut by £ 270,000. No reasons were given for the downgrading and, in corresondence, the Council refused to give reasons or to permit any appeal. The institute sought judicial review, contending, *inter alia,* that the Council had acted unfairly in failing to give reasons or, alternatively, that in the absence of reasons its decision ought to be regarded as irrational.

Held, dismissing the application, that no duty would be imposed in the present case. Sedley J reviewed the arguments for and against the requiring of reasons in any given case as follows:

> The giving of reasons may among other things concentrate the decision maker's mind on the right questions; demonstrate to the recipient that this is so; show that the issues have been conscientiously addressed and how the result has been reached; or alternately alert the recipient to a justiciable flaw in the process. On the other side of the argument, it may place an undue burden on decision makers; demand

> an appearance of unanimity where there is diversity; call for the articulation of sometimes inexpressible value judgments; and offer an invitation to the captious to comb the reasons for previously unsuspected grounds of challenge.

In *Doody*, the nature and impact of the decision itself called for reasons as a routine aspect of procedural fairness. In *Cunningham*, there was a 'trigger factor'; the court could readily evaluate the different between what the board had awarded and what an industrial tribunal would have awarded. The court was unable, in the present case, to judge whether the decision of the Council was extraordinary or not; it lacked the necessary academic expertise. In summary, Sedley J said:

> (1) There is no general duty to give reasons for a decision of case where there is such a duty.
>
> (2) One such class is where the subject matter is an interest so highly regarded by the law for example, personal liberty - that fairness requires that reasons, at least tor particular decisions, should be given as of right.
>
> (3) (a) Another such class is where the decision appears aberrant. Here, fairness may require reasons so that the recipient may know whether the aberration is in the legal sense read (and so challengeable) or apparent.
>
> (3) (b) It follows that this class does not include decisions which are themselves only challengeable by reference to the reasons for them. A pure exercise of academic judgment is such a decision.

6

PROPORTIONALITY

EXPLICIT DISCUSSION OF DISPROPORTIONALITY AS A GROUND OF REVIEW

The principle as an area for the future development of the common law

***Council of Civil Service Unions v Minister for the Civil Service* (1985) HL**

Per Lord Diplock:

> Judicial review has I think developed to a state today when without reiterating any analysis of the steps by which the development has come about, one can conveniently classify under three heads the grounds on which administrative action is subject to control by judicial review. The first ground I would call 'illegality', the second 'irrationality' and the third 'procedural impropriety'. That is not to say that further development on a case by case basis may not in the course of time add further grounds. I have in mind particularly the possible adoption in future of the principle of 'proportionality' which is recognised in the administrative law of several of our fellow members of the European Economic Community.

Current judicial attitudes to the principle

***R v Secretary of State for the Home Department ex p Brind* (1991) HL**

In October 1988, the Secretary of State, acting under the

Broadcasting Act 1981, issued directives to the BBC and the IBA prohibiting the broadcasting of 'words spoken' by members or apparent adherents of organisations proscribed under prevention of terrorism legislation. The appellants, who were journalists, alleged that the ban infringed their rights to freedom of expression, as guaranteed by the European Convention on Human Rights, and that it was disproportionate to the ends sought to be achieved.

Held that proportionality was not yet a distinct ground of judicial review. Lord Lowry and Lord Ackner rejected it, generally on the ground that it would inevitably involve consideration of the merits of the decision challenged - a matter entrusted to the decision maker and not to courts of supervisory jurisdiction. Lord Lowry added that to accept it would be to encourage a rush of unmeritorious applications for judicial review. Lord Bridge and Lord Roskill accepted that proportionality might in time become an independent ground of review, but denied its application to the present case, Lord Bridge considering that review on the ground of irrationality would achieve a similar end. Lord Templeman, according similar importance to irrationality as a ground of review, noted that proportionality is required by the European Court of Human Rights, and held 'applying these principles' that the Secretary of State's decision was justifiable.

IMPLICIT USE OF PROPORTIONALITY IN JUDICIAL REASONING

R v Secretary of State for Transport ex p Pegasus Holdings (1988)

The applicants chartered aircraft and flying crews from the Romanian airline Tarom. Tarom held a permit from the Secretary of State for this purpose. Five of its pilots voluntarily took flying tests conducted by the British Civil Aviation Authority. Four of them failed for the reason that they displayed an inability to manoeuvre the aircraft. The Secretary of State provisionally withdrew Tarom's licence within a matter of hours of the results of the tests becoming known. This caused the applicant package holiday company great difficulties in transporting its customers.

The applicant claimed that the Secretary of State had failed to grant it a fair hearing before withdrawing the licence.

Held that, on the facts, there had been no breach of the rules of natural justice or of a duty of fairness. The requirements of fairness had to be considered in all the circumstances of the case. *Per* Schiemann J:

> One has in the context of fairness to bear in mind, on the one hand, the no doubt substantial economic damage to the applicants and perhaps the irritation and inconvenience that I do not doubt the passengers suffered. On the other hand, one has to bear in mind the magnitude of the risk ...

PROPORTIONALITY AND THE *WEDNESBURY* TEST

R v Chief Constable of Sussex ex p International Trader's Ferry Ltd (1999) HL

The company transported livestock to the continent from the Sussex port of Shoreham. The activities of animal rights protesters led to a very great investment of police resources in order to ensure the safety of the company's lorries. The Chief Constable decided to reduce the police presence, informing the company that operations at the port were adversely affecting the policing of the rest of the county, and that export activities would be reduced on police orders if they would not be safety accomplished with a reduced police presence. The company sought certiorari to quash the Chief Constable's decision, on the grounds that it was unreasonable as a matter of domestic law, and contrary to Arts 34 and 36 of the EC Treaty, since it amounted to a quantitative restriction on exports. The Divisional Court rejected the imputation of unreasonableness but allowed the application on the European law point. The Court of Appeal held that the Chief Constable's decision was justifiable under Art 36 of the Treaty. The company appealed to the House of Lords.

Held, dismissing the appeal, that, as far as domestic law was concerned, the right to trade lawfully was not absolute. In the circumstances, therefore, it had been proper for the Chief Constable to balance a number of factors. He had not been shown to have considered irrelevant factors or have overlooked relevant ones. In reviewing his decision, the court would respect his margin of appreciation. As a matter of European law, the question was whether the steps taken by the Chief Constable were proportionate. Lord Slynn held that they were, and commented:

> In *Ex p Brind* [above], the House treated *Wednesbury* unreasonableness and proportionality as being different. So in some ways they are, although the distinction between the two tests in practice is in any event much less than is sometimes suggested. The cautious way in which the European Court usually applies this test, recognising the importance of respecting the national authority's margin of appreciation, may mean that whichever test is adopted, and even allowing for a difference in onus, the result is the same.

THE EUROPEAN CONVENTION FOR THE PROTECTION OF HUMAN RIGHTS AND FUNDAMENTAL FREEDOMS

The Convention and the UK courts

Statutory discretion need not be exercised in conformity with the Convention

R v Secretary of State for the Home Department ex p Brind (1991) HL

In addition to their claim that the consequences of the Secretary of State's decision were disproportionate to the end which he sought to achieve the applicants argued that Art 10 of the European Convention on Human Rights was a relevant consideration to which the Secretary of State was bound to have proper regard. Section 29(3) of the Broadcasting Act 1981 conferred on the Secretary of State a discretion to prohibit broadcasting which was otherwise unfettered.

Held that the acceptance of the applicants' submission would result in the effective incorporation of the Convention into English law, and that, since Parliament had refused many opportunities to incorporate it by legislation, Parliament's intention must be deemed to be that the Convention should retain its current status. Lord Ackner acknowledged that reference could be made to the Convention in order to resolve ambiguities in UK legislation, but denied that there was any ambiguity in s 29(3):

> The limit placed upon the discretion is simply that the power is to be used for the purposes for which it was granted by the legislation (the so called *Padfield* doctrine) and that it must be exercised reasonably in the *Wednesbury* sense. No question of the construction of the words of s 29(3) arises ...

Accordingly, the authorities in which reference had been made to the Convention for the resolution of statutory ambiguity in accordance with the deemed intention of Parliament were insufficient to justify the applicants' submission that the Secretary of State should have had regard to it here. *Per* Lord Ackner:

> The fallacy of this submission is however plain. If the Secretary of State was obliged to have proper regard to the Convention, that is, to conform with Art 10, this inevitably would result in incorporating the Convention into English domestic law by the back door. It would oblige the courts to police the operation of the Convention and to ask themselves in each case, where there was a challenge, whether the restrictions were 'necessary in a democratic society' ... applying the principles enunciated in the decisions of the European Court of Human Rights. The Treaty, not having been incorporated in English law, cannot be a source of rights and obligations and the question: 'Did the Secretary of State act in breach of Art 10?' does not therefore arise.

R v Morrisey, R v Staines (1997) CA

The appellants, who had been convicted of participation in a financial offence, appealed on the ground that answers given by them in the course of an investigation into the offences had rendered the proceedings unfair, and should have been excluded. The answers had been given to an inspector appointed under the Financial Services Act 1986, which provided (by s 177) that such answers should be admissible in evidence. The appellants' argument for exclusion rested on the discretion to exclude contained in s 78 of the Police and Criminal Evidence Act 1984, and on remarks made in *R v Saunders* (1996). In that case, the Court of Appeal had remarked that, if the appellant were to appeal successfully to the European Court of Human Rights (which he later did), consideration would have to be given to implementing the effect of that decision in domestic law.

Held, dismissing the appeal, that s 177 raised a statutory presumption that the evidence in question was admissible. To exclude the evidence in deference to the decision in the European Court of Human Rights would amount to a purported judicial repeal of the domestic law. The European Convention on Human Rights, as interpreted by the Court of Human Rights, remained unenforceable in the English courts. Their Lordships were in express agreement with the appellants' submission that the resulting position was very unsatisfactory, but had no choice but to dismiss the appeal.

***R v Director of Public Prosecutions ex p Kebilene and Others* (1999)**

The applicants sought judicial review of the decision of the Director of Public Prosecutions (DPP) to consent to their prosecution for alleged offences under ss 16A and 16B of the Prevention of Terrorism (Temporary Provisions) Act 1989. They argued *(inter alia)* that, pending commencement of the provisions of the Human Rights Act 1998 (incorporating the European Convention on Human Rights into domestic law), they had a legitimate expectation that the DPP would exercise his prosecutorial discretion to refuse consent to any prosecution which might be held unsafe after the Convention's incorporation.

Held that the claimed expectation did not arise, since the express provisions of the 1998 Act postponing incorporation of the central provisions of the Convention were repugnant to it. However, the compatibility of the Convention with the offences changed was (in the judgment of Lord Bingham ol Cornhill CJ) a matter which a conscientious and rational DPP would wish to take into account when exercising his prosecutorial discretion, since an appeal against conviction might well be heard after incorporation of the Convention. On the hypothesis of inconsistency between the offences charged and the Convention, such appeals would be likely to be successful. The DPP had in fact received legal advice on the question of compatibility between the offences and the Convention. It was proper for the court to review the soundness of that advice. In the judgment of Laws LJ, the DPP was obliged to take the compatibility question into account and, since this was a question of law, it was the duty of a court of review to address and decide that issue.

Both judges concluded that the offences were likely to Convention. The parties were invited to make submission as to appropriate relief, and leave to appeal to the House of Lords was granted in respect of all the questions raised.

Q Reconcile this decision with the opinion of Lord Ackner in *Brind* (above).

Circumstances justifying reference to the Convention as persuasive authority

Derbyshire County Council v Times Newspapers Ltd (1992-93) CA and HL

The County Council brought a libel action against the publishers, editor and two journalists of *The Sunday Times*. The newspapers had printed allegedly defamatory articles concerning the council's management of its superannuation fund. The defendants applied to strike out the statement of claim as disclosing no reasonable cause of action. For the claim to succeed, it was necessary for the plaintiffs to establish that a body corporate should be able to sue for libel. The defendants argued that it should not have that right, since it would be enabled thereby to suppress legitimate criticism of its activities. The defendants submitted that this would be contrary to Art 10 of the European Convention, and did not come within the derogation to Art 10. It was unnecessary in a democratic society protect for a body corporate to have the right to sue for libel since it could protect its reputation by suing for malicious falsehood, or by bringing a prosecution for criminal libel. At first instance, the defendants' submissions were rejected. They appealed to the Court of Appeal.

Held, allowing the appeal, that a corporate public authority had no right Common law to sue for libel. In so holding, the court considered Art 10 of the Convention. On the admissibility of the Convention in English courts, Balcombe LJ remarked that, although it had not been incorporated into domestic law, the authorities recognised its relevance in three situations:

(1) Article 10 may be used for the purpose of the resolution of an ambiguity in English primary or subordinate legislation [see *Brind* above].

(2) Article 10 may be used when considering the principles upon which the court should act in exercising a discretion, for example, whether or not to grant an interlocutory injunction (see *AG v Guardian Newspapers Ltd (No 1)* [see 22 below]).

(3) Article 10 may be used when the common law (by which I include the doctrines of equity) is uncertain. In *AG v Guardian Newspapers Ltd* (No. 2) the courts at all levels had regard to the provisions of Art 10 in considering the extent of the duty of confidence. They did not limit the application of Art 10 to the discretion of the court to grant or withhold an injunction to restrain a breach of confidence.

Even if the common law is certain, the courts will still, when appropriate, consider whether the UK is in breach of Art 10.

(As authority for this proposition, Balcombe LJ cited *Ex p Choudhury*.

The plaintiffs appealed to the House of Lords.

Held, dismissing the appeal, that the judgment of the Court of Appeal would be upheld, but without reliance on the Convention. In the field of freedom of speech, there was no difference in principle between English law and Art 10 of the Convention. Lord Keith added that he found it satisfactory to be able to conclude that the common law of England was consistent with the obligations assumed by the Crown under the Convention in this field.

COMMON LAW PROCEDURES FOR THE VINDICATION OF FUNDAMENTAL RIGHTS

The intensity of judicial review of a decision may be increased proportionately to the importance of the rights which it determines

R v Secretary of State for the Home Department ex p Bugdaycay (1987) HL

The appellants obtained leave to enter the UK by false statements as to their purposes and as to the time for which they intended to stay. In fact, they intended to seek asylum in the UK and, upon being granted entry, each unsuccessfully did so. Orders for their removal were made by the Secretary of State, on the ground that the appellants were illegal entrants since they had failed to disclose material facts when entering the UK. The appellants denied that the facts concealed by them were material, in that they were not facts which would have caused the immigration officer to refuse leave to enter. They further claimed that the court had jurisdiction to make a finding on their entitlement to asylum.

Held that the appeals would be dismissed on both grounds. *Per* Lord Bridge:

> [The courts are entitled, within limits] to subject an administrative decision to the more rigorous examination, to ensure that it is in no way flawed, according to the gravity of the issue which the decision determines. The most fundamental of all human rights is the individual's right to life and when an administrative decision under challenge is said to be one which may put the applicant's life at risk, the basis of the decision must surely call for the most anxious scrutiny.

The decision maker's failure to maintain a reasonable balance between human rights and competing interests may be subject to review on *Wednesbury* principles

R v Secretary of State for the Home Department ex p Brind (1991) HL

With reference to his conclusion that, in the absence of

legislation incorporating the Convention into English law, the Secretary of State's decision could not be impugned on the grounds that it did not properly take into consideration Art 10, Lord Bridge added:

> But I do not accept that this conclusion means that the courts are powerless to prevent the exercise by the executive of administrative discretions, even when conferred, as in the instant case, in terms which are on their hue unlimited, in a way which infringes fundamental human rights. Thus, Art 10(2) of the Convention spells out and categorises the competing public interests by reference to which the right to freedom of expression may have to be curtailed. In exercising the power of judical review, we have neither the advantages or the disadvantages of any comparable code to which we may refer or by which we are bound. But, again, this surely does not mean that in deciding whether the Secretary of State, in the exercise of his discretion, could reasonably, impose the restriction he has imposed on the broadcasting organisations, we are not perfectly entitled to start from the premise that any restriction of the right to freedom of expression requires to be justified and that nothing less than an important competing public interest will be sufficient to justify it. The primary judgment as to whether the particular competing interest justify the particular restriction imposed falls to be made by the Secretary of State to whom Parliament has entrusted the discretion. But we are entitled to exercise a secondary judgment by asking whether a reasonable Secretary of State, on the material before him, could reasonably make that primary judgement.

The common law requires a substantial public interest justification for the infringement of fundamental rights

R v Cambridge Area Health Authority ex p B (1995) Divisional Court and CA

The applicant, a girl aged 10 years, applied through her father as next friend for certiorari to quash the Authority's decision to refuse her further medical treatment. She suffered from leukaemia, and was virtually certain to die in the very near future if the treatment were withheld. Her chances of recovery with the treatment were put at 10-20%.

Held, *per* Laws J, granting the order and remitting the matter to the authority, that it had not taken into consideration the wishes of the father and, further, that it had taken a decision which interfered with the applicant's right to life. Respect for that and other fundamental human rights was not merely a matter of international obligation under the European Convention. It was of the same substance as the English common law. Decisions assaulting such rights could only be justified on substantial public interest grounds. The Authority had not sufficiently explained the priorities which had led it to deprive the applicant of her chance to life. On this (and other) grounds, an order of certiorari would be granted.

Held, on appeal to the Court of Appeal, that the order would be discharged, since the legality of the Authority's decision could not be faulted. The court did not refer to the reasoning of Laws J summarised above.

R v Ministry of Defence ex p Smith and Others (1996) CA

The test for irrationality proposed by counsel for three of the appellants (and approved by the Court of Appeal) included a direction to take account of human rights issues:

> The court may not interfere with the exercise of an administrative discretion on substantive grounds save where the court is satisfied that the decision is unreasonable in the sense that it is beyond the range of responses open to a reasonable decision maker. But in judging whether the decision maker has exceeded this margin of appreciation, the human rights context is important. The more substantial the interference with human rights, the more the court will require by way of justification before it is satisfied that the decision is reasonable in the sense outlined above.

The Court of Appeal did not comment at length on the differential intensity of review made explicit by this approach. In the Divisional Court, however, Simon Brown LJ cited the authorities on judicial review in the human rights context, and stated that:

> ... they emphasise that, within the limited scope of review open to it, the court must be scrupulous to ensure that no recognised ground of challenge is in truth available to the applicant before rejecting his application. When the most fundamental human rights are threatened, the court will not, for example, be inclined to overlook some perhaps minor flaw in the decision making process, or adopt a particularly benevolent view of the Minister's evidence, or exercise its discretion to withhold relief...[However] even where fundamental human rights are being restricted, 'the threshold of unreasonableness' is not lowered. On the other hand, the Minister on judicial review will need to show that there is an important competing public interest which he could reasonably judge sufficient to justify the restriction and he must expect his reasons to be closely scrutinised. Even that approach, therefore, involves a more intensive review process and a greater readiness to intervene than would ordinarily characterise a judicial review challenge.

R v Secretary of State for Home Department ex p McQuillan (1995)

The applicant, a former member of the Irish Republican Socialist Party, sought review of the decision of the Secretary of State to refuse to revoke successive exclusion orders made against him under the Prevention of Terrorism (Temporary Provisions) Act 1989. He argued that the effect of the order, barring him from entering Great Britain, was to confine him to the one part of the UK where his life and his family's safety were most at risk.

Held that, if the court were possessed of the information held by the Secretary of State, its task would be to determine whether the Secretary of State's decision lay within the band of rational decisions available in a case which potentially called in question the right to life. Sedley J stated that rationality would be measured in this context by (among other things) asking whether, in the light of its impact, the exclusion order could reasonably be considered an expedient response by a Home Secretary who has given proper weight to the fundamental right thereby put at risk. However, this approach was not available in the present case, where the Crown's evidence had to be regarded in the light of authority as sufficient to invoke national security interests precluding further review.

The applicant had claimed rights under European law. Questions affecting the extent of those rights had already been referred to the European Court of Justice, and the present application would be stayed (without stay of the exclusion order) pending the outcome of those references.

> Q In its reference to an 'expedient' response, is the test suggested by Sedley J in fact a measure of rationality or proportionality?

R v Lord Seville of Newdigate and Others ex p A and Others (1999)

General statutory words are deemed insufficient to permit the infringement of fundamental rights

Pierson v Secretary of State for the Home Department (1997) HL

The appellant was serving two mandatory life sentences for the murder of his parents. The Home Secretary's predecessor increased the tariff period of the sentence beyond that recommended by the judiciary to 20 years on the mistaken view that the murders had been characterised by certain aggravating features. His successor, although aware of the error, left the tariff period unaltered. The appellant sought judicial review of the latter decision. The Court of Appeal overturned a first instance decision in the appellant's favour.

Held, by a majority, that the appeal would be allowed. While s 35(2) of the Criminal Justice Act 1991 entrusted the power to take decisions relating to the release of life prisoners to the Home Secretary and was wide enough to authorise the fixing of a tariff, it did not follow that it was wide enough to permit a retrospective increase in the level of punishment once the tariff had been fixed and communicated to the prisoner. The Home Secretary's power was to be subject to the interpretive principle of legality, which was explained by Lord Browne-Wilkinson (dissenting) in the following words:

> A power conferred by Parliament in general terms is not to be taken to authorise the doing of acts by the donee of the power which adversely affect the legal rights of the citizen or the basic principles on which the law of the United Kingdom is based unless the statute conferring the power makes it clear that such was the intention of Parliament.

The principle applied in cases such as *Cooper v Wandsworth Board of Works* and *Doody v Secretary of State for the Home Department* to justify the presumption that Parliament must have intended the executive to act in accordance with common law principles of procedural fairness. It applied with equal force to protect substantive basic or fundamental rights.

THE ATTITUDE OF THE EUROPEAN COURT OF JUSTICE

Nold v Commission of the European Communities Case 4/73 (1974)

In 1969, the Commission authorised the merger of the mining companies of the Ruhr into a single company, Ruhrkohle. At a later date, the Commission promulgated new trading rules fixing the conditions required to be met for acquisition of the status of direct wholesaler of coal. Among the conditions was the requirement to buy at least 6,000 tonnes of coal from Ruhrkohle. Nold, a coal wholesaler and building merchant, complained that it could not attain this minimum quota. It claimed that it was the victim of discrimination, since, unlike its competents, it would now have to deal to its disadvantage through an intermediary. It further argued that its fundamental rights had been violated, namely, the right to free development of the personality and the right to freedom of economic action. In the result, its very existence was endangered.

Held that Nold had been treated no differently from any other undertakings, and that it had therefore not been the victim of discrimination. With regard to the matter of fundamental rights, Nold had no more than a commercial interest, the uncertainties of which were part of the very essence of economic activity. It was for Nold to acknowledge the changes which had taken place and to carry out the necessary adaptations. The action would be dismissed. The court included the following observations in the course of its judgment:

> As the court had already stated, fundamental rights form an integral part of the general principles of law, the observance of which it ensures.
>
> In safeguarding these rights, the court is bound to draw inspiration from constitutional traditions common to the Member States, and it cannot therefore uphold measures which are incompatible with fundamental rights recognised and protected by the constitutions of those States.
>
> Similarly, international treaties for the protection of human rights on which the Member States have collaborated or to which they are signatories, can supply guidelines which should be followed within the framework of Community law.

7
PUBLIC ASSEMBLY

RESTRICTION FOR THE AVOIDANCE OF PUBLIC DISORDER

Beatty v Gillbanks (1882)

The Salvation Army organised processions in the streets of Weston-Super-Mare. The processions were accompanied by another organised body called the Skeleton Army, which opposed itself to the Salvation Army. Factions supporting each of the two groups developed, and violent disorder broke out. After a major disturbance, a justices' notice requiring the cessation of assemblies to the disturbance of the public peace was posted in the town and served on the appellant organisers of the Salvation Army. The Salvation Army continued to march. They were met and stopped by the police, who told the appellants that they must obey the notice. The appellants refused, were arrested, and as a result of being charged with 'unlawfully and tumultuously assembling with others to the disturbance of the public peace, and against the peace of the Queen', were bound over to find sureties to keep the peace. They appealed to the Queen's Bench Divisional Court.

Held, allowing the appeal, that, as regarded the appellants themselves, there was no disturbance of the peace. The appellants' aims were wholly lawful, if not indeed laudable. The disturbance which had taken place had been caused entirely by the unlawful and unjustifiable interference of the Skeleton Army. *Per* Field J:

> I entirely concede that everyone must be taken to intend the natural consequences of his own acts, and it is clear to me that, if this disturbance of the peace was the natural consequence of the acts of the appellants, they would be liable, and the justices would have been right in binding them over. But the evidence set forth in the case does not support this contention; on the contrary, it shows that the disturbances were caused by other people antagonistic to the appellants, and that no acts of violence were committed by them ... The law relating to unlawful assemblies, as laid down in the books and the cases, affords no support to the view of the matter for which the learned counsel for the respondent was obliged to contend, viz, that persons acting lawfully are to be held responsible and punished merely because other persons are thereby induced to act unlawfully and create a disturbance.

Duncan v Jones (1936)

A meeting was to be held outside an unemployed training centre in Deptford to protest against the Incitement to Disaffection Bill. The appellant had addressed a meeting at the same location more than a year previously, and on that occasion there had been disturbances at the centre. The appellant, who intended to address the present meeting, was told by a police inspector that it could not be held at the intended venue, but could take place some 175 yards away in a different street. The appellant told the inspector that she was going to hold the meeting in any event, stepped onto a platform, and began to address the audience. The inspector then arrested her, to which she submitted without resistance. She was charged with obstructing the inspector in the execution of his duty contrary to s 12 of the Prevention of Crimes Act 1871. Upon conviction, she appealed to the London Quarter Sessions. The Deputy Chairman of Quarter Sessions held, dismissing the appeal:

(1) that in fact (if it be material) the appellant must have known of the probable consequence of her holding the meeting - namely, a disturbance and possibly a breach

of the peace - and was not unwilling that such consequences should ensue;

(2) that in fact the respondent reasonably apprehended a breach of the peace;

(3) that in law it thereupon became his duty to prevent the holding of the meeting; and

(4) that in fact, by attempting to hold the meeting, the appellant obstructed the respondent when in the execution of his duty.

The appellant appealed by way of case stated to the King's Bench Divisional Court.

Held that the deputy chairman had been entitled to come to the conclusion to which he came on the facts which he had found. The case was a plain one. The *ratio* of *Beatty v Citibanks* (above) was not in point, and the judgments in that case did not carry the matter any further. *Per* Lord Hewart CJ:

> There have been moments during the argument in this case when it appeared to be suggested that the court had to do with a grave case involving what is called the right of public meeting. I say 'called', because English law does not recognise any special right of public meeting for political or other purposes. The right of assembly, as Professor Dicey puts it (Dicey's *Law of the Constitution*, 8th edn, p. 499), is nothing more than a view taken by the court of the individual liberty of the subject. If I thought that the present case raised a question which has been held in suspense by more than one writer on constitutional law - namely, whether an assembly can properly be held to be unlawful merely because the holding of it is expected to give rise to a breach of the peace on the part of persons who are opposed to those who are holding the meeting - I should wish to hear much more argument before I expressed an opinion. This case, however, does not even touch that important question.

Thomas v Sawkins (1935)

A public meeting to protest against the Incitement to

Disaffection Bill was held on private premises. The organisers of the meeting had previously made it clear to the police that they were not welcome. Police officers nevertheless attended, and the appellant took hold of one of them in order to eject him. The officer resisted, and the appellant brought a private prosecution for assault. At first instance, the case was dismissed, and the appellant appealed to the Divisional Court.

The question arose whether the police officers had been lawfully on the premises.

Held that the decision to dismiss the case would be upheld. The police had been lawfully on the premises in the exercise of a power to enter and remain order to deal with a breach of the peace or to prevent an anticipated breach of the peace. The court rejected the appellant's argument that no such power existed where a breach was merely expected by the police, and was not yet occurring. *Per* Avory J:

> I think it is very material in this particular case to observe that the meeting was described as a public meeting, that it was extensively advertised, and that the public was invited to attend. There can be no doubt that the police officers who attended the meeting were members of the public and were included in that sense in the invitation to attend. It is true that those who had hired the hall for the meeting might withdraw their invitation from any particular individual who was likely to commit a breach of the peace or some other offence, but it is quite a different proposition to say that they might withdraw the invitation from police officers who might be there for the express purpose of preventing a breach of the peace or the commission of an offence ... I am satisfied that the justices had before them material on which they could properly hold that the police officers in question had reasonable grounds for believing that, if they were not present, seditious speeches would be made and/or that a breach of the peace would take place. To prevent any such breach of the peace the police were entitled to enter and to remain on the premises.

Q In view of Avory J's opinion that the police had power to enter and remain in order to prevent an anticipated breach of the peace, was it 'very material to observe that the meeting was described as a public meeting'?

Jordan v Burgoyne (1963)

The respondent was a leader of the extreme right wing National Socialist movement. He addressed a rally in Trafalgar Square. A group of communists, Campaign for Nuclear Disarmament (CND) supporters and Jewish activists attended the rally, intending to prevent it taking place Jordan used the following words:

> ... more and more people every day are opening their eyes and coming to say with us 'Hitler was right'. They are coming to say that our real enemies ... were not Hitler and the National Socialists of Germany, but world Jewry and its associates in this country.

At this point, there was turmoil, and the police stopped the rally. Jordan was convicted of using insulting words whereby a breach of the peace was likely to be occasioned, contrary to s 5 of the Public Order Act 1936. His appeal to quarter sessions was allowed on the ground that, although his words had been insulting, they would not have been likely to lead ordinary, reasonable people to commit a breach of the peace. The prosecutor appealed to the Divisional Court.

Held, allowing the appeal, that it was difficult to imagine any reasonable person not being provoked beyond endurance by the respondent's words, but that there was no room for any test as to whether any member of the audience was a reasonable man or an ordinary citizen. *Per* Lord Parker CJ:

> This is ... a Public Order Act, and if in fact it is apparent that a body of persons are present - and let me assume in the defendant's favour that they are a body of hooligans - yet if words are used which threaten, abuse or insult them - all very strong words - then that person must take his audience as he finds them, and if those words to that audience are likely to provoke a breach of the peace, then the speaker is guilty of an offence.

RESTRICTION IN THE INTEREST OF PRIVATE RIGHT

***Hubbard v Pitt* (1975) CA**

The defendants, who were opposed to property redevelopment in Islington, organised a campaign against the plaintiffs, a firm of local estate agents. They assembled outside the plaintiffs' offices with placards and leaflets, stating that they would continue this picketing until the plaintiffs complied with their demands. The picketers were orderly and peaceful, co-operated with the police, and left sufficient room for pedestrians to pass along the pavement. The plaintiffs obtained an injunction to prevent the defendants from 'besetting' their offices, claiming that it was substantially interfering with their business. The defendants appealed.

Held, by a majority, that the appeal would be dismissed. The balance of convenience was in favour of maintaining the injunction until full trial. *Per* Lord Denning MR (dissenting):

> Finally, the real grievance of the plaintiffs is about the placards and leaflets. To restrain these by an interlocutory injunction would be contrary to the principle laid down by the court 85 years ago in *Bonnard v Ferryman* and repeatedly applied ever since. That case spoke of the right of free speech. Here we have to consider the right to demonstrate and the right to protest on matters of public concern. These are rights which it is in the public interest that individuals should possess; and, indeed, that thy should exercise without impediment as long as no wrongful act is done. It is often the only means by which grievances can be brought to the knowledge of those in authority -- at any rate with such impact as to gain a remedy...As long as all is done peaceably and in good order without threats or incitement to violence or obstruction to traffic, it is not prohibited: see *Beatty v Gillbanks* [above]. I stress the need for peace and good order. Only too often violence may break out: and then it should be firmly handled and severely punished. But, so long as good order is maintained, the right to demonstrate must be preserved. In his recent inquiry on the Red Lion

Square disorders, Scarman LJ was asked to recommend 'that a positive right to demonstrate should be enacted'. He said that it was unnecessary: 'The right of course exists, subject only to limits required by the need for good order and the passage of traffic.'

RESTRICTION IN THE INTEREST OF PUBLIC RIGHT

Hirst and Agu v Chief Constable of West Yorkshire (1986)

The appellants, who were animal rights activists, carried on a protest outside a shop selling animal furs. They stood in various parts of the street outside the shop, holding a banner and handing out leaflets. The street was a spacious but busy pedestrian precinct. They were convicted of obstructing the highway contrary to s 137 of the Highways Act 1980 and appealed to the Divisional Court by way of case stated.

Held, allowing the appeal, that the Crown Court had been wrong to regard the appellants' activities as unlawful merely because they were not incidental to the lawful use of the highway to pass and re-pass. Where the activity on which the charge was based was not of itself contrary to law, a court should consider: (a) whether a more than negligible obstruction had been caused; (b) whether the obstruction was deliberate; and (c) whether it was caused without lawful authority or excuse. In answering the third question, the court was to consider, as a question of fact, whether the activity was reasonable.

Director of Public Prosecutions v Jones (1999) HL

The appellants, who had held what was agreed to have been a peaceful and non-obstructive demonstration on the verge of the A344 adjacent to the perimeter fence of Stonehenge, were convicted of taking part in a trespassory assembly' on a highway in respect of which an order prohibiting such assemblies had been made, contrary to s 14B(2) of the Public Order Act 1986 (as inserted by s 70 of the Criminal Justice and Public Order Act 1994). They appealed successfully to the Crown Court, but their convictions were reinstated following an appeal by the DPP to the Divisional Court. The appellants appealed to the House of Lords.

Held, allowing the appeal, that the case raised a point of fundamental constitutional importance, namely, the limits of the public's rights of access to the public highway. The common law contained observations to the effect both that the right of the public upon a highway was limited to passing and re-passing over it, and that there may be reasonable or usual (and therefore non-trespassory) uses of the highway which are not limited or ancillary to mere passage. The latter were to be preferred. *Per* Lord Irvine of Lairg LC:

> In truth very little activity could accurately be described as 'ancillary' to passing along the highway; perhaps stopping to tie one's shoe lace, consulting a street-map, or pausing to catch one's breath. But I do not think that such ordinary and usual activities as making a sketch, taking a photograph, handing out leaflets, collecting money for charity, singing carols, playing in a Salvation Army band, children playing a game on the pavement, having a picnic, or reading a book, would qualify. These examples illustrate that to limit lawful use of the highway to that which is literally 'incidental or ancillary' to the right of passage would be to place an unrealistic and unwarranted restriction on commonplace day to day activities. The law should not make unlawful what is commonplace and well accepted.

The Divisional Court had regarded the order prohibiting trespassory assemblies on the road as prohibiting all assemblies. This approach was incompatible with Art 11 of the European Convention, which conferred a right to freedom of peaceful assembly and therefore created a presumption of lawfulness, while allowing the state to restrict the right. Had it been necessary, Lord Irvine would have clarified or developed the common law to realise the approach of the Convention.

ARTICLE 11 OF THE ECHR

(1) Everyone has the right to freedom of peaceful assembly and to freedom of association with others, including the right to form and to join trade unions for the protection of his interests.

(2) No restrictions shall be placed on the exercise of these rights other than such as are prescribed by law and are necessary in a democratic society in the interests of national security or public safety, for the prevention of disorder or crime, for the protection of health or morals or for the protection of the rights and freedoms of others. This Article shall not prevent the imposition of lawful restrictions on the exercise of these rights by members of the armed forces, of the police or of the administration of the State.

8

PUBLIC ORDER

Brutus *v* Cozens (1973) HL

During a tennis match at Wimbledon which involved a South African player, the appellant stepped onto the court blowing a whistle, threw leaflets around, attempted to give one to a player and sat down on the court. Other protesters then made their way onto the court. Play was stopped. The appellant was charged with using insulting behaviour whereby a breach of the peace was likely to be caused, contrary to s 5 of the Public Order Act 1936. The magistrates held that the appellant's behaviour could not be described as 'insulting'. The prosecutor appealed to the Divisional Court, which defined the word 'insulting' and held that the evidence established that the appellant had used insulting behaviour. The appellant appealed to the House of Lords.

Held, allowing the appeal, that the meaning of the word 'insulting' was a matter of fact, not law, and that the question for the Divisional Court had therefore been whether the magistrates had acted unreasonably in holding that the appellant's behaviour was not insulting. They had not so acted. The Divisional Court had defined 'insulting' behaviour as that which affronted others and tended to evidence a disrespect or contempt for their rights. *Per* Lord Reid:

> I cannot agree with that. Parliament had to solve the difficult question of how far freedom of speech or behaviour must be limited in the general public interest. It would have been going much too far to prohibit all speech or conduct likely to occasion a breach of the

> peace because determined opponents may not shrink from organising or at least threatening a breach of the peace in order to silence a speaker whose views they detest.

R v Howell (1982) CA

In the course of attempting to disperse a group of people who had congregated on the street and were behaving in a disorderly manner, police arrested the appellant. During his arrest, the appellant struck a police officer in the face. He was convicted of an assault occasioning actual bodily harm. On appeal, he argued that there had been no breach of the peace before the arrest, that the arrest was consequently unlawful, and that he had used reasonable force to prevent it.

Held that the appeal would be dismissed. In so holding, Watkins LJ considered the definition of 'breach of the peace':

> A comprehensive definition of the term 'breach of the peace' has very rarely been formulated ... The older cases are of considerable interest but they are not a sure guide to what the term is understood to mean today, since keeping the peace in this country in the latter half of the 20th century presents formidable problems which bear upon the evolving process of the development of this branch of the common law. Nevertheless, even in these days when affrays, riotous behaviour and other disturbances happen all too frequently, we cannot accept that there can be a breach of the peace unless there has been an act done or threatened to be done which actually harms a person, or in his presence his property, or is likely to cause such harm, or which puts someone in fear of such harm being done. There is nothing more likely to arouse resentment and anger in him, and a desire to take instant revenge, than attacks or threatened attacks upon a person's body or property ...

We are emboldened to say that there is a breach of the peace whenever harm is actually done or is likely to be done to a person or in his presence to his property or a person is in fear of being so harmed through an assault, an affray, a riot, unlawful assembly or other disturbance. It is for this breach of the peace when done in his presence or the reasonable apprehension of it taking place that a constable, or anyone else, may arrest an offender without a warrant ..

R v Chief Constable of Devon and Cornwall ex p CEGB (1982) CA

The Central Electricity Generating Board was obstructed by demonstrators in its attempts to exercise its statutory powers to survey land for suitability as a site for a nuclear power station. The police attended at the site, but refused to intervene, on the grounds that there was no actual or threatened breach of the peace. The CEGB sought an order of mandamus to compel the police to remove or to assist in the removal of the demonstrators.

Held that it would not be appropriate to order mandamus. Lord Denning MR, however, considered that there had been or was likely to be a breach of the peace. It might be constituted either by the physical steps taken by CEGB employees to prevent the obstruction, whether or not such reaction might be justified as a matter of self-help, or by the conduct of the demonstrators themselves. Lord Denning MR continued:

> ... the lifting up of a recumbent obstructor would be a battery unless justified as being done in the exercise of self-help. But in deciding whether there is a breach of the peace or the apprehension of it, the law does not go into the rights and wrongs of the matter - or whether it is justified by self-help or not. Suffice it that the peace is broken or is likely to be broken by one or another of those present. With the result that any citizen - and certainly any police officer - can intervene to stop the breach.

If I were wrong on this point, if there were here no breach of the peace nor apprehension of it, I would give a licence to every obstructor and every passive resister in the land. He would be able to cock a snook at the law as these groups have done. Public works of the greatest importance could be held up indefinitely. This cannot be. The rule of law must prevail.

Q May lawful behaviour constitute a breach of the peace, or would it be more accurate to say that lawful behaviour may give rise to a breach of the peace? Which formulation is suggested by Lord Denning's *dictum?*

The police as victims of public order offences

Director of Public Prosecutions v Orum (1989)

The DPP appealed to the Divisional Court by way of case stated from the dismissal of charges against the respondent for offences under s 5(l)(a) of the Public Order Act 1986 (causing harassment, alarm or distress) and s 51(1) of the Police Act 1964. The respondent had used threatening and abusive language to police constables who were intervening in an altercation between the respondent and his girlfriend, and he had later assaulted one of the constables. The only persons present had been the respondent, his girlfriend, and the two police constables.

Held, allowing the appeal, that the question requiring determination by the court was whether a police officer could be a person who was likely to be caused harassment, alarm or distress by the threatening, abusive or insulting words or behaviour of an accused. There was nothing in the Act to enforce the conclusion that as a matter of law he could not. As a matter of fact, words or behaviour which would have such an effect on an ordinary member of the public would often have little emotional impact on a police officer other than that of boredom. However, that was a question of fact for the magistrates to decide in the light of all the circumstances.

PROTECTION OF PRIVACY

The absence of a general right to privacy at common law

Kaye v Robertson (1991) CA

The plaintiff, a well known television actor, was seriously injured when debris fell on his car. He underwent head and brain surgery. As he was recovering in hospital, a journalist and photographer from the *Sunday Sport* entered his room, interviewed him and took photographs of his injuries. The plaintiff obtained an injunction against publication of the interview or the photographs, basing his application upon claims for libel, malicious falsehood, trespass to the person and the tort of passing off since the law recognised no general right to privacy. The defendants applied to the Court of Appeal for the discharge of the injunction.

Held, allowing the appeal in part, that the injunction had wrongly been granted on the basis of the claim of libel, though it would be upheld in modified form on the basis of the malicious falsehood claim. *Per* Leggatt LJ:

> We do not need a First Amendment to preserve the freedom of the press, but the abuse of that freedom can be ensured only by the enforcement of a right to privacy. This right has so long been disregarded here that it can be recognised now only by the legislature. Especially since there is available in the US a wealth of experience of the enforcement of this right both at common law and also under statute, it is to be hoped that the making good of this signal shortcoming in our law will not be long delayed.

Breach of confidence

The development of the equitable doctrine of breach of confidence

Albert v Strange (1849)

Queen Victoria and Prince Albert made etchings of their children. The Royal Family kept them privately, although a few copies were given to friends. The plates of the etchings were entrusted to a printer for further copies to be made. Without the printer's knowledge, one of his employees made further copies. The defendant purchased them. He intended to exhibit them, and to prepare a catalogue listing and describing them. The plaintiff obtained an injunction to prevent the exhibition and the publication of the catalogue. In further proceedings, the defendant applied for the variation of the injunction to permit him to publish the catalogue, although he accepted that the exhibition should not be held. On appeal, counsel for the defendant contended that the injunction could be based only on breach of trust or on the property rights of the plaintiff.

Held that a breach of trust, the protection of property rights, contract or a breach of confidence would justify the continuance of the injunction as originally made. The plaintiff undoubtedly had property rights in his own work. On the evidence adduced by the plaintiff and the absence of any explanation from the defendant, the court was bound to assume that the possession of the etchings by the defendant had been obtained in breach of trust, breach of an implied contract, or in breach of confidence.

The doctrine is independent of other legal rights

***Duchess of Argyll v Duke of Argyll* (1967)**

Following the failure of his marriage to the plaintiff, the duke intended to publish in *The People* a series of articles relating to the couple's married life. The first two instalments were published, and the plaintiff sought injunctions against the duke and against the editor and publisher of *The People* to restrain further publication of 'secrets ... relating to her private life, personal affairs or private conduct, communicated to the first defendant in confidence during the subsistence of his marriage to the plaintiff and not hitherto made public property'.

Held, following a review of the authorities, that obligation of confidence could arise from property rights or from contract, but that these were not the only grounds on which a court could intervene. *Per* Ungoed-Thomas J:

> These cases, in my view, indicate:
>
> (1) that a contract or obligation of confidence need not be expressed but can be implied;
>
> (2) that a breach of confidence or trust or faith can arise independently of any right of property or contract other, of course, that any contract which the imparting of the confidence in the relevant circumstances may itself create;
>
> (3) that the court in the exercise of its equitable jurisdiction will restrain a breach of confidence independently of any right at law.

The confidential nature of a marital relationship was of its essence, and so obviously implicit in it that it did not need to be expressed. In the protection of that confidence:

> ... the court is not to be deterred merely because it is not already provided with fully developed principles, guides, tests, definitions and the full armament for judicial decision. It is sufficient that the court recognises that the communications are confidential, and their publication within the mischief which the law as its policy seeks to avoid, without further defining the scope and limits of the jurisdiction; and I have no hesitation in this case in concluding that publication of some of the passages complained of is in breach of marital confidence...

Factors affecting the availability of the protection

Rights to confidentiality are incompatible with interests in publicity

Woodward v Hutchins (1977) CA

The plaintiffs were members of a well known pop group. The defendant, their press relations agent, contracted with a national newspaper to write a series of articles about the group, giving details of its members' personal lives. The plaintiffs sued for libel, breach of contract and breach of confidence. At first instance, an injunction was granted to prevent breach of confidence, but not on the other two grounds. The defendants appealed to the Court of Appeal.

Held that the injunction would be discharged. *Per* Lord Denning:

> There is no doubt whatever that this pop group sought publicity. They wanted to have themselves presented to the public in a favourable light so that audiences would come to hear them and support them. Mr Hutchins was engaged so as to produce, or help to produce, this favourable image, not only of their public lives but of their private lives also. If a group of this

> kind seek publicity which is to their advantage, it seems to me that they cannot complain if a servant or employee of theirs afterwards discloses the truth about them. If the image which they fostered was not a true image, it is in the public interest that it should be corrected. In these cases of confidential information, it is a question of balancing the public interest in maintaining the confidence against the public interest in knowing the truth ...

Other considerations

Stephens v Avery (1988)

A man was convicted of manslaughter for the killing of his wife, whom he had found in a compromising position with another woman. The plaintiff told the defendant, expressly in confidence, that she had had a lesbian relationship with the wife. The defendant allegedly informed *The Mail on Sunday*, which then stated in print that the plaintiff was the woman who had been found with the wife. The plaintiff brought proceedings for breach of confidence, and the defendant applied for the claim to be struck out as disclosing no reasonable cause of action. The defendant argued: (a) that the law did not protect information which related to grossly immoral behaviour; (b) that the law did not protect mere tittle-tattle or trivial gossip; (c) that information relating to sexual contact was inevitably known to both parties to it, and therefore not confidential; and (d) that, in the absence of a legally enforceable contract or a pre-existing relationship such as that of employer and employee, doctor and patient or priest and penitent, no legal duty of confidence arose. The master refused to strike out the claim, and the defendants appealed.

Held that the appeal would be dismissed. It was correct to say that the law afforded no protection to information about grossly immoral conduct, but there was no longer any generally recognised code of sexual morality to which a judge would be justified in making reference. The triviality of the information sought to be protected went to the exercise of the court's discretion to afford an equitable remedy, and not to the nature of the plaintiff's right. Furthermore, the information in the present case either was not trivial or could not be judged to be so until trial. The mere fact that two people knew a secret did not deprive it of its quality of secrecy. *Attorney General v Guardian Newspapers (No 2)* was authority for the proposition that information only ceased to be capable of protection as confidential when it was in fact known to a substantial number of people. No legally enforceable contract or pre-existing relationship was required by law. *Per* Sir Nicholas Browne-Wilkinson VC:

> The basis of equitable intervention to protect confidentiality is that it is unconscionable for a person who has received information on the basis that it is confidential subsequently to reveal that information. Although the relationship between the parties is often important in cases where it is said that there is an implied as opposed to express obligation of confidence, the relationship between the parties is not the determining factor. It is the acceptance of the information on the basis that it will be kept secret that affects the conscience of the recipient.

The defence of public interest compelling disclosure

Francome v Mirror Group Newspapers (1984) CA

The first plaintiff was a well known jockey. He was approached by journalists who wished to confirm the authenticity of tapes of his telephone conversations. The tapes, which had been made by other unidentified persons, were said to reveal that he had breached the rules of racing. They had been made by the tapping of his telephone without his knowledge. The plaintiff brought proceedings against the journalists and the newspaper for which they wrote, claiming, *inter alia,* damages for breach of confidence. He obtained an interlocutory injunction to restrain publication based on the tapes until trial. On appeal, the defendants sought the discharge of the injunction. They argued in defence to breach of confidence that they had acted in the public interest in revealing the plaintiff's suspected wrongdoing.

Held that an injunction had properly granted, but would be upheld in amended terms. It was indeed in the public interest that the allegations against the plaintiff should be investigated by the proper authorities, and the injunction would be varied to permit the disclosure of the tapes to such authorities with the permission of the appropriate minister of the Crown. The editor of the *Daily Mirror* had asserted a right in the public interest to publish a story based on the tapes, although he admitted that publication would probably be an offence under s 5(b) of the Wireless and Telegraphy Act 1949. Sir John Donaldson MR regarded this as a claim to be bound by the law only in so far as it remained expedient in the public interest (as conceived by the editor) to be so bound, and rejected it in forceful terms. Reviewing the circumstances in which a subject might feel obliged to break the law, he added:

> .... I nevertheless recognise that, in very rare circumstances, a situation can arise in which a citizen is faced with a conflict between what is, [sic] in effect, two inconsistent laws. The first law is the law of the land. The second is a moral imperative, usually, but not always, religious in origin ... However, I cannot over-emphasise the rarity of the moral imperative. Furthermore, it is almost unheard of for compliance with the moral imperative to be in the financial or other best interests of the persons concerned ...
>
> The 'media', to use a term which comprises not only the newspapers, but also television and radio, are an essential foundation of any democracy. In exposing crime, antisocial behaviour and hypocrisy and in campaigning for reform and propagating the views of minorities, they perform an invaluable function. However, they are peculiarly vulnerable to the error of confusing the public interest with their own interest... In the instant case, it is impossible to see what public interest would be served by publishing the contents ot the tapes which would not equally be served by giving them to the police or to the Jockey Club.

Revelation of wrongdoing is not the only acceptable rationale for disclosure

Lion Laboratories Ltd v Evans (1985) CA

The plaintiffs were the manufacturers of the Lion Intoximeter

3,000, used by the police for measuring the blood alcohol levels of motorists suspected of drink-driving offences. Two former employees of the plaintiff passed company documents detailing the plaintiff's and the Home Office's doubts about the Intoximeter to the *Daily Express*. The plaintiff applied for and received an *ex parte* injunction to prevent publication of the documents, claiming breach of copyright or breach of confidence. The *Daily Express* subsequently published an article based on the documents. The defendants appealed against the injunction.

Held, allowing the appeal and discharging the injunction, that the issue raised by the defendants was a serious question concerning the life and the liberty of an unascertainable number of Her Majesty's subjects. Although the information regarding the working of the Intoximeter was confidential and had been unlawfully taken in breach of confidence, the defendants would not be restrained from putting that information before the public. In the evidence before the court, no misconduct was alleged against the plaintiffs. However, it was incorrect to assert that the publication of confidential information would be in the public interest only if it revealed wrongdoing on the part of the person to whom it was confidential. The revelation of wrongdoing was merely one instance of an occasion on which there might be just cause for breaching confidence.

Malone v Metropolitan Police Commissioner (No 2) (1979)

Sir Robert Megarry VC addressed, *inter alia,* the contention that the tapping of the plaintiff's telephone had contravened his right of privacy. He observed that there was no general right of privacy recognised by English law, but added that, if the existing rules, in combination with the requirements of justice and common sense, pointed to the existence of such a right, a court would not be deterred from acknowledging it. The creation of a wholly new right was a different matter, however, and a court would have to bear in mind that its function was judicial, not legislative. Further, the right claimed was broad in its scope:

> The wider and more indefinite the right claimed, the greater the undersirability of holding that such a right exists. Wide and indefinite rights, while conferring an

advantage on those who have them, may well gravely impair the position of those who are subject to the rights. To create a right for one person, you have to impose a corresponding duty on another. In the present case, the alleged right to hold a telephone conversation in the privacy of one's own home without molestation is wide and indefinite in its scope ... In any case, why is the telephone to be subject to this special right of privacy when there is no general right?

Q What is the duty which corresponds to the right to hold a telephone conversation without molestation? Is it accurately described as a duty?

Article 8 of the ECHR

(1) Everyone has the right to respect for his private and family life, his home and his correspondence.

(2) There shall be no interference by a public authority with the exercise of this right except such as is in accordance with the law and is necessary in a domocratic society in the interests of national security, public safety or the economic well being of the country, for the prevention of disorder or crime, for the protection of health or morals, or for the protection of the rights and freedoms of others.

9

FREEDOM OF EXPRESSION

Schering Chemicals Falkman Ltd (1982) CA

The plaintiff, the manufacturer of a pregnancy-testing drug, sought an injunction to prevent the broadcasting of a television documentary which concerned allegations that the drug had caused abnormalities in children born to women who had used it. The plaintiff claimed that the producer of the documentary, who was formerly its employee, had used material confidential to the plaintiff.

Held, by a majority, that the injunction granted to the plaintiff would be upheld. Although the material in question was said already to be in the public domain, its re-publication would cause further damage to the plaintiff. *Per* Lord Denning MR (dissenting):

> The freedom of the press is extolled as one of the great bulwarks of liberty. It is entrenched in the constitutions of the world. But it is often misunderstood. I will first say what it does *not* mean. It does not mean that the press is free to ruin a reputation or to break a confidence, or to pollute the course of justice or to do anything that is unlawful. I will next say what it *does* mean. It means that there is to be no censorship. No restraint should be placed on the press as to what they should publish ... The press is not to be restrained *in advance* from publishing whatever it thinks right to publish. It can publish whatever it chooses to publish. But it does so at its own risk. It can 'publish and be

> damned'. Afterwards—after the publication—if the press has done anything unlawful -it can be dealt with by the courts. If it should offend—by interfering with the course of justice—it can be punished in proceedings for contempt of court. If it should damage the reputation of innocent people, by telling untruths or making unfair comment, it may be made liable in damages. But always afterwards. Never beforehand. Never by previous restraint.

Attorney General v Guardian Newspapers (No 1) (1987) HL

Peter Wright, a former member of the British security service MI5, sought to publish a book in Australia giving an account of his experiences in the service. The Crown obtained an interim injunction in New South Wales against publication in Australia, and injunctions to prevent the publication of extracts from the book in British newspapers. Contempt of court proceedings were also prosecuted against newspapers which had published in disregard of the injunctions. Certain of the newspapers applied for the discharge of the injunctions, arguing that the contents of the book were now in the public domain. By the time the appeals reached the House of Lords, the book had been published in its entirety in several countries, and no attempt was made to prevent individuals from freely importing copies into the UK.

Held, by a majority, that the injunctions would be upheld and broadened. *Per* Lord Bridge (dissenting):

> . . . now that the original aim of preventing disclosure of secret material can no longer be attained, the deterrent argument can only carry minimal weight.
>
> What of the other side of the coin and the encroachment on freedom of speech? Having no written constitution, we have no equivalent in our law to the First Amendment to the Constitution of the United States of America. Some think that puts freedom of speech on too lofty a pedestal. Perhaps they are right. We have not adopted as part of our law the European Convention for the Protection of Human Rights and Fundamental Freedoms to which this country is a

> signatory. Many think that we should. I have hitherto not been of that persuasion, in large part because I have had confidence in the capacity of the common law to safeguard the fundamental freedoms essential to a free society including the right to freedom of speech which is specifically safeguarded by Art 10 of the Convention. My confidence is seriously undermined by your Lordships' decision ...

Freedom of speech is always the first casualty under a totalitarian regime. Such a regime cannot afford to allow the free circulation of information and ideas among its citizens. Censorship is the indispensable tool to regulate what the public may and what they may not know. The present attempt to insulate the public in this country from information which is freely available elsewhere is a significant step down that very dangerous road.

COMPATIBILITY OF ENGLISH LAW AND THE CONVENTION

Attorney General v Guardian Newspapers (No 2) (1990) HL

The Attorney General sought permanent injunctions to prevent the publication of material obtained directly or indirectly from Mr Wright, a general injunction against the future publication by certain newspapers of material derived from Mr Wright or other members of the security service, and an account of profits made by another newspaper which had begun to serialise the book.

Held, on the first issue by a majority only, that the permanent injunctions would not be granted because publication would not be contrary to the public interest. This was because the information in question was already in the public domain. The Crown was entitled to an account of the profits from that part of the serialisation which had already been published, but not with regard to future serialisation. The claim for general injunctions would be refused. In the course of his speech, Lord Goff considered the compatibility of the English law on confidentiality with Art 10 of the European Convention on Human Rights.

> Finally, I wish to observe that I can see no inconsistency between English law on this subject and Art 10 of the

European Convention on Human Rights. This is scarcely surprising, since we may pride ourselves on the fact that freedom of speech has existed in this country perhaps as long as, if not longer than, it has existed in any other country in the world. The only difference is that, whereas Art 10 of the Convention, in accordance with its avowed purpose, proceeds to state a fundamental right and then to qualify it, we in this country (where everybody is free to do anything, subject only to the provisions of the law) proceed rather upon an assumption of freedom of speech, and turn to our law to discover the established exceptions to it. In any event, I conceive it to be my duty, when I am free to do so, to interpret the law in accordance with the obligations of the Crown under this Treaty. The exercise of the right to freedom of expression under Art 10 may be subject to restrictions (as are prescribed by law and are necessary in a democratic society) in relation to certain prescribed matters, which include 'the interests of national security' and 'preventing the disclosure of information received in confidence'. It is established in the jurisprudence of the European Court of Human Rights that the word 'necessary' in this context implies the existence of a pressing social need, and that interference with freedom of expression should be no more than is proportionate to the legitimate aim pursued. I have no reason to believe that English law, as applied in the courts, leads to any different conclusion.

ARTICLE 10 OF THE ECHR

(1) Everyone has the right to freedom of expression. This right shall include freedom to hold opinions and to receive and impart information and ideas without interference by public authority and regardless of frontiers. This Article shall not prevent States from requiring the licensing of broadcasting, television or cinema enterprises.

(2) The exercise of these freedoms, since it carries with it duties and responsibilities, may be subject to such formalities, conditions, restrictions or penalties as are prescribed by law and are necessary in a democratic society in the interests of national security, territorial integrity or public safety, for the prevention of disorder or crime, for the protection of health or morals, for the protection of the reputation or rights of others, for preventing the disclosure of information received in confidence, or for maintaining the authority and impartiality of the judiciary.

10

FREEDOM OF RELIGION

THE DEFINITION OF 'RELIGION'

Barralet v Attorney General (1980)

The South Place Ethical Society had as its objects: (i) 'the study and dissemination of ethical principles'; and (ii) 'the cultivation of a rational religious sentiment'. In pursuit of both these objects, the society had as its aim to rely on the methods of reason, rather than on instruction by supernatural revelation and, in the second of its objects, the word 'religious' was used in a sense devoid of supernatural content. By an originating summons, the society asked the court to declare whether or not its objects were charitable. The court considered whether the objects fell under the charitable heads of the advancement of religion, the advancement of education, or whether they were for purposes beneficial to the community.

Held that the society's objects came under the latter two heads, but could not be brought under the first head. The society had contended that a sincere belief in ethical qualities was religious, because such qualities as truth, love and beauty were sacred, and the advancement of any such belief was the advancement of religion. Although it was true that such beliefs might occupy a place in the minds of their possessors parallel to that of religious beliefs, the two could not be equated. *Per Dillon* J:

> In a free country ... it is natural that the court should not desire to discriminate between beliefs deeply and

> sincerely held, whether they are beliefs in a god or in the excellence of man or in Platonism or some other scheme of philosophy. But I do not see that that warrants extending the meaning of the word 'religion' so as to embrace all other beliefs and philosophies. The two are not the same, and are not made the same by sincere inquiry into the question, what is God ... There is a further point. It seems to me that two of the essential attributes of religion are faith and worship.

THE EXTENT OF THE ASSOCIATION BETWEEN CHRISTIANITY AND THE LAW

Bowman v Secular Society (1917) HL

The society's objects included the following: '... to promote ... the principle that human conduct should be based upon natural knowledge, and not upon supernatural belief, and that human welfare in this world is the proper end of all thought and action.' The appellants challenged the validity of a testamentary gift to the society on the grounds that acts done in pursuance of its objects were illegal.

Held, by a majority, dismissing the appeal, that such acts would not now be regarded as contrary to the law. Lord Sumner stated that the case gave rise to the question whether Christianity was part of the law of England, and if so, in what sense it was. While it was true that England was a Christian State, that the national religion was Christianity and that the English family was built on Christian ideals, the maxim that 'Christianity was part of the law of England' was rhetoric and not law. Lord Sumner continued:

> English law may well be called a Christian law, but we apply many of its rules and most of its principles, with equal justice and equally good government, in heathen communities, and its sanctions, even in courts of conscience, are material and not spiritual ... In the present day, reasonable men do not apprehend the dissolution or downfall of society because religion is publicly assailed by methods not scandalous. Whether

> it is possible that in the future irreligious attacks, designed to undermine fundamental institutions of our society, may come to be criminal in themselves, as constituting a public danger, is a matter that does not arise. The fact that opinion grounded on experience has moved one way does not in law preclude the possibility of its moving on fresh experience in the other; nor does it bind succeeding generations, when conditions have again changed.

THE LAW OF BLASPHEMY

The protection of Christianity

Whitehouse v Lemon (1979) HL

The magazine *Gay News* published a poem entitled The Love that Dares to Speak its Name'. This, in the words of Lord Diplock, purported 'to describe in explicit detail acts of sodomy and fellatio with the body of Christ immediately after His death and to ascribe to Him during his lifetime promiscuous homosexual practices with the Apostles and with other men'. A private prosecution was brought against the magazine and its editor by Mary Whitehouse. Although the common law offence of blasphemous libel had been thought to have become a 'dead letter' (described thus by Lord Denning in *Freedom Under the Law* (1949)), the defendants were convicted. They appealed to the House of Lords on the grounds that to sustain a conviction, it was necessary to prove the accused's specific intent to shock believing Christians.

Held, by a majority, that the appeal would be dismissed. The Court of Appeal had correctly concluded that blasphemous libel was a crime of strict liability. It was sufficient to show an intent to publish the material in question; the motive for publication was irrelevant. Although the judge at first instance had stated that he would have been prepared if necessary to extend the protection of the law against blasphemous libel to other religions, the House made it clear that, at present, it applied exclusively to Christianity. It was not for the judiciary to broaden it. *Per* Lord Scarman:

> My Lords, I do not subscribe to the view that the common law offence of blasphemous libel serves no

> purpose in the modern law. On the contrary, I think that there is a case for legislation extending it to protect the religious beliefs and feelings of non-Christians. The offence belongs to a group of criminal offences designed to safeguard the internal tranquillity of the kingdom. In an increasingly plural society, it is necessary not only to protect the differing religious beliefs, feelings and practices of all but also to protect them from scurrility, vilification, ridicule and contempt.

The position of other religions

R v Chief Metropolitan Stipendiary Magistrate ex p Choudhury (1991)

The applicant sought judicial review of the Chief Magistrate's refusal to issue a summons alleging blasphemous libel and seditious libel against the publisher of Salman Rushdie's novel *The Satanic Verses*.

Held, refusing the application, that, on the present state of the law, the offence of blasphemous libel did not extend to protect any religion other than Christianity. If the law was to be changed in this respect, it was for Parliament and not the courts to change it. Were it open to the present court to change it, it would not in any event do so, since the extension of the protection would give rise to difficult questions of definition, and put the issue of the libel itself beyond the common understanding of a jury. Furthermore, in so far as the protection afforded by the common law of blasphemous libel was discriminatory, Watkins LJ (re-stating and apparently approving the submissions of counsel for the publisher) considered that state of affairs objectively justified:

> The offence of blasphemous libel is an offence of strict liability ... If the offence is extended to cover attacks upon religious doctrines, tenets, commandments, or practices of religions other than Christianity, the existence of such an extended law of blasphemy would encourage intolerance, divisiveness and unreasonable interference and interferences with freedom of expression. Fundamentalist Christians, Jews or Muslims

> could then seek to invoke the offence of blasphemy against each other's religion, doctrines, tenets, commandments, or practices; for example denying the divinity of Jesus Christ; or for denying that the Messiah has yet to come; or for denying the divine inspiration of the Prophet Mohammed, and so on. An extended law of blasphemy which applied to all religions could be used as a weapon between Protestants and Roman Catholics in Northern Ireland, or by fringe religions, such as the Church of Scientology. The fact that the offence was committed only in cases of scurrilous attacks would mitigate, but would not eliminate, the resulting intolerance, divisiveness, and unreasonable interference with freedom of expression ...
>
> Would it be preferable to maintain the status quo, or to abolish the offence of blasphemous libel, or to extend it to all religions, or to extend it and re-define its *mens rea* to require blameworthy motivation?

Religious discrimination and testamentary freedom

Blaythwayt v Baron Cawley (1976) HL

A testator who died in 1936 had settled property upon certain persons, subject to a forfeiture clause providing that, if any person who became entitled as tenant for life or tenant in tail male to possession of the estate should 'be or become a Roman Catholic ... the estate hereby limited to him shall cease and determine and be utterly void and my principal estate shall thereupon go to the person next entitled ...'. The question arose whether this clause was void for reasons of public policy.

Held that it was not. Lord Wilberforce noted that the European Convention referred to freedom of religion and to enjoyment of that and other freedoms without discrimination on the ground of religion. He acknowledged that conceptions of public policy should move with the times, but was of the opinion that to introduce a rule of law avoiding the clause would be to uphold one freedom only at the cost of a substantial reduction in another - the freedom of testamentary disposition. The provision in question was a matter of choice, not of discrimination, and private choice was not a matter of public policy. *Per* Lord Cross of Chelsea:

> Turning to the question of public policy, it is true that it is widely thought nowadays that it is wrong for government to treat some of its citizens less favourably than others because of differences in their religious beliefs; but it does not follow from that that it is against public policy for an adherent of one religion to distinguish in disposing of his property between adherents of his faith and those of another. So to hold would amount to saying that, though it is in order for a man to have a mild preference for one religion as opposed to another, it is disreputable for him to be convinced of the importance of holding true religious beliefs are the true ones.

Q Should a distinction be drawn in terms of public policy between a will which disentitles all but those of a given faith, and one which disentitles none but those of a given faith?

ARTICLE 9 OF THE ECHR

(1) Everyone has the right to freedom of thought, conscience and religion; this right includes freedom to change his religion or belief, and freedom, either alone or in community with others and in public or private, to manifest his religion or belief, in worship, teaching, practice and observance.

(2) Freedom to manifest one's religion or beliefs shall be subject only to such limitations as are prescribed by law and are necessary in a democratic society in the interests of public safety, for the protection of public order, health or morals, or for the protection of the rights and freedoms of others.

FREEDOM OF MOVEMENT

Freedom to travel abroad

Immigration Act 1971

1 (1) All those who are in this Act expressed to have the

right of abode in the UK shall be free to live in, and to come and go into and from, the UK without let or hindrance except such as may be required under and in accordance with this Act to enable their right to be established or as may be otherwise lawfully imposed on any person.

2 (1) A person is under this Act to have the right of abode in the UK if: (a) he is a British citizen ...

Exclusion orders: legal challenge

R v Secretary of State for the Home Department ex p Stitt (1987)

The applicant sought judicial review of the Secretary of State's refusal to revoke an exclusion order made under the Prevention of Terrorism (Temporary Provisions) Acts 1976 and 1984. Additionally, he applied to order the Secretary of State to give reasons for the making of the exclusion order.

Held, refusing the application, that the 1976 Act was comprehensive in its provision of rights to those against whom the legislation operated, and no such rights of the applicant had been breached. Further, the Secretary of State's refusal to give reasons was based on considerations of national security. Once there was *bona fide* evidence that security was involved, the court would not examine the strength of justification for the Secretary of State's actions.

Deportation

Considerations governing the discretion to make a deportation order after conviction

R v Nazari (1980) CA

Following their convictions for various offences, the three defendants, all of whom were immigrants, were recommended to be deported. The Court of Appeal laid down the following principles for general application in cases where there was jurisdiction to make a deportation order:

(1) the court was to consider whether the offender's continued presence in the UK would be to the country's detriment. The country had no use for criminals of

other nationalities. The more serious the crime and the longer the offender's criminal record, the more obvious it was that a deportation order should be made;

(2) the court would not be concerned with the political systems operating in the country to which the offender would be deported. This was a matter for the Home Secretary to take into account at the end of the offender's sentence of imprisonment in this country;

(3) the court would consider the effect that an offender's deportation would have on innocent persons not before the court, such as the offender's family;

(4) where an offender states his intention to return to his country voluntarily at the end of his sentence, the court would be unwise to allow such a statement much weight;

(5) where an offender is found to be an illegal immigrant, a deportation order should normally be made.

Legal challenge to the decision to deport

R v Governor of Brixton Prison ex p Soblen (1963) CA

Soblen was convicted of espionage in the USA. He absconded while on bail pending an appeal. During a flight returning him from Israel to the US, he inflicted wounds upon himself as the plane neared London, in order to force it to land. A deportation order was made against him by the Secretary of State, who let it be known that he intended Soblen to be placed on a flight to the US. Soblen sought a writ of habeas corpus on the grounds, *inter alia,* that the deportation order was calculated to amount to extradition, and that the Secretary of State had accordingly acted for an improper purpose; no power to extradite in fact existed with respect to Soblen's offence. At first instance, Soblen's application was refused.

Held, dismissing the appeal, that two principles were to be weighed together. First, the Crown had power to surrender a fugitive offender to another country only in so far as it might do so in accordance with the Extradition Acts. Secondly, the Secretary of State could deport an alien it he considered it to be conducive to the public good. It was necessary to inquire what the Secretary of State's purpose had been in making the order. If the deportation order was a mere sham, designed to achieve an unlawful extradition, then the court could overturn it. Here however, there was no evidence that the Secretary of State had acted to achieve an improper purpose, and there were grounds on which he could genuinely have come to the conclusion that Soblen's deportation would be to the public good.

R v Secretary of State for the Home Department ex p Hosenball (1977) CA

The applicant, a US citizen, had been working in the UK as an investigative journalist. He was informed by the Secretary of State that he was to be deported on the ground of national security. The applicant sought further information from the Secretary of State, who considered the request but stated that it was to be refused in the interests of national security. By the terms of the Immigration Rules and of an undertaking given by the Secretary of State to the House of Commons, a person proposed to be deported was to be given a hearing and such particulars of the allegations against him as would not entail disclosure of sources of evidence. The applicant received a hearing, but was given no particulars of the case against him. He sought judicial review of the subsequent decision to issue a deportation order against him, on the grounds that the Secretary of State was required either by the principles of natural justice or by the Rules or undertaking to distinguish between disclosable and non-disclosable allegations upon which the order was based.

The application was dismissed at first instance, and the applicant appealed to the Court of Appeal.

Held, dismissing the appeal, that the demands of national security could prevail over the requirements of natural justice. The balance between the demands of national security and natural justice was a matter for the Secretary of State. He had considered the applicant's request for further information, and he was entitled to refuse it. He would be answerable to Parliament, and not to the courts, for his judgment. *Per* Lord Denning MR:

> There is a conflict here between the interests of national security on the one hand and the freedom of the

> individual on the other. The balance between these two is not for a court of law. It is for the Home Secretary. He is the person entrusted by Parliament with the task. In some parts of the world national security has on occasions been used as an excuse for all kinds of infringements of individual liberty. But not in England.

R v Secretary of State for the Home Department ex p Cheblak (1991) CA

Shortly after the outbreak of hostilities in the Gulf in 1991, the applicant, a Lebanese citizen and a known pacifist, was arrested and served with a notice of the Home Secretary's intention to make a deportation order against him on the grounds of national security. The risk was later stated by the Home Department to arise from the applicant's association with an organisation which, it was believed, might indulge in terrorist activity in the UK. The Secretary of State subsequently stated in an affidavit that national security prevented the disclosure of further details of the case in favour of deportation. The applicant, arguing that the Secretary of State's decision was contrary to natural justice, irrational, and made in disregard of relevant considerations, sought judicial review and a writ of habeas corpus. Both applications were refused at first instance, and the applicant appealed to the Court of Appeal.

Held, dismissing the appeal, that the challenge failed on all three grounds. Concluding his judgment, Lord Donaldson MR noted that responsibility for decisions made on grounds of national security rested not with the courts, but with government; the courts would intervene if the Secretary of State were to be shown to have acted in bad faith or to have exceeded his statutory powers. Otherwise, the court would accept that the Secretary of State had good grounds for his decision without requiring him to adduce evidence to that effect. Although it was true that tensions might arise between considerations of individual liberty and the requirements of national security, and that there would be cases where the latter would prevail over the former, it was relevant to remember that national security was in fact the foundation of all civil liberties.

Deportation and the rights of third parties

Singh v Immigration Appeals Tribunal (1986) HL

The applicant, a Sikh musician, overstayed his leave to remain in the UK by more than three years. He appealed unsuccessfully to an immigration adjudicator and thence to the Immigration Appeals Tribunal against a deportation order made against him by the Secretary of State. He then sought judicial review of the tribunal's decision. Before the House of Lords, he contended that the damaging effect of his deportation on the Sikh community was either a compassionate circumstance or part of the relevant circumstances which the immigration authorities were bound by the 1982 Immigration Rules to take into account in considering an appeal against a deportation order.

Held, allowing the appeal, that the respondent tribunal had misdirected itself in law. The prejudice to third parties which would be caused by the applicant's deportation was a relevant factor under the Immigration Rules. Further, under principles of general law, it was a factor which the Secretary of State had been bound to consider by virtue of its bearing on the matter before him. It was therefore a matter which the tribunal should have directed itself to consider, since it was bound by s 19(1)(a) of the Immigation Act 1971 to decide whether the Secretary of State's decision was 'in accordance with the law'.

Protocols 4 and 7 of the ECHR

Protocol 4, Art 2:

(1) Everyone lawfully within the territory of a State shall within that territory, have the right to liberty of movement and freedom to choose his residence.

(2) Everyone shall be free to leave any country, including his own.

(3) No restrictions shall be placed on the exercise of these rights other than such as are in accordance with law and are necessary in a democratic society in the interests of national security or public safety, for the maintenance of 'order public', for the prevention of crime or for the protection of the rights and freedoms of others.

(4) The rights set forth in para 1 may also be subject, in particular areas, to restrictions imposed in accordance with law and justified by the public interest in a democratic society.

Protocol 7, Art 1:

(1) An alien lawfully resident in the territory of a State shall not be expelled therefrom except in pursuance of a decision reached in accordance with law and shall be allowed:

 (a) to submit reasons against his expulsion;

 (b) to have his case reviewed;

 (c) to be represented for these purposes before the competent authority or a person or persons designated by that authority.

(2) An alien may be expelled before the exercise of his rights under para l(a), (b) and (c) of this Article, when such expulsion is necessary in the interests of public order or is grounded upon reasons of national authority.

11
PRISONERS' RIGHTS

Judicial review is available to vindicate the residual rights of prisoners

R v Board of Visitors of Hull Prison ex p St Germain (No 1) (1979) CA

As a result of their part in riots at Hull Prison, the applicants were subjected to various disciplinary penalties by the Board of Visitors. They sought orders of certiorari to quash the disciplinary awards, on the grounds that the board had failed to observe the rules of natural justice. Their applications were refused by the Divisional Court, on the preliminary ground that the determinations of the Board of Visitors in these circumstances could not be subject to judicial review, but concerned merely internal and domestic disciplinary matters. Further, recognition of the right of prisoners to apply for judicial review of decisions relating to prison discipline would render the position of the prison authorities intolerable. The applicants appealed to the Court of Appeal.

Held, allowing the appeals and remitting the case to the Divisional Court, that the supervisory jurisdiction of the High Court was, in principle, sufficiently broad for an order of certiorari to issue against the disciplinary award of a Prison Board of Visitors. Shaw LJ cited provisions of the Prison Rules 1964, made under the Prison Act 1952, and concluded that '... despite the deprivation of his general liberty, a prisoner remains invested with residuary rights appertaining to the nature and conduct of his incarceration'. He continued:

> Now the rights of a citizen, however circumscribed by a penal sentence or otherwise, must always be the concern of the courts unless their jurisdiction is clearly excluded by some statutory provision. The courts are in general the ultimate custodians of the rights and liberties of the subject whatever his status and however attenuated those rights may be as the result of some punitive or other process ... Once it is acknowledged that such rights exist, the courts have function and jurisdiction. It is irrelevant that the Secretary of State may afford redress where the rules have been infringed or their application has been irregular or unduly harsh. An essential characteristic of the right of a subject is that it carries with it a right of recourse to the courts unless some statute decrees otherwise.

R v Deputy Governor of Parkhurst Prison ex p Hague; Weldon v Home Office (1991) HL

The applicant in the first case sought judicial review of the prison governor's decision to transfer him between prisons and to segregate him from other prisoners, and included a claim for damages for false imprisonment. The Court of Appeal granted his application in part, but held that a claim for damages by a prisoner for breach of the Prison Rules did not lie, and a claim for false imprisonment would be maintainable only if the prisoner had been deprived of his residual liberty in bad faith, or the conditions of his imprisonment were 'intolerable'. In the second case, a prisoner claimed damages against the Home Office for assault and battery, and for false imprisonment. The Home Office appealed to the House of Lords from the Court of Appeal's refusal to strike out the part of the claim relating to false imprisonment. The House heard the cases as conjoined appeals.

Held, dismissing the prisoner's appeal in the first case and allowing the Home Office's appeal in the second case, that a prisoner had no claim for damages arising from a breach of the Prison Rules, and could not maintain an action for false imprisonment on either of the grounds identified by the Court of Appeal. The second of these claims rested on the proposition that a prisoner had, despite his confinement, a residual liberty amounting to a right which the law would protect. That was incorrect. While it was true that the law would provide a remedy where the prisoner's conditions of detainment were intolerable, the remedy thus granted would be one which would not impugn the legality of the detainment.

Rejecting the concept of residual liberty, Lord Bridge said as follows:

> Can the prisoner then complain that his legal rights are infringed by a restraint which confines him at any particular time within a particular part of the prison? It seems to me that the reality of prison life demands a negative answer to this question. Certainly, in the ordinarily closed prison, the ordinary prisoner will at any time of day or night be in a particular part of the prison, not because that is where he chooses to be, but because that is where the prison regime requires him to be ... Thus, the concept of the prisoner's 'residual liberty' as a species of freedom of movement within the prison enjoyed as a legal right which the prison authorities cannot lawfully restrain seems to me quite illusory. The prisoner is at all times lawfully restrained within closely defined bounds and if he is kept in a segregated cell, at a time when, if the rules had not been misapplied, he would be in the company of other prisoners at the workshop, at the dinner table or elsewhere, this is not the deprivation of his liberty of movement, which is the essence of the tort of false imprisonment, it is the substitution of one form of restraint for another.

Prisoners' rights of access to legal advice and to the courts

Raymond v Honey (1983) HL

Raymond, a prisoner, applied to commit the prison governor for contempt of court. The governor had intercepted and decided not to forward a letter written by Raymond to his solicitor which related not only to pending legal proceedings, but also contained allegations against an assistant governor. Raymond's application to commit the governor was also intercepted by him. Orders made under s 47 of the Prison Act (PA) 1952 permitted correspondence between a prisoner who was party to any legal proceedings and his solicitor, and gave the prison governor power to stop letters containing allegations against prison officers, requiring him to explain the correct complaints procedure to the prisoner. The Divisional Court held that the stopping of the first letter did not constitute contempt of court, but that the stopping of the second letter did. The governor appealed, and Raymond cross-appealed.

Held that both the appeal and the cross-appeal would be dismissed. Two principles governed the case. The first was derived from *R v Gray* (1900). Any act calculated to obstruct or interfere with the course of justice, or the lawful process of the courts, was a contempt of court. The second principle, stated in *R v Board of Visitors of Hull Prison ex p St Germain (No 1)*, was that a convicted prisoner retained all civil rights which were not expressly or by necessary implication taken from him. The PA 1952 did not confer power to make regulations which would deny or interfere with a prisoner's right to have unimpeded access to a court. The orders made under s 47 of the PA 1952 would be interpreted narrowly in order to avoid ascribing to them that effect (which would have rendered them *ultra vires*). The governor had temporarily denied Raymond's access to the court by stopping the second letter, and had therefore committed a contempt.

R v Secretary of State for the Home Department ex p Leech (No 2) (1993) CA

The appellant, a prisoner, sought certiorari to quash the power of a prison governor under the Prison Rules 1964 to censor inmates' correspondence with their solicitors in respect of legal proceedings not yet commenced. At first instance, the court rejected the contention that the relevant part of the Rules (r 33(3)) was *ultra vires* s 47(1) of the PA 1952, which conferred power to make rules for the regulation and management of prisons'. The prisoner appealed to the Court of Appeal.

Held, allowing the appeal, that it was necessary to consider whether there was an objective need for a rule as wide as r 33(3), which empowered a prison governor to stop any letter or communication on the grounds that its contents were objectionable or that it was of inordinate length. While both a power to examine correspondence between prisoners and then legal advisors to ascertain whether it was *bona fide,* and a power to stop objectionable correspondence could be justified, neither the distinction between proceedings already begun and those contemplated, nor the reference to the length of the correspondence were required. Since r 33(3) was therefore wider than necessary and created a substantial impediment to the exercise of the prisoner's basic rights as expounded in *Raymond v Honey* (above), it was *ultra vires,* so far as it purported to apply to correspondence between prisoners and their legal advisers.

R v Secretary of State for the Home Department ex p Simms (1999) HL

Two prisoners serving life sentences, who claimed that they had been the victims of miscarriages of justice, sought interviews with journalists in order to publicise their grievances. It was the policy of the Home Secretary, relying on paras 37 and 37A of the Prison Service Standing Order 5A (made under s 47(1) of the PA 1952) to allow the interviews only if the journalists signed undertakings not to use any part of the interviews for professional purposes. The justification for the policy was that the interviews would tend to undermine discipline and control within the prison environment. The journalists refused to sign the undertakings, and the prisoners sought judicial review of the policy as a fetter upon their access to justice. They were successful at first instance. The Court of Appeal allowed an appeal by the Home Secretary. The prisoners appealed to the House of Lords.

Held, allowing the appeal, that investigative journalism had been shown on the evidence to play an important role in leading to the detection and remedy of miscarriages of justice. It was hard to conceive of a more pressing justification for the assertion of a right to free speech. The fact that fundamental and basic rights were being invoked mandated the application of the principle of legality to the construction of paras 37 and 37A. So interpreted, the two paras were not *ultra vires* s 47(1) of the PA 1952, but to base upon them an absolute rule against the publication of interviews was unlawful.

THE COURTS AND POLICE POWERS

Police duties and the nature of the citizen's duty to assist the police

Rice v Connolly (1966)

In the early hours of the morning, police constables were patrolling an area of Grimsby in which a number of burglaries had taken place the same night. The officers saw the appellant behaving suspiciously, and asked him where he was going, where he was coming from, and his name and address. The appellant gave only partial (although accurate) details and refused to provide more information. When he refused to accompany the constables to a police box to confirm his identity, he was then arrested on the grounds that he had wilfully obstructed a police constable in the exercise of his duty. The appellant was convicted and appealed to the Divisional Court.

Held that the appeal would be allowed. It was clear that the appellant had obstructed the police, and that the police had been acting throughout in accordance with their duty. It was part of the obligations and duties of a police constable (*per* Lord Parker CJ):

> ... to take all steps which appear to him necessary for keeping the peace, for preventing crime or for protecting property from criminal injury. There is no exhaustive definition of the powers and obligations of the police, but they are at least those, and they would further include the duty to detect crime and to bring an offender to justice.

However, it was necessary for the prosecution to prove that the obstruction was 'wilful', which in the context meant not merely 'intentional', but connoted something which was done without lawful excuse. Here, the question was whether the appellant had a lawful excuse for failing to answer the questions which had been put to him. In the judgment of Lord Parker CJ, he had; while every citizen had a moral or social duty to assist the police, there was no legal duty to that effect, and the appellant was therefore within his rights to refuse to answer the questions put to him. *Per* Marshall J:

In order to uphold this conviction, it appears to me that one has to assent to the proposition that where a citizen is acting merely within his legal rights, he is thereby committing a criminal offence.

The requirement of legal justification for police action

R v Waterfield and Lynn (1964)
Per Ashworth J:

In the judgment of this court, it would be difficult, and in the present case it is unnecessary, to reduce within specific limits the general terms in which the duties of police constables have been expressed. In most cases, it is probably more convenient to consider what the police constable was actually doing and in particular whether such conduct was *prima facie* an unlawful interference with a person's liberty or property. If so, it is then relevant to consider whether (a) such conduct falls within the general scope of any duty imposed by statute or recognised at common law, and (b) whether such conduct, albeit within the general scope of such a duty, involved an unjustifiable use of powers associated with the duty.

The exercise of specific powers

Arrest
The meaning of 'reasonable suspicion'

Castorina v Chief Constable of Surrey (1988) CA
Section 2(4) of the Criminal Law Act (CLA) 1967 provided as follows: 'Where a constable, with reasonable cause, suspects that an arrestable offence has been committed, he may arrest without warrant anyone whom he, with reasonable cause, suspects to be guilty of the offence.' Detectives, who reasonably suspected that the burglary of a company's premises was an inside job, interviewed the respondent and arrested her. They had been informed that the documents taken by the burglar would have been useful to a person who had a grudge against the company. The respondent was, detained at the police station for three and a quarter hours, interrogated, and released without charge. She claimed damages for wrongful arrest and detention. The court at

first instance upheld her claim, holding that 'reasonable cause' required an 'honest belief founded on reasonable suspicion leading an ordinary cautious man to the conclusion that the person arrested was guilty of the offence'. It was further stated that an ordinary man would have sought more information from the suspect before arresting her, including an examination of whether she held any grudge against the company. The respondent was awarded £ 4,500. The Chief Constable appealed to the Court of Appeal.

Held, allowing the appeal, that, in objective terms, there was sufficient information available to the arresting officers to give them reasonable cause to suspect that the respondent was guilty of the burglary. The remaining question therefore was whether, before arresting her, the officers should have sought further information and explanation from her. Purchas LJ reviewed the authorities and concluded that they imposed no such requirement. Although the failure to follow an obvious course of questioning might, in exceptional circumstances, render the decision to arrest subject to challenge under the *Wednesbury* principle *(Associated Provincial Picture Houses Ltd v Wednesbury Corp*, the court should have been concerned in the present action only to establish whether the arresting officers had reasonable cause for suspicion, and not with any further inquiries which the officers might have carried out. The judge at first instance had not so confined himself, and had therefore directed himself wrongly in law in applying the provisions of the CLA 1967.

The requirement to inform the suspect of the grounds for his arrest

Christie v Leachinsky (1947) HL

The appellant was a rag merchant. He was arrested by two police officers of the Liverpool police force and charged under the Liverpool Corporation Act 1921 with the unlawful possession of a bale of cloth. He was detained in Custody for a day, brought before a magistrate and twice remanded for periods of a week. At the hearing, he was discharged, but was re-arrested later the same day. The Leicester police then charged him with larceny and took him to Leicester in order to commit him for trial. The Leicester magistrates dismissed the charge. The appellant brought an action against the Liverpool police officers for false imprisonment and for trespass to the person.

Held that, under the Liverpool Corporation Act 1921, the police could arrest without a warrant in these circumstances only if the name and address of the suspect were unknown and could not be ascertained. That was the case here, and the arrest was therefore unlawful. Further, the common law power of arrest was limited to arrest on a specific charge. Viscount Simon considered that the authorities established the following propositions:

(1) If a policeman arrests without warrant on a reasonable suspicion of felony, or of other crime of a sort which does not require a warrant, he must in ordinary circumstances inform the person arrested of the true ground of arrest. He is not entitled to keep the reason to himself or to give a reason which is not the true reason. In other words, a citizen is entitled to know on what charge or on suspicion of what charge he is seized.

(2) If the citizen is not so informed, but is nevertheless seized, the policeman, apart from certain exceptions, is liable for false imprisonment.

(3) The requirement that the person arrested should be informed of the reason why he is seized naturally does not exist if the circumstances are such that he must know the general nature of the alleged offence for which he is detained.

(4) The requirement that he should be so informed does not mean that technical or precise language need be used. The matter is a matter of substance, and turns on the elementary proposition that in this country a person is, *prima facie,* entitled to his freedom and is only required to submit to restraint on his freedom if he knows in substance the reason why it is claimed that this restraint should be imposed.

(5) The person arrested cannot complain that he has not been supplied with the above information as and when he should be, if he himself produces the situation which makes it practically impossible to inform him, for example, by immediate counter-attack or by running away.

An originally unlawful arrest may become lawful

Lewis and Another v Chief Constable of the South Wales Constabulary (1991) CA

The appellants were arrested for burglary. They were not informed of the reason for the arrest until their arrival at the police station. This took place 10 minutes after arrest in the case of the first appellant and some 23 minutes after arrest in the case of the second appellant. Section 28(3) of the Police and Criminal Evidence Act (PACE) 1984 provided that 'no arrest is lawful unless the person arrested is informed of the ground for the arrest at the time of, or as soon as practicable after, the arrest'. The appellants brought an action against the Chief Constable for wrongful arrest and false imprisonment. The trial judge held that the arrest, although originally unlawful, was a continuing action and became lawful once the appellants were told the reasons for it. The jury awarded each appellant £200 in damages. The appellants argued on appeal that the arrest was a nullity, that an originally unlawful arrest could not later become lawful, and that they were accordingly entitled to damages in respect of the entire period of detention (some five hours).

Held, dismissing the appeal, that the authorities showed that arrest was to be regarded as an ordinary English word, and not a legal concept. Therefore, the question whether a person had been arrested depended on the fact of deprivation of liberty, and not on the legitimacy of the arrest The case of *Holgate-Mohammed v Duke* (below) showed that arrest was a continuing act, and remained good law in the light of the PACE 1984. There was nothing inconsistent with s 28(3) in holding that, from the time the appellants had been informed of the reason for their arrest, the arrest became lawful.

Limits on restraint of suspects outside arrest

Kenlin v Gardiner (1967)

Two plainclothes police officers became suspicious of the behaviour of two boys, who were visiting the homes of members of their school rugby team in order to remind them about a forthcoming match. One of the officers approached the boys, asked them what they were doing, and showed his warrant card. The boys nevertheless failed to realise that the men were police officers, and one of the boys attempted to run away. The officer took hold of the boy by the arm in order to prevent his escape. A struggle then took place, one of the officers was struck, and the boys ran away. They were charged under s 51(1) of the Police Act 1964, and appealed against conviction.

Held that the appeal would be allowed. Winn LJ considered whether the officer had been entitled in law to take hold of the boy by the arm, and continued:

> I feel myself compelled to say that the answer to that question must be in the negative. This officer might or might not in the particular circumstances have possessed a power to arrest these boys. I leave that question open, saying no more than that I feel some doubt whether he would have had a power of arrest; but on the assumption that he had a power of arrest, it is to my mind perfectly plain that neither of these officers purported to arrest either of these boys. What was done was not done as an integral step in the process of arresting, but was done in order to secure an opportunity, by detaining the boys from escape, to put to them or to either of them the question which was regarded as the test question to satisfy the officers whether or not it would be right in the circumstances, and having regard to the answer obtained from that question, if any, to arrest them. I regret to say that I think there was a technical assault by the police officer ...

RV Inwood (1973) CA

The appellant was charged with assaulting a police constable in the exercise of his duty. He had attended voluntarily at a police station for questioning in connection with alleged thefts. During this procedure, a detective constable had told the appellant that he proposed to charge him with theft and handling stolen goods, and had cautioned him. The police then carried out the formalities associated with arrest, including finger-printing the appellant. The appellant later attempted to leave the police station. The police sought to prevent his departure, and in the ensuing struggle, two officers were injured. At trial, the judge directed the jury that the appellant had been legally arrested. The appellant was convicted.

Held, allowing the appeal, that the question whether it had been made clear to the appellant that he was under arrest was one of fact and should have been left to the jury. It would depend on the circumstances of individual cases whether enough had been done to demonstrate that a man had been arrested, and no particular formula would suit every case. Different procedures might have to be followed with different persons depending on their age, ethnic origin, knowledge of English, intellectual qualities or mental disabilities. In every case, there would be an obligation to make it plain to the suspect by what was said and done that he was no longer a free man. Here, without the judge's direction, the jury might or might not have found sufficient to have been done. The conviction would therefore be quashed.

Pedro v Diss (1981)

The appellant was charged with an assault on a police constable in the course of his duty, contrary to s 51(1) of the Police Act 1964. The officer had seen the appellant in the doorway of a house, and suspected that he might be in possession of house breaking implements or property stolen from the house. He searched the appellant. In response to further questioning, the appellant walked away. When the officer took the appellant by the arm and told him that he wanted him to return to the house, the appellant tried to pull away, swore at the officer, and hit him. At trial the appellant argued that the officer was acting unlawfully by detaining him without arresting him. The officer contended that s 66 of the Metropolitan Police Courts Act 1839 gave him power to detain. The appellant was convicted.

Held, allowing the appeal, that officer had not been acting in the course of his duty. There had been no arrest, and in order lawfully to detain the appellant under s 66, the officer should have communicated to him that he was no longer a free man, and the ground for the detention.

Challenge to the exercise of statutory powers of arrest

Holgate-Mohammed v Duke (1984) HL

A police officer suspected the appellant of the theft of jewellery, but considered that he needed further evidence in order to secure the appellant's conviction. Rather than interviewing the appellant under caution, the officer decided to arrest her and take her to a police station for questioning. The county court judge found the officer's intention was to subject the appellant 'to the greater stress and pressure involved in arrest and deprivation of liberty in the belief that if she was going to confess she would be more likely to do so in a state of arrest' (though it was not suggested that any impropriety took place). The judge awarded the appellant £1,000 damages for false imprisonment. The Court of Appeal allowed an appeal by the Chief Constable. The appellant to the House of Lords.

Held, dismissing the appeal, that the powers under which the arrest had been made were not common law powers, but derived from s 2(4) of the Criminal Law Act 1967. Accordingly, the court was concerned with the exercise of a discretion conferred by statute. It could be challenged only by reference to the *Wednesbury* principles. Applying those principles, Lord Diplock noted that it had been found as fact by the county court judge that the officer had acted in good faith. The court therefore had only to determine whether the officer's exercise of his discretion had been reasonable. This depended on whether the officer's motivation constituted an irrelevant consideration. Lord Diplock was of the opinion that it did not. Accordingly, the arrest was lawful.

Other powers

A suspect's rights may not be infringed unless that necessity appears on the facts of the individual case

Lindley v Rutter (1981)

The appellant was arrested for disorderly behaviour while drunk. She was taken to a police station, where she refused to be searched. Two women police officers then forcibly searched her and removed her brassiere. In the course of the search, the appellant assaulted one of the officers. The officers believed that they were acting in accordance with standing orders of the Chief Constable, which they understood to require them to search every female prisoner and remove her brassiere for her own protection. The appellant argued that the woman police officer had not been acting in the course of her duty when the appellant assaulted her.

Held, allowing the appeal, that the appellant's argument was correct, since the officer had exceeded her duty at the time of the assault. *Per* Donaldson LJ:

> It is the duty of the courts to be ever zealous to protect the personal freedom, privacy and dignity of all who live in these islands. Any claim to be entitled to take action which infringes these rights is to be examined with very great care. But such rights are not absolute. They have to be weighed against the rights and duties of police officers, acting on behalf of society as a whole. It is the duty of any constable who lawfully has a prisoner in his charge to take all reasonable measures to ensure that the prisoner does not escape or assist others to do so, does not injure himself or others, does not destroy or dispose of evidence and does not commit further crime such as, for example, malicious damage to property. This list is not exhaustive, but it is sufficient for present purposes. What measures are reasonable in the discharge of this duty will depend upon the likelihood that the particular prisoner will do any of these things unless prevented ... What can never be justified is the adoption of any particular measures without regard to all the circumstances of the particular case. This is not to say that there can be no standing instructions ... But the officer having custody of the prisoner must always consider, and be allowed and encouraged to consider, whether the special circumstances of the particular case justify or demand a departure from the standard procedure either by omitting what would otherwise be done or by taking

> additional measures. So far as searches are concerned, he should appreciate that they involve an affront to the dignity and privacy of the individual. Furthermore, there are degrees of affront involved in such a search. Clearly, going through someone's pockets or handbag is less of an affront than a body search. In every case, a police officer ordering a search or depriving a prisoner of property should have a very good reason for doing so.

A suspect must be informed of the reason for an infringement of his rights

Brazil v Chief Constable of Surrey (1983)

The appellant was asked but refused to leave a public house, and was arrested by police officers for conducting herself in a way likely to cause a breach of the peace. Upon being taken to the police station, she was informed by a woman police officer that everyone brought into the police station had to be searched for their own safety. The appellant then assaulted the officer. At this stage, the police did not suspect the appellant of being in possession of controlled drugs. The officer in charge of the police station, Acting Inspector Martin, subsequently ordered the appellant to be searched by force. She then assaulted the woman police officer who was carrying out the search. Acting Inspector Martin did suspect the appellant of being in possession of controlled drugs, but he did not inform her that this was the reason for the search. The appellant contended that the first assault could not be an assault on a police officer in the execution of her duty because the justification given for the search as not a proper justification. With regard to the second search, the appellant argued, *inter alia,* that it was unlawful because she had not been informed of the reason for it.

Held, allowing the appeal and quashing the appellant's convictions, that both submissions were correct. In so holding, the court applied the reasoning of Donaldson LJ in *Lindley v Rutter* (above) in respect of the first search, and obtained guidance from *Christie v Leachinsky* (above) in respect of the second.

Protection of the subject through the exclusion of evidence

The considerations governing exercise of the common law discretion to exclude evidence

Jeffrey v Black (1978)

The respondent was arrested by members of the police drug squad for the theft of a sandwich from a public house. He was taken to a polite station. Before he was charged, he was asked to give his consent to his flat being searched. The respondent accompanied the police to his flat and unlocked the door. In the course of the search, the police found cannabis and cannabis resin. The magistrates found as fact that the respondent had not given his consent to the search of his flat. They therefore exercised their common law discretion to exclude evidence found as a result of the search, and dismissed the charges. The prosecution appealed by way of case stated to the Divisional Court, asking, *inter alia:* '... were the justices right in ruling that the evidence of the finding of the articles was inadmissible if they found that the respondent had not given his consent to the search?'

Held that there was no discretion to exclude relevant evidence solely on the ground stated, and the case would be sent back to be re-heard before a different bench. The test for the admissibility of evidence was whether the evidence was relevant to the matters in issue. The magistrates, in common with any other English court, had a general discretion to decline to allow any evidence to be called by the prosecution if they thought that it would be unfair or oppressive to allow that to be done. However, it would be appropriate to exercise the discretion only in exceptional circumstances. *Per* Lord Widgery CJ:

> ... if the case is exceptional, if the case is such that not only have the police officers entered without authority, but they have been guilty of trickery or they have misled someone, or they have been oppressive or they have been unfair, or in other respects they have behaved in a manner which is morally reprehensible, then it is open to the justices to apply their discretion and decline to allow the particular evidence to be let in as part of the trial.

There is no discretion to exclude evidence on the ground that it was obtained by entrapment

R v Sang (1980) HL

In the course of the appellant's trial on charges of conspiracy in connection with counterfeit bank notes, his counsel sought to persuade the judge to rule against the admissibility of the prosecution's evidence on the ground that it related to offences which the appellant would not have committed unless he had been induced to do so by police officers acting as *agents provocateurs*. The judge ruled that he had no discretion to exclude evidence on this ground, and therefore refused to hear the evidence by which the entrapment was intended to be established. The appellant then changed his plea to one of guilty. His appeal against the judge's ruling was dismissed by the Court of Appeal. He renewed it before the House of Lords.

Held, dismissing the appeal, that the judge's ruling had been correct. The court was concerned not with how evidence was gathered, but rather with the use made of it at the trial. To allow the exclusion of evidence on the basis for which the appellant contended would effectively be to introduce into English law a defence of entrapment. No such defence existed. *Per* Lord Diplock:

> ... the function of a judge at a criminal trial as respects the admission of evidence is to ensure that the accused has a fair trial according to the law. It is no part of a judge's function to exercise disciplinary powers over the police or prosecution as respects the way in hich evidence to be used at the trial is obtained by them. If it was obtained illegally there will be a remedy in civil law; if it was obtained legally but in breach of the rules of conduct for the police, this is a matter for the appropriate disciplinary authority to deal with ...

Statutory exclusion of evidence

R v Keenan (1989) CA

Police officers stopped the appellant's car, arrested the appellant for taking and driving the car away without authority, and searched the car in the appellant's absence. They found a homemade spear in it. The appellant was charged with driving offences, and with possession of an offensive weapon. After his committal, at which the only evidence relating to the spear was provided by the officers who had found it, further evidence was served in which two other officers alleged that the appellant had been asked about the spear. They stated that he had admitted that he knew it was in the car, but denied it was his. In breach of provisions of the Code of Practice for the Detention, Treatment and Questioning of Persons by Police Officers issued under s 66 of the Police and Criminal Evidence Act 1984, the alleged interview had not been properly recorded or documented by the police. The appellant maintained that it had never taken place. He was convicted, and appealed on the ground that evidence of the alleged interview should not have been admitted.

Held, allowing the appeal and quashing the conviction, that the breaches of the code had been serious and substantial. To admit the evidence was to penalise the appellant if he intended to exercise his right to remain silent at the trial, or to force him to challenge it and thereby open his past record to cross-examination or to put him at a disadvantage since there was no contemporaneous record of the interview. The evidence should therefore have been excluded under s 78 of the 1984 Act. *Per* Hodgson J:

The provision [of the 1984 Act and the Codes of Practice issued under it] will only be workable if and when compliance with them becomes the habitual practice of the police... It is to be hopeds that in future no police officer will display the ignorance of even the important provisions in issue in the case as these officers did.. We think that, in case where there have been significant and substantial' breaches of the 'verballing' provisions of the Code, the evidence so obtained will frequently be excluded. We do not think that any injustice will be caused by this. It is clear that not every breach or combination of breaches of the code will justify the exclusion of interview evidence under s 76 or s 78: see *R v Hallett* (1989). They must be significant and substantial. If this were not the case, the courts would be undertaking a task which is no part of their duty; as Lord Lane CJ said in *R v Delaney* ((1989) at: 'It is no part of the duty of the court to rule a statement inadmissible simply in order to punish the police for failure to observe the Codes of Practice.'

Article 5 of the ECHR

(1) Everyone has the right to liberty and security of person. No one shall be deprived of his liberty save in the following cases and in accordance with a procedure prescribed by law:

(a) the lawful detention of a person after conviction by a competent court;

(b) the lawful arrest or detention of a person for non-compliance with the lawful order of a court or in order to secure the fulfilment of any obligation prescribed by law;

(c) the lawful arrest or detention of a person effected for the purpose of bringing him before the competent legal authority on reasonable suspicion of having committed an offence or when it is reasonably considered necessary to prevent his committing an offence or fleeing after having done so;

(d) the detention of a minor by lawful order for the purpose of educational supervision or his lawful detention for the purpose of bringing him before the competent legal authority;

(e) the lawful detention of persons for the purpose of the prevention of the spreading of infectious diseases, of persons of unsound mind, alcoholics or drug addicts, or vagrants;

(f) the lawful arrest or detention of a person to prevent his effecting an unauthorised entry into the country or of a person against whom action is being taken with a view to deportation or extradition.

(2) Everyone who is arrested shall be informed promptly, in a language which he understands, of the reasons for his arrest and of any charge against him.

(3) Everyone arrested or detained in accordance with the provisions of para 1(c) of this Article shall be brought promptly before a judge or other officer authorised by law to exercise judicial power and shall be entitled to trial within a reasonable time or to release pending trial. Release may be conditioned by guarantees to appear for trial.

(4) Everyone who is deprived of his liberty by arrest or detention shall be entitled to take proceedings by which the lawfulness of his detention shall be decided speedily by a court and his release ordered if the detention is not lawful.

(5) Everyone who has been the victim of arrest or detention in contravention of the provisions of the Article shall have an enforceable right to compensation.

GLOSSARY

Act of State - an action authorised or adopted by the executive in the conduct of its relations with another State or its subjects.

Applicant - the party which applies to court for judicial review of a public authority's decision or action.

Attorney General - the government's principal legal advisor and representative, responsible for the supervision of criminal justice and competent in all cases to vindicate public rights.

Caution - a statement required to be made to a person suspected by the police of an offence, indicating that his answers or silence in response to questioning may be given in evidence in a criminal prosecution.

Certiorari - a remedy available in judicial review proceedings, bringing up and quashing the decision which is subject to challenge.

Collective ministerial responsibility - the convention that government ministers should not disagree publicly with government policy.

Common law - (as contrasted with statute) the entire corpus of binding judicial decisions and the legal principles to which it gives rise.

Constitutionalism - the principle that the legal power of government should derive from and be limited by a higher form of law.

Constitutionality - the conformity of actions, practices, decisions or legislation with a formal constitution.

Conventions - non-legal rules derived from practice, serving to define the constitutionally proper exercise of power.

Declaration - a non-coercive remedy available in judicial review proceedings, consisting of a formal statement of the law as it applies to the facts before the court.

Delegated legislation - *see* Subordinate legislation.

Entrenchment - the conditional or absolute protection of a legislative measure from subsequent repeal.

12

TRIBUNALS, INQUIRIES AND THE OMBUDSMEN REMEDY

SUMMARY

This chapter considers several ways in which disputes may be resolved by means other than recourse to the courts. It commences by examining tribunals and inquiries. These are now a part of everday life given the ever-increasing role that the state plays the life of the individual, and the potential which that creates for things to go wrong. Their characteristics are considered in a general manner, and an attempts is made to draw some distinctions between both them and the courts. The chapter concludes by considering the ombudsmen remedy. Since the office of the Parliamentary Commissioner was established in 1967, there has been expansion in the areas in which ombudsmen may investigate compalaints of maladministration. The discussion will therefore focus on some of the more established ombudsmen, as well as on a recent arrival to the ombudsman fold.

Tribunals and inquiries

At the outset, it is necessary to distinguish between tribunals and inquiries. Whilst a tribunal is a permanent body which sits periodically, an inquiry is something which is established on an ad hoc basis. Inquiries are set up as a response to a particular event eg the Southall Rail Crash. They may sit for many months and perhaps even years, especially where their remit has been extended, but they are not permanent bodies. A further distinction which can be made relates to the decision-making powers of the two bodies. Whilst tribunals are empowered to make decisions which are binding on those parties subject to their jurisdiction, inquiries generally do not have formal decision-making powers. The end of an inquiry will often be marked by the publication of a report containing the inquiry's recommendations. It will generally be a matter for the appropriate minister to decide whether or not to act on these recommendations.

Broadly speaking, therefore, we can see that tribunals are concerned with matters of fact and law, whereas inquiries are concerned with wider policy issues. In the case of planning inquiries, however, it may be argued that they cut across the divide. They involve matters of law and policy and they are able to reach decisions rather than merely make recommendations, subject to a right of appeal to the Secretary of State.

Tribunals

The resolution of disputes is of course a task which our courts perform on a daily basis. However, courts are not the only forum for dispute resolution. Given the ever-increasing role of government within the modern state, as evidenced by initiatives such as the creation of the welfare state, the potential for disputes has been greatly increased Accordingly, it has been necessary to establish specialist tribunals to determine disputes arising in their own areas of expertise. Examples of these specialist tribunals include: Industrial Tribunals, Mental Health Review Tribunals and Social Security Appeal Tribunals. The former is concerned with disputes relating to employment eg unfair dismissal claims, discrimination in the workplace on the grounds of race or sex. Mental Health Review Tribunals were established under the Mental Health Act 1959. They currently exercise the jurisdiction to review the compulsory detention of patients in hospital under the terms of the Mental Health Act 1983. By virtue of s 72 of that Act, they have the power to direct that a patient be discharged provided that they are satisfied that a pre-condition laid down in the statute applies. Social Security Appeal Tribunals are primarily concerned with hearing appeals against a refusal to pay social security benefits. They also hear appeals relating to the overpayment of benefit to a claimant.

Tribunals and courts distinguished

Although it is clear that both courts and tribunals perform as adjudicative role, they are distinct bodies. In *A-G v BBC* (1981), where the point at issue was whether a local valuation court was an 'inferior court' and hence protected by the law of contempt of court, the HL drew a distinction between the two. Lord Scarman observed that:

> 'I would identify a court in (or "of") law, ie a court of judicature, as a body established by law to exercise, either generally or subject to defined limits, the judicial power of the state. In this context judicial power is to be contrasted with legislative and executive (ie administrative) power. If the body under review is established for a purely legislative or administrative purpose, it is part of the legislative or administrative system of the state, even though it has to perform duties which are judicial in character.'

It is normally the case that the name accorded to a body will indiicate whether it is a court or tribunal. However, it is the nature of the functions which the body performs which is important. Thus in *A-G v BBC* (1981), the HL held that a local valuation court was in fact a tribunal because it performed administrative functions. Conversely, despite its name, the Employment Appeal Tribunal is in fact a court.

Characteristics of tribunals

In 1955, following the 'Crichel Down Affair', the Committee on Administrative Tribunals and Enquiries was set up under the chairmanship of Sir Oliver Franks. Its remit was to consider and make recommendations on the constitution and working of tribunals and the holding of enquiries.

The Franks Committee reported in 1957 (Cmnd 218). In its opinion, the tribunal system should reflect what it described as three 'closely linked characteristics': openness, fairness and impartiality. The committee later expanded on this theme when it observed that:

> 'In the field of tribunals openness appears to us to require the publicity of proceedings and knowledge of the essential reasoning underlying the decisions; fairness to require the adoption of a clear procedure which enables parties to know their rights, to present their case fully and to know the case which they have to meet; and impartiality to require the freedom of tribunals from the influence, real or apparent, of departments concerned with the subject-matter of their decisions'.

With regard to the choice between either a court or tribunal as the ajudicator in a particular dispute, the Franks Committee noted that 'tribunals have certain characteristics which often give them advantage over the courts'. These characteristics were: cheapness, accessibility, freedom from technicality, expedition and, expert knowledge of the particular subject. However, as a general principle, the committee considered that 'a decision should be entrusted to a court rather than to a tribunal in the absence of special considerations which make a tribunal more suitable'. These five characteristics merit further consideration.

Cheapness

It is patently the case that tribunals provide a cheaper means resolving disputes than the courts. There is no equivalent of a court fee to be paid and often, legal representation will be unnecessary. Where an individual is legally represented, the costs are likely to be less than in respect of court proceedings given that tribunals generally resolve disputes more quickly. This is important when it is remembered that Legal Aid is not generally available for disputes dealt with by tribunaes.

Accessibility

Tribunals are more accessible than the courts. Whilst there are several tribunals which meet only in one location, it is generally the case that tribunals will endeavour to sit in places which are convenient for those who wish to use them. Thus tribunals will often form local committees which meet across the country. Alternatively, a tribunal may travel around the country hearing cases.

Freedom from technicality

Whilst we need to be aware of the dangers of over-generalisation, it will often be the case that tribunal hearings are conducted in a more informal manner than court proceedings. Tribunals do not have the power to administer oaths and, generally, they do not adhere to the rules of evidence which are applied in the courts. The actual hearing itself is unlikely to be conducted in the formal manner of a court proceeding. The parties may all sit around the one table, and legal representations will often be unnecessary where legal points are not at issue.

Expedition

Court proceedings can be slow and protracted. Tribunal hearings, by contrast, are generally more expeditious. In part this is due to the fact that the remit of a tribunal is narrower than that of a court, which may have to deal with a wide range of matters. It is also due to the fact that the expertise of the tribunal may enable it to quickly identify the issues and resolve them to the satisfaction of the parties.

Expert knowledge of the particular subject

With the exception of the chairperson of a tribunal, who is normally a lawyer, the other members of a tribunal are all likely to have expertise in the particular field. This expertise will often mean that the facts of the case are rapidly understood, especially where they are similar to those of cases already heard by the tribunal. Although the court system does allow for a degree of judicial specialisation, judges will still be required to hear cases which cut across a number of subject areas. Moreover, it is unlikely that a judge will have expertise on the facts of a case before the court.

The statutory framework

The Tribunals and Inquiries Act 1992 consolidated the Tribunals and Inquiries Act 1971 and certain other enactments relating to tribunals and inquiries. It provides the statutory framework for the composition and procedure of tribunals. It also makes provision for the judicial control of tribunals.

Composition and procedure

The Council on Tribunals (see below) may make general recommendations to the appropriate minister as to the making of appointments to membership of any of the tribunals specified in Sch 1 to the Act (s 5). The minister must have regard to these recommendations, although he need not follow them. The appointment of tribunal chairpersons is a matter for the minister (s 6). They are selected by the minister from a panel of persons appointed by the Lord Chancellor. The minister also has the power to terminate a person's membership of one of the tribunals specified in Sch 1 to the Act (s 7). This is only exercisable, however, with judicial consent from the Lord Chancellor, the Lord President of the Court of Session or the Lord Chief Justice of Northern Ireland, depending on where the tribunal sits. The procedural rules under which Sch 1 tribunals operate can be made, approved, confirmed or concurred in by the minister, the Lord President of the Court of Session, the Commissioners of Inland Revenue or the Foreign Compensation Commission (s 8).

Judicial control

Section 10 of the 1992 Act imposes a general duty on Sch 1 tribunals (and ministers) to give reasons for their decisions. The statement of reasons may be furnished either orally or in writing. Reasons need not be given, however, on the grounds of national security or to a person not primarily concerned with the decision. The general duty may also be overridden by, amongst other things, specific statutory provision for the giving of reasons. Where reasons are given, whether in accordance with s 10 or some other statutory provision, they form part of the final decision of the tribunal.

Section 11 confers a right of appeal on a point of law in respect of the decisions of certain of the tribunals specified in Sch 1 to the 1992 Act. The appeal is to the HCt in the first instance, although a further appeal to the CA may be brought with the leave of the HCt or the CA. It must not be forgotten that in addition to a statutory right of appeal, the decisions of tribunals will be subject to judicial review. Thus the decision of a tribunal may be quashed where it has, for example, acted outside its statutory powers or contrary to the rules of natural justice. Moreover, if it has refused to exercise its jurisdiction, it may be compelled to do so by the grant of an order of mandamus.

The Council on Tribunals

The council was established under the Tribunals and Inquiries Act 1958. It now operates under the terms of the Tribunals and Inquiries Act 1992. By virtue of s 1 of that Act, the main functions of the council are:

- to keep under review the constitution and workings of the tribunals specified in Sch 1 to the Act, and from time to time to report on their constitution and working;
- to consider and report on matters referred to the council under the Act with respect to tribunals other than the ordinary courts, whether or not specified in Sch 1 of the Act; and
- to consider and report on such matters, or matters the council may consider to be of special importance, with respect to administrative procedures which involve or may involve the holding of a statutory inquiry by or on behalf of a minister.

The council has between 10 and 15 members appointed by the Lord Chancellor and Lord Advocate. The Parliamentary Commissioner for Administration (see below) is an ex officio member of the Council. It performs a lot of its functions by committee. Presently there are six committees apart from the Scottish Committee, which is expressly provided for in the 1992 Act. Its membership is determined by the Lord Advocate. He may designate members of the council as members of the Scottish Committee, or alternatively he may appoint non-council members to the committee.

The Council on Tribunals produces an annual report on the various aspects of its work during the course of that year. This is laid before Parliament in accordance with s 4(7) of the 1992 Act. In the annual report for 1997/98 (HC 45), for example, the Council considered, amongst other things, the implications for tribunals of the Human Rights Act 1998. Clearly this is an important issue for tribunals given that they will be required to determine cases where convention rights have been asserted, and to interpret legislation in a way which is compatible with the convention (s 3 of the 1998 Act). In so doing, they will have to have regard to the jurisprudence of the convention institutions (s 2 of the 1998 Act). Moreover, the definition of 'public authority' in s 6 of the 1998 Act encompasses tribunals. Therefore, tribunals must strive to ensure that they do not act unlawfully by acting in a way which is incompatible with a convention right, unless they are required to do so by primary legislation. In order for tribunals to properly perform these tasks, there will be a need for education and training both prior to and after the bulk of the Human Rights Act 1998 is brought into force in October 2000.

Criticisms of the tribunal system

The tribunal system has clearly been much improved since the publication of the Franks Report. Many of the concerns voiced by that committee have subsequently been addressed eg most tribunal chairpersons are now legally qualified. However, the system does still give rise to concerns. In the annual reports of the Council on Tribunals, there are sometimes criticisms of the way in which particular tribunals have operated. At a more general level, the council has continued to express its support for an adversarial as opposed to an inquisitorial approach to the resolution of disputes. Whilst a tribunal should always avoid immersing itself in a dispute to the extent that it is no longer able to perform an adjudicative function in an independent and impartial manner, arguably tribunals ought to be rather more proactive than the courts. This is particularly appropriate in a forum where legal representation is often absent.

With regard to the independence of tribunals, it ought not to be forgotten that their members are appointed by the government. Given that they resolve disputes which are often between the state and the individual, it is perhaps a cause for concern that their membership is not determined by an independent appointment panel. This having been said, the operation of the tribunal system to date does not indicate that decisions have been tainted with bias.

Inquiries

Inquiries may take one of two main forms: statutory inquiries ie inquiries held in pursuance of a duty imposed by a statutory provision; and non-statutory inquiries.

Statutory inquiries

These may be held in a variety of different contexts. For example, such inquiries are quite common in the planning arena. By virtue of s 78 of the Town and Country Planning Act 1990, an applicant for planning permission who is aggrieved by the decision of the local planning authority has the right to appeal to the Secretary of State. In order to assist him in the determination of that appeal, the Secretary of State may cause a local public inquiry to be held. Where such an inquiry is held, it will be conducted by a planning inspector in accordance with the Town and Country Planning (Inquiries Procedure) Rules 1992 (SI No 2038). If however, a particular planning matter raises questions of national or regional importance, or the scientific or technical aspects of the proposed development are of an unfamiliar nature, s 101 of the 1990 Act provides for the referral of the matter to a Planning Inquiry Commission (PIC). Where a referral is made, the functions and procedure to be followed by the PIC are set out in Part 1 of Sch 8 to the 1990 Act.

It is evident from the above, that the procedure to be followed in a statutory inquiry will often be determined in an Act of Parliament or by rules or regulations made under that Act. However, where no such provision has been made, s 9 of the Tribunals and Inquiries Act 1992 confers a general power on the Lord Chancellor to make rules regulating Inquiries procedure. This power is exercisable following consultation with the Council on Tribunals.

Inquiries have generally been regarded as being a part of the decision-making process rather than the decision-makers. However, in the case of local planning inquiries, it is now commonplace for a decision to be made by a planning inspector in the exercise of powers delegated by the Secretary of State.

Non-statutory public inquiries

Such inquiries are set up by the government to look into matters of public interest or concern. Usually these entail public scandals or major disaster involving the loss of life. Thus more recently, the government has set up inquiries into amongst other things: 'Arms to Iraq' (chaired by Sir Richard Scott VC); BSE (chaired by Lord Phillips); and the Paddington Rail Crash (chaired by Lord Cullen). Despite the diverse nature of these inquiries, they do share a common feature; they all were or are being chaired (the last two are ongoing) by senior members of the judiciary. This has been a common practice over the years. In some cases, it has meant that a senior judge has presided over a number of public inquiries. Lord Cullen, for example, who is the Lord justice Clerk and President of the Second Division of the Court of Session in Scotland, presided over the inquiries into the Piper Alpha Oil Rig Disaster (1988-90) and the shootings at Dunblane (1996) prior to his appointment to chair the Paddington Rail Crash Inquiry.

Non-statutory public inquiries may be established under the Tribunals of Inquiry (Evidence) Act 1921. This provides for a more formal inquiry to deal with matters of urgent public importance. In the years 1921-1984, only 22 such inquiries were held.

The origins of Ombudsmen

The term 'ombudsman' is Scandanavian in origin. Essentially it means a 'grievance man' or 'complaints officer'. The first modern ombudsman appeared in Sweden in 1809. However, the most significant development in terms of the spread of the ombudsman concept occurred in 1955, when Denmark elected its first ombudsman. The initial holder of that office, Professor Hurwitz, acted as something of a ambassador during his tenure. He made several trips to Britain which so captivated the public imagination that he received complaints from British citizens about the way in which they had been treated by public bodies in this country. His visits coincided with a growing feeling in Britain that something needed to be done in order to protect the individual against the increasing power of central government and the conduct of government officials.

Incorporation in the UK

During his visits, as Stacey has noted, the Danish ombudsman spoke at meetings organised by 'Justice', a group of lawyers committed to the idea of an ombudsman for the UK. He also had discussions with Sir John Wyatt who, as Director of Research for the Justice Committee, produced a report in 1961 which recommended that the UK should have an ombudsman. The Wyatt Report stimulated considerable interest in both the academic and popular press. Nevertheless, the government of the day rejected the idea of an ombudsman on the basis that the office would interfere with the prompt and efficient dispatch of business.

In its election manifesto prior to the general election of 1964, the Labour Party committed itself to the establishment of an ombudsman for central government 'with the right and duty to investigate and expose any misuse of government power as it affects the citizen'. Once elected, the new government set about drawing up legislative proposals which would fulfil its manifesto commitment However, as Stacey notes, progress on the Bill was slow. This was partly due to the fact that many of the government departments represented on the relevant cabinet subcommittee took advantage of the opportunity to make a case for excluding their own department from the ombudsman's remit. Nevertheless, the Parliamentary Commissioner Act received Royal Assent on 22 March 1967.

The Parliamentary Commissioner

The first thing to note about the Parliamentary Commissioner for Administration (the PCA) is the title of the office. Despite the fact that the holder of the office performs the role and functions of what would be called an ombudsman in a different jurisdiction, in the UK, PCA is the preferred title. In the years following the creation of the PCA, the ombudsman concept has spread domestically with the result that ombudsmen have appeared in other fields such as local government and the National Health Service. The holders of these offices are also known as commissioners rather than ombudsmen. More recently, however, we have seen the advent of ombudsmen in name as well as function. Thus, for example, the Courts and Legal Services Act 1990 established the office of the Legal Services Ombudsman.

The functions of the PCA

The role of the PCA is to investigate complaints of 'injustice' resulting from 'maladministration'. Despite the key nature of these concepts, neither is defined by the 1967 Act However, during the passage of the Bill before Parliament the minister responsible, Richard Crossman, observed in the HC that 'maladministration' meant:

'Bias, neglect, inattention, delay, incompetence, ineptitude, perversity, turpitude, arbitrariness and so on.'

Maladministration

The 'Crossman catalogue' represents the classic statement on the meaning of 'maladministration'. Nevertheless, as the words 'and so on' clearly indicate, it is not an exhaustive definition. Other forms of conduct not expressly referred to may also come within the definition of maladministration. A precise statutory definition would seem to have been avoided on the ground that it may have been unduly restrictive. Thus in the absence of a statutory definition, the PCA has a measure of flexibility in the conduct of his investigations. Doubtless each person who has held the office since its creation has had their own working definition of what constitutes maladministration.

In *R v Local Comr for Administration for the North and East Area of England, ex p Bradford Metropolitan City Council* (1979), the CA gave some consideration to the meaning of maladministration'. Although each judge expressed himself slightly differently, a common thread emerges from the judgments: maladministration is concerned with the manner in which decisions are reached and the manner in which they are or are not implemented. It is not concerned with the nature, quality or reasonableness of the decision itself.

Criticisms have been levelled at the term 'maladministration'. In the Justice-All Souls Report on Administrative law (1988), it was noted that the Commission for Local Administration in England felt that councillors and officials disliked the term. Moreover, that body argued that the term meant little to those who wished to lodge a complaint. One alternative may be to dispense with the term and instead allow the PCA to investigate any action which is 'unreasonable, unjust or oppressive' like his New Zealand counterpart. This suggestion was made by Justice in its publication *Our Fettered Ombudsman.*

Injustice in consequence of maladministration

By definition, the wording implies that maladministration may exist without injustice and that injustice may occur in the absence of maladministration. However, in order for a complaint to be investigated, it is imperative that the complainant has personally suffered injustice as a consequence of maladministration. The link between the two concepts is therefore very important. It limits the class of persons who may have a complaint of maladministration investigated by the PCA and in this sense acts in a not dissimilar manner to the need to demonstrate a sufficient interest in order to bring an application for judicial review.

Bod decisions and bad rules

In its Second Report for the session 1967-68 (HC 350), the Select Committee on the PCA urged the PCA to investigate complaints which related to either 'bad decisions' or 'bad rules'. As stated previously, the PCA is not concerned with the quality of the decision itself. Nevertheless, if the PCA finds that the effects of a decision are thoroughly bad, he may infer from that that there has been an element of maladministration.

Bad decisions may result from the implementation of a bad rule. Where, however, the rule itself does not breach the Crossman catalogue, it would seem that the PCA would be precluded from intervening. Nevertheless, it is possible for the PCA to circumvent this objection by taking the view that if the proper implementation of a rule results in a decision which is bad (ie causes injustice), there may be something wrong with the rule itself. Although this will by no means always be the case, the greater the number of bad decisions, the stronger is the justification for thinking that there is something wrong with the rule from which they originate.

Jurisdiction of the PCA

The bodies that are subject to the jurisdiction of the PCA are listed in Sch 2 to the 1967 Act. They include central government departments such as the Ministry of Defence, the Foreign and Commonwealth Office, the Home Office and the Lord Chancellor's Department, together with ministers and officials of such departments. Also included in the Schedule are a variety of other organisations, such as the Charity Commission, the Inland Revenue and the Royal Mint, all of which are subject to a degree of ministerial responsibility.

The PCA's jurisdiction also extends to non-departmental public bodies which have executive or administrative functions that directly affect individuals and which would have been within the PCA's jurisdiction if carried out by a government department. In addition to these requirements, the bodies must also be subject to some degree of ministerial responsibility. Included in this category, therefore, are the Commission for Racial Equality, the Arts Council and the English and Scottish Tourist Boards. From time to time, as bodies are either established or abolished, references to them may either be inserted or deleted from Sch 2 as appropriate. Alternatively where a body is already listed, the description of that body may be altered.

Matters excluded from the PCA's jurisdiction

These are provided for in s 5 and Sch 3 to the 1967 Act Essentially they fall into two categories: matters where a complainant has an alternative remedy available to him from a tribunal or court; or the matters specified in Sch 3. Certain matters may of course be excluded on both grounds. In the case of the former category, the bar on an investigation does not apply if the PCA is satisfied that the circumstances are such that it is not reasonable to expect the person aggrieved to resort to the alternative remedy. Clearly, therefore, the PCA has a discretion in the matter. In *R v Comr for Local Administration, ex p Croydon London Borough Council* (1989), Woolf LJ (as he then was) observed that in exercising this discretion, the ombudsman should not be concerned with whether or not the complainant would succeed in court, but rather whether the court was the appropriate forum.

Moreover, the availability of an alternative remedy was a matter to be considered both before and during the course of an investigation.

Writing extra-judicially on the same theme, Lord Woolf has expressed the view that the PCA and his local government counterpart ought to have the power to refer a matter to court either before, during or on the completion of an investigation. Such a power would be exercisable where a significant point of law was involved or where the courts were in a better position than the ombudsman to grant a remedy. In the PCA's annual report for 1980, the then holder of the office explained that:

> 'As a matter of practice, where there appears on the face of things to have been a substantial legal wrong for which, if proved, there is a substantial legal remedy, I expect the citizen to seek it in the courts and I tell him so. But where there is doubt about the availability of a legal remedy or where the process of law seems to be cumbersome, slow and expensive for the objective to be gained, I exercise my discretion to investigate the complaint myself.'

Schedule 3 matters

Some matters are regarded as being outside the jurisdiction of the PCA even though on the face of it, they fall within the scope of his function. They are exhaustively set out in Sch 3 to the 1967 Act. For present purposes, they may be summarised as follows:

- foreign affairs, including consular matters, matters relating to the dominions and extradition;
- action taken by or with the authority of the Secretary of State for investigating crime or protecting state security (including passport matters);
- the commencement or conduct of civil or criminal proceedings before any court;
- the prerogative of mercy;
- action taken by or on behalf of the Minister of Health or Secretary of State by a Regional, Area or District Health Authority or various specified hospital boards;

- contractual or commercial transactions of a government department or authority to which the Act applies, except (i) the compulsory purchase of land, or (ii) the disposal of land so acquired;
- personnel matters; or
- the grant of honours, awards or privileges within the gift of the Crown.

Whether or not all of these exclusions are justified is a moot point. In the case of the prerogative of mercy, for example, the effect of the exclusion is lessened by the fact that in principle, its exercise is justiciable in the light of *R v Secretory of State for the Home Department, exp Bentiey* (1994). Personnel matters are more problematic. The justification for their exclusion is that they may be resolved by other means eg before a tribunal. In the words of the PCA in his Annual Report for 1988, his 'proper concern was with complaints qua citizen, and not with complaints qua employee, or qua supplier of goods or services to a department or public body'. Nevertheless, on several occasions, the Select Committee on the PCA has recommended that public service personnel matters should fall within the PCA's jurisdiction, as they do in the case of his New Zealand counterpart.

The MP 'filter'

By virtue of s 5 of the 1967 Act, a person who claims to have suffered injustice in consequence of maladministration must complain in writing to an MP. An investigation by the PCA will only take place, however, where the MP has referred the complaint to him (with the consent of the complainant) and has requested an investigation. Normally the expectation would be that an aggrieved person would complain to his constituency MP. This view is reinforced by the PCA's website which helpfully provides a list of all MPs, by name and constituency, for those who may be in doubt as to the identity of their MP. It also accords with the convention that MPs do not involve themselves in the affairs of another constituency. Nevertheless, since the 1967 Act is not prescriptive on this matter, it follows that a complaint could be made to an MP other than the complainant's constituency MP.

Unlike almost all other ombudsmen (Sri Lanka and France have a similar stipulation), the public have no direct access to the PCA. In the White Paper which preceded the 1967 Act, the government of the day stressed that it had no intention to 'create any new institution which would erode the functions of Members of Parliament'. Instead, by creating the PCA, it wished to provide MPs with 'a better instrument which they can use to protect the citizen'. In effect, therefore, the purpose of the MP filter was to allay fears that the PCA would disturb the relationship that had traditionally existed between an MP and his constituents. The requirement does ensure that an MP is kept in touch with the problems which his constituents are faced with in their contact with the machinery of the state. Additionally, it may serve as a means of sparing the PCA; from needless work since complaints which are received may be capable of being resolved by the MP himself.

In its First Report of 1993-94 (HC 33), the Select Committee on the PCA noted that in response to a questionnaire which it sent to MPs, 38.4% of the 333 who responded were in favour of direct access to the PCA, whereas 58% were against it. On this basis, the Select Committee observed that:

> '... many Members value their role as champions of their constituents' complaints and are unwilling to see this constitutional function in any way by-passed or diminished'. (HC 33, para 58).

Despite the support within the HC for the preservation of the status quo, a number of objections can be levelled against the MP filter. These were summarised by the Select Committee in its 1993-94 report as follows:

- direct access to the PCA should be a matter of right for the public
- the filter is an anomalous, almost unique feature of the UK ombudsman system
- potential complainants may be unwilling to approach an MP although they desire the assistance of the PCA
- whether or not a complaint is referred to the PCA by

an MP will depend upon the views and practice of the particular MP

- the filter is an obstacle to the PCA effectively promoting his services
- the filter creates an unnecessary bureaucratic barrier between the PCA and the complainant which consumes both the time and resources of the PCA and his office.

In practice, it has not been uncommon for the PCA to receive complaints directly from members of the public. Originally, the PCA's response would be to inform the complainant that he must contact his MP. Since 1978, however, the practice has been to reply to the complainant offering to refer the matter to the complainant's MP if the complainant so wishes. This pragmatic solution has the advantage of avoiding the delay which would otherwise arise if the complainant was required to submit his complaint to his MP. It is also a stratagem which has the support of the Select Committee.

It is apparent from the figures that in recent years, there has been a steady increase in the number of complaints that the PCA has received annually. In 1990, for example, 704 complaints were received, whereas by 1996, this figure had risen to 1,920. Nevertheless, even this higher figure falls well below the expected caseload of 6,000-7,000 per annum when the office was first established. It also compares unfavourably with ombudsmen in other jurisdictions. For example, in 1992, the PCA received 945 complaints whereas in Australia, the Commonwealth Ombudsman received 17,153 complaints that year. Such disparities may of course in part be explained by the scope of the respective ombudsman's jurisdictions. Nevertheless, they do suggest that the PCA is an under-utilised remedy.

An under-utilised remedy

Under-utilisation of the remedy may be because there is a lack of public awareness of the office. The publication of annual reports does help to keep the public informed of the nature and scope of the PCA's work, but in truth these are unlikely to be read by people other than those with a particular interest in the field. Occasionally a particular investigation may generate interest amongst the media, as was the case with the Channel Tunnel Rail Link (see below). Additionally, maintaining pages on the World Wide Web represents a further means by which the work of the PCA can reach a wider audience.

Time limit

Section 6(3) of the 1967 Act provides that a complaint must be made to an MP no later than 12 months from the date on which the person aggrieved first had notice of the matter alleged in the complaint, This time limit, which is more generous than the three months provided for in respect of bringing an application for judicial review, runs from when the person became aware of the matter rather than from the date on which the matter arose. Several months may therefore pass before the person aggrieved has the relevant knowledge.

The PCA has the discretion to investigate complaints not made within the 12-month time limit where he considers that special circumstances make it proper to do so. If, for example, the aggrieved person's poor health had prevented him from making the complaint within 12 months, the PCA may nevertheless decide to investigate the complaint. The danger in extending the time limit too greatly is that the complaint losses its freshness. Memories may fade and the facts of the complaint may become distorted with time. In practice, it is likely that the PCA will carry out a preliminary examination of a time-barred case, to determine whether it has any merit, before exercising his discretion to overlook the time limit.

Screening

Once a complaint has been referred to the PCA by an MP, a decision must be made as to whether or not to carry out a full investigation. This will be preceded by an initial screening of the complaint by the PCA's officers. The screening process must be carried out in a careful manner. It will often involve the officers working their way through voluminous papers and files in search of evidence to support the complaint. It will also necessitate that they have an understanding of the relevant statutory provisions, and it may require them to make informal enquiries of the department or authority whose actions are the subject of the complaint. Where more information is required before a decision can be made as to whether or not to conduct a full investigation, the PCA's officers will contact the complainant and invite him to send the information direct to the PCA. On occasion, it will be necessary to reject a complaint. This may be because it has been made against a body which falls outside the PCA's jurisdiction. Alternatively, as was previously suggested, a complaint may be rejected because an alternative means of redress is available to the complainant.

The screening process is time-consuming. In his annual report for 1997-98, the PCA noted that on 31 December 1996, 272 cases had been in screening for more than three months. The PCA considered that this was unacceptable and therefore set about improving matters. The efforts of the PCA and his officers appear to have been rewarded since at 31 March 1998, only eight cases had been in screening for more than 12 weeks.

Procedure for investigating a complaint

Where the PCA has determined that a complaint has been duly made under the 1967 Act, he may propose to conduct an investigation. If this is the case, s 7(1) requires him to afford an opportunity to those who are the subject of the allegations either personally, or as principal officer of the department or authority concerned, to comment on the allegations contained in the complaint. The PCA and his officers therefore carry out an active investigation into the complaint. Unlike court proceedings, which typically involve a judge hearing representations on both sides of an argument and then adjudicating on the matter, the complainant need play no further role in the investigation once it has begun. Moreover, an investigation also differs from court proceedings, which are generally held in public, in that it is conducted in private.

In terms of the conduct of the investigation itself, the PCA has a wide discretion as to the procedure to be followed. He may require any person, including any minister or officer of the department or authority concerned, who is able to furnish information or produce documents relevant to an investigation, to do so. He also enjoys the same powers as the courts in terms of the attendance and examination of witnesses and the production of documents. It is an offence to obstruct an investigation without lawful excuse or to behave in a manner which would, if the investigation was a court proceeding, constitute a contempt of court (s 9).

Reports

On the completion of an investigation, s 10 of the 1967 Act requires the PCA to send a report of his findings to the MP who referred the complaint to him, or if that person is no longer an MP, to another appropriate MP. This requirement ensures, therefore, that the MP is kept informed of the outcome of his constituent's complaint. Similarly, an MP will receive a statement of reasons from the PCA when it has been decided not to investigate a complaint. In both cases, the MP will need to make this information available to the complainant since the Act does not require the PCA to provide the complainant with a report. In practice, the PCA sends the MP an additional copy for him to send on to the complainant. Where an investigation has been conducted, a report of its findings must also be sent to the head of the department or authority concerned and to any person alleged to have been responsible for the action which was the subject-matter of the complaint.

Generally speaking, where an investigation has found in favour of the complainant ie that there has been injustice in consequence of maladministration, that injustice will be remedied by the relevant authority or department. Nevertheless, it should be noted that the PCA does not have enforcement powers to ensure that his recommendations are complied with. If the PCA believes that an injustice has not or will not be remedied, he may lay before Parliament a special report on the case (s 10(3)). This additional publicity may have the desired effect. In 1995, the PCA exercised this power for only the second time since his office was established. He did so in relation to the Channel Tunnel Rail Link. The PCA found that there had been maladministration in failing to consider whether ex gratia payments ought to be made to persons suffering hardship and distress because they were unable to sell their properties due to the uncertain status of the project during a five-year period. The Department of Transport rejected his finding, hence the special report. Ultimately the government of the day proposed certain forms of redress which were acceptable to the PCA, but not before a report had been published by the Select Committee on the PCA in support of his findings.

Section 10(4)of the 1967 Act requires the PCA to lay an annual report before Parliament detailing the work of his office during that year. Statistics relating to the number of complaints received during the period are included. These will be further broken down into the numbers of complaints that were rejected, subject to pre-investigation resolution or investigated fully. Additionally, the PCA's annual report is likely to contain comments on particularly noteworthy cases that have been investigated.

The Health Service Commissioner

Complaints relating to the National Health Service hospitals were excluded from the jurisdiction of the PCA by Sch 3 to the 1967 Act. This was by no means a popular decision. In the years that followed, bodies such as the Select Committee on the PCA recommended that the Commissioner should be entitled to investigate complaints about hospitals. However, when the government decided to act, it chose a different option to that advocated by the Select Committee. Instead of extending the jurisdiction of the PCA, the government opted to establish a separate Health Service Commissioner for Scotland, England and Wales. This was achieved by the National Heath Service (Scotland) Act 1972 and the National Health Service Reorganisation Act 1973, respectively. Ironically, despite the creation of the separate posts, they have in fact been held jointly by the PCA since 1973. This is due to the fact that the office of the PCA has received fewer complaints than was originally expected.

Jurisdiction

The jurisdiction of the Health Service Commissioner (HSC) was originally somewhat limited. In addition to the customary exclusion in respect of personnel matters, the HSC was excluded from investigating complaints relating to clinical decisions or family health service practitioners ie general medical practitioners, dentists, opticians and pharmacists. The exclusion of clinical decisions meant that from the outset, the HSC had to reject large numbers of complaints that he received. More recently, however, the jurisdiction of the HSC has been expanded. The consolidating Health Service Commissioners Act 1993 was amended in 1996 with the result that the HSC may now investigate complaints relating to clinical decisions and family health service practitioners. In the case of the former, internal professional advises (a GP, hospital consultants, a nurse, a dentist and a pharmacist) play a crucial role in the consideration of a case. They identify cases where external professional advice needs to be obtained which, according to the HSC's Annual Report 1998-99, will always be necessary where a clinical investigation is carried out. When considering the clinical judgments of clinicians, the HSC is 'not looking for leading edge practice'. The standard which he applies 'is whether they have acted reasonably, in a way that a patient has a right to expect from a competent clinician' .

In common with the PCA and the Local Government Commissioners, the HSC is not entitled to conduct an investigation where a complainant has a right of appeal to a tribunal or a remedy before a court of law. However, he may do so if he considers that in the particular circumstances, it is not reasonable to expect the complainant to pursue an alternative remedy. Potential difficulties arise here given that complaints relating to clinical decisions may also form the basis of a medical negligence action. The HSC has taken the view that in these circumstances, it is for the complainant to decide which route to take. If the complainant expresses an intention to take legal proceedings, this precludes an investigation by the HSC.

Alternative complaints procedure

There is also a presumption in the 1993 Act that a complaints should first be pursued through the NHS complaints procedure (Hospital Complaints Procedure Act 1985) before the HSC can investigate the matter. One again, however, this presumption may be overridden if the HSC considers that it is not reasonable to expect this to have happened. In practice, the HSC receives many complaints that have not exhausted and may not even have embarked upon the NHS procedure. These are seldom investigated unless the HSC takes the view that the NHS procedure is unlikely to resolve the complaint. Thus of the 2,869 complaints received in 1998-99, 1,184 were referred back to the complainant for this reason.

Procedure for complaints

A complaint must be made in writing to the HSC either by the person aggrieved or where that person has died, by a personal representative, a family member or by some other suitable representative of the deceased. Thus unlike the PCA or the Local Government Commissioners, complaints to the HSC do not have to be made through an elected representative. The time limit for making a complaint is one year from the date on which the complainant became aware of the maters complained of. This time limit may be extended if the HSC considers that it is reasonable to do so. An investigation may follow if the complained has suffered injustice or hardship due to:

- a failure in a service provided by a health service body;
- a failure of such a body to provide a service which it was the function of the body to provide; or
- maladministration connected with any other action taken by or on behalf of such a body.

Assuming that an investigation is carried out and that the complaint is found to be justified, the HSC may seek an apology for the complainant. Alternatively, he may seek to ensure that a decision is changed or that an administrative practice is no longer followed. Damages are not a remedy recommended by the HSC and therefore if this is what a Complainant really seeks, they ought to pursue legal proceedings.

The Local Government Commissioners

Complaints relating to local authorities were not included in the jurisdiction of the PCA under the 1967 Act. This amounted to a significant void which was the subject of criticism from Justice, amongst other. Eventually that void was filled by the establishment of the Commission for Local Administration in accordance with Part III of the Local Government Act 1974. In practice, therefore, complaints against local government are dealt with in England by three Commissioners who operate on a regional basis, and in Wales by one Commissioner.

Jurisdiction

The Local Government Commissioners (LGCs) exercise functions which are broadly comparable with those of the PCA. Like the PCA, they are empowered to investigate complaints where it is alleged that a member of the public has sustained 'injustice in consequence of maladministration'. Originally, complaints had to be referred to a LGC by a member of the local authority involved with a request that the matter be investigated. Now, however, as a consequence of an amendment made by the Local Government and Housing Act 1989, it is possible to by pass this equivalent of the 'MP filter' and complain in writing direct to the LGC.

As with complaints to the PCA, there is a 12-month time limit on the bringing of a complaint, although this can be extended where the LGC considers it reasonable to do so (s 26(4) of the 1974 Act). Prior to initiating an investigation, the LGC must be satisfied that the complaint has been brought to the attention of the authority to which the complaint relates and that the authority has been given a reasonable opportunity to investigate, and reply to the complaint (s 26(5)).

Restrictions on the conduct of investigations

The LGCs are precluded by statute from carrying out an investigation into a complaint where:

- there is a right of appeal to a tribunal or minister (s 26(6)(a) and (b))
- the person aggrieved has a remedy by way of proceedings in a ccourt of law (s 26(6)(c))
- it affects all or most of the inhabitants of the local authority (s 26(7)).
- it involves a matter or subject specified in Sch 5 to the 1974 Act (s26(8)).

Schedule 5 matters can be summarise as follows:

- the commencement or conduct of civil or criminal proceedings before any court of law
- action taken by an authority in connection with the investigation or prevention of crime
- action relating to contractual or certain specified commercial transactions
- action in respect of appointments on renewals, pay, discipline, superannuation or other personnel matters.
- action concerning the giving of instruction or conduct, curriculum, internal organisation, management or discipline in any school or other educational establishment maintained by the local education authority.

Result of an investigation

Assuming that a LGC has decided to carry out an investigation into a complaint, the procedure to be followed is much the same as that relating to PCA investigations. In many cases, a local authority will accept that it has acted wrongly, and the matter can be settled locally. Where it, does not accept that it is in the wrong, it will be necessary to publish an adverse report. Like the PCA, the LGCs do not have the power to enforce their reports. However, these reports will be drawn to the attention of the public because the local authority is under an obligation to give notice in newspapers that copies are available for public inspection. A local authority has three months from the date of issue of the report to inform the LGC of the remedial action which it proposes to take. If the LGC is not satisfied with this, he may publish a further report containing recommendations for remedial action. A local authority is required to reply to this further report. If the LGC is still not satisfied after considering the reply, he may require the authority to publish a statement in a newspaper setting out his findings and why he takes the view that the authority's response is unsatisfactory.

Good practice guidance

Since 1989, the LGCs have been in a position to issue guidance to local authorities on good practice in the light of their investigations. To date, six such guides have been issued. They deal with the following: devising a complaints system; good administrative practice; council housing repairs; members' interests; disposal of land and remedies.

Complaints

Between them, the LGCs receive approximately 15,000 complaints each year. In 1998-99, the complaints could be categorised as follows: housing (37.5%); planning (20.7%); highways (7.2%); education (9.0%); social services (7.1%); local taxation (5.8%); environmental health (3.6%); land (2.2%); and, other (6.9%). Thus, not surprisingly, the majority of complaints received related to two key responsibilities of local authorities; housing and planning. Approximately a third of the complaints received in 1998-99 were rejected on the basis that there was no maladministration. More than 4,000 were rejected as being premature, and a combined total of in excess of 3,700 were rejected by the LGCs either in the exercise of their discretion not to pursue a complaint or on the basis that they were beyond their jurisdiction. Given that local settlements accounted for nearly 2,300 complaints, the actual number where maladministration was found to have caused injustice was 331.

Review of public sector ombudsmen

In March 1999, the government announced that a review of the public sector ombudsmen in England ie the PCA, the HSC and tne LGCs, is to be conducted by a team in the Cabinet Office. This will consider a number of issues, such as whether the present arrangements are in the best interests of complainants and whether they hinder the attainment of a more efficient, effective and economical service. The review will also consider the potential interaction between the ombudsmen and other independent complaints authorities. Recommendations relating to the statutory powers and duties of the ombudsmen will be a further aspect of the review.

Ombudsmen and the courts

Whether or not ombudsmen are subject to judicial review in the exercise of their functions has been an issue in several cases. In *Re Fletcher's Application* (1970), for example, the CA decided that the appellant should not have leave to move for an order of mandamus. The appeal committee of the HL subsequently refused leave to take the application to the HL. It did so on the ground that there was no jurisdiction to investigate a complaint because s 5(1) of the Parliamentary Commissioner Act 1967 conferred a wide discretion on the PCA as to whether or not to investigate a complaint.

Two later cases concerned the office of the Commissioner for Local Administration. In *R v Comr for Local Administration, ex p Eastleigh Borough Council* (1988), the CA ruled that where the ombudsman had exceeded his jurisdiction in reporting a complaint against a local authority, his report was subject to judicial review. The CA arrived at this conclusion on the basis of the public law character of the ombudsman's office, and because the Local Government Act 1974 did not provide a right of appeal against the findings in an ombudsman's report. Judicial review was thus available to fill the statutory void. In *R v Comr for Local Administration, ex p Croydon London Borough Council* (1989), the QBD granted the authority a declaration that the ombudsman's report was void where, on the facts, there was no justification for his finding of maladministration.

These two cases were essentially concerned with the exercise of the ombudsman's powers. In both cases, it was alleged that he had contravened the requirements of the Local Government Act 1974. Thus in neither case did the courts address the issue as to whether or not the exercise of the LCG's discretionary powers was subject to review. It appears to be the case, however, in the light of the ruling in *R v Parliamentary Comr for Administration, ex p Dyer* (1994) and certain obiter remarks made in that case, that both the PCA and the LGC's decisions are subject to judicial review. In *ex p Dyer*, in answer to the proposition that the 1967 Act indicated that the PCA was solely answerable to Parliament for the way in which he performed his functions, Simon Brown LJ noted that there was:

> 'nothing about the PCA's role or the statutory framework within which he operates so singular as to take him outside the purview of judicial review.'

The decision in ex *p Dyer* is less far-reaching than might at first glance appear to be the case. It establishes that the PCA, and by analogy the LCGs, are subject to review, but it does not establish that all ombudsmen fall within the supervisory jurisdiction of the courts. Thus in *R v Parliamentary Comr for Standards, ex p At Fayed* (1998), the CA rejected the argument that the Parliamentary Commissioner for Standards was subject to review. Although the CA accepted that there were a number of similarities between his office and that of the PCA, such as the fact that they are both subject to the supervision of standing committees of Parliament and that they both report to Parliament, a significant distinction' existed between the two roles: the PCA investigates administrative matters, the activities of government; the Commissioner for Standards investigates the activities of Parliament. The courts are thus constitutionally debarred from using their powers of review in respect of the Commissioner for Standards by virtue of art 9 of the Bill of Rights 1688.

Equally as important as the foregoing is the fact that although *ex p Dyer* establishes that the courts have the jurisdiction to review the decisions of the PCA, it is a jurisdiction which will rarely be invoked. Applications for judicial review are unlikely to succeed, save in exceptional cases, because the courts readily acknowledge the wide measure of discretion accorded to ombudsmen by Parliament. Thus in *R v Comr for Local Administration, exp H (a minor)* (1998), Turner J upheld a decision of the LGC not to investigate a complaint where a remedy had already been sought by judicial review proceedings. In these circumstances, it was thought that Parliament could not have intended that the applicant should have an additional right to ventilate a grievance by complaining to the LGC. For an example of a successful application, however, see *R v Parliamentary Comr for Administration, ex p Balchin* (1999), where it was held that the PCA had failed to take into account a factor which was potentially decisive to the question whether or not the applicants had suffered injustice as a consequence of maladministration.

European Ombudsman

By virtue of art 195(2) (138e(2)) of the Treaty of Rome, the European Parliament is required to appoint an ombudsman after each election of the Parliament for the duration of its term of office. On 2 July 1995, the Parliament complied with this obligation when it elected Mr Jacob Soderman (formerly the Finnish National Ombudsman) as the first European Ombudsman. Mr Soderman was later re-elected Ombudsman by the Parliament following the 1999 European elections.

The European Ombudsman is required to be completely independent in the performance of his duties. He must not take instructions from any body as to the performance of those duties and during his term of office, he is not allowed to engage in any other occupation, whether paid or not. He is assisted by a staff which comprises a Secretary General, principal legal officers, legal officers, an information officer, assistants and secretaries. The ombudsman's principal office is in Strasbourg, with a branch in Brussels.

Jurisdiction

By virtue of art 195 (I) (138e(1), the ombudsman is:

> 'empowered to receive complaints from any citizen of the Union or any natural or legal person residing or having its registered office in a Member State concerning instances of maladministration in the actions of the Community institutions or bodies, with the exception of the Court of Justice and the Court of First Instance acting in their judicial role.'

'Maladministration' is therefore a central concept with regard to the work of the Ombudsman. Nevertheless, in common with UK legislation, the term has not been defined by the EC Treaty. The Ombudsman himself has generally expressed a lack of concern at the absence of a definition, noting in passing that the experience of national ombudsmen suggests that it is better not to attempt a too rigid definition of what amounts to maladministration. However, in response to a European Parliament resolution calling for a clearer definition of 'maladministration', the Ombudsman stated in his 1997 Annual Report that the term could be applied to:

> 'administrative irregularities, administrative omissions, abuse of power, negligence, unlawful procedures, unfairness, malfunction or incompetence, discrimination, avoidable delay and lack or refusal of information.'

In several important respects, the jurisdiction of the ombudsman is wider than that of the PCA. Thus a complaint for which there is an alternative remedy is not beyond his remit. Moreover, unlike the PCA, the Ombudsman may act on complaints made directly to him (as well as through a member of the European Parliament) and he also has the ability to act on his own initiative. This ability is in common with most national ombudsmen. In the Ombudsman's first Annual Report, it was explained that own initiatives would only be taken where many complaints had been received on the same issue and it was considered to be an effective way to seek a possible solution. One such initiative into public access to documents held by Community institutions and bodies has resulted in the adoption of rules on public access by the institutions and bodies concerned.

Petitions and complaints

The 'right' to complain to the Ombudsman is in addition to the right enjoyed by all EU citizens and any natural or legal person residing in or having its registered office in a member state to address 'a petition to the European Parliament on a matter which comes within the Community's fields of activity and which affects him, her or it directly (art 194 (8d)). Any petitions that are received are assigned to the Parliament's Committee of Petitions. Given that there is a close relationship between a petition and a complaint, it has been necessary for the ombudsman and the committee to clarify their respective functions and to co-operate fully with one another. It is therefore possible for cases received by either to be transferred to the other provided that the complainant or petitioner agrees. Moreover, it has been agreed that the Ombudsman will not accept complaints which are, or have been, before the committee.

Once a complaint has been received by the Ombudsman, it will be necessary to determine whether or not it is admissible. A complaint may be ruled inadmissible because the body or institution against which it was made does not fall within the Ombudsman's jurisdiction. Further reasons for declaring a complaint inadmissible include:

- the object or matter of the complaint was not identified;
- the two-year time limit for bringing a complaint has been exceeded;
- internal remedies have not been exhausted in staff cases; or
- the case is being dealt with or has been settled by the Court of Justice.

Where a complaint is admissible, an investigation will follow. To date, many such investigations have resulted in a finding of no maladministration. Where, however, an instance of maladministration is revealed, the statute of the ombudsman obliges him to seek a friendly solution between the parties. If this cannot be reached, the Ombudsman may either close the file with a critical remark to the institution or body concerned, or he may make a formal finding of maladministration accompanied by draft recommendations. The body or institution has three months to respond. If it refuses to accept the recommendations and no other solution to eliminate the maladministration can be found, the Ombudsman may send a special report with possible recommendations to both the Parliament and the body or institution concerned. The Parliament is thus presented with an opportunity to look for a way to solve the maladministration. In common with the PCA, the Ombudsman has no powers of enforcement.

FURTHER READING

S Bailey, B Jones and A Mowbray *Cases and Materials on Administrative Law* (3rd edn, 1997).

P Leyland and T Woods *Textbook on Administrative Law* (3rd edn 1999).

N Parpworth and K Thompson 'The European Ombudsman' [1998] CIL 157.

Z Segal 'Tribunals of Inquiry: A British Invention Ignored in Britain' [1984] PL 207.

M Seneviratne *Ombudsmen in the Public School* (1994).

F. Stacey *The British Ombudsman* (1971).

Lord Woolf *Protection of the Public - a new challenge* (1990).

13

FREEDOMS AND LIBERTIES IN THE UK

SUMMARY

In this chapter we are concerned with how freedoms and liberties might be protected in the UK. The chapter commences with an attempt to distinguish between rights and liberties whilst recognising that this is by no means a straightforward task. Some consideration is also given to the way in which rights and liberties have been traditionally protected in English law. The main body of the chapter is concerned with the European Convention on Human Rights institutions, rights, procedures and jurisprudence) and the Human Rights Act 1998. The treatment in this chapter therefore looks at the Act from a human rights perspective.

Human rights and civil liberties distinguished

There are essentially two schools of thought as to where human rights are derived from. On the one hand, the 'natural law' school believes at human rights are derived from natural law; they are rights which people enjoy simply by virtue of being human. On the other, the 'legal "positivist" school holds that rights are derived from legal systems; they are conferred by positive laws.

It is important to appreciate that human rights and civil liberties are extremely closely related. In some cases, it may be difficult to distinguish one from another; to identify where one ends and the other begins. The closeness of this relationship is further evidenced by the fact that the terms are often used interchangeably, implying that they are synoymous. However, is it possible to distinguish between a 'right' and a 'liberty'?

There have been many attempts to analyse what we mean by 'rights' and 'liberties'. In the case of a 'right', it is acknowledged that we may distinguish between a right which is moral and a right which is legal Moreover, as Dworkin has noted in *Taking Rights Seriously* (1977), by asserting that one has a 'right' to do something, the word 'right' is being used in a stronger sense than if we were to observe that a particular course of action was the 'right' thing to do. The variety of meanings which lawyers may ascribe to the word 'right' have been analysed by Hohfeld. He contends that when we talk of a 'right', we may mean: right or claim; privilege; power; or immunity. For Hohfeld, the essential characteristic of a 'right' or 'claim' is that it imposes a duty on another. He underlines the point with the aid of an example. A person who owns land has a right to exclude others from entering that land. Those who are thereby excluded are under a corresponding duty not to enter that land. In the Hohfeldian analysis, this is the only proper use of the word 'right'.

The concepts of 'power' or 'immunity' need not detain us further. For present purposes, it is 'privilege' which is of interest. This is because in Hohfeld's analysis, a privilege amounts to a freedom to do something, the exercise of which cannot be prevented by another because they do not have the right to do so. It differs from a right because there is no corresponding duty on another to act or refrain from acting. In this sense, therefore, it may be argued that Hohfeld's 'privilege' closely resembles a 'liberty'.

In the light of the above, it may be possible to distinguish between 'rights' and 'liberties' on the basis that rights are of a more fundamental nature than liberties. They impose duties on others rather than merely requiring that they are not interfered with. Thus when we talk of the 'right to life', we are concerned with a fundamental human right which imposes a duty on others not to take that life away. It may be argued, therefore, that respect for human rights demands more of the individual and society as a whole than does respect for civil liberties.

The suggestion made in the previous paragraph is necessarily tentative. It may be possible to distinguish between human rights and civil liberties, but it is by no means certain that this is the case. What is clear is that English courts and lawyers have traditionally talked in terms of liberties and freedoms rather than human rights when faced with claims that the 'rights' of the individual have been abused. This may of course now change given the enactment of the Human Rights Act 1998.

Political and social or economic rights

Political rights are a common feature of human rights documents. They involve matters such as: the right to life; equality of treatment before the law; freedom of expression; freedom of peaceful assembly and association; and freedom from discrimination. It will later become apparent that the European Convention on Human Rights (ECHR) is primarily concerned with the protection of civil and political rights.

Social and economic rights are rather different in nature. They are concerned with matters such as: the right to work; the right to equal pay for equal work; and the right to education. The Universal Declaration of Human Rights, which was adopted and proclaimed by the General Assembly of the United Nations on 10 December 1948, is an amalgam of political and social and economic rights. In addition to those social and economic rights already mentioned, the Declaration states in art 24 that:

> Everyone has the right to rest and leisure, including reasonable limitation of working hours and periodic holidays with pay.'

Moreover, art 25(1) of the Declaration provides that:

> 'Everyone has the right to a standard of living adequate for the health and well-being of himself and of his family, including food, clothing, housing and medical care and necessary social services, and the right to security in the event of unemployment, sickness, disability, widowhood, old age or other lack of livelihood in circumstances beyond his own control."

The key distinction between political rights and social and

economic rights is evident in this provision. Whilst the former tend not to require much in the way of government expenditure for their enjoyment, social and economic rights clearly place financial burdens on the state. In order for the terms of art 25(1) to be fully complied with a comprehensive welfare and social security system would need to be in place.

The traditional means of protecting civil liberties in the UK

The task of protecting civil liberties in the UK has traditionally fallen to both Parliament and the courts. However, given the susceptibility of Parliament to the dictates of a strong executive, it is unwise to think of it as playing anything more than a minor role in this connection. Thus we must turn to the courts.

Civil liberties have been protected in the UK by the courts. Judges have long been concerned by attempts on the part of the executive to interfere with the rights of the individual. Thus the courts have shown themselves willing, on occasion, to act as defender of the individual against unauthorised state intervention. We have already seen in the case of *Entick v Carrington* (1765) how the lack of legal authority ensured that the King's Messengers were trespassers at the relevant time. A rather more recent example of the courts acting to protect the rights and freedoms of the individual is to be found in a case concerned with freedom of speech.

Redmond-Bate v DPP (1999). Mrs R-B was preaching to passers-by on the steps of a cathedral. She was approached by a police officer who informed her and other preachers that they were not to stop people. On his return, the officer found that a crowd of more than a hundred had gathered and that some of the people were behaving in a hostile manner towards the preachers. He feared that a breach of the peace would occur if they did not stop preaching. The preachers refused to comply with his request to stop and were accordingly arrested. They were convicted by magistrates of wilfully obstructing an officer in the execution of his duty contrary to s 89(2) of the Police Act 1996. An appeal to the Crown Court was unsuccessful. DC held: Whether or not the offence had been committed depended upon whether the officer was acting within the execution of his duty at the material time. This itself turned on whether there were reasonable grounds for apprehending a breach of the peace. It was both illiberal and illogical to proceed from the fact that the women were preaching about God and morality to the view that there was a reasonable apprehension that violence would erupt if action were not taken. There was nothing in the situation as perceived by the officer which entitled him to apprehend a breach of the peace.

The concept of breach of a peace will be considered. The decision in *Redmond-Bate v DPP* highlights how the courts might protect freedom of speech, a freedom which Lord Denning one referred to, in conjunction with freedom of assembly, as 'among our most precious freedoms'. It has not always been thus. In *A-G v Guardian Newspapers Ltd* (1987), Lord Bridge remarked that the decision of the majority of the HL to uphold an interim injunction preventing the sale of the 'Spycatcher' book had 'severely undermined' his confidence in the 'capacity of the common law to safeguard the fundamental freedoms essential to a free society including the right to freedom of speech'.

European Convention on Human Rights

Introduction

The European Convention on Human Rights and Fundamental Freedoms (ECHR) was very much a by-product of the Second World War and the desire to promote unity within Europe and to ensure that human rights were properly respected and protected thereafter. Its drafting by the Council of Europe marked a shift in attitude from the pre-Second World War belief that human rights and fundamental freedoms were internal political matters beyond the reach of the wider international community. The original text of the convention, which owed much to the efforts of British draftsmen, was signed in Rome by 15 states on 4 November 1950. It did not take effect, however, until it had been ratified by 10 of its signatories. This was achieved on 3 September 1953.

It ought to be stressed at the outset that the Council of Europe is not an institution of the EC and that therefore, the

ECHR does not amount to an EC Treaty. Although all 15 member states of the EC have signed the convention, it has also been signed by 26 non-EC states such as Turkey, Iceland, Romania and Albania which are nevertheless members of the Council of Europe. The ECHR is therefore served by its own institutions which are separate and independent of those which serve the EC.

Institutions

The ECHR was originally served by three institutions: the European Commission of Human Rights; the European Court of Human Rights; and the Committee of Ministers. Each performed its own particular functions (although there was some overlap) which to a greater or lesser extent assisted in ensuring that rights guaranteed by the convention were upheld within the signatory states. The Commission, for example, was the initial point of contact for all those who claimed to be the victim of an infringement of a convention right. It registered the complaints that were received, it investigated them and, it determined whether a complaint satisfied the admissibility criteria. In this sense, therefore, the Commission acted as a filter. Where a complaint was ruled admissible, the Commission was charged with the responsibility of brokering a friendly settlement between the parties (see below). If no settlement could be reached, the complaint would sometimes be referred to the European Court of Human Rights for its determination, but not before the Commission had itself expressed an opinion as to whether there had been a violation of the convention.

Institutional reform

The years that followed the ratification of the ECHR saw a steady and more recently, a rapid increase in the workloads of both the Commission and the Court. This can be attributed to a number of different factors, including the widespread acceptance of the right of individual petition (see below) and the growing public awareness that Strasbourg may provide a remedy for a grievance when all the domestic avenues have been exhausted. Almost inevitably, increasing workloads were attended by delays. Both the Commission and the Court were confronted by a backlog of cases which meant that in practice, disputes could take between five and six years to pass through their various stages at Strasbourg. Delays of this length were unacceptable and therefore institutional reform became a necessity.

A number of states advocated the retention of a two-tier system with the Commission becoming a Court of First Instance and the original Court acting as a Court of Appeal. However, the preferred option of the majority was the creation of a single unified Court which would perform the functions of both the Commission and the original Court.

Protocol 11

On 1 November 1998, Protocol 11 to the ECHR entered into force. This introduced major procedural and institutional changes to the convention machinery, not least of which was the demise of the Commission. This occurred on the expiry of a one-year transitional period during which the Commission continued to deal with applications pending at the time that the protocol was implemented. Accordingly, the ECHR is now served by two institutions: the Committee of Ministers and the Court of Human Rights.

The Committee of Ministers

The Committee of Ministers is essentially a political body. It is composed of the Ministers of Foreign Affairs for each of the states which is a member of the Council of Europe. When not in formal session, ministerial deputies act as state representatives. Despite the political nature of the committee, it performed a judicial function prior to the entry into force of Protocol 11. This entailed determining whether the convention had been violated in those cases where it had received a Commission report as to the merits of the case and the case had not been referred to the Court. Although in practice the committee did not deal with important cases, it was at the very least questionable whether a political body ought to be performing a judicial function. Accordingly under the new system, the Committee of Ministers no longer has the jurisdiction to determine cases not going to the Court. Its role under the ECHR is therefore now confined to supervising the execution of the Court's judgments (art 46).

The European Court of Human Rights

A key reform introduced by Protocol 11 has been the establishment of a single unified European Court of Human Rights which functions on a permanent, full-time basis. The Court currently consists of 41 judges (a number equal to that of the High Contracting Parties) all of whom sit in their individual capacity. In order to stand for election by the Parliamentary Assembly, a candidate must be of high moral character and 'must either possess the qualifications required for appointment to high judicial office or be jurisconsults of recognised competence' (art 21). During a term of office, a judge is forbidden from engaging in any activity which is incompatible with their independence, impartiality or the demands of full-time office.

Judges are elected for a period of six years (formerly it was nine), although they may stand for re-election. Before taking up office, each elected judge must either swear or declare that: 'I will exercise my functions as judge honourably, independently and impartially and that I will keep secret all deliberations'. Once in office, a judge enjoys security of tenure. He is required to retire when he reaches the age of 70, but he cannot be dismissed from office unless the other judges agree by a two-thirds majority that he has ceased to fulfil the required conditions (art 24). Rule 7 of the Rules of the Court (RoC) further elaborates on the subject of dismissal. Before being dismissed, a judge must first be heard by the Plenary Court Moreover, any judge of the Court may set in motion the procedure for dismissal from office.

It is worth noting that in Mowbray's opinion, the process of appointing judges to the new Court 'did not operate with sufficient rigour, consistency or smoothness'. He identifies two main reasons why this was the case. First, because individual governments were given a wide measure of discretion as to the selection and privatisation of their judicial candidates. Secondly, Mowbray argues that the Parliamentary Assembly's 'scrutiny of candidates was rather secretive and selective'.

With regard to the former, it is unfortunate that the independence of some candidates can be questioned given the emphasis that both the ECHR and the judicial oath place upon the need for independence. However, Professor Schermers, a former Commissioner, has argued that 'the nominations of several governments convey the impression that political arguments play too important a role in nominations'. The danger of a politicised Court is self-evident. The decisions of the Court should be based on legal considerations alone. If it was widely believed that decisions of the Court were as much dependent upon the identity of the state concerned and the national mix of the judges hearing the case as upon the force of the legal argument, the convention system would fall into disrepute.

The second criticism of the appointment process, that the scrutiny of the candidates was not what it ought to have been, relates to the first in that it may have resulted in some bad appointments. Concerns were sometimes expressed in the past about the old Court and whether or not all of its members had the necessary qualities to be good judges. In the UK, government criticism of the Court reached its zenith when it decided in *McCann v UK* (1995) that the UK had breached art 2 of the ECHR in relation to the killing of three suspected IRA terrorists by the SAS on the island of Gibraltar. Protocol 11 thus represented an opportunity for thoroughgoing reform of the Court. Unfortunately, however, Professor Schermers has observed in respect of the appointment of the new Court that 'some of the members finally chosen hardly know the Convention, let alone the case law of the Commission and Court'.

Plenary Court

The function of the Plenary Court is not to determine cases brought under the convention. Instead, it is concerned with matters such as: the election of a President of the Court and one or two Vice-Presidents for a period of three years; the setting up of chambers for a fixed period of time and the election of their Presidents; and the adoption of the rules of the Court. Under these rules, the Court is divided into four sections. The composition of each section reflects a geographical and gender balance, and takes account of the different legal systems of the various High Contracting Parties. The Presidents of the sections are the two Vice-Presidents of the Court and the two Presidents of the Chambers. A section will exist for a period of three years.

The judicial business of the Court is undertaken by committees, chambers and the Grand Chamber.

Committees

These are set up by chambers within each of the Court's sections for a fixed period of time. They consist of three judges who have the jurisdiction to determine the admissibility of individual applications brought under art 34 of the ECHR. Acting unanimously, a committee may declare an application inadmissible or strike it out of its list of cases. Any decision that it does reach is final. In this sense, therefore, the committees carry out the task of filtering applications which was formerly undertaken by the Commission. Where the committee does not reach a decision, the admissibility of an application will be determined by a chamber.

Chambers

As was noted above, chambers are established by the Plenary Court. They consist of seven judges and will include: the President of the section to which the case has been allocated; an ex officio member, the judge elected in respect of the state party concerned (or an equivalent); and, such other judges from the relevant section as are appointed by the President. Chambers decide on the admissibility and merits of individual and state applications. The decision on admissibility is to be taken separately, unless the Court decides that the exceptional nature of the case demands otherwise.

In certain specified circumstances, and subject to neither party objecting, a chamber may relinquish its jurisdiction in a case in favour of the Grand Chamber at any time before it has given judgment (art 30). The specified circumstances are that:

- the case raises a serious question affecting the interpretation of the convention or the protocols thereto; or
- the question before the chamber might have a result inconsistent with a previous judgment of the Court.

The judgment of a chamber is not necessarily final. It only becomes so:

- when the parties declare that they will not request that the case be referred to the Grand Chamber under art 43 (see below);
- three months have passed since the judgment was delivered and no request for a referral has been made; or
- the panel of the Grand Chamber has rejected the request for an art 43 referral.

Grand Chamber

This is the most important of all the Court's guises. The Grand Chamber consists of 17 judges together with an ex officio member (see above). It includes the President of the Court, the Vice-Presidents, the Presidents of the Chambers and other judges chosen in accordance with the rules of the Court. In addition to having the power to determine individual or inter-state applications passed to it by a chamber, the Grand Chamber may hear cases referred to it under art 43 of the ECHR. This provides that in exceptional cases, either party may request within three months of the date of a chamber's decision that the matter be referred to the Grand Chamber. A panel of five judges of the Grand Chamber is required to accept the request if it:

- raises a serious question affecting the interpretation or application of the convention or the protocols thereto; or
- raises a serious issue of general importance.

Where a request is accepted, the Grand Chamber will give judgment in the case. If the panel rejects the request, the decision of the chamber is thereby rendered final. There is no right of appeal against a panel's determination. The Grand Chamber also has the power to consider requests for advisory opinions submitted in accordance with art 47 of the ECHR (see below)."

Jurisdiction and functions of the Court

The Court's jurisdiction extends to all matters concerning the interpretation and application of the convention and the protocols thereto. In the event of a dispute as to whether or not the Court has jurisdiction, the Court will decide the issue.

By virtue of art 36, a High Contracting Party whose national is an applicant has the right to submit written comments and to take part hearings before either a chamber or the Grand Chamber. At any stage the proceedings, the Court may strike out an application from its list cases if, for example, the matter has been resolved or the applicant does not intend to pursue his application. A struck out application may be restored to the list if the Court considers that the circumstances justify such a course of action.

The Court's hearings are held in public, unless exceptional circumstances justify otherwise. Similarly, documents deposited with the Court's registrar are accessible to the public unless the President of the Court decides otherwise. Where the Court finds that there has been a violation on of the convention, and the domestic law of the High Contracting Party concerned allows for only partial reparation to be made, art 41 empowers the Court to award 'just satisfaction' where necessary. The practice of the Court thus far has been that 'satisfaction' is achieved by the award of monetary compensation.

Article 45 of the ECHR requires that reasons shall be given for judgments of the Court as well as for decisions as to the admissibility of an application. Where the whole or part of a judgment is not the unanimous decision of the Court, any judge is entitled to deliver a separate opinion.

Articles 47-49 of the ECHR make provision for the giving of advisory opinions by the Court. These opinions, which are given at the request of the Committee of Ministers, are on legal questions relating to the interpretation of the convention and its protocols. They are not concerned, however, with the content or scope of the substantive rights and freedoms defined in s 1 of the ECHR (see below). Whether or not the request for an advisory opinion falls within the Court's jurisdiction is a matter for the Court to decide. If an opinion is given, it will be accompanied by reasons and it will be communicated to the Committee of Ministers.

Substantive rights

Section 1 of the ECHR details the various rights and freedoms which the High Contracting Parties are required to guarantee to everyone within their jurisdiction. These rights and freedoms may be summarised as follows:

- the right to life (art 2)
- freedom from torture and inhuman or degrading treatment (art 3)
- freedom from slavery and forced labour (art 4)
- the right to liberty and security of the person (art 5)
- the right to a fair trial (art 6)
- freedom from retrospective criminal laws or increased sentencing (art 7)
- the right to respect for private and family life (art 8)
- freedom of thought, conscience and religion (art 9)
- freedom of expression (art 10)
- freedom of assembly and association (art 11)
- the right to marry and found a family (art 12)
- the right to an effective remedy in national law where convention rights or freedoms have been violated (art 13)
- freedom from discrimination in the enjoyment of convention rights and freedoms (art 14).

It is apparent from this catalogue that the rights and freedoms contained in the ECHR are essentially civil and political in nature. There is no real mention of social or economic rights, such as the right to work or the right to be paid a fair wage, which sometimes feature in other human rights documents. Moreover, to state the nature of the rights and freedoms in the manner above is partly misleading since it implies that all such rights and freedoms are absolute. This is by no means the case.

The only absolute freedoms in the ECHR are the freedom from torture and inhuman or degrading treatment (art 3) and the freedom from slavery or servitude (art 4). All other rights and freedoms are subject to some form of qualification. Thus in the case of the right to life (art 2), a person may be deprived of this right 'in the execution of a sentence of a Court following his conviction of a crime for which this penalty is provided by law'. Similarly, there are various exceptions to the right to liberty and security of the person (art 5). These include imprisonment after conviction by a competent court and the lawful arrest or detention of a person for the purpose of bringing him before a court. In the case of arts 8-11 of the ECHR, provision is made for quite wide-ranging exceptions to the rights and freedoms contained therein. Thus these rights and freedoms may be interfered with, limited or restricted in accordance with or as prescribed by law where it is 'necessary in a democratic society in the interest of: national security; public safety; for the protection of health or morals; or for the protection of the rights and freedoms of others.

These exceptions are common to each of arts 8-11. Further more specific exceptions exist in respect of these articles. Thus the right to respect for private and family life (art) may be interfered with in accordance with the law where it is necessary for the 'economic well being of the country'. Similarly, art 11 (freedom of assembly and association) does 'not prevent the imposition of lawful restrictions of the exercise of these rights by members of the armed forces, of the police or of the administration of the State'.

Protocols

To end a discussion of the substantive rights guaranteed by the convention at this juncture would be to overlook an important factor, namely that these rights have been added to over the years by a number of protocols. Protocols thus allow the ECHR to reflect changing attitudes towards the content and protection of human rights. In Protocol 1. for example, arts 1, 2 and 3 are concerned with the protection of property and the rights to education and free elections, respectively. This protocol was ratified by the UK a number of months after it was opened for signature in early 1952. Protocol 6, which provides for, among other things, the abolition of the death penalty, was ratified by the UK on 20 May 1999 despite the fact that it had been made in 1983. Protocols 4 and 7 which are concerned with matters such as: a prohibition on imprisonment for debt; freedom of movement; a prohibition on the expulsion of nationals; procedural safeguards relating to the expulsion of aliens; the right to an appeal in criminal matters; compensation for wrongful conviction; the right not to be tried or punished twice in respect of the same offence; and equality between spouses, have never been ratified by the UK although they were opened for signature in 1963 and 1984 respectively.

At the time of writing, 21 of the 41 High Contracting Parties have ratified all the extant protocols (those referred to above). The UK is therefore not alone in having failed to ratify them all. It should be noted, however, that of all the High Contracting Parties not to have ratified more than one protocol, the UK was the first to ratify the convention itself. The protocols that have not been mentioned were largely concerned with amending the enforcement machinery of the ECHR. They ceased to have effect when Protocol 11 came into force.

Derogation

In times of war or other public emergency threatening the life of the nation, a High Contracting Party may, by virtue of art 15 of the ECHR, take measures derogating from its obligations under the convention. Derogation is only permitted to 'the extent strictly required by the exigencies of the situation' and the measures adopted must not be inconsistent with a Contracting Party's other obligations under international law. In the case of art 2, except where death results from lawful act of war, and arts 3, 4(1) and 7, no derogation is permitted under art 15. Where a High Contracting Party wishes to exercise the right to derogate, it must keep the Secretary-General of the Council of Europe fully informed of the measures taken and reasons for them. When such measures have ceased to operate and the convention rights have been fully restored, the Secretary-General must be informed.

Article 15 has been invoked by the UK on a number of occasions in the context of Northern Ireland. Despite several legal challenges to such derogations eg *Ireland v UK* (1978), the Strasbourg authorities have ruled that they have been justified by the circumstances. In so doing, it is apparent that the Court has accepted that a state should be allowed a wide margin of appreciation (see below) in such matters. At the time of writing, the UK has a derogation entered in respect of art 5(3).

Right of individual petition

The right of an individual to petition the Commission where they claimed to be the victim of the violation of a convention right was not an automatic right that arose on the ratification of the convention. It was dependent upon a declaration from a High Contracting Party that it recognised the competence of the Commission to deal with petitions from its citizens. Thus in the case of the UK, declarations were issued on a five-yearly basis following the Wilson government's acceptance of the right of individual petition in 1966. There were occasions when it was suggested that a declaration ought not to be renewed, most notably following the decision in *McCann v UK* (1995). However, when it came to reforming the convention system, the Conservative government advocated the retention of an optional and renewable right of individual petition to the new Court. The new arrangements do not allow for this.

By virtue of art 34, the right of individual petition has been elevated to the status of a compulsory requirement. Thus individuals now enjoy a mandatory right of access to the Court and the High Contracting Parties have undertaken 'not to hinder in any way the effective exercise of this right'.

Inter-state applications

Article 33 of the ECHR states that:

> 'Any High Contracting Party may refer to the Court any alleged breach of the provisions of the Convention and the protocols thereto by another High Contracting Party.'

This provision largely restates the original art 24 of the

ECHR, although the reference is now made to the Court rather than to the Commission. A state will not be the 'victim' of an alleged breach of the convention by another state, but it may be that one of its citizens has been. Accordingly, this article provides for the possibility of the state acting on the citizen's behalf.

In practice, applications under the original art 24 were extremely rare. One example was *Ireland v UK* (1978), where the Irish government alleged, inter alia, that detention without trial and the use of various interrogation techniques on suspected terrorists in Northern Ireland were contrary to arts 3 and 5 respectively of the ECHR. Given that such applications have the potential to threaten the unity of the Council of Europe, it seems unlikely that they will be much pursued in the future. It is far more likely that human rights disputes between High Contracting Parties will be resolved behind closed doors, away from the glare of publicity which would inevitably attend an inter-state application.

Admissibility criteria

Determining whether or not an application was admissible was formerly a task for the Commission. This task is now to be performed by a chamber of the Court in the case of inter-state applications, or by a committee or chamber of the Court for individual applications, in accordance with the criteria laid down in art 35 of the ECHR. The decision as to whether an individual application is dealt with by a committee or a chamber is made by a Judge Rapporteur following a preliminary. examination of the case.

For the Court to be able to deal with an application:

- all domestic remedies must have been exhausted; and
- no more than six months must have passed from the date on which the final decision was taken.
- In the case of individual applications made under art 34, further admissibility criteria apply. These require that an application:
- must not be anonymous:

- must not be substantially the same as a matter that has already been examined by the Court or has already been submitted to another international investigative body;
- must not be incompatible with the provisions of the convention or the protocols thereto; and
- must not be manifestly ill-founded or an abuse of the right of application.

The admissibility criteria which apply to both types of application are essentially procedural. In the case of individual applications, however, the requirements that the application must not be manifestly ill-founded or an abuse of the right of petition will involve considering the merits of the case, even though art 29 of the ECHR refers to admissibility and merits as separate issues.

Friendly settlements

Where the Court has declared an application admissible, it must then examine the case which may entail undertaking an investigation. At the same time, art 38(1)(b) of the ECHR requires the Court to:

> 'place itself at the disposal of the parties concerned with a view to securing a friendly settlement of the matter on the basis of respect for human rights as defined in the Convention and the protocols thereto.'

Friendly settlement negotiations are confidential and without prejudice to the parties' arguments before the Court. By virtue of Rule 62(2) of the RoC, no written or oral communication and no offer or concession made whilst trying to secure a friendly settlement may be referred to or relied on before the Court. Such settlements thus amount to a resolution of the case short of a formal court hearing. An applicant who is concerned about the costs of or indeed the length of time that his case is taking may be attracted by a friendly settlement. It may involve the applicant being financially compensated by the state and, in addition or as an alternative to compensation, the state may undertake to amend an offending law or change an administrative practice.

For the state, the attraction of a friendly settlement lies in the fact that it is a way of avoiding a formal court hearing and the possibility of being found to have violated the convention. The publicity which would inevitably surround such a ruling may be damaging to a state's reputation as a guarantor of human rights. Moreover, friendly settlements often include a clause at the insistence of the state to the effect that the settlement is without prejudice to its submission that there has been no violation of the convention. In other words, a settlement has been reached without admission of liability.

Doctrine of a margin of appreciation

This doctrine has evolved in the jurisprudence of the European Court of Human Rights. Its importance lies in its recognition of the fact that a High Contracting Party may be in a better position than the Court to determine when a departure from a convention right is justified by the circumstances. In *Handyside v UK* (1976), the Court observed that

> 'By reason of their direct and continuous contact with the vital forces of their countries, state authorities are in principle in a better position than the international judge to give an opinion on the exact content of those requirements [of morals] as well as on the "necessity" of a "restriction" or "penalty" intended to meet them'

The doctrine of a margin of appreciation is thus significant in terms of the exceptions to arts 8-11 referred to above. It also has a role to play in the context of art 15 of the ECHR. In *Brannigan and McBride v UK* (1993), the Court noted that the High Contracting Party was best placed to decide on the presence of an emergency situation and to determine the nature and scope of the measures necessary to avert it. The Court therefore felt that with regard to art 15, 'a wide margin of appreciation should be left to the national authorities'.

Clearly there is an inherent danger with the doctrine: if a High Contracting Party is allowed too much latitude, there is a danger that it may ride roughshod over the rights which it purports to have guaranteed to its citizens. Accordingly, it ought to be noted that the operation of the doctrine is subject to supervision by the European Court. Where necessary, the Court will be prepared to rule that a state measure has gone beyond that which was required by the circumstances ie that it is disproportionate to the aim pursued.

Incorporation of the Convention into English law

Incorporation: the judges' view

In the 45 or so years which marked the period between the ratification of the ECHR by the UK and its incorporation into domestic law by the Human Rights Act 1998, attitudes amongst the senior judges appear to have changed on the question of incorporation. The Lord Chancellor at the time of ratification, Lord Jowitt, was firmly opposed to such a course of action, and yet the current Lord Chancellor, Lord Irvine, piloted the Human Rights Bill through the HL. Why the change in attitude towards the ECHR?

There is no simple answer to this question. At one level, it might be argued that the change in attitude owes as much to individual personalities as to anything else. Lord Denning, whose judicial career in both the CA and the HL spanned approximately 30 years of the relevant period, once argued against a Private Members' Bill to incorporate the convention on the basis that it would lead to much litigation brought by 'disgruntled people who will bring proceedings before the courts challenging the orderly system of our society'. Lord Elwyn-Jones, the Lord, Chancellor at the time (1976), objected to incorporation for similar reasons and because he considered that the ECHR was 'framed in such wide and general terms'. However, his successor, Lord Hailsham, took a contrary view in his The *Dilemma of Democracy* (I978) where he considered that incorporation may be advantageous to the UK.

At another level, it might be argued that the need for incorporation started to become apparent to certain judges when the common law, that traditional tool for the protection of liberties and freedoms, no longer seemed capable of performing the task to their satisfaction. For example, the remarks of Lord Bridge in *A-G v Guardian Newspapers Ltd* (1987), suggest a faltering confidence in the common law's ability to protect civil liberties.

Such views were not confined to statements made in court. Extra-judicial writings and lecture became a vehicle for expressing views on the convention and whether or not it ought to be incorporated into UK law. The then Máster of the Rolls, Lord Bingham, forcefully argued for the incorporation of the ECHR during a lecture on the subject in 1993. In his opinion, there was no task 'more central to the judicial function, than that of seeking to protect, within the law, the basic human rights of the citizen, against invasion by other citizens or by the state itself. The need to incorporate the ECHR was due to a number of factors which included:

- the increasing power of the executive;
- the unreliability of Parliament as a guardian of human rights in practice;
- the ever-lengthening list of occasions when the UK was found to be in breach of the convention either by the Commission or the Court;
- the common law as it stood was unable to give citizens the same protection as the convention; and
- the fundamental rights protected by the convention are part of Community law which in turn is part of UK law.

There are obviously very close links between certain of these factors. The fact that the UK's system of government has become an 'elective dictatorship' ensures that a legislature which is in theory supreme is ultimately controlled by the executive. Moreover, the inability of the common law to protect human rights to the same degree as the ECHR partly explains the adverse rulings from Strasbourg. However, the fifth factor is perhaps the most interesting of all. Whilst Lord Bingham considered it to be an argument in favour of incorporation, might it not be argued that it is just as much an argument against the need for incorporation?

Alternatives to incorporation

The most obvious alternative to incorporation would have been to preserve the status quo. However, given that there was an increasing awareness of the need to secure the better protection of human rights In the UK, this was not really an option. Several alternatives to incorporation may have achieved the desired purpose.

One such alternative was pre-legislative scrutiny. Kinley has suggested that this could take the form of two joint committees of both Houses which would examine Bills and statutory instruments respectively in order to ensure compliance with the convention. The joint committees would report their findings to both Houses which would then be better informed as to the human rights issues raised by the particular piece of legislation. Alternatively, the Hansard Society Commission took the view that there was no need for the establishment of a new committee to perform this function. In its opinion, the HL Select Committee on the Scrutiny of Delegated Powers could carry out a pre-legislative scrutiny of Bills. A further alternative might have been the establishment of a Human Rights Commission or Commissioner to scrutinise new legislation and to carry out investigations into particular issues or legal areas where there was cause for concern.

Incorporation: a brief history

Attempts to directly incorporate the ECHR into UK law occurred quite regularly during the 1970s and 1980s as members of the HL and backbench MPs introduced Bills before Parliament to this effect. Lord Wade, for example, introduced several Bills of Rights, but all such attempts were unsuccessful. It was apparent that the prospects for incorporation would be greatly enhanced if it were to become the policy of one of the major political parties. This occurred prior to the last general election when the Labour Party published its proposals to 'bring rights home to British people'. Essentially, it argued that incorporation would reduce costs, reduce the time taken to pursue legal proceedings and give power back to the British courts. These were all factors which made incorporation necessary. With regard to the latter, the Labour Party argued that it was not right that other European citizens could have convention rights dealt with by the courts in their own country whilst British citizens had to go abroad to seek justice. The increasingly poor record of the UK in terms of the numbers of admissible cases brought against it, the occasions on which it was actually found to have violated the convention, and the generally serious nature of these complaints was also cited as a justification for incorporation. Thus the Labour Party fought the 1997 general election with a manifesto commitment to incorporate the ECHR, if elected. Success at the polls gave the Labour Party the mandate that it had wanted.

The Human Rights Act 1998

The Human Rights Act (HRA) received Royal Assent on 9 November 1998. At the time of writing, many of its provisions have yet to come into force. The government has indicated that 2 October 2000 will be the key date in this regard. The key constitutional aspects of the HRA have already been discovered. Thus, the focus will be upon the human rights issues raised by the Act.

Convention rights

Section 1 of the 1998 Act gives effect in UK law to what the Act refers to as 'convention rights'. These are defined as being: arts 2-12 and 14 of the ECHR; arts 1-3 of the First Protocol; and, arts 1 and 2 of the Sixth Protocol. Article 1 is therefore omitted from the definition, as is art 13 of the ECHR. In the case of the former, this is not surprising given that it does not confer a substantive right on individuals. In the case of art 13, however, the same argument cannot be applied. This requires that:

> 'Everyone whose rights and freedoms as set forth in this Convention are violated shall have an effective remedy before a national authority notwithstanding that the violation has been committed by persons acting in an official capacity.'

The exclusion of art 13 from the definition of 'convention rights' was defended by the Lord Chancellor during the passage of the Bill on the basis that it was otiose. In his opinion, the power which s 8(1) of the 1998 Act invests in the courts to 'grant such relief or remedy, or make such order, within its powers as it considers appropriate' rendered the inclusion of art 13 unnecessary.

Interpreting convention rights

When interpreting convention rights, s 2 of the 1998 Act requires domestic courts to 'take into account' the jurisprudence of the European Court of Human Rights together with the opinions and decisions of the Commission and the Committee of Ministers. This clearly makes sense. It would be foolhardy if judges who are not necessarily familiar with the text of the convention did not have regard to the judgments and decisions of the convention's institutions in respect of the rights contained therein. However, s 2 does not oblige domestic courts to reach an interpretation which is consistent with the views from Strasbourg. Nevertheless, if English courts were to significantly depart from the interpretation accorded to convention rights by the Strasbourg authorities, it will still be possible to apply to the European Court of Human Rights. That Court may arrive at a different conclusion to the domestic courts, in which case its view would prevail. Would this undermine the status of the HL as the supreme court in the UK? In Lord Bingham's opinion, such an eventuality would:

> '... do nothing to undermine the authority or dignity of the House of Lords as our supreme court that, in matters arising from interpretation or application of a multilateral international treaty, the final decision is accorded to the body established as the ultimate authority on those questions.'

Freedom of expression and freedom of thought, conscience and religion

Of all the convention's substantive rights, the only two such rights specifically mentioned in the main body of the 1998 Act (the convention rights appear in Sch 1 to the Act) are those enshrined in arts 9 and 10: freedom of thought, conscience and religion; and freedom of expression. Sections 12 and 13 of the HRA 1998 require the courts to have particular regard to these rights when considering granting relief or allowing for a development in the law which would have an impact on these rights, Although this does not amount to according these rights a special status, it does reflect the fact that they are potentially vulnerable to the development of other rights based on the terms of the ECHR. Thus as Duffy and Stanley have noted, s 12(4) of the Act acknowledges the impact which the development of a tort of privacy will have upon freedom of expression. It therefore requires a court to have this in mind in respect of proceedings to prevent the publication of material which the respondent claims is 'journalistic, literary or artistic". In the case of s 13, the importance of the right to freedom of thought, conscience and religion is evident where an applicant seeks to enforce a 'right' which would run contrary to religious teachings eg where a gay couple wished to be married in church (Duffy and Stanley).

Public authorities

By virtue of s 6 (1) of the 1998 Act:

> 'It is unlawful for a public authority to act in a way which is incompatible with a Convention right.'

A public authority will not be acting unlawfully, however, if the terms of primary legislation require it to act in a way which is incompatible with a convention right (s 6(2)). For the purposes of the HRA, a 'public authority' includes: a court or tribunal; any person certain of whose functions are functions of a public nature. This definition is clearly not exhaustive. It will fall to the courts to determine whether or not a particular person or body is a public authority. There are some persons or bodies which English, and now European law, have long recognised as being public authorities eg government departments, local authorities, prisons and the police. However, s 6 of the Act makes it clear that it is the nature of a person's or body's functions which is the key issue. This incorporates the test laid down in *R v Panel on Take-overs and Mergers, ex p Datafin* (1987), although it provides no further guidance as to what a function of a public nature might be. Parliament is expressly excluded from the definition of 'public authority', although the exclusion does not extend to the HL when acting in a judicial capacity. Thus if Parliament were to enact a law which was contrary to a convention right, it would not be acting unlawfully under s 6 of the 1998 Act.

Proceedings

Where it is claimed that a public authority has acted contrary to s 6, or that it proposes to do so, s 7 provides that a person may bring proceedings against that authority. Moreover, in proceedings brought against a person, they may rely on the convention right or rights concerned. Thus the claim that a public authority has acted contrary to a convention right may be used as either a sword or a shield. However, for the purposes of s 7, the allegation that a public authority has acted unlawfully can only be invoked by a person who is, or would be, a 'victim' of that act.

Standing under the Human Rights Act

Standing or locus standi in respect of judicial review proceedings already been considered in this book. By of art 34 of the ECHR, complaints under the convention can only be brought by a 'person, non-governmental organisation or group of individuals claiming to be a victim of a violation'. Under the HRA, this 'victim test' takes precedence over the sufficient interest test where the proceedings are brought in an application for judicial review (s 7(3)). In other words, an applicant alleging the breach of a convention right would have to establish that he is a victim of that breach. He will not be deemed to have a sufficient interest unless he is able to do so.

This victim test has been interpreted in a fairly restricted manner by the European Court. Since English courts are required to take the court's jurisprudence into account when determining questions relating to convention rights (s 2), it follows that they may also interpret the test restrictively. Marriott and Nicol have argued that the possible outcome will be that the 'representative plaintiff, by which they mean pressure groups, trade unions and trade associations, 'will be denied direct access to judicial review on fundamental rights matters'. Whilst this may be the likely outcome and whilst it may be unfortunate that, as they point out, 'our domestic standing requirements should hang on the outcome of inter-state negotiations conducted half a century ago', a counter-argument may exist. Signatories to the ECHR are required to guarantee the rights contained therein to their citizens. Enforcing those rights thus becomes a matter for individuals, hence the right of individual petition which is now automatic. Violations of convention rights are, on the whole, unlikely to have the broad impact that an unlawful public decision may have. Individuals rather than large groups are likely to be affected and, therefore, it might be argued that it is right to have a test for standing which is unlikely to be satisfied by the representative plaintiff. As Marriott and Nicol acknowledge, such groups may still have an indirect role to play in the domestic context in that they may provide advice and support (financial or otherwise) for the victims of alleged breaches of human rights.

The issue of standing under the 1998 Act is perhaps less clearcut than might at first glance appear to be the case. Whilst the Act itself adopts the 'victim test' from the ECHR, it does not preclude the right of a person to rely upon 'any other right or freedom conferred on him by or under any law having effect in any part of the United Kingdom' (s 11 (a)). Since fundamental human rights are principles of both the common law and EC law, it follows that a party may be able to rely upon them in legal proceedings where their standing has been determined on the basis of sufficient interest rather than the victim test. This may be an attractive option for a 'representative plaintiff unable to satisfy the victim test. If this does prove to be the case then, in the words of Marriott and Nicol, 'the victim requirement may well induce further "back-door incorporation" of the substance of the ECHR into the common law'.

Judicial remedies

Where a court finds that an act of a public authority is, or would be, unlawful, it may grant such relief or remedy as it considers appropriate, provided that it has the power to do so (s 8). This proviso is important because it precludes the possibility of the courts developing new remedies for acting contrary to a convention right. It is worth noting, however, that by virtue of s 7(11), a minister may add to the relief or remedies which a tribunal may grant for the violation of a convention right.

Damages may be awarded under s 8 of the Act, although there are limits on the exercise of this power. Thus by virtue of s 8(2), 'damages may be awarded only by a court which has power to award damages, or to order the payment of compensation, in civil proceedings'. In other words, the jurisdiction to award damages is restricted to those courts which currently award damages: the civil courts. If in criminal proceedings a court held that there had been a violation of a convention right, the 'victim' could not be compensated by order of that court. He would have to pursue separate proceedings in the civil courts. Moreover, damages are not an automatic entitlement under the 1998 Act. This much is evident from s 8(3) which provides that:

'No award of damages is to be made unless, taking account of all the circumstances of the case, including-

(a) any other relief or remedy granted, or order made, in relation to the act in question (by that or any other court), and

(b) the consequences of any decision (of that or any other court) in respect of that act,

the court is satisfied that the award is necessary to afford just satisfaction to the person in whose favour it is made.'

Thus a court may take the view that damages are unnecessary given the nature of the relief already granted. In deciding whether or not to award damages, or the quantum of damages, a court must take into account the principles applied by the European Court of Human Rights to the award of 'just satisfaction' under art 41 of the ECHR. As Duffy and Stanley point out, strictly speaking there are no principles given that art 41 case law has yet to develop. However, the article is broadly the same as the old art 50 under which 'just satisfaction' was awarded. Thus this respect, s 8(3) is rather like s 2 in that it requires UK courts to have regard to the jurisprudence of the European Court of Human Rights, although it stops short of compelling them to follow it.

As the definition of 'public authority' makes clear, a court is a public authority for the purposes of the Act. Courts may therefore act unlawfully by acting contrary to a convention right, in which case they may be liable in damages. However, by virtue of s 9(3), damages may not be awarded where a judicial act has been done in good faith, unless it is necessary to compensate a person in accordance with art 5(5) of the ECHR. This entitles everyone who has been the 'victim of arrest or detention' in contravention of art 5 to compensation. By necessary implication, therefore, excepting the situation covered by art 5(5), damages will only be awarded in respect of a judicial act which can be shown to have been done in bad faith. Proving judicial bad faith is likely to be a difficult task.

Remedial orders

Subject to the provisos laid down in s 10(1)(a)(i) - (iii), which relate to appeals, if a minister believes that there are compelling reasons for doing so, he may amend by order legislation declared to be incompatible with a convention right under s 4 of the HRA. In other words, the minister has the power to amend primary legislation by making secondary legislation. Such provisions which, as we saw, are known as 'Henry VIII' clauses, confer a wide and important power on members of the executive. The parliamentary scrutiny to which they are subject may be limited. Generally, a draft of the order must be approved by each House of Parliament in accordance with the procedure laid down in Sch 2 to the 1998 Act. In urgent cases, however, a draft order need not be laid before Parliament. Given the importance of this power, its use needs to be limited. In the present context, the use of remedial orders is clearly circumscribed and in any event, it is a use for the promotion of rather than a restriction on human rights. A remedial order may also be made where in the light of a ruling made against the UK by the European Court of Human Rights, it appears that a legislative provision 'is incompatible with an obligation of the United Kingdom arising from the convention' (s 10(1)(b)).

Derogations and reservations

Given that the UK has an art 15 derogation in place in respect of art 5(3), s 14 of the 1998 Act provides for what it terms 'designated derogations'. These are the derogation in respect of art 5(3) and any other derogations which the Secretary of State may by order designate. Thus under the HRA 1998, art 5(3) of the ECHR will have effect in domestic law subject to the terms of the derogation. In *Rights Brought Home: The Human Rights Bill* (1997) Cm 3782, the government explained the position thus:

> 'We are considering what change might be made to the arrangements under the prevention of terrorism legislation. Substituting judicial for executive authority for extensions, which would mean that the derogation could be withdrawn, would require primary legislation. In the meantime, however, the derogation remains necessary' (para 4.3).

Reservations are permitted under art 57 of the ECHR. This provides that:

> 'Any State may, when signing this Convention or when depositing its instrument of ratification, make a reservation in respect of any particular provision of the Convention to the extent that any law then in force in its territory is not in conformity with the provision. Reservations of a general character shall not be permitted under this Article.'

The UK has a reservation in place in respect of art 2 to the First Protocol of the ECHR. This is concerned with the right to education. The second principle of art 2 states that in exercising any functions in relation to education and teaching, the state shall respect the right of parents to ensure that such education and teaching is in conformity with their own religious and philosophical convictions. The reservation (entered in March 1952) makes it clear that the UK accepts this principle to the extent that it is compatible with the provision of efficient instruction and training, and the avoidance of unreasonable public expenditure. Since the government has concluded that the reservation should be kept in place, s 15 makes provision for 'designated reservations'. These include the current reservation (HRA 1998, Sch 3, Part II) and any other reservations which the Secretary of State may by order make. A designated reservation which is withdrawn wholly or in part ceases to be a designated reservation.

FURTHER READING

Lord Bingham 'The European Convention on Human Rights: Time to Incorporate' (1993) 109 LQR 390.

Lord Bingham 'The Way We Live Now: Human Rights in the New Millenium' [1998] I Web JCL

P Duffy and P Stanley Human *Rights Act 1998* (Current Law Annotated Statutes).

D. Feldman 'Remedies for Violations of Convention Rights under the Human Rights Act' [1998] EHRLR 691.

W Hohfeld 'Some Fundamental Legal Conceptions as Applied in Judicial Reasoning' (1913) 23 Yale Law Journal 16.

D Kinley *The European Convention on Human Rights: compliance without incorporation* (1993).

J Marriott and D Nicol 'The Human Rights Act, Representative Standing and the Victim Culture' [1998] EHRLR 730.

A Mowbray, The composition and operation of the new European Court of Human Rights' [1999] PL 219.

H G Schermers 'Election of Judges to the European Court of Human Rights'(1998) EL Rev 568.

SELF-TEST QUESTIONS

1. How might we distinguish between civil and political rights on the one hand, and social and economic rights on the other?
2. What criticisms can be levelled at the traditional means of protecting, rights and liberties in English law? Did their shortcomings make incorporation of the ECHR inevitable?
3. Do you agree with the view that the doctrine of a margin of appreciation is 'essential to retain state confidence in the operation of the system'?
4. Alternatively, is it the case that the margin of appreciation is a 'conclusory label which only serves to obscure the true basis on which a reviewing court decided whether or not intervention in a particular case is justifiable'?
5. Could the rights contained within the ECHR have been properly respected and upheld in the UK by a means other than incorporation?
6. What will be the nature of the role performed by the courts under the Human Rights Act 1998?

14

FREEDOM OF EXPRESSION

SUMMARY

Freedom of expression is a right guaranteed under the ECHR (art 10). It is widely regarded as being a necessary feature in any state which purports to be a democracy. In this chapter, we shall consider the extent to which English law places restrictions on the freedom of expression where the exercise of that freedom would involve the publication etc of that which is obscene or indecent, or would prejudice the Administration of justice. There are other examples of restrictions on freedom of expression which will not be considered here eg the Official Secrets Acts of 1911 and 1989. The present chapter is confined to the law relating to 'obscenity and indecency and contempt of court on the basis that they share an important characteristic; they are regulated by both statute and the common law.

Control of obscenity and indecency

This is not the occasion on which to embark upon a discussion as to the arguments both for and against the control of obscene or indecent material. There are too many shades of opinion on matters such as pornography and whether or not it has a place in society for them to be considered here. For present purposes, it must be acknowledged that Parliament has seen fit to impose restrictions on access to such material and to impose criminal sanctions in the event of a person being convicted of publishing or displaying obscene or indecent material. The law on obscenity and indecency is thus to be found in a number of statutes. The principal enactment is the Obscene Publications Act 1959 as amended by the 1964 Act of the same name. This Act will therefore be the focus of our attention in the following discussion, although reference to other relevant enactments will be made, where appropriate. In addition, it should be noted that the common law offence of obscene libel has not actually been abolished by the 1959 and 1964 Acts and neither do the statutes prevent a prosecution on a charge of conspiracy to corrupt public morals or to outrage public decency.

Publication of obscene matter

Section 2(1) of the Obscene Publications Act 1959 (as amended) provides that it is an offence where:

> '... any person who, whether for gain or not, publishes an obscene article or who has an obscene article for publication for gain (whether gain to himself or gain to another)...'

Section 1 (2) of the Obscene Publications Act 1964 provides that where a person has been charged with an offence under s 2 of the 1959 Act, they:

> '... shall be deemed to have an article for publication for gain if with a view to such publication he has the article in his ownership, possession or control.'

Section 1 (5) of the 1964 Act further provides that 'publication for gain' means:

> '...any publication with a view to gain, whether the gain is to accrue by way of consideration for the publication or in any other way.'

It is apparent from these provisions, therefore, that the essence of the offence is the publication of an obscene article. The test of 'obscenity' will be considered in the next section. For present purposes, it is necessary to consider what is meant by 'publication' and 'article'. Section 1 (3) of the 1959 Act provides that for the purposes of the Act, a person publishes an article who:

'(a) distributes, circulates, sells, lets on hire, gives, or lends it, or who offers it for sale or for letting on hire; or

(b) in the case of an article containing or embodying matter to be looked at or a record, shows, plays or projects it, or, where the matter is data stored electronically, transmits that data.'

An 'article' is defined by s 1(2) of the 1959 Act as:

> 'any description of article containing or embodying matter to be read or looked at or both, any sound record, and any film or other record of a picture or pictures.'

The definitions of 'publication' and 'article' are patently quite wide. In *A-G's Reference (No 5 of 1980)* (1980), the CA held that a video cassette was an article within the meaning of s 1 (2). In order to commit an offence under s 2(1), however, an article which is published must be obscene.

Test of obscenity

Section 1 (1) of the Obscene Publications Act 1959 provides that:

> '... an article shall be deemed to be obscene if its effect or (where the article consists of two or more distinct items) the effect of any one of the items is, if taken as a whole, such as to tend to deprave and corrupt persons who are likely, having regard to all relevant circumstances, to read, see or hear the matter contained or embodied in it.'

The test of obscenity is therefore the tendency that the article will have to 'deprave and corrupt' the minds of those likely to read it etc. The phrase 'deprave and corrupt' was borrowed from the case of *R v Hicklin* (1868) where Lord Cockburn defined 'obscenity' as a tendency:

> 'to deprave and corrupt those whose minds are open to such immoral influences, and into whose hands a publication of this sort may fall.'

In *DPP v Whyte* (1972), Lord Wilberforce observed that this test requires the magistrates or jury 'to ascertain who are likely readers and then to consider whether the article is likely to deprave and corrupt them'. It is therefore no longer permissible to presume a tendency to deprave and corrupt from a finding that an article is obscene, as was formerly the case. In performing this task, the statute provides no further assistance as to what is meant by 'deprave and corrupt'. In a trial on indictment, this will be a matter which is left to the jury, although the trial judge may provide some guidance in his summing-up or in response to a request from the jury. Where a judge does give guidance, it was suggested by the CA in *R v O'Sullivan* (1995) that it should entail reading the relevant provisions of the 1959 and 1964 Acts 'without attempting to improve or re-define the wording of the Acts'. Underlying this advice is the concern that by embellishing upon the statutory definition, a trial judge may be in danger of misdirecting a jury. In *R v Penguin Books Ltd* (1961), where the publishers of *Lady Chatterley's Lover* by D H Lawrence were prosecuted under the 1959 Act, Byrne J stated that:

To deprave means to make morally bad, to pervert, to debase or corrupt morally. To corrupt means to render morally unsound or rotten, to destroy the moral purity or chastity, to pervert or ruin a good quality, to debase or defile'.

Expert evidence will not generally be permitted as to whether a particular article was likely to deprave or corrupt, although in *DPP v A and B C Chewing Gum Ltd* (1968), such evidence was allowed where the alleged obscene matter, which depicted violence, was directed at very young children. Similarly in *R v Skirving* (1985), the CA upheld the decision of the trial judge to allow expert evidence where the case related to a pamphlet in which instructions were given on drug taking. Expert evidence was permissibls in this instance since it was felt that the average person was unlikely to have knowledge or experience of the matters dealt with in the pamphlet.

The decisions in these last two cases highlight a further feature of the obscenity test: it is not confined to the publication of sexually explicit material. Material which deals with extreme violence or drug taking, or which is racially offensive (*Britton v DPP* (1996)) may also be obscene for the purposes of the 1959 Act. As with sexually explicit material, it is not necessary to prove that such material actually depraved and corrupted its readers; it is enough that it has a tendency to do so.

The definition or test of obscenity has been much criticised. Thus in 1954, Norman St John-Stevas (as he then was) submitted that 'the time for abandoning the *Hicklin* formula is long overdue'. In *DPP v Whyte,* Lord Wilberforce observed that: 'It can only have been the pressure of Parliamentary compromise which can have produced a test so difficult for the courts'. In a later report into, inter alia, the laws of obscenity and indecency, the Williams Committee recommended that terms such as 'deprave' and 'corrupt' should be dispensed with since they were too vague and uncertain to serve any useful purpose (1979, Cmnd 7772). Nevertheless, the test for obscenity has remained unaltered. An alternative to the test may be to simply provide that an article is obscene if it relates to or is concerned with any one of a number of specified activities. This approach was adopted by the Earl of Halsbury in his Obscenity Bill which received a Second Reading in the HL on 9 March 1999. The Schedule to the Bill contained a list of some 40 or so activities, the depiction etc of any one of which would render an article obscene.

The likely readers etc

Since an article is obscene for the purposes of the 1959Act if it has a tendency to deprave or corrupt those persons likely to read it, it follows that an article is not obscene in itself. It is its effect on the minds of its likely readers which is what matters. In *R v Calder & Boyars Ltd* (1969), Salmon LJ observed that:

> This court is of the opinion that the jury should have been directed to consider whether the effect of the book was to tend to deprave and corrupt a significant proportion of those likely to read it.'

What is a significant proportion will be a matter for the jury to determine. Although trial judges ought to refrain from redefining the words used in the Acts, in *R v O'Sullivan* (1995), the CA felt that it would be permissible to make 'some reference to the fact that the persons likely to be corrupted should amount to more than a negligible number'. In *DPP v Whyte,* Lord Cross observed that: 'A significant proportion of a class means a part which is not numerically negligible but which may be much less than half. A recent study into pornography trials in the Crown

Court in England and Wales carried out by Edwards has confirmed that, for the relevant period, trial judges gave no direction to the jury as to the meaning of 'significant proportion'.

A further issue arises with regard to the likely readers of an article. What if they are habitual consumers of obscene material? Does this mean, therefore, that a defence may be run to the effect that the likely readers could not be depraved and corrupted because they already were depraved and corrupted? In *DPP v Whyte,* the magistrates who heard the prosecution came to the conclusion that the relevant articles were not obscene on the basis that the booksellers' regular customers were inadequatr, pathetic, dirty minded men... whose morals were already in a state of depravity and corruption'. Nevertheless, on appeal, the HL concluded by a majority of 12 that the magistrates should have convicted the defendants. In the words of Lord Wilberforce, who was in the majority.

The Act is not merely concerned with the once and for all corruption of the wholly innocent; it equally protects the less innocent from further corruption, the addict from feeding or increasing his addiction.'

The aversion argument

In several of the leading cases, defence counsel have sought to argue that far from encouraging its readers to perform the acts which it describes or depicts, an article may in fact so revolt or disgust its readers as to discourage them from participating in such activities. This line of reasoning has become known as the aversion argument. In effect, it is a contention that the article has the reverse effect of tending to deprave and corrupt its likely readers; it is a 'turn off rather than a 'turn on'. The failure to direct the jury about this argument was one of the reasons why the CA upheld the defendants appeal against conviction in *R v Colder & Boyars Ltd.* Such a failure amounted to a 'serious defect in the summing up'. Similarly in *R v Anderson* (1971), convictions under the 1959 Act were quashed on the basis, inter alia, that the failure to properly explain to the jury defence counsel's use of the aversion argument amounted to 'a very substantial and serious misdirection'. In the later case of *R v Elliott* (1996), however, the

CA thought that it would be difficult to effectively advance such an argument in respect of a private cinema showing sex videos, where the material shown 'was clearly being offered as being attractive primarily at least to men'.

Article considered as a whole

In determining whether or not an article is obscene for the purpose of the 1959 Act, s 1 (1) requires that its effect is taken as a whole. Where, however, the article consists of two or more items, it is the effect of any one of those items when taken as a whole which matters. Accordingly, if the application of the test shows one item to be obscene, it follows that the whole article is obscene. The legal position was described by Lord Widgery CJ in *R v Anderson* (1971) in the following manner:

> 'A novelist who writes a complete novel and who cannot cut out particular passages without destroying the theme of the novel is entitled to have his work judged as a whole, but a magazine publisher who has a far wider discretion as to what he will, and will not, insert by way of items is to be judged under the Act on what we call the "item by item" basis.'

It is the article or articles themselves which must be the focus of attention in obscenity proceedings. They must be examined and their effect on their likely readership must be considered in, order to determine whether or not they are obscene. It is not permissible, therefore, for a defendant to show that other articles which are currently in circulation are not materially different from those which are the subject of the prosecution. On the basis of the decision in *R v Reiter* (1954), these other articles would be considered to be irrelevant.

Defences

Several defences to a charge under the 1959 Act are provided for in the statute itself. Of these, the most significant is the defence of public good (s 4). This provides that a person shall not be convicted of a s 2 offence and a forfeiture order shall not be made under s 3 if they can show that:

> '... publication of the article in question is justified as being for the public good on the ground that it is in

> the interests of science, literature, art or learning, or of other objects of general concern.'

In effect, therefore, s 4 allows for the publication of an article which satisfies the obscenity test on the basis that publication is for the public good. The burden of proof rests with the defence. Expert evidence may be allowed as to the literary, artistic, scientific or other merits of an article, although the final decision as to whether any of these merits outweighs the obscene nature of the article is a matter for the court or jury to decide. It would seem that for the publication of an article to be justified under s 4, it would have to contain something new or special; that which merely reproduces the commonplace would not fall within the scope of s 4: *Britton v DPP* (1996).

In *A-G's Reference (No 3 of 1977)* (1978), the CA held that 'learning' was used in s 4 as a noun rather than a verb and that therefore it meant the 'product of scholarship'. It did not include teaching or any form of education, including sex education. In *DPP v Jordan* (1977), the HL ruled that the phrase 'other objects of general concern' was a mobile phrase, the content of which would change as society changes. Nevertheless, it was related to the specified objects in s 4 and did not therefore cover pornographic material which was claimed to have a therapeutic value for some members of the public.

A person charged with a s 2 offence may also be acquitted if he can show that he did not examine the obscene article and that he had no reasonable cause to suspect that its publication would make him liable to be convicted of an offence under the section (s 2(5) of the 1959 Act). In practice, this defence is only likely to be made out by a person who has unknowingly distributed obscene material and who was prevented from examining it by its packaging.

Powers of search and seizure

Under s 3 of the 1959 Act, the police may obtain a warrant to enter and search premises or to search a stall or vehicle for obscene materials. A warrant must specify that the search which it authorises is for 'obscene material'. In *Darbo v DPP* (1992), it was held that the expression 'any other material of a sexually explicit nature' was too wide since it encompassed material which would not be obscene for the purposes of the Act. A magistrate will only grant a warrant where he is satisfied that the police have reasonable grounds for suspecting that obscene material is being kept for publication for gain. Section 3 does not apply, therefore, to a private collection of obscene material. During the conduct of a search, the police have the power to seize and remove any articles which they reasonably believe to be obscene and kept for publication for gain.

Forfeiture

Once allegedly obscene articles have been seized, three courses of action lie open to the police: the articles may be returned to the occupier of the premises or the user of the stall or vehicle; the articles may be used as evidence in a prosecution for an offence under s 2 of the 1959 Act; or, as is quite often the case, the police may decide to bring forfeiture proceedings in respect of the seized articles. With regard to the latter, if the court is satisfied that any of the articles are obscene, they shall order that those articles are forfeited. In practice, the quantity of allegedly obscene articles which are the subject of forfeiture proceedings may be enormous. A search of a warehouse or garage, for example, may lead to the seizure of thousands of magazines and books. In these circumstances, as Professor Stone has noted, a sample of the materials seized by the police would be put before a magistrate. The sample itself would have been agreed by both the prosecution and the defence. However, as he points out, whilst this serves to expedite matters, it is not a practice that strictly accords with the wording of s 3. This refers to a finding of obscenity in respect of an article as the justification for its forfeiture. Forfeiting articles on the basis that they are like articles which have been found to be obscene thus strains the wording of the statute, even if it is an understandable solution to the problem of examining huge piles of material.

Further statutory provision for obscenity and indecency

Obscenity offences

Parliament's battle against obscenity has not been confined to the publication of obscene articles. It has extended into other realms, such as the theatre and postal communications. Thus it is an offence under s 2 of the Theatres Act 1968 to present or direct an obscene performance of a play. The obscenity test which the 1968 Act adopts is the same as that found in the Obscene Publications Acts ie the tendency of the performance to deprave and corrupt persons likely to attend it. The same cannot be said of the Post Office Act 1953. Section 11(1)(b) of this Act makes it an offence to send or attempt to send a postal packet which:

> 'encloses any indecent or obscene print, painting, photograph, lithography, engraving, cinematograph film, book, card or written communication, or any indecent or obscene article whether similar to the above or not.'

The purpose of this provision is to preclude the use of post office services for the distribution of indecent or obscene material: *R v Bremner and Joy* (1984). It is not aimed at protecting postal workers from the risk of accidentally opening a package containing such material. Whether or not any of the items mentioned in s 111(1)(b) is obscene for the purposes of the 1953 Act depends not upon its tendency to deprave and corrupt, but upon the dictionary definition of 'obscene'. In *R v Anderson* (1971), which concerned prosecutions brought under both the Obscene Publications Act 1959 and the Post Office Act 1953, the court accepted that 'obscene' may mean 'repulsive', 'filthy', 'loathsome' or 'lewd'. However, as Professor Stone has pointed out, difficulties arise with these two contrasting approaches as to what constitutes obscenity. Under the 1953 Act, an item which is repulsive may therefore be obscene. In a prosecution under the 1959 Act, however, the defence may seek to argue that an article is repulsive (the aversion argument) in order to get D acquitted. This anomaly has the potential to cause confusion amongst a jury. It would therefore need to be clearly explained by the trial judge in his summing-up.

In *R v Stamford* (1972), the CA noted that in common with the Obscene Publications Acts, the task of determining whether or not an article is indecent or obscene for the purposes of the 1953 Act is a matter for the jury. The CA accepted counsel for the appellant's argument that:

'... one way of expressing the test of indecency or obscenity which are at either end of the scale common to both, was that a matter is obscene if it is one that offends against recognised standards of propriety, and it may be that the same test applies to a matter alleged to be indecent, bearing in mind, as the courts have said, that those are different concepts, different steps on the scale of impropriety, obscenity being the graver of the two.'

Indecency offences

There are several statutory offences involving indecency. In addition to s 11 (1)(b) of the Post Office Act 1953, s 1 of the Protection of Children Act 1978 makes it an offence to take, permit to be taken, distribute, show or have in one's possession with a view to distributing or showing, indecent photographs or pseudo-photographs of children. For the purposes of this offence, it was held in *R v Fellows* (1997) that although a computer disk is not itself a photograph, it contained data which could be converted into a screen image and then printed in such a way as to reproduce the original photograph. The data was therefore a photograph within the meaning of the Act. Moreover, in order to be convicted of this offence, it is not necessary for the prosecution to show that D knew that the indecent photograph was a photograph of a child: *R v Land* (1999). Section 1 of the 1978 Act also makes it an offence to publish an advertisement which conveys the idea that the advertiser shows or distributes indecent photographs, or that he intends to do so.

Possession of an indecent photograph or pseudo-photograph of a child is in itself an offence contrary to s 160 of the Criminal Justice Act 1988. 'Indecent' is not defined in these statutory provisions and must therefore be given its ordinary and natural meaning. In *Knuller v DPP* (1973), Lord Reid observed that 'indecent' meant 'anything which an ordinary decent man or woman would find to be shocking, disgusting or revolting'.

Section 1 of the Indecent Displays (Control) Act 1981 makes it an offence to publicly display or to cause or permit the public display of any indecent matter. In deciding whether any matter (not including an actual human body or part thereof) is indecent for the purposes of the Act, the section requires that any part of the matter not exposed to view 'must be disregarded, and that account may be taken of juxtaposing one thing with another. In *R v South Western Magistrates' Court, ex p Heslop* (1994), it was held that an Underground station manager had not committed an offence contrary to s 1of the 1981 Act where a poster remained on public display despite a complaint having been received. The poster, which depicted a model in her underwear, had the following graffiti written on it: 'I've been sitting here for six months in my underwear and my bum smells'. In the opinion of the stipendiary magistrate, with which the QBD agreed, although this was in extremely bad taste, it was not indecent.

The common law

Section 2(4) of the 1959 Act provides that:

> 'A person publishing an obscene article shall not be proceeded against for an offence at common law consisting of the publication of any matter contained or embodied in the article where it is of the essence of the offence that the matter is obscene.'

This section is therefore aimed at the common law offence of obscene libel. Although it does not abolish that offence, it does assert the primacy of the statutory provisions. In *Shaw v DPP* (1962), the HL effectively created a new common law offence - conspiracy to corrupt public morals. It did so on the basis that the *actus reus* of the offence, the conspiracy, did not consist of the publication of the booklet (a directory of the names and addresses of prostitutes), but of an agreement to corrupt public morals by means of the booklet, which might never be published. In *Knuller v DPP* (1973), the HL held that *Shaw* had been rightly decided or that if it had not, it should remain until altered by Parliament. Moreover, it was accepted by the HL that the authorities established a common law offence of conduct which outrages public decency. Their Lordships felt that it would also be an offence to conspire or agree to do the illegal act (outrage public decency).

In *R v Rowley* (1991), where D left notes in public places in Brighton expressing a need for a 'pretend son' or a boy 'to collect and deliver secret messages', the CA held that the offence of outraging public decency 'consists in the deliberate commission of an act which is per se of a lewd, obscene or disgusting nature'. Therefore, D had not committed the offence since there was nothing in the notes themselves that was capable of outraging public decency. Where a person is charged with this offence, the prosecution do not need to prove that D intended to outrage public decency. It is enough that D did a deliberate act which was found by the jury to outrage public decency: *R v Gibson* (1990).

It might be argued that given the statutory offences which have been created in respect of that which is indecent or obscene, it is unfortunate that the common law has been used as the vehicle to develop offences which are beyond the reach of the statutory safeguards. The defence of public good (s 4 of the 1959 Act), for example, does not apply to either of the common law offences. Nevertheless, the offences we preserved by s 5(3) of the Criminal Law Act 1977, and they may continue to be charged, although in the case of corrupting public morals, this rarely happens.

Contempt of court

Introduction

The law relating to contempt of court is diverse and by no means entirely clear. It consists of a statute, the Contempt of Court Act 1981, various substantive criminal offences, such as perjury or perverting or obstructing the course of justice, and the common law (see below). A further distinction exists between civil and criminal contempts. Civil contempts essentially amount to disobeying a court order: see, for example, *M v Home Office* (1993).

Criminal contempts are of greater interest in the context of freedom of expression. Essentially they amount to conduct which represents an interference with the administration of justice. Criminal contempts may therefore take a variety of forms, including publications which are prejudicial to a fair trial, publications which interfere with the course of justice as an ongoing process and, contempt in the face of the court. In exercising the contempt jurisdiction, it is necessary for the courts to strike a balance between freedom of expression on the one hand and the administration of justice on the other. The reporting by the press and the media generally of the proceedings in court, and the discussion of issues of public concern arising in those proceedings is clearly important. However, when the effect of the publication is to prejudice the administration of justice, the courts may and often will find those responsible for the publication guilty of contempt.

Open justice

Open justice is an important principle in English law. In the leading case *Scott v Scott* (1913), the principle was stated to require that justice be done in public. Subsequently in *A-G v Leveller Magazine Ltd* (1979), Lord Diplock observed that there were two aspects to the application of the principle of open justice:

> '... as respects proceedings in the court itself it requires that they should be held in open court to which the press and the public are admitted and that, in criminal cases at any rate, all evidence communicated to the court is communicated publicly. As respects the publication to a wider public of fair and accurate reports of proceedings that have taken place in court the principle requires that nothing should be done to discourage this.'

Public participation in the administration of justice is therefore central to the principle of open justice. In several cases, the beneficial effect of a public presence in the courts has been vigorously asserted by senior judges. Thus in *R v Socialist Worker Printers and Publishers Ltd, ex p A-G* (1975), Lord Widgery C J remarked that:

The great value of having the public in our courts is that discipline which the presence of the public imposes upon the court itself. When the court is full of interested members of the public... it is bound to have the effect that everybody is more careful about what they do, everyone tries just that little bit harder and there is a disciplinary effect on the court which would be totally lacking if there were no critical members of the public or press present.'

Similarly in *A-G v Leveller Magazine Ltd* (1979), Lord Diplock observed that open justice 'provides a safeguard against judicial arbitrariness or idiosyncrasy and maintains the public confidence in the administration of justice'. More recently in *R v Legal Aid Board*, ex p *Kaim Todner (a firm)* (1999), Lord Woolf MR observed that the principle of open justice was:

> '... necessary because the public nature of the proceedings deters inappropriate behaviour on the part of the court. It also maintains the public confidence in the administration of justice. It enables the public to know that justice is being administered impartially. It can result in evidence becoming available which would not become available if the proceedings were conducted behind closed doors or with one or more of the parties' or witnesses' identity concealed. It makes uninformed and inaccurate comment about the proceedings less likely.'

Open justice is not, however, an absolute principle. It is subject to exceptions which, in the words of Viscount Haldane LC in *Scott v Scott* (1913) are 'the outcome of a yet more fundamental principle that the chief object of the courts of justice must be to ensure that justice is done'. In other words, there will be circumstances where a departure from the principle is justified in the interests of the administration of justice. One such departure may involve an *in camera* hearing ie in the absence of the press or public. However, given that *in camera* proceedings represent a wide departure from the principle of open justice, they will only be justified by exceptional circumstances. Thus if a case involved trade secrets or matters of national security, for example, a court may be justified in exercising its power to exclude the public from the proceedings.

In *R v Malvern Justices, ex p Evans* (1988), where D pleaded guilty to a charge of driving after having consumed excess alcohol, the magistrates decided to sit *in camera* to hear details of D's personal life which were said to explain why she had turned to drink and why she should not be disqualified from driving. The DC dismissed an application for judicial review of that decision which was brought by a journalist and a local newspaper. However, in the opinion of Watkins LJ, proceedings should only be heard *in camera* where there were 'compelling reasons' for such a course of action. Although the DC did not hold that the magistrates had been wrong to sit in private in the present case, the general tenor of the court's judgment suggests that it considered it doubtful whether it had been appropriate in the circumstances of the case.

The Contempt of Court Act 1981

The Contempt of Court Act 1981 (CCA 1981) was introduced by Lord Hailsham LC as a liberalising measure. It has not codified the law on contempt; instead, it provides for strict liability in respect of contempts committed within the scope of the Act. The Act itself owes a number of its provisions to recommendations made by the Phillimore Committee on Contempt of Court (Cmnd 5794 (1974)). However, the catalyst for reform was not the publication of the recommendations themselves, but the ruling of the European Court of Human Rights in *Sunday Times v UK* (1979). In short, the European Court concluded that injunctions granted to prevent the publication of newspaper articles which were critical of a company which had distributed the thalidomide drug amounted to a violation of art 10 of the Convention which guarantees freedom of expression. In order to ensure that UK law subsequently complied with the convention, the CCA 1981 was enacted.

Strict *liability* The principal feature of the CCA 1981 is the strict liability rule. Section 1 of the Act thus provides that:

> '... conduct may be treated as a contempt of court as tending to interfere with the course of justice in particular legal proceedings regardless of intent to do so.'

Thus it is unnecessary for the prosecution to prove that D intended to commit a contempt of court or that he was reckless as to whether or not a contempt would be committed in order to secure a conviction. It will have to prove, however, that D intended to publish that which constitutes the contempt. Strict liability offences are not the norm in criminal law. Generally, there is a presumption in favour of *mens rad* forming part of a statutory offence. This presumption may be rebutted, however, especially where the statute is silent on this matter. In the case of the CCA 1981, a publication will only fall foul of the strict liability rule where it:

> 'creates a substantial risk that the course of justice in the proceedings in question will be seriously impeded or prejudiced" (s 2(2)).'

This then, is the *actus reus* of the offence. What amounts to a 'substantial risk' is not defined by the statute, although in *A-G v BBC* (1997), Auld LJ observed that:

> '... the threshold of risk is not high, simply of more than a remote or minimal risk of serïous prejudice.'

Similarly, the statute offers no guidance as to when proceedings can be said to have been 'seriously' impeded or prejudiced. Nevertheless, it would seem that the purpose underlying the use of the adverb 'seriously' is to ensure that the CCA 1981 only applies to contempts which are more than trivial in nature.

The strict liability rule only applies to publications as defined by s 2(1) of the Act. Thus there will be certain types of contempt, such as contempt in the face of the court, which do not involve a publication and which do not therefore fall within the scope of the Act. Moreover, the Act only applies where the relevant proceedings are 'active' at the time of the publication. For the purposes of s 2, Sch 1 to the CCA 1981 states when criminal, civil, or appellate proceedings are active. Thus in the case of criminal proceedings, they will become active where, for example, a person has been arrested without warrant. Criminal proceedings will be concluded where D is acquitted, sentenced, some other verdict is passed which puts an end to the proceedings, the proceedings are discontinued or are concluded by operation of law.

Defences Where a person has been charged with contempt of court contrary to the CCA 1981, one of several defences may be raised in argument. Section 3 of the Act provides that a publisher is not guilty of contempt under the strict liability rule if at the time of the publication, having taken all reasonable care, he does not know and has no reason to suppose that the relevant proceedings are active. A distributer of a publication may rely on an equivalent defence under s 3. In effect, these defences amount to innocent publication or distribution. The real nature of these defences is underlined by the fact that the burden of proof rests with D. In practice, the need to take all reasonable care will mean that D will have to show that proper inquiries were made of a case at the time of publication in order to ensure that proceedings were not active. This may entail making contact with the police in order to get up-to-date reports as to the status of a criminal investigation.

Section 4(1) of the CCA 1981 states that a person is not guilty of contempt under the strict liability rule 'in respect of a fair and accurate report of legal proceedings held in public, published contemporaneously and in good faith'. In other words, responsible journalism will not fall foul of the contempt laws. Where an order has been made pursuant to s 4(2) (see below), a publication is contemporaneous for the purposes of sub-s (1) if it is made as soon as practicable after the order has expired.

The final 'defence' is found in s 5 of the Act. This provides that:

> 'A publication made as or as part of a discussion in good faith of public affairs or other matters of general public interest is not to be treated as a contempt of court under the strict liability rule if the risk of impediment or prejudice to particular legal proceedings is merely incidental to the discussion.'

In truth, it is not really a defence as such since it will be for the prosecution (in the form of the Attorney-General) to show that the risk of prejudice to a fair trial was not merely incidental to the discussion of the matter dealt with by the article.

A-G v English (1983). A doctor was being tried for the murder of a baby with Down's syndrome. On the third day of the trial, an article was published in the *Daily Mail* which expressed support for the candidature of a woman standing for Parliament who had been born without arms. It was suggested in the article that had she been born at the time of writing, 'someone would surely recommend letting her die of starvation, or otherwise disposing of her'. Proceedings were instituted for contempt and D, the editor, was found guilty despite relying on s 5 of the CCA 1981. HL held: the appeal against conviction would be allowed. Section 5 does not take the form of a proviso or an exception to s 2(2). It stands on an equal footing with it. It was clear that the article was capable of prejudicing the jury in the trial, but it was also clear that it fell within s 5.

What is a court? The 1981 Act is, as its short title indicates, concerned with contempts of court. By virtue of s 19 of the Act, a 'court' is defined as including:

> 'any tribunal or body exercising the judicial power of the State.'

The key aspect of this definition is thus that the body in question must be exercising a judicial function. In *A-G v BBC* (1981) the HL made it clear that labels can be misleading. The mere fact that a body is called a court, in that case a local valuation court, does not necessarily mean that it is a court for the purposes of the 1981 Act. What matters is the nature of its function. Thus a body which is performing an administrative function will not be a court. Tribunals may exercise the judicial power of the state and hence be courts within the meaning of s 19. In *Pickering v Liverpool Daily Post and Echo Newspapers* (1991), for example, a Mental Health Review Tribunal was held to be a court. Similarly in *Peach Grey & Co v Sommers* (1995), an industrial tribunal was a court for the purposes of the law of contempt. However," in *General Medical Council v BBC* (1998), the CA held that a Professional Conduct Committee of the CMC was not a court despite the fact that it performed a recognisably judicial function.

Restrictions on reporting

The CCA 1981 provides for two types of order which constitute restrictions on the reporting of legal, proceedings. By virtue of s 4(2), a court may:

> 'where it appears to be necessary for avoiding a substantial risk of prejudice to the administration of

> justice in those proceedings, or in any other proceedings pending or imminent, order that the publication of any report of the proceedings, or any part of the proceedings, be postponed for such period as the court thinks necessary for that ' purpose.'

Section 11 of the Act provides that:

> 'In any case where a court (having power to do so) allows a name or other matter to be withheld from the public in proceedings before the court, the court may give such directions prohibiting the publication of that name or matter in connection with the proceedings as appear to the court to be necessary for the purpose for which it was so withheld.'

Several distinctions can thus be made between these two orders. The first of these concerns the duration of the relevant order. A s 4(2) order amounts to a postponement of the reporting of the legal proceedings; that postponement is at the discretion of the court and may last for some time where it has been made in order to protect proceedings which are pending or imminent. However, there will be a point in time in the future when reporting will be permitted. In practice, where a s 4(2) order is made, it is required to state the time at which it will cease to have effect. A s 11 order, by contrast, imposes a prohibition on the reporting of the particular matter eg the identity of a victim or witness. It is not likely to cease to have effect at some point in the future. A further distinction relates to the scope of the orders which must be stated in the orders themselves. The scope of a s 4(2) order is clearly wider than that of a s 11 order. It precludes 'any report of the proceedings' whilst it is in force and as such amounts to a 'blanket ban' on media coverage of the case. Section 11 is rather more limited in that the proceedings may still be reported, provided that the matter to which the order relates is not disclosed.

Section 4(2) orders In *MGN Pension Trustees v Bank of America National Trust and Savings Association* (1995), Lindsay J held that in considering whether to make an order under s 4(2), a court should adopt a three-stage approach. This would entail asking itself:

- whether there was a substantial risk of prejudice to the administration of justice in the proceedings;
- was an order necessary for avoiding the risk; and
- whether the court in its discretion ought to make any and, if so, what order.

As was previously noted in the context of s 2(2) of the 1981 Act, 'substantial risk' means more than a remote or minimal risk: *A-G v BBC* (1997). Once it has been concluded that reporting would result in a substantial risk of prejudice to the administration of justice, the second stage requires a court to consider whether an order is in fact necessary to avoid that risk. This involves a balancing exercise on the part of the court taking into account the need for a fair trial by an unprejudiced jury on the one hand, and the requirement of open justice on the other. The mere fact that an individual faces several trials does not necessarily mean that a s 4(2) order will be granted in respect of the first trial.

R v Beck, ex *p Daily Telegraph plc* (1993). Three social workers were charged with serious offences involving the sexual and physical abuse of children in local authority care. The number of charges was such that the case was divided into three indictments. At the trial of the first indictment, the trial judge made a s 4(2) order at the request of B's counsel. The order extended to the reporting of the first trial up to and including the verdicts. A number of national newspapers appealed against the order under s 159 of the Criminal Justice Act 1988. CA held: that there was a substantial risk of prejudice to the administration of justice if the trial on the first indictment were to be reported. However, given the widespread public concern caused by the trial and the issues which it raised about local authority care, it would not be right for the trial to proceed without the public having an opportunity of knowing what was going on.

The decision in *Beck* illustrates the CA carrying out the balancing exercise and deciding it in favour of open justice and legitimate public concern as to the nature of the allegations. It also illustrates the fact that the press as 'a person aggrieved' have the right to appeal against a s 4(2) order by virtue of s 159(1)(a) of the Criminal Justice Act 1988. Indeed, the press may have a role to play in the actual process of deciding whether or not to grant a s 4(2) order.

R v Clerkenwell Metropolitan Stipendiary Magistrates, ex p Telegraph plc, (1993). The Serious Fraud Office laid an information before a stipendiary magistrate alleging that T had committed an offence contrary to s 2(13) of the Criminal Justice Act 1987. The information was heard in private. T's counsel applied for a s 4(2) order to be granted on the basis that T had already been charged with other offences and that publication of the s 2(13) charge would involve a substantial risk of prejudice to those proceedings. The order was made. The newspapers believed that the s 2(13) proceedings were a matter of public interest and that reporting them would not involve such a risk. They sought to make representations to the magistrate as to why the order should be discharged. The magistrate declined to hear representations from them on the basis that he had no power to hear anyone other than the parties to the proceedings. The newspapers sought judicial review of the decisions to make the s 4(2) order and to refuse to hear their representations. QBD held: the court had a discretionary power to hear representations from the press or the news media when considering whether to make a s 4(2) order. However, given that they were best qualified to represent the public interest in reporting the proceedings, a court ought normally to hear representations from the press or news media whenever they asked to be heard and whenever the court was of the opinion that their representations would be of assistance.

Where there is no substantial risk of prejudice to the administration of justice in proceedings, it follows that a s 4(2) order should not be granted: MGN *Pension Trustees Ltd v Bank of America National Trust and Savings Association* (1995) and *Re Central Independent Television plc* (1991). In the latter case, where a trial judge made an order under s 4(2) prohibiting the reporting of a trial by radio or television on the evening that the jury had to spend the night in a hotel, so that the jurors could watch television or listen to the radio free from the possibility of being prejudiced by media reports, the CA held that such an order had not been appropriate. Had there been a substantial risk of prejudice, which there was not, it would have been possible to insulate the jury from the media by means other than a s 4(2) order eg deprive them of television and radio for the night.

Section 11 orders Section 11 of the CCA 1981 does not confer a power to make a direction prohibiting the publication of a name or other matter; it merely recognises that it may be exercised by a court which has the power to do so. At common law, the power has been used, for example, to confer anonymity on witnesses in blackmail trials or where matters of national security are involved.

R v Socialist Worker Printers and Publishers Ltd, ex *p A-G* (1975). During D's trial for blackmail, the judge directed that the two victims of the alleged blackmail be referred to as Mr Y and Mr Z. Prior to the end of the trial, the names, addresses and other particulars of the victims were published in the *Socialist Worker*. The A-G sought orders of committal for contempt of court against the publishers of the article and its author. DC held: by publishing the names of the witnesses in defiance of the judge's direction, the respondents were committing all blatant affront to the authority of the court. They were therefore in contempt of court.

In delivering the judgment of the court in the *Socialist Worker* case, Lord Widgery CJ noted that anonymity for victims in blackmail cases had been commonplace for many years. It was justified:

> '... not out of any feelings of tenderness towards the victim of the blackmail, a man or woman very often who deserves no such consideration at all. The reason why the courts in the past have so often used this device in this type of blackmail case where the complainant has something to hide, is because there is a keen public interest in getting blackmailers convicted and sentenced, and experience shows that grave difficulty may be suffered in getting complainants to come forward unless they are given this kind of protection.'

It is apparent from Lord Widgery's remarks, therefore, that a s 11 order is only to be granted where it is necessary in the interests of the administration of justice. Thus in *R v Evesham Justices*, ex *p McDonagh* (1988), where magistrates made an order under s 11 in respect of D's home address because he feared that he would be further harassed by his ex-wife, the DC granted a declaration that the magistrates' decision was unlawful. In the words of Watkins LJ:

> There are undoubtedly many people who find themselves defending criminal charges who for all manner of reasons would like to keep unrevealed their identity, their home address in particular... But s 11 was not enacted for the benefit of the comfort and feelings of defendants.'

Similarly in *R v Dover Justices, ex p Dover District Council* (1991) where it was alleged that D's restaurant had breached food hygiene regulations, the DC rejected economic loss to the business as justifying the grant of a s 11 order. The situation in relation to professions is, therefore, that in general they will not be granted anonymity even where they are concerned that publicity will cause damage and may seriously prejudice a reputation.

Thus in *R v Legal Aid Board, ex p Kaim Todner (a firm)* (1999), where a firm of solicitors sought to challenge a decision of the Legal Aid Board to terminate its franchise and applied to have its identity kept secret in the judicial review proceedings, the CA dismissed an appeal against a refusal to grant a s 11 order. In delivering the judgment of the court, Lord Woolf MR stated nine reasons as to why kay J had been correct in refusing to grant the order save on an interim basis. The eighth reason is of particular interest in that Lord Woolf sought to draw a distinction between a plaintiff, a defendant and a third party with regard to the grant of an order of anonymity. In the case of the plaintiff, he contended that 'it is not unreasonable to regard the person who initiates the proceedings as having accepted the normal incidence of the public nature of court proceedings'. A defendant was in a slightly better position given that he had not initiated the proceedings. However, it was the witness who had no interest in the proceedings who 'has the strongest claim to be protected by the court if he or she will be prejudiced by publicity'. Nevertheless, in Lord Woolf's opinion, the general approach was that:

'... parties and witnesses have to accept the embarrassment and damage to their reputation and the possible consequential loss which can be inherent in being involved in litigation. The protection to which they are entitled is normally provided by a judgment delivered in public which will refute unfounded allegations.'

The common law

Despite the enactment of the CCA 1981, the common law may still apply in respect of publications that are 'intended to impede or prejudice the administration of justice' (s 6(c) of the CCA 1981). Clearly the need to prove intention on the part of D makes it more difficult for 'the prosecution to secure a conviction under the common law than under the strict liability rule. However, there are certain advantages in bringing a prosecution under the common law.

The first of these relates to the status of the proceedings in respect of which a contempt has allegedly been committed. Whereas those proceedings must be 'active' under the CCA 1981, under the common law, there is some uncertainty as to whether proceedings must be 'pending or imminent' for a contempt to have been committed. In *A-G v News Group Newspapers* (1989), Watkins LJ appeared to doubt whether this was a necessary requirement and in *A-G v Span Newspapers* (1992), Bingham LJ and Hodgson J reached different conclusions on this issue. This uncertainty is by no means satisfactory from the point of view of an editor or publisher of a newspaper who is contemplating whether or not to publish a particular article. If common law contempt continues to be used, this issue needs to be clarified.

With regard to the risk of prejudice to legal proceedings created by a publication, the common law requires that the risk must be real *R v Thomson Newspapers Ltd, ex p A-G* (1968). This is therefore a less stringent standard than that required under the CCA 1981, where the risk must be 'substantial'. Finally, where proceedings are brought under the common law for contempt, the statutory defences under ss 4 and 5 of the CCA 1981 will not apply. In *A-G v Hislop* (1991), for example, it was held that the intention to impede or prejudice the administration of justice by publishing an article amounted to common law contempt. The existence of the intention was also held to negative the 'good faith' aspect of the defence under s 5 of the 1981 Act. Since the defences under ss 4 and 5 amount to important constraints on the scope of contempt and hence serve to uphold the freedom of the press, it is unfortunate that they may be by-passed in this manner.

Thus common law contempt may apply in circumstances where the strict liability rule may not. However, it need not necessarily be simply an alternative. Where proceedings are 'active', it would be possible for an article to fall foul of both the common law and the CCA 1981: *A-G v Hislop* (1991).

FURTHER READING

S Bailey, D Harris and B Jones *Civil Liberties: Cases and Materials* (4th edn, 1995).

M Beloff 'Fair Trial - Free Press? Reporting Restrictions in Law and Practice'[1992] PL 92.

S Edwards 'On the Contemporary Application of the Obscene Publications Act 1959' [1998] Crim LR 843.

CJ Miller 'Some Problems of Contempt' [1992] Crim LR 107.

N St John-Stevas 'Obscenity and the Law' [1954] Crim LR 817.

R Stone Textbook on *Civil Liberties* (2nd edn, 1997).

SELF-TEST QUESTIONS

1. What are the arguments both for and against the retention of the statutory definition of 'obscenity' in the Obscene Publications Act 1959? Is the compilation of a list of activities the depiction etc of any one of which would be obscene a better alternative?

2. Is it acceptable in a trial for an offence contrary to the 1959 Act that the defence may seek to establish that the publication was deliberately repulsive so as to discourage people from the activities described rather than promote them?

3. On what basis might it be argued that Professor Stone is correct when he asserts that: The English law relating to the control of obscenity and indecency is a mess'?
4. If you were asked to make a case for the reporting by the press and media generally of court proceedings and the discussion of issues arising in those proceedings, what arguments would you advance?
5. Conversely, what is the nature of the arguments for restricting comments or reports on actual or pending legal proceedings?
6. What is the *actus reus* of contempt under the CCA 1981?
7. Will it always be the case that any prejudice to proceedings brought about by a newspaper report will have a detrimental effect on the defence alone? Can you think of any circumstances in which the prosecution may be prejudiced by a report in the press?

15

POLICE POWERS

SUMMARY

The principal focus of this chapter is on the powers of the police to: stop and search; arrest; and enter, search and seize items. Although it is acknowledged that specific powers to do any of these things may be provided for in other enactments, the chapter will examine the Police and Criminal Evidence Act 1984 (PACE) powers In addition, the exercise of police discretion will be considered together with the extent to which this is subject to review by the courts. The chapter ends by looking at two specific offences which may be committed against a police officer: assaulting an officer; or wilfully obstructing an officer, both of which can only be committed if the officer is acting within his or her duty at the relevant time.

Police Discretion

It will become apparent from the discussion that follows that the Police and Criminal Evidence Act 1984 confers many powers upon the police. Whether or not a particular power is exercised will, of course, be a matter of discretion for an individual officer. Thus, for example, he may decide to stop and search a person or to arrest them where he believes that either course of action is appropriate in the circumstances. However, although the powers of the police are wide, they are not unlimited. Their exercise is subject to the supervisory jurisdiction of the courts. Thus where a police officer has exceeded his or her powers, the courts will be prepared to intervene.

Lindley v Rutter (1981). D was arrested for disorderly behaviour whilst drunk and taken to a police station. She was placed in a cell and, following a struggle, searched. Two women police officers removed her brassiere. They did so in purported compliance with a standing order from the chief constable. This recommended such a course of action so as to prevent a defendant from harming herself. In respect of the struggle D was charged with assaulting a police officer in the execution of her duty. She was convicted and therefore appealed. DC held: that the police officer had failed to properly exercise her discretion in the present case. No account had been taken of D's particular circumstances before deciding to remove her brassiere. At the material time, therefore, the police officer was not acting within the execution of her duty.

Judicial review of police action on the basis of the *Wednesbury* principles is, therefore, a possibility. In *R v Chief Constable* of Sussex, ex *p International Trader's Ferry Ltd* (1999), where ITF sought to challenge the chief constable's decisions on the policing of animal rights protesters at a port which had a detrimental impact on their business of exporting livestock, Lord Slynn observed that:

> 'My Lords, it is clear that, although the duty to keep the peace is that of the chief constable, what he does may be reviewed by the courts; if his act is clearly unlawful it will be quashed and he may be ordered to do something else; he may have to pay damages.'

On the facts, the HL concluded that the police were acting within the scope of their discretion. Restricting the days on which the port would be policed was justified given the financial and manpower resource implications of policing the port in the face of large-scale demonstrations.

In addition to considering the lawfulness of police conduct, the courts are also prepared to hear challenges brought against police inactivity. Indeed, there may be circumstances in which a court will compel the police to perform a duty that they owe to the general public.

R v Metropolitan Police Comr, ex p Blackburn (1968). The Commissioner issued a policy decision to his officers stating that they were not to attempt to enforce a provision of the Betting, Gaming and Lotteries Act 1963. The rationale for this was the uncertain state of the law at the time and the resource implications of keeping gaming clubs under observation. B sought an order of mandamus. The DC dismissed the motion. B appealed. CA held: that the wide discretionary powers enjoyed by the police were not beyond the review of the courts.

Mandamus was not necessary in the present case since the Commissioner had given an undertaking to the court that the policy decision would be revoked. However, had this not been the case, the court would have been prepared to grant the order sought on the basis that the police are under a clear legal duty to enforce the law.

In *R v Chief Constable of Devon and Cornwall, ex p CEGB* (1982) the CA took the view that the circumstances of the case made it inappropriate to grant an order of mandamus. Lord Denning MR observed that it was 'of the first importance that the police should decide on their own responsibility what action should be taken in any particular situation'. Applying this general principle to the circumstances of the case, Templeman LJ stated that:

> '... it is for the police and the board to co-operate and decide on and implement the most effective method of dealing with the obstructors. The court cannot tell the police how and when their powers should be exercised, for the court cannot judge the explosiveness of the situation or deal with the individual problems which will arise as a result of the activities of the obstructors.'

The Police and Criminal Evidence Act 1984 (PACE 1984)

When introducing a revised and amended Police and Criminal Evidence Bill before the HC in November 1983, the then Home Secretary, Leon Brittan, declared that the measure was necessary for a number of reasons:

> 'First, the present state of the law is unclear and contains many indefensible anomalies. Secondly, the

> police need to have adequate and clear powers to conduct the fight against crime on our behalf and the public need to have proper safeguards against any abuse of such powers if they are to have confidence in the police. Thirdly, these measures play an essential part in an overall strategy designed to create more effective policing' (*Hansard*, HC vol 48, col 25).

The need for legislation did not mean, however, that Parliament was prepared to accept whatever it was given by the government of the day. Considerable parliamentary time was spent both on the floor of the House and in the committee rooms in moulding the second version of the Bill into what was desired. Indeed, the process of enactment has been described by Professor Zander as 'an example of the democratic system working. The resultant Act is a very important piece of legislate. Although it does not amount to a codification of police powers, it does form the basis of many of the powers exercised by the police on a daily basis.

Codes of Practice

Sections 60 and 66 of PACE required the Secretary of State to issue codes of practice in connection with the exercise of various powers accorded to the police under PACE. To date, five such codes have been drafted. They are concerned with:

- powers of stop and search (Code A);
- searching premises and the seizure of property (Code B);
- detention, treatment and questioning of suspects (Code C);
- identification matters (Code D); and
- tape-recording interviews with suspects (Code E).

A failure to comply with a code does not in itself render a police officer liable to any criminal or civil proceedings (s 67(10)). Nevertheless, the codes serve an important purpose in that they provide the police with additional guidance, which is sometimes clearer than that given in PACE itself, as to how they are to exercise their powers under the Act. Each code must therefore be readily accessible at all police stations so that it may be consulted by anyone who wishes to do so. Moreover, the fact that they are codes rather than statutory provisions ensures that they may be more easily revised, either wholly or partly, when the need arises. In practice the Secretary of State achieves this by laying a draft of the revised code before Parliament, considering representations made to him about it, and modifying it accordingly. The revised code is then brought into effect by order eg the Police and Criminal Evidence Act 1984 (Codes of Practice No 5) Order I999, SI 1999/291.

Police Powers of Stop and Search

The police have the power to stop and search persons under a variety of different enactments. Thus, for example, under s 23(2) of the Misuse of Drugs Act 1971, a police officer may search any person whom he has reasonable grounds to suspect to be in possession of a controlled drug in contravention of the Act. A similar power entitles a police officer to search a vehicle or vessel for a controlled drug. For the purposes of the 1971 Act, a 'controlled drug' is a substance or product specified in Sch 2 to the Act. These include cocaine and diamorphine (the medical name for heroin), both of which are Class A drugs, and amphetamine and cannabis (Class B drugs). A police officer has the power to seize and detain anything which he finds as a consequence of a s 23 search which appears to him to be evidence of an offence under the Act (s 23(2)(c)).

There are several powers of stop and search available to the police which are not based on the need for reasonable suspicion. Thus s 60 of the Criminal Justice and Public Order Act 1994 is concerned with powers to stop and search in anticipation of violence. Where it is believed that serious violence may take place in the locality, or that persons are carrying dangerous instruments or offensive weapons in the locality, a police officer of the rank of inspector or above may authorise the use of the s 60 search powers during the course of a 24-hour period. These entitle the police to stop and search any pedestrian, any vehicle, the driver of the vehicle or any of its passengers for offensive weapons or dangerous instruments. There is no need for a police officer to reasonably suspect that an individual is in possession of these weapons or articles.

PACE

The main power that the police have to stop and search persons or vehicles is to be found in s 1 of PACE 1984. This provides that a person or vehicle may be detained (the Act does not use the word 'stop') in a public place for the purpose of conducting a search for stolent or prohibited article or articles, in relation to which a person has committed or is committing or is going to commit an offence under s 139 of the Criminal Justice Act 1988. For the purposes of the Act, 'prohibited articles' are an offensive weapon ie an article made or adapted for causing injury to persons, or an article used in connection with offences such as burglary or theft eg a jemmy.

The power to stop and search may only be exercised where a constable has 'reasonable grounds' for suspecting that he will find one of these articles. 'Reasonable grounds for suspecting' is not defined by the Act. Some guidance as to its meaning is to be found in Code of Practice A. Accordingly, there must be some objective basis for the existence of reasonable grounds for suspicion. This may consist of information received which indicates, for example, that gang members habitually carry knives or weapons or controlled drugs. However, it can never be supported on the basis of personal factors alone, such as a person's colour, age, hairstyle or manner of dress. Neither can it be founded on the basis of stereotyped images of certain persons or groups as more likely to be committing offences.

A police officer who has detained a person or vehicle in order to conduct a search need not carry it out if it subsequently appears that it is unnecessary or impracticable (s 2(2)). However, where a search is to be conducted, prior to its commencement, a police officer who is not in uniform must provide documentary evidence of his identity. Additionally, whether he is in uniform or not, he must take reasonable steps to bring to the attention of the appropriate person (ie the person to be searched or the person in charge of the vehicle):

- his name and the name of the police station to which he is attached;
- the object of the proposed search; and
- the officer's grounds for proposing to make it.

The Act gives little guidance as to the nature of a search. It does state, however, that s 1 does not authorise an officer to require a person to remove any of his clothing in public other than an outer coat, jacket or gloves (s 2(9)(a)). Where a police officer has carried out a search, he is required by s 3(1) of PACE to make a written record of it unless it is not practicable to do so. If it is not practicable at the time of the search, a record shall be made as soon as practicable after its completion. The record of a search must state:

- its object
- the grounds for making it
- the date and time when it was made
- the place where it was made
- whether anything, and if so, what was found
- whether any, and if so what, injury to a person or damage to property has resulted from the search
- the identity of the police officer making it.

If a record of a search has been made, the person searched is entitled to a copy on request within a period of 12 months from the date of the search.

Arrest

The most important power that the police possess is the power to arrest members of the public. In *Spicer v Holt* (1977), Viscount Dilhome stated that:

> 'Arrest' is an ordinary English word...Whether or not a person has been arrested depends not on the legality of the arrest but on whether he has been deprived of his liberty to go where he pleases.'

Later, in *Holgate-Mohammed v Duke* (1984), Lord Diplock observed that:

> '... arrest is a continuing act: it starts with the arrester taking a person into custody (sc by action or words restraining him from moving anywhere beyond the arrester's control), and it continues until the person so restrained is either released from custody or, having been brought before a magistrate, is remanded in custody by the magistrate's judicial act.'

It would seem that these statements continue to reflect the position with regard to arrest. In *Lewis v Chief Constable of South Wales Constabulary* (1991), Balcombe LJ described an arrest as 'a matter of fact'. In his opinion, 'it is not a legal concept (though it clearly has legal consequences) and is a continuing act.'

In order for an arrest to be lawful, it is necessary for the police (and members of the public) to show that they are exercising a power that is derived from lawful authority. In the case of the police, one such form of authority may be a warrant for an arrest issued by a magistrate in accordance with s 1 of the Magistrates' Courts Act 1980. Moreover, at common law, the police have the power to arrest any person who has committed or is about to commit a breach of the peace. However, the most common source of authority for effecting an arrest is statute. Numerous Acts of Parliament confer powers of arrest on the police. Thus, for example, ss 3(6), 4(3), 4A(4), and 5(4) of the Public Order Act 1986 entitle a police officer to arrest a person where he reasonably believes that an offence is being committed under the relevant section. Nevertheless, the most important statutory powers of arrest are those found in ss 24 and 25 of the PACE 1984.

Section 24

This section confers a general power of arrest without warrant in respect of 'arrestable offences'. For the purposes of the Act, an 'arrestable offence' is an offence for which:

- the sentence is fixed by law; and
- persons over the age of 21 who have not previously been convicted may be sentenced to five years' imprisonment.

Thus arrestable offences are serious in nature. They include offences such as grievous bodily harm, theft, robbery, riot and violent disorder. Other offences, such as treason, murder, manslaughter, rape and kidnapping are also clearly arrestable offences. For the purposes of 116 of PACE, however, this latter category are labelled 'serious arrestable offences'.

There are certain offences which do not satisfy the requirements referred to above. However, by virtue of s 24(l)(c) of PACE, these offences (listed in sub-s (2)) are arrestable offences for the purposes of the 1984 Act. They include publishing an obscene article contrary to s 2 of the Obscene Publications Act 1959, any offence under the Football (Offences) Act 1991 and the offence of having an article with a blade or point contrary to s 139(1) of the Criminal Justice Act 1988.

The s 24 power of arrest may be exercised by either a police officer or a member of the public. A citizen's arrest is only authorised under this section, however, where:

- a person is in the act of committing an arrestable offence (s 24(4)(a)); or
- there are reasonable grounds for suspecting that person to be committing an arrestable offence (s 24(4)(b)); or
- an arrestable offence has been committed and the person is guilty of the offence or there are reasonable grounds for believing him to be guilty of the offence (s 24(5)(a) and (b)).

Before a member of the public decides to exercise the power of arrest in s 24(5), it is as well to remember that they will be acting without lawful authority if D is subsequently acquitted.

R v Self (1992). D was suspected of having stolen a bar of chocolate from a shop. He assaulted a shop assistant and a member of the public before he was arrested by the latter. He was charged with theft and two counts of assault with intent to prevent his lawful detention contrary to s 38 of the Offences Against the Person Act 1861. At his trial, D was acquitted of the theft charge but convicted of the assault charges. On appeal, D argued that his acquittal on the theft charge meant that there was no power to arrest under s 24(5) of PACE 1984. He argued, therefore, that he should not have been convicted of the s 38 offences because at the relevant time, he was seeking to break free from an unlawful arrest. CA held: allowing D's appeal, that the s 24(5) power of arrest required as a condition precedent that an offence had been committed. Since no offence had been committed in the present case, there was no power to apprehend or detain D.

The police enjoy wider powers of arrest under s 24 than ordinary members of the public. In addition to those already mentioned, where a police officer has reasonable grounds for suspecting that an arrestable offence has been committed, he may arrest without a warrant anyone whom he has reasonable grounds for suspecting to be guilty of the offence (s 24(6)). The outcome in *R v Self* may have been rather different had this power of arrest been available to the public. A police officer may also arrest without a warrant:

- anyone who is about to commit an arrestable offence; or
- anyone whom he has reasonable grounds for suspecting is about to commit an arrestable offence (s 24(7)(a) and (b)).

Reasonable suspicion

It is evident that a number of the s 24 powers of arrest are exercisable where a police officer (or member of the public) reasonably suspects that an arrestable offence has been, is being or will be committed. The phrase 'reasonably suspects' is not defined in the 1984 Act. However, some guidance as to its meaning has been given by the courts. Thus in *Castorina v Chief Constable of Surrey* (1988), Woolf LJ (as he then was) suggested that where it was alleged that there had been an unlawful arrest, three questions needed to be answered:

- Did the arresting officer suspect that the person who was arrested was guilty of the offence?
- Assuming that the officer had the necessary suspicion, was there reasonable cause for that suspicion?

- If the answer to both these questions is 'yes', then the officer has a discretion which entitles him to make an arrest, and he has exercised that discretion in accordance with the *Wednesbury* principles.

From the above, it is clear that the answer to the first question depends upon a subjective assessment of the police officer's state of mind at the relevant time. The second question introduces an objective element into the equation in that it requires an assessment of whether or not the officer's suspicion was 'reasonable' in the circumstances. This will be a matter for a court to decide. The requirement that the suspicion is 'reasonable' represents a safeguard against the abuse of the s 24 power of arrest.

In *O'Hara v Chief Constable of the Royal Ulster Constabulary* (1997), where D was arrested under s 12(1) of the Prevention of Terrorism (Temporary Provisions) Act 1984 on the basis that a police officer had reasonable grounds for suspecting him to be a terrorist, it was held that the reasonable suspicion has to be in the mind of the arresting officer. Moreover, the HL was of the opinion that an officer's suspicion need not be based on his own observations but could be based on what he had been told or on an anonymous 'tip-off. In *Fox v UK* (1990), the European Court of Human Rights held that the arrest of a suspected terrorist under s 11 of the Northern Ireland (Emergency Provisions) Act 1978 was contrary to art 5(1) of the ECHR because although the suspicion was genuine, there was insufficient evidence to support the view that the suspicion was reasonable.

Section 25

The power of arrest under this section applies in respect of non-arrestable offences. It is exercisable where such an offence has been or is being committed or attempted and an officer believes that the service of a summons would be impracticable or inappropriate because any one of the general arrest conditions is satisfied. The 'general arrest conditions' are listed as follows in s 25(3):

- the name of the relevant person is unknown to and cannot be readily ascertained by the officer; or

- the officer has reasonable grounds for doubting whether a name furnished by the relevant person is in fact his real name; or
- the relevant person has failed to furnish a satisfactory address for service; or
- the officer has reasonable grounds for doubting whether an address furnished is a satisfactory address for service; or
- the officer has reasonable grounds for believing that arrest is necessary to prevent the relevant person-
- causing physical injury to himself or another;
- suffering physical injury;
- causing loss or damage to property;
- committing an offence against public decency;
- causing an unlawful obstruction of the highway; or
- the officer has reasonable grounds for believing that arrest is necessary to protect a child or other vulnerable person from the relevant person.

It is clear from this list that the 'general arrest conditions' fall into two distinct categories: the identity and address of the relevant person; and the behaviour of that person. With regard to the former, a person who has an unusual name or who shares their name with a celebrity or fictional character may fall foul of s 25 where they have committed a non-arrestable offence and do not have some form of identification with them to corroborate the fact that the name stated is their real name. As far as the relevant person's behaviour is concerned, it is possible, inter alia, to arrest a person in order to prevent them causing harm to themselves or another. In *Moulding v DPP* (1996), it was stated, obiter, that a police officer may therefore arrest a person under s 25 in order to prevent himself from being harmed by that person. Section 25 also allows for a person to be arrested so as to prevent them suffering physical injury. Protective custody may be necessary, for example, where a person has been questioned by police in connection with an offence which has aroused public feeling in the local community.

The two-stage process for determining whether an officer had reasonable suspicion to arrest under s 24 of PACE also applies in respect of s 25: *Edwards v DPP* (1993). Thus it is an officer's state of mind at the relevant time which is the important factor. Accordingly, where an officer arrests a person and gives a reason for that arrest that makes no reference to any of the s 25 general arrest conditions, it will not be possible to infer that the officer had any one of these conditions in mind at the relevant time.

Information to be given on arrest

Where a person is arrested, s 28 of PACE requires that they are informed that: they are under arrest (sub-s (1)); and, the ground for the arrest (sub-s (3)). This information, which broadly reflects what was required under the common law (see *Christie v Leachinsky* (1947)), is to be given as soon as is practicable. Where D was arrested by being detained in a car which had been specially adapted by the police to trap any person who attempted to steal it, it was held, inter alia, that s 28 had been complied with by the arresting officers who arrived quickly on the scene: *Dowes v DPP* (1994). However, Kennedy LJ was of the opinion that had the officers been slow to respond, a court may not have taken the view that the information had been given as soon as was practicable. If this were indeed the case, the arrest would have been unlawful.

In *Edwards v DPP* (1993), Evans LJ observed that: 'giving correct information as to the reason for an arrest is a matter of the utmost constitutional significance in a case where a reason can be and is given at the time'. Thus giving a person the wrong or an invalid reason for his arrest will also fall foul of s 28 and hence render the arrest unlawful.

In several cases, it has been necessary for the courts to determine the legal consequences of an unlawful arrest.

DPP v Hawkins (1988). A police officer took H by the arm and informed him that he was under arrest. A struggle ensued which made it impracticable for the officer to inform H of the ground for the arrest. It became practicable to comply with s 28(3) of PACE on H's arrival at a police station, but it was found as a matter of fact by magistrates that he either was not informed or that he was given the wrong reason. They therefore dismissed informations against him for offences contrary to s 51(1) of the Police Act 1964 and s 5 of the Public Order Act 1986. The prosecutor appealed by way of case stated. DC held: at the material time, the officers were acting in the execution of their duty. The offences were committed when it was impracticable to comply with the requirement laid down in s 28(3). The fact that compliance was later practicable meant that the arrest only became unlawful from that point in time onwards.

Lewis v Chief Constable of the South Wales Constabulary (1991). Two women were arrested and taken to a police station. They were not informed of the reasons for their arrest (suspicion of burglary) until they arrived at the police station. They were detained for five hours and then released without charge. They sued the chief constable for wrongful arrest and false imprisonment. They sought damages for the entire time that they were detained. The trial judge ruled that their arrests were unlawful from the time that they could have been given the reasons for their arrests to the time when they were given the reasons - 10 minutes and 23 minutes respectively. They were each awarded £200 damages by the jury. They appealed. CA held: that the trial judge had been right. The effect of telling a person, who was initially arrested without being given the reasons, those reasons at a later time was that the arrest became lawful from that moment. The women had therefore been unlawfully arrested for a number of minutes rather than hours.

These cases illustrate the effect that the s 28(3) requirement can have upon the lawfulness of an arrest. An unlawful arrest can become lawful, and a lawful arrest can become unlawful, where s 28(3) has been or has not been complied with. In practice, a failure to comply with s 28 is likely to be rectified at the police station, where the arrested person is brought before the custody sergeant. This is in part because the law does not require that the person who made the arrest need necessarily be the person who supplies the s 28 information. Moreover, in *DPP v L* (1999), where a custody sergeant recorded that *L* had been arrested on the grounds of 'Public Order, s 5 Public Order Act resisting arrest', the DC took the view that this 'regularised' the arrest. In other words, despite the fact that there was no evidence that *L* had actually been informed of the grounds for her arrest, it was presumed that this must have been the case since the entry had been made on the custody record in her presence.

Powers to Enter Property

It was stated by Lord Camden in *Entick v Carrington* (1765) that:

> 'No man can set his foot upon my ground without my licence, but he is liable to an action, though the damage be nothing ... if he admits the fact, he is bound to shew by way of justification, that some positive law has empowered or excused him.'

In effect, Lord Camden's remarks encapsulate what is widely understood to be the principle of legality; that interference with a person or their property can only be justified by the existence of some lawful authority which permits such interference. This authority may take one of several different forms. In terms of entering a property, this may of course take place with the express permission of the owner. Alternatively, the law recognises that a person may have an implied licence to enter a property.

Implied licence

All those persons with lawful business on a property will have an implied licence to enter. Thus, for example, the deliverers of milk, newspapers or mail will all be able to enter in the absence of express permission to do so. Similarly, a police officer making house-to-house enquiries would have an implied licence to enter a property. In the Australian case *Halliday v Nevill* (1984), the High Court stated that:

> 'A passer-by is not a trespasser if, on passing an open driveway with no indication that entry is forbidden or unauthorised, he or she steps upon it either unintentionally or to avoid an obstruction such as a vehicle parked across the footpath. Nor will a passer-by be a trespasser if, for example, he or she goes upon the driveway to recover some item of his or her property which has fallen or blown upon it or to lead away an errant child.'

An implied licence to enter does not, however, give unlimited access to the property in question. Whilst a path or a driveway may represent a 'bridge or thoroughfare' between the highway and a private dwelling *(Halliday v Nevill)*, an implied licence will not extend to going beyond the front door of a house or to trying to obtain access to a rear garden. Express permission would be needed in these circumstances. Similarly in the case of a shop, the implied licence to enter would only extend to the public parts of the premises. In practice, the distinction between the public and private areas in a shop is normally made clear through the use of signs or notices.

An implied licence to enter may be revoked by the owner of the property. Revocation can take one of two forms: verbal; or written ie a sign or notice. In either case, the words used must be sufficiently clear to convey the fact of revocation. On several occasions, the courts have treated expressions such as 'Fuck Off as vulgar expletives rather than as a revocation of an implied licence: see, for example, *Snook v Mannion* (1982) and *Gilham v Breidenbach* (1982). Where an implied licence has been revoked, a person who remains on the property without some other form of lawful authority will have become a trespasser.

Davis v Lisle (1936). Two police officers suspected that the driver of a lorry had obstructed the highway contrary to s 54(6) of the Metropolitan Police Act 1839. They entered a garage into which the lorry had been driven in order to pursue their enquiries. They did so without the express permission of the owner. Neither officer was in possession of a search warrant. The owner of the garage said to the officers 'Get outside - you can't come in here without a search warrant'. Nevertheless, the officers made no attempt to leave and one of them sought to produce his warrant card. They were therefore forcibly removed from the garage. In respect of his conduct, the owner was convicted of (i) assaulting a police officer in the execution of his duty (ii) wilfully obstructing a police officer in the execution of his duty, and (iii) unlawfully, wilfully and maliciously damaging a police tunic. He appealed against his convictions. DC held: allowing the appeal against the convictions for offences (i) and (ii) but upholding the conviction for offence (iii), that in respect of the first two offences, at the material time, the officers were not acting within the execution of their duty. They had been told to leave and therefore they became trespassers when they did not do so. The act of producing a warrant card amounted to an attempt to assert a right to remain on the premises which the officers did not have.

Once an implied licence has been revoked, a licensee does not immediately become a trespasser. He or she must be given a reasonable time in which to leave the property. In *Robson v Hallett* (1967), where a police sergeant who had been invited into a house was asked to leave, and was then assaulted as he attempted to do so, the DC held that he was acting within the execution of his duty at the time of the assault. This would not have been the court's finding had the sergeant attempted to assert some right to remain which he did not possess, as in *Davis v Lisle*.

Under statutory authority

In addition to entering a property under an express or implied licence, a police officer may be authorised to enter contrary to the owner's wishes. The authority in question will normally be derived from statute, although it may be authorised by the common law where it is necessary in connection with an actual or apprehended breach of the peace.

Entry under a search warrant

Following the receipt of an application from the police, magistrates may issue a warrant to search premises under s 8 of PACE. The application itself must state: the ground on which it is made; the enactment under which the warrant would be issued; the premises which it is desired to enter and search; and, so far as possible, the articles or persons to be sought (s 15(2)). An application is made ex parte and supported by written information (s 15(3)). A magistrate may issue a search warrant under s 8(1) where he is satisfied that there are reasonable grounds for believing that:

- a serious arrestable offence has been committed; and
- there is material on the premises likely to be of substantial value to the investigation; and
- the material is likely to be relevant evidence; and

- it does not consist of or include items subject to legal privilege, excluded material or special procedure material; and
- any of a number of specified conditions apply.

The specified conditions referred to above include that entry to the premises will not be granted in the absence of a warrant or, that the purpose of the search will be frustrated or seriously prejudiced if immediate entry cannot be secured (s 8(3)(c) and (d)).

It is apparent from the terms of s 8(1)(d) that a warrant under this section cannot authorise a search for certain specified items. Those items which are subject to legal privilege are defined in s 10 of PACE. Essentially they amount to communications between a legal adviser and his client, or his client's representative, relating to the giving of legal advice or in connection with or in contemplation of legal proceedings. 'Excluded material' encompasses personal records (eg records relating to a person's physical or mental health), human tissue or tissue fluid, and journalistic material (ie material acquired or created for the purposes of journalism). 'Special procedure material' is defined in s 14 of PACE. It consists of journalistic material other than that which is excluded, and items which are neither legally privileged nor excluded material, but which have been acquired or created in the course of a person's work, or for the purpose of any paid or unpaid office, and which are held in confidence.

Whereas legally privileged material is beyond the search powers of the police, access to excluded material or special procedure material may be obtained by the police for the purposes of a criminal investigation. The special procedure for obtaining access is prescribed in Sch 1 to PACE. It involves making an application to a circuit judge who may order that the material should be produced, or access granted to it, provided that one or other of the sets of access conditions is fulfilled. These are set out in paras 2 and 3 of the Schedule. The first set, which only applies to special procedure material, contains several conditions broadly similar to those specified in s 8(1) in respect of searches for non-protected materials. In addition, reference is made to, inter alia, the fact that other methods of obtaining the material have been tried without success and, that production or access is in the public interest due to the benefits that would accrue to the investigation.

The second set of access conditions apply to either special procedure or excluded material. They are satisfied if there are reasonable grounds for believing that the relevant material is on the premises, that but for s 9(2) of PACE a search for that material could have been authorised by a warrant issued under a pre-PACE enactment and that the issue of such a warrant would have been appropriate.

Entry and search without search warrant

A warrant is by no means always required to carry out a search. Section 17 of PACE authorises the police to enter and search any premises without a search warrant where their purpose is to: arrest a person (sub-s (1) (a), (b), (c) and (ca)); recapture a person (sub-s (1) (cb) and (d)); or, save life or limb or prevent serious damage to property (sub-s (1)(e)).

Since s 17 empowers the police to enter a property despite the owner's objections, it is a power which must be exercised with care.The mere possession of lawful authority does not absolve the police from the need to first request the permission of the owner to enter. This is evident from the decision in *O'Loughlin v Chief Constable of Essex* (1998) where three police officers forced an entry into a house in order to speak to the plaintiffs wife about criminal damage that had been done to a neighbour's car. In giving judgment, the majority of the CA held that refusing a request to enter premises does not thereby render the use of force necessary. Force would only be necessary where: an officer has stated the grounds on which he intends to enter the premises; the grounds give him a right of entry recognised by law; and his request has been refused. In *O'Loughlin* itself, the fact that the officers wished to enter the premises to question the woman rather than to arrest her meant that their entry did not fall within the terms of s 17 of PACE. Without the necessary lawful authority, they were therefore trespassers.

Section 17 (1)(d) of PACE empowers the police to enter premises for the purpose of:

> 'recapturing [any person whatever] who is unlawfully at large and whom he is pursuing.'

As Professor Zander has noted, this provision reproduces the power which formerly existed at common law. It entitles the police to enter premises in order to recapture a person who has escaped from prison, a court, police custody or detention in a mental hospital. However, for the power to be exercisable, the police must be pursuing the escapee.

D'Souza v DPP (1992). Mrs D was admitted to hospital under the Mental Health Act 1983 for psychiatric assessment. Following a visit from her husband, she left the hospital without leave being granted under the Act and returned home. Several hours later two uniformed police officers went to the house to take her back to the hospital. Mrs D's daughter refused to admit them and they therefore forced an entry pursuant to s I7(1)(d) of PACE. The daughter and father then attacked the officers. They were charged with assaulting an officer in the execution of his duty. Both were convicted and their convictions were upheld by the Crown Court. The daughter's appeal to the DC was dismissed. She therefore appealed to the HL. She argued that the police did not have the power to enter under s I7(l)(d) and that therefore at the material time, the officers were not in the execution of their duty. HL held: allowing the appeal, that the s 17 power was exercisable where the pursuit was almost contemporaneous with the entry into the premises. Since the officers had merely resorted to the premises where they believed that they might find Mrs D, they had not been pursuing her and therefore they were not within the execution of their duty at the time of the assaults.

Entry and search after arrest

Where a person is under arrest for an arrestable offence, s 18 of PACE entitles a police officer to enter and search any premises occupied or controlled by that person provided that he has reasonable grounds for suspecting that there is on the premises evidence relating to: the arrestable offence; or some other arrestable offence which is connected with or similar to that offence. The Act does not define what is meant by 'occupied or controlled', but the expression clearly covers the arrested person's abode and quite possibly their workplace. Similarly, there is no definition of what are 'similar' or 'connected' arrestable offences. In *Jeffrey v Black* (1978), it was held that arresting D for the theft of a sandwich did not entitle the police to carry out a search for drugs. Since these offences were neither similar nor connected, if the police wished to search for drugs, they ought to have arrested D for a separate arrestable offence in which case a s 18 search would have been permissible.

Subject to the proviso in sub-s (5), the s 18 powers may only be exercised where an officer of the rank of inspector or above has authorised them in writing. In the light of the decision in *R v Badham* (1987), it would seem that a written record of a verbal authorisation would be insufficient to comply with the requirement in s 18(4). Compliance would be achieved, however, by an independent document in which the authorisation was recorded in writing. The proviso applies where the presence of the arrested person at a place other than a police station is necessary for the effective investigation of the offence.

Section 32(2)(b) of PACE provides a further power to enter and search premises following an arrest. Unlike s 18, the power of search is not limited to premises 'occupied or controlled by the person under arrest. Instead, it authorises the search of premises where D was at the time of the arrest, or immediately prior to the arrest. These premises may therefore be owned by an entirely innocent third party. The s 32(2)(b) power is only exercisable where a police officer has reasonable grounds for believing that there is evidence on the premises relating to the offence for which D was arrested. Thus s 32(2)(b) is narrower than s 18 in terms of the purpose of the search. It is wider, however, in the sense that the relevant offence need not be an arrestable offence.

General power of seizure

Section 19 of PACE confers a general power of seizure on a police officer who is lawfully on any premises. The power of seizure is exercisable where the officer has reasonable grounds for believing that the item:

- has been obtained in consequence of the commission of an offence (s 19(2)); or
- is evidence in relation to an offence which he is investigating or any other offence (s 19 (3)).

In both cases, seizure is only authorised where it is necessary to prevent the item being concealed, lost, altered or destroyed. In the case of the s 19(2) power, seizure may also be necessary to prevent the item being damaged. Section 19(4) provides for the seizure of information stored in a computer. This is achieved by requiring the information to be produced in a form which can be taken away eg a disk copy. The power is exercisable in the circumstances provided for in s 19(2) and (3), save that seizure will not be necessary to prevent the information being altered or damaged, but it may be necessary to prevent it being tampered with.

Code of Practice B reinforces several of the provisions in s 19 of PACE, including the fact that no item may be seized which is subject to legal privilege (para 6.2 and s 19(6)). Where a police officer decides not to seize property because of an explanation given by the person holding it, but he nevertheless has reasonable grounds for believing that it has been obtained in consequence of the commission of an offence by some person, para 6.3 of Code B requires the officer to inform the holder of his suspicions. It also requires the officer to inform the holder that if he disposes of the property, he may be liable to civil or criminal proceedings.

Where the power of seizure has been exercised, the item may only be retained for as long as is necessary in the circumstances (para 6.6). It may be retained for purposes which include: for use as evidence at a trial for an offence; for forensic examination or for other investigation in connection with an offence; or, where there are reasonable grounds for believing that it has been stolen or obtained by the commission of an offence, in order to establish its lawful owner. In the case of the first and second purposes, retention is unnecessary if a photograph or copy would suffice (para 6.7).

Assault on or wilful obstruction of a police officer

By virtue of s 89 of the Police Act 1996, a person commits an offence where he assaults a police officer in the execution of his duty or a person assisting the officer in the execution of his duty (sub-s (1)). Section 89 further provides that it is an offence to resist or wilfully obstruct a police officer in the execution of his duty or a person assisting him in the execution of his duty (sub-s (2)). These offences are re-enactments of earlier statutory provisions, such as s 51 of the Police Act 1964. In order for a person to be convicted of either offence, it is therefore necessary that an assault or wilful obstruction occurred, and that at the material time, the police officer was acting in the execution of his duty. If he was not so acting, neither offence may be committed, although D could be charged with a lesser offence such as common assault. The meanings of the terms 'assault', 'wilful obstruction' and 'in the execution of his duty' are therefore of central importance to the determination of guilt under s 89.

Assaulting a police officer

'Assault' is not defined in s 89 of the 1996 Act. Accordingly, it must be accorded the meaning that it has at common law. Strictly speaking, an assault is committed where a person intentionally or recklessly causes another to apprehend immediate unlawful violence to the person. The application of force, whether that be a punch, kick, or the merest unwanted touching, amounts to a battery. It is not uncommon, however, for the term 'assault' to be used in an imprecise manner so as to denote conduct which is in truth a battery. In order to be guilty of an offence under s 89(1), it is unnecessary for the prosecution to prove that D either knew or believed that the victim of the alleged assault was a police officer: *R v Forbes and Webb* (1865). Despite the antiquity of this decision it remains good law. Indeed in *Blackburn v Bowering* (1994), Sir Thomas Bingham MR contended that the ruling 'makes good sense'. Do you agree?

In order to be convicted of a s 89(2) offence, it is necessary that D's conduct not only amounted to an obstruction but also that it was wilful. Since neither of these terms is defined by the 1996 Act, it has been necessary for the courts to consider what is meant by 'wilful obstruction'.

Rice v Connolly (1966). R was approached by a police officer who believed him to be behaving in a suspicious manner in an area where there had been a number of burglaries. R only gave partial answers to the questions that he was asked and he refused to accompany the officer to a police box where it was hoped he would be properly identified. R was arrested and charged with wilfully obstructing an officer in the execution of his duty contrary to s 51 (3) of the Police Act 1964. DC held: allowing his appeal, that to obstruct in the context of s 51 (3) was to do any act which made it more difficult for an officer to carry out his duty. 'Wilful' meant 'intentionally' or without lawful excuse. Thus although R's conduct did amount to obstructing the police, that obstruction was not wilful. R had a lawful excuse; he was under no legal obligation to answer the questions put to him.

Hills v Ellis (1983). D witnessed a fight between two men whilst leaving a football ground. He intervened when he saw a police officer arresting what he believed to be the innocent party. In order to make his point he grabbed the officer's elbow. He was told to desist by another officer, but he ignored the warning and was therefore arrested and charged with a s 51(3) offence. DC held: dismissing his appeal against conviction, that a private citizen had no lawful excuse to interfere with a lawful arrest by a police officer. The fact that D had an innocent motive for obstructing the officer was irrelevant. The criminal law was concerned with intention rather than motive. D intended to do the acts which amounted to obstructing the officer, and he was therefore guilty of the offence.

Lewis v Cox (1985). D's friend was arrested by the police and placed in the back of a van. D opened the van's door to inquire of his friend where he was being taken. He was told by an officer that he would be arrested for obstruction if he continued to open the door. D ignored the warning and opened the door once again as the van was about to pull away. He was arrested and charged with a s 51(3) offence. DC held: upholding the prosecutor's appeal against the magistrates' dismissal of the charge, that the magistrates ought to have asked themselves whether by opening the van door, D intended to make it more difficult for the police to carry out their duties even though that may not have been his predominant intention. Had they done so, they would have concluded that, on the evidence, D was guilty of the offence.

The *actus reus* of the s 89(2) offence, the obstruction, has thus been broadly defined by the courts. Often an obstruction will be active (see *Hills v Ellis* and *Lewis v Cox),* but a passive obstruction will also fall within the scope of the provision, such as where a person refuses to comply with a police officer's order: *see Johnson v Phillips* (1975). The mens rea ingredient of the offence, that the obstruction was wilful, can be further illustrated with the aid of an example. If D was asked questions by a police officer and he invented a 'cock and bull story' (see *Rice v Connolly),* his conduct would amount to a wilful obstruction in that he had intentionally made it more difficult for the officer to carry out his duties. If, however, D answered honestly but as it later proved to be, incorrectly, any obstruction that occurred could not be said to be wilful because it was committed with an absence of intent.

Within the execution of his duty

In order for a s 89 (1) or (2) offence to have been committed, it is necessary that at the time of the assault or wilful obstruction, the police officer was acting within the execution of his duty. A number of cases have therefore turned on this issue.

Kenlin v Gordiner (1967). Two schoolboys were performing an innocent errand when they aroused the suspicion of two plain clothes police officers. The officers approached the boys and one of them displayed his warrant card. The boys did not believe that they were policemen. One boy was held by the arm as he attempted to run away and a struggle ensued during which he punched and kicked the officer. The other boy was also physically restrained. They were both charged with assaulting an officer in the execution of his duty contrary to s 51(1) of the Police Act 1964. DC held: in quashing their convictions, that although the boys had undoubtedly assaulted the officers, their use of force was justified in that it was an act of self-defence in respect of earlier assaults by the officers. Since the boys had not been physically detained for the purpose of arresting them, but in order to question them, the officers were acting outside their duty at the material time.

Collins v Wilcock (1984). A woman suspected of soliciting for the purposes of prostitution was asked to get into a police car. She refused and walked away. A police woman followed D in order to question her and possibly issue a caution. D again refused to speak to the officer who consequently took her by the arm in order to prevent her from continuing to walk away. A struggle ensued during which D scratched the policewoman. D was charged with a s 51 (1) offence. DC held: in allowing D's appeal against conviction, that the policewoman had taken hold of D's arm in order to restrain her. Since this was not done for the purpose of arresting D, the restraint amounted to a battery and was therefore unlawful. At the material time, therefore, the policewoman was not acting within the execution of her duty.

Donnelly v Jackman (1970).D was walking along the street when he was asked to stop by a police officer who wished to speak to him about an offence he was investigating. D ignored the officer and continued walking. The officer tapped D on the shoulder, but it was apparent from D's general behaviour that he had no intention of stopping. Nevertheless, the officer tapped him on the shoulder once again, whereupon D struck him. D was charged with a s 51 (I) offence. DC held: dismissing D's appeal against conviction, that it is not every trivial interference with a citizens' liberty that amounts to a course of conduct sufficient to take an officer outside the execution of his duty. The facts of the case were such that the officer could be said to have been acting within the execution of his duty at the material time.

Mepstead v DPP (1995). D returned to his van to find that one of two policemen was issuing him with a fixed penalty notice in respect of a parking offence. D became agitated and abusive and therefore one of the officers took him by the arm and uttered reassuring words in order to calm him down. Violence ensued and D was charged with assaulting an officer in the execution of his duty. DC held: dismissing D's appeal against conviction, the degree of physical contact in the present case did not exceed that which is permissible by the ordinary standards of everyday life ie it was not a battery. The police officer's purpose in taking D's arm was not to detain him and thus at the material time, he was acting within the execution of his duty.

These four DC cases illustrate the considerations which need to be taken into account when determining whether or not an officer was within the execution of his duty in respect of the alleged commission of a s 89 offence. To detain a person for a purpose other than arrest clearly takes an officer outside the execution of his duty, save where the detention takes place in order to prevent a breach of the peace: see *Albert v Lovin* (1982). Other physical contact which is, prima facie, a battery, may nevertheless be permissible provided that an officer has acted with an appropriate purpose in mind. It would seem, however, that the longer an arm is held (for example), the more difficult it will be to argue that detention was not the officer's purpose. The decision in *Donnelly* has subsequently been doubted, but not actually overruled. Accordingly, it should be confined to its own particular facts.

It is possible to identify in judgments such as Kenin something approaching judicial regret that defendants who have reacted violently towards policed officers may nevertheless escape conviction or have their convictions quashed because the officer was outside the execution of his duty at the material time. In *Bentley v Brudzinski* (1982), a case which involved the unlawful detention of a person by a police officer for the purpose of asking further questions and eliciting an identity, Donaldson LJ suggested that prosecutors should charge D with common assault as an alternative to the statutory equivalent of a s 89 (1) offence. If this approach were adopted, D may still be convicted, albeit of a lesser offence, even where the officer was outside the execution of his duty at the time of the assault.

FURTHER READING

S Bailey, D Harris and B Jones *Civil Liberties: Cases and Materials* (4th edn. 1995).

H Fenwick *Civil Liberties* (2nd edn, 1998).

R Stone Textbook on *Civil Liberties* (2nd edn, 1997).

M Zander *The Police and Criminal Evidence Act 1984* (3rd edn,1995).

SELF-TEST QUESTIONS

1. To what extent have the courts shown themselves willing to intervene in respect of the exercise of police discretion?
2. What purpose do the Codes of Practice made under Pace Serve?
3. Why is it particularly important that the police are always able to demonstrate that they have authority for their actions? What might be the source of that authority?
4. What is meant by the doctrine of implied licence? How might as implied licence be revoked?
5. Where the police have a statutory power to enter premises, what does the case law tell us about how this power should be revoked?
6. Where a defendant is charged with an offence under either s 89(1) or (2) of the Police Act 1996, what requirements must be satisfied in order for the defendant to be convicted?

16
FREEDOM OF ASSEMBLY AND PUBLIC ORDER

SUMMARY

This chapter is concerned with freedom of assembly and the powers that the police have at common law and under statute for maintaining public order. The concept of a breach of the peace is therefore discussed, together with the circumstances in which the police may take action in order to prevent a reasonably apprehended breach from occurring. The chapter also focuses on the offences under Part I of the Public Order 1986 and the statutory powers available to the police for dealing with processions and assemblies under Part II of that Act.

Rights and Freedoms

The traditional means of protecting the rights and freedoms of the individual in English law. For present purposes, it is worth noting that from time to time, English judges have filled of a 'right' to protest. Thus in *Hirst and Agu v Chief Constable of West Yorkshire* (1986), Otton J remarked that:

> The court have long recognised the right of free speech to protest on matters of public concern and to demonstrate on the one hand and the need for peace and good order on the other.'

However, if we think of the 'right' to protest or to demonstrate in Hofeldian terms, it may be that it is more appropriately described as a privilege. In truth, the individual is free to protest or to demonstrate provided that they do so in a peaceable manner and do not contravene any existing law, such as obstruction of the highway.

Breach of the peace

The concept of a breach of the peace has a long history in the criminal law of England. Nevertheless until recently, it was not entirely clear what type of conduct could be said to amount to a breach of the peace. Thus in 1954, Professor Glanville Williams referred to the 'surprising lack of authoritative definition of what one would suppose to be a fundamental concept in criminal law'. The courts had a tendency to refer to the concept in a way that suggested that it was so well understood as not to require definition. Moreover, there may have been a reluctance to define the concept because the courts 'are constantly under the temptation to make it do far too much work' (Professor Glanville Williams). However, when two differently constituted Courts of Appeal did define the concept in 1981, the result was not a uniform definition.

R v Howell (1982). A disturbance occurred in the street due to an overspill from a party. In response to complaints made by local residents, the police warned the partygoers that they would be arrested for breach of the peace unless they returned home. H verbally abused an officer and than struck him whilst being arrested. H was convicted of assault occasioning actual bodily harm. On appeal he argued, inter alia, that the force had been necessary in order to free himself from an unlawful arrest because there had been no breach of the peace. CA held: dismissing the appeal, that both the police and the ordinary citizen have a power of arrest when there is a reasonable apprehension of an imminent breach of the peace, or where a breach of the peace has been committed. A breach of the peace occurs whenever harm is actually done, or is threatened to be done, to a person or in his presence to his property.

R v Chief Constable of Devon and Cornwall, ex p Central Electricity Generating Board (1982). The CEGB sought to survey a piece of land for the purpose of determining whether to construct a power station. Protesters sought to prevent this by obstructing

CEGB's employees, by, for example, chaining themselves to machinery on the site. Despite requests from the CEGB, the chief constable refused to intervene. He claimed that the police had no statutory or common law power to arrest, not least because there had been neither a breach, nor an apprehended breach of the peace. The CEGB sought an order of mandamus to compel the police to remove the protesters. CA held: not granting the remedy, that there is a breach of the peace whenever a person who is lawfully carrying out his work is unlawfully and physically prevented by another from doing it (Lord Denning).

The tenor of these judgments is really quite different. In *Howell,* the CA emphasised the need for violence or the threat of violence before there will be a breach of the peace. In *CEGB,* Lord Denning considered that criminal obstruction itself amounted to a breach of the peace. This latter opinion ought to be approached with caution. It was the opinion of one judge, albeit a very distinguished judge who was at the time the Master of the Rolls, and it was not shared by the other judges who heard the appeal. In subsequent cases, the test laid down in *Howell* is the one which has been preferred. Thus in *Percy v DPP* (1995), a case which decided that civil trespass did not amount to a breach of the peace, Collins J observed that:

> 'In our judgment, breach of the peace is limited to violence or threats of violence as set out in *R v Howell* and any observations which indicate something wider ought not to be followed.'

Reasonable apprehension

Where a police officer apprehends that a breach of the peace is imminent, preventive action is only justified where that apprehension is reasonable. In short, that must be some basis in fact for that apprehension: a mere assertion that a breach of the peace was apprehended is not enough. Whether or not an apprehension was reasonable will be a matter of fact for the court to decide.

Past events may create a reasonable apprehension of a breach of the peace. Thus previous violent confrontations between rival groups, as in *Beatty v Gillbanks* (1882), may create a reasonable apprehension. Similarly, provocative conduct at the relevant time may create a reasonable apprehension of an imminent breach of the peace. Since the reasonable apprehension requirement is a safeguard against unjustified police interference with the freedom of the individual, it is essential that the courts interpret the requirement narrowly. This has not always been the case.

McLeod v Metropolitan Police Comr (1994). The former husband of M had obtained a court order for the return of certain furniture and effects. Three days before the order was due to expire, he went to M's house accompanied by his brother and sister, a solicitors' clerk and two police officers. The officers were there at the request of the husband's solicitors. M was not at the house. The party was admitted by M's mother. They proceeded in loading furniture into a van. Whilst carrying out this operation for a second time, M returned. She demanded that the furniture be put back in the house. One of the officers intervened. He insisted that the van should remain loaded and that the husband should be allowed to drive away. He indicated that any disputes should be later resolved by the parties' solicitors. M took criminal proceedings against her former husband and his relatives for theft. These were dismissed. She also pursued civil proceedings against the solicitor; her former husband and his relatives; and the police. In the action against the police, M sought damages for trespass and breach of duty. Tuckey J dismissed the claim on the basis that the police had been carrying out their duty in order to prevent an apprehended breach of the peace. M appealed. CA held: at common law the police had the power to enter private premises without a warrant to prevent a breach of the peace occurring. This was provided that they reasonably apprehended that the breach was likely to occur. The power needed to be exercised with care. The facts supported the argument that the police had a lawful excuse for entering M's house.

When the case was heard at Strasbourg, however, the European Court of Human Rights took a rather different view of the matter. In *McLeod v UK* (1999), it held that the police officers' entry amounted to a breach of art 8 of the ECHR. This was because it was disproportionate to the legitimate aim pursued ie action taken for the prevention of disorder or crime. In the opinion of the Court, the officers' entry was not justified since at the material time M was not even present at the house. There was therefore no basis for forming a reasonable apprehension of an imminent breach of the peace.

More recently, it has been possible to discern a more robust approach by English courts when determining whether or not an apprehension was reasonable in the circumstances. Thus in *Foulkes v Chief Constable of the Merseyside Police* (1998), Beldam LJ expressed the view that: There must, I consider, be a sufficiently real and present threat to the peace to justify the extreme step of depriving of his liberty a citizen who is not at the time acting unlawfully'. Similarly in *Redmond-Bate v DPP* (1999), the DC concluded that there was nothing in the situation as perceived by the police officer which entitled him to apprehend a breach of the peace.

Private Premises

The decision of the CA in *McLeod* also illustrates the fact that a breach of the peace may occur on private as well as public premises. Thus in *McConnell v Chief Constable of Greater Manchester Police* (1990), where a police officer arrested a person who attempted to re-enter a carpet store after having been asked to leave the manager's office, the CA accepted that authorities such as *R v Chief Constable of Devon and Cornwall, ex p CEGB* (1982) made it clear that a breach of the peace could occur on private land. In the words of Purchas LJ in *McConnell:*

> 'Clearly a purely domestic dispute will rarely amount to a breach of the peace. But, in exceptional circumstances, it might very well do so. Whether those particular circumstances which come to pass on private premises are sufficient to support a reasonable apprehension that a breach of the peace was about to occur will depend on the circumstances in which the preventive steps called for under the Justices of the Peace Act 1361 are taken.'

Given that the police have the power at common law to enter a private house in order to prevent a breach of the peace, such a power must be exercised with care. This is especially important since any entry is likely to be contrary to the owner's wishes.

Binding over

Where a person has been found to have breached the peace, or to have engaged in conduct likely to cause a breach of the peace, magistrates have the power to 'bind over' that person under s 115 of the Magistrates' Courts Act 1980, under the common law, and under the Justices of the Peace Act 1361. 'Binding over' amounts to a person agreeing to keep the peace and/or be of good behaviour for a specified period of time on pain of forfeiting a sum of money (a recognizance) fixed by the court if they fail to comply with the order. A refusal to agree to a binding-over order may result in the person being imprisoned. Nevertheless, the binding over order itself is not a criminal conviction: *R v County of London Quarter Sessions Appeal Committee, ex p Metropolitan Police Comr* (1948).

In February 1994, the Law Commission published a report, 'Binding Over' (Law Com No 222) in which it stated that:

> 'We are satisfied that there are substantial objections of principle to the retention of binding over to keep the peace or to be of good behaviour. These objections are, in summary: that the conduct which can be the ground for a binding-over order is too vaguely defined; that binding-over orders when made are in terms which are too vague and are therefore potentially oppressive; that the power to imprison someone if he or she refuses to consent to be bound over is anomalous; that orders which restrain a subject's freedom can be made without the discharge of the criminal, or indeed any clearly defined, burden of proof; and that witnesses, complainants or even acquitted defendants can be bound over without adequate prior information of any charge or complaint against them'.

In the light of the above objections, the Law Commission recommended that the power to bind over be abolished. The vagueness of binding-over orders was referred to by the European Court of Human Rights in *Steel v UK* (1998). In that case, which was concerned with, amongst other things, the issue of whether binding-over orders were specific enough to be described as 'lawful orders of a court' within the meaning of art 5.1 (b) of the ECHR, the court observed that:

> '... the orders were expressed in rather vague and general terms; the expression "to be of good behaviour" was particularly imprecise and offered little guidance to the person bound over as to the type of conduct which would amount to a breach of the order.'

Binding-over orders were again at issue before the European Court of Human Rights in *Hashman and Harrup v UK* (1999), a case involving hunt saboteurs. Although the facts of the case reveal that it was concerned with behaviour which was *contra bonos mores* ie conduct which is wrong in the judgment of the majority of contemporary fellow citizens, it is nevertheless of interest in the present context since the power to bind over extends to such behaviour. The European Court's finding that the order was too imprecise to comply with art 10.2 is significant. Given that binding-over orders which are made following a breach of the peace may be similarly vague and imprecise, there is a danger that they may fall foul of the ECHR at some point in the future. In order to avoid this possible development, there is a need for binding-over orders to give far clearer guidance to the person bound over as to the type of conduct which would amount to a breach of that order.

Common Law Preventive Powers

The duties of the police have never been exhaustively defined either by statute or the common law. Nevertheless, it is clear that one such duty is the preservation of the peace. Once this is accepted, it follows that the police will require powers in order to carry out this duty. The existence of preventive powers raises difficult issues, not least of which is the scope of those powers. In what circumstances is it justifiable to allow an officer to interfere with the freedom of the individual when no offence has been committed? In a number of cases, the courts have accepted that interference may be justified, even where a person is not acting unlawfully, in order to preserve the peace and maintain public order.

Humphries v Connor (1864). H, a protestant, walked through a predominantly catholic area wearing a party emblem, an orange lily. A number of people who were provoked by the emblem followed H and threatened her with violence. C, a police officer, removed the lily from H in order to preserve the peace. H sued C for assault. Court of Queen's Bench in Ireland held: that although what H did was a perfectly legal act, C's actions, which were an assault in law, were necessary in order to prevent a breach of the peace. C therefore had a defence to the proceedings.

Beatty v Gitibanks (1882). B, a captain in the Salvation Army, led a procession through the streets. On previous occasions, there had been violent clashes with the Skeleton Army, an organisation antagonistic to the Salvationists. B was informed by a police sergeant that he must obey a magistrates' notice directing all persons to abstain from assembling, and disperse at once. He refused to comply and was arrested. B was subsequently bound over to keep the peace for 12 months. DC held: that the appeal would be allowed. The appellants were acting lawfully and therefore could not be guilty of an unlawful assembly merely because other persons were thereby induced to threaten a breach of the peace.

Wise v Dunning (1902). The appellant, a protestant, preached in the streets of Liverpool dressed with beads hung around his neck and waving a crucifix above his head. He used expressions which were insulting to the catholic population. Disturbances and riots had been caused by his conduct on previous occasions. The magistrate found that his language was provocative and bound him over to keep the peace and be of good behaviour. DC held: the decision of the magistrate was correct. The natural consequence of the appellant's conduct was illegality ie a breach of the peace.

Duncan v Jones (1936). D proposed to address a gathering of about 30 persons in a street, near to the entrance of an unemployed training centre. Approximately a year before, D had addressed a meeting on the same spot. Later that same day, a disturbance had taken place in the centre. The centre's superintendent had attributed it to the meeting. Thus a year on, when D attempted to address the gathering, she was told by a police officer that she would have to move to a neighbouring street some 175 yards away. D failed to comply with the direction and was arrested and charged with wilfully obstructing an officer in the execution of his duty. She appealed. DC held: dismissing the appeal, the case stated clearly indicated a causal connection between the earlier meeting and the disturbance at the centre. This was a sufficient basis for the officer to reasonably apprehend a breach of the peace if D were allowed to address the gathering in the street. It was his duty to seek to prevent a breach of the peace, and he had therefore been obstructed while taking steps in accordance with that duty.

A number of noteworthy points emerge from these cases. First, although he did not dissent from the ruling of the court in *Humphries v Connor* (1864), Fitzgerald J did express severe reservations about a principle which entitled a constable to interfere with another's person where that person was neither about to commit a breach of the peace nor perform an illegal act. In sanctioning such conduct in order to prevent a breach of the peace by others, Fitzgerald J considered that the court was making 'not the law of the land but the law of the mob supreme'. Do you agree?

The principle established in *Humphries v Connor* has been extended by *Duncan v Jones* (1936). Whilst the former established that what might otherwise be a tort would not be so if it was done in order to prevent an apprehended breach of the peace, the latter case established that it is an offence to fail to comply with a direction given in order to prevent a breach of the peace. When viewed in this light, *Duncan v Jones* represents a significant incursion into the liberty of the individual. It accords the police wide powers for dealing with apprehended breaches of the peace, subject only to the limited safeguard that the apprehension must be reasonable (see above).

The decision in *Beatty v Gillbanks* (1882) raises some interesting questions. In *Duncan v Jones,* Lord Hewart CJ referred to it as a 'somewhat unsatisfactory case'. He did so on the basis that despite the observations of Field J to the effect that an individual would be liable for the natural consequences of his own acts, the court in *Beatty v Gilibanks* concluded that the disturbances were caused not by the Salvation Army but by the antagonistic Skeleton Army. The issue of causation is a difficult one in the context of public order. Given that disturbances had occurred on previous occasions and that therefore future disturbances were a foreseeable event, could it be said that the Salvation Army had caused those later disturbances? Is it possible to reconcile the decisions in *Beatty V Gillbanks* and *Wise v Dunning?* Might it be argued that the court's sympathies were aroused by the Salvation Army but not by Dunning?

Whether or not the decision in *Beatty v Gillbanks* was correct on its facts, it does represent a blow in favour of freedom of expression and the 'right' to assemble. If the natural consequence of A's lawful actions is that B will act unlawfully, ought A to be prevented from acting as he intended? *Wise v Dunning* indicates that the answer to this question may be 'yes', but is there an alternative way of preserving the peace and maintaining public order?

Public Order Act 1986

Background

Prior to the enactment of this piece of legislation, there had been several rather high profile instances of the breakdown of public order in English towns and cities. Rioting had occurred in places such as London, Liverpool and Bristol. These events were followed by inquiries, most notably those chaired by Lord Scarman into the Red Lion Square Disorders (1974) and the Brixton Riots (1981), which sought to identify the reasons for the disturbances and to make recommendations in order to prevent a recurrence. Additional impetus for reform came in form of a Law Commission Report (*Criminal Law: Offences Relating to Public Order*, Law Com No 123 (1983)) and government Green and White Papers (*Review of the Public Order Act 1936 and related legislation,* Cmnd 7891 (1980) and *Review* of *Public Order Law,* Cmnd 9510 (1985)).

The Public Order Act 1986 was thus greatly influenced by the various suggestions and recommendations made in these reports. Although the Act confers a number of powers on the police so as to enable them to maintain public order, it is not a codification of the law in this area. As we have already seen, the police retain the power at common law to deal with actual and apprehended breaches of the peace. Moreover, certain public order offences are still to be found in order enactments. Section 1 of the Public Order Act 1936, for example, has survived the passage of its 1986 successor. It provides that it is an offence for a person to wear a 'uniform signifying his association with any political organisation or with the promotion of any political object' in any public place or at any public meeting. In *O'Moran v DPP* (1975), the DC was of the opinion that whether or not an article of dress amounted to a uniform depended upon the circumstances of the case. In that particular case, the wearing of berets, dark glasses and dark clothing by a number of men at a funeral did amount to the wearing of a uniform for the purposes of the 1936 Act.

The offences

In accordance with recommendations made by the law Commission, s 9 of the Public Order Act 1986 abolished the common law offences of riot, rout, unlawful assembly and affray. In their place, it created a number of new statutory offences which will be considered further below. For ease of explanation, these will be divided into two categories: riot, violent disorder and affray on the one hand, and ss 4, 4A and 5 on the other. Those features which are common to each of the offences within a category will be highlighted, as will those features which make an offence distinctive.

Riot, violent disorder and affray

These offences have the following common characteristics:

- the conduct which they prohibit must be such as would cause a person of reasonable firmness present at the scene to fear for his personal safety;

- no such person need actually be, or be likely to be, present at the scene;
- a person must intend their conduct to be violent or threaten violence or must be aware that his conduct may be violent or threaten violence; and
- they may be committed in private as well as public places.

Riot is made an offence by s 1 of the Public Order Act 1986. It is the most serious of the public order offences in that a person convicted of the offence may be sentenced to up to 10 years' imprisonment. In the case of violent disorder (s 2) and affray (s 3), the maximum sentences are five years and three years respectively. Unlike riot and violent disorder therefore, affray is not an arrestable offence. This explains why s 3(6) of the 1986 Act empowers a constable to arrest anyone whom he 'reasonably aspects' committing affray.

The offences of riot and violent disorder are committed in a group context. In the case of riot, where 12 or more persons who are present together use or threaten unlawful violence for a common purpose, each person using unlawful violence for the common purpose is guilty of the offence. The requirement of a 'common purpose' is a distinctive feature of the offence of riot. It may be inferred from the conduct of the group taken as a whole. Thus a group of persons who attack police officers during a demonstration could be said to be acting for a common purpose. In the case of violent disorder, three or more persons must be gathered, together and must be using or threatening unlawful violence, though this need not be simultaneous. Unlike riot, however, where it is only those who actually use violence who will be guilty of the offence, violent disorder may be committed by the use or the threat of unlawful violence.

The numerical requirement for the offence of violent disorder is vitally important. It follows, therefore, that if three persons were charged with violent disorder and one of them was acquitted, the remaining two would not be guilty of the offence (although they may be found guilty of a s 4 offence, see s 7(3) of the 1986 Act). This assumes that there were only three persons present If, however, a jury is satisfied that there were others present at the scene not mentioned in the indictment, a conviction may still stand.

In its *Offences against Public Order,* Working Paper No 82, the Law Commission observed that:

> 'The essence of affray lies ... in the fact that the defendant participates in fighting or other acts of violence inflicted on others of such a character as to cause alarm to the public: it is essentially an offence against public order.'

Thus a person may be charged with affray where they have participated in a street fight, even though there is insufficient evidence to charge them with a more specific offence, such as assault occasioning actually bodily harm. Affray involves the use or the threat of violence, although for the purposes of s 3, 'a threat cannot be made by the use of words alone (s 3(3)). Therefore in *R v Robinson* (1994), the making of a threat in an aggressive tone of voice did not satisfy s 3(3) because there was no conduct beyond the use of words.

Sections 4, 4A and 5

These offences share the following common characteristics:

- they involve the use of threatening, abusive or insulting words or behaviour or the display of any writing, sign or other visible representation which is threatening, abusive or insulting;
- they may be committed in a public or a private place, although no offence is committed where D is inside a dwelling and the other person is also inside that or another dwelling;
- a constable may arrest without warrant anyone whom he reasonably suspects is committing an offence under the relevant section;
- the basic offences are all summary in nature; and
- they may be racially aggravated under s 31 of the Crime and Disorder Act 1998.

In order to commit an offence under s 4 of the 1986 Act, D's behaviour must be directed at another person with intent to cause that person to believe that immediate unlawful violence will be used against him or another by any person, or to provoke the immediate use of unlawful violence by that person or another, or whereby that person is likely to believe that such violence will be used or that it is likely that such violence will be provoked. By virtue of s 6(3) of the 1986 Act, D will only be guilty of a s 4 offence if he intended his words, behaviour etc to be threatening, abusive or insulting, or he was aware that it may have such an effect.

Atkin v DPP (1989). Two customs officers and a bailiff went to A's farm to recover VAT which was owed. The bailiff remained outside in a car whilst the customs officers spoke with A inside the farmhouse. A became angry when he was informed that if he could not pay the money owed, the bailiff would have to enter in order to distrain on his goods. On several occasions he stated that: 'If the bailiff gets out of the car he's a dead un'. The customs officers noticed a gun in the house and accordingly left. They informed the bailiff of the threats that had been made against him and all three left the farm. A was convicted by magistrates of an offence contrary to s 4 of the Public Order Act 1986. He appealed on the basis that for such an offence to be committed, the person against whom the threats have been made must actually be physically present at the material time. DC held: quashing his conviction, that for the purposes of s 4(1)(a), the bailiff could not be the relevant person because he was not in earshot and the words were not directed towards him. Moreover, since the words used could only be directed at the customs officers, it followed in the light of s 4(2) that no offence was committed since at the material time, all concerned were within a dwelling.

The terms of s 4(2) underline the public order nature of the offence. D may commit an offence where his behaviour falls within the scope of s 4(1), he is inside a dwelling, and his behaviour is directed at a person who is not in that or another dwelling. However, no offence is committed where D and the victim are in the same or different dwellings. In *Atkin v DPP*, Henry J remarked that the wording of s 4(2) evidenced a clear intention on the part of Parliament to 'exclude domestic quarrels conducted within the home even in circumstances where such words or behaviour would, if repeated outside the dwelling, create an offence'.

For a s 4 offence to be committed, it is necessary that D's behaviour causes another person to fear immediate unlawful violence. In *R v Horseferry Road Metropolitan Stipendiary Magistrate, ex p Siadatan* (1991), it was alleged that Viking Penguin Books Ltd had committed an offence under s 4 (1) of the 1986 Act by distributing Salman Rushdie's *The Satanic Verses.* However, the DC dismissed an application for judicial review of the stipendiary magistrate's decision not to issue a summons on the information laid by the applicants before the magistrates' court. In so doing, the DC observed that the word 'immediate' in s 4(1) prior to the words 'unlawful violence' did not mean that the violence needed to be instantaneous for an offence to be committed. Instead, 'immediate' connoted:

> '... proximity in time and proximity in causation, that it is likely that violence will result within a relatively short period of time and without any other intervening occurrence.'

In the later case of *Valentine v DPP* (1997), V, whilst standing outside a prison officer's house, shouted that the 'next time you go on duty we're going to burn your house. You're all going to ... die'. The magistrates convicted V of a s 4(1) offence and he duly appealed. It was argued on his behalf that the condition precedent on the attack taking place, the prison officer's absence from the family home, amounted to an intervening occurrence and that therefore the violence was not going to be immediate in the sense of a relatively short time interval. However, the DC held that the finding was one to which the magistrates were properly entitled to come. The factual basis supported the magistrates' conclusion that the victims did believe that immediate unlawful violence would be used on them, in the sense of during the same night as the threats were issued.

The words 'threatening, abusive or insulting' which are common to the offences in ss 4, 4A and 5 of the 1986 Act are not defined in the statute. In the absence of a statutory definition, the words should therefore be accorded their ordinary and natural meaning.

Brutus v Cozens (1973). Anti-apartheid protesters walked onto a tennis court at the Wimbledon Tennis championships. They distributed leaflets, blew a whistle and waved placards and banners in front of the crowd. Play was stopped for several minutes whilst police removed the protesters. The appellant was charged with using insulting behaviour whereby a breach of the peace is likely to be occasioned contrary to s 5 of the Public Order Act 1936 (now repealed). The insult in question was said to have been directed at the crowd. The magistrates dismissed the information against him, but the respondent's appeal to the DC was successful. HL held: the word 'insulting' was intended to have its ordinary and natural meaning. Although their lordships were referred to a dictionary definition of 'insulting', it was felt that an ordinary sensible man knows an insult when he sees or hears it. The conduct of the appellant was deplorable and probably it ought to be punishable. It was not, however, insulting.

Where D is convicted of the basic s 4 offence, he may be sentenced to up to six months' imprisonment, a fine or both. However, by virtue of s 31 (1) (a) of the Crime and Disorder Act 1998, D will be guilty of an offence if he commits a s 4 offence which is 'racially aggravated'. An offence is 'racially aggravated' for the purposes of the 1998 Act if:

> '... at the time of committing the offence, or immediately before or after doing so, the offender demonstrates towards the victim of the offence hostility based on the victim's membership of a racial group' (s 28(1)).

Parliament's condemnation of racially aggravated offences is evident in the fact that the maximum sentence for a s 4 offence committed under s 31 of the 1998 Act is two years (s 31 (4)). Where D is tried for the racially aggravated offence and found not guilty, the jury may nevertheless convict him of the basic offence (s 31 (6)).

R v Miller (1999). A senior train conductor approached M and asked to see his ticket. M did not have a ticket although he pretended that he had lost it. When pressed by the conductor, M became abusive. He referred to the conductor as a 'Paki' and continued his racial abuse after he was ordered to leave the train. At one point, M observed that he felt like head-butting the conductor. The conductor had considered that he was going to be hit and he was upset by the incident. He signed off sick when the train reached its terminus. M was arrested and subsequently found guilty by magistrates of aggravated threatening words and behaviour and travelling on a railway without a ticket. He was committed to the Crown Court for sentencing where he received sentences of 18 months and one month respectively. He appealed against the 18-month sentence. CA held: that this was a bad example of a racially aggravated offence. Although the sentence was severe, it was justified by the need to reflect public concern about conduct which damages good race relations within the community and to take account of M's previous convictions for public order and allied offences.

Whilst s 5 is also a summary offence, it is a less serious offence than s 4. This is evident from the fact that in the event of a conviction, the maximum penalty is a fine not exceeding level 3 on the standard scale. The *actus reus* of the s 5 offence entails using threatening, abusive or insulting words or behaviour, or disorderly behaviour etc 'within the hearing or sight of a person likely to be caused harassment, alarm or distress thereby'. In other words, it is the mental rather than the physical reaction to the words or behaviour which is what matters. The *mens rea* of the offence consists of intending or being aware that the words or behaviour etc may be threatening, abusive, insulting or disorderly. In *DPP v Orum* (1988), the DC held that a police officer could be a person who is likely to be caused harassment, alarm or distress by threatening, abusive or insulting words or behaviour. Nevertheless, Glidewell LJ did observe that: 'Very frequently, words and behaviour with which police officers will be wearily familiar will have little emotional impact on them save that of boredom'. Whether or not the words or behaviour do cause harassment, alarm or distress will be a question of fact to be determined by the trial court.

Several distinctions can be made between the s 4 and s 5 offences in addition to that relating to severity. The first of these is concerned with 'disorderly behaviour'. Disorderly behaviour can be the *actus reus* of a s 5 offence, but not of a s 4 offence. The term is not defined in the 1986 Act and therefore it has been left to the courts to determine what is meant by 'disorderly behaviour'.

Chambers and Edwards v DPP (1995). C and E were protesters against a motorway link road. On the day in question, a land engineering surveyor was using a theodolite to take measurements. It was operated by emitting an infra-red beam. C held his hand in front of the theodolite to obstruct the beam. He continued to do so after being warned by the police that his conduct was disorderly and was causing harassment, alarm or distress to the persons working there. E walked in front of the theodolite carrying a placard. He was given the same warning by the police as that received by C. However, he repeated his protest. C and E were arrested and jointly charged with an offence contrary to s 5 of the Public Order Act 1986. They were both convicted by magistrates. Their convictions were upheld by the Crown Court. They further appealed. DC held: the absence of a statutory definition of 'disorderly behaviour' suggested that Parliament had intended that such words be given their ordinary meaning. This was the approach which had been adopted in *Brutus v Cozens* (1973). Whether behaviour on a particular occasion was properly characterised as 'disorderly' was a question of fact for the trial court to determine. There need not be any element of violence, present or threatened, for there to be disorderly behaviour. In the present case, deliberate and persistent conduct which rendered ineffective a machine which the surveyor was attempting to operate in the course of his employment was capable of amounting to disorderly behaviour.

In *Chambers v DPP,* Keene J noted that Parliament had provided certain safeguards in respect of s 5 so as 'to avoid criminalising behaviour unnecessarily and interfering with normal peaceful demonstrations'. In addition to the *mens rea* requirement (s 6(4)), he drew attention to s 5(3) of the 1986 Act. This provides that:

'It is a defence for the accused to prove-

- that he had no reason to believe that there was any person within hearing or sight who was likely to be caused harassment, alarm or distress, or
- that he was inside a dwelling and had no reason to believe that the words or behaviour used, or the writing, sign or other visible representation displayed, would be heard or seen by a person outside that or any other dwelling, or

that his conduct was reasonable.'

The defences provided for in s 5(3) thus represent a further distinction between this section and s 4. One such defence was at issue in a case concerned with a protest outside an abortion clinic.

DPP v Clarke (1991). Anti-abortion protesters gathered outside a licensed clinic. Each protester displayed photographs of aborted foetuses to both police officers and passers-by. They were requested to stop but failed to do so. They were therefore arrested and charged with an offence contrary to s 5 of the Public Order Act 1986. It was held by the magistrates that the protesters could not rely on the s 5(3) defence because their conduct was not reasonable. However, the informations against them were dismissed on the basis that they had not intended the photographs to be threatening, abusive or insulting. The DPP appealed. DC held: dismissing the appeal, that the justices had applied the correct tests in respect of ss 5(3) (objective) and 6(4) (subjective).

Section 4A was inserted into the 1986 Act by s 154 of the Criminal Justice and Public Order Act 1994. It is broadly similar to s 5 although in order to be guilty of the offence, D must intend to cause a person harassment, alarm or distress. Moreover, the victim must actually be caused harassment, alarm or distress. The more serious nature of the s 4A offence is evident in the fact that a person found guilty may be sentenced to up to six months' imprisonment (two years, if racially aggravated, s 31 (4)(b) of the Crime and Disorder Act 1998). By contrast, a person convicted of a s 5 offence can only be fined, even where the offence is racially aggravated (s 31 (5)).

Processions and assemblies

Part II (ss 11-16) of the Public Order Act 1986 provides for the statutory control of processions and assemblies. For the purposes of the Act, a 'public procession' is defined as being 'a procession in a public place' (s 16). This circular definition sheds no light on what amounts to a procession. Accordingly, it is necessary to look to a case decided under the Public Order Act 1936. In *Flockhart v Robinson* (1950), where D appealed against his conviction for organising a public procession contrary to s 3(4) of the 1936 Act, the KBD held by a majority that the conviction should stand. In giving judgment, Lord Goddard CJ observed that:

> 'A procession is not a mere body of persons; it is a body of persons who are moving along a route. Therefore, the person who organises the route is the person who organises the procession.'

It is clear from the above, therefore, that in order to be a procession, there must be movement of a body of persons along a defined route. This contrasts with a public assembly which is a static gathering of persons. For the purposes of the Public Order Act 1986, a 'public assembly' is:

> 'an assembly of 20 or more persons in a public place which is wholly or partly open to the air' (s 16).

Thus s 16 places a numerical limit upon a 'public assembly' which is absent from the definition of a 'public procession''. However, like the definition of a 'public procession', it requires that the gathering has occurred in a 'public place'. For the purposes of the 1986 Act, a 'public place' means any highway and:

> 'any place to which at the material time the public or any section of the public has access, on payment or otherwise, as of right or by virtue of express or implied permission.'

The distinction between a public procession and a public assembly is of practical importance given that the 1986 Act imposes stricter controls over the former.

Written notice for processions

By virtue of s 11 of the Act, the organiser of a public procession is required to give the police advance written notice where the intended purpose of the procession is to: demonstrate support for or opposition to the views or actions of any person or body of persons; or to publicise a cause or campaign; or to mark or commemorate an event. The requirement of advance written notice does not apply where: it is not reasonably practicable to give such notice; the procession is commonly or customarily held (eg the Durham Miners' Gala); or it is a funeral procession organised by a funeral director.

It is worth emphasising that the requirement of advance written notice does not amount to a request for permission to hold a procession. The police do not have the power to permit some processions to take place and refuse others. Instead, the s 11 requirement serves as a means of establishing a dialogue between the police and the organisers of a procession so that a march can take place without public order being compromised. Given that there wili be occasions when a large police presence is necessary, the 1986 Act requires that at least six days' advance notice should normally be given by the organiser of a procession. Such notice must specify: the date of the procession; the start-time; the route; and the name and address of the organiser(s) (s 11(3)). The numbers expected to participate in the procession is a notable absentee from this list. However, in practice, it seems likely that this is a piece of information which the police will request of an organiser if it has not already been provided.

It is an offence for an organiser of a procession to fail to comply with the notice requirement in s 11 or to hold a procession where the date, start-time, or route differs from that stated in the written notice (s 11 (7)). D may have a defence, however, if he can show that he did not know of and neither suspected nor had reason to suspect the failure to satisfy the s 11 requirements (s 11 (8)). Moreover, where the alleged offence relates to a difference in the date, time or route of the procession it is a defence to show that the difference is due to circumstances beyond D's control or that it has been done with the agreement of a police officer or by his direction (s 11 (9)).

Imposing conditions on processions

Section 12 of the 1986 Act empowers the police to impose conditions on a procession. It is a power which may be exercised either prior to a procession being held or during the course of a procession. In the case of the former, it will be exercised by the chief officer of police. Where the procession is ongoing, the most senior officer present at the scene is invested with the power to impose conditions. Conditions may only be imposed on a procession in certain specified circumstances. Thus having regard to the time, place and route of a procession, a police officer is only entitled to impose conditions where he reasonably believes that the procession may result in:

- serious public disorder;
- serious damage to property;
- serious disruption to the life of the community; or
- the purpose of the organisers is the intimidation of others.

Where any one of these pre-conditions applies, a police officer may impose such conditions as appear to him to be necessary to prevent such an eventuality. The Act itself refers to conditions relating to the route of a procession or prohibiting it from entering a specified public place (s 12(1)). However, the power to impose conditions extends beyond these two statutory examples. It may be exercised, for example, in respect of the start-time of a procession.

Banning processions

With the exception of the City of London and the metropolitan police area, the police do not have the power to ban processions. The s 13 power is generally exercised by a local council, with the consent of the Secretary of State, following an application from the chief officer of police for the area. In the City of London and the metropolitan police area, it will be exercised by the chief police officer with the consent of the Secretary of State.

Applying for a banning order is a measure of last resort. It is only to be sought by a chief officer where he reasonably believes that the power in s 12 of the 1986 Act is insufficient to prevent a procession from resulting in serious public disorder. A fear that a procession will give rise to any of the other three pre-conditions for exercising the s 12 power does not therefore justify an application for a banning order. Where a banning order is made, it will apply in respect of all pubic processions or of a specified class of processions within the area. A 'blanket ban' on processions in an area is therefore permissible under the Act. Whilst such a step amounts to a significant infringement of civil liberties, it does avoid allegations that the police are guilty of political bias when seeking a s 13 order. A banning order may last for up to three months.

In *Kent v Metropolitan Police Comr* (1981), the Campaign for Nuclear Disarmament sought judicial review of a decision by the Commissioner to impose a ban on all processions in his area, save for those traditionally held on 1 May to celebrate May Day and those of a religious character customarily held, for a period of 28 days. In giving his judgment, Ackner LJ stated that:

> 'Blanket bans on all marches for however short a time are a serious restriction of a fundamental freedom, and the courts will always be vigilant to see that the power to impose such a ban has not been abused.'

Nevertheless, the CA refused to declare that the ban was ultra vires. In the court's opinion, recent disturbances at marches held in the Commissioner's area meant that it had been open to him to conclude that there was 'a tinderbox situation where a month's respite from all marches was essential to prevent public disorder'.

It is an offence to organise a procession which D knows to be contrary to a banning order (s 13(7)). Moreover, D commits an offence where he participates in a procession which he knows to be banned under s 13, or where he incites another to participate (s 13(8) and (9)).

Imposing conditions on assemblies

There is no equivalent of ss 11 or 13 in respect of public assemblies. In the White Paper *Review of Public Order Law* (1985)

(Cmnd 9510), which preceded the 1986 Act, the government of the day felt that bans on public assemblies should not be imposed because:

> 'Meetings and assemblies are a more important means of exercising freedom of speech than are marches: a power to ban them, even as a last resort, would be potentially a major infringement of speech (especially at election time)' (para 5.3 at pp 31 -2).

The power to impose conditions on public assemblies is to be found in s 14 of the 1986 Act. It is activated by any one of the four pre-conditions previously mentioned in the context of public processions (see above). Where the power is exercised, either before or during the course of a public assembly, the conditions which may be imposed under s 14 are more limited than those under s 12. They relate to: the place at which the assembly may be held; its maximum duration; or the maximum number of persons permitted to attend. Whilst a ban on public assemblies would indeed be 'a major infringement of speech', it has to be noted that in truth something tantamount to a ban can be achieved by the imposition of very restrictive conditions. In *DPP v Baillie* (1995), where B was the purveyor of information as to the time and place of a free festival, a s 14 notice was served on him by police. It contained a number of conditions relating to the time, place and duration of the public assembly, as well as requiring that any event must be licensed in accordance with the Local Government (Miscellaneous Provisions) Act 1982. In the opinion of the Crown Court, 'the police drafted this notice so as to stop the event, not simply regulate it. On appeal by the DPP the DC accepted that there was 'just sufficient evidence' that B was the organiser of a public assembly for the purposes of the 1986 Act. However, the appeal was dismissed on the basis that the uncertain nature of the arrangements with regard to time and place made it impossible to decide whether the free festival would be a 'public assembly' within the meaning of s 14(1).

Trespassory assemblies

Sections 14A, 14B and 14C were inserted into the Public Order Act 1986 by ss 70 and 71 of the Criminal Justice and Public

Order Act 1994. They make provision for prohibiting trespassory. assemblies; offences in respect of trespassory assemblies; and stopping persons from proceeding to trespassory assemblies. The phrase 'trespassory assembly' is not actually defined in these new provisions, although by reading s 14A(1) and (9) together, it is possible to determine what a trespassory assembly is. Essentially it involves a gathering of more than 20 persons on land to which the public has no right of access or a limited right of access. To be a trespassory assembly it is likely to be held without the permission of the landowner, or in excess of any permission and may result in serious disruption to the life of the community or significant damage to land, a building or monument which is of historical, architectural, archaeological or scientific importance.

The police may apply to the local council to grant an order prohibiting trespassry assemblies in their area for a specified period (s 14A(1)). Where an order is granted by the council with the consent of the Home Secretary (in the City of London and the metropolitan police district it will be made by the Metropolitan Police Commissioner with the Home Secretary's consent) it is subject to temporal and spatial limits: it must not last for longer than four days; and it does not extend beyond a radius of five miles from a specified centre. It is an offence to organise an assembly which D knows to be prohibited under s 14A (s 14B(1)). Moreover, it is an offence to take part in an assembly which D knows to be prohibited or to incite another to take part (s 14B(2) and (3)).

DPP v Jones (1999). The defendants were part of a gathering of more than 20 persons on a grass verge adjacent to a perimeter fence at Stonehenge. The area was subject to an order under s 14A(1) of the Public Order Act 1986. Most of the gathering had moved at the request of a police officer. The defendants refused to do so and were arrested and charged with an offence contrary to s 14B(2) of the 1986 Act. They were convicted by magistrates. On appeal to the Crown Court, the convictions were quashed. They were reinstated by the DC. The defendants appealed to the HL. HL held: by a majority of 3:2, that the appeal be allowed. The public had the right to use the public highway for such reasonable activities, including peaceful protest, as were not inconsistent with and did not obstruct the general public's primary right of passage along the highway. The use in the present case had been reasonable and therefore the offence of trespassory assembly had not been committed.

An individual's civil liberties are further restricted by the terms of s 14C of the Public Order Act 1986. This confers a power on the police to restrict a person's freedom of movement by stopping him and directing him not to proceed where the officer 'reasonably believes' that: the person is on his way to an area covered by a s 14A order; and that the assembly is prohibited by that order (s 14C(1)). It is an offence to fail to comply with a direction given under sub-s (1) (s 14C(3)).

FURTHER READING

S Bailey, D Harris and B Jones *Civil Liberties: Cases and Materials* (4th edn, 1995).

D Bonner and R Stone 'The Public Order Act 1986: Steps in the Wrong Direction?' [1987] PL 202.

K Kerrigan 'Breach of the Peace and Binding Over - Continuing Confusion' (1997) 2(1) J Civ Lib 30.

R Stone Textbook on *Civil Liberties* (2nd edn, 1997).

P Thornton *Public Order Law* (1987).

C Townsend *Making the peace: public order and public security in modern Britain* (1993).

SELF-TEST QUESTIONS

1. Why is 'breach of the peace' an important concept in English law?
2. What purpose is served by the requirement that a police officer must reasonably apprehend a breach of the peace before he/she can exercise the power of arrest to prevent a breach from occurring?
3. Why do you think that Parliament saw fit to treat processions and assemblies differently when enacting the Public Order Act 1986?

4. How do the conditions which may be imposed under ss 12 and 14 of the 1986 Act differ? Do the criteria for their application differ?

5. Do the powers under the Public Order Act 1986 mean that the common law powers for preserving public order are now redundant?

17

THE SUABILITY OF THE SOVEREIGN

Closely connected with the sovereignty of the State are the matters of the amenability of the State itself or of its chief executive to judicial process, and the circumstances under which subordinate officers or private individuals may plead, in justification of otherwise illegal acts—tortious or contractual—executive authorization by the State. The first of these questions we shall consider under the title "The Suability of the Sovereign"; the second under the rubric "Acts of State."

As regards the suability of the Sovereign the distinction between the State, as the sovereign political person or entity, and its Government is to be kept steadily in mind, as is also the distinction between the chief executive of the State, often termed its "sovereign," and the State itself.

Non-Suability of the Chief Executive of the State. Historically, the conception of Sovereignty first attached itself to the ruling monarch rather than to the State, and it was not until the rise of modern republican governments with popularly elected chief executives that publicists began to draw a clear line of distinction between the status and powers of the ruler and those of the State he represented. Indeed, at the present time, according to the forms and phraseology of English law, sovereignty inheres in the King; he is the fountain, the original repository of all legal justice; it is his will, acting through Parliament, that creates law; and it is personal allegiance to him that British citizenship connotes.

As is well known, English public law rests, historically, upon feudal law, and it early became a principle of that law that a lord could be sued only by his own peers. Consequently, when the head of a Kingdom obtained a status superior to that of all the other feudal lords, there were no peers who might sue him, and, with the rise of monarchical absolutism this deduction from feudal law, became reinforced by doctrines of divine or patrimonial right.[1]

Blackstone, in his *Commentaries,* states the established rule, together with its reasons,—a rule which has not been since changed,—as follows:

"Our King is equally sovereign and independent within these his dominions, as any emperor is in his empire, and owes no kind of subjection to any other potentate upon earth. Hence it is, that no suit or action can be brought against the King, even in civil matters, because no court can have jurisdiction over him. For all jurisdiction implies superiority of power: authority to try would be vain and idle, without any redress, and the sentence of a court would be contemptible, unless that court had power to command the execution of it; but who, says Finch, shall command the King? Hence it is likewise, that by law the person of the King is sacred, even though the measures pursued in his reign be completely tyrannical and arbitrary: for no jurisdiction upon earth has power to try him in a criminal way; much less to condemn him to punishment. If any foreign jurisdiction had this power, as was formerly claimed by the Pope, the independence of the Kingdom would be no more: and, if such a power were Vested in any domestic tribunal, there would be an end of the constitution, by destroying the free agency of one of the constituent parts of the sovereign legislative power."

As is well known, this doctrine that "the King can fo no wrong," that is, no legal wrong, is, and for many years has been supplemented by the constitutional practice that the King can exercise his governing powers only through some adviser or public official who thereby assumes political responsibility for the advice he gives and personal responsibility, civil and criminal, for the act, which responsibility may be enforced in the ordinary courts, and he cannot justify an act, otherwise illegal, by pleading the command of the Crown. Furthermore, in matters not of tort, the citizen legally aggrieved by the act of his State is permitted, even though not as a matter of strict legal right, that is, *ex debito justitice,* to obtain relief, in most cases, by petition of right or *monstrans de droit.*

Whether or not the Chief Executive of a popular or representative government has an immunity from judicial control with respect to his personal acts has not been certainly determined in the United States, but it appears to be reasonably certain that this is the case. Of course, in his case, such an immunity cannot be rested upon the premise that he has a divine or historical or patrimonial right of absolute rulership, nor upon any basis of feudal theory; rather, the doctrine, so far as it has been asserted, has been upon grounds of practical expediency or of necessity. This is shown by the reasoning of Chief Justice Chase in an opinion rendered in the case of *Mississippi v. Johnson,*[2] in which a motion for leave to file a bill of injunction had been sought by the State of Missisippi to restrain President Johnson from executing in the State certain acts of Congress asserted to be unconstitutional in character. The Chief Justice said: "The Congress is the legislative department of the Government; the President is the Executive Department. Neither can be restrained in its action by the Judicial Department; though the acts of both, when performed, are, in proper cases, subject to its cognizance. The impropriety of such interference will be clearly seen upon consideration of its possible consequences. Suppose the bill filed and the injunction prayed for allowed. If the President refuse obedience, it is needless to observe that the court is without power to enforce its process. If, on the other hand, the President complies with the order of the court and refuses to execute the Acts of Congress, is it not clear that a collision may occur between the Executive and Legislative Departments of the Government? May not the House of Representatives impeach the President for such refusal? And, in that case, could this court interfere in behalf of the President, thus endangered by compliance with its mandate, and restrain by injunction the Senate of the United States from sitting as a court of impeachment? Would not the strange spectacle be offered to the world wonder of an attempt by this court to arrest proceedings in that court? These questions answer themselves. . . . We are fully satisfied that this court has no jurisdiction of a bill to enjoin the President in the performance of his official duties; and that no such bill ought to be received by us.

"It has been suggested that the bill contains a prayer that, if the relief sought cannot be had against Andrew Johnson, as President, it may be granted against Andrew Johnson as a citizen of Tennessee. But it is plain that relief as against the execution of an Act of Congress by Andrew Johnson is relief against its execution by the President. A bill praying an injunction against the execution of an Act of Congress by the incumbent of the presidential office cannot be received, whether it describes him as President or as a citizen of a State."

In the trial of Aaron Burr for treason Chief Justice Marshall, who presided, is reported to have said: "I suppose it will not be alleged in this case that the President ought to be considered as having offered a contempt to the court in consequence of his not having attended, notwithstanding the subpoena was awarded agreeably to the demand of the defendant. The court would indeed not be asked to proceed as in the case of an ordinary individual." And again, in the same case, Marshall said: "In no case of this kind would the court be required to proceed against the President as against an ordinary individual. The objections to such a course are so strong and obvious that all must acknowledge them."[3]

That actions against the President personally for tort or crime, while he is in office, will not lie cannot be said to be certainly established; but at any rate, no such case is to be found in the American reports.[4]

However, the principle is well established that no public official or private individual can justify an act upon his part by a command of the President, or of the Governor of a State, which the President or Governor, by existing constitutional or statute law has not the authority to give. Thus in *Little v. Barreme*,[5] the United States Supreme Court, speaking through Chief Justice Marshall, held that a commander of an American ship of war, in obeying directions of the President acted at his peril, and was personally responsible for the consequences of his act, if the President was not legally authorized to issue the instructions.

Marshall said: "I confess the first bias of my mind was very strong in favor of the opinion that though the instructions of the executive could not give a right, they might excuse from damages. I was much inclined to think that a distinction ought to be taken between acts of civil and those of military officers; and between proceedings within the body of the country and those on the high seas. That implicit obedience which military men usually pay to the orders of their superiors,[6] which indeed is indispensably necessary to every military system, appeared to me strongly to imply the principle that those orders, if not to perform a prohibited act, ought to justify the person whose general duty it is to obey them, and who is placed by the laws of his country in a situation which in general requires that he should obey them. . . . But I have been convinced that I was mistaken, and I have receded from this first opinion. I acquiesce in that of my brethren, which is, that the instructions cannot change the nature of the transaction, or legalize an act which, without those instructions, would have been a plain trespass."

Again, in *United States v. Lee*[7] in which was sustained an action of trespass against certain military officers of the United States in possession of the Arlington estate, formerly belonging to Robert E. Lee, and claimed by the Federal Government as a result of certain confiscation proceedings, the court said: "This right [of the heirs of Lee to possession] being clearly established we are told that the court can proceed no further, because it appears that certain military officers, acting under orders of the President, have seized this estate, and converted one part of it into a military fort and another into a cemetery. It is not pretended, as the case now stands, that the President had any lawful authority to do this, nor that the legislative body could give him any such authority, except upon payment of just compensation. The defense stands here solely upon the absolute immunity from judicial inquiry of everyone who asserts authority from the executive branch of the Government, however clear it may be made that the executive possessed no such power. . . . No man in this country is so high that he is above the law.

No officer of the law may set that law at defiance, with impunity. All the officers of the Government, from the highest to the lowest, are creatures of the law and are bound to obey it."

It scarcely need be said, however, that, in determining the legal validity of orders given by the President, the courts will not attempt to control the political or other discretionary powers that are constitutionally vested in him. This is illustrated by the case of *Durand v Hollins,*[8] which was an action of trespass against an officer of the United States Navy for destroying by bombardment from a naval vessel certain property at Greytown in Nicaragua. In defense, the defendant urged that he was an officer of the United States Navy and acted under orders of the President of the United States and the Secretary of the Navy. Upon demurrer, the court, in the course of its opinion, said: "The principal ground of objection to the pleas ... is that neither the President nor the Secretary of the Navy had authority to give the orders relied on to the defendant, and hence that they afford no ground of justification. . . . The interposition of the President abroad, for the protection of the citizen, must necessarily rest in his discretion; and it is quite clear that, in all cases where a public act or order rests in executive discretion, neither he nor his authorized agent is personally civilly responsible for the consequences [quoting *Marbury v. Madison,* 1 Cr. 165]. . . . The question whether it was the duty of the President to interpose for the protection of the citizens at Greytown against an irresponsible marauding community that had established itself there, was a public political question, in which the Government, as well as the citizens whose interests were involved, was concerned, and which belonged to the Executive to determine; and his decision is final and conclusive and justified the orders given through the Secretary of the Navy."

Actes de Governement in French Law

In the present treatise the writer has not sought to extend his inquiries for illustrations of general principles of public law beyond the jurisprudential systems of Great Britain and the United States. It is, however, worth while to make at least a reference to certain respects in which the French doctrine as to the suability of State functionaries different from that of American and English law.[9]

First of all it is to be observed that the French law does not hold personally responsible, in civil damages, officials, who, while acting as officials, nevertheless without legal right. The State, in such a case, may be held liable, but not the individual. Mr. Walton points out that this doctrine is based upon a juristic theory more subtile than that of the English doctrine of principal and agent or master and servant. "The State is not a master who gives instructions to his servants. It is a moral [corporate] person which, like other moral [corporate] persons, acts by its 'organes'. . . . When a physical person employs a servant there are two persons and two wills to be considered. But when the organs of a moral person act for it, and act within the range of the operations prescribed by law for the moral person, we may disregard altogether the personality of these organs. The will which they manifest is not their will, it is the will of the moral person."

When a French functionary is not acting officially is personally responsible, civilly and criminally, for acts, but it is often a difficult matter for the courts to determine what is, and what is not a *fait personnel.*

The French judicial tribunals exercise the right to refuse to impose penalties upon individuals for violations of administrative ordinances which are illegal because beyond the legal competence of the authorities issuing them. The Council of State *(Conseil d'Etat)* also exercises the right to annul administrative orders if deemed *ultra vires.* Until recently, however, the Council of State made a distinction between simple ordinances emanating from the President, which did not, and "ordinances of public administration" *(reglements d'administration pu-bligue)* which did have to be submitted to the Council for its advice before promulgation. Only the first of these classes of ordinances, it held, might be annulled for excess of power. In 1907, however, this distinction was abandoned by the Council of State, and both classes of ordinance held subject to annulment if in excess of power. "The far-reaching effect of the decision can only be fully appreciated," says Garner, "when we remember that a very considerable and important part of French legislation today is being enacted not by the legislature but by the President in the form of ordinances of public administration, issued in pursuance of legislative delegation. In recent years there has been an increasing tendency on the part of the legislature to abdicate its functions and to delegate its powers of legislation to the executive. Almost every important act of parliament today concludes with the familiar clause: 'An ordinance of public administration shall determine the measures proper for assuring the execution of the present law.' "

The French courts still refuse to question the validity of Acts of Parliament upon the ground of their incompatibility with the provisions of the "Constitutional Laws," or for any other reason. And, as regards executive acts, there are still several classes which wholly escape from judicial control. Thus, as might be expected, and as is generally true in all constitutional States, the courts do not attempt to control such acts of the President as the summoning and closing of sessions of Parliament, the dissolution of the Chamber of Deputies (with the approval of the Senate), and his acts in respect to the conduct of foreign relations. Also, as yet, the Council has not claimed the right to annul ordinances of the President with regard to the colonies, though, as Garner points out, there is now, since the decision in 1907, no logical reason why it should not do so.

There still remains, however, immune from judicial control the class of acts termed by French publicists *Actes de Gouvernement*, which, in a general way, correspond to what in the United States are known as "Political Acts," but which, by some writers at least, include acts which become such by reason of the urgent public need which causes their commission, and which, therefore, would, according to American law, demand justification either under the "war powers" of the Government, or under what is known as the "Police Power" of the State, but which would not give them that immunity from judicial control which "Political Acts" enjoy.

As regards the definition of *Actes de Gouvernement* different writers have expressed different views. As quoted by Garner, Tessier says: "To *govern* is to oversee the functioning of the public authorities, to assure the execution of the laws, to carry on relations with foreign Powers; to *administer* is to assume the daily application of the laws and to watch over the relations of the citizens with the public authorities and the relations between the different administrative authorities."[10] Other writers, however, have defined the class so broadly as to make it possible to exclude from judicial control almost any abuse of official authority, and, specifically, governmental acts for protection against invasion, epidemics, floods, riots, insurrections, etc. "The whole theory," says Garner, "is an arbitrary one; it is hardly consistent with the liberal and enlightened jurisprudence of the Council of State and is condemned by some of the most distinguished jurists of France." This may be true as regards those acts which are sought to be removed from judicial control because of the conceived urgency of the public need for them, but it is not true of those acts which are "political" in the American sense of the word. These, it would seem, are by their very nature, and irrespective of the special circumstances under which they may happen to be exercised, such as to justify the courts in refusing to subject them to judicial control.[11]

Actes de Gestion (Fisc) in French Law.

In French law, and, indeed, generally, in Continental law, a distinction is drawn between the acts of the State with reference to matters essentially political or public in character, and those in which the State appears as the owner of property, or the conductor of business enterprises. When acting in this latter capacity, the acts of the State are known in French law as *Actes de Gestion*, and these in turn are divided into two classes, acts of public *Gestion* and acts of private *Gestion.* As to both classes the State is held responsible in tort or contract, for unlawful acts, in the former class by means of administrative litigation; in the latter class in the ordinary courts. Acts of public *Gestion* relate to the operation by the State of public works. Acts of private *Gestion* are those that grow out of the state ownership or management of property or business enterprises of a character or in a manner similar to that of property or enterprises in the hands of private individuals.

In Germany these commercial or proprietary interests of the State are grouped under the term Fisc or Fiskus, a term inherited from the Roman Law. "In Germany," says Borchard, "the activity of the Fiskus, for which liability is admitted in principle, includes what the French designate as acts of *Gestion,* both public and private. The German State, or, strictly speaking, its Treasury, is liable as a Fiskus, in its character as the owner of real property, of public works, domains, forests, roads, and provision magazines; when it emits loans or derives money from various sources of revenue, notably commerce in tobacco and salt, or establishes a lottery, operates a railroad or telegraph service (though here the officer rather than the State is made liable), or when through its officers it enters into contracts or other acts necessary to the administration or development of these various undertakings. In Germany, Austria and Switzerland the private law of obligations, including contractual and non-contractual liability, is applied to the State to a much greater extent than in France, although, as a matter of fact, while the French administrative courts firmly deny the applicability of the principles of the Civil Code, the doctrines of liability of private law are nevertheless generally applied."[12]

Suability of the State in Domestic Courts.

From the question as to the suability of the Chief Executive or titular sovereign of a State we turn now to the amenability to judicial process of the sovereign State itself. Here, in Anglo-American law, we find no dispute as to the doctrine. Questions have often arisen, in specific in stances, as to whether or not the judicial proceeding or writ is, in substance, against the State or personally against its officials,[13] but the former having been determined to be the case, American and English courts, without exception or hesitation, repudiate jurisdiction, unless the State has expressly or implicitly consented to be sued. Questions also arise as to whether certain bodies-politic, such as the member States of the American Union, or their municipal corporations, or the dependencies of a sovereign State, such, for example, as the Colonies and Dominions of Great Britain, the Indian Empire, or the Native States of India, or the so-called protectorates of international law, have a status such as to bring them within the operation of the doctrine of the non-suability of bodies-politic.[14]

The carrying over of the doctrine of the non-suability of the ruling monarch or titular sovereign of a State to the State itself was effected without difficulty when the proposition was accepted that sovereignty is not an inherent personal or patrimonial right of the monarch.. At first it was sought to locate sovereignty in the citizen body viewed as an organized unit. Later, however, the now prevailing conception was adopted which ascribes this supreme legal status to the State abstractly viewed as a political person. In other words, the State person, as regards the doctrine under consideration, takes the place occupied by the King or Emperor. Thus we find the English Court of Appeals in Chancery, in the case of *United States of America v. Wagner*[15] saying:

"It is contended that this foreign State, being a republic, cannot sue in its own name, and must either associate with it as plaintiff, or proceed in the name of the President of the Republic, or some other officer of state .... It was contended, then, that when a monarch sues in our courts, he sues as the representative of the State of which he is the sovereign; that the property claimed is looked upon as the property of the people or State and that he is permitted to sue, not as for his own property, but as the head of the executive government of the State to which the property belongs: and it was contended, in like manner, that when the property belongs to a republic, the head of the executive, or in other words the President, ought to sue for it. This argument, in my opinion, is founded on a fallacy. The sovereign, in a monarchical form of government, may, as between himself and his subjects, be a trustee for the latter, more or less limited in his powers over the property which he seeks to recover. But in the courts of Her Majesty, as in diplomatic intercourse with the Government of Her Majesty, it is the sovereign, and not the State, or the subjects of the sovereign, that is recognized. From him, and as representing him individually, and not his State or Kingdom, is an ambassador received. In him individually, and not in a representative capacity is the public property assumed by all other States, and by the courts of other States, to be vested. In a republic, on the other hand, the sovereign power, and with it the public property, is held to remain and to reside in the State itself, and not in any officer of the State. It is from the State that an ambassador is accredited, and it is with the State that the diplomatic intercourse is conducted."

Grounds Upon Which the Doctrine of Non-Suability is Rested

It is often the case in law that a doctrine, originally deduced from certain premises, comes to be defended upon wholly different grounds. Thus we find the doctrine of the non-suability of the sovereign State supported by arguments, practical or dogmatic in character, which have little reference to its actual historical origin.

In the early American case of *Briggs v. Lightboats*,[16] Justice Gray made an extended inquiry into the history of the doctrine of the non-suability of the sovereign as developed in English and American law, but supplemented its historical basis by the following dictum as to its practical utility: "It would be inconsistent with the very idea of supreme executive power, and would endanger the performance of the public duties of the sovereign, to subject him to repeated suits as a matter of right, at the will of any citizen, and to submit to the judicial tribunals the control and disposition of his public property, his instruments and means of carrying on his government in war and peace, and the money in his treasury."

In the case of *United States v. Lee*,[17] which has been earlier referred to, Justice Miller declared of this doctrine: "It seems most probable that it has been adopted in our courts as a part of the general doctrine of publicists that the supreme power in every State, wherever it may reside, shall not be compelled, by process of courts of its own creation, to defend itself in those courts."

In a comparatively recent case [18] in the same court we find Justice Holmes saying: "A sovereign is exempt from suit, not because of any formal conception or obsolete theory, but on the logical and practical ground that there can be no legal right as against the authority that makes the law on which the right depends." [19]

This proposition that a sovereign State cannot logically be conceived of as itself the "subject" of legal rights and duties, that is, as the entity in which they inhere, it will be remembered. It will also be remembered that this is a proposition that is relevant only in national or municipal jurisprudence. In the field of International Law it is pre-eminently the States that are envisaged as the subjects as well as the objects of such rights and obligations as international jurisprudence is able to create or impose.

Suability of Sovereigns or of Sovereign States in Foreign Courts

Thus far we have been speaking of the non-suability of sovereign bodies-politic without their consent in their own courts. As a matter of universally observed international comity, municipal courts do not assert jurisdiction over foreign States or their chief executives.

A leading case as to sovereign rulers is *Da Haber v. Queen of Portugal,*[20] decided in 1851, in which the court, by Lord Chief Justice Campbell, said: "It is quite certain, upon general principles, and upon the authority of the case of *Duke of Brunswick v. King of Hanover,* recently decided in the House of Lords, that an action cannot be maintained in any English court against a foreign potentate, for anything done or omitted to be done by him in his public capacity as representative of the nation of which he is the head; and that no English court has jurisdiction to entertain any complaints against him in that capacity. Redress for such complaints affecting a British subject is only to be obtained by the laws and tribunals of the country which the sovereign rules, or by the representations, remonstrances or acts of the British Government. To cite a foreign potentate in a municipal court, for any complaint against him in his foreign capacity, is contrary to the law of nations, and an insult which he is entitled to resent."

It will be observed that, in the quoted statement, the court refers to suits based upon acts of a foreign sovereign in his public or official character. The rule, is, however, the same as to proceedings based upon the sovereign's private acts, and also as to proceedings against his property.

In the *Parlement Beige,*[21] decided in 1878, the British Court of Appeals declined jurisdiction in an action *in rem* against a vessel which, it appeared, though operated, to an extent at least, commercially, was the property of the King of Belgium. The court said: "It is admitted that neither the sovereign of Great Britain nor any friendly sovereign can be adversely personally impleaded in any court of this country. It is admitted that no armed ship of war of the sovereign of Great Britain, or of a foreign sovereign can be seized by any process whatever, exercised for any purpose by any court of this country. . . . Having carefully considered the case of the *Charkieh,*[22] we are of opinion that the proposition deduced from the earlier cases in an earlier part of this judgment is the correct exposition of the law of nations, viz., that as a consequence of the absolute independence of every sovereign authority and of the international comity which induces every sovereign State to respect the independence of every other sovereign State, each and every one declines to exercise by means of any of its courts any of its territorial jurisdiction over the person of any sovereign or ambassador of any other State, or over the public property of any State which is destined to its public use, or over the property of any ambassador, though such sovereign ambassador or property be within its territory, and therefore, but for such common agreement, subject to its jurisdiction."

This same doctrine was recognized by the United States Supreme Court in the early case of *The Exchange,*[23] and has never since been questioned. Another case in which the whole doctrine was exhaustively discussed was that of *Briggs v. Lightboats*[24] earlier referred to.

Still another carefully considered American case is that of *Mason v. Intercolonial Railway of Canada?*[25] decided in 1908. A fairly modern English case is that of *Mighell v. Sultan of Johore,*[26] decided in 1893.

It has been seen that in the *Parlement Beige* the court refused to entertain proceedings *in rem* against a vessel owned by a foreign sovereign but devoted in part to ordinary commercial purposes. As to just how far the immunity from attachment or other judicial process will be applied in the case of property, especially ships, owned by a State or its sovereign, and wholly devoted to commercial purposes, the British and American courts are not in full agreement, nor can either of them be said to have established a hard and fast doctrine.

In *The Maipo*[27] it was held that a naval transport, owned by a foreign government and in its possession, through a naval captain and crew, although chartered to a private individual for commercial purposes, was not subject to seizure under a process of an admiralty court of the United States. The *Parlement Beige* was the chief authority relied upon in determining the general principle of public law. In a second case dealing with the same vessel,[28] in which the action was advanced by a stranger and based upon a tort, Justice Hough said: "Why was a war vessel exempt from seizure? Not because it was a war vessel, but because it was a part of the exercise or manifestation of sovereign power. Why is any other vessel exempt? Why may any other piece of property be exempt? For the same reason, just as the sovereign himself is exempt.... If the Republic of Chile considers it a governmental function to go into the carrying trade, as would appear to be the case here, that is the business of the Republic of Chile; and if we do not approve of it, if we do not like it, if we do not wish any longer to accord that respect to the property so engaged, which has hitherto been accorded to government property, then we must say so through diplomatic channels, and not through the judiciary."

This general subject has been recently examined in an able article by Mr. Charles H. Weston,[29] who summarizes as follows the results reached by him from an examination of the cases.

REFERENCES

1. There is some authority for the statement that the Saxon Kings were suable, and that this rule continued until the time of Edward I.
2. Wallace 475.
3. This immunity from judicial control thus predicated of the President has been ascribed in some of the States of the American Union to their respective Governors. In other States it has been denied. As to compelling the Governor by mandamus to perform a purely ministerial act the State courts are in conflict. See 6 L. R. A. n. s. 750, and 32 L. R. A. n. s. 355. And the same is true as to enjoining action upon his part. Cf. Burdick, *Law of the American Constitution*, p. 127, note 3.

   Goodnow in his *Principles of the Administrative Law of the United States* (p. 108), says: "What has been said with regard to the remedies against the action of the

President may be repeated with regard to the remedies against the action of the Governor. The Governor is held, for example, not to be subject to the process of the courts, but he may be personally liable after the expiration of his term of office for acts done in office. (*Druecker v. Salomon*, 21 Wis. 621.) The State Courts also are almost as careful not to come into personal conflict with the Governors as the United States courts are not to come into personal conflict with the President. The better rule is that they will not attempt to exercise a control over him personally. (*People v. Morion*, 156 N. Y. 136; *Darrett Petitioner*, 32 Maine 508.) The only exception to this rule is in the case of the *quo warranto*. There are several cases where the quo warranto has been issued to the Governor. (*Atty.-Gen. v. Barstow*, 4 Wis. 567; *Morris v. Bulkley*, 61 Conn. 287.) The courts have, however, very little hesitation about declaring an act of the Governor, in which it would appear that he exercises considerable discretion, null and void. (*People v. Curtis*, 50 N. Y. 321; *People v. Brady*, 56 N. Y. 182; *Dullam v. Wilson*, 53 Mich. 392; *People v. Platt*, 50 Hun, 454.) The courts will not, however, interfere with acts of the Governor which they regard as political in character."

4. Mechem, *Law of Public Officers*, p. 396. See also Cooley *On Torts*, 1st ed., p. 377.

5. 2 Cr. 170.

6. The United States Constitution provides that the President of the United States shall be the Commander-in-Chief of the army and navy. Art. II, sec. 2.

7. 106 U.S. 196.

8. 4 Blatch. 451 (1860).

9. The observations which follow are largely based upon two excellent articles, by J. W. Garner, entitled "Judicial Control of Administrative and Legislative Acts in France," published in *The American Political Science Review*, November, 1915 (vol. IX, p. 637), and "French Administrative Law" in the *Yale Law Journal*, April;

1924; and an article by F. P. Walton, entitled "The French Administrative Courts and the Modern French Law as to the Responsibility of the State for the Faults of its Officials: A Comparison with the Common Law," which appeared in the *Illinois Law Review*, October-November, 1918. See also F. J. Goodnow, *Comparative Administrative Law*, vol. II, pp. 149-177.

10. *La Responsibilite de la Puissance Publique*, p. 42.

11. Of course the courts properly assert the right to determine for themselves whether or not a particular act is "political" in character.

12. *The Diplomatic Protection of Citizens Abroad*, p. 137. Cf. Sections 31 and 89 of the German Civil Code. See Borchard, *passim*, for the principles of State liability recognized in other European States.

13. See especially the study of Singewald, *The Doctrine of the Non-Suability of the State in the United States* (Johns Hopkins Univ. Studies in Historical and Political Science, vol. XXVIII, No. 3, 1910); and Willoughby, *The Constitutional Law of the United States*, vol. II, chap. LIV.

14. As to the French doctrine of the suability of the State, Garner says: "Originally the doctrine of the non-liability of the State was the rule in France, but it has long since been abandoned, at least as far as its responsibility for the acts of administrative agents is concerned. The new principle of State responsibility was the result, in part, of the growth of the democratic conception that the State is a moral person possessing duties as well as rights; and, in part, of the enormous expansion of the activities of the State by which it came to be the largest employer of labour. ... In response to this change of sentiment there has been developed in France an elaborate body of jurisprudence, mainly the work of the Council of State and the Tribunal of Conflicts, which definitely fixes the responsibility of the State and which assures to the injured individual reparation such as is entirely unknown in. Anglo-Saxon countries. The basic principles of this jurisprudence is

that the State is liable to the individual not only in contract but also in tort where the tortious act of the agent is not a purely personal act; that is, the State is liable where the injury is due to a fault of service *(faute de service).* The fault may be due to error, an omission, an act of negligence or even want of judgment on the part of the agent. On the other hand, if the injury is done by the agent in his personal and unofficial capacity, that is, if it results from a *fait personnel,* he and not the State is liable." *Yale Law Journal,* April, 1924, p. 616.

15. 1867, L. R. 2 Ch. App. 582.

16. 11 Allen 157.

17. 106 U. S. 196.

18. *Kawananakoa v. Polyblank,* 205 U.S. 349.

19. In this case the court held that the Territory of Hawaii partook sufficiently of the nature of a sovereign State, to render it immune from suit without its consent. It would seem, however, that a better ground for this holding would have been that the Territory, as to the matter in dispute, stood in the stead of the sovereign United States.

20. Q. B. 196.

21. L. R. 5 Prov. Div. 197.

22. L. R. 4 Adm. & Eccl. 59. This case was an action against the ship *Charkieh* for damages arising out of a collision occurring in the river Thames. In bar it was pleaded that the ship was the property of Ismail Pasha, Khedive of Egypt. The court held that Egypt, at that time, had not the sovereign or international status that would entitle its Khedive to the immunity which was claimed. In fact the court had received from the British Foreign Office the statement "that the Khedive has not been and is not now recognized by Her Majesty as reigning sovereign of the State of Egypt."

23. Cranch 116.

24. 11 Allen (Mass.) 157.

25. 197 Mass. 349.
26. L.R. (1849) 1 Q.B. 149.
27. 252 Fed. Rep. 627.
28. *The Maipo*, 259 Fed. Rep. 367.
29. "Action against the Property of Sovereigns," *Harvard Law Review*, vol. XXXII, p. 266.

INDEX

Q

R

S

T

❑❑❑

ENCYCLOPAEDIA OF
ADMINISTRATIVE LAW

ENCYCLOPAEDIA OF ADMINISTRATIVE LAW

Vol. 4

Administrative Law in Asia and Australia

Edited by

S.R. Sharma

ANMOL PUBLICATIONS PVT. LTD.
NEW DELHI - 110 002 (INDIA)

ANNMOL PUBLICATIONS PVT. LTD.
4374/4B, Ansari Road, Daryaganj
New Delhi - 110 002
Ph.: 23261597, 23278000
Visit us at: www.anmolpublications.com

Encyclopaedia of Administrative Law

First Edition, 2003

ISBN 81-261-1478-9 (Set)

PRINTED IN INDIA

Published by J.L. Kumar for Anmol Publications Pvt. Ltd., New Delhi - 110 002 and Printed at Mehra Offset Press, Delhi.

CONTENTS

Preface

In the modern political era administrative law has taken on a preeminent role in regulating relations between the machinery of government and the individual citizen. At its core is the control of power specifically the review by the judiciary of the way in which executive power has been used. Consequently the subject embraces a huge range of issues, some of them highly politicized. In recent years these have included the legality of a ban on blood sports, whether the courts can order a minister to suspend the operation of a primary Act of Parliament, whether a minister can ban certain types of interview from being broadcast, the powers of local authorities to spend public money, or to refuse to do so, the scope of the discretion vested in the police officers to determine policing policy, the scope of the powers vested in the Home Secretary regarding parole for prisoners convicted of murder, whether the courts could declare invalid an exercise of prerogative power, and the availability of damages in respect of unlawful action by public bodies. It will be seen that it is largely the product of judicial activity, although its existence is increasingly recognised in statutory provisions.

The growth in administrative law has to a large extent mirrored the increase in the level of state involvement in many aspects of every day life during the twentieth century, generating the need for a coherent and effective body of rules to govern relations between individuals and the state. Students of constitutional law will readily recognise that administrative law is in reality an out growth of the doctrine of the separation of powers. It is evidence of the judiciary acting as a check on the powers of the executive, and perhaps even the legislature, in some respects. It should not be assumed, however, that any such coherent and effective body of rules actually exists yet. Administrative law is a constantly evolving subject.

In view of the above consideration in mind about the administrative law, that a comprehensive encyclopaedia has been prepared which focuses on the comparative dimensions of administrative law.

The editor is extremely grateful to the British Council Library in New Delhi, the American Information Centre, New Delhi, and the Central Secretariat Library, New Delhi for their valuable assistance in preparing the encyclopaedia. The editor is equally beholden to Shri J.L. Kumar, Managing Director, Anmol Publications Pvt. Ltd., New Delhi for publishing the encyclopaedia in a very short time.

—Dr. S.R. Sharma

1

ROLE OF PUBLIC ADMINISTRATION IN A WELFARE STATE[1]

The study of how a Government functions is not new in this country. How rulers and their servants should conduct themselves is a subject, which repeatedly engaged the attention of our ancestors many centuries ago. I need only mention in this connection Kautilya's famous Arthasastra. The immediate importance of these studies and treatises has to some extent disappeared, but much of what they contain has considerable force even today. We must, however, remember that in those days, the kings were absolute monarchs and could rule at will. The people lived happily when the rulers were bad. During the regime of the British, a system grew up which continued some of the features of the old Indian administration. The administrators were however first of all tax-collectors or perhaps traders . To create the conditions conducive to successful trade, they had to keep the country quiet. In order to facilitate its exploitation, they introduced a few economic and administrative reforms and they brought about a certain degree of modernisation by introducing a network of roads, railways, telegraphs etc. Basically, however, their administrative system was designed to keep the country under control in their own interests rather than to develop it for the welfare of its inhabitants.

Today, there prevails a democratic form of Government in which the people administer themselves through elected representatives, ministers selected by these representatives and civil servants appointed by the Ministers. Outwardly, there has not been much change in the administrative machinery since the British left our country. The Deputy Commissioners, the Judges, the Policemen and the paraphernalia of Government appear to continue as before; but the important thing that we should remember is that all these officials no longer derive their authority from the Crown but from the people of the country. Again the objective of the administration has changed completely. Today, the function of the administration is to secure the welfare of the whole body of citizens and to enforce the rights of every individual, whereas prior to Independence, the objective was to make the State prosperous, the ruler's authority strong, and his coffers well-filled irrespective of the happiness and well-being of the inhabitants of the country. In a Welfare State, one can never under-estimate the importance of the role the administration is called upon to play and we must constantly examine how it functions and whether it is really serving our purpose. To put it in a nut-shell, the affairs of our country are conducted through elected bodies, which function through an executive, subject to the checks and safeguards of an independent judiciary. The Parliament and the State Legislatures decide what should be done, the Ministers and their officers carry out these programmes, and the Judiciary is there to see that they do not over-step the bounds of their authority. Executive authority is wielded at top level by a Cabinet of Ministers; but obviously, the Cabinet, however large and competent, cannot do everything by itself and the actual implementation of its decisions are left to a large body of Government servants ranging from the Chief Secretary down to the village Accountant. These officials, who form the administration proper, function according to certain laws and regulations. Now in dealing with the administration and administrative problems, we must always remember that the administration and the administrative machinery are not in themselves an end but only the means towards the establishment of a welfare State. It is, therefore, of the utmost importance that we study the working of this machinery and see whether it usefully fulfils our purpose, whether it should not be modified or altered and if so, in what manner.

As I have just said we have inherited a frame-work from the British. Superficially, we do not appear to have carried out many alterations; a closer examination will however, show that we have introduced certain important changes. I would quote only three instances; firstly, the large number of Advisory Committees we have set up to enable us to formulate our policies after taking their opinion into consideration; secondly, the Community Development organisation, which has been created in order to bring new life to the country-side and to instil a spirit of progress amongst the millions, who live in the rural areas and, lastly, our new three-tier system of democratic decentralisation. What will eventually be the pattern of administration is not a matter on which I can only conjecture at present. If our organisation is to remain dynamic and if we are to progress, there will be changes— in fact, there must be changes. From time to time, our conception of a Welfare State will change and to achieve this altered pattern, we shall have to forge new administrative systems to suit our purpose.

As I said at the beginning, the study of public administration is not new in this country; but, unfortunately, from about the 16th century for about 400 years, administrators and educationists in our country paid but little attention to it. Even in foreign countries, which witnessed great industrial and scientific progress, sufficient attention was not paid to the study of administration. Towards the end of the last century, however, the importance of these studies dawned on thinking people and, gradually, Government officials, University Teachers and prominent business executives began to devote more attention to administrative problems. This trend has gained increased momentum after the last war. In our case, in view of the fact that we are pursuing a system of planned economy, an efficient administration attuned to the needs of our Plans is a sine-qua-non and that is why the last decade has witnessed the establishment of a number of institutes, staff colleges and training schemes both for Government officials and business executives. Several Universities have already started suitable courses on the subject and I am glad that the Karnataka University has joined their ranks.

In a short inaugural address, I cannot hope to cover all the points which you will do during a course of studies leading to a Diploma. I shall not enter into the academic question of what is administration. We all come into contact with it in one form or another every day: the Post Office, the Railways, the Police, the various departments which collect taxes, to quote but a few examples. I would, however, like to deal with one or two administrative problems. The British created an administrative frame-work to suit their purpose, within which all public activity took place. It had, as model, the English System of Civil Services. In England, however, the Civil Services frunction against the background of an elected and sovereign Parliament and a democratic net-work of local authorities in the shape of Municipal Boroughs and Country Councils. You may perhaps not know it, but in England, law and order, and the control of the Police force is a subject which vests in Municipal and District authorities, all of which are elected. In England, the Civil Service advises and carries out orders, but never rules. In India, however, the old Civil Service was there to rule. One of the biggest problems which faced us in 1947 was how to make use of a very efficient machinery geared to work in a particular direction and how to re-orientate it to suit the requirements of democracy. As you know, human beings do not change their habits at once and officials are human beings and you cannot expect them to change their attitude over-night. Our people also were accustomed to see the administration as an instrument of control in the hands of foreign rulers. They too had to be made to understand that the body of officials, who were to serve their needs, could not function without their positive cooperation. It was a very difficult task indeed. Fortunately, our leaders at the helm of affairs acted firmly and wisely, and, this was how, instead of destroying an edifice, which had been built up at considerable expense, they made it serve the interests of the nation. There were some, who sought to exploit the changed situation but by and large, owing to firmness and tact, our officials, who are after all our own kith and kin, adjusted themselves to the changed circumstances. The success of our Plans, the vast changes we have brought about in the lives of our people, the numerous reforms, which have been introduced, which in the days of the British, one could not even think of, enactments designed to raise the standard of living of our people, bear witness to the success with which we have been able to make use of the administrative machinery we inherited from a foreign ruler. These achievements are too numerous to catalogue; but to illustrate my point, I would only mention a few, namely, the extension of telephone facilities to so many small towns and villages; the spread of primary education; the establishment of new universities; the eradication of malaria; Tenancy reform; the removai of untouchability, and the creation of numerous industries in the Public Sector.

I just mentioned to you that there was a large measure of local self-government in England. In India too, when the British left, we had District Boards, Municipalities and here and there, a Panchayat or two, but the powers wielded by these authorities were generally few and they were constantly subject to official control—which is not a bad thing—but also to official interference, which is not desirable. We are now trying to build up a new type of local self-Government suitable to our political and economic conditions, not with a view to multiplying authorities and organisations, but in order to make democracy a reality. If the country is to move forward and to move quickly, Parliament and the Legislatures cannot do the job. Distances are very great and whilst Bangalore is nearer to you than Delhi, it is still very far away to the vast majority of our people, to whom travel is an expensive luxury in terms of time and money. People must not come to the Government; Government must go to them and this involves decentralisation not merely of powers to officials but also of the authority to decide, and this decentralisation will not be effective unless it is brought right down to the village level. That is the purpose of our recent reforms in the field of local self-Government. How this democratic decentralisation, as it has been called, must function, is one of the most important matters which we have to study. We have redeployed the machinery for taking decisions so as to vest effective power at a level at which it can be exercised by the man in the street himself. We have entrusted wide powers to Panchayats and Taluk Boards and we shall progressively handover more and more functions to them as soon as they can get themselves organised and begin to function effectively.

There is another aspect of our activity which merits your attention. The Welfare State, which we envisage, has, in view of the economic backwardness of the country and in view of the undesirability of concentrating economic power in the hands of a few people, entered the field of industry and set up a number of undertakings in what is called the public sector. This has been done by taking over certain essential undertakings such as the generation and distribution of electric power and transport. Here we had to nationalise a number of concerns, where the prime motive was profit, for which we have substituted service. In addition to these, we have had to set up in the industrial field a large number of factories. In the exploitation of our natural resources, we have had to constitute boards and organisations to extract and market our reserves of mineral ores, oil, gas and manufactures. The rapid expansion of our activities in all these sectors has brought in its wake a large number of problems. As far as raw materials and man power are concerned, we are more than self-sufficient. The question is how to make the fullest use of these raw materials. We have, therefore, had to start schemes of training in the country itself besides sending a large number of our young men abroad for higher technical education. This is no easy task. To work out their training programmes, to set up various organisations required to exploit our raw materials and then to run these organisations, we need a very great number of competent administrators. I can tell you from my own experience, as Minister in charge of industry, that raw materials, engineers and machines alone are of no use in successfully running an industry, unless we have competent administrators to guide and co-ordinate our activities. From where are we to get these administrators? We have been lucky enough to find some among our civil servants, who can successfully adapt themselves to an ever-changing pattern of activity. But running a Government Department is not quite the same as the management of a large business concern. It requires more flexibility in out-look and greater adaptability. Even private industrial undertakings have recognised the importance of management for the success of an enterprise. If our public sector undertakings are to succeed, if our private industry is to prosper and if we are to catch up with more advanced countries, we shall have to train up thousands of industrial executives. I, therefore, earnestly hope that the new course leading to a diploma in Public Administration will devote sufficient attention not merely to administration in Government Departments but also to the art of management in the industrial sector and thereby help us in meeting the shortage of trained administrators.

In conclusion, I would like to emphasize once again the importance of the study of administration. There is a controversy whether administration is an art or a science, or whether administrators are born or made. The important thing in administration is to find out how best we can do a particular job. We can do this by study and by detailed examination; but in order to attain the objective set, we must have a real sense of function. Our Prime Minister has recently stated, in his Presidential address to the Indian Institute of Public Administration, that no administrator or anyone else for that matter can do first class work without a sense of function or without some measure of crusading spirit.

It is my earnest hope, that imbued as our youth is, with a desire to serve, this course in public administration will help us to solve our administrative problems and to produce young men equipped to take their full share in the establishment of a Welfare State, which is our objective.

— *B. D. Jatti*

REFERENCE

1. This paper is a virtual reproduction of the speech delivered by Shri B. D. Jatti, then Chief Minister, while inaugurating the Diploma Course in Public Administration, Karnataka University, Dharwar, on 6th August, 1961.

2

THE DECISION PROCESS IN KOREA

LAW AS A PROCESS OF DECISION

In another context I have characterized the Korean tradition as "alegal,"[1] and there are several reasons for this characterization. First was the traditional aversion to, and the low estimate of, law as a set of rules for punishment. Law as a body of standards applying physical violence in the form of penal sanctions has been a negation of common decency in man. Coercive sanction represented an unpleasant necessity that had to be called into operation with utmost reluctance when the object of its application renounced his humanity by reverting to a state of violence or by injuring the basic fabric of social life. Physical violence, no matter what its justification, has always stood for a negation of culture, humanity, and virtue.[2] On the other hand, a man of culture regulated his conduct according to the code of propriety—the Confucian *li*—which appealed to human decency, not to fear of punishment. So long as he lived by that code, there was no need to concern himself with legal norms.

Second was the Korean preference for mediation and compromise rather than adjudication. Koreans have abhorred the black-and-white designation of one party to a dispute as right and his opponent as wrong. Assigning all blame to one for the sake of rendering a judgment has been repugnant to the fundamental valuation of harmony, because such a judgment has retarded swift restoration of broken harmony.[3] The ultimate ideal has been a complete absence of dispute and conflict. But if discord could not be avoided, society demanded the quickest restoration of broken concord. For this purpose mediation has been preferred, because it does not require the fixing of blame. Parties themselves formulate the solution by mutual agreement, thus obviating the need for an external sanction.[4] Since mediation is possible only when both sides are willing to compromise, each side has to give a little and to be satisfied with less than complete victory.

Third was what Max Weber called the "patrimonial" nature of justice in Korea.[5] "Formal rationality," which he so strenuously emphasized as characteristic of Occidental capitalism, could not be more conspicuously absent than it is in Korea. The Korean perspective has been so thoroughly "substantive-oriented" that it is more often "irrational" than "rational."[6] The Korean approach to decision-making has rather depreciated "rational rules" in favour of special equities and circumstances unique to the individual case. Even when the perspective is said to be "rational" in Weber's sense, the guiding principle involved is "substantive," that is, the so-called non-legal considerations are dominant. "Logically formal rationality," which demands adherence to "rules" and use of abstract concepts created by adjudication specialists, is least characteristic of the Korean approach. No specialist in adjudication has been counted among Korea's national heroes, and no professionalization of such specialists has materialized. A series of elaborate codifications of rules has never been rigorously separated from other value systems such as ethics, religion, or politics. In other words, adjudication never attained that degree of formal rationality that Weber considers central to the modern legal thought of the Occident.

Having cherished a non-formalistic mode of decision in which concrete ethical and other practical considerations have always prominently figured, the Korean process has neither achieved a high degree of logical rationality nor has it considered such a perspective desirable. "Affects," considered by Weber as typical of irrationality,[7] are precisely the things that render life worth living for Koreans, since these are concrete expressions of interpersonal commitment. According to Weber, such traditional value-preferences as loyalty, filial piety, human-heartedness, righteousness, good faith, and affection all clearly fall outside the realm of the legally relevant.[8] Yet these sentiments have been the basic goals of the community and have constituted the ideological basis of Korean decision-making.

Therefore, unless we broaden the focus of our inquiry to include these considerations, we, as students of an Oriental legal system, will have precious little on which to focus. For that reason we must proceed beyond "judicial process" and center on the "decision process" in Korea.

Because every man is a decision-maker, and life itself is a series of decisions, the type of decision in which we are interested is the "authoritative decision." A decision is authoritative when it is in conformity with the community expectations of authority, that is, a particular type of decision is to be made by certain individuals in a manner expected of them. Moreover, the process of decision must be effective if it is to be called "law,"[9] and effectiveness requires sanctions or "deprivations."[10] But the sanction need not be violence; it can be physical, psychological, or both, and it need not be "statal."[11] With such a concept of law, a student of Korea's legal system can proceed with his inquiry.

COMMUNITY PERSPECTIVES OF AUTHORITY[12]

As we have seen, law as a body of rules for the application of penal sanctions has traditionally been associated in Korea with the failure of human decency. A man who was able to sustain his humanity only because of his fear of punishment typified barbaric subhumanness. On the other hand, a man who regulated his conduct according to the dictates of propriety was civilized and virtuous. Indifference to the requirements of law was, therefore, a mark of human decency. This traditional negative perspective toward law is still largely visible among the Korean people as Table 2.1 indicates. Although some Koreans thought that a man who adhered to the traditional code of propriety in the present era of "dehumanized" interpersonal relations was either stupid or doomed, most of them felt that it was better for a man to live without fear or resort to the law.

Table 2.1: Virtue v. Law

A man is said to be one capable of living without law. What kind of man do you think he is?

		N	Per cent
(a)	a good and gentle man	745	57
(b)	a foolish man	222	17
(c)	a man who cannot go on living in today's world	96	7
(d)	other	33	2
(e)	no response	205	16
	Total	1301	99

One might think that the courthouse, as an arena of modern justice, would evoke a feeling of pleasant reverence and awe in the minds of the Korean people. The vast majority of the population, however, has never been to a courthouse. Furthermore, they were proud of that fact. Many of the respondents felt insulted when they were asked such a question, because they regarded it as tantamount to being asked whether they had ever been convicted of a crime. The older respondents in rural areas vehemently protested that they had not only had no occasion to go near such a place, but that they also never had had any need to go near a police station or a government building. On the other hand, younger respondents in urban areas felt proud to answer that they had indeed visited a courthouse on a field trip as a student.

Table 2.2: Visit to a Courthouse

Perchance, have you been to a courthouse?

		N	Per cent
(a)	no	950	73
(b)	yes	281	22
(c)	no response	70	5
	Total	1301	100

The general reaction to this question indicates that to the average Korean the courthouse still symbolizes a dehumanized mode of sanctioning the public order. He feels happy and relieved that he has so far escaped the necessity of getting involved with the process of decision that goes on inside the courthouse. He simply wants to keep away from it as much as possible. He does not even care to be a spectator to the "thrilling human dramas" that are staged inside the hall of justice.

Table 2.3: Urbanization and Courthouse

	Courthouse visitors N	*Per cent*	*Total sample N*	*Per cent*	*Per cent difference (courthouse visitors minus total sample)**
Metropolitan areas	91	32	236	18	+14
Cities	66	24	190	15	+09
Towns	17	06	115	9	–03
Rural areas	107	38	760	58	–20
	281	100	1301	100	

* *These differences between courthouse visitors and the total sample, when scaled according to the urbanization dimension, are statistically significant when tested by Chi Square.*

Table 2.3 analyzes 281 respondents who had been to a courthouse according to urbanization categories.[13] More than one-third of the metropolitan sample (91 out of 236, 39 per cent) had been to a courthouse, whereas less than one-seventh of the sample from rural areas (107 out of 760, 14 per cent) had done so. This is an indication that law in Korea is still an urban phenomenon. Another indication is percentage differences shown in the last column of Table 2.3, which form a clear urbanization scale. It may also be noted here that only 4 per cent of the total sample (51 out of 1301) had been there as a party in civil suit.

When a "legal" settlement of a dispute is proposed, the Korean reaction is less than favourable. According to the modern Occidental myth, it is highly desirable to settle litigation.[14] But as far as a Korean is concerned, a declaration of intention to resort to the law is a declaration of war. Such a declaration signifies a complete breakdown of the traditional mode of restoring broken social harmony. It means that the disrupted interpersonal relationship cannot be rehabilitated within the normal framework of social interaction. Now hostility is taken out of the ordinary context of community living. Even if the proposed adjudicatory process would come to an end, there could never be a "settlement" in the real sense of the term. The ruptured relation would remain unrepaired and perpetuate itself under an official imprimatur, thus barring reconciliation. Koreans believe that war or other combat cannot produce genuine peace; thus open conflict cannot result in settlement. A man who wants a "legal" settlement of a dispute is not seeking a "settlement" but a fight. The unfavourable reactions of the Koreans, indicated in Table 2.4, go beyond any general disinclination toward litigation based on considerations of loss of time and money.

Table 2.4: Perspectives toward Lawsuits

When you are involved in a quarrel or a dispute with another person and he declares to you. "I am going to settle this legally," how would you feel?

	N	*Per cent*
(a) bad	733	56
(b) indifferent	189	14
(c) good	235	18
(d) other	23	2
(e) no response	121	9
Total	1301	99

The Korean preference for non-legal settlement of disputes can be illustrated in many ways. This preference is especially strong when the dispute is between two relatives.[15] When a disagreement reaches an impasse, a settlement has to be sought outside of the immediate family. In such a situation, nearly a third of our respondents chose the legal mode of settlement, as shown in Table 2.5. And yet the majority still chose non-legal modes of settlement. Some of the respondents (52 out of 1301, 4 per cent) had such strong feelings about two relatives going to the law to settle their differences that they could see no way of settling the matter.

Informal mediation whereby the parties themselves formulate a solution through mutual agreement is still the most popular form of settlement. The mediator does not impose his own solution. Since the mediator has a detailed and intimate knowledge of the equities involved and the totality of the circumstances under which the disagreement initially developed and a resolution is presently sought, he can keep the channels of communication open and can assist the parties in formulating an acceptable solution. He does not assign fault or blame, but he does encourage concessions. He is also a channel through which the community expectation for a speedy settlement can be communicated. The community makes it clear through him that peace and harmony must be restored as quickly as possible, and that the parties to the dispute are an object of community disapprobation as potential provokers of open conflict and even violence.

Table 2.5: Lawsuits between Relatives

A dispute concerning a piece of land has arisen among relatives and it has gotten to a point where it is no longer possible to find solution within the family. If one has to turn to an outsider for help in this kind of situation, to whom should he look for help?

		N	Per cent
(a)	to the law	419	32
(b)	since one cannot turn to the law, there is no way to settle the dispute	52	4
(c)	to village (neighbourhood) elders	296	23
(d)	to clan meetings	384	30
(e)	other	8	1
(f)	no response	142	11
	Total	1301	101

If we analyze Table 2.5 according to the urbanization categories, we again find "legalization" closely related to urbanization. More than one-half (122 out of 236) of the metropolitan sample were willing to resort to the law. But only one-quarter (191 out of 760) of the rural sample were similarly inclined.

The Korean reaction to personal injury situations contrasts sharply with that of American "claim-consciousness." Although it is invalid to explain the contrast solely in terms of a single factor, it is nevertheless clear that the difference in community expectations of the two cultures is an important element accounting for the contrast. It has often been pointed out that Americans are so claim-conscious because of the existence of a large-scale and comprehensive liability insurance system. But it seems there is no reason why an equally strong argument cannot be made in favour of explaining the development of a liability insurance scheme as an institutional response to the claim-consciousness of the people. Given the "litigiousness" of the American people, it would be foolhardy indeed not to carry liability insurance. This is especially true since the American claim-consciousness is not always focused exclusively on those who are insured. Tables 2.6 through 2.9 illustrate the contrast.

Table 2.6: Traffic Accidents and Law

The driver of a bus or a truck wrongfully injures you severely. What would you do?

		N	*Per cent*
(a)	nothing I can do	46	4
(b)	it is up to him to do whatever is necessary and right	149	12
(c)	negotiate and compromise	534	41
(d)	go to the law	436	34
(e)	other	6	0
(f)	no response	130	10
	Total	1301	101

In Table 2.6, most of the respondents wanted to know whether the driver "intended" to injure them or not. If the driver did not intend to cause injury, many of them did not see why the poor man should be dragged through a legal proceeding. Legal technicalities such as holding the owner of the vehicle (who may not be a poor man like the driver but a wealthy corporation head) liable rarely occurred to them. It should perhaps be added that very few respondents mentioned consulting a lawyer in any of the situations covered by the questionnaire.[16]

Table 2.7 analyzes, according to urbanization categories, 195 respondents in Table 2.6 who either could do nothing or were willing to accept whatever was offered. Thus, with respect to the passive surrendering of one's claim in Table 2.6, the difference between the metropolitan and rural areas is again pronounced.

Table 2.7: Urbanization and Claim-Consciousness

	Apathetic		*Total sample*		*Per cent difference (apathetic minus total sample)**
	N	*Per cent*	*N*	*Per cent*	
Metropolitan areas	17	09	236	18	–09
Cities	28	14	190	15	–01
Towns	25	13	115	9	+4
Rural areas	125	64	760	58	+06
	195	100	1301	100	

* *Statistically significant differences.*

Here, the legal action was for medical expenses only. Even this limitation of the claim allowed only 10 per cent of the sample to choose the alternative of suing. The typical rural response was that, having taken the risk deliberately, there was no one but oneself to blame for the mishap, for it was careless not to have stayed away from the dangerous bridge. Moreover, most of them expressed bewilderment as to whom they could possibly sue. A more enlightened response was to notify the appropriate governmental authority so as to facilitate a speedy repair of the bridge without suing anyone.

Table 2.8: Government Liability

A bridge on a public highway is in disrepair. While you are crossing that bridge, you fall through a hole and severely injure yourself. What would you do?

		N	*Per cent*
(a)	sue for medical expenses	135	10
(b)	nothing I can do, because it was my fault that I was injured	954	73
(c)	other	79	6
(d)	no response	133	10
	Total	1301	99

Table 2.9: Urbanization and Claims against Government

	Medical claimants		*Total sample*		*Per cent difference (medical claimants minus total sample)**
	N	*Per cent*	*N*	*Per cent*	
Metropolitan areas	55	41	236	18	23
Cities	17	13	190	15	—02
Towns	10	7	115	9	–02
Rural areas	53	39	760	58	–19
	135	100	1301	100	

* *Statistically significant differences.*

Table 2.9 contains the analysis by urbanization categories of the 135 respondents who were willing to sue for medical expenses in Table 2.8. As would be expected from our prior findings, metropolitan residents are decidedly more claim-conscious than the rural dwellers.

In no society has the concept of property ownership attained "absoluteness" from the beginning. As Weber points out, even the Roman concept of *dominium* achieved the status of "a particularly abstractly ordered institution" rather late in the development of the legal system.[17] The individualistic, common law concept of "title" is of relatively recent origin. In the case of Korea, the concept of property ownership lacks the logically formal abstractness it has in the West. Property rights of the individual are still determined largely on the basis of mutual compromise and practical utility, not in terms of abstract law. The exercise of property right is still subject to "particularistic" considerations involved in each concrete case. Table 2.10 illustrates the point.

Table 2.10: Sympathy v. Property Right

(A) During a severely cold winter, a destitute family in desperate need of shelter secretly erects a shanty on a piece of land you own. What would you do when you discover this fact?

		N	*Per cent*
(a)	let them stay on	1044	80
(b)	make them move out	93	7
(c)	other	38	3
(d)	no response	126	10
	Total	1301	100

(B) Now, you have to use the land in a hurry. You tell them to move out. But they refuse to do so. What would you do?

		N	*Per cent*
(a)	nothing I can do	370	28
(b)	take legal action	192	15
(c)	pay them some money and have them move out	529	41
(d)	forcibly evict	0	0
(e)	other	42	3
(f)	no response	168	13
	Total	1301	100

The overriding concern in the minds of the Koreans is to maintain one's humanity. Many a Korean would rather suffer loss of property in order to preserve basic decency as a neighbour, i.e. his "face." If a man is driven by hunger and cold to invade another's property right, humanitarian sentiments demand that the owner let the trespasser stay. That is especially true if the property is not being put to use. Also, from a more utilitarian vantage point, the owner expects to retain community approval of him as a decent human being, although at the same time he hopes the destitute trespasser will reciprocate by moving out quickly if requested. But even when the squatter refuses to reciprocate the favour of the owner, the latter is still reluctant to take legal action.

As Table 2.10 indicates, it is customary for the Korean property-owner to give some money to the squatter so that he might settle elsewhere. Of course, it should be noted that squatting is much more an urban than a rural phenomenon. The metropolitan areas of Korea are being swamped with former rural dwellers seeking a better life. Not a small proportion of these newcomers, however, are those who have found themselves compelled to discontinue their rural life under circumstances that indicate their inability to conform to rural community standards of rectitude. Consequently, landowners in urban centers have had to put up with this problem, and the result has been some bitterness on their part. But the practice of paying the squatter to leave the land is still a standard one.[18]

Nearly one-third of our metropolitan sample (78 out of 236, 33 per cent) were willing to resort to the legal process while less than one-tenth of the rural sample (74 out of 760, 10 per cent) were willing to do so. Thus, we see once again that "legal consciousness" or the consciousness of one's legal rights and willingness to act on them increases with urbanization.

The particularistic concept of justice also prevails in criminal law. That happens partly because once a matter is placed in the hands of the police, the normal procedure for achieving reconciliation is rendered unavailable. If there is a theft, a Korean sees the wrong as done to the victim, not to the state; thus he must decide whether the thief should be prosecuted. For that reason, some Koreans find it difficult to report a thief to the police. It is hard for a man with a criminal conviction to regain standing in the community. According to the traditional way of thinking, he has, for the most part, lost his humanity in the eyes of the community. Penal sanction has always been a very serious matter. It is not humane to take a wrongdoer to the police; better to let him have an opportunity to atone for his wrong. Since the Korean concept of guilt is interpersonal rather than transcendental, the atonement is with the victim, not with God or the law. If the victim is willing to forgive, there can be reconciliation without the intervention of law, which only formalizes and perpetuates the ruptured social harmony. The traditional procedure of freezing the offender out of the community through ostracism leaves the door open for atonement and reconciliation.

From an Occidental perspective, the particularistic mode of criminal justice appears to be amorphous and wishy-washy. A strong sense of injustice seems to be totally lacking among Koreans. A guilty man usually is allowed to come back to society without being compelled to "pay his debt to the society." It is clear that under the particularistic system of criminal justice the "debt" a criminal owes to his society is never clearly specified. The size of the debt varies considerably from person to person according to a host of factors that have to be taken into account. Since the application of a universalistic standard in the specification of the debt itself is strongly resisted, the concept of guilt always remains personal, relative, and amorphous.

During the interviews it was apparent that many respondents were trying to give the "right" answers rather than what they genuinely thought they would do under the circumstances. But it is significant that a surprisingly large proportion of the sample admitted their reluctance to volunteer information to the police. As soon as the element of the thief's poverty and the contrasting wealth of the victim was injected into the consideration, there was a dramatic shift in the pattern of response. Now a clear majority admitted their unwillingness to bring the wretched thief to justice. The percentage is especially significant if we take into account that such an admission was a "wrong" response to make to an outsider. It should also be added that at the time the government had been conducting a gigantic propaganda campaign throughout the country exhorting people to give active assistance to the authorities in apprehending Communist saboteurs and spies smuggled into the country from the north. The government was also offering large sums of money for information leading to such an apprehension.

Table 2.11: Hunger and Theft

(A) If you saw a man steal, what would you do?

		N	*Per cent*
(a)	would report him to the police	740	57
(b)	would be difficult to report him to the police	415	32
(c)	other	20	2
(d)	no response	126	10
	Total	1301	101

(B) A man who is extremely poor and on the verge of starvation goes into a rich man's house and steals. You happen to see him steal. What would you do?

		N	*Per cent*
(a)	would report him to the police	402	31
(b)	would be difficult to report him to the police	748	58
(c)	other	13	1
(d)	no response	138	11
	Total	1301	101

COMMUNITY DEMANDS ON THE DECISION-MAKER

Included in community perspectives of authority are the demands of the community on the decision-maker to make socially relevant decisions in conformity with community expectations. Such demands need not be formally expressed through institutionalized procedures of decision-making. As an important part of community authority, the ability to comply with demands becomes an important factor in the evaluation of the competence and the authority of the decision-maker. It has often been pointed out that in an informally structured setting, the authority of the decision-maker in terms of his ability to conform to the community perspectives is of crucial importance. In a formally structured setting, such as a highly rationalized bureaucracy, the mere fact of appointment to a position often gives the decision-maker sufficient authority or "legitimacy." But a mediator or arbitrator who disregards the demands of the community not only loses his authority in the instant decision, he also loses it for future decisions. A mediator could scarcely be said to be acting authoritatively if he insists on specifying the legal rights of the parties or otherwise attempts to apply a universalistic standard in a community where he is expected merely to assist the parties to reach an agreement or a settlement. In this connection, Table 2.12 is of interest. It should be noted that the question was which of the two was a better *policeman,* not a better *man.* A decision-maker, even a policeman, who insists on strict application of formal law is not acting in conformity with the community perspectives of authority.

Table 2.12 Strictness and Leniency

One policeman uncovers each and every infraction of the law and has the offender punished in each and every case. Another policeman tries to be lenient in most cases, seeking prosecution of only gross offenders. Which of these two policemen do you think is the better policeman?

		N	*Per cent*
(a)	one who strictly enforces the law	437	34
(b)	one who tries to be as lenient as possible	674	52
(c)	other	8	1
(d)	no response	182	14
	Total	1301	101

To gain an understanding of the current Korean perspectives of authority, it is useful to delineate the traditional ones. For this purpose, the book, *Oknangchachon,* which was popular among the common people of Korea in the eighteenth and nineteenth centuries, will be summarized. As was customary in the other popular stories of the period, the novel's author is unknown. Typical also is the didactic aim of *Oknangchachon.* It is presented here because it deals with the Korean "judicial decision" process in a criminal prosecution and illustrates traditional Korean perspectives of authority. The story attempts to narrate in all seriousness what was thought to be the "ideal" mode of administering the criminal process at that time.

A girl named Konang is engaged to a young man in a distant village. The young man sets out for the girl's house to be married and to bring back the bride to his home. On the way, the groom's entourage gets into trouble with a group of obnoxious servants of a local nobleman. In the ensuing scuffle, one of the hostile servants is killed by the groom's servants. As the man responsible for the killing, the groom is arrested and put in jail, awaiting his trial and sentence. The girl hears the tragic news, and after a suitable interval of lamentation and grief, she secretly decides to rescue her betrothed. She dresses as a young man, travels a considerable distance to the jail, and bribes the jail-keeper to permit her to take the place of her lover. The young man at first refuses to go along with this foolhardy scheme. But the girl insists that since she has promised to be his wife, she is now his spouse for all practical purposes. Should her betrothed be executed or otherwise punished, she would become a widow or a wife of a convicted killer. By taking his place in jail, she will be exchanging her miserable future as a widow for the life of a convicted woman, while her betrothed would be saved from infamy. She also insists that, as a female, her life is much less valuable than his, for he is a young man with a promising future. The young man finally agrees to the scheme and runs away, leaving his fiancee behind. All those who have witnessed the scene, including the bribed jail-keeper, are deeply moved by the noble deed of self-sacrifice and loyalty.

A few days later in the courtyard of the government house the public trial begins, and almost immediately it is discovered that the prisoner is an imposter. The girl confesses her deeds in detail. Upon hearing the moving story, the" magistrate is overwhelmed by the sheer beauty and goodness of the loyalty and virtuous devotion of the girl. He forgives not only the girl but her betrothed as well. He is overjoyed that such goodness and virtue manifested themselves in his jurisdiction. He sends a report to the royal court, which in turn is very much pleased by the glad tiding. The king grants the couple an audience and appoints the young man to a local magistracy. The couple's virtue so permeates the entire jurisdiction that dissension and immorality disappear from the populace. The agricultural harvest in the jurisdiction continues to be bountiful for years. The people are happy and content. The hero is eventually promoted to the governorship of a large province. His virtuous wife also receives a title of honor commensurate with the exalted position of her husband. The couple rules by such virtuous example that prosperity reigns throughout the province. Harmony and virtue among the people are such that the government house becomes desolate and officials have no business to transact. Finally, the entire kingdom is filled with peace, virtue, and prosperity.

It is clear from this that the logically formal rationality of the judicial decision is not a part of the demand placed upon the decision-maker by the Korean people. It is precisely such "legally irrevelant" factors as ethical integrity and virtuous example that are relevant in the decision-making. The ultimate goal was the "non-activity" of the decision process—a process wherein formal rationality has little relevance.

PROCESS OF DECISION: THE TRADITIONAL MODE

Conciliation and mediation are still the most popular and prevalent forms of settling disputes in Korea today. A distinction could be drawn between these two forms of settlement on the basis of the degree of participation by a third party in the decision process. In the case of conciliation, the disputants themselves achieve agreement with little participation by a third party. In the case of mediation, participation by a mediator is an important feature. But the two forms share a fundamental similarity in that they both presuppose the disputants themselves to be the principal decision-makers. Even in the case of mediation the role of the mediator is not that of a judge. He merely assists the disputants in formulating a solution that is acceptable to both sides. Although the processes of decision involved in conciliation and mediation have received systematic attention from scholars even in the Asian context, we shall briefly outline the principal features of these processes in Korea. Because mediation involves a third party as a decision-maker, it comes closer to the "judicial" decision process, so we shall narrow our focus to mediation for the purpose of facilitating a comparative analysis between the traditional and the new processes.

The whole process of mediation is marked by informality. Outside such westernized, special fields as labour and commercial legislation that affect a small segment of the nation in urban centers, there is no formal institutionalization of this process. Nor are there professional specialists in mediation. In spite of a few very recent attempts to institutionalize mediation as a part of the formal judicial process, it remains informal in Korea.

As a rule, no formal qualification is required of a mediator. But it is essential that he be a decent human being. The degree of decency is, of course, left amorphous; the ultimate test is the acceptance by the disputants of him as a mediator. Even if a man possesses great wealth and education, he could still turn out to be an ineffectual mediator. In this respect, the earthy wisdom of an uneducated farmer may be better equipment than a university degree. A high social status may be helpful, but it can militate against the mediator's effort to establish rapport with the disputants if the disparity between them is substantial. By the force of his authority, he may impose his wishes upon the parties. But if he does so, he can not be considered an ideal mediator. Age may be another factor that affects the mediator's performance. To be sure, a chronological seniority always entitles a man to a certain amount of deference from his juniors. But a disparity in age can be a handicap just as much as political honour. Effective mediators are men who have affable personalities, patience, experience in mediation, knowledge of the background of the dispute, and compatibility with both sides in terms of social class, age, and wealth.

The disputants do not always select a mediator. A man might appoint himself as mediator, provided, of course, that he is accepted by both parties. Indeed, some meddlesome characters offer their good offices unsolicited, but they are usually soon informed that their services are unwanted. Inasmuch as a successful mediation enhances a man's stature considerably, every Korean feels an urge to try his hand. Sometimes a total stranger may be invited to mediate so long as the disputants like the stranger's personality. It is not so much his lack of prejudice or partiality that is important, for impartiality is not a prerequisite. The fact that a man is in a special relationship with one side of the dispute may make him a better mediator because he can be more persuasive with this party.

An effective mediator does not try to impose his decision. He only suggests a solution. Any amount of coercion he may exercise is directed toward compelling the parties to get together and reach some sort of agreement. The reactions of the community are an important criterion by which to evaluate the reasonableness and the good intention of the parties. The mediator will be quick to point out whether, under the circumstances, a particular solution proposed by one side conforms to the community standard of reasonableness. Other members of the community will make their views known to the mediator. What is reasonable and appropriate under the circumstances of the particular case will be gradually clarified by the community through the mediator.

In this process the central concern is to discover what is proper and decent, not so much what is legal. There is no codified criterion of what is right or wrong. A good, and therefore a right, solution is what the parties can agree on and approve. In this sense "the law" is what the disputants approve through mediation.[19] There is little concern that the settlement be a good example for the future. The particular solution need not even be socially just. As long as it is approved by the parties of this particular case, it is a just and good solution. Since no two disputes can be identical in all respects, the solution for this particular case is not, and ought not to be, intended for solving future disputes. The parties to future disputes must specify their own solutions anew in the light of the particular circumstances in which they find themselves.

A successful settlement must be accompanied by a full restoration of the amicable relationship that had existed between the parties before the development of the dispute. In fact, the restored relationship may be much more cordial than the one that had existed. An aloof relationship may be turned into a warm and affectionate one because of a dispute and its successful resolution. The degree of success or failure of a mediation will thus be determined by the quality of the relationship between the disputants subsequent to the settlement. A successful settlement in Korea will be customarily celebrated by a festive repast and sealed by convivial drinking.

It has been pointed out that such a traditional mode of dispute settlement as mediation cannot long remain effectual in communities larger than the village. In view of the rapidity with which traditional village life is disintegrating in Korea, it may be argued that the traditional mode of dispute settlement is doomed even there. As we have seen, mediation is a decision process by means of which the whole community enforces its standards of propriety and decency by making its standards tangible through the compromises reached by the mediator and the disputants themselves. This presupposes the existence of a defined set of norms and values that are amenable to complex processes of adjustments, and equilibrations required by the infinite number of variations involved in considering each dispute. If we examine the number of combinations made possible by balancing the social statuses of two disputants, it is easy to realize the complexities involved in achieving some kind of consensus when familial, biological, economic, educational, biographical, and personality factors are also added to the scale.

Such a complex task of equilibration is not too difficult so long as the community standards retain strength and vitality. As soon as they begin to fluctuate, however, it becomes very difficult. Nevertheless, the vitality of the community preference for mediation remains amazingly strong in Korea notwithstanding that the country is undergoing a rapid change in every aspect of community life. The stability of the community standards has been successively undermined by the Japanese colonization, the division of the country, and the military occupation by the Soviet and the United States armies immediately following the departure of the Japanese. The Korean War contributed its share of disruptive effects. But in spite of these and other forces conspiring to upset the viability of the traditional perspectives, the Korean partiality for conciliation and mediation remains, at least in South Korea, very much alive and strong.

PROCESS OF DECISION: THE EMERGING MODALITY

Faced with a strong native proclivity to eschew law and adjudication in favour of more informal procedures of mediation, the modern Korean legal system of European origin has been subjected to a process of indigenization almost in spite of itself. So long as were strict our observation to the formal provisions of the written laws and official organizational structures, we find little that could be suggestive of the on-going process of adaptation to the indigenous milieu. Those specialists who participate in the judicial decision process are, in their professional capacity, invariably reluctant to acknowledge the significance or even the existence of such a process of adjustment. To them, such modification adulterates the advanced model. They are apprehensive of such regression and reversion. They even feel ashamed to admit the tenacity of "feudal" vestiges. As custodians of the modern system, these specialists feel they have an obligation to prevent "backsliding."

An attempt will now be made to delineate the emerging pattern of the judicial decision process in Korea on the basis of experience and observation of those who have participated in that process. The attempt is necessarily preliminary and tentative because of the lack of systematic empirical data. There are several reasons for this. First is the relatively minor importance attached to the judicial process in Korea. As a part of the community power process, the courts have been allowed only an insignificant role. With respect to wealth, family, and other values, the Korean courts have been able to affect a very small segment of the community life. The decisions of the highest court are rarely reported in the press. Only spectacular family scandals and murder trials excite the curiosity of the public.

Second is a feeling among students of the power process, as well as among the legal profession, that the judicial process in Korea has not yet reached that stage of development where it can be considered sufficiently "mature." It is often observed that, having had less than two decades of self-government and a large portion of that wasted by war, the Korean judiciary has not yet been able to emerge with its own developed personality. As a result, students of Korean power process have been wary of attempting to delineate the "Korean" judicial process. But even if it be true that this judicial process has not yet matured, the process of maturation itself should be of keen interest to the student of law and society. Moreover, the Korean judiciary does seem to be emerging in very recent years with its own distinct personality.

The scarcity of dissent is a more serious obstacle to empirical analysis of judicial behavior.[20] In Korea lower courts dissent is almost unknown, and before 1960 there was little dissent in the Supreme Court. Since 1960 a few dissents have begun to appear, though their number is not large enough for any meaningful analysis. During the past few years, one Supreme Court judge in particular has come to be identified as a dissenter. But a tradition of "great dissent" has not yet been established. In fact, one can detect a certain note of annoyance when the alleged propensity to dissent is pointed out. Furthermore, the "dissenter" himself would consider such a designation rather detractive.

The reason for the paucity of dissenting opinions, of course, does not lie in any legislative injunction against dissent. On the contrary, the Court Organization Law provides that each judge of the highest court who participates in a decision is to write his opinion (Art. 20).[21] The law also contains a detailed provision for voting among the judges, the basic principle being the decision by a simple majority (Art. 59). The current practice is for a dissenting judge to append his signed opinion at the end of the majority decision. The twelve judges of the Supreme Court are divided into three petty benches composed of four judges each. Therefore, when a petty bench is evenly divided, another bench joins the divided group to break the tie.

The general prevalence of unanimity in the Korean judicial decision process can better be explained if we turn once again to the traditional perspectives of authority. The Koreans have never accepted the notion that a decision can be legitimated by a numerical superiority of its supporters. A military battle may be won by a numerical superiority, but a dispute cannot be settled by dissension among the decision-makers. Jeopardized harmony can be repaired only through consensus. To Koreans, a majority decision can achieve only a temporary lull, never a viable peace. It must be remembered that what the Koreans have traditionally sought is not a judgment. No one needs to win to end a dispute, for the aim of settlement is not a dichotomous fixing of blame. A group of decision-makers who are unable to achieve unanimity do not presently satisfy community expectations.

This strong preference for unanimity has been one of the reasons why conciliation or mediation has been preferred to adjudication or arbitration. With the former, unanimity is indispensable. Unanimity makes such a form of settlement effective, and restored social equilibrium tends to be more lasting. It is small wonder that the Korean judicial decision-makers have had to retreat from the statutory majority rule, faced as they have been with such strong community demands for unanimity. To be sure, majority rule is democratic; it is modern; it conforms more closely to the logically formal rationality of the modern legal system of which the decision-makers are an essential part. But they realize that their decision does not take place in the exhilarating realm of rational abstraction and universalistic logic. Their decisions are a part of the process of community interaction. If those decisions, already labouring under a disadvantage due to the alien origin of the system, are to be effective, they cannot go squarely counter to the community perspectives, and presently they cannot be adequately legitimated by a juristic science of European origin.

The community demand for unanimity in decision processes puts such a strong pressure upon the decision-makers that they will go a long way to achieve consensus. With a great deal of negotiation and compromise taking place, the result is almost invariably a unanimous decision. When a dissenter does insist on his right to differ, he must in fact be willing to vitiate to a large extent the authority of the decision of the majority. A preliminary indication would be that there must have been a very strong reason why the minority could not acquiesce in the decision. If the majority decision could not obtain the agreement of the minority, it can hardly command the acquiescence of the people. This means that, unless the minority is willing to impair the authority not only of the instant decision but the decision unit itself, dissent will be avoided as much as possible. In this sense a dissent is liable to be viewed as disruptive, un-co-operative, and unproductive. A man cannot be a consistent dissenter and yet remain a member of a particular decision unit. That he is consistently opposing the majority decision means that he has a serious doubt about the legitimacy or the good faith of the majority. Under such circumstances he cannot in good conscience remain a member of such a decision unit. On the other hand, the majority cannot long tolerate a participant who not only remains un-co-operative but also jeopardizes the authority of the decision process.

This willingness to go to great lengths to produce unanimity entails several important consequences. The most readily apparent is the difficulty of making an important decision. It often develops that the only alternative to unanimity is no decision at all, not to mention the inevitable delay and loss of time. Moreover, no decision is indeed preferred in many cases to an open acknowledgment of dissension. A corollary to this indecisiveness is a strong propensity to secrecy. Inasmuch as the mere fact of disagreement among the decision-makers is sufficient to undermine their authority, the decision-makers who participate in the decision process show strong inclination to keep this process of interaction secret, for fear of betraying themselves by the dissension that might develop. Until a consensus is made up and unanimity is assured, the decision-makers are loath to carry on their deliberations in public. Consequently, any public assembly of decision-makers for open debate and deliberation tends to be either a theatrical demonstration of unanimity for the purpose of bolstering the authority of the decision process, or a petulant brawl and vituperation for the purpose of acting out the frustration engendered by the protracted period of indecision and the inability to create a consensus.[22]

The third consequence is the factional schism that ineluctably follows dissent. A consistent dissenter cannot remain a member of the decision process for long without causing a factional division. The pressure upon him to forego dissent is such that the "trouble-maker" has either to withdraw from the decision unit or to rally support in the form of a faction of his own.[23]

The fourth consequence is what may be called the "facelessness" of the decision behaviour. When a group of decision-makers makes a unanimous decision, it is impossible for non-participants to know exactly the role each decision-maker played in arriving at the "unanimous" decision. Where not only dissents but concurring opinions are also available it is possible for an observer to decipher with some degree of accuracy the exact standing of each decision-maker on various issues. From this the observer can make predictions as to the general nature of future decisional outcomes by the same unit, and going a step further, he can even attempt to make meaningful policy recommendations. No such intellectual tasks are possible for an observer faced with "faceless" unanimity.

Finally, what may perhaps be the most important consequence is the "fractioning" of the decision-making function that in practice sanctions individual decision-making. Given the predisposition of the participants toward unanimity, one naturally expects that the decision rendered unanimously will reflect a high degree of agreement and intense interaction among the decision-makers. The reality of the process belies such an expectation. Unanimity, in fact, masks "minority decision." What emerges from the practice of the participants is individual decision-making on the basis of either specialization or rotation. One member of the decision unit is assigned to a case according to his specialized competence. Where no special expertise is considered necessary, the members rotate assignments to equalize the work load. The member who is assigned to a case assumes primary responsibility and leadership in conducting hearings and research. He makes the initial decision. He then prepares a draft of the opinion. When the decision unit gathers together for a final decision, the individual member in charge reports his decision. At this point, the other members of the unit usually accept their colleague's decision as a matter of course. It is rarely necessary for a member to defend his decision or persuade his colleagues to accept his disposition of the case. It almost appears as if the members have made a tacit pact among themselves not to oppose each other's decision. So long as a member does not dissent from others, others will not disagree with him when his turn comes up.[24]

To be sure, there are cases in which a senior member might suggest a change in phraseology of the draft opinion. In most cases, however, those who are not directly involved do not even bother to acquaint themselves with the case or the draft opinion. Even in politically important cases, the Court will go along with the members who have the primary responsibility. In those rare cases where some members feel compelled to disagree, such a dissent is confined to the inner walls of the conference room. As soon as there is dissent, the subtle process of creating consensus is set in motion. Aggressiveness is taboo; there is no quicker way to gain an enemy. Sarcasm, wit, indifference to seniority and age, and rudeness are strictly out of place. Exhibition of superior erudition in "legal dogmatics," especially on the part of a junior member, is in very bad taste. Strict legal logic occupies but a small place in the discussion. Every member is presumed to know the law and can justify his conclusion in terms of the formal logic of juristic science.

The discussion tends to emphasize the particularistic elements unique to the case. Ideological, sociological, or ethical considerations occupy the central position in the discussion. One of the more convincing arguments would be to point up the importance of winning approval from colleagues, friends, and society as a whole. If a member can convince his colleagues that the proposed decision would seriously impair his relationship with those whom he considers important in his professional and social life, he can be confident of a major concession in his favour.

Another feature of the Korean judicial decision process worth noting is the mediational role the judicial process plays "unofficially." Whether a lone policeman in the rural police box or a judge in Seoul, the role of a mediator comes to him naturally. In many cases these official decision-makers do not hesitate to exert pressure on the parties to settle their disputes non-juridically. It is interesting to note that these decision-makers are somewhat furtive about their mediational role. They feel that they are being unfaithful to their official duties by indulging in their "feudal" propensities. This is in sharp contrast to Occidental systems that encourage out-of-court settlements through pre-trial conferences and so forth as a means of reducing the congestion of dockets and for saving time and money.

It is ironic that the best argument that can be made by the official decision-makers to persuade the disputants is to convince them of the "horrors" of judicial process. By convincingly describing the worst possible "deals" a man can get at the hands of the court, the mediation-minded official decision-makers can frighten the disputants into mediation. In this sense there may be good reason for the official decision-makers to feel somewhat guilty about their preference for mediation.

CONCLUSION

The foregoing has examined the judicial decision process of Korea in the context of its interaction with the community perspectives of authority. It attempts to delineate both the traditional and the current patterns of decision-making. The latter is in a state of flux, since it is a product of both the traditional and the Occidental. Thus, the Korean judicial process is in a "mixed" state. Formally it is a "modern" legal system in which a logically formal rationality of the Continental European variety is supposed to prevail. But the participants in this process bring with them a set of perspectives and values that are "patrimonial" and traditional. Beneath the modern institutional facade, the interaction between traditional perspectives and essentially Occidental institutions goes on. It has been nearly eight decades since this interaction first began. If one looks at the process of interaction in evolutionary terms, he will conclude that the Korean judicial decision process is at a transitional stage. This of course assumes that every legal system inevitably develops from the traditional to the Occidental. According to this view, the Korean judicial process will lose more of the traditional and particularistic aspects and, as Korean society develops, become more similar to the process now prevailing in the Occident.

However, even if the Korean judicial process were destined to become more Occidental, it is doubtful that it would ever become identical with the judicial decision process of the Occident. In view of the large number of non-Occidental societies that have decided to work with a modern legal system of Occidental origin, it is important to gain a sound understanding of the process of indigenization and adaptation that is taking place in these societies. Korea provides an interesting case for study. Its traditional jural values and perspectives of authority have in a sense been an exact opposite of those of the modern Occident. The tension thus created between the old and the new has given rise to a type of judicial behavior that is neither Occidental nor traditional. For the present the traditional perspectives of the community have been tipping the scale in their favour. In terms of degree, it may be argued that present Korean judicial behaviour is much closer to the traditional type than to Weber's ideal type. The Korean perspectives of authority will have to undergo a profound change before the judicial decision process can begin to assume significance as part of the community power process in Korea.

— *Pyong-Choon Hahm*

REFERENCES

1. P. C. Hahm, *The Korean Political Tradition and Law* (Seoul: Hollym, 1967), p. 6.
2. This facet of the Korean perspective sets Korea apart from its neighbour, Japan. In Japan, physical violence occupied a fundamentally different position in the value system. If superbly disciplined and victorious, physical violence could attain "beauty." Disciplined and victorious violence served as a symbol of virtue and goodness in man. This is the basic tenet of *bushido*, the

ideology of the Japanese military elite of the past. The art of violence has also imparted to them a value-orientation that emphasizes achievement and performance.

3. Cf. Paul Bohannan's discussion of the fundamental importance of the "restoration of the *tar*," in processes of adjudication, of self-help, and of ritual preparation, among the Tiv in post-World War II Nigeria, in his *Justice and Judgment Among the Tiv* (New York: Oxford University Press, 1957), pp. 208. 14; and cf. Paul Bohannan (ed.), "Part II: The Ethnography of Law: The Judicial Process," in *Law and Warfare: Studies in the Anthropology of Conflict* (Garden City: Doubleday, 1967).

4. F. S. C. Northrop, "Mediational Approval Theory of Law in American Realism," *Virginia Law Review*, 44 (1958), 347-63, especially 351.

5. M. Weber, *Religion of China* (Glencoe, III.: The Free Press, 1951), pp. 100-104 and *Law in Economy and Society* (Cambridge, Mass.: Harvard Univ. Press, 1954), pp. 61-64, 304-5.

6. See Glendon Schubert, "Behavioral Jurisprudence," *Law and Society Review*, 2 (June 1968), 417, Table 3.

7. M. Weber, *The General Theory of Social and Economic Organization* (trans.), A. M. Henderson and T. Parsons (New York: Free Press, 1964), p. 92.

8. Weber clearly pits "ethical" concepts against "juristic" ones. Weber, *Law in Economy and Society*, p. 309. To Weber the legal system is "where the facts of life are juristically 'construed' in order to make them fit the abstract propositions of law and in accordance with the maxim that nothing can exist in the realm of law unless it can be 'conceived' by the jurist in conformity with those 'principles' which are revealed to him by juristic science." Ibid. p. 307.

9. M. S. McDougal, "Law as a Process of Decision: A Policy-Oriented Approach to Legal Study," *Natural Law Forum*, 1 (1956), 53-72, especially 58.

10. H. D. Lasswell and A. Kaplan, *Power and Society* (New Haven: Yale University Press), 1950, pp. 74-75.

11. Weber, *Law in Economy and Society*, p. 16.

12. Some of the observations in this paper are based on the results of a field investigation which was conducted during the period from December 1, 1963, to June 15, 1964. About a year's preparation had preceded the actual field survey and the analysis of the results. The study was financed by a grant from the Asia Foundation. The schedule of questions used for the survey was composed after a pre-test conducted in the capital city and in a remote rural village. Out of the voting population of 12,985,015, determined on the basis of the voting list compiled by the National Election Commission for the presidential election held on October 15, 1963, 1301 respondents were selected according to a modified form of stratified random sampling.

    The interviews were conducted on a nation-wide scale throughout South Korea with the chosen sample. The interviewers had been given training in advance, and they performed their task conscientiously and efficiently. The collected data were coded and tabulated by ISM machines at the Statistics Bureau of the Economic Planning Board of the Republic of Korea. A preliminary report was submitted to the Asia Foundation on August 15, 1964. A complete analysis of the data collected by this study has not yet been made public.

13. The two metropolitan areas, Seoul and Pusan, are called Special Cities. Seoul had a population of a little more than 3 million and Pusan a little more than 1 million. The "cities" had populations of between 50,000 and 800,000. The "towns" had populations of between 14,000 and 49,000.

14. A. K. R. Kiralfy, *Potter's Outline of English Legal History* (London: Sweet and Maxwell, 1958), pp. 4-5.

15. It must be pointed out that the concept of "relation" itself is much broader in Korea than in the Occident.

16. In a study that scales fifty-one societies on a dimension that is interpreted to correspond to the development of legal institutions (with the Western judicial system as the goal toward which social evolution has been developing, in the countries in the sample), Korea is scored in the second category. That is, it is scored among those relatively (to the pre-literate and primitive tribes which were the subjects of the ethnographic studies from which most of the data were drawn) developing countries that have mediation and police, but lack the institutionalization of counsel. See Richard D. Schwartz and James C. Miller, "Legal Evolution and Societal Complexity," *American Journal of Sociology,* 70 (1964), 159-69, especially 164.

17. Weber, *Law in Economy and Society,* pp. 220-23.

18. P. C. Hahm, "The Korean People and Their Property Rights," *American Journal of Comparative Law,* 12 (1963), 61-71.

19. Northrop, "Mediational Approval Theory of Law in American Realism," p. 350.

20. There are no official reports of Supreme Court decisions. A couple of unofficial reports are available of which one put out by Omungak, a publisher in Seoul, is most readily available. These unofficial publications report only selected cases. A committee set up by a Supreme Court Regulation (No. 42, August 12, 1958) makes an initial selection of decisions to be published. The reporters then may make their own selections out of those chosen by the committee. The reason for the "screening" of cases to be published seems to be because a complete reporting of every decision would serve no useful purpose in view of the current practice of the Supreme Court's reviewing every case submitted to it on appeal as a matter of course.

    In more than a thousand cases decided before 1962 as reported by Omungak no dissenting opinion can be found. The absence of dissent may be due to the editorial policy of both the committee and the reporter. However, in more recent reports the same reporter includes about nine civil cases in which dissenting opinions were formally expressed with one case containing a concurring opinion. The decisions date from the period subsequent to 1964. Two criminal cases and one administrative law case are reported with concurring opinions while three administrative law cases contain dissenting opinions. These cases were also decided after 1964. From this, one might anticipate a trend toward more frequent published dissent.

21. The present wording of Article 20 of the Court Organization Law is the product of an amendment dated August 12, 1961. Before this amendment the formal expression of dissent by a Supreme Court judge was left entirely to his discretion.

22. It may be noted that the former is characteristic of the Soviet system and the latter of the Asian parliamentary systems, including Japan. In the latter a desire to fix blame upon the opponent for the indecision operates strongly. It can also rightly signify a beginning of belligerency between the opposing groups.

23. If we follow this line of logic a little further in the context of the Korean power process as a whole, a political group in Korea has little capacity to tolerate dissent. Any form of dissent quickly hardens into a minority faction. Formal division frequently follows. As soon as a dissenter appears, a faction is formed around him and before long he will be forming his own group. On the other hand, this strong pressure for unanimity too often fails utterly to function in an intergroup situation. This failure is especially pronounced among political groups formed out of factional divisions. Inasmuch as unanimity has already proven impossible, there is no way for them to make any decision except by a naked power struggle. In the absence of an alternative principle that can guide the intergroup behavior, political opposition tends to become a personal enmity against members of the opposing group. Because compromise is possible only after a protracted period of negotiation, bitter hostility

among groups effectively militates against any decision based on compromise and consensus in intergroup situations. In the result, the impasse tends to be broken by "radical" or extremist elements in the dominant group who become impatient with concessions and delay.

24. Individual decision-making also entails individual responsibility. This is graphically illustrated by Hahn Bae-ho in his study of the decision by Syngman Rhee's government to close down an opposition newspaper: Hahn Bae-ho and Kim kyu-taik, *Inter-Group Conflicts and Political Decision-Making in Korea,* Yonsei University, 1965 (mimeographed), pp. 35, 37, 43-44. Although the decision had been made unanimously by the Cabinet, the Senior Minister found himself denying any involvement by declaring that the decision "had nothing to do with the Cabinet." This meant that the responsibility for the decision by individually with the Director of the Office of Public Information, and not Collectively with the Cabinet. Every member of the Cabinet was individually responsible for those decisions affecting matters under his jurisdiction. Unanimity was a mere formality. Although the fractioning of decision function and responsibility is not so apparent in the case of the judicial process as in the "political" process, such a fractioning is nonetheless an important feature of the judicial decision process in Korea.

3

EMPIRICAL JURISPRUDENCE IN JAPAN

Before World War II, Japan had few empirical studies of the judicial process. Neither law professors nor attorneys had any special interest in such studies because they were concerned solely with analyzing cases and interpreting statutes. Social scientists gave no attention to analyzing the empirical aspects of the courts, in part, probably, because of the sanctity attributed to the Imperial courts. Candor, however, compels the admission that the lack of adequate research techniques to study the judicial process in a scientific manner also impeded such inquiry. However, it does not follow that pre-war Japan did not have practical problems and theoretical issues to be solved. Quite the contrary, much *should* have been done, because the structure of the judicial system which had been introduced from Western countries (especially from Germany) in the early Meiji Era was not well suited to Japanese social conditions. The Japanese people had outside of the formal judicial system handier, more convenient, and less expensive devices to solve their disputes. However, these informal processes of conflict resolution, which usually stemmed from feudal Japan, might have become obstacles to the modernization of the judicial system.

This discrepancy between the official system and informal dispute-settling devices, combined with the hiatus between the imported Continental codes and legal practices, and the indigenous Japanese legal system, eventually provoked among legal scholars a new approach to the study of law. Indeed, even before the war a few Japanese law professors showed enthusiasm for the developing trends in jurisprudence abroad, such as the sociology of law, the jurisprudence of interests, and the free law movement in Continental Europe, and their American equivalents which likewise criticized the conceptual basis for and the doctrinaire nature of traditional jurisprudence. Japanese academic society before the war was aware of the identity of most proponents of these new trends, but actual empirical studies of the judicial process had to await, in my opinion, the acquisition of essential research skills and greater methodological sophistication.

THE INFLUENCE OF FOREIGN SCHOLARSHIP

Important changes have occurred, however, during the last two decades. Both academic and practicing lawyers began to undertake empirical research in the judicial process, using scientific methods. During the first stage, many foreign studies were either translated, or else introduced, by Japanese proponents. Law students thereby could gain access to such studies in their own language. A pioneer in these endeavors is Takeo Hayakawa, professor of Anglo-American law at Kobe University. A leading legal empiricist himself, Hayakawa has energetically introduced realist and behavioural studies from abroad, and especially those produced in the United States. Most of his articles have appeared in Japanese journals. In 1958, he discussed the opinions of such celebrated Anglo-American lawyers as Jerome Frank and Fred Rodell, concerning the law-making function of the judicial process.[1] In 1960, he discussed mainly the Brandeis brief and the United States Supreme Court's decision in the School Segregation cases, in order to show the importance of relating social science techniques to fact-finding processes in court proceedings.[2] These two articles were followed by his endeavour to give Japanese readers a more general view of empirical research in foreign countries. In 1963[3] and 1966,[4] for example, he published articles on American empirical work. Both appeared in the popular law magazine, *Horitsujiho*. He also commented upon American developments relating law and the use of electronic computers (jurimetrics).[5] In 1965, after having visited several Scandinavian countries, Professor Hayakawa wrote a brief introduction to the socio-legal studies that were an outgrowth of Scandinavian legal positivism.[6]

Besides these panoramic introductions to foreign empirical studies Hayakawa also published several articles in which he discussed particular methodological approaches to the study of the judicial process, including Sidney Ulmer's scalogram analysis of the judicial behavior of United States Supreme Court justices[7] and C. Herman Pritchett's bloc analysis.[8]

Jurimetric studies from the United States were introduced also by other scholars. Tomoyuki Ohta, a legal scholar who has applied symbolic logic to analyze case law in Japan,[9] introduced[10] Fred Kort's series of articles on statistical prediction of judicial decisions.[11] Fumio Saito, in 1963 and 1965, discussed Schubert's judicial behavior studies.[12] Hiroyuki Nose, a law student interested in applying cybernetic methods to the analysis of judicial decisions, has discussed Reed Lawlor's methods of predicting decisions[13] which combine Boolean algebra and computer technology, Nose also translated into Japanese, with a brief comment, an article by Professor of Law Thomas Cowan.[14] The present author published in 1965 an article commenting upon American empirical studies arising particularly in political (science) jurisprudence and sociology.[15]

Some of the new trends in eastern European countries, including the Soviet Union, were introduced into Japan after 1963 by specialists in Soviet law. Tsuneo Inako discussed new trends in Soviet jurisprudence involving attempts to apply the theory and method of cybernetics to legal study,[16] with particular reference to the work of Djangir A. Kerimov.[17] Hideya Kageyama tried to give a general view concerning what is actually going on in the U.S.S.R.,[18] and he also has introduced the work of the East German legal scholar Victor Knapp.[19]

SOME INDIGENOUS EXAMPLES OF EMPRICAL JURISPRUDENCE

In 1959, Hiroo Murata published a pioneering work.[20] The author is a psychologist (and non-lawyer) who works in the field of criminology. In this ambitious book he tried to establish an empirical science of judicial process by using research techniques that had been developed in various fields other than law, such as cybernetics, information theory, and the philosophical approach that is known in Europe and America as "logical positivism." He emphasized that the judicial process is double-structured in the sense that its evaluative aspect can be distinguished from its fact-finding aspect. The empirical approach could be conducted only in regard to the factual aspect of the judicial process. Murata speaks primarily of the role of courts in criminal trials, and although he attempts to show the theoretical relevance of a variety of methods and approaches, there are virtually no empirical data presented as examples of the research that he advocates.

The topics he discussed range widely. He described the fact-finding process of criminal trials as a communications system with counsel for both parties sending messages to the judge. He discussed the quality of these messages in terms of the range of evidence presented to the court, and the sequence of its presentation. In so doing, Murata used information theory and techniques, communication theory, and linear programing. He also discussed the strategic aspects of judicial decision-making processes, using game theory and related approaches. Furthermore, his analysis included psychological aspects of the judicial process. He discussed the psychology of the accused, in confessions both inside and outside the courtroom, the testimony of witnesses, and indirect evidence.[21]

It is only fair to point out that Murata was rather far in advance of the profession for which he wrote at the time his book was published. But because very few lawyers could fully understand the author's goals, to say nothing of his techniques, as yet no concrete studies following his suggestions have been published. It seems likely, however, that the next generation of students involved with the empirical study of the judicial process will follow Murata's lead and he will then be given greater credit for his ground-breaking contributions in this field.

In 1959 also, Kosuke Kobayashi discussed the function of the new rule in the Judicature Act of 1947, adopted with the support of the American occupation authorities, which required that individual opinions be given by each judge in Supreme Court decisions.[22] Although the then prevailing opinion emphasized the probable positive advantages that could be anticipated under, and the progressive nature of, the new policy on judicial dissent, Kobayashi sought to underscore the disadvantages of having judges criticize each other's work in public. So his article was Bonnative rather than empirical. Several years later, Katsuyoshi Sakurada undertook an historical analysis of the rule and practice of judicial unanimity before the war, and of the legislative background of the enactment of the new policy on dissent, together with the arguments of legal scholars pro and con.[23] A few dissenting and concurring opinions had begun to appear by the time Sakurada wrote, so he was able to give several examples of minority opinions for the period from 1958 to 1962. He did not, however, attempt to make a rigorous, systematic analysis of judicial dissent.

In 1960, Hayakawa published his own research on the judicial behavior of Japanese Supreme Court justices in the decision of civil liberties cases, using scalogram analysis to replicate similar studies in the United States; this study was reprinted in English, both in Japan and in the United States.[24]

Hiroyuki Nose's study of 1964[25] is, although a tentative one, the first example which applied electronic computer techniques drawn from information theory directly to the empirical analysis of case law. He analyzed one hundred cases decided at Sapporo summary court and involving criminal trials of defendants charged with responsibility for having caused death or bodily injury through negligence in connection with traffic accidents during the first quarter of 1963 (viz., offences under Article 211 of the Criminal Code of Japan).

To analyze these cases, the author tried to describe the judicial decision-making process in relation to the communications from the public prosecutor to the tribunal. The dependent variable (or output) of the process is the conviction of the defendant.

The messages which are carried in these cases are classified by the author into nine patterns. For each pattern he shows a flow diagram of the information. These diagrams suggest that if the message involves any kind of several combinations of information such that it is possible for the current of the circuit to be on," then the predicted decision will be output. But these circuits do not convey information concerning the "quantity" of the flow of messages, that is, about the level of efficiency of the communication; the output of the circuit is related only to "whether the defendant is culpable or not." Other possible outputs are ignored. But this is merely a tentative design, and further and more detailed study is expected to make possible a more subtle analysis of decisional outputs.

Especially after the war, as I have shown, foreign empirical researches were either translated or introduced in abridged form into Japan, and attracted considerable attention from those interested in the scientific study of law. Nevertheless, few similar concrete studies were conducted by Japanese scholars. It is ironic to observe that thus far the study of empirical jurisprudence has borne very few indigenous empirical fruits.

SENTENCING STUDIES IN JAPAN

There is one aspect in which there have been substantial developments in empirical research on the judicial process. In Japan, studies of sentencing behaviour of judges can be readily traced back to the pre-war era. Even then some of the foreign studies on sentencing, such as those by Franz Exner or by Sheldon and Eleanor Glueck were well known among Japanese academics, and particularly among specialists in criminal law and criminology. Exner's book[26] was translated into Japanese in 1940.[27] Probably stimulated by Exner's study, Takeo Fuwa, a professor of criminal law, published a pioneering study.[28] He analyzed about twelve thousand criminal decisions of the Keijo (now Seoul, Korea) district court from 1933 to 1937. Fuwa emphasized the important role of judges in criminal sentencing, saying that the judge's decision in sentencing was not analytical, but rather was intuitive and subjective. He recognized, of course, individual differences in the criminal sentencing of judges, but he tried to show the existence of some general tendencies. There was a standard type of penalty assessed by a judge for a certain type of offense, which in turn corresponded to a standard type of offender's *conduct* as determined by the indictment for the offence. On the basis of empirical data Fuwa tried to show that judges made the penalty "fit the crime." For example, in cases of infanticide, the standard type of offender's conduct is as follows: a widow has worked very hard to bring up her children. After they are grown she falls in love again and becomes pregnant; but she does not want to marry her paramour and she is annoyed at her own misconduct, so she decides to kill the baby at birth. The standard sentence for this standard crime of infanticide was, according to Fuwa's data, a suspended sentence of two years' imprisonment. Other crimes analyzed by Fuwa included homicide, larceny, wounding, and arson. Fuwa's analysis remained, however, at the level of statistical description. He attempted neither causal statistical analysis nor scientific interpretation of his empirical data. Nevertheless the study had a strong influence on criminal law practice and administration in Japan because his tabulations of data, though not drawn from mainland Japan, could be used as a basis for prediction by lawyers, and as a guide by judges, for sentencing practices in criminal cases. Thus it was a kind of prediction study, albeit a primitive one. Furthermore this study stimulated various similar types of studies among the practitioners, and particularly among the public prosecutors. More than a dozen other such empirical studies have been especially appreciated by Japanese legal practitioners and listed in the Appendix at the end of this chapter. This work clearly has been important because of both its popularity and its amenability to direct, practical application. It can also be seen as perhaps a necessary stage of pre-scientific inquiry and the precursor of more rigorous theoretical work.

Work more scientific in nature in Japan stems from the influence of Sheldon Glueck, whose predictive studies of crime had been introduced in Japan before the war. The Japanese studies which followed Glueck were of two main types: (1) prediction studies in the field of criminology, and (2) prediction studies of judicial behaviour in sentencing. Glueck himself published in 1956 an article on sentencing which suggested the applicability of the same method, as had been previously used to predict criminal behaviour, for predicting behavior of judges in sentencing criminals.[29] Glueck' s article was translated into Japanese[30] shortly

Table 3.1: Characteristics of Defendants Guilty of Assault, and Their Punishment

Variable	*Division*	*Total*	*Defendants imprisoned at forced labour*		*Defendants who were fined*		*Weight*
			155 persons	*A(100 per cent)*	*268 persons*	*B(100 per cent)*	
I	No precious record		42	27.1	131	48.9	35.7
Record of same	Arrested but not prosecuted		20	12.9	52	19.4	39.9
type of previous	1 previous offence		40	25.8	55	20.5	55.7
offense	2 previous offence		14	9.0	10	3.7	70.9
	3 previous offence		39	25.2	20	7.5	77.1
II	No previous record		54	34.8	136	50.7	44.5
Record of different	Arrested but not prosecuted		32	20.6	49	18.3	
type of previous	1 previous offence		17	11.0	38	14.2	
offense	2 previous offence		20	12.9	23	8.6	51.1
	3 previous offence		32	20.6	22	8.2	71.5
III	No		122	78.7	233	86.9	47.5
Delinquent grouping	Yes		33	21.3	35	13.1	61.9
IV	No		99	63.9	263	98.1	39.4
Serious wounding	Yes		56	36.1	5	1.9	95.0

V	10 days or less	34	21.9	193	72.0	23.3
Time required for	11-15 days	30	19.4	56	20.9	48.1
medical treatment	16-31 days	62	40.0	16	6.0	87.0
	over 1 month	29	18.7	3	1.1	94.4
VI	Hand, leg, etc.	28	18.1	182	67.9	21.0
Method of assault	Dull weapon	58	37.4	69	25.7	59.3
	Edged tool	69	44.5	17	6.3	87.6
VII	To a certain degree pardonable	2	1.3	10	3.7	26.0
Motive inferred	Ordinary	73	47.1	218	81.3	36.7
	Bad	80	51.6	40	14.9	77.6

after its first appearance in the American research literature. The first attempt to put Glueck's hypothesis to an empirical test was made by a public prosecutor in 1961. Yoshiro Kamei constructed a prediction table for the division of indictment and non-indictment decisions in larceny cases.[31] He had collected, as samples, one hundred cases each for both indicted and non-indicted defendants, from the public prosecutor's office at Gifu during the five years from September 1955 to 1960. Examining these samples and using the Chi-square test for significance, he denoted eight evaluative factors relevant to the differences between the two groups. Each factor was divided into two or more subcategories and scored by using Glueck's so-called weighted score method. A score level was then determined which distinguished between the two groups of defendants, with the non-indicted group below, and the indicted group above, the cutting point provided by the critical score.

Similar studies appeared in 1963 and 1964, by Masayoshi Honda and Yataro Inoue,[32] and by Chihiro Katakura and Yasuko Sato,[33] also basically following Glueck's method. For present purposes I shall discuss the latter study as an example.

Katakura and Sato were interested in finding a method by which it will be possible to evaluate quantitatively the standards of judgment invoked by judges for sentences of imprisonment at forced labour or fining in the assessment of penalty for the crime of wounding.[34] The first group comprised 155 defendants who had been accused of wounding and who were sentenced after public trial to imprisonment at forced labour by the Tokyo district court, whose irrevocable decisions became effective during the period from April 1, 1960, to March 31, 1961. A second group included two defendants who had been accused of wounding and who were sentenced after public trial by the same court during the same period to pay only a fine, as well as a much larger subgroup of 266 defendants, with the same characteristics except that they were processed by judges of the summary courts in the jurisdictional area of Tokyo during November 1960.

Fourteen characteristics of defendants defined the set of variables presumed to be relevant to the difference in sentencing (imprisonment at forced labour as distinguished from a fine). These include: "age," "place of residence," "record of same type of previous offence," "record of different type of previous offence," "delinquent grouping," "whether or not wounding was serious (that which endangered life and that which resulted in serious physical handicap)," "length of time required for medical treatment," "method of assault," "motive inferred," "number of victims," "whether or not the offender had an accomplice," "whether or not the offender had drunk liquor," "whether or not the other party counterattacked," and "mutual settlement and compensation." Each variable has been scaled into two or more subdivisions. The standard for classification in regard to each subdivision has been operationalized so that each of the 423 defendants (items) has been assigned to one of the subdivisions of each of the fourteen variables.

The distribution of the defendants, grouped according to the two categories of punishment, for each of the fourteen variables, was then tested for statistical significance. Chi square was used, and the 5 per cent level of significance was the criterion accepted. Half (7) of the variables showed a significant difference between the two groups; these appear, together with the frequencies (and corresponding percentages) observed for their subdivisions, in Table 3.1. By calculating for each subdivision the ratio of the proportions for both groups, a series of weights was derived (last column). Evidently, those variable subdivisions for which there is a low proportion of imprisonments and a high proportion of fines are assigned relatively low weights; and conversely, a high proportion of imprisonments and a low proportion of fines result in a high weight. And—as we shall shortly see—a combination of high weights results, from the point of view of defendants, in the likelihood of being a member of the imprisonment group.

Table 3.2 reports the summation weights, for defendants in both groups, based upon their respective weights on each of the seven variables found to be statistically significant. The range of total weights is 303.4 — 543.3 for the imprisonment group, and 237.4—436.9 for the fined group. As the table shows, a total weight of 340 discriminates well between the two groups, with more

Table 3.2: Defendants Characteristics, Summary Weights, and Form of Punishment in Assault Cases

Sum of weights	*Defendants imprisoned at forced labour*		*Defendants who were fined*	
	155 persons	*(100 per cent)*	*268 (100 per cent) persons*	
230-239			1	49(18.3)
240-249			48	
250-259			26	
260-269			14	62(23.1)
270-279			22	
280-289			29	
290-299		2(1.3)	23	66(24.6)
300-309	2		14	
310-319			36	
320-329		13(8.4)	8	65(24.3)
330-339	13		21	
340-349	5		5	
350-359	10	26(16.8)	8	14(5.2)
360-369	11		1	
370-379	15		2	
380-389	16	39(25.2)	2	8(3.0)
390-399	8		4	
400-409	7		2	
410-419	9	23(14.9)	1	3(1.1)
420-429	7			
430-439	11		1	
440-449	11	27(17.4)		1(0.4)
450-459	5			
460-469	4			
470-479	4	15(9.7)		
480-489	7			
490-499	2			
500-509	5	7(4.5)		
510-519				
520-529				
530-539	2	3(1.9)		
540-549	1			

than 90 per cent of the imprisonment group falling above, and more than 90 per cent of the fined group falling below, that criterion level. The remaining 10 per cent of each distribution can be considered—and was explicitly so discussed by the authors, in the original report of this research—to be error variance.

Honda and Inoue's study of the evaluation of penalties in larceny cases offers another example of the same type of research as the article by Katakura and Sato. Honda and Inoue examined 534 larceny offenders handled by the Tokyo Public Prosecutors' Office during the period from February to April 1961. The cases studied were divided into two groups: (1) prosecuted (169 persons), and (2) unprosecuted (365 persons). The authors constructed a prediction table using eight variables: (1) method of committing the crime, (2) frequency of crimes, (3) amount of damages, (4) motive or cause for the crime, (5) behavior of the offender, (6) past criminal record of the offender, (7) whether or not the offender had fixed abode or occupation, and (8) offender's family background.

Honda and Inoue examined the number of those belonging to the prosecuted groups, and discovered that a total weight of four hundred discriminated between the two groups as follows:

Table 3.3: Larceny Defendant Characteristics, and the Decision to Prosecute

	399.9 or less	*400 or more*
Prosecuted group	23 (13.7 per cent)	146 (86.3 per cent)
Unprosecuted group	317 (86.9 per cent)	48 (13.1 per cent)

In an attempt to improve their differentiation of the two groups, the authors experimented in the construction of alternative tables by adding two other variables. With (9: the feeling of the victim), the cutting level is 450, with 12.5 per cent errors for the prosecuted group and 11.3 per cent for the unprosecuted group. With (10: whether or not any person undertakes supervision of the offender), the cutting level is 440, with 10.7 per cent errors for the prosecuted group, and 12.0 per cent for the unprosecuted group. Using all ten variables, the cutting level is 490, with 9.5 per cent errors for the prosecuted group and 10.7 per cent for the other one. As usually is the case with designs such as this, the inclusion of additional variables does improve slightly the discriminating (and, potentially, the predictive) power of the array.

Public prosecutor Haruo Abe, a proponent of Glueck's methods,[35] has also been an advocate of the application of scientific methods to the study of judicial process.[36] In 1962 he published, with Teruo Yamamoto, a paper[37] which criticized earlier sentencing studies on the grounds that they were of no practical value to the prediction of individual sentences in explicit, actual cases. Although the criticized studies could convey general trends in the sentencing behaviour of judges, for particular crimes, nevertheless these studies were merely descriptive. What was needed, they argued, was a method that would make it possible to predict sentencing outcomes in particular, and as yet undecided, cases.

Abe and Yamamoto used 155 cases of defendants judged guilty of the crime of wounding, decided by the Tokyo district court from May to December 1960. Using Glueck's method, they chose five scaled variables, each of which was scored as zero, one, or two, as follows: (1) remedial period: *a.* within two weeks (0), *b.* within one month (1), c. more than one month (2); (2) motivation given by victim: *a.* exists (0), *b.* not clear (1), *c.* does not exist (2); (3) reconciliation and restitution: *a.* exists (0), *b.* not clear (1). r. does not exist (2); (4) gang association: *a.* does not exist (0). *b.* not clear (1), *c.* exists (2): *(5)* previous criminal career: *a.* none (0), *b.* different type (1). *c.* same type (2).

Thus a five-variable prediction table was constructed, with non-weighted scoring. The sentence in any individual case could be predicted by counting the total scores given to each item, and referring to a correlation table.

Toshiro Maeda, a professor of criminology, has done several prediction studies of the effect of Kyukei upon sentencing. In one of these, Maeda constructed a prediction table for Kyukei.[38] According to the Code of Criminal Procedure of Japan (Article 293 No. 1), after the evidence for proving the facts constituting the offence have been examined, the public prosecutor must express his opinion ("Kyukei") about the application of the law and about the appropriate length of the penalty. In the Penal Code of Japan the difference between possible maximum and minimum penalties is very great. The judge has considerable discretion in affixing either the maximum or the minimum penalty, or something in between. Therefore the prosecutor's recommendation (Kyukei) will have some psychological influence upon the judge. The Code certainly intends the prosecutor's personal viewpoint to influence to some extent the judge's

Table 3.4: Prediction Table for Sentences in Cases of Criminal Fraud

Variable	Sub-divisions	Score
(a) age	up to 30	1
	more than 30	0
(b) private settlement	success	1
	no success	0
(c) previous imprisonment	no	1
	yes	0
(d) fraud recidivist	no	1
	yes	0
(e) number of previous criminal offenses	0-4	1
	5 or more	0
(f) criminal personality	no	1
	yes	0
(g) whether one can sympathize with his motivation or not	yes	1
	no	0
(h) 1. damages of more than 500,000 yen	neither applies	1
2. luxury accounts to an extent for both the motivation of fraud and the use of money	either applies	0
(i) whether, after committing fraud, he did anything which aggravated it or not	No	1
	yes	0

sentencing decision. The author tries to make this hypothesis scientifically testable. In order to do so, he chooses the variables relevant to the prosecutor's Kyukei behaviour by using a chi-square test, and he next divides each variable into two sub-categories, using the same non-weighted scoring method as had been employed in Abe and Yamamoto's study. His sample of 163 cases was taken from those defendants found guilty by the Tokyo District Court from May 1 to November 30, 1963. Prosecutor's recommendations are classified according to the length of the proposed sentence: under a year; one year; from thirteen to thirty months; and more than two and one-half years.

In a second study, Maeda analyzed 102 criminal fraud cases selecting his sample from criminal defendants pronounced guilty by the Tokyo district court, during the period from June 1 to November 30, 1964.[39] The two groups for analysis included those who received (1) suspended and (2) executed sentences Using procedures that are by now familiar to us (chi square, and 0, 1, 2 scoring), Maeda constructed a prediction table (Table 3.4).

By combining different variables the author made up several prediction tables. His best discriminaiton came from the use of eight variables(a, b, c, e, f, g, h, i,). A summated score of four or less resulted in an excuted sentence, whereas a score of five or more signified a suspended sentence. The error variance for this table was only 6.9 per cent of the cases examined.

In a third study, also involving the prediction of suspended and executed sentences in fraud cases, Maeda used a weighted score method to analyze the same sample that was used in the second study.[40] Here he built upon his observation of a high correlation between variable b (above) and each of the other variables. Maeda divided sub-categories of variable b by the sub-categories of each other variable. These ratios were hypothesized to have a high correlation with the difference between suspended and executed sentences. The percentages of suspended sentences, for each of the ratios of sub-categories, were calculated as in Table 3.5. The discrimination level of 170 differentiates the two types of sentences with an error variable of only 7.8 per cent.

This particular prediction table was applied by a different researcher to the result of trials in the Kyoto district prosecutor's

Table 3.5: The Calculation of Weighted Scores (Maeda's Method)

Prediction ratio	*Sub-category*	*Weighted score in percentage points*
b/a	b1/a1	98
	b1/a2	97
	b2/a1	44
	b2/a2	24
b/c	b1/c1	97
	b1/c2	97
	b2/c1	47
	b2/c2	8
b/d	b1/d1	98
	b1/d2	94
	b2/d1	47
	b2/d2	8
b/c	b1/e1	98
	b1/e2	89
	b2/e1	50
	b2/e2	7
Total score	Suspended sentence	Executed sentence
171 and over	74	3
170 and under	5	20

office, and it was found for that sample to be more than 80 per cent correct.

In 1966 a similar type of study was done by assistant judges Ritaro Naka and Toshimaro Kojo, analyzing other types of crime such as larceny and wounding.[41] They used a weighted scoring method, based on Pearson's coefficient of contingency. The samples were divided according to the suspension/execution of sentences, to the length of prison term assigned, and also according to the grant or denial of probation. The cases, decided by the

Tokyo district court, had the following sample sizes: 300 larceny cases in 1960; 271 wounding cases in 1960; and 103 cases decided during January 1959 to January 1961 involving involuntary manslaughter for negligent operation of an automobile.

Morio Miyahara, an attorney, published a research paper in 1966 which analyzed 105 train accident (criminal) cases, decided at various levels of the judiciary and selected from all over Japan, and decided between 1944 and 1965.[42] Using the chi-square test and a Pearsonian correlation table, he analyzed the relation between the seriousness of the crime (measured in terms of the number of people killed in the accident), and the sentence (suspended or executed). This was perhaps the first example of research using empirical methods to be published by a practical lawyer. Miyahara is now conducting other types of empirical research, in collaboration with some legal scholars, on other automobile accident (personal injury) cases.

SUMMARY

The sentencing studies discussed in this paper were mostly conducted by public prosecutors. We have noted only a few exception in which the report was authored by either a judge or a criminologist. This might be because these studies were initiated under the strong influence of seeking a better understanding of crime, and for social engineering purposes. Their intent was to Standardize the sentencing practices of judges throughout Japan, therby providing more equal treatment for defendants. Consequently the authors were less interested in focusing upon the differences, in sentencing behaviour, among individual judges;[43] rather, their intention was to minimize individual differences in either the sentences of judges or in the Kyukei of public prosecutors, for the same crime, in order to guarantee equal justice in criminal sentences. Therefore no one could expect these studies to be very theoretically sophisticated. No hypotheses were formulated by the authors; and no theoretical argument concerning the judicial behaviour of the judges of criminal courts has been forthcoming. They may prove, however, to have laid the groundwork for more rigorous future study of judicial process and behaviour, an approach which has just begun in Japan.

— *Zensuke Ishimura*

REFERENCES

1. "Shihokatei ni okeru rippo no keiki" (The Judicial Process in Its Law-Making Aspects), Hotetsugaku Nempo (Annual Report of Legal Philosophy), (I958), pp. 105-37.
2. "Shihokatei ni okeru shakai-kagaku" (Social Science in the Judicial Process), *Hotetsugaku Nempo* (1960), pp. 29-56.
3. "Ho to kodokagaku" (Law and the Behavioural Sciences), *Horitsujiho,* 35 (July 1963), 20-56.
4. "Amerika ni okeru shihokatei to kodokagaku" (Judicial Process and the Behavioural Sciences in America), *Horitsujiho,* 38 (March 1966), 14-25.
5. "Amerika ni okeru hogaku to denshi-keisanki" (Jurisprudence and the Electronic Computer in America). *Jurist,* 328 (August 15, 1965), 31-39.
6. "Hokuo no Hoshakaigaku" (Sociology of Law in North European Countries), *Horitsujiho,* 37 (June 1965), 39-45.
7. S. Sidney Ulmer, "Supreme Court Behaviour and Civil Liberties," *Western Political Quarterly,* 13 (1960), 295, translated by T. Hayakawa, as "Saikosaibansho no kodo to jinken, Horitsujiho shiryo-ban" *(Sourcebook* to *Horitsujiho),* (December 1960, January 1961); T. Hayakawa. "Saikosaibansho jinken-han-ketsu no shakudohyo bunseki" (Scalogram Analysis of Supreme Court Decisions with Reference to Civil Liberties Cases), *Jurist,* 256 (1962), 46-54.
8. C. H. Pritchett, *The Roosevelt Court: A Study in Judicial Politics and Values, 1937-1947* (New York: Macmillan, 1948); Pritchett, *Civil Liberties and the Vinson Court* (Chicago: University of Chicago Press, 1954); T. Hayakawa, "Shihokodo no Bloc bunseki—Shihokatei no jisshoteki kenkyu" (Bloc Analysis of Judicial Behaviour—Positive Study of the Judicial Process), and *Eibei-shiho Ronshu, Suenobu Sensei Kanreki Kinen Ronbunshu* (Essays on Anglo-American Private Law, to Commemorate the 60th Birthday of Professor Suenobu), (Tokyo: Tokyo University Press, 1963), pp. 389-410.

9. Tomoyuki Ohta, "Tojisha ni okeru shoyuken iten: Bunsekitetsugaku teki hoho ni yoru kenkyu no kokoromi" (The Moment When the Right of Ownership Shall Be Shifted: An Example of Legal Study Using the Method of Analytical Philosophy), *Keiso* (1963); T. Ohta, "Horitsugaku ni okeru keikenho-gaku-teki hoho—Seiteiho no shakaitosei kino o ketteisuru shoyoin ni tsuite" (An Empirical Approach in Jurisprudence—Factors Controlling the Function of Statutes as a Means of Social Control), *Horitsujiho*, 37 (April 1965), 36-40; T. Ohta, "Gendaihogaku to kigoronri" (Contemporary Jurisprudence and Symbolic Logic), *Koza Gendaiho* (Series in Contemporary Law) 15 (1966), 285-320.

10. T. Ohta, "Fred Kort, 'Saibankan iken no naiyobunseki to hokihan' " (Fred Kort: Content Analysis of Judicial Opinions and Rules of Law), *Hotetsugaku Nempo* (1965), pp. 157-75.

11. "Content Analysis of Judicial Opinions and Rules of Law," in Glendon Schubert (ed.), *Judicial Decision-Making* (New York: Free Press, 1963), pp. 133-76; "A Quantitative Restatement of Legal Rules," *Modern Uses of Logic in Law* (retitled *Jurimetrics Journal),* 3 (June 1963), pp. 87-97; and "Simultaneous Equation and Boolean Algebra," in H. W. Baade (ed.) "Jurimetrics," a symposium comprising the Winter 1963 issue of *Law and Contemporary Problems*, 28. 1-270. also reprinted by Basic Books (New York: 1963).

12. Fomio Saito, "Amerika ni okeru shihokodo no kodokagakuteki bunseki" (A Behavioural Approach to the Judicial Process in America), Shakaikagaku Roshu (Studies in Sodal Sciences), (Kyushu University, Division of Liberal Arts), 3 (March 1963), 75-97; 5 (March 1965), 45-79.

13. Hiroyuki Nose, "Computer ni yoru hanketsu no bunseki to yosoku-Tokuni Read Lawlor no hoho ni tsuite" Lawlor's Method for the Analysis and Prediction of Judical Decisions by Means of Computers), *Hokkaido-hogaku-ronshu* (Hokkaido Law Review), 15, No. 3 (1965), 101-24.

14. "Decision Theory in Law, Science, and Technology," *Science*, 140 (June 1963), 1065-75. Nose's translation appears in *Hokkaido Law Review*, 15, No. 2 (1964),195-234. 195-234.

15. Zensuke Ishimura, "Amerika ni okeru saiban kenkyu" (Empirical Studies in the Judicial Process in America), *Koza Gendaiho* (Series in Contemporary Law). 15 (1966). 184-217.

16. Tsuneo Inako, "Cybernetics to horitsu" (Cybernetics and Law), *Horitsujiho*, 36 (May 1964), 31-36.

17. D. A. Kerimov, "Cybernetics and the Law," *Soviet State and Law*, 21 (1962), printed in the Russian language. Printed in English as "Cybernetics and Soviet Jurisprudence," *Law and Contemporary Problems*, 28 (1963), 71-77, and "Future Applicability of Cybernetics to Jurisprudence in the U.S.S.R.," *Modern uses of Logic in Law* 3 (1963), p. 153.

18. "Cybernetics to horitsugaku" (Cybernetics and Jurisprudence), *Hokeironshu* (The Journal of the Association of Legal, Political, and Economic Science), 46 (October 1964), 97-138, and 47 (February 1965), 111-69.

19. Ibid. 45 (July 1964), 155-99; Victor Knapp, "Uber die Moglichkeit der Anwendung Kybernetischen Methoden in Recht" (On the Possibility of Applying Cybernetics in the Domain of Law), *Staat und Recht*, 4, 613ff.

20. Hiroo Murata, *Saiban kagaku* (Judicial Science), Keiso, 1959, pp. 1-277.

21. Cf. Hans Toch (ed.), *Legal and Criminal Psychology* (New York: Holt, Rinehart, and Winston, 1961).

22. Kosuke Kobayashi, "Saikosaibansho no tasuiken to shosuiken" (Majority and Minority Opinions in the Supreme Court of Japan), *Horitsujiho*, 31 (November 1959), 35-56.

23. Katsuyoshi Sakurada, "Shosuikenron, Saibanshoho 11 jyo seitei to sono *igi* (Theory and Practice of the Dissenting Opinion at the Japanese Supreme Court), *Hogaku*, 28, No. 4 (December 1964), 407-77.

24. T. Hayakawa, "Shihoteki kodo no shakudohyo bunseki—Shihokatei no jisshoteki kenkyu" (Legal Science and Judicial Behaviour—With Particular Reference to Civil Liberties in the Japanese Supreme Court); *Kobe University Law Review*, 2 (1962), 1-27; and reprinted in Glendon Schubert (ed.), *Judicial Behaviour: A Reader in Theory and Research* (Chicago: Rand McNally, 1965), pp. 325-34; see also the editor's comment, p. 315, contrasting Hayakawa's study with the early work by Pritchett.

25. Hiroyuki Nose, "Shihojyo no kettei to Communication" (Judicial Decision and Communication, for the Computerized 'Strafbefehlsverfahren'), *Hokudaiho-gakuronshu* (Hokkaido Law Review) 15, No. 1 (1964), 119-54.

26. Franz Exner, *Studien uber die Strafzumassungpraxis der Deutschcn* (Gerichte, 1931).

27. "Doitsu saibansho ni okeru kei no ryotei no jissai" (trans.), Haruyo Shinohara, *Shihoshiryo* (Materials for Criminal Justice) 263 (1940).

28. Takeo Fuwa, *Kei no ryotei ni kansuru jisshoteki kenkyu* (Positive Study of the Assessment of Penalties in Criminal Sentencing), (Ganshodo: 1939), pp. 1-362.

29. S. Glueck, "The Sentencing Problem," *Federal Probation*, 20, No. 4 (December 1956).

30. "Kei no ryotei no mondai" (trans.). Haruo Abe and Takaki Kobayashi, with brief comment by Abe, *Horitsu no hiroba* (Plaza of Law), 9, No. 12 (1956), and 10, No. 1 (1957).

31. Yoshiro Kamei, *Kiso fukiso no hyotei-ho* (Method of Division of Indictment and Non-Indictment), *Homusogokenkyusho-kenkyubu shiryo* (Materials of the Criminological Research Department, No. 5). Not officially published.

32. "Shogaizai no ryokei ni kansuru kenkyu: Choeki bakkin kubun no kijyun" (Research Concerning the Division of Imprisonment at Forced Labour and of Fine in the Assessment of Penalty for the Crime of Wounding).

Homusogoken-kyusho-kenkyubu kiyo (Bulletin of the Criminological Research Department), (1963), pp. 123-52.

33. "Settozai ni taisuru kei no ryotei ni kansuru kenkyu: Dai-ippo, Kiso fukiso no kijyun" (A Study of the Evaluation of Penalties in Larceny Cases: The First Report, Standards of Judgment Prosecutors as to Whether to Prosecute . or not). *Ibid.* (1964), pp. 171-93.

34. Cf. Edward Green, *Judicial Attitudes in Sentencing* (New York: St. Martin's Press, 1961); and Schubert, *Judicial Behaviour,* Chap. 4B.

35. Haruo Abe and Kokichi Higuchi, "Glueck hanzai yosoku nyumon" (An introduction to Glueck's Prediction of Crime), *Ichiryusha* (1959), pp. 1-178.

36. Haruo Abe, "Saiban no kagakuteki kisei ni tsuite" (Scientific Control of the Judicial Process), *Horitsujiho,* 29 (April 1957), 18-27.

37. "Sokanhyo no oyo ni yoru ryokei no kagakuteki kenkyu" (A Scientific Study of Sentencing by the Use of Correlation Tables), *Jurist,* 248 (1962), 36-48.

38. Toshiro Maeda, "Kyukei yosokuhyo shiron: Sagihan no kyukei ruikei ni kansuru yosoku" (Tentative Article on Prediction Tables of Kyukei: The Kyukei Patterns for the Crime of Fraud), *Jochihogakuronshu* (Sophia Law Review) 7,Nos. 1-2 (1963), 113-72.

39. T. Maeda, "Ryokeiyosoku kenkyu jyosetsu: Sagihan no shikko jikkei ni kansuru keiryo keijigakuteki kubun" (Introduction to Research on Predicting Sentences: The Difference Between Suspension and the Execution of a Sentence of Fraud, According to Criminometrics), *Jochihogakuronshu,* 8, No. 1 (1964), 105-51.

40. T. Maeda. Sagihan shikkoyuyo yosokuhyo sairon: Kakushu yosokuhyo no yorestu" (Four Addition Tables for Predicting Suspended Sentences Involving Fraud) Jochihogakuronshu, 9, No. 2 (1965), 85-203.

41. Ritaro Naka and Toshimaro Kojo, "Ryokei no jisshoteki kenkyu" (Positive Study of Judicial Sentencing),

Shihokenkyuhokoku (Research Report of the Institute of Judicial Training). 15.No.1 (1966).

42. Morio Miyahara, "Resshajiko ni keru chuigimu to ryokei" (The Duty _of Attention in a Train-Accident Criminal Case, and Its Sentence), *Hanrei Times* (case Law Times). 192 (August 1966). 86-109.

43. Cf. Albert Somit, Joseph Tanenhaus, and Walter Wilke, "Aspects of Judicial Sentencing and Behaviour, "*University of Pittsburgh Law Review*, 21 (1960), 613-21 and reprinted in Schubert (ed.) *Judicial Behaviour*, pp. 389-94.

APPENDIX: DESCRIPTIVE (A THEORETICAL) STATISTICAL SENTENCING STUDIES IN JAPAN

Takahashi, Masami. "Sosho-sagi ni kansuru ryokei no jissai" (Sentencing in Soshosagi (Prozessbetrugl), *Hosokai zasshi* (Journal of the Bar Association) 18, Nos. 5-6 (1940), 41-79, 47-70.

Koga, Toshiro. "Kei no ryotei ni kansuru jisshoteki kenkyu-tokuni tosei jihan no ryo kei ni kanshite" (Positive Study on Sentencing—Particularly with Reference to Cases Related to Law of the Controlled Economy), *Shihokenkyu-hokokusho* (Research Report of Institute of Judicial Training), 29,No. 14 (1941), 1-261.

Kosetsu, Shizuhiko, *Kei no ryotei no jisshoteki kenkyu* (Positive Study on Sentencing) (KyowaTosho Shuppan Co., 1948), pp. 1-226.

Takahashi, Masami, "Ryokei no hensen ni kansuru tokei" (Statistics of Change in Sentencing), *Keijisaiban-shiryo* (Materials for Criminal Justice), 59 (1951), 1-263.

Takahashi. Masami, "Ryokei no hensen ni tsuite" (Changes in Sentencing), in *Keijiho no riron to genjitsu, Ono hakushi kanreki* slinkuga (Theory and Practice in Criminal Law, Essays to Commemorate the Sixtieth Birthday of Seiichiro Ono. LL.D.) 2 (1951), 351-403. Also in

Keijisaiban-shiryo (Materials for Criminal Justice). 65 (1952).

Takahashi, Masami. "Settozai ni taisuru ryokei no chiikisa ni tsuite" (On the Regional Difference of Sentencing for the Crime of Larceny), Keihozashi (Journal of Criminal Law). 3, No. 3 (1953). 364-87. Also in *Keijisaiban-shiryo*, 76, 1-191.

Shoda, Mitsusaburo and Takahashi, Masami, "Shogaichishizai ni taisuru ryokei no jisshoteki kenkyu" (Positive Study on Sentencing for the Crime of Death through Bodily Injury), *Horitsujiho*, 30 (May. August, November 1958) 71-77, 74-80, 68-81; and 31 (January 1959), 87-100.

Irie, Masanobu, "Satsujin no tsumi ni kansurti ryokei shiryo" (Statistics for the Crime of Homicide), *Shihokenkyusho-chosa-sosho* (Material Report of the Institute of Judicial Training), 5-1 (1959). 1-227: 5-2 (1959). 1-801.

Irie, Masanobu. "Shogaichishi no tsumi ni kansuru ryokei shiryo" (Statistics for the Crime of Death through Bodily Injury), *Shihokenkyusho-chosa-sosho* 6 (1959), 1-328.

Takeyasu. Masamitsu, "Eikoku, Seidoku to ni okeru boryoku hanzai no torishimari to kei no ryotei" (Crackdown on Violent Crime and Sentencing for it in the United Kingdom and West Germany), *Horitsujiho*, 31 (February 1959), 68-74, and (March 1959), 72-79.

Takeyasu, Masamitsu and Fuzihiro, Kizo, "Seimeihan ni taisuru kei no ryotei" (Study on the Evaluation of Penalties for Offenses against Human Life), *Homusogokenkyusho-kenkyubu-kiyo* (Bulletin of the Criminological Research Department) (1962), pp. 81-146.

Takeyasu, Masamitsu and Tokoro, Kazuhiko. "Nichi Ei Doku ni okeru seimeihan ni taisuru kei no ryotei" (Study on the Evaluation of Penalties for Offences against Human Life in Japan. United Kingdom, and Germany),

Homusogokenkyusho-kenkyushiryo (Research Materials of the Criminological Research Department), 10, (1962).

Takeyasu, Masamitsu and Tokoro, Kazuhiko. "Nichi Ei Doku Futsu oyobi Suis ni okeru kei no ryotei no gaikyo" (A Summary of the Evaluation of Penalties for Offences against Human Life in Japan, Germany, the United Kingdom, France, and Switzerland), *Homusogo-kenkyusho-kenkyubu-kiyo* (1963), pp. 49-82; and Takeyasu, Masamitsu, "Seimeihan ni taisuru kei no ryotei ni kansuru jisshoteki kenkyu" (Positive Study on the Evaluation of Penalties for Offences against Human Life), ibid., pp. 83-121.

Takeda, Kunio and Hanyu. Masanori, "Jidoshajiko ni yoru gyomujyo kashit-suchishizai ni taisuru ryokei no kosatsu" (Consideration of the Assessment of Punishment for Involuntary Manslaughter by Negligence in an Automobile Accident, Based on a Case at Urawa District Court). *Shihoken-kyushoho* (Law Journal of the Legal Training and Research Institute), 29 and 31 (1966), 20-56, 58-84.

Takahashi, Masami, "Satsujinzai ni taisuru ryokei no jisshoteki kenkyu" (Positive Study of the Assessment of Penalties for the Crime of Homicide), *Shihokenkyuho-kokusho* (Research Report of the Institute of Judicial Training), 17, No. 5 (1967), 1-276.

Onitsuka, Kentaro, "Kei no ryotei ni kansuru jisshoteki kenkyu: gokanzai" (Positive Study of the Assessment of Penalty: Rape), *Shihokenkyuhokokusho*, 17, No. 3 (1967), pp. 1-296.

4

MEASURING ATTITUDES ACROSS CULTURES: A FACTOR ANALYSIS OF THE REPLIES OF JAPANESE JUDGES TO EYSENCK'S INVENTORY OF CONSERVATIVE-PROGRESSIVE IDEOLOGY[1]

Recognizing the necessity of cross-cultural comparison was at one time fundamental to most social research, but until recently, behavioural scientists have neglected this and instead concentrated almost exclusively on the development and testing of hypotheses within a single country, notwithstanding the endeavours of students of "comparative government."[2]

Only recently have problems of cross-cultural generalization begun to be faced squarely again.[3] The difficulties of genuine crosscultural research are manifold. In this paper we deal with only one of the most perplexing aspects—stimulus (questionnaire, attitude-measurement) construction—and specifically ask: "Can an attitude inventory, developed in England[4], and apparently used successfully in England, Germany, Sweden,[5] and the United States,[6] be applied in the measurement of the attitudes and ideology of Japanese Supreme Court and High Court Judges?"[7]

In attempting to develop a scientific study of politics, we presumably seek to determine common patterns of political attitudes, behavior, and institutions. At least we look for standardized criteria which can be applied in measuring precisely whatever differences and similarities in attitudes, behaviour, and institutions we actually observe.

One of the most popular notions that political scientists and other political commentators have used in describing and analyzing political phenomena in the United States and in other countries is that of the attitude continuum labeled liberal (or progressive, or radical) and conservative. Many inventories attempting to measure this dimension in the United States and elsewhere have been constructed,[8] and one of the most widely used is that developed by the British psychologist, Hans Eysenck.[9]

Eysenck has posited a four-step hierarchical model of attitude organization. At the lowest level he spoke of *specific opinions:* "opinions which are not related in any way to other opinions . . . and which are not reproducible in the sense that if the same or a similar question were asked again under different circumstances, the answer might be different. Such opinions do not go beyond themselves and they do not throw any light. . . on the personalities or on the ideologies of the people holding them."[10]

At the next higher level Eysenck described "opinions which are reproducible and which form a relatively constant part of an individual's make-up."[11] These he called *habitual opinions.* The third level he designated *attitudes,* the term he gave to "a large number of ... opinions on the same issue which in combination define [one's] attitudes toward that issue."[12] The example he gave was of opinions which he labeled anti-Semitic.

"But," Eysenck further observed, "even attitudes of this kind are not independent. . . . Attitudes themselves are correlated and give rise to what might be called super-attitudes or *ideologies.*"[13]

This then is Eysenck's model of attitude organization:[14]

IDEOLOGY	(Conservatism)
↑	
ATTITUDES	(Anti-Semitic)
↑	
HABITUAL OPINIONS	("Jews are inferior.")
↑	
SPECIFIC OPINIONS	("Finkelstein is a dirty Jew!")

Eysenck further points out that different types of measurement are suitable for these different levels of organization: public opinion polls generally tap the habitual opinion level; unidimensional, linear scales measure attitudes; while factor analysis and other more complex statistical procedures are appropriate for the measurement of ideologies.[15]

The question of whether or not specific opinions cluster sufficiently to be decriebed as attitudes, and whether attitudes in turn should be called ideologies, can be resolved empirically. One technique involves the construction of inventories (i.e. sets of opinion-statements which are presumed to deal with the same attitude and/or ideology) which are administered to respondents who express agreement r disagreement with the statements. The responses are then measured by appropriate statistical tests of the amount of intercorrelation among the opinions which leads to inferences about the attitudes of the respondents.

EYSENCK'S ORIGINAL TWO-FACTOR PATTERN

Eysenck followed such a procedure in developing and testing a forty-item inventory which he considered to be a measure of radicalism or conservatism.[16] He constructed his inventory by surveying earlier pre-mid-1940's) attitudinal research, selecting appropriate items from these studies, and then adding other items of his own that he deemed significant and timely.[17] Respondents were asked to indicate (by a Likert scale) whether they strongly approved of the statement, approved on the whole, disapproved on the whole, or strongly disapproved. Indecision and non-response were assigned neutral weights of zero. The respondents were also asked to provide certain demographic information concerning their sex, age, profession, income, education, and political party affiliation.

The inventory was administered to students at the University of London, extension students, and to their friends, and 750 responses were selected from middle-class subjects divided equally among Conservative, Liberal, and Socialist party supporters.[18] These 750 replies, when scored and factor-analyzed, were found to load most highly on two unrotated factors,[19] the first of which Eysenck identified as radical-conservative and second as tough-minded and tender-minded.[20]

Our interest here does not lie—as well it might—in a comparison of the numerical values of the factor loadings of the replies of Eysenck's British respondents with those of his German, Nagel's American, and my Japanese subjects. Indeed, were we to compare the specific factor loadings on the first two factors for each of the groups for whom we have data, we would see very great discrepancies. Rather, we are interested—as was Eysenck himself—with the *pattern* which results when the first two factors are plotted in two-dimensional space. The assumption here is that such a method results in better comprehension of the ideological configuration of the respondents than does reliance upon the loadings of any single item or factor alone. For all

Table 4.1 Item Loadings of the First Two Factors for Five Groups of Respondents

Item	*Eysenck British*	*Eysenck German*	*Nagel Judge*	*Tanaka Japan*	*Dator Judge*
1	*2*	*3*	*4*	*5*	*6*
		FACTOR I			
1	47	—35	42	—51	51
2	—33	30	54	44	—10
3	51	60	02	—52	33
4	—57	57	—52	23	—16
5	—62	16	—44	05	—38
6	—53	—	—47	—	—22
7	—13	36	—12	42	24
8	—22	21	—45	31	—38
9	—68	90	—29	66	—60
10	45	—62	19	—49	57
11	46	—20	47	—42	30
12	50	—57	29	—45	35
13	—30	35	—31	49	—11

Contd...

1	2	*3*	*4*	*5*	*6*
14	—46	42	—55	29	39
15	72	—64	30	—55	27
16	47	—36	16	—61	58
17	—53	33	—46	21	05
18	41	—54	23	37	29
19	23	—50	—17	—40	56
20	55	—70	17	68	41
21	—29	44	11	64	—38
22	36	—33	15	12	—11
23	—60	70	—51	17	—54
24.	21	—45	29	—55	64

FACTOR II

1	32	06	51	—73	36
2	15	—06	—05	—44	58
3	32	—17	26	—30	02
4	—22	42	—02	31	56
5	—23	24	—09	08	07
6	49	—	40	—	37
7	—27	—19	61	50	—32
8	20	—16	10	—12	15
9	01	—27	12	75	50
10	39	—28	35	39	—15
11	—65	52	—21	41	—02
12	17	—05	29	—47	32
13	—09	08	04	67	—20
14	47	—14	26	—35	23
15	11	—04	21	51	06
16	—34	21	27	38	—10
17	56	—42	21	—31	20
18	16	—19	17	37	35
19	25	—20	62	—63	34
20	23	—22	66	26	52
21	—03	—12	02	—59	23
22	—42	34	—07	—22	—18
23	—20	16	09	22	26
24	07	—02	41	—52	14

subjects, the first two factors accounted for significantly more of the variance than did a combination of any other two factors, and, as I shall seek to demonstrate, the pattern of the first two factors in each instance is sufficiently similar to Eysenck's original pattern to encourage me to rest my analysis on the first two factors alone.

Nagel's study of American judges, and my study of Japanese judges, did not use all forty of Eysenck's original items. Instead, Nagel selected twenty-four items, presumably in order to have a shorter questionnaire.

As I shall show, Eysenck's radical-conservative continuum seems to be composed of attitudes which cluster in eight sub-categories:

1. Socialist Sympathy
2. Pro-War
3. Rehabilitation of Offenders
4. Religious Sympathy
5. Ethnocentrism
6. Sexual Freedom
7. Democratic Sympathy
8. Male Superiority

Nagel chose twenty-four items (with some changes) from Eysenck's inventory so that each of the eight sub-categories had three items each relating to it.[21] I adopted Nagel's inventory, also making some changes that I felt the Japanese situation demanded.

In the discussion to follow, including the presentation of Eysenck's findings, I shall rely on the twenty-four Nagel items only. The items are given in Table 4.2 in an English back-translation of the form I used on the Japanese judges. Eysenck's original numbers for these items are given in parentheses. I shall refer to the items according to their numbers *without* parentheses in the discussion which follows, however, so care should be taken if reference is made to Eysenck's studies. Also, since I will make considerable use of the clusters, I have chosen to display the items according to the eight sub-categories and not in simple numerical order, although this may cause some inconvenience to the reader in re-checking the exact wording of a specific item.

Thus, using the loadings exactly as Eysenck reported them for his first two factors,[22] I have plotted the twenty-four items as shown in Figure 4.1. It will be seen that the items fall in neat clusters into four quadrants which from now on I will refer to, in counter-clockwise position from upper right to upper left, lower left, and lower right, as quadrants I, II, III, and IV respectively.

*Table 4.2: Back-Translation (from Japanese to English) of the Questionnaire Used for a Sample of Japanese Judges**

Sexual Freedom

14 (23). Divorce laws should be altered to make divorce harder [easier]. (C)

17 (29). Men and women have the right to find out whether they are sexually suited before marriage (e.g. by companionate marriage). (L)

22 (35). Birth control, except when medically indicated, should be made illegal. (C)

Religious Sympathy

6 (9). Religious [Sunday]-observance is old-fashioned, and should cease to govern our behavior. (L)

11 (16). Only by going back to religion can civilization hope to survive. (C)

16 (28). It is right and proper that ethical [religious] education in schools should be compulsory. (C)

Socialist Sympathy

2 (2). Present laws favour the rich as against the poor. (L)

9 (12). Ultimately, private property should be abolished, and complete socialism introduced. (L)

15 (27). The nationalization of the great industries is likely to lead to inefficiency, bureaucracy, and stagnation. (C)

Rehabilitation of Offenders

4 (6). Our treatment of criminals is too harsh; we should try to cure, not to punish them. (L)

18 (30). The principle "It is bad to pamper your child" [Spare the rod and spoil the child] has much truth in it, and should govern our methods of bringing up children, (C)

23 (36). The death penalty is barbaric, and should be abolished. (L) *Democratic Sympathy*

8. (11). Unrestricted freedom of discussion on every topic is desirable in the press, in literature, on the stage, etc. (L)

13 (20). There should be far more controversial and political discussion over the radio and television. (L)

24 (40). Only people with a definite minimum of intelligence and education should be allowed to vote. (C)

Pro-War

3 (3). War is inherent in human nature. (C)

5 (8). In the interest of peace, we must give up part of our national sovereignty. (L)

10 (13). A person who refuses to defend his country cannot be called a patriot. [Conscientious objectors are traitors to their country, and should be treated accordingly.] (C)

Ethnocentrism

1 (1). Koreans [Coloured people] are innately inferior to Japanese [white people]. (C)

12 (17). Marriages between Japanese [white] and Koreans [coloured people] should be strongly discouraged. (C)

20 (33). Foreigners [The Jews] have too much power and influence in this country. (C)

Male Superiority

7 (10). It is right [wrong] that men should be permitted greater sexual freedom than women by society. (C)

19 (31). Women are not the equals of men in intelligence, organizing ability, etc. (C)

21 (34). Differences in pay between men and women doing the same work should be abolished. (L)

* *The bracketed words are the language of Eysenck's original inventory. The symbols in parentheses, following the items, denote their presumed directionality, liberal or conservative. On Item 7, the direction is L for Eysenck; on Item 14, the direction is L for both Eysenck and Nagel.*

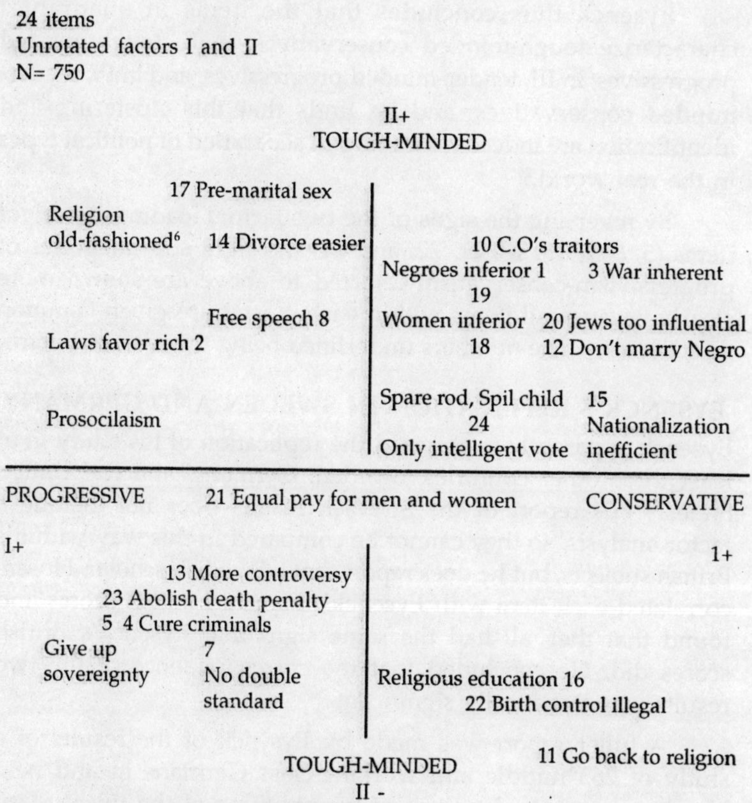

Figure 4.1 *Eysenck's British Subjects*

First we note that all of the items on the right of the vertical axis, whether in quadrants I or IV, are "conservative" items, while all to the left are "progressive" (I shall generally use these terms throughout, though Eysenck prefers "radical" and Nagel uses "liberal"). Thus the horizontal axis, which is Factor I, can clearly be labelled, from left to right, progressive-conservative. Eysenck names the vertical axis, or Factor II, tough-minded (at the top) and tender-minded (bottom), though he admits that "other interpretations of this . . . factor are of course possible. One set of opinions appears to be dominated by ethical, moralistic, superego, altruistic values; the other by realistic, worldly, egoistic values."[23]

Eysenck thus concludes that the items in quadrant I characterize tough-minded conservatives; in II, tough-minded progressives; in III, tender-minded progressives; and in IV, tender-minded conservatives; and he finds that this clustering and identification are indeed a meaningful separation of political types in the real world.[24]

By reversing the signs of the two factors loadings for eight items (5, 6, 7, 15, 18, 21, 22, and 24) the eight sub-categories of progressivism-conservatism referred to above are shown more clearly because all items within each cluster are given common directionality. The numbers underlined being the reversed items.

EYSENCK'S REPLICATION IN SWEDEN AND GERMANY

Eysenck apparently supervised the replication of his study in at least three other countries: Sweden, Germany, and the United States.[25] His report of the Swedish results does not include a factor analysis, so they cannot be compared in this way with his British subjects, but he does report that a Swedish scholar, Husen, correlated each item with Eysenck's Factors I and II scores and found that they all had the same signs that Eysenck's British scores did. He concluded that the correspondence of the two results was statistically significant.[26]

A fuller report was made by Eysenck of the results of a study of 263 middle and working-class Germans in and near Hamburg, and the loadings of twenty-three of the twenty-four items we are interested in were given for the first two factors (apparently item 6, "Sunday observance is old-fashioned . . ." was not included). The representation of these two factors, with the signs of all but seven of the factor loadings reversed so as to place conservative responses on the right and the progressive on the left while the rest remained unchanged to highlight the patterning of the clusters. While the correspondence between Eysenck's British and German patterns is very close, still we see that the clustering is not nearly as "neat" for the Germans as it was for the British. Since our interest here is primarily with the Japanese data, I shall refrain from commenting on the specific variations found, and simply note that they exist and that they may be due in no small measure simply to linguistic (stimulus) differences. I shall amplify this last point below.

FACTOR PATTERN OF NAGEL'S AMERICAN JUDGES

The American political scientist Stuart Nagel in 1960 mailed a twenty-four item inventory, adapted from Eysenck's, to all 313 state and federal Supreme Court judges who were serving in 1955. One-hundred and eighteen usable responses were returned. In order to make the inventory more applicable for the American situation, the wording of five items was changed:

Item 7. "It is wrong that men . . ." was changed to "it is right . . ." Thus, we should expect to have to reverse the factor loading of this item to keep it in its original cluster.

Item 9. The sentence was entirely changed from a reference to socialism to read instead: "More collectivism, like the TVA, should be introduced into our society." This American version would seem to be decidedly less extreme than Eysenck's wording, but the item should be found in the same cluster for both groups.

Item 15. This was changed from reading, "nationalization of the great industries," in Eysenck's form to, "nationalization of any industry," in Nagel's. We would not expect the item to be located in a significantly different position because of this.

Item 16. This was altered from a simple reference to "religious education" to "non-sectarian religious education." I expect no cluster change.

Item 17. Finally, the phrase, "e.g. by companionate marriage," was eliminated from Nagel's inventory, thereby perhaps having the effect of increasing the assumption that the statement referred to irresponsible pre-marital sexual intercourse rather than to the more restrained relationship implied by "companionate marriage." I am less certain how this should affect the position of the item, but I doubt there should be a change.

The question can legitimately be asked whether or not Nagel's inventory is identical to Eysenck's and whether some variation between the replies of the British and American respondents should be attributed to actual ideological pattern differences between them, or to differences in the inventories.[27]

Eysenck's inventory had forty items and Nagel's but twenty-four. While the shorter form might have heightened the return rate for Nagel's judges, did it have any effect on the replies themselves? If the length of the inventory is unrelated to the patterning of the answers, why did Nagel choose three items from each of the eight sub-groups of liberalism-conservatism, and not (more simply) one or two?

Nagel's inventory followed the same item order as Eysenck's, but excluded sixteen items. What effect does item order have on the pattern of replies, especially considering the (perhaps) threatening nature of the first item (colored people are inferior)? Does the inclusion or exclusion of the sixteen items affect the pattern of replies? Should the order of the twenty-four items have been randomized on the inventories to control for this? Should Nagel have done so even though Eysenck did not?

To what extent are Nagel's item wording changes necessary, desirable, or harmful? Do they result in items which are more *similar* because of cultural differences than they would have been if they had not been changed? On the other hand, are there some other items that *should* have been altered? Consider item six. What does "Sunday observance" mean to an American? Does it mean the same for a British citizen?

Are there some items that are only of marginal significance to conservatism-liberalism in the United States, however important they might be in England, and are some crucial items (e.g. states' rights) omitted? If so, would it have been better, worse, or of no consequence if Nagel had added specifically appropriate items?

There are other things as well which can be suggested as having an effect on the replies of the American respondents sufficient to alter their pattern without there in fact being a basic ideological difference between the same two groups. Sampling, as I suggested, could be one. Eysenck's subjects were university and extension students (and their friends) who personally were administered the inventory. Nagel mailed his inventory to the American judges, and only about 38 per cent returned usable responses. Are we safe in making statements about American judges generally on the basis of these returns? Of course, Nagel uses the replies of the American judges not so much for this purpose, but rather to show that a judge's position on the inventory as either a liberal or a conservative correlates significantly with his judicial decisions in criminal, business regulation, motor vehicle accident, and employee compensation cases.[28] Nonetheless, other readers are strongly tempted to generalize from Nagel's data to the ideology of American judges.

The pattern of responses for Nagel's American judges, and is derived by plotting the items, according to their loadings (items 5, 6, 15, 18, 21, 22, and 24 were reversed) on the first two (of nine) factors as determined by my own factor analysis of Nagel's data.[29]

Recall that the wording of three of Nagel's items (15, 16, and 17) differed somewhat from Eysenck's; in one (9) Nagel used an entirely new sentence; and in another (7), the direction of the sentence was completely reversed. Yet, in spite of thesechanges, there is a relatively stable pattern of replies. The Male Superiority cluster altered its quadrant location from I to II. Items in the Democratic Sympathy, Rehabilitation of Offenders, Male Superiority, and Religious Sympathy clusters are rather widely separated, but we conclude that the modified Eysenck inventory measures substantially the same major dimensions for the British, German, and American respondents, though the clustering of items in the sub-categories is not as tight for the German and American respondents as it was for the original British subjects.

The variations can be explained in a number of ways. Alterations in the wording of the items may account for some. Differences in the sampling procedure and in the mere number and type of subjects themselves may account for others. The passage of time (Eysenck's British and German data were gathered in the late 1940's, Nagel's in 1960) may account for yet more. And finally, the pattern differences may be due to actual differences in the arrangement of ideological space among the various groups.

FACTOR PATTERN OF A JAPANESE SAMPLE

Eysenck's inventory has been used twice in Japan. It was administered to a mixed group of 355 Japanese university students, their relatives, labor union representatives, and Christian women.[30] The forty-item inventory was directly translated, save for one statement that was omitted (our item 6) concerning Sunday observance. A few of the items were also considerably altered, but of the twenty-four which Nagel selected, only two were modified: Item 10, concerning conscientious objection, was rejected and a statement favoring the rearmament of Japan was inserted, and item 20 was changed from one referring to "Jews" having too much power to "America" (not *Americans).* The rest of the twenty-four items were not altered, thus leaving such statements as "colored people are inferior to white people" to perplex the Japanese who, while vaguely recognizing that they are "colored," generally consider themselves to be a superior people.[31]

The loadings on the two factors of the Japanese subjects, with the signs of all items but 5, 7, 15, 18, 21, 22, and 24 reversed as in the case of the Germans to place the conservative replies on the right and to clarify the clusters. We observe a cluster pattern which, in spite of considerable scattering, is still relatively similar to Eysenck's original.

The change in wording of item 20 ("America" for "Jews") has shifted that item radically. Item 21 is separated from the Male Superiority cluster and seems to be part of the Religious Sympathy cluster. Item 18 ("Spare the rod") may also be a religious item here, and item 22 ("Birth control is illegal") may be part of the Rehabilitation of Offenders cluster.

FACTOR PATTERN OF JAPANESE HIGH COURT JUDGES

In 1964, while I was teaching in the College of Law and Politics of Rikkyo University, Tokyo, the students of my seminar in judicial behavior and I translated the twenty-four items of Eysenck's inventory which Nagel used and sent them to the fifteen Supreme Court and 193 High Court (Court of Appeals) judges who were on the Japanese bench in 1964.[32]

The translation proved to be extremely difficult. A number of items (e.g. "Jews are too powerful in this country.") were clearly inappropriate. Others ("Only persons with a minimum of education and intelligence should be allowed to vote.") were argued by my Japanese colleagues as not being major aspects of conservatism-progressivism in Japan while important Japanese issues were omitted in Eysenck's inventory. To translate the phrase, "Spare the rod and spoil the child," directly into Japanese would have rendered it meaningless. Problems relating to the items (1 and 12), referring to coloured and white people, have been mentioned.

Our group spent days on the translation of each item, and we consulted a number of Japanese sociologists, psychologists, and political scientists[33] before deciding on what we felt was an "equivalent stimulus" (rather than direct) translation:

> We changed "coloured people" to "Koreans" and "white people" to "Japanese" (1 and 12) in the belief that this is a similar, even if not identical, problem to the race question in the United States and England. We decided to replace "Jews" with "Foreigners" (20) for the same reason.
>
> Because Japan now has a very simple divorce procedure (considerably more liberal than any American state or England, we believe), we changed item 14 from making divorce "easier" to "harder."
>
> We retained Nagel's reversal of item 7, stating that greater male sex freedom was "right" rather than "wrong."
>
> Because purely religious education in the schools has never been an issue while ethical education decidedly is, we replaced "religious" with "ethical" in item 16. Item 10 also was especially perplexing because Japan (as far as I can determine) has had nothing equivalent to conscientious objection to war as a recognized principle. (Tanaka and Matsuyama also had trouble with this item, and discarded it entirely in favor of an item stating that Japan should be rearmed.) We here said, roughly, "A person who refuses to defend his country cannot be called a patriot," which sounds rather weak thus stated in English, and certainly is less extreme than Eysenck's item about conscientious objectors being traitors, but we felt it was the closest we could come, given the Japanese historical situation, and that it was superior

to Tanaka and Matsuyama's decision because it was somewhat closer to Eysenck's item.

We chose Eysenck's version of item 9 because socialist sympathy is a viable political option in Japan, even though Nagel may have felt it was not in the United States.

Deciding that "Sunday observance" in item 6 probably meant simply "religious observance" for most Americans and not what it signified for British citizens anyway, and noting that it was omitted from the German and the earlier Japanese translations, we decided that it would be tapping roughly the same dimension that it did in America if we substituted "religious" for "Sunday."

We adopted Nagel's shortening of item 17 (pre-marital sex, omitting "companionate marriage") as well.

Finally, we chose to substitute a different phrase in item 18. Rather than translating "spare the rod and spoil the child," which apparently has no equivalent in Japanese, and hence does not have the epigrammatic quality it has in English, we chose another well-known Japanese saying which we felt was closest, though by no means identical because it lacked reference to physical punishment. This can rather inadequately be rendered in English as "it is bad to pamper your child." The term "pamper" is *amaeru* and we felt it was the best that could be done.[34]

In sum, we altered the wording of seven items (1 , 6, 10, 12, 16, 18, 20), adopted Nagel's alteration for two (7 and 17) and Eysenck's rather than Nagel's for two (9 and 15). I reversed one item (14), differently from both Eysenck and Nagel, and I retained Nagel's reversal, from Eysenck, of another (7). The remaining twelve were left unchanged from the form used by both Eysenck and Nagel. It should be noted that we apparently had translation difficulties with two items, in spite of our pre-test procedures: "birth control" was apparently interpreted by some respondents as including abortion, while it was meant to designate only contraception. The word "controversial" also caused trouble in item 13, and more judges (23 per cent) omitted or declined to answer that item than any other, claiming they did not understand its meaning.

The item distribution for the first two (of ten) factors which were derived when I factor analyzed the replies of all judges (N = 71) who omitted no more than five items (11 of the 82 judges who returned otherwise usable inventories were thus excluded from the analysis).

Once again, in spite of certain item difficulties, we find a pattern which corresponds broadly with that encountered before. The Male Superiority cluster is modified with both item 7 (changed from stating that the double standard is "wrong" to "right") and item 21 ("Abolish pay differences between men and women," having been reversed to indicate, *do not* abolish differences) falling near the Religious Sympathy cluster as item 21 also did for Tanaka and Matsuyama's subjects. Save for item 18, the Rehabilitation of Offenders cluster has shifted from quadrant III to II. The placement of the Sexual Freedom items is also quite different for the judges. The patterning of the other clusters is generally what we have encountered before.

We conclude, then, that the Eysenck inventory of progressive-conservative ideology displays remarkable consistency over the four cultures where it has been used. For the British, German, American, and Japanese subjects (with but a few discrepancies) the items on the right of the figures (positioned in accordance with their factor loadings on the first two factors) are conservative while those on the left are progressive.

Even more significantly, the eight sub-categories of progressive-conservative ideology also seem to be generally stable over the four cultures. The general positioning is indicated in Figure 4.2. Ethnocentrism, Pro-war, and Male Superiority items cluster in quadrant I; Sexual Freedom in quadrant II; Socialist and Democratic Sympathy in quadrants II and III, Rehabilitation of Offenders in quadrant III, and Pro-religious Sympathy in quadrant IV.

The question does arise, nonetheless, whether or not it is desirable to attempt to define different clusters of items for the Japanese judges than the eight derived from Eysenck's subjects. It is possible that the items should be differently clustered to explain better the components of progressivism-conservatism in

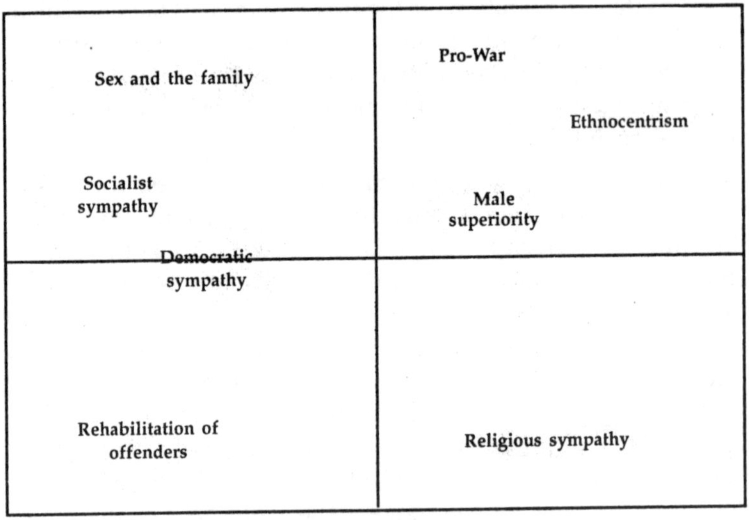

Figure 4.2 *General Position of the Eight Sub-Categories of Progressive-Conservative Ideology in Four Countries*

a given country or for a given set of respondents. Recognizing this, I have reclustered the items for the Japanese judges.

We see first that agreement with items on the right of the vertical axis can be considered to indicate support for "traditional" Japanese values while agreement with those on the left evidences adherence to "modern" or "Western" values. This, of course, is also consistent with a progressive-conservative identification.

Concerning the naming of specific clusters, we see that the seven items in quadrant I might all be said to be tapping a "Superiority" dimension, and that under that general label, we can discern Japanese Superiority (1, 12, 20). Male Superiority (14 and 19), Intellectual Superiority (24), and Adult Superiority (18).

The five items in or near quadrant IV might be called Pro-religion and Traditional Ethics, while those in quadrant III, I feel, are best identified as Confused Item Wording. These were the two items about which many of the judges evidenced misunderstanding.

The six items farthest to the left all seem to be favoring Freedom and Equality, while both items 7 and 17, near the center of the figure, seem to indicate an Anti-Sex dimension. Finally, items 2 and 4, both falling near the vertical axis, appear to relate to the Status of Current Law.

I feel that this reclustering does not at all invalidate the earlier contention that the eight sub-categories found in Eysenck's analysis can also be said to be a part of progressive-conservative ideology in Japan. Indeed, I am struck by the relative immobility of the Ethnocentric, Religious, Pro-war, Socialist, and Democratic clusters. Rather, because of differences in the wording of the items and the various subjects involved, we should expect some variation. The re-clustering of the items might help indicate more precisely just what these differences are and what, according to a culture-specific basis, they might mean.

For the Japanese judges, I feel that the re-clustering indicates that the inventory taps Superiority-Equality and Pro-religious dimensions as its dominant themes, with certain items (7 and 17) indicating a negative evaluation of sex, and others (2 and 4) the appropriateness of current Japanese law.

That these are major dimensions of progressive-conservative (modern-traditional) ideology in Japanese culture, as far as an elite such as the Japanese judges is concerned, is understandable. As is well known, Japan is very much a status-oriented country, and several conservative-progressive inventories constructed by Japanese for use in Japan focus precisely on this fact.[35] It is of considerable significance that Eysenck's inventory does include items which focus on superiority-inferiority *v.* equality in human relations, and that the Japanese judges seemed to have responded to it in this manner.

Second, the persistence of the Religious Sympathy cluster in all the cultures surveyed, and its dominance in our re-clustering of the Japanese responses, is a finding of unusual interest. The judges indicated greater religious affiliation than is found in the Japanese population generally.[36] Yet, 61 per cent agreed that religion was old-fashioned, and but 41 per cent agreed that the only way civilization can be saved is by returning to religion (this latter is the lowest per cent of agreement of all the groups studied). In many ways, Japan can be considered as a non-religious (not anti-religious) nation.

Yet the Japanese, and especially the elites, are very much concerned with ethics. Ninety-six per cent of the judges agreed that ethical education in the public schools is necessary, and ethical education (which was banned by the Occupation and remained proscribed until the mid-1960's) has been re-introduced. More recently, the Ministry of Education has been urging that even more attention be devoted "to teaching of the fundamentals necessary to develop moral responsibilities in children."[37]

In addition, while most Japanese generally do not consider themselves to be members of any religious organization, the political party which is well on its way to becoming the third largest party in Japan, the *Komeito* (Clean Government Party), is closely affiliated with and derives its intellectual, financial, and electoral support from the *Soka Gakkai*, a Nichiren-Buddhist group which is the largest religious organization in Japan. Moreover, the government itself (or at least a major faction of the ruling Liberal Democratic Party) is moving to re-introduce some of the traditional religious symbols. Thus. *Kigensetsu*, the day when Japan was supposedly founded, has been reinstated as an official holiday. State support for Yasukuni and other important Shinto shrines is being seriously discussed by the government.

These attempts to bring back religion and traditional ethics as conservative, governmentally manipulated institutions are, however, being staunchly resisted by the "progressive" elements of the Japanese population. We should not be surprised, therefore, that the religious dimension has considerable importance as a factor in progressive-conservative ideology in Japan as elsewhere.

Not only the revised item clustering but also the comments of the Japanese judges themselves[38] lead us to conclude that at least two of the items (2 and 4) were viewed by the judges primarily as relating directly to their work as judges and as supporters (or critics) of the law. It is very significant that the only other group reported here for whom items 2 and 4 were found to lie together was that of Nagel's American judges! It is not surprising that the judges of both cultures should view these items in a quite different way than would ordinary citizens.

Finally, the history of Japanese adjudication relative to sex[39] and the fact that only two of the Japanese judges agreed that pre-marital sexual relations were permissible while 87 per cent *disagreed* that men should be allowed greater sexual freedom than women, encourages us to identify these two items which fall nearest the center of the figure (7 and 17) as tapping an Anti-Sex dimension. Moreover, because of the judicial consensus against sexual activity, and the concentration of these items near the zero point on the figure, we conclude that pro-sex *v.* anti-sex —at least for the judges — is not a progressive-conservative problem. Progressives and conservatives alike are opposed to sexual liberality.

INVENTORY SCORES AND POLITICAL PARTY AFFILIATION OF JAPANESE JUDGES

One of the reasons I chose Eysenck's inventory was that it was essentially the same as Nagel's: I intended to see if a judge who held a "liberal" (or conservative) ideology tended to render a "liberal" (or conservative) judicial decision. Unfortunately, I am unable to find this out for two reasons. (1) Only two Japanese Supreme Court justices (both retired) returned completed inventories. True, one was a well-known liberal and the other a conservative, and they scored appropriately on Eysenck's inventory, but two justices do not substantiate a hypothesis. (2) Although Japanese high court decisions are reached by a multi-judge court, and the decisional vote distribution is a matter of public record, how each individual judge voted, is not. I tried through a number of different contacts to have this material made available to me, but I was unable to determine how individual judges voted on specific cases. Without examining split decisions on multi-judge courts, we cannot be sure whether a judge is being influenced by his ideology when he renders a liberal or conservative decision, or whether the facts of the case themselves are such.

Failing that, I fell back on Eysenck's original method. I divided the judges into two ideological groups according to three different scoring methods. The first method was (as Eysenck's) simply to assign a zero each time a judge either responded in a conservative direction to an item or omitted it, and 1 when he gave a progressive answer. Next the numbers were totalled and the judges were ranked from high to low. As a second method, I took into account the different intensities of agreement and disagreement by assigning 1 for a very conservative response, 2 for a simple conservative one, 3 for don't know or no answer, 4 for a simple progressive choice, and 5 for a very progressive one.

Finally, following the method used by Nagel,[40] I utilized the Japanese judges' item loadings on Factor I (the conservative-progressive factor) to determine which items seemed to be most strongly progressive or conservative and which least so, in order to allow those items which loaded higher to weigh more than those which loaded lower. Thus, for items 1, 9, 10, 16, 19, 21, 23, and 24 I scored a very conservative response 1, conservative 2, don't know 5, progressive 8, and very progressive 9.[41] For items 3,5,8, 11, 12, 14, 20, I scored, on the same basis, 2-3-4-7-8, and for the remaining nine I scored 3-4-5-6-7.

The results are found in Figures 4.9, 4.10, and 4.11 respectively. We see that regardless of the scoring method, the Japanese judges as a whole were essentially conservative. Several of them scored at the "very conservative" end of the scale, and none at the "very progressive" end. Most were on the conservative side of the theoretical mid-point (the vertical dotted line on the figures).

We do see confirmation, however, of my contention that the Eysenck inventory measures conservative-progressive ideology for the Japanese judges. I asked the judges to state their political party preferences. Liberal Democrats (the ruling conservative political party) were in the preponderance (40 per cent) and if we combine all judges who specifically mentioned that they had supported some progressive political party (Socialist, Social Democrat, or some combination with a left-wing party—none mentioned the Communist Party), 27 per cent can be classified as progressive party supporters (labeled on the figures as "Socialist"). Thirty-three per cent of the judges either declined to name their party affiliation (17 per cent), said they did not vote (two gave this answer), or said they voted for various candidates without regard for their political party (14 per cent). We classified these on the figures as "other."

We then used a point biserial correlation to test the significance of the difference in the distribution of Liberal Democrats and Socialists on either side of the mid-point. The difference was significant beyond the .01 level for all three scoring methods.

Thus we can see that regardless of the scoring method used to rank them, the supporters of the Liberal Democratic party were overwhelmingly conservative and the Socialist parties were progressive, while the "others" were spread throughout the scale.

I conclude with some confidence, then, that by this test, the Eysenck inventory has validity in Japan as a measure of conservative and progressive ideology.

CONCLUSION

In the preceding pages I sought to determine whether or not Eysenck's inventory of conservative and progressive ideology, developed in the late 1940's in England, could be used as a currently valid instrument in Japan. I believe that it can. Similarities in the clusters of twenty-four of Eysenck's original forty items for the first two factors lead me to conclude that the ideological space of progressivism-conservatism may be such that Eysenck's inventory can be used in different countries and for different groups of persons.[42]

In addition to this factor pattern similarity, in the United States, England, and Japan, independent criteria (American judges' decisions on certain types of cases, and both the British subjects' and the Japanese judges' political party affiliations) enable me to affirm that the inventory can be used as a satisfactory measure by which people can be (1) classified as either conservatives or progressives, (2) ranked according to their degree of progressivism or conservatism, or (3) perhaps even have their degree of conservatism-progressivism compared in absolute numerical terms with that of persons not only in their own but in other countries.

I did not undertake to demonstrate this latter function here. This will be the main task of a proposed multiple scalogram analysis: to decide whether or not it is possible to extract a set of items from the twenty-four that will scale satisfactorily for all respondents so that we can make meaningful absolute comparisons of their ideologies. At the present time, though I feel that for a one-sample case the inventory satisfactorily classifies persons as progressives or conservatives, and ranks them along a progressive-conservative continuum, I have no confidence that the inventory as it now stands can do so for persons from two or more independent groups. That is, though something can be said about item percentage differences or about variations in the total number of conservative and progressive items chosen between groups, as both Nagel and I have done, I am reluctant to conclude, for example, that the Japanese judges are more or less conservative than the American judges, and am even less willing to declare how much more or less. But I feel we will eventually be able to undertake this kind of attitude measurement and comparison.

In conclusion, one additional thing must be made clear. I am not contending that Eysenck's inventory is the best possible one for cross-cultural purposes. I have not examined others in the detail I have this one. Neither am I contending that it is the best inventory for any one country. My Japanese colleagues were probably correct when they protested that inventories constructed specifically for Japan would be better for measuring conservatism-progressivism in that country. What I am urging is that, as a tried and proven instrument, this inventory be replicated in as many different countries and on as many different groups as possible. Its success with judges seems demonstrated, and because of the advantages of small groups, public vote, and (often) public decision and explanation which the study of judicial behavior has, judicial behavior holds an especially privileged and obligated place in comparative political research. It seems to me, then, that it is primarily through the development, testing, and replication of measures cross-culturally that the excessively parochial, episodic, and sterile tradition of political science can be overcome.

While additional, locally relevant items may be included; while care must be taken in the translation of items; while we must not cling to the inventory after it, like all the tools of science, becomes obsolete or superseded; while all the true but perhaps needlessly inhibiting warnings about cross-cultural research need to be heard: I believe that priority should be given to truly comparative judicial research and to the replication and improvement of proven instruments.

— *James Allen Dator*

REFERENCES

1. The factor analyses reported in this paper were financed by a grant from the Division of Research, Virginia Polytechnic Institute. I wish to thank Mark Swerdlin and Tony Springhall of the Virginia Tech Computing Center for their programing assistance.

2. This charge is certainly not new. See Roy Macridis, *The Study of Comparative Politics* (New York: Random House, 1955); Gunnar Heckscher, *The Study of Comparative Government and Politics* (London: Alien and Unwin, 1957); and Sigmund Neumann, "Comparative Politics—A Half-Century Appraisal," *The Journal of Politics*, 19 (1957), 369-90.

3. Some examples: Gabriel Almond and Sydney Verba, *The Civic Culture* (Princeton: Princeton University Press, 1963); Richard Merritt and Stein Rokkan, *Comparing Nations* (New Haven: Yale University Press, 1965); Bruce Russett, et al., *World Handbook of Political and Social Indicators* (New Haven: Yale University Press, 1964); F. W. Moore (ed.), *Readings in Cross-Cultural Methodology* (New Haven: HRAF Press, 1961); J. David Singer (ed.), *Quantitative International Politics* (New York: Free Press, 1967).

4. Hans J. Eysenck, *The Psychology of Politics* (London: Routledge and Kegan Paul, 1954), especially Chap. 4.

5. Hans J. Eysenck, "Primary Social Attitudes: A Comparison of Attitude Patterns in England, Germany, and Sweden," *Journal of Abnormal and Social Psychology*, 48 (1953), 563-68.

6. Stuart Nagel, "Off-the-Bench Judicial Attitudes," in Glendon Schubert (ed.), *Judicial Decision-Making* (New York: Free Press, 1963), pp. 29-54. Nagel has reported other aspects of this study in a number of professional journals as well. See note 28, below.

7. James Alien Dator, "The Life History and Attitudes of Japanese High Court Judges," *Western Political Quarterly*, 20 (June 1967), 408-39. Kunio Tanaka and Yasuo Matsuyama, "Shakaiteki Taido no Sokuteiron-teki Kenkyu" ("Research in the Measurement of Social Attitudes"), in Okichi Endo (ed.), *Sengo Nihon Shinrigaku no Tenbo [A View of Psychology in Postwar Japan]* (Tokyo: Sanitchi Shobo, 1954), pp. 215-19, also report on the use of Eysenck's inventory in Japan.

8. Nagel cites nine such inventories, "Off-the-Bench Judicial Attitudes," p. 44, n. 11, and discusses why he believes Eysenck's scale is superior to each.

9. Eysenck, *The Psychology of Politics*, p. 129.

10. Ibid, p. 111.

11. Loc. cit.

12. Ibid. p. 112.

13. Ibid. p. 113.

14. Rokeach also indicates that above the ideological level is a "belief system" which psychologically integrates all of the lower items. As fundamentally important as they may be, we are not concerned with belief systems here. See Milton Rokeach, *The Open and Closed Mind* (New York: Basic Books, 1960), especially Chap. 2, p. 35.

15. Eysenck, *Psychology of Politics*, p. 113.

16. The following statement of Eysenck's procedure is from *Psychology of Politics*, pp. 121-43.

17. This is one way to construct an attitude inventory. For others, see Warren Torgerson, *Theory and Methods of Scaling* (New York: Wiley, 1958), Chap. 3, and Herbert McClosky, "Conservatism and Personality," *American Political Science Review*, 52 (March 1958), 27-45. Rokeach, *Open and Closed Mind*, p. 72, used a method similar to that of Eysenck.

18. Since Eysenck was interested in identifying and measuring ideological space-patterns themselves and not in generalizing about the attitudes and/or

ideologies of all or a sub-group of British citizens, this method is justifiable. See Hans Eysenck, "Primary Social Attitudes: 1. The Organization and Measurement of Social Attitudes," *International Journal of Opinion and Attitude Research,* 1 (1947), 51-58, and Eysenck, "Primary Social Attitudes: A Comparison of Attitude Patterns," pp. 563-568. However, that Eysenck's British, Swedish, and German (and later, Tanaka and Matsuyama's Japanese) subjects are mainly university students, while Nagel's American and my Japanese respondents are political elites, should be kept in mind in comparing differences found both for specific items and the attitude/ideological patterns.

19. Eysenck justifies basing his analysis on unrotated rather than rotated factors in his "Primary Social Attitudes: 1," pp. 62-64. The question of when, and by what method, to rotate is a thorny one and in my factor analysis of Nagel's American and my Japanese judges' replies, I found that utilization of the unrotated factors was preferable to the orthogonal Varimax rotation solution I chose as part of my factoring routine. I do not know whether a different method of rotation—for example, an oblique rotation—would have resulted in a more interpretable rotated structure. The point of much of what follows, however, in each instance based on unrotated factors, is to show the considerable similarity of the first two factors for all sets of respondents. On this basis alone, we feel Eysenck's argument is vindicated.

20. In his "Primary Social Attitudes: 1," pp. 59 ff, Eysenck mentions third and fourth factors which he labels Feminism and Humanitarianism respectively, and an unspecified (though apparently there were six, see p. 62) number of "doublet factors": "*i.e.,* correlations between two statements too large to be accounted for by sampling errors." (Loc. cit.) Unrotated Factor I accounted for 18 per cent of the variance, II for 8 per cent, III and IV had 2 per cent each, and the remaining six (?) 3 per cent all together. Thus Eysenck's discussion centered on the first two unrotated factors.

Andrew Comrey and John Newmeyer ("Measurement of Radicalism-Conservatism," *Journal of Social Psychology*, 67 (December 1965), 357-69, note that, if left unrotated, first-order factors are typically identified as liberal-conservative, but when rotated, liberal-conservatism vanishes, and in its place are several distinct sub-variables, such as religiosity, humanism, nationalism, and the like. I do not know what the situation in Eysenck's studies was, but my own factor analyses of Nagel's American and my Japanese judges found this definitely to be the case. It was not always possible to decide upon a satisfactory identification of the rotated factors, however. The items which loaded highest on the second (of ten) rotated factors for our Japanese judges, for example, were 1, 12, and 20 (Koreans are inferior; Don't marry Koreans: and Foreigners have too much influence.) This is plainly an "ethnocentric" factor. Similarly, items 6 (Religion is old-fashioned) and 11 (Go back to religion) and only those two loaded on rotated Factor VI. This is obviously a "religiosity" factor. But what is the best name for rotated Factor X, upon which items 5 (Give up sovereignty), 17 (See if sexually suited), and 24 (Only intelligent vote) loaded highest? There were similar problems in naming the rotated factors for Nagel's judges.

21. Nagel, "Off-the-Bench Judicial Attitudes," p. 30.
22. Eysenck, *Psychology of Politics*, p. 129.
23. Eysenck, "Primary Social Attitudes: 1," p. 61.
24. Eysenck. *Psychology of Politics*, pp. 133-42.
25. I have not been able to find a detailed reference to nor any information about Eysenck's supposed American replication. He specifically mentions such a study in *Psychology of Politics*, p. 132. Although he describes what he *expects* to be the results of the use of his inventory in the United States, on the basis of F scale and similar studies (in "Primary Social Attitudes: Comparison," pp. 563 f.), he does not give any details.
26. Eysenck, "Primary Social Attitudes: Comparison," p. 564.

27. The following questions will apply later to the Japanese version of Eysenck's inventory, and will not be specifically repeated again.

28. In addition to the "Off-the-Bench" article previously cited, see Nagel's articles, "Political Party Affiliation and Judges' Decisions," *American Political Science Review*, 55 (December 1961) 843-50; "Ethnic Affiliation and Judicial Propensities," *Journal of Politics*, 24 (February 1961), 92-110; "Judicial Backgrounds and Criminal Cases," *Journal of Criminal Law, Criminology, and Police Science*, 53 (September 1962), 333-39; and "Testing Relations Between Judicial Characteristics and Judicial Decisions," *Western Political Quarterly*, 15 (September 1962). 425-37.

29. Judges with more than five Don't Know or No Answer responses were eliminated, hence N = 101. I wish to thank Professor Nagel for making his data cards available to me.

30. Tanaka and Matsuyama, "Shakai-teki Taido no Sotteiron Kenkyu," pp. 215-19.

31. See Joichi Suetsuna, et al., *Nihonjin no Kokuminsei [Japanese National Character]* (Tokyo: Shiseido, 1961), English resume, p. 27, and my discussion on this point in Dator. "Life History and Attitudes of Japanese Judges," pp. 430 f.

32. A detailed analysis of the replies can be found in Dator, "Life History and Attitudes of Japanese Judges," pp. 420-35.

33. I would like to thank Dean Tsunahiro Kikui, Professors Norio Ogata, Jiro Kamishima, Masaaki Ikeda. Takao Sawaki, Michitoshi Takabatake, and Paul Matsushita, all of Rikkyo University, and Joji Watunuki of Tokyo University, and Yasumasa Tanaka of Gakushuin University for their advice on the translation and administration of the inventory. Members of the seminar on judicial behavior were Yutaka Ashino, Toshiro Baba, Satoshi Fujino, Yoshitake Maki, Noritaka Nemoto, and Toshiaki Yoshimoto. Special thanks are

due to Mr. Yoshiaki Sakai who worked on the translation. The guidance of Dr. Roderick B. Dugliss, then of International Christian University, is also gratefully acknowledged. None of these people is in any way responsible for the errors in the inventory.

For discussion on the techniques of translation, see Reuben Brower (ed.), *On Translation* (Cambridge: Harvard University Press, 1959); John Catford, *A Linguistic Theory of Translation* (New York: Oxford University Press, 1965); Susan Erwin and Robert Bower, "Translation Problems in International Surveys," *Public Opinion Quarterly*, 16 (Winter 1953), 595-604; Joyce Hertzler, *A Sociology of Language* (New York: Random House, 1965), especially pp. 128-31; Dell Hymes, "Linguistic Aspects of Cross-Cultural Personality Study," in Bert Kaplan, (ed.), *Studying Personality Cross-Culturally* (New York: Row and Peterson, 1961), pp. 313-59; Eugene Nida, *Toward a Science of Translation* (Leiden: E. J. Brill, 1964).

On the general problem of inventory construction for comparative research, see Bruce Anderson. "On the Comparability of Meaningful Stimuli in Cross-Cultural Research." *Sociometry*, 30 (June 1967), 124-36. and Roy Carter, Jr., "Some Problems and Distinctions in Cross-Cultural Research," *American Behavioral Scientist*, 9 (March 1966), 23 f. Specifically concerning the use of American-derived scales in Japan, see Leonard Gordon and Akio Kikuchi, "American Personality Tests in Cross-Cultural Research—A Caution," *Journal of Social Psychology* 69 (August 1966), 179-83, and Akio Kikuchi and Leonard Gordon, "Evaluation and Cross-Cultural Application of a Japanese Form of the Survey of Interpersonal Values," *Journal of Social Psychology*, 69 (August 1966), 185-95.

34. A brief justification, with more complete citations, is found in Dator, "Life History and Attitudes of Japanese Judges," p. 427.

35. See, for example, the inventories for Tsuneo Muramatsu, et al., *Nihonjin* [*The Japanese*] (Tokyo:

Reimei Shobo, 1960), and Tajiro Hayasaka, *Shinko Shukyo ni Kansuru Shakai Shinrigaku-teki Kenkyu* [*A Study of the Social Psychology of New Religions*] (Tokyo: Mimeographed, 1965).

36. Dator, "Life History and Attitudes of Japanese Judges," p. 417.

37. *Japan Times Weekly*, July 29, 1967, p. 2.

38. Dator, "Life History and Attitudes of Japanese Judges," pp. 423 and 427.

39. For example, see the Japanese Supreme Court decision on its *Lady Chatterley's Lover* case in John Maki(ed.),*Court and Constitution in Japan* (Seattle: University of Washington Press, 1964), Chap. 1.

40. Nagel, "Off-the-Bench," pp. 50 f. It should be noted that Nagel used Eysenck's British factor loadings and not those derived from a factor analysis of the American judges. Comparison of the factor loadings of Eysenck's British subjects with those from my analysis of Nagel's American judges shows that if Nagel had utilized this factor analysis of his judges' responses rather than Eysenck's, the weighting would have been different for all items except 1, 4, 7, 11, 13, 18, and 23.

41. Although item 21 had a loading of only —.38, it loaded higher on un-rotated Factor I than on any other single factor. Thus I included it as a "conservative-progressive" item.

42. That it might very well be inappropriate in certain countries—for example, developing areas—should be tested, but not be taken for granted until it has been.

5

INDIVIDUALISM IN DECISION-MAKING IN THE SUPREME COURT OF JAPAN[1]

Japan's Court Organization Law, which became effective in 1947 during the Allied Occupation, provided for some important reforms of the Japanese judicial system. One of them was Article 11, which states: "The opinion of every Supreme Court justice shall be expressed in written decisions." This was a radical departure from the practice of the *Daishin-in*, which was Japan's highest court before the Occupation. Following the Continental practice, the *Daishin-in* announced only per curiam decisions that were ostensibly unanimous. If there were dissents, or individual opinions disagreeing with those announced, they were kept strictly secret.[2] Thus the 1947 reform was an epoch-making event in the history of the Japanese judiciary. It might even be described as revolutionary, because it secularized judicial decision-making by showing the Japanese people that Supreme Court justices, like other men, disagreed among themselves.

Viewed in historical perspective, the reform has an even deeper meaning. In traditional Japanese culture, an ongoing group was expected to render unanimous decisions, and it was regarded as undesirable and improper for one member of a group to maintain an opinion that differed from the opinion of the others. For that reason, voting as a decision-making procedure was assiduously avoided. Decision-making in the *Daishin-in* took place, therefore, without open dissent. Thus an examination of the impact of Article 11 on the behaviour of the justices will indicate the extent to which they conformed to or deviated from traditional decision-making practices.

Another important reform in the Court Organization Law is a provision for the recruitment of the Supreme Court's fifteen justices from the ranks of lawyers, law professors, and administrative officials as well as from among career judges.[3] As a result of this sharp break with previous practice, the Supreme Court, since 1947, has included approximately one-third career judges, one-third lawyers, and one-third law professors and administrative officials. This change is interesting because its relationship to the expression of dissent and individual opinions can be examined by correlating decisional behaviour with professional careers (and also, of course, with other background characteristics).

This study focuses on the impact these two reforms—the legitimation of dissent, and diversification in recruitment—had on the behavior of Japanese Supreme Court justices. The method is largely statistical and seeks to ascertain relations between dissenting and other opinion behavior and pre-Court occupation, criminal and civil law specialization, and liberalism and conservatism. It also seeks to ascertain trends in dissenting and other opinion behavior. The analysis that follows is, however, exploratory and tentative; it is primarily a pilot study for future research on the Supreme Court of Japan.

DATA

The principal data for this study are cases, decided by the Supreme Court of Japan from 1947 through 1962, in which at least one justice expressed an individual opinion (that is, an opinion in addition to the one presenting the views of the majority of justices comprising "the Court") in the decision. There were 589 criminal cases and 161 civil cases in which such non-unanimous decisions occurred, a total of 750 constituting the complete sample. All of these cases are reported in *Saiko Saibansho Saibanshu,* which is the most comprehensive official publication of the Court's decisions.[4] If several cases raise the same issue and are decided unanimously, only one of them is published, but as a rule all cases are published in which one or more justices express individual opinions. Thus, as a practical matter, the data for this study embrace virtually all non-unanimous cases decided by the Supreme Court from 1947 through 1962.

In the official reports of the Court's decisions, the terms "majority opinion," "supplementary opinion," "minority opinion," and "opinion" are used.[5] Those categories are inapposite for the present analysis; so instead I used the following: "majority opinion," "concurring opinion," and "dissenting opinion." A "majority opinion" is the opinion of the Court. A "concurring opinion" is an opinion that agrees with the result reached by the majority but disagrees with its reasons. A "dissenting opinion" is an opinion that disagrees with the result reached by the majority. I classified all opinions in these terms, and recorded the vote of each participating justice in all non-unanimous decisions as either "majority," "concurring," or "dissenting."

Because there was considerable turnover in the Court's membership from 1947 to 1962, the data were partitioned into periods in which no more than six of the fifteen justices change. This yielded four periods, each covering four years: I (1947-50), II (1951-54), III (1955-58), and IV (1959-62). Table 5.1 shows the justices who served during each period and indicates the frequencies of their majority, concurring, and dissenting votes in criminal and civil cases. There were 4729 votes in criminal cases and 987 votes in civil cases.

If we examine the previous occupations for all of the justices in the sample (Table 5.1), it is clear that the Court Organization Law has been followed reasonably well, and that the anticipated tri-partite professional representation on the Court obtains. Twelve of the justices in Table 5.1 (34 per cent) were former judges; twelve (34 per cent) had been lawyers; and eleven (31 per cent) used to be administrators or professors.

VARIABLES

The dependent variables in this study are the majority, concurring, and dissenting votes of the justices. Because participation varied considerably, as Table 5.1 shows, three ratios were used to measure individual differences in voting behavior. They are the dissenting ratio (DSR), concurring ratio (CCR), and difference ratio (DFR).

Table 5.1: *Frequency of Votes in Divided Decisions by Chronological Period, Type of Opinion, Prior Career, Ideoogy, and Specialization of Japanese Supreme Court Justices, 1947-62*

Priority of appoint-ment	Name		Chronological Period and Type of Opinion I(1947-50)			II(1951-54)			III(1955-58)			IV(1959-62)			Total
			M	D	C	M	D	C	M	D	C	M	D	C	
1.	Mibuchi	X	7	0	0										7
	(1)	Y	0	0	0										0
2.	Tsukazaki	X	64	21	4	3	5	2							99
	(2)	Y	5	0	0	0	0								5
3.	Hasegawa	X	97	3	1	36	1	0							138
	(2)	Y	5	2	0	0	0	0							7
4.	Sawada	X	41	44	23	47	17	3							175
	(3)	Y	8	1	0	2	0	0							11
5.	Shimoyama	X	87	1	2	74	14	2	1	0	0				181
	(1)	(Y)	5	0	0	15	6	0	2	0	0				28
6.	Inoue	X	49	41	4	50	44	14	5	1	4				212
	(1)	(Y)	6	0	1	10	4	3	0	1	2				27
7.	Kuriyama	X	41	31	12	49	14	32	69	6	9				263
	(3,M)	Y	4	0	0	17	3	2	9	2	1				38
8.	Mano	X	53	11	27	50	51	15	47	30	3				287
	(2,L)	Y	1	2	5	5	2	6	3	0	6				30

Contd....

Contd. Table 5.1

Priority of appointment	Name		Chronological Period and Type of Opinion I(1947-50)			II(1951-54)			III(1955-58)			IV(1959-62)			Total
			M	D	C	M	D	C	M	D	C	M	D	C	
9.	Shono	X	8	1	1										10
	(2)	Y	0	0	0										0
10.	Kotani	X	48	17	7	78	15	6	93	33	9	18	5	3	332
	(2,L)	Y	5	0	0	20	2	1	17	8	2	12	6	3	76
11.	Shima	X	95	3	0	96	8	2	94	8	1	15	2	2	326
	(1,M)	(Y)	6	1	0	14	1	1	16	2	3	11	4	0	59
12.	Y. Saito	(X)	42	7	54	83	29	11	31	50	10	17	5	3	342
	(3,C)	Y	7	2	0	6	2	5	10	3	2	10	3	4	54
13.	Fujita	X	87	2	4	87	13	3	112	16	3	24	9	7	367
	(1,L)	(Y)	4	0	1	16	4	2	18	7	3	21	6	7	79
14.	Iwamatsu	x	92	2	1	106	4	7	41	2	4	0	0	0	259
	(1,M)	(Y)	9	0	0	7	3	2	4	2	0	2	0	0	29
15.	M.Kawamura	X	96	1	0	84	2	10	88	13	1	35	1	6	338
	(4,M)	Y	7	0	0	16	0	0	20	1	0	14	2	1	61
16.	Hozumi	X	22	16	2	6	3	0							49
	(4)	Y	6	0	0	0	0	0							6

Contd....

Contd. Table 5.1

Priority of appointment	Name		*Chronological Period and Type of Opinion* I(1947-50)			II(1951-54)			III(1955-58)			IV(1959-62)			Total
			M	*D*	*C*	*M*	*D*	*C*	*M*	*D*	*C*	*M*	*D*	*C*	
17.	Tanimura	X				4	15	4	70	14	4				111
	(2,L)	Y				16	3	1	5	5	1				31
18.	K.Tanaka	X	5	0	0	29	14	0	35	36	1	6	3	1	130
	(4,C)	Y	4	0	0	12	0	2	14	1	2	7	1	2	45
19.	Kobayashi	X				22	14	14	59	27	15	1	1	0	151
	(2,L)	Y				11	2	0	11	5	2	0	0	0	31
20.	Motomura	X				32	15	0	37	26	0				110
	(2,C)	Y				15	0	0	8	2	0				25
21.	Irie	X				33	0	2	78	3	4	29	5	6	160
	(3,M)	Y				9	0	0	14	1	1	12	3	3	43
22.	Ikeda	X				1	0	0	47	38	7	28	15	4	140
	(3,M)	Y				0	0	0	16	3	2	22	4	3	50
23.	Tarumi	Ⓧ							38	10	13	29	8	16	114
	(1,M)	Y							16	3	0	12	1	5	37
24.	D. Kawamura	X							20	10	1	40	10	3	84
	(2,L)	Y							6	2	4	25	5	6	48

Contd....

Contd. Table 5.1

Priority of appointment Name		Chronological Period and Type of Opinion I(1947-50)			II(1951-54)			III(1955-58)			IV(1959-62)			Total
		M	D	C	M	D	C	M	D	C	M	D	C	
25. Shimoiizaka	ⓧ							15	1	3	24	12	2	57
(1,C)	Y							5	2	3	9	2	7	28
26. Okuno	X							23	2	4	30	7	16	82
(1,L)	ⓨ							12	0	1	17	7	11	48
27. Takahashi	X							10	2	0	21	3	2	38
(2,C)	Y							7	0	0	14	1	0	22
28. Takagi	X							1	0	0	18	17	3	39
(2)	Y							0	0	0	13	3	1	17
29. Ishizaka	ⓧ							1	0	0	22	19	3	45
(1)	Y							0	0	0	11	5	1	17
30. K. Yokota	X										21	0	2	23
(4)	Y										4	1	1	6
31. Yamada	X										11	7	3	21
(2)	Y										6	3	4	13
32. Gokijo	X										18	0	0	18
(1)	Y										3	1	0	4

Contd....

Contd. Table 5.1

Priority of appointment	Name		Chronological Period and Type of Opinion I(1947-50) M	D	C	II(1951-54) M	D	C	III(1955-58) M	D	C	IV(1959-62) M	D	C	Total
33.	M. Yokota	X										13	1	1	15
(1)		Y										1	1	0	2
34.	K.Saito	X										3	0	1	4
(3)		Y										0	0	0	0
35.	Kusaka	(X)										1	0	0	1
(3)		Y										0	0	0	0
			934	201	142	970	278	127	1015	328	96	424	135	80	4730
			82	8	7	191	32	25	213	50	35	226	59	59	987
Total			1016	209	149	1161	310	152	1228	378	131	650	194	139	5717

legend:

Ideology:
L=Liberal
M=Moderate
C=Conservative

Prior career: Type of Opinion:
1=Judge
2=Lawyer
3=Administrator
4=Professor

M=Majority
C=Concurring
D=Dissenting

Types of Issues:
X=Criminal cases
Y=Civil cases
(If the judge is a specialist in either field, X or Y is circled.)

DSR is the ratio of each justice's dissenting votes to his participation in non-unanimous decisions, and CCR is the ratio of his concurring votes to his participation. DFR is the ratio of the sum of each justice's dissenting and concurring votes to his non-unanimous decisions; that is, DSR + CCR = DFR. Table 5.2 reports the empirical values of these ratios for twenty-seven justices who participated in at least forty decisions.

For the purposes of this analysis, the remaining variables are viewed as being independent. They are based on nominal classification of either cases or justices. In regard to cases, they are the four chronological periods mentioned and the type of litigation (civil or criminal). In regard to justices, they are prior career (judge, lawyer, professor, or administrator), ideology (conservative, moderate, or liberal), and specialization (civil or criminal law). Type of litigation was determined by the official designation of a case as civil or criminal in the official reports. Prior career was ascertained by examining biographical sources. Ideological identification was based on Hayakawa's scalogram analysis of the Supreme Court for the 1955-60 period.[6] Specialization was ascertained by examining biographical sources. Table 5.1 shows the justices' prior careers, ideology, and specialization.[7]

The independent variables are probably not statistically independent of each other, but the sample sizes and, especially, the quality of measurement are not adequate to determine the extent of empirical intercorrelation among them. Table 5.3 shows the cross-tabulation of the nineteen justices for whom joint observations are possible for prior career and ideology. Five of the seven liberals were lawyers. Most former judges and administrators are classified as moderates. Certainly the representation of law professors and administrators had not by 1962 had the effect of making the court a more *liberal* group. Cross-tabulation of the data concerning prior career and specialization shows that all six civil specialists are former career judges; and of the five criminal specialists, three are former career judges and two are former administrators—both ex-prosecutors. Data for ideology are particularly sparse, but it can be observed

*Table 5.2 Dissenting, Concurring, and Difference Ratios, 1947-62**

DFR rank	*Name*	*DSR*	*CCR*	*DFR*
1	Sawada	.38	.16	.54
2	Inoue	.38	.12	.50
3½	Mano	.30	.18	.48
3½	Y.Saito	.25	.23	.48
5	Ishizaka	.39	.06	.45
6	Kobayashi	.26	.18	.44
7	Takagi	.36	.07	.43
8.½	Ikeda	.32	.08	.40
8½	Tarumi	.16	.24	.40
10½	Hozumi	.35	.03	.38
10½	Shimoiizaka	.20	.18	.38
12½	Kuriyama	.19	.18	.37
12½	Okuno	.12	.25	.37
14	K. Tanaka	.32	.04	.36
15	Motomura	.32	.00	.32
16½	D.Kawamura	.20	.11	.31
16½	Tsukazaki	.25	.06	.31
18	Kotani	.21	.07	.28
19	Tanimura	.20	.06	.26
20.	Fujita	.13	.06	.19
21	Irie	.06	.08	.14
22	Takahashi	.10	.03	.13
23.	Shimoyama	.11	.01	.12
24½	M.Kawamura	.06	.04	.10
24½	Shima	.08	.02	.10
26	Iwamatsu	.05	.04	.09
27.	Hasegawa	.04	.01	.05
	Means	.21	.10	.31

* *For justices participating in forty or more decisions.*

Table 5.3 Ideology and Prior Career

Prior career	*Canservatives*	*Ideology:* *Moderates*	*Liberals*	*N*
Judges	1	3	2	6
Lawyers	2	0	5	7
Administrators	1	3	0	4
Professors	1	1	0	2
N	5	7	7	19

that no civil specialists were conservative, and no criminal specialists were liberal.

Hypotheses

1. *Change in the Articulation of Individual Opinion*

Article 11 resulted in statistically significant increases in individualistic behaviour of Japanese Supreme Court justices from 1947 through 1962.

2. *Prior Careers and Individualism*

Differences in prior careers are significantly related to differences in decisional behavior.

3. *Ideology and Individualism*

Liberals and conservatives are more individualistic in their behavior than are moderates.

4. *Specialization of Justices in Relation to Cases*

Specialists tend to be most individualistic in decisions concerning their former fields of expertise. Therefore,

(A) Criminal specialists are more individualistic in criminal cases than civil specialists.

(B) Civil specialists are more individualistic in civil cases than criminal specialists.

(C) Criminal specialists are more individualistic in criminal cases than in civil cases.

(D) Civil specialists are more individualistic in civil cases than in criminal cases.

In all of these hypotheses, "individualism" is defined operationally to mean any judge's ratio of concurring, dissenting, and concurring plus dissenting votes to his total participation in split decisions, for any given sample or subsample.

ANALYSIS

Table 5.2 shows that the justices tended to dissent approximately twice as often as they concurred. The means for DSR and CCR are respectively .21 and .10. A comparison of individual dissenting and concurring ratios indicates that only three justices (Okuno. Tarumi, and Irie) concurred more than they dissented. A reading of their opinions shows that for Okuno and Tarumi, both of whom were former judges, the differences between DSR and CCR (.13 and .08) are greater and both appear to be greatly concerned about legal doctrine and its development, therefore, they can be characterized as juridically oriented. There are six justices—Ishizaka, Takagi, Hozumi, K. Tanaka, Motomura, and Tsukazaki—whose dissenting ratios are relatively much larger than their concurring ratios. These justices can be characterized as result-oriented. With the exception of Ishizaka, they were all former lawyers or professors.

Okuno was the most doctrine-oriented of these justices, and Motomura, who dissented relatively often but never concurred, was the most result-oriented. The data on background characteristics are much too scanty to prove this, but cross-tabulation shows that most of the concurrence-oriented (doctrinaire) justices were former judges or administrators; whereas most of the dissent-oriented (toward results) justices were lawyers or—what may surprise some readers—professors. The political ideology data are even scantier than those for previous occupations, because observations are not available for almost half of the justices in this sample, but the data that are available are consistent: the doctrinaire (concurrence) oriented justices are attitudinally liberals or moderates, whereas the result (dissent) oriented justices are conservatives. A few justices—Y. Saito,

Shimoiizaka, and Kuriyama—concur about as often as they dissent; and despite asymmetries in the opinion behavior of many of the justices, DSR and CCR are related and apparently measure the same phenomenon. The Pearsonian correlation between the DSR and CCR columns of Table 5.2 is a moderate and highly significant +.63 (p<.001). Thus DFR (which is DSR + CCR) will be interpreted as an index of individualistic behavior, which is the key dependent variable in most of the hypotheses to be tested.

Table 5.4 Dissenting, Concurring, and Difference Ratios for All Justices by Period, 1947-62

		Criminal cases			*Civil cases*			*Tatal cases*		
Period		*DSR*	*CCR*	*DFR*	*DSR*	*CCR*	*DFR*	*DSR*	*CCR*	*DER*
I.	1947-50	.16	.11	.27	.08	.07	.15	.15	.11	.26
II.	1951-54	.20	.09	.29	.13	.10	.23	.19	.09	.28
III.	1955-58	.23	.07	.30	.17	.12	.29	.22	.08	.29
IV.	1959-62	.21	.13	.34	.17	.17	.34	.20	.14	.34

Table 5.4 was constructed to test the null alternative to Hypothesis 1. If individualistic behavior (defined in terms of DFR) increased significantly over the sixteen-year period covered by this study, then the null hypothesis must be rejected and H1 remains plausible. On the other hand, if the null hypothesis cannot be rejected, then of course H1 must be. H1 assumes that there was a progressive increase in individualistic behavior, which is explained on the basis that as Article 11 became accepted, individualistic opinion behavior became more common among the justices. As Table 5.4 shows, the overall DFR scores increase progressively over the four periods, but the crucial question is whether those increases could have occurred by chance. Using the z test[8] to determine the significance of the differences in DFR scores between periods, the following values were obtained: I-II, z=1.46; II-III, z=0.51; III-IV, z=2.45. A z value of 1.64 is significant at the .05 level and a z of 2.33 is significant at the .01 level. Hence only the difference between DFRs for the last two periods is clearly significant. But because the DFRs increase progressively over all periods, it is legitimate to test the hypothesis by determining the

significance of the difference between DSRs for the first and last periods. That difference is significant beyond the .01 level (z=4.05). Another way of testing the hypothesis is to combine the data for the first and second periods and compare them with the combined data for the third and fourth periods. The difference between these DFRs is also significant beyond the .01 level (z=3.18).

Still another way of testing the null hypothesis is to determine whether the distribution of individual (dissenting plus concurring) and majority votes over the four periods could have occurred by chance. The chi square test is appropriate for this purpose and yields a chi square value of 17.2, which is significant beyond the .01 level. In view of the progressive increase in individualistic behaviour over the four periods and the results of the z and chi square tests, the null hypothesis to H1 must be rejected.

In regard to type of litigation, there were almost five times as many criminal decisions as there were civil decisions. The percentage of votes cast in civil cases increased from 7 per cent in the first period to 15 per cent in the second; it continued to increase slightly to 17 per cent in the third period; and then rose sharply to 38 per cent in the final period.

Although H1 did not extend to possible trend differences between criminal and civil cases, it is readily possible to categorize the data on this basis, as Table 5.4 does, for descriptive purposes. Table 5.4 shows that incremental change consistently was in the positive direction for both criminal and civil DFR ratios, so that we can appropriately infer that H1 cannot be rejected for either criminal or civil cases; we already have observed that H1 cannot be rejected for the combined sample of criminal and civil cases. There are, however, differences between the trends in dissenting and concurring ratios, as these relate to the two sub samples of criminal and of civil cases. Dissenting ratios are consistently higher than concurring rates in criminal cases,[9] whereas there is no significant difference between dissenting and concurring rates in civil cases. Moreover, dissent is significantly higher in criminal than in civil cases (with t = 7.35 and p<.01), although the corresponding difference is not significant for concurrence. We observe also that the difference in the expression of individualism is greatest during the initial period (when DFR for criminal cases is .12 more than for civil cases), and it is negligible by the third period; indeed, the observed t of 1.73 for the two series shows that overall there is no significant difference between the expression of individualism in criminal and in civil cases. Evidently, this result can be attributed primarily to the increase in the articulation of dissent and concurrence in civil cases, with both DSR and CCR more than twice as large for the fourth as for the first period.

Hypothesis 2 was tested initially by comparing the DFR means of administrators, judges, lawyers, and professors, which were respectively .39, .29, .30, and .28.[10] Variance analysis showed that differences among these means are not statistically significant. A similar test of DSR means for the four career groups also failed to show any statistically significant differences. There are, however, significant differences in concurring rates between administrators (.15), lawyers and judges (.09 and .11), and professors (.04). The null hypothesis appears to be correct for dissenting, but not for concurring, opinion behaviour. In support of H2, however, are statements made by former career judges that when they first came to the Court in 1947 they were hesitant to dissent, but as time went on they did so and regarded the dissenting opinion as a desirable innovation in judicial decision-making.[11] Their statements are plausible because, of the four career groups analyzed, the career judiciary was the most likely to be committed to traditional decision-making practices.

By comparing the dissenting ratios of career judges and non-judges over the four periods, we can make a further partial test of both H1 and H2 (Table 5.5). The difference between these two series of DFR rates is significant at .05 (with t - 3.94). Clearly there was no significant change in the individualistic opinion behavior of the non-judges, but there was a significant change for the judges, especially between the first and second, and between the third and fourth, periods. More detailed examination of Table 5.5 shows that although non-judges initially dissented and concurred at a level almost three times as great as that of the judges, the latter nearly doubled their rates for both dissenting and concurring during the second period; and the judges concurred at the same rate as the non-judges by the third period, and dissented at the same rate by the fourth period. The dissenting rate for judges doubled, and their concurring rate increased six-fold during the period of this study. Moreover, if one focuses upon the three judges whose tenure extends into all four periods, again we see that the changes we described as having occurred in the opinion behavior of the judges career type *cannot* be attributed to personnel changes, because the extent of increase in both dissenting and concurring rates is not only in the same direction as that for the group of eight judges; for Shima, Fujita, and Iwamatsu the increases are even more extreme (and therefore, of course, significant at a lower probability level) than for the other five justices in the judges category.

Table 5.5 Prior Careers and Ratios of Individualistic Opinion Behaviour, by Major Periods

		Lawyers, administrators, and professors			*All former judges*			*Former judges with continuing tenure*		
Period		*DSR*	*CCR*	*DFR*	*DSR*	*CCR*	*DFR*	*DSR*	*CCR*	*DER*
I.	1947-50	.18	.16	.34	.10	.03	.12	.03	.02	.05
II.	1951-54	.21	.11	.32	.17.	.06	.22	.09	.05	.13
III.	1955-58	.26	.07	.33	.11	.09	.20	.11	.04	.15
IV.	1959-62	.20	.10	.30	.19	.19	.38	.19	.15	34

The available evidence, inadequate though it is, suggests that the occupation authorities may have erred in their presumption about the liberalizing effect of the appointment of professors and administrators. When lawyers, and civil Jaw specialists, are compared (in terms of political ideology classifications) with professors, administrators, and criminal law specialists, we find that the lawyers and civil law specialists include seven liberals, two moderates, and two conservatives; whereas for the other group, there are no liberals, five moderates, and three conservatives. Deleting the moderates and focusing upon the difference between liberals and conservatives, we can arrange the data in the form of a four-fold contingency table for which the correlation, between being in the first group and being classified as liberal, is +.68, a coefficient which is statistically significant at the .05 level. Moreover, Hayakawa's own observation of his data confirms that lawyers and civil law specialists tend to be sympathetic toward fair procedure claims of criminal defendants, and (to the lesser extent that these are included in the scale) toward civil liberties claims; while administrators, criminal law specialists, and professors tend to be more conservative in their attitude toward such issues.[12]

Hypothesis 3 is based on the assumption that liberals and conservatives tend to dissent and concur more than moderates because, since liberals and conservatives are at ideological extremes, their positions are more intensely held. The alternative or null hypothesis was tested by comparing the DFR means of conservatives, moderates, and liberals. For civil and criminal cases combined they are: conservatives, .34; moderates, .23; liberals, .34 (Table 5.6). Although the pattern is consistent with H3, variance analysis showed that the difference between DFR scores for extremists (liberals and conservatives together) and moderates is not statistically significant. When civil and criminal cases are separated, however, the difference in DFR scores for the three ideological groups in civil cases is significant at the .05 level using the F test (F=3.83); and a t test (one-tailed) showed that the difference between extremists and moderates in civil cases is significant between the .05 and .10 levels (t=1.42). Moreover, although there is no significant difference between the concurring rates of moderates, and of extremists, the corresponding difference in DSRs is significant at .01 when the contingency table of frequencies is tested by chi square.

When the group rates are calculated directly from the grouped frequency data, the DSR for extremists is .22, twice as great as the .11 for moderates. Even the difference *between* conservatives, .26, and liberals, .21, when calculated in this way, is significant at .02. This finding suggests that there is a scale of ideology in relation to dissenting behavior, with conservatives the most individualistic, liberals next, and moderates least. H3

Table. 5.6 Average Ratios of Individualistic Opinion Behavior, by Ideological Type

Ideology	Ratios: *DSR*	CCR	DFR
Liberal	.20	.14	.34
Moderate	.13	.10	.23
Conservative	.24	.10	.34

must be deemed rejected only in part, and that in relation to concurring behaviour.

Table 5.7 shows that of the four hypotheses relating to previous legal specialization, and opinion behavior analyzed according to similar categorizations of the decisions, two (H4A and H4D) cannot be rejected; one (H4B) is rejected; and the other (H4C) is rejected in part.

The criminal specialists have significantly higher ratios, in criminal cases, than do civil specialists, for DSR, CCR, and DFR. But the contrary does not hold: civil specialists do *not* have significantly higher ratios than criminal specialists do in civil cases; indeed, the DSR difference is minimal, and that for CCR is in the direction contrary to that predicted.

Table 5.7 Average Ratios of Individualistic Opinion Behaviour by Legal Specialization and Legal Issues in Cases

Prior	*Types of Issue:* *Criminal*			*civil*			*Totals*		
specialization	*DSR*	*CCR*	*DFR*	*DSR*	*CCR*	*DFR*	*DSR*	*CCR*	*DFR*
Criminal	.25	.21	.46	.17	.20	.37	.24	.20	.44
Civil	.14	.05	.18	.18	.11	.28	.14	.06	.20

The criminal specialists have higher dissenting (and therefore difference) ratios in criminal than in civil cases. The concurring difference is in the predicted direction, but it is too small to be significant. The civil specialists have higher concurring (and therefore difference) ratios in civil than in criminal cases, and the dissenting difference just misses being significant at the .05 level.

Although we made no predictions, Table 5.7 shows also that criminal specialists are more than twice as individualistic as civil specialists, especially in their concurring behavior. These differences are significantly greater than what one would expect to observe on a chance basis.

The tendency for civil specialists to manifest increased individualistic behavior in civil cases and criminal specialists to do (relatively) the same in criminal cases is intuitively plausible, since justices who are supposed to have special knowledge in some field can be expected to stand apart from the majority when cases in their specialties are decided.

CONCLUSION

This study showed that there has been a progressive rise in individualism in the Japanese Supreme Court during its first sixteen years. This rise did not occur by chance and it appears to be directly related to the enactment and acceptance of Article 11 of the Court Organization Law. Individualism increased gradually, but that is what one would expect in view of the traditional approach to decision-making in Japan.

Attempts to relate differences in individual behaviour to the variables of prior career, ideology, and specialization were only partly successful. The findings concerning prior career and ideology suggest, however, further research is needed concerning these variables. In such research it is necessary to specify ideology more precisely and collect data in regard to it for all justices in the universe being studied. Specialization appears more closely related to the expression of individualism than either prior career or ideology. This apparent relationship merits further investigation using larger samples of specialists; and other types of specialization, for example, administrative law, also merit investigation.

Almost inevitably, an exploratory study such as the present one raises more hypotheses than it verifies, but the hypotheses raised here are researchable, and data are, or will be, available to test them. Thus this study makes a modest beginning for further research on individualism in the Japanese Supreme Court.

— *Takeyoshi Kawashima*

REFERENCES

1. I owe a special debt of gratitude to the co-editors of this volume, who gave me most valuable advice and suggestions. I Also express sincere thanks to Mr. Kahei Rokumoto, graduate student, Mr. Koichi Takatsu, research assistant, Mr. Takao Tanase, research assistant, Mr. Minoru Ishida, research assistant, all at the University of Tokyo, who extended generous assistance and co-operation for this study.
2. It has been said, however, that when *Daishin-in* judges disagreed with the Court's opinion, they sometimes put their seals upside down on it. See David J. Danelski, "The Supreme Court of Japan: An Exploratory Study," Chap. 6, p. 137.
3. Court Organization Law, Art. 41. *Daishin-in* judges were recruited only from lower court judges and procurators.
4. This collection of Supreme Court decisions is the most complete available. It contains almost all of the Court's decisions from 1947-1951, all of them for 1952 and 1953, and thereafter those selected for publication by a special committee of the Court. There is another collection, *Saiko Saibansho Hanreishu* (Collection of Supreme Court Precedents), which contains those decisions selected by a committee of the Court with the intention of officially recognizing them as precedents. See Kentaro Mibuchi, "Hanreishu Hensan no Genjo" (Present State of Editing Hanreishu), *Horitsu Jiho*, 34 (1962). No. 1, 54-58. This latter is the collection that is generally available.
5. "Supplementary opinions" are usually concurring opinions; "minority opinions" and "opinions" can be either dissenting or concurring opinions.
6. Takeo Hayakawa, "Saiban no Shakudohyo Bunseki" (Scalogram Analysis of Judicial Decisions), in B. J. George, Ryuichi Hirano, and Hiroshi Tamiya (eds.), *Keiken Hogaku Nyumon* [Readings on Empirical Jurisprudence] (Tokyo: Tokyo University Press, 1966),

pp. 298-99. An earlier version of the same scale is contained in Takeo Hayakawa, "Legal Science and Judicial Behavior, with Particular Reference to Civil Liberties in the Japanese Supreme Court," *Kobe University Law Review,* 2 (1962), 1-27; reprinted in Glendon Schubert (ed.), *Judicial Behavior* (Chicago: Rand McNally, 1964), pp. 325-334. Four justices shown in the revised scale were eliminated from the analysis because they participated in seven or less decisions. Of the remaining justices, the first seven were classified as liberals, the next seven as moderates, and the remaining five as conservatives. The partitioning was based in part on intuitive considerations and hence is not entirely objective. Furthermore, the data are not entirely adequate for present purposes because they were measured ordinally. Of course, this admission is in no sense (nor is it intended to be) a criticism of the research study from which I have borrowed, or of the author to whom I am much indebted.

7. In a few instances, justices could have been placed in more than one prior-career category. Mibuchi was formerly legal counsel to a business firm, a law professor, as well as a judge; Okuno was formerly an administrator as well as a judge; and Y. Saito was formerly a judge as well as an administrator (prosecutor).

8. For the z test, see Joy P. Guilford, *Fundamental Statistics in Psychology and Education* (New York: McGraw-Hill, 1956), p. 221.

9. Using a t test for correlated samples, t = 4.27, which is significant at the .05 level. See Joy P. Guilford, *Fundamental Statistics,* p. 220.

10. In testing this hypothesis, only the justices shown in Table 5.2 were considered. The means mentioned were calculated by averaging the ratios in Table 5.2. The means shown in Tables 5.4 and 5.5 were calculated from voting frequencies.

11. These statements were made in interviews conducted by Professor Danelski in January, 1966. See Danelski, "The Supreme Court of Japan," Chap. 6, p. 136.

12. In Schubert (ed.), *Judicial Behaviour,* at p. 334, n. 22

6

THE SUPREME COURT OF JAPAN AN EXPLORATORY STUDY[1]

The study is exploratory in a double sense: it views *terra incognita,* and it suggests hypotheses for further research. The ultimate goal of the inquiry is to develop a cross-cultural theory of judicial behaviour. This study is, however, only a tentative step in that direction. I have chosen to study the Supreme Court of Japan because of my general interest in the dynamics of decision-making in collegial courts. The Japanese Court fits these interests, for, like its American counterpart, it has the power of judicial review and a collegial decision-making process in which there are face-to-face discussions, majority rule, and the right to dissent publicly. Despite such similarities, the courts operate differently in their societies. To explain why that is so, it is necessary to develop a general cross-cultural theory of judicial behaviour.

This chapter is a partial report of ongoing research on the Supreme Court of Japan. The first section deals with the broadest research problem—the Court's societal context. Appointment to the Court is then considered, followed by a general discussion of the Court's decisional process; the final section is an empirical analysis of decision-making by the Court's Grand Bench during Kotaro Tanaka's chief justiceship (1950-60)

THE SOCIETAL CONTEXT

The Supreme Court of Japan stands at the apex of a legal system that until recently was greatly influenced by Continental, especially German, approaches to law and judicial decision-making.[2] The Court exists in its present form mainly because of the American victory in World War II and subsequent allied Occupation of Japan. On the surface, the legal reforms of the Occupation were monumental—especially the establishment of a democratic constitution and the creation of an independent Supreme Court to interpret the constitution and protect human rights through the exercise of judicial review. Whether these reforms will have a significant impact on Japanese political behaviour turns in large part on the men who constitute the Japanese judiciary, and in the period immediately following the Occupation, they were code-oriented civilians, products of a society that differed in important respects from the society from which the reform-minded Occupation lawyers had come. That is not to say that the Occupation lawyers were insensitive to societal considerations or that they sought to impose American institutions just because they seemed to work in their own society. On the contrary, the lawyers sought to attain a synthesis of what they considered to be desirable and compatible in both legal systems. How successful their work was depends ultimately upon the compatibility between Japanese society and the reforms. In regard to the Supreme Court, this means the presence of societal conditions appropriate for the exercise of judicial power.

No more than a beginning can be made in specifying those conditions, and the specification is, of course, no more than a set of hypotheses. The kind of society in which I think the conditions are present is characterized by more or less impersonal contract relations among its members who perceive each other as separate, self-determining individuals.[3] In Maruyama's terms, it is a society in which "individuation" has occurred.[4] For purposes of entering into and benefiting from these relationships, adult members of such a society are generally assumed to be equal. Rights are regarded as more important than obligations; thus the phenomenon of "rights consciousness" on the part of the society's members. Formal legal rules are also regarded as important, and major disputes are usually resolved by impersonal legal processes such as litigation. For that reason, formal legal skills are highly valued, and those who possess them, especially judges, are accorded considerable prestige. The society described, approximates Sir Henry Maine's idea of a society based on the concept of contract. Japan is presently taking on some of the characteristics of such a society. It is, in Maine's celebrated phrase, moving *"from Status to Contract."*[5]

Traditional Japan was characterized by status relations among its members, who perceived each other in terms of a network of group and family ties. Those hierarchical relationships constituted the society's main connective threads relating men to each other and ultimately to the state.[6] Obligations were far more important than rights; indeed originally the Japanese had no equivalent word for "rights," and if one "asserted his rights," in the sense the expression is used in the West, he was regarded as a troublemaker.[7] Disputes were usually settled by processes involving personal intermediaries. Conciliation was typical; litigation was rare.[8] There were statutes, of course, and other legal rules, but such formal law was regarded as little more than *denka no hoto,* that is, a sword handed down from generation to generation as a family treasure, perhaps important as a symbol, but not something for actual use, except as a last resort.[9] Thus formal legal skills were neither highly valued nor much in demand.

Japan is still to some extent a status society, but individuation, especially in the metropolitan areas, has been underway for some time.[10] The Japanese are becoming more rights-conscious, and individualism and egalitarianism, especially among younger citizens, appear to be on the rise. Conciliation is still an important means of dispute resolution, but there is evidence indicating an increasing willingness to resort to the courts.[11] Newspaper coverage of court proceedings has increased since the 1930's, which probably indicates a growing legal consciousness.[12] Formal legal skills are also now more in demand, and although the Japanese bar, by Western standards, is relatively small (about 7400 members), it is becoming an increasingly attractive profession. There has been a remarkable upward trend in the number of students taking the National Law Examination. In 1950, there were less than 5000 applicants; in 1964, more than 12,000. Less than 5 per cent of the applicants pass the examination, which is a prerequisite for admission to the Legal Training and

Research Institute. At the Institute, which is under the jurisdiction of the Supreme Court, all members of the legal professions—judges, procurators, and lawyers—receive the same training, at the end of which they choose their initial career positions. There has been an upward trend in choosing the bar over other careers—in 1949, less than 20 per cent; in 1965, more than 70 per cent.[13]

One of the reasons for the effectiveness of the U.S. Supreme Court is the prestige of the judiciary and the legal profession generally. The American bar appears to be an important link connecting the people and the Court. Since judges and lawyers (including prosecuting attorneys) are members of the same profession, they participate in and benefit from the same prestige hierarchy that has at its apex the Supreme Court, and opinion surveys have consistently shown that Supreme Court justices occupy one of the most prestigious positions in American society.[14] Although the situation is different in Japan, judges do have considerable prestige. A survey conducted in six of Japan's largest cities showed that, in terms of occupational prestige, district judges ranked third, just under prefectural governors and university professors.[15] But the prestige of Japanese judges, apparently, stems not so much from the possession of professional legal skills as from their positions as government officials. Official position is also the source of prestige of public procurators, who are regarded as members of a separate profession having equivalent legal status with judges.

The history of the Japanese bar can be characterized as the history of a quest for prestige.[16] Lawyers were not members of the same profession as judges and procurators, and in pre-Occupation Japan could not aspire to those positions the way lawyers in the United States and Great Britain could. Because of the non-litigious character of the society and its emphasis on informal and personal means of dispute resolution, the lawyer's skills were neither especially needed nor valued. Japan's movement in the direction of a contract society in recent years and the Occupation's legal reforms have helped in raising the status of lawyers. Appointment to the bench—even to the Supreme Court—is now a possibility for them. The prestige of the lawyer in Japan seems to be on the rise, but compared with his American counterpart, he still has a long way to go.

Judges in Japan may enjoy relatively high prestige, but there is considerable psychological distance between them and the people. This is, of course, true in practically every society, including the United States, but in Japan the phenomenon seems more pronounced. The major reason for this again appears to be societal —informal dispute resolution and awe of high officials—but if the Supreme Court is to act effectively in its governmental role, psychological links between citizens and the Court are necessary. The constitutional provisions requiring popular review of appointments of Court members provides a means for such linkage. Although the provision has been criticized as meaningless since every justice has been approved by a majority of about 90 per cent, it is not meaningless if it creates a public awareness of the Court and its significance.[17]

Despite popular review of judicial tenure, there was little public interest in the Court until the late 1950's. In 1947, a newspaper said that the problem would eventually take care of itself. Once the Court exercised judicial review in an important case, "the public's concept of the importance of the Supreme Court will quickly undergo revolutionary change. All that is needed is a dramatic object lesson."[18] In 1959 there were two dramatic decisions—in the *Matsukawa* and *Sunakawa* cases—that gave the Court unprecedented popular visibility. The former was a criminal prosecution of twenty defendants for murder of three persons killed in a train derailment believed to have been inspired by Communists. Seventeen of the defendants were convicted and four received the death penalty. On the day the Court's decision was announced, thousands of persons from all parts of Japan were marching to Tokyo for the purpose of converging on the Supreme Court and demanding acquittal of the defendants. While a cordon of 3000 policemen surrounded the Court, "as a precautionary measure against demonstrations by either leftist or rightist elements," thousands of persons waited outside of the Supreme Court building to hear the Court's decision, which was to remand the case for retrial.[19] The Japanese Communist Party hailed the Court's decision as "a victory of the people's unity and struggle,"but it had harsh words for the justices who had dissented, especially the Chief Justice. "We must," declared the Party's central committee in a public statement, "impeach Chief Justice Tanaka."[20]

Four months later, in the *Sunakawa* case, the Court reversed District Judge Date's decision that the stationing of U.S. troops in Japan was unconstitutional. Although there was substantial public support for the Supreme Court's unanimous decision, there were also a considerable number of protests. The Socialists, who had issued a favourable statement concerning the *Matsukawa* case, now said they would launch a campaign against the justices in the *Sunakawa* case when they came up for popular review at the polls. Especially interesting about the *Sunakawa* case was the number of statements made by interest groups. In favor of the decision were such groups as the Japan Wounded War Veterans' Association and the National Association of Towns and Villages, and against the decision were such groups as the General Council of Japan Labour Unions and the Jurists' Council for Research on the Security Treaty.[21] Clearly, the mass-media coverage of the *Matsukawa* and *Sunakawa* cases aroused public interest in the Court and showed in a dramatic way its importance.

But public awareness of the Court is not the same thing as a public support for it. There is some negative feeling on the part of liberal lawyers and intellectuals, who maintain that the Court has not fulfilled its role as protector of human rights, that it has been too conservative, and that it has exercised too much judicial restraint. For these reasons, apparently, young liberal judges are resigning and graduates from the Legal Institute are increasingly choosing the bar over the judiciary for their careers. Some of these lawyers and intellectuals maintain that Japan is not yet sufficiently westernized for the Supreme Court to act like its American counterpart. Others say that the problem stems from the appointment of '"safe" conservatives to the Court — men who. as one writer put it, "are more conservative than the conservative party."[22] Since conservatives have controlled the government during most of the Court's life and therefore have appointed most of the justices, the statement is plausible. Certainly the Court's behaviour and its significance in Japanese society depend, in large part, on the men who are appointed to it.

APPOINTMENT

The cabinet has formal power to appoint all justices and to designate the Chief Justice.[23] The Chief Justice, like the prime minister, is officially appointed by the Emperor.[24] Any person possessing "broad vision and extensive knowledge of law," who is beyond the age of forty, may be appointed to the Court, but ten of the fifteen Court members must have had at least ten years' experience as a regular judge or a total of twenty years' experience as a summary court judge, lawyer, procurator, or law professor. No legal experience is required for the remaining five members.[25] These are only the formal rules. To understand the operating rules regarding appointments to the Court, it is necessary to look, as Holmes has said, at "a page of history."

In 1947, when the initial Court was appointed by the Katayama Socialist Coalition cabinet, the Court Organization Law provided for an advisory committee on Supreme Court appointments. A few months earlier such a committee had been convened by the Yoshida Cabinet, but it had been dissolved soon after the 1947 election.[26] The Katayama advisory committee was selected as follows: four members of the career judiciary were chosen by a nationwide vote of the judges; four lawyers were chosen by a similar election of the bar; four "learned men" were selected from the universities by the prime minister; the procurator general, the president of the House of Councillors, and speaker of the House of Representatives brought the committee total to fifteen.[27] This committee submitted a list of thirty candidates for the Court, including some names of members of the committee. A reliable source reports that the cabinet, upon receipt of the list of nominees, felt bound by it, lest the committee members "lose face."[28] In terms of career backgrounds, the composition of the initial Court closely resembled the composition of the advisory committee: five career judges, five lawyers, one procurator who had formerly been a judge, one member of the then existing Administrative Court, one former diplomat, one professor, and one man who had been a judge, law lecturer, and legal counsel to an important business firm.

In 1948, the advisory committee was abolished, but its initial work was viewed as establishing a precedent that judges, lawyers, and "men of learning and experience"[29] (mostly law professors, procurators, and legal bureaucrats) are to be equally represented in the Court. In 1949, when former Tokyo University law professor Shigeto Hozumi replaced Justice Shono, formerly a lawyer, the bar associations argued that there had been a breach of the unwritten rule established when the Court was set up. Other breaches of the rule have occurred, but the rule is still recognized. Of the forty-three justices appointed from 1947 through 1965, the period analyzed here, thirteen have been career judges, fifteen have been lawyers, and fifteen have been men of learning and experience (five law professors, three procurators, two legal bureaucrats, one judge of the old Administrative Court, one diplomat, one legal bureaucrat who earlier had been a career judge, one procurator who also had been a judge, and one who had a varied career as judge, law lecturer, and legal counsel). The average tenure of career judges has been 5.5 years; of lawyers, 5.1 years; and of men of learning and experience, 6.6 years.

Hierarchy appears to be one of the main underlying principles in appointments to the Court. It is a social phenomenon as well as a bureaucratic phenomenon in regard to career judges. The ladders to the Court are fairly well defined; they are also long, and rungs are seldom skipped. In regard to the judiciary, the first and crucial rung, at least up to 1966, was graduation from the law faculty of Tokyo University. Graduation from Tokyo is probably significant to a judge's rise because of influential school cliques *(gakubatsu)* in the judicial bureaucracy, and the Tokyo cliques apparently have controlled promotions through the years.[30] After graduation from Tokyo University, the typical steps upward are: assistant judge, district judge (a long stay in Tokyo is helpful), high court judge, president of one of the lesser high courts, president of the Tokyo High Court, and finally the Supreme Court. Assignment to the Supreme Court as research official *(chosakan)* early in a judge's career is helpful, and selection as president of the Legal Training and Research Institute is even better. Sometimes a president of one of the larger high courts, such as Osaka's, has been appointed to the Supreme Court. Although not every president of the Tokyo High Court has gone to the Supreme Court, when there is a vacancy in the Court the Tokyo High Court president is usually the most visible candidate.

Hierarchy appears also to operate in the appointment of lawyers to the Court. Seven out of the first eight lawyers appointed have been presidents of Tokyo or Osaka bar associations, and the eighth was chairman of an important committee of the Japanese Federation of Lawyers. Japanese lawyers told me that when a lawyer on the Court retires, the presidents of the Tokyo and Osaka bar associations are almost invariably considered; but often, it has been said, they have declined appointment in recent years on the ground that it would entail financial sacrifice, more work, and a less interesting life. Different hierarchical patterns to a position on the Court now seem to be developing such as teaching at the Legal Training and Research Institute, working in the Supreme Court Secretariat, or taking a high court appointment. In other words, the appointment of lawyers is becoming bureaucratized. Graduation from Tokyo University helps a lawyer in his rise to the Court, but it is not a necessity. Two-thirds of the lawyers appointed up to the end of 1966 were graduates of Chuo (3), Kyoto (2), Nihon (2), Meiji (1), Hosei (1), and Waseda (1). The remaining five were Tokyo graduates, but lawyers as a group have accounted for ten of the twelve non-Tokyo graduates who have served on the Court in this period.

And hierarchy appears to be important in the appointment of men of learning and experience. Procurators work their way up their own career ladder and come to the Supreme Court when they reach superintendent procurator-general of a large district, or, as in one case, assistant procurator-general. Law professors, with a single exception, have been members of the most prestigious academic group in Japan—the Tokyo University law faculty. The others have risen high in their professions—the former diplomat to the level of ambassador and the legal bureaucrats to the level of director of legislative bureaus in the Diet. All were graduates of Imperial Universities—thirteen from Tokyo and two from Kyoto.

Apparently, because hierarchy is important and age gives status, the average appointment age has been high—61.4 years. In the initial Court there were seven justices who began service in their fifties; only four of the twenty-eight justices appointed from 1948 to the end of 1965 have been less than sixty years of age. The Supreme Court has become the top rung of a number of career ladders. Thus presidents of high courts come to the Supreme Court when they are near the brink of compulsory retirement, at age sixty-five, and continue their careers until they are seventy, the compulsory retirement age for Supreme Court justices. The same is true of procurators whose retirement age is sixty-three or sixty-five, depending on the position they hold. Since compulsory retirement for Tokyo University professors is set at the age of sixty, it is not surprising that their average age of appointment has been little more than sixty-one. Lawyers in private practice, of course, have no retirement age, but their average age when appointed to the Court has been more than sixty-two.

The precise significance of place of birth in regard to appointments is not clear. In the period considered in this chapter-- 1947-65—thirty of Japan's forty-six prefectures had been represented in the Court. Five prefectures contributed more than one justice—Tokyo (9), Aichi (3), Osaka (2), Kyoto (2) and Saga (2). Except for Saga, these prefectures can be characterized as urban, and they have been among the five most populous prefectures since 1908. For Tokyo, more than population must be taken into account in explaining why 20 per cent of the appointees were born in that prefecture, since its population has never exceeded 10 per cent of the national population. Perhaps the reason for a higher percentage of Tokyo-born justices is that a disproportionate percentage of Japan's elite live in Tokyo, and they were more likely to go to Tokyo University (which was established to train Japan's governmental elite) and thereby gain access to such elite positions as those of judges. The importance of admission to Tokyo University cannot be overemphasized. One justice told me that when he received word that he had been admitted to Tokyo University, his father, who had been a professional man in a rural prefecture, decided that the whole family would move to Tokyo so that his son could live at home while carrying on his law studies.

Family and marriage ties appear to be significant. This was evident in the selection of Kotaro Tanaka for the chief justiceship in 1950. At one point in the appointment process, the leading candidates were Tanaka, Justices Mano and Hozumi, and Shinzo Koizumi, former president of Keio University. Prime Minister Yoshida is said to have favored Koizumi and offered him the post, but it was declined.[31] A week later Tanaka was appointed. Since Tanaka had been Education Minister in Yoshida's first cabinet for a period of about five months, one might have thought that was the basis for the appointment. That probably had something to do with it, for the two men usually saw eye to eye on important matters. But reliable persons with whom I spoke in Japan maintain that also important in the appointment was the intercession of Tanaka's father-in-law, Joji Matsumoto, a lawyer and a scholar of considerable status who had served with Yoshida in the Shidehara cabinet. Matsumoto was not only Tanaka's father-in-law; he was also Koizumi's brother-in-law. It is often said in Japan that power and status are consolidated by well-planned marriages, and that these ties are frequently politically significant.[32] For that reason genealogies and biographical dictionaries were examined. In one biographical dictionary, there is a special section on relationships contracted through marriage and adoption of "a selected group of Japanese notables."[33] Nine of the forty-three justices, including Chief Justice Tanaka, were included. These justices were shown to be tied by marriage to persons important in universities, government, business, and the nobility—roughly in that order.

The organized bar has undoubtedly played an important role in some appointments to the Court, especially when its members have been considered for vacancies. When the initial Court was selected in 1947, the three Tokyo bar associations polled their members concerning the qualifications of the candidates nominated by the advisory committee, and the results of the poll were submitted to the cabinet.[34] I already have pointed out that the bar associations have staunchly defended the informal rule that the bar should have one-third representation in the Court. In 1960, when a successor to Chief Justice Tanaka was being discussed, the Japan Federation of Bar Associations supported Tadashi Hanai, a former attorney general, and opposed former Tokyo University professor Sakae Wagatsuma for the position because Wagatsuma reportedly said in a speech that "Japanese lawyers are less studious than Japanese women."[35]

Relatively little is known about the extent to which members of the Supreme Court get involved in the appointment of fellow colleagues. There is evidence, however, that in the early 1950's a Court member was consulted by the government concerning an appointment.[36] And about the same time, three justices called on the attorney general to ask reconsideration of a decision to appoint a certain government official to the Court.[37]

THE DECISIONAL PROCESS

Each year approximately 4500 cases are appealed to the Supreme Court of Japan.[38] All cases come before one of the Court's three divisions, which are designated Petty Benches I, II, and III.[39] Each division usually consists of five justices, three of whom constitute a quorum.[40] If a case is found to involve a constitutional question not already settled by the Court or by some other issue that is important or complicated, it will be referred to the Grand Bench, which is the entire Court sitting *en banc*. Nine Court members constitute a quorum of the Grand Bench, and, if a law, regulation, or executive action is declared unconstitutional, a majority of the Grand Bench (eight members) must so agree. Cases are not transferred between divisions.

Research officials *(chosakan,* play an important role in the disposition of cases. There are presently thirty of them assigned to the Court.[41] Their functions are analogous to those of the law clerks in the U.S. Supreme Court, but there the similarity ends. American law clerks are usually recent graduates of leading law schools chosen by the justices to assist them for a year or two. Research officials, on the other hand, are themselves judges who have had from ten to twenty years' trial or appellate experience. Presently the chief research official is a high court judge; all of the others are district judges. Chosen for their ability, they are likely to rise high in the judicial hierarchy after serving the usual four or five years with the Supreme Court. Indeed, one of the present justices — Makoto Iwata — was formerly a research official. There is some specialization among research officials: fourteen handle only civil cases; another fourteen handle only criminal cases; and two are specialists in administrative law. Unlike law clerks in the U.S. Supreme Court, research officials are not assigned to particular justices. The civil and administrative research officials are assigned cases in the order they are docketed and work with the justices to whom they have been assigned on the same basis. Research officials who specialize in criminal law are divided into three groups—each group working with one of the petty benches for a period of four months, after which it is assigned to another petty bench. Criminal cases assigned to justices of a given petty bench arc assigned by rotation to research officials then working with that petty bench. Since cases are also assigned to the justices in sequence according to the order in which they are docketed, each of the research officials has an opportunity to work with each of the justices.[42]

After counsel has been appointed in certain criminal cases and briefs have been printed, the typical case in the Supreme Court goes to the research official who has been assigned to it. He is referred to as the "research official in charge of the case." His first task is to determine whether it is an "important case," that is, one worthy of extensive research and careful consideration by the justices, or a "simple case," usually a frivolous appeal. If it is the latter, he will stamp an "X" on it, which means, as a practical matter, dismissal. Since approximately 80 per cent of the civil cases and 90 per cent of the criminal cases fall into the latter category, he spends a good part of his time sifting appeals to find those that are meritorious. When he determines a case to be important, he often does exhaustive research—reading and digesting voluminous records and depositions and briefing the relevant statutes and precedents. His report, which is printed, sometimes attains the size of a large book. The report is usually objective; if there is more than one plausible decision for a case, the basis for each is given in the report. Sometimes the research official gives his opinions, although this is said to be infrequent.[43] In working on research reports, it is common for research officials to consult one another, and such consultation is officially encouraged. It is, in fact, institutionalized in the "joint meeting" of research officials that is held several times a month for the purpose of studying common problems and ensuring uniformity of decisions in cases involving identical or similar issues before different petty benches. A research official typically devotes about ten clays to an important case.

When the research report is completed, it goes to the justice who has been assigned the case, and his assignment, like the research official's, is based on rotation. He is referred to as the "justice in charge of the case." After studying the report, and perhaps consulting with the research official, he sets a date for its consideration at a petty bench conference. These conferences are held weekly, and twice a month there is a special conference. At the conference, the justice in charge of the case presides over its discussion. Although the conferences are secret, the research official, unlike his counterpart in the U.S. Supreme Court, may be present to give further information or to clarify some aspects of his report. Discussion usually proceeds in light of the report, which all of the justices have received and read before the conference. Informality is the rule in the conference: there is no prescribed order in regard to speaking or voting. Sometimes the positions of the justices are so clear from the discussion that no vote is taken. If it is evident that the appeal cannot be sustained, the action of the petty bench will be to dismiss, but if it looks as though reversal is possible, the appellee will be asked to file a brief and the case will be set for oral argument. When an appellant is informed that the Court desires to hear argument, he knows that he has at least a fifty-fifty chance of winning, for about 80 per cent of the civil cases and 50 per cent of the criminal cases that go to oral argument are reversed. The rate of reversal is lower in the criminal cases because if they involve a capital offense or a serious disturbance of the public peace, oral argument is ordered as a matter of course.[44]

The amount of time allotted for oral argument of a case depends upon its importance. Sometimes many hours are given to a single case. Oral argument in Japan is not like it is in the United States. There is less questioning by the justices and practically no give-and-take between counsel and the Court. As one Tokyo University professor put it, "The justices sit like Buddha until the lawyer finishes."

After the case has been argued, there is another conference for further discussion and decision. Unless the justice in charge dissents, which is rare, he writes the Court's opinion. If he does dissent, then the majority justices decide among themselves who will write the opinion, often choosing the justice who was most vocal in conference. Although it seldom happens, sometimes a justice is assigned an opinion because of his expertise in a particular area of the law.[45]

The principal differences between the Grand Bench and petty bench consideration of cases are livelier discussions in conference and greater manifestation of dissent.[46] The Grand Bench conferences, like those of the petty benches, are held each week, but they tend to last longer, and it is not uncommon to carry the discussion of a case over from one meeting to another. The justices discuss the case without any time limitation, and in this respect, according to former Chief Justice Tanaka, they are perhaps unique among collegial bodies in Japanese government. It is almost impossible, said Tanaka, to control the free speech of the justices.[47] Although the chief justice presides, the justice in charge of the case plays a leading role in its discussion, for usually his opinion is the basis for it. Discussion again is informal and so is voting.

Because a great number of the cases before the Grand Bench involve constitutional questions, the values of the justices are inevitably manifested in conference discussion and later in their written opinions, especially dissenting and supplementary opinions. In conference, attempts are made at persuasion, and at times they are successful. This may be viewed as task-leadership behavior.[48] The concept of task leadership must, however, be understood in a Japanese context. Such leadership in the Court is far more subtle and less aggressive than it is in the Supreme Court of the United States. What is involved is complex interpersonal communication that operates at a non-verbal as well as at a verbal level. In discussing this matter in more general terms, Ike has written that many Japanese "are prevented by training and social custom from saying what they think and of revealing their real and innermost feelings and thoughts. The pressure for social harmony and for outward unanimity is too strong. Individuals who grow to maturity in such an environment must learn to fathom another's thoughts, feelings, and intentions by reading between the lines, by observing indirect signs, and by resorting to a kind of intuitive process."[49] When disagreements among justices come to the surface in conference, their colleagues characteristically seek to reconcile opposing positions, thus manifesting social-leadership behaviour.[50] As one retired justice told me, "We collaborated to harmonize our views; that is what we all wanted." Despite the high value placed on harmony, the right to dissent is highly respected in the Court. In cases involving matters of principle, at least, there is no expectation of compromise.[51]

After the Grand Bench reaches a decision the research official in charge of the case usually assists in writing the Court's opinion, but the amount of work he does depends on the justice in charge. Justice Mano, for example, seldom availed himself of the research official's service. On the other hand, some justices are said to have relied so heavily on the research official that he was virtually author of the Court's opinion. A number of the research officials have taken graduate work in law in Europe or the United States, and thus many of the references to foreign precedents may be attributed to them.[52] The authors of the Court's opinion are usually not identified, but after retirement, justices are willing to acknowledge their authorship.

The right to express individual views in the form of dissenting and supplementary opinions is highly prized by members of the Court. The dissenting opinion was a remarkable post-war innovation in view of the previous Continental practice of announcing only unanimous Court decisions. It also runs counter to the value placed on consensus in Japanese society: Japanese cabinet decision-making still proceeds in terms of consensus without votes being taken, and there is no right to dissent in the district and high courts. At first, some members of the career judiciary in the Court doubted the wisdom of the expression of dissent, but after coming to the Supreme Court, they were persuaded of the usefulness of the practice. One justice said the right to individual expression of views makes for greater alertness and responsibility on the part of the Court. Another said that if he had not the right to dissent, he could not in good conscience have remained on the Court after his first disagreement with the majority. In preparing a dissenting opinion in a very important case in which the Court was sharply divided, one justice worked so hard that he became and when he finished the opinion, he had to be taken to the hospital. In the same case, another justice devoted similar effort in writing his dissenting opinion, and when he finished he was moved to write a *haiku* about the case, the first he had ever written.

Reference individual and reference group behaviour appears to be present in the Japanese Supreme Court, as it does in the U.S. Supreme Court, especially when justices are writing dissenting opinions. In view of the selection of justices in terms of occupations—career judge, lawyer, procurator, professor—it is not surprising that the justices would wonder what their former colleagues would think of their positions in certain cases. One justice —a former professor—said that he had dissented by himself in a certain case and was gratified to learn that another professor, to whom he had sent his opinion, fully agreed with him. I was told by a venerable Japanese scholar that in the old *Daishin-in*, where public expression of dissent was prohibited, dissenting judges would sometimes put their seals upside down on the Court's opinion so that they could later prove to former colleagues that they did not agree with the judgment. This is an excellent example of reference group behavior.

After the opinions are written, they are circulated and sometimes elicit further opinions—usually supplementary opinions that take issue with the views of the dissenters. When the opinion writing is completed and the Court's judgment is finally approved in conference, the justices place their personal seals on the opinions that represent their views, and the opinions are publicly announced by the Chief Justice.

AN EMPIRICAL ANALYSIS OF GRAND BENCH DECISIONS

One of the distinguishing features of the Grand Bench is its relatively high rate of non-unanimous decisions—in recent years, approaching 50 per cent.[53] In a society in which consensus, harmony, and unanimity are important values, such a high rate of dissent must be meaningful. Just as analysis of non-unanimous decisions has provided the basis for significant insights into decision-making in the Supreme Court of the United States, so it does in regard to the Japanese Supreme Court.[54] There are methodological problems, however, in studying Grand Bench decision-making. One problem arises from the small number of cases it reports each year—as few as nine and seldom more than fifty. An obvious way of coping with that problem is to study the decisions over a relatively long period of time, say, ten years. But then another problem arises, and that is the high non-participation rate because of relatively rapid turnover of justices on the Court.

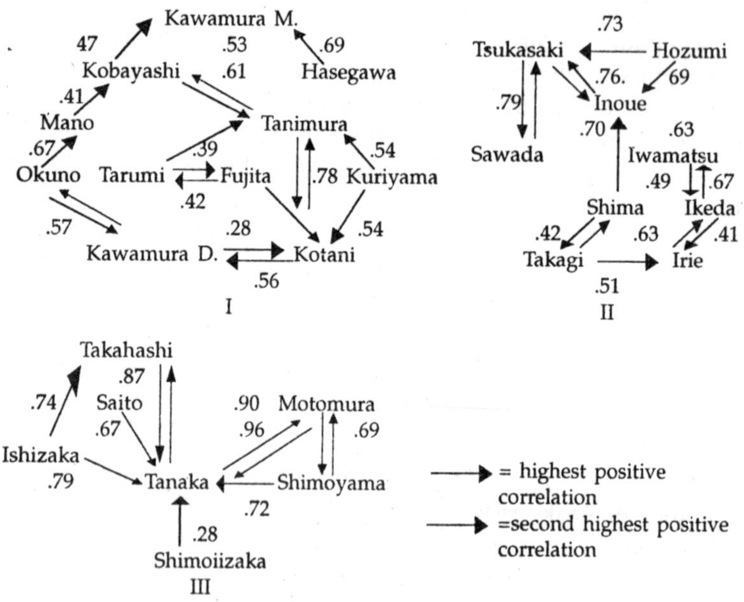

Figure 6.1 *Linkage Analysis, Grand Bench, 1959-60*

Table 6.1 Major Values of Kotaro Tanaka as Disclosed by Content Analysis of Essays Written in 1945 and 1946

Values	*Incidence*	*Intensity*	*Value score**
Positive			
Natural Law	27	1.96	52.92
Order, harmony	23	1.61	37.03
Spiritual Life	18	2.00	36.00
Humanity	14	1.64	22.96
Absolute justice	10	1.80	18.00
Emperor, Emperor system	6	2.67	67.02
Democracy	11	1.45	15.95
National political ideology	8	1.50	12.00
Turth	4	3.00	12.00
Reason	8	1.37	10.96
Orthodoxy	6	1.34	8.04
Limitation of freedom	8	1.00	8.00
National characteristics	5	1.60	8.00
Common sense	5	1.60	8.00
Feeling of shame	4	2.00	8.00
Intellectuality	4	1.50	6.00
God's will	4	1.25	5.00
Freedom	5	1.00	5.00
Social progress	4	1.00	4.00
Negative			
Anarchy	10	1.90	19.00
Naturalism, epicurianism	7	1.57	10.99
Disctatorship, fascism	7	1.29	9.03
Positivism	5	1.60	8.00
Chauvinism	4	2.00	8.00
Professional politicians	5	1.75	7.00
Power politics	5	1.40	7.00
Marxism	5	1.20	6.00
Miitarism	4	1.00	4.00

* *Value score=incidence times intensity.*

With these problems in mind, divided Grand Bench decisions of Kotaro Tanaka's Chief Justiceship—specifically those announced between March 15, 1950, and October 19, 1960-were chosen for analysis.[55] For purposes of this analysis, a divided decision was defined as any decision (other than one clearly involving a jurisdictional matter) in which at least one justice disagreed with the disposition decided upon by a majority of his colleagues. Typically, the disposition of a case required one decision, but in a few instances a single case raised two issues that were voted on separately. In those cases, each decision was counted separately. The total universe consisted of 127 divided decisions in which twenty-seven justices cast a total of 1684 votes.

In an effort to obtain an overview of the voting patterns for the entire period, votes of the justices were intercorrelated by pairs, and the phi correlation coefficients obtained were arranged in a 27 by 27 matrix. The matrix was then analyzed by linking justices with each other in terms of their highest and second highest positive correlation coefficients.[56] The results of the analysis are shown in Figure 6.1. Three well-defined clusters of justices emerge. The first cluster, containing the largest number of justices—eleven—is the most loosely intercorrelated. The second cluster, containing nine justices, is somewhat more tightly intercorrelated. The third cluster contains the smallest number of justices—seven—and they are highly intercorrelated.

Figure 6.1 appears to indicate that ideology is the basis for division in the Court. Japanese lawyers and scholars whom 1 interviewed almost invariably identified Tanaka and Saito as "conservatives" and Mano and Fujita as "liberals."[57] In an effort to verify that judgment concerning Tanaka, a systematic content analysis of some of his pre-Court statements was made by a Japanese research assistant, using Japanese texts.[58] Table 6.1, which reports the analysis, shows a portrait of a spiritually oriented Japanese conservative. Some liberal values are present, but the preference for order over freedom is clear, and especially significant are such traditional values as the Emperor system, orthodoxy, and the feeling of shame.[59] If the ideological characterizations of Saito, Mano, and Fujita by the lawyers and scholars are also correct, then the first cluster appears to be associated with liberalism and the third cluster with conservatism. Independent empirical support for this interpretation is contained in data collected by Dator in his survey of attitudes of Japanese high court and Supreme Court judges,[60] and also in Hayakawa's scalogram analysis of the Japanese Supreme Court.[61]

There are more sophisticated methods for analyzing correlation matrices. One of them is smallest space analysis, which is a type of multi-dimensional scaling developed by Guttman and Lingoes.[62] It compares the ordinal ranks of variables in a matrix and then shows them as points in multi-dimensional space. In order to meet the assumptions of the method, however, all the cells of a matrix must contain correlation coefficients. This means that a matrix covering a decision-making period shorter than ten years had to be used. Thus the universe of 127 Grand Bench decisions was divided as equally as possible—one part (63 decisions) covering the period from March 15, 1950, to June 22, 1955, and the other (64 decisions) covering the period from July 18, 1955, to October 19, 1960. The justices' votes for each period were intercorrelated by pairs and the phi correlation coefficients were arranged into two matrices in which each cell was filled. To accomplish this, it was necessary to eliminate nine justices from the analysis.

The results of the smallest space analysis for each period are presented three dimensionally in Figures 6.2 and 6.3. The similarity of the figures and their consistency with the linkage analysis are remarkable. Since each dimension is an ordered metric, the analysis begun in Figure 6.1 now can be extended with greater precision.

The most important dimension in Figures 6.2 and 6.3 is the first one, which appears to be measuring the same phenomenon in both periods. The Spearman correlation (rho) between the rank orders of the twelve justices, who are in both figures, is .84, which is significant at the .01 level. The first dimension in Figure 6.3 clusters the justices the same way as the linkage analysis. With a single exception (Shima), Figure 6.2 does the same. Thus, if in the linkage analysis the first cluster consists of liberals and the third of conservatives, the second cluster must be composed of justices who are ideologically between—that is, moderates.[63]

In an effort to determine the ideological content of the first dimension of Figure 6.3, the justices were ranked in terms of the percentage of votes they cast in favor of criminal defendants during the 1955-60 period. The correlation between that rank order and the rank order of the justices on the first dimension in Figure 6.3 is .97, which is significant considerably beyond the .01 level. The rho between those rank orders for the 1950-55 period, however, is .71, considerably lower than the rho for the following period but still significant at the .01 level. The lower rho for the 1950-55 period was apparently due to a series of seven decisions that raised the same issue concerning the constitutionality of convictions based solely on confessions made in court. Because the issue had been initially decided before 1950, at least some of the justices apparently felt bound by the precedent, and they divided somewhat differently in these decisions than they did in other criminal cases. Whether that was due to precedent-orientation or an attitudinal variable other than the one measured by the first dimension in Figure 6.2 is a question I am unable to answer, but if those seven decisions are eliminated from the analysis, the rank-order correlation rises from .71 to .92. Thus the first dimension in Figures 6.2 and 6.3 is apparently related to a general attitude toward the rights of criminal defendants and their punishment.

That a majority of the justices in both periods are positively related to this dimension is not surprising, for there has been a trend in the Japanese judiciary toward increased leniency with criminal defendants, especially in matters of punishment. One of the reasons for the trend, according to Abe, is "an awareness of human rights—a humanitarian impulse" on the part of judges. Indeed, some "modern" judges, he says, "believe that the most important role of the judiciary lies in the protection of offenders from severe and unreasonable punishment."[64] The issue of punishment is, in a sense, present in every criminal case, but it was especially salient in the cases before the Tanaka Court involving such matters as the death penalty and sentences based on convictions for violation of Occupation laws that were no longer in force. Undoubtedly, more than "humanitarian impulse" was involved in the decision of some criminal cases such as those in which Communists were defendants. The voting patterns in those decisions are the same as those in divided criminal decisions generally, but I suspect that anti-Communist attitudes reinforced the general anti-criminal attitude as the basis for votes against criminal defendants.

The first dimension in Figures 6.2 and 6.3 can therefore be identified as a form of liberalism, but it is important to indicate what this dimension does not appear to include. Schubert, in his study of the U.S. Supreme Court, identified five sub-components of political liberalism—political freedom, political equality, religious freedom, the right to a fair procedure, and the right to privacy.[65] The dimension identified in the Japanese Supreme Court resembles only the sub-component dealing with fair procedure. If liberalism and conservatism in the Japanese Supreme Court are defined in this limited sense, then the clusters in the linkage analysis can be labeled as follows: I, liberal; II, moderate; and III, conservative.

The remaining dimensions disclosed by the smallest space analysis are more difficult to identify. To begin with, the second dimension in Figure 6.2 appears to be measuring something other than the second dimension in Figure 6.3, since the rank-order correlation between them is not statistically significant. In the 1950-55 period, the second dimension divides conservatives, moderates, and liberals in increasing order of magnitude. It shows the unlikely trio of Mano, Iwamatsu, and Saito adjacent to each other with relatively high scores on the dimension. An examination of the patterns of agreement among them suggests that the dimension is related to the confession cases mentioned earlier. Other decisions are also apparently related to it. For example, Mano, Iwamatsu, and Saito voted together in two land reform decisions, casting three of the four dissents in those cases. The fourth dissenter was Inoue, but he is further from them on the dimension because he had consistently disagreed with them in the confession cases in which they were the majority. The second dimension in the 1955-60 period is primarily the basis for division among the liberals, and again it is difficult to identify. It is worth noting, however, that Fujita's and Tarumi's proximity on this dimension is related to three cases, involving freedom of conscience and freedom of assembly, in which they jointly stood against the rest of the Court. This suggests incipient development of another dimension of liberalism in which political freedom is a principal component. Three cases, however, are slender evidence upon which to base such a conclusion. The main reason for difficulty in identifying dimensions beyond the first dimension is that the analyses presented here are based on relatively small universes of decisions.

The third dimension in Figures 6.2 and 6.3 may be measuring the same phenomenon, for the correlation between the rank orders of justices aligned on them is .69, which is significant at the .05 level. In the 1955-60 period, the dimension appears to be related to seven decisions involving smuggling and confiscation issues in which the moderates invariably voted together, sometimes with the conservatives, sometimes with the liberals. The conservatives always voted together in those decisions, but the liberals were usually divided. In the 1950-60 period, there was one decision similar to the smuggling decisions of the later period, and in that case the moderates and conservatives, joined by one of the liberals, voted together. Again the small number of cases in these universes precludes identification of the dimension.

Despite the small universes used in the smallest space analyses, it is remarkable that the same justices cluster in relatively the same way and in relatively the same areas of the three-dimensional spaces. It is highly improbable that this could occur by chance and suggests that generally the same variables account for much of the justices' voting behavior in both periods. At least one of the variables appears to be ideological, but the cohesiveness manifested may also be related to other variables such as petty bench membership, pre-Court occupation, university education, prefecture of birth, and age.

One might infer from the linkage analysis in Figure 6.1 that there is at least slight relation between voting cohesiveness and petty bench membership, since sixteen of the twenty-seven justices in the figure are linked with members of their petty benches. Of the fifty-two primary and secondary links indicated, nineteen connect members of the same petty benches. This is only two more than the seventeen links one would have expected if they were divided equally among the three benches, but the figure is more significant than it appears, because a justice cannot be linked with himself; thus his chances of being linked with justices of the other petty benches are 20 per cent higher. This hypothesis deserves further exploration and testing especially in relation to cohesiveness in petty bench voting.

Table 6.2 Petty Bench Membership and Ideology

	Petty Benches		
	I	II	III
Liberals	1	6	4
Moderates	4	2	3
Conservatives	3	1	3

Different sorts of hypotheses arise from a consideration of Table 6.2, which shows the distribution of liberals, moderates, and conservatives in terms of petty bench membership. It indicates that liberals dominated the second petty bench, and conservatives and moderates dominated the first petty bench. If liberals are scored 3, moderates 2, and conservatives 1, trends in the ideological composition of the petty benches can be observed over the ten-year period. The first petty bench began with an average score of 1.8, which remained the same with the first appointee; it then decreased to 1.6 and finally to 1.4. The trend was just the opposite in the second petty bench; it began with an average score of 2.4 that increased to 2.6 and finally to 2.8. The third petty bench maintained an average score of 2.4 until the last two years of the period when it decreased to 2.0. The trends in the first and second petty benches suggest two hypotheses: (1) Justices who have no strong ideological commitments when they come to the Court take on the ideological coloration of their petty bench. This makes for harmony and consensus in the primary work group and undoubtedly makes petty bench decision-making more pleasant. (2) Retiring justices arc replaced with men whose outlook and values are similar to their predecessors.

Table 6.3: Pre-Court occupation and Ideology

	Lawyers	*Judges*	*Professor*	*Procurators*	*Other*
Liberals	6	3	1	0	1
Moderates	2	3	1	1	2
Conservatives	2	3	1	1	0

Table 6.3 shows the pre-Court careers of liberals, moderates, and conservatives. Except for the lawyers, the distribution is fairly even. Why former lawyers were disproportionately more liberal than justices coming from other backgrounds is not easy to answer. One hypothesis is that practically all of them were not recruited from the ranks of the government bureaucracy and hence were willing, perhaps, to proceed less conservatively than most of their colleagues on the bench. If that is so, a corollary hypothesis is that lawyers who enter the judicial bureaucracy and are recruited from it will tend to be less liberal than the typical lawyer who served on the Tanaka Court. Another hypothesis is that liberalism is related to education as much as to former occupation, since four of the six liberal lawyers were graduates of non-Imperial universities. They are the same four liberal justices indicated in Table 6.4 which shows an even distribution among the ideological clusters except for non-Imperial universities.

Table 6.4 University Education and Ideology

	Tokyo	*Kyoto*	*Non-imperial universities*
Liberals	7	0	4
Moderates	7	1	1
Conservatives	6	1	0

Prefecture of birth appears to be related to ideology in the Tanaka Court, as Table 6.5 shows. Of the nine justices who were born in the metropolitan prefectures of Tokyo. Kyoto, and Aichi, five were liberals and four were moderates. The conservatives all came from prefectures that, in the period when the judges were growing to manhood, could be characterized as rural.[66] Two came from Saga, which is in Kyushu; three from the northern Honshu prefectures of Aomori, Yamagata, and Miyagi; and the remaining two came from Toyama and Okayama. More precise data concerning the justices' early socialization—for example, whether they lived in cities even though they had been born in rural prefectures—is needed for verification of hypotheses concerning the impact of region on ideology and voting behaviour.

Table 6.5: Prefecture of Birth and Ideology

	Metropolitan	*Non-metropolition*
Liberals	5	6
Moderates	4	5
Conservatives	0	7

There may be a relation between age and liberalism in the Tanaka Court. The average year of birth for the liberals was 1888, for moderates, 1889, and for conservatives, 1891. What the hypothesis suggests is not that age makes for liberalism, but that liberalism and conservatism are related to the climate of political opinion prevailing during the critical periods of the justices' political socialization. Some of the retired justices and high court judges whom I interviewed suggested the hypothesis in discussing their student days. They pointed to the significance of the early Taisho Democracy and the World War I period in regard to the development of their general ideological orientation. If there is anything to the hypothesis, one would expect the conservative trend to continue because justices coming to the Court in the late 1960's were born about 1910 and hence came of age in an era when military leadership was ascendant in Japan. One would also expect, however, that the trend would eventually be reversed when the influence of post-World War II democracy is manifested in appointments to the Court.[67]

The conservative trend in the Court during the 1950's may have been due to conservatism of the cabinets of that period and the abolition of the advisory committee in 1948. To determine whether the hypothesis was tenable, Tanaka Court justices who were recommended by the advisory committee and appointed by the Katayama cabinet in 1947 were compared with the justices appointed thereafter by conservative cabinets. Table 6.6 indicates that liberals on the Tanaka Court had been favoured in the initial appointments, but after that appointment of liberals, moderates, and conservatives in almost equal numbers resulted in a substantial increase of conservatives. An almost certain prediction is that if the Socialists come to power in Japan, the Court will become increasingly more liberal and also probably more activist, especially when a majority of the justices are Socialist appointees and the (conservative) Liberal Democratic Party is in power. Indeed, if this happens in the near future, the Court will attract more public attention than it has had heretofore and may thereby acquire political significance more like that of the tribunal after which it was modelled in 1947.

Table 6.6 : Appointment and Ideology

	1947	*1948-58*
Liberals	6	5
Moderates	5	4
Conservatives	2	5

— *David J. Danelski*

REFERENCES

1. This chapter was originally a paper presented at the 1966 annual meeting of the American Political Science Association. Grateful acknowledgement is made to the Concilium on International Studies at Yale University for a travel grant to Japan, to the Social Science Research Council for research assistance, and to the East-West Center for an appointment as a senior specialist. Special thanks are due to Professors Takeo Hayakawa, Takeshi Ishida, Hideo Wada, James A. Dator, John M. Maki, and Chitoshi Yanaga, who helped in facilitating the research for the paper and who were good enough to read an early draft. Alfred C. Oppler, Glendon Schubert, Robert Ward, Laurence Beer, and Jens-Uwe G.

Jungnickel also read and commented on the paper. I should like to thank them and my co-workers—Takao Yamada, Michiko Sekino, Noriko Palmer, Edward Tufte, and my wife Jill. I should like to name all those persons in Japan who gave so generously of their time for interviews, but space and other considerations do not permit it. I cannot refrain, however, from commenting on the enjoyable hours I spent on several occasions with the late Kenzo Takayanagi. Finally I must acknowledge indebtedness to two works on Japan that were crucial to this study: Arthur Taylor von Mehren (ed.), *Law in Japan: The Legal Order in a Changing Society* (Cambridge: Harvard University Press, 1963), and John Maki, *Court and Constitution in Japan* (Seattle: University of Washington Press, 1964). Also useful in revising this paper for publication was Jens-Uwe G. Jungnickel's B.A. thesis, "A Bloc Analysis of Non-Unanimous Decisions of the Grand Bench of the Japanese Court," International Christian University, 1966.

2. When I visited the Legal Training and Research Institute in Tokyo in 1966, I was struck by the number of German law books in its library. Later I found exact figures for its foreign language books as of 1963: German, 7634; English, 2363; French 332: others, 49. "Some Information about the Legal Research and Training Institute," unpublished manuscript. Harvard Law Library.

3. The term "contract" is used here in its broadest sense and includes the notions of legal contract, social contract, covenant, and agreements of all kinds.

4. See Masao Maruyama, "Patterns of Individuation and the Case of Japan: A Conceptual Scheme," in Marius B. Jansen (ed.). *Changing Japanese Attitudes Toward Modernization* (Princeton: Princeton University Press, 1965), pp. 489-531.

5. *Ancient Law* (London: Oxford University Press. 1931), p. 141.

6. Ruth Benedict. *The Chrysanthemum and the Sword* (Boston: Houghton Mifflin Co., 1946), Chap. 3.

7. Takeyoshi Kawashima, "The Notion of Law, Right and Social Order in Japan," in Charles A. Moore (ed.). *The Status of the Individual in East and West* (Honolulu: University of Hawaii Press, 1968), pp. 429-47; and Chap. 2, *supra,* describing a similar point of view among Koreans.
8. See Dan Fenno Henderson, *Conciliation and Japanese Law: Tokugawa and Modern,* 2 vols. (Seattle: University of Washington Press, 1965).
9. Kawashima, "The Notion of Law."
10. Maruyama, "Patterns of Individuation."
11. Yoshio Sasaki. "Civil Conciliation in Rural Districts" (in Japanese), *Horitsu Jiho,* 32 (No. 10, 1960), 59-73.
12. Kawashima, "The Notion of Law," p. 13.
13. Supreme Court of Japan, *The Japanese Legal Training and Research Institute* (Tokyo: The Legal Training and Research Institute, 1965), pp. 9. 16, 31-32.
14. See Albert J. Reiss, Jr., *Occupations and Social Status* (New York: Free Press, 1961), p. 50; Alex Inkeles and Peter H. Rossi, "National Comparisons of Occupational Prestige," *American Journal of Sociology,* 61 (1955), 329-39.
15. Japanese Sociological Association, "Social Stratification and Mobility in Japan," in International Sociological Association, *Transactions of the Second World Congress of Sociology,* 2 (1954), 414-31. In subsequent surveys by the same group, respondents were not asked about the prestige of judges. See Kunio Odaka and Sigeki Nishihira. "Social Mobility in Japan," *East Asian Cultural Studies,* 4 (1965). 83-126.
16. Richard W. Rabinowitz, "The Japanese Lawyer—A Study in the Sociology of the Legal Profession," unpublished Ph.D. thesis (social science), Harvard University, 1955. A portion of this thesis was published as "The Historical Development of the Japanese Bar," *Harvard Law Review,* 70 (1956), 61-81. See also Takaaki Hattori, "The Legal Profession in Japan: Its Historical Development and Present State," in von Mehren (ed.), *Law in Japan,* pp. 111-52.

17. See David J. Danelski, "The People and the Court in Japan," in Joseph Tanenhaus and Joel Grossman (eds.), *The Frontiers of Judicial Research* (New York: Wiley, 1968), pp. 45-72.
18. *The Nippon Times,* August 5, 1947.
19. *The Japan Times,* August 11, 1959.
20. *Akahata;* August 11, 1959.
21. *The Japan Times,* December 17, 1959.
22. Hideo Shimizu, *The Law Faculty of Tokyo University: The Mammoth Base of the Japanese Elite* (in Japanese), (Tokyo, 1965), p. 115. For a defense of judicial restraint by former Chief Justice Kisaburo Yokota, see "Political Questions and the Supreme Court in Japan" (in Japanese), *Hoso jiho,* 16 (No. 1, 1964), 1-11.
23. Japan, *Constitution,* Art. 79, Sec. 1; Art. 6.
24. Ibid.
25. Japan, *Court Organization Law,* Art. 41, Sec. 1.
26. Hideo Wada, "Appointment of Supreme Court Justices and People's Review," [in Japanese] *Jurist,* 289 (1964), 251-61; Supreme Commander for the Allied Powers (S.C.A.P.), *Political Reorientation of Japan* (Washington: U.S. Government Printing Office, 1948), pp. 235-36.
27. Ibid. See also Secretariat of the Commission on the Constitution *Comments and Observations by Foreign Scholars on the Problems Concerning the Constitution of Japan,* 1956 (Tokyo: Secretariat of the Commission on the Constitution, 1964), p. 268.
28. Alfred C. Oppler, "Japan's Courts and Law in Transition," *Contemporary Japan, 21* (1952), 29.
29. The classification of justices, at the time of their appointment, as "lawyers," "judges," and "men of learning and experience" was suggested by Professor Takeo Hayakawa of Kobe University. I am indebted to him for partitioning among these three categories the forty-three justices discussed here. They were partitioned as follows: judges—Iwamatsu, Shimoyama, Fujita, Inoue, Shima, Tarumi, Shimoiizaka, Ishizaka, M.

Yokota, Ishida, Matsuda, Iwata, Shimomura; lawyers—Mano, Tsukazaki, Kotani, Shono, Hasegawa, Tanimura, Motomura, Kobayashi, D. Kawamura, Takahashi, Takagi, Yamada, Gokijo, Kido, Kashihara; men of learning and experience—Mibuchi, Sawada, Y. Saito, Kuriyama, M. Kawamura, Hozumi, K. Tanaka, Irie, Ikeda, Okuno, K. Yokota, K. Saito, Kusaka, Osabe, J. Tanaka.

30. See Shimizu, *The Law Faculty of Tokyo University*, pp. 63-64; Allan B. Cole, *Japanese Society and Politics: The Impact of Social Stratification and Mobility on Politics* (Boston: Graduate School of Boston University, 1956), pp. 20-25.

31. *The Nippon Times*, February 23, 1950.

32. Ties of blood and marriage also appear to be important in the appointment of U.S. Supreme Court justices. See David J. Danelski, *A Supreme Court Justice Is Appointed (New York:* Random House. 1964). pp. 159-61.

33. *Japan Biographical Encyclopedia and Who's Who, 1964-65* (Tokyo: Rengo Press, 1965).

34. S.C.A.P., pp. 242-43.

35. *Tokyo Shimbun*, April 11, 1960.

36. Oppler, "Japan's Courts and Law in Transition," 30.

37. Confidential interview.

38. This section is based primarily on confidential interviews of former justices and others connected with the Court, and on a speech Chief Justice Kisaburo Yokota gave at the Second Asian Judicial Conference in 1965. A mimeographed copy of the speech, which is untitled, was made available to me.

39. A difficult problem that the Court has faced through the years concerns keeping abreast with its docket. In a speech *(supra)* delivered in 1965, Chief Justice Yokota said that in the previous year the Court disposed of about half as many cases as were docketed, and that it had a one-year backlog of civil cases and a five-month backlog of criminal cases.

40. Chief Justice Tanaka did not sit with the first petty bench, which was his official assignment, except in a few cases where it was necessary to constitute a quorum.

41. The Supreme Court's predecessor, the *Daishin-in,* was a court of forty-five judges, and because of the present Court's heavy work load, there has been some discussion of enlarging the Court to its pre-war size. When the number of research officials is added to the number of justices, the sum is exactly the number of judges comprising the *Daishin-in.*

42. Yokota, "Speech," pp. 19-20.

43. Ibid. p. 22.

44. Ibid. pp. 14-16, 24.

45. Ibid. p. 15.

46. Ibid. p. 16.

47. Kotaro Tanaka, "Reflecting upon the Past Ten Years as Chief Justice of the Supreme Court" (in Japanese), *Hoso,* 120 (1940), 1-2.

48. For a discussion of leadership in the Supreme Court of the United States, see David J. Danelski, "The Influence of the Chief Justice in the Decisional Process," in Walter F. Murphy and C. Herman Pritchett, *Courts, Judges, and Politics* (New York: Random House, 1961), pp. 497-508. In Japan, as in the United States, chief justices, or candidates for the chief justiceship, are discussed in terms of leadership qualities. One person told me that Chief Justice Tanaka was not a strong leader because he lacked a forceful personality, and that stronger personalities (such as Justice Mano's) overpowered him in conference discussion. This source suggested, however, that more than personality was involved in Tanaka's failure to lead his Court. Other factors were that he was a scholar and not a judicial type, and that he was a Catholic, and so Western in his ways that his colleagues, it was said, were not completely at ease with him. When Tanaka approached retirement in 1960, former Attorney General Tadashi Hanai, a leading

candidate to succeed him, was not given much of a chance for the appointment because, as one newspaper reported it: "Some people within the Court fear that he will be too gentle as Supreme Court Chief Justice." *Tokyo Shimbun*, April 11, 1960.

49. Nobutaka Ike, *Japanese Politics* (New York: Knopf, 1957). p. 267. During the Court's early years, however, there was occasional aggressive behavior in conferences on the part of a few justices. See Saburo Iwamatsu, *The Path of a Judge* [in Japanese] (Tokyo: Nihon Hyoron Sha, 1967), pp. 257-62.

50. In regard to social leadership, see Danelski, "The Influence of the Chief Justice in the Decisional Process."

51. Tanaka, "Reflecting upon the Past Ten Years as Chief Justice of the Supreme Court."

52. Some justices, however, read the foreign literature precedents relevant to the case in their charge. In writing the Court's opinion in the case involving the constitutionality of the death penalty, Justice Mano consulted one of Samuel Smiles' books. The first few sentences of the opinion after the statement of the lawyer's argument are directly from Smiles. See Tsuyoshi Mano, "Eleven Years of the Supreme Court" (in Japanese), *Trial and Modern Age* (Tokyo: Nihon Hyoron Sha, 1964).

53. Yokota, "Speech," p. 18.

54. See Glendon Schubert, *The Judicial Mind* (Evanston: Northwestern University Press, 1965).

55. Data for this analysis were collected, at Tokyo University by Japanese research assistants, from *Saiko Saibansho Hanreishu* (Collection of Supreme Court Precedents). This collection reports all cases selected by a committee of the Court for publication. The Court has a more complete collection of reports entitled *Saiko Saibansho Saibanshu* (Collection of Supreme Court Decisions). In an effort to ascertain the number of divided decisions not reported in *Hanreishu*, permission was granted from the Court's Secretariat in 1966 to

examine all the cases in *Saibanshu* decided between June 1, 1958, and October 31, 1960. Only two additional divided decisions were disclosed, both by petty benches. Court officials have said that *Saibanshu* contains virtually all of the Court's divided decisions. Although the universe of divided Grand Bench decisions analyzed here is assumed to be relatively complete, it is safer to regard it as a sample of important decisions made by the Tanaka Court. After this chapter was written, the Supreme Court gave Tokyo University a set of *Saibanshu,* which Professor Kawashima used for his study in Chapter 5, *supra.*

56. See Louis L. McQuitty, "Elementary Linkage Analysis for Isolating Orthogonal and Oblique Types and Typal Relevancies," *Educational and Psychological Measurtment,* 17 (1957), 207-29; "Elementary Factor Analysis," *Psychological Reports,* 9 (1961), 71-84. Correlation coefficients less than .25 were not used in the analysis. Hence Hasegawa and Shimoiizaka have only one link in Figure 6.1. Hasegawa's secondary link is with Fujita (.22), and Shimoiizaka's is with Ikeda (.18).

57. Eight Japanese lawyers and fifteen scholars were interviewed in Japan in January 1966.

58. The essays analyzed were "A New Political Ideology and the Law of Nature" and "Freedom and Order." They are contained in Tanaka's *Education and Politics* (in Japanese), (Tokyo: Kogaku-sha Publishing Co., 1946). Table 6.1 reports the top 83 per cent of the evaluations in the essays. In regard to the method used, see Ralph K. White, *Value-Analysis* (Glen Gardner, N.J.: Society for the Psychological Study of Social Issues, 1953). In view of the small sample of statements analyzed by only one coder. Table 6.1 cannot be regarded as anything more than suggestive of Tanaka's value system.

59. These values were articulated in the Supreme Court's opinion in the *Fukuoka Patricide* case and the case involving D.H.Lawrence's *Lady Chatterley's Lover.* See Maki, *Court and Constitution in Japan,* pp. 3-17, 130-34.

Natural law, which is perhaps overemphasized in the analysis because one of the essays deals specifically with that subject, is intimately connected with the fact that Tanaka is a Roman Catholic convert. It serves to link the spiritual, intellectual, and conservative values and also provides a symbol to rationalize them. I think that is precisely the way natural law was used in the Court's *Patricide* opinion, which Tanaka wrote, and I think it is used in the same way generally in Tanaka's approach to the Constitution. See Tanaka, "Democracy and Judicial Administration in Japan," *Journal of the International Commission of Jurists*, 2 (1959-60). 11.

60. James Alien Dator,"The Life History and Attitudes of Japanese High Court Judges," *Western Political Quarterly*, 20 (1967), 408-39; and Chapter 4, *supra*. Two Supreme Court justices responded to Dator's questionnaire. In terms of his analysis, one was a liberal and the other a conservative. The former is in the first cluster here: the latter, in the third.

61. Takeo Hayakawa, "Legal Science and Judicial Behavior, with Particular Reference to Civil Liberties in the Japanese Supreme Court," *Kobe Law Review* (International Edition, No. 2, 1962), 1-27; reprinted in Glendon Schubert (ed.), *Judicial Behavior* (Chicago: Rand McNally, 1964), pp. 325-34.

62. "Gunman-Lingoes Smallest Space Analysis" programme (SSA1 for symetrical matrices), Hebrew University, modified 5.VIII.66, was made available to me by Professor Glendon Schubert at the University of Hawaii. Except for minor modifications, this is the programme described by James C. Lingoes, "An IBM-7090 Programme for Guttman-Lingoes Smallest Space Analysis-I," *Behavioral Science*, 10 (1965), 183-84. See Glendon Schubert, "The Dimensions of Decisional Response: Opinion and Voting Behavior of the Australian High Court." in Tanenhaus and Grossman (ed.), *The Frontiers of Judicial Research*, pp. 163-95.

63. In Chapter 5, *supra*, Professor Kawashima's designation of justices (as liberal, moderate, and conservative) is

consistent with Fig. 6.1, except for M. Kawamura, Kuriyama, and Tarumi, who are labelled by Kawashima as moderates instead of liberals. The difference in designation can be accounted for by our use of different methods of analysis, and time periods.

64. Haruo Abe, "The Accused and Society: Therapeutic and Preventaire Aspects of Criminal Justice in Japan," in von Mehren, *Law in Japan*, p. 338.

65. Schubert, *The Judicial Mind*, Chap. 6.

66. In 1903, 79 per cent of the Japanese population lived in districts of less than ten thousand persons. If a higher percentage is used as an indicator of rural prefectures, the conservatives were born in rural prefectures. See Irene B. Taeuber, *The Population of Japan* (Princeton: Princeton University Press, 1958), p. 48.

67. In his study of attitudes of Japanese high court judges, Dator found that generally "judges in their 30's and 40's were more liberal than those older. But judges in their 50's were more conservative than those in the 60-year-old bracket." Dator, "The Life History Attitudes of Japanese High Court Judges," p. 436. His finding is consistent with the hypothesis discussed.

7

THE PHILIPPINE SUPREME COURT: A STUDY OF JUDICIAL BACKGROUND CHARACTERISTICS, ATTITUDES, AND DECISION-MAKING

INSTITUTIONAL FRAMEWORK

In formal structure, powers, and procedures, the Philippine Supreme Court is strikingly similar to the Supreme Court of the United States. Both courts operate within a presidential form of government with implied recognition of the separation of powers. Both are constitutional tribunals that stand at the apex of an independent judicial hierarchy. Both are courts of last resort, and both have the power of judicial review. Yet it would be naive to assume that the Philippine and U.S. Supreme Courts play the same roles. Their formal structures are similar, but the dynamic and cultural elements that underlie the political systems in which they operate are vastly different.

Traditional analyses of the Philippine Supreme Court—its organization, powers, and decisions—are not wanting. There is, however, a lack of empirical studies dealing with the behaviour and role of judges in the Philippines. It is submitted that an inquiry into actual characteristics and decision-making of Supreme Court justices will add a new perspective to the study of Philippine political process. That is what this study attempts to do. It explores the background characteristics, attitudes, and decision-making of Philippine Supreme Court justices, and compares the findings with those contained in similar studies of the Supreme Court of the United States.

One of the objectives of this study is a comparison of the background characteristics of the Supreme Court justices who served during the three major periods of recent Philippine political history — the American Colonial administration (1901-35), the Commonwealth period (1935-46), and the Republic (1946-66). For this purpose, data for seventy-eight justices were collected on paternal occupations, ethnic origins, religion, education, career patterns, marital affinities, as well as social, professional, and political affiliations. Another objective of this study is an analysis of the voting records of the justices of the Colonial, Commonwealth, and Republic Courts, with particular focus on decisional trends in relation to three important fields — civil liberties, economic liberalism, and judicial activism. The study thus examines the attitudinal behaviour of individual justices as inferred from their opinions and voting responses, and considers institutional constraints and external influences in the decision-making process of the Philippine Supreme Court.

THE JUDICIAL STRUCTURE

The Constitution provides that "the judicial power shall be vested in one Supreme Court and in such inferior courts as may be provided by law."[1] This basic law provides also that all justices and judges shall be appointed by the President with the consent of the Commission on Appointments, and shall hold office during good behaviour until they reach the age of seventy.[2]

The legal and judicial system in the Philippines has evolved under the mixed influence of Spanish and American elements with a "sub-stratum of native customary law."[3] The hierarchy of courts during the American period, patterned after that of the Spanish regime, has continued in its basic form up to the present. At the bottom of the judicial hierarchy are the justice of the peace courts in the municipalities and municipal courts in the cities.[4] Appeals from the decisions of these courts are brought to the courts of first instance; the latter courts, which are grouped into sixteen judicial districts, also have original jurisdiction over certain classes of civil and criminal cases. In the City of Manila, moreover, is a juvenile and domestic relations court.[5] The next higher court is the Court of Appeals. Originally established in 1936 "to provide a court of last resort for a review of the decisions of the lower courts on questions of fact,"[6] the Court of Appeals consists of a presiding justice and seventeen associate justices.[7] The court is usually partitioned into six divisions for decision-making purposes, although it occasionally hears and decides some cases and proceedings not enumerated by law as the exclusive jurisdiction of the Supreme Court to review.[8]

The Supreme Court is the highest Philippine judicial tribunal. Originating in the Audiencia Territorial de Manila (highest court under the Spanish colonial administration), the Supreme Court was re-established by the military government after the United States took over Manila,[9] and soon after was re-organized by the Philippine Commission in 1901.[10] Initially composed of seven justices, the Court's membership was increased to nine in 1917 and to eleven by the end of the American period.[11] The number of justices was then reduced to seven shortly after the inauguration of the Commonwealth;[12] but in 1945, after the liberation of the country from the three-year Japanese occupation, the size of the Court was again increased to eleven by the President of the Philippines in exercise of his emergency powers.[13]

FUNCTIONS OF THE SUPREME COURT

The Supreme Court is composed of a Chief Justice and ten associate justices. It has been described as "the most important legitimizing institution in the Philippines."[14] The Court has original jurisdiction over cases affecting diplomatic and consular officials; also all petitions for the issuance of writs against the Court of Appeals must be brought before it. Another important function of the Supreme Court is to review the orders or decisions of administrative bodies like the Court of Industrial Relations and the Public Service Commission. Above all, it has exclusive power to review final judgments or decrees of inferior courts involving (a) the constitutionality of a treaty, law, or regulation; (b) the legality of a tax or assessment; (c) the jurisdiction of an inferior court; (d) criminal offenses for which the penalty of death or life imprisonment has been imposed; (e) civil cases in which the value in controversy exceeds 50,000 pesos: and (f) all other cases in which errors or questions of law are involved.

The Supreme Court also promulgates rules concerning pleading, practice, and procedure for all courts, as well as admission to the practice of law. Its approval is necessary before a judge may be assigned or transferred from one district to another. In addition, some members of the Court have important functions vis-a-vis the executive and legislative departments. If the President was ever impeached, his trial (as in the United States) by the Senate would be presided over by the Chief Justice.[15] In case of protests contesting the election of a President or Vice-President, the Court's role is to act as a Presidential Electoral Tribunal to determine the outcome.[16] Furthermore, three Supreme Court justices, designated by the Chief Justice, are among the nine members constituting, for each House of Congress, an electoral tribunal; the senior justice acts as chairman.[17]

RECRUITMENT OF SUPREME COURT JUSTICES

During the American regime, appointments to the Philippine Supreme Court were made by the President of the United States, with the consent of the U.S. Senate. Under the Commonwealth and later the Republic, Supreme Court justices have been appointed by the President of the Philippines, with the consent of the Commission on Appointments.[18] To be eligible for appointment to the Supreme Court, one must be at least forty years of age, a Philippine citizen for not less than five years, and have ten or more years of experience as a judge or law practitioner in the Philippines.

Actual recruitment policies and practices may be inferred from an analysis of the background characteristics and career patterns of those who have been appointed to the Supreme Court. Many men who have gained distinction or seniority in the bureaucracy, in the lower courts—particularly in the Court of Appeals—in legal practice, in teaching, or in politics have aspired to appointment to the Supreme Court. Their aspirations have had varied support from political leaders such as those of the dominant political party, interest or professional groups like the Philippine Bar Association, regional associations, and congressional blocs or factions. The President's perception and appraisal of these diverse influences or pressures, as modified by his own personal preferences and attitudes, largely determine who will be appointed. In the last decade or so, many Supreme Court appointees were promoted from the position of incumbent presiding justice of the Court of Appeals. Recent appointments have included a former politician, who had served in the cabinet as executive secretary, and a law professor-practitioner who had also been a presidential legal advisor.

THE PROCESS OF DECISION-MAKING

In hearing and determining cases within its jurisdiction, the Court sits *en banc.*[19] Six justices constitute both a quorum and the minimal concurrence necessary to judgment. However, eight concurrent votes are essential to declare a statute or treaty unconstitutional, or to review and decide on a death penalty imposed by the trial court.

Either original or appellate cases may be brought before the Supreme Court. In all cases, notice to all parties is essential. Printed or typewritten copies of the record on appeal, transcripts, and briefs in appealed cases and in original pleadings, memoranda, and reports in original cases must be sufficient in number not only for the use of the parties, but also for each member of the Court.[20]

A case is usually calendared for hearing after filing the respondent's brief or after the expiration of the time for such filing. In the hearing, each party is entitled to a half-hour period for oral argument before the whole Court, and if necessary his time may be extended at the discretion of the Court. Individual justices often direct questions to the counsel making oral argument.

The Court usually deliberates before announcing its decision, although some urgent motions (e.g. a petition for habeas corpus, or a motion to annul the proclamation of elected candidates under controversial circumstances) often receive more speedy judicial response.

Conclusions regarding a case are made in consultation among the justices. After a decision of the body is reached, a member is assigned to write the opinion of the Court. Any justice may write a concurring opinion, he may concur and dissent in part, or may dissent entirely from the decision of the majority. The Constitution requires that the decision of the Court must express distinctly the facts and the law on which the decision is based, and any member who dissents from it must state the reasons for his dissent. The extent to which dissent has been articulated in the Court during the different periods of Philippine political history will be discussed later.

SOCIAL AND PROFESSIONAL BACKGROUNDS OF JUSTICES

Ethnic Origins

About one-third (eleven) of the thirty-two justices who sat in the Supreme Court during the American regime were Filipinos; but there was less turnover among them than among the twenty-one Americans who constituted the remainder. Actually, there was a well-established policy throughout the period of American administration to maintain marginal but majority control by allocating five seats to Americans and four (including the Chief Justiceship) to Filipinos. One reason for such policy may be deduced from a confidential cablegram sent in 1909 from the American Governor-General of the Philippines to the U.S. Secretary of War:

> Believe that the appointment of Filipinos to the Supreme Court, making the majority of that body native, would have very disastrous effect upon capital and those proposing to invest here. . . .[21]

About a decade later, however, Francis B. Harrison, incumbent American Governor-General, initiated a vigorous programme to "Filipinize" the government service. One of his proposals was to provide for a Filipino majority in the Supreme Court by the appointment of a Filipino justice in place of an American. But U.S. Secretary of War Baker opposed Harrison's recommendation "until such time as we are ready to give

Table 7.1: Ethnic Origins of Filipino Justices

Ethnic group	*Colonial Court* Per cent*	*(N)*	*Commonwealth Court Per cent*	*(N)*	*Republic Court Per cent*	*(N)*	*Totals Per cent*	*(N)*	*Philippine population** Per cent*	*Per cent difference (col. 4 minus col.5)*
Tagalog	33	(3)	25	(6)	40	(14)	34	(23)	21.0	+13
Ilongo (Hiligaynon)	22	(2)	38	(2)	17	(6)	25	(17)	10.4	+15
Pampango	11	(1)	13	(3)	11	(4)	12	(8)	3.2	+9
Pangasinan	0	(0)	8	(2)	14	(5)	10	(7)	2.5	+7
Ilocano	11	(1)	4	(1)	9	(3)	7	(5)	11.7	–5
Waray-Warray	11	(1)	0	(0)	0	(0)	2	(1)	5.5	–4
Cebuano	0	(0)	4	(1)	3	(1)	3	(2)	24.1	–21
Bicol	11	(1)	4	(1)	0	(0)	3	(2)	7.8	–5
Others	0	(0)	4	(1)	6	(2)	4	(3)	13.8	–10
Total	99	(9)	100	(24)	100	(35)	100	(68)	100.0	

* *The twenty-one Americans who served in the Colonial Court, including five of them who continued to serve briefly (a year or less) in the Commonwealth Court, were excluded. In addition, two Commonwealth justices (including one who had also served in the Colonial Court) were not included in the sample due to lack of valid data.*

***Based on the 1960 Census of the Philippines on Population and Housing, which sets the total inhabitants at 27,087,685 (Table II, p. 2).*

independence to the islands."[22] And Woodrow Wilson re-affirmed the old policy, writing that "my heart pulls one way (namely, in the direction of Governor Harrison's recommendation) and my head in the other, in the direction of your own judgment. I suppose I must follow my head in this case. . . ,"[23]

This policy continued, evidently, in the desire to "ensure an American interpretation of the Philippine Organic Act."[24] In 1933, the Philippine leaders' request for the appointment of Filipinos to two vacancies in the Supreme Court to make a Filipino majority was endorsed by Governor-General (subsequently, U.S. Supreme Court Justice) Frank Murphy, but was not favorably considered by Franklin D. Roosevelt's New Deal administration in Washington.[25] It was only after the inauguration of the Philippine Commonwealth in 1935 that the old colonial policy on Supreme Court membership was reversed to the extent of having an all-Filipino membership of the Court.

Almost all Filipinos are of Malay blood, i.e. more or less Mongoloid racial stock. Nonetheless, there are in various parts of the country fifty-five ethnic groups, which differ in customs, language or dialect, and ways of living.[26] Inasmuch as Filipino justices of the Supreme Court come from one common racial stock, their composition may be more meaningfully examined in terms of their identity with the different ethnic groups.[27]

Table 7.1 indicates that more than one-half (59 per cent) of the Filipino justices were Tagalogs and Ilongos, although the two ethnic groups to which they belong constitute less than a third of the Philippine population. Likewise, the Pampango and Pangasinan justices account for 22 per cent of all those who have served in the Supreme Court, although they make up only 5.7 per cent of the national population.

The Ilocanos were fairly well represented in the Colonial Court (11 per cent), but this has not been true since the Commonwealth. The Warays, Cebuanos, and Bicolanos make up 37.4 per cent of the Philippine population, but the justices who came from these three groups composed only 8 per cent of the justices appointed to the Supreme Court. The three remaining justices (4 per cent) came from the province of Zambales in West Central Luzon.

The above data indicate that appointments to the Supreme Court have been dominated by the Tagalogs and Ilongos, followed by the Pampangos and Pangasinenses. From among these four ethnic groups, which make up a little over a third of the total national population, four-fifths of all Filipino justices have been recruited. Clearly, the most underrepresented group has been the Cebuanos.

PATERNAL ORIGINS AND OCCUPATIONS

Paternal origins of Philippine justices during the Republic indicate that almost half (48 per cent) came from upper-middle-class families of lawyers, physicians, businessmen, or small landowners, and of these about a third married into wealthy, upper-class families. On the other hand, more than a third (37 per cent) of the justices had lower-middle-class origins with fathers who were small merchants, clerks, and so forth. Only a tenth (11 per cent) were born in upper-class families of big landowners; but even fewer (4 per cent) came from the laboring or lower class.

In summary, only about three-fifths (59 per cent) of the Philippine justices came from the upper social classes, whereas comparable data for the United States show that eight-tenths (82 per cent) of the total of 91 justices who were members of the Supreme Court from 1789 to 1957 came from that strata of society. From 1933 to 1957, 81 per cent of the U.S. Supreme Court's membership were of upper- or upper-middle-class origins.[28] These findings suggest that the U.S. Supreme Court has been less democratic in its demographic bias than its Philippine counterpart.

There are also comparisons in certain paternal occupations. About 11 per cent of both the Philippine and the American justices had fathers who were judges. The fathers of 22 per cent of the Philippine justices held elective posts; a slightly higher proportion of the American justices (30 per cent) had fathers who held public office (other than state judge). One difference is that one-fifth of the Philippine justices (19 per cent) had fathers who were physicians; only half as many American Supreme Court justices were doctors' sons.

PLACE OF BIRTH

We can also compare Philippine and American justices with regard to the national sub-culture in which they were socialized. About 30 per cent of the Philippine Colonial justices came from urban centers and 70 per cent came from small towns. The Commonwealth and Republic Courts (1935-66) in the Philippines were constituted almost identically in terms of their members' birthplaces: 43 per cent from urban centers and 57 per cent from small towns. Similarly, 44 per cent of American Supreme Court justices from 1933 to 1957 had been born in urban communities, 50 per cent in small towns, and 6 per cent in rural areas.[29]

AGE AND TENURE

During the Philippine Colonial and Commonwealth periods, many justices were appointed while in their mid-thirties or forties. The average age of Supreme Court appointees was forty-six years during the Colonial era and forty-nine years during the Commonwealth period. Under the Republic, the trend has continued toward the appointment of older men. The average age of appointees during the early years of the Republic was fifty-four years, increasing to fifty-seven years in the 1960's. Conversely, the average tenure of the justices in the Supreme Court has steadily decreased from 14.6 years during the Colonial regime to 10.7 years during the Commonwealth to 8.8 years during the Republic. Accordingly, the average age of incumbent justices remained remarkably stable at about fifty-four years until quite recently when it increased by almost ten years. At present, the average age of justices in the Philippine Supreme Court appears to be higher than that of the justices of either the United States or Australia, whose average age is around sixty-one years.[30]

RELIGION AFFILIATION AND EDUCATION

There is practically no differentiation in the religious affiliation of Filipino justices. It is true that a considerable number of the Colonial justices (mostly Americans) were Protestants, but almost all justices during the Commonwealth and Republic have been Roman Catholics. Also during the last two periods, two Protestants, a Mason, and a member of the Philippine Independent Church have served in the Supreme Court.

Table 7.2: Ages of Justices

	Age at appointment			*Age at given year*		
	Range	*Median*	*Mean*	*Range*	*Median*	*Mean*
Colonial Court (1918)	35-60	45	46.3	38-75	58.5	56.7
Commonwealth Court (1938)	43-60	45	48.7	44-67	59	55.8
Early Republic Court (1948)	43-69	54	54.2	53-69	58	58.1
Recent Republic Court (1964)	45-66	58	57.0	54-69	67	65.0

Regarding social or professional affiliations, a considerable number of the justices are members of upper-class social clubs and of professional associations in the Philippines and abroad. Since 1954, six members of the Civil Liberties Union have been appointed to the Court.

A large majority of the Filipino justices in the Colonial Court were products of Catholic high schools or seminaries,[31] and obtained their collegiate and legal education in Catholic universities. On the other hand, the American justices of the Colonial Court were predominantly alumni of private non-sectarian colleges and state universities, which accounts for the figures in Table 7.3 showing that only one-fourth of the justices during the Colonial period received their legal education from Catholic universities; a third of them took up post-graduate degrees, mostly from private non-sectarian and state educational institutions.

With the inauguration of the Commonwealth and the Filipinization of the Supreme Court, there was a noticeable shift toward secular education. During the Commonwealth, less than a third (29 per cent) of the justices graduated from Catholic high schools and about two-fifths (42 per cent) took their pre-law studies in Catholic colleges. The percentage of justices with public secondary and pre-law college education, on the other hand, increased in the Republic: 46 per cent in the secondary and 40 per cent in pre-law collegiate levels.

Table 7.3: Educational Background of Justices

Level of education	Kind of institution attended	Colonial Court N=24 Per cent	(N)	Commonwealth Court N=24 Per cent	(N)	Republic Court N=35 Per cent	(N)	Total* N=83 Per cent	(N)
Secondary	Catholic	17	(4)	29	(7)	40	(14)	30	(25)
	Private non-sectarian	4	(1)	25	(6)	14	(5)	15	(12)
	Public	4	(1)	33	(8)	46	(16)	30	(25)
	Unidentified	75	(18)	17	(4)	0	(0)	27	(22)
College pre-law	Catholic	33	(8)	42	(10)	40	(14)	39	(32)
	Private non-sectarian	21	(5)	17	(4)	14	(5)	17	(14)
	Public	13	(3)	21	(5)	40	(14)	27	(22)
	Unidentified	33	(8)	17	(4)	6	(2)	17	(14)
Law school	Catholic	25	(6)	33	(8)	23	(8)	27	(22)
	Private non-sectarian	79	(19)	29	(7)	23	(8)	41	(34)
	State university	33	(8)	38	(9)	54	(19)	43	(36)
Post-graduate	Catholic	4	(1)	21	(5)	23	(8)	17	(14)
	Private non-sectarian	17	(4)	21	(5)	14	(5)	17	(14)
	State university	13	(3)	0	(0)	0	(0)	4	(3)

**Seven Colonial justices, another Colonial justice who also served in the Commonwealth, and one Commonwealth justice were excluded from the sample for lack of valid data. Justices with overlapping terms were counted in the two different courts in which they served, except the five American justices in the Colonial Court who served very briefly (a year or less) in the Commonwealth Court; they were not counted in the latter body.*

In the law schools, secularized education made its greatest gains among Filipino justices. While the American majority in the Colonial Court were mostly alumni of state or non-sectarian law schools, the Dominican-run University of Santo Tomas virtually monopolized the legal education of Filipino justices in the colonial period. In contrast, only 33 per cent of the Commonwealth justices obtained their legal education in Catholic universities; a slightly smaller number (29 per cent) completed their law training in private non-sectarian institutions. A notable development in the educational background of the justices is indicated by the fact that 38 per cent of the Commonwealth justices graduated from the College of Law, University of the Philippines.

The proportion of Republic justices who were graduates of Catholic law schools was considerably less than that of the Commonwealth Court, while the percentage of those who studied in private non-sectarian law schools decreased slightly. The University of the Philippines, on the other hand, further established its dominant position as contributor to the legal education of Court members, with 54 per cent of the Republic justices graduating from its law school.

With respect to post-graduate law degrees awarded to justices, however, the Catholic educational institutions, particularly the University of Santo Tomas, have even improved on their position. About a third of the Colonial justices took up post-graduate studies and, of this group, almost all were graduates of private non-sectarian and state universities. The proportion of justices with master's or doctoral degrees in the Commonwealth and Republic Courts increased from 35 per cent to 42 per cent, but not one of them received a higher degree from state universities. Some justices have taken advanced studies at such leading American law schools as Harvard or Yale, but a larger number did their post-graduate work at the University of Santo Tomas.

CAREER PATTERNS

What are the professional backgrounds and career patterns of those who have sat in the highest tribunal? In some countries, previous judicial experience is considered to be essential for appointment to the Supreme Court. Gadbois, in his study of the indian Supreme Court, noted that all appointees to the Court since 1950 previously were judges of the High Courts.[32] Available data on American Supreme Court justices, on the other hand, tent to show that only a fourth of them had previous experience as federal, and about half as state, judges.[33]

The Philippine experience stand midway between the Indian and American practice. As Table 7.4 indicates, nearly two-thirds of the Colonial and Commonwealth justices served as trial judges before their elevation to the Supreme Court. But the percentage of appointees with such judicial experience in lower courts decreased to 48 per cent under the Republic.

Table 7.4: Previous Professional Background of Justices

Previous experience	*Colonial Court 100 per cent (17)*	*Commonwealth Court 100 per cent (27)*	*Republic Court 100 per cent (31)*	*Total* 100 per cent (75)*
Trial Judge	64 (11)	60 (9)	48 (15)	46 (35)
Private Practitioner	41 (7)	46 (7)	58 (18)	42 (32)
Law Professor	58 (10)	40 (6)	45 (14)	40 (30)
Administrator	29 (5)	46 (7)	45 (14)	34 (26)
Prosecuting Attorney	41 (7)	33 (5)	38 (12)	32 (24)
Politician	17 (3)	40 (6)	25 (8)	22 (17)
Editor	11 (2)	13 (2)	6 (2)	8 (6)

**Based on a sample of 61 out of 78 justices who had been appointed to the Supreme Court up to 1966. Four Filipino colonial justices continued to serve in the Commonwealth Court, while 10 Commonwealth justices carried on to the Republic Court; all of them were counted in both courts in which they served. On the other hand, five Americans who sat in the Colonial court and served very briefly in the Commonwealth Court were not counted in the latter.*

The percentage of justices with previous background as attorneys-general or prosecuting attorneys has slightly decreased:

41 per cent in the Colonial Court; 33 per cent in the Commonwealth Court; and 38 per cent in the Republic Court. Most of these former prosecutors became trial judges before they reached the Supreme Court.

On the other hand, the number of justices who had been administrators has increased from 29 per cent in the Colonial period to 46 per cent and 45 per cent in the Commonwealth and Republic, respectively. This development may be significant in the light of the comments of Ulf Torgersen. In discussing the Norwegian Supreme Court, he observed: "Judges, who . . . have been recruited from the administration, tend to feel loyalty to the state administration, and are somewhat reluctant to act against the government when faced with the problem of determining the legality of some measures."[34]

Considerably more law professors became justices during the American regime than during the two other periods. The comparative figures are: Colonial, 58 per cent; Commonwealth, 40 per cent; and Republic, 45 per cent. The higher percentage may be explained by the common practice of government prosecutors, judges, and even justices to teach part-time (usually evening classes) in the law schools. Only a few of the justices, however, were primarily engaged in academic work.

The appointments to the Supreme Court in the last decade have been marked by the increasing proportion of those who had been private law practitioners. Thus, 57 per cent of justices in the Republic Court had practiced privately as compared to 41 per cent and 46 per cent of the Colonial and Commonwealth Courts, respectively; but a majority of these justices had practiced law before entering the government bureaucracy or judiciary. Only a few justices (8 per cent) had experience as newspaper editors.

It is especially interesting to ascertain how many members of the court were formerly politicians, since in the Philippines politics is considered a "national pastime," and sharing political power is often considered a stepping stone to professional advancement. In the Colonial period, 17 per cent of the justices had been politicians previously. Appointments to the Supreme Court, by a nationally elected Filipino President under the

Commonwealth, included several politicians, thereby increasing their number to 40 per cent of the whole Court. Since independence, the trend has been towards the recruitment of relatively fewer politicians so that only 28 per cent of the Republic justices had been "partisans in politics." Furthermore, a majority of them reached the Supreme Court after "retiring" from politics and serving in the judiciary or the bureaucracy.

In any case, the percentage of Philippine justices who had been politicians is substantially less than that of justices of the U.S. Supreme Court. Part of this difference may be because in the Philippines, justices of the peace or local judges are not elected posts, and serious attempts have been made to establish an independent, politically neutral judiciary at lower levels. In fact, very few of the justices have well-known party affiliations. This does not necessarily mean, however, that candidates for appointment to the Philippine Supreme Court need less political support than their counterparts in the United States. They probably need as much, if not more.

DECISIONS: ISSUES AND TRENDS

We shall now analyze the responses and records of the Supreme Court in three important fields of public policy: civil liberties, economic liberalism, and judicial activism.

Civil liberties or political liberalism includes such issues as freedom of speech, press, and association; due process; equal protection; religious liberty; and other claims to personal rights and freedoms, whether based upon constitutional provisions or upon statutory or judicial norms.[35]

Analysis of economic liberalism is focused on labour-management or tenant-landlord relations, governmental regulation of economic or business activities, the power of eminent domain, and taxation.[36]

A third field explored in this study concerns judicial activism and restraint. The Court's perception of its "judicial" role vis-avis other departments or instrumentalities of government is examined, and cases indicating the Court's willingness or reluctance to decide issues affecting the status, decisions, or activities of the executive, legislative, and administrative branches of government and to uphold, limit, and expand judicial power are analyzed.

Cases in these three fields should be viewed first in the context of the total decisional output of the Supreme Court. For this purpose, we shall examine all Supreme Court decisions in four selected years: 1928, 1938, 1948, and 1954. Table 7.5 indicates the total number of decisions in the three fields of particular interest and also the totals for the four terms sampled.[37]

The average proportion of civil liberties cases is only 7 per cent of the total number of cases. In contrast, the percentage of civil liberties cases in the U.S. Supreme Court is much higher, averaging about a third of all decisions during the past decade.[38]

The number of cases related to economic liberalism or judicial activism is even smaller. Economic liberalism cases average only 6 per cent of the total cases in the sample; decisions reflecting the degree of judicial activism or restraint exercised by the Court average also 6 per cent. On the other hand, a large majority of Supreme Court cases have to do With civil and commercial law suits. In this latter group, however, the issues involved were generally not so controversial.

Table 7.5: Reported Decisions of the Supreme Court in Selected Years

Category of cases	1928		1938		1948		1954		Averages	
	Per cent	*Number*	*Per cent*	*Number*	*Per cent*	*Number*	*Per cent*	*Number*	*Per cent*	*Number*
Civil liberties	8	(16)	5	(12)	13	(31)	5	(18)	7	(19)
Economic liberalism	3	(5)	11	(24)	5	(13)	4	(15)	6	(14)
Judicial activism	4	(7)	7	(15)	8	(21)	4	(15)	6	(14)
Others	86	(165)	77	(171)	73	(177)	88	(332)	81	(211)
Total	101	(193)	100	(222)	99	(242)	101	(380)	100	(259)

Table 7.6 shows the breakdown of divided cases or dissensual decisions of the Supreme Court as related to the case

totals for four-year sample periods of the different stages of Philippine political history—the American regime, Commonwealth, Early Republic, and Recent Republic. It is significant to note that a large and increasing proportion of dissensual decisions (33-45 per cent) involves the three issues of civil liberties, economic liberalism, and judicial activism.

Table 7.6: Dissensual Decisions in Relation to Total Decisions for Selected Periods

	Dissensual Decisions										
Period	*Civil liberties*		*Economic liberalism*		*Judicial activism*		*Others*		*Dissensual*	*Total*	*Percentage of dissensual decisions to total*
	Per cent	*(N)*	*Per cent*	*(N)*	*Per cent*	*(N)*	*Per cent*	*(N)*	*decisions*	*decisions*	*decisions*
1927-30	12	(19)	11	(18)	10	(16)	67	(109)	162	792	20
1937-40	17	(12)	9	(6)	9	(6)	65	(45)	69	943	7
1947-50	25	(69)	8	(20)	12	(32)	55	(146)	267	1114	24
1954	16	(3)	5	(1)	21	(4)	58	(11)	19	380	5
1963-66	6	(1)	13	(2)	25	(4)	56	(9)	16	1906	1

The Philippine Supreme Court decides more cases than its American counterpart. This judicial output, as Table 7.6 shows, increased by 41 per cent from the time of the American regime to the early years of independence, and since then it has nearly doubled. There appears, however, to be greater consensus among justices of the Philippine Court, although the rate of unanimity has varied in the different stages of political development. During American colonial rule, when the Americans maintained a bare majority in the Court, about a fifth of the total cases were non-unanimous. With an all-Filipino membership, the Commonwealth Court registered a much lower amount of dissent: only 7 per cent of the total cases were divided. Disturbed political, social, and economic conditions after the war, aggravated by the dissident activities of the Hukbalahap, may have had some effects on the rate of unanimity in the Early Republic Court; the percentage of non-unanimous cases rose to 24 per cent. In the 1960's, the relative economic and political stability may have contributed to the remarkably high rate of unanimity in the highest tribunal. Of 1,906 cases adjudicated from 1963-66, in only 16 decisions, or 1 per cent of the total, was the Court divided. The extent to which the Court's rate of unanimity is influenced by the values and attitudes of the individual justices will be discussed in a later section.

Next we shall compare the collective records of the Supreme Court in years sampled. Table 7.7 presents positive and negative responses of the Court as a body in cases involving civil liberties, economic liberalism, and judicial activism. A decision in a civil liberties case is considered to be positive when it strengthens or favors individual claims for personal rights or freedom; it is negative when it weakens or denies such claims. With regard to economic liberalism cases, a decision is assumed to be positive when it supports the claims of labor unions against management, favours government regulation of business, or upholds tax laws and ordinances for community services and welfare; otherwise, it is negative. A positive response in a judicial activism case broadens judicial power or the jurisdiction of the Court by allowing it to inquire into the legality of a court martial, to review the decision of an administrative tribunal, to take cognizance of what is claimed to be a political question, or to uphold the power of the courts to adjudicate international, electoral, or admistrative problems. A response that restricts the jurisdiction of the Supreme Court or weakens judicial power is viewed as negative.

Except in 1948, the Court's decisions generally strengthened free speech, due process, equal protection, and privacy. But the Commonwealth (1938) and Republic (1954) Courts showed higher positive response than the Colonial (1928) Court. It is interesting to note, however, that a sharp increase in the number of civil liberties cases in 1948 was accompanied by a sharp drop in the percentage of positive decisions. These changes indicate a conservative judicial response to early post-war issues or problems such as political collaboration, treason, and the Huk rebellion.

Table 7.7: Positive and Negative Responses in Liberalism and Activism Cases for Selected Years

Category of cases and years	*Decisions and types of responses*			
	Positive decisions	*Negative decisions*	*Total decisions*	*Per cent of positive decisions to total decisions*
Civil liberties				
1928	9	7	16	55
1938	8	4	12	67
1948	11	20	31	35
1954	11	7	31	35
Economic liberalism				
1928	1	4	5	20
1938	17	7	24	71
1948	7	6	13	54
1954	8	7	15	53
Judicial activism				
1928	3	4	7	43
1938	4	11	15	27
1948	8	13	21	38
1954	7	8	15	47

Regarding economic liberalism, the 1938 Court had the highest percentage of cases favouring labour rights, broadening the taxing power, and strengthening administrative regulation of banks and public utilities. To a lesser extent, the post-independence Courts (1948 and 1954) were also inclined to support economic liberalism. But the Court during the American regime (1928) was very conservative in this regard.

During the last four decades, the Philippine Supreme Court has exercised considerable judicial restraint. Each of the four Courts studied gave more decisions restricting than broadening judicial power, and the Commonwealth Court (1938), which had the highest positive response to civil liberties and economic liberalism, acted with greatest restraint. Only 27 per cent of its decisions broadened judicial power, compared with 47 per cent for the 1954 Court.

VOTING BEHAVIOUR AND CUMULATIVE SCALES

Having considered the decisions of the Supreme Court as a collective body, we may now direct attention to the voting responses of the individual justices with a view to determining their respective attitudes regarding civil liberties or political liberalism, economic liberalism, and judicial activism. Efforts were made to construct cumulative scales of Court behaviour for each of the above variables and for each of four-year sample periods for different political periods in Philippine history, namely, 1927-30 for the American regime, 1937-40 for the Commonwealth period, 1947-50 for the Early Republic years, and 1963-66 for the Recent Republic period. The technique used was Guttman's cumulative scaling as adapted by Glendon Schubert for the scaling of the votes of Supreme Court justices.[39]

Scales could not be constructed for all the categories for each period, In the 1963-66 period there was only one divided civil liberties case. Likewise, there were not enough economic liberalism and judicial activism cases in the 1937-40 and 1963-66 periods to construct scales. Thus there were only seven groups of cases involving the three variables in the four periods sampled which were large enough to attempt cumulative scaling.

To ascertain "unidimensionality," Guttman's coefficient of reproducibility (R) was used; an R of .90 is generally considered as indicating unidimensionality. In addition, Menzel's coefficient of scalability (S) was also computed; an S of "somewhere between .60 and .65," is generally considered as indicating scalability.

Table 7.8 summarizes the computations for R and S. All the cases in the three case categories for the period 1927-30 resulted in non-scales, while quasi-scales were constructed from the political liberalism cases in 1937-40 and the economic liberalism cases 1947-50. On the other hand, marginal scales were developed for the civil liberties cases and the judicial activism cases for 1947-50.

POLITICAL LIBERALISM

The only scale for civil liberties cases was found for those decided in the period 1947-50 (Figure 7.1). In terms of the scale, Justice

Table 7.8: Measures of Consistency for the Cumulative Scales[40]

	C Scale		*E Scale*		*A Scale*	
Periods	*R*	*S*	*R*	*S*	*R*	*S*
	Non-scale		Non-scale		Non-scale	
1927-30	.832	.438	.829	.500	.800	.351
	Quasi-scale					
1937-40	.857	.583				
	Scale		Quasi-scale		Scale	
1947-50	.892	.664	.881	.622	.895	.700

Perfecto, who had spent many years as a national legislator before coming to the Court, was an extreme political liberal. He had only three negative votes (two of which were inconsistent) out of fifty-seven participations. Justice Hilado, a former private law practitioner and trial judge, was the second most favourably inclined toward civil liberties, although he registered five inconsistent votes in twenty-eight participations. Also favourably disposed, but to a less degree, were Justices Paras, Briones, and Feria, whose scale ranks were third, fourth, and fifth, respectively. Like Hilado, both Paras and Briones had five inconsistent votes but they had participated in considerably more cases. Paras and Briones had been members of Congress; the former also had served a long term as trial judge, and the latter had served on the Court of Appeals. Justice Feria was elevated directly to the Supreme Court after a long career as a law professor.

On the other end of the scale were Justices Tuason and Padilla, both former administrators and prosecuting attorneys. In addition, Padilla taught law, and Tuason later served as a trial judge. While Tuason had six inconsistent votes in sixty-four participations, Padilla had only one inconsistent vote in forty-five decisions. Justice Hontiveros, who had a varied career pattern as private law practitioner, politician, and judge, was also near the conservative end of the C scale, but since he had participated in only six decisions, there is room for doubt about the degree of his political conservatism.

Considering their scale ranks, Justices Pablo, Moran, and Bengzon might be considered moderate conservatives. Justice

Pablo (a former private law practitioner and politician) and Justice Moran (a former law professor) had short stints as prosecuting attorneys before their long service as trial judges. In contrast, bureaucrat-professor Bengzon's first judicial experience was in the Court of Appeals. He had the highest number of inconsistent votes: seven in sixty-three decisions, in which he voted negatively on civil liberties claims forty-six times.

In the middle of the C scale were Justices Reyes, Ozaeta, and Montemayor. Ozaeta, reappointed to the Supreme Court after serving as secretary of justice, had been a private law practitioner, administrator, prosecuting attorney, and trial judge. Reyes and Montemayor were new appointees to the Court; both had been bureaucrats and trial judges. In addition, Reyes used to be a professor and prosecuting attorney. Justice Torres, with his minimal participation, was also located at mid-scale; he had been a prosecuting attorney, administrator, and trial judge.

Table 7.9: C Scale (Political Liberalism) Ranks of the Justices

Non-scale	*Colonial 1927-30*	*Quasi-scale*	*Commonwealth 1937-40*	*Scale*	*Republic 1947-50*
1	Romualdez				
2	Malcolm			1	Perfecto
3	(Villa-real)			2	Hilado
4	Johnson	1	Imperial	3	Paras
5	Street	2	Laurel	4	Briones
6	Villamor	3	Abad Santos	5	Feria
7	Avancena	4	Avancena	7	Reyes, Ozaeta, Montemayor
8	Johns	5	Diaz	9	Torres
9	Ostrand	6.5	(Villa-real)	10	Bengzon
		6.5	Moran	11	Moran
		8	Concepcion	12	Pablo
				13	Hontiveros
				14	Padilla
				15	Tuason

The C scale ranks of the justices are summarized in Table 7.9, which shows that during the Colonial period. Chief Justice Avancena was one of the more conservative members of the Court. A decade later, Avancena occupied a more modal rank. This trend continues under the Republic, as evinced by Justice Moran whose quite conservative rank during the Commonwealth was relatively more moderate a decade later after he became Chief Justice. A possible implication of this trend is that more and more conservative justices had been appointed to the Supreme Court since the inauguration of the Commonwealth. Considering, however, the comparative backgrounds, views, and records of the justices in the three different political periods, this explanation is highly dubious, for many political liberals were appointed to both the Commonwealth and Republic Courts. A more likely explanation for the trend is that sharper issues of liberalism came before the Court in the latter period.

ECONOMIC LIBERALISM AND JUDICIAL ACTIVISM

The only other cases that formed a scale were the judicial activism decisions for 1947-50, shown in Figure 7.2. On the other hand, the cases involving economic liberalism, during the same period, resulted in only a quasi-scale. A moderately high positive correlation was found between the E quasi-scale and the A scale. At least from a statistical point of view, E and A could be combined into one scale, and such a scale was constructed for 1947-50.

A comparison of the C Scale and the E/A scale is revealing. Justice Perfecto, who ranked first in the C Scale, was also on top of the E/A Scale. Other political liberals, Justices Briones and Paras, were also found to be economic liberals and judicial activists, holding ranks between second and fourth in both scales. On the other hand, Justice Feria (a moderate political liberal who ranked fifth on the C Scale) joined Justices Moran and Bengzon (both moderate political conservatives) to form the group of moderate conservatives in the fields of economic liberalism and judicial activism. Conversely, Justice Pablo (moderate political conservative) who ranked twelfth in the C scale, demonstrated more positive response toward economic liberalism and judicial activism. Just as in the C Scale, Justices Ozaeta, Reyes, and

Montemayor maintained their mid-scale ranks in the E/A Scale. They were joined by Justice Hilado, a political liberal who held number two ranking in the C Scale. Justice Padilla, and to a slightly less degree, Justice Tuason, were most strongly inclined toward extreme economic conservatism and judicial restraint. Their bottom ranks in the E/A Scale were equally matched by their political conservatism, with Justice Tuason holding the last rank in the C Scale.

On the whole, it is noteworthy that the C Scale and E/A Scale are moderately correlated at a rho of .72, which is somewhat higher than the rho of .61, which Schubert reported to obtain between C and E scales in his study of the American Supreme Court.[41] Indeed, it is apparent that except for three most deviant justices (Pablo, Feria, and Hilado), one might with some justification have been able to combine all three scales into a single para-attitudinal (ideological) dimension of liberalism and conservatism. Omitting Pablo, the correlation between C and E/A rises to .91; and omitting also Feria and Hilado, it rises to a remarkably high .98. Certainly, it is an important finding of this study that even when the E and A scales were separately constructed on the basis of an *a priori* hypothesis about content boundaries and differences, the empirical evidence of isomorphism suggests that these are better conceptualized as a single atti-tudinal dimension of economic liberalism *and* judicial activism.

SUMMARY

The Philippine Supreme Court decides a much larger number of cases annually than its American counterpart. That this number has increased by two and a half times from the Colonial Court to the Republic Court is indeed striking. For it is indicative of an increasingly greater reliance on the Supreme Court as the nation's "most important legitimizing institution" to settle disputes in this developing country. Concurrently, there appears to be a long-term trend toward an institutional sublimation of dissent within the highest tribunal. With the exception of the politically unstable and economically difficult years of post-war and early independence, the percentage of dissensual cases in the Supreme

Court has decreased from 20 per cent in 1927-30 to 7 per cent in 1937-40, to 5 per cent in 1954, and finally, to a mere 1 per cent in 1963-66. This trend toward greater consensus among the justices may be traced to several factors. First of all, some differences between the Colonial justices, on one hand, and the Commonwealth and Republic justices, on the other hand, may be recalled. Although the Colonial Court was composed of a majority of Americans, many of whom were Protestants, there was generally greater homogeneity in the Commonwealth and Republic Courts, which had all-Filipino and predominantly Catholic memberships.

Another possible factor may be traced to the marked increase in the number of justices who had previous experiences as administrators. Whereas less than a third of the Colonial justices were former bureaucrats, nearly one-half of the Commonwealth and Republic justices had been government administrators, apparently with some similarities in values and orientation, especially in reacting to issues involving governmental action or measures. In this connection, the educational background among the justices may also be related. In the Colonial Court, the slight American majority had primarily a secular education, whereas the Filipino members were products of Catholic seminaries. colleges. The pattern radically changed after independence: The legal education of Filipino justices during the Colonial years was monopolized by the Dominican University of Santo Tomas, whereas 28 per cent of the Commonwealth justices and 27 per cent of the Republic justices completed their law in Catholic colleges. The majority (55 per cent) of the Republic justices were law graduates of the University of the Philippines.

But why did the drop continue, although to a smaller degree, in the proportion of dissensual Supreme Court cases from the Commonwealth to the present? Some hypotheses may be posited from an examination of differences between the Commonwealth and Republic justices. One point of difference is age: the Republic justices tend, on the average, to be a decade older than the Commonwealth justices. Furthermore, there is a greater disparity of ages among the Commonwealth justices (44-67) than among the Republican justices (54-69); but the Colonial Court had the widest range of 38-75 years. There also has been a continuing trend toward a court that is more homogeneous from a generational point of view. From these findings, we may hypothesize that, *ceteris paribus,* (a) the wider the age range in the Supreme Court, the greater is the amount of dissent; and (b) the older the Court members and the narrower their age range, the greater is the tendency toward consensus.

A case in point is the scale ranking of Chief Justices Avancena and Moran in the field of civil liberties. In Table 7.9, we noted that each of these justices held a conservative rank in the previous court and then assumed a more modal rank in the latter court. We rejected the idea that this finding necessarily implied that more conservative men have been appointed to the Supreme Court. Rather, we sought to explain this finding as the result of more extremely liberal issues which arose after national self-government and independence.

This may be exemplified further by the Supreme Court's responses to issues of liberalism. In Table 7.7, the political socialization of Supreme Court members in the tenets of constitutional government, with its notion of natural individual rights and separated or limited powers, is evident in the high proportion of positive responses to civil liberties cases in all the sampled years, except 1948. In the latter year, the sharp drop in the number of positive decisions in political liberalism cases can be clearly attributed to the many controversial issues and complex problems following the end of World War II, such as emergency powers, Huk rebellion, suspension of the writ of habeas corpus, and reaction to political collaboration or treason during the Japanese occupation.

In the area of economic liberalism, the highest percentage of positive decisions was recorded by the Commonwealth Court (1938) which also registered the highest percentage of former politicians among its members. It was also during the Commonwealth period that a more active participation or intervention of government in economic and business activities began to be widely accepted.[42]

This favorable inclination toward economic liberalism continued, to a slightly less degree, in the Republic Court. In contrast, the Colonial Court was characterized by an extreme economic conservatism. It is reasonable to deduce that the philosophy of free enterprise was a powerful weapon of the Colonial Court, with its small American majority, "to ensure an American interpretation of the Philippine Organic Act" and thus protect the interests of foreign investors in the islands.

The foregoing analysis suggests the need for further verification and amplification of our findings and conclusions, which are offered here mainly as hypotheses of judicial behaviour. It is evident that the degree of consensus and the brand of liberalism of the Supreme Court depends not only on the backgrounds and personalities of its members, but also on the varying case content, constraints, interactions, and conditions—both internal and external—that constitute the aggregate stimuli of judicial decision-making.

— *Abelardo G. Samonte*

REFERENCES

1. Philippine Constitution, Art. VII, Sec. 1.
2. Ibid., Art. VIII, Sees. 5 and 9. The Commission on Appointments consists of twelve Senators and twelve Congressmen elected by each House, respectively, on the basis of proportional representation of the political parties.
3. Joseph R. Hayden, *The Philippines: A Study in National Development* (New York: Macmillan, 1950), pp. 242-43.
4. The primary statutory basis for the present structure of Philippine courts is Republic Act 296, June 17, 1948, as amended by Republic Act 2613, August 1, 1959.
5. Republic Act 1401, September 9, 1955.
6. First Annual Report of the President of the Philippines (1936), pp. 20-23. In 1938, the membership of the Court of Appeals was increased from eleven to fifteen (Commonwealth Act 259, April 7, 1938).
7. Republic Act 296, as amended by Republic Act 1605, August 23, 1956. In 1945, the Court of Appeals was abolished by presidential decree (Executive Order 37,

series of 1945) but was recreated by the Congress a year later (Rep. Act 5).

8. Republic Act 296, Sec. 29.
9. General Order 20, May 29, 1899.
10. Act 136, June 11, 1901.
11. Act 2711, March 10, 1917; Hayden, *The Philippines,* p. 242.
12. Commonwealth Act 3, December 31, 1935.
13. Executive Order 40, series of 1945.
14. Jean Grossholtz, *Politics in the Philippines* (Boston: Little, Brown, 1964), p. 127.
15. Constitution, Art. IX, Sec. 3.
16. R.A. 1793, June 21, 1957.
17. Constitution, Art. VI, Sec. 11.
18. See Philippine Constitution, Art. VI, Sec. 12.
19. The Constitution provided an alternative for the Court to sit in two divisions unless otherwise provided by law. In accordance with this constitutional provision, the alternative for divisional decision-making was ruled out by the Judiciary Act of 1948, which provides that all cases within the Court's jurisdiction shall be decided in full court. As a matter of historical note, during the last two decades of the American regime (1917-35) the Supreme Court sat either in full court or in divisions (Act 2711, Sec. 138).
20. The New Rules of Court, Rule 56, effective January 1, 1964.
21. Cablegram from Governor-General Forbes to the U.S. Secretary of War, dated May 13, 1909. (U.S. National Archives, Washington, D.C.)
22. Letter of Secretary of War Baker to President Wilson, August 17, 1917. (U.S. National Archives, Washington, D.C.)
23. Reply of President Woodrow Wilson to the Secretary of War, August 21, 1917. (U.S. National Archives, Washington, D.C.)

24. Testimony of Speaker Manuel Roxas of the Philippines House of Representatives, at a hearing before the Committee on Immigration and Naturalization, U.S. House of Representatives, April 1930. (U.S. National Archives, Washington, D.C.)
25. Cablegram from Governor-General F. Murphy to the Secretary of War, July 13, 1933. (U.S. National Archives, Washington. D.C.)
26. Marcelo Tangco, "The Christian Peoples of the Philippines," *Natural and Applied Science Bulletin*, 11, No. 1 (January-March, 1951), 12-13.
27. Most of the American justices who were members of the Colonial Court came from the Midwest and South of the United States.
28. John Schmidhauser, "The Justices of the Supreme Court: A Collective Portrait," *Midwest Journal of Political Science*, 3 (1959), 7-8.
29. Ibid. p. 17.
30. See Glendon Schubert, "Judges and Political Leadership," in Lewis Edinger (ed.), *Political Leadership in Industrialized Societies* (New York: Wiley, 1961), p. 255.
31. Data on the secondary education of many American members of the Court could not be ascertained.
32. George Gadbois, Jr., "The Paramount Judiciary in India: 1937-64," unpublished doctoral dissertation, Duke University, 1965, p. 127. See also Law Commission of India, *Fourteenth Report: Reform of Judicial Administration* (New Delhi, 1958), Vol. 1, p. 35.
33. S. Sidney Ulmer, "Public Office in the Social Background of Supreme Court Justices," *American Journal of Economics and Sociology*, 21 (1962), 63.
34. Ulf Torgersen, "The Role of the Supreme Court in the Norwegian Political System," in Glendon Schubert, *Judicial Decision-Making* (New York: Free Press, 1963), pp. 228-29.
35. Glendon Schubert, *The Judicial Mind* (Evanston: Northwestern University Press. 1965). pp. 101-2.

36. Ibid. p. 127. See also Herman Pritchett, *The Roosevelt Court* (New York: Macmillan, 1948), p. 257.

37. Data on unreported cases in 1928 and 1938 were not available because of the loss of records during the war. There were seven unreported cases in 1948 and 146 cases in 1954. Most of these were relatively minor and decided by unanimous vote. For the period from July 1, 1947. to June 30, 1951, for instance, there was a total of 106 unreported cases; only five justices dissented and each in only four instances or less.

38. Schubert, *The Judicial Mind, p.* 148.

39. For the basic procedures, see Glendon Schubert, *Quantitative Analysis of Judicial Behaviour* (New York: Free Press, 1959), pp. 269-90. In the scales reported in Figures 7.1-7.3, the titles of cases have been omitted; and the cases are cited by two-digit volume number, followed by a slash bar and then the beginning page number.

40. C for political liberalism, E for economic liberalism, and A for judicial activism.

41. *The Judicial Mind,* p. 173, Table 27.

42. See Abelardo G. Samonte, "The Role of Public Enterprise in Philippine National Development," *International Review of Administrative Sciences,* 33 (1967), 140-41.

Appendix: Individual Attributes of Supreme Court Justices in Sampled Periods

Judges: Cases:	Perfecto	Hilado	Paras	Briones	Feria	Reyes	Ozaeta	Montemayor	Torres	Bengzon	Moran	Pablo	Hontiveros	Padilla	Tuason	Total
82/524	+		+	+	∅			+			+	+		+	+	7-1
87/641			+			+		∅		+		∅			+	5-2
80/418	+	∅	+	+	+					+	+	∅			+	7-2
87/418			+			+	+	∅		∅	+	+			+	6-2
85/711			+			+	+	+		+	+	+		+	-	8-1
78/112	+	+	+	+	+					+	+	+		+	-	9-1
82/23	+		+	+						+	+	+		+	-	7-1
78/820	+	+	+		+					∅	+	+	+	-	∅	8-2
79/629	+	∅	+	+	+					+	+	+		-	-	7-2
82/789	+			+	+	+				+		+			-	6-1
83/551	+		+	+	+					+	+	+			-	7-1
80/71	+	∅	+	+	+					+	+	+			-	7-2
80/859	+	+	+		+							+		-	-	5-2
79/283	+	∅	+	+	∅					+	+	+		-	-	6-4
82/723	+		+	+	+					+	+	-			-	6-2
84/525			+		+	+	+	+	+	-	-				-	6-3
85/431			+			+	+	+		-	-	-		-	-	4-5
84/161			+		+	-	-	-		-	-	-			⊕	3-6

Contd...

Contd...

Judges: Cases:	*Per-fecto*	*Hilado*	*Paras*	*Briones*	*Feria*	*Reyes*	*Ozaeta*	*Monte-mayor*	*Torres*	*Beng-zon*	*Moran*	*Pablo*	*Honti-veros*	*Padilla*	*Tuason*	*Total*
83/267	+		+	∅	+	-		-			-			-	-	3-6
87/493			+		+	-	-	-		-	-	-			-	2-7
84/219	+		+		+	-				-	-	-		-	⊕	4-5
78/431	+									-		-		-	-	1-4
80/1	+	∅	+	+	-					⊕	-	-		-	-	4-6
78/599	+	+	∅	+	-					⊕	-	-		⊕	-	5-5
82/230	∅		+	+	-					-	-	-			-	2-6
82/828	+		∅	+	-						-				-	2-4
84/722			+		-	-	-	⊕	-	⊕	-	-		-	-	3-8
84/714	+		+			-	-	-		-	-	-			-	2-7
84/306			+		-	-	-	-		-	-			-	-	1-8
85/495			+			-	-	-		-	-	-		-	-	1-8
85/845			+			-	-	-		-	-	-		-	-	1-8
81/258	+	+	+	-	-					-	-	-		-	-	3-7
77/1053	+			-	-					-	-	⊕		-	-	2-6
83/267	∅		+	-	-	-		-		-	⊕	-			⊕	3-7
81/261	+	+	-	-						-		-		-	-	2-6
80/407	+	+	-	-	-					-	-	-		-	-	2-8
79/3	+	+	-	-	-					-	-	-		-	-	2-8

Contd...

Contd...

Judges: *Cases:*	*Perfecto*	*Hilado*	*Paras*	*Briones*	*Feria*	*Reyes*	*Ozaeta*	*Montemayor*	*Torres*	*Bengzon*	*Moran*	*Pablo*	*Hontiveros*	*Padilla*	*Tuason*	*Total*
77/927	+	+	-	-	-					-	-	-		-	-	2-8
77/983	+	+	-	-	-					-	-	-		-	-	2-7
77/993	+	+	-	-	-					-	-	-		-	-	2-8
83/662	+		-	-	-	-		-		-	-	-			-	1-9
83/755	+		-		-	-	-	-		-	-	-			-	1-9
83/662	+				-	-	-	-		-	-	-			-	1-8
81/682	+		-	⊕	-					-	-	-			-	2-6
81/640	+		-	-	⊕					-	-	-			-	2-6
81/183	+		-	-	-					⊕		-		-	-	2-6
78/418	+		-							-		-		-	-	1-5
78/497	+		-							-		-		-	-	1-4
80/187	+		-	-	-					-	-	-		-	-	1-8
81/218	+		-	-	-					-		-		-	-	1-7
81/361	+		-	-	-					-		-		-	-	1-7
81/377	+		-	-	-					-		-		-		1-6
78/392	+		-	-						-				-	-	1-5
81/517	+		-	-	-					-	-	-				1-6
81/404	+		-	-	-					-		-		-	-	1-7
80/541	+	-	-	-	⊕					-		-		-	⊕	3-6

Contd...

Contd...

Judges: Cases:	Perfecto	Hilado	Paras	Briones	Feria	Reyes	Ozaeta	Montemayor	Torres	Bengzon	Moran	Pablo	Hontiveros	Padilla	Tuason	Total
79/780	+	-	-	⊕	-					-	-	⊕		-	⊕	4-6
80/383	+	-	-	⊕	-					-	-	-		-	-	2-8
78/366	+	-	⊕	-	-					-	-	-	-	-	-	2-9
77/1018	+	-	⊕	-	-					-	-	-	-	-	-	2-9
81/128	+	-	⊕	-	-					-	-	-		-	-	2-8
79/165	+	-	-	-	-					⊕	-	-		-	-	2-8
78/226	+	-	-	-	-					-	-	-	-	-	-	1-10
78/249	+	-	-	-	-					-	-	-	-	-	-	1-10
80/488	+	-	-	-						-	-	-		-	-	1-8
81/741	+	-	-	-	-					-	-	-		-	-	1-9
78/766	-	-		⊕	-						-	-		-	-	1-7
Total	54-3	11-17	33-30	19-30	17-37	6-13	4-9	5-13	1-1	17-46	14-40	14-49	1-5	5-40	10-54	211-387
Scale Ranks	1	2	3	4	5	7	7	7	9	10	11	12	13	14	15	

R = 1 - 41/379 = .892 S = 1 - 43/128 = .664

Note: Circle indicates inconsistent vote.

Figure 7.1 The C Scale of Political Liberalism and Conservatism, 1947-50

Appendix: Individual Attributes of Supreme Court Justices in Sampled Periods

Judges: Cases:	Perfecto	Briones	Pablo	Paras	Hilado	Ozaeta	Reyes	Montemayor	Feria	Moran	Bengzon	Tuason	Padilla	Total
81/476	+	+	+	+					ø		+	+	+	7-1
79/352	+	+		ø	+				+	+		+	+	7-1
83/518	+	+	+	+	+				ø	+	+	+		8-1
80/297	+	+	+	+	+				ø	+	+	+		8-1
77/873	+	+	+	+	+				+	+	+	-	-	8-2
80/506	+	+	ø	+	+				+	+	-	⊕	-	7-3
80/722	+	+	+	ø	ø				+	+	-	-	-	5-5
81/577		+	+	+		+			+	-	-	-	-	5-4
78/1	+	+	ø	+	+				+	-	-	-	-	5-5
83/813	+	+	+	+		+	+	+	-	⊕	-	-		8-3
82/756	+		+	+	+	+		-		-	-	-		5-4
84/292	+			+		-	-	-	-	-	-	-	-	2-8
77/909	+	ø	+	+	-				-	-	-	-	-	3-7
79/68	+		ø	+	-				-	-	-	-	-	2-7
81/566	+	ø	+	-		-			-	-		-	⊕	3-6
83/17	+	+	-	-		-		-	-	⊕	-	⊕		4-6
81/685	+	+	-	-		-			-	-	-	⊕		3-6
81/512	+	+		-	-				-	-		-		2-5
87/29			-	-		-	-	-			-	⊕		1-6

Contd...

Contd...

Judges: / *Cases:*	*Per-fecto*	*Briones*	*Pablo*	*Paras*	*Hilado*	*Ozaeta*	*Reyes*	*Monte-mayor*	*Feria*	*Moran*	*Beng-zon*	*Tuason*	*Padilla*	*Total*
84/313	+			-			-	-	-	-	-	-		1-7
79/122	+	-	-	-	-				-	-	-	-	-	1-9
83/85	+	-	-	-			-	-	-	-	-	-		1-7
83/171	+	-	-				-	-	-	-	-	-		1-8
81/614	+	-	-	-					-		-	-		1-6
80/845	+	-	-	-	-				-	-	-	-	-	1-9
81/286	+	-	-	-					-		-	-	-	1-7
80/533	+	-	-	-	-				-	-	-	-	-	1-9
80/488	+	-	-	-	-					-	-	-	-	1-8
80/272	+	-	-	-	-				-	-	-	-	-	1-9
Total	27-0	13-11	10-15	12-16	7-9	3-5	1-4	1-6	7-20	7-17	4-22	8-21	3-14	103-160
Scale Ranks	1	2	3	4	5.5	5.5	7.5	7.5	9	10	11	12		13

R = 1-14/133 = .895 S = 1-18/60 = .700

Note: The negative votes of Justice Hontiveros in the 9th and 14th cases were excluded.

Figure 7.2 The A Scale of Judicial Activism and Restraint, 1947-50

Appendix: Individual Attributes of Supreme Court Justices in Sampled Periods

Judges: / *Cases:*	*Per-fecto*	*Briones*	*Pablo*	*Paras*	*Hilado*	*Ozaeta*	*Reyes*	*Monte-mayor*	*Feria*	*Moran*	*Beng-zon*	*Tuason*	*Padilla*	*Total*
81/476	+	+	+	+					ø		+	+	+	7-1
79/352	+	+		ø	+				+	+		+	+	7-1
83/518	+	+	+	+	+				ø	+	+	+		8-1
80/297	+	+	+	+	+				ø	+	+	+		8-1
77/873	+	+	+	+	+				+	+	+	-	-	8-2
83/559	+	+	+	+	+			+	+	+	+	-		9-1
83/663	+	+	+	+	+			+	+	+	+	-		9-1
83/108	ø	+	+	+	+			+	+	+	+	-		8-2
80/506	+	+	ø	+	+				+	+	-	⊕	-	7-3
80/722	+	+	+	ø	ø				+	+	-	-	-	5-5
78/846	+		+	ø	+					+	-	-	-	4-4
81/577		+	+	+		+			+	-	-	-	-	5-4
78/1	+	+	ø	+	+				+	-	-	-	-	5-5
79/176	+	+	+	+	+				-	ø	-	ø	-	7-3
77/1066	+	ø	+	+	+				-	-	-	-	-	4-6
83/813	+	+	+	+		+	+	+	-	⊕	-	-		8-3
82/756	+		+	+	+	+		-		-	-	-		5-4
84/292	+			+		-	-	-	-	-	-	-	-	2-8
77/909	+	ø	+	+	-				-	-	-	-	-	3-7

Contd...

Judges: Cases:	Per-fecto	Briones	Pablo	Paras	Hilado	Ozaeta	Reyes	Monte-mayor	Feria	Moran	Beng-zon	Tuason	Padilla	Total
80/848	+	+	+	+	-				⊕	⊕	-	-	⊕	7-3
79/68	+		ø	+	-				-	-	-	-	-	2-7
81/566	+	ø	+	-		-			-	-		-	⊕	3-6
81/203	ø	+	+	-					-		-	-	-	2-6
79/80	+	ø	+	-					-	-	-	-	-	2-7
79/819	+	+	-	-	-				-	-	-	-	-	2-8
83/17	+	+	-	-		-		-	-	⊕	-	⊕		2-8
81/685	+	+	-	-		-			-	-	-	⊕		3-6
83/297	ø	+	-	-	-				-	-	-	-	-	3-6
81/512	+	+		-	-				-	-		-		2-5
87/29			-	-		-	-	-			-	⊕		1-6
84/313	+			-			-	-	-	-	-	-		1-7
79/122	+	-	-	-	-				-	-	-	-	-	1-9
83/85	+	-	-	-					-	-	-	-		1-7
80/835	+	-	-	⊕	-				-	-	-	-	-	2-8
80/776	+	-	-	-	-				-	-	-	-	-	1-9
79/409	+	-	-	-	-				-	-	-	-	-	1-9
83/171	+	-	-				-	-	-	-	-	-		1-8
81/614	+	-	-	-					-		-	-		1-6
80/845	+	-	-	-	-				-	-	-	-	-	1-6

Contd...

Judges: *Cases:*	*Per-* *fecto*	*Briones*	*Pablo*	*Paras*	*Hilado*	*Ozaeta*	*Reyes*	*Monte-* *mayor*	*Feria*	*Moran*	*Beng-* *zon*	*Tuason*	*Padilla*	*Total*
81/286	+	-	-	-					-		-	-	-	1-7
80/533	+	-	-	-	-				-	-	-	-	-	1-9
80/488	+	-	-	-	-					-	-	-	-	1-8
80/272	+	-	-	-	-				-	-	-	-	-	1-9
Total	38-3	21-16	19-20	19-23	13-15	3-5	1-4	4-6	11-29	13-24	7-33	9-34	4-24	162-236
Scale Ranks	1	2	3	4	5.5	5.5	7.5	7.5	9	10	11	12		13

R = 1 - 24/218 = .899 S = 1 - 30/91 = .670

Note: The votes of Justice Hontiveros in four cases, which were all negative, were not included.

Figure 7.3 Combined E and A Scale of Economic Liberalism and Judicial Activism, 1947-50

Appendix: Individual Attributes of Supreme Court Justices in Sampled Periods

Justices	Age: When appo-inted	Age: At mid period	Ethnic identity	Paternal occupation	Setting of birth	Religion	Education: Catholic(C) Private non-sectarian(N) Public or state(S): High school	pre-law college	law school	post-grad-uage	Previous Experience: Trial judge	private practi-tioner	law profe-ssor	Admini-strator	Govt. prose-cuting attorney	Politi-cian	Journ-alist	Term in Supreme Court
1	2	3	4	5	6	7	8	9	10	11	12	13	14	15	16	17	18	
Colonial Court (1927-30)																		
Avancena (Chief Justice)	45	56	Ilongo	landowner	urban	Catholic	C	C	C		x			x	x			1917-41
Johns	64	71	American South		rural	Methodist		N	N		x	x				x		1921-32
Johnson	43	68	American Midwest	judge	small town			N	S	S			x			x		1903-33
Malcolm	36	47	American Midwest		Small town	Mason		S	S	S			x	x				1917-36
Ostrand	49	56	Norwegian American Midwest		Small town	Lutheran			S		x	x						1921-33
Romualdez	46	53	Waray	government adminis-trator	large town	Catholic					x		x		x	x		1921-32

Street	45	56	American South		small town			S	S	S		x		x		x	1917-35
Villamor	57	65	Ilocano		large town	Catholic	C	C	C	C	x	x	x	x	x		1920-33
Villa-real	45	48	Pampango	farmer, trader	small town	Catholic	S		N		x			x			1925-30
*Commonwealth Court (1937-40)**																	
Abad Santos	52	52	Pampango	average landowner	large town	Catholic	S	N	S	N				x			1938-41
Avancena (Chief Justice)	45	66		(For other data, see Colonial Court, supra.)													
P. Concepcion			Tagalog			Catholic		C	C	C	x	x	x	x			1936-40
Horilleno	60	60	Ilongo		large town	Catholic	C		N		x	x			x		1938-44
Imperial	51	58	Bicol		large town			C	N		x				x	x	1931-44
Laurel	45	48	Tagalog	lawyer	large town	Catholic	S	C	S	N (Yale. Oxford)			x	x		x	1936-42
Moran	43	44	Pangasinan	merchant	large town	Catholic	N	N	N	C	x		x		x		1938-51

Contd...

1	2	3	4	5	6	7	8	9	10	11	12	13	14	15	16	17	18
Early Republic Court (1937-50)																	
C. Bengzon	45	52	Panagasinan	justice of the peace	large town	Catholic	C	C	S				x	x			1941-66
Briones 1945-49	51	54	Cebuano	farmer	urban	Catholic	C	C	N						x	x	x
Feria	61	64	Ilongo		urban	Catholic	C	C	C	C			x	x	x		1945-53
Hilado	54	57	Ilongo	lawyer	urban	Catholic	S		S			x	x				1945-48
Hontiveros	52	59	Ilongo		small town	Catholic	N		C			x	x			x	1941-44 1946-48
Montemayor	58	58	Pangasinan	town mayor	large town	Catholic	S	S	S	N (Harvard)	x		(public school teacher)	x			1948-60
Moran (Chief Justice)	43	53		(For other data, see Commonwealth Court, supra.)													1938-51
Ozaeta	50	57	Tagalog	landowner	small town	Catholic	S	S	N		x	x		x			1941-45 1948-50
Villa-real	45	58	(For other data, see Colonial Court, supra.)														

**Data on Justice Diaz unavailable.*

Pablo	59	62	Tagalog		small town		N	N	N	N	x	x			x	x		1945-55
Padila	52	54	Pangasinan	legislator, physician	urban	Catholic	C	C	S	N-C (Columbia, UST)	x	x	x	x			1946-64	
Paras	50	57	Tagalog	governor, landowner	urban	Catholic	S	S	S	N	x					x		1941-61
Perfecto	54	57	Ilongo		urban	Catholic	C	C	C							x	x	1945-49
A. Reyes	60	-	Tagalog		urban	Catholic	S	S	S		x	x	x	x	x		x	1949-59
Torres	69	-	Tagalog	judge prosecuting attorney	urban	Catholic	C	C	C		x			x	x			1949-50
Tuason	62	64	Tagalog	village head	large town	Catholic	S	S	C		x		(public school teacher)	x	x			1946-54

1	2	3	4	5	6	7	8	9	10	11	12	13	14	15	16	17	18
Recent Republic Court (1963-66)																	
C. Bengzon (Chief Justice to 1965)	45	67	(For other data, see Early Republic Court, supra.)														
J. Bengzon	66	66	Pangasinan	government emplyee	large town	Catholic	C	C	S			x	x	x	x	x	1964-present
Barrera	63	68	Pampango	phsician, politician	large town	Catholic	S	S	S	C	x	x		x			1959-66
Bautista Angelo	54	68	Tagalog	JP, physician	large town	Catholic	C	C	S	C	x			x	x	x	1950-66
Ruiz Castro	52	-	Ilcano	dentist	large town	Catholic	S	S	S					x	x	x	1966-present
R.Concepcion (chief Justice since 1965)	51	61	Tagalog	government employee	urban	Catholic	C	C	C			x	x		x		1954-present
Dizon	59	63	Pampango	big landowner	large town	Catholic	C	C	S		x	x	x				1960-present
Labrador	58	70	Zambal	JP	small town	Catholic	S	S	S		x		x	x		x	1952-64
Makalintal	52	54	Tagalog	physician surgeon	small town	Catholic	S	S	S		x	x	x	x			1962-present

Padilla	52	70	(For other data, see Early Republic Court, supra.)														1946-64
Paredes	65	69	Ilocano	Prosecuting attorney, politician	large town	Catholic	S	N-S	S	C	x	x	x	x	x		1960-65
Regala	65	67	Pampango	small merchant	large town	Protestant	S	S	S	N (yale, Chicago)	x		x	x			1962-67
J.B.L. Reyes	52	62	Tagalog	physician	urban	Catholic	C	C	S	C-N (UST, Central de Madrid)		x	x		x		1954-present
Sanchez	66	-	Tagalog	small landowner	large town	Catholic	S	N	N	C	x	x	x		x		1966-present
Zaldivar	60	60	Ilongo	JP, landowner	small town	Philippine Independent Church	S	S	S			x	x	x		x	1964-present

8

TWO SURVEYS OF SIMULATED JUDICIAL DECISION-MAKING: HAWAII AND THE PHILIPPINES[1]

This chapter compares some aspects of the attitudes of judges of two former American territories in the Pacific Basin region, one of which has become an American state during the post-World War II era, and the other an independent republic. The work here stems from an earlier study of Hawaii judges by Theodore L. Becker and seeks to replicate that study to some extent. In both studies the primary objective was to investigate how the attitudes of judges, toward their institutional roles and the policy issues that confront them for resolution, interrelate in their decision-making. Initially, data are presented bearing upon cultural influences and attitudinal variables that purport to measure the role parameters of these judges and their decisions. The Philippine data are interpreted first in relation to a causal model of judicial decision-making and then in terms of a pattern analysis.

THE JUDICIAL STRUCTURES

The research was focused upon judges in the Philippines and in Hawaii because of the similarity between these two polities in terms of insularity, political acculturation, political structure, language, and judicial structure.[2] Both Hawaii and the Philippines were territories of the United States during most of the first half of the twentieth century. The Philippine Islands were ceded by Spain to the United States in 1898, the same year that Hawaii was voluntarily annexed. The Philippines became an independent republic on July 4, 1946, and Hawaii became a state on August 21 1959; each patterned her constitution upon the model provided by the Constitution of the United States.

Although the Philippine judicial system reflects a blend of the Spanish and American cultures, the *structure* of the judiciary plainly reflects the American prototype. It has already been described in detail in the previous chapter. Thus it is sufficient to say here that it consists of a Supreme Court, a Court of Appeals, provincial courts of first instance, municipal courts, and justice of the peace courts.

In the Philippines, judges are dispersed among eleven major islands, whereas in Hawaii judges are located on four principal islands, each of which has one circuit court to which judges are appointed to six-year terms by the governor. Honolulu has eight circuit judges who are assigned to four divisions (civil, criminal, probate, and family courts). Circuit courts have both original and appellate jurisdiction, with appeals coming from district courts.[3]

Article V of the Hawaiian Constitution provides for a Supreme Court, circuit courts, and "such inferior courts as the legislature may from time to time establish." The Supreme Court consists of one Chief Justice and four associate justices nominated by the governor of the state with the advice and consent of the Senate. Justices serve a seven-year term, unless they reach seventy or become incapacitated before their term is up.

THE RESEARCH DESIGN

The purpose of the Hawaiian study[4] was to determine the relation between individual perceptions of institutional role and attitudes toward policy issues. Three levels of questions were asked: (1) What kinds of influences (including both precedent and policy components) were most important to the respondents in making their official decisions? (2) Were their own policy preferences, on an abstract question of socio-economic policy, relatively liberal ("enlightened," in Decker's words) or conservative? (3) How would a judge vote when that abstract policy was explicitly related in an hypothetical case to an array of strictly conservative precedential decisions?

The judicial respondents were also asked to specify, on a five-point Likert scale, the extent to which each considered himself to be influenced, in his decision-making as a judge, by several hypothesized independent variables, including:

> (a) the position argued by a highly respected advocate (as a lawyer); (b) his own view of justice in the case; (c) what the public needs, as the times may demand; (d) precedent, when clear and directly relevant; (e) common sense; (f) the views of a highly respected advocate (as a member of the community); (g) what the public demands; and (h) other.

Analysis focused upon a distinction between (d) and the other categories. Respondents who scored higher on (d) than on other categories were classified as precedent oriented; those who scored higher on any other category than on (d) were classified as value oriented; and the remainder were deemed to be of mixed orientation.

The attitudinal measures were related to a nominal scale of decision-making in a hypothetical case, which was so designed that the outcome dictated by judicial precedents was opposite to the outcome that was hypothesized to correspond to the value preference of the respondents. The former outcome (consistent with precedent) was designated "objective," and the other outcome (inconsistent with precedent) "subjective." It was then possible to compare the extent to which "precedent-oriented" and other judges made "objective" decisions in the hypothetical case.

The hypothetical case, *Charney v. Mercy Hospital,* involved a suit by a patient against a hospital, claiming damages for the negligence of a nurse operating within the scope of her employment.[5] In Table 8.1 the data are regrouped in such a way as to focus upon the tails of the distribution of attitudinal responses, thereby disregarding temporarily the responses of judges who gave replies that indicated no marked preference for *either* precedent *or* personal beliefs, as the most influential variables in their decision-making. These data were grouped differently by Theodore Becker in his report of the Hawaiian data.[6] However, for present purposes, it seems more useful to compare the judges who claimed to be most strongly influenced by precedent, with those most strongly influenced by their views concerning the merits of the substantive policy issue, in relation to the precedential consistency of their preferences in the decision of the hypothetical case. Becker indicated that his principal research hypothesis required that judges, who had policy issue preferences that were inconsistent with precedent, decide the hypothetical case "objectively"—that is, in accord with precedent and contrary to their own respective issue preferences.[7] Stated in more operational language, Becker's hypothesis requires that judges, whose own strong policy preference would be to hold the hospital liable for its employee's negligence,[8] nevertheless would vote, in accord with precedent, to hold the hospital legally irresponsible for employee negligence. In relation to Table 8.1, the best examples of such judges (because they would have the strongest policy views) would fall in cell b. As the table shows, however, *no* persons in this subsample behaved as Becker had hypothesized they should.[9]

Table 8.1: Judicial Attitudes and Simulated Decisions (Hawaiian Sample)

	Dominant role orientation:	
	Precedential (d is most important)	*Policy (b,c,or e are Most imporatant)*
outcome:		
Objective" (agrees with precedent)	4 a	0 b
"Subjective" (disagrees with precedent)	c 2	d 5

On the other hand, it certainly is not implausible to entertain the alternative hypothesis, that judges who claim to believe most in precedent will tend to vote consistently with precedent, and that judges who claim to be more influenced by their policy views will vote in accord with their policy views. Tables 8.1 and 8.2 were constructed to test this alternative hypothesis, which assumes that judges act consistently with their beliefs; and inasmuch as we specify the direction of the relation that we expect to find, a one-tailed test of significance is appropriate to evaluate the statistical likelihood of the null hypothesis that the sampling distribution reported in Table 8.1 might readily be accounted for by chance. Using Fisher's probability test, the Table 8.1 tetrad is significant at the .05 level. The expected cell frequencies for Table 8.2 are too small to permit a test of statistical significance.

As Table 8.1 shows, nine of the eleven judges voted in accord with the stated substantive hypothesis. The two who did not were judges who, in diametrical opposition to Becker's own original hypothesis, voted *against* the hospital (and therefore, contrary to precedent) even though they had claimed to be most strongly influenced by precedent. An examination of the response patterns for these two judges (i.e., J and N in Table I of Becker's article[10]) shows only that both scored "common sense" as influential, although it was clearly less so than precedent. On the available evidence, one must conclude that these two judges voted, in the hypothetical case, inconsistently with their responses to the question concerning what influenced them *most*. It is interesting to observe, however, that the zero cell (b) identifies this contingency table as one which is consistent with the hypothesis of a cumulative scalar relation[11] between the two variables, "dominant role orientation" and "outcome." From the latter perspective, the clear implication of the table is that even relatively moderate substantive policy preferences outweigh strong beliefs in the obligation to follow precedent, when a judge experiences cognitive dissonance because of conflict between his concepts of professional role, and of wise social policy. This iconoclastic inference—it can hardly be called a "finding," with such scanty evidence—is so contrary to Becker's own expectations, and to his earlier writing on this subject, which uses data from law student samples and a similar survey instrument, that no doubt the strongest finding that can justifiably be based on Table 8.1 is that these data do *not* support Becker's hypothesis about the importance of *stare decisis* as the major operating component in judicial role concepts. These data *do,* however, support with statistical significance the hypothesis that those judges who think precedents are most important follow them, and those judges who do not think precedents are most important do *not* follow them.

Table 8.2: Judicial Attitudes, Policy Preferences, and Simulated Decisions (Hawaiian sample)

	Dominant role orientation:		
Outcome:	*Precedential*	*Mixed*	*Policy*
agrees with precedent	4	2 [+1]	0
disagrees with precedent	2	5 (+3)	3 (+2)

Note: Sixteen of these respondents favoured a policy of joint responsibility for hospitals and their employees; the positions of the remaining six are indicated within parentheses, if they favoured the more liberal policy of exclusive hospital liability. The brackets are for the one Hawaiian judge who favoured the conservative policy of absolving the hospital from all legal liability.

Table 8.2, although not amenable to a test of statistical significance,[12] is presented because it clearly supports the findings based on Table 8.1. As is evident in note 9, the one respondent, out of Becker's entire sample of twenty-two Hawaiian judges, who favoured the relatively conservative policy of holding the nurse alone liable voted consistently with his views, just as the five who thought that only the hospital should be liable voted consistently with their views, precedents to the contrary notwithstanding. The remaining sixteen whose policy views, though relatively moderate, were in conflict with the precedents, constitute the primary sub-sample analyzed in Table 8.2. Clearly there was a tendency for judges who thought that precedents were most important to follow them; and for those who thought that policy preferences were of at least equal importance to follow their preferences. And most of those whose orientation was mixed paid more respect to their policy bias than they did to the precedents.

The Philippine replication will permit us to re-examine Becker's hypothesis in relation to the survey responses of a larger sample of judges for whom the *content* of substantive preference on the policy issue differs from that for the Hawaiian sample, and for whom it was possible to obtain more extensive data in regard to attitudes toward precedent.

Twenty-six of the thirty Hawaiian judges who were solicited responded to the questionnaire, although four of the responses were later found to be unsuitable for coding.[13] In the Philippines, on the other hand, a sample of sixty-four of the universe of one hundred and sixty-four judges were contacted: fifty-nine responded to at least parts of the interview schedule; of these, forty-seven gave complete responses; and thirty-nine who gave substantive responses to all parts of the questions constitute the subsample for the three variables discussed below.[14] The Philippine sample is not a random one because the research design sought to attain the complete universe of judges.

Because the Manila area is the most heavily populated and easily accessible, and is the seat of both the Supreme Court and the Court of Appeals, it became over-represented in the sample. It can, however, be argued that Manila plus three regions (Central Luzon, the Tagalog Provinces, and the Visayan Provinces) constitute the most politically influential regions in the Philippines[15] and therefore *should* be over-represented in the sample. In any event, the sample is limited to ten of the sixteen judicial districts. The non-sample districts, to which are assigned about a third of the total judges, include the geographic areas of northcentral, eastern, and northeastern Luzon; the Polillo Islands; and Mindanao Island.

Filipino judges were asked, as were those in the Hawaiian sample, to decide a hypothetical case in which precedent was opposed to the postulated personal policy preference of the respondents. (See Appendix A.) The judges' simulated decisions in this case are the dependent variable in the causal model described below. As in the Hawaiian study, the independent variables coded for the Filipino sample included the respondent's conception of the importance of precedent, and his personal value predisposition toward the abstract policy issue of tort liability of hospitals, which confronted him in more explicit form in the hypothetical case.

HYPOTHESIS

The hypothesis tested is one that Becker has proposed, and which has motivated much of his earlier research:

> *General Hypothesis.* Once a legal precedent reaches a point of being clearly controlling in a dispute presented in an appellate litigational context, it will inhibit a substantive value preference of the decision-maker who assumes the judicial role, thus resulting in an objective decision.[16]

Stated in more operational terms, this study seeks to investigate the empirical validity of the proposition that judges will follow institutional precedents rather than their personal policy preferences, when asked to make a decision in which the precedents and their own policy preferences are in conflict.

DATA

In addition to the seven items Becker had used in his Hawaiian study to measure the relative importance attributed by the respondents to the influence of precedents, the Philippine question included an eighth item (relating to the influence of the *ratio decidendi* of a case). This item was intended to provide an alternative observation of attitudes toward precedent, just as there were several items (b, c, and e in Table 8.1) which provided alternative observations of attitudes toward policy. The five points on the Likert scale used for scoring the intensity of each item of this question, ranged from 0 (minimally influential) to 4 (maximally influential). To construct one of the independent variables, X (attitude toward precedent), that entered into the correlational analysis described below, the intensity scores of each respondent for both items d (precedent, when clear and directly relevant) and h *(ratio decidendi)*, were added together to form a *stare decisis* index. This index ranged from an empirically unobserved theoretical minimum of zero to a frequently attained maximum of eight, denoting both the attribution of extreme influence for precedents deemed relevant, and a consequent predisposition to uphold the legal principle of non-responsibility of hospitals for employee torts, given precedents that held for this.

Another independent variable, Z (attitude toward policy), was scaled in such a way that its directionality, in theory, was the same (from the point of view of outcome in terms of legal principle) as that attributed to variable X. The response that only the employee should be held liable for her own tort, which was supportive of the principle of non-liability of the hospital, was scored as three points; the response that both the employee and the hospital should be held liable was scored as two points; and the response that only the hospital should be held liable (in Becker's view this was the most "enlightened" or liberal response) was scored as one point. The positive direction of this variable was to favour conservative policy, which in principle would lead to the same choice in the hypothetical case as would the positive direction (or *pro-stare decisis)* in the instance of variable X, because either of these alternative bases should lead to favouring the immediate financial interests of the hospital in the simulated decision. It is interesting to note that one clear cultural difference between Hawaii and the Philippines showed up in the responses to this particular question. As Table 8.3 shows, in Hawaii the effective division in attitude is between exclusive hospital liability and joint liability; but in the Philippines, which is less economically and socially progressive, the effective division is between joint liability and exclusive employee liability. As a class, therefore, Hawaiian judges tended to be more liberal in their policy views on this issue than were Filipino judges.

Table 8.3: Attitudes of Hawaiian and Filipino Judges toward the Policy Issue of Tort Liability on the Part of Hospitals and Their Employees

Liability favoured for:	*Respondents:*		*Evaluation of choice:*	
	Hawaiian	*Filipino*	*Effect*	*Score*
Employee only	1	16	H+	3
Both employee and hospital	15	21	H0	2
Hospital only	6	2	H–	1

Note: The frequencies above are too small to warrant calculation of a test of statistical significance.

The dependent variable, Y (simulated decision in the hypothetical case, *St. Mary's Mercy Hospital v. Pedro)* was scored three points for a reversal (an H+ choice in favour of the hospital) and one point for an affirmance (an H— choice in favour of Pedro's widow). Y also was aligned, therefore, in a conservative or pro-hospital direction.

The observed scores for the sample of thirty-nine respondents are reported in Appendix B. Evidently, these scores can be treated as interval data; indeed, they must be considered in this way if causal analysis is to be attempted.[17] Using these data from Appendix B, Pearsonian correlation coefficients were calculated for the relation between each pair of the three variables; and the associated unstandardized regression coefficients (slopes), partial (first-order) correlation coefficients, and partial regression coefficients (both b's and Betas) were also calculated. Of these, the ones that enter into the discussion below are reported in Table 8.4.

Table 8.4: Measures of Relation among Attitudes toward Stare Decisis (X), Attitudes toward Policy (z), and Simulated Decisions (Y) (Philippine Sample)

	Zero-order:				*First-order:*		
		r	b			r	b
Variables:	YZ	.46	.40	*Variables:*	YZ.X	.41	.35
	YX	–.30	–.09		YX.Z	–.19	–.06
	ZX	–.29	–.10				
	XZ		–.79				

CAUSAL ANALYSIS

Figure 8.1 portrays a paradigm of the correlation between the two independent variables, and between each of them and the dependent variable. As Blalock,[18] Alker, and others have discussed recently, an important scientific question is posed by the problem of inferring causality among these variables. Of course, the designation of X and Z as independent variables, and of Y as a dependent variable, implies a hypothesis about the directionality

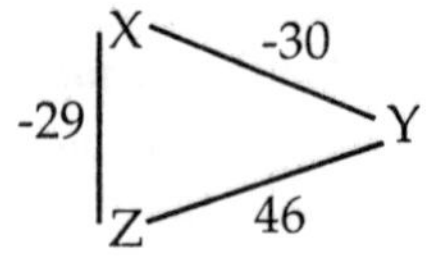

Figure 8.1 *Zero-Order Intercorrelations among Three Variables of State Decisis (X), Policy Bias (Z), and Decisional Preference (Y) (Philippine Sample)*

of causation, at least as between X and Y, and Z. and Y. The hypothesis is, of course, that the arrows should be drawn as indicated in Figure 8.2. The appropriateness of such a hypothesis

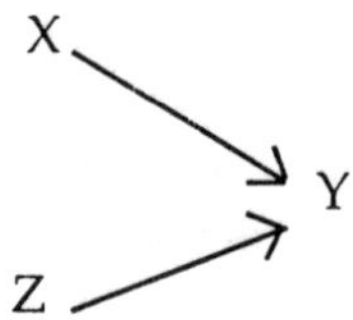

Figure 8.2 *Double Causation*

for testing by these data is confirmed by the structure of the interview instrument employed in their collection: the questions were asked in the sequence Z, X, Y, so that from a chronological approach to causation there is empirical justification for the assumption that a respondent's simulated decision in the hypothetical case could not have "caused" him to have expressed the attitude that he did, toward either *stare decisis* (X) or the policy issue (Z). Of course, by the same logic, one might argue that X could not have caused Z because the response to Z was chronologically prior; but that interpretation is not preferred because it would completely resolve the problem on the basis of the chronology of the causation. It can be countered, for example, that the manifest content of the two questions upon which these variables were based is such that neither could directly affect the other; that is, the two are independent of each other from a logical as well as from a statistical point of view. Statistical independence presumes, however, that the zero-order correlation between X and Z, error variance and other possible effects of outside variables apart, ought to be zero as Figure 8.2 indicates. An observed correlation other than zero might be demonstrated to be spurious; or it could be in that event that our hypothesis of independence is false, and X causes Z or Z causes X, or even that double

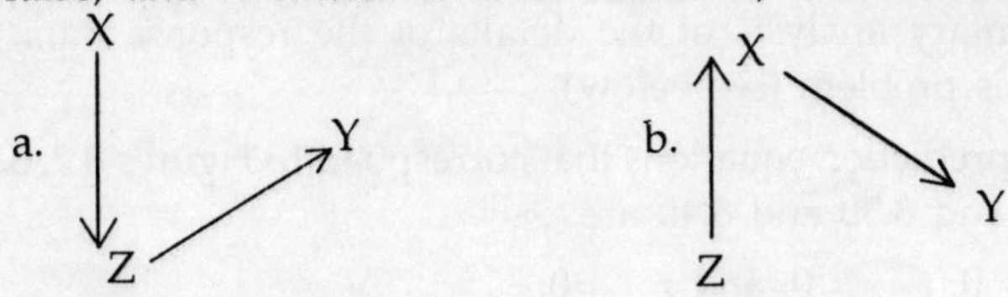

Figure 8.3 *Development Sequence*

causation obtains and each affects the other. Hence, we cannot without more choose among the alternative models depicted in Figures 8.2, 8.3, 8.4, and 8.5. It is necessary, therefore, to make additional assumptions which will permit the elimination of one

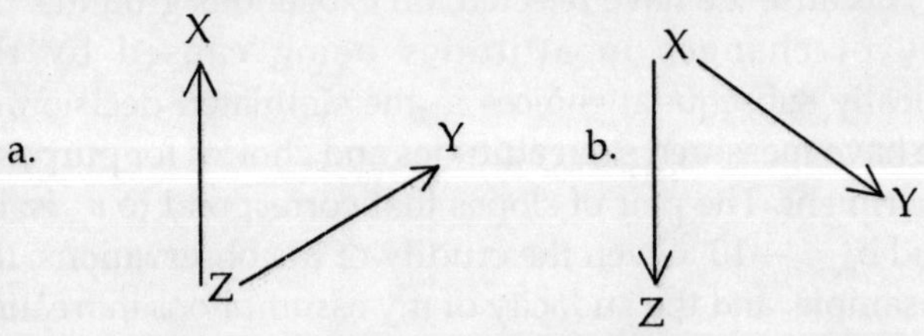

Figure 8.4 *Spurious Correlation*

of the three causal links, so that we can focus attention upon the relatively simpler models which it might be possible to fit to the data at hand. In Alker's terminology, Figure 8.2 presents a model with independent variables which have an effect of double causation upon Y; Figure 8.3 presents two alternative developmental models and Figure 8.4 portrays a pair of models of spurious correlation; but because of the double-headed arrow

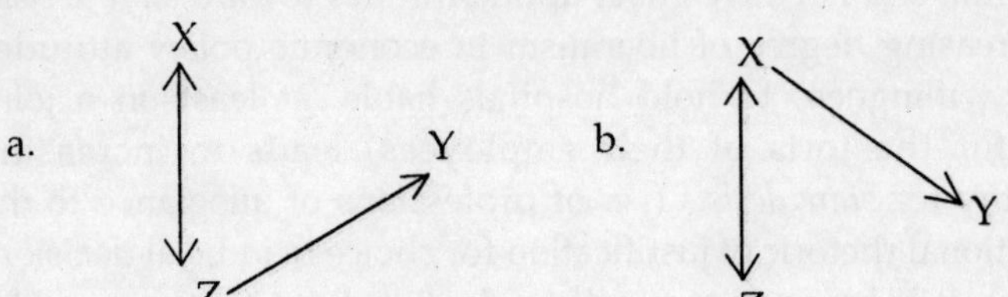

Figure 8.5 *Reciprocal Causation*

between X and Z, Figure 8.5 can be analyzed only in part by the Simon-Blalock methods of causal analysis that have been worked out to date, although an attempt will be made, on the basis of the supplementary analysis of the details of the response data, to resolve this problem (see below).

The prediction equations that correspond to Figures 8.2; 8.3a and 8.4a; and 8.3b and 8.4b are:

r_{xz}, = 0, $r_{yx.z}$ = 0, and $r_{yz.x}$ =0.

In fact, as we observe from both Table 8.4 and Figure 8.1, the empirical correlations are:

r_{xz} = —.29, $r_{yx.z}$ = —.19, and $r_{yx.z}$ = .41.

So we must go further, and turn our attention to the unstandardized regression coefficients (slopes). In doing so, we disregard b_{xy} and b_{zy}, because we have rejected, on exogenous grounds, the possibility of changes in attitudes being caused by the chronologically subsequent choices in the simulated decision, at least as we have measured such attitudes and choices for purposes of this experiment. The pair of slopes that correspond to r_{xz} is: b_{xz} = — .79 and b_{zx} = —10. Given the crudity of the observations, the size of the sample, and the audacity of my assumptions in treating these responses as interval-level data, it does not seem too much more to make the additional assumption that any coefficient of a value $\leq \pm .10$ should be deemed, in the light of what is probably the large amount of error variance obtaining, to be an approximation of zero. This statistical decision entails the rejection, as inappropriate, of the models in Figures 8.3a, 8.4b, and 8.5. Consequently, this pair of slopes shows that attitudes toward *stare decisis* have no causal effect upon attitudes toward the policy issue; but that, conversely, attitudes toward policy have a substantial and negative effect upon attitudes toward *stare decisis.* An increasing degree of liberalism in economic policy attitudes (i.e. of willingness to hold hospitals liable, at least on a joint basis, for the torts of their employees) leads to increasing sympathy for *stare decisis* (i.e. of professions of allegiance to the conventional rhetoric of justification for choice in judicial decision-making). It is by no means self-evident, at least to persons who have been socialized into the American lego-political culture, that attitudes of economic liberalism among judges ought to be the cause of seeming *legal* conservatism in those same judges. Further explanation of this relationship is necessary.

The slopes for the effect of *stare decisis* upon decision and for the effect of policy upon decisions are b_{yx} = —.09 and b_{yz} — .40, indicating that X has no effect upon Y, but that Z has a moderate positive causal effect upon it. *Stare decisis,* therefore, had no effect upon the decisional choices of the Filipino judges in the sample; their attitudes toward the policy issue evoked by the hypothetical case, on the other hand, function as a partial cause of their simulated decisions. This finding requires the rejection of the models of Figures 8.2, 8.3b, 8.4b, and 8.5b as inappropriate for these empirical data.

The elimination of these four models clearly suggests that the most appropriate model must be the remaining one, Figure 8.4a, which shows Z to be the joint cause of both X and Y, and reveals the apparent correlation between X and Y to be spurious. This interpretation can be further tested by observing the partial b's: if Figure 8.4a is the correct model, then we ought to predict that $b_{yx.z} = 0$ and $b_{yz.x} \neq 0$. As Table 8.4 shows, the empirical coefficients are — .06 and .35, respectively, which can be viewed as satisfying the predictions. The first of these partials shows that when the effect of Z is held constant, changes in X produce no changes in Y;[25] the second partial shows that when X is controlled, changes in Z continue to lead to moderate changes in Y. That is to say that economically conservative policy attitudes were (in regard to simulated decisions in this hypothetical case) a direct partial cause of economically conservative judicial decisions, which were also pro-hospital in effect and precedentially consistent choices. Economically conservative policy attitudes tend also to cause low estimates of the importance of *stare decisis*—or else—and this would have the same statistical consequence for the correlation—economically liberal policy attitudes tend to cause high estimates of the importance of *stare decisis.* We cannot choose between these alternative possible explanations on the basis of the correlational data; to do that, we must examine the contingency tables which summarize the basis upon which the response data of Appendix B affect the correlations.

PATTERN ANALYSIS

Although the correlations which we have been discussing are Pearsonian and are based, at least for Z and X, upon more than two scale categories, it is useful for present purposes to group the data into nominal scales for both X and Z, as shown in Table 8.5. One effect of so doing is to reduce the effect of the low scores upon the *stare decisis* variable (which, of course, as an interval scale has the broader range): five of the eight respondents who fall in cell c of Table 8.5 have scores of 4 or less on X, and they account for *half* of the total of squared deviances (100.44) from the average score (6.59) on X. The effect of these five individuals in Table 8.5 is no different from that of any of the other 34 in the table; so it is not surprising that a correlation coefficient (phi) based upon Table 8.5 would be somewhat lower than the Pearsonian r of which it is an estimate (ϕ = —. 15; r = —.29). On the other hand, phi correlations for similar tables, relating the nominalized X and Z scales to Y, would result in slight *overestimations* of the Pearsonian correlations. It is desirable to be aware of such gross implications of the reduction of the data to the summary form of a contingency table; but it is instructive to note more particularly the pattern types of respondents who are partitioned among the cells of the table.

Table 8.5 The Relation between Attitudes toward Policy and Precedent (Philippine Sample)

	Z	
Scores:	3	1-2
Scores:		
7-8	8 (*a*)	15 (*b*)
X 2-6	8 (c)	8 (*d*)

Cell a includes six judges for whom the three variables of the set are perfectly linearly related. These are respondents who scored 3 on Z, 7 or 8 on X, and 2 on Y: their conservative beliefs in a policy of non-liability for hospitals and in the sanctity of precedents were mutually reinforcing so that, in the hypothetical case, they experienced no cognitive dissonance whatever in voting to free the hospital from liability. Since they had no problems we can learn nothing relevant from them about the ways in which persons who *do* experience dissonance resolve their problem. The other two judges who fall in cell a (#20 and #25) evidently were confused by the questionnaire; their voting pattern (3,8,1) reveals them to be *stare decisis-respecting* economic conservatives who chose to vote in the hypothetical case contrary to both policy and precedential attitudes. It is therefore appropriate to view them as sources of error variance in the correlations.

Cell d, also in the major diagonal, includes four justices who are the functional counterparts of the six untroubled conservatives of cell a: these four also manifest a linear pattern, with scores (2, 6, 1) that indicate relatively liberal policy views, moderate sympathy for *stare decisis,* and liberal (anti-hospital) votes in the case. To the extent that these four were cross-pressured, we can assume that they experienced a lesser degree of dissonance than did the others to whom we shall turn presently. Of the remaining four judges in this cell, three were liberals (with patterns of 2, 6, 2 or 1, 6, 2) who appeared to sublimate their policy views to their moderate sympathy for *stare decisis* by voting pro-hospital in the case. These three judges might be designated as the hard-core precedent followers, and they are the respondents (in this sample) who come closest to substantiating Becker's "general hypothesis" about the importance of *stare decisis* in judicial decision-making. There is also another confused respondent (#27) in this cell. Although he was liberal on the policy question and not very deferential to *stare decisis* (with a pattern of 2, 4, 2), he voted in favour of the hospital in the hypothetical case.

Cell c includes seven economic conservatives who (with patterns of 3, 4-6, 2) were presumably neither much reinforced nor much restrained by precedential considerations, and who therefore were relatively free to vote their policy bias, and did so. Also in this cell is a solitary but evidently confused economic conservative (with a pattern of 3, 2, 1) whose policy views and minimal deference to *stare decisis* should have led him to vote like the other seven. But for no reason that could be discovered by this questionnaire, #4 voted to hold the hospital liable. This is another case of error variance.

This leaves cell b, which is by far the most interesting one in the table. This cell includes the fifteen judges who were maximally cross-pressured by a combination of liberal views on the policy question and maximum respect for *stare decisis,* and were confronted with a simulated case for which all of the direct, clear, and relevant precedents pointed to an outcome opposite to their own policy preference. These are the judges who provide the best test of Becker's hypothesis. To provide evidence in support of that hypothesis, at least an overwhelming majority should have voted "objectively" (as Becker puts it), in deference to the precedents and contrary to their own "sense of justice," and to reverse so that the integrity of the legal principle of non-liability of hospitals, for employee torts, would be respected. But these Filipino judges did the opposite: only two voted to reverse, and the remaining thirteen—a full third of the entire sample, all with identical patterns of 1-2, 7-8, 1—resolved their dissonance by following their own policy preference and voting to hold the hospital liable, legal precedents to the contrary notwithstanding.[26]

Clearly, economic liberalism is associated with precedential respect much more than economic conservatism is associated with a low regard for *stare decisis,* because cell b in Table 8.5 is almost twice as large as cell c.

In Table 8.6 we focus on the 35 respondents whose behavior seems to have been rational, omitting those four who apparently were confused. This table shows the relation to all three variables of the half-dozen major pattern-types which emerged from our consideration of Table 8.5. Thus, cell a contains the reinforced conservatives and cell d the unrestrained conservatives. Cells e and b contain the only five respondents who provide support for Becker's hypothesis. These are judges whose liberal policy views are dominated by their moderate to strong sympathy for *stare decisis.* Cell f contains the unrestrained liberals, and cell c contains the critical group of cross-pressured liberals. It is evident that c is by far the most populous cell, and this group of respondents

Table 8.6: The Relations between Attitudes toward Policy and Precedent, and Simulated Decisions (Philippine Sample)

Scores:	Z Scores: 3	Z 1-2	Z 1-2
X 7-8	6 a	2 b	13 c
X 2-6	d 7	e 3	f 4
Y	2	2	1

is critical in the sense that it is clear that this group is responsible for the negative correlation between Z and X, for the positive correlation between Z and Y, and for the spurious correlation between X and Y.

Table 8.7 enfolds Table 8.6 in the ways appropriate to focus on the dyadic relationships of those four-fold contingency tables which demonstrate the kind of effect that these thirteen policy-

Table 8.7: The Relations between Policy and Precedent, Policy and Decisions, and Precedent and Decisions, Excluding Irrational Responses, and with the Cross Pressured Bloc of Liberal Respondents in Parentheses (Philippine Sample)

Scores:	Z: 3	Z: 1-2
X 7-8	6	(13) +2
X 2-6	7	7

	Z: 3	Z: 1-2
Y 2	13	5
Y 1		(13) +4

	X: 7-8	X: 2-6
Y 2	8	10
Y 1	(13)	4

dominant liberals have on the various correlations. If they had voted so as to confirm Decker's hypothesis there would, of course, have been no change in the four-fold or correlation for X and Z, but then the other two tables would appear as shown in Table 8.8. The clear correlational consequence, when we include the four bracketed sources of error variance that affected the Pearsonian correlations, would have been a reduction in ryz to approximately zero (—.02), while converting the correlation

Table 8.8: The Relations between Policy and Decisions, and Precedent and Decisions, if Precedent Had Dominated Policy in the Decisions of the Cross-Pressured Bloc of Liberal Respondents (shown in parentheses), Including the Irrational Responses (shown in brackets) (Phillipine Sample)

Z

Scores:		3	1-2
Y	2	(13) 13	+5 [+1]
	1	[+3]	4

X

		7-8	2-6
Y	2	(13) +8	10
	1	[+2]	4 [+1}

between X and Y from low negative to low positive (+ .29). If Filipino judges had *not* followed their policy preferences they *would* have paid greater respect to precedent. But this was not the case. Instead we observe that these thirteen Filipino judges opted for contemporary concepts of social justice rather than for the policy preferences of their imputed predecessors. It is explicitly the sophisticated lip service, which they paid to the conventional legal norm of *stare decisis,* that provides both a necessary and a sufficient explanation for the spurious correlation that we observed to obtain between *stare decisis* and decision-making in this survey of judicial attitudes.

APPENDIX A

HYPOTHETICAL CASE (PHILIPPINE SAMPLE)

Please decide the following case as a justice of the highest court in your country should:

St. Mary's Mercy Hospital v, Pedro

Mr. Pedro was seriously injured in an automobile accident. He was rushed to the St. Mary's Mercy Hospital where an emergency blood transfusion was found to be necessary. In the handling of the blood, one of the nurses of the hospital made an error and supplied the doctor with the wrong type of blood. It was proved at the trial that this error was directly responsible for the death of Mr. Pedro. Pedro's widow sued the hospital for negligence for 300,000 pesos. Negligence was clearly established by the evidence and the judge returned a verdict for the plaintiff. Mrs. Pedro. The hospital appeals.

The law of the jurisdiction is based on several cases. *Juanillo v. Gutierrez* (1940) held, in reversing a verdict for the plaintiff, that a charitable organization is not responsible for damages occasioned by the negligence of its employees, if the negligent act is done while the employee was pursuing the course of employment. The case of *Lacson vs. Rodriguez* (1904) held that a hospital could not be sued in a breach of contract action because it was a charitable, nonprofit organization, and because there was no fraud found to exist on the part of the hospital. The case of *Gonzaga v. Morales* (1958) held that an overdose of barbiturates given to the plaintiff-patient by an intern in a hospital did not constitute a breach of warranty in a sale and, therefore, the private hospital employing the intern was not liable for damages to the plaintiff.

Reverse the lower court decision (for the Hospital)

Affirm the lower court decision (for Pedro in the full amount)

Reasons:

Appendix B: Scores on Variables Measuring Attitudes toward Policy (Z), Attitudes toward Stare Decisis (X), and Simulated Decisions (Y) (Philippine Sample)

Respondent No.	*Z*	*X*	*Y*	*Respondent No.*	*Z*	*X*	*Y*
2	2	5	1	29	3	8	2
4	3	2	1	30	3	4	2
6	3	8	2	31	2	8	1
7	3	4	2	32	2	8	2
10	2	8	1	33	2	8	1
11	2	6	2	34	2	7	1
13	2	8	2	35	3	4	2
15	2	7	1	36	2	6	1
16	2	8	1	38	1	8	1
17	2	8	1	40	2	6	1
18	3	4	2	43	2	8	1
20	3	8	1	50	3	6	2
21	2	6	1	52	2	7	1
22	3	8	2	53	2	8	1
23	1	6	2	54	3	7	2
24	3	8	2	55	2	7	1
25	3	8	1	56	3	7	2
26	2	8	1	57	3	5	2
27	2	4	2	59	2	6	2
28	3	5	2				

Note: Scores signify the following responses.

Z
- 3 = employee liable
- 2 = both hospital and employee liable
- 1 = hospital liable

X
- 8 = maximal respect for *stare decisis*
- 2 = minimal respect for *stare decisis*

Y
- 2 = reverse (hospital not liable)
- 1 = affirm (hospital liable)

— *Victor E. Flango & Glendon Schubert*

REFERENCES

1. The research design and the data collection for this article were carried out exclusively by Mr. Flango. The co-author's participation was limited to the later stages of analyzing and presenting the data, and writing the research report. Mr. Flango would like to take this opportunity to thank Dr. Theodore L. Becker, who both guided the field research in the Philippines, and also generously permitted use of his own data on Hawaiian judges; Miss Nena Eslao, Institute of Philippine Culture, Ateneo de Manila, who co-ordinated this project in the Philippines; Mrs. Marilu del Rosario, also of the Institute of Philippine Culture, who conducted the bulk of the interviews; and the judges of both Hawaii and the Philippines without whose co-operation this project could not have been undertaken. Mr. Schubert thanks Edward J. Weissman for his incisive and helpful comments on the several drafts of this chapter.
2. Compare Glendon Schubert, "Judges and Political Leadership," in Lewis Edinger, *Political Leadership in Industrialized Societies: Studies in Comparative Analysis* (New York: Wiley, 1967), pp. 220-65, which compares the political leadership role of the Supreme Courts of the United States, the Philippines, Australia, and Japan.
3. *Constitutions of the United States: National and State* (New York: Oceana Publications, 1962), and Wilfred C. Tsukiyama, "New Angles in Court Administration—Hawaii" (New York: Institute of Judicial Administration, 1961). p. 2.
4. See Theodore L. Becker, "A Survey Study of Hawaiian Judges: The Effect on Decisions of Judicial Role Variations," *American Political Science Review*, 60 (1966), 677-80.
5. For further details on this case and on scoring procedures, see Becker, *Political Behavioralism and Modern Jurisprudence* (Chicago: Rand McNally, 1965), Chaps. 3-5, and Appendix A-3.
6. For a discussion of the statistical analysis that Becker based upon his own grouping of the data, see the

exchange of correspondence between S. Sidney Ulmer and Theodore L. Becker, in "Communications to the Editor," *American Political Science Review*, 61 (1967), 1098-1101.

7. In Becker's own words, "The basic fact I wished to describe was the number of judges who would *adhere to clear precedent which dictated that they come to a decision contrary to their own personal opinions* (this is simply my definition of objective decision)." "Communications to the Editor," p. 678, n. 3. (Italics in original.)

8. Becker does not report the empirical responses to the question which asked for attributions of liability from the employee, the hospital, or both. He does state, however, that "It was hypothesized (quite correctly) that the great majority of judges would have a decisional propensity to decide for a claimant against a hospital." "Communications to the Editor." In fact, of the eleven judges who constitute the subsample for Table 8.1, only three (all of whom fall in cell d) did favour the relatively liberal policy of holding the hospital exclusively responsible for its employee's acts; the other eight favoured the more moderate policy of joint responsibility for the hospital and its employee. But all eleven agreed that the hospital should be held at least jointly responsible—and such a policy result would be contrary to the precedents in the hypothetical case. Flango has reproduced these data in his mimeographed paper "The Cross Cultural Judicial Decision" (1966), p. 37.

9. Of the remaining eleven judges in Becker's sample, who indicated that they were influenced equally strongly by precedential and by policy considerations, only three voted "objectively" and the other eight made "subjective" (anti-precedential) choices in the hypothetical case. Clearly, these judges with "mixed" attitudinal orientations towards policy and precedent did not tend to sublimate their substantive views and follow the perceived obligations of their judicial role, as they should have done in order to provide support

for Becker's hypothesis. The one judge who favoured holding the nurse exclusively responsible voted "objectively" (pro-hospital and pro-precedent) in the hypothetical case; three who favoured the opposite goal of exclusive hospital responsibility voted "subjectively" (anti-hospital and anti-precedent); and of the remaining seven whose moderate policy preferences favoured joint responsibility for the hospital and nurse, only two voted (consistent with Becker's hypothesis) "objectively."

10. Becker, "A Survey Study of Hawaiian Judges." p. 679.

11. See Edgar F. Borgatta, "On Analyzing Correlation Matrices: Some New Emphases," *Public Opinion Quarterly,* 22 (Winter 1958-59), 520.

12. Sidney Siegel, *Nonparametric Statistics for the Behavioural Sciences* (New York: McGraw-Hill, 1956), p. 110.

13. Cf. Theodore L. Becker, "Surveys and Judiciaries, Or Who's Afraid of the Purple Curtain," *Law and Society Review,* 1 (1966), 141.

14. Most judges were very co-operative and generous with their time. Although some judges qualified their answers heavily, evaded direct questions, or declined to respond to portions of the interview schedule, most judges seemed quite willing to be interviewed. One Filipino judge remarked that he was "willing to be interviewed at any time, and for any length of time, either in my office or at my residence." Most of the reasons advanced for declining to answer the schedule centered around either the pressure of work or the impropriety of offering advance opinions on legal questions that could possibly come up for decision in the future. One judge declined to respond, however, because the questionnaire reminded him of an examination. Cf. David L. Grey, "Interviewing at the Court," *Public Opinion Quarterly,* 2 (1967), 285-89.

15. Dante C. Simbulan, "A Study of the Socio-Economic Elite in Philippine Politics, 1946-1963." Microfilm (Canberra: Australian National University Library, 1965), p. 197.

16. Theodore L. Becker, *Political Behavioralism and Modern Jurisprudence*, p. 100.

17. Under a more cautious assumption, one would consider X to be scaled at the ordinal level only, and Y at the nominal level, in which event one would use as a measure of their degree of association the coefficient of differentiation, theta. Similarly, he would use a coefficient of rank correlation (such as rho or tau) to measure the association between Z and X. But putting aside the not inconsiderable problem of what meaning could be attributed to intercomparisons involving different measures of association, none of the ones mentioned would support the causal analysis attempted here.

18. Hubert M. Blalock, Jr., *Causal Inferences in Nonexperimental Research* (Chapel Hill: University of North Carolina Press, 1961).

9

TWO CAUSAL MODELS OF DECISION-MAKING BY THE HIGH COURT OF AUSTRALIA[1]

A recent development of considerable importance in American political science has been the burgeoning professional interest in both mathematical models and statistical designs for the analysis of political decision-making processes. The importance of this trend toward positive theory lies in its significance as an index to the development (including the socialization generally, and the formal education particularly) of the profession along such lines that have made serious scientific study of politics possible.[2] One component of this trend toward "harder"—as distinguished from "softer," but not necessarily "easier"—political theory is represented by game theoretic type approaches.[3] Another component begins (so far as political science is concerned) with Herbert Simon's work in the early fifties,[4] which was carried forward and refined by sociologist Hubert Blalock a decade later,[5] and converges with the work of Sewall Wright as adapted by Warren Miller and Donald Stokes.[6] More recently this component has attracted a quickening and extension of professional awareness among political scientists, as the consequence of the work of Hayward M. Alker, Jr.,[7] and the publication of several reports of empirical research employing the theory and method of causal analysis.[8] It is not surprising that many of these initial empirical applications were secondary analyses of survey and aggregate data on the American national electorate and legislature,[9] because it is in these fields of political science that the quality of measurement and construction of at least partially tested empirical theory are most advanced.

In this chapter I shall endeavor to discuss the use of causal inference theory in an attempt to analyze my own data as reported in a series of recent articles on the decision-making behaviour of justices of the High Court of Australia.

Earlier papers that I have written on the subject of Australia's High Court[10] are: a law review article focusing on voting behaviour in relation to attribute and participational differences;[11] an article, intended primarily for a political science audience, on the latent ideological causes of manifest voting differences;[12] an article for a sociology journal, on sociometric choices in opinion behaviour in relation to attribute and participational differences;[13] and in a political science book on research in the judicial process a chapter on the isomorphism and ideological equivalence of voting behaviour and opinion behaviour.[14] In each of these papers an analysis in detail was made of the empirical aspects of the denoted relationships, but only incidental attention was given to causal analysis in the more technical and rigorous sense. These earlier substantive findings can be deemed, therefore, subject to qualification in the light of what a systematical causal investigation of these intervariable relationships may reveal.

A principal constraint on this effort lies in the very small size of my sample, and the relatively crude observations that underlie the measurements upon which I have to rely.[15] However, it is my hope that the present exploration will have the effect not only of suggesting the utility of the approach in application to the kinds of substantive problems canvassed in this book, but also of stimulating the production of better quality data by demonstrating the effects of their lack.[16]

When writing the other articles which report my research on the High Court of Australia, I had decided in advance to await their completion before undertaking the causal analysis, which comprises this chapter. In part this decision reflected my impression of the appropriateness of different levels of analysis to various media of publication, but I thought it also desirable—so that this chapter could be confined to feasible length—first to publish elsewhere the description and empirical analysis of the variables dealt with here. Therefore, I present below only a cursory description of the data and the minimal necessary information concerning the operationalization and substantive content of the relevant variables. Similarly, I assume that causal modeling is by now an approach sufficiently within the domain of the profession that it is no longer necessary to reiterate the fundamentals of the approach as a prelude to every report of its empirical application.

DATA

The sample for analysis consists of all decisions of the High Court reported in the *Commonwealth Law Reports* for the decade extending from Chief Justice John Latham's de facto retirement, on May 11, 1951, to the appointment of Justice Francis Owen, on September 22, 1961. The only personnel changes occurred during the winter of 1958, when Douglas Menzies (appointed June 12, 1958) replaced William Webb (resigned May 16, 1958), and Victor Windeyer (appointed September 8, 1958) replaced Dudley Williams (resigned July 31, 1958). We have therefore two stable sub-groups of seven justices each. One group acted during an earlier and longer period of seven years, and the other group acted during a later and shorter period of three years. Five justices (Owen Dixon. Alan Taylor, Edward McTiernan, Wilfred Fullagar, and Frank Kitto) were members of both groups and participated in the decisions of the Court throughout all (or substantially all) of the ten-year period. There are a total, therefore, of nine judges in the sample, and from a sociological point of view there are two different "courts," because of the change in the composition of the decision-making group.

For present purposes, I define a decisional outcome to be a set of votes (and associated opinions) by the justices participating in the disposition of a particular case. A case is a real or feigned conflict of interests between two or more parties litigant who, through the agency of their lawyer-spokesmen (barristers), seek to induce a majority of the justices to support their respective claims. A justice's vote is his support of a litigant's claim or claims, as inferred from the observation of the order that he proposes for disposition of the case. An opinion is the statement that a justice (usually) writes to justify his voting position. The total of participations is equal to the total of votes for any set of decisions, but participation implies only membership in the group of decision-makers impaneled for the disposition of a particular case, while a vote has directionality in relation to the outcome of the group decision.

Table 9.1: Universe of Observations

	Nonunanimous:			*Total:*		
Period	*Decisions*	*Opinions*	*Votes*	*Decisions*	*Opinions*	*Votes*
1951-58	129	629	627	510	2321	2141
1958-61	058	284	284	200	0927	0836
Totals	187	913	911	710	3248	2977

The frequencies of decisions, participations, and opinions observed in the sample are reported in Table 9.1, with a breakdown for the two periods. Both the ratio of opinions to decisions (4.2) and the mean panel size (4.6) are the same for both periods. The High Court acts through a continuously shifting series of ad hoc committees or panels of two to six members; and it infrequently—11 to 12 per cent of the time—uses *en banc* (or, as Australian lawyers call it, "full Court") decisions of the entire group of seven justices. Panels of five make a majority of the decisions and panels of three are next in popularity, for the reason, it has been suggested, of avoiding the possibility of an equal division of votes. The ratio of opinions to votes, which measures change in the relative frequency of individual articulation of opinion, is the same for both periods, .92 and .90. These findings stand in sharp contrast to the corresponding ones for the United States Supreme Court, whose average ratio of participation is much higher and ratio of opinions to participation is much lower. This reflects the differences in customs and institutional roles that have obtained for these two courts, at least during the period of their co-existence. During the same ten-year period as that for our High Court sample, the Supreme Court decided on the merits 1749 cases, of which 946 (54 per cent) were split decisions, whereas only 187 (26 per cent) of the High Court decisions were non-unanimous. The Supreme Court decided more than twice as many cases in absolute terms and it divided in voting twice as often as did the High Court. Consequently, the corresponding sample of split decisions available for the study of the Supreme Court is five times larger than this High Court sample. On the other hand, the Supreme Court had seven changes in personnel during the same period as that of our sample in which for the High Court there were only two changes. The personnel turnover rates were 78 per cent and 29 per cent respectively. Indeed, from the point of view of the totals of split decisions for stable courts, the High Court provides better samples of voting data than does the Supreme Court.

Disregarding, for the moment, the impact of cultural norms governing the disclosure of differences in viewpoint, we can observe that disagreement in opinions is more widespread than that concerning outcomes. This is so because dissenters, almost without exception, *disagree* with the opinions of justices who vote in the majority, while majority justices by no means necessarily *agree* upon their reasons for reaching the same result. For the same reason, opinion differences can be observed in decisions for which the vote as to outcome is unanimous. Such "unanimous" decisions in the High Court are more numerous than split decisions. Thus, the observation of inter-agreement in opinions makes possible the discrimination of differences among the justices in the overwhelming majority which consists of unanimous decisions, as well as in the remaining minority of split decisions.

VARIABLES

Each of the earlier reports of this research emphasized the relationships in a pattern for one among several different subsets of the universe of variables postulated to be relevant, and each brought to bear a different theoretical focus. In order to discuss these differences, it is necessary to distinguish among three classes of variables: exogenous, intervening, and dependent. The alternative classification system and terminology previously employed involved a distinction among attribute, participation, attitudinal,and social deference variables. Interval scales for these variables during each of the two chronological periods into which the data were partitioned are reported in Table 9.2. This table describes three exogenous variables that I assume to function as indices of ideology: socialization [age] (A), culture [domicile] (D), and political orientation [socio-economic-political conservatism] (S). Each of these variables represents, at the theoretical level, a behavioural concept; and at the empirical level, an observable surrogate that I have hypothesized to be a manifest index of the latent variable. Age signifies what pattern of cultural norms was dominant when the judicial subjects were growing up and were being socialized into a particular phase in the development of Australian political society.[17] In Australia, as in Japan,[18] this means, so far as it concerns judges of the present and immediate past generation, that younger men are apt to be *more* conservative than older ones—the euphoric soporifics of eternal progress toward liberalism, which some social soothsayers have proffered, to the contrary notwithstanding. Domicile signifies the variation in sub-cultural differences that have implications for political ideology, such as the cultural parameters of the milieu in which adult learning and reinforcement[19] took place for the judges in my sample. An American example of this variable in operation would be to compare the boyhood of Mark Twain with that of James Russell Lowell, or to compare the boyhood of Robert E. Lee with that of Ulysses S. Grant. The third variable, S, is a linear and additive index of four component background characteristics of political orientation: political party affiliation, the partisan character of the government appointing the judge to the High Court, his father's economic and social status, and his own religious affiliation. All of these components were so aligned, in relation to Australian cultural parameters, that the positive direction of the index is hypothesized to be that of socio-economic-political conservatism. The chronological age of each judge in my sample is readily available information,[20] and these data can be appropriately scaled intervally. Domicile, however, could only be trichotomized,[21] although I have scaled the three states (which define the sub-cultural regions) along a longitudinal dimension (*viz*-Queensland, New South Wales, Victoria), hypothesizing that the southern is the conservative end of the scale. Of course, such a crudely differentiated scale is not a very desirable one for the calculation of Pearsonian correlations, but I knew of no better alternative. I have reported elsewhere[22] the details of the index of socio-economic-political orientation (with conservatism the positive direction) as scores on S, which are reported in Table 9.2.

Table 9.2. Empirical Scores for Variables

	Sample:	*Class:* *Exogenous*			*Participational*		*Attitudinal*		*Dependent*
		A	S	D	Ps	Pt	X	Y	O
1951-58	Dixon	68.7	1	2	.27	.36	.62	.82	11
	Fullagar	62.1	3	2	—.06	.01	—.34	1.13	—03
	Kitto	51.4	2	2	.14	.13	—.28	.46	61
	McTiernan	62.9	—4	1	—.14	—.24	—1.44	—.34	—12
	Taylor	53.1	1	1	—0.4	—.05	—.30	—.42	02
	Webb	67.9	—2	0	.04	.02	.71	—.49	—04
	Williams	65.0	3	1	—.24	—.23	.77	—.89	05
1958-61	Dixon	73.7	1	2	.18	.31	.98	.62	11.5
	Fullagar	67.1	3	2	.11	—.01	—.58	.66	01
	Kitto	56.4	2	2	—0.6	—.01	—.18	.45	04
	Mctiernan	67.9	—4	1	—.14	.19	1.03	.00	—03
	Taylor	58.1	1	1	—.24	—.22	—.56	—.02	—03.5
	Menzies	52.3	4	2	.16	.06	—.75	1.11	—08
	Windeyer	59.4	5	1	—0.2	0.5	.96	52	—02

There are two intervening variables: participation and attitudes. Participation is a measure of the extent to which, in the assignment of the judges to the Court's decision-making panels, individual judges made decisions and therefore voted more or less frequently than the participational mean for the group.

The two attitudinal variables are collectivism (X) and authoritarianism (Y).[23] Both are Guttman scales of voting data for the non-unanimous decisions during the periods sampled. X is predominantly concerned with voting differences in cases raising issues of economic and social egalitarianism. The positive or collectivistic direction of the scale is the liberal direction. Y is concerned with political and psychological issues. The pro-authoritarian (positive and conservative) direction of the scale involves the support of the strict interpretation of legal norms, the upholding of judicial review and of both judicial and federal centralization, and the support of governmental fiscal interests. Of course, empirical cumulative scales for X and for Y discriminate only rank differences among the respondent judges. However, by observing the analogue vectors for X and Y, in the multi-dimensional (four) space derived from a smallest space analysis of phi correlations, it is possible to observe an interval scale of differences in regard to these two attitudinal dimensions.[24] The correlations measure assent-dissent differences among the justices in all of the non-unanimous decisions for each period sampled, and the scale analogues are equivalent to Guttman's first principal components[25] of these cumulative scales. The scores reported in Table 12.2 for X and Y are the distances from the origin, along these vectorial dimensions, of the respective projections from the configuration of points that represent the judges in the space.[26]

The dependent variable, social deference (O), is a measure of interagreement among the judges in the writing of opinions to rationalize their votes, in unanimous as well as in split decisions. The scores for this variable in Table 9.2 are based on an index that combines both positive and negative deference. The positive direction of the scale is that of agreement (positive deference).[27] On the scale of opinion deference, those judges whose opinions gained most acceptance rank highest, and those whose opinions attracted the least support from others rank lowest. I have discussed elsewhere the statistical and other methodological problems that are posed by the large amounts of missing data, brought about, in regard to both the voting and the opinion scales, by the High Court's system of using panels for decision-making purposes.[28]

THE HYPOTHETICAL MODEL

Figure 9.1 presents the model of causal relationships that, on the basis of the research that has been done to date in the field of judicial behaviour, seems to me to be most plausible to assume. In general, the model indicates that the exogenous variables (A, D, and S) are not independent, but rather are intercorrelated;[29] that participation (P) intervenes between the exogenous and the other decisional variables (X, Y, and O); and that the two attitudinal variables (X and Y) are independent of each other, but they both, together with P, are causes of variation in O. All of the arrows predict that non-zero correlations will be observed, and that the direction of *causation* will be as indicated by the arrowheads. The direction of *correlation* (positive or negative) is not predicted: all three exogenous variables are hypothesized to be aligned in the same direction (conservative), but X and Y are aligned oppositely (the negative direction is conservative on X, and the positive direction is conservative on Y). The theory did not predict directionality, in terms of the liberalism/conservatism continuum, for either P or O.

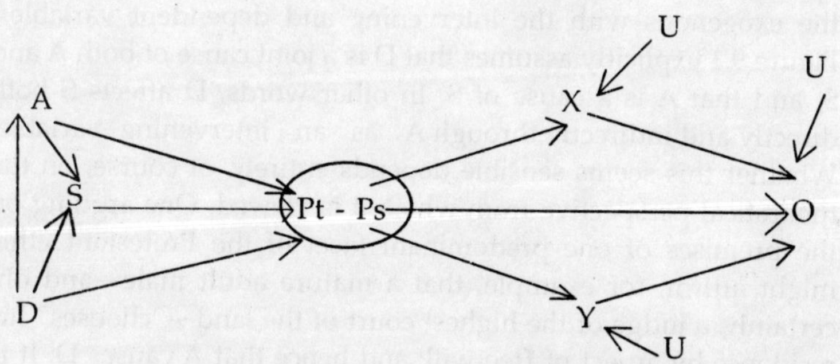

Figure 9.1 *The Predicted Model Structure (Hypothetical)*

I assume that the direction of causation, between the exogenous variables and participation, is from the former to the latter. From the point of view of the chronology of the decision-making process it could not be otherwise. The judges become acculturated and socialized, and develop their social affiliations and identifications as mature and established barristers long before they become members of the High Court—which is without exception in late middle life—and hence available for assignment to the decision-making panels of the Court. The same reasoning applies to the direction of causation between the exogenous variables and either the attitudinal variables or the dependent opinion behaviour variable. I assume further that the attitudinal variables are causally, as they most certainly are chronologically in the decision-making process, prior to the social choices involved in the rationalization of the votes that articulate the attitudinal preferences. It is true that one can quite plausibly hypothesize the possibility of feedback loops from opinions to attitudes, and from attitudes to participation, and from any of these to the exogenous variables; but we focus here upon the most important, obvious, and empirically observable paths of causation. Analysis of the feedback system must be postponed until we have a better understanding of the static patterns of causation.

The inference of the direction of causation, in the bilateral relationships among the three exogenous variables, may not appear to be so intuitively obvious as do the paths connecting the exogenous with the intervening and dependent variables. Figure 9.1 explicitly assumes that D is a joint cause of both A and S; and that A is a cause of S. In other words, D affects S both directly and indirectly through A, as an intervening variable. Whether this seems sensible depends entirely, of course, on the theoretical perspective from which it is viewed. One arguing on the premises of one predominant facet of the Protestant ethic might affirm, for example, that a mature adult male—and oh! certainly, a judge of the highest court of the land—"chooses" his residence by an act of free will; and hence that A causes D. It is necessary to recall, therefore, the particular definitions that have been given here to the latent ideological variables for which the empirically observed A, D, and S serve as surrogates. Domicile stands for the dominant cultural pattern of a region—such as what are perceived to be the socio-political and economic differences between New England and the American South, for example—and particularly, for this sample of Australian judges, the differences between the sub-cultures of Victoria and of New South Wales. Age is presumed to provide access to what are in effect time-slices of cultural developmental changes, or the particular pattern of cultural norms that was dominant in the country as a whole—modified, to be sure, by the sub-regional differentiations that D is assumed to measure—at the time of each judge's youth when he was socialized into the belief systems of his society. The third variable, political orientation (S), measures, albeit crudely, social affiliations and identifications of the adult judge, and supposedly differentiates what might be called his basic ideological predisposition as a conservative or a liberal.[30] Given these theoretical premises, it is indispensable to assume that the culture of the region where a judge resides is a cause of his political orientation toward that culture, directly as well as indirectly through the intervention of childhood learning and societal induction processes.

It will be noted that the model assumes recursiveness: that only unidirectional causation obtains between pairs of variables in the model. Such a simplifying assumption, like all simplifying assumptions, undoubtedly reduces the potential congruity between the model and empirical reality. The relevant question, however, is not whether this model is an "oversimplification," but whether, by making such an assumption, can one gain certain partial knowledge about causality in the empirical domain that would not otherwise be attainable to all—given the difficult problems of statistical theory and method associated with attempts to study reciprocal causation non-experimentally. Moreover, the assumption of one-way causation is not intuitively implausible, as applied to most of the relationships in this model. It hardly seems sensible to argue, for example, that a judge's age—at least when our interest focuses upon his chronological age as an index to childhood acculturation—is "caused" by his attitudes toward policy issues, by his participation in decisions, or by the extent to which there are differentials in the deference that he shows to his colleagues in the process of rationalizing those decisions. To be sure, his decision-making behaviour at time *t* may affect his health, which in turn functions in a feedback loop to set psychophysiological parameters[31] that affect his subsequent decision-making behaviour at time *t+1*.[32] But such refinements lie beyond the scope of the present exploratory endeavor. And only by efforts to work with the present model will it become possible to develop the professional skill necessary to carry out the more complicated causal analysis such as the health feedback loop implies.

Ten arrows are missing. No direct links are predicted between any of the three exogenous variables and any of the three variables on the other side of participation in Figure 9.1. It is explicitly hypothesized that all of these zero-order correlations will be spurious, and due to the intervening effect of participation on the other decisional variables. It is expected, therefore, that the first-order correlation, controlling for participation, will in each of these instances vanish; *viz.* that $r_{AX.P} = 0$, $r_{AO.P} = 0$, $r_{AY.P} = 0$, r_{SXP},. - 0, $r_{so.p} = 0$, $r_{sy.p} = 0$, $r_{DX.P.} = r_{DO.P'} = 0$, $r_{DY.P} = 0$. It is also hypothesized that any zero-order correlation between X and Y must be spurious, and due to the joint effects of P; this prediction is that $r_{XY.P}$— 0. In spurious correlation, the apparent zero-order correlation between two variables can be completely accounted for by a third variable, which affects them both and creates an ostensible association between them, although that seeming association is due entirely to either the intervening or else double effect of the third variable.[33]

Attention is now directed to the isotopes of the participation variable, Pt and Ps. Votes, the data on the basis of which the X and Y scales were constructed, were inferred from the subset of non-unanimous decisions (Table 9.1). Opinions, the data on the basis of which the O scale was constructed, were observed from the total universe of reported decisions (both unanimous and non-unanimous). Ps (participation in non-unanimous, *viz.*, split, decisions) is, therefore, a proper subset of Pt (participation in both unanimous and split decisions).[34] Both scales are reported (Table 9.2) as ratios of deviation from the average of participation for the group (court) in the subset and universe of decisions, respectively. The scales appear to be very similar. The earlier smallest space study, which was designed to measure the degree of bias in Ps as a sample of Pt, demonstrated that the voting behaviour of the judges in the split decisions was considerably better representative of their opinion behaviour in all decisions (for the time periods included in the analysis, of course) than most *a priori* speculators have presumed would be the case.[35] Consequently, this model hypothesizes that the only difference between Ps and Pt will be due to random variation (in the content of unanimous, as distinguished from split, decisions); and explicitly, that the correlation between Ps and Pt will be unity, except for error variance. In Figure 9.1, the arrows have been drawn from Ps to X and to Y, and from Pt to O, because this attribution corresponds precisely to the data sets. Of course, it is possible to use the correlations from the exogenous variables to either Pt or Ps, but the former seems preferable as a measure of the more general relationship.

With better data, it would be conventional to accept as an approximation of zero (or of unity) any empirical correlation falling within the range of ± .05. Given the substantial error variance (both observational and measurement) that contaminates these correlations, I shall use the much weaker criterion of ± .15.

Table 9.3 Zero-order Pearsonian Correlation Coefficients (Decimals Omitted)

		1951-58							
		A	S	D	Ps	Pt	X	Y	O
	A		—258	—286	007	081	659	—041	086
	S	—488		573	040	252	—698	351	666
	D	040	335		410	508	—466	818	392
	Ps	223	454	777		964	—262	610	470
1958-61	Pt	331	422	628	852		—360	698	615
	X	599	—383	—395	—031	279		477	—308
	Y	613	—025	—010	—041	221	434		205
	O	683	099	420	326	640	414	740	

Table 9.3 presents the zero-order correlation matrices for the Pearsonian correlations among the scales reported in Table 9.2 for both periods. The table shows that the correlation between Pt and Ps is .96 in the first period, and .85 in the second. These are sufficiently high and positive correlations, averaging more than +.90, so that I accept their evidence as confirmation of the prediction that $r_{PtRs} = 1.00$, subject to the extent that the empirical correlations have been depressed by random error variance. Certainly there were no important empirical differences, so far as the extent of their participation in split and in unanimous decisions is concerned, for the judges in these samples during either period.[36]

We turn now to the empirical evidence bearing upon the prediction of ten spurious correlations, between the exogenous variables and X, O, and Y, and between X and Y, controlling for participation. As Table 9.4 shows, these predictions are only 30 per cent correct in either period. There are differences for the clusters of partials, however. Half of the partials for relationships between the exogenous variables and O vanish, although more often in the first than in the second period. Political orientation influenced opinion behaviour directly in both periods, although in opposite directions. Domicile affected opinion behaviour only indirectly, in the sense that when the Chief Justice's assignments to panels (the proximate cause of participation differentials) associated together groups of judges from the same state, they then tended to agree with each other somewhat more frequently—the zero-order correlations are $r_{DO(1)}$ = .40, $r_{DO(II)}$ = .42—than they agreed with the opinions of judges from other states. Age affected opinion behaviour only indirectly in the early period; but later age exerted a relatively strong influence upon O, which was largely direct rather than through the intervening participation variable.

Table 9.4: First-Order Partial Correlations Predicted to Vanish. Controlling for Participation (Decimals Omitted)*

Variables	*Period:* 1951-58	1958-61
AO.Pt	05	65
SO.Pt	67	—53
DO.Pt	12	03
AX.Ps	68	62
SX.Ps	—71	—41
DX.Ps	—41	—59
AY.Ps	—06	64
SY.Ps	41	01
DY.Ps	79	04
XY.Pt	34	40

**The coefficients that are deemed to have vanished are printed in italics*

None of the partials for correlations with the X scale vanish. Evidently we must infer that all three exogenous variables maintained substantial direct influence upon the collectivism scale in both periods. Contrary to our hypothetical model, differences in participation in decision-making do not intervene between our indexes of age, domicile, and political orientation, and this judicial attitude. In other words, these exogenous influences were so strong in their impact on attitudes toward questions of socio-economic policy, that the social context provided by the composition of the decision-making panels made little difference. The situation in regard to the Y scale is quite different, however. Here, half of the predictions are correct, and they are better in the later than in the early period. Age has no direct effect upon authoritarian attitudes in the early period, but it does in the later period. To the contrary, political orientation and domicile have a direct effect upon authoritarianism in the early period, but in the later they have only an indirect effect through participation. We might infer from this that reinforcement from being in the cultural-plurality subgroup of a panel[37] is a much more important consideration when ideological conservatism is brought to bear upon the questions of politico-legal policy that provided the substantive content of the Y scale.

The prediction of independence between the scales also fails in both periods. Not only do the partials fail to vanish, but they do not even reduce very impressively the values of the zero-order correlations ($r_{XY(I)}$, = -.47, $r_{xy.Pt(I)}$ = —.34; $r_{XY(II)}$ = .43, $r_{xy.Pt(II)}$ = .40). However, our observation of the direct effects of the exogenous variables on both attitudinal variables, but especially upon *X*, readily explains why controlling for participation alone does not suffice to demonstrate the spuriousness of the link between X and Y. An examination of the partials, controlling for the set of ideological indicators, is at least suggestive of what one ought to be able to demonstrate with better measurements of the exogenous variables. Controlling for D in the first period, for example, reduces r_{xy} to —.188; not quite enough to satisfy our criterion, to be sure, but certainly approaching it. And in the later period, controlling for A brings the partial down to .106, lower than our criterion. I did not, of course, hypothesize that controlling for any of the exogenous variables would result in a demonstration of spuriousness for r_{XY}, and so I do not claim that the observation of these other partials confirms any hypothesis. But it suggests a path that may be fruitful for future research. Moreover, my present findings of, for example, direct links between all three of the ideological indexes and collectivism, directly imply that a test of first-order partials is not the most appropriate one in any event. What we ought to observe would be $r_{XY\ ASDPt}$—a fourth-order partial correlation coefficient. It is hardly necessary to point out that there is no possibility of calculating any such coefficient, with any meaningful results, given the poor quality of the measurement of the data presently at hand. I did calculate a few second and higher order partials; and it is piquing to observe that $r_{DX.SA(I)}$ = .023, for example, which implies that domicile has only a spurious association with collectivist attitudes, *except* to the extent that sub-cultural variation influences childhood socialization and adult political orientation—but mostly even the second order partials tended to blow up in spurious magnitude, because of the piling up of the excessive degree of error variance that undoubtedly is contained in the zero-order correlations. Moreover, it should be noted how unstable the correlation between X and Y appears to be, swinging from —.48 in this early period to +.43 in the later period, a combined range of more than .90. We would expect such instability, of course, in a correlation that was truly spurious in both instances. Finally, it makes no theoretical sense to assume that either of these two attitudes *could* "cause" the other one. And from the points of view of both the multidimensional statistical theory and the social psychological theory of belief systems,[38] the two attitudes are jointly affected by ideological variables. They do not cause each other.

Certain supplementary evidence can be noted about the predictions for X, Y, and O, individually. In the first period, for example, not only do the partials vanish for r_{AO} and r_{AV}, but they vanish also for the zero-order correlations, which are .09 and —.04, respectively. In the later period, the same is true of r_{SY} = .03, and r_{DY} = .01. There is also one partial ($r_{DX\ (I)}$) [39] that does not disappear when controlled for participation, but does disappear (with $r_{DX.S\ (I)}$ = —.11) when the control is for political orientation.

(It was, incidentally, the observation of this first-order partial which suggested the calculation of the second-order partial noted above.) The observed $r_{DX.S(I)}$ does not "prove" that the hypothetical model is correct in predicting a spurious correlation between domicile and collectivism. It does, however, indicate that a model which predicted a direct effect of political orientation upon collectivism would fit these data better. We might infer tentatively that although authoritarian attitudinal differences in Period I can be attributed directly to the effect of sub-cultural variation, such regional influences are mediated for the issues of economic policy by judicial ties of social and political affiliation (which, one might presume, provide a continuing source of reinforcement that they do *not* provide regarding the more psychological and lego-political issues of the Y variable).

Table 9.5 Predicted Causal Relations in the Hypothetical Model (in Decimals)*

Variables	*Period:* 1951-58	1958-61
XO	—31	*01* ($r_{OX.A}$)
YO	*—4* ($r_{OY.A}$)	74
PtO	62	64
PsX	*—09* ($r_{XPs.D}$)	*—03*
PsY	61	*—04*
PtPs	96	85
APt	*08*	33
SPt	*—06* ($r_{SPt.D}$)	42
DPt	51	63
AS	—26	—49
DS	57	33
DA	—29	*04*

**Non-causal relations that are deemed to have vanished are printed in italics.*

Note: All correlations are zero-order, except for the four first-order partials which are specified.

We are concerned with more than one kind of predictive error, however. In addition to those predictions that err because partial correlations do not vanish, we must contend with correlations that are zero when the model predicts causal links. Table 9.5 shows that there are four such instances in each period, and all these must be counted as misfits of our model. In the early period, the zero-order correlation between age and participation is r_{APt}=.081 (and r_{APs} =.007): and in the later period, the correlation between domicile and age drops to .04, while the total correlation between participation and each of the attitudinal variables disappears, with r_{PsX} = —-.03, r_{PsY} = —.04. Clearly, the latter three instances all represent what are direct relationships in the model. We must, therefore, infer that the model is in error to the extent that, during the later period, age is independent of domicile, and participation has no effect upon judicial attitudes but only upon opinion deference. The latter inference tends to reinforce one of our earlier inferences: that the ideological indexes operated directly upon *X* in both periods, and without the intervention of P. Certainly the —.03 correlation confirms this inference for the later period. On the other hand, the —.04 for r_{PSY} might seem hardly consistent with the vanishing partials for $r_{SY.Ps}$ and $r_{DY.Ps}$, were it not that the zero-order correlations here are also zero, as previously noted. In strictly empirical terms what the Iow negative correlation between domicle and age during the early period meant was that, on a manifest level, the Victorian judges tended to be younger than the average for the Court during this period. On a latent level, what the correlation implies is that there was a slight tendency for the non-Victorian (New South Wales, and Queensland, *viz.* the more northern states) regional subcultures to have a predominant influence upon the early socialization of the judges, and hence for the Court in a collective or aggregative sense to have been reared in a somewhat more liberal political ethos.

There are also four instances in which the first-order partials vanish for correlations for which the controls to be specified are appropriate to apply, given the structure of our hypothetical model. In the early period, $r_{PSX.D}$) = —.09, adding further confirmation to our previous discussion of the relative unimportance of participation as an intervening variable in relation to X. The other two instances in the early period are $r_{YO.S}$ = —.04, and $r_{SPt.D}$ = —.06, indicating that the authoritarian attitude has no effect on opinion behaviour, given the direct link between political orientation and O, and controlling for S; and that the apparent influence of S on Pt disappears, with a control for domicile. In the later period, $r_{XO.A}$ = .01, indicating that the collectivist attitude has no effect on opinion behaviour, given the direct effect that age does have, and controlling for age.

THE EMPIRICAL MODELS

We are now in a position to consider the empirical model that emerges, in each period, as a modification of the hypothetical model with which we began our analysis. Direct attention to the non-causal relationships, including both the successful predictions (based on Figure 9.1) that arrows would vanish, and the unsuccessful predictions (also based on Figure 9.1) that causal relations would be observed. Then, present the causal models, for both periods, that the foregoing analysis has indicated to fit best the present data.

We turn now to a more general interpretation of Figure 9.4. Domicile appears to be the most influential exogenous variable, among those measured and included within this system, during the early period of analysis. The regional sub-culture variable directly affects age (socialization), political orientation, decisional participation, and authoritarian attitudes. Indirectly, through the intervention of age, political orientation, and participation, domicile affects the other two variables, opinion deference and collectivistic attitudes (which itself intervenes between age and political orientation, and opinion deference). Directly or indirectly, domicile influences variation in all of the other variables in the model. The two other variables that were initially assumed to be exogenous variables function additionally in intervening roles, during this period. Age affects political orientation and collectivism; the political orientation variable affects collectivism and opinion deference. Two of the three variables that were assumed to intervene do so. The attitudinal variable of collectivism intervenes between age and political orientation, and opinion deference; and participation intervenes between domicile, and the attitude of authoritarianism, and opinion deference. The third variable that was assumed to be intervening, the authoritarian attitude, does not perform that function in this model. Instead it operates as a dependent variable, subject to the conjoint effects of participation, political orientation, and domicile. The opinion deference variable, which was hypothesized to be a dependent variable, affected jointly by the participational and by both attitudinal variables, appears in this period to be affected only by participation and by the one attitudinal variable, collectivism. Stated otherwise, opinion behaviour is biased by differences in participation in decision-making, and opinion behaviour serves to rationalize attitudinal differences that relate to issues of collectivism. Acting both directly and indirectly, the three variables that were hypothesized to be exogenous influence both judicial attitudes and opinion behaviour, but only the domicile variable affects participation in decision-making. (Translated into somewhat more empirical language this means that Chief Justice Owen Dixon, who assigned his colleagues as well as himself to the decisional panels during both periods covered in the present study, showed a notable and consistent tendency to place Victorians in decision-making roles more frequently than he did judges who hailed from New South Wales.) The arrow connecting the U to each of the dependent variables is intended to remind us of the unspecifiable (including error) variance which, though presumed to be operating independently upon each dependent variable, nevertheless must be taken into account in an analysis of what causes change in the variation of each.

The model, analogous to that of Figure 9.4, for the later period, 1958-61. This is also a recursive model. Therefore, as in the case of Figure 9.1, only unidirectional causation is assumed.

What evidently has happened is that X and Y have exchanged roles in the causal structure. In this later period, it is Y rather than X that intervenes between A and O and it its X. rather than Y, that functions as a dependent variable. The other principal changes from the earlier period are that all three exogenous variables jointly affect participation; that participation now intervenes only between the three exogenous variables and the dependent opinion variable; and that age substitutes for the political orientation variable, as a direct influence upon opinion behaviour.

Domicile has no causal effect upon age during this later period. The observed correlation ($r_{DA} = .04$) for the later period signifies, in relation to the earlier period, that neither sub-culture had a predominant influence upon the socialization process for the later sample of judges. In empirical terms, what happened was that the third oldest judge, a New South Walesman, was replaced by another New South Walesman, who was the fourth oldest judge during the later period. Clearly this change was minimal, and insufficient to have reduced the correlation to zero. It was the other personnel change that produced the change in the correlation. The second oldest judge during the early period was the only Queens-lander in either sample, and therefore the one who scored lowest on the domicile scale. He was replaced by a Victorian who was both twenty years junior to his predecessor and also the youngest judge on the Court. A close look at Table 9.2 suggests that the small negative zero-order correlation during the early period (when $r_{DA} = —.29$) is probably a statistical artifact of the small sample and discrete scale categories; and it might be better to consider domicile to have been uncorrelated with age in both periods. The increase in the negative correlation between A and S, and the decrease in the positive correlation between D and S, show that the effect of the two personnel changes was to increase the influence of youth, and to decrease that of the Victorian subculture, upon social conservatism among the judges. But these differences are not great, and they certainly reflect no greater sampling variation than we should expect to get when two persons are replaced in a small seven-man group.

One other major change is that age now appears to be the most influential exogenous variable, and the relative importance of domicile and political orientation is correspondingly attenuated. All three of the exogenous variables act jointly to affect participation although domicile—which was the only one of the three to maintain a direct influence upon participation during the earlier period—retains a higher level of association than either of the other two. But if older, more conservative, Victorians are the judges who participate most frequently in decision-making, and who tend to prefer each other in opinion interagreement, it is the older judges, those who are *less* conservative, and the New South Walesmen who jointly are most influential in affecting attitudes toward collectivism (which operates as a dependent variable in this later period). And opinion deference is paid to those who share a relatively authoritarian attitude, those judges who are older, and those who participate most frequently in decisions.

If we now compare Figures 9.4 and 9.5, looking for the patterns common to them both, it is evident that we have focused upon two static models of a process that is quite dynamic. Our two periods combined extend over a decade; and what these models do, in effect, is to examine the means of variation during each period. Not only are these means an average of more than five years apart; it also is clear that the second group differs in several important respects from the first. The Dixon Court, with Windeyer and Menzies, was not the same as the Dixon Court with Williams and Webb. The influence of the Victorian subculture became somewhat less, and that of age became somewhat greater (although the Court's physical age remained almost constant, in a collective sense);[40] the earlier partial influence of participational bias on attitudes disappeared leaving only the effect on opinion behaviour; and authoritarianism displaced collectivism as the attitude influntial on opinion behaviour. However, in both periods domicile and age together influence political orientation; domicile affects participation, and both political orientation and age affect collectivism; and participation affects opinion behaviour. In both periods, participation and one of the attitudinal variables intervene between the exogenous and the hypothesized dependent (opinion) variable. However, one of the attitudinal variables, contrary to what was hypothesized, acts as a dependent variable in each period; and also contrary to what was hypothesized, some of the exogenous variables maintain direct causal influence upon both of the dependent variables in each period.

A CAUSAL CRITIQUE OF NON-CAUSAL FINDINGS

In this concluding section, we turn to an evaluation of the substantive findings, or assumptions, of the earlier articles in the series,[41] to the extent that these can be reappraised in the light of the present causal analysis. After appraising the most general set of findings that emerge from the group of articles together, we shall turn to a seriatim review of the reliability of the substantive contributions made by each article.

The earlier papers assumed that participation had an important influence upon voting behaviour, and that the attribute variable with the greatest effect upon participation is domicile. A related finding was that political orientation bears an important influence upon voting behaviour, reinforcing that of participation. The preceding discussion here enables us to be both more precise and more confident in our assessment of these relationships. Clearly, participation is *not*, in general, an important influence on *voting* behaviour—although it is important as an influence upon opinion behaviour. However, it is correct that domicile acts to influence voting behaviour, both directly and indirectly through political orientation and participation. And causal analysis makes explicit *why* political orientation seemed, in the evaluation of the earlier papers, to have such an important influence upon voting behaviour. As Figures 9.4 and 9.5 both show, political orientation is the only attribute variable that directly affects both attitudinal variables in both periods; and in addition, both of the other attribute variables (age and domicile) themselves act in-directly through political orientation to complement their respective alternative paths of causation. Political orientation is a conduit, therefore, not only for the substantive content that I formerly had attributed to it, but also in part for the other two attribute variables. In regard to the general tenor of the prior conclusions, it would appear that they were wrong about the importance of participational differences, but right otherwise.

The initial article is concerned mostly with reporting empirical observations, ordered by cumulative scaling analysis. It concludes with an attempt to extrapolate, in the customary nonrigorous and quasi-causal manner, inferences from the face of the zero-order correlation matrices. But these are matrices of rank order (rho)—and even of phi—correlations, because the level of measurement employed was either ordinal or nominal. There are, of course, differences between the values of these rho and phi coefficients and the Pearsonian ones reported here, but the change in level of measurement does not lead to any important changes in the substantive conclusions reached earlier except in one respect—and this is no doubt the most important one. Many of the earlier judgments about causal influences upon the two attitudinal scales, X and Y, must be revised in the light of the present analysis. These correlational differences reflect, in turn, the substitution here of the ordered metric scales, derived from smallest space measurements, for the strictly ordinal scales that were correlated for the law review article. It makes a substantial difference whether account is taken not only of the sequencing of the judges along the attitudinal dimensions, but also of their relative spacing along those dimensions; causal analysis presumes the latter degree of precision in measurement.

The second article is primarily a study of the relationship between judicial attitudes and ideology, relating the cumulative scales to each other and to the point configuration of the judges in three-dimensional spaces generated by smallest space analysis. The most explicit articulation of any of the earlier papers, to the present causal analysis, occurs in the concluding paragraph of the section entitled "Attributes and Participation," of the political science journal article, in which an attempt was made to use causal analysis to test a hypothesis about the relationships among the three exogenous variables, participation in split decisions, and the two attitudinal scales. The level of measurement was ordinal or nominal, as in the law review article; and the correlations were, therefore, rho's or phi's. The use of rho or phi coefficients of correlation, as the basis for causal analysis, violates at least one (interval level measurement) of the basic assumptions of the latter approach. Nevertheless, this second article correctly eliminated the arrows between D and Y, and S and Y, for the later period, on the grounds that the first-order partials (ρ_{DYPs} = —.03; $\rho_{SY.Ps}$ = .06) disappeared. In this chapter using Pearsonian correlation and an ordered metric scale for Y, the equivalent partial correlations indicate the same conclusion: in Table 9.3, $r_{DY.Ps}$ = .04, and $r_{SY.Ps}$ = —.01. No conclusion was reached about the other paths directly from exogenous to attitudinal variables, during either period, except that none could be eliminated on the basis of partial correlation coefficients calculated from the rho/phi matrices. However, the path from A to Y could have been eliminated for the earlier period, because the zero-order correlation was .00. Our analysis here would agree with the dropping of AY, but it also deletes AO (on the grounds of the partial, controlling for participation) for the earlier period; and DO in both periods (on the same grounds). The one important difference between the findings of the second article, and those reached now, involves (again) the key relationships to the cumulative scales, here in regard to participation. Again, the difference between the present and earlier findings reflects both levels of measurement and method of correlation. Table 9.3 shows that for the later period the zero-order correlations between split decisional participation and the attitudinal scales are both approximately zero. The rho correlations used in the earlier study are $\rho_{PSX} = -.18$ and $\rho_{PsY} = .34$. It does not appear that the partial correlations, controlling for the possibility of spurious correlation between participation and attitudes due to the effect of one or more of the exogenous variables, were examined in the earlier study. If they had been examined, one might have observed that $\rho_{PsX.s} = .06$, indicating that the manifest $\rho_{PSX} = -.18$ was indeed spurious. None of the partials for ρ_{PSY} would have vanished, however. And what seems important is that the cruder levels of measurement and correlation, employed initially, precluded the detection of the absence of any direct influence of participation upon the attitudinal variables, a finding which we were able to make in the present analysis.

The third article in the series focused on the association between the exogenous variables and the dependent opinion variable, with (total) participation hypothesized to function as the intervening variable. The implicit design was, from a mathematical point of view, a set of independent, linear, two-variable equations, with opinion behaviour as the dependent variable. If the linear equations in this set are combined in a multivariate design, then we have the models shown here, in Figures 9.4 and 9.5, except with two-way causation and no arrows removed.

It was recognized that the level of measurement and correlation involved so much error variance that little confidence could be placed in the conclusions reached; and a few of the detailed findings (*viz.* that the correlation between domicile and participation decreases during the later period, or that age is negatively correlated with participation during the later period) appear, in the light of present findings, to have been erroneous, and a product of the error variance in the earlier work. More importantly, however, the principal conclusion reached by the third article was one of impasse:

> We cannot . . . account for the differences in opinion agreement on the basis of age (whatever our assumption about its direction and substantive significance), or on the basis of differences in the major subcultures from which these men were drawn, or in their relative conservatism (at least, as I was enabled to measure it), or even (through participation differentials) in their relatIve degrees of exposure to group esteem.[42]

Needless to say, it is precisely to answer questions such as these that causal analysis has been employed, and I believe usefully, in the present *post hoc* re-analysis of the same empirical observations, on the basis of which we have determined that age acted directly upon opinion agreement in the later period, and indirectly in the earlier one; that domicile affected opinion agreement indirectly during both periods; that political orientation affected opinion agreement directly during the first period and indirectly during the second; and that participation was a direct cause of opinion agreement during both periods. Consequently, we can conclude that the causal analysis employed here adds in an important way to the simpler guides to statistical inference that were relied upon for understanding these relationships in the initial analysis of the data in the sociology journal article.

The fourth and final paper focused upon the relation between voting and opinion behaviour, comparing point configurations (generated from voting data, and opinion data, respectively) in four-dimensional smallest space analyses. Six of the principal findings of this fourth article can be reexamined now, in the light of the present findings. The first of these findings is that "Y is the more fundamental [scale], in the sense that the rank positions on it are more representative of the general positions of the justices in multidimensional space."[43] Figures 9.4 and 9.5 here cannot be said to disconfirm that finding, but neither can they be said to confirm it. There is no apparent basis, in these two causal models, for concluding that either attitudinal scale is more important or "fundamental" than the other one. The second finding was that Y fit the opinion spaces perfectly in both periods, and better than X did; this finding might be restated to mean that YO should be correlated more highly and positively than XO in both periods. This proposition is confirmed by the present data: r_{YO} is .21, and r_{xo} —.31, in the earlier period; and r_{yo} is .74, and r_{xo}.41, in the later period. The third finding was that both XO and YO are more highly positive correlations during the later than in the earlier period: evidently, the present data confirm this finding. The fourth finding is that both X and Y causally effect O in both periods. The present evidence contradicts that finding, because Figures 9.2 and 9.3 show that the correlation between Y and O during the earlier period, and that between X and O during the later period both are spurious. The fifth finding is that the structure of the relation between the two attitudinal scales, and between them and the opinion variable, is less complex in the earlier than in the later period. The causal model neither confirms nor disconfirms that finding; the apparent complexity of the two models is equivalent, both in general (each involving a dozen causal paths among a set of seven variables) and in particular relationships to the X and Y variables (which have reciprocally complementary roles, as between the two periods). The sixth and final finding was that the samples of unanimous and non-unanimous data are substantially the same; and our finding that Ps = Pt provides at least partial (if inferential) confirmation that there are no relevantly important differences between the decisional sample used for measuring opinion behaviour and that used for measuring voting behaviour. In sum, many of the major findings of the smallest space analysis are confirmed by the present causal analysis. Other findings do not find confirmation, but neither are they disconfirmed by the present analysis. The major difference between the findings of the two studies concerns the effect of attitudinal on opinion behaviour. This latter is, however, a most basic matter in the framework of either analytical approach. Causal analysis raises serious doubts concerning the earlier conclusion: that opinion behaviour was a rationalization of (*viz.* was caused by) both attitudinal variables in both periods. The alternative finding indicated by causal analysis is that certain attitudes are among the joint causes of opinion behaviour at some but not at all times. The implication of this finding for future research is that all three classes of variables—exogenous/ideological, intervening (attitudinal, and participational/group interaction), and dependent (voting and opinion behaviour)—must be accommodated in models that will prove useful in extending our knowledge about judicial decision-making behaviour beyond the present frontiers of research achievement. The continuing concern with the problem of measurement error variance, which has haunted our discussion (as it did also in the four earlier articles), implies a corollary prescription: that greater efforts to make use of experimental controls, in the design of our research, can be expected to yield a handsome payoff in terms of increased confidence in the validity and reliability of the findings that are produced by future causal analyses of judicial behaviour. In sum, work with more rigorous theory will impel a greater concern for problems of method; the requirements of more rigorous methodology will direct attention to the quality and level of measurement, and therefore of observations; and sensitivity to the latter requirements will result in more refined research designs that will be *a priori* rather than *post hoc* empirical investigations. The upshot will be data better suited to the needs of future causal analysts than are the data examined in the present study.

— *Glendon Schubert*

REFERENCES

1. Although they are in no way responsible for what appears in the published version of this chapter, I am deeply indebted to Hayward R. Alker, Jr., and Hubert M. Blalock, for their incisive and helpful comments on

an earlier and considerably different draft. I am similarly indebted to Edward J. Weissman for his comments, advice, and assistance on successive drafts of this chapter.

2. Harry Woolf, *Quantification: A History of Measurement in the Natural and Social Sciences* (Indianapolis: Bobbs-Merrill, 1961), especially pp. 31-63 and 204-22; Hubert M. Blalock, Jr., "The Measurement Problem: A Gap Between the Languages of Theory and Research," in Hubert M. Blalock, Jr., and Ann B. Blalock (eds.), *Methodology in Social Research* (New York: McGraw-Hill, 1968), Chap. 1, pp. 5-27; and Hayward M. Alker, Jr., "The Long Road to International Relations Theory: Problems of Statistical Nonadditivity," *World Politics*, 18 (1966), 623-55; and S. Sidney Ulmer, "Mathematical Models for Predicting Judicial Behaviour," in Joseph L. Bernd and Archer Jones (eds.), *Mathematical Applications in Political Science, III* (Charlottesville: University of Virginia, 1967), Chap. 1, pp. 67-95.
3. L. S. Shapley and Martin Shubik, "A Method for Evaluating the Distribution of Power in a Committee System," *American Political Science Review*, 48 (1954), 787-92; William H. Riker, *The Theory of Political Coalitions* (New Haven: Yale University Press, 1963), and "Bargaining in a Three-Person Game," *American Political Science Review*, 61 (1967), 642-56; Walter Murphy, *The Elements of Judicial Strategy* (Chicago: University of Chicago Press, 1964); Glendon Schubert, "Policy without Law: An Extension of the Certiorari Game," *Stanford Law Review*, 14 (1962), 284-327.
4. Herbert A. Simon, "Spurious Correlation: A Causal Interpretation," *Journal of the American Statistical Association*, 49 (1954), 467-79, reprinted as Chapter 2 in his *Models of Man: Social and Rational* (New York: Wiley, 1957).
5. Hubert M. Blalock, Jr., *Causal Inferences in Nonexperimental Research* (Chapel Hill: University of North Carolina Press, 1961); Blalock, "Four-Variable Causal Models and Partial Correlations," *American*

Sociological Review, 68 (1962), 182-94 and 510-12; Blalock, "Causal Inference, Closed Populations, and Measures of Association," *American Political Science Review*, 61 (1967), 130-36; Blalock, "Theory Building and Causal Inferences," in Blalock and Blalock (eds.), *Methodology in Social Research*, Chap. 5, pp. 155-98.

6. Sewall Wright, "The Method of Path Coefficients," *Annals of Mathematical Statistics*, 5 (1934), 161-215; Wright, "Path Coefficients and Path Regressions: Alternative or Complementary Concepts?" *Biometrics*, 16 (1960), 189-202; Wright, "The Treatment of Reciprocal Interaction, with or without Lag, in Path Analysis," *Biometrics*, 16 (1960), 423-45; Warren B. Miller and Donald E. Stokes, "Constituency Influence in Congress," *American Political Science Review*, 60 (1966), 45-56.

7. Hayward M. Alker, Jr., *Mathematics and Politics* (New York: Macmillan, 1965), Chap. 6; Alker, "Causal Inference and Political Analysis." in Joseph L. Bernd (ed.), *Mathematical Applications in Political Science, II* (Dallas: Southern Methodist University, Arnold Foundation Monographs), 14 (1966), 7-43; Alker, "Statistics and Politics: The Need for Causal Data Analysis," (a paper presented at the Annual Meeting of the American Political Science Association, Chicago, September 5-8, 1967).

8. Robert D. Putnam, "Toward Explaining Military Intervention in Latin American Politics," *World Politics*, 20 (1967), 83-110; Donald J. McCrone and Charles F. Cnudde, "Toward A Communications Theory of Democratic Political Development: A Causal Model," *American Political Science Review*, 61 (1967), 72-79.

9. Charles F. Cnudde and Donald J. McCrone, "The Linkage Between Constituency Attitudes and Congressional Voting Behaviour: A Causal Model," *American Political Science Review*, 60 (1966). 66-72; Arthur S. Goldberg, "Discerning A Causal Pattern among Data on Voting Behaviour," *American Political Science Review*, 60 (1966), pp. 913-22; and cf. Aage R. Clausen,

"Measurement Identity in the Longitudinal Analysis of Legislative Voting," *American Political Science Review*, 61 (1967), 1020-35.

10. The initial report of the research was my paper, "The High Court and the Supreme Court: Two Styles of Judicial Hierocracy," (presented at the Annual Meeting of the American Political Science Association, New York City, September 10, 1966).

11. Schubert, "Judicial Attitudes and Policy-Making in the Dixon Court" *Osgoode Hall Law Journal, 7:* No. 1 (forthcoming, October 1969).

12. Schubert, "Political Ideology on the High Court," *Politics* (The Journal of the Australasian Political Studies Association), 3 (1968), 21-40.

13. Schubert, "Opinion Agreement Among High Court Justices in Australia," *The Australian and New Zealand Journal of Sociology, 4* (1968), 1-16.

14. Schubert, "The Dimensions of Decisional Response: Opinion and Voting Behaviour of the Australian High Court," in Joel Grossman and Joseph Tanenhaus (eds.), *The Frontiers of Judicial Research* (New York: Wiley, 1968), Chap. 6, pp. 163-95.

15. See Hubert M. Blalock, Jr., *Causal Inferences in Nonexperimental Research* (Chapel Hill: University of North Carolina Press, 1961), pp. 143-62: "Measurement Error in Nonexperimental Studies"; Paul M. Siegel and Robert W. Hodge, "A Causal Approach to the Study of Measurement Error," in Blalock and Blalock (eds.), *Methodology in Social Research*, Chap. 2, pp. 28-59.

16. In the analysis in this chapter, the most obvious such effect is the large quantum of floating residual error variance, one consequence of which is to confine correlational analysis almost completely to zero and first-order partials, thereby precluding investigation into the more complex multivariate relationships which would need to be explored for better understanding.

17. For a brief presentation of the traditional view—presently under attack —of the historical development

of Australian society, see Russel Ward, *Australia* (Englewood Cliffs, N. J.: Prentice-Hall, 1965); for a contemporary analysis, see A. F. Davies and S. Encel, *Australian Society: A Sociological Introduction* (Melbourne: F. W. Cheshire, 1965), and Robert Alford, *Party and Society* (Chicago: Rand McNally, 1963), Chap. 7.

18. David J. Danelski, "The Japanese Supreme Court: An Exploratory Study," (a paper presented at the 1966 Annual Meeting of the American Political Science Association, New York City, September 10, 1966), p. 17.

19. See my "Behavioural Jurisprudence," *Law and Socitey Review*, 2 (I968). pp. 407-28.

20. The birth dates of the judges in the present sample are: Dixon (Chief Justice), 1886; Webb, 1887; Williams. 1889; McTictnan, February 16, 1892; Fullagar, November 16, 1892; Windeyer, 1900; Taylor, 1901; Kitto, 1903; and Menzies, 1907. In Table 9.2. the age of each judge is scored, to the nearest tenth of a year, up to January 1, 1955, and January 1, I960, the approximate midpoints of the two periods.

21. Actually, there was only a single tally for a third category which was for Webb, a Queenslander, during the 1951-58 period. For the other judges, however, the sample was dichotomized, with Victoria coded as +2 and New South Wales as +1, as Table 9.2 shows.

22. "Judicial Attitudes and Policy-Making in the Dixon Court," Table 1.

23. For a detailed discussion of these scales, see my "Judicial Attitudes and Policy-Making in the Dixon Court," especially Figures 1-4. My original research design called for field interviews which would have provided me with a direct measure of the attitudes of the judges in my sample. However, I did not succeed in attracting at an appropriate time the necessary support for this projected phase of the research. Consequently, I have had to rely, for present purposes, on the cumulative voting scales, a more indirect and

inferential measure of judicial attitudes. Cf. Harry S. Upshaw, "Attitude Measurement," in Blalock and Blalock (eds.), *Methodology in Social Research,* Chap. 3, pp. 60-111.

24. See my "The Dimensions of Decisional Response," especially Table 6.7 and Figures 6.1-6.2, at pp. 183, 187, 188.

25. Louis Guttman, "The Principal Components of Scalable Attitudes," in Paul Lazarsfeld (ed.), *Mathematical Thinking in the Social Sciences* (New York: Free Press, 1954), Chap. 5, p. 225.

26. For a discussion of the theory and method of this procedure, see my *The Judicial Mind: Attitudes and Ideologies of Supreme Court Justices, 1946-1963* (Evanston: Northwestern University Press, 1965), Chaps. 2 and 3.

27. See my "Opinion Agreement Among High Court Justices," especially Figure 1 and Table IV. at pp. 7 and 8.

28. Ibid, and op. cil. n. 14, *supra.*

29. This statistical assumption is certainly plausible, given my substantive assumption that each of these exogenous variables is an index of conservative ideology.

30. For a general discussion of liberal ideology, by an Australian political scientist, see Kenneth R. Minogue, *The Liberal Mind* (New York: Random House, 1964).

31. See my "Behavioural Jurisprudence," pp. 411-14 and Figure 1.

32. Cf. the discussion of dynamic models in Edward J. Weissman, "Mathematical Theory and Dynamic Models," Chap. 13, *infra.*

33. Hubert M. Blalock, Jr., *Social Statistics* (New York: McGraw-Hill, 1960), pp. 329-43; and Hayward M. Alker, Jr., *Mathematics and Politics* (New York: Macmillan, 1965), p. 126. Both references give the formula for partial correlation.

34. For further detail see my "Judicial Attitudes and Policy-Making in the Dixon Court, " Table2.

35. See my "The Dimensions of Decisional Response."
36. See the section on "Participation" in my "Judicial Attitudes and Policy-Making in the Dixon Court."
37. Bernard Berelson and Gary A. Steiner, *Human Behaviour: An Inventory of Scientific Findings* (New York : Harcourt, Brace & World, 1964), "Face-to-Face Relation in small Groups," Chap.8.
38. Hans J. Eysenck, *The Psychology of Politics* (London: Routledge and Kegan Paul, 1954), pp. 111-14; and my "Idologies and Attitudes, Academic and Judical,"*Journal of Politics, 29* (1967), 3-40.
39. At the zero-order level of correlation, $r_{DX=-.}$466, signifying that judges from Victoria are less collectivist in their attitudes than are judges from New South Wales.
40. Because the two new judges were much younger than predecessors, the court's average age increased only slightly, from 61.6 to 62.1. However, five of the seven judges were, as individuals, each five years older during the second period (on the average) than they were during the first.
41. See my "Judicial Attitudes and Policy-Making in the Dixon Court," "Political Ideology on the High Court," "Opinion Agreement Among High Court Justices in Australia," and "The Dimensions of Decisional Response."
42. Schubert, "Opinion Agreement Among High Court Justices." p. 15.
43. Schubert,"The Dimensions of Decisional Response," p. 188.

10

MATHEMATICAL THEORY AND DYNAMIC MODELS[1]

Methodological elegance and statistical rigor have increasingly become hallmarks in empirical research in judicial behavior.[2] This degree of sophistication is characteristic only of the ways in which the data are manipulated, which is also the case with much research in political science generally. Theorizing and theory-building have remained largely verbal. Thus, while the substance of behavioral theories is quite different from the more traditional formulations,[3] the method of theorizing remains basically the same. This concern with verbal theories serves, unfortunately, to widen the gap between theory and measurement.[4] Complex, abstract, and wide-ranging schema are difficult, if not impossible, to operationalize.[5] More serious is the ambiguity which inheres in verbal formulations. In the process of operationalizing some verbal concepts, one is forced to deal with the problems of precision and measurement at the same time. Given the usual problems of measurement in political science, one is forced, if one is to do empirical research at all, to compromise the ideal of perfect measurement. More serious than the amount of error which poor measurement introduces into the analysis, is the problem of loss of precision which this entails. If the theory is expressed verbally, we are in the position of never being precise. An example will illustrate the point.

At a conceptual level, systems theory may be helpful even if it is not testable.[6] The benefits of theorizing explicitly are lost when the theory may be expressed in such a loose fashion. Thus, deductive theorizing is only marginally better than relying on intuitions and guesses. In some instances, one is forced to guess at the meaning of theoretical constructs as well as to ignore the question of validity of the operational measures. While one can never completely close the gap between theory and research, it is possible to make our theories much more precise. Through the use of mathematical formulations, we can maximize two important goals: theoretical precision, and the retention of abstract theory.

At this time, inductive theorizing suffers from a similar set of problems. Divergent findings from one or from different studies are often synthesized verbally. Whenever the literature is reviewed it often resembles more a bibliographical essay than an exercise in theory-building. If our theories are expressed as a set of equations, we can then present our formulations with a set of unknowns. Predictions may be either in the form of a precise specification of the value of an unknown, or in a more general statement as to sign. In this way, similarities both between and among theories are made apparent. One might, for example, notice that a given theory is a "special case" of another formulation. In addition, by explicitly noting the differences and similarities among theories, we can concentrate the empirical research on the differences in order to decide between "competing" theories. In comparative politics, mathematical theories serve to integrate the vast amount of data which must, because of the enormity of the domain under investigation, be collected by many scholars over long periods of time. These mathematical formulations are abstract so that different operational theories may be used in different cultures.[7] In addition to providing a focus for research, a general mathematical model provides an organizing device for its findings.

CROSS-CULTURAL RESEARCH AND THEORIES OF CHANGE

A second issue in theorizing about comparative political behavior is the type of theory we need to guide our research. One strategy would call for typologies of regimes or systems.[8] Theories are often confined to the syslems which fall within the categories of analysis. As such, one finds a special theory for economically developed democracies, another for Communist regimes, another for former colonial possessions, and so forth. However, one might well contend that a lesser problem with typologies is that they are not consistent, i.e. the problem is not the typologies themselves, but adequate typologies as opposed to inadequate ones.[9] It would seem, though, that typologies, no matter how elegant, serve to concentrate research on within-category variation and thus leave important questions in a never-never land between types. That is to say, one ignores the problems of the study of change. One is led to a teleologial perspective in which the developing nations are postulated as moving, on some dimension, in the direction of the developed nations. In this sort of model, one's comparisons are among sets of static models. That is, one studies different polities that are assumed to be at different stages of development. The linkage is provided by the assumption of an "end-state" of development. But the result is a contradiction—a static theory of change. One reason for this failure to deal with change as the central concern of our theories is the lack of a general theoretical model. In addition, mathematical models and empirical research have been largely based on algebra. Differential equations, however, are more appropriate to the study of change. We must increasingly turn from algebra to calculus, both to formulate and to test theories of change. As I shall argue later, even if we are interested in stability, we shall need dynamic formulations to test whether the system under study will ever reach the conditions for the stability that we wish to study.[10]

It would seem that there are a number of issues that are closely tied to the formulation of dynamic models. Let us briefly note the ways in which they are interrelated. First, mathematical formulations can serve as conceptual ordering tools. That is, through mathematical notions of change and stability, we can better deal with these concepts as they relate to the phenomena we study. Mathematical formulations—especially differential equations—allow us to study change, which increasingly is becoming of interest to students of comparative politics. We might note, as an example, the growth of the field of political development.[11] Mathematical formulations can be of use for speculating because they have two advantages over verbal theorizing: they are precise; and through various sorts of manipulations, we can see some of the implications of the speculations.

Theories of change, as now formulated, are adequate only for the study of within-model change; they cannot go beyond a given model. Let us be explicit. Assume a typical multiple regression equation such as this one:

$$Y = A + B_1X_1 + B_2X_2 + B_3X_3 + e \quad (1)$$

We can account for change in Y by changes in the values of the independent variables (X_1, X_2, X_3). But even if the error term is not large, we cannot account for deviations from the model. And if we move to recursive causal models,[12] they also cannot account for such deviations. There is no way to account for the fit of different sets of data to different models unless we deal with these different data in terms of a more general model. It would appear to be desirable to develop models which can account for the observed differences between lower-order models. In this sense, theories of change can be introduced.

This chapter is concerned with the presentation of a dynamic model of judicial behaviour as a guide to future comparative research. The model, expressed as a series of differential equations, appears to be applicable to a wide variety of empirical situations and might well serve as a guide for further theorizing as well as for research. Before we deal with the model, it is necessary to show how it was developed out of a series of static models formulated by this author as a result of their apparent inadequacies. It is to these that we now turn. We shall first discuss the state of empirical research in judicial behavior and how this led to the formulation of a series of static models. Then from these models, we shall move to a consideration of a dynamic model.

SOCIAL BACKGROUNDS AND JUDICIAL DECISIONS

It is not surprising that developments within the field of political science have reached a point such that causal modeling techniques now are being applied to the study of social background characteristics and decisional behavior of judges. In one sense, these causal models serve to make explicit the concerns of earlier research. Such work tended to begin with operational concepts far removed from the sophisticated constructs that they purported to tap. In one form or other, the available biographical data was converted into variables. Given the low level of conceptualization and the poor quality of the measurements, most of the findings were negative.[13] That is, social background characteristics tended to be weakly correlated with various conceptualizations of voting variables.[14] In addition to the questions raised by their cross-sectional and static character, three other problems were present in these research projects.

The first, already noted, was the failure at the conceptual and theoretical level to decide just what concepts were being operationalized and measured. This included the failure to measure the dependent decisional variables at a level of sophistication greater than that of dichotomized categories of cases. The second problem involved a failure to specify the relations among the variables. By and large, the research reports consisted of a series of two-variable measures of association. Thus, questions about the relations among the independent variables and the conceptual communalities of the operationally discrete categories of cases were ignored.[15] Finally, the problems of measuring stimuli were either ignored or treated in an ad hoc fashion. In many studies, there was no way of knowing whether judges of different courts were being asked the same questions.[16] Yet, some analysts assumed (probably incorrectly) that this was the case. In more general methodological terms, an important unmeasured variable which could perhaps account for the observed differences among judges was ignored.

For the problem at hand, three partial solutions were adopted. Causal model analysis served as a means of dealing with the relations of the variables in the system. Cumulative scales of cases expressed within the common metric of a factor analysis of all dissensual decisions served conceptually to organize the dependent variables.[17] Finally, the problem of measuring the stimuli (cases) was controlled out by studying just one court. This had the disadvantage of reducing the size of the samples to a point where sampling error was enormous.

I have previously formulated some recursive causal models of decision-making by the United States Supreme Court. Using some data from this project for examples, I shall illustrate some uses for causal modeling techniques in dealing with unmeasured variables in static models, and how the results of these manipulations lead to a formulation of a more general dynamic model.

RECURSIVE CAUSAL MODELS

Within the restrictive assumptions of recursive causal models,[18] it is possible to make some tests of relations among variables. It is also possible, if we make some further assumptions, to infer the relation between unmeasured variables and those which are explicitly included in the system. In terms of the usual problems of data collection in comparative research, this allows us to make inferences about relations which we cannot directly observe. In addition, our discussion of these inferences will serve to illustrate a problem with recursive causal models. This problem results from the disparities from among a set of causal models. When we formulate a dynamic model, this will allow us to sub-stantively account for these changes in the relations among variables, and to test some of the assumptions which have been made in the recursive models. Thus, a dynamic model will account for change if this is indeed the case, or it will allow us to explain the variance between the models as the result of incorrect assumptions which must be made if we use recursive models. In short, dynamic models can account for change and do not require as restrictive a set of assumptions as recursive models.

In this section, we shall illustrate a new use for causal modelling and at the same time use some of the findings to formulate a dynamic model. In social background studies of judges, a crucial intervening variable—ideology—is frequently omitted. This is the result of two problems: how to measure ideology directly; and the static character of social background formulations. With the exception of the surveys conducted by Nagel[19] and Dator,[20] discussions of judicial belief systems have been confined to various psychometric techniques for inferring belief systems from observed behaviours.[21] In terms of causal models, including such psychometric measures along with the decisional outcomes would be tautological. As such, this inferential method of measuring judicial attitudes and ideologies must be rejected. Moreover, as they presently are conceptualised, social background variables are designed for static analyses. That is to say, a theory of judicial behavior in which social background variables, with values due to a judge's pre-judicial experience, are the independent variables cannot account for change in the behavior of a judge when he is on the court. Thus, we need a measure of ideology that is not a function of the observed votes and which, at the same time, can change in value so that we can account for changes in a judge's behaviour over time.

Given these problems and given also that recursive causal models require that error terms be uncorrelated, we shall show how we can make some estimates about the relations between social background variables and decisional variables, with ideology as an intervening variable. Let us begin by describing our three measured variables. Party-liberalism (Pa) is based on data collected by John Schmidhauser in his study of social backgrounds of U.S. Supreme Court Justices.[22] As conceptualized and measured here, it taps the party identification and wing of that party, both regional and ideological, with which a justice was associated. It is scaled so that it would be hypothesized to correlate positively with liberal voting behavior. The two dependent variables are the C (civil liberties) and E (economic liberalism) scales (measured as factorial projections on the scale axes) taken from three periods of the U.S. Supreme Court. These periods were defined by stable membership on the Court. They are: Period I: 1946-49; Period II: 1949-53; and Period III: 1953-54. The two voting scales are based on the data, grouped by terms, collected and reported by Glendon Schubert in his book *The Judicial Mind*.[23] In my earlier paper on which this analysis is based, it was found that the relatively long periods of time did not add any systematic biases to the results of either the factor analysis or the Guttman scaling. In fact, it was concluded that the longer periods of time had the advantage of providing larger samples of cases with which to work. Figure 10.1 presents the correlations among these variables for the three periods.

With recursive causal models, one must decide a priori which variable causes which. It did not appear reasonable to assume that civil liberties voting behavior caused voting behaviour in economic liberties cases or vice versa. But such a framework of one way causation created problems for the analysis in which the correlation between C and E could not be accounted for by Pa. However, if we are willing to sacrifice (temporarily, of course)

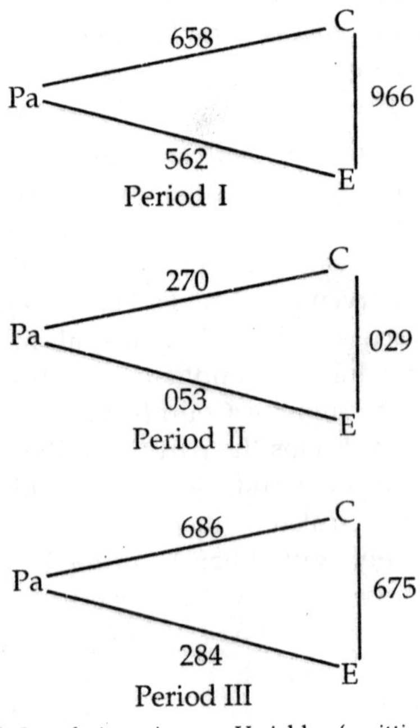

Figure 10.1 Observed Correlations Among Variables (omitting decimals)

our ability to test a model, and are willing instead to be satisfied with greater information about a model we assume to be true, then we can make certain causal inferences about the influence of ideology on the decisional variables (C and E). Let us assume that the relation between C and E is spurious. Mathematically, we can express this in terms of the correlation coefficients, $r_{CE} = (r_{IC}) (r_{IE})$, in which I = Ideology and C and E are defined as above. Empirically, we have one known (r_{IC}) and two unknowns (r_{IC} and

r_{IE}). If we assume, in addition to the usual assumptions of causal models, that C and E are perfectly measured and that I explains as much of C as it does of E, we can solve the equation. The first assumption could be relaxed if we work with the unstandardized regression coefficients and assume that measurement error were only random.[24] Since we are attempting to illustrate more than to test our method, the correlation coefficients should suffice. We should remember that C and E are ordered metrics which are treated as interval scales. Later, too, when we bring in Pa, it should be remembered that Pa is also an ordinal scale that is being treated as interval.

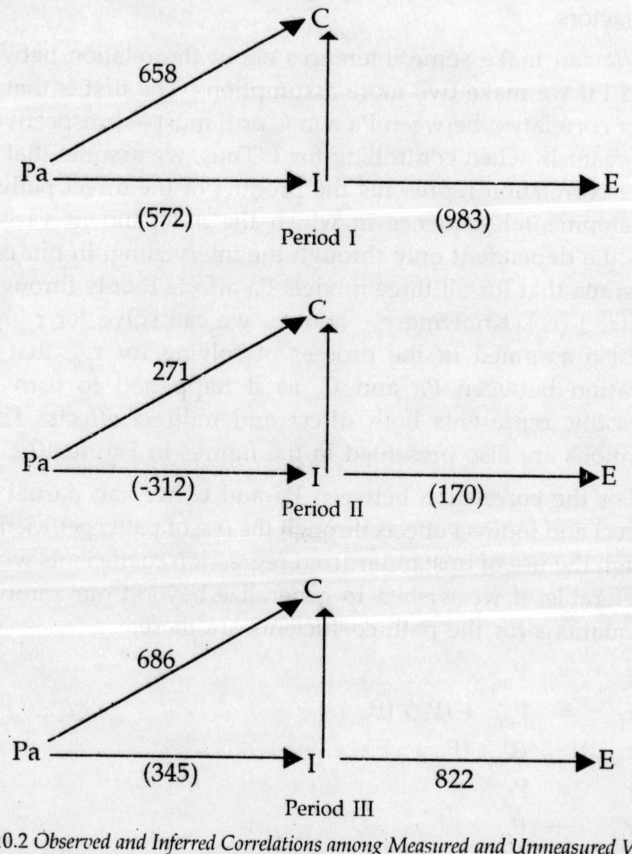

Fig 10.2 *Observed and Inferred Correlations among Measured and Unmeasured Variables (omitting decimals; inferred correlations for unmeasured variable inparentheses*

The second additional assumption, equality of correlation, would seem reasonable in light of some of the findings in *The Judicial Mind.* For the seventeen-year period covered in that book, there was an approximately equal number of C and E cases.[25] In addition, the first factorial (inferred ideological) dimension tended to be equally correlated with both scale axes.[26] Inasmuch as we have assumed that $r_{CE} = (r_{IC})\ (r_{IC})$ and that $r_{IC} = r_{IE}$, simple algebraic manipulations inform us that $r_{IC} = \sqrt{(r_{IC})\ (r_{IE})}$ as does r_{IE}. The empirical solutions are presented in Figure 10.2. Our spuriousness model is analogous to a factor analytic model in which the observed correlations are assumed to be accounted for by one or more factors.

We can make some inferences about the relation between Pa and I if we make two more assumptions. The first is that the smaller correlation between Pa and C or E must— irrespective of sign— vanish, when controlling for I. Thus, we assume that the weaker correlation represents the product of the direct paths in a developmental sequence in which the independent variable affects the dependent only through the intervening. In our case, we assume that for all three models Pa affects E only through I: $I_{PaE} = (r_{PaI})\ (r_{IE})$. Knowing r_{PaE} and r_{IE}, we can solve for r_{PaI}. We have also assumed in the process of solving for r_{PaI}, that the correlation between Pa and C, as it happened to turn out empirically, represents both direct and indirect effects. These correlations are also presented in the figures in Figure 10.2.

For the correlation between Pa and C, we can partial out the direct and indirect effects through the use of path coefficients,[27] although the use of unstandardized regression coefficients would be preferable, if we wished to generalize beyond our sample.[28] The equations for the path coefficients are these:

$$
\begin{aligned}
r_{PaI} &= P_{IPa} \\
r_{Pac} &= P_{CPa} + (P_{CI})\ (P_{IPa}) \\
r_{PaE} &= (P_{EI})\ (P_{IPa}) \\
r_{Ic} &= P_{CI} \\
r_{IE} &= P_{EI} \\
r_{CE} &= (P_{EI})\ (P_{CI})
\end{aligned}
\qquad (2)
$$

The only path coefficient that differs from the correlation coefficients in Figures 10.1 and 10.2 is the direct path between C and Pa. Instead of presenting all the path coefficients, which would be largely repetitious, let us present P_{CPa} for each of the three periods in order. They are .096, .324, and .402. These can be compared with the indirect effects of Pa on C which can be calculated by multiplying r_{PaI} by r_{IC}. The later results are the same as the zero-order correlation between Pa and E or, empirically, .562, —.053, and .284.

We can attempt to interpret substantively our results, realizing the huge weight which lies on our assumptions—some of which we know have not been met. In the first period, ideology appears to determine decisional responses almost completely. We might note that this relates to the statistical problem of multi-collinearity, which is a special case of the mathematical problem of identification. This means that when variables are highly correlated, the sampling error approaches infinity. Or, geometrically, a perfect correlation can be expressed by two vectors occupying the same line. Thus, this one line can be placed anywhere in an N-dimensional space without changing the relationship. As correlations approach unity, there are more ways in which they can overlap; whereas, correlations of zero must be expressed as two vectors at right angles to each other. A more intuitive explanation of multi-collinearity is that when two variables are highly correlated, we have no way of knowing that they are separate variables.

Given this, we might note that this period was one in which the Court was made up of two relatively cohesive blocs—one liberal (4) and one conservative (5).[29] The direct path between Pa and C is relatively trivial, reflecting the little that is left after ideology has done its work. In the second period, ideology is relatively unimportant (.17) and the direct path between Pa and C assumes greater import than does the indirect path through I. This might be interpreted as a result of the McCarthy era, in which political events directly influenced decisionai outcomes. We might also note that Pa ceased to be as important as it was in Period I, and most of the influence of party-liberalism was direct, in terms of our model, on C.

The third period is a hybrid since it is between the two other periods. In terms of magnitudes of the correlation coefficients, it resembles the model for the first period. P_{CPa} is not as trivial as it was in Period I and it is even greater than the same coefficient for the second period; however, the indirect path (through I) between Pa and C is greater in value than the direct path, as was the case in Period I. All this might be interpreted in the light of the waning years of the McCarthy era, when the junior Senator from Wisconsin was down but not out.

Needless to say, these interpretations are tentative. A dynamic model will allow us to test for the stability conditions which we assumed when we used algebraic manipulations. Most of our inferences have been based on observations of correlations, which we assumed to be spurious. As such, we must note that mathematically we were assured of some solution to the equations: thus we cannot call our results findings, since we could not have failed to obtain some estimates for the non-observed correlations. That these results were readily interpretable may make our large set of assumptions appear reasonable or they may indicate a very fertile imagination on the part of this analyst. From here we turn to the dynamic model. This section, however, was necessary for two reasons. First, it retraced my own thinking that led up to the dynamic formulation, and thus it is to be hoped that the dynamic model will make more sense, since we have examined some of its intellectual history. Without this, we would be jumping off into differential equations with little or no introduction. The second reason for this section is that it serves to illustrate a possible use for more conventional causal modeling in ways which have not been presented in earlier research or exposition.

FROM STATIC TO DYNAMIC MODELS

Until now we have been working with static models and have assumed one-way causation. The questions of static models and of reciprocal causation are separate issues. However, the formulation of a dynamic model — that is, a model in which time is introduced as an essential notion[30] — will include reciprocal causation. In fact, through the use of time-lags, we will be able to handle reciprocal causation. We replace the methodological simplicity of earlier models with the methodologically more complex, but theoretically more realistic, introduction of reciprocal causation. It must be remembered that this is not simply a movement toward a "better" model. That is to say, the introduction of reciprocal causation into the model is not to be viewed as simply a refinement of an earlier model. Rather, if the data fit such a complex model, the earlier models which had ruled out reciprocal causation by assumption must be rejected and the inferences drawn are not simply insufficient, they are mathematically and statistically biased. They are mathematically biased because one has more unknowns than equations — meaning that one is unable to obtain unique estimates for the coefficients. They are statistically biased in that least-squares procedures give biased estimates. These are two separate problems. The first is the problem of identification. The second involves the lesser problem of statistical estimation. If we can identify the equations, the second problem becomes one of finding and using other estimation techniques.

An illustration is necessary to elucidate the point that the models which allow for reciprocal causation and feedback replace rather than supplement recursive models. An example of supplementation in the field of judicial behavior is illustrated by the change from the one-dimensional model of the Supreme Court assumed by C. Herman Pritchett in his book *The Roosevelt Court*[31] to the multi-dimensional model presented by Glendon Schubert in *The Judicial Mind*.[32] I can best illustrate the point in terms of the problem in factor analysis of when to stop extracting factors. Pritchett had what can be viewed the first factor—general liberalism. The model which Schubert has presented continued the factoring to the third and fourth principal components.[33] In this sense, the multi-dimensional model provided a better fit to the data than a one-dimensional model. The question, in factor analysis, of when the fit is "good enough" appears to have been solved by the apparently ad hoc preference of analysts as well as computer programers for setting the cut-off at eigen values of less than unity, which makes mathematical, but not necessarily theoretical, sense. This is more generally the problem when one is adding refinements to a model and when one has begun to describe everything as unique, i.e. there are as many factors as variables in the analysis. Returning to the general discussion, the Schubert model does not falsify the Pritchett model. Rather it adds to Pritchett's model and provides a better fit to the data (it explains more of the variance). Pritchett's model is not incorrect; it is merely incomplete. With it, we face a different sort of problem. If there is a significant amount of reciprocal causation, and I shall leave "significant" undefined, then our recursive models are not incomplete, as was Pritchett's; they are an artifact. We cannot meet the assumptions for recursive models and the results are not mathematically interpretable.

Because we have made the assumptions for our static models does not mean that we ought to have made them. If, to a major degree, our assumptions were unwarranted, then we must build more complex models. These models will have the incidental advantage of allowing us to test *some* of our earlier assumptions. Perhaps, as a result, we will be dealing with more realistic assumptions.[34]

Another problem with the earlier models is that important variables may have been omitted. This is not necessarily a problem. However, if any of the variables which we have left out are related to more than one of the included variables (except as through the other variables explicitly in our system), then we have violated the vital assumption of uncorrelated error terms. This is of substantive importance in that we might have left out a variable or variables which are creating spurious relations both between and among the variables in the model. Methodologically, the problem is of greater import. If our error terms are correlated, we run into the problem of identification. That is to say, we cannot get unique estimates. This illustrates how the substantive problem of unmeasured variables and the substantive problem of reciprocal causation are intimately related to the fundamental methodological and mathematical problem of identification. We now turn to a brief discussion of the identification problem.

The Identification Problem[35]

$$25 = A + B + C \tag{3}$$

This simple equation illustrates the identification problem. There are an infinite number of solutions that are mathematically correct for A, B, and C. Although this is not the place to discuss the problem in great detail, it is important to discuss how it relates to model building. With recursive models and the assumption of uncorrelated error terms, there are enough equations and the unknowns are so distributed among the equations that we can obtain unique estimates for the coefficients. In addition, we can use least-squares estimates. To test the recursive models, we must go further and set some of the b's equal to zero. These are the predictions. Because we have identified the equations, we can get unique estimates. Comparing these estimates with the prediction, we can evaluate the model. Needless to say. it would also be possible to set some of the b's equal to any other number. At this stage, however, our hypotheses and body of theory are too small and not adequate enough to make such precise predictions possible.

If, in fact, there is sizeable reciprocal causation or the error terms are correlated, the equations can no longer be identified. Our least squares estimates are an artifact. One solution to the identification problem is to search for new variables that enter into the model. This must be done by assumption and be handled in such a way that we no longer have the problem of excess unknowns. It then becomes a question of finding new variables which are related to only some of the endogenous variables in the system. It is entirely possible that we might wind up with a situation in which we can identify only some of the equations. Depending on what and how much we wish to test, this might serve as a partial solution. The major problem is finding such new variables. These variables — the exogenous ones — must, by assumption, be related to the endogenous variables in such a way that we can meet the necessary and sufficient conditions for identification.

Another way in which we can bring in new variables is by allowing for limited reciprocal causation and feedback. We can create new variables which are, in fact, lagged endogenous variables in which time is continuous. We can have X_1 at time 0 affecting X_2 at time 0 which in turn affects X_1 at time 1 , if we assume discrete time. In short, we can deal with the problem of reciprocal causation either by finding exogenous variables which allow us to identify the equations for the endogenous variables or by reconceptualizing the relations among the endogenous variables in terms of lagged variables or else by some combination of both of these approaches.

Needless to say, we must still make some untestable assumptions. However, these assumptions are not as restrictive as those of the recursive models. At bottom, we must make a major epistomological assumption. We cannot allow everything to cause everything else at one time. Such a situation or hypothesis is mathematically insoluable if one wants to obtain unique values. We must assume that the world is bloc recurtive. That is to say, there may be reciprocal causation within blocs of variables as well as one-way causation between such blocs. The next question should be: what are the necessary conditions for identification? I cannot deal with this exceedingly complex subject here, other than by directing attention to a discussion of it by several leading social statisticians and econometricians.[36]

DYNAMIC MODELS

As noted, one solution to the identification problem (which is the result of reciprocal causation and the failure of the phenomena to meet the assumptions of recursive models) is to deal with reciprocal causation in terms of time-lags. This means that we move from static models to dynamic models. Mathematically we must move from algebraic equations, which assume instantaneous effects, to differential equations and calculus. This latter mathematical representation assumes change is continuous.

Algebraic equations make the assumption that the system of variables is in equilibrium. As noted earlier, the shocks from the environment must be assumed to leave the system in an equilibrium. Allowing for reciprocal causation means that shocks which come into the system of endogenous variables could reverberate through the system back and forth among the variables with the possibility that stability is never attained. An increase in X may lead to an increase in Y which leads to an increase in Z which increases X, spiralling, until the system explodes. We must, in constructing dynamic models, be concerned with whether the stability conditions have been met.

It might be argued that dynamic models are important to know about if one is interested in the process of change. However, if one is interested in the study of equilibria, it is not necessary to study dynamic models. For instance, if we assume that during the 1937 court-packing fight the time in the U.S. was one of disequilibrium in which the Court was subjected to great disturbing influences from the environment, it might be argued that the time before 1937 was a conservative period for the Supreme Court and was a time of equilibrium and stability (among the variables). In addition, it might be argued that the post-New Deal Court (the "liberal" Supreme Court) is a period in which a new equilibrium has been reached with a period of stability. Such a model would serve the important function of precisely defining what we mean by the "old" and "new" Court. In fact, it would appear that this would serve as an operational definition of what is meant by "periods" in the history of the Supreme Court. On this level, such an argument would be quite acceptable. Indeed, this would serve as an interesting hypothesis. However, it might be argued that the major interest of the scholar is in stability. The court-packing plan was a once-in-a-lifetime or at least once-in-a-generation affair. Such a position would indicate that studies should involve only the periods of stability. Technically, such a research strategy would option the study of comparative statics. As Blalock has pointed out, following the discussion by Samuelson and others, comparative statics can be studied only if they are embedded within a dynamic model.[37] With a dynamic model, even if we are not interested in how stability is obtained, we can determine whether the necessary and sufficient conditions for stability have been met. In this way, we can test whether the system does, in fact, achieve stability. Thus, in simplest terms, a dynamic model is necessary if we are to discover whether there are any static situations to study. Of course, if our interest is in change, then no other justification for dynamic models is necessary.

FORMULATING THE MODEL

Of greatest substantive interest, as noted in our static models, were the relations and variables close to the decision-making process itself. As noted, there are a number of alternative hypotheses to explain the differential results for the different time periods. One hypothesis is that due to variables of exogenous shocks (either Senator McCarthy, et al., or personnel changes on the Court), the relations among the variables were in disequilibrium. Perhaps it took several years for an equilibrium to be established. In such a model, we must take into account questions of stability. Our task in this section is to formulate such a model and then specify what the stability conditions are. We shall confine ourselves to linear differential equations and the necessary conditions for stability.

One variable, or set of variables, which was left out of our previous model was the sociometric relations among the judges. These interactions might be hypothesized to intervene between ideology and decisional outcomes. Such a variable might well be reciprocally related to both ideology and decisions. That is, patterns of interactions are determined by and also determine ideology. In addition, patterns of interaction determine outcomes, and perhaps also are determined by the outcomes. In the latter case, for example, the relations between two justices might not be affected by their ideological positions. They are prepared to allow their brethren to "keep scrubbing,"[38] even when, as Holmes contended, their position "won't wash." What might affect interactions is that one side won—not that they were wrong. Because many judges have served in the political wars for many years, and because the courts are political institutions, it would seem reasonable that politization, which involves socialization into the political and bargaining milieu, would be explicitly a variable to be included within the system. Figure 10.3 presents a model which gives the possible inter-relationships. While the entire four-variable model forms a loop, there is reciprocal causation between ideology (I) and group interactions (G), as well as between the latter and decisions (D). The one-way path between D and politization (P) and the path between P and I close the loop. The small closed loops represent feedback. They denote our ignorance. They represent other variables which form loops between the specific variable and themselves.

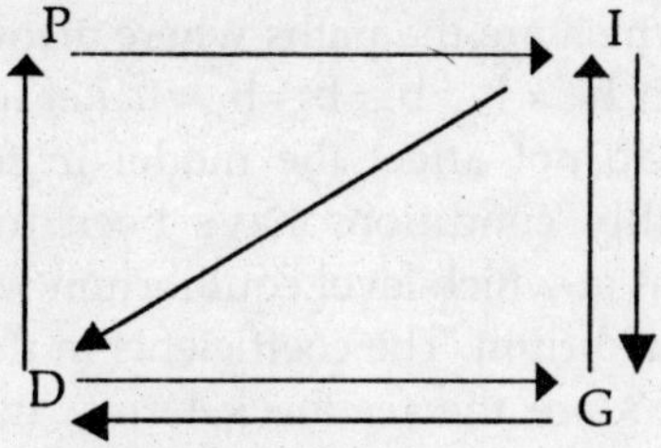

Figure 10.3 *A Dynamic Model*

A major assumption is that effects are lagged. For instance, ideology may affect group interactions which later affect ideology. For instance, the famous feud between Justices Jackson and Black[39] involving, on the manifest level, the Jewell Ridge Coal case[40] subsequently affected politization and possibly ideology: witness Jackson's return to economic conservatism with the failure of his political ambitions.[41] This might well have continued to reverberate through the system, because of the feedback loops or the relations among the variables, until the system exploded. Since this did not occur (although Jackson's telegrams might be viewed as a sort of minor explosion), we might infer that stability conditions were met.

Remembering that we must change notation (since conventional notation is least-squares notation and least-squares estimates are inappropriate here), we can number our variables from 1 to 4. Let $P=X_1$, $I=X_2$, $G=X_3$, $D=X_4$. We can write the differential equations for the model:

$$\frac{dX_1}{dt} = b_{11}X_1 + b_{14}X_4$$

$$\frac{dX_2}{dt} = b_{21}X_1 + b_{22}X_2 + b_{23}X_3$$

$$\frac{dX_3}{dt} = b_{32}X_2 + b_{33}X_3 + b_{34}X_4 \quad (4)$$

$$\frac{dX_4}{dt} = b_{42}X_2 + b_{43}X_3 + b_{44}X_4$$

The remaining b's (which are the paths where arrows have been left out) are set to zero: $b_{12} = b_{13} = b_{24} = b_{31} = b_{41} = 0$. Let us ignore the constants since they do not affect the model in terms of whether or not the stability conditions have been met. The constants would only tell us at which level equilibrium would be reached—if there were equilibrium. The coefficients in the major diagonal of a matrix of b's are the feedback terms. In matrix form, the b's are as follows:

$$\begin{vmatrix} b_{11} & 0 & 0 & b_{14} \\ b_{21} & b_{22} & b_{23} & 0 \\ 0 & b_{32} & b_{33} & b_{34} \\ 0 & b_{42} & b_{43} & b_{44} \end{vmatrix} \qquad (5)$$

The first necessary condition for stability is that the sum of the feedback terms be negative. The second condition is that the determinant of the slope matrix $|b_{ij}|$ be positive since we have an even number of variables. Solving for $|b_{ij}|$, we get:

$$\begin{vmatrix} b_{11} & 0 & 0 & b_{14} \\ b_{21} & b_{22} & b_{23} & 0 \\ 0 & b_{32} & b_{33} & b_{34} \\ 0 & b_{42} & b_{43} & b_{44} \end{vmatrix} = b_{11} \begin{vmatrix} b_{22} & b_{23} & 0 \\ b_{32} & b_{33} & b_{34} \\ b_{42} & b_{43} & b_{44} \end{vmatrix} - b_{14} \begin{vmatrix} b_{21} & b_{22} & b_{23} \\ 0 & b_{32} & b_{33} \\ 0 & b_{42} & b_{43} \end{vmatrix}$$

$$= b_{11}\,(b_{22}\,b_{33}\,b_{44} + b_{23}\,b_{34}\,b_{42} - b_{22}\,b_{34}\,b_{43} - b_{23}\,b_{32}\,b_{44}) - b_{14}\,(b_{21}\,b_{32}\,b_{43} - b_{21}\,b_{33}\,b_{42}) \qquad (6)$$

The first condition is met if all feedback is negative. However, if the negative coefficients are larger than the positive coefficients, then the first necessary condition can be met even if some of the feedback loops are positive. This can be illustrated by the Black-Jackson feud. The negative feedback terms would simply imply that strong institutional pressures, from both within and without the Court, dampened the overt conflict. The appointment of Vinson as a "peace-making" Chief Justice would be an example of such a negative feedback. Some positive feedback might be tolerated within the first necessary condition for stability. However, there is also the problem of the sufficient conditions for stability which might be violated if some of the feedback is positive.

The second necessary condition for stability is that the determinant in equation six be positive. What we can observe is that the negative terms in the equation must be less than the positive terms. Specifically, b_{21} b_{32} b_{43} must be a very weak path, that is, the loop which runs from politization through ideology and group interactions to decision-making. Presumably this could be achieved by a weak link between P and I. This makes greater sense in light of the rest of the equation. For stability, the feedback term of politization must be negative (condition 1); however, it cannot be a strong negative value because it is the multiplier for the first part of the determinant, which must be greater than zero (condition 2). What appears to be intuitively reasonable in this model is that, in general, stability must be attained in the relationships among J, G, and D. P must be weak enough that it does not "disturb" the equilibrium among the other three variables. The path which closes the grand loop (p_{14}) must be fairly weak or the system will not be stable. This assumes a great deal about the other coefficients. However, as we shall see, it comports with what we might expect. Of greater importance to stability is the feedback term b_{33} which, if it is strongly negative, will lead to stabilized relationships among I, G, and D.

Up until now, we have been dealing with lagged endogenous variables as a solution to the identification problem—a problem which was made explicit by the introduction of reciprocal causation and feedback. Remembering that feedback terms are a summary of variables which we have not included (or have not thought of), we can begin to look for variables which are part of the feedback terms. In addition, we can attempt another solution to the identification problem by looking for some exogenous variables that allow us to identify the coefficients of the endogenous variables. By assumption, we shall introduce the stimuli (cases) as an exogenous variable affecting G. That is to say, the relevant issues—dimensions and "facts" of the cases—are established through the group decision-making process.

This implies that the sociometric relationships among the judges structure the issue. Consequently, a consensual judgment is reached as to where the stimulus is located in a multidimensional space. Such an introduction complicated our model to a fairly important extent since the relation between ideology and stimuli is not additive. Rather, it is multiplicative. Conceptualizing the relation between i and j points as a dominance relation, we can allow the stimuli to take on the value of zero and one (i>j and j>i, respectively). Conceptualizing a conservative vote as zero and a liberal vote as one, we can deal with the relation between stimuli and ideology as a binary multiplicative relation. This introduction complicates our model because non-additive (non-linear) systems of differential equations are more difficult to evaluate. There are no general solutions for non-linear differential equations.[42]

To summarize these speculations, we can find that a rigorous statement (in terms of differential equations) of more complex models is an aid to an intuitive understanding of some of the phenomena we wish to grasp. Because our initial speculations are stated as equations, it is most important that the movement to more rigorous statements and to the eventual testing of such models is made much easier.

The model presented here might serve as an interesting starting point. It was originally drawn on the basis of some fairly diffuse hunches. More and more, as I played around with the equations and thought of empirical examples which would fit the model, it appeared to fit some intuitive notions which one finds in much of the literature.[43] While I do not contend that this tests the intuitive notions, nor would it be reasonable to say that my intuitive notions are better than more traditional speculations, it does seem that speculating with these sorts of models has the advantage that the models are explicit about what the relations are. In addition, the mathematical framework will serve as the framework for testing the models when measurement and sampling error are less of a problem then they are now. Then, also, we can begin to worry about estimation procedures.

An example of an interesting speculation is the role of group decision-making processes. As we saw, stability depends to a large extent on the feedback term b_{33}. This simply means that the conference serves as a stabilizing influence on the decision-making of the U.S. Supreme Court. As we know, during the period around the court-packing plan and for some time before, the conference system broke down. Caucuses of the four conservatives and the three liberals served as sub-group conferences in which the important group decisions were made.[44] What this means, in terms of our model, was that b_{33} was probably close to zero. Mathematically, stability conditions could not be met. And then the court became involved in its greatest crisis in history. Perhaps, we can similarly interpret the Black-Jackson feud. The import is that these sorts of models begin the task of moving us beyond verbal speculations and theories.

CONCLUSIONS: MATHEMATICAL MODELS AND EMPIRICAL RESEARCH

Despite the introduction of mathematical language into the discussion of judicial behaviour, the model presented remains quite distant from empirical testing. In an attempt to show how testing might be brought in, ascertaining the relevance of the model may be viewed as a first step. More specifically, we shall attempt to show how this model relates to some of the research reported in other chapters of this book.

Taken on its own terms (the theoretical level), the model is weakest in defining the variables included in it. In fact, one might view each of the four variables as a bloc of highly interrelated variables. In addition, the feedback loops (b_{11}, b_{22}, b_{33}, b_{44}) include unmentioned as well as unmeasured variables. We shall assess the relevance of the model on the level of measurement. Following that, we shall view the bi-variate and multi-variate relations presented in earlier chapters as they relate to the relations included in the dynamic model.

Most of the chapters here begin with a discussion of the setting or the milieu. The institutional and cultural parameters of the various judicial bodies and judiciaries are discussed on the verbal level. Conceptually, we may view these parameters as part of the undefined feedback loops. For instance, Hahm's discussion of the community pressures for unanimity[45] may be viewed as part of the feedback loop b_{33}. His chapter suggests the importance of looking at the path from politization to ideology to group decision-making. He notes that the paths are quite weak and that some of the signs are negative. The data suggest that the path b_{14} is negative and that the feedback loop around politization (b_{11}) is quite strong and negative.

Measuring the four variables, we find that most of the chapters have explicitly dealt with one or more of the variables in question. Table 10.1 reports how they relate to the variables in the dynamic model. Ideology is the most frequently discussed variable. However, with the exceptions of the Flango-Schubert and the Dator chapters, the measures are not independent of other variables in the system. In most cases, the ideological variables are inferred from the decisional outputs of the Court. Among this latter group (Kawashima, Danelski, Samonte, Gadbois, Fouts, and Peck), we find two different approaches to the components of the broad ideology variable. One group deals with the variables included within the ideology rubric seriatim (Samonte, Fouts, and Peck). The others (with the exception of Kawashima, who deals with only one component of ideology) attempt to relate the components to each other. The dependent decisional variables in Schubert's chapter are components of the ideology variable expressed within a common framework. Dator's chapter attempts both a discussion of components and their relations, with the advantage that the measurement is independent of the decisional variables.

The other variables in the model are discussed mostly in verbal terms. In the case of some discussions, the feedback loops are the focus. In these cases, they begin to specify the content of the feedback loops and thus suggest ways in which we might improve the model. Finally, we might note that decisions (as a variable) are probably the most difficult to measure apart from their use in inferring other variables in the system. In other words, work is needed on uncontaminated measures of decisions. As the situation now stands, decisions are used primarily to infer ideology (see above) or as manifestations of the group decision-

Table 10.1 The Relations between Empirical Vaiables and Variables in the Model

Author	*Variable*	*Measured*[46]	*Relations to Dynamic Model*
1	*2*	*3*	*4*
Hahm	Politization	Indirect	discriptive discussion of cultural tradition and distribution of attitudes toward adjudication.
	Group decision making	indirect	discussion of forces affecting unanimous decisions.
Ishimura	Decision	direct	decisions as result of exogenous variables: revant to X_4 and b_{44}.
Dator	Ideology	direct-survey	independent measures of X_2.
Kawashima	Backgrounds	direct	exogenous variables.
	Ideology	indirect	inferred from decisions.
	Decisions	direct	suggests effect of X_3 on X_4 as well as the effects of the American Occupation in Japan as an exogenous shock into the through X_1.
Danelski	Backgrounds	direct	exogenous variables.
	Politization	indirect	discussion of effect of exogenous variables on X_1.
	Ideology	indirect	inferred from decisions.
	Ideology	direct	content analysis of speeches.
Samonte	Backgrounds	direct	exogenous variables.
	Ideology	indirect	inferred from decisions—includes change data.
Gadbois	Backgrounds	direct	exogenous variable.
	Ideology	indirect	inferred from decisions.
Flango and Schubert	Ideology	direct-survey	independent measure of a component of X_2.

1	2	3	4
	Decisions	direct-simulated	X_4.
Fotus	Backgrounds	direct	exogenous variable.
	Ideology	indirect	inferred from decisions.
Peck	Ideology	indirect	inferred from decisions.
Schubert	Backgrounds	direct	exogenous variables.
	Ideology	indirect	inferred from backgrounds and from decisions.

making process (see Kawashima's chapter). As a result, it becomes impossible to assess the effects of these variables on each other.

In terms of the bi-variate and multi-variate relationships discussed in certain chapters, we find that multi-variate analysis tends to be confined to measuring components of the ideology variable with the exception of the Flango-Schubert and the Schubert chapters. Table 10.2 reports the links between and among variables expressed in terms of the b's in the dynamic model.

We might also inquire into the methodological relevance of the chapters to the perspective of the dynamic model. Most

Table 10.2: Relations between the Model and Other Chapters

Author	*Relations relevant to model*
Hahm	descriptive
Ishimura	descriptive
Dator	descriptive
Kawashima	b_{32}, b_{42}
Danelski	b_{42}
Samonte	b_{42}
Gadbois	b_{42}
Flango and Schubert	b_{42}
Fouts	b_{42}
Peck	b_{42}
Schubert	b_{32}, b_{42}, b_{43}

relevant are mose chapters which explicitly use causal models (Flango-Schubert, and Schubert). These are followed by those chapters which use multi-variate analysis (Danelski, Dator, and Gadbois). The chapters by Samonte, Fouts, Peck, and Kawashima deal with bi-variate relations; and the chapters by Hahm and Ishimura are largely descriptive.

Our discussion thus far has ignored the social background variable which appears in many of the chapters. This is the major exogenous variable under discussion. It is most frequently conceptualized in terms of a developmental sequence in which ideology is an intervening variable and decisions are the dependent variable. The dynamic model suggests that the relations are a great deal more complex and that this static conceptualization of the social background variable is probably unduly limited.

One major use of any model is heuristic. We can evaluate the model on this basis because it allows us to bring together in a common framework a diverse set of chapters. The model appears to make explicit the differences among the chapters and to suggest their communalities as well. In addition, the feedback loops provide a summary way of dealing with variables and phenomena which are frequently discussed verbally. Given this, we obtain a mathematical representation for some of the looser ideas and concepts while, at the same time, focusing on explicit relations that we postulate as being more important.

— *Edward J. Weissman*

REFERENCES

1. I wish to acknowledge two major intellectual debts to Hubert M. Blalock. Jr.. and to Glendon Schubert. Without their tutelage, I could never have written this paper. I thank James Stimson for his most helpful comments on an earlier draft.

2. See among others, Glendon Schubert, *The Judicial Mind: The Attitudes and Ideologies of Supreme Court Justices, 1946-1963* (Evanston: Northwestern University Press, 1965); Walter F. Murphy and Joseph Tanenhaus, "Public Opinion and Supreme Court: The Goldwater

Campaign," *Public Opinion Quarterly*, 32 (1968), 31-50; S. Sidney Ulmer, "Mathematical Models for Predicting Judicial Behaviour," in Joseph L. Bernd and Archer Jones (eds.), *Mathematical Applications in Political Science, III* (Charlottesville: University of Virginia Press, 1968), Chap. 4. This list is only suggestive and is, of course, in no way exhaustive.

3. Walter Murphy, *Elements of Judicial Strategy* (Chicago: Chicago University Press, 1964); Theodore L. Becker, *Political Behavioralism and Modern Jurisprudence* (Chicago: Rand McNally, 1964). In Murphy's book, certain game theoretic notions are treated and discussed on the verbal level. Becker's book attempts to test some traditional notions in a somewhat experimental design.

4. Hubert M. Blalock, Jr., "The Measurement Problem: A Gap Between the Languages of *Theory* and Research," in Hubert M. Blalock, Jr., and Ann Blalock (eds.), *Methodology in Social Research* (New York: McGraw-Hill, 1968), Chap. 1.

5. This is particularly true of some of the structural-functionalists. Cf. Gabriel A. Almond and James S. Coleman, *The Politics of the Developing Areas* (Princeton: Princeton University Press, 1960), pp. 3-64.

6. David Easton, *A Systems Analysis of Political Life* (New York: Wiley, 1965).

7. For a discussion of a general or main theory which is tested in different ways in different situations (auxiliary theories) see Blalock, "The Measurement Problem."

8. See Almond, *The Politics of Developing Areas;* David Apter, "A Comparative Method for the Study of Politics," *American Journal of Sociology*, 64 (1958), 221-37; Almond and G. Bingham Powell, Jr., *Comparative Politics: A Developmental Approach* (Boston: Little Brown, 1966), Chaps. 9 and 10.

9. This sort of critique is made by Arthur L. Kalleberg. "The Logic of Comparison: A Methodological Note on the Comparative Study of Political Systems." *World Politics*, 19 (1966), 69-82.

10. Hubert M. Blalock, Jr., *Theory Construction* (Englewood Clifts: Prentice-Hall, forthcoming).
11. See Almond and Powell, *Comparative Politics.*
12. See Hubert M. Blalock. Jr., *Causal Models in Nonexperimental Research* (Chapel Hill: University of North Carolina Press. 1964).
13. Cf. the conclusions to Don R. Bowen, "The Explanation of Judicial Voting Behavior from Sociological Characteristics of Judges," (unpublished Ph.D. Dissertation, Yale University, 1965); see also Joel Grossman. "Social Backgrounds and Judicial Docision Making: Notes for a Theory, "*Journal of Politics*, 29 (1967), 334-51.
14. Cf. Bowen, "The Explanation of Judicial Voting Behaviour;" Sheldon Goldman, "Voting Behaviour on the United States Courts of Appeals, 1961-1964," *American Political Science Review* 60 (1966), 374-83; Stuart S. Nagel, "Judicial Characteristics and Judicial Decision-Making" (Unpublished Ph.D. Dissertation, Northwestern University, 1961).
15. Cf. Nagel, "Judicial Characteristics," and Bowen. "The Explanation of Judicial Voting Behavior."
16. Nagel attempts to solve this problem by using a sort of deviation score (from court means) approach. Goldman attempts to explain the problem away. Bowen is led into some questionable conclusions as a result of ignoring the problem. See Bowen, "Judicial Characteristics," pp. 45-46.
17. Cf. Schubert, *The Judicial Mind.*
18. Cf. Blalock, *Causal Models in Nonexperimental Research.* These assumptions are: linearity and additivity, no reciprocal causation, uncorrelated error terms, interval measurement and (by deduction) only random measurement error in only the non-control variables.
19. Stuart S. Nagel, "Off-the-Bench Judicial Attitudes," in Glendon Schubert (ed.). *Judicial Decision-Making*, Vol. 4 of the International Yearbook of Political Behaviour Research (New York: Free Press, 1963), Chap. 2.

20. James A. Dator, "The Life History and Attitudes of Japanese High Court Judges," *Western Political Quarterly*, 20 (1967), 408-39; Dator, "Measuring Attitudes Across Cultures: A Factor Analysis of the Replies of Japanese Judges to Eysenck's Inventory of Conservative-Progressive Ideology," Chapter 4.
21. See Schubert, *The Judicial Mind.*
22. John R. Schmidhauser, "The Justices of the Supreme Court: A Collective Portrait," *Midwest Journal of Political Science.* 3 (1959), 1-57. These data were made available by the Inter-University Consortium for Political Research.
23. Schubert, *The Judicial Mind,* Chap. 5.
24. Cf. Blalock, *Causal Models in Nonexperimental Research,* Chap. 5.
25. Schubert, *The Judicial Mind,* Chap. 5.
26. Ibid, Chap. 7.
27. O. Dudley Duncan, "Path Analysis: Sociological Examples," *American Journal of Sociology,*72 (1966), 1-16.
28. Hubert M. Blalock, Jr., "Causal Inferences, Closed Populations, and Measures of Association," *American Political Science Review,* 61 (1967), 130-36.
29. Schubert, *The Judicial Mind,* pp. 103-13.
30. Frisch, cited in Blalock, *Theory Construction,* Chap. 5.
31. (New York: Macmillan, 1948).
32. *The Judicial Mind,* Chap. 7.
33. The fourth factor is named and discussed in Glendon Schubert, "Simulating the Supreme Court: An Extension of the Tenth Man Game," *Journal of Legal Education* (forthcoming).
34. See Franklin Fisher, *The Identification Problem in Econometrics* (New York: McGraw-Hill, 1966).
35. This discussion is taken from Blalock, *Theory Construction,* Chap. 6.
36. See The *Identification Problem in Econometrics;* Carl F.

Christ, *Econometric Models and Methods* (New York: Wiley, 1966), Chaps. 5 and 6.

37. Blalock, *Theory Construction*, Chap. 6; Paul A. Samuelson, *Foundations of Economic Analysis* (Cambridge: Harvard University Press, 1947), Chap. 3. See also the references cited in Blalock, ibid.

38. This interchange is quoted in Murphy. *Elements of Judicial Strategy*, p. 84.

39. See ibid, p. 55; Eugene Gerhart, *America's Advocate: Robert H. Jackson* (Indianapolis: Bobbs-Merrill, 1958), Chap. 15; John P. Frank, *Mr. Justice Black: The Man and His Opinions* (New York: A. A. Knopf, 1948), Chap. 7. Each of the biographers takes the side of his subject.

40. *Jewell Ridge Coal Corporation v. Local No. 6167, United Mine Workers of America, et al.*, 325 U.S. 161 (1945). See also Jackson's concurring opinion in the denial of the motion for rehearing, *Jewell Ridge Coal Corporation* v. *Local No. 6167, United Mine Workers of America*, 325 U.S. 897 (1945).

41. See Glendon Schubert, "Jackson's Judicial Philosophy: An Exploration in Value Analysis," *American Political Science Review*, LIX (1965), 963.

42. Blalock, *Theory Construction*, Chap. 6.

43. This was especially true of my reading of Murphy, *Elements of Judicial Strategy*.

44. Ibid. 79.

45. Pyong-Choon Hahm, "The Decision Process in Korea," p. 40, Chap. 2.

46. Empirical variables that maintain the distinction among variables in the dynamic model are classified as being directly measured; those which blur the distinction among theoretical variables are classified as indirectly measured.

INDEX

ENCYCLOPAEDIA OF ADMINISTRATIVE LAW

ENCYCLOPAEDIA OF ADMINISTRATIVE LAW

Vol. 2

Indian Administrative Law

Edited by

S.R. Sharma

ANMOL PUBLICATIONS PVT. LTD.
NEW DELHI - 110 002 (INDIA)

ANMOL PUBLICATIONS PVT. LTD.
4374/4B, Ansari Road, Daryaganj
New Delhi - 110 002
Ph.: 23261597, 23278000
Visit us at: www.anmolpublications.com

Encyclopaedia of Administrative Law

First Edition, 2003

ISBN 81-261-1478-9 (Set)

PRINTED IN INDIA

Published by J.L. Kumar for Anmol Publications Pvt. Ltd., New Delhi - 110 002 and Printed at Mehra Offset Press, Delhi.

CONTENTS

Preface

In the modern political era administrative law has taken on a preeminent role in regulating relations between the machinery of government and the individual citizen. At its core is the control of power specifically the review by the judiciary of the way in which executive power has been used. Consequently the subject embraces a huge range of issues, some of them highly politicized. In recent years these have included the legality of a ban on blood sports, whether the courts can order a minister to suspend the operation of a primary Act of Parliament, whether a minister can ban certain types of interview from being broadcast, the powers of local authorities to spend public money, or to refuse to do so, the scope of the discretion vested in the police officers to determine policing policy, the scope of the powers vested in the Home Secretary regarding parole for prisoners convicted of murder, whether the courts could declare invalid an exercise of prerogative power, and the availability of damages in respect of unlawful action by public bodies. It will be seen that it is largely the product of judicial activity, although its existence is increasingly recognised in statutory provisions.

The growth in administrative law has to a large extent mirrored the increase in the level of state involvement in many aspects of every day life during the twentieth century, generating the need for a coherent and effective body of rules to govern relations between individuals and the state. Students of constitutional law will readily recognise that administrative law is in reality an out growth of the doctrine of the separation of powers. It is evidence of the judiciary acting as a check on the powers of the executive, and perhaps even the legislature, in some respects. It should not be assumed, however, that any such coherent and effective body of rules actually exists yet. Administrative law is a constantly evolving subject.

In view of the above consideration in mind about the administrative law, that a comprehensive encyclopaedia has been prepared which focuses on the comparative dimensions of administrative law.

The editor is extremely grateful to the British Council Library in New Delhi, the American Information Centre, New Delhi, and the Central Secretariat Library, New Delhi for their valuable assistance in preparing the encyclopaedia. The editor is equally beholden to Shri J.L. Kumar, Managing Director, Anmol Publications Pvt. Ltd., New Delhi for publishing the encyclopaedia in a very short time.

—Dr. S.R. Sharma

1

ADMINISTRATIVE EVOLUTION IN INDIA — A REVIEW

Administration is a process common to all group effort, public or private, civil or military, large or small scale. It is a process at work in every organised and purposeful activity, and it varies in forms and objects. Although the administration of public and the administration of private affairs differ on many points, there is an underlying similarity, if not identity, in the process of such administration. We are here concerned with public administration and it may be defined approximately as comprising all those purposeful operations and processes for the fulfilment of recognised objectives and the enforcement of public policy. Another clear definition is also given as follows:—

"The system of public administration is the composite of all the laws, regulations, practices relationships, codes and customs that prevail at any time in any jurisdiction from the fulfilment or execution of public policy. The art of administration is the direction, co-ordination and control of many persons to achieve some purpose or objective. It is a dynamic art taking the human and physical resources available in a system of administration and bending them to the achievement of some required goal. An administrator is one who directs, co-ordinates and controls the activities."

Brooks Adams' definition is also interesting. "The administration is the capacity of co-ordinating many and often conflicting social energies in a single organism so adroitly that they shall operate as a unity. This pre-supposes the power of recognising the series of relations between numerous special social interests with all of which no man can be intimately acquainted. Probably no very highly specialised class can be strong in this intellectual quality because of the intellectual isolation incident to specialisation. Yet administration or generalisation is not only the faculty upon which social stability rests but is possibly the highest faculty of the human mind."

The field of administration, therefore, lies wherever any work has to be done. As a philosopher has remarked "the laws do not administer themselves automatically." The practice of the art of administration is comparable to the practice of medicine. Skill and wisdom in handling men, matters and materials are not easily acquired but when successfully acquired their importance and utility are great. The ends of administration are the ultimate objects of the State, the maintenance of peace and order, achievement of social justice, instruction of the young and the adults, protection against disease and its cure, safety and security, adjustment and compromise of conflicting groups and interests, economic and social development, the attainment of higher standard of life and all that ensures full and proper life for all its citizens. What administration is called upon to do has varied in the different stages of human civilisation. While little was expected from administration in the centuries gone by, which have faded into the dim past, and while at one stage people expected to be let alone in their activity, now the expectations from administration cover a wide range of services and protection. The demands made by people upon Government have greatly increased. One main reason for increased reliance upon Government has been the historical process of the transfer of power to Government from absolute kings through various types of aristocracy to the people through democracy. Administration has increasingly become a common agency through which mutual interests approximating to good principles can be explored and preserved, and competing and conflicting interests adjusted. It is through administration that such policy adjustments are made effective and the highest possible standard of human welfare attained.

On the interesting question whether administration is a science or an art W.F. Willoughby wrote:

"In administration there are certain fundamental principles of general application analogous to those characterising any science which must be observed if in the ends of administration, efficiency in operation is to be secured and these principles are to be determined only by the rigid application of the scientific method to their investigation."

Another observation on this matter is as follows:— "On the question of whether administration is chiefly art or science it must be said that while it is and must be both, it is steadily coming to be more than an art and like all other sciences the developing science of administration has several branches. By established usages public administration has come to signify primarily organisation, personnel, practices and procedure essential to the effective performance of all the functions entrusted to the executive branch of the Government. Right throughout, even from historical times, the administration has always been the servant of policy."

Whatever policies have been laid down either by absolute kings or by aristocracies in power or by elected representatives of the people administration has been the instrument and machinery to implement all such policies. The practical tasks of Government have increased many-fold ever since the ancient saying indicating its essentials as "sufficient food, sufficient forces and the confidence of the people." Administration has, therefore, great responsibilities and duties.

Tracing the history of administration in our country from ancient times, it may be said that the concept of complete identity of the State with the king was then predominant. Later development was that the king was not the State but merely a part of it. The State was conceived of as an organic whole with its different constituent parts. The administrative function of the State then was an essential one of protecting the people. Protection not only included the defence of the territory against all possible enemies and the protection of the people against internal disorder or injustice, but also enforcement of protection afforded by customs and traditions of religion and morality. Even land taxation was on this basis. No taxation without protection. Protection was so much needed and so important.

The best illustration of this picture of the State activity including practically every activity is in Kautilya's Arthasastra. The normal form of Government then was Monarchical, the king presiding over the Executive and the Judicial functions, with his ever ready role of the Commander-in-Chief expected to take the lead in the field of battle. The king was having the assistance of his ministers. As Kautilya has put it, "Sovereignty is possible only with assistance, for a single wheel can never move". The king was having his Mantries and also the Mantri Parishad. There were various heads of Departments and Kautilya mentions two very high officials viz., (Sannidhata) and the Samahartha. The former whose designation literally indicated one who attended upon the king was in charge of the Treasury, including the stores, and the latter was the Collector of General Revenues. Among other officials of administration were the Senapathy, the Durgapala (Governor of Forts) and the Anthapala (Governor of Frontier). Village was the Administrative Unit and was under a Gramika. The king appointed the headmen of villages.

A very interesting and instructive chapter in the history of Indian administration is the one relating to the period of ancient Mauryas. The Mauryan empire reached its zenith under Ashoka, grandson of Chandragupta. Ashoka's views of just administration were carved on pillars or rocks throughout his dominions. It is worthy to note one of Ashoka's edicts dealing with the prompt despatch of administrative business. "A long period has elapsed during which in the past business was not carried on or information brought in at all times; when I am eating, or in the ladies' apartments or in my private rooms, or in my conveyance or in the pleasure grounds, everywhere, the persons appointed to give information should keep me informed about the affairs of the people."

"And in all places I attend to the affairs of the people, and if per chance by word of mouth I personally command a donation or injunction or again when a matter of urgency has been committed to the high officers, and in that matter a division or adjournment takes place in the council, then without delay information must be given to me in all places. Such is my command."

His famous edict of toleration is here reproduced:

"His sacred and gracious Majesty the King does reverence to men of all sects, whether ascetics or householders by gifts and various forms of reverence."

His sacred Majesty, however, cares not so much for gifts or external reverence as that there should be growth of the essence of the matter in all sects. The growth of the essence of the matter assumes various forms but the root of which is restraint of speech, to wit a man must not do reverence to his own sect only or disparage that of another without reason. The sects of other people all deserve reverence for one reason or another. By thus acting a man exalts his own sect and at the same time does service to the sects of other people. Such was the broad tolerant and pious injunction enjoined on his administration with a view to securing for all sects recognition, equal and proper treatment.

The Mauryan Empire was divided into a Home Province under the direct control of the Central Government and 4 or 5 outlying provinces each under the rule of a Viceroy who was himself responsible to the Central Government. The administration was highly centralised, elaborately organised and operated by a vast well-trained, and highly paid Bureaucracy. It impinged upon the life of the ordinary man at all points. It prohibited the town-dwellers from being out of doors after a fixed time at night, it regulated prices, it levied tolls, it issued passports, it prescribed the degree of chastisement for offences. Espionage and Intelligence Departments were very well-organised. Spying was not limited to the discovery of offences but the content or discontent of subjects was also engaging the activities of the spy who had also to ascertain and furnish information regarding the leakage of revenue. The required fear and government check on the activities of the officials were provided in an intelligent and widespread measure, contributing to the integrity of the public service.

The king was assisted by a Council which consisted of high officers of the State in charge of various departments, and the Council was concerned with all aspects of administration. Each of the great departments of the State was under the charge of a Minister.

In the Gupta period the pattern and form of Administration was generally similar to that of the Mauryas and was ultimately based on the administration of each village by a Headman with whom was associated the Village Assembly. The Village Assembly appears to have been composed of the representatives and acknowledged leaders of the entire population of the village. Even in the subsequent period Monarchy was in the ascendent and was the dominant force in Administration. The Muslim invasion and the Establishment of the Pathan Kingdom strengthened the earlier trend towards the magnification of the position of the Kings. The power of the King became increasingly based on the military strength rather than on the will of the people. The King combined in his person the Legislative, Judicial, Administrative and Military functions at the highest level. The one element of continuity throughout the ages was provided by the village communities which, to a great extent, managed their own affairs.

We will now move on to witness some of the important aspects of Moghal Administration. By far the best view into this vista could be had in the period of Akbar. The most important authority on this period is the Aine-Akbari or Institutes of Akbar written by the Emperor's wise and devoted councillor Abul Fazal "Allami". Another important authority is the contemporary annalist known as "Albedavni." Another remarkable testimony is that of the European Traveller, the famous French Physician Francois Barnier. The characteristics of this administration were the increasing power of the King till it reached its zenith, and that the Emperor's will as Law in the most literal sense had permeated the organisation. The administration was on military lines. The rank in the Imperial Government was closely correlated to the number of troops maintained by the Nobles, and even officials employed wholly in civil duties were graded in the Military Hierarchy. Every important official had been assigned to him the responsibility for maintaining and commanding the stated number of troops. The Commanders were known as Mansabdars or Place Holders and were graded as Mansabdars of 10,000, 5,000 and 1,000 and so on to 10. The Provincial Governorships were held Mansabdars of high rank. "The Ministers were only the Emperor's advisers when he chose to consult them and his

Assistants in whatever branch of administration he delegated to them." The Chief amongst these Ministers was the Vakil (the Emperor's Lieutenant in all matters connected with the Realm and the Household). Next came the Vazir or Dewan, who, in modern terms may be described as the Finance Minister. Abul Fazal has catalogued the qualities of a Vazir as follows:— "Skilful Arithmetician, free from avarice, circumspect, warm-hearted, abstinent, active in business, pleasing in his style, clear in his writing, truthful, man of integrity, condescending, zealous in his work", and then brings the reader to an anti-climax by writing that "the Vazir is in reality a Book-keeper." The other important Ministers were the Sadar, who combined in himself the work of a Chief Justice and the Chief Inquistor, and the Chief Bhakshi who was the Pay-Master General and Chief Recruiting Officer.

In the towns law and order was maintained by Kothwal on who many responsibilities were placed. He was to organise Night Patrols, keep a Register of Houses, take note of comings and goings of strangers and according to "Ain" observe the Income and Expenditure of the various classes of men". Investigation and recovery of stolen property were enforced by the effective administrative rule, "The Kothwal shall discover thieves and the goods they have stolen, or be responsible for the loss." During Akbar's time, the Empire was divided into Subas, under a Subedar, and the Subas were divided into Sircars or districts which were under the charge of Fauzdars who combined the functions similar to those of a Magistrate, a Collector and a Military Commander. Quazi was the Judicial Officer.

A few words about the Revenue Administration which formed the foundation of all Administrations will be quite relevant here. In the ancient period, the accepted basis of land-holding was "that the duty of the person was to cultivate, the obligation of the King was to protect him and the duty of the cultivator in return for this protection was to pay a customary share of the produce of the soil." Whether this was paid as rent to the King in the capacity of the owner of all land in his Kingdom or whether it should be regarded as Tax paid to the State is an interesting subject of wider range, which need not be considered here. Suffice it to say that the cultivator in the ancient period had a great measure of security of tenure. In the ancient period actual sharing of the produce of the land and collection based on a standard figure of yield appeared to have been in use.

Both in ancient and mediaeval India the revenue system was based on the immemorial theory that the King was entitled to a share of produce of all land, that he might realise it either by direct collection or by assignment. Under Akbar, this theory was crystallised into a well-defined set of regulations which not only specified the rights of the King but also laid down the standard obligation of the individual cultivator. The office of the provincial Dewan was intimately and effectively associated with the collection of revenue and had already been a powerful instrument of administration. Such provincial dewans had been linked by Akbar to the Imperial Revenue Ministry. The Dewans developed the zamindari which was responsible not only for collecting the revenue on behalf of the local representative of the King, but also one which exercised civil and military jurisdiction and was a creation mainly for easy and ready revenue administration and collection.

In the 16th Century the adoption of the standard yield, the principle of taking the State share on estimates of normal yield from good, bad and middling land were adopted. Akbar took up the task of organising a pattern for commuting grain-payment into cash by adopting the practice of applying local prices of grains instead of a single Empire price. This was further developed into the system of payment based on the settlement for 10 years. The revenue payment ceased to be expressed in terms of grains and became a cash payment per unit area cultivated and fixed for each locality under consideration on average yield and average price, the settlement being fixed for a definite period. The difficulty of direct collection of revenue over a large area together with the necessity of remunerating the State Officers in some convenient way led to the growth of the practice of assignment. Particular areas of territory was assigned to important individuals who were not only authorised to collect and appropriate portions of the revenue but also to exercise many of the functions of the King and to maintain law and order in their assignments. Barring a portion of revenue of such an assignment, the chief was supposed to collect the revenue from the Zamindars and forward it to the King. The system later deteriorated into one of Revenue Farming and Auctioning of the right of collection. The reforms of Raja Todarmall, a man equally distinguished as a soldier and a Civil Administrator, eradicated the gross abuses that had grown up in the system of revenue administration by instituting Audit Procedure, Measurement and Settlement, and remarkably improved the situation.

The origin of the British administration in India has rightly to be traced from the establishment of the East India Company. A small body of Englishmen trading in the East had then no need of a detailed administration except that concerned with the buying and selling, and with the governance of its members. The early charters of the East India Company had given it the authority to make reasonable laws, constitution, orders and ordinances for the benefit of its limited administration and to punish offences committed by its servants. It gave it no territorial jurisdiction.

The great expansion of its jurisdiction and the consequent increase in responsibility and duties pertaining to administration in the following hundred years were achieved by three different processes, namely acquisition of Zamindari rights, conquest or cessation of territory and assumption of the Dewani. A significant step in the enlargement of the Company's administration was in the year 1698 when in Bengal the Company bought Zamindari rights at first of the three villages of Suttanati, Calcutta and Govindpur.

The East India Company obtained permission from the then Rulers to acquire the Zamindari rights. In Madras, the position was different; instead of the limited authority obtained in Bengal from the rulers the Company had obtained the full powers of Government. The subsequent step was that the Company decided to "Standforth as Dewan and take over the revenue administration of the country instead of merely holding the Zamindari rights. Courts were established. In 1773 by the Regulating Act the then Supreme Court was set up in Bengal. The Office of the Collectors, Magistrates and Judges came into existence.

The early organisation of the Company in India was naturally suitable to a purely trading organisation. Each Factory or Trading Establishment was under the control of a President, later called Governor and a Council consisting of senior servants of the Company in the Factory. The President was in very much the same position as the Chairman of a Board of Directors. He took the chair and naturally gave the lead though he was bound by the view of the Council. The Commercial Factories which had presidents of a Council came to be called Presidencies. In the History of the East India Company, the important question which cropped up now and then and was ultimately settled according to historical circumstances, was whether the administration of the country should be in the hands of a trading Corporation which looked primarily to dividends or was the real authority to be exercised by the English Parliament.

By the Regulating Act of 1773, which may be regarded as the first serious attempt by the English Parliament to control the administration in India, the Presidencies of Bombay and Madras were subjected to the control of the Presidency of Bengal. The subsequent important measure was that of Pitt's Act of 1784 which established a Board of Control including the Chancellor of the Exchequer and the Secretary of the State.

The Office of the Collector was created by the Company to collect the revenue and govern the village. He was the Magistrate and the Head of the Police Force. For some time he was also the District Judge. Later, Cornwallis introduced the system whereby Revenue Administration was kept distinct from Judicial and Police functions. But these administrative tendencies were soon reversed and power began to be concentrated in the hands of Collectors. After 1757, the Revenue, Magisterial and Police functions were united under the control of Collectors while major criminal matters were considered by the District Judge. The Collector became the "Ma Bap" or Mother and father of the District. In 1863 one civilian had humorously written about the Collector; "The Collector, man of equal might, reports all day and corresponds all night". With the efflux of time the District Officer, Collector, became the centre of the Administrative system. His duties varied from his primary work of collecting revenue to devoting his energies to suppression of crime and in tranquil times concentrated on development work. Above all, it increasingly became his duty to know people in his district and press their needs and difficulties for redress by the Government. The concept of equality of all men before law and the rule of law progressed.

In Revenue Administration, the significant changes were from the Revenue Farming or hereditary Zamindary to that of permanent Settlement. Recognising the agency, the amount of payment and the period of the settlement of land revenue led to the proprietary rights of the Zamindars. Under the Permanent Settlement, the law was that an estate should be sold if the revenue was not paid by sun-set on the latest day. This was known as the "Sun-set-Law". It resulted in the breaking up of bigger Estates. A new race of land-lords was created. The Ryot, who was the actual cultivator, was left an easy prey to exploitation. The subsequent history, in this direction, is one of conferring more and more rights on the actual cultivators and security of their tenures. As a contrast to the Zamindary System there also developed a Ryotwari settlement which favoured direct settlement with individual cultivators. Under this system the Ryots had the right to pay or transfer or sub-let their belongings and were not to be evicted, provided they paid their rents. Remarkable progress was also made with the development of Administration to meet the travails of Famines. This was the development of famine administration. Whenever drought and failure of rains brought widespread distess, the famine administration was geared up to meet the situation.

The Act of 1833 abolished the trading monopoly of the Company and completely stopped its commercial activities. This Act introduced a highly centralised system of administration. The event of 1857 completed the dissolution of East India Company. Morley-Minto Reform of 1900 was the first step towards the association of the people with the Administration though it was nothing more than benevolent despotism. The Great War hastened the process of increasing the association of the people with every branch of administration. The concept of a Government by the representatives of the people, for the people rapidly took shape.

Bureaucracy and Democracy were strangely mixed and closely associated with each other by implementing the Act of 1919. It was the birth and progress of the Dyarchical Government. Even though unitary form of state was maintained, the spheres of central and provincial Governments were demarcated. In simple, any Dyarchical Government meant division of the Government into two sections; one of them fully bureaucratic and the other popular to a great extent. Both the sections had to work under the Governors of the provinces who had ordinary and extraordinary powers. Taxation became to a great extent provincial. The central and provincial spheres of administration were demarcated by this Act, and a large measure of independence was given to the provinces. The provincial subjects were divided into two groups; the reserved half to be administered where irrevocable council, existed and the transferred subjects were to be administered by Ministers, selected by the Government from among the elected members of the Provincial Legislative Council, who were fully responsible so that chamber for their actions and policies. In the Central Executive Council, more of our countrymen, took their places.

Then came the Act of 1935 with its constitutional structure based on the concept of Provincial Autonomy and Federation. The Executive Authority of each province extended to matters with respect to which the Legislature of the Province had power to make Laws. The main source of income of the Province were enumerated as Land Revenue, Excise Duties, Taxes on Agricultural Income, Taxes on lands and buildings, Taxes on profession, Taxes on Civilian Goods etc., with certain other sources of revenue as mainly central. The Chief Executive Head of the Province was the Governor who had three fold classification of his powers; those he had to exercise in his discretion, in his individual judgment, or on the advice of ministers responsible to the Legislature. He had considerable powers in matters of finance, and though the budget was subject to the vote of the Legislature in respect of the votable portion, the Governor had the discretion to restore the cuts. The administrative departments of Revenue and Police, had increasingly to attend the numerous items of work pertaining to administration and welfare of the people. The

Development Department which had been created as and when administration required them, progressed improving upon their tradition and techniques and methods of service and administration. Education came to take an increasing role not only in advancing the cultural, spiritual and mental horizons but in economic advancement. The Members of the Indian Civil Service continued to occupy all important posts or Administration with increasing recruitment of the Indian to this service. One of the most important factors in the administrative impact of Britain on India has been the development of the Imperial and Provincial Services. The admission to this Service which was first by nomination was thrown open to competition by talent.

We will now move on to the situation subsequently in August 1947 which heralded the new trends in administration. We became fully independent under our own Constitution; with complete and full responsible Government based on the principle of collective responsibility of the Cabinet. The development of All-India and Province services, and the increasing responsibilities and duties of administration, are an important feature. It may be a proper finale to this recapitulation of the history of administration if the present pattern of our administration is very briefly indicated. The foundation, the guiding ideals and the inspiring force of our administration are based on the principles of our Constitution which are so secure to citizens "Justice social, economic and political, liberty of thought, expression, belief, faith and worship, equality of status and of opportunity and to promote among them all Fraternity, assuring the dignity of the individual and the unity of the nation". The Union and State Governments, the Union and the State Legislatures, the Supreme Court and the High Courts, the Army, the Navy and the Air Force, the All-India and the State services, the Public Service Commission, their functions rights, powers, duties and responsibilities, are all clearly defined, and the hierarchy of administration in each department from village unit upwards, the objectives and their spheres of service are all well-known. Democratic decentralization of powers and functions is the pattern of our village administration. Administration is constantly working to achieve the Rule of Law, and higher levels of efficiency. The practical tasks of administration have now become manifold and numerous. In addition to the time-honoured and traditional functions it is now entrusted with tasks pertaining to increase of material prosperity, social services, Industrial and labour management and organisation, State trading and Civil Supplies, communications and charge of public utility concerns, assistance in formulation of policies, administration of Corporations etc., functions which have far exceeded the limits visualised in the past for administration. Administration more than ever before is determined and coordinated action in pursuit of common purpose calling forth in those charged with the affairs of administration qualities and habits such as business-like methods, organising capacity, adaptability to different conditions, readiness to take responsibility, hard and concentrated work integrity, character, devotion and loyalty, contentment efficiency, intelligence and an all-round discernment and understanding, permeated with principles of service and justice.

"Since the memory of man runneth not to the contrary the art of administration has been one of the essential human possessions." Modern trends have made this possession not only large and diversified in content but of increasing value. An appreciation of this Art is in no small measure an encouragement and improvement of the Artist.

— M. Rahamathulla

2

THE GROWTH OF STATE ADMINISTRATION IN INDIA[1]

The present Constitution of India has ushered in a federal polity called the Union of States embracing the original Provinces, and the Princely States which, subsequent to the partition of the country, became integrated into the Republic. Generally Federations are formed by bringing together a number of autonomous states for achieving a common end. A Federation normally presupposes the existence of a number of States enjoying independence, and possessing individuality and consciousness of it. Naturally a Federation would be the result of a desire on the part of such States for Union, though not for unity, and for an alliance between states to federate. As a result of such an alliance is created a new state to which the hitherto sovereign states surrender their sovereignty and become its components. Such a dual polity serves the twin purposes of national unity and the preservation of the identity of the states, as, in the words of Prof. Dicey, "Federation is a political contrivance intended to reconcile national unity with the maintenance of State rights", i.e., the desire for national unity and determination of each individual unit to maintain its identity and autonomy.

Judged from these standards the Indian Union did not possess the right type of material for the formation of a Federal Polity capable of undergoing the traditional process, in spite of the fact that Federation was already mooted under the scheme of the Government of India Act, 1935, which was in turn a culmination of a long-drawn out process of administrative decentralisation that had been going on in India for so many years. The material then was to make the Federal structure in India was varied and diverse from any standard that could be applied. So the Constitution that ushered in the Federal Union had also at the same time to create the constituent States. This was achieved in different stages, and eventually homogeneous political institutions came to be evolved.

The problem of moulding the right type of components of our Federation was further complicated by the different types of administrative units that were functioning on the eve of Independence. There were the British Indian Provinces which enjoyed provincial autonomy under the Act of 1935, comprising what was called 'British Indian', and as many as 562 Princely States constituting the 'Indian India'. The British India was "governed by the Crown according to the Statutes of the (British) Parliament and enactments of the Indian Legislature, and the Indian States (Indian India) under the suzerainty of the Crown and still for the most part under the personal rule of the Princes."[2] The degree of political experience, the system of administration, the extent of area, population and material resources of different provinces and the Princely States varied greatly. This divergence could not escape being reflected in the new Constitution of India. Under Article I of the constitution as it originally stood, Indian Union comprised three different categories of States. The first category of States was Part 'A' States comprising those States which were designated as Governors' Provinces under the Government of India Act of 1935, including the truncated provinces of Assam, the Punjab and West Bengal (parts of which went to Pakistan as a result of the Partition of the Country in terms of the Indian Independence Act of 1947). The second category of States was the Part 'B' States which were the former Princely States. A few of the former Princely States like Mysore and Hyderabad, which retained their separate identity in the beginning. Many of these States were merged and Unions of States like the Union of Rajasthan were created. Finally, there were the Part 'C' States which comprised the Chief Commissioner's Provinces of the Government of India Act, 1935, and a few Princely States either as individual or as corporate units. As these were under the direct control of the President of India, strictly speaking, they were not constituent units of the Federation. The territories of the Andaman and Nicobar Islands were also directly Administered by the President of India.[3]

Such a distinction between the constituent units of a Federation was highly repugnant to the principle of the equality of States, which is essential in a true Federation. But the Constitution of India had to accept such a discrimination due to the peculiar situation in which the Federation was shaped and also due to the legacy that was inherited. It only indicates that neither the formation of the administrative units in India under the strongly centralised rule of the British was scientific not the system of administration that was evolved uniform. The States Reorganisation Commission testified to them when it said "the existing structure of the States of the Indian Union (before the Reorganisation of States, 1956 is partly the result of accident and the circumstance attending the growth of the British Power in India and partly a by-product of the historic process of the integration of former Indian States. The division of India during the British period was itself fortuitous and had no basis in Indian history. It was a mere accident that as a result of the abandonment, after the upheaval of 1857 of the objective of extending the British dominion by absorbing princely territories, the surviving States escape annexation. The map of the territories annexed as directly administered by the British was also not shaped by any rational or scientific planning."[4] But "it was shaped by the military, political or administrative agencies or conveniences of the moment and with same regard to the natural affinities or wishes of the people".[5] Moreover, the British rule, in its early stages, did not required an elaborate organization in view of the very limited scope of activity of the East India Company. It had "merely trading stations without territorial sovereignty, and it was only gradually that wider authority came to be exercised".[6]

With the gradual replacement of trading activities by territorial acquisition and wielding of governmental functions, and with political motives overshadowing the desire for commercial gains, the company had to think of organising their newly acquired areas into administrative units to serve certain specific purposes. "The provincial organisation of British India was meant to serve a two-fold purpose: to uphold the direct authority of the supreme power in areas of vital economic and strategic importance and to fill the political vacuum arising from the destruction or collapse of the former principalities. Of these two, the first was obviously the primary objective, and it required the suppression of the traditional regional and dynastic loyalties. This was sought to be achieved by erasing old frontiers and by creating new provinces which ignored natural affinities and common economic interests. The administrative organisation of these provinces was intended to secure their subordination to the Central Government, which was the agent and instrument of imperial control exercised from London. This process inevitably led to the formation of units with no natural affinity".[7] It is now proposed to examine some of the main features of this gradual development that took place in India under the British rule with reference to the formation of the several units of administration from time to time; and the growth of the administrative machinery in those units.

EVOLUTION OF INDIAN PROVINCES

The British control over Indian soil was acquired and extended piece-meal. It started with small trading settlements, particularly on the coastal regions during the 17th Century. It took a long time for the British authority to acquire territories and expand further into the country. The three principal settlements of the East India Company were Bombay, Madras and Bengal, Bombay was leased to the Company by Charles II, and was given to him as a part of the dowry of Katherine of Braganza of Portugal in 1661; Madras was got by the Company in 1640 on payment of tribute; and Bengal in 1757 at the Battle of Plassey. Any fresh territory that was acquired was added on to one of these three Presidencies. The term 'Presidency' was applied to the whole tract over which their authority extended.[8] The Presidencies were administered by a President and a Council composed of servants of the Company.

After the Battle of Plassey, in 1772, the territorial power of the Company in Bengal was extended and consolidated. The

Company got Zamindari rights in the District of 24 Paraganas adjoining Calcutta. So the Battle of Plassey and Buxar practically invested the company with territorial sovereignty over Bengal, Bihar and Orissa. The Diwani Rights (the right to collect revenue) were granted to the Company by Emperor Shah Alam in August 1761.

The origin of different provinces in India is related to the gradual expansion of British authority over more and more areas through a policy of conquest, annexation, purchase etc. Bengal was the first Province to attain importance over Bombay and Madras. As the premier presidency, Bengal was enriched at various dates, by the additions of Agra in 1805, Assam 1825, Oudh in 1856; the Central Provinces in 1853 and part of Burma (1825-53) Bihar and Orissa also formed part of Bengal originally, though they came to be separated in 1911.[9] Bengal came to be created a separate Province in 1853 when the Governor-General was relieved from the charge of the Governership of Bengal. The North-West Frontier Provinces were created in 1836. The Governor-General, further to rid himself of the direct administration of Bengal including Bihar and Orissa, created the Lieutenant-Governorship of Bengal.

Madras was one of the provinces to reach the rank of a distinct presidency along with Bombay and Bengal. It attained its shape and size that remained more or less intact all along, with minor boundary alterations from time to time, since the defeat of Tipu Sultan of Mysore, in 1799.

The Presidency of Bombay completely assumed its shape by 1818, when the last of the Peshwas was finally overcome and the Maratha Empire became a thing of the past. Sind was added to Bombay in 1843 just because it had an easy and convenient access from Bombay by sea.

Punjab, which was under a board of administration in the beginning and then under a Chief Commissioner, was annexed in 1849. It became a Lieutenent-Governorship when Delhi was transferred to it. In 1856 Oudh was annexed and placed under a Chief Commissoner. But it was merged with the North-West Provinces and became renamed the United Provinces of Agra and Oudh in 1901, when some of the districts separated from the Punjab adjoining the Indo-Afghan Frontier were made into a new province called the North-Western Frontier Province in 1901 for purposes of political security. It remained to Chief Commissionership upto 1932 and became a Governor's Province under the Act of 1935. The Central Provinces, formed out of portions of North-West Province and certain lapsed territories were, placed under a Chief Commissioner in 1861. In 1903 Berar was linked to the Central Provinces which became a Governor's Province in 1920, called the Central Provinces and Berar. In 1826 Assam was annexed and added to Bengal from which was again separated and made a Chief Commissioner Province in 1874. In 1905 the partition of Bengal led to the conversion of the eastern half of Bengal together with Assam into the Lieutenant-Governorship of Bengal. This partition of Bengal was vehemently opposed. Lord Curzon justified the measure on the plea that the Province as it existed then was too unwieldy for administration under a single charge and partition was necessary in the interest of efficient and effective administration. "But the dividing line was so crudely drawn that it meant the splitting of the Province into two communal blocs; the one in which the Hindus were in the majority, and the other in which the Muslims predominated. The measure was construed as an attempt on the part of Lord Curzon to cripple the new renaissance in Bengal, and for the first time, agitation went beyond the accepted methods, namely of prayer, petition and protest".[10] The partition evoked further resentment when the radical wing of the Congress Party accepted a policy of the boycott of the British goods as a part of their protest against the partition of Bengal. The partition of Bengal was annulled in the course of the announcement during the Delhi Durbar of 1911 and the arrangement was modified in 1912 when Assam once again became a Chief Commissionership; Bengal a Presidency, and Bihar and Orissa a Lieutenant-Governorship. Assam was made a Governor's Province in 1920. British Baluchistan was formed into a Chief Commissionership in 1887. Coorg which was annexed in 1834 was administered by the Resident in Mysore. Similarly, Ajmer ceded in 1818 and was administered by the Agent to the Governor-General in Rajputana. Delhi comprised a small area enclosing the new capital city which was created a separate Province under a Chief Commissioner in

1912 in accordance to the announcement on the eve of the King Emperor's Durbar.

So, by the time the Montagu-Chelmsford Reforms were to be implemented there were nine major Provinces and six lesser charges. The major Provinces were the three Presidencies of Bombay, Madras and Bengal; the four Lieutenant Governorships of the United Provinces, the Punjab, Burma, Bihar and Orissa; and the 2 Chief Commissionerships of the Central Provinces and Assam. The lesser charges were the North-West Frontier Province, British Baluchistan, Coorg, Ajmer, the Andamans, and Delhi. The Government of India Act, 1935 classified the Provinces into only 2 categories: (i) Governors' Provinces which were 11 in all; and (ii) the five Chief Commissioners' Provinces, Madras, Bombay, Bengal the United Provinces, the Punjab, Bihar, the Central Provinces and Berar, Assam, the North-West Frontier Province Orissa, and Sind were the Governors' Provinces.[11] The Chief Commissioners' Provinces were: as laid down in Section 94 of the Act, British Baluchistan, Delhi, Ajmer Merwara, Coorg, and the Andaman and Nicobar Islands. The Governors' Provinces were to become autonomous and the Chief Commissionerships administered by the Governor-General acting through a Chief Commissioner.

It is seen from the above list of provinces that two provinces, —Orissa and Sind, came to be separated from Bihar and Bombay respectively and established in 1936 as separate provinces in pursuance of the recommendation made by the Indian Statutory Commission in its Report and accepted by the Joint Select Committee of Lord Linlithgow. Sind was separated from Bombay as a result of the agitation for a separate province on linguistic and cultural grounds. So also Orissa. When these province were conceded, naturally it was taken for granted the other linguistic areas, tagged on to different province against their will should also press for the formation of separate linguistic provinces, so much so that it gave to spur to the agitation for the creation of linguistic province in India'. This demand for re-drawing the map of India on the basis of language became more vociferous from time to time as expressed in a number of resolutions passed by various provincial legislatures.

When power came to be transferred to Indians and the question of satisfying the claims for a separate State for Muslims on the basis of religion came to be examined, the Provincial structure of India had to be disturbed obviously. It was decided, after a series of hectic negotiations between the Indians and the representatives of the British Government, to accept the proposals made in the course of the famous 'Mountbatten Plan' or 'the June 3, Plan' which actually cut the Gordian knot on transfer of power. The June 3 Plan suggested the partition of the two Provinces of Bengal and Punjab. Sind was to take a decision of its own in a special meeting of the legislative Assembly. The North-Western Frontier Province and the Muslim-majority district of Sylhet in Assam were to decide by a referendum as to their future. The Plan also provided for the setting up of a Boundary Commission to settle the details of the boundaries in case partition of the country was decided upon. This had become almost inevitable by then as the only solution to the deadlock. On the Plan being accepted by the All-India Congress and the Muslim League, the Indian Independence Act was passed by the British Parliament on July 18, 1947. The object of this last but the 'noblest and greatest law' ever enacted by the British Parliament on Indian affairs was to give legal effect to the Mountbatten Plan. It Provided for the partition of India and the establishment of the two Dominions of India and Pakistan with Legislative supremacy separately for both. This partition of the country resulted in the partition of the two Provinces of Punjab and Bengal. West Punjab, East Bengal, North-Western Frontier Province, Sind, Baluchistan and the district of Sylhet joined Pakistan. So the remaining territories, the eight Governors' Provinces including the truncated Provinces of Bengal and Punjab (West Bengal and East Punjab) and the Four Chief Commisionerships, came to constitute the Dominion of India which was the nucleus for the coming Indian 'Union of States'.

THE PROBLEM OF THE PRINCELY STATES

But there was also the menacing problem of the Indian States, which constituted 'Indian India', to be faced by the architects of new India. It would not be out of place here to refer briefly to the status and privilege assigned to these nearly 562 Princely States whose integration was tackled and achieved with admirable courage and statesmanlike approach by the late Sardar Vallabh Bhai Patel—the steel-man of Indian Politics.

The Princely States of India, which were under the suzerainty of the Crown and for most part under the personal rule of the princes, covered an area of 598,138 square miles. They could be grouped into three distinct classes.[12]

Princely States

Class of State, Estate, etc.	*Number*	*Area in square miles*	*Popula-tion*	*Revenue in Crores of ruppes*
1. States the rulers of which were members of the Chamber of Princes in their own right.	108	514,886	59,847,186	42.16
2. States the rulers of which were represented in the Chamber of Princes by 12 members of their order elected by themselves.	127	76,846	8,004,114	2.89
3. Estates, Jagirs and others	327	6,406	801,674	.74

As can be made out from the above classification there was nothing in common among the states except that they were not a part of British India. From the point of view of development in the political, economic and administrative fields also they had great variations. There were 'constitutional states' like Mysore and Travancore, and States which 'were under purely autocratic administration'[13], lingering in the mediaeval atmosphere. But some of them did try to catch up with the modern trend of progress. They tried to improve their administration. As the Indian States Committee observed,[14] "Of the 108 Princes in Class I, 30 have established legislative councils, most of which are at present of a consultative nature only; 40 have constituted High Courts more or less on British Indian models; 34 have separated the executive from judicial functions; 56 have a fixed privy-purse; 46 have started regular graded Civil list of officials; and 54 have Pension or Provident Fund schemes".[15] This clearly indicates the sense of responsibility exhibited by some rulers toward their people for good government and their increasing association with the government.

The relation between the Crown and these Princely States was based on the concept of the 'Paramount Power' which means 'the Crown acting through the Secretary of State for India and the Governor-General in council, we are responsible to the Parliament of Great Britain'. The Paramountcy of the Crown was based upon treatment engagnements and sanads, supplemented by usage are sufferance and by decisions of the Government of India and the Secretary of State. The Paramount Power come interfere with the States 'in its own interests as responsible for the whole of India, in the interests of the States, and in the interests of the people of the States'[16]. Intervention in the affairs of the States, as in the case of Hyderabad, Baroda, Mysore and Manipur, became an accepted practice almost, which was at its height during the Viceroyalty of Lord Curzon.

The status of the Princely States was described in the Report on Indian Constitutional Reforms of Montagu-Chelmsford as follows.[17]

"The States are guaranteed security from without, the Paramount Power acts for them in relation to foreign Powers and other States, and it intervenes when the internal peace of their territories is seriously threatened. On the other hand the States' relations to foreign Powers are those of the Paramount Power; they share the obligation for the defence; and they are under a general responsibility for the good government and welfare of their territories".

Naturally the States had no international status. So the position of the States was one of 'subordinate isolation' and Lord Hardinge look upon their rulers as 'helpers and colleagues in the great task of imperial rule'. They were the 'subordinate allies' of the Crown.

The Montagu-Chelmsford Report recommended, among other things, the codification and standardisation of the political practice in the states and the creation of the Chamber of Princes, with a standing Committee, which fructified in terms of the Royal Proclamation of February 8, 1921. This was a first step in the direction of establishing some connection with the Indian political system on different lines altogether. When an All-India Federation was contemplated under the Government of India Act, 1935, the rulers of the Princely States were given a privileged position. When all the Provinces were to join the Indian Federation automatically, the States were given an option either to join or to remain outside. Those States which would choose to join would do so through an Instrument of Accession executed by the ruler of the State in favour of the Crown on acceptance of which only, the State would become an unit of the Federation. So the Crown could also reject an Instrument of Accession if its terms were found inconsistent with the scheme of the Federation and also the terms of these Instruments of Accession could vary from State to State. The States were also given the power to veto changes in the Federation constitution affecting their position. Above all, the accession of the rulers of States with at least half the total population of all the States in India was made a condition precedent to the establishment of the Federation. This condition was particularly calculated to use the States as forces which would prevent a Federal Polity from coming into existence. So the Federal Scheme that was contemplated under this Act remained on paper. It did not materialise.

The rulers of the Princely States were thus encouraged to insist on this privilege of theirs to be honoured in and future scheme for the formation of a Union of States. They claimed a right to stay out and form a separate Union or Unions among themselves as the non-accedings Provinces. The claim was in fact conceded by Sir Stafford Cripps!

The Cabinet Mission Scheme made a departure from the line of policy that was pursued with regard to the States. Though it suggested certain freedom to the Princes to determine the manner of their entry, implying an opportunity to have the most favourable conditions of accession, yet it expressed the hope that "the Prince consent would not unreasonably be withheld from and change which might emerge as a result of negotiations". It also made it clear that Paramountcy would not be transferred to any new government but would 'lapse'.

The Indian Independence Act, 1947, accordingly terminated the Paramountcy of the Crown over the States. This, however, was not the end of the problem but a beginning of a series of problems on the Princely states as all the Princely states were deemed to have become free and all treaties and covenants ceased to be operative. They could decide to join either the Dominion of India, or Pakistan, or remain independent even! This possibility of a State or States thinking of remaining independent was referred to with concern by Mr. Attlee when he said "it would be, I think, unfortunate if, owing to the severance of their Paramountcy relations with the Crown, they were to become islands cut off from the rest of India", which would have been fatal to all concerned. Naturally, the Interim Government gave priority to the problem of Integration of States and set up the States Ministry on July 5, 1947, to deal with the problem, with Sardar Vallabh Bhai Patel as Minister in charge and Mr. V. P. Menon as the Secretary of the Ministry.

The integration of the Princely States was achieved through a three-fold process of merger, consolidation and integration, which can be described as a silent and peaceful revolution. As a result of an appeal to the Princes issued by the States Ministry requesting them to join in the work of the Constituent Assembly and accede to the Indian Union, not only in their own interest but also in the larger interests of the unity and solidarity of the nation, most states acceded to India before August 15 itself in regard to the three subjects—Defence, Foreign Relations and Communication. Only three States, Junagadh, Hyderabad and Kashmir, posed some problem, which has been solved by the Government of India to preserve the Unity of the nation. The accession of the States became full-fledged by 1949 by which time they signed fresh Instruments of Accession extending Federation jurisdiction in all matters. The political map of India therefore, came to be completely redrawn by the time the new constitution was inaugurated. As many as 216 State were merged with the adjoining Governors' Provinces, the States were taken over as centrally administered area and 275 States were united to form the five States Unions. Only Mysore, Hyderabad, Jammu and Kashmir were retained in their original form. Out of a conglomeration of 562 Princely States emerged 13 sizable units which became the components of the Indian Federation along with the other parts of British India. Needless to point out, this was the result of the untiring efforts of Sardar Patel who is rightly acknowledged the architect of Free India.

THE TERRITORIAL ARRANGEMENT UNDER THE NEW CONSTITUTION

The new Constitution of India in its original form listed in the First Schedule the States and territories of India which were grouped into three categories. There were 9 Part A States, 8 Part B States and 10 Part of States, and the territories of the Andaman and Nicobar Islands. This was bound to be a temporary arrangement in a period of transition and it was still open for the Indian Parliament to create new states or alter the boundaries of States according to Article 3 of our Constitution. Within a short time after the inauguration of the constitution, under popular pressure for linguistic State and particularly due to the coercive steps taken by the Andhras, a separate linguistic State of Andhra came in existence on October 1, 1953, though the same right was denied to others in the south, in spite of their long-standing and peaceful demand.

The feeling that all is not well with the territorial distribution of India, which was not based on any sound principle, and which disregarded particularly the linguistic and cultural considerations, was growing very strong even after the new constitutional arrangement. The then existing units were heterogeneous in their composition with people speaking different languages and having different cultures put under the control of a State government just because it was so even in the past. The agitation for linguistic provinces, particularly in the South, was growing from strength to strength and the Congress Party in power, as it was already committed to the creation of Linguistic Provinces, had a special obligation to take steps for the creation of provinces on linguistic principle. When the situation was drifting towards an agitational approach the Government of India announced the appointment of a High Power Commission called the States Reorganisation Commission in December 1953[18] to examine: "objectively and dispassionately" the whole question of reorganisation of States, in all its aspects and make recommendations in regard to the broad principles which should govern the solution of this problem. The Commission submitted its Report in September 1955. Based on the recommendations of this Commission with some modifications a Bill was drafted and introduced in the Union Parliament which was passed as the States Reorganisation Act, 1956. Steps were taken to bring into existence states mostly formed of linguistic principles. This opportunity was also taken to wipe out distinctions and the old categorisation among the states of the Indian Federation. There came into existence 14 States and 5 Union Territories in the place of 27 States. The States Reorganisation Act, 1956 did not set at rest the linguistic states' controversy as bi-lingual Bombay was retained as one of the States. The Maharashtrians and the Gujarathis naturally remain dissatisfied till the bifurcation of Bombay into two State Maharashtra and Gujarat, under the Bombay Reorganisation Act 1960, once again after unfortunate incidents in the State Consequent to the re-organisation of States the Indian Union is at present made up of the territories of the following 15 States: Andhra Pradesh, Assam, Bihar, Maharashtra, Gujarat, Kerala, Madhya Pradesh, Madras, Mysore, Orissa, Punjab, Rajasthan, Uttar Pradesh, West Bengal, Jammu and Kashmir; and the Union Territory of Delhi, Himachal Pradesh, Manipur, Tripura, the Andaman and Nocobar Islands, and the Laccadive Minior and Amindiv Islands.[19] The Nagaland,[20] and the territory of Goa, Daman and Diu are also being centrally administered for the present as Union Territories.

In this fashion the political map of India has been completely changed after a number of troubles and tribulations for the people from time to time. But one can realise that the political strength that was supplied to the various parts of the country by the British administration for the first time in our history was not only preserved but further increased through a wise and well-planned process of integration, merger and consolidation of our territory and by the adopting of a more rational principle in redistributing the territories of states. Thus has emerged a reorganised. India paving the way for an effective national integration.

The historical recapitulation of the changes that were effected in the shaping of the several units of administration would not be completed without some reference to the development in the administration. Hence it is proposed at this stage to refer to the changes that were brought about in the administrative set-up at the Provincial level. As there was some continuity and uniformity maintained in the case of British Indian Provinces it is desirable and proper to restrict the treatment to the Provincial set-up only. It is, however, impossible to refer to the administrative set-up of the princely states in the Indian India as there was nothing in common to them except the autocracy of the rulers. At the end it is proposed to deal with the Union-State relations under the new Constitution of India.

THE EVOLUTION OF THE ADMINISTRATIVE SYSTEM IN THE STATES

It has been pointed out earlier that the East India Company acquired the Diwani Rights in Bengal, Bihar and Orissa in 1765 which virtually established a dual authority in these areas viz., of the Company and also of the Nawab, which led to anarchy. Though this anomalous plan of 'Double Government' worked successfully for some time under Clive, it failed miserably under his successors. Describing the evil effects of Double Government, Richard Becher—the Resident at the Nawab's Court, himself wrote in 1769 "It must give pain to an Englishman to have reason to think that since the accession of the company to the Diwani the condition of the people of this country has been worse than it was before; and yet I am afraid the fact is undoubted .....this fine country which flourished under the most despotic and arbitrary Government, is verging towards its ruin....."[21] In the circumstances the British Parliament was obliged to intervene because the Company was under the control of the state with overriding authority in all affairs relating to higher branches of government, leaving to the Company its monopoly of trade and disposal of patronage. The result of the assertion of the control of the State over the company at this hour of distress was the Regulating Act, 1773, which was 'an Act for establishing certain Regulations for the better management of the affairs of the East India Company, as well in India as in Europe'. It was the first Act of Parliament which prescribed a definite system of government for managing the affairs of India.

1773 TO 1857

The Regulating Act provided for the appointment of a Governor-General and a Council of four members for the government of the Presidency of Bengal with powers to superintend and control the Presidencies of Madras and Bombay, and full powers of administration over Bihar, Bengal and Orissa. This arrangement under the Act of 1773 became the nucleus of Central Government in India with the Governor-General-in-Council as the chief authority according to the Charter Act of 1833, and also of the Provincial governments. The Governor-General in Council was to make, regulations from time to time 'for the good order and civil government of the Company's settlement at Fort William'. The Act also provided for the creation of a Supreme Court with a Chief Justice and three puisne judges with civil, criminal, admiralty and ecclesiastical jurisdiction. Though the Act could claim to be the first of its kind in providing for an administrative machinery in India, yet it could not claim to have set up a perfect system. It was full of defects. It did not clearly define the jurisdiction of the Governor-General and the Supreme Court which resulted in friction; and the Act created a Governor-General who was powerless before his own Council as he was to take decisions on the basis of the majority opinion in the Council. However, the Act was important as it made a beginning in the system of a written constitution for British India and for having improved the status of the Presidency of Bengal by placing it on a different footing altogether from other Presidencies. The machinery of Government that was created under this Act got modified from time to time under the subsequent enactments of the British Parliament in 1781, 1784, 1786, 1793, 1813 and 1858.

In the early stages of British rule it would be very difficult to distinguish between the administrative set-up in the Provinces and at the Central level, and these again from the constitutional set-up. When gradually it was established that the Governor-General of Bengal has special powers to visit a Presidency and exercise with the local Council his authority as with the Council of Bengal that there was a tendency to model government outside Bengal on that system. "The Presidency governments were constructed on the basis of the Central Government, the Governor being aided by a Council of two Civil member to whom was added the Commander-in-Chief of the local forces. He had the same power to override his Council and until the passing of the Act of 1833 had legislative as well as executive powers, subject in the case of legislation intended to apply to those within the jurisdiction of the Supreme Court to registration therein"[22].

For purposes of administration the earlier acquisition of the Company were treated as extensions of Bengal and the regulations of that Presidency were applied thereto with modifications and were treated as the 'regulation districts'. But the areas taken from Nepal and the Delhi territories and all later acquisitions mained outside the former areas and came to be classified as 'non-regulation' areas for whose administration the Governor-General issued on his executive authorities such orders as he thought fit, and he used such officers as were necessary.

The administrative and judicial reforms of Cornwallis were made applicable in full measure in the regulation districts. The measures had taken into account the need for defining the functions of different officers and branches clearly. For instance the Collector[23] was confined to revenue functions, and his civil, judicial and magisterial functions were taken away and vested in the District Judge subject to the Provincial Courts of Appeal and Circuit, which were subject to the Sadr Diwani and Sadr Nizamat Adalats at Calcutta as the Central Criminal and Civil Courts respectively. But this separation of the executive and judiciary was found impracticable, and the magisterial functions were restored to the Collector in 1816. In the case of non-regulation areas authority came to be concentrated in the hands of the district officer styled the Deputy Commissioner. In his hands were concentrated the executive, magisterial and judicial powers subject to the appellate and supervisional care of the Commissoner... under the Governor-General full powers of government rested with a board of administration of three members, who controlled the eight divisions under Commissioners, and the twenty four districts under deputy commissioners, which again were divided into small areas under Indian Tahasildars..."[24]. District, therefore, came to be the unit of administration as it is so even now.

The Charter Act of 1833 brought about many fundamental charges which affected both the Central and the Provincial administrative arrangement. The keynote of this Act was centralisation of power and authority in all governmental activity. It made the Governor-General of Bengal the Governor-General of India. The Governor-General in Council could exercise complete control over other Presidencies and territories as and when they were acquired. The provincial governments were obliged to spend only that amount of money as was approved by the Governor-General in Council as it was presumed that all revenues were to be raised under the authority of the Central Government. The Provincial governments were also under an obligation to carry out the orders of the Central Government. The net result was that the Central government could give directions, and criticise the Provincial governments in all matters, so much so that the Presidencies of Bombay and Madras were reduced to subordinate position. They lost their right to make the own laws as the Governor-General in Council became the only law-making body in India on all subjects.

1858 TO 1919

The transfer of Government in India from the Company to the Crown with the passage of the Act of 1858 'for the better Government of India', brought about changes the administration of the country. The provisions of the Act of 1858 applied almost solely to the Government England, and the Government in India was carried on before. The Act created a new office of the Secretary of State for India with a Council to exercise the function hitherto held by the Board of Control. The Secretary .State became a Minister for Indian affairs in the British Cabinet. It was left to the

Act of 1861 to make further changes as something had to be done to reform the administrative structure in India for better administration.

The Act of 1861 brought about important changes both in the Central and Provincial governments in India, the frame of which was retained for a long time to come. The constitution of the Executive Governments in Madras and Bombay was not altered by this Act, but they continued to retain some signs of their former dignity and partial Inpendence. They had the sole privilege of corresponding directly with the Secretary of State on certain matters, which was not possessed by other provincial governments. The power of legislation, which was taken away from Madras and Bombay by the Act of 1833, was restored in. 1861. However, all the laws passed by the Provincial legislatures required the sanction of the Governor-General and could be disallowed by the Crown. The Provincial legislatures were left to deal with subjects of provincial and local interest though there was no strict distinction between the central and provincial subjects. The Act of 1861 had only mentioned that measures concerning Public Debt, Finances, Currency, and Copyrights were to be ordinarily considered by the Central government. The system of assigning specific responsibilities to individual members of the Council was also introduced, which was the origin of the 'Portfolio' system.

In the other great Provinces of India the Executive governments were differently constituted from those of Madras and Bombay. Bengal, the United Provinces of Agra and Oudh, the Punjab, and Burma were administered by Lieutenant-Governors drawn from the ranks of officers in the service of the Crown. They were appointed by the Governor-General with the approval of the Crown. The Lieutenant-Governors had no Councils for executive business as it was thought that the personal supervision and complete responsibility of the Governor-General in Council were essential. But the Governor-General in Council could establish in each Province a Council for legislative purposes only as provided for in the Act of 1861. The Government of Central Provinces and Assam were administered by the Chief

Commissioners. For Provinces without legislatures, laws were made by the Governor-General in Council.

It is evident from the foregoing analysis that from the point of view of the relation between the Centre and the Provinces, the position of the Provincial Governments was essentially one of complete subordination in legislation and administration to the Centre, which also exercised full financial control. They were the 'agents' of the Central government. There was no clear-cut demarcation of functions as it was never attempted or found necessary. The Provinces were ordinarily concerned with internal administration, police, civil and criminal justice, assessment and collection of revenue, education, forests, control over Municipal and Rural Boards etc., though the Centre had always the privilege of having active supervision to the extent of appointing Commissions of inquiry whenever necessary with regard to the administration of these subjects. In financial matters the position was that all revenues went originally into the coffers of the Central government and that all but the most trifling expenditure had to be defrayed under its order. The Government of India completely controlled all taxation. A Province would refer a taxation proposal to the Central Government first for approval. So the trend was towards concentration of authority in the hands of the Central Government, probably due to the severe experiences of the Indian Mutiny.

But since 1870 a great and beneficial change has been brought about in the relations between the central and provincial governments. The spirit was to give to each Province Government with more independent power as it was realised the provincial governments necessarily possessed far more knowledge of the local requirements and conditions than the Central authority. There were measures of financial decentralisation as initiated by Lord Mayo in 1870, mainly due to that change in outlook. There was an increasing realisation on the part of the British observers that Indians should to taken into confidence by giving them greater opportunities for association with higher levels of authority and responsibility. The spirit of nationalism was taking shape in India with the spread of education, liberal ideas and the birth of the Indian National Congress. There was every-where demand for change in the composition and functions of the legislatures at all levels.

The Councils Act of 1892 provided for enlarged Councils at the Centre and the Provinces with greater non-official element. The members were given the right of sending questions on matters of public importance "subject to such conditions and restrictions as may be prescribed in rules made by the Governor-General or the Provincial Governors." Though these concessions were 'very paltry and miserable' yet the legislative Councils were slowly taking shape. But the measures were not at all adequate to satisfy the Indian demand for greater participation. The appointment and the recommendations the Royal Commission on Decentralisation at this state was a significant event. The Minto-Morley Reform, the Government of India Act, 1909, were yet another important measure which increased the representation element in the legislative Councils and extended the powers. Morley felt that there was no need to have a official majority in the Provincial Councils. So in all case the elected element came to be substantial though the method of election was far from being satisfactory. Apart from the composition, the functions of the legislature were also extended to include even discussion of the Finances, the moving of resolutions etc. But the need for devolution of authority to the provinces in a great measure was still there.

1919 TO 1950

At the time the Montagu-Chelmsford Reforms were to be introduced, every province except Bombay had the provincial headquarters, for the purpose of supervising the Revenue administration, a Board of Revenue or in equivalent, a Financial Commissioner. They constituent the chief revenue authority of the Province, which also formed the core of departmental administration. In the judicial capacity they formed an appellate court for the increasing volume of revenue and often rent suits. For other purposes than Revenue, the provincial government dealt chiefly with its Commissioners and Collectors. The Province was divided into several Divisions, each Division placed in charge of a Commissioner. Four to five district ordinarily made a Division.

Districts which were in the charge of the Collectors were further divided into subdivisions with deputy collectors, and sub-divisions into Taluks. The district continued to the chief unit of administration, as ever.

The Central Government insisted on retaining control over provincial governments, which was largely shaped by financial considerations. The Government of the country was treated as one. The provincial governments were merely the 'agents' with powers delegated to them because 'no single' administration could support the Atlantean burden'. The practice of the provincial governments referring to the respective Departments of the Government of India certain matters for supervision and also as appellate authority, continued. In all those spheres of business which were primarily the concern of the Local (provincial) governments, the Government of India exercised an unquestioned right of entry, either on their own or on appeal. The degree of interference varied with circumstances. This administrative practice continued in spite of future changes.

So till the introduction of the Reforms of 1919 there were three cardinal features of the structure of government. They were, as observed by the Indian Statutory Commission: 1). The centralisation of authority at the centre; 2) the control over legislative functions, exercised by the Executive; and 3) the ultimate responsibility of Parliament (British) for the whole of Indian Governement.[25]

This spirit of concentration and control by the centre came to be radically changed by the Montagu-Chelmsford Reforms as embodied in the Government of India Act 1919, which struck a new path in the direction of centralisation, though the step was taken with great caution and hesitancy. The new policy of the then coalition Government was announced in Parliament on August 20, 1917, by the then Secretary of State for India, Montagu. The opening sentence of this declaration stated: "The policy of His Majesty's Government... that of increasing association of Indians in every branch of the administration and the gradual development of the governing institutions with a view to the progressive realisation of responsible government in India as an integral part of the British Empire." The Joint Report of Mr. Montary and Mr. Chelmsford believed in the necessity of applying to India the traditions of British democracy and said "further development is possible unless we are going to give the people of India some responsibility for their own government."[26] The Report also laid down four governing principles which were to be embodied in the next constitutional structure. One of the principles was the "the Provinces are the domain in which the earlier step towards the progressive realisation of responsible government should be taken. Some measure of responsibility should be given at once and our aim is to give complete responsibility as soon as conditions permit. This involved at once the giving to the Provinces of the largest measure to independence, legislative, administrative and financial of the Government of India, "which is compatible with the due discharge by the latter of its own responsibilities".[27]

The outcome was the introduction of 'Dyarchy' in the executive government of the Provinces; the devolution of legislative authority by the centre to the provinces and the relaxation of the control of the Secretary of State; expansion and reconstitution of both the central and provincial legislatures; and appointment of a larger number of Indians to the Executive Councils. With these changes, the Government of India Act, 1919, is said to have begun a new era in the development of representative institutions in India.

Since the new system brought about changes in the provincial administrative machinery it is necessary to deal with it in some detail. The term Dyarchy was used for the first time by Mr. Lionel Curtis to signify that form of provincial executive in which there is "the separation of functions into two classes, one called the Reserved departments, which the Governor, with the help of his Executive Council, administers under the control and supervision of the Governor-General and the Secretary of State, and the other called Transferred departments which are administered by the Governor with the help of the Ministers responsible to the elected Legislature of his Province."[28] The object of such division was to introduce an element of parliamentary responsibility in certain subjects so that the legislature will have an opportunity to control and direct the administration at the provincial level. This was however an innovation.

For this structure of provincial government to work there was a compelling need to define the sphere of activity of the Central and Provincial governments. Such a division of subjects was brought about for the first time. 'Centre Subjects' and 'Provincial Subjects' were listed in a Schedule to Rule 3 of the Devolution Rules according to which the Central Subjects were: Defence, External Relations, Relations with States in India, Political Charges, Communications, Shipping and Navigation, Commerce, Currency and Coionage, All-India Services, the Public Service Commission etc. The Provincial Subjects, which were further classified into 'Reserved subjects' and Transferred Subjects were: (a) Transferred Subjects: Local Self-Government Medical Administration, Public Health, Education, Public Works, Agriculture, Co-operative Societies, Forests, Excise Religious and Charitable Endowments, Development of Industries etc. (b) Reserved Subjects: Water Supply including irrigation and Canals, Water Storage, Land Revenue Administration, Administration of Justice, Development of Mineral Resources, Finance, Police, Elections etc.[29] There were in all 47 entries under the Central subjects; 51 entries under Provincial Subjects of which 21 entries were Transferred and 30 Reserved ones. The residuary powers rested with the Central Government. The Act also set up a unicamera legislatures called the Legislative Council in the Governor's Provinces with 70 per cent members elected, not more than 20 per cent to be official members, and the remaining nominated.

The Dyarchical executive was introduced in the Governors' Provinces in the year 1921, and it continue to be in operation till 1937. In the course of the sixteen years of its functioning, Dyarchy just managed to survive, as it was handicapped by so many factors from within and without. The members of the Executive Council were nominated by the Governor and the Ministers were chosen from among the elected members of the Legislative Council by him. In theory, they held the office during the pleasure of the Governor, much more so in practice, but the confidence of the Council was also essential to their retention of office. If ministerial government could not function smoothly, there was provision for drastic action by the Governor who could transfer back the subjects to the position of the reserved subjects, with, of course, the prior sanction of the Governor-General in council and the Secretary of State. The Provincial Governor had many occasions on which he could choose to exercise such a control, amounting to a curtailment of the little freedom of action the Ministers had. The Governor was not to be a mere constitutional head. The Report had not made any secret of this intention. It said that the Governor was not to over-rule them in every case when his judgement differed from theirs, but he was to "refuse assent when the consequences of acquiesence would clearly be serious" and "not to accept without hesitation and discussion proposals which are clearly seen to be the result of inexperience."[30] So it boiled down to the point that the Ministers were members of the Executive government but not members of the Executive Council. Their position was that of glorified Secretaries. Further, there was no scope for joint deliberation under Dyarchy. The Governor could appoint and dismiss ministers individual as there was nothing like the joint responsibility of the ministers. The Act created a Governor who combined in himself both ordinary and extraordinary powers and duties. He was not only a part of day-by-day administration but was also the 'authority-in-reserve'.

Dyarchy, created as it was under hostile conditions in India, had to face a rough political weather. The political climate in the country was charged with distrust as suspicion, not congenial for even a fair trial for this new system. This added to the difficulties of Dyarchy in the working, which arose out of its own inner defects like the unnatural division of governmental subjects, lack of harmony between the two halves of the provincial government, and the presence of a strong and powerful Government with overriding powers. The observations of the Statutory Commission are noteworthy in this context: "The intention of Dyarchy was to establish, within a certain definite range responsibility to an elected legislature. If this intention is not carried out, the justification for the constitution bifurcation and for all the complications which it brings in its train is difficult to find."[31] Naturally the Commission recommended the abolition of Dyarchy in the Provinces.

With all its inherent defects, Dyarchy had its own benefits, though rather limited. It gave an opportunity to Indians to associate themselves as Ministers at the provincial level. They did achieve good results inspite of severe handicaps. The Statutory Commission had admiration for the work of the Ministers who "have shown themselves notably energetic in several of the spheres of administration committed to their charge. In some provinces they have made interesting experiments on which a bureaucratic government might have hesitated to embark. The results may not always have been successful, but a quickened public interest has certainly been achieved."[32] With this experience gained, the ground was prepared for the grant of autonomy to the provincial governments, which was the culmination of that process of decentralisation that was already in progress.

The Government of India Act, 1935, was based on the principles that were embodied in the report of the Statutory Commission and the Joint Select Committee of the Parliament. As a result of the cry that was raised for 'decentralisation' and for a larger measure of association of elected Indians in the legislatures, provincial self-government was conceded in the Act of 1935.

This act claimed to have effected further improvement over the four cardinal principles that were laid down in the Montagu-Chelmsford Reforms. The Act mooted an All-India federation, providing for a greater degree of decentralisation with all the British Indian Provinces joining automatically and the Indian Princely States joining at their option. It also provided for Dyarchy at the centre and bicameral legislatures. It created a Federal Court with jurisdiction over the provinces and the States. The Act lessened the control of the Home Government over Indian Affairs. But the most important provision of the Act was the provision for Provincial Autonomy. This was a definite improvement, however, on the previous system, but the Act did not establish a full-fledged responsible government in the Provinces.

The Provincial Government, according to Section 48 of the Act, consisted of a Governor appointed by a commission from His Majesty, and a Council of Ministers. It was laid down in

Section 51 that "the Governor's Ministers shall be chosen and summoned by him..... and shall hold office during his pleasure" They should also be members of either house of the provincial legislature. There was no bar on the nominated members being appointed as ministers. There was no scope for developing collective responsibility among the Ministers even under this Act.

The Governors' position deserves explanation. They could act in three different capacities: 1) ordinarily according to the advice of the Ministers; 2) in their individual judgement while fulfilling their special responsibilities regarding maintenance of peace and tranquillity in the Provinces, safeguarding the rights of the public servants, minorities etc., when the Ministers' advice could be disregarded; and 3) in their own discretion—in matters like appointing and dismissing of Ministers, issuing of Ordinances, appointing members of Public Service Commission, deciding the charged items of expenditure upon the Provincial revenues etc. The Governors were given, under Section 93 of the Act, the authority to suspend the constitution and take over the administration in their own hands. The Governors were allowed to preside over the meetings of the Council of Ministers, which added to the powerful position of the Governors. They enjoyed substantial powers which were intended to be exercised. So the position of the Governors was not one of a constitutional nead but one of a real head of the provincial executive with a Ministry whose powers were greatly circumscribed. Such a powerful Governor was created only to preserve the British control and hold over Indian Administration which, naturally, stifled the growth of responsible government. Provincial autonomy was intended to work hand in hand with the autonomy of the Governors, which was practically impossible.

The Act attempted a distribution of legislative powers, and enumerated three lists of subjects: Federal, Provincial and Concurrent for legislation by the concerned legislatures. The Federal Legislature could make laws for the whole or any part of British India for any Federated state, and a Provincial Legislature could make laws for the Province or any part thereof on the subjects enumerated in the respective lists. The residuary powers were vested with the Governor-General. But this does not mean that executive power was co-extensive with this legislative power. Throughout the Act an effort was made to retain effective authority in the hands of the Federal Government. For instance, under section 126 the supremacy of the Federal Executive was expressly provided for to the extent of constituting a Federal Inspectorate to issue directions etc., which has become an undesirable precedent. There was, for the first time, a clear division of the sources of revenue and expenditure between the Federation and the Provinces in the Schedule VII to the Act, with the result that several Provinces could never meet their obligations from their own resources, and some though they could do so, could not develop their territories well. Moreover, there were a number of restrictions of a constitutional character, which came in the way of Provincial Legislatures having any real power over the purse. Considerable amounts were 'charged' on the provincial revenues. Such expenditure in regard to the functions of Governors' Special responsibility also was forced on the Provincial Legislature. So they could not embark upon any development projects.

Reference should also be made at this point to the arrangement in the Act of carrying on the actual work of administration in the Provinces. Various Public Servants were classified into: (i) All-India Services which consisted of the Indian Civil Service, the Indian Police Service, the Foreign Service, the Service of Engineers, the Medical Service (Civil), Educational Service (certain branches), the Agricultural Service, and the Veterinary Service; (ii) and (iii), Central Services Class I and II; (iv) and (v)—Railway Services Class I and II; (vi)—Provincial Services. Appointments to Provincial Services were made by the Governor or any other Provincial authority as directed by the Governor. In spite of the waning practice of recruitment by open competition, the Act provided for the appointment of Public Service Commissions, for the Federation as well as for such Provinces as may desire to adopt this method for recruiting. There was also scope for a Common Public Service Commission for several Provinces. A provincial Public Service Commission was to consist of a Chairman and such other members as appointed by the Governor in his discretion. The Governor could lay down regulations to govern the working of these Commissions. Their position was reduced to that of the 'agents' of the Governors without real influence of their own to bear on the policy of recruitment.

So in all fields of Provincial activity the Governor, and the Federal Government through the Governor-General, dominated the scene. To quote Prof. K. T. Shah "the scope of action open to Provincial Governments was so narrow, that there can be no real autonomy in the Provinces; much less a real independence of the Indian Government."[33] The Provincial autonomy as provided for in the Act of 1935 was more illusory than real since the Governor could become a virtual dictator of the Province in all respects.

The Federal part of the Act was never implemented, though the Provincial part was implemented with the forming of popular Ministries in the Provinces in 1937 after the General Elections. But the Congress Ministries which were functioning in six of the Provinces resigned in October 1939 on the issue of the Second World War. Though the machinery set up by the Act broke down, the provisions of the Act however were supposed to be in force with modifications till they were replaced by the present Constitution of India.

THE ARRANGEMENT UNDER THE NEW CONSTITUTION

The working Constitution of India is largely shaped on the basis of the scheme of its predecessor, the Government of India Act, 1935. Many provisions have been taken bodily and incorporated, though the basis has changed completely. Sovereignty is shifted from the British Parliament to the People of India.[34] It has a Federal polity providing for the Federal governmental structure and of the States in the same body-constitution.

There is an elaborate apparatus of government in all the constituent States covering the three divisions of sovereign power—the executive, legislative, and judicial. The Executive of the State is made up of the Governor as the constitutional head and a Council of Ministers who are members of the State Legislature, appointed by the Governor according to Article 163 of the Constitution. The Governors are appointed by the President of India and hold office during the pleasure of the President. Ordinarily their term of office is 5 years. They have been Invested with Legislative, Executive, and Judicial Powers which they normally discharge on the advice of their Ministers. The old system of the Governor acting in his discretion has now been taken away. The position of the Chief Minister in the State is that of the real executive. He in charge of the administration of the state and acts as a link between the Governor and the public. But much also depends on his personality and the party-backing he has both at the State and national level. It might also be remarked that his position is mostly what he makes of it.

The Constitution provides for a bicameral legislature in certain states only — and in certain others only one House. The two Houses of the State Legislature are the Legislative Assembly and the Legislative Council.

According to Article 214, there shall be a High Court for each State with a Chief Justice and such other judges as the President may appoint from time to time. Every High Court is a court of record and shall have all the powers of such a court including the powers to punish for contempt of itself. Appointments of persons other than District Judges to the judicial services of a State are made by the State Governor in accordance with the rules made by him in consultation with the State Public Service Commission and the High Court. There shall be an Advocate-General for the state appointed by the Governor.

The Constitution of India makes provision for different categories of Services. There are All-India Services, the Central or Federal Services and the State Services. According to Article 309 the recruitment and conditions of service of the persons appointed to Public Services in connection with the affairs of the Union or States are to be regulated under rules by the appropriate legislature. Article 315 provides for an Union Public Service Commission for each State or a Joint Public Service Commission for two or more States if they so desire. The Chairman and members of the U. P. S. C. and Union Public Service Commissions, if any, are appointed by the President and in case of a State P. S. C., the Governor makes the appointments.

RELATIONS BETWEEN THE UNION AND THE STATES

The problem of the relations between the States and the Union under the Constitution assume special importance, as there is a lot of controversy and criticism as to the true nature of our Federation. Critics observe that our Federation is not at all a true form of Federation; it is a Unitary State with subsidiary federal features, or as K. C. Wheare puts it, it is a 'Quasi-Federal State', to which list of descriptive titles may now be added that of a 'Paramount Federation'.[35] The chief point is that there are greater points in favour of a highly centralised Union Government being created and the powers that are given to the States are purely devolutionary in character. This can be better appreciated by an examination of the relations between the Union and the-States in the Legislative, Administrative and Financial fields.

The Seventh Schedule of the Constitution contains three lists of subjects: the Union List-with 97 topics; the State List-with 66 topics, the Concurrent List-with 66 topics, the Concurrent List-with 47 topics. The residuary power is with the Union Government. These legislative powers of the different authorities also grant powers in the executive field co-extensively in our constitution, that is to say, the executive Government of the Union can deal with all those matters on which the Union Parliament can legislate, and similarly the States' Executives. With regard to topics in the concurrent list both the Union and States have jurisdiction. In case there is a conflict between the two, the Union law shall prevail. In the legislative field the constitution provides for the Union Parliament to legislate on a topic in the State list temporarily in the interest of the nation, provided the Rajya Sabha passes a resolution with 2/3 majority of the members present and voting. It shall also be competent for the Parliament to make laws for any part or the whole of the country when there is the proclamation of an emergency, or for implementing a treaty or agreement with any other country.

The administrative relations range from the Union Government giving directions to a State to entrusting a State with some duties to be carried on by the State on behalf of the Union Government, though in theory "the administrative autonomy of the States is almost equal to the administrative autonomy of the Centre".[36]

The Union Parliament may decide, by a resolution to that effect in the Rajya Sabha, to create more All-India Services, besides the existing ones. The personnel of these services serve in the States also but the State Governments have no power to take disciplinary action of a serious nature against them. The Union Parliament may also provide for the adjudication of disputes between States with regard to the sharing of Inter-State river waters. The Inter-State water Disputes Act, 1956, is already on the statute book. An Inter-State Council may also be created for making recommendations on better co-ordination. In certain matters among States. It is also to be noted that according to Section 15 of the States Reorganisation Act, 1956, Zonal Councils are formed with membership for two or more States in each Zone. The meetings of all the Zonal Councils are to be presided over by the Union Minister for Home Affairs, who is nominated for the purpose by the President. Besides, there has been a network of agencies like the Central Board of Education, Transport etc.

The financial relations between the Union and the States are determined largely on the model of the Government of India Act, 1935. There are some taxes exclusively given to the Union; some exclusively given to the States, some are levied by the Union and collected by the States, some are to be levied and collected by the Union but given to the States. Taxes levied and collected by the States belong to them. States also receive grants-in-aid from the Union Government in certain cases. The question of distribution of the proceeds of income-tax etc., are to be referred to the Finance Commission from time to time. In respect of taxes levied and collected by the Union and the States, the Parliament makes the allocations. These provisions only indicate the grip the Union Government possesses over the States.

Finally, the working of the Planning Commission—which is not known to the constitution — the Election Commission, and the powers of the President to declare emergency only contribute to a closer control which the Union Government can exercise over the States. Critics feel that there is not much change in the position of the States in the new set-up except the change. So the States occupy a status of equality with the Union Government in certain matters, which are very few; a status that may be described as inferior in certain other matters; and finally one of subordination in many respects.[37]

In conclusion a few observations may be made. The growth of the administrative machinery of the Indian and the State Governments has been so intricately connected with the constitutional development that has taken place all along in the British period that it is hardly possible to examine them independently of each other. The trend in the earlier stages was in the direction of insisting on greater control and on ultimate power being retained in the hands of the Central authority, and the administrative machinery was particularly expected to serve the needs of the Imperial authority. It is only under the stress of the nationalist movement that the British Parliament conceded, in small measure from time to time, devolution of authority to Provinces. After Independence the whole outlook had to be naturally changed. The Federal principle, though adopted, was under severe reservations with regard to a strong Centre —a Centre growing at the cost of the States — because of the special problems faced by the country.

— A.M. Rajasekhariah

REFERENCES

1. In this paper the term "State" is used to mean (*i*) non-sovereign administrative units of the unitary British Government in India including the Provinces (referred to as Local Government), and the Princely States; and (*ii*) non-sovereign units of the Indian Federation later on.
2. Report of the Indian States Committee, 1928-29, p. 10.
3. The distinction and categorisation among states is wiped out according to the Constitution Amendment. (Seventh) Act, 1956, (States Reoganisation Act, 1956).
4. Report of the States Reorganisation Commission, 1955, Para 14.

5. Report on the Indian Constitutional Reforms, 1918, Para 39.
6. A Constitutional History of India, 1600-1935, A.B. Keith, p. 28.
7. Report of the States Reorganisation Commission, 1955, Para 15.
8. India—Its Administration and Progress—Sir John Stratchey 1903, p. 43.
9. Provincial Autonomy, 1937, K.T. Shah. p. 12.
10. The Transfer of Power in India—V.P. Menon, p. 6.
11. Government of India Act, 1935, Section—46, (Burma and Aden were excluded from India under Section. 268 of the said Act.).
12. Report of the Indian States Committee, 1928-1929, p. 10.
13. *Ibid.*, p. 11.
14. This Committee was appointed in December, 1927 to investigate the relationship between the Paramount Power and the States and to make recommendations for the adjustment of financial and economic relations between British India and the States. The Committee submitted its Report in March, 1929.
15. *Ibid.*, p. 12.
16. *Ibid.*, p. 15.
17. M/C Report—quoted in the Indian States Committee Report, p. 20.
18. The Commission was appointed under a Resolution of the Government of India in the Ministry of Home Affairs, with Mr. Fazl Ali as the Chairman, and its two other members were Pandit Hridayanath Kunjaru and Sardar K.M. Panikkar.
19. First Schedule to the Constitution as amended by Section of the Constitution (seventh Amendment) Act, 1956; and the Bombay Reorganisation Act, 1960.
20. A Bill has been introduced in the Indian Parliament for the constitution of a separate State of Nagaland.
21. Indian Constitutional Documents A.C. Banerji, Vol. I. p. 10.

22. A Constitutional History of India—A.B. Keith, p. 12.
23. Officials called the Supervisors were appointed in 1769 by Warren Hastings to supervise the collection of revenue by native Zamindars and to report on the state of the country—its produce, trade etc. They were made the Collectors of revenue in 1772 and entrusted with official and police administration. But these officals were withdrawn in 1774 only to be reappointed in 1786 since when they have been the one of Indian Administrative system.
24. *Ibid.*, p. 153.
25. Report of the Indian Statutory Commission—1930, Vol. 1, p. 111.
26. Report on the Indian Constitutional Reforms—1918, Para 17.
27. *Ibid*—Paras 188, 189, 190, 191.
28. The Working of Dyarchy in India—Kerala Putra, p. 18.
29. Report of the Indian Statutory Commission, Vol. I p. 126.
30. Report on the Indian Constitutional Reforms, 1918, Para 219.
31. Report of the Indian Statutory Commission, 1930, Vol. I p. 214.
32. *Ibid.*, p. 212.
33. Provincial Autonomy—K.T. Shah, p. 45.
34. See the Peamble to the Constitution of India.
35. Union and State Relations in India—K. Santhanam.
36. Union and State Relations in India—K. Santhanam, p. 25.
37. *Ibid*; Page 8.

3

THE GOVERNOR AND THE STATE ADMINISTRATION

It is now for more than twelve years that the present Indian Constitution has been working. There have been a few amendments to the Constitution; but they have not affected in any way the governor and his powers and position. The provisions in this behalf in the Constitution therefore, hold good in the very form and spirit in which they obtained on 26th January 1950, the day of the inauguration of the present Constitution of the Union of India.

Twelve years of working the Constitution in some thing like fifteen States and, that too, for more than two terms of office of five years each in each State has brought in its train various experiences and situations both for the respective Governors concerned as well as for the Chief Ministers and the people of those particular States. This does not mean that all kinds of permutation and combination of situations have arisen during this period and that they are all exhausted, though, of course, during this period roughly speaking, something like fortyfive Governors and as many Chief Ministers and one hundred and eighty Governor-years have been involved. There has not been much scope yet for very peculiar or impossible situations which could strain the Constitutional provisions. This has been so mainly because the Congress has been the All-India ruling party at the centre and only once in one State has an opposition party secured power and ruled for about twenty-eight months. The law and order and other situations there, that is in Kerala, deteriorated and the Governor had to use his special powers. Even so, the Governor as well as the Chief Minister were working with mutual understanding and cordiality even during the twenty-eight months of Communist regime.

The real test and strain on the present Constitutional provisions can be visualised only when the Central Government belongs to one party and when there is in power in a State a really powerful party which holds quite different views and the Governor belongs to the ruling party in the Centre. Such a situation can arise, for instance, in Tamil Nadu if the D. M. K. Party comes to power. Somewhat difficult situations can arise when the Chief Minister and his party treats the Governor as a superfluity or as something unnecessarily imposed. It may similarly be imagined that a Governor with experience and maturity on his side may look upon an over-ambitious Chief Minister with ridicule. Personal equations have much to do in such circumstances. These are not matters so much for the Constitution to solve as for adjustment between the persons concerned.

It may be said that the Constitution has yet to stand the test even as regards the powers and position of the President of the Union. There was recently a public controversy regarding the President's powers, though it is obvious that the Parliament is the supreme authority in all matters. Even the slightest encroachment on it under any circumstances would be an infringement of the Constitution and a mockery of democracy. Fortunately, no public controversy has yet arisen about any Governor's powers; though there have been many and varied internal clashes, which have been ultimately settled amicably by mutual understanding or by bowing to the interpretation of Law and the Constitution by competent authorities.

The constitution-makers discussed the question of the appointment of Governors for States and their position and powers vis-a-vis the President on the one hand and the Chief Minister of the State on the other. It was ultimately decided that he should be the constitutional head of the State and the Government should be carried on in his name and that he was to be representative of the President. He was not to be elected, but to be appointed by the President and was to hold office during his pleasure. His position in the State is analogous to that of the President at the Centre except that he has no responsibilities as regards the diplomatic or the military departments. But the Chief Minister is the real repository of power as he is the leader of the elected majority party in the Legislature. The State Legislature is really the supreme authority in the State just as the Parliament is in the Union.

Though the facts are as stated above, it is the Governor, according to the Constitution, who summons addresses, prorogues, adjourns and dissolves the Assembly and the Council, if any, of the State. It is he who appoints and calls upon the Chief Minister to form the government. The Council of Ministers is supposed to be appointed by him and all of them are to hold office during his pleasure. Analogous to the President's powers and responsibilities in the Union, the Governor's also include the power to cause the annual financial statements to be placed before the State Legislature and of making demands for grants and of recommending 'money bills' He has also the power of issuing Ordinances when the Legislature is not sitting. He can veto bills and/or reserve them for the consideration of the President. No Act though passed can become operative unless the Governor consents to it. He has the power of pardon also.

But all these powers have to be exercised in the capacity of the constitutional Head of the State and not in his discretion, nor in his individual capacity. This makes the whole position clear and ordinarily he has to be only the mouth-piece and the constitutional instrument of the Chief Minister of the State.

The Governor of a State is the ex-official Chancellor of the Universities in the State except, of course, of the National Universities. But here too, he is supposed to act not in his discretion as is usually understood, but according to the advice tendered by the Chief Minister. Thus there is very little scope for independent judgement or action for a Governor in matters with which he has to deal as a constitutional head.

Apart from the constitutional provisions and demarcation of powers of the Governor on the one hand and the President on the other, sometimes differences might have arisen in some cases as regards leave and going out of the state and such other smaller matters. But since the President is the supreme authority, the Governor has no choice but to bow to his superior. As regards the powers as between the Governor and the Chief Minister, differences have sometimes arisen as regards, (a) pardon, (b) appointment of judges of the High Court, (c) appointment of the Vice-Chancellors, (d) nomination of Members of the University to the Legislative Council, (e) Governor's confidential report to the President, (f) Governor's report as regards the Scheduled Castes and Tribes in the State, (g) submission of certain papers to the Governor, and (h) provisions in bills under legislation. This means that whenever there has been the slightest vestige of discretion to the Governor and some choice of action, there have occurred differences of opinion. The Chief Minister has often enough carried the day except when he has allowed the Governor to please himself. Thus the Governor is at a disadvantage and fights a losing battle often enough. But he can save himself all embarrassment if he realises the constitutional position and knows exactly what is meant by the term 'Constitutional Head'. Except in Assam, no Governor has any direct powers or responsibility save in emergencies. Only in Assam the Governor has direct responsibility regarding the NEFA area. But even there, the Chief Ministers have not been happy about these powers.

Does it mean then that he is a non-entity or that he has no useful functions to perform? No, that is not the case. His most important role is that he represents and acts in the name of the impersonal authority of the State and of the Union and not of any person or individual or any political party, and is equally approachable by all parties and groups. He is supposed to be above all parties and groups. His role is most significant when there is any impending break-down of the normal working of the Constitution. He immediately steps in and takes over as the agent of the President and carries on till normal conditions are restored. A few such crises have occurred during the last twelve years, as in Kerala, Orissa and so on, when the Governor took over and carried on till normal elections took place.

The Governor's role in a State in fields other than politics and administration can be a very significant and abiding one, if the person occupying the position is one who loves work and intensely wishes to be useful to the people among whom his lot has been cast. Social welfare in general and cultural activities can be the special fields of a governor's extra-official duties. In every State, since they are all welfare states, such activities are carried on a large scale by various official and non-official bodies. A welfare state cannot but have such activities. For instance, there are children's welfare societies, women's councils, Red Cross Societies, literary and other art societies, charitable hospitals, physical culture associations, research and study groups and so on and so forth.

The Governor has special advantages, if he makes up his mind to play an active role in these fields. He is the highest dignitary of the State, and its head. He is usually an elderly and experienced person and is honoured and respected everywhere. He is the highest paid officer in the State. He has resources and facilities for organising and for travelling around in the whole state as no one else has. The Chief Minister as well as other officers of state are usually ever willing to give extra time and attention to such activities, especially when they are sponsored or encouraged by the Head of the State.

It may be said to the credit of the President of the Union that some very healthy conventions have been developed as regards the choice and appointment of Governors. They have been men of experience and standing. With very few exceptions, persons of the same state have not been appointed as Governors. It may be mentioned that a Governor from outside the State has a distinct advantage. The term of office has been seldom extended in the same State beyond one term, that is five years. Rarely have Governors been allowed to be absent from their respective States for long periods. They have never been appointed without the consent of the Chief Ministers concerned. The annual meet of the Governors has been a regular feature. Seldom has any Governor failed to rise to the occasion and to act up to the expectations of the people of the State.

But after all is said and done, no hard and fast rule can be laid down for the mutual relationship and the conduct of Governors and Chief Ministers in States. If there is mutual goodwill and if there is a strong desire to take the fullest advantage of the Governor or the Chief Minister as the case may be, in the interest of the good of the people, the best results and lasting achievements can follow. If, on the other hand, the Raj Bhavan becomes an isolated spot and the Governor has seldom any occasion to enter the life of the people of the State, the Governor as well as the people may be said to be very unfortunate. It should not really be so. From whatever State or region the Governor may come, it is his duty to identify himself immediately with the people. Since he has to be there for five years, he must learn their language, respect their susceptibilities and strive to do good to them. In the same way, the Chief Minister and his people must make the Governor feel at home and see that opportunities are given to him, apart from routine official duties, to serve the people. That is the only way to make the institution of the Governor not merely constitutional but also useful.

— R.R. Diwakar

4

REVENUE ADMINISTRATION IN INDIA — A BACKGROUND

With more than 70% of the total population of the State deriving their livelihood from agriculture and allied occupations, it is but natural that the Revenue Departments comes into contact directly with the largest number of citizens. Successive governments had also to devote special attention to the organisation of the Revenue Department, as Land Revenue accounted for the bulk of the revenues of Provinces and States, till the thirties of this century, the only other important sources of revenue being Excise and Forest. During the last 25 years, however, the Provinces and States have been exploiting new sources of revenue and Land Revenue now occupies a comparatively minor place among the sources of revenue to the States. In the earlier days Revenue Officers were in charge of almost all items of work done on behalf of Government in the Districts and Taluks. Now most of the Districts and Taluks have got specialist officers of each Department but the load of miscellaneous work on Revenue official has not diminished. It is not possible to discuss all the items of work handled by Revenue Officers in this brief account. Hence this paper will be confined to Revenue administration proper, viz. to the relations between Government and the persons having an interest in land. It will be convenient to discuss these relations under the following sub-heads:

(*a*) Initial fixation and periodical revision of assessment on land.

(*b*) Recovery of land revenue.

(c) Agricultural Income-tax.

(d) Land Reform Legislation.

(e) Changes in the organisation and set up of the Revenue Department.

Before taking up a discussion of these topics, in the order mentioned above, I propose to give a brief historical background on the levy of land in India, to enable a better understanding of the present system.

Almost all over the world the State arranges to secure for itself by some form of a levy, a portion of the income derived by those who utilize land for various purposes. The methods adopted, however, vary considerably. In India, there is no uniformity in the system even in the areas which constituted British India upto 1947 and were under one Central Government. Almost each province had a different system. Experts who have examined the systems have opined that many of the complexities of Land Revenue can be traced to the fact that the Indian systems are the result of a gradual process of evolution from indigenous practices. These indigenous practices were moulded into their present shape by British Officers, quite independently of one another, to suit local circumstances in different provinces.

From time immemorial, it has been customary in India for the rulers to collect land revenue from those who cultivated land. It is, however, difficult to say when precisely this levy originated and in what form it was charged. According to the description given by Manu of the fiscal administration of an ancient Hindu State, the main source of the State revenue was a share of the gross produce of all land. This share was generally one sixth of the gross produce i.e. of the grain heap made up at the threshing floor. This share could, however, be raised to one fourth in times of war or during other emergencies. The share of produce due to the ruler was assessed upon a village as a whole. Its payment was the joint responsibility of the whole village community. The village headman who represented the community allocated this share among the individual owners with due regard to the condition and quality of the land cultivated by them. This simple method of assessment admirably suited the condition prevailing in those days. Being a share of the produce, its determination did not require any complicated calculations based on fertility of the land, and cost of production. Whatever was produced was heaped on the floor and the division was made in the presence of the King's Officers. In a bad year when the crops failed and there was no produce, relief was automatic.

Between the village headman and the King there was a chain of civil officers, consisting of lords of single villages, lords of 10 villages, lords of 100 villages and lords of thousand villages. These were responsible for the collection of the revenue. They were remunerated by fees in kind, by a portion of the King's produce or by holding land, free of revenue, in virtue of their office.

Difficulties, however, came to be experienced with the growth of population and extension of cultivation. The division of the share of the produce could not be properly supervised. The peasantry also often practised concealment. The King's officers also began to cheat both their master and the peasantry.

In the earlier days of the Muslim administration, the State share of the produce demanded by the Hindu Kings was converted into Khiraj or tribute payable on land in countries ruled by Muslims. The share taken was, however, greater than before. The existing agency of collection was also utilised. When some of the Muslim kingdoms expanded rapidly, the method of assessment was changed. The King's share of the produce was determined in accordance with the estimates framed on the standing crops. Later even this method was found unsuitable and the King's share came to be assessed in monetary terms. The system of payment of land revenue in cash thus came into vogue. Attempts at reforming system were first made by Sher Shah. A major change was brought about only during the reign of Akbar. With the assistance of his Minister Raja Todar Mal, Akbar laid the foundation of a system which furnished the basis for land revenue policy for generations thereafter. Under this system all the land was measured by a uniform standard and the average produce per bigah of land was ascertained. Land was classified into four categories according to soil and fertility and the gross produce was calculated on the basis of the produce grown during the preceding ten years. The average gross produce thus obtained for any particular piece of land was then commuted into cash on the basis of the prevailing prices in the previous thirteen years. The King's share was fixed at one third of this. The assessment so made was intended to continue unchanged for ten years. Actually it continued indefinitely as there were so regular revisions.

With the expansion of the Mogul Empire central authority became less effective. The provincial officers became powerful and exploited the landholders. Some of them important additional levies on the land in the form of cesses or abwah With the decline of the empire and during the anarchy they followed these officers openly flouted the central authority and assumed full control over the territory they administered.

Todar Mal's system involved the maintenance of a elaborate set of accounts and the employment of a host of tax gatherers, who intervened between the cultivator and the Supreme Government. One of these was the Zamindar, who was unknown to the early Hindu system. Originally he was merely a tax collector or farmer of the revenue, contracting to contribute a lump sum from the country allotted to him. With the expansion of the empire and the decline of the authority and the Central Government, these middlemen employed for collection of land revenue became stronger and exploited the pleasure ruthlessly. They paid lumpsum amounts to the Government or the provincial governor and appropriated and excess receipts for themselves. In course of time the middlemen claimed ownership of the lands also. They recovered large amounts in the form of rent and cesses and paid only the fixed land revenue to Government. The rulers and the chieftains did not much care what happened to the peasantry. They found the system of farming and land revenue collections suitable as they were saved the trouble of maintaining a large amount of tax-collector. They were also assured of regular receipts.

The East India Company after the acquisition of the 'Diwani' of Bengal, Bihar, and Orissa in 1765, continued for sometime the prevailing land revenue system and tried to collect its revenue through supervisors or collectors. These were shortly replaced by a Committee of Circuit who were instructed to tour the province, conduct auctions and make land revenue settlements with the highest bidders, the period of settlement being fixed at 5 years. The new system, however, proved unworkable. The old Zamindars and farmers who wished to retain possession of their lands had to bid higher and pay much more revenue than their estates could yield. Arrears accumulated and the income from land revenue went down. The disastrous famine of 1770 further worsened the condition of the peasantry.

PERMANENT SETTLEMENTS

It was about this time that the East India Company waged wars of conquest in different parts of India. A regular inflow of revenue was absolutely necessary to enable the company to consolidate its position and to expand its activities. The collection of land revenue direct from a large number of cultivators raised several problems at that time when the means of communication were poor and there was paucity of trained staff and lack of reliable records. It was also necessary for the company, which wanted to consolidate its position in India, to create a class of vested interests upon whose loyalty and devotion it could rely in times of difficulty. The Company was also interested in the extension of cultivation in order to increase its receipts and it hoped that settling the land revenue on a permanent basis would encourage such extension of cultivation and improvement of land. All these considerations led the East India Company to decide in favour of a permanent settlement of land revenue in the areas now covered by Bengal and parts of Bihar and Orissa. Under the 'permanent settlement' it was guaranteed that the land revenue then fixed would continue in perpetuity and the Zamindars were thus assured of the benefits of any future increments in the value of and income from lands. Actually, however, the permanent assessments were determined at about ten-elevenths of the rents received by the Zamindars. Similarly, though the Zamindars were given proprietary rights over the lands and were armed with powers over the person and property of the ryot, their estates were liable to be sold for arrears of revenue if they were not paid within the prescribed date. Therefore, in the period immediately following the permanent settlement, the Zamindars suffered heavily through excessive burden of land revenue assessment. The Bengal Land Revenue Commission, 1938, describes this period in the following words:—

"The period immediately after the permanent settlement and indeed for three or four decades, was one during which the Zamindars were struggling for their existence against the sale law. At that time, one third of the total area of Bengal according to Lord Cornwallis, two-thirds according to Colebrooke and four-fifths according to Grant, was uncultivated; and the only way in which the Zamindars could improve their assets was by bringing waste land under cultivation. The competition was not for lands, but for tenants to cultivate it. Consequently, if the ryots withheld their rent, or abandoned their holdings, the Zamindar was hard put to it to pay a revenue amounting to ten-elevenths of his assets. The records of that period and the Fifth Report show that more than half the estates in Bengal were sold for arrears of revenue; many of the large Zamindars were dismembered; and most of the original Zamindars reduced to poverty."

As time went on, however, cultivation was extended, prices rose and the rents increased. The burden of assessment on the Zamindars became lighter. Many of the Zamindars sublet their Zamindari or portions thereof to others and avoided even this trouble of directly collecting rents from their tenants.

MAHALWARI AND RYOTWARI SETTLEMENTS

There is little doubt that after a lapse of time permanent settlement led to expansion of cultivation. From the point of view of Government, there was the advantage that it ensured a regular inflow of land revenue. For that reason, it was extended to other parts of the country, viz. Benares and parts of Madras and Assam. Later, when the Company's rule was more securely established, the view gained ground that the State would benefit more from periodical settlements. Further, in certain parts of the Company's territories, viz. the U. P. (now Uttar Pradesh) and the Punjab, there, were well organised village communities and, barring a portion of the U.P., there were no local chieftains or large farmers of land in this area. These areas thus presented a different problem, and settlement was concluded with village communities and the villagers were held jointly and severally responsible for the payment of revenue. This came to be known as the Mahalwari system of land revenue, as the land revenue was assessed on the 'Mahal'. In some parts of Madras, the land revenue was directly settled with individual ryots in view of the difficulty of making settlement with the whole villages. This initiated the ryotwari system which was later introduced in Bombay and other neighbouring provinces. Both these systems—Mahalwari and Ryotwari—involved a detailed survey of fields and classification of lands according to soil. The assessments were fixed not in perpetuity but for definite period.

DISTINCTIONS BETWEEN DIFFERENT SYSTEMS

The different systems of settlements that were thus evolved in India can be broadly classified as (i) permanent or those in which assessment was fixed in perpetuity and (ii) temporary or those in which assessment was fixed for definite period. They can also be classified as (i) Zamindari, in which assessment was fixed on a village or Mahal jointly and severally on the whole village community and (iii) ryotwari, in which assessment was fixed on the holding of a ryot.

The main distinction between settlements with landlords in possession of single estates and settlement with proprietary bodies for group of estates on the one hand and the ryotwari system on the other hand is that in the former there is an intermediary between the actual cultivator and the Government, whereas in the latter there is none. Unlike in the Mahalwari tenure, in the ryotwari no joint responsibility is placed on all holders in a village and one land holder cannot be called upon to make good the default in payment of land revenue of any other land-holder in the village. The ryot cannot be evicted from his land so long as he continues to pay the assessment and he can transfer his rights in the land to others by a sale, gift, partition etc. He is also free to relinquish his holding or any part of it on giving due notice to Government.

DISPARITIES BETWEEN DIFFERENT STATES

Though the general pattern of land revenue settlement and assessment in India broadly follows the description given above, the development of the different systems has not been on the same lines in all the States. This disparity has been further widened with the integration of the former princely States where, except in a few States administered by retired or deputed officers from (British) India, there were no regular settlements or systems of land revenue. The result is that, at one end there were States like Punjab, Bombay (before the merger in it of certain princely States), Madras, Assam and former Mysore in which practically all the land had been surveyed, measured and settled on some definite principles. At the other there were States like Rajasthan, former Saurashtra and former Madhya Bharat where there were still large portions of unsurveyed and unsettled land and where settlements made in the past followed no scientific principles and had been more or less the result of political conditions prevailing in the State at the time. In between, there were States like Uttar Pradesh, and Madhya Bharath where there had been settlements on regular lines, but owing to the prevalent Zamindari system several intermediaries had crept in. Recently, these intermediaries have been eliminated and the former tenants have become occupants of land directly responsible to the State Governments for payment of revenue. But the revenue realised from these former tenants is the same as the revenue paid by them previously to the intermediaries and has now been revised on the abolition of the intermediaries. The lands have not been resettled on the hitherto accepted principles of revenue assessment, viz. productivity of the land, cost of cultivation, economic facilities etc. It appear that in these states, considerations such as past history, political expediency, and the administrative difficulties mostly influenced the rates of land revenue and these as likely to continue for a time. Conditions in the States of West Bangal, Bihar and Orissa are more or less similar and organised in quite a large part of these States, there was no organise land revenue administration at the lower level because of the permanent settlement. The records of lands were therefore in most cases not complete and accurate.

SETTLEMENTS AND RESETTLEMENTS

The system of assessment through settlements for a definite period and a revision of assessment after the period prevails generally in all parts of India except in the permanently settled areas or in certain insecure rivers tracts in some States, where a system of fluctuating land revenue is in force. Under the periodical settlement system, an area for which a settlement is undertaken cadastrally surveyed and classified according to fertility. The rate of revenue is then worked out by taking the consideration the yield of the principal crops, the price of agricultural produce, the rental and sale value of the land and ordinary expenses of cultivation. Other considerations like physical configuration, climate and rainfall, proximity to markets, means of communication and standard of husbandry also figure in the determination of the assessment at the time of the settlement. The assessment so determined is fixed for a term of years, varying from 15 to 20 years; the usual period is 30 years. When the revision of a settlement becomes due, the various changes that have occurred since the last settlement, in the conditions and circumstances relevant to the assessment of land revenue, are taken into consideration. The necessity for periodical revision of settlement arises mainly because of changes in—

(a) the area of the land and holdings; and

(b) the prices and yields of agricultural produce.

Many of the, states had fixed limits for increase of assessment at a revision settlement. Such limits were made applicable in Bombay, Hyderabad and Mysore State by executive instructions through the statute prescribed on such limits. The recent trend has been to remove such links on enhancement assessment due to revision.

DIFFERENT BASES OF LAND REVENUE

In calculating the land revenue payable to Government, different States adopt different methods. On the basis of the principles adopted, these methods can be classified as follows:

(i) net assets or economic rents,

(ii) net produce or annual value,

(iii) empirical,

(iv) rental value,

(v) capital value, and

(vi) gross produce.

(i) Net Assets or Economic Rents

Net assets form the basis of assessment in Punjab, Uttar Pradesh, Madhya Pradesh and certain of the erstwhile part B and C States like Pepsu, Himachal Pradesh, Ajmer and Delhi. Similar principles are followed in the temporarily settled areas of Bihar, Orissa and West Bengal. Net assets have been defined as the 'estimated average annual surplus of an estate or group of estates remaining after deduction of the ordinary expenses of cultivation as ascertained or estimated'. In other words, it is rent less all costs incurred in earning the rent. This is calculated by estimating the gross produce and deducting from it the cost incurred by the landlord. The gross produce is valued in terms of money at the commutation rate which is usually the average price of a particular crop for the preceding twenty years or more.

(ii) Net Produce or Annual Value

The former Madras Presidency and the Chief Commissioner's Province of Coorg were the only areas whereas produce was adopted as the basis of land revenue assessment. In the Districts of Bellary, South Karanra and Coorg and Kollegal Taluk of present Mysore State the assessment now in force has been fixed on the basis of an income.

The land revenue assessment is not to exceed fifty per cent of the net produce. To determine this the grow produce is first ascertained and valued at average prices and the cost of cultivation, etc., are then deducted. The terms usually included in the estimate of cost of cultivation are:

(1) Ploughing cattle. (2) Agricultural implements. (3) Seed. (4) Manure. (5) Labour required for ploughing, sowing, weeding, reaping, threshing etc.

A resettlement generally takes the shape of an enquiry into the economic conditions of a tract and the average into variations in prices of foodgrains. Except for special reasons, no re-classification of soil and no fresh calculation of grain out-turn, cultivation expenses, allowance for vicissitudes of seasons, etc., are made at a resettlement. The term of settlement is thirty years.

(iii) Empirical

The empirical basis of assessment was adopted in the former States of Bombay, Hyderabad and Mysore and also some of the smaller States. Sixteen out of the nineteen Districts of present Mysore State have had their land revenue assessment fixed on the empirical basis. This systems is so called because several factors are taken into consideration by the Settlement Officer at the time of the settlement or revision. The assessment is ultimately based to the subjective impressions of the Settlement Officer.

The system originally introduced by Mr. Pringle in the Poona District was more or less similar to that of Madras, but it broke down completely, partly owing to its complexity, but mainly because the assessments were too high. A new system devised by Mr. Goldsmith and Lieutenant Wingate was introduced about the year 1840 in Poona, and then with slight modifications extended to the rest of the Bombay Presidency. The procedure adopted by these two officers has been concisely described in a joint report submitted by them in 1840.

"The present condition of the agricultural classes, the state of particular villages, the amount of the Government realisations, the prices of produce and similar considerations, compared with those of preceding years, afford us the chief ground work for determining satisfactorily what abatement or addition should be made to the existing Jumma. We also by a similar process arrive at an opinion of what the rates of the different soils should be, and by applying these to the ascertained area and classification we find what amount of Jumma these rates will produce, and by examining whether this is as much in abatement or excess of the existing Jumma as our previously formed opinions had led us to think necessary we are enabled to correct our first estimate of the approximate amount of the Jumma and thereby finally settle our rates."

At the original survey the lands were classified after careful enquiries as to their fertility into several groups and their relative values expressed in fractions of a rupee 16 annas representing the best class of soil. The classification of the soils was not made with the object of basing the assessment on the net produce, but merely served as a basis for the apportionment of the total demand determined for the area on general considerations.

The determination of the assessment involved them distinct operations. The talukas were first grouped according to "marked and permanent distinctions", such as climate, situation and the general condition of cultivation. The next process was the determination of the total demand for the area under settlement by an examination of the revenue and economic history of the tract. The third and final operation was the distribution of the aggregate thus determined over the individual survey numbers with reference to the soil classification described above. The settlement officer's final decision thus depends "not upon the formal working out of results based on theory, but rather upon the subjective impressions of local knowledge and experience."

The same system was adopted by Hyderabad and Maysore States with some minor changes.

(iv) Rental Value

The main emphasis in all the above States except Madras is on rental value. Though the basis of assessment in these States is net assets or is empirical, the general method adopted is to determine by enquiry the actual rents received by the landholders and then to fix the assessment after allowing for certain deductions. The recent trend in tenancy legislation is to fix the maximum rents payable by the tenants, and it seems clear that rental value cannot, in future, be relied upon for determining the land revenue.

(v) Capital Value

Capital value has not been adopted as a basis of assessment in any State in India, though in practically all the State, the sale and mortgage values of the land form one of the factors taken into consideration at the time of settlement.

(vi) Gross Produce

Before the more scientific methods of assessment were evolved, gross produce formed the basis of assessment is almost all States in India. In Assam, this basis still continues and the limit of assessment for any tract has been fixed at ten per cent of the value of gross produce of that tract.

LAND REVENUE ADMINISTRATION

The administrative machinery for the collection of land revenue is more or less of a uniform pattern in all States, except in areas under permanent settlement. The usual practice is for States to be divided into division and districts, with Commissioners in charge of the divisions and Collectors or Deputy Commissioners in charge of the districts. The districts are again divided into tehsils or talukas, each in charge of a Tehsildar with one or two Naib-Tehsildars to assist him. Below these there is a well organised system of village officers who actually collect the land revenue, prepare accounts and keep records. Hitherto most of the village officers held their posts on a hereditary basis. The recent trend however, is to replace them by paid officials. The village officers are "lambardars" or "patils" who collect the land revenue and patwaris are village accountants. The functions of the lambardar or patil are:—

(1) to collect and pay into the treasury the land revenue and all sums recoverable as land revenue; and

(2) to aid in carrying out harvest inspections, surveys and in maintaining the record of mutations.

In some States, the patil is sometimes also assigned certain quasi-magisterial duties. The duties of a patwari or a village accountant are —

(1) to make surveys for field inspection, record of crops, revision of maps, and to furnish reports relating to mutations, partitions, takavi advances etc;

(2) to report calamities affecting crops, including crop positions, to assist the Revenue and other officers visiting his taluka in the performance of their duty; and to assist generally in collection of land revenue.

In the permanently settled areas, there has been till recently no elaborate administrative machinery at the village level for the collection of land revenue as it was paid direct into the State treasury by the estateholder or the zamindar. In the initial stages of the introduction of permanent settlement, Kanungoes and Patwaris were appointed to supervise the accounts and to help the zamindars, gumastas or agents for making local collections. But later, when Government ceased to look into the details of local collections and concerned themselves only with the lumpsums payable by the zamindars, the posts of Kanungoes were abolished, while the Patwari became a servant of the zamindar. The introduction of the recent agrarian reforms abolishing the zamindari tenures in these areas has, however, necessitated a change in the revenue administration. The State Government concerned with these areas have in most cases already reorganised their administrative machinery to suit the changed conditions.

During the second half of the 19th century when the principles of land revenue assessment still in vogue were finalised, the main anxiety appears to have been to levy a fixed sum in respect of each land, the amount being fixed for a long period, generally 30 years. It was then felt that by fixing the assessment for long periods, the cultivator who was mostly illiterate can be saved from unlawful extortions of the local revenue officers, which would be easy under a fluctuating system. The fixed levy was no doubt so calculated that it would not work as hardship over a period of years as the average out-turn of crops was considered. This concept of an average which would leave some surplus in good years for being carried over to bad years, is itself inapplicable when the bulk of the cultivators are small holders, working at the bare subsistence level. The bulk of the agricultural classes had thus no surplus even in very good years.

The inadequacies of the existing systems of levying land revenue have been recognised from a long time. Nearly 40 years back the Indian Taxation Enquiry Committee pointed out that if the canons of taxation are applied to land revenue only the canon of certainty is satisfied. The canon of convenience is not fully satisfied. The application of the canon of economy is found difficult as the exact proportion of the expenditure relating to District and Taluk administration relating to land revenue alone cannot be determined. It is, however, clear that even if only the cost of the establishment at lower levels dealing mainly with the assessment and collection of land revenue is taken into consideration the cost of collection constitutes. A greater percentage of the receipts than in the case of later levies like income-tax and sales tax. The canon of ability too fails but the doctrine of progression was held by the committee to be inapplicable to land revenue which was considered essentially as a tax on things and not on persons. It was pointed out that land revenue viewed scheme of taxation is not only not progressive but actually tends in the opposite direction. The system of periodical settlement was recommended to be continued, the basis and pitch of assessment being made definite and the procedure as simple and cheap as possible. An element of progression was also suggested. To secure these essentials the Committee recommended that the basis of Settlement should be annual value which was defined as the gross produce less cost of production, including the value of the labour actually expended by the farmer and his family on the holding and the return for enterprise. The rate of assessment was not to exceed 25% of the annual value. Progression in the case of the large holder was to be secured through an income tax on agricultural incomes or by levy of succession duty or both. Exemption of tax to the poorest cultivator was ruled out as land revenue was deemed to be a tax in rem.

These recommendations of the Taxation Enquiry Committees were not, however, implemented by any Province or State till the attainment of Independence. It is likely that the Economic Depression of the thirties was one of the reasons for shelving this question. Moreover, ever since the Bardoli Satyagraha, revision of land revenue assessment became a political issue. The story of Bardoli by Mahadev Desai contains some of the family budgets of the agriculturists of Bardoli. According to these cultivation by itself left the agriculturists with a deficit in more of the cases. The surplus, if any, came from non-agricultural pursuits such as sale of milk products. And reform to base land revenue assessment on annual value was therefore inopportune.

The first Congress Ministry of former Bombay State which assumed office in 1937, was among the earliest to tackle the question of revising the system of land revenue assessment. The amendment to the Bombay Land Revenue Code effected by Bombay Act XX of 1939 brought to it Statute book for the first time the underlying principles of settlement of land revenue. The principles of assessment methods of valuation, the pitch of assessment, the principle of revision; and the linking of assessment to the prices specified produce were incorporated in the Bombay Law Revenue Code. The rental value was made the basis for working out the assessment. The main features of the amendment were as follows:

1. The maximum limit of assessment was fixed at per cent of the rental value of lands;
2. Enhancement of assessment was limited to 30 per cent as maximum;
3. Reduction or increase in assessment by rebate or placing a surcharge on the assessment was to be made with reference to prices of special agricultural produce;
4. Provision was made for exemption from assessment for water charges;
5. Factors for determining assessment were clearly stated;
6. Settlement reports were to be placed on the tables of legislature for information of M.L.A's. and M.L.C's.
7. Provision was made for reference to the B. R. Triburinal.

It will, however, be seen that the Bombay Act of 1939 did not introduce any new principles of importance but merely crystallised the considerations which had guided Settlement Officers for a period of nearly 100 years.

The only change of a fundamental character effected prior to the achievement of independence was in the princely State of Travancore. In this State as in Madras the assessment originally levied was a share of the yield from the land, after deducting the cultivation expenses. This system was changed in 1946 and the levy of a uniform tax (originally about 14 annas per acre; now Rs. 2.00 per acre) on all lands irrespective of whether it is dry or wet or garden and irrespective of the tenure, was introduced. Agricultural income-tax was also introduced on all agricultural incomes exceeding Rs. 2000/-. After the merger of Cochin and Travancore States, the basic tax was extended to the area of former Cochin State also and in 1957 the levy of basic tax was extended to all the areas of Kerala State. The Supreme Court held that the levy of a uniform tax on all land, irrespective of its productivity, violates the constitution. Kerala State has passed a new law in 1961 which also imposes basic tax at two rupees per acre per annum on all lands of whatever description and held under whatever tenure but provides at the same time for relief in respect of lands whose gross income is less then ten rupees per acre, by reducing the rate of basic tax to one fifth of the gross income from the land.

DEVELOPMENTS SINCE INDEPENDENCE

The integration of Princely States and their merges (some with erstwhile Part A States, some with erstwhile Part B States and some in erstwhile Part C States) and the implementation of Land Reforms relating to the abolitions of intermediaries set new and important tasks to the revenue administrations of States. In the formerly princely States, the degree of political and administrative efficiency varied greatly. Consequently, there was great diversity in the land revenue system in those areas. Thus in most of the areas of former princely States which merged a former Bombay State, the assessments were much higher than those prevailing in the neighbouring areas, of the Bombay State. To give relief to the people of these merged States, the Bombay Government provided that when the assessment in the merged areas exceeded that in the premerged part by 20% the excess over that percentage should be remitted. The areas of Ramdurg, Jamkhandi, Jath, Mirs Senior, Miraj Junior, Kolhapur, Kurundwas Senior, Kurundwas Junior, Sangli, Mudhol, Aundh and Savanur now in the Districts of Bijapur, Belgaum and Dharwar got relief.

With the abolition of intermediaries the question of the rate of land revenue for the individual cultivators holding assumed importance. In many States the whole class of tenants and the outgoing intermediaries in respect of land allowed to be retained by them continued to pay the old rates of rent and assessment. The Mysore, Madras and Hyderabad Acts for abolition of intermediaries, however, provided for recovery of only levy the land revenue assessment proper fixed on the basis of general principles .of settlement for the land in question. In the interim period till fixation of such assessment, the rates applicable in adjoining areas already brought under settlement it were levied.

In the post-independence period, taxation of land used for agricultural as well as non-agricultural purposes was reviewed in detail by the Taxation Enquiry Commission 1953-'54. The Commission has pointed out that in perspective of the vast changes in agricultural economy, including the big upward movement in agricultural prices, land revenue has shrunk in dimensions and also that a simple fiscal system with land revenue as its main feature has been transformed into the complex system of the present day in which several other Central and State taxes occupy a far more important place than that occupied by land revenue. While recognising that agricultural income-tax in addition to land revenue will make land taxation as whole more equitable, the Commission opines that agricultural income-tax cannot replace land revenue in the sense of constituting roughly an equivalent source of revenue for State Governments. A combination of basic tax at a flat rate with agricultural income-tax was also ruled out as an alternative to land revenue. Replacement of land revenue by levy of sales tax on primary agricultural produce was not considered feasible in view of several administrative and financial difficulties. The Commission recommended that the future pattern of settlement and revision should be largely similar to the existing ryotwari system but should make a departure from it in significant respects.

The Commission regarded survey classification and initial settlement as evolved with minor differences in many States as indispensable operations but felt that the same could not be said of revision settlements, in to manner in which they had been conducted in the past. In view of the administrative effort involved and the requirements of trained personnel for tackling all the land where resettlements are overdue, the Commission recommended that the present method of resettlements may be abandoned. It was pointed out that local condition distinguished from prices and even of local prices increased to have the same significance as in the past for its fixation of assessment levels. The Commission recommended that land revenue should be revised once in a years with reference to the changes in the price level. Such revision was to be effected for smaller units as under the present system. Similarly price levels for the State in whole or for the regions should be considered and in local prices. The revision upward, or downward, was to be within strictly defined limits and effected with reference to changes in the price level. The increase or reduce was not, however, to be proportionate to the price change. No changes were to be made for moderate fluctuation i.e. changes up to 25% in either direction. Even who appreciable variation occurred, the adjustments in the revenue should be only a moderate proportion of the point changes, as any change in the incidence of land revenue would be justified only if related to the change in the income of the cultivator, and normally the cost of production also varies in the same direction as prices. Moreover, the scale adopted for making adjustments was to such as to leave ample margin for the cultivator. The relief given in the event of a fall in prices was to be general than the enhancement for a rise in prices in the same proportion.

The following illustrative scale was suggested by the Commission for enhancement and reduction of land revenue on the basis of price levels are given on the next page.

Before introducing this system of decennial review of assessment in a State as a whole or in a homogeneous region of a State, on the basis of prices, the present land of assessment had to be standardised, having regard to different assessment levels of different areas of the land settled or resettled at different times. It was recognised that the process of such standardisation would only and in reducing disparities to the extent practicable and not by any means one of eliminating them. Complete elimination of disparities was considered neither fixed nor necessary. A maximum limit had·to be postulaed for the increase and decrease also if the question of reduction did actually arise. Standardisation was to be wide, simple and *ad hoc.* The increase had to be gained

Rise in Prices	*Land Revenue Increase in land Revenue*
Upto 25 per cent (4 annas in the rupee)	Nil
Above 25 per cent (4 annas in the rupee) but not above 31¼ per cent 5 annas in the rupee	$3\frac{1}{8}$% (half annas in the rupee).
Above 31¼ per cent (5 annas in the rupee) but not above 37½ per cent 6 annas in the rupees)	6¼% (one annas in the rupee)
Above 37½ per cent (6 annas in the rupee) but not above 43¾ per cent (7 annas in the rupee)	$9\frac{3}{8}$% (one and a half annas in the rupee)

Fall in prices	*Reduction in land revenue.*
Upto 25 per cent (4 annas in the rupee)	Nil
Above 25 per cent (4 annas in the rupee) but not above 31¼ per cent 5 annas in the rupee)	6¼% (one annas in the rupee)
Above 31¼ per cent (5 annas in the rupee) but not above 37½ per cent (6 annas in the rupee)	12¼% (two annas in the rupee)
Above 37½% per cent (6 annas in the rupee) but not above 43¾ per cent (7 annas in the rupees)	18¾% (three annas in the rupee)
Above 43¾% per cent (7 annas in the rupee)	25% (four annas in the rupee)

in relation to the price period relevant to the settlement and resettlement at which the existing assessment was fixed. The maximum increase of 25% was to be in respect of the settlement units where the existing assessment was with reference to the prices during 1880-1899. There to be no increase in settlement units where existing assessment was based on the prices subsequent to 1940. It increase was to be 12½% in settlement units where existing assessment was fixed on the basis of prices during 1900-1920 and 6¼ in settlement units which had adopted the price during 1920-1939.

Levy of agricultural income tax on all agricultural incomes above Rs. 3,000/- was also recommended by the Commission to bring greater equity into the system.

The recommendations relating to land revenue of yet to be implemented in most of the States. The State of Bombay, however, amended its Land Revenue Code 1936 to bring the Settlement System in conformity with the recommendations of the Taxation Enquiry Commission. Under the new procedure introduced by this amendment:

(1) The area to be settled has to be constituted into Zones, consisting of Taluks or parts which are homogeneous in respect of physical configuration, climatic condition, rainfall principal crops grown in the area and soil characteristics.

The lands in each Zone have to be divided into groups, on a consideration of the following factors: (i) Physical configuration, (ii) Climate and rainfall (iii) Prices and (iv) Yield of principal crops. The law provides for the following additional factors also being taken to consideration in forming groups if deemed necessary.

(a) Markets *(b)* Communications *(c)* Standard of husbandry *(d)* population and supply of labour *(e)* agricultural resources *(f)* variations in area of occupied and cultivated lands during the last 30 years *(g)* wages *(b)* ordinary expenses of cultivating principal crops, including wages of the cultivator for his labour in cultivating the land and *(i)* sales of land used for the purpose of agriculture.

In respect of each class of land in each group the standard rates have to be fixed by the Settlement Officer. Standard rate with reference to any particular class of land in a group has been defined as the value of one sixteenth of the average yield of crops per acre of land in that class of sixteen annas classification value. The land revenue assessment of individual survey numbers and subdivisions divisions is to be based on their classification. After every ten years from a settlement the Government can enhance or reduce the assessment on land in any and by placing a surcharge or granting a rebate on the assessment by reference to the alteration of prices of principal crops in that zone.

— K. Balasubrahmaniam

5

THE PUBLIC SERVICE COMMISSION, ITS POWERS AND FUNCTIONS— A CRITICAL ASSESSMENT

The idea of a Public Service Commission in India was first mooted in 1919 in the Despatch on the Indian constitutional reforms, and the Government of India Act, 1919, contained a provision for the establishment of Public Service Commission. No action was, however, to set up the Commission. The Royal Commission in the Superior Civil Services in India, known as the Lee Commission, observed in their report, "Wherever democratic institutions exist, experience has shown that to assure an efficient Civil Service, it is essential to protect it, so far as possible, from political or personal influences and to give it that position of stability and security which universal to its successful working as the impartial and sufficient instrument by which Governments, of whatever political complexion, may give effect to their policies" and recommended that the statutory Public Service Commission contempted by the Government of India Act, 1919, should be established without delay. A Central Public Service Commission known as the "Public Service Commission (India)" was set up in 1926 for the all-India and higher Services. The Simon Commission recommended establishment of Public Service Commission in all provinces in order to relieve Ministers from the technical work of recruitment and to prevent them from being exposed to the charge of using their positions to prompt family or communal interest at the expense of efficient or just administration, of the Services. The Government of India Act, 1935, provided for the establishment

Federal and Provincial Public Service Commission. There were several unsatisfactory features in the position of members of these commissions, which effected the independence. Important matters such as the tenure members and the method of the termination of the service were left to be determined by regulations to framed by the executive governments. Members was eligible for extension and, except the Chairman, for the employment in government service, after retirement with the consent of government. The Constitution of India, framed after independence, has done away with the imperfections and the position of the commissions is not broad-based on a statutory foundation.

The new Constitution provides for the establishment of a Public Service Commission at the Centre, known to the Union Public Service Commission and one for each for or a group of two or more States. Their main features as:

(*i*) Appointment of members (a member including the Chairman) by the President in the case of U.P.S.C. or a Joint Commission and by the Governor in the case of a State Commission.

(*ii*) Fixed tenure of office of a member for six year or until the attainment of the age of 65 years in the case of the Union Commission or 60 years in the case of Union Public Service Commissions.

(*iii*) Determination of the number of members of the Commission and their conditions of service is left to the President or the Governor, as the case may be, provided that the conditions of service of a member shall not be varied to his disadvantage after his appointment.

(*iv*) A member of any Public Service Commission can only be removed from his office by the President on the ground of misbehaviour in consultation with the Supreme Court, or if he is adjudged insolvent, or engages during his term of office in any paid employment outside the duties of his office, or is, in the opinion of the President, unfit to continue in office by reason of infirmity of mind or body.

(*v*) The entire expenses of the Commission are charged to the Consolidated Fund of India or the State concerned, as the case may be, that is to say, they are not required to be submitted to the vote of Parliament or the State Legislature.

(*vi*) All regulations made by the President or Governor excluding any matter from the purview of the Commission have to be laid before Parliament or the State Legislature for such modification as it may deem fit to make.

(*vii*) Placing of the annual report of the Commission by Government before the legislature together with a memorandum explaining, as respects the cases, if any, where the advice of the Commission was not accepted, together with the reasons for such non-acceptance.

(*viii*) Further employment of a member is severely restricted as indicated below:

(*a*) The Chairman of the Union Commission is completely debarred from further employment under the Central or State Government.

(*b*) The Chairman of a State Commission may be appointed as Chairman or member of the Union Commission or as Chairman of any other State Commission.

(*c*) A member of the Union Commission (other than Chariman) may be appointed as Chairman of the Union Commission or any State Commission.

(*d*) A member of a State Commission (other than Chariman) may be appointed as Chairman or member of the Union Commission or as Chairman of that or any other State Commission.

The Commission is in a very strong position from a constitutional point of view. Like the Executive and Legislature, it is created by the same sovereign authority namely, the Constitution of India. It is thus in no way subordinate to the legislature or the executive. The framers of the Constitution have provided for all reasonable safeguards to make the Commissions in India Immune from all undue influences, and to enable them to carried out their allotted duties with impartiality, integrity and independence, without fear or favour.

POWERS AND FUNCTIONS OF COMMISSIONS

The .functions (which include power) of the Commissions are:—

(*i*) to advise Government on all matters relating to the method of recruitment and the principles to be followed in making appointments to civil services and civil posts, and in making promotions and transfer from one service to another and on the suitability of candidates for such appointments, promotions or transfers.

(*ii*) to conduct examinations for appointment to the services;

(*iii*) to advise on disciplinary matters affecting Government servants;

(*iv*) to advise on claims for costs of legal proceedings instituted against a Government servant and on the claims for pension in respect of injuries sustained by a Government servant while on duty;

(*v*) to advise on any other matter specifically referred to them by the President or the Governor.

There is a provision for extending the functions of the Commission by Parliament or a State Legislature not only in respect of Government Services, but also in respect of services under Local Authorities, Corporations and other public institutions.

It will be observed that the Commission, as envisaged in the Constitution, is a purely advisory body. In this connection, it is interesting to recall the following observations made by Sir Samuel Hoare, the then Secretary of State for India, in the British Parliament during the passage of the Government of India Bill, 1935:

"It was the definite view of the Joint Select Committee, and it is the definite view of my advisers here and in India, that the Public Service Commission had much better be advisory. Experience goes to show that they are likely to have more influence if they are advisory than if they have mandatory powers. The danger is that if you give them mandatory powers, you then set up two Governments in a Province, and two Governments at Centre, and there is everything to be said against a procedure of that kind. From many points of view, it is much better that they should be advisory."

It is open to Government either to accept or reject the advice tendered by the Commission, but there is a provision, as stated above, requiring the Government, while presenting the Commission's annual report to the legislature, to explain the reasons why in particular cases the advice of the Commission was not accepted. This is a safeguard against arbitrary action by them in disregared and of the Commission's advice.

I shall now attempt to make a critical assessment of the position, powers and functions of a State Commission in this country. The constitutional independence given to the Commission is largely vitiated by vesting the appointment of members in the hands of the Governor, i.e., the Chief Minister in actual practice. The Chief Minister often appoints persons on political, communal regional and other grounds, and not solely on merit, and human nature being what it is, such persons usually find it difficult to resist ministerial pressure and influence in carrying out their duties in an independent and impartial manner.[1] Things would certainly improve if the appointments are made by the President in consultation with the Chief Justice of India, as in the case of High Court Judges. This would also being accordance with the general principle that the appointing and removing authority should be the same. When the Government of India was considering amendments to the Constitution, the Madhya Bharat Commission suggested an amendment to vest the appointments in the President, but was told in reply that the State Governments did not agree to the proposal. They would not naturally like to shed their power of patronage and of indirectly controlling recruitment of services. It would be further desirable if one or two members of the Commission are chosen from outside the State; as this will enhance its reputation for impartiality in the eyes of the general public.

There is no rational basis for the difference in the retirement of the members of the Union Commission and the State Commissions, especially as it is rarely that members of the State Commissions are promoted to the Union Commission. There is a similar difference in the case of the High Court and Supreme Court Judges, but it is now proposed to raise the superannuation age of the High Court Judges to 62, even though the recruitment to the Supreme Court is usually done from among the High Court Judges. The question, therefore, of increasing the age limit of the members deserves consideration. The Constitutional provision which operates invidiously against the members of the Commission is the embargo on their further re-employment in Government Service after retirement. Although the High Court and the Commission enjoy almost the same constitutional position and importance in a State, there is no such embargo on the re-employment of Judges and there have been recently several instances of Judges appointed as Governors and Ambassadors, after retirement. The idea behind the embargo is said to be to ensure the independence of members. Does this mean that the independence of Judges is of less importance than that of the members? Again, even with the present embargo, can it be said that the members, as a class, have maintained their independence? Independence depends solely on the character of the person appointed, and if unsuitable person are chosen, no amount of constitutional provisions would preserve their independence. I do not urge that the disqualification should be removed but I do advocate that the invidious distinction between the Judges and the members should be removed. It is an oversight in the Constitution for which there is no justification. Though such an embargo deprives the nation of the services are some experienced and highly trained persons, it is necessary as there can be no guarantee that only suitable persons will be appointed on the Bench or the Commission.

Though the Commission is an advisory body, its advice is considered, by way of convention, as mandatory on Government in all democratic countries. There has not been a single instance in living memory in the United Kingdom where the Civil Service Commission's advice was flouted by Government. In our country, however the Union and State Governments were inclined, in the early years of independence, to reject the advice if it was not to their liking, and, with the sure majority at their back, were not unduly perturbed at the constitution provision that reasons for such non-compliance have to be placed before the legislature concerned. One Union Home Minister stated on the floor of Parliament that the Government was not a rubber stamp of the Union Public Service Commission, while one of the Chief Minister declared in the Assembly that the Ministers should have become the last word in making appointments, as they were the elected representatives of the people. If this argument is valid, the decisions of judges who are also not elected representatives of the people should not be binding on Governments. Though the position has much improved at the Centre, it leaves much to be desired in most of the States. In other countries also, the obligation to accept the advice of the Commissions is, as stated above, more of the nature of a convention, but an indirect statutory safeguard also exists in some. For example, in the United Kingdom, the Superannuation Act of 1859 contains provision that no civil servant can draw a pension unless his appointment had been made with the concurrence of the Civil Service Commission. Some such statutory safeguard should be provided in this country also to check the tendency to depart from the advice of the Commissions.

Proviso to clause (3) of Article 320 of the Constitution empowers the President as regards the all-India services and other services and posts in connection with the affairs of the Union and the Governor as regards the services and posts in the State to make regulations to specify the matters in which it shall not be necessary for Public Service Commission to be consulted. These regulations are called "Limitation of Functions Regulations." Though clause (5) of the Article requires that such regulations shall be laid before the legislature concerned as soon as possible after they are made and shall be subject to such modifications as the legislature may make, this safeguard has been found to be ineffective in preventing Governments from abusing this power, either because of the mechanical majority at their command in the legislature or because of the absence of a vigorous Opposition. This power, which was obviously intended to enable a Government to employ specialists on a contractual basis or to make temporary appointments for political reasons, has been often used to withdraw from the purview of the Commission many posts and even wholesale departments. Instances have been known in which Government used this power to withdraw a particular post from the preview of the Commission, appoint its nominee to it and then restore it to the Commission. A recent example of the abuse of this power is the notification[2] issued by the Mysore Government, removing Class III and IV posts from the jurisdiction of the State Commission. The Government was stated to have issued the order to give relief to the Commission which was overburdened with work, though the Commission had never complained of overwork and had protested strongly against the Government's move.

These posts form the bulk of Government jobs and it is estimated that this order will take away nearly 80% of the Commission's work. If a Commission is considered incompetent or dilatory, appropriate remedies can be applied instead of assuming powers which properly belong to the Commission under the Constitution. If the power is to be used in this arbitrary fashion to deprive a Commission of the bulk of its work, a better course would be for the Government to undertake recruitment of the personnel and to abolish the Commission. If such an extreme step is considered improper, any serious reduction of the Commission's authority is equally improper. There are also no grounds for discriminating between the higher and lower classes of Government posts, as far as recruitment is concerned. As this is not a solitary instance and as similar notifications were issued in the Punjab, the former Madhya Bharat and elsewhere, it is necessary to amend the Constitution to delete this proviso and to provide that recruitment to all posts and services is undertaken by the Commissions, except in cases provided for separately in the Constitution such as the appointment of Judges, as in the United Kingdom. It is clear that the retention of this power to limit the functions of the Commissions is not justified in a democratic set-up of Government.

Another favourite method of the executive to encroach on the legitimate sphere of the Commission is to misuse the power enjoyed by it under the Limitation of Functions Regulations to make temporary appointments for periods not .exceeding six months or so. This power, which was obviously intended to make appointments in emergencies so that Government work should not suffer, has often been used too indiscriminately by Governments and has been a constant source of friction between them and the Commissions. The annual-reports of the various Commissions are replete with complaints that posts have been filled by appointment of departmental nominees on the ostensible ground that the posts were temporary though they were most likely to continue beyond the period permissible under the Regulations and that these nominees were kept in office far in excess of the period without a reference to the Commission with the result that the experience which they gain of the duties of the post given them an undue advantage over candidates from the open market. The gross abuse of this power of making temporary appointments can be effectively checked by making it obligatory to prepare departmental annual forecasts of personnel requirements in terms of which the Commission would make recruitment, with holding the salaries of candidates after the expiry of the permissible period by the Accountant-General and by sending departmental monthly returns to the Commission showing the temporary appointment made during the month.

Another cause for friction between the Government and the Commission is the question of promotion. Clause (3) (b) of Article 320 of the constitution requires that the Commission shall be consulted on the principles to be followed "in making promotions and transfers from one service to another and on the suitability of candidates for such promotions or transfers." It is contended to Governments that this provision requires them to consult the Commissions only if promotion is to be made first one service to another and not in the same service. This would mean that if an overseer in the Public Working Department is to be promoted to the post of Assistant Engineer, the Commission will be consulted, but consultation is necessary if an Assistant Engineer is promoted to various higher posts right up to the Engineer. In the absence of a comma after the 'promotion' in the clause, Government's contention seems to be right, but it is improper that such an important thing as promotion even in the same service, should be excluded from the purview of the Commission. Even now, the Commission is consulted for promotion in the same service in some States like Bombay and Orissa. The position at the Centre is that the Government of India, while not considering it obligatory to consult the Union Commission as regards promotion in the same service, have introduced the system of Departmental promotion Committees which deal with all promotions to be made on the basis of selection. These Committees consist of a member of the Commission who presides and officers of the department concerned who have personal knowledge of the work of the officers to be considered for promotion. The fact that a member of the Commission presided at the meetings does not obviate the necessity of Government's referring to the Commission for approval their recommendations in regard to promotions which are with in the purview of the Commission. The recommendations of the Committee regarding promotions which are outside the Commission's purview need not be referred to the Commission for approval unless the member attending the Committee desires them to be so referred. The association of a member of the Commission with the Committee ensures proper consideration and objective assessment of the claims of all persons eligible for promotion. The State Governments would be well-advised to follow the practice prevailing at the Centre and to set up such Committees for all promotions.

One of the most important functions of a Commission is to hold open competitive examinations for appointment to the services. Such examinations are held by all the commissions except the Madhya Pradesh Commission for all regularly constituted services. The written test is usually combined with a viva voice test or interview which is designed primarily to assess those mental qualities which may be said to constitute 'personality', brain or intelligence being left to be assessed by the written examination. There is now no prescribed minimum standard at the only test and the combined marks of the written and oral tests determine a candidate's place in the result sheet. Formerly, minimum qualifying marks were necessary in the oral test for recruitment to the I. A. S. and allied services, but this has been now done away with in view of public criticism. The change may be all right for the Income Tax, Accounts and other services for which personality is not essential There may be also differences of opinion on the conduct and content of a personality test, but the possession of a minimum personality qualification is essential for administrative services such as the I. A. S. and I. P. S., if we want to maintain efficiency in administration. For posts outside the regularly constituted services, selection is made only on the basis of interviews, as the number of vacancies is very small. For such interviews, the Commission invites a representative of the department concerned to assist it. It also usually invites an outside expert for assistance in recruitment to posts requiring technical, scientific or specialised qualifications. Though the members of the Commission take into account the opinion of the departmental or expert adviser, the selection entirely rests with them. The practice followed by some Commission to select more candidates than the number of posts advertised gives a loophole to the executive to upset the order of priority given by the Commission and to choose the candidates it likes from the list. The interviews held by the Union Commission for the all-India services like the I.A.S., and the I. P. S., include psychological tests and group discussions, but those held by the State Commissions are simple and last for about 10 to 15 minutes per candidate. At these interviews, candidates are asked questions about their qualifications, training, experience and general knowledge, but in the absence of a proper job analysis' the interviews tend up to be general and académic in character. Dr. Paul Appleby is, therefore, correct in his criticism that the selection method in India possesses too much academic and 'intellectuality' orientation and is not much concerned with the actual requirements of the job. But from my experience as a Chairman for about five years, I may say that though the present method may have resulted in faulty selections, it has, on the whole, worked in a fairly reasonable manner, and it generally succeeds in selecting the best candidate or candidates out of those called for interview. Selection by mere interviews for the Provincial Civil Service and other regularly constituted services, as is done in Madya Pradesh, is to be strongly deprecated as it gives more scope for nepotism and executive interference than when the interviews are combined with a written test. Again the reliability of the oral test conducted under the best of conditions tends to be lower than that of a well-designed written examination. Besides, even if such selections may be just and impartial, they will not appear to be so to the candidates or the general public.

The above account will give a fairly good idea of the relations that exist at present between the various State Governments and their Service Commissions. The Commissions perform a very important and vital function in a democracy, as the personnel recruited by them man the administration for the next thirty years or so. Though the Ministers may lay down policy, the actual implementation of that policy rests with the officials. It has been rightly said that policy-making is 10% and administration 90% of the governmental work. It is no exaggeration to say that on a just and impartial recruitment to government services and posts depends, to a large extent, the progress of the country and the happiness and prosperity of the people. The Commissions also greatly help maintain the morale of government servants by protecting them from unjust and unmerited punishments. By taking over the work of recruitment to civil services and for civil posts, the Commission save the Ministers from their friends, relatives and political supporters who are in need of jobs either for themselves or for others. But this is not generally appreciated by the average Minister who looks upon the Commission as a nuisance as it comes in the way of his patronage and power. This dislike finds expression in his adoption of certain techniques to bypass the Commission or to reduce its usefulness. Some of these techniques have been described above. Others are to draft advertisements in such a way as to limit the field of recruitment to some particular candidates, to make appointments and subsequently exclude the posts from the purview of the Commission, to make undue delay in issuing orders of appointment to candidates selected by the Commission, etc. Fortunately, the relations between the Government and the Commission now much improved at the Centre and will no doubt gradually improve in the States also. Even in the United Kingdom with its homogeneous population and centuries-old democratic traditions, there were constant bickerings between Government and Civil Service Commission for about 15 years in the beginning. We, who have only recently taken to democracy and have to surmount our age-old tendencies to casteism and nepotism, are bound to take a little longer to appreciate the work of the Commission and accept its advice in all cases without a single exception.

The present powers and functions of the Commissions, excepting in the case of recruitment, are inadequate for realising their basic purpose of establishing and strengthening the civil services, free from personal and political influences, and of helping in improving personnel standards and practices. Excepting recruitment, the Commissions' other functions are of a negative character in the sense that they deal only with such cases as are referred to them. The informal but deciding factors in promotion, the suppression of serious disciplinary cases, political, caste and communal influences on personnel decisions and the ubiquitious favouritism and corruption within the ministries and departments are matters which can hardly be noticed by the Commissions. In the context of the enormous expansion of our public services and the vital role they are called upon to play in the building up of a New India, it is becoming increasingly necessary to introduce' merit system principles' in the public services. This need can be realised by giving more authority and functions to an independent service authority like the Commission, so that the Commission can contribute to the creation and strengthening of an efficient and contested public service. For this purpose, the Commission should have the power to develop standards of promotions disciplinary control, government-employee relations and other conditions of service and exercise supervision on the application of these standards by the departments.

I am not, however, in favour of investing the State Commissions with these and other enhanced powers until the Constitution is amended to vest the appointment of the members in the President. Looking to the nature of duties and responsibilities which the members have to perform, it is essential that they should possess certain qualities, such as integrity, judicial temper, freedom from personal and social prejudices and preferences and fearlessness. The Royal Commission on the Superior Civil Services in India wrote, "We would venture to emphasise the paramount importance of securing as members of the Commission, men of the highest public standing who will appreciate the vital and intimate relationship which should exist between the State and its servants. These Commissioners should be detached so far as practicable from all political associations." The object of the Constitution in establishing Service Commissions will be defeated if proper care is not taken to appoint suitable and deserving persons on them.

— **D.V. Rege**

REFERENCES

1. It is to be noticed that most non-official Governors in India have been politicians who were either defeated in elections or not wanted in Delhi or in the States.—Ed.
2. En passant, it may be observed Mr. A.D. Gorwala, generally acknolwdged as an incisive student of Indian administration, suggested in the Report on Mysore Administration he submitted in 1958, that it would be advisable for the Commission to devote itself to the recruitment of gazetted personnel. Also it is now known that it is not true to say that the Commission did not complain of over-work.

[Editor]

6

LANGUAGE AND ADMINISTRATION

All I propose to do in this paper is to give you some hints on how to use English language for purposes of administration, on the basis of a brief note I could prepare.

Before I examine the subject in detail, I should like you to realise that there is no source material available on this subject. I looked up all the libraries I could, and was unable to find such material. Anyway administration has to be done in some language or other and unless you pick up the rudiments of that particular language, you will not be able to achieve efficiency in administration—a topic on which we have heard so much spoken these days. It is important to use the right and best language in administration. Every branch of science and every branch of knowledge has developed its own vocabulary, and the language used in every branch has become conventionalised and standardised. In such specialised vocabularies, particular words are used in particular senses only. In administration also particular words are used in such special senses. Unless you are familiar with the special senses in which words are used in administration, it would be difficult for you to follow, on the one had, the correspondence within the Government and, on the other hand, to conduct it with the public. The Government may be described here as the sayer and the public as the sayee, if I may coin words. The sayee is the common citizen. He may be a villager or a highly educated person coming from urban areas. In both cases he is an uninitiated sayee, so far as administrative language is concerned. You cannot expect him to be familiar with the intricacies of the administrators. You will have to use a language which he can follow. This means there are two kinds of language—one kind for purely Departmental correspondence or that with the Government of India, and quite another for correspondence with the sayee or sayees. The question whether the language of administration should be the language used in the particular area shall not be discussed here. It is a controversial issue with which I am not now concerned here. Opinions vary on the issue. Some think that the language of administration must be in the regional language. My concern is to discuss the language now is actual use in administration, that is, the English language at the Government level and probably the regional language at the taluka level or the Panchayat Raj level. Of course, I have my private views on the subject, but I shall not bring them in here.

Administration is carried on by what are called personnel. When they first enter the portals of administration they are full of freshness and the originality of as idealist. But soon they find that the language there is unusual and even unintelligible. The problem of an administrator, so far as language is concerned, is two-fold. Firstly, the language used should be intelligible to your higher officials. Secondly, it must be intelligible to the ordinary citizen. If he deviates from the accepted offical vocabulary, he is frowned upon by his superior officers. If his letters and communications are not understandable to ordinary men, he will be equally considered inefficient by the ordinary men. In other words, he has to pick up what is called the official jargon. I am reminded of what Ivor Brown has said about writers. According to him, every craftsman chooses his tools excepting the writer. But in his case, if he is carelesss, his writing will become unintelligible. The public will become indifferent and that will be his penalty. But in official domain there is no such penalty for wrong use of language. The Government letters are not thrown away simply because they are difficult to understand. The administrator has to be careful while dealing with his masters, the people. He has to be equally careful with his official bosses. Even if you deviate a little, the superior officer will say that you have not picked up the official language. If you write in the official language to the villager, you will not be understood. When trying to use official language, use discretion, intelligence and resourcefulness. I cannot give you an extensive list of words already in use as well as of newly coined words. Old words will have to be changed to keep pace with living language. New words will have to be carefully examined as to whether they are generally understood. Some times old words emerge with altogether new meanings. We are constantly called upon to discard old words and use new words. But we cannot be ahead of our masters, and we cannot lag behind them. Be careful about accepting new words and do not be deaf to the call of new words. We have to use today's words and not be deaf to the call of new words. We have to use today's words because we have to use today's language. The language of administration is neither that of yesterday nor that of tomorrow. In official language there is no room for circumlocution. The language has got to be simple and intelligible.

Let me now illustrate how new words are formed nowadays. We have a large number of words which are formed by the use of prefixes and suffixes such as "dis" and "ise". There can be alternatives. New words should be used where there are no proper alternatives. New words must be brought in to occupy vacant seats. You cannot unseat those words which are already adequate. For example, take the word "incentive". The opposite of this word is "deterrent". Then where is the need for coining "disincentive"? So you should not coin new words when existing words are sufficient. The only rules that should govern the admission of new words can be whether there is a need for it, and whether it will be accepted by a large section of the people. You should always avoid any unnecessary or redundant words in offical language. Be simple, direct and brief, while corresponding with the common man. There are so many types of correspondence such as circulars, memorandums, notices, official letters etc. I have left out legal and legislative drafting, because this has become highly specialised and will have to be handled separately. Now it is accepted that this language has nothing to do with the language of general administration. So far as the administrator is concerned, his duty is only to explain legislative language in a simple and understandable way. He has nothing to do with its technical interpretation. Here the real problem of the administrator would seem to be to find a language which is intelligible to the common man, without sacrificing the substance of the law. As far is possible, administration should avoid old and hackneyed words. There are a few practical tips. In case of words which are closely related in meaning, do not separate them too much. If you do so, the meaning may be distorted. In official language do not use words which are too new or words which are too old. Now before you start writing a letter, you have to make certain preparations. Firstly you must try to understand fully the request of the correspondent. It has been my own experience that as many as 50% of the mistakes in official correspondence are due to this lack of understanding the correspondent. Secondly, there is the fear of taking responsibility. This results in vagueness in correspondence. Sometimes you do not know your master's mind, and then you try to formulate vague replies. This will cause further unnecessary queries and explanations. This must be avoided. So my first suggestion is that you should study carefully what the correspondent wants, and use imagination in constructing sympathetically what kind of a person he is. If you do that, your replies are likely to bear fruit .One way of increasing efficiency is to improve the official language. You may ask me whether a proper study will not take time and cause delay. Believe me, time spent on such a study is time saved, if you take the longer view. If you eliminate ambiguity you increase efficiency by reducing the delay. Simple and direct language will mean quick disposal. The reason why letters come back for back-references is that there is lack of clarity in correspondence. So, please study the original papers adequately, bestow attention on the problem of a proper reply, and then you will have less delay.

I have some important suggestions as to how to conduct official correspondence. (i) Be sure that you know what your original correspondent is asking before you answer him. This is a golden rule to bear in mind. Always imagine the human context of the case, by trying to imagine yourself in the correspondent's situtation (ii) Begin by answering his question directly. Do not beat about the bush. (iii) As far as possible confine yourself to the facts of the case. (iv) Do not drag in any irrelevant matter. (v)

Avoid the formal frame-work. Do not mix methods such as the direct and indirect, or active and passive. Try to be personal as far as possible. (vi) When you start a correspondence in the indirect speech, stick to it throughout. (vii) Be careful to mention nothing that might give the correspondent the impression that you are trying to avoid trouble. (viii) Use no more words that are necessary for the job. (ix) Do not use a new paragraph to end a letter. (x) Explain technical terms in a simple language, intelligible to the common man. Avoid such terms, if you can.

While writing official correspondence you should prefer the concrete word to the abstract, the direct to the circumlocutary. This is what the best authorities I have consulted such as Fowler, Quiller-Couch and Gower have suggested. You should always prefer transitive verbs. Use the familiar words as far as possible, and the far-fetched must be used only when absolutely essential. Use the familiar words and avoid the vaguer ones. Superfluous words should be cut out. Nowadays people are in the habit of using adjectives indiscriminately. Adjectives should be used to denote kind, not degree. Adverbs at adverbial forms must be sparingly used. Such redundant pharses as "the fact is that", "to be borne in mind", "as such" etc., should be avoided. There are also certain verb-phrases like "to draw up" etc. that should be avoided. You must aim at brevity and avoid padding. We must be careful to use correctly prepositions, articles and members. Nowadays there is a tendency to import the journalistic habit of headline language. This would create confusion. What is good journalese may not be good officialse. These are some of the pitfalls and traps of official language.

— Siddayya Puranik

7

ALL-INDIA SERVICES

The constitutional sanction for the creation of All-India Services is as follows:

'If the Council of States (Rajya Sabha) has declared by a resolution supported by not less than two thirds of the members present and voting that it is necessary of expedient in the national interest to do so, Parliament-may by law provide for the creation of one or more All-India services common to the Union and the States and subject to the other provisions of the Constitution, regulate the recruitment and the conditions of Service of persons appointed to any such services.'[1]

The All-India Services are thus created by the Union Government with the consent of the States. The constent of the States is a very important factor, as there should be harmony between the Union and the State governments if the All-India services have to achieve their primary objective of national unity. The consent of the states is important from yet another angle, namely, the officers of the All-India cadre posted to the States should be given whole hearted welcome by the State governments; otherwise the position of the officers would be very difficult in the matter of executing policies.

Besides, in the absence of the consent of the States, the unifying element of the All-India services is likely to be destroyed. So the States play an important part in assisting the Union government in the creation of All-India Services, by exercising their privilege of 'consent'.

Recommending the creation of more All-India Services, the Official Language Commission has pointed out: 'The *raison d'etre* of creating All-India Services individually or in groups is that officers on whom the brunt of the responsibility for administration will inevitably fall may develop a wide and All-India outlook.' They have recommended that 'as far as possible about fifty per cent of the new entrants in any cadre of the All-India Services existing or to be newly created should be from outside the State concerned on computation, fifty per cent being made after deducting the number of posts in any state to be filled by promotion.' As regards the constitution of further All-India Services they have made recommendations as under:

'We also consider that apart from the I.A.S. and the I.P.S. some more All-India Services should now be constituted. The question of reconstituting All-India cardres for certain technical departments and particularly the suggestion that the India Service of Engineers should be revived, as we understand, has been under the consideration of the Union Ministries concerned for some time. The Central and State governments have to work in very close co-operation in executing important development projects, which necessitates that technical personnel should be recruited and trained on a common basis and that they should have uniform standards of efficieny and the feeling of belonging to common and important cadres.'

'We recommend therefore that the following services, namely the Indian Service of Engineers, the Indian Forest Service and the Indian Medical Health Service should now be constituted.[2]

A resolution to this effect was passed in the Rajya Sabha on December 6, 1961. The Times of India stated: 'The Rajya Sabha to-day passed a resolution calling legislation to create three new All-India services.' The Indian Service of Engineers, the Indian Forest Service, and the Indian Medical Health Serivce.

'This is the first time that the Rajya Sabha has adopted a resolution as provided for under article 312 of the constitution, in regard to the creation of All-India Services. The resolution says that it is necessary and expedient in the national interest that Parliament should provide for the creation of three services.'

The Resolution was approved by 109 votes to I wish one absentation.'[3]

The arguments in favour of creating more All-India Services are mamy. The requirements of modern administration stand in glaring contrast with the Bureaucratic State in the past, interested in maintaining law and order and collecting revenue. The state to-day has to tackle many economic and social problems in order to do away with illiteracy, poverty and unemployment. This naturally requires a large number of officials to shoulder the new responsibilities of the state. Hence the need for more All-India Services. Secondly, the All-India Services stand for 'unity in diversity. They assist the Union Government in formulating policies and also their execution.

Thirdly, the All-India services contribute to the simplification of administration and also to its flexibility. Fourthly, they assist the Union government in modifying and adjusting policies in accordance with the changing needs of the country. Lastly, they lead to uniformity of laws and constitutional procedures as far as administration is concerned. There would be no confusion as regards the assumption of responsibility and the proper discharge of duties. They lead to unified administration, checking the unhealthy tendencies of duplication of work and confusion. They help in correcting the particularist trends and also in securing greater inter-state harmony in implementing efficiently all-India policies.

The arguments advanced against the creation of All-India Services are as follows:

The tendency of posting I. A. S. people to all key position in administration does not appear to be sound. In peferring officers of the All-India cadre to hold key positions, the claims of experts are ignored. To illustrate, the secretary of Public Works Department. (P. W. D.) is to be an engineer himself if he is to contribute in great measure to administrative efficiency. Similarly if the Director of Public Instruction (D. P. I.) is a qualified educationist he would administer much better than an I.A.S. officer. Thus the claims of I. A. S. officers to hold all key positions in administration, may not be accepted in the interests of better administration. In view of this argument there does not seem to be any need for creating more All-India Services.

As a matter of fact there are critics who argue that there is no justification for the existence of All-India Services, because it was hastily conceived by our leader when the country was passing through a great crisis. Many English I. C. S., officers retired from service on the eve of the transfer of power, and some Muslim I.C.S. officer opted for Pakistan and the Union Government thought in maintaining the unity of the country, by replacing the I.C.S.,.with a new service or services. It was that consideration which prompted the makers of the constitution to include the provision in the constitution empowering the Union government with the consent of the states to create All-India Services. The former I.C.S. and the I. P. S. which were existing at the commencenes of the constitution, were deemed to be All-India Service created by Parliament under the constitution. It is clear therefore that the two types of All-India Services were constituted as a measure of expediency in national interest which is nowhere defined in the constitution.

Now, India has successfully faced the situation and things have settled down. We have achieved political unification, economic unity and administrative stabilising. The question therefore is: Is there real need to continue the Services and to create more All-India Services, which do not fit in with the federal structure envisaged in the constitution? The creation of more All-India Services definitely a violation of the federal principle. "The greatest disadvantage in setting up All-India Services is the creation of too many classes and grades in the same departmnet which destory the homogeneity of the Service. In all highly devloped public administrations the need has been felt to minimise the number of grades to ensure greater definition of responsibility and efficiency. Further, All-India Services will mean very much higher emoluments which would add to the pay-bill of the states' budgets. The danger of creating too large a proportion of All-India officers would be that after selection to such services there would be no competition in promotions and the like.

As their future is assured, and this might detract from genuine efficiency. The differential scales of pay between the officers of the All-India and the State Services also create dissatisfaction and destory morale. The management also tends to debar state service officers from 'top posts'. The notion that only All-India Services bring about national intergration is wrong. On the other hand, it might lead to discontent and disintegration. Further, this tendency of creating more and more All-India Services on the basis of more pay etc., is opposed to Mahathma Gandhi's conception of Sarvodaya State."[4]

Moreover, to presume that there were no efficient services in the country in Provinces and States is not direct. As a matter of fact, Bombay, Madras and Bengal had built up efficient provincial services and best administrative traditions. Some States like old Mysore had also evolved a good administrative system. This being the case, to claim that one of the objectives of the All-India Services is to supply officers for states in order to tone to administrative process may not be fair from the point of view of many States.

There is an argument that if 'outsiders' hold key positions in States, there would be more objectivity and impartiality in administration. It is true that there is justification for utilising All-India Services in the States. But there is no justification for monopolising the States administration by appointing officers of the All-India cadre for all key posts. The multiplication of All-India Services leads to a unitary system of government with it highly centralised bureaucracy. They are likely to suppress the initiative and importance of State services. The spoil the vitality of the State administration by imposing centrally recruited officers to conduct the administration of States. Finally they would dwarf the State Public Service Commissions by paralysing the significance of State services.

Regarding the argument that local officers are biases or likely to be biased and to that extent, they will not be impartial, critics point out that people coming from outside may not evince any interest in the administration of the State. Further, they are likely to be guided by some subordinates and it would be very dangerous. Further situated as we are, we are trying to build a welfare state and we require top officers to galvanise the people to create enthusiasm and secure their co-operation. Unless officers know the language of the people, understand the customs and traditions and identify themselves with the masses, the administration will not be successful in implementing welfare schemes such as community development. Therefore it may be desirable to utilise the services of the officers of the State, instead of importing members of All-India Services to State administration.

This does not mean that there should be no exchange of administrative personnel. By all means, services of officers may be lent on request from State services to the Union or from the Union to the States according to the needs of each. This co-operation between States and States, and between States and Union is necessary. But to impose officers on State Administration or Union Administration is not desirable.

There is a controversy whether there is more efficiency in All-India Services or State Services. Of course efficiency does not depend upon scales of pay only. Efficiency really means loyalty of the officer to the cause he is serving, sincerity of purpose and quick execution. Unless officers have sympathy for the people their intellectual equipment book knowledge alone will not accelerate the development Projects. The requirements of the welfare state must be considered when we talk of efficiency. Viewed in this light neither the Union nor the State can exclusively claim to be the repository of efficiency.

One more controversy about the creation of the three more All-India Services is 'why have the Union Government selected these services alone?—the Indian Services of Engineers, the Indian Forest Service, and the Indian Medical and Health Service.' If these services are important from the national point of view, they may be transferred from the State list to the Union list. Can anyone say that education is not of national interest, especially university education. Can we say that Agriculture which has been neglected so far is not of national interest? Thus we do not seem to be clear in our thinking. The present method of tinkering with the problem of creating more and most All-India Services does not seem to be good.

Critics point out that there is no justification for creating more All-India Services. Further, it would be more realistic to fix the quota for all the States as is done in the case of the U. N. O. for the member states, became in practice some States are poorly represented in the Services. There cannot be national integration unless every State is enabled to participate in the All-India Services. This is not retrograde step but it would bring better national solidarity. Thus the existing I. A. S. and I. P. S. may be continued provided suggestions of the above type accepted. But the creation of more All-India Services not certainly favoured by the States. Although the Ministers' Conference has recently agreed to the proposed it is doubtful how far their stand is backed by all to State legislatures and public opinion in the States.

QUOTA SYSTEM

The lack of a rational principle in the represention of States in the I. A. S. and the I. P. S. raises the problem of fixing quota for each State. Along with this, adoption of large number of linguistic media also intense the need for fixing 'quotas'. It has been pointed out to experts that the causes for the poor representation of States in the All-India competitions are falling standard of university education and lack of knowledge of English on the part of students who fail to express themselves properly in the written examination. It has been felled popular circles that this language difficulty should never be the cause of depriving the country of bright people coming from different States, from taking up responsible posts in the All-India services. Yet another justification for the quota system is equality of opportunities for all, is the matter of employment, which is enshrined in Article 16 of the Constituation under the chapter on 'Fundamental Rights'.

But the arguments advanced against the Quota system are numerous. It has been pointed out by critics that the object of open competition for All-India Services is to seek merited young graduates, but the regional quota system would smash the guiding factor of 'merit'. Besides this the quota system would also harm the national unity in administration. The arguments of the Official Language Commission are worth quoting in this respect. The report reads as follows:

"A quota system in the All-India services would be de-facie abhorrent to most persons and quite understandably.

The All-India Services are a profoundly important link in the unity and integrity of the country and one would hate to consider any such fragmentation of the process selection or derogation of the principle of an open All-India competition for recruitment which has maintained for these services for such a long time. A consideration of the quota system of recruitment does not necessary mean the allotment of candidates drawn from regions exclusivly to the respective States of regions. The policy of alloting about fifty per cent of the new entrants in any State of an All-India Service from outside the State as recommended by the States Reorganisation. Commission could still be achieved theoretically speaking in spite of a quota system of recruitment. Furthermore it will be noticed, that a quota system with any measure of safeguard about minimum quality would still entail the common listing of candidates who have answered in different languages in an open general list for the purpose of enforcing minimum standards of attainment.'

The Commission further says: 'Apart from these point there are other strong reasons which impel us to the view that a quota system of recruitment to the All-India Service should not be countenanced. It might result in to deterioration in the standards of candidates recruited, and at time when we expect that administrative personnel will be taxed even more than it has been hither to as a consequence of the programmes of economic and other development which the country has launched upon. It may be recalled in this connection that for the Indian Police Service for a while a system of limited competition on a province basis was tried and has since been given up, we understand because among other things this system did not yield good enough quality in the personnel recruited. In the case of the administrative services this factor is likely to be even more significant. Recruitment to All-India Service by a system of quotas, whatever the version adopted would amount to a fragmentation of the All-India compitition into so many provincial competitions in essence of particulars indistinguishable from similar competition held under the auspices of the State Public Service Commissions, for recruitment to the provincial cadres of the different States. The provincial services have already channel for induction into the All-India Services in the shape of the promotion posts that is to say the proportion of posts In the cadres of All-India Services. The introduction of the quota system would thus lead to a fragmentation of the All-India Services and to the provincialisation of the fragments.'[5]

The notification of the Ministry of Home affairs with regard to the quota system reads as follows:

'The question of introducing the quota system of recruitment to the All-India or Union services on the basis of languages has not even been considered by the Government of India, nor can such a suggestion be considered seriously as it would be completely contrary to the basic idea of an All-India competition. The Government of India appreciates that there are difficulties in arranging for satisfactory moderation of answer papers if they are written in a number of languages. Whether this difficulty is insuparable and that the idea of answers being written in different languages should be abandoned or whether any system could be devised to get over the difficulties and arrange for moderation of answer papers, and if so what these arrangements should be, are matters which the Government of India will have to consider in due course in the light of views expressed by the Official Language Commission.'

Hence it is clear that whatever the pretext, whether the lack of knowledge of English and of free expression of views through it or the question of conducting competitive examinations in many linguistic media, the quota system cannot be encouraged as it militates against the spirit of All-India Services. In the national interests it is necessary that responsible posts of the All-India cadre should be taken up by the best candidates, rather than by candidates of meagre ability in the name of state representation. Since capacity is the prime consideration for All-India Services, best candidates should be the keynote of All-India Services and not equal share in the volume of employment concerning the All-India Services.

TRAINING

The training of public servants is one of the important problems to be tackled in order to produce quality personnel to manage the All-India Services. The I.A.S. probationers are sent to the National Academy of Addministration at Mussoorie for training. During this period they are required to study the Constitution and Five-Year Plans of India, the Criminal Law of the country, Indian History in its social and political aspects, General Principles of Economics and their application to Indian conditions, Principles of Public Administration and Organisation of Government Institutions.

Hindi and the regional language of the State to which a candidate is allotted are also taught. Proficiency in these subjects is tested by the Union Public Service Commisson and confirmation in the Service follows on the passing of this examination and the completion of a year of service.

The recruits to the I. P. S. are trained in the Central Police Training College at Mount Abu. Here the recruits learn the handling of weapons etc, more directly related to the normal work of a police officer than in the case of the I. A. S. These probationers are also expected to pass a final examination conducted by the Union Public Service Commission after a year's training. But on the completion of this institutional training they are no more fitted to assume the responsibility of an A. S. P., than an I. A. S. officer is fit to hold charge of a sub-division.[6]

Training at these institutions generally seeks to provide probationers a theoretical induction to, and acquaintance with, the content and nature of their future work and environment with special emphasis on the organisationl, legal, procedural and operational aspects of their duties. It is imparted to them at school and the university. Once on the job, they grow with it on the ladder of practical experience with its achievements and failures, the challanges of getting along with colleagues above, below, and at the same levels and reckoning with outside elements, and administrative and other considerations in carrying out their duties as public servants.[7]

But now the question is: Is training imparted in these institutions sufficient to fit them to the responsible posts to which they are posted ? The general opinion is, the method of training specially for I. P. S. is not effective, as it fails to give them practical training which is very important. But of course we cannot gainsay the fact considering the vast number of recruits who are sent to the National Academy of Administration every year. But the one appreciable feature of the training is that in order to compensate for the lack of practical training, they are conducting study tours, visits to important universities, offices, courts, district and divisional headquarters regularly, in order to impart practical training to wider their outlook and a better understanding of the social pressures.

The chief objectives of the training programme are the imparting of skill and preliminary knowledge of administration in the probationers. Shri S. B. Bapat speaking on training pointed out: 'The generally accepted conception of training is a compound of several distinct elements. In one sense training means the imparting of knowledge of facts and their inter-relations, knowledge essentially of the specialised or professional nature. This is the sense at which the doctors, engineers and teachers are trained. In another sense training involves the teaching of techniques which require the coordinated handling of tools and appliances and physical facilities rather than of ideas.This is the sense in which one speaks of trained artisans and mechanics. In still another sense training entails the formation of mental and physical habit patterns to ensure that the same stimuli would always produce the same automatic responses. Training implies 'what a good gardener does to the growing, sapling, pruning of the unwanted bits, supporting the weaker limbs, generally giving shape and direction but otherwise leaving the plant free to grow to its full natural status. While all other aspects of training were duly allowed for, it was this last aspect which has been most emphasised in the pattern evolved for the basic training of the I. A. S. probationers.[8]

The former I. C. S. the predecessor of I. A. S., had established a good repute, as the young probationers were emarked for their loyalty and devotion to duty. But the one distinct advantage which the I. A. S. officers have over their I. C. S. counterparts is, they are no more the agents of alien masters, but at best they could act as the servants of our people doing good for our own country. More important than power and authority and handsome salary is the spirit of public service. Every officer of All-India cadre has to think of his career in terms of public service. The Preamble to the Constitution, the Fundamental Rights and the Directive Principles enshrined in the Constitution demand a new type of administrative machinery with a different outlook, to work under the influence of a new social, political and economic ideology. The officers besides being faithful to the constitutional procedures of law, have to carry out manifold welfare activities. The goal of welfare state which has been envisaged calls for effective implementation by the officers of the All-India cadre.

Unlike under the I. C. S., to-day we have a changed political set-up under the Constitution; we have popularly elected ministers both at the central and state level, and decision-making finally rests with them. The I. A. S. personnel can no longer exercise the privileges of its bureaucrats in the old regime—I. C. S.,—in executing the policies and programmes enunciated by the popularly elected cabinets and legislatures. It is indeed a happy augury that the National Academy of Administration in organising its training is trying to inculcate into the mind of probationers, the fundamental principles governing the administration of the country. This is very important from the point of view of their assuming the responsibilities of administration. Not merely this; they are giving basic training as regards personal and public conduct by maintaining the virtues of integrity, justice and fairplay. This is very essential because they should serve as ideals to the ordinary citizens as far as their conduct is concerned.

Shri N. K. Bhojwani in his article 'Training of Public Servants in a Developing Economy' has discussed in detail the various problems connected with training. He has remarked, 'for some, experience accumulated through the years turns them into administrative geniuses, such persons may well be described as born administration. But experience does not dole out its favours equally. For many administrators experience may indeed not be even cumulative. It may amount to doing jobs in a given field reasonably well and perhaps making the same mistakes through force of habit. At the same time the spirit of public administration no less than its objective mechanics and horizons keep changing, calling for higher technical competence and imposing heavier burdens of accountability—on public servants inherent in a democratic form of government, free press and more exacting demand to the administration from the public, for the fulfilment of their anticipations of a better life promised by freedom and economic planning. How are administrators to recognise the meaning of and react to such changes? Are previous education and training during the probationery period adequate for all time ? What about numerous other public servants who do not undergo any training whatever as probationers e. g. engineers, scientists and doctors?

New concepts of training have developed round these questions based on the premise that the past liberal education at the University and probationary training are no longer enough for all time for civil servants of to-day and tomorrow. They generally aim at providing fresh orientation to experienced administrators to further develop their potential, widen their horizons and enable them to keep pace with the changes in a modern administration. It is this concept of training of public servants which is important.'

Bhojwani has further stated, 'even to the extent that emotional acceptance of the Importance and necessity training of public servants has developed, it appears to be subject to certain deliberate or subconscious mental reservations such as an attitude that while training is an excellent thing, it is for others or a belief that no adequate and mechanics of formal training can be worked out to appeal to and be of practical value to grown-up public servants with practical experience. This latter relief is obviously the basis for the view that there is no adequate substitute for experience on the job and learning through doing in the making of good administrators. The executive training scheme of the Government of India under which members of certain services are depute for training in district and field administration through secondment to local officers is obviously based on the view. Such attitudes and belief have naturally lengthened the time-lag between the recognition and the application of the idea of a formal and systematic training for public servants."[9]

But the practical training begins when the officers of the All-India cadre are appointed as junior Officers. This short duration of the Junior grade imparts them to training, which is of utmost importance. The experience which they gain during this period enables them to manage the administration at a district level, department level and so on. This experience prepares them for handling administrative problems, particularly to co-ordinate During the probationary period they get training only in general administration but the valuable part of the training constitutes the period of their confirmation. However great may be the benefit given by training, there is valuable substitute for the practical experience. At last training only imparts the preliminary knowledge of administration and nothing more.

Commenting on the defects of the method of traning followed in India, Shri C. D. Deshmukh, in his discussion on 'Morale in the Public Services' opines: 'Although have not heard any complaint about favouritism, so for recruitment is concerned, but I believe the present system of training for the new probationers not only in the administrative services, but for the central services also, does not seem to be very effective. Before Independence, a great deal of attention used to be paid to the training of young officers in the districts and for some time fresh entrants only watched their senior officers doing the job. I believe even now the same system could be evolved in attracting at least a handful of fresh entrants to senior officers.'[10]

Similar views have been expressed by Kumari Kusum Kapur and Shri A. K. Mitra, in their article— 'Administrative Reorganisation in India'. They remark: "The Young I.A. S. officers sent out for field training to-day are definitely at a disadvantage in comparison with their predecessors. The likelihood of the presence of a suitably senior and really experienced colleague to whom they can be attached is not very great. Naturally, their training suffers inasmuch as they can no longer draw on their senior colleagues' experience and have to learn work mostly through the trial and error method. As Mr. Gorwala says 'in I. A. S. there is undoubtedly good material but if in the years to come it does not bear comparison with the best men of the past, one reason will be failure in training. So it is desirable that suitable senior officers should be posted in some of the districts, despite their seniority with a view to making these districts training ground for the young officers'. This initial training will, of course have to be supplemented by further special courses and refresher courses. But this initial in-service training must be sound and for that purpose they must be attached to a really experienced senior officer from whose experience they can freely draw."[11]

At this juncture it is necessary to draw our attention to a recent change. It reads: 'The Government of India has decided to increase the probationary period for entrant's to the I. A. S. from one year to two years. A probationer shall be discharged, if he is found lacking qualities of mind and character needed for the I. A. S, of the constructive outlook and human sympathy needed and the public services generally.'[12] Along with this measure it is to be hoped that in future a more comprehensively scheme of training with great emphasis on practical experience would be introduced for the purpose of All-India Services.

— Smt. R.V. Aryamane

REFERENCES

1. Article 312 of the Constitution.
2. Report of the Official Language Commission 1956. Chapter XI. The Union Language and the Public Service Examinations' p. 11.
3. The Times of India—Daily Newspaper. December, 7, 1961 column—Call to create New Service' p. 13.
4. Shri N. Murugesan Mudaliar, The Hindu, Madras, dated 23rd December, 1961.
5. Report of the Official Language Commission 1956, Chapter XII—The Union Language and the Public Services Examinations.' p. 192-206.
6. Seminar Papers. Part II Training of Civil Servants p.

158. Ind. Jl. of Pub. Admn. Vol. III, April—June 1957.

7. N.K. Bhojwani-Training of Public Servants in a Developing Economy. Ind. Jl. of Pub. Admn. vol. VII. Oct.—Dec., 1961. pp. 447-48.

8. Shri S.B. Bapat 'The Training of the I.A.S. The Indian Journal of Public Adminstration Vol. I, April, June, 1955 p. 119-127.

9. N.K. Bhojwani—'Training of Public Servants in a Devloped Economy' pp. 447-72. The Indian Journal of Public Administration, vol. VII Oct.-Sept. 1961.

10. Shri. C.D. Deshmukh—Discussion on 'Morale in Public Service' Report of a Conference, Jan. 3-4-'59. p. 13., Indian Institute of Public Administration, New Delhi.

11. Kumari Kusum Kapur and Shri A. K. Mitra. — 'Administrative Reorganisation in India' Chapter IV, p. 209.

Journal of the National Academy of Administration, Mussoorie Vol, VI. Jan. 1961.

12. News feature—'Recent Developments in Public Administration in India' p. 550.

The Indian Journal of Public Administration, Vol. VII, October-December. 1961.

8

SELECTION, BACKGROUND CHARACTERISTICS, AND VOTING BEHAVIOUR OF INDIAN SUPREME COURT JUDGES, 1950-1959

The Supreme Court of India presently consists of fourteen members and sits in New Delhi at the summit of a pyramidal, integrated judicial system. Although the formal political structure of the Indian Republic is federal, its judicial structure is unitary. Both union and state laws are interpreted in a single court system; there is no division of judicial business between the central and state governments. The Supreme Court has the power of judicial review, and its decisions are binding on India's sixteen High Courts as well as on all trial courts. Its formal jurisdiction is considerably broader than that of the Supreme Court of the United States. It has two types of original jurisdiction, the first relating to disputes among the states, and the second to claims of infringement of constitutionally protected "fundamental rights." A large number of important cases have been decided by the Court through the exercise of the second type of original jurisdiction. The Court also has broad appellate jurisdiction, and it may give advisory opinions if they are requested by the President of India.

Compared with courts in other developing countries, the Indian higher judiciary is exceptionally strong, and the judges of the Supreme Court have played a central role in sustaining constitutional government in India. This is one reason why they merit careful, systematic, empirical study. This chapter is an initial effort in that direction, and I hope that it will stimulate similar studies by others, especially in India. It focuses on the Court's first decade—1950 to 1959 —and explores three topics: selection of judges, their background characteristics, and their voting behaviour.

SELECTING THE JUDGES

Although the Indian Constitution provides that judicial appointments be made by the President after consultation with the Chief Justice of India and any judges of the Supreme Court and High Courts the President deems necessary, appointments are actually made by the Prime Minister and the cabinet, and the President simply announces them. In all Supreme and High Court appointments, with the exception of the Chief Justiceship, the Chief Justice must be consulted, but his concurrence is not a constitutional requirement. There is evidence, however, that he is very much involved in the appointment process. In 1959, Home Minister Pant informed the Lok Sabha (the Lower House of the legislature) that "since 1950, 17 judges have been appointed to the Supreme Court and every Time one of those Judges was nominated and recommended by the Chief Justice of India." This statement has been corroborated, at least in part, by two former Chief Justices. Mehr Chand Mahajan, who served as Chief Justice in 1954 , and the only member of the Supreme Court who published an autobiography, wrote that as Chief Justice he "had a say in the appointment of judges of the High Court and of my colleagues in the Supreme Court whenever vacancies occurred." And B. P. Sinha, who occupied the Chief Justiceship longer than anyone else (1959-64) told me in 1963 that the Chief Justice has the initiative in the selection process.

In order to be considered for a Supreme Court judgeship, one must (a) have served for at least five years as a High Court judge, or (b) have been for at least ten years a High Court advocate, or (c) be a "distinguished jurist." During the decade under consideration, twenty-three judges, including five Chief Justices, served on the Supreme Court, and all of them had been promoted from High Courts. Ten had come from the High Courts of Bombay, Calcutta, and Madras—the three oldest and most prestigious tribunals in India. Of these ten only one, Das Gupta, was Chief Justice when he accepted an appointment to the Supreme Court. Of the remaining thirteen judges, ten had served or were serving as Chief Justice of these other High Courts. The practice is to offer judgeships to the senior judge (the Chief Justice) of a particular High Court, so it is interesting that no Chief Justice of the Bombay or Madras High Court, and only Das Gupta of the Calcutta High Court, has accepted a position on the Supreme Court. This suggests that the Chief Justices of these High Courts considered their position to be one of greater prestige and importance than an associate judgeship on the Supreme Court.

Although members of the bar and distinguished jurists were eligible for appointment, none was appointed. According to the Law Commission, members of the bar have been excluded from the field of selection because of the government's view that "it will be somewhat hazardous to appoint to the Bench a person straight from the Bar without previous judicial experience." The government, while acknowledging that it "desires to appoint those who have much experience," claims to have offered Supreme Court judgeships to "at least two advocates," but both refused the appointment because they were reluctant to sacrifice lucrative practices for a less remunerative Supreme Court post. In explaining why no academic lawyers were appointed during the decade, the Law Commission stated that "we have not produced in our country academic lawyers and jurists of note who could, as in the United States, be honoured with seats on the Supreme Court Bench." Thus, although the field of selection established by the constitution offered the executive a good deal of latitude, the custom now of appointing only senior High Court judges has the effect of narrowing the field down to them.

Communal considerations appear important in making appointments to the Supreme Court. When one speaks of communalism in India, he is usually referring to the distinction made between Hindus and Muslims. It is customary to have at least one Muslim on the Court at all times. Saiyed Fazl Ali was one of the original six members of the Suprerne Court. When he left the bench in 1952, he was replaced by Ghulam Hasan, a retired judge of the Allahabad High Court. Hasan died in late 1954, and the vacant Muslim seat was filled within a few weeks by Syed Jafer Imam, who at the time of his elevation was Chief Justice of the Patna High Court. When the Court was increased to ten associate judges, Mohammed Hidayatullah was appointed, so there were two Muslims on the bench in the late 1950's. This custom of always having a Muslim on the highest tribunal dates from the colonial period, for the British made certain there was always a Muslim on the Federal Court, which was the predecessor of the Supreme Court.

Table 1 Religion of Supreme Court Judges, IAS Entrants and Total Population (in Percentages)

	Supreme Court judges (1950-59)	*I A.S entrants (1948-60)**	*Total population (1951-61)***
Hindu	78	90	84
Muslim	18	02	10
Christian	04	03	02
Sikh	00	04	02

* Data from R. K. Trivedi and D. N. Rao. "Regular Recruits to the IAS—A Study," *Journal of the National Academy of Administration, V (I960), 50-80,* and Ralph Braibanti, "Reflections on Bureaucratic Reform in India," in Braibanti and Joseph J. Spengler (eds.), *Administration and Economic Development in India* (Durham: Duke University Press, 1963), p. 54.

** Data from *India: A Reference Annual, 1965* (Delhi: Government of India, Ministry of Information and Broadcasting, Publications Division, 1965), p. 19. Columns two and three total less than one hundred per cent because several small religious groups are omitted.

The twenty-three judges include, in addition to the four Muslims, eighteen Hindus and one Christian (Vivian Bose). Table 1 shows the religious affiliation of the judges compared with new officers entering the Indian Administrative Service (the elite bureaucratic cadre), and with the population at large. These religious background data show that both the judges and the bureaucrats reflect quite closely the religious composition of the nation. Muslims are almost as much over-represented on the Supreme Court as they are under-represented in the bureaucracy, and the reverse is the situation with the Hindus. It is somewhat surprising, in view of the over-representation of Sikhs in many other fields, that none has ever served on the Supreme Court.

Regional loyalties, based especially on language, but also on ethnic and caste considerations, long have been strong in India, and have increased in political significance in recent years. Thus it is not surprising that regionalism is important in making appointments to the Supreme Court. Of the fourteen states of India during this period (since the States Reorganization Act of 1956, state boundaries correspond closely to the major linguistic boundaries), the twenty-three judges represented ten. Five of the judges served on two different High Courts, and counting them twice, the High Court regional representation is as follows: Bombay (6), Madras (5), Calcutta (4), Patna (4), Punjab (3), Allahabad (2), and one judge from each of the High Courts of Andhra Pradesh, Rajasthan, Orissa, and Madhya Pradesh. Unrepresented on the bench were Assam, Jammu and Kashmir, Mysore and Kerala. Assam is one of India's least developed states, its population is small, it is relatively insignificant politically, and its High Court, composed of but three judges, is one of the two smallest in India. The other High Court that has only three judges is Jammu and Kashmir, but the special status of this state probably explains its non-representation more than the size of its High Court or population. I do not know why no one from the Mysore High Court was elevated to the Supreme Court during the decade. This leaves Kerala, which did not have a High Court until 1956. In a sense, however, Kerala was represented by P. Govinda Menon, who was born in Kerala and served on the Madras High Court (whose jurisdiction included Kerala until 1956) for nine years before he was promoted to the Supreme Court.

There is other compelling evidence of the significance of regional considerations in making appointments. During the period covered by this study, thirteen judges either retired, died, or resigned. Their successors, more often than not, were men from the same geographic region and, in several cases, from the same High Court. For example, the first vacancy was created when Chief Justice Kania, formerly of the Bombay High Court, died on November 6, 1951. The next appointee to the Court was N. H. Bhagwati, also of the Bombay High Court. N. C. Aiyar, of the Madras High Court, retired early in 1953, and the next appointee was B. Jagannadhadas who, although at the time was Chief Justice of the Orissa High Court, was educated in Madras and had practised for several decades before the Madras High Court. When Chief Justice Sastri, who had come to the Supreme Court from the Madras High Court, retired on January 3, 1954, the vacancy was filled the following day by T. L. V. Ayyar, also from the Madras Court. Clearly, it is customary to follow both regional and religious criteria of representation along with High Court seniority.

Executive influence in the selection process, which has been condemned by the Law Commission, seems to be restricted chiefly to communal and regional considerations, and does not appear to embrace partisan political or ideological criteria. Neither members of the Law Commission nor, to the knowledge of this writer, anyone else, has suggested that the government sought to appoint to the Supreme Court men whose ideology is the same as the governing elite's. All but two judges (Kania and Fazl Ali, who were appointed to the Federal Court just prior to national independence) were appointed by Congress Party governments, since the Indian National Congress has controlled the central government since independence. But only one of these judges (Jagannadhadas) appears to have been at any time an active member of the Congress Party, and none has played a role of any known significance in the independence movement. Indeed, the senior judiciary in India is composed of men whose careers have been remarkably non-political. This is in marked contrast to the situation in the United States where more than 90 per cent of all appointees to the federal judiciary have been members — in many instances active members — of the same political party as the President who appointed them.

Special informal rules govern the selection of the Chief Justice of India. During the decade, the Chief Justiceship was vacant five times, and in each case it was filled by the associate judge who had served longest on the Court. So the Chief Justice is not appointed; he is invariably promoted on the basis of seniority. As a result, there is a rapid turnover in the office, for the senior associate judge is always in his sixties and must retire at sixty-five. In 1954, there were three different Chief Justices: Sastri retired in January; he was replaced by Mahajan, who reached retirement age in December; and then Mukherjea took over.

The fact that the senior associate justice is promoted to the Chief Justiceship means that when a High Court Chief Justice or judge is offered an associate justiceship on the Supreme Court, he can calculate rather quickly whether or not he will become Chief Justice of India and how long he will serve in that position. B. P. Sinha, for example, in relinquishing the Chief Justiceship of the Nagpur High Court in 1954 to become the most junior Supreme Court judge, knew that when S.R. Das reached retirement age on September 30, 1959, he would then be the senior justice and therefore become Chief Justice of India.

The Law Commission has argued that mere seniority should not be the sole criterion for selecting the Chief Justice, and has recommended that the most qualified man available be selected, whether he be from the Supreme Court, a High Court, or the bar. The custom of promoting whoever happens to be next in line does offer one distinct advantage in a country where various political, communal, caste, regional, and other considerations are publicly perceived as criteria employed whenever appointments are made by the executive. At least no one can allege that any such extraneous considerations play a direct part in selecting India's highest judicial officer.

The mandatory retirement age for Supreme Court judges is sixty-five. The British introduced the practice of mandatory retirement during the colonial period, and several members of the Constituent Assembly also expressed concern that some judges might prolong their service on the Court beyond their years of mental alertness and physical stamina unless a retirement age was made mandatory.

Mandatory retirement, together with the practice of appointing High Court Chief Justices and judges on the basis of seniority, has led to frequent turnover in the Supreme Court. The ages of the twenty-three judges considered here ranged, at the time of their promotion, from just under fifty-three to sixty-two, the average appointee being fifty-seven. Nine of the twenty-three reached retirement age during the decade, three died while serving, and another resigned just short of his retirement date because of poor health. The average tenure of these thirteen was 5.3 years. Obviously those involved in appointing Supreme Court justices have placed a premium on extensive High Court experience and seniority. Since an advocate is rarely invited to accept a High Court judgeship until he is in his late forties, the average High Court service of these judges was ten years. Advanced age is therefore placed at a premium; and more than two-thirds of the judges in this sample were born in the nineteenth century.

BACKGROUND CHARACTERISTICS

The preceding discussion has shown that Indian Supreme Court judges are homogeneous in terms of previous High Court experience and advanced age. But beyond these characteristics, what manner of men are they? The answer to this question is not easy, in part because of the inadequacy of biographical sources, but also because of the widespread belief in India that "legal acumen," "learning in the law," "proper legal equipment," and so forth are the only appropriate traits to consider when discussing judges.

In recent years there has developed, particularly among some students of the Supreme Court of the United States, an empirical interest in the political sociology of judges. The research purposes of these scholars vary, but one of the principal areas of inquiry concerns the relations between background characteristics of judges and judicial decision-making. A hypothesis for which there is some confirmation maintains that certain background characteristics, such as the political party, ethnic, and religious affiliations of judges, correlate with their decisions. Prerequisite to such a study is the systematic collection of biographical data on the judges, which for Indian judges has not yet been done.

I have attempted a collective portrait of the present twenty-three judges based upon available sources of information. Data concerning the social, economic, and political background of these individuals are not readily available from standard biographical sources. Indeed, the only standard biographical source is *The Times of India Directory and Year Book Including Who's Who,* All but two of the justices (Bose and Jagannadhadas) have biographical entries in this *Who's Who,* but each entry is limited simply to date of birth, current position, some previous positions held, and some information concerning education. Beyond this source there is little else. Occasionally one of the law journals carries a brief note on the career of a newly appointed or deceased judge and sometimes the *Supreme Court Reports* includes a eulogy delivered by the Chief Justice honouring a deceased colleague, or an encomium to a retiring colleague. Only two biographies have been written, and only one judge has written an autobiography. As a result, one attempting to prepare a collective portrait on the basis of published materials must work with fugitive data.

Information concerning the educational backgrounds of the judges is relatively complete. All but five (Bose, Imam, Kapur, Hidayatullah, and Das Gupta, who received degrees from English universities, earned baccalaureate degrees in India, and virtually all of these degrees were awarded by institutions of high standing. All had substantial formal legal training, except two (S.K. Das and Wanchoo) of the three judges who were members of the Indian Civil Service. Thirteen graduated from one of the law colleges in India, and eight from one of the Inns of Court in London. Table 2, which presents in summary form a profile of the judges, shows that nearly all of those with Indian law degrees attended law schools of the highest standing, and nine of the thirteen received their legal education at Madras, Calcutta, or Bombay Universities. All six justices from South India received their entire education there, graduating from the Law College of Madras University. Similarly, each of the three judges who came up from the Bombay High Court received all of his education in India. But of the four from the Calcutta High Court, three were British-educated barristers. None received any portion of his education in the United States.

Because caste is so important in Indian society, it would be of interest to know the caste background of the eighteen Hindu judges. Such information is not easily obtained, but in a number of instances the family name is also a caste name, which makes identification easier. Ayyar and Sastri are South India Brahmin names; hence T. L. V. Ayyar, N. C. Aiyar, and M. Patanjali Sastri, all from the State of Madras, are Brahmin Hindus. Mahajan is almost invariably a Bania (trader or shopkeeper caste) name, Sinha is usually Kayasth (caste of scribes), and Menon is a name which belongs to the Nair community of Kerala. The caste affiliation of others, however, is less easy to determine. Table 2 identifies caste affiliations to the extent permitted by available sources of information.

Nine of the eighteen Hindu judges are identified as Brahmins even though Brahmins constitute only about one-fifteenth of the Hindu population. That at least half of the Hindu judges are Brahmins is not surprising, because Brahmin ascendency has long been a feature of Indian life. This group quickly accepted modern education during the British period and they were predominant among Indians in the Indian Civil Service. Their hold on senior government positions continues to be greatly disproportionate to their percentage of the population; in 1956, for example, thirteen of the twenty-three Hindus in the late Prime Minister Nehru's cabinet were Brahmins. Although Brahmins are least numerous in South India and proportionately most numerous in North India, two-thirds of the Supreme Court judges from South India, all of whom are Hindu, are Brahmin Hindus, whereas less than half of the judges from North India are Brahmins.

Information on the career patterns of these men is quite complete. All except the three Indian Civil Service judges enrolled as High Court advocates shortly after completing their education, and spent an average of more than twenty years practicing law before they were offered a High Court judgeship. Moreover, the intensity of the regional identification of these men is emphasized by the evidence that all but Jagannadhadas spent more than two decades as advocates before the same High Court on which they eventually sat. Jagannadhadas, born in what is today part of Orissa State, spent some thirty years as a Madras High Court advocate

Table 2 Profile of Judges Who Served on Supreme Court of India, 1950-59

Name	*Date of birth*	*Religion*	*Caste*	*Baccalaureate*	*Legal*	*High Court experience*	*Date appointed to Supreme Court*	*Age at appoint-ment*	*Date of retirement*
1	*2*	*3*	*4*	*5*	*6*	*7*	*8*	*9*	*10*
Kania, Harilal Jaikisondas	11/3/1890	Hindu	Brahmin	India	Bombay Law College	Bombay High Court,1933-46	6/20/1946	55	11/6/1951[a]
Faz Ali, Saiyed	9/19/1886	Muslim	–	Allahabad University (Uttar Pradesh)	Middle Temple	Patna High Court, 1928-47; Chief Justice, 1943-47	6/9/1947	60	9/18/1951[b]
Sastri, M. Pantanjali	1/4/1889	Hindu	Brahmin	Pachaiyappa's College (Madras)	Madras Law College	Madras High Court, 1939-47	12/6/1947	58	1/3/1954
Mahajan, Mehr Chand	12/23/1889	Hindu	Non-Brahmin (Bania)	Government College, Lahore	Punjab Law College	Lahore High Court, 1943-47; East Punjub High Court, 1947-48	10/4/1948	58	12/22/1954
Mukherjea, Bijan Kumar	8/15/1891	Hindu	Brahmin	Hooghly College (Bengal)	Calcutta Law College	Calcutta High Court, 1936-48	10/14/1948	57	2/1/1956[c]
Das, Sudhi Ranjan	10/1/1894	Hindu	Non-Brahmin	Calcutta University	Gray's Inn	Calcutta High Court, 1942-49; Punjab High Court, 1949-50	1/20/1950	55	9/30/1959

Contd.

1	2	3	4	5	6	7	8	9	10
Aiyar, Nagapudi Chandrasekhara	1/25/1888	Hindu	Brahmin	Christian College (Madras)	Madras Law College	Madras High Court, 1941-48	9/23/1950	62	1/24/1953[d]
Bose, vivian	6/9/1891	Christian	—	Pembroke College, Cambrige	Middle Temple	Nagpur High Court, 1936-56; Chief Justice 1949-51	3/5/1951	59	6/8/1956[e]
Bhagwati, Harilal	8/7/1894 Natvarlal	Hindu	Brahmin	Baroda (Gujerat)	Government College College, Bombay	Bombay High Law	9/8/1952 Court, 1944-52	58	8/6/1959
Hasan, Ghulam	7/3/1891	Muslim	—	Uttar Pradesh	Allahabad Law College	Allahabad High Court, 1948-51[F]	9/8/1952	61	11/5/19548[g]
Jagannadhadas, B.	7/28/1893	Hindu	Brahmin	Madras Presidency College	Madras Law College	Orissa High Court, 1948-53; Chief Justice, 1951-53	3/9/1953	59	7/27/1958
Ayyar, T. L. Venkatarama	11/25/1893	Hindu	Brahmin	Madras	Madras Law College	Madras High Court, 1951-53	1/4/1954	60	11/24/1958[h]
Sinha, Bhuvaneshwar Prasad	2/1/1899	Hindu	Non-Brahmin (Kayasth)	Patna College (Bihar)	Patna Law College	Patna High Court, 1943-51; Chief Justice, Nagpur High Court, 1951-54.	12/3/1954	55	2/1/1964
Imam, Syed	4/18/1900	Muslim	—	Trinity College Cambridge	Middle Temple	Patna High Court, 1943-55; Chief Justice, 1953-55	1/10/1955	54	2/1/1964[i]

Das, Sudhansu Kumar	9/3/1898	Hindu	Non-Brahmin	Presidency College (Callcutta), and London School of Oriental Studies	Indian Civil Service	Patna High Court, 1945-56; Chief Justice, 1955-56	4/30/1956	57	9/2/1963
Menon, P Govinda	1896	Hindu	Non-Brahmin (Nair)	Presidency College (Madras)	Madras Law College	Madras High Court, 1947-56	9/1/1956	59	10/16/1957[j]
Kapur, Jeevan Lal	12/13/1897	Hindu	Non-Brahmin	Magdalene College, Cambridge	Inner Temple	Punjab High Court, 1949-57	1/14/1957	59	12/12/1962
Gajendragadkar Pralhad Balacharya	3/16/1901	Hindu	Brahmin	Decan College (Poona)	Poona Law College	Bombay High Court, 1945-57	1/15/1957	55	3/15/1966
Sarkar, Anal Kumar	6/29/1901	Hindu	Non-Brahmin (Kayasth)	Scottish Churches and Bangabhasi Colleges (Bengal)	England	Callutta High Court, 1949-57	3/4/1957	55	6/28/1966
Subba Rao, Koka	7/15/1902	Hindu	Non-Brahmin (Naidu)	Government Arts College, (Andhra Pradesh)	Madras Law College	Madras High Court, 1948-54; Andhra Pradesh High Coúrt, 1954-58; Chief Justice, 1956-58	1/37/1958	55	4/16/1978[k]
Wachoo, Kailas Nath	2/25/1903	Hindu	Brahmin	Muir Central College (Allahabad)	Indian Civil Service	Allahabad High Court, 1947-51; Chief Justice, Rajasthan High court, 1951-58	8/11/1958	55	2/24/1966

Contd.

1	2	3	4	5	6	7	8	9	10
Hidayatullah, M.	12/17/1905	Muslim	—	Morris College (Nagpur), and Trinity College, Cambridge	Lincoln's Inn	Nagpur High Court, 1946-56; Chief Justice, 1954-56,Chief Justice of Madhya Pradesh High Court, 1956-58	12/1/1958	52	12/16/1970[l]
Das Gupta, Kaluda Charan	1/3/1900	Hindu	Non-Brahmin (Kayasth)	Calcutta University; Magdelene College, Cambridge	Indian Civil Service, and Barrister-at-Law	Calcutta High Court, 1948-59; Chief Justice, 1958-59	8/24/1959	59	1/2/1965

a Date of death.
b Reappointed for the period from October 15, 1951, to May 30, 1952.
c Date of resignation because of ill health.
d Reappointed for the period from September 5, 1955, to October 31, 1955 and from December 1, 1955, to May 11, 1956.
e Reappointed for the period from September 9, 1957, to September 30, 1958.
f Hasan earlier (1940-48) had been a judge of the Oudh Chief Court, and its Chief Judge from 1946-48. Although not technically a High Court, it had the status of a High Court during those years.
g Date of death.
h Reappointed for the period from March 1, 1961, to April 30, 1961.
i Date of resignation because of ill health.
J Date of death.
k On this date Subba Rao, who was then Chief Justice of India, resigned to contest the election for the Presidency of India as the candidate of the parties which combined to oppose the Congress party candidate.
l Due to retire on this date.

and was appointed an original member of the Orissa High Court when it was created in 1948. The three I.C.S. judges, upon completion of their training in England, embarked immediately upon careers in the judicial side of the civil service, and after more than thirty years of experience in lower judicial positions, moved up to the Supreme Court. Of the twenty for whom the practice of law was their principal career before joining a High Court, all but N. C. Aiyar held no judicial post prior to appointment as a High Court judge. Four others (Mukherjea, Sinha, Imam, Hidayatullah) served in various governmental law-officer capacities for brief periods, and two of these (Imam and Hidayatullah) served in the early 1940's as advocate-general for their state governments.

Thus a central ingredient of the prototype of a Supreme Court judge is more than twenty years of law practice before the High Court of the state of his birthplace. When he reached his late forties, he would accept an appointment to the bench of that High Court. After a High Court tenure averaging ten years, he would move on to the Supreme Court, remaining there until reaching mandatory retirement age.

Whereas Schmidhauser could write that the pattern of recruitment of U.S. Supreme Court judges "is one which emphasizes the intimacy of judicial and political affairs," the pattern in India is precisely the opposite. Indeed, the aims of the appointment criteria and procedures established by the constitution are to minimize the possibility of partisan political appointments. The available evidence points quite clearly to the conclusion that Indians who were publicly identified with particular political parties have not been appointed to the Supreme Court. Unlike U.S. Supreme Court appointees, all but one of whom since 1789 held some political post before his appointment to the high bench, the judges of the Indian Supreme Court have been men who have eschewed politics as either a vocation or as an avocation throughout their careers. This is especially important if we are to understand the ethos of the senior judiciary in India. Eschewing political activities entailed, for almost all the judges, having little or nothing to do with the pre-1947 agitation for national independence. Thus there was, and continues to be, little overlapping between the national political elite, led during most of the past half-century by Gandhi and Nehru (both, incidentally, British-educated barristers), and the senior judiciary. That is one reason for a number of clashes between politicians and judges since 1950, exemplified by the late Prime Minister Nehru's caustic remark that the function of an Indian judge "is not merely to sit in wig and gown for a number of hours a day and look very learned."

Although these general comments concerning the apolitical character of the background of Supreme Court judges apply to the prototypic judge, one of the twenty-three — Jagannadhadas — apparently was overtly associated with the Congress Party. He joined the Indian National Congress in the 1920's and was interned in the early 1940's by the British for agitational activities connected with the "Quit India" movement. But he was not a leader in the freedom struggle. Three other judges briefly held positions of a political nature, two prior to Indian independence, and one immediately following it. Former Chief Justice Sastri was an appointed member of the Madras Legislative Council, apparently in the 1930's. Around the same time, Ghulam Hasan was a member of the United Provinces Legislative Assembly. Mehr Chand Mahajan, who served as Chief Justice in 1954, was Acting Prime Minister of Jammu and Kashmir from September 1947 until early 1948. Before 1947, Mahajan had been a judge for four years on the Lahore High Court, which was located after August 15, 1947, in the new nation of Pakistan. His tenure as Acting Prime Minister, though brief, spanned the most critical post-partition months, and during this time Mahajan was a central figure in the accession of Kashmir to India. As Mahajan's autobiography makes clear, he was a most enthusiastic spokesman in behalf of Indian interests in Jammu and Kashmir; very clearly he "sided openly with India and was for the state's accession to India." He allocates nearly fifty pages of his autobiography to his brief tenure as Acting Prime Minister, leaving only nine (in a book of 285 pages) for his later role as Chief Justice of India.

One judge's overt involvement in politics occurred not before but after his appointment to the Supreme Court. K. Subba Rao, who joined the Court in 1958 and became Chief Justice in 1966, resigned the Chief Justiceship on April 11, 1967 (three months before reaching the mandatory retirement age) to become the United Opposition's candidate for the presidency of India. The United Opposition was a conglomerate of seven parties, ranging from the Communist Party on the left to the Jan Sangh and Swatantra on the right, allied in an effort to defeat Dr. Zakir Husain, the Congress Party candidate. Although the Congress Party nominee had never received less than 98 per cent of the vote in earlier elections, the race between Husain and Subba Rao was a close one, with Husain winning by a margin of 471,244 to 363,971. Not unexpectedly, because of the posture expected of judges regarding politics, Subba Rao's attempt to gain the presidency was almost unanimously condemned by newspapers, bar associations, and law journals.

Among the criteria available for the attribution of social status, paternal occupation is widely accepted as the most trustworthy clue to the determination of social origin. Such data are not readily obtainable for these Indian judges, but the available information suggests that the typical judge came from a high status family. Sastri came from a "stock of Pandits renowned for their learning and culture," and Mukherjea's father was a Sanskrit scholar. S. R. Das came from a family of lawyers; and one of his uncles, in particular, enjoyed a wide reputation as a wealthy and successful attorney. Something is known about the wives of four others. In India marriage tells a good deal about social status, because it is unusual for either partner to marry out of his (or her) parents' social class. Kania married the daughter of an ex-member of the Executive Council of the Governor of Bombay; Hasan was married to the daughter of a District and Sessions Judge; Menon was married to the daughter of the Chairman of the Air Transport Licensing Board; and Subba Rao's father-in-law was the Chief Justice of the Mysore High Court. Thus all four married into families of relatively high social status, and there is no evidence to suggest that their own backgrounds were not similar. Mahajan, however, did not come from a socially prominent family. His father was a mukhtar, an advocate without formal legal training but entitled to practice law in the lower courts. It seems appropriate to conclude that generally speaking, the typical

Supreme Court judge emerged from a high social status background.

It seems equally likely (though supportive evidence is not easy to adduce) that the typical judge's parents enjoyed comfortable economic circumstances. That all of them enjoyed opportunities for advanced education, and that ten received part of their education several thousand miles distant in England, is sufficient to establish that their parents were among the small minority of economically advantaged in India.

The composite picture of the typical judge of the Supreme Court of India includes being a Hindu, birth in a socially prominent and economically comfortable family, legal education at a prominent Indian university or at one of the Inns of Court in London, more than two decades of private law practice before the High Court of the state of his birthplace, non-involvement in active politics, and ten years of experience with consequent seniority as a member of a High Court. Such a combination of characteristics defines the population from which justices are drawn; but to be selected an individual needs finally to enjoy the good fortune of being next in line when a particular type of seat (i.e. Muslim seat or regional seat) becomes vacant.

EXPLORATORY EMPIRICAL ANALYSIS OF DIVIDED DECISIONS

The remainder of this chapter consists of an exploratory empirical analysis of decision-making in non-unanimous cases decided by the Supreme Court from its establishment on January 26, 1950, to September 30, 1959, the date on which Chief Justice S. R. Das, the last member of the original appointees, reached retirement age. The decisional data consist of all the split decisions reported in the official *Supreme Court Reports.* Although not all decisions of the Court are officially published, I believe that all divided decisions are reported. Apparently most unreported decisions are brief rulings that involve no major nor new questions of law.

Nine hundred and sixty-three decisions, including two advisory opinions, were reported during the decade; sixty-eight

(7 per cent) of these were non-unanimous. Table 3 presents these data on an annual basis.

The largest single category of non-unanimous decisions concerns interpretation of the Indian Bill of Rights, or "Fundamental Rights" (to use the constitutional language). There were twenty-seven divided decisions, two-thirds of which were decided during the first half of the decade, and they involved, in particular, assertions of equal protection of the law, the right to personal liberty, freedom of speech or press, and property rights.

Table 3 Decisional Data, 1950-59

Year	*Total decisions*	*Unanimous*	*Non-unanimous*	*Per cent non-unanimous*
1950	43	33	10	23
1951	62	54	8	13
1952	79	73	6	08
1953	99	93	6	06
1954	126	123	3	02
1955	83	74	9	11
1956	88	86	2	02
1957	113	107	6	05
1958	145	135	10	07
1959	125	117	8	06
Totals:	963	895	68	Avg: 07

The only other significant categories of divided rulings are ten income tax decisions (typically a dispute between the state income tax commissioner and a business firm over what should be assessed for tax purposes), and six sales tax cases (typically resulting in a ruling on the circumstances in which a state could impose a sales tax on businesses engaged in inter-state trade).

Fifty-two, or 76 per cent of these divided decisions are characterized by a single dissenting vote. In thirteen others, there were dissents by two judges, and in the remaining three decisions there were three dissents. Although there were eleven justices (including the Chief Justice) on the Court after 1956, not more than seven judges participated in any one of these decisions and, as Table 4 indicates, the typical non-unanimous case was decided by a bench of five judges.

Table 4 Voting Divisions in Non-Unanimous Cases

Voting division	*Number of cases*
6-1	2
5-1	3
4-1	31
3-1	2
2-1	14
5-2	2
4-2	3
3-2	8
4-3	3

Unlike the Supreme Court of the United States, which decides all cases by a full Court, the Indian Supreme Court employs the divisional bench system. During the 1950's there were usually three benches functioning simultaneously, one to handle civil appeals, another for criminal appeals, and a third to hear constitutional cases. The size and composition of these benches are determined at the discretion of the Chief Justice; the only constitutional constraint is that at least five judges must sit to decide any case involving a substantial question of constitutional law, or for an advisory opinion. The Chief Justice can assign all the judges to hear a particular case, but that is very rarely done now. During most of the first year, however, when the Court consisted of only six justices (including the Chief), it was not uncommon for all to participate together as the constitutional bench. Since 1951 there were only three non-unanimous decisions *en banc* in which all judges participated.

Because of these data inadequacies, and consequent methodological difficulties, the findings reported in my analysis of divided decisions, below, must be treated as tentative. The fact that 93 per cent of the Court's decisions were unanimous may well be related to the homogeneity of the judges. But when a tribunal's work is divided among several benches, and the Chief Justice determines the composition of each bench, the actual attitudinal differences among the judges cannot be completely reflected in the non-unanimous decisions. When litigation raises policy issues over which there is actual disagreement among the judges, this potential voting division may thus be concealed by the bench assignments. The power of the Chief Justice to manipulate the composition of each bench is (ex hypothesis) the power to bias both the decision-making process and, necessarily, also the decisional policy output.

Table 5 shows that S. R. Das, the only judge who could have participated in all of the sixty-eight decisions because he was a member of the court throughout the period, did not participate in nearly one-third as a consequence of the divisional bench system. The average rate of participation was even lower (56 per cent); and only one-quarter (26 per cent) of the votes in split decisions were dissents.

There was considerable variation in how much individual judges participated. At one extreme is Gajendragadkar, reputed to be one of contemporary India's most distinguished jurists. A member of the Court during the last thirty-three months, he participated in only one of the twenty-four divided rulings made during this period. At the other extreme is Sastri, who was a participant in twenty-nine of the thirty divided rulings made during his tenure on the Court. There were also pronounced individual differences concerning frequency of dissent. Only once in the seventeen divided cases in which he participated was Kania in the minority, while Jagannadhadas was in the minority seven times in the nine divided rulings in which he participated. Together Bose and Mahajan account for more than one-quarter of all the dissenting votes cast during the decade.

Table 5 Individual Voting Records in Non-Unanimous Cases

	Judge	Number of cases partici-pated in	Number of times in dissent	Per cent of time in dissent	Number of non-partici pations	Per cent of non-partici-pation
1.	Das Gupta	0	0	0	0	0
2.	Menon	0	0	0	4	100
3.	Hidayatullah	2	0	0	7	78
4.	Gajendragadkar	1	0	0	23	96
5.	Kania	17	1	6	1	6
6.	Imam	13	1	8	22	63
7.	Aiyar, N. C.	13	1	8	15	48
8.	Das, S. K.	13	1	8	10	43
9.	Das, S. R.	47	6	13	21	31
10.	Hasan	8	1	13	2	20
11.	Bhagwati	21	4	19	24	53
12.	Mukherjea	26	5	19	10	28
13.	Sinha	18	4	22	17	49
14.	Wanchoo	4	1	25	8	67
15.	Sastri	29	8	28	1	3
16.	Ayyar, T. L. V.	14	4	29	15	52
17.	Fazl Ali	15	6	40	8	35
18.	Bose	29	12	41	14	33
19.	Kapur	12	5	42	12	50
20.	Sarkar	10	5	50	11	52
21.	Mahajan	22	11	50	11	33
22.	Subba Rao	7	4	57	11	61
23.	Jagannadhadas	9	7	78	12	57
		330	85	26[a]	256	44[b]

a Computed by dividing 85 (column 2) by 330 (column 1).

b Computed by dividing 256 (column 4) by 586 (columns 1 and 4).

Table 6 shows how each of the five Chief Justices voted during his tenure. It is apparent that the Chief Justices very rarely —four occasions out of fifty-one participations—were in the minority. Indeed, they were in the majority in 92 per cent of the divided cases; and they also wrote majority opinions in nearly half (45 per cent) of those cases.

Table 6 Voting of Chief Justices in Non-Unanimous cases

Chief Justice	*Number of cases partici pated in*	*Number of times in dissent*	*Per cent of time in dissent*	*Number of non-partici-pations*
Kania (1950-51)	17	1	6	1
Sastri (1951-54)	11	3	27	1
Mahajan (1954)	2	0	0	1
Mukherjea (1954-56)	2	0	0	0
Das, S. R. (1956-59)	19	0	0	13
Totals:	51	4	8	16 [a]

a There was one divided decision in which Chief Justice Mukherjea did not participate because he was ill.

The small number of non-unanimous cases, the rapid turnover of judges, and the use of the divisional bench system (which institutionalizes non-participation) combine to make quantitative analysis of these data more difficult as well as more tenuous, but they do not preclude exploratory analysis. The sixty-eight divided decisions are distributed evenly over the decade (Table 3). However, the composition of the Court and its benches was more stable before 1955, so the data are more adequate during the 1950-54 period (i.e. up to Chief Justice Mahajan's retirement on December 22, 1954) than thereafter. Fifteen of the thirty-three split decisions of the early period (1950-54) dealt with civil liberties questions. In each of these, an individual was asserting that one or more of his constitutionally guaranteed freedoms had been violated by some executive action or legislation. Five involved arrests under the Preventive Detention Act; five others involved state ordinances and enactments establishing "special courts" designed to enable the executive to bring about a "speedier trial" of certain offenses; three were free speech/free press cases; one involved an externment order, the effect of which was to require that the petitioner leave Delhi and stay away for three months; and the other concerned the freedom of movement of Indian citizens from Pakistan into India.

Cases	*Bose*	*Mahajan*	*Hasan*	*Aiyar, N.C.*	*Mukherjea*	*Kania*	*Ali*	*Das, S.R.*	*Sastri*	*Jagannadhadas*	*Bhagwati*	*Ayyar, T.L.V.*	*Votes*
50/594		+			+	+	∅	+	+				5-1
50/605		+			+	+	∅	+	+				5-1
52/284	+	+		+	+		+	+	—				6-1
52/710	NP	+		+	+		NP	+	—				4-1
54/933	+	+	+		+			—		NP	NP	NP	4-1
51/167		NP		+	+	+	+	—	—				4-2
50/519		+			+	—	—	NP	—				2-3
50/88		+			—	—	⊕	—	—				2-4
52/435	+	+		+	—		—	—	—				3-4
51/451	+	+		+	NP		NP	—	NP				2-3
53/589	+	NP	+	—	—			NP	—		NP		2-3
52/612	NP	+		—	—		NP	—	—				1-4
54/30	+	NP	—		—			NP	—	—	NP		1-4
51/621	+	—		NP	NP	—	NP	—	—				1-4
51/228 2-5		—		—	⊕	—	⊕	—	—				
Total partici-pation	7	12	3	7	13	8	8	12	14	1	0	0	85
Incon-sistent votes	0	0	0	0	1	0	4	0	0	0	0	0	5

Coefficient of scalability: .78

Legend: + For the Civil liberties claim

— Against the claim, less liberal position

NP Non-participation

Blank Retired, deceased, not yet appointed

Figure 1 Scalogram Analysis of Civil Liberties Cases January 26, 1950, to December 22, 1954

Scalogram analysis was used to investigate the possibility of significant attitudinal differences among the judges. The hypothesis to be tested is that the responses of the judges to the questions raised in these cases are functions of one dominant variable—their attitude toward deprivations of civil liberties.

Figure 1 reports only a quasi-scale; there are too many non-participations (with consequent indeterminancy) and too few split decisions with more than a single dissenter to meet the requirements of cumulative scale theory. However, the coefficient of scalability of .78 suggests that with a more adequate sample of data, a civil liberties scale could probably have been determined. The figure indicates that Bose and Mahajan are the most favourable toward civil liberties claims. Both had consistent voting patterns which demonstrate a predisposition to vote against governmental efforts to restrict individual freedoms. Sastri and Das, on the other hand, consistently failed to support the libertarian position. Instead they upheld both legislation restrictive of civil liberties and the executive's interpretation and application of such legislation. The logical hypothesis to infer is that the psychological content of the underlying scale, implied by this quasi-scale, is that of political liberalism. Bose and Mahajan are the most liberal, and Sastri and Das are the least liberal of the judges in this sample. Four of the five inconsistent votes are attributed to Fazl Ali, a Muslim judge who participated in only eight of the decisions. Although we are entitled to infer that his voting behavior in these cases was inconsistent with that of his colleagues, we do so with less confidence than we would if we had more observations available of his voting behaviour.

Eight decisions of this early period (1950-54)—too few to test as a separate scale—raised economic issues including: action taken by an agricultural income-tax commissioner against a farmer, an appeal by a privately owned bank against a pro-labor ruling by the Industrial Tribunal, the claim of a large private business that a state sales tax was unconstitutional, an appeal by an individual convicted under the Bombay Prohibition Act, acquisition of privately owned land for a public purpose by the Bombay government, the takeover of a large private business by the central government, and finally, the constitutional validity of

Cases	*Bose*	*Mahajan*	*Aiyar, N.C.*	*Mukherjea*	*Hasan*	*Kania*	*Ali*	*Das, S.R.*	*Sastri*	*Jagannadhadas*	*Bhagwati*	*Ayyar, T.L.V.*	*Votes*
50/605		+		+		+	Ø	+	+				5-1
50/594		+		+		+	Ø	+	+				5-1
52/284	+	+	+	+			+	+	—				6-1
52/710	NP	+	+	+			NP	+	—				4-1
51/167		NP	+	+		+	+	—	—				4-2
55:1/313*	+	+		+	+			--		NP	NP	NP	4-1
54/933	+	+		+	+			—		NP	NP	NP	4-1
52/889*	NP	+	+	+			NP	—	—				3-2
50/519		+		+		—	—	NP	—				2-3
50/621*		+		+		—	—	—	—				2-4
50/869*		NP		—		—	—	⊕	⊕				2-3
50/88		+		—		—	⊕	—	—				2-4
52/435	+	+	+	—			—	—	—				3-4
51/451	+	+	NP	NP		—	NP	—	—				2-3
54/842*	+	+		NP	—			—	—				2-3
54/30	+	NP		—	—			NP	—	—	NP		1-4
53/1069*	+	NP		—	—			NP	—		—		1-4
52/612	NP	+	—	—			NP	—	—				1-4
53/589	+	NP	—	—	⊕			NP	—		NP		2-3
50/459*		+		—		—	—	NP	—				1-4
50/435*		+		—		NP	—	—	—				1-4
51/621	+	—	NP	NP		—	NP	—	—				1-4
51/228		—	—	⊕		—	⊕	—	—				2-5
Total participation	10	18	8	20	6	11	12	18	21	1	1	0	126
Inconsistent votes	0	0	0	1	1	0	4	1	1	0	0	0	8

Coefficient of scalability: .75

Legend: + For the individual claim (anti-government)
— Against the individual claim (pro-government)
NP Non-participation
Blank Retired, deceased, not yet appointed
* Economic issue

Figure 2 Scalogram Analysis of Civil Liberties and Economic Cases, January 26, 1950, in December 22, 1954.

two comprehensive state land-reform laws. It seemed worth testing the composite group of twenty-three civil liberties plus economic decisions because they all had one thing in common: the government (some level or one of its branches or agencies) was the appellant or respondent in each case, and a private interest (an individual, landlord, or privately owned business) was involved either as appellant or respondent in each. The attitudinal dimension hypothesized for investigation by cumulative scaling was individualism (versus government authority).

Figure 2 shows the results. Although this is also a quasi-scale, it does suggest that the scalable dimension underlying the voting behaviour in these cases is one that involves both economic and political liberalism. Certainly no significance can be attributed to the drop in the coefficient of scalability from .78 in Figure 1 to .75 in Figure 2.

What these figures clearly show is that there is one consistent ordering for seven of the nine judges (excluding Jagannadhadas, Bhagwati, and T. L. V. Ayyar) on political and economic issues. Ranging from the most individualistic judge, that ranking includes (in the sequence indicated): Bose, Mahajan, N. C. Aiyar, Kania, Ali, Das, and Sastri. The first two are the most consistently individualistic and the last two the most collectivistic. Both of the two remaining judges of this group of nine whose participation is sufficient to permit this tentative interpretation are in the middle of the scale.

Bose participated in ten of the cases (seven civil liberties, three economic), but not once did he support the government position. Mahajan participated in eighteen, and in sixteen of these cases he too rejected the government position and supported the individual or private interest claim; moreover, in all six cases raising economic issues in which he participated, he rejected the government position. Combining the civil liberties and economic cases led to no inconsistent responses for Bose or Mahajan, whom we can designate as *classical* liberals. In the English and American cultures, classical liberalism represents a point of view typical of the mid-nineteenth rather than of the mid-twentieth century. Classical liberalism sought protection for the individual against intervention or regulation by the state. Thus it was essentially negative in character. It opposed restrictions on civil liberties as well as opposing governmental intervention in the economic sphere, and advocated instead a laissez-faire economic policy. Recognition of this latter point is central to understanding what the implied scale suggests. An economic liberal in a contemporary Western industrialized society would generally support the claims of the economically underprivileged, upholding such forms of government intervention in the economy as land reform and the regulation of private business to prevent monopoly and uphold consumer or underdog interests.

The positions of Sastri and Das also have remained unchanged. In eighteen cases out of twenty-one, Sastri upheld whatever action the government took to restrict individual freedoms. And in thirteen cases out of eighteen, S. R. Das acted similarly. Of the eight economic cases added to the initial quasi-scale Das participated in six, and in only one of these did he vote against governmental action restrictive of claimed property rights; Sastri participated in seven, and he also departed only once from his customary predisposition toward accepting whatever the government had done. These two judges voted as economic liberals, but as political conservatives, an attitudinal combination that corresponds with classic conservatism. Neither classic liberalism nor classic conservatism constituted a point of view found in the United States Supreme Court during the past generation.

If we define a liberal as one who believes in maximizing individual personal liberties, while at the same time accepting the position that individual property rights are not sacrosanct, then only Fazl Ali comes close to being a modern liberal. No Indian Supreme Court judge of this period was what we think of as a modern conservative. In the combined civil liberties-economic liberalism quasi-scale, Fazl Ali remains responsible for four inconsistent votes on civil liberties issues. He was perfectly consistent in the economic cases, in all of which he upheld governmental action restrictive of individual property rights. Examination of the eight civil liberties cases discloses that governmental policy restrictive of activities of the Communist Party of India was at issue in five, and official efforts to stem the post-independence communal bloodshed between Hindus and Muslims figured in two others. In four of the five Communism cases, Fazl Ali voted disapproval of the methods being used by the government to restrict the disruptive activities of the Communists. In both the communalism cases (and, of course, in the other Communism case) Fazl Ali upheld the restrictions on individual freedom. One of these communalism cases concerned Dr. Khare, the President of the All-India Hindu Mahasabha. This is a reactionary and extremist Hindu communal political party, and Dr. Khare had been ordered to leave Delhi because of speeches "tending to excite hatred" between Hindus and Muslims. The other case involved Brij Bhushan, the publisher of *Organizer,* an English language weekly organ of Hindu communal extremism which contained "highly objectionable" articles which served to fan the flames of communal rioting between Hindus and Muslims. As the only Muslim on the Court, it is hardly surprising that Fazl Ali approved of the government's efforts to restrict the activities of Hindu extremists.

The scalograms present one kind of systematic ordering of voting inter-agreement. An alternative ordering is provided by calculating the correlation coefficients based on tetrads of agreement/disagreement for each pair of justices, to the extent that they participated together in the entire sample of split decisions. This provides a standard statistical measure of both the degree and direction of voting inter-agreement and disagreement. The resulting matrix is found in Table 7.

Table 7 Phi Correlation Matrix: All Divided Decisions

	Bose	*Aiyar*	*Mahajan*	*Kania*	*Mukherjea*	*Ali*	*Sastri*	*Das*
Boss	1.000	.612	.267	–.316	–.316	–.333	–.522	–.311
Aiyar	.612	1.000	.632	.000	–.125	–.408	–.333	–.167
Mahajan	.267	.632	1.000	.255	.033	–.657	–.606	–.380
Kania	–.316	.000	.255	1.000	–.213	–.302	–.161	–.113
Mukherjea	–.316	–.125	.033	–.213	1.000	.123	–.089	–.073
Ali	–.333	–.408	–.657	–.302	.123	1.000	–.185	–.378
Sastri	–.522	–.333	–.606	–.161	–.089	–.185	1.000	.387
Das	–.311	–.167	–.380	–.113	–.073	–.378	.387	1.000

Linkage analysis resulted in three clusters of judges (Figure 3). Most strongly positively correlated are Mahajan and Aiyer; Fazl Ali and Mukherjea show only low positive correlation. Mukherjea, consistent with his middle position in the scalograms, was not strongly correlated with any other judge. The pair who disagreed most frequently was Mahajan and Fazl Ali, at —.657. They participated together twelve times in non-unanimous cases, disagreeing ten times. Their background characteristics were also very different: Fazl Ali was an English-educated (and knighted) barrister from a wealthy, urban, Muslim family; while Mahajan came from a less advantaged, rural, orthodox Bania Hindu background.

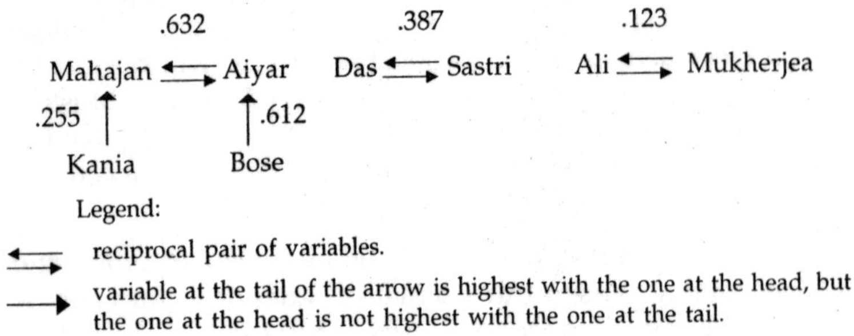

Fig 3 Elementary Linkage Analysis

Table 8 Factor Loadings

	I	*II*	*III*
Mahajan	.87	—.12	.34
Aiyar, N. C.	.81	—.11	—.23
Bose	.73	.16	—.60
Kania	.18	—.35	.78
Mukherjea	—.17	.33	.30
Das	—.41	—.68	—.27
Ali	—.51	.82	.01
Sastri	—.67	—.51	—.20

The assumptions of factor analysis are not completely satisfied by the data, but we can note the results of such an investigation of the correlation matrix. The loadings on the first factor (Table 8) seem to correspond in a general way with the cumulative scale positions of the major clusters of judges—positive, neutral, and negative toward individualism.

Figure 4 shows the three pairs of two-dimensional plots of these factorial loadings. The individualism scale (from Figure 2) is, according to Figure 4, perfectly positively correlated with factor I, and it is moderately positively correlated (at about +.5) with factor II. The scale is uncorrelated with factor III, which I assume to represent the other 30 per cent of the non-unanimous decisions that are not included in the scale for this period. As the plot for the first two factorial axes shows, a vector that passed through Fazl Ali would be orthogonal to the individualism scale, and I infer, in accordance with my earlier designation of Fazl Ali as probably the only modern liberal on the Court during this period, that this orthogonal vector is one that represents the ideological position of modern liberalism—favouring *both* political and economic liberalism. It is apparent, from Figure 4, that these two vectors, for individualism and for modern liberalism, are equivalent to a counterclockwise rotation of about 30° of reference axes I and II, respectively. Because I have only the one scale (which is uncorrelated with factor III), and I have not discovered any correspondingly rigorous systematic basis for scaling the 30 per cent of the split decisions that are not in Figure 8.2, I must, for present purposes at least, leave the third factor unidentified.

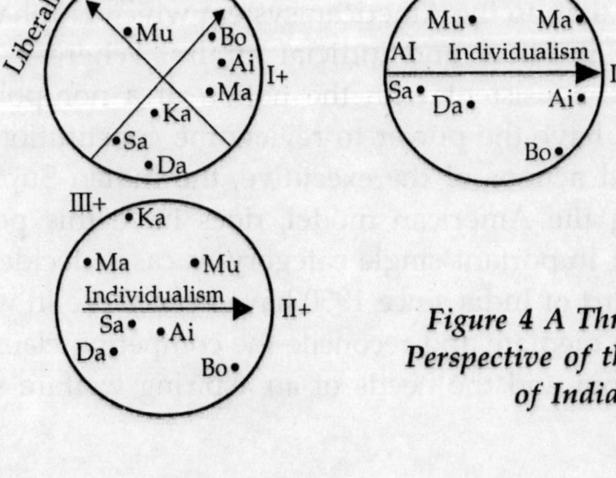

Figure 4 A Three Dimensional Perspective of the Supreme Court of India, 1950-54

CONCLUSION

The constitutional norms governing the process of selecting Supreme Court judges, and the norms determining the criteria an individual must meet in order to be appointed, reflect the zeal which characterized the efforts of the framers to keep political criteria out of the selection process, and to keep politicians off the supreme bench. Implicit in these norms and explicit in the debates of the Constituent Assembly is the view that a judge should be steeped in technical legal skills, that the task of constitutional interpretation and adjudication require the specialized skills of one "learned in the law," and that a judge should be and should have long been detached from active, partisan politics.

The discussion of the career patterns and background characteristics of those who sat on the Supreme Court during the 1950's indicates that there weie no gross deviations from the constitutional norms. The background of the twenty-three judges registers the broad religious and sectional pluralism of the Indian nation, but not one of them before his appointment had had an essentially political career, and all had first gained rather lengthy judicial experience as High Court judges. Indeed, the most common denominators among them on the eve of their elevation to the Supreme Court were seniority on their respective High Courts, and non-involvement in the great issues of the day.

Thus, the recruitment process at the Supreme Court level in India is more akin to the system operative in many European democracies where judges are members of the career civil service, and where promotions are determined by merit and not by political criteria, than to the American system which emphasizes the intimacy of political and judicial affairs. Whereas most European courts, consistent with the notion of a non-political judiciary, do not have the power to review the constitutionality of legislation and actions of the executive, the Indian Supreme Court, following the American model, does have this power. Indeed, the most important single category of cases decided by the Supreme Court of India since 1950 have been those in which the Court had to mediate and reconcile the competing claims of individual freedom and the needs of an aspiring welfare state.

The decisions of the Court in this area were clearly of great political significance, and yet they were made by men who were not drawn from community affairs—men who, in the course of their careers, had generally maintained a posture of aloofness from what went on about them.

— George H. Gadbois, Jr.

9

FINANCIAL HAND BOOK OF THE CONSTITUTION OF INDIA

A PRELIMINARY SURVEY

A. Some Salient Features of the Indian Constitution

The Preamble to the Constitution proclaims India a Sovereign Democratic Republic. It emphasises the sovereignty of the people and the fact that all powers of the Government are derived from the people. Justice, Liberty, Equality and Fraternity which are the essential characteristics of a democratic government have been set out in the Preamble in unambiguous terms as the very most important objective of the Constitution. The Constitution is republican in character as the executive head of India is not a hereditary monarch. It is an elaborate written statement containing 395 Articles and nine Schedules.

The Constitution is essentially Federal in structure although it describes India as a Union of States and the word Federation is absent. The Union is really a Federal Union resembling the American or Canadian Federation and not a mere League of States; nor are the Union and State Governments related to each other as Principal and Subordinate. The peculiar feature of Indian Constitution is that although, being a Federation, it should have a dual polity, its real endeavour is to have unformity in all basic matters for the sake of consolidation of the Union. Thus the Constitution does not admit of a dual citizenship as the American Constitution does; there is only a single citizenship throughout the Union namely the Indian citizenship. The Constitution provides for a single integrated judiciary, uniformity in civil and criminal law and special All-India Services common to the Union and States. No State has the right to secede from the Union or to frame its own constitution.

The Indian Constitution is a flexible constitution. It does not suffer from such faults and weaknesses as all other federal Constitutions do, .namely, rigidity, conservatism and legalism. All federal constitutions are generally so framed that they can not in any circumstances change their form and shape and can never be unitary. To reduce the disadvantages arising from such rigidity and legalism, the Indian Constitution has, like the Australian Constitution made a number of provisions which are to remain in force only until the Parliament by law, otherwise provides and has conferred on Parliament concurrent powers with respect to no less than forty seven subjects. Moreover, greater facility is provided for the amendment of the Constitution to avoid the rigidity and conservatism as is found in other constitutions.

Another special feature is that the Indian Constitution can be both unitary as well as federal as the circumstances require. In normal times it is designed to work as a federal system but in times of wai and other national emergencies, the whole country becomes converted into a single unitary state. This is based on the principle that in an emergency, when conflicting interests may arise, the ultimate allegiance can not be divided and that the Federation, which alone can work for the general welfare of the country as a whole in such an emergency and not the states, must command the residual loyalty of the citizens.

Although the word 'President' is used to denote the head of the state, the form of Government is modelled not on the Presidential system of government of the United States but on the cabinet form of Government of the British Constitution. Under the Presidential system of America, the President is the head of the Executive; the entire administration is vested in him. Under the Indian Constitution the President occupied the position similar to that of the king under the English Constitution. He is the head of the state but acts only on the advice of his ministers, while the President of the United States is not bound to accept any advice tendered to him by any of his secretaries.

B. The Constitution is an EPITOME.

PREAMBLE

The Preamble does not form an integral part of the Constitution but is merely an introduction without any legal significance. It is only a statement of purposes whose object is to serve two important ends (i) it states the great object which the Constitution and the government established by are expected to promote; and (ii) it indicates the source from which the'Constitution derives its authority.

The Preamble of the Indian Constitution resolves to establish a "Sovereign Democratic Republic". This sovereignty invested in the people of the country. Being a democratic republican government, India is not governed by a king but by the people's representative. The preamble also refers to justice, liberty, equality and fraternity to which all Indians are entitled.

TERRITORY AND EXTENT

There are four categories of states :—

1. *Part 'A' States*—There are in India ten States each with a governor as its, head namely Assam, Bihar, Bombay, Madhya Pradesh, Madras, Orissa, Punjab, Uttar Pradesh, West Bengal, and Andhra. These are known as Part 'A' States.
2. *Part 'B' States—There* are other 8 States and States Unions under a Rajpramukh namely Hyderabad, Jammu and Kashmir, Madhya Bharat, Mysore, Patiala and East Punjab States. Union, Rajasthan, Saurashtra and Travancore-Cochin.. These are known as Part 'B' States.
3. *Part 'C' States*—Third group of administrative units comprise 10 small States and are known as Part 'C' States. Such States are Ajmer, Coorg, Bhopal, Bilaspur,

Himachal Pradesh, Delhi, Kutch, Manipur, Tripura, Vindhya Pradesh.

4. *Part 'D' States* include Andaman and Nicobar Islands under a Chief Commissioner.

Parliament has authority to admit into the Union or establish new States on such terms and conditions as it thinks fit. It may also increase, diminish or alter the name or boundaries of any State on the recommendation of the President and the wish of the states to be affected by such alteration.

Citizenship

The Indian Citizens are, as follows— (1) Those domiciled in India; (2) Displaced persons, who have migrated to India from Pakistan; and (3) Indians overseas.

The first category includes persons resident of India who have their domicile in the territory of India, who or one of whose parents were born in this country or who have been ordinarily living in it for a perrod of five years .from the day preceeding the commencement of the Constitution.

Second category consists of those who have migrated to India from Pakistan or who have come to India from Pakistan under permanent permits granted to them by the Indian authorities.

In the third category falls the prisons of Indian origin residing outside India. If they meant to retain their Indian citizenship, all they need to do, is to apply for it.

In regard to citizenship, the Constitution deliberately adopts the principle of single citizenship for the whole of India. It means that no person is entitled to claim that he is a citizen of two countries.

Fundemental Rights

The enunciation of fundamental rights is a feature in many written constitutions. These rights are regarded as a solemn declaration of the high purposes round which public opinion may rally and supply a moral standard for acts and omissioins on the part of the State. It is a unique feature of the Indian

Constitution that it sets out in the constitution itself the most elaborate declaration of human rights yet framed by any State. The fundamental rights enumerated in the constitution fall under the following categories :—

(1) Right to equality (2) Right to freedom (3) Right against exploitation (4) Right to freedom of religion (5) Cultural and educational rights (6) Right to property and (7) Right to constitutional remedies.

1. *Right to equality*—Discrimination against any citizen on grounds of religion, race, caste, sex or place of birth is prohibited. In public employment, Constitution assures equality of opportunity for all. It has established social equality by abolition of title, local and foreign. The State is not to deny to any person equality before law or the equal protection on law.
2. *Right to freedom* guarantees rights (*a*) to freedom of speech and expression; (*b*) to assemble peacefully and without arms; (*c*) to form associations or unions; (*d*) to move free throughout the territory of India; (*e*) to reside and settle in any part of the territory of India; (*f*) to acquire, hold and dispose of property; and (*g*) to practise any profession or to carry of any occupation, trade or business.
3. *Right against exploitation*—Traffic in human beings declared punishable offence. So too is *begar* (forced labour except without payment) or any form of forced labour except compulsory service for the State for public purposes. Under Art. 24, no child below the age of fourteen years shall be employed to work in a factory or mine or engaged in any hazard employment.
4. *Religious freedom*—Subject only to public order, morality, health and some other essential provisions, all persons are equally entitled to freedom of conscience and the right to profess, practise and propagate religion freely..
5. *Cultural and educational rights*—The Constitution provides for the protection of the interests of linguistic, cultural and religious minorities and their right to

establish and administer their own educational institutions.

6. *Right to property*—No person shall be unlawfully deprived of his property movable or immovable.
7. *Right to Constitutional remedies*—The Constitution guarantees the right to every citizen to move the Supreme Court for enforcement of fundamental rights. And for that purpose the Supreme Court is given general powers to safeguard these rights as well as the power to propose particular remedies such as habeas corpus, mandamus etc.

Directive Principles of State Policy

The word directive is used to lay down certain allocations to the future legislature and the executive showing the manner in which they have to exercise their authority. They are meant to be codes of constitutional propriety which will govern the future government in relation to the people. These principles are not enforceable by law. Following are some of the principles of policy which the State should secure.

1. Adequate means of livelihood.
2. Fair distribution of wealth.
3. Equal pay for equal work.
4. Prevention of exploitation of child and adult labour.
5. Right to work, to education and public assistance in certain cases.
6. Right to receive free and compulsory education within a period of ten years from the commencement of the Constitution for all children upto the age of fourteen.
7. Public assistance in case of unemployment, old age, sickness, disability and other cases of deserved want.
8. The right to a living wage.
9. Conditions of work assuring a decent standard of life and full enjoyment of leisure and social and cultural opportunities.

10. Raising the level of nutrition and the standard of living of its people and the' improvement of public health.
11 Promoting with special care the educational and economic interests of the scheduled castes and the scheduled tribes and other less favoured sections of the community and protecting them from social injustice and all forms of exploitation.

UNION EXECUTIVE

President—The President is the head of the Indian Republic. He is elected indirectly by an electoral college consisting of the elected members of both Houses of Parliament and the Legislatures of the States.

The qualification of the office of the President—He (1) should be a citizen of India; (2) must have completed the age of 35 years; (3) qualified for election as a member of the House of the People. He will not be eligible for election if he holds a job in Government giving him financial rewards.

Term of office—The President holds office for five years and is eligible for re-election: but he can resign and hand over the charge to the Vice-President.

Salary and allowances—The President draws a salary of Rs. 10,000/- per mensem plus usual allowances. He shall also be granted a pension after he retires from office.

Impeachment—The President can be impeached for "the violation of the Constitution". The procedure for impeachment is as follows—A charge can be brought against him in either House of Parliament. But it should be passed by a majority of not less than two-thirds of the total membership of the House. If such a resolution is passed by two-third majority, the President is forthwith removed from the office.

Powers of the President—Legally, the President of India is the head of the executive. The entire executive action of the Government is vested in him and shall be exercised by him either directly or through officers subordinate to him in accourdance with the Constitution. He has the supreme command of the Defence Forces of the Union. He appoints the Prime Minister and the other Ministers are appointed by him on the advice of the Prime, Minister. The appointments of Judge of the Supreme Court, of the High Courts, in the States, the Attorney General of India, the Comptroller and Auditor General, the Governors of States and Members of the Public Service Commission require his previous sanction. In the field of legislation, his previous consent is necessary for the introduction of certain bills on certain subjects. Without his assent no bill passed by the Parliament can become law. In short, there is no limit to the authority possessed by the President. With all that, however, Art. 74 (1) of the Constitution states that in the exercise of all the, powers and functions belonging to him under the Constitution, he is under an obligation to consult the Council of Ministers of which the Prime Minister is the head. The Constitution however does not specifically state that the President is always bound to accept the advice of the Prime Minister. No doubt he will not be able to interfere in day-to-day administration as this will result in frequent constitutional deadlocks. But in extraordinary situations, it is evident that the President may choose to act in his discretion without accepting the Ministerial advice. If he also, happens to be a great personality, he will certainly be able to greatly influence the decisions of the Ministry. The President's powers may for the sake of convenience be summed up as follows—

(*a*) Executive Powers; *(b)* Emergency Powers; *(c)* Legislative Powers; *(d)* Financial Powers; and *(e)* Judicial Powers.

(a) The President, being the executive head of the Union will be in supreme command of the Defence Forces of the Union and will thus have the power of declaring war and concluding peace. All the executive action of the Government of India will be expressed to be taken in the name of the President.

(b) The President has been given very wide powers to meet situations in emergencies, arising out of war or internal aggression, emergencies arising out of the failure of constitutional machinery in the States as also in times of financial distress in the country.

(c) All Bills passed by the Parliament require the assent of

the President before they become law. He can withhold his assent from all Bills other than Money Bills. But if the same Bill is passed by Parliament for the second time with or without amendment, the President must not withhold his consent therefrom. In any case of disagreement over a Bill (other than a Money Bill) the President may summon a joint sitting of both the Houses. Moreover at any time except when both the Houses of Parliament are not in session, the President will have the power *of* issuing Ordinances which will have the same force as Acts of Parliament.

(d) The President has been authorised to lay before Parliament at the beginning of every financial year, a financial statement showing the estimated receipts and expenditure of the Union for that year. In the case of failure of constitutional machinery of the states, he is given the right to sanction expenditure from the Consolidated Fund of the State.

(e) The President has the power to grant pardons, reprieves or remissions of punishment of any person convicted of any offence.

Vice-President is the ex-officio chairman of the Council of States. Any citizen of India aged thirty five years and above and qualified for the membership of the Council of States can be elected to this office by both the Houses of Parliament. When the President is ill, if he resigns or dies or is removed or is for any reason absent, his place will be taken by the Vice-President till a new President is elected.

Council of Ministers—The Constitution provides that the President should have a Council of Ministers to assist him. The Council of Ministers is the real executive of the Indian Republic with the President as its leader. The Council will "aid and advise" him in the exercise of his functions. The President appoints the Prime Minister and other members of his cabinet on the advice of the Prime Minister. The Ministers are collectively responsible to the Lower House. It is the duty of the Prime Minister to communicate to the President all the decisions by the Cabinet.

The Prime Minister provides the link between the Cabinet and the President. The Ministers are required to take oaths of office and secrecy and their salaries and allowances will be determined by the Parliament.

UNION LEGISLATURE *i.e.* PARLIAMENT

Parliament consists of the President and two Houses known respectively as the Council of States and the House of the People.

Council of States is a permanent body elected indirectly and has a maximum strength of 250 members but as nearly as one third of the members shall retire every second year. Among these 12 will be nominated by the President. The nominated members should be men of learning and wide experience such as artists, writers, scientists and social workers. A member of Council of States must be a citizen of India and must not be less than 30 years of age. The Vice President of India shall be ex-officio chairman of the Council of States.

The **House of the People** will consist of not more than 500 members. These members are directly elected by the voters in the several States. Every adult or grown-up citizen of India is given the right to vote. The electoral constituencies are so divided that each member in this House represents not less than 500,000. There will be no nomination to the House of the People. The normal life of the House is five years. The minimum age for membership is 25 years for the Lower House.

The difference between the Council of States and the House of the People :

The difference is not merely in their size. The powers given to them are not the same. The function of both is to legislate but the greater part of this responsibility will be borne by the Lower House. A bill has to be passed by both the Houses before it becomes law. In the case of a disagreement between the two Houses, a joint session of the two Houses is summoned to resolve the deadlock. The opinion of the Lower House will ultimately prevail owing to its numerical majority. But it is to be noted that the procedure regarding deadlock relates only to Bills other than Money Bills for, as regards Money Bills, the provision of the

Constitution is that sole power shall belong to the Lower House. Money Bills cannot be introduced in the Council of States. They must as a rule originate in the House of the People.

There is freedom of speech in Parliament subject to certain provisions of the Constitution and rules and standing orders of Parliament. For a period of 15 years from 26. 1. 1950, the business of the Parliament can be transacted either in English or Hindi but after the end of 15 years, the business will have to be conducted in Hindi alone.

UNION JUDICIARY

The Indian Constitution provides for a single (and not dual as in America) Judiciary with the Supreme Court at its head. Below the Supreme Court, there are various High Courts for each State and below the High Courts, there are various subordinate courts.

Supreme Court of India—The Supreme Court consists of a Chief Justice who is appointed by the President and not more than seven other judges (but Parliament can sanction a larger number) who are also appointed by the President in consultation with the Chief Justice. A Judge may hold office until he attains the age cf 65 years.

The Supreme Court decides disputes between the Government of India and any State or States or between two or more States involving any question of law or fact. Civil and criminal appeals of a certain kind from High Courts will also be heard by it. The Supreme Court is also competent to order the enforcement of Fundamental Rights. It has also advisory jurisdiction by which the President can refer to it any question of public importance. The law declared by it is binding on all courts of the country.

High Courts in the States—There is a High Court for each State. It consists of Chief Justice and such other Judges as the President, from time to time deem it necessary to appoint. Every High Court has superintendence over all Courts subordinate to it throughout the territory excepting any court constituted for Armed Forces of India.

Subordinate Courts—Appointments, promotions and posting of District Judges shall be made by the Governor in consultation with the High Court of the State.

ATTORNEY-GENERAL

For expert legal advice in the performance of its functions, the President appoints an Attorney-General of India to tender legal advice to the Government of India and perform other duties of legal character.

COMPTROLLER AND AUDITOR GENERAL

The Comptroller and Auditor-General is appointed by President to perform duties and exercise powers relating to the accounts of the Union and the States. His main duty is to keep careful watch on the finances of the Union and of the States and specially to see that the expenses voted by the Parliament or the Legislature of a State and laid down in the Appropriation Act are not exceeded or varied.

PART A STATES

There will be a Governor for each State in whom all executive power is vested. He is appointed by the President and holds office during his pleasure. Any citizen of India who has completed 35 years of age is eligible for appointment as Governor. Governor holds office for a term of five years unless he resigns earlier. Besides official residence, Governor draws a salary of Rs. 5,000 per month and other allowances, and enjoys certain privileges.

The Governor will be assisted by a Council of Ministers with Chief Minister at the head of the Council to aid and advise the Governor. The Chief Minister is appointed by the Governor and the other Ministers are also appointed by him on the advice of the Chief Minister. Ministers hold office during the pleasure of the Governors. The Council of Ministers is collectively responsible to the Legislative Assembly of the State.

Every State has a Legislature. Some States have two chambers while others have only one chamber. Where there are two chambers, one is known as Legislative Council and the other as Legislative Assembly and where there is only one House, it is known as Legislative Assembly.

Those with two Houses are Bombay, Bihar, Madras, Punjab, Uttar Pradesh and West Bengal. In all the States, the Lower House is called Legislative Assembly and the Upper House is known as Legislative Council.

Legislative Assembly of each State shall be composed of members elected by direct election on the basis of adult franchise. The total number of members of the Assembly shall in no case be more than 500 or less than 60. The actual strength is to be determined on the ratio of one to every 75,000 of the population of the State. Its normal life is five years. Some seats may be reserved for Scheduled tribes and Scheduled castes. The Governor may also nominate the representative of Anglo-Indian Community.

The total number of members of the Legislative Council of a State is not to exceed one fourth of the total members in the Legislative Assembly but in no case it is to be less than 40. This is a permanent body and one-third of its members will retire every second year. Half of its members will be elected from local bodies from among the graduates of three years standing and teachers who have worked at least for three years. A third of the members will be elected by the Legislative Assembly from among non-members and the rest will be nominated by the Governor from among men of eminence in literature, art, science or social service.

PART B STATES

Rulers of Part B States are known as Rajpramukhs. They are appointed in accordance with the agreements made between the States and Government of India. The executive power of the State is vested in Rajpramukh. There is a Council of Ministers to aid or advise him. For ten years or such period as may be fixed by the President, the governments of these States will function under the general control of the Government of India.

PART C STATES

These States are administered by the President through a Chief Commissioner or Lt. Governor. The Parliament may create a Council of Advisers or Ministers for these States.

DISTRIBUTION OF POWERS

For the purposes of distributing legislative powers between the Centre and the States, three comprehensive lists have been drawn up. These lists are (1) Union List, (2) Concurrent List and (3) State List.

The Parliament has "exclusive power" to make laws in regard to the matters mentioned in the Union List. The Concurrent List means that matters are shared between the Union and the States for the purpose of legislation such as criminal law, civil procedure, preventive detention, marriage and divorce, transfer of property other than agricultural lands, contracts bankruptcy etc.

There are 66 items in the State List. Some of them are Police, Administration of Justice, Prisons, Local Governments, Public Health and Sanitation, Forests, Fisheries etc. The Legislature of a State has "exclusive power" to make laws in matters mentioned in this list.

Jurisdiction over all other matters not mentioned in the Concurrent and State Lists will belong to Parliament. This means that the Centre will acquire "residualy powers."

FINANCE, PROPERTY, CONTRACT & SUITS

No tax can be levied or collected except by authority of law. There are provisions for the creation of several funds. The general fund is the Consolidated Fund of India into which all income of the Government of India with the specified exceptions should go and a Consolidated Fund for each State. In addition, there is a Public Account of India and a Public Account for each State. The next fund is the Contingency Fund of India and of each State at the disposal of the President of India and the Governor or Rajpramukh of a State respectively.

TRADE, COMMERCE & INTERCOURSE WITHIN INDIA

There will be freedom of trade, commerce and intercourse throughout the territory of India but Parliament may impose certain restrictions on the freedom of trade, commerce and intercourse between one State and another in the public interest.

PUBLIC SERVICES

The Constitution provides for a Public Service Commission for the Union and one for each State; and it permits two or more States to have a Joint Public Service Commission. The main functions of the Union and State Public Service Commissions are to recommend candidates for appointment and to conduct examinations for recruitment to the Central and State services.

ELECTIONS

The superintendence, direction and control of elections to Parliament and Legislature of every State and of President and Vice-President including appointment of election tribunals shall be vested in a Commission known as Election Commission.

There shall be only one general electoral roll for every territorial constituency and no person will be ineligible for inclusion in such roll on grounds only of religion, race, caste, sex or any of them.

There is no property qualification of voters. Every person who is a citizen of India and who is not less than twenty one years of age and who is not otherwise disqualified is entitled to vote at the elections of the House of the People and the Legislative Assemblies of States.

SPECIAL PROVISIONS FOR CERTAIN CLASSES

There are special provisions regarding reservation of seats for Scheduled Castes, Scheduled Tribes and representation of Anglo-Indian Community and other benefits intended for them.

LANGUAGES

Hindi in Devnagri script shall be the official language of the Union and the form of numerals for official use shall be the international form of Indian numerals. The English language shall continue for all official purposes of the Union for a period of 15 years but the President may authorise, during the said period, the use of Hindi in addition to English language. If at the end of 15 years, it is found that Hind will not be able to replace English wholly, Parliament may provide for the use of English for such purposes as may be specified by law.

The Constitution recognises the use of Assamese, Bengali, Gujarati, Hindi, Kannada, Kashmiri, Malayalam, Marathi, Oriya, Punjabi, Sanskrit, Tamil, Telugu and Urdu any one or more of which may be used as the regional languages of the union.

AMENDMENT OF THE CONSTITUTION

The Constitution shall stand amended when the President gives assent to any Bill for the purpose after it is passed in each House of Parliament by a majority of not less than two thirds of the members of the House present and voting. Exception is however made in the case of amendments of certain particular provisions, in which cases any amendment will in addition require the ratification by not less than one half of the States in Part A and Part B before such Bill is presented to the President for assent.

10

PUBLIC FUNDS

A. CREATION OF VARIOUS FUNDS

There are various provisions in the Constitution for the creation of several funds. The general fund is the *"Consolidated Fund of India"* into which all income of the Government of India with the specified exceptions should go and a *"Consolidated Fund of each State"*. In addition there is a *"Public Account of India"* and a *"Public Account of each State"*. The next fund is the *"Contingency Fund of India and of each State"* at the disposal of the President of India and the Governor or Rajpramukh of the State respectively.

The word "State" used above does not include Part 'C' States whose receipts of revenues and all other public moneys are credited in the Union accounts. The finances of Coorg are, however kept separate under Article 242 of the Constitution.

Provision has also been made for the creation of District and Regional Funds in connection with the administration of Tribal Areas in Assam. (*Vide* Para 7 of the Sixth Schedule to the Constitution).

In order to enable a proper appreciation of the situation in which these various funds were created, a knowledge of the historical background is considered necessary and a brief description thereof is given below:—

Historical Background

Before the Government of India Act, *1935* came into force, the Governor-General in Council was the custodian of the Public

Account which was a single account for the whole of India. All the financial transactions of Provincial Governments were effected through the Central balances and their first effective record was when they were classified by the Accountants General. The account of each Provincial Government was only a subsidiary account and the balance of each Provincial Government was only an account balance which was worked out by the Accountant General concerned. Consequent on the coming into force of the Government of India Act 1935, the balances of the Provincial Govts. were from 1-4-1937 physically separated from that of the Central Government and a separate Public Account was set up for each Government into which all moneys received by a Government whether on revenue,or other account were paid and credited and from which all disbursements of or on behalf of that Government were made.

In so far as the financial set-up in the Union and Part A States is concerned, the position under the Government of India Act 1935 was maintained upto 31-3-50. Part B States in which the financial set-up varied from one State to another were brought into the Indian pattern of accounting system from 1-4-50 (from 13-4-50, in the case of PEPSU) on integration of their federal finances with those of the Indian Union.

The object of the creation of a consolidated fund in place of the previous 'revenues of India' is to prevent the possibility of the proceeds from particular taxes being appropriated by particular items of expenditure without regard to the general financial necessities of the Government as a whole. An Appropriation Act is therefore newly introduced whereby not a pie from the Consolidated Fund can be spent without the authority of the lower House. Formerly when any Money Bill was passed, it was the prerogative of the Governor-General to certify the Bill before it could become law. Under the Constitution, this procedure of certification is done away with and the President possesses no such power.

B. CONSOLIDATED FUND

The Constitution provides for a Consolidated Fund of India and a Consolidated Fund for each State. Art. 266 (1)

1. Definition

(a) *"The Consolidated Fund of India"*. Excepting the following two items *viz.*

(i) Sums payable into "the Contingency Fund of India";

and

(ii) the whole or part of the net proceeds of certain taxes and duties assigned to States.

(1) all revenues received by the Government of India (including those received by Part C States);

(2) all loans raised by that Government by the issue of treasury bills, loans or ways and means advances;

and

(3) all moneys received by that Government in repayment of loans are credited into one separate consolidated fund entitled *"the Consolidated Fund of India"*.

(*b*) *"the Consolidated Fund of the State"*, Excepting such sums as are payable into "the Contingency Fund of the State";

(1) all revenues received by the Government of a State (Part A and Part B States only),

(2) all loans raised by that Government by the issue of treasury bills, loans or ways and means advances,

and

(3) all moneys received by that Government in repayment of loans

are credited into one separate consolidated fund entitled *"the Consolidated Fund of the State"*.

2. Appropriation of moneys out of the Fund

Art. 266(3)

The following are the three essential conditions which govern the appropriation of moneys out of the Consolidated Fund of India or the Consolidated Fund of a State :—

(*i*) It must be in accordance with law. No money can be withdrawn without an Appropriation Act having been passed by the competent Legislature. This is however subject to the provisions relating to the Supplementary, Additional or Excess Grants and Votes on account, Votes of credit and Exceptional Grants.

Arts. 114 (3), 204 (3)

(*ii*) The purpose for which the grant is made must be one authorised by the Constitution.

(*iii*) The procedure laid down for the purpose with respect to the passing of Appropriation Bills in Articles 112 to 116 and 202 to 206 should be strictly followed.

3. Custody etc.

Art. 283

(*a*) *"the Consolidated Fund of India".*

The following matters are to be regulated by law made by Parliament and until provision in that behalf is so made, by rules made by the President :—

(*i*) The custody of the Consolidated Fund of India.

(*ii*) The payment of moneys into such Fund.

(*iii*) The withdrawal of moneys therefrom.

and

(*iv*) All other matters connected with or ancillary to the above matters.

(*b*) *"the Consolidated Fund of the State."*

The following matters are to be regulated by law made by the Legislature of the State and until provision in that behalf is so made, by rules made by the Governor or Rajpramukh of the State :—

(*i*) The custody of the Consolidated Fund of the State.

(*ii*) The payment of moneys into such Fund.

(*iii*) The withdrawal of moneys therefrom.

and

(*iv*) All other matters connected with or ancillary to the above matters.

Note—The rules made by the President to regulate the aforesaid matters in respect of the Consolidated Fund of India as well as Public Account of India which have been promulgated under the Min. of Law Notification No. 374I-B II/50 Dt. 31-3-50 provide that the aforesaid matters shall be regulated

(*a*) as respects moneys held or received in a Part B State other than in a Treasury of the Central Government, by the rules in force in that State regulating such matters in relation to moneys received on account of the revenues of the State; and

(*b*) in other cases, by the rules made by the Central Government or by any person authorised by it in that behalf under Sec. 151 of the Government of India Act, 1935 and in force on 25-1-50 insofar as these rules are not inconsistent with the provisions of the Constitution. These rules are to be read with subject to all necessary modifications.

The various State Governments have also made similar Rules to keep alive the position as on 25-1-50.

4. Expenditure charged upon the Fund

The *main characteristic* of the expenditure charged upon the Consolidated Fund of India or the Consolidated Fund of the State is that it is not subject to vote of Parliament or the State Legislature although there is nothing in the Constitution to prevent a discussion on it.

Art. 113 (1), Art. 203 (1)

(1) The following expenditure is *charged on the Consolidated Fund of India* :— Art. 112 (3)

(*a*) (*i*) the emoluments and allowances of the President and (*ii*) other expenditure relating to his office;

(*b*) the salaries and allowances of (*i*) the Chairman and the Deputy Chairman of the Council of States and (*ii*) the Speaker and the Deputy Speaker of the House of the People;

(*c*) (*i*) debt charges for which the Government of India is liable including interest :

(*ii*) sinking fund charges and redemption charges;

(*iii*) any other expenditure relating to the raising of loans and the service and redemption of debt;

(*d*) (*i*) the salaries, allowances and pensions payable to or in respect of Judges of the Supreme Court;

(*ii*) the pensions payable to or in respect of Judges of the Federal Court;

(*iii*) the pensions payable to or in respect of Judges of any High Court which exercises jurisdiction in relation to any area included in the territory of India or which at any time before the commencement of the Constitution exercised jurisdiction in relation to any area included in a Province corresponding to a State specified in Part A of the First Schedule;

(*e*) the salary, allowances and pension payable to or in respect of the Comptroller and Auditor General of India;

(*f*) any sums required to satisfy any judgment, decree or award of any court or arbitral tribunal;

(*g*) any other expenditure declared (*i*) by the Constitution or (*ii*) by Parliament by law to be so charged.

The following expenditure, in addition, has been declared by the Constitution to be so charged :—

(*h*) the administrative expenses of the Supreme Court including all salaries, allowances and pensions payable to or in respect of the officers and servants of the Court; Art. 146 (3).

(*i*) the administrative expenses of the office of the Comptroller and Auditor General including all salaries, allowances and pensions payable to or in respect of persons serving in that office; Art. 148 (6).

(*j*) annual Grants-in-aid of the revenues of the States of

Assam, Bihar, Orissa and West Bengal in lieu of assignment of any share of the net proceeds in each year of export duty on jute and jute products to those States; Art. 273 (1).

(*k*) Grants-in-aid from the Union to certain States in need of assistance; Art. 275.

(*l*) contribution towards adjustment in respect of certain expenses and pensions; Art. 290.

(*m*) any sums the payment of which has been guaranteed or assured by the Government of the Dominion of India to any Ruler of a State as privy purse; Art. 291.

(*n*) any sums required for the purpose of making loans to any State; Art. 293 (2).

(*o*) the expenses of the Union Public Service Commission including any salaries, allowances and pensions payable to or in respect of the members or staff of the Commission. Art. 322.

(2) The following expenditure is *charged on the Consolidated Fund of the State:*— Art. 202 (3).

(*a*) (*i*) the emoluments and allowances of the Governor and (*ii*) other expenditure relating to his office;

Note—The above item relates to Part A States. For corresponding item in respect of Part B States, see item (*l*) below.

(*b*) the salaries and allowances of

(*i*) the Speaker and the Deputy Speaker of the Legislative Assembly; and

(*ii*) in the case of a State having a Legislative Council, also of the Chairman and the Deputy Chairman of the Legilslative Council;

(*c*) (*i*) debt charges for which the State is liable including interest,

(*ii*) sinking fund charges redemption charges, and

(*iii*) other expenditure relating to the raising of loans and the service and redemption of debt;

(*d*) expenditure in respect of the salaries and allowances of Judges of any High Court;

(*e*) any sums required to satisfy any judgment, decree or award of any court or arbitral tribunal;

(*f*) any other expediture declared by (*i*) the Constitution or (*ii*) by the Legislature of the State by law, to be so charged.

The following expenditure, in addition, has been declared by the Constitution to be so charged :—

(*g*) the administrative expenses of a High Court including all salaries, allowances and pensions payable to or in respect of the officers and servants of the Court; Art. 229 (3)

(*h*) in the case of the State of Travancore-Cochin, a sum of fifty-one lakhs of rupees required to be paid annually to the Devaswom fund under the covenant entered into before the commencement of the Constitution by the Rulers of the Indian States of Travancore and Cochin for the formation of the United State of Travancore and Cochin; Art. 238 (10) (*ii*)

(*i*) contribution towards adjustment in respect of certain expenses and pensions; Art. 290

(*j*) contribution made by the State to the Government of India in adjustment of the amount of privy purse previously paid by the latter. Art. 291 (2)

(*k*) the expenses of the State Public Service Commission including any salaries, allowances and pensions payable to or in respect of the members or staff of the Commission. Art. 322

(*l*) in the case of the Part B States—

the allowances of the Rajpramukh and other expediture relating to his office as determined by the President by general or special order.

Art. 238 (10)

Note—For corresponding item in respect of Part A States, see item (*a*) above.

5. Expenditure from the Consolidated Funds : Provisions to secure effective financial control by the Legislature

The Constitution contains a number of provisions designed to secure effective control by the Parliament and State Legislatures over the finances of the Governments concerned. The system of financial control envisaged in the Constitution prevents the frittering away of the Consolidated Funds and preserves it in tact to meet only the authorised lawful expenditure. The various provisions made in this respect are stated below. The relevant Articles of the Constitutions are quoted against each item.

(1) *In respect of the Consolidated Fund of India.*

(*a*) A Bill is deemed to be a Money Bill if it contains only provisions dealing with all or any of the following matters, viz.

(*i*) the custody of the Consolidated Fund of India, the payment of moneys into or the withdrawal of moneys from such Fund;

(*ii*) the appropriation of moneys out of the Consolidated Fund of India;

(*iii*) the declaring of any expenditure to be expenditure charged on the Consolidated Fund of India or the increasing of any amount of any such expenditure;

(*iv*) the receipt of money on account of the Consolidated Fund of India or the custody or issue of such money;

and

(*v*) any matter incidental to the above

Art. 110 (I) (c) (d) (e) (f) & (g)

(*b*) A Bill or amendment making provision for any of the matters specified in sub-clauses (*i*) to (*iv*) of item (*a*) above can not be introduced or moved except on the recommendation of the President and a Bill making such provision, cannot be introduced in the Council of States. Art. 117 (1)

(*c*) A Bill which, if enacted and brought into operation, would involve expenditure from the Consolidated Fund of India shall not be passed by either House of Parliament unless the President has recommended to that House the consideration of the Bill. Art. 117(3)

(*d*) Subject to the provisions regarding Supplementary, Additional or Excess Grants and 'Votes on account', 'Votes of credit' or Exceptional Grants, no money can be withdrawn from the Consolidated Fund of India except under appropriation made by law passed in accordance with the provisions relating to Appropriation Bills, Art. 114 (3)

(*e*) No amendment can be proposed to any Appropriation Bill in either House of Parliament which will have the effect of varying the amount or altering the destination of any grant made or of varying the amount of any expenditure charged on the Consolidated Fund of India except under appropriation made by law in the prescribed manner. Art. 114 (2)

(*f*) No money out of the Consolidated Fund of India shall be appropriated except in accordance with law and for the purposes and in the manner provided in the Constitution. Art. 266 (3)

(*g*) The procedure regarding the passing of Appropriation Bills have been made equally applicable in the case of Supplementary, Additional or Excess Grants and Votes on account, Votes of credit and Exceptional grants. Arts. 115, 116

(2) *In Respect of the Consolidated Fund of the State,* there are also corresponding provisions as stated below—

(*a*) A Bill is deemed to be a Money Bill if it contains only provisions dealing with all or any of the following matters namely—

(*i*) the custody of the Consolidated Fund of the State,

the payment of moneys into or the withdrawal of moneys from the Fund;

(*ii*) the appropriation of moneys out of the Consolidated Fund of the State;

(*iii*) the declaring of any expenditure charged on the Consolidated Fund of the State or the increasing of the amount of any such expenditure;

(*iv*) the receipt of money on account of the Consolidated Fund of the State or the custody or the issue of such money;

(*v*) any matter incidented to the above. Art. 199 (I) (c) (d) (e) (f) and (g)

(*b*) A Bill or amendment making provision for any of the matters specified in sub-clauses (i) to (iv) of item (a) above cannot be introduced or moved except on the recommendation of the Governor and a Bill making such provision cannot be introduced in a Legislative Council. Art. 207 (I)

(*c*) A Bill, which if enacted and brought into operation, would involve expenditure from the Consolidated Fund of a State shall not be passed by a House of the Legislature of the State unless the Governor or Rajpramukhhas recommended to that House the consideration of the Bill. Art. 207 (3)

(*d*) Subject to the provisions relating to the Supplementary, Additional or Excess Grants and 'Votes on account' 'Votes of credit' and Exceptional Grants, no money can be withdrawn from the Consolidated Fund of the State Without an Appropriation Act. Art. 204 (3)

(*e*) No amendment can be proposed to a Bill in the Legislature which will have the effect of varying the amount or altering the destination of any grant so made or of varying the amount of any expenditure charged on the Consolidated Fund of the State. Art. 204 (2)

(*f*) No moneys out of the Consolidated Fund of a State shall be appropriated except in accordance with law and for the purposes and in the manner provided in the Constitution. Art. 266 (3)

(*g*) The procedure regarding the passing of Appropriation Bills have been made equally applicable in the case of Supplementary, Additional or Excess Grants and Votes on account, Votes of credit and Exceptional Grants. Arts. 205, 206.

(*h*) In order to ensure that the expenses voted by the Legislatures are not exceeded or varied and money expended was legally available for and applicable to the purpose or purposes to which it has been applied, there is provision for the office of the Comptroller and Auditor-General of India whose independence and freedom has been safeguarded in a variety of ways. The report of the Comptroller and Auditor-General is to be laid before each House of the Parliament and Legislature of the State as provided in the Constitution.

(*i*) "Rules of Procedure and Conduct of Business in Parliament" provide for the Parliamentary control to be exercised through two committee viz. Committee on Public Accounts and Committee on Estimates, who are entrusted with the examination of the Appropriation Accounts and Estimates respectively.

Note :—For detailed description of the functions of these Committees, please see the chapter 'Procedure in Financial Matters.'

(*j*) Rule 57 of the Rules of Procedure and Conduct of Business in Parliament enjoins that a Bill shall be accompanied by a financial memorandum which shall invite particular attention to the clauses involving expenditure and shall also give an estimate of the recurring and non-recurring expenditure involved in case the Bill is passed into law and that clauses or provisions in Bills involving expenditure from public funds shall be printed in thick type or in italics.

There are similar rules made by the various State Legislatures also.

6. Power of the President to authorise expenditure from the Consolidated Fund of a State Art 357(2)

Art. 357(2) provides that in the case of failure of Constitutional machinery in a State, the President may authorise, when the House of the People is not in session, expenditure from the Consolidated Fund of the'State pending the sanction of such expenditure by Parliament.

7. Proceeds of certain duties and taxes belonging to the Union List not to form part of the Consolidated Fund of India —

In the following cases, the proceeds of certain duties and taxes as specified below which although belong to the Union List, do not form part of the Consolidated Fund of India but are assigned to the States under the arrangements made for the distribution of revenues :—

(*i*) The proceeds in any financial year of the following duties leviable within any State do not form part of the Consolidated Fund of India (but are assigned to that State)- Art. 268 (2)

(*a*) Stamp duty in respect of bills of exchange, cheques, promissory notes, bills of landing, letters of credit, policies of insurance, transfer of shares, debentures, proxies and receipts. —Item 91 Union List

(*b*) duties of excise on medicinal and toilet preparations containing alcohol, opium, Indian hemp and other narcotic drugs and narcotics, —Item 84 Union List

(*ii*) The net proceeds in any financial year of the following duties and taxes except insofar as those proceeds represent proceeds attributable to Part C States do not form part of the Consolidated Fund of India— Art. 269 (2)

(*a*) Duties in respect of succession to property other than agricultural land. —Item 88 Union List (*b*) Estate duty in respect of property other than agricultural Land. —Item 87 Union List

(*c*) Terminal taxes on goods or passengers carried by railway, sea or air. —Item 89 Union List

(*d*) Taxes on railway fares and freights. —Item 89 Union List

(*e*) Taxes other than stamp duties on transactions in stock exchanges and futures markets. —Item 90 Union List

(*f*) Taxes, on the sale or purchase of newspapers and on advertisements published therein. —Item 92 Union List

(*iii*) Such percentage as may be prescribed, of the net proceeds in any financial year of "Taxes on income other than agricultural income excluding Corporation tax" (Vide Item 82 Union List) except insofar as those proceeds represent proceeds attributable to Part C States or to taxes payable in respect of Union emoluments does not form part of the Consolidated Fund of India. —Art. 270 (2)

The Parliament has, however, a right to levy a surcharge on the duties and taxes mentioned at items (ii) & (iii) above for the purposes of the Union and in that case, the whole proceeds of any such surcharge shall however form part of the Consolidated Fund of India. —Art. 271

8. Fees taken by the Supreme Court and High Courts

(*a*) Any fees or other moneys taken by the Supreme Court form part of the Consolidated Fund of India. Art. 226 (3)

(*b*) Any fees or other moneys taken by the High Courts form part of the Consolidated Fund of the State.—Art. 229 (3)

9. Borrowing on the Security of Consolidated Funds

(*a*) The Union can raise money by borrowing upon the security of the Consolidated Fund of India within such

Limits, if any, as may be fixed by Parliament by law. Art. 292

(b) The state can raise money by borrowing within the territory of India upon the security of the consolidated Fund of the same within such limits of any, as may be fixed by legistature of such state by law.

10. Transitional Provisions regarding moneys received or raised or expenditure incurred between the commencement of the Constitution and 31st March 1950—

The provisions of the Constitution relating to the Consolidated Fund of India or the Consolidated Fund of any State and the appropriation of moneys out-of either of such Funds is not applicable in relation to moneys received or raised or expenditure incurred by the Government of India or the Government of any State between the commencement of the Constitution *i.e.* 26-1-50 and 31-3-50 (both days inclusive).

Any expenditure incurred during the above period shall be deemed to be duly authorised if the expenditure was specified in a schedule of authorised expenditure authenticated in accordance with the provisions of the Government of India Act, 1935 by the Governor General of the Dominion of India or the Governor of the corresponding Province or is authorised by the Rajpramukh of the State in accordance with such rules as were applicable to the authorisation of expenditure from the revenues of the corresponding Indian State immediately before such commencement; Art. 390

C. PUBLIC ACCOUNT

1. Definition

The Constitution provides for a Public Account of India and a Public Account for each State.

(*a*) *Public Account of India.* All public moneys other than those credited to the Consolidated Fund or the Contingency Fund of India which are received by or on behalf of the Government of India are credited to *"the Public Account of India"* Art. 266 (2) (*b*) *Public Account of the State.* All public moneys other than those credited to the Consolidated Fund or the Contingency Fund of the State which are received by or on behalf of the Government of the State are credited to *"the Public Account of the State."* Art. 266 (2).

2. Custody etc.

(1) *Public Account of India.* The following matters are to be regulated by law made by Parliament and until provision in that behalf is so made by rules made by the President:-

(*i*) the custody of public moneys other than those credited to the Consolidated Fund or the Contingency Fund of India received by or on behalf of the Government of India;

(*ii*) their payment into the Public Account of India;

(*iii*) the withdrawal of moneys from such account;

and

(*iv*) all other matters connected with or ancillary to the above matters.

(2) *Public Account of the State.* The following matters are to be regulated by law made by the Legislature of the State and until provision in that behalf is so made, by rules made by the Governor or Rajpramukh of the State :—

(*i*) the custody of public moneys other than those credited to the Consolidated Fund or the Contingency Fund of the State which are received by or on behalf of the Government of the State;

(*ii*) their payment into the Public Account of the State;

(*iii*) the withdrawal of moneys from such account;

and

(*iv*) all other matters connected with or ancillary to the above matters. Art. 283

Note:—For rules made by the President and Governors or Rajpramukhs, please *see* the Note below item 2 under Consolidated Funds in this chapter.

Custody of suitors' deposits and other moneys received by public servants and Courts Art. 284

(1) There shall be paid into the *Public Account of India* the following :—

(*i*) All moneys received by or deposited with any officers employed in connection with the affairs of the Union in his capacity as such, other than revenues or public moneys raised or received by the Government of India;

and

(*ii*) All moneys received by or deposited with any Court within the territory of India to the credit of any cause, matter, account or persons relating to the affairs of the Union.

(*a*) There shall be paid into the *Public Account of the State* the following :—

(*i*) All moneys received by or deposited with any officer employed in connection with the affairs of the State in his capacity as such, other than revenues or public moneys raised or received by the Government of the State;

and

(*ii*) All moneys received by or deposited with any Court within the territory of India to the credit of and, cause, matter, account or persons relating to the affairs of the State.

3. Legislation relating to Public Account.

(*a*) *Relating to the Public Account of India-*

(1) A Bill is deemed to be a Money Bill if it contains only provisions dealing with the receipt of money on account of the Public Account of India or the custody or issue of such money or any matter incidental to the above. Art.110 (1) (f) & (g)

(2) A Bill or amendment making provision for the receipt of money on account of the Public Account of India or the custody or issue of such money

cannot be introduced or moved except on the recommendation of the President and a Bill making such provision cannot be introduced in the Council of States Art. 117(1)

(*b*) *Relating to the Public Account of the State—*

(1) A Bill is deemed to be a Money Bill if it contains only provisions .dealing with the receipt of money on account of the Public Account of the State or the custody or issue of such money or any matter incidental to the above. Art. 199 (1) (f) & (g)

(2) A Bill or amendment making provision for the receipt of money on account of the Public Account of the State or the custody or issue of such money cannot be introduced or moved except on the recommendation of the Governor or Rajpramukh and a Bill making such provision cannot be introduced in a Legislative Council. Art. 207 (1)

D. CONTINGENCY FUND

1. Definition

The Constitution provides for the establishment of a Contingency Fund of India and a Contingency Fund of each State.

(*a*) *"The Contingency Fund of India"*. "The Contingency Fund of India" is the title given to the Contingency Fund established by Parliament by law which is in the nature of an imprest and into which are paid from time to time such sums as may be determined by such law. The said Fund is placed at the disposal of the President to enable advances to be made by him out of the Fund for the purposes of meeting unforesees expenditure pending authorisation of such expenditure by Parliament by law, (under Article 115 or Article 116). Art. 267 (1)

Note : Article 115 details the procedure in Parliament relating to Supplementary, Additional or Excess grants.

Article 116 details the procedure in Parliament relating to Votes on account, Votes of credit and Exceptional grants.

(*b*) *"The Contingency Fund of the State"*. "The Contingency Fund of the State" is the title given to the Contingency Fund established by the Legislature of the State by law which is in the nature of an imprest and into which are paid from time to time such sums as may be determined by such law. The said Fund is placed at the disposal of the Governor or Rajpramukh of the State to enable advances to be made by him out of such Fund for the purposes of meeting unforeseen expenditure pending authorisation of such expenditure by the Legislature of the State by law (under Article 205 or Article 206). Art. 267 (2)

Note : Article 205 details the procedure in State Legislatures relating to Supplementary, Additional or Excess grants.

Article 206 details the procedure in State Legislature relating to Votes on account, Votes of credit and Exceptional grants.

2. Custody etc.

(*a*) *"The Contingency Fund of India"*. The following matters are to be regulated by law made by Parliament and until provision in that behalf is so made, by rules made by the President:—

(*i*) the custody of the Contingency Fund of India;

(*ii*) the payment of moneys into such Fund;

(*iii*) the withdrawal of moneys therefrom;

and

(*iv*) All other matters connected with or ancillary to jhe above matters. Art. 283 (1)

(*b*) *"The Contingency Fund of the State"*. The following matters are to be regulated by law made by the Legislature of the State and until provision in that behalf is so made, by rates made by the Governor or Rajpramukh of the State :—

(*i*) the custody of the Contingency Fund of the State;

(*ii*) the payment of moneys into such Fund;

(*III*) the withdrawal of moneys therefrom;

and

(*iv*) all other matters connected with or ancillary to the above matters, Art, 283 (a)

3. Legislation relating to Contingency Fund

(*a*) *Relating to the Contingency Fund of India.*

(1) A Bill is deemed to be a Money Bill if it contains only provisions dealing with the custody of the Contingency Fund of India, the payment of moneys into or the withdrawal of moneys from any such Fund or any matter incidental to the above. Art. 110 (I) (c) & (g)

(2) A Bill or amendment making provision for the custody of the Contingency Fund of India, the payment of moneys into or the withdrawal of moneys from the Fund cannot be introduced or moved except on the recommendation of the President and a Bill making such provision cannot be introduced in the Council of States. Art. 117 (I)

(*b*) *Relating to the contingency Fund of the State.*

(1) A Bill is deemed to be a Money Bill if it contains only provisions dealing with the custody of the Contingency Fund of the State, the payment of moneys into or the withdrawal of moneys from the Fund or any matter incidental to the above. Art. 199 (I) (c) & (g)

(2) A Bill or amendment making provision for the custody of the Contingency Fund of the State, the payment of moneys into or the withdrawal of moneys from the Fund cannot be introduced or moved except on the recommendation of the Governor or Rajpramukh and Bill making such provision cannot be introduced in a Legislative Council. Art. 207 (2)

11

PROCEDURE IN FINANCIAL MATTERS—BUDGET, GRANTS AND APPROPRIATION

A. EXPLANATION OF THE TERMS

Budget

Annual Financial Statement or the Budget—The President or the Governor or the Rajpramukh of the State, in respect of every financial year, causes to be laid before the Legislature concerned a statement of the estimated receipts and expenditure of the Government for that year. This "annual financial statement" is popularly known as "the Budget." In this statement the sums required to meet expenditure charged upon the Consolidated Fund of India or the Consolidated Fund of the State and the sums required to meet other expenditure proposed to be made from the Fund are shown separately, the expenditure on revenue account being distinguished from other expenditure.

Arts. 112, 202, 238.

As provided in Para 13 of the Sixth Schedule to the Constitution, the estimated receipts and expenditure pertaining to an autonomous district in tribal areas of Assam, which are credited to or is to be made from the Consolidated Fund of the State of Assam is shown separately in the annual financial statement of the State to be laid before the Legislature thereof.

Presentation of the Budget in Parts—The Budget can also be presented in two or more parts and when such presentation takes place, each part shall be dealt with in accordance with the rules as if it were the Budget.

(Rule 134 of the Rules of Procedure and Conduct of Business in Parliament framed under Art. 118.)

Grants

Demands for Grants

So much of the estimates embodied in the annual financial statement as relates to expenditure other than the expenditure charged upon the Consolidated Fund of India or the Consolidated Fund of the State is submitted to the Legislature concerned in the form of *'Demands for Grants'* on the recommendation of the President or the Governor or the Rajpramukh of the State as the case may be.

When the 'Demands for Grants' are presented to the Legislature, the Legislature may either

(*a*) assent to the demands;

or

(*b*) refuse to assent to any demand;

or

(*c*) assent to any demand subject to a reduction of the amount specified therein. Arts. 113, 203, 238.

The demands for grants are presented to the Legislature in such form as the Finance Minister may, after considering the suggestions, if any of the Estimates Committee settle but ordinarily, a separate demand is proposed for each Ministry. Each demand contains first, a statement of the total grant proposed and then a statement of the detailed estimate under each grant divided into items.

(Rule 131 of the Rules of Procedure and Conduct of Business in Parliament framed under Art. 118 of the Constitution)

Supplementary Grant—(1) If the amount authorised by the Appropriation Act to be expended for a particular service for the current financial year is found to be insufficient for the purposes of that year;

or

(2) when a need has arisen during the current financial year for supplementary expenditure upon some new service not contemplated in the "annual financial statement" for that year,

a supplementary statement showing the estimated amount of that expenditure is laid before the Legislature. This supplementary statement is then dealt with in the same way as the "annual financial statement."

Arts. 115, 205, 238

Additional Grant—When a need has arisen during the current financial year for additional expenditure upon some new service not contemplated in the "annual financial statement" for that year, a supplementary statement showing the estimated amount of that expenditure is laid before the Legislature. This supplementary statement is then dealt with in the same way as the "annual financial statement." Arts. 115, 205, 238.

Excess Grant—If any money has been spent on any service during a financial year in excess of the amount granted for that service and for that year, a demand for such excess is presented to the Legislature. This demand for the excess is then dealt with in the same way as the "annual financial statement." Arts. 115, 205, 238.

Token Grant—When funds to meet proposed expenditure on a new service can be made available by re-appropriation, a demand for the grant of a token sum may be submitted to the vote of the Legislature and if the Legislature assents to the demand, funds may be so made available.

(Rule 138 of the Rules of Procedure and Conduct of Business in Parliament framed under Art. 118.)

"Votes on Account"—The House of the People (in the case of Parliament) and the Legislative Assembly (in the case of State Legislatures) have power to make any grant in advance in respect of the estimated expenditure for a part of any financial year pending the completion of the procedure prescribed for the voting of such grant and the passing of the law authorising appropriation

of moneys out of the Consolidated Fund of India or the Consolidated Fund of the State to meet that expenditure. Such grants are called *"Votes on Account"*.

The withdrawal of moneys from the Consolidated Fund of India or of the State for the purpose for which these grants are made, will be authorised by an Act of the appropriate Legislature. In respect of the grants, the procedure in Parliament/State Legislature with respect to Estimates and Appropriation Bills will be followed. Arts. 116, 206, 238.

"Votes of Credit" The House of the People (in the case of Parliament) and the Legislative Assembly (in the case of State Legislatures) have power to make a grant for meeting an unexpected demand upon the resources of India or of the State when on account of the magnitude or the indefinite character of the service, the demand cannot be stated with the details ordinarily given in an "annual financial statement." Such grants are called *"Votes of Credit"*.

The withdrawal of moneys from the Consolidated Fund of India or the State for the purposes for which these grants are made, will be authorised by an Act of the appropriate Legislature. In respect of these grants, the procedure in Parliament State Legislatures with respect to Estimates and Appropriation Bills will be followed. Arts. 116, 206, 238.

Exceptional Grant—The House of the People (in the case of Parliament) and the Legislative Assembly (in the case of State Legislatures) have power to make an *"exceptional grant"* which forms no part of the current service of any financial year.

The withdrawal of moneys from the Consolidated Fund of India or of the State for the purposes for which these grants are made will be authorised by an Act of the appropriate Legislature. In respect of these grants, the procedure in Parliament/State Legislatures with respect to Estimates and Appropriation Bills will be followed. Arts. 116, 206, 238.

Appropriation

Appropriation Bill—After the grants have been made by the Legislature, a Bill is introduced to provide for the appropriation out of the Consolidated Fund of India or of the State of all moneys required to meet—

(*a*) the grants made by the Legislature; and

(*b*) the expenditure charged on the Consolidated Fund of India or of the State but not exceeding in any case the amount shown in the statement previously laid before the Legislature.

This Bill is called "the Appropriation Bill".

No amendment can be proposed to any such Bill in the Legislature which has the effect of

(*a*) varying the amount of any grant;

or

(*b*) altering the destination of any grant so made;

or

(*c*) varying the amount of any expenditure charged on the Consolidated Fund of India or of the State,

and the decision of the person presiding whether an amendment is inadmissible is final.

No money can be withdrawn from the Consolidated Fund, until this Bill is passed by the Legislature.

This Bill when passed by the Legislature becomes the "*Appropriation Act*". Arts. 114, 204, 238.

B. PROCEDURE IN FINANCIAL MATTERS

The procedure in financial matters in Parliament as well as in State Legislature laid down in the Constitution resolves itself into the following three stages—

(*a*) Presentation of the "Annual financial statement" and the expenditure mentioned therein. Arts. 112, 202.

(*b*) Submission of the Estimates and "Demands for grants." Arts. 113, 203

and

(*c*) Law to be made authorising the appropriation of moneys out of the Consolidated Fund of India or of the State. Arts. 114, 204.

In respect of Supplementary, Additional and Excess grants, the provisions regarding financial statement and expenditure or demand and law to be made authorising the appropriation of moneys out of the Consolidated Fund of India or of the State mentioned at items (a) (b) & (c) above are equally applicable.

Similarly, the provisions regarding grants and law to be made authorising the appropriation of moneys mentioned at items (b) and (c) above applies to 'Votes on account', 'Votes of credit' and Exceptional grants. The detailed provision of the Constitution are furnished below :—

In Parliament

I. *(a) Annual Financial Statement or Budget—*

(1) The President, in respect of every financial year, causes to be laid before both the Houses of Parliament, a statement of the estimated receipts and expenditure of the Government of India for that year which is called the "Annual Financial Statement" popularly known as "Budget". Art. 112.

(2) The estimates of expenditure embodied in the annual financial statement shows separately—

(*i*) the sums required to meet expenditure charged upon the Consolidated Fund of India; and

(*ii*) the sums required to meet other expenditure proposed to be made from the Consolidated Fund of India;

and distinguishes expenditure on revenue account from other expenditure. Art. 112

(b) Procedure in Parliament with respect to estimates—

(1) So much of the Estimates as relates to expenditure charged upon the Consolidated Fund of India is not submitted to the vote of Parliament but nothing in this clause shall be construed as preventing discussion in either House of Parliament of any of those estimates. Art. 113.

(2) So much of the estimates as relates to other expenditure is submitted in the form of *demands for grants* to the House of the People and the House of the People have power

(*i*) to assent;

or

(*ii*) to refuse to assent to any demand;

or

(*iii*) to assent any demand subject to a reduction of the amount specified therein.

(3) No demand for a grant is made except on the recommendation of the President. Art. 113

(*c*) *Appropriation Bills*—

(1) As soon as may be after the grants have been made by the House of the People, there is introduced a Bill to provide for the appropriation out of the Consolidated Fund of India of all moneys required to meet—

(*i*) the grants so made by the House of the People, and (ii) the expenditure charged on the Consolidated Fund of India but *not exceeding in any case* the amount shown in the statement previously laid before Parliament.

(2) No amendment can be proposed to any such Bill in either House of Parliament which will have the effect of

(*i*) varying the amount of the grant;

or

(*ii*) altering the destination of any grant so made;

or

(*iii*) varying the amount of any expenditure charged on the Consolidated Fund of India;

and the decision of the person presiding as to whether an amendment is inadmissible, is final.

(3) Subject to the provisions regarding Supplementary, Additional or Excess grants and 'Votes on account,' 'Votes of credit' and Exceptional grants, no money can be withdrawn from the Consolidated Fund of India except under appropriation made by law passed in accordance with the above provisions. Art, 114.

II. *Supplementary, additional or excess grants—*

(1) The President

(*a*) (i) if the amount authorised by the Appropriation Act to be expended for a particular service for .the current financial year is found to be insufficient for the purposes of the year,

or

(*ii*) when a need has arisen during the current financial year for supplementary or additional expenditure upon some service not contemplated in the annual financial statement for that year.

or

(*b*) if any money has been spent on any service during a financial year in excess of the amount granted for that service and for that year,

causes to be laid before both the Houses of Parliament another statement showing the estimated amount of that expenditure or causes to be presented to the House of the People a demand for such excess, as the case may be.

(2) The provisions relating to the Annual financial statement, Procedure in Parliament with respect to Estimates and Appropriation Bills have effect in relation to any such statement and expenditure or demand and also to any law to be made authorising the appropriation of moneys out of the Consolidated Fund of India to meet such expenditure or the grant in respect of such demand as they have effect in relation to the annual financial statement and the expenditure mentioned therein or to a demand for a grant and the law to be made for the authorisation of appropriation

of moneys out of the Consolidated Fund of India to meet such expenditure or grant. Art. 115

III. *'Votes on account, 'Votes of credit'* and *exceptional grants—*

(1) The House of the People have power

(*a*) to make any grant in advance in respect of the estimated expenditure for a part of any financial year pending the completion of the procedure for the voting of such grant and the passing of the law in accordance with the provisions relating to Appropriation Bills in relation to that expenditure;

(*b*) to make a grant for meeting an unexpected demand upon the resources of India when on account of the magnitude or the indefinite character of the service, the demand cannot be stated with the details ordinarily given in an annual financial statement;

(*c*) to make an exceptional grant which forms no part of the current service of any financial year;

and Parliament have power to authorise by law the withdrawal of moneys from the Consolidated Fund of India for the purposes for which the said grants are made.

(2) The provisions relating to the Procedure in Parliament with respect to Estimates and Appropriation Bills in Parliament, have effect in relation to the making of any grant under clause (1) above and to any law to be made under that clause as they have effect in relation to the making of a grant with regard to any expenditure mentioned in the annual financial statement and the law to be made for the authorisation of appropriation of moneys out of the Consolidated Fund of India to meet such expenditure. Art. 116

VI. *For Special Provisions as to Financial Bills*— Art. 117

Please see under chapter 'Bills.'

In State Legislatures

I. (*a*) *Annual Financial Statement or Budget—*

(1) The Governor, or the Rajpramukh, in respect of every financial year, causes to be laid before the House or Houses of the Legislature of the State, a statement of the estimated receipts and expenditure of the State for that year which is called "the Annual Financial Statement" popularly known as "Budget".

(2) The estimates of expenditure embodied in the annual financial statement shows separately—

(*i*) the sums required to meet expenditure charged upon the Consolidated Fund of the State; and

(*ii*) the sums required to meet other expenditure proposed to be made from the Consolidated Fund of the State;

and distinguishes expenditure on revenue account from other expenditure.

Art. 202

(b) *Procedure State in Legislatures with respect to Estimates*—

(1) So much of the estimates as relates to expenditure charged upon the Consolidated Fund of a State is not submitted to the vote of the Legislative Assembly but nothing in this clause shall be construed as preventing the discussion in the Legislature of any of those estimates.

(2) So much of the said estimates as relates to other expenditure is submitted in the form of *demands for grant* to the Legislative Assembly, and the Legislative Assembly have power

(*i*) to assent;

or

(*ii*) to refuse to assent to any demand;

or

(*iii*) to assent to any demand subject to a reduction of the amount specified therein.

(3) No demand for a grant shall be made except on the recommendation of the Governor or Rajpramukh as the case may be.

Art. 203

(c) *Appropriation Bill —*

(1) As soon as may be, after the grants have been made by the Assembly, there is introduced a Bill to provide for the appropriation out of the Consolidated Fund of the State of moneys required to meet—

(i) the grants so made by the Assembly;

and

(ii) the expenditure charged on the Consolidated Fund of the State but not exceeding in any case the amount shown in the statement previously laid before the House or Houses.

(2) No amendment shall be proposed to any such Bill in the House or either House of the Legislature of the State which will have the effect of

(i) varying the amount of the grant;

or

(ii) altering the destination of any grant so made;

or

(iii) varying the amount of any expenditure charged or the Consolidated Fund of the State;

and the decision of the person presiding as to whether as amendment is inadmissible under this clause shall be final.

Art. 204.

(3) Subject to the provisions relating to the Supplementary, Additional or Excess grants and Votes on account, Votes of credit and Exceptional grants, no money shall be withdrawn from the Consolidated Fund of the State except under appropriation made by law passed in accordance with the provisions relating to Appropriation Bills.

II. *Supplementary, Additional or Excess grants.*

(1) The Governor or Rajpramukh

(a) (i) if the amount authorised by the Appropriation Act to he expended for a particular service for the current financial year is found to be insufficient for the purposes of that year,

or

(ii) when a need has arisen during the current financial year for supplementary or additional expenditure upon some new service not contemplated in the annual financial statement for that year,

or

(b) If any money has been spent on any service during a financial year in excess of the amount granted for that service and for that year,

cause to be laid before the House or the Houses of the Legislature of the State another statement showing the estimated amount of that expenditure or causes to be presented to the Legislative Assembly of the State a demand for such excess as the case may be.

(2) The provisions relating to the "annual financial statement," procedure in State Legislatures with respect to Estimates and Appropriation Bills mentioned above have effect in relation to any such statement and expenditure or demand and also to any law to be made authorising the appropriation of moneys out of the Consolidated Fund of the State to meet such expenditure or the grant in respect of such demand as they have effect in relation to the "annual financial statement" and the expendture mentioned therein or to a demand for a grant and the law to be made for the authorisation of appropriation of money out of the Consolidated Fund of the State to meet such expenditure or grant. Art. 205.

II. *'Votes on account', 'Votes of credit' and Exceptional grants—*

(1) The Legislative Assembly have power—

(a) to make any grant in advance in respect of the estimated expenditure for a part of any financial year pending the completion of the procedure prescribed for the voting of such grant and the passing of the law in accordance with the provisions relating to Appropriation Bills in relation to that expenditure;

(*b*) to make a grant for meeting an unexpected demand upon the resources of the State when on account of. the magnitude or the indefinite character of the service, the demand cannot be stated with the details ordinarily given in an annual financial statement;

(*c*) to make an exceptional grant which forms no part of the current service of any financial year; and the Legislature of the State have power to authorise by law the withdrawal of moneys from the Consolidated Fund of the State for the purposes for which the said grants are made.

(2) The provisions relating to the procedure in State Legislatures with respect to Estimates and Appropriation Bills in State Legislatures have effect in relation to the making of any grant under clause (1) above and to any law to be made under that clause as they have effect in relation to the making of a grant with regard to any expenditure mentioned in the "annual financial statement" and the law to be made for the authorisation of appropriation of money out of the Consolidated Fund of the State to meet such expenditure. Art. 206

Note—"Special provisions as to Financial Bills". Art. 207 *Phase see under chapter 'Bills'.*—

C. FINANCIAL CONTROL BY LEGISLATURES: ESTIMATES COMMITTEES AND PUBLIC ACCOUNTS COMMITTEE

The financial control by the Parliament and State Legislature over the expenditure from the Consolidated Fund of India or of the State is exercised in two stages *viz.*

(*i*) Control of Committee on Estimates;

and

(*ii*) Control of Committee on Public Accounts.

(i) Committee on Estimates.

After the commencement of the first session of Parliament State Legislatures, every year, a Committee on Estimates is constituted

(*a*) to examine such of the estimates as may seem fit to the Committee;

and

(*b*) to suggest economies consistent with the policy underlying the estimates.

The Committee continues its examination of the estimates from time to time throughout the financial year and report to Parliament as its examination proceeds. It is not incumbent on the Committee to examine the entire estimates of any one year. The demands for grants may be finally voted notwithstanding the fact that the Committee has made no report.

Rule 145 of the Rules of Procedure and Conduct of Business in Parliament.

Note :—Similar provisions exist in the Legislatives Rules of the States.

(ii) Committee on Public Accounts.

After the commencement of the first session of Parliament State Legislatures every year, a Committee on Public Accounts is constituted.

The *function* of the Committee is to examine the accounts showing the appropriation of the sums granted by Parliament State Legislature to meet the expenditure of the Government and such other accounts laid before Parliament State Legislature as the Committee may think fit.

Control of Public Accounts Committee.

(1) In scrutinising the Appropriation Accounts and the report of the Comptroller and Auditor-General thereon, it is the *duty* of the Committee to satisfy itself—

(*a*) that the moneys shown in the accounts as having been disbursed were legally available for and applicable to the service or purpose to which they have been applied or charged;

(*b*) that the expenditure conforms to the authority which governs it; and

(*c*) that every re-appropriation has been made in accordance with the provisions made in this behalf in the Appropriation Act or under rules framed by Competent authority under the provisions of the said Act,

(2) It shall also be the duty of the Committee on Public Accounts—

(*a*) to examine such trading, manufacturing and profit and loss accounts and balance sheets as the President or the Governor or the Rajpramukh may have required to be prepared and the Comptroller and Auditor General's report thereon; and

(*b*) to consider the report of the Comptroller and Auditor General in cases where the President or the Governor or the Rajpramukh may have required him to conduct an audit of any receipts or to examine the accounts of stores and stock.

Rules 143 & 144 of the Rules of Procedure and conduct of Business in Parliament.

Note :—Similar provisions also exist in the Legislature Rules of the States.

D. REGULATION BY LAW OF PROCEDURE IN LEGISLATURE IN RELATION TO FINANCIAL BUSINESS.

Regulation by law of Procedure in Parliament and State Legislature in relation to financial business—

Art. 119 & 209

Please see under Chatper 'Bills'.

12

FINANCIAL ARRANGEMENT

The subject-matter of the financial arrangements between the Union and the States as embodied in the Constitution can be divided into the following four categories:—

A. DISTRIBUTION OF REVENUES

It includes provisions regarding—

I. Distribution of proceeds of certain duties and taxes;

II. Grants-in-aid;

III. Agreement with Part B States; and

IV. Safeguarding provisions.

B. SETTLEMENT OF EXTRA COSTS

(*a*) resulting from the direction given by the Union to States; and

(*b*) resulting from the conferment of powers and imposition of duties by the Union on States.

C. ADJUSTMENT OF CONTRIBUTIONS

(a) in respect of expenses and pensions in connection with the services of any Court or Commission; and

(b) in respect of privy purse sums of Rulers.

D. EMERGENCY PROVISIONS

There are also *emergency provisions in respect of the distribution of revenues.*

A. DISTRIBUTION OF REVENUES BETWEEN THE UNION AND THE STATES (PART A AND PART B ONLY)—

The sources of revenue and taxation of both Part A and Part B States are to a large extent, different from those of the Union. The financial arrangements embodied in the Constitution for the distribution of revenues between the Union and the States embrace, however, the following kinds of provisions:—

I. *Distribution of the proceeds of certain duties and taxes. which includes provisions regarding*

(*a*) Duties levied by the Union but collected and appropriated by the States — Art. 268

(*b*) Taxes levied and collected by the Union but (*i*) assigned to the States; — Art, 269

(*ii*) distributed between the Union and the States

and

Art. 270

(*iii*) which may be distributed between the Union and the States; and

Art. 272

(*c*) Surcharge on certain duties and taxes for purposes of the Union, — Art. 271

II. *Grants-in-aid* — Arts. 273, 275

III. *Agreement with Part B States with regard to certain financial matters.* — Art. 278

IV. *Safeguarding provisions.*

I. Distribution of the proceeds of certain duties and taxes.

The particulars as well as the arrangements made for the levy, collection and distribution of proceeds of certain duties and taxes, as provided in the Constitution, are summed up below:—

(*a*) *Duties levied by the Union but collected and appropriated by the States.*

Art. 268.

Particulars—

(*a*) Stamp duty in respect of bills of exchange, cheques, promissory notes, bills of lading, letters of credit, policies of insurance, transfer of shares, debentures, proxies and receipts; Item 91 Union List

and

(*b*) Duties of excise on medicinal and toilet preparations containing alcohol, opium, Indian hemp and other narcotic drugs and narcotics. Item 84 Union List

Levy—The above duties are levied by the Government of India,
Collection—These are collected

(*a*) in the case where such duties are leviable within a Part C State, by the Government of India,

and

(*b*) in other cases, by the States within which such duties are respectively leviable.

Distribution— The proceeds in any financial year of any such duty leviable within any State do not form part of the Consolidated Fund of India but are assigned to that State.

(*b*) (*i*) *Duties and Taxes levied and collected by the Union but assigned to the States.* Art. 269

Particulars—

(*a*) Duties in respect of succession to property other than agricultural land; Item 88 Union List

(*b*) Estate duty in respect of property other than agricultural land; Item 87 Union List

(*c*) Terminal taxes on goods or passengers carried by railway, sea or air; Item 89 Union List

(*d*) Taxes on railway fares and freights. Item 89 Union List

(*e*) Taxes other than stamp duties on transactions in stock exchanges and futures markets; Item 90 Union List

and

(*f*) Taxes on the sale or purchase newspapers and on advertisements published therein. Item 92 Union List

Levy—The above duties and taxes are levied by the Government of India.

Collection—These are collected also by the Government of India.

Distribution—The net proceeds in any financial year of any such duty or tax, except insofar as those proceeds represent proceeds attributable to Part C States, do not form part of the Consolidated Fund of India but are assigned to those States within which that duty or tax is leviable in that year and are distributed among those States in accordance with such principles of distribution as may be formulated by Parliament by law.

(*ii*) *Taxes levied and collected by the Union but distributed between the Union and the States.* Art. 270.

Particulars—Taxes on income other than agricultural income excluding Corporation tax. Item 82 Union list

Levy—The above taxes are levied by the Government of India.

Collection—They are also collected by the Government of India.

Distribution—(1) Such percentage, as may be prescribed, of the net proceeds in any financial year of any such tax except in so far as those proceeds represent proceeds attributable to Part C States or to taxes payable in respect of Union emoluments, does not form part of the Consolidated Fund of India but is assigned to the States within which that tax is leviable in that year and is distributed among those States in such a manner and from such time as may be prescribed.

(2) In each financial year, such percentage as may be prescribed, of so much of the net proceeds of taxes on income as does not represent the net proceeds of taxes payable in respect of Union emoluments is deemed to represent proceeds attributable to Part C States.

Note: For the definition of "Union emoluments", please see chapter "Appointments under the Constitution"

(*iii*) *Taxes which are levied and collected by the Union and may be distributed between the Union and the States.*

Art: 272

Particulars—Duties of excise on tobacco and other goods manufactured or produced in India except—

(*a*) alcoholic liquors for human consumption;

(*b*) opium, Indian hemp and other narcotic drugs and narcotics;

(*c*) medicinal and toilet preparations containing alcohol or any substance included in sub-para (*b*) above.

Levy—The above duties are levied by the Government of India.

Collection—These are also collected by the Govt. of India.

Distribution—If Parliament by law so provides, there shall be paid out of the Consolidated Fund of India to the States to which the law imposing the duty extends, sums equivalent to the whole or any part of the net proceeds of that duty and those sums shall be distributed among those States in accordance with such principles of distribution as may be formulated by such law.

(*c*) *Surcharge on certain duties and taxes for purpose of the Union.* Art. 271

Though the net proceeds or a share of the net proceeds of the following duties and taxes which are levied and collected by the Government of India, are distributed among the States, as mentioned above, Parliament has a right to increase any of such duties or taxes by a surcharge for purposes of the Union and the whole proceeds of any such surcharge form part of the Consolidated Fund of India: —

(*a*) Duties in respect of succession to property other than agricultural land;

(*b*) Estate duty in respect of property other than agricultural land;

(*c*) Terminal taxes on goods or passengers carried by railway, sea or air;

(*d*) Taxes on railway fares and freights;

(*e*) Taxes other than stamp duties on transactions in stock exchanges and futures markets;

(*f*) Taxes on sale or purchase of newspapers and on advertisements published therein;

(*g*) Taxes on income other than agricultural except Corporation Tax.

II. *Grants-in-aid.*

(*a*) *Grants in lieu of export duty on jute and jute products.*

Art. 273

There is charged on the Consolidated Fund of India in each year as grants-in-aid of the revenues of the States of Assam, Bihar, Orissa and West Bengal, in lieu of assignment of any share of the net proceeds in each year of export duty on jute and jute products to those States, such sums as may be prescribed.

The sums so prescribed shall continue to be charged on the Consolidated Fund of India so long as any export duty on jute or jute products continues to be levied by the Government of India or until the expiration often years, whichever is earlier.

(*b*) *Grants from the Union to certain States.* Art. 275

(1) Such sums as Parliament may by law, provide is charged on the Consolidated Fund of India in each year as grants-in-aid of the revenues of such States as Parliament may determine to be in need of assistance and different sums may be fixed for different States.

(2) There is payable out of the Consolidated Fund of India as grants-in-aid of the revenues of a State such capital and recurring sums as may be necessary to enable that State to meet the costs of such schemes of development as may be undertaken by the State with the approval of the Government of India for the purpose of promoting welfare of the Scheduled Tribes in that State or raising the level of administration of the Scheduled Areas therein to that of the administration of the rest of the Areas of that State.

(3) There is also payable out of the Consolidated Fund of India as grants-in-aid of the revenues of the

State of Assam sums, capital or recurring, equivalent to—

(*a*) the average excess of expenditure over the revenues during the two years immediately preceding the commencement of the Constitution in respect of the administration of the tribal areas;

(*b*) the costs of such schemes of development as may be undertaken by that State with the approval of the Government of India for the purpose of raising the level of administration of the said areas to that of the administration of the rest of the areas of that State.

Until provision is made by Parliament, the powers conferred on Parliament are exercisable by the President by order made after considering the recommendations of the Finance Commission.

III. *Agreement with Part B States with regard to certain financial matters.* Art.278

The Government of India have a right to enter into an agreement with the Government of a Part B State with respect to the following matters, *viz.*

(*a*) the levy and collection of any tax or duty levialable by the Government of India in such State and for the distribution of the proceeds thereof otherwise than in accordance with the provisions laid down in the Constitution;

(*b*) the grant of any financial assistance by the Government of India to such State in consequence of the loss of any revenue which that State used to derive from any tax or duty leviable under the Constitution by the Government of India or from any other source;

(*c*) the contribution by such State in respect of any payment ment made by the Government of India as Privy Purse.

When an agreement is so entered into, the provisions made in the Constitution regarding the above matters shall in relation to such State have effect subject to the terms of such agreement.

The agreement shall continue in force for a period not exceeding ten years from the commencement of the Constitution but the President may at any time after the expiration of five years from such commencement terminate or modify any such agreement if after consideration of the report of Finance Commision, he thinks it necessary to do so.

IV. *Safeguarding Provisions.*

(*i*) *Prior recommendation of President required to Bills affecting taxation in which State are interested.* Art. 274.

No Bill or amendment which

(*i*) imposes or varies any tax or duty in which States are interested,

or

(*ii*) varies the meaning of the expression "agricultural income" as defined for the purposes of enactments relating to Indian Income-Tax,

or

(*iii*) affect the principles on which moneys are or may be distributable to States

or

(*iv*) imposes any such surcharge for the purposes of the Union,

shall be introduced or moved in either House of Parliament except on the recommendation of the President.

Note : For meaning of the expression "Tax or duty in which States are interested," please see chapter "Taxation."

(2) *For other provisions viz,*

(*a*) Calculation of net proceeds— Art. 279

(*b*) Taxes on professions, trades, callings and employments Art. 276

(*c*) Savings— Art. 277

Please see chapter "Taxation"

B. SETTLEMENT OF EXTRA COSTS

Provision has been made in the Constitution if [vide Art. 257 (4) and 258 (3)] for the settlement of extra costs incurred by the State resulting either from (*a*) the direction given by the Union to the State or (*b*) conferment of powers and imposition of duties by the Union on States.

(*a*) *Extra cast resulting from, the direction, given, by the Union to the State—* Art. 257 (4)

Where in carrying out any direction given to a State as the construction and maintenance of any means of communication or as to measures to be taken for the protection of any railway [under Art. 257 (2) and (3) of the Constitution], costs have been incurred in excess of those which would have been incurred in the discharge of the normal duties of the State if such direction had not been given, Art. 257 (4) of the Constitution provides for the payment by the Government of India to the State such sum as may be agreed or in default of agreement, as may be determined by an arbitrator appointed by the Chief Justice of India, in respect of the extra costs so incurred by the State.

(*b*) *Extra cost resulting from the conferment of powers and imposition of duties by the Union on States—* Art. 258 (3)

Where under Art. 258, powers and duties have been conferred or imposed upon a State or officers or authorities thereof the Constitution provides for the payment by the Government of India to the State such sum as may be agreed or in default of agreement, as may be determined by an arbitrator appointed by the Chief Justice of India, in respect of any extra costs of administration incurred by the State in connection with the exercise of those powers and duties.

C. ADJUSTMENT OF CONTRIBUTIONS

(*a*) *Adjustment in respect of certain expenses and pensions.*

Art. 290

Where under the provisions of the Constitution, the expenses of any Court or Commission or the pension payable to or in respect of a person who has served before the commencement of the Constitution under the Crown in India or after such commencement in connection with the affairs of the Union or of a State are charged on the Consolidated Fund of India or the Consolidated Fund of a State, then if

(*i*) in the case of a charge on the Consolidated Fund of India, the Court or Commission serves any of the separate needs of a State or the person has served wholly or in part in connection with the affairs of a State;

or

(*ii*) in the case of a charge on the Consolidated Fund of a State, the Court or Commission serves any of the separate needs of the Union or any other State or the person has served wholly or in part in connection with the affairs of the Union or another State, there shall be charged on and paid out of the Consolidated Fund the State, or as the case may be, the Consolidated Fund of India or the Consolidated Fund of the other State, such contribuition in respect of the expenses or pension as may be agreed, or as may in default of agreement be determined by an arbitrator to be appointed by the Chief Justice of India.

(*b*) *Privy Purse sums of Rulers.* Art. 291

(1) Where under any covenant or agreement entered into by the Ruler of any Indian State before the commencement of the Constitution, the payment of any sums, free of tax, has been guaranteed or assured by the Government of the Dominion of India to any Ruler of such State as Privy Purse—

(*i*) such sums shall be charged on and paid out of the Consolidated Fund of India; and

(*ii*) the sums so paid to any Ruler shall be exempt from all taxes on income.

(2) When the territories of any such Indian State are comprised within a Part A or B State, there shall be charged on and paid out of the Consolidated Fund of that State such contribution, if any, in respect of the payments made by the Government of India and for such period as may, subject to any agreement entered into in that behalf, be determined by order of the President.

D. EMERGENCY PROVISIONS

Application of provisions relating to distribution of revenues while a Proclamation of Emergency is in operation .— Art. 354

The President may, while a Proclamation of Emergency is in operation, by order direct that all or any of the provisions relating the distribution of revenues shall, for such period, not extending in any case beyond the expiration of the financial year in which such Proclamation ceases to operate, as may be specified the order, have effect subject to such exceptions and modifications as he thinks fit. Every order shall be laid before each House of Parliament as soon as it is made.

13

TAXATION

A. DEFINITIONS

(1) **"Taxation"**—includes the imposition of any tax or impost, whether general or local or special; and

"Tax" shall be construed accordingly. Art. 366 (28)

(2) "Tax on income" includes a tax in the nature of an excess profits tax. Art. 366 (29).

(3) **"Corporation Tax"** means any tax on income, so far as that tax is payable by companies and is a tax in the case of which the following *conditions* are fulfilled:—

(*a*) that it is not chargeable in respect of agricultural income;

(*b*) that no deduction in respect of the tax paid by companies is, by any enactments which may apply to the tax, authorised to be made from dividends, payable by the companies to individuals;

(*c*) that no provision exists for taking the tax so paid into account in computing for the purposes of Indian income-tax, the total income of individuals receiving such dividends, or in computing the Indian income tax payable by, or refundable to, such individuals. Art. 366 (6)

(4) **"Estate'Duty"** means a duty to be assessed on or by reference to the principal value, ascertained in accordance with such rules as may be prescribed by or

under laws made by Parliament or the Legislature of a State relating to the duty, of all property passing upon death or deemed, under the provisions of the said laws, so to pass. Art. 366 (9)

(5) **"Agricultural income"** means agricultural income as defined for the purposes of the enactments relating to Indian income-tax. Art. 366 (1)

(6) **"Goods"** includes all materials, commodities, and articles. Art. 366 (12)

(7) **"Tax or duty in which States are interested"** means

(*a*) a tax or duty the whole or part of the proceeds whereof are assigned to any State; or

(*b*) a tax or duty by reference to the net proceeds whereof, sums are for the time being payable out of the Consolidated Fund of India to any State.

Art. 274 (2)

(8) **"Net Proceeds"**— *Please see item 'C' of this chapter.*

B. IMPOSITION OF TAXES

1. Taxes not to be imposed save by authority of law.

Article 265 of the Constitution provides that "no tax shall be levied or collected except by authority of law." Art. 265.

2. Compensation clause under "Right to Property" not to affect the imposition of taxes.

The requirements of Art. 31 (2) of the Constitution relating to the Fundamental Right *viz.* "Right to Property" to the effect that the law authorising the acquisition of property must provide for compensation cannot be deemed to affect the provisions of any law which the State may make for the purpose of imposing or levying any tax or penalty. Art. 31 (5) (b) (i)

3. Restrictions on the powers of State Governments for imposition of taxes and exemptions from taxation.

In the following cases, the powers of State Governments

to impose taxes have been restricted as shown below :—

(*a*) *Restriction as to imposition of tax on the sole or purchase of goods.*—

(1) No law of a State shall impose, or authorise the imposition of a tax on the sale or purchase of goods where such sale or purchase takes place-

(*i*) outside the State; or

(*ii*) in the course of the import of the goods into, or export of the goods out of, the territory of India.

Explanation-A sale or purchase is deemed to have taken place in the State in which the goods have actually been delivered as a direct result of such sale or purchase for the purpose of consumption in the State; nowithstanding the fact that under the general law relating to sale of goods, the property in the goods has, by reason of such sale or purchase, passed in another State.

(2) Except insofar as Parliament may by law otherwise provide, no law of a State shall impose or authorise the imposition of, a tax on the sale or purchase of any goods where such sale or purchase takes place in the course of inter-State trade or commerce:

[Provided that the President may, by order, direct that any tax on the sale or purchase of goods, which was being lawfully levied by the Government of any State immediately before the commencement of the Constitution shall, notwithstanding that the imposition of such tax is contrary to the provisions of this clause, continue to be levied until 31. 3. 51].

Note :—The directions of the President under this Clause were issued, by order *viz.* "The Sales Tax Continuance Order, 1950."

(3) No law made by the Legislature of a State imposing or authorising the, imposition of a tax on the sale or purchase of any such goods as have been declared by Parliament by law to be essential for the life of community shall have effect unless it has been reserved for the consideration of the President and has received his assent. Art. 286.

(*b*) *Exemption from taxes on electricity.—*

Save insofar as Parliament may by law otherwise provide no law of a State shall impose or authorise the imposition of a tax on the consumption or sale of electricity (whether produced by a Government or other persons) which is—

(*a*) consumed by the Government of India or sold to the Government of India for consumption by the Government; or

(*b*) consumed in the construction, maintenance or operation of any railway by the Government of India or railway company operating that railway or sold to that Government or any such railway company for consumption in the construction, maintenance of operation of any railway.

and any such law imposing or authorising the imposition of tax on the sale of electricity shall secure that the price of electricty sold to the Government of India for consumption that Government or to any such railway company for consumption in the construction, maintenance or operation of any railway shall be less by the amount of the tax than the price charged to other consumers of a substantial quantity of electricity. Art. 287

(c) *Exemption from taxation by States in respect of water and electricity in certain cases.—*

(1) Save insofar as the President may by order otherwise provide, no *"law of a State in force"* immediately before the commencement of the Constitution shall impose or authorise the imposition of a tax in respect of any water or electricity stored, generated, consumed, distributed or sold by any authority established by any existing law or any law made by Parliament for regulating or developing any inter-State river or river-valley.

Explanation.—"Law of a State in force" includes a law of a State passed or made before the commencement of the Constitution and not previously repealed, notwithstanding that it or parts of it may not be then in operation either at all or in particular areas.

(2) The Legislature of a State may by law impose or authorise the imposition of, any such tax as is mentioned in clause (1), but no such law shall have effect unless it has, after having been reserved for the consideration of the President, received his assent; and if any such law provides for the fixation of the rates and other incidents of such tax by means of rules or orders to be made under the law by any authority, the law shall provide for the previous consent of the President being obtained to the making of any such rule or order. Art. 288.

The following further *exemptions from taxation* have been provided for, in the Constitution:—

(*d*) *Exemption from property of the Union from State taxation.*—

(1) The property of the Union is, save insofar as Parliament may by law otherwise provide, exempt from all taxes imposed by a State or any authority within a State.

(2) Nothing in clause (1) shall, until Parliament by law otherwise provides, prevent any authority within a State from levying any tax on any property of the Union to which such property immediately before the commencement of the Constitution liable or treated as liable, so long as that tax continues to be levied in that State.

Art. 285.

(*e*) *Exemption of property and income of a State from Union taxation.*—

(1) The property and income of a State is exempt from Union taxation.

(2) This, however, does not prevent the Union from imposing or authorising the imposition of any tax to such extent, if any, as Parliament may by law provide in respect of a trade or business of any kind carried on by or on behalf of the Government of a State or any operations connected therewith,

or any property used or occupied for the purposes of such trade or business, or any income accruing or arising in connection therewith.

(3) The provisions made in Cl. (2) above, does not apply to any trade or business or to any class of trade or business which Parliament may by law, declare to be incidental to the ordinary functions of Government. Art. 289.

(*f*) *Privy purse sums of Rulers.—*

Where under any covenant or agreement entered into by the Ruler of any Indian State before the commencement of the Constitution, the payment of any sums, free of tax, has been guaranteed or assured by the Government of the Dominion of India to any Ruler of such State as privy purse, the sums so paid to any Ruler are exempt from all taxes on income. Art. 291.

4. Taxes on professions, trades, callings and unemployments.—

(1) Notwithstanding the provisions relating to the subject matter of laws made by Parliament and by the Legislatures of States (Art. 246), no law of the Legislature of a State relating to taxes for the benefit of the State or of a municipality, district board, local board or other local authority in respect of professions, trades, callings or employments shall be invalid on the ground that it relates to a tax on income.

(2) The total amount payable in respect of any one person to the State or to any one municipality, district board, local board or other local authority in the State by way of taxes on professions, trades, callings and employments shall not exceed two hundred and fifty rupees per annum:

Provided that if in the financial year immediately preceding the commencement of the Constitution, there was in force in the case of any State or any such municipality, board or authority, a tax on professions, trades, callings or employments, the rate or the maximum rate, of which exceeded two hundred and fifty rupees per annum, such tax may continue to be levied until provision to the contrary is made by Parliament by law, and any law so made by Parliament may be made either generally or in relation to any specified States, municipalities, boards or authorities.

(3) The power of the Legislature of a State to make law as aforesaid with respect to taxes on professions, trades, callings and employments shall not be construed as limiting in any way the power of Parliament to make laws with respect to taxes on income accruing from or arising out of professions, trades, callings and employments. Art. 276.

5. **Taxes, duties, cesses or fees levied by the State or any local body and in force on 25-1-50 to continue.**

Any taxes, duties, cesses, or fees which immediately before the commencement of the Constitution were being lawfully levied by the Government of any State or by any municipality or other local authority or body for the purposes of the State, mucipality, district or other local area may, notwithstanding that those taxes, duties, cesses or fees are mentioned in the Union List, continue to be levied and to be applied to the same purposes until provision to the contrary is made by Parliament by law; Art. 277

6. **Power of certain Part B States to impose restrictions on trade and commerce.**

Notwithstanding anything in the Constitution, any of the Part 'B' States which before the commencement of the Constitution was levying any tax or duty on the import of goods into the State from other States or on the export of goods from the State to other States may, if an agreement in that behalf has been entered into between the Government of India and the Government of that State, continue to levy and collect such tax or duty subject to the terms of such agreement and for such period not exceeding ten years from the commencement of the Constitution, as may be specified in the agreement:

Provided that the President may, at any time after the expiration of five years from such commencement, terminate or modify any such agreement, if after consideration of the recommendations of the Finance Commission, be thinks it necessary to do so. Art. 306.

7. Imposition of taxes on goods imported from other States.

Provisions regarding the imposition of taxes on goods imported from other States are contained in Articles 304 and 306 of the Constitution.

Art. 304 empowers a State Legislature to impose by law, on goods imported from other States any tax to which similar goods manufactured or produced are subject, so, however, as not to discriminate between goods so imported and goods so manufactured or produced.

Under Art. 306, a Part 'B' State can impose such a tax provided before the commencement of the Constitution, such tax or duty was being levied by that State and an agreement in that behalf has been entered into between the Government of India and the Government of that State. Such agreement is, however, subject to termination or modification after the expiration of five years from the date of commencement of the Constitution by the President.

8. Special provisions relating to the administration of Tribal Areas in Assam—Powers to impose taxes.

(1) The Regional Council and District Council have power to levy and collect taxes on lands and buildings and tolls on persons resident within such areas.

(2) The District Council for an autonomous district have the power to levy and collect all or any of the following taxes within such district:—

(*a*) taxes on professions, trades, callings and employments;

(*b*) taxes on animals, vehicles and boats;

(*c*) taxes on the entry of goods into a market for sale therein and tolls on passengers and goods carried in ferries; and

(*d*) taxes for the maintenance of schools, dispensaries or roads.

(3) A Regional Council or District Council, as the case may be, may make regulations to provide for the levy and collection of any of the taxes specified in sub-paras (1) and (2) above.

Art. 242 (2); Sch. VI Para 8.

C. CALCULATION OF "NET PROCEEDS"

(1) **"Net Proceeds"** means in relation to any tax or duty the proceeds thereof reduced by the cost of collection.

For the purposes of the distribution of revenues, the net proceeds of any tax or duty in or attributable to any area is required to be ascertained and certified by the Comptroller and Auditor-General of India whose certificate is final.

(2) Subject to the express provisions made in the Constitution, a law made by Parliament or an order of the President may, in any case where the proceeds of any duty or tax are or may be assigned to any State, provide for the manner in which the proceeds are to be calculated, for the time from or at which and the manner in which, any payments are to be made for the making of adjustments between one financial year and another, and for any other incidental or ancillary matters. Art. 279

D. DISTRIBUTION OF LEGISLATIVE POWERS RELATING TO TAXATION.

The matters relating to taxation as enumerated in the Union, State and Concurrent Lists are extracted below. While the Parliament and the State Legislatures have exclusive power to make laws with respect to the matters enumerated in the Union and State Lists respectively, the matters enumerated in the Concurrent List are shared by both of them for the purpose of legislation.

Residuary Powers of legislation—

The residuary powers of legislation resting with Parliament include the power of making any law imposing a tax not mentioned either in the Concurrent List or State List.

Art. 248 (2)

Extract from the Union List—

Entry 82. Taxes on income other than agricultural income.

83. Duties of customs including export duties.

84. Duties of excise on tobacco and other goods manufactured or produced in India except

(*a*) alcoholic liquors for human consumption;

(*b*) opium, Indian hemp and other narcotic drugs and narcotics; but including medicinal and toilet preparations containing alcohol or any substance included in sub-para (b) of this entry.

85. Corporation tax.

86. Taxes on the capital value of the assets exclusive of agricultural land of individuals and companies; taxes on the capital of companies.

87. Estate duty in respect of property other than agricultural land.

88. Duties in respect of succession to property other than agricultural land.

89. Terminal taxes on goods or passengers carried by railway, sea or air; taxes on railway fares and freights.

90. 'Taxes other than stamp duties on transactions in stock exchanges and futures markets.

91. Rates of stamp duty in respect of bills of exchange, cheques, promissory notes, bills of

lading, letters of credit, policies of insurance, transfer of shares debentures, proxies and receipts.

92. Taxes on the sale or purchase of newspapers and on advertisements published therein.

97. Any tax not mentioned either in State List or Concurrent List.

Extract from the State List—

Entry 46. Taxes on agricultural income.

47. Duties in respect of succession to agricultural land.

48. Estate duty in respect of agricultural land.

49. Taxes on lands and buildings.

50. Taxes on mineral rights subject to any limitations imposed by Parliament by law relating to mineral development.

51. Duties of excise on the following goods manufactured or produced in the State and countervailing duties at the same or lower rates on similar good manufactured or produced elsewhere in India-

(*a*) alcoholic liquors for human consumption;

(*b*) opium, Indian hemp and other narcotic drugs and narcotics;

but not including medicinal and toilet preparations containing alcohol or any substance included in sub para (b) of this entry.

52. Taxes on the entry of goods into a local area for consumption, use or sale therein.

53. Taxes on the consumption or sale of electricity.

54. Taxes on the sale or purchase of goods other than newspapers.

55. Taxes on advertisements other than advertisements published in newspapers.
56. Taxes on goods and passengers carried by road or on inland waterways.
57. Taxes on vehicles whether mechanically propelled or not, suitable for entry on roads including tramcars subject to the provisions of entry 35 of List III.
58. Taxes on animals and boats.
59. Tolls.
60. Taxes on professions, trades, callings and employments.
61. Capitation taxes.
62. Taxes on luxuries including taxes on entertainments, amusements, betting and gambling.
63. Rates of stamp duty in respect of documents other than those specified in the Union List with regard to rates of stamp duty.

Extract from the Concurrent List—

Entry 43. Recovery in a State of claims in respect of taxes.

44. Stamp duties other than duties or fees collected by means of judicial stamps but not including rates of stamp duty.

E. FREEDOM AS TO PAYMENT OF TAXES

for Promotion of any Particular Religion.

The fundamental right *viz.* "Right to Freedom of Religion" guaranteed to the citizens under the Constitution includes "Freedom as to payment of taxes for promotion of any particular religion." Art. 27 of the Constitution provides as follows:-

"No person shall be compelled to pay any taxes, the proceeds of which are specifically appropriated in payment of expenses for the promotion and maintenance of any particular religion or religious denomination."

F. PROVISIONS AS TO TAXATION BILLS

1. Prior recommendation of President required to Bills affecting taxation in which States are interested.

Bills or amendments which impose or vary any tax or duty in which 'States are interested or which vary the meaning of the expression "agricultural income" as defined for the purposes of enactments relating to Indian income-tax or which affects the principles on which moneys are or may be distributable to States or which impose any surcharge for the purposes of the Union require the prior recommendation of the President for their introduction or moving in either House of Parliament.

Art. 274

Other Provisions:—

2. (a) *Relating to the Union—*

(1) A Bill if it contains only provisions dealing with the imposition, abolition, remission, alteration or regulation of any tax or any matter incidental thereto is deemed to be a Mony Bill.

A Bill is however not deemed to be a Money Bill by reasons only that it provides for

(*i*) the imposition of fines or other pecuniary penalties; or

(*ii*) the demand or payment of fees for licences or fees for services rendered; or

(*iii*) the imposition, abolition, remission, alteration or regulation of any tax by any local authority or body for local purposes.

Art. 110 (1) (a) & (g) and (2).

(2) A Bill or amendment making provision for the imposition, abolition, remission, alteration or regulation of any tax as mentioned at item (1) above cannot be introduced or moved except on the recommendation of the President and a Bill making such provision cannot be introduced in the Council of States.

No recommendation is however required for the moving of an amendment making provision for the reduction or abolition of any tax. Art. 117 (1)

(*b*) *Relating to the States—*

(1) A Bill if it contains only provisions dealing with the imposition, abolition, remission, alteration or regulation of any tax or any matter incidental to the above is deemed to be a Money Bill.

A Bill is however not deemed to be a Money Bill by reason only that it provides for

(*i*) the imposition for fines or other pecuniary penalties; or

(*ii*) the demand or payment of fees for licences or fees for services rendered; or

(*iii*) the imposition, abolition, remission, alteration or regulation of any tax by any local authority or body for local purposes. Art. 199 (1) (a) & (g) and (2)

(2) A Bill or amendment making provision for the imposition, abolition, remission, alteration or regulation of any tax as mentioned at item (i) above cannot be introduced or moved except on the recommendation of the Governor or Rajparamukh and a Bill making such provision cannot be introduced in a Legislative Council.

No recommendation is however required for the moving of an amendment making provision for the reduction or abolition of any tax. Art. 207 (1)

G. MISCELLANEOUS

(1) For *"Distribution of the proceeds of certain duties and texes as well as for the arrangement for their levy and collection,"* kindly see the chapter "Financial Arrangement."

(2) *Surcharge on certain duties and taxes for purposes of the Union*-please see under chapter "Financial Arrangement."

FINANCE COMMISSION

(1) Interpretation—

"Finance Commission" means a Finance Commission constituted under Art. 280 (vide infra).

"State" does not include a State specified in Part 'C' of the First Schedule. Art. 264

(2) Constitution—Art 280 (1) of the Constitution provides as follows:—

"The President shall, within two years from the commencement of the Constitution and thereafter at the expiration of every fifth year or at such earlier time as the President considers necessary, by order, constitute a Finance Commission which shall consist of a Chairman and four other members to be appointed by the President." Art. 280 (1)

Note—The report of the first Finance Commission has already been published. The constitution of the second Finance Commission is likely to be announced soon.

(3) Qualification and selection of members.

Parliament may by law determine the qualifications which shall be requisite for appointment as members of the Commission and the manner in which they shall be selected. Art. 280 (2)

(4) Duties

The duty of the Finance Commission is to make recommendations to the President as to—

(*a*) the distribution between the Union and the States of the net proceeds of taxes which are to be or may be divided between them and the allocation between the States of the respective shares of such proceeds;

(*b*) the principles which should govern the grants-in-aid of the revenues of the States out of the Consolidated Fund of India;

(*c*) the continuance or modification of the terms of any agreement entered into by the Government of India with the Government of any Part 'B' State; and (*d*) any other matter referred to the Commission by the President in the interest of sound finance.

Art. 280 (3)

(5) Procedure and Powers of the Commission

The Commission determine their procedure and have such powers in the performance of their functions as Parliament may by law confer on them. Art. 280 (4)

(6) Disposal of the recommendations of the Finance Commission

The President shall cause every recommendation made by the Finance Commission together with an explanatory memorandum as to the action taken thereon, to be laid before each House of Parliament. Art. 281

The Constitution requires the President to issue orders in the following cases only after considering the recommendations of the Finance Commission :—

(1) Prescribing percentage for the distribution of the proceeds of taxes on income other than agricultural income— Art. 270;

(2) Prescribing sums as grants-in-aid in lieu of export duty on jute and jute products to the revenues of certain States— Art. 273;

(3) Prescribing sums as grants-in-aid of the revenues of States in need of financial assistance— Art. 275;

and

(4) Terminating or modifying the agreement entered into with Part 'B' States— Arts. 278 & 306.

EMERGENCY PROVISIONS

Proclamations

Emergency Provisions contained in the Constitution provide for the following three kinds of Proclamations :—

I. Proclamation of Emergency— Art. 352;

II. Proclamation as to the failure of Constitutional machinery in States— Art. 356;

and

III. Proclamation as to financial emergency— Art. 360;

The nature, duration and effect of each of them is described below:—

I. Proclamation of Emergency

(1) *Nature and Definition*—

"Proclamation of Emergency" means a Proclamation issue under clause 1 of Article 352 which is reproduced below :—

"Art 352 (1)—If the President is satisfied that a grave emergency exists whereby the security of India or of any part of the territory thereof is threatened, whether by war or external aggression or internal disturbance, he may, by Proclamation, make a declaration to that effect." Art. 366 (18)

(2) *Duration*—A Proclamation of Emergency subsists until

(*i*) it is revoked by a subsequent Proclamation; or

(*ii*) it ceases to operate at the expiration of two months unless before the expiration of that period, it has been approved by resolutions of both Houses of Parliament:

Provided that if any such Proclamation is issued at a time when the House of the People has been dissolved or the dissolution of the House of the People takes place during the period of two months referred to in cl. (ii) and if a resolution approving the Proclamation has been passed by the Council of States, but no resolution with respect to such Proclamation has been passed by the House of the People before the expiration of that period, the Proclamation shall cease to operate at the expiration of thirty days from the date on which the House of the People first sits after its reconstitution unless before the expiration of the said period of thirty days, a resolution approving the Proclamation has been also passed by the House of the People. Art. 352 (2)

(3) *Effect*—While a Proclamation of Emergency is in operation, then—

(*a*) notwithstanding anything in the Constitution, the executive power of the Union shall, extend to the giving of directions to any State as to the manner in which the executive power thereof is to be exercised;

(*b*) the power of Parliament to make laws with respect to any matter shall include power to make laws conferring powers and imposing duties or authorising the conferring of powers and the imposition of duties, upon the Union or officers and authorities of the Unïon as respects that matter, notwithstanding that it is one which is not enumerated in the Union List. Art. 353

(4) *Application, of provisions relating to distribution of revenues while a Proclamation of Emergency is in operation.*

(*a*) The President may while a Proclamation of Emergency is in operation by order, direct that all or any of the provisions relating to the distribution of revenues shall for such period, not extending in any case beyond the expiration of the financial year in which such Proclamation ceases to operate, as may be specified order, have effect subject to such exceptions or modifications as he thinks fit.

(*b*) Every order made under cl; (a) shall as soon as may be after it is made, be laid before each House of Parliament. Art. 354

II. Proclamation as to Failure of Constitutional Machinery in States.

If the President on receipt of a report from the Governor or Rajpramukh of a State or otherwise, is satisfied that a sitution has arisen in which the Government of a State cannot be carried on in accordance with the provisions of the Constitution, he may, by Proclamation assume to himself all or any of the functions of the Government of that State other than the powers of High Court and declare that the powers of the Legislature of the State shall be exercisable by or under the authority of Parliament. Every such Proclamation requires the approval of Parliament within two months from the date of its issue and no such Proclamation will continue to remain in force for more than six months without the further approval of Parliament and in no case can any such Proclamation remain into force for a period exceeding three years. If the dissolution of the House of the People takes place during any such period of six months and a resolution approving the continuance of such Proclamation is passed by the Council of States but no such resolution has been passed by the Lower House, the Proclamation shall cease to operate at the expiration of thirty days from the date on which the House of the People first sits after its reconstitution unless before the expiration of that period a resolution approving the continuance of such Proclamation has also been passed by the House of the People.

Where a Proclamation is issued, it shall be competent for Parliament to confer on the President, the power of the Legislature of the State to make laws or he may delegate such power subject to conditions as he may think fit to impose, to any other authority to be specified by him in that behalf. It shall also be competent for the President to authorise, when the House of the People is not in session, expenditure from the Consolidated Fund of the State pending the sanction of such expenditure by Parliament.

Arts. 356 & 357

III. Proclamation as to Financial Emergency.

(1) *Nature.* If the President is satisfied that a situation has arisen, whereby the financial stability or credit of India or of any part of the territory thereof is threatened, he may, by a Proclamation, make a declaration to that effect.

(2) *Duration*—As in the case Proclamation of Emergency mentioned ibid.

(3) *Effect*—During the period any such Proclamation is in operation, executive authority of the Union shall extend to the giving of directions to any State to observe such canons of financial propriety as may be specified in the directions and to the giving of such other directions as the President may deem necessary and adequate for the purpose.

Notwithstanding anything in the Constitution—

(a) any such direction may include—

(*i*) a provision requiring the reduction of salaries and allowances of all or any class of persons serving in connection with the affairs of a State;

(*ii*) a provision requiring all Money Bills or other Bills to be reserved for the consideration of the President after they are passed by the Legislature of the State;

(*b*) it shall be competent for the President during the period any Proclamation issued under this Article is in operation, to issue directions for the reduction of salaries and allowances of all or any class of persons serving in connection with the affairs of the Union including the Judges of the Supreme Cout and the High Courts.

Art. 360

14

MONEY BILLS AND OTHER FINANCIAL BILLS

A. CLASSIFICATION OF BILLS FROM THE VIEW-POINT OF LEGISLATIVE PROCEDURE

From the view-point of the Legislative Procedure laid down in the Constitution for the introduction and passing of Bills in Parliament as well as in State Legislatures, Bills may be classified into the following categories:—

(*i*) Bills generally

(ii) Money Bills and

(iii) Other financial Bills.

B. DEFINITIONS

(1) "Money Bills."

(i) Money Bills in Parliament:—

A Bill is deemed to be a Money Bill, if it contains only provisions dealing with all or any of the following matters, namely—

(*a*) the imposition, abolition, remission, alteration or regulation of any tax;

(*b*) the regulation of the borrowing of money or the giving of any guarantee by the Government of India or the amendment of the law with respect to any financial obligations undertaken or to be undertaken by the Government of India;

(*c*) the custody of the Consolidated Fund or the Contingency Fund of India, the payment of money into or the withdrawal of moneys from any such Fund;

(*d*) the appropriation of moneys out of the Consolidated Fund of India;

(*e*) the declaring of any expenditure to be expenditure charged on the Consolidated Fund of India or the increasing of the amount of any such expenditure;

(*f*) the receipt of money on account of the Consolidated Fund of India or the public account of India or the custody or issue of such money or the audit of the accounts of the Union or of a State; or

(*g*) any matter incidental to any of the matters specified in sub-clauses (*a*) to (*f*) above.

A Bill is not deemed to be a Money Bill by reason only that it provides for the imposition of fines or other pecuniary penalties, or for the demand or payment of fees for licences or fees for services rendered or by reason that it provides for the imposition, abolition, remission, alteration or regulation of any tax by any local authority or body for local purposes.

If any question arises whether a Bill is a Money Bill or not, the decision of the Speaker of the House of the People thereon, shall be final.

There shall be endorsed on every Money Bill when it is transmitted to the Council of States and when it is presented to the President for assent, the certificate of the Speaker of the House of the People signed by him that it is a Money Bill.

Art. 110

(ii) Money Bills in State Legislatures

A Bill is deemed to be a Money Bill, if it contains only provisions dealing with all or any of the following matters, namely—

(*a*) the imposition, abolition, remission, alteration or regulation of any tax;

(*b*) the regulation of the borrowing of money of the giving of any guarantee by the State or the amendment of the law with respect to any'financial obligations undertaken or to be undertaken by the State;

(*c*) the custody of the Consolidated Fund or the Contingency Fund of the State, the payment of moneys into or the withdrawal of moneys from any such Fund;

(*d*) the appropriation of moneys out of the Consolidated Fund of the State;

(*e*) the declaring of any expenditure to be expenditure charged on the Consolidated Fund of the State or the increasing of the amount of any such expenditure;

(*f*) the receipt of money on account of the Consolidated Fund of the State or the public account of the State or the custody or issue of such money; or

(*g*) any matter incidental to any of the matters specified in sub-clauses (*a*) to (*f*) above.

A Bill is not deemed to be a Money Bill by reason only that it provides for the imposition of fines or other pecuniary penalties or for the demand or payment of fees for licences or fees for services rendered, or by reason that it provides for the imposition, abolition, remission, alteration or regulation of any tax by any local authority or body for local purposes.

If any question arises whether a Bill introduced in the Legislature of a State which has a Legislative Council is a Money Bill or not, the decision of the Speaker of the Legislative Assembly of such State thereon, shall be final.

There shall be endorsed on every Money Bill when it is transmitted to the Legislative Council and when it is presented to the Governor or Rajpramukh for assent, the certificate of the Speaker of the Legislative Assembly signed by him that it is a Money Bill. Art. 199

(2) "Finance Bill"

"Finance Bill" means the Bill ordinarily introduced in each year to give effect to the financial proposals of the Government for the next following financial year and includes a Bill to give effect to supplementary financial proposals for any period.

Note :—The above definition is not given in the Constitution but is based on Rule 140 of "the Rules of Procedure and Conduct of Business in Parliament" framed under Art. 118 of the Constitution.

(3) Financial Memorandum to Bills and Money Clauses in Bills

Rule 57 of "the Rules of Procedure and Conduct of Business in Parliament" framed under Article 118 of the Constitution requires that a Bill should be accompanied by a financial memorandum which should invite particular attention to the clauses involving expenditure and should also give an estimate of the recurring or non-recurring expenditure involved in case the Bill is passed into law.

Clauses or provisions in Bills involving expenditure from public funds is to be printed in thick type or in italics.

(4) "Appropriation Bills"

Please see under the chapter "Procedure in Financial Matters—Budget, Grants and Appropriation".

(5) "Financial business"

includes any business which the Speaker holds as coming within this category under the Constitution.

(Rule. 142 of the Rules of Procedure and Conduct of Business in Parliament.)

C. LEGISLATIVE PROCEDURE— A COMPARATIVE STUDY

Wheres there are any special procedure or provision prescribed or made in respect of the Money Bills or Financial Bills, the same has been indicated in the respective columns below. The other provisions under the Bills generally also apply to Money Bills and other Financial Bills unless expressed otherwise.—

(a) *In Parliament*—

Arts. *107, 108, 111.* General provisions as to introduction and passing of Bills and assent thereto.	**Art. 109** Special Procedure in respect of Money Bills	**Art. 117** Special provisions as to financial Bills
(1)	(2)	(3)
Introduction— A Bill other than a Money Bill or other financial Bill may originate in either House of Parliament. (Art. 107 (1))	(1) A Money Bill shall not be introduced in the Council of States.	(1) A Bill or amendment making provision for any of the matters specified below is not introduced or moved except on the recommendation of the President and a Bill making such provision is not introduced in the Council of States:— (*a*) the imposition, abolition, remission, alteration or regulation of any tax: Provided that no recommendation is required for the moving of an amendment making provision for the reduction or abolition of any tax ; (*b*) the regulation of the borrowing of money or the giving of any guarantee by the Government of India or the amend-

(1)	(2)	(3)
		ment of the law with respect to any financial obligations undertaken or to be undertaken by the Goverment of India ; *(c)* the custody of the Consolidated Fund or the Contingency Fund of India, the payment of moneys into or the withdrawal of moneys from any such Fund ; *(d)* the appropriation of moneys out of the Consolidated Fund of India ; *(e)* the declaring of any expenditure to be expenditure charged on the Consolidated Fund of India or the increasing of the amount of any such expenditure; *(f)* the receipt of money on account of the Consolidated Fund of India or the Public Account of India or the custody or issue of such money or the audit of the accounts of the Union or of a State.

(1)	(2)	(3)
		(2) A Bill or amendment is however not deemed to make provision for any of the matters aforesaid by reason only that it provided for (*i*) the imposition of fines or other pecuniary penalties; or (*ii*) the demand or payment of fees for licences or fees for services rendered; or (*iii*) the imposition, abolition, remission, alteration or regulation of any tax by any local authority or body for local purposes.
Passing— Subject to the provisions regarding joint sitting of both Houses in certain cases as mentioned below and passing of Money Bills, a Bill is not deemed to have been passed by the Houses of Parliament unless it has been agreed to by both Houses, either without amendment or with such amend-	(2) After a Money Bill has been passed by the House of the People, it is transmitted to the Council of States for its recommendations and the Council of States within a period of fourteen days from the date of its receipt of the Bill returns the Bill to the House of the People with its recommendations and the House of the	(3) A Bill which, if enacted and brought into operation, would involve expenditure from the Consolidated Fund of India shall not be passed by either House of Parliament unless the President has recommended to that House, the consideration of the Bill.

(1)	(2)	(3)
ments only as are agreed to by both Houses. (Art. 107 (2)) *Joint sitting of both Houses in certain cases.* (Art. 108) (1) If after a Bill has been passed by one House and transmitted to the other House— (*a*) the Bill is rejected by the other House, or (*b*) the Houses have finally disagreed as to the amendments to be made in the Bill, or (*c*) more than six months elapse from the date of the reception of the Bill by the other House without the Bill being passed by it, the President may, unless the Bill has lapsed by reason of a dissoution of the House of the People, notify to the Houses by message if they are sitting or by public notification if they are not sitting, his in-	People may thereupon either accept or reject all or any of the recommendations of the Council of States. (3) If the House of the People accepts any of the recommendations of the Council of States, the Money Bill is deemed to have been passed by both Houses with the amendments recommended by the Council of States and accepted by the House of the People. (4) If the House of the People does not accept any of the recommendations of the Council of States, the Money Bill is deemed to have been passed by both Houses in the form in which it was passed by the House of the People without any of the amendments recommended by the Council of States.	

(1)	(2)	(3)
tention to summon them to meet in a joint sitting for the purpose of deliberating and voting on the Bill. *Provided that nothing in this clause applies to a Money Bill.* (2) In reckoning any such period of six months, no account is to be taken of any period during which the House is prorogued to adjourned for more than four consecutive days. (3) Where the President has notified his intention of summoning the Houses to meet in a joint sitting; neither House shall proceed further with the Bill, but the President may at any time after the date of his notification summon the Houses to meet in a joint sitting for the purpose specified in the notification and if he does so, the Houses shall meet accordingly.	(5) If a Money Bill passed by the House of the People and transmitted to the Council of States for its recomdations is not returned to the House of the People within the said period of fourteen days, it is deemed to have been passed by both Houses at the expiration of the said period in the form in which it was passed by the House of the People.	

(1)	(2)	(3)
(4) If at the joint sitting of the two Houses, the Bill with such amendments if any, as are agreed to a joint sitting, is passed by a majority of the total number of members of both Houses present and voting, it shall be deemed for the purposes of the Constitution to have been passed by both Houses. Provided that at a joint sitting— (*a*) if the Bill, having been passed by one House, has not been passed by the other House with amendments and returned to the House in which it originated, no amendment shall be proposed to the Bill other than such amendments (if any) as are made necessary by the delay in the passage of the Bill (*b*) If the Bill has been so passed and		

(1)	(2)	(3)
returned, only such amendments as aforesaid shall be proposed to the Bill and such other amendments as are relevant to the matters with respect to which the Houses have not agreed and the decision of the person presiding as to the amendments which are admissible under this clasue, shall be final. (5) A joint sitting may be held under this Article and a Bill passed thereat, notwithstanding that a dissolution of the House of the People has intervened since the President notified his intention to summon the Houses to meet therein. *Assent*— When a Bill has been passed by the Houses of Parliament, it is presented to the President and the President declares either that he assents to the Bill or		

(1)	(2)	(3)
that he withholds assent thereform; Provided that the President may, as soon as possible after the presentation to him of a Bill for assent return the Bill *if it is not a Money Bill* to the Houses with a message requesting that they will reconsider the Bill or any specified provisions thereof and, in particular, will consider the desirability of introducing any such amendments as he may recommend in his message, and when a Bill is so returned, the Houses shall reconsider the Bill accordingly and if the Bill is passed again by the Houses with or without ammendment and presented to the President for assent, the President shall not withhold assent therefrom. Art. 111		

Other general provisions.

(1) A Bill pending in Parliament shall not lapse by reason of the prorogation of the Houses. Art. 107 (3)

(2) A Bill pending in the Council of States which has not been passed by the House of the People shall not lapse on a dissolution of the House of the People. Art. 107 (4)

(3) A Bill which is pending in the House of the People or which having been passed by the House of the People is pending in the Council of States shall subject to provisions regarding "Joint sittings of both Houses in certain cases", lapse on a dissolution of the House of the People. Art. 107 (5)

(*b*) *In State Legislatures—*

Arts. 196, 197, 200 & 201 General Provisions as to introduction and passing of Bills and Assent thereto.	**Art. 198** Special procedure in respect of Money Bills	**Art. 207** Special provisions as to financial Bills.
(1)	(2)	(3)
Introduction— A Bill other than a Money Bill or other Financial Bill, may originate in either House of the Legislature of a State which has a Legislative Council. [Art. 196 (1)]	(1) A Money Bill shall not be introduced in a Legislative Council.	(1) A Bill or amendment making provision for any of the matters specified below is not introduced or moved except on the recommendation of the Governor or Rajpramukh and a Bill making such provision is not introduced in a Legislative Council—

(1)	(2)	(3)
		(*a*) the imposition, abolition, remission, alteration or regulation of any tax: Provided that no recommendation is required for the moving of an amendment making provision for the reduction or abolition of any tax; (*b*) the regulation of the borrowing of money or the giving of any guarantee by the State, or the amendment of the law with respect to any financial obligations undertaken or to be undertaken by the State; (*c*) the custody of the Consolidated Fund or the Contingency Fund of the State, the payment of moneys into or the withdrawal of moneys from any such fund; (*d*) the appropriation of moneys out of the Consolidated Fund of the State; (*e*) the declaring of any expenditure to

(1)	(2)	(3)
		be expenditure charged on the Consolidated Fund of the State or the increasing of the amount of any such expenditure; (*f*) the receipt of money on account of the Consolidated Fund of the State or the public account of the State or the custody or issue of such money. (2) A bill or amendment is however not deemed to make provision for any of the matters aforesaid by reason only that it provides for (*i*) the imposition of fines or other pecuniary penalties; (*ii*) or the demand or payment of fees for licences or fees for services rendered; or (*iii*) the imposition, abolition, remission, alteration or regulation of any tax by any local authority or body for local purposes. (3) A Bill, which if

(1)	(2)	(3)
Passing— Subject to provisions regarding "Restriction on powers of Legislative Council as to Bills *other than Money Bills*" as mentioned below and "passing of Money Bills", a Bill is not deemed to have been passed by the Houses of the Legislature of a State having Legislative Council unless it has been agreed to by both Houses, either without amendment or with such amendments only as are agreed to by both Houses. [Art. 196 (2)] *Restriction on powers of Legislative Council as to Bills other than Money Bills.* (Art. 197). (1) If after a Bill has been passed by the Legislative Assembly of a State having a Legislative Council and transmitted to the Legislative Council— (*a*) the Bill is rejected by the Council; or	(2) After a Money Bill has been passed by the Legislative Assembly of a State having a Legislative Council, it shall be transmitted to the Legislative Council for its recommendations, and the Legislative Council shall within a period of fourteen days from the date of its receipt of the Bill return the Bill to the Legislative Assembly with its recommendations, and the Legislative Assembly may there upon either accept or reject all or any of the recommendations of the Legislative Council. (3) If the Legislative Assembly accepts any of the recommendations of the Legislative Council, the Money Bill is deemed to have been passed by both Houses with the amendments recommended by the Legislative Council	enacted and brought into operation, would involve expenditure from the Consolidated Fund of a State shall not be passed by a House of the Legislature of the State unless the Governor or Rajpramukh has recommended to that House the consideration of the Bill.

(1)	(2)	(3)
(*b*) more than three months elapse from the date on which the Bill is laid before the Council without the Bill being passed by it; or (*c*) The Bill is passed by the council with amendments to which the Legislative Assembly does not agree, the Legislative Assembly may, subject to the rules regulating its procedure, pass the Bill again in the same or in any subsequent session with or without such amendments, if any, as have been made, suggested or agreed to by the Legislative Council and then transmit the Bill as so passed to the Legislative Council. (2) If after a Bill has been so passed for the second time by the Legislative Assembly and transmitted to the Legislative Council— (*a*) the Bill is rejected by the Coun-	and accepted by the Legislative Assembly. (4) If the Legislative Assembly does not accept any of the recommendations of the Legislative Council, the Money Bill is deemed to have been passed by both Houses in the form in which it was passed by the Legislaive Assembly without any of the amendments recommended by the Legislative Council. (5) If a Money Bill passed by the Legislative Assembly and transmitted to the Legislative Council for its recommendations is not returned to the Legislative Assembly within the said period of fourteen days, it is deemed to have been passed by both Houses at the expiration of the said period in which it was passed by the Legislative Assembly.	

(1)	(2)	(3)
cil; or (*b*) more than one month elapses from the date on which the Bill is laid before the Council without the Bill being passed by it; or (*c*) the Bill is passed by the Council with amendments to which the Legislative Assembly does not agree, the Bill shall be deemed to have been passed by the Houses of the Legislature of the State in the form in which it was passed by the Legislative Assembly for the second time with such amendments, if any, as have been made or suggested by the Legislative Council and agreed to by the Legislative Assembly.		
(3) *Nothing in this article applies to a Money Bill.*	The provisions of Art. 197 are not applicable to Money Bills.	
Assent— When a Bill has been passed by the Legislative Assembly of a State or in the case of a State		

(1)	(2)	(3)
having a Legislative Council, has been passed by both Houses of the Legislature of the State, it is presented to the Governor or Rajpramukh and the Govenor or Rajpramukh declares either (*i*) that he assents to the Bill; or (*ii*) that he withholds assent therefrom; or (*iii*) that he reserves the Bill for the consideration of the President: Provided that the Governor or Rajpramukh may, as soon as possible after the presentation to him of the Bill for assent, return the Bill *if it is not a Money Bill* together with a message requesting that the House or Houses will reconsider the Bill or any specified provisions thereof and in particular, will consider the desirability of introducing any such amendment as he may rec-		

(1)	(2)	(3)
ommend in his message and when a Bill is so returned, the House or Houses reconsider the Bill accordingly and if the Bill is passed again by the House or Houses with or without amendment and presented to the Governor or Rajpramukh for assent, the Governor or Rajpramukh shall not withhold assent therefrom: Provided futher that the Governor or Rajpramukh shall not assent to, but shall reserve for the consideration of the President, any Bill which in the opinion of the Governor or Rajpramukh would, if it became law, so derogate from the powers of the High Court as to endanger the position which that Court is by the Constitution designed to fill. Art. 200 *Bills reserved for consideration—*		

(1)	(2)	(3)
When a Bill is reserved by a Governor or Rajpramukh for the consideration of the President, the President either declares that he assents to the Bill or that he withholds assent therefrom: Provided that, where the Bill is *not a Money Bill,* the President may direct the Governor or Rajpramukh to return the Bill to the House or as the case may be, the Houses of the Legislature of the State together with a message and when a Bill is so returned, the House or Houses shall reconsider it accordingly within a period of six months from the date of receipt of such message and if it is again passed by the House or Houses with or without amendment, it shall be presented again to the President for his consideration. Art. 201		

Other general provisions—

(1) A Bill pending in the Legislature of a State shall not lapse by reason of the prorogation of the House or Houses thereof. Art. 196 (3)

(2) A Bill pending in the Legislative Council of a State which has not been passed by the Legislative Assembly shall not lapse on a dissolution of the Assembly. Art. 196 (4)

(3) A Bill which is pending in the Legislative Assembly of a State or which having been passed by the Legislative Assembly is pending in the Legislative Council, shall lapse on a dissolution of the Assembly. Art. 196 (5)

D. MONEY BILLS AND FINANCIAL BILLS TO BE RESERVED FOR THE CONSIDERATION OF THE PRESIDENT DURING FINANCIAL EMERGENCY

The direction given by the Union to a State during the operation of a financial emergency may provide that all Money Bills or Financial Bills be reserved for the consideration of the President after they are passed by the State Legislature. Art. 360 (4)

E. PROCEDURE OF CERTIFICATION IN RESPECT OF MONEY BILLS UNDER GOVT OF INDIA ACT, 1935 DONE AWAY WITH

Formerly under the Govt. of India Act 1935, when any Money Bill was passed, it was the prerogative of the Governor General to certify the Bill before it would become law. Under the Constitution this procedure of certification has been done away with and the President possesses no such power.

F. INTRODUCTION OF BILLS AFFECTING TAXATION IN WHICH STATES ARE INTERESTED

Prior recommendation of President required to Bills affecting taxation in which States are interested—

No Bill or amendment which

(*i*) imposes or varies any tax or duty in which States are interested;

or

(*ii*) varies the meaning of the expression "agricultural income";

or

(*iii*) affects the principles laid down in the Constitution on which moneys are or may be distributable to States;

or

(*iv*) imposes any such surcharge for the purposes of the Union,

shall be introduced or moved in either House of Parliament except on the recommendation of the President.

Art. 274

Note: For the meaning of the expression "tax or duty in which States are interested", please see under "Definitions" in chapter "Taxation".

G. REGULATION BY LAW OF PROCEDURE IN LEGISLATURES IN RELATION TO FINANCIAL BUSINESS

Articles 119 and 209 of the Constitution provide that the Parliament Legislature of a State may, for the purpose of the timely completion of financial business, regulate by law the procedure of, and the conduct of business in the House or Houses of the Legislature in relation to any financial matter or to any Bill for the appropriation of moneys out of the Consolidated Fund of India or the State and, if and so far as any provision of any law so made is inconsistent with any rule made by a House of the Legislature or with any rule or standing order having effect in relation to the Legislature, such provision shall prevail.

H. TRANSITIONAL PROVISIONS

Art. 389 contains transitional provisions according to which Bills pending in the Dominion Legislature or in the Legislatures of Provinces and Indian States may be continued in Parliament or the Legislature of the corresponding State unless there is anything to the contrary.

15

AUDIT AND ACCOUNTS

A. COMPTROLLER AND AUDITOR-GENERAL OF INDIA.

(1) *Appointment*—Art. 148 (1) of the Constitution provided for a Comptroller and Auditor-General of India, who shall be appointed by the President by warrant under his hand and seal.

(2) *Oath or affirmation*—Every person appointed to be the Comptroller and Auditor-General of India shall, before he enters upon his office, make and subscribe before the President or some person appointed in that behalf by him, an oath or affirmation in the following form set out for the purpose :—

"I, A.B., having been appointed Comptroller and Auditor-General of India do *swear in the name of God/ solemnly affirm* that I will bear true faith and allegiance to the Constitution of India as by law established, that I will duly and faithfully and to the best of my ability, knowledge and judgement, perform the duties of my office without fear or favour, affection or illwill and that I will uphold the Constitution and the laws." — Art. 148 (2) & Third Schedule.

(3) *Salary and other conditions of service*—The provisions as to the salary and other conditions of service of the Comptroller and Auditor-General are contained in the Second Schedule to the Constitution. These provisions are effective until they are determined otherwise by

Parliament by law under the provisions of clause (3) of Article 148 of the Constitution. The Comptroller and Auditor-General (Conditions of Service) Act, 1953 (No.21 of 1953) has since been passed by Parliament to regulate certain conditions of service of the Comptroller and Auditor-General viz. (a) Term of office and (b) Pension payable to him. Except these, the other conditions of service specified in the Second Schedule still hold good.

(*i*) *Salary*—The Comptroller and Auditor-General of India is entitled to a salary at the rate of four thousand rupees per mensem. In addition to this, the person who was holding office immediately before the commencement of the Constitution as Auditor-General of India and became Comptroller and Auditor-General of India under the transitional provisions of the Constitution is entitled to receive as special pay, an amount equivalent to the difference between the salary so specified and the salary which he was drawing as Auditor-General of India immediately before such commencement.

(*Vide* Part E Para. 12(1) & (2) of the Second Schedule).

(*ii*) *Term of office*—A Comptroller and Auditor-General of India holds office for a term of six years from the date on which he enters upon his office :

Provided that he may at any time by writing under his hand addressed to the President resign his office.

Note—The term of six years in respect of the 1st Comptroller and Auditor-General under the Constitution is computed from 15.8.1948.

(*iii*) *Pension*—A Comptroller and Auditor-General of India shall on his retirement, be eligible

(*a*) (*i*) in the case of the first Comptroller and Auditor-General under the Constitution, to such pension as may be admissible to him under the rules for the time being applicable to the service to which he belonged at the date on which he became the Comptroller and Auditor-General; or

(ii) in the case of any other Comptroller and Auditor-General who was in the service of the Government at the date of his appointment, to such pension as may be admissible to him under the rules for the time being applicable to the Service to which he belonged at the date of his appointment;

the serivce as Comptroller and Auditor-General in either case, being reckoned for the purposes of the relevant rules as service for pension; and

(b) to an additional pension of six hundred rupees per annum in respect of each, completed year of service as Comptroller and Auditor-General, such service in respect of the 1st Comptroller and Auditor-General under the Constitution being computed from 15.8.1948.

Provided that the aggregate of all pensions payable to the Comptroller and Auditor-General shall not

(i) in the case of a member of the Indian Civil Service, exceed one thousand pounds sterling per annum;

or

(ii) in the case of a member of any other service, exceed twelve thousand rupees per annum.

(*Vide* Sections 2 and 3 of the Comptroller and Auditor-General (Conditions of Service) Act, 1953.)

(iv) *Leave and other conditions of service.*—Under sub para (3) of para. 12 of the Second Schedule to the Constitution, the rights in respect of leave of absence and the other conditions of service shall be governed or continue to be governed, as the case may be, by the provisions which were applicable to the Auditor-General of India immediately before the commencement of the Constitution. These provisions are contained in the Audit and Accounts Order, 1936 as adapted by the India (Provisional Constitution) Order, 1947. All references in those provisions to the Governor-General shall be construed as references to the President.

Neither the salary of a Comptroller and Auditor-General nor his rights in respect of leave of absence, pension or age of retirement shall be varied to his disadvantage after his appointment. (*Vide* Proviso to Clause (3) of Art. 148

The Comptroller and Auditor-General shall not be eligible for further office either under the Government of India or under the Government. of any State after he has ceased to hold office.

Art. 148 (4)

(4) *Removal*—The Comptroller and Auditor-General shall only be removed from office in like manner and on the like grounds as a judge of the Supreme Court. It means that the Comptroller and Auditor-General shall not be removed from his office except by an order of the President passed after an address by each House of Parliament supported by majority of the total membership of that House and by a majority of not less than two-thirds of the members of that House present and voting, has been presented to the President in the same session for such removal on the ground of proved misbehaviour or incapacity; the procedure for the presentation of the address or for the investigation and proof of the misbehaviour or incapacity being regulated by Parliament by law.

Art. 148 (i) read with Art. 124 (4) and (5)

B. PROVISIONS TO SAFEGUARD THE INDEPENDENCE AND FREEDOM OF THE COMPTROLLER & AUDITOR-GENERAL OF INDIA.

The Constitution has installed the Comptroller and Auditor-General as a high independent statutory authority who has his own judgement to look to and who has no frowns or favours to be guided from outside. He is the one dignitary who sees on behalf of the Legislature that the expenses voted by them are not exceeded or varied and the money expended was legally available for and applicable to the purpose or purposes which it has been applied. Nothing can fetter his discretion on or judgement in any manner as to matters which he may bring to the notice of the Legislatures in the discharge of his duties. He is placed beyond the political and party influences of the day. For the purpose of securing the hihest standards of financial integrity of the administration and watching the interest of the tax-payer and also for purposes of Legislative control over the entire executive Government and its officers, the Constitution safeguards the independence and freedom of the Comptroller and Auditor-General in a variety of ways as will be clear from the following provisions: —

(1) The Comptroller and Auditor-General shall be appointed by the President under his hand and seal and shall only be removed from office in like manner and on the like grounds as a Judge of the Supreme Court. Art. 148 (1)

(2) His oath of office under the Constitution requires him to uphold the Constitution and the laws and to discharge his duties without fear or favour, affection or illwill. Art. 148 (2)

(3) Neither the salary of a Comptroller and Auditor-General nor his rights in respect of leave of absence, pension or age of retirement shall be varied to his disadvantage after his appointment. Art. 148 (3)

(4) The Comptroller and Auditor-General shall not be eligible for further office either under the-Government of India or under the Government of any State after he has ceased to hold office. Art. 148 (4)

(5) The conditions of service of persons serving in the Indian Audit and Accounts Department and the administrative powers of the Comptroller and Auditor-General shall be such as may be prescribed by rules made by the President after consultation with the Comptroller and Auditor-General. Art. 148 (5)

(6) The administrative expenses of the office of the Comptroller and Auditor-General, including all

salaries, allowances and pensions payable to or in respect of persons serving in that office, shall be charged upon the Consolidated Fund of India.

Art. 148(6)

(7) The salary, allowances and pensions payable to or in respect of the Comptroller and Auditor-General of India have been declared by the Constitution to be a charged expenditure on the Consolidated Fund of India.

Art. 112 (3)

C. DUTIES AND POWERS OF THE COMPTROLLER AND AUDITOR-GENERAL.

The functions of the Comptroller and Auditor-General are derived in the main from the provisions of Articles 149 to 151 of the Constitution. The Constitutional provisions relating to his duties and powers are described below—

(*a*) *Art. 149*—"The Comptroller and Auditor-General shall perform such duties and exercise such powers in relation to the accounts of the Union and of the States and of any other authority or body as may be prescribed by or under any law made by Parliament and until provision in that behalf is so made, shall perform such duties and exercise such powers in relation to the accounts of the Union and of the States as were conferred on or exercisable by the Auditor-General of India immediately before the commencement of the Constitution in relation to the accounts of the Dominion of India and of the Provinces respectively."

Article 149 of the Constitution as reproduced above envisages an Act of Parliament to regulate the duties and powers of the Comptroller and Auditor-General in relation to the accounts of the Union and of the States and of any other authority or body and until such a provision is made, it lays down that the Comptroller and Auditor-General shall perform such duties and exercise such powers in relation to the accounts of the Union and of the States as were conferred on or exercisable by the Auditor-General of India immediately before the commencement of the Constitution in relation to the accounts of the Dominion of India and of the Provinces respectively. The duties and powers of the Auditor-General of India in relation to the accounts of the Dominion of India and of the Provinces immediately before the commencement of the Constitution were prescribed in the Audit and Accounts Order, 1936 as adapted by the India (Provisional Constitution) Order, 1947 and in the Initial Subsidiary Accounts Rules issued by the Governor-General in pursuance of Para 11 (3) of the former Order. By virtue of the provisions of Art. 149 of the Constitution, the relevant provisions of the former Order and the Initial and Subsidiary Accounts Rules continue in force and regulate the duties and powers of the Comptroller and Auditor-General in relation to the accounts of the Union and of the States until an Act is passed by Parliament under this Article. In applying the said Order and Rules under the Constitution, references to the Auditor-General, Dominion, Province, Governor-General and Governor are deemed to refer to the Comptroller and Auditor-General, Union, States, President, Governor Rajpramukh respectively.

Besides the duties and functions relating to the keeping and auditing of and reporting upon the accounts of the Union and of the States, the Comptroller and Auditor-General may be entrusted with duties and functions in relation to the accounts of any other authority or body as may be prescribed by or under any law made by Parliament. It has been held the expression "any other body" used in the above Article does not include private commercial and quasi-commercial undertakings in which Governments in India may be participating.

(*b*) *Art. 150—"Power of the Comptroller and Auditor-General to give direction as to accounts*—The accounts of the Union and of the States shall be kept in such form as the Comptroller and Auditor-General of India may, with the approval of President, prescribe."

This Article empowers the Comptroller and Auditor-General with the approval of the President to prescribe the from in which the accounts of the Union and of the States are to be kept. It has been held that the power to prescribe the form includes the power to give any directions with regard to the methods or principles in accordance with which any accounts are to be kept. This provision is designed to secure the maximum degree of uniformity in accounting amidst the immense volume and variety of financial transactions of different Governments in India. The Comptroller and Auditor-General has also power to prescribe the form of initial and subsidiary accounts and of the accounts rendered to his offices, besides under this Article with the approval of the President, under the Initial and Subsidiary Accounts Rules on his sole authority.

(*c*) *Administrative and financial* powers.—The Comptroller and Auditor-General is the administrative head of the Indian Audit and Accounts Department. His administrative powers will be governed by rules made by the President after consultation with the former as provided in cl. (5) of Art. 148 of the Constitution. He derives his financial powers by delegation from the Union Government.

(*d*) Under Article 279 (1) of the Constitution, the Comptroller and Auditor-General is also to ascertain and certify the net proceeds of any tax or duty or of any part of such tax or duty in or attributable to any area for the purpose of distribution of revenues between the Union and the States.

(*e*) *Art. 151—"Audit Reports—* (I) The reports of Comptroller and Auditor-General of India relating to the accounts of the Union shall be submitted to the President who shall cause them to be laid before each House of Parliament.

(2) The reports of the Comptroller and Auditor-General of India relating to the accounts of a State shall be submitted to the Governor or Rajpramukh of the State, who shall cause them to be laid before the Legislature of the State,"

D. AUDIT REPORTS

After the completion of the year's accounts, the results of audit are reported to the Governments concerned and their Legislatures through the medium of Audit Reports under Art. 151 of the Constitution. In relation to the accounts of the Union and of each of the States, the Comptroller and Auditor-General submits the two reports *viz.* (I) Audit Report on the Appropriation Accounts; and (2) Audit Report on the Finance Accounts. The form of these reports is determined by the Comptroller and Auditor-General who, in doing so, gives due weight to the views and requirements of Governments and Legislatures.

The reports relating to the accounts of the Union are submitted to the President, who causes them to be laid before the Parliament and the Reports relating to the accounts of States are submitted to the Governor or Rajpramukh of the State, who causes them to be laid before the Legislature of the State.

The procedure which Parliament and the State Legislatures will follow in dealing with these Reports, will be regulated by rules framed by them under Articles 118 (1) and 208 (1) of the Constitution. The procedure in Parliament, till the new rules are framed, will be regulated by a set of rules known as "the Rules of Procedure and Conduct of Business in Parliament."

The existing rules provide, inter alia, for the consideration of the Appropriation Accounts and the connected Audit Report by a Committee of the Legislature known as the Committee on Public Accounts.

Note :—For functions of Public Accounts Committee, please see chapter "Procedure in Financial Matters".

E. TRANSITIONAL PROVISIONS

Art. 377 of the Constitution provides that the Auditor-General of India holding office immediately before the commencement of the Constitution shall, unless he has elected otherwise, become on such commencement the Comptroller and Auditor-General of India and shall, thereupon, be entitled to such salaries and to such rights in respect of leave of absence and pension as are provided in respect of the Comptroller and Auditor-

General of India and be entitled to continue to hold office until the expiration of his term of office as determined under the provisions which were applicable to him immediately before such commencement.

F. BILLS RELATING TO AUDIT

(1) A Bill if it contains only provisions dealing with *"the audit of the accounts of the Union or of a State or any matter incidental thereto"* is deemed to be a Money Bill in Parliament. Art. 110 (1) (f) and (g).

(2) A Bill or amendment making provision for *"the audit of the accounts of the Union or of a State"* cannot be introduced or moved except on the recommendation of the President and a Billl making such provision cannot be introduced in the Council of States.

Art. 117(1).

G. LEGISLATIVE COMPETENCE IN RESPECT OF AUDIT MATTERS

(*i*) *"Audit of the accounts of the Union and of the States"* is a Union subject (vide Entry No. 76 of List I of the Seventh Schedule to the Constitution).

(*ii*) *"The salaries, allowances and rights in respect of leave of absence and other conditions of service of the Comptroller and Auditor-General"* have also been included in Entry No. 75 of List I of the Seventh Schedule to the Constitution. As such, the Parliament has *"exclusive power"* to make law with regard to any of the above matters.

H. POWER OF HIGH COURTS TO PRESCRIBE FORMS OF ACCOUNTS FOR SUBORDINATE COURTS

The High Court has power to prescribe forms in which books, entries ard accounts shall be kept of any such courts or tribunals in relation to which it exercises jurisdiction.

Art. 227 (2) (b).

I. POWER OF DISTRICT COUNCIL TO MAKE REGULATIONS FOR THE MAINTENANCE OF ACCOUNTS BY NON-TRIBAL MONEY-LENDERS IN TRIBAL AREAS IN ASSAM.

The District Council of an autonomous district set up in connection with the administration of tribal areas in Assam may, by regulation, provide for the maintenance of accounts by non-tribal money-lenders and for the inspection of such accounts by officers appointed in that behalf by the District Council.

Schedule VI, Para 10.

BORROWING

A. Definitions

(1) **"Borrow'** includes the raising of money by the grant of annuities;

and

(2) **"Loan"** shall be construed accordingly. —Art 366 (4)

(3) **"Debt"** includes any liability in respect of any obligation to repay capital sums by way of annuities and any liability under any guarantee;

and

(4) **"Debt charges"** shall be construed accordingly.

Art 366 (8)

(5) **"Guarantee"** includes any obligation undertaken before the commencement of the Constitution to make payments in the event of the profits of an undertaking following short of a specified amount. Art 366 (13)

(6) **"Securities"** includes stock. Art. 366 (26)

B. Borrowing by the Union and States.

(*a*) Borrowing by the Government of India.

"*Power and its extent:*—The executive power of the Union extends borrowing upon the security of the Consolidated Fund of India within such limits, if any, as may from time to time be fixed by Parliament by law and the giving of guarantees within such limits, if any, as may be so fixed. Art. 292.

(b) Borrowing by States.

Power and its extent :—The executive power of a State extends to borrowing within the territory of India upon the security of the Consolidated Fund of the State within such limits, if any, as may from time to time be fixed by the Legislature of such State by law and to the giving of guarantees within such limits as may be so fixed. This is however subject to the following provision:

A State may not, without the consent of the Government of India, raise any loan if there is still outstanding, any part of a loan which has been made to the State by the Government of India or by its predecessor Government or in respect of which a guarantee has been given by the Government of India or by its predecessor Government. The Government of India may grant the consent subject to such conditions as its may think fit to impose. Art. 293

C. Power of the Govt of India to make loans to any State:

Art. 293 (2) of the Constitution provides that the Government of India may, subject to such conditions as may be laid down by or under any law made by Parliament, make loans to any State or so long as any limits fixed by Parliament by law are not exceeded, give guarantees in respect of loans raised by any State and any sums required for the purpose of making such loans shall be charged on the Consolidated Fund of India.

D. Bills relating to borrowing.

In respect of the Union.—

(1) A .Bill, if it contains only provisions dealing with "the regulation of the borrowing of money or the giving of any guarantee by the Government of India or the amendment of the law with respect to any financial obligations undertaken or to be undertaken by the Government of India, or any matter incidental to the above" is deemed to be a Money Bill.

Art. 110(1) (b) &(g)

(2) A Bill or amendment making provision for "The regulation of the borrowing of money or the giving of

any guarantee by the Govt. of India or the amendment of the law with respect to any financial obligations undertaken or to be undertaken by the Govt. of India" can not be introduced or moved except on the recommendation of the President and a Bill making such provision can not be introduced in the Council of States. Art. 117 (1)

In respect of the States.—

(1) A Bill, if it contains only provisions dealing with "the regulation of the borrowing of money or the giving of any guarantee by the State, or the amendment of the law with respect to any financial obligations undertaken or to be undertaken by the State or any matter incidental to the above" is deemed to be a Money Bill. Art. 199 (1) (b) (g)

(2) A Bill or amendment making provision for "the regulation of the borrowing of money or the giving of any guarantee by the State or the amendment of the law with respect to any financial obligations undertaken or to be undertaken by the State" cannot be introduced or moved except on the recommendation of the Governor or Rajpramukh and a Bill making such provision cannot be introduced in a Legislative Council. Art. 207 (1).

E. Legislation in respect of Public Debts

The Parliament has exclusive power to make laws with regard to the *"Public Debt of the Union"* and the State Legislature with .regard to the *"Public Debt of the State."*

Schedule VII, Lists 1-35 & 11-43.

16

PROPERTY

The various Articles of the Constitution relating to "Property" can conveniently be divided into the following categories :—

A. Definitions.

B. Articles governing the vesting of property in the Union or States.

C. Articles providing for the exemption of property from taxation.

D. Article relating to the executive power of the Government to acquire property.

E. Articles providing for

(*a*) fundamental rights in relation to property; and

(*b*) compulsory acquisition of property.

F. Articles providing for legislation relating to property.

G. Miscellaneous.

A. DEFINITIONS

1. **"Estate"**—The expression "estate" shall, in relation to any local area, have the same meaning as that expression or its local equivalent has in the existing law relating to land tenures in force in that area and shall also include any jagir, inam or muafi or other similar grant. Art. 31A (2)

2. **"Rights"**—The expression "rights" in relationt to an estate, shall include 'any 'rights vesting in a proprietor, subproprietor, under-proprietor, tenure-holder or other intermediary and any rights or privileges in respect of land revenue. Art. 31A (2)

B. PRINCIPLES GOVERNING THE VESTING OF PROPERTY IN THE UNION OR STATES

In Articles 294 to 298 of the Constitution, certain principles have been enunciated to determine whether a particular property vests in the Union or a State. The provisions made in this respect cater for the following kinds of cases :—

(1) Succession to property and assets.

(2) Property accruing by escheat or lapse or as *bona vacantia.*

(3) Things of value lying within territorial waters.

(4) Acquired property.

(1) Succession to property and assets

Articles 294 and 295 lay down the mode of succession in repect of the property and assets which prior to the commencement of the Constitution belonged to the

(*i*) Dominion of India,

(*ii*) Provinces, and

(*iii*) Indian States.

Art. 294 provides that as from the commencement of the Constitution and subject to any adjustment made or to be made by reason of the creation before the commencement of the Constitution of the Dominion of Pakistan and of the Provinces of West Bengal, East Bengal, West Punjab and East Punjab,

(*i*) all property and assets which immediately before such commencement were vested in His Majesty for the purposes of the Government of the Dominion of India shall vest in the Union;

and

(*ii*) all property and assets which immediately before such commencement were vested in His Majesty for the purposes of the Government of each Governor's Province shall vest in the corresponding State.

Art. 295 deals with the succession to property falling within third category *i.e.* belonging to an Indian State. It provides that

(*iii*) (*a*) as from the commencement of the Constitution and subject to any agreement entered into by the Government of India with the Government of the State, all property and assets which immediately before such commencement were vested in any Indian State corresponding to a Part 'B' State shall vest in the Union, if the purposes for which such property and assets were held immediately before such commencement will thereafter be purposes of the Union relating to any of the matters enumerated in the Union List;

(*b*) all other property and assets not vested in the Union as referred to in clause (a) above, shall vest in the corresponding Part 'B' State as from the commencement of the Constitution.

Note :—For *"Succession to rights, liabilities and obligations"* please see the next chapter on Services.

(2) Property accruing by escheat or lapse or as bona vacantia

Any property in the territory of India which if the Constitution had not come into operation, would have accrued to His Majesty or as the case may be, to the Ruler of an Indian State by escheat or lapse, or as *bona vacantia* for want of a rightful owner shall, if it is property situated in a State, vest in such State and shall, in any other case, vest in the Union:

Provided that any property which at the date when it would have so accrued to His Majesty or to the Ruler of an Indian State was in the possession or under the control of the Government of India or the Government of a State shall, according as the purposes for which it was then used or held were purposes of the Union or of a State, vest in the Union or in that State. Art. 296

(3) Things of value lying within territorial waters invest in the Union.

All lands, minerals and other things of value underlying the ocean within the territorial waters of India shall vest is the Union and be held for the purposes of the Union.

Art 297

(4) Acquired property.—

All property acquired for the purposes of the Union or of a State shall vest in the Union or in such State, as the cast may be.

Art. 298

C. PROVISIONS AS TO EXEMPTION OF PROPERTY FROM TAXATION

'The exemption of property of the Union from State taxation' and *'the exemption of property of a State from Union taxation'* has been provided for as follows in Articles 285 and 289 of the Constitution respectively :—

(1) Exemption of property of the Union from State taxation.—

The property of the Union shall, save insofar as Parliment may by law otherwise provide, be exempt from all taxes imposed by a State or by any authority within a State. This, however, cannot be deemed to prevent any authority from levying any tax on the property of the Union to which such property was immediately before the commencement of the Constitution liable or treated as liable, so long as that tax continues to be levied in that State. —Art. 285

(2) Exemption of property of a State from Union taxation.—

The property of a State shall be exempt from Union taxation.

The Union can however impose or authorise the imposition of any tax in respect of any property used or occupied for the purpose of a trade or business carried on by, or on behalf of the Government of a State. Art. 289.

D. EXECUTIVE POWER OF THE GOVERNMENT TO ACQUIRE PROPERTY

The executive power of the Union and of each State extends, subject to any law made by the appropriate Legislature, to the grant, sale, disposition, or mortgage of any property held for the purposes of the Union or of such State, as the case may be, and to the purchase or acquisition of property for those purposes respectively and to the making of contracts. Art. 298 (1).

E. FUNDAMENTAL RIGHTS RELATING TO PROPERTY

(*i*) *Provisions under "Right to Freedom."*—

Part III of the Constitution contains the Fundamental Rights guaranteed to the citizens. In Article 19 thereof, while enumerating the rights under "Right to Freedom", it has been provided as follows :—

"*Art. 19 (1) (f)*—All citizens shall have *the right to acquire, hold and dispose of property.*"

In order to enable the imposition of reasonable restrictions on the exercise of the above right, in clause (5) of the said Article, it has been further provided that nothing in Art. 19 (I) (f) as cited above shall affect the operation of any existing law insofar as it imposes or prevent the State from making any law imposing reasonable restrictions on the exercise of the above right either in the interests of the general public or for protection of the interests of any Scheduled Tribe.

(*ii*) *Provisions under "Right to Property,"*—

The fundamental right known as "Right to Property" has been jealously safeguarded in Art. 31 of the Constitution by making the compulsory acquisition of property a difficult process. The provisions in this respect are stated below :—

"*Art. 31 (1)*—No person shall be deprived of his property save property by authority of law.

Art. 31 (2)—No property shall be compulsorily acquired or requisitioned save for a public purpose and save by authority of a law which provides for compensation for the property so acquired or requisitioned and either fixes the amount of the compensation or specifices the principles on which, and the manner in which, the compensation is to be determined and given, and no such law shall be called in question in any court on the ground that the compensation provided by that law is not adequate.

(2A)—Where a law does not provide for the transfer of the ownership or right to possession of any property to the State or to a corporation owned or controlled by the State, it shall not be deemed to provide for the compulsory acquisition or requisitioning of property, notwithstanding that it deprives any person of his property.

Art. 31 (3)—No such law as is referred to in clause (2) made by the Legislature of a State shall have effect unless such law, having been reserved for the consideration of the President, has received his assent."

(*iii*) *Provisions under "Right to Freedom of Religion."*-

Every religious denomination or any section thereof shall have the right (1) to own and acquire movable and immovable property and (2) to administer such property in accordance with law. Art. 26 (c) & (d)

(b) Compulsory acquisition of Property

In order to effect compulsory acquisition of property, the following conditions must be fulfilled :—

(1) There must be the authority of law to deprive a person of his property.

(2) The purpose for which the acquisition or requisition is made must be a public purpose.

(3) The law authorising the acquisition or requisition must provide for compensation for the property to be taken over and either fix the amount of the compensation or specify the principles on which and the manner in which, the compensation is to be determined and given. No such law can be called in question in any court on the ground that the compensation provided by that law is not adequate.

(4) The law authorising the acquisition if made by the Legislature of a State and having been reserved for the consideration of the President, must have received the assent of the President. —Art. 31 (I) (2) & (3)

As the requirements of a public purpose and payment of compensation as embodied in clause (2) of Art. 31 of the Constitution was likely to come in the way of this Government in the carrying out of certain reforms, proper discharge of executive functions and fulfilment of certain other obligations, the following clauses were further inserted in the said Article :—

Clause (4)— If any Bill pending at the commencement of the Constitution in the Legislature of a State has, after it has been passed by such Legislature, been reserved for the consideration of the President and has received his assent, then notwithstanding any thing in the Constitution, the law so assented to, shall not be called in question in any court on the ground that it contravenes the provisions of clause (2).

Clause (5)—Nothing in clause (2) shall affect

(*a*) the provisions of any existing law other than a law to which the provisions of clause (6) (vide infra) apply;

or

(*b*) the provisions of any law which the State may hereafter make—

(*i*) for the purpose of imposing or levying any tax or penalty, or

(*ii*) for the promotion of public health or the prevention of danger to life or property, or

(*iii*) in pursuance of any agreement entered into between the Government of the Dominion of India or the Government of India and the Government of any other country or otherwise with respect to property declared by law to be evacuee property.

Clause (6)—Any law of the State enacted not more than eighteen months before the commencement of the Constitution may, within three months from such commencement, be submitted to the President for his certification; and thereupon if the President by public notification so certifies, it shall not be called in question in any court on the ground that it contravenes the provisions of clause (2) of this Article (Art. 31) or has contravened the provisions of sub-section (2) of Sec. 299 of the Government of India Act, 1935."

Note :—In sub-section (2) of Sec. 299 of the Government of India Act, 1935, a provision was made to the effect that there shall be no law for acquisition of any property for public purposes without providing for payment of compensation.

The provisions made in clauses (4), (5) and (6) as reproduced above did not, however, prove effective to serve the intended purpose and necessitated amendment of the constitution. As a result, Articles 31 A and 31 B were inserted by the Constitution (First Amendment) Act, 1951 providing for the "Saving of laws providing for the acquisition of estates etc.," and "Validation of certain Acts and Regulations" respectively Article 31A has again recently been amended by the Constitution (Fourth Amendment) Act, 1955. The contents of the these two Articles are given below :—

Article 31 A—Saving of laws providing for acquisition of estates etc.

(1) Notwithstanding anything contained in article 13, no law providing for—

- (*a*) the acquisition by the State of any estate or of any rights therein or the extinguishment or modification of any such rights, or
- (*b*) the taking over of the management of any property by the State for a limited period either in the public interest or in order to secure the proper management of the property, or
- (*c*) the amalgamation of two or more corporations either in the public interest or in order to secure the proper management of any of the corporations, or
- (*d*) the extinguishment or modication of any rights of managing agents, secretaries and treasurers,

managing directors, directors or managers of corporations, or of any voting rights of shareholders thereof, or

(*e*) the extinguishment or modification of any rights accruing by virtue of any agreement, lease or licence for the purpose of searching for, or winning, any mineral or mineral oil, or the premature termination or cancellation of any such agreement, lease or licence.

shall be deemed to be void on the ground that it is inconsistent with, or takes away or abridges any of the rights conferred by article 14, article 19 or article 31 :

Provided that where such law is a law made by the Legislature of a State, the provisions of this article shall not apply thereto unless such law, having been reserved for the considetion of the President, has received his assent.

(2) In this article.—

(*a*) the expression "estate" shall, in relation to any local area, have the same meaning as that expression or its local equivalent has in the existing law relating to land tenures in force in that area, and shall also include any jagir, inam or muafi or other similar grant and in the States of Madras and Travancore-Cochin, any *janmam* right;

(*b*) the expression "rights", in relation to an estate, shall include any rights vesting in a proprietor, sub-proprietor, under-proprietor, tenure-holder, *raiyat, under-raiyat* or other intermediary and any rights or privileges in respect of land revenue.

Art. 31B— Validation of certain Acts and Regulations.

Without prejudice to the generality of the provisions contained in article 31 A, none of the Acts and Regulations specified in the Ninth Schedule nor any of the provisions thereof shall be deemed to be void, or ever to have become void, on the ground that such Act, Regulation or provision is inconsistent with or takes away or abridges any of the rights conferred by, any provisions of this Part, and notwithstanding any judgment, decree or order of any court of tribunal to the contrary, each of the said Acts and Regulations shall, subject to the power of any competent Legislature to repeal or amend it, continue in force.

The fundamental rights may be suspended during the operation of a Proclamation of Emergency. Arts. 358 & 359.

F. LEGISLATION RELATING TO PROPERTY

(*a*) The following items occur in the *Union List* and as such, Parliament has 'exclusive power' to legislate on them :—

1. Property of the Union and the revenue therefrom but as regards property situated in a Part 'A' or Part 'B' State, subject to legislation by the State save insofar as Parliament by law otherwise provides. Sch. VII, List I-32

2. Acquisition or requisitioning of property for the purposes of the Union. Sch. VII, List I-33

(*b*) The following items occur in the *State List* and as such the State Legislatures have 'exclusive power' to legislate on them:—

1. Acquisition or requisitioning of property except for the purposes of the Union subject to the provision of entry 42 of List III relating to legislation recompensation (videinfra).
Sch. VII, List II-36.

2. Transfer and alienation of agricultural land.
Sch. VII, List II-18

(*c*) The following items occur in the *Concurrent List* and as such both *i.e.* the Parliament as well as the State Legislatures are competent to legislate on them:—

1. Transfer of property other than agricultural land.
Sch. VII, List III-6

2. Custody, management and disposal of property

(including agricultural land) declared by law to be evacuee property. Sch. VII, List. III-41

3. Principles on which compensation for property acquired or requisitioned for the purposes of the Union or of a State or for any other public purpose is to be determined and the form and the manner in which such compensation is to be given. Sch. VII, List III-42

G. MISCELLANEOUS

(1) For *"assurances of property"*, please see the Heading "Contract" of this chapter.

(2) *Valuation of property to determine appellate jurisdiction of the Supreme Court. —*

If the property involved in some claim or question which is the subject-matter of some judgement, decree or final order values Rs. 20,000 (or such other sum as may be specified by law) or more, it becomes appealable to the Supreme Court. Art. 133 (b)

(3) *Provisions relating to property*

(*a*) *as to the administration and control of Scheduled Areas and Scheduled Tribes —*

The Governor or Rajpramukh may by regulations

(*i*) prohibit or restrict the transfer of land by or among members of the Scheduled Tribes in such area; and

(*b*) regulate the allotment of land to members of the Scheduled Tribes in such area;

Art. 244 (1) & Sch. V, Para. 5(2)

(*c*) *as to the administration of Tribal Areas in Assam. —*

The District and Regional Councils have power to make locus with respect to

(1) the allotment, occupation or use or the setting apart of land other than any land which is a reserved forest for the purpose of agriculture or grazing as for residential or other non-agricultural purposes or for any other purpose likely to promote the interests of the inhabitants of any village or town :

Provided that such laws shall not be deemed to prevent the compulsory acquisition of land for public purposes by the Government of Assam; and

(2) the inheritance of property.

Art. 244 (2) & Sch. VI, Para 3.

SUCCESSION TO RIGHTS, LIABILITIES AND OBLIGATIONS

Articles 294 and 295 lay down the mode of succession in respect of the rights, liabilities and obligations of the

(*i*) Dominion of India,

(*ii*) Provinces, and

(*iii*) Indian States.

Art. 294 provides that as from the commencement of the Constitution and subject to any adjustment made or to be made by reason of the creation before the commencement of the Constitution of the Dominion of Pakistan and of the Provinces of West Bengal, East Bengal, West Punjab and East Punjab,

(*i*) all rights, liabilities and obligations of the Government of the Dominion of India whether arising out of any contract or otherwise shall be the rights, liabilities and obligations of the Government of India;

and

(*ii*) all rights, liabilities and obligations of the Government of each Governor's Province, whether arising out of any contract or otherwise shall be the rights, liabilities and obligations of the Government of each correspoinding State.

Article 295 deals with the succession to the rights, liabilities and obligations falling within the third category *i.e.* those of an Indian State. It provides that

(*iii*) (*a*) as from the commencement of the Constitution, all rights, liabilities and obligations of the Goverment of any Indian State corresponding to a Part 'B' State, whether arising out of any contract or otherwise, shall be the rights, liabilities and obligations of the Government of India, if the purposes for which such rights were acquired or liabilities and obligations were incurred before such commencement will thereafter be purposes of the Government of India relating to any of the matters enumerated in the Union List. This is however subject to the agreement entered into in that behalf by the Government of India with the Government of the State;

(*b*) all rights, liabilities and obligations other than those referred to in clause (*a*) above, whether arising out of any contract or otherwise shall devolve on the Government of the corresponding Part 'B' State as from the commencement of the Constitution.

Note. For *"Succession to property and assets"*, please see the beginning of this chapter.

CONTRACTS

1. **Power for the making of contracts.**—The executive power of the Union and of each State extends to the making of contracts. Art. 298 (i);

2. **Execution of contracts.—Clause (i)** of Art. 299 provides that all contracts made in the exercise of the executive power of the Union or of a State shall be expressed to be made by the President or by the Governor or Rajpramukh of the State, as the case may be and all such *contracts* and all *assurances of property* made in the exercise of that power shall be executed on behalf of the President or the Governor or the Rajpramukh by such persons and in such manner as he may direct or authorise.

   Note :—The directions of the President made under the above Article have been promulgated under the Ministry of Law Notification No. F. 35-I/50-L dt. 26-1-50 and F. 35-IV 150-L dt. 8-3-50. It contains the details of contracts and the officers competent to execute them on behalf of the President.

3. **Liability in respect of any contract or assurance of property.**—Clause 2 of Article 299 of the Constitution provides that neither the President, nor the Governor nor the Rajpramukh shall be personally liable in respect of any contract or *assurance* made or executed for the purposes of the Constitution or for the purposes of any enactment relating to the Government of India which was in force prior to the commencement of the Constitution, nor shall any person making or executing any such contract or *assurance* on behalf of any of them be personally liable in respect thereof.

4. **Devolution of contractual rights, liabilities and obligations on the commencement of the constitution.**

As from the commencement of the Constitution,

(*i*) all contractual rights, liabilities and obligations of the Government of the Dominion of India and of each Governor's Province have been devolved on the Government of India and of each corresponding State respectively; and

(*ii*) all contractual rights, liabilities and obligations of the Government of any Indian State have devolved as follows :—

(*a*) on the Government of India if the purposes for which such rights were acquired or liabilities and obligations were incurred before such commencement will thereafter be the purposes of the Government of India;

(*b*) on the corresponding Part 'B' State in cases other than those mentioned at clause *(a)* above. Art. 294

5. **Legislation relating to contract :**—The Parliament as well as the State Legislatures, both are competent to legislate on "Contracts, including partnership, agency, contracts of carriage and other special forms of

contracts, but *not including* contracts relating to agricultural land"; this item having been included in the Concurrent List Vide Entry No. 7 of List III of the Seventh Schedule to the Constitution.

Legislation on the "transfer and alienation of agricultural land" is the exclusive jurisdiction of the State Legislatures.

(*Vide* Sch. VII, List II-18).

6. **Contracts for appointments.**—A contract under which a person is appointed to hold a civil post under the Union or a Sate may, if the President or the Governor or the Rajpramukh deems it necessary in order to secure the services of a person having special qualifications, provide for the payment to him of compensation, if before the expiration of an agreed period, that post is abolished or he is for reasons not connected with misconduct on his part, required to vacate that post.

Art. 310 (2).

17

SERVICES

The provisions relating to services made in the Constitution are susceptible to the following divisions *viz.*

A. Definitions;

B. General Provisions as to services;

C. All-India services;

D. Judicial services;

E. Fundamental rights relating to employments;

F. Special provisions relating to certain classes;

G. Legislation relating to services; and

H. Reduction in salaries and allowances.

A. DEFINITIONS

1. **"Pension"** means a pension, whether contributory or not, of any kind whatsoever payable to or in respect of any person and includes retired pay so payable, a gratuity so payable and any sum or sums so payable by way of the return, with or without interest thereon or any other addition thereto, of subscriptions to a provident fund. Art. 366 (17).

2. **"Union emoluments"** includes, all emoluments and pensions payable out of the Consolidated Fund of India in respect of which income-tax is chargeable. Art. 270 (4) (c).

3. **"Chief Justice"** — the expression "Chief Justice" includes an acting Chief Justice. Schedule II, Part D.

4. **"Judge"** — A Judge includes an Ad hoc Judge. Schedule II, Part D.

5. **"Actual Service"** includes

   (*i*) time spent by a Judge on duty as a Judge or in the performance of such other functions as he may at the request of the President undertake to discharge;

   (*ii*) vacations including any time during which the Judge is absent on leave; and

   (*iii*) joining time on transfer from a High Court to the Supreme Court or from one High Court to another. Schedule II, Part D.

6. **"District Judge"**—The expression' "District Judge" includes (1) judge of a city civil court (2) additional district judge (3) joint district judge (4) assistant district judge (5) chief judge of a small causes court (5) chief presidency magistrate (6) additional chief presidency magistrate (7) sessions judge (8) additional sessions judge and (9) assistant sessions judge. Art. 236 (a)

7. **"Judicial Service"**—The expression "Judicial Service" means a service consisting exclusively of persons intended to fill the post of district judge and other judicial posts inferior to the post of district judge. Art. 236 (b).

8. **"Union Pensions"** means pensions payable by the Government of India or out of the Consolidated Fund of India. —Entry 71 of the Union List, Sch. VII.

9. **"State Pensions"** means pensions payable by the State or out of the Consolidated Fund of the State. —Entry 42 of the State List, Schedule VII.

B. GENERAL PROVISIONS AS TO SERVICES.

The Chapter on "Services" in the Constitution makes provision in respect of the following matters :

(*a*) *Persons serving in connection with the affairs of the Union or of a Slate : —*

(1) Recruitment and conditions of service;

(2) Tenure of office;

(3) Dismissal, removal or reduction in rank of persons employed in civil capacities;

(4) Transitional provisions, regarding:

(*i*) Pre-Constitution laws to continue in force;

(*ii*) Protection of existing officers of certain services.

(*b*) *All India Services*—Please see next item "C" of this chapter.

Persons serving in connection with the affairs of the Union or of a State—

(1) Recruitment and conditions of service.

Under Article 309 of the Constitution, the recruitment and conditions of service of persons appointed to public services and posts in connection with the affairs of the Union of any Part A or B State will be regulated by Acts of the appropriate Legislature. But until provision in this behalf is made by an Act of the appropriate Legislature, it has been provided that it shall be competent for the President or such person as he may direct in the case of services or posts in connection with the affairs of the Union and for the Governor or Rajpramukh of a State or such person as he may direct in the case of services or posts in connection with the affairs of a State to make rules regulating the recruitment and the conditions of service of persons appointed to such services and posts. Such rules will however have effect subject to the provisions of any such Act.

(2) Tenure of office.

(*i*) Every person who is a member of a defence service or of a civil service of the Union or an All-India service or holds any post connected with defence or any civil post under the Union, holds office during the pleasure of the President. Art. 310 (1) (*ii*) Every person who is a member of a civil service of a State or holds any civil post under a State, holds office during the pleasure of the Governor or as the case may be, of the Rajpramukh of the State. —Art. 310 (1)

(*iii*) *Special provision for appointments under contracts*—Notwithstanding that a person holding a civil post under the Union or a State holds office during the pleasure of the President, or as the case may be, of the Governor or Rajpramukh of the State, any contract under which a person, not being a member of a defence service or of an All-India service or of a civil service of the Union or a State is appointed under the Constitution to hold such a post may, if the President or the Governor or the Rajpramukh as the case may be, deems it necessary to secure the services of a person having special qualifications, provide for the payment to him of compensation, if before the expiration of an agreed period that post is abolished or he is for reasons not connected with misconduct on his part, required to vacate that post. Art. 310 (2)

(3) Dismissal, removal or reduction in rank of persons employed in civil capacities—

Art. 311 of the Constitution prescribes two essential conditions to be fulfilled in order to effect a legal and valid dismissal, removal or reduction in rank of persons employed in civil capacities under the Union or a State. Those are

(*i*) the dismissal, removal or reduction in rank must be ordered by the competent authority;

and

(*ii*) except in certain cases, the person affected must have been given a reasonable opportunity of showing cause against the action proposed to be taken in regard to him.

The provisions made in this connection are stated below:—

"Art. 311 (1)—No person who is a member of a civil service of the Union or an all-India service or of a civil service of a State or holds a civil post under the Union or a State shall be dismissed or removed by an authority subordinate to that by which he was appointed.

(2)—No such person as aforesaid shall be dismissed or removed or reduced in rank until he has been given a reasonable opportunity of showing cause against the action proposed to be taken in regard to him."

The following cases have, however, been laid down as *exceptions* to the requirement of reasonable opportunity by means of a Proviso :—

(*a*) Where a person is dismissed or removed or reduced in rank on the ground of conduct which has led to his conviction on a criminal charge;

(*b*) Where an authority empowered to dismiss or remove a person or to reduce him in rank is satisfied that for some reasons to be recorded by that authority in writing, it is not reasonably practicable to give that person an opportunity to show cause. It has further been provided in clause (3) of this Art. (Art. 311) that if any question arises whether it is reasonably practicable to give to any person an opportunity of showing cause, the decision thereon of the authority empowered to dismiss or remove such person or to reduce him in rank as the case may be, shall be final;

(*c*) Where the President or Governor or Rajpramukh, as the case may be, is satisfied that in the interest of the security of the State, it is not expedient to give to that person such an opportunity.

(4) Transitional provisions—

(*i*) *Pre-Constitution laws to continue in force—*

Under Article 313 of the Constitution, until other provision is made in this behalf, all the laws in force immediately before the commencement of the Constitution and applicable to any public service or any post which continues to exist after such commencement as an all-India sevice or as service or post under the Union or a State shall continue in force so far as consistent with the provisions of the Constitution.

(*ii*) *Protection of existing officers of certain services*—

In Art. 314, protection has been given to the existing officers of certain services in respect of their conditions of service, rights etc. It has been laid down in this Article that every person who having been appointed by the Secretary of State or Secretary of State in Council to a civil service of the Crown in India continues on and after the commencement of the Constitution to serve under the Government of India or of a State shall be entitled to receive from the Government of India or the Government of the State which he is from time to time serving, the same conditions of service as respects remuneration, leave and pension and the same rights as respects disciplinary matters or rights as similar thereto as changed circumstances may permit, as that person was entitled to immediately before such commencement.

C. ALL-INDIA SERVICES.

Power for the Creation. — If the Council of States has declared by resolution supported by not less than two-third of the members present and voting that it is necessary or expedient in the national interest so to do, Parliament by law provide for the creation of one or more All-India services common to the Union and the States. Art. 312 (1)

Services Created.—Art. 312 (2) of the Constitution provides that the services known at the commencement of the Constitution as the Indian Administrative Service and the Indian Police Service shall be deemed to be all-India services created by Parliament.

Recruitment and conditions of service of persons appointed to an all-India service:

Parliament may by law regulate the recruitment and the conditions of service of persons appointed to any such service.
Art. 312 (1)

Tenure of office.—Every person who is a member of an all India service holds office during the pleasure of the President.
Art. 310 (1)

Dismissal, removal or reduction in rank.—The provisions of Art. 311 ibid is equally applicable in the case of a member of an all-India service.

Transitional provisions.—By virtue of the provisions of Art. 313, all laws relating to all-India services continue in force unless otherwise provided by Parliament.

D. JUDICIAL SERVICE.

The provisions with regard to judicial service have been continued in Articles 234, 235 and 236 of the Constitution.

The expression 'judicial service' has been defined in Art. 236 (*b*) as follows :—

"The expression 'judicial service' means a service consisting exclusively of persons intended to fill the post of district judge and other civil judicial posts inferior to the post of district judge."

Recruitment of persons other than district judges to the judicial service.—Art. 234 provides that the appointments of persons other than district judges to the judicial service of a State shall be made by the Governor or Rajpramukh of the State in accordance with rules made by him in that behalf after consultation with the State Public Service Commission and with the High Court exercising jurisdiction in relation to such State.

Postings, promotion etc. of persons belonging to the judicial service.—Under Art. 235, the High Court is entrusted with the power of control over district courts and courts subordiniate thereto. Such control includes the posting and promotion of, and the grant of leave to, persons belonging to the judicial service of a State and holding any post inferior to the post of district judge. This can not, however, be deemed as taking away from any such person any right of appeal which he may have under the law regulating the conditions of his service or as authorising the High Court to deal with him otherwise than in accordance with the conditions of his service prescribed under such law.

E. FUNDAMENTAL RIGHTS RELATING TO EMPLOYMENTS.

(*a*) Provisions under "Right to Equality"—

(*1*) Under "Right to Equality" which is a Fundamental Right guaranteed to the citizens under the Constitution,

Art. 16 provides for "Equality of opportunity in matters of public employment". The relevant provisions in this respect are follows :

Equality of opportunity in matters of public employment.—

Art. 16 (1)—There shall be equality of opportunity for all citizens in matters relating to employment appointment to any office under the State.

(2) No citizen shall on grounds only of religion, race caste, sex, descent, place of birth, residence or any of them be ineligible for or discriminated against in respect of any employment or office under the State.

In order, however, to reserve certain powers to prescribe residence and religious qualifications in certain cases, as well as to provide for reservation of appointments or posts in favour of backward classes, the following provisions have been further inserted—

"(3) Nothing in this Article shall prevent Parliament from making any law prescribing in regard to a class or classes of employment or appointment to an office under any State specified in the First Schedule or any local or other authority within its territory, any requirement as to residence within that State prior to such employment or appointment.

(4) Nothing in this Article shall prevent the State from making any provision for the reservation of appointments or posts in favour of any backward class of citizens which, in the opinion of the State is not adequately represented in the services under the State.

(5) Nothing in this Article shall affect the operation of any law which provides that the incumbent of an office in connection with the affairs of any religious or denominational institution or any member of the governing body thereof shall be a persons professing a particular religion or belonging to a particular denomination.

(*ii*) Under Art. 18 (4), no person holding any office of profit or trust under *the State* shall without the consent of the President, accept any present, emolument or office of any kind from or under any foreign State.

Note :—Unless the context otherwise requires, *"the State"* includes the Government and Parliament of India and the Government and the Legislature of each of the States and all local or other authorities within the territory of India or under the control of the Government of India.

(b) Provisions under "Right against Exploitation"—

No child below the age of fourteen years shall be employed to work in any factory or mine or engaged in any other hazardous employment. Art. 24.

Note :—The Items (*a*) (*ii*) and (*b*) mentioned above are in the nature of restrictive provisions.

F. SPECIAL PROVISIONS RELATING TO CERTAIN CLASSES.

In the Constitution, special provisions have been made regarding appointments of Scheduled Castes, Scheduled Tribes and Anglo-Indians to the various services and posts. Art. 335 lays down that the claims of the members of the Scheduled Castes and the Scheduled Tribes shall be taken into consideration consistently with the maintenance of efficiency of administration in the making of appointments to services and posts in connection with the affairs of the Union or of a State.

Under Art. 336, reservation of posts for members of Anglo-Indian community in respect of appointment to posts in the (*i*) railway (*ii*) customs (*iii*) postal and telegraph services of the Union has been granted as follows :—

(*a*) During the first 2 years after the commencement of the Constitution—Appointments to be made on the same basis as adopted immediately before 15.8.47.

(*b*) During every succeeding period of 2 years—Reservation to be less by 10% (or as nearly as possible) than the numbers reserved during the immediately preceding period of 2 years.

(*c*) At the end of 10 yrs.— Reservation shall cease.

The above provisions do not, however, constitute a bar to appointments of Anglo-Indians to unreserved posts if otherwise qualified.

G. LEGISLATION RELATING TO SERVICES

Items relating to services included in the Legislative Lists are extracted below :—

The Parliament and the State Legislature have exclusive legislative jurisdiction with respect to matters included in the Union and State Lists respectively.

Extract from the Union List

Entry 70. Union public services; All-India Services; and Union Public Service Commission.

71. Union Pensions.

73. Salaries and allowances of the Members of Parliament, the Chairman and the Deputy Chairman of the Council of States and the Speaker and the Deputy Speaker of the House of the People.

75. Emoluments, allowances, privileges and rights in respect of leave of absence of the President and Governors; salaries and allowances of the Ministers of the Union; and

the salaries, allowances and rights in respect of leave of absence and other conditions of service of the Comptroller and Auditor-General.

Extract from the State List—

Entry 41. State public services; and State Public Service Commission.

38. Salaries and allowances of Members of the Legislature of the State, of the Speaker and Deputy Speaker of the Legislative Assembly

and if there is a Legislative Council, of the Chairman and Deputy Chairman thereof.

40. Salaries and allowances of Ministers for the State.

42. State pensions.

H. REDUCTION IN SALARIES AND ALLOWANCES

The directions given by the Union to a State during the operation of a financial emergency may provide for the reduction of salaries and allowances of all or any class of persons serving in connection with the affairs of a State or the Union including the Judges of the Supreme Court and the High Courts. Art. 360 (4)

18

PUBLIC SERVICE COMMISSIONS

1. CONSTITUTION

The Constitution provides for a Public Service Commission for the Union and a Public Service Commission for each State. Two or more States may, however, agree that there shall be one Public Service Commission for that group of States, and if a resolution to that effect is passed by the House or where there are two Houses, by each House of the Legislature of each of those States, Parliament may by law provide for the appointment of a Joint Public Service Commission to serve the needs for those States. The Public Service Commission for the Union, if requested so to do by the Governor or Rajpramukh of a State, may, with the approval of the President, agree to serve all or any of the needs of the State. Art. 315

2. APPOINTMENT AND TERM OF OFFICE OF MEMBERS

(1) The Chairman and other members of a Public Service Commission are appointed.

(*i*) in the case of the Union Commission or a Joint Commission by the President; and

(*ii*) in the case of a State Commission, by the Governor or Rajpramukh of the State.

This is, however, subject to the proviso that as nearly as may be, one half of the members of every Public Service Commission shall be persons, who at the dates of their respective appointments have held office for at least ten years either under the Government of India or under the Government of a State and in computing the said period of ten years, any period before the commencement of the Constitution during which a person has held office under the Crown in India or under the Government of an Indian State shall be included.

(2) Unless resigned or removed from service earlier, a member of a Public Service Commission holds office for a term of six years from the date on which he enters upon his office or until he attains, in the case of the Union Commission, the age of 65 years and in the case of a State Commission or a Joint Commission, the age of 60 years whichever is earlier.

(3) A person who holds office as a member of a Public Service Commission, on the expiration of his term of office becomes ineligible for reappointment to that office. Art. 316

3. RESIGNATION, REMOVAL AND SUSPENSION OF A MEMBER OF A PUBLIC SERVICE COMMISSION

Resignation—A member of a Public Service Commission may, by writing under his hand addressed, in the case of the Union Commission or a Joint Commission to the President and in the case of a State Commission, to the Governor or Rajpramukh of the State resign his office. Art. 316 (2) (a)

Removal—A member of a Public Service Commission may be removed from his office in the following manner—

The Chairman or any other member of a Public Service Commission shall only be removed from his office by order of the President on the ground of misbehaviour after the Supreme Court on reference being made to it by the President has, on enquiry held in accordance with the procedure prescribed in that behalf, reported that the Chairman or such other member as the case may be, ought on any such ground to be removed.

Notwithstanding the above provision, the President may, by order, remove from office the Chairman or any other member of a Public Service Commission if the Chairman or such other member as the case may be—

(*a*) is adjudged an insolvent; or

(*b*) engages during his term of office in any paid employment outside the duties of his office; or

(*c*) is in the opinion of the President, unfit to continue in office by reason of infirmity of mind or body.

Arts. 316 (2) (b), 317 (1) & (3)

Although no exhaustive illustrations as to what constitutes 'misbehaviour' have been given, it has been expressly provided in the Constitution that if the Chairman or any other member of a Public Service Commission is or becomes in any way concerned or interested in any contract or agreement made by or on behalf of the Government of India or the Government of a State or participates in any way in the profit thereof or in any benefit or emoluments arising therefrom otherwise than as a member and in common with the other members of an incorporated company, he shall be deemed to be guilty of misbehaviour. Art. 317 (4)

Suspension : The President in the case of the Union Commission or a Joint Commission, and the Governor or Rajpramukh in the case of a State Commission, may suspend from office the Chairman or any other member of the Commission in respect of whose alleged misbehaviour, a reference has been made to the Supreme Court, until the President has passed orders on receipt of the report of the Supreme Court on such reference.

Art. 317 (2)

4. POWER TO MAKE REGULATIONS AS TO CONDITIONS OF SERVICE OF MEMBERS AND STAFF OF THE COMMISSION.

In the case of the Union Commission or a Joint Commission, the President and, in the case of a State Commission, the Governor or Rajpramukh of the State may by regulations

(*a*) determine the number of members of the Commission and their conditions of service;

and

(*b*) make provision with respect to the number of members

of the staff of the Commission and their conditions of service :

Provided that the conditions of service of a member of a Public Service Commission shall not be varied to his dis-advantage after his appointment. Art. 318

5. PROHIBITION AS TO THE HOLDING OF OFFICES BY MEMBERS OF COMMISSION ON CEASING TO BE SUCH MEMBERS.

On ceasing to hold office—

(*a*) the Chairman of the Union Public Service Commission shall be ineligible for further employment either under the Government of India or under the Government of a State;

(*b*) the Chairman of a State Public Service Commission shall be eligible for appointment as the Chairman or any other member of the Union Public Service Commission or as the Chairman of any other State Public Service Commission, but not for any other employment either under the Government of India or under the Government of a State;

(*c*) a member other than the Chairman of the Union Public Service Commission shall be eligible for appointment as the Chairman of the Union Public Service Commission or as the Chairman of a State Public Service Commission but not for any other employment either under the Government of India or under the Government of a State;

(*d*) a member other than the Chairman of a State Public Service Commission shall be eligible for appointment as the Chairman or any other member of the Union Public Service Commission or as the Chairman of that or any other State Public Service Commission but not for any other employment either under the Government of India or under the Government of a State.

Art. 319.

6. FUNCTIONS OF PUBLIC SERVICE COMMISSIONS.

The functions of Public Service Commissions laid down in the Constitution include the performance of the following kinds of duties:—

(*a*) Duties in connection with the recruitment for and appointment to the Services; Art. 320 (1) and (2)

(*b*) Duties in connection with the matters referred to them for consultation; Art. 320 (3).

(*c*) Duties in connection with the presentation of the Report. Art. 323.

There is also provision enabling the Parliament or State Legislatures to provide for, by enactment, the exercise of *additional functions* by the Union or State Public Service Commissions. Art. 321.

The detailed provisions in this connection are stated below :—

(*a*) *Duties in connection with the recruitment for and appointment to the services —*

It shall be the duty of the Union and State Public Service Commissions to conduct examinations for appointments to the services of the Union and the services of the State respectively. Art. 320 (1)

It shall also be the duty of the Union Public Service Commission, if requested by any two or more States so to do, to assist those States in framing and operating schemes of joint recruitment for any services for which candidates possessing special qualifications are required. Art. 320 (2).

(*b*) *Duties in connection with the matters referred to them for consultation—*

The Union Public Service Commission or the State Public Service Commission as the case may be, shall be consulted—

(*a*) on all matters relating to methods of recruitment to civil services and for civil posts;

(*b*) on the principles to be followed in making appointments to civil services and posts and in making promotions and transfers from one service to another and on the suitability of candidates for such appointments, promotions or transfers;

(*c*) on all disciplinary matters affecting a person serving under the Government of India or the Government of a State in a civil capacity including memorials or petitions relating to such matters;

(*d*) on any claim by or in respect of a person who is serving or has served under the Government of India or the Government of a State or under the Crown in India or under the Government of an Indian State in a civil capacity, that any costs incurred by him in defending legal proceedings instituted against him in respect of acts done or purporting to be done in the execution of his duty should be paid out of the Consolidated Fund of India or as the case may be, out of the Consolidated Fund of the State;

(*e*) on any claim for the award of a pension in respect of injuries sustained by a person while serving under the Government of India or the Government of a State or under the Crown in India or under the Government of an Indian State in a civil capacity and any question as to the amount of any such award.

and it shall be the duty of a Public Service Commission to advise on any matter referred to them and on any other matter which the President or as the case may be, the Governor or Rajpramukh of the State may refer to them :

Provided that the President as respects the All-India services and also as respects other services and posts in connection with the affairs of the Union, and the Governor or Rajpramukh, as the case may be, as respects other services and posts in connection with the affairs of a State, may make regulations specifying the matters in which either generally or in any particular class of cases or in any particular circumstances, it shall not be necessary for a Public Service Commission to be consulted. Art. 320(3)

A Public Service Commission need not be consulted as respects the manner in which any provision for the reservation of appointments or posts in favour of any backward class of citizens may be made or as respects the manner in which effect may be given to the claims of Scheduled Castes and Scheduled Tribes to services and posts. Art. 320 (4)

(c) *Duties in connection with presentation of the Report—*

(1)It shall be the duty of the Union Commission to present annually to the President a report as to the work done by the Commission

(2) It shall be the duty of a State Commission to present annually to the Governor or Rajpramukh of the State a report as to the work done by the Commission and it shall be the duty of Joint Commission to present annually to the Governor or Rajpramukh of each of the States the needs of which are served by the Joint Commission, a report as to the work done by the Commission in relation to that State. Art. 323

Additional functions—

Power to extend functions —

An Act made by Parliament or as the case may be, the Legislature of a State may provide for the exercise of additional functions by the Union Public Service Commission or the State Public Service Commission as respects the services of the Union or the State and also as respects the services of a local authority or other body corporate constituted by law or of any public institution. Art. 321

7. REPORTS OF PUBLIC SERVICE COMMISSIONS

The Union Public Service Commission presents annually to the President, a report as to the work done by the Commission. On receipt of such report, the President causes a copy thereof together with a memorandum explaining, as respects the cases, if any, where the advice of the Commission was not accepted, the reasons for such non-acceptance to be laid before each House of Parliament.

Similarly, a State Public Service Commission presents annually to the Governor or Rajpramukh of the State, a report as to the work done by the Commission and a Joint Public Service

Commission presents annually to the Governor or Rajpramukh of each of the States the needs of which are served by the Joint Commission, a report as to the work done by the Commission in relation to that State. In either case, the Governor or Rajpramukh as the case may be, on receipt of such report causes a copy thereof together with a memorandum explaining as respects the cases, if any, where the advice of the Commission was not accepted, the reasons for such non-acceptance to be laid before the Legislature of the State.

8. MEASURES TO SECURE INDEPENDENCE OF PUBLIC SERVICE COMMISSIONS—

In order to secure the independence of Public Service Commissions, the Constitution provides for certain measures as mentioned below :—

(1) Art. 316 (3) provides that a person who holds office as a member of a Public Service Commission shall, on the expiration of his term of office, be ineligible for re-appointment to that office.

(2) There is a special procedure prescribed in Art. 317 (*vide supra*) for the removal of a member of a Public Service Commission.

(3) It has been provided in Art. 318 (*vide supra*) that the conditions of service of a member of a Public Service Commission, shall not be varied to his disadvantage after his appointment.

(4) There are certain prohibitions laid down in Art. 319 (*vide supra*) as to the holding of offices by members of the Union and State Commissions on ceasing to be such members.

(5) All regulations made by the President or the Governor or Rajpramukh specifying the matters in which either generally or in any particular class of cases or in any particular circumstances, it shall not be necessary for a Public Service Commission to be consulted are required to be laid for not less than fourteen days before each House of Parliament or the House or each House

of the Legislature of the State as the case may be, as soon as possible after they are made and thereupon, they shall be subject to such modifications, by way of repeal or amendment as both Houses of Parliament or the House or both Houses of the Legislature of the State may make during the session in which they are so laid. Art. 320 (5)

(6) *Expenses of Public Service Commissions*—Art. 322 provides that the expenses of the Union or a State Public Service Commission, including any salaries, allowances and pensions payable to or in respect of the members or staff of the Commission, shall be charged on the Consolidated Fund of India or as the case may be, the Consolidated Fund of the State.

9. POWER OF THE PRESIDENT/GOVERNOR OR RAJPRAMUKH TO MAKE CONSULTATION OBLIGATORY IN THE CASE OF CERTAIN APPOINTMENTS.

(*i*) *Appointment of officers and servants of the Supreme Court*—The President may by rule require that appointments to any office connected with the Supreme Court shall not be made except after consultation with the Union Public Service Commission. Art. 146 (1)

(*ii*) *Appointment of officers and servants of the High Court*—The Governor or Rajpramukh may by rule require that the appointment to any office connected with the High Court can be made only after consultation with the State Public Service Commission. Art. 229 (1)

10. TRANSITIONAL PROVISIONS

Under Art. 378, the members of the Public Service Commission for the Dominion of India and of a Province became after the commencement of the Constitution the members of the Public Service Commission of the Union and of the corresponding State unless elected otherwise.

19

APPOINTMENTS UNDER THE CONSTITUTION—CONDITIONS OF SERVICE, SALARIES, ALLOWANCES, PENSIONS ETC.

Scheme of arrangement followed—

A. Appointments of Dignitaries—

(a) *Union*

(1) President.

(2) Vice-President.

(3) Ministers including Prime Minister for the Union.

(4) The Attorney-General for India.

(5) Officers of Parliament.

(*a*) Speaker of the House of the People;

(*b*) Deputy Speaker of the House of the People;

(*c*) Chairman of the Council of States.

(*d*) Deputy Chairman of the Council of States.

(6) Members of Parliament.

(7) Judges of the Supreme Court: Chief Justice, Acting Chief Justice, Ad-hoc Judges.

(8) Comptroller and Auditor-General of India.

(b) States

(9) Governor.

(10) Ministers including Chief Minister for the State.

(11) The Advocate General for the State.

(12) Officers of the State Legislature—

(*a*) Speaker of the Legislative Assembly;

(*b*) Deputy Speaker of the Legislative Assembly;

(*c*) Chairman of the Legislative Council.

(*d*) Deputy Chairman of the Legislative Council.

(13) Members of the State Legislature.

(14) Judges of the High Court.

(15) Rajpramukh.

(16) District Judges.

B. Appointments of Staff

(*a*) *Union.*

(1) Parliament Secretariat.

(2) Officers and servants of the Supreme Court.

(3) Persons serving in the Indian Audit and Accounts Department.

(*b*) *States.*

(4) Secretariat of the State Legislature.

(5) Officers and servants of High Court.

(6) Application of Constitutional provisions and rules made thereunder in respect of persons belonging to Judicial Service to certain class of Magistrates.

(7) Provisions as to the administration and control of Scheduled Areas and Scheduled Tribes.

(8) Provisions as to the administration of Tribal areas in Assam.

C. Appointments of Commissions, Councils, Committees, Authorities etc. under the Constitution.

(1) Finance Commission.

(2) Public Service Commission.

(3) Election Commission.

(4) Commission for the administration of the Scheduled Areas and welfare of the Scheduled Tribes in Part A and B States.

(5) Commission for the backward classes.

(6) Commission of Parliament on official language.

(7) Committee of Parliament on official language.

(8) Inter-State Council.

(9) Authority for Trade, Commerce, and Intercourse.

(10) Special officer for Scheduled Castes and Scheduled Tribes.

Appointments of Dignitaries.

(*a*) *Union.*

1. PRESIDENT

Term of office—5 years from the date of entering upon office But (i) he may resign earlier;

(*ii*) he may be removed from office by impeachment for violation of the Constitution; and

(*iii*) notwithstanding the expiration of his term, he may continue to hold office until his successor enters upon his office. Art. 56 (1).

Qualifications for election—A person in order to become eligible for election as President

(1) must be a citizen of India;

(2) must have completed the age of 35 years;

(3) must be qualified for election as a member of the House of the People; and

(4) must not hold any office of profit under the Government of India or the Government of any State or under any local or other authority subject to the control of the said Governments.

Explanation—A person shall not be deemed to hold any of profit by reason only that he is the President or Vice-President of the Union or the Governor or Rajpramukh or Uprajpramukh of any State or is a Minister either for the Union or for any State.

Art. 58.

Conditions of office—

(1) The President shall not be a member of either House of Parliament or of a House of the Legislature of any State.

(2) He shall not hold any other office of profit.

(3) He shall be entitled

(1) to the use of his official residences without payment of rent; and

(2) to such emoluments, allowances and privileges as may be determined by Parliament by law and until provision in that behalf is so made, to the following emoluments, allowances and privileges:—

Emoluments—Rs. 10,000 p. m. plus

Allowances as were payable to the Governor-General of the Dominion of India immediately before commencement of the Constitution.

Privileges—Same privileges to which the Governor-General was entitled immediately before the commencement of the Constitution.

2. OFFICERS OF PARLIAMENT

(*a*) **Chairman of the Council of State.**

(*b*) **Deputy Chairman of the Council of States.**

(*c*) **Speaker of the House of the People.**

(*d*) **Deputy Speaker of the House of the People.**

The Chairman and. the Deputy Chairman of the Council of States and the Speaker and the Deputy Speaker of the House of the People is entitled to such salaries and allowances as may be respectively fixed by Parliament by law and until provision in that behalf is so made, to such salaries and allowances as are specified below :—

Speaker of the House of the People and Chairman of the Council of States	to such salaries and allowances as were payable to the Speaker of the Constituent Assembly of the Dominion of India immediately before the commencement of the Constitution.
Dy. Speaker of the House of the People and Dy. Chairman of the Council of States	to such salaries and allowances as were payable to the Dy. Speaker of the Constituent Assembly of the Dominion of India immediately before the Commencement of the Constitution.

Art. 97, Schedule II, Part C

3. MEMBERS OF PARLIAMENT

Members of either House of Parliament are entitled to receive such salaries and allowances as may from time to time be determined by Parliament by law and until provision in that respect is so made, allowances at such rates and upon such conditions as were immediately before the commencement of the Constitution applicable in the case of members of the Constituent Assembly of the Dominion of India. Art. 106

4. JUDGES INCLUDING CHIEF JUSTICE OF THE SUPREME COURT

Appointment—Every Judge of the Supreme Court shall be appointed by the President by warrant under his hand and seal after consultation with such Judges of the Supreme Court and of the High Courts in the States as the President may deem necessary for the purpose. In the case of appointment of a Judge other than the Chief Justice, the Chief Justice of India shall always be consulted. Art. 124 (2)

Term of Office—Every Judge shall hold office until he attains the age of 65 years, unless resigned or removed from service earlier. Art. 124 (2)

Qualifications for appointment — A person in order to be qualified for appointment as a Judge of the Supreme Court (*i*) must be a citizen of India, (*ii*) has been for at least 5 years a Judge of a High Court or of two or more such Courts in succession;

or

has been for at least ten years an advocate of High Court or two or more such Courts in succession;

or

is, in the opinion of the President, a distinguished jurist. Art. 124 (3)

Salaries etc.

(1) The Judges of the Supreme Court are entitled to, in respect of time spent on actual service, the following salary—

The Chief Justice —Rs. 5000 p. m.

Any other Judge —Rs. 4000 p. m.

Provided that if a Judge of the Supreme Court at the time of his appointment is in receipt of a pension (other than a disability or wound pension) in respect of any previous service under the Government of India or under the Government of a State or any of their predecessor Governments, his salary in respect of service in the Supreme Court shall be reduced by the amount of the pension.

(2) Every Judge is entitled to such privileges and allowances and to such rights in respect of leave of absence and pension as may from time to time be determined by or under law made by Parliament and until so determined, to such privileges, allowances and rights as are specified below :—

(*a*) Every Judge of the Supreme Court is entitled without payment of rent to the use of an official residence. A Judge who was holding office as the Chief Justice or any other Judge of the Federal Court and on commencement of the Constitution became the Chief Justice or any other Judge of the Supreme Court is not, however, entitled to this benefit during the period he holds office as such Chief Justice or other Judge.

(*b*) On the other hand, every Judge who so became the Chief Justice or other Judge of the Supreme Court shall in respect of time spent on actual service, be entitled to receive in addition to the salary specified in the Constitution *i. e.*, Rs. 5,000 p. m. for Chief Justice and Rs. 4,000 p. m. for any other Judge, as *special pay* an amount equivalent to the difference between the above salary and the salary payable to the Chief Justice or any other Judge of the Federal Court immediately before such commencement.

(*c*) Every Judge of the Supreme Court is entitled to receive such reasonable allowances to reimburse him for expenses incurred in travelling on duty within the territory of India and is also entitled to be afforded such reasonable facilities in connection with travelling as the President may from time to time prescribe.

(*d*) The rights in respect of leave of absence (including leave allowances) and pension of the Judges of the Supreme Court are governed by the provisions which, immediately before the commencement of the Constitution were applicable to the Judges of the Federal Court.

Neither the privileges nor the allowances of a Judge nor his rights in respect of leave of absence or pension shall be varied to his disadvantage after his appointment. —Art. 125 & Schedule II, Part D.

Note : -For meaning of the expression *"Chief Justice"*, *"Judge"* and *"actual service"*, please see the definitions under the chapter "SERVICES"

Acting Chief Justice

Appointment— Art. 126 provides for the appointment of one of the Judges of the Supreme Court to act as the Chief Justice when the office of the latter is vacant or he is unable to perform the duties of his office by reason of absence or otherwise.

The provisions re: salaries, allowances etc. applicable to the Chief Justice equally apply to the acting Chief Justice.

Ad Hoc Judges

Appointment—Art. 127 provides for the appointment of a Judge of a High Court duly qualified for appointment as a Judge of the Supreme Court to be an ad-hoc Judge for certain period in order to complete the quorum of the Judges of the Supreme Court. Such appointments are to be made by the Chief Justice of India with the previous consent of the President and after consultation with the Chief Justice of the High Court concerned. While attending the sittings of the Supreme Court, the ad-hoc Judge shall have all the jurisdiction, powers and privileges of a Judge of the Supreme Court. Art. 128

Retired Judges acting as a Judge of the Supreme Court—

The Chief Justice of India may at any time with the previous consent of the President request any retired Judge of the Supreme Court or Federal Court to sit and act as a Judge of the Supreme Court.

Every such person while so sitting and acting shall be entitled to such *allowances* as the President may by order determine and shall have all the jurisdiction, powers and privileges of but shall not otherwise be deemed to be, a Judge of the Supreme Court. Art. 128.

5. COMPTROLLER AND AUDITOR-GENERAL OF INDIA

Please see under the chapter "Audit and Accounts."

(*b*) *States*

6. GOVERNOR

Appointment—The Governor of a State shall be appointed by the President by warrant under his hand and seal. Art. 155

Term of office—(1) The Governor holds office during the pleasure of the President.

(2) The Governor may resign his office.

(3) Subject to the above, the Governor shall hold office for a term of 5 years from the date of entering upon office. Notwithstanding the expiration of his term, he may however continue to hold office until his successor enters upon his office. Art. 156

Qualifications for appointment—A person to be eligible for appointment as Governor

(1) must be a citizen of India; and

(2) must have completed the age af 35 years —Art. 157

Conditions of office—(1) The Governor shall not be a member of either House of Parliament or a House of the Legislature of any State.

(2) The Governor shall not hold any other office of profit.

(3) The Governor shall be entitled without payment of rent to the use of his official residences.

(4) The Governor shall be entitled to such emoluments, allowances and privileges as may be determined by Parliament by law and until so determined to the emoluments, allowances and privileges as specified below— *Emoluments*—Rs. 5,500/- p. m. plus.

Allowances as were payable to the Governors of the corresponding Provinces immediately before the commencement of the Constitution.

Privileges—Same privileges throughout the term of office to which the Governors of the corresponding Provinces were entitled immediately before the commencement of the Constitution.

(5) The emoluments and allowances of the Governor shall not be diminished during his term of office.

Art. 158 & Schedule II, Part A

Emoluments, allowances and privileges of the person discharging the functions of a Governor—

Any person discharging the functions of a Governor shall be entitled to the same emoluments, allowances and privileges as the Governor, —Schedule II, Part A, Para. 4

7. MINISTERS (INCLUDING CHIEF MINISTER) FOR THE STATES (PARTS A AND B)

(1) The Chief Minister shall be appointed by the Governor or Rajpramukh and the other Ministers shall be appointed by the Governor or Rajpramukh on the advice of the Chief Minister.

(2) The Ministers hold office during the pleasure of the Governor or Rajpramukh.

(3) A Minister who for any period of six consecutive months is not a member of the Legislature of the State shall, at the expiration of that period cease to be a Minister.

(4) The salaries and allowances of Ministers shall be such as the Legislature of the State may from time to time by law determine and until so determined, the same as were payable to such Ministers for the corresponding Province or the corresponding Indian State as the case may be immediately before the commencement of the Constitution. Art. 164 and Schedule II, Part B

Note :- It has been provided in Arts. 164 & 238 (b) that in the States of Bihar, Madhya Pradesh, Orissa, and Madhya. Bharat, there shall be a Minister in charge of tribal welfare who may in addition be in charge of the welfare of the Scheduled Castes and backward classes or any other work.

8. THE ADVOCATE-GENERAL FOR THE STATE.

The Governor or Rajpramukh of each State shall appoint a person who is qualified to be appointed a Judge of a High Court to be Advocate-General for the State.

The Advocate-General shall hold office during the pleasure

of the Governor or Rajpramukh and shall receive such remuneration as the Governor or Rajpramukh may determine. Art. 165

9. OFFICERS OF THE STATE LEGISLATURE

(*a*) **Speaker of the Legislative Assembly;**

(*b*) **Deputy Speaker of the Legislative Assembly;**

(*c*) **Chairman of the Legislative Council;**

(*d*) **Deputy Chairman of the Legislative Council.**

The Speaker and the Deputy Speaker of the Legislative Assembly and the Chairman and the Deputy Chairman of the Legislative Council shall be entitled to such salaries and allowances as may be fixed by the Legislature of the State by law and until so fixed, such officers of Part A and Part B States shall be entitled respectively to such salaries and allowances as are specified below :—

Part 'A' States—

The Speaker and the Deputy Speaker	The same salaries and allowances as were payable to the Speaker and the Deputy Speaker of the Legislative Assembly of the corresponding Province immediately before the commencement of the Constitution.
The Chairman and the Deputy Chairman	The same salaries and allowances as were payable to the President and the Deputy President of the Legislative Council of the corresponding Province immediately before the commencement of the Constitution and where the corresponding Province had no Legislative Council immediately before such commencement, to such salaries and allowances as the Governor may determine.

Art. 186, Schedule II, Part C.

Part B States —

The Speaker and the Deputy Speaker; The Chairman and the Deputy Chairman	As may be determined by the Rajpramukh of the State. —Art. 186 read with Art. 238 (8).

10. MEMBERS OF THE LEGISLATIVE ASSEMBLY AND THE LEGISLATIVE COUNCIL.

Salaries and allowances—As may from time to time be determined by the Legislature of the State by law and until so determined, salaries and allowances at such rates and upon such conditions as were immediately before the commencement of the Constitution applicable in the case of members of the Legislative Assembly of the corresponding Province and in the case of Part B States as may be determined by the Rajpramukh. Art. 195 and Art. 238 (9)

11. JUDGES OF THE HIGH COURTS.

Appointment—Every Judge of a High Court shall be appointed by the President by warrant under his hand and seal after consultation with the Chief Justice of India, the Governor or Rajpramukh of the State and in the appointment of a Judge other than the Chief Justice, the Chief Justice of the High Court.

Art. 217

Term of office— Every Judge shall hold office until he attains the age of 60 years, unless resigned or removed or his office being vacated earlier. Art. 217

Qualifications for appointment—A person in order to be qualified for appointment as a Judge of a High Court

(1) must be a citizen of India; and

(2) must have 10 years experience of a judicial office in India or as an Advocate of a High Court. Art. 217.

Art. 376 however provides that the existing Judges including Judges who were not citizens on the date when the institution came into operation shall continue as Judges if so choose. According to sec. 13 of the Constitution first Amendment) Act,

1951, any such Judge, notwithstanding that he is not a citizen of India, be eligible for appointment Chief Justice or other Judge of any other High Court.

Salaries etc.—

(*a*) *In respect of Part 'A' States*—

The Judges of the High Court of each Part A State are entitled to a salary as mentioned below in respect of time spent on actual service—

The Chief Justice —Rs. 4,000 p. m.

Any other Judge —Rs. 3,500 p. m.

The persons who were holding offices as the Chief Justice or as any other Judge of the High Court in any Province immediately before the commencement of the Constitution and became after such commencement the Chief Justice or a Judge of the High Court in the corresponding State under the transitional provisions, shall in respect of time spent on actual service as such Chief Justice or other Judge, be entitled to receive in addition to the above salary as *special pay* an amount, if any, by which the above salary falls short of the salary payable to the Chief Justice or other Judge of the High Court in the Province immediately before the commencement of the Constitution.

Art. 221 (i) & Schedule II, Part D

Allowances and rights—Every Judge is entitled to such allowances and to such rights in respect of leave of absence and pension as may from time to time be determined by or under law made by Parliament, and until so determined to such allowances and rights as are mentioned below—

(*i*) Every Judge is entitled to receive such reasonable allowances to reimburse him for expenses incurred in travelling on duty within the territory of India and is also entitled to such reasonable facilities in connection with travelling as the President may from time to time prescribe.

The rights in respect of leave of absence (including less allowances) and pension of the Judges of the High Court any

State shall be governed by the provisions which immediatley before the commencement of the Constitution was applicable to the Judges of the High Court in the, corresponding Province.

Neither the allowances of a Judge nor his rights in respect of leave of absence or pension, shall be varied to his disadvantage after his appointment. —Art. 221 (2) and Schedule II, Part

Note :—For the meaning of the expressions *"actual service "Chief Justice" "Judge"*, please see under definitions in the Chapter "SERVICES"

Chief Justice includes acting Chief Justice.

(*b*) *In respect of Part 'B' States—*

(1) The Judges of each High Court of a Part B State and entitled to such salaries as may be determined by the President in consultation with the Rajpramukh.

(2) Every Judge shall be entitled to such allowances as to such rights in respect of leave of absence and pension as may from time to time be determined by or under law made by Parliament and until so determined, to such allowances and rights as may be determined by President after consultation with the Rajpramukh.

Neither the allowances of a Judge nor his rights in respect of leave of absence or pension shall be varied to his disadvantage after his appointment, Art. 23

Salaries and allowances of a Judge on his transfer from one High Court to another —

When a Judge is transferred from one High Court to any other High Court in India, he shall, during the period serves as a Judge of the other Court, be entitled to receive addition to his salary such compensatory allowance as may be determined by Parliament by law and until so determined such compensatory allowance as the President may by order for. Art. 222.

Allowances of Retired Judges acting as Judges of a High Court

Every retired Judge while sitting and acting as a Judge of a High Court shall be entitled to such allowances as The President may by order determine and have all the jurisdiction, answer and privileges of, but shall not otherwise be deemed to be a Judge of that High Court. Art. 224

12. RAJPRAMUKH

Conditions of Rajpramukh's office.

(1) The Rajpramukh shall not be a member of either House of Parliament or of a House of the State Legislature.

(2) The Rajpramukh shall not hold any other office of profit.

(3) The Rajpramukh shall, unless he has his own residence the principal seat of Government of the State, be entitled without payment of rent to the use of an official residence and shall be also entitled to such allowances and privileges as the President may, by general or special order determine.

(4) The allowances of the Rajpramukh shall not admonished during his term of office. Art. 238 (4) read with Art. 158

13. DISTRICT JUDGES.

Appointment—Appointment of persons to be, and the posting and promotion of, district judges in any State shall be made by the Governor or Rajpramukh of the State in consultation with the High Court exercising jurisdiction in relation to such State. Art. 233 (1).

Notifications—A person not already in the service of the Union or of the State shall only be eligible to be appointed a district judge if he has been for not less than 7 years an advocate or a pleader and is recommended by the High Court for appointment. Art. 233 (2).

Note :—For the definition of the expression *"District Judge"* please see Definitions in this chapter.

Appointments of Staff

Union

(I) Secretariat of Parliament

Art. 98 of the Constitution provides for the establishment of a separate secretarial staff in respect of each House of Parliament with power to create posts common to both Houses of Parliament.

The recruitment and the conditions of service of persons appointed to the secretarial staff of either House of Parliament will be regulated by law made by Parliament and until provision in that behalf is so made, by rules made by the President after consultation with the Speaker of the House of the People or the Chairman of the Council of States as the case may be. Such rules shall have effect subject to the provisions of any law so made.

(2) Officers and Servants of the Supreme Court.

Art. 146 provides that the *appointment* of officers and servants of the Supreme Court shall be made by the chief Justice of India or such other Judge or officer of the Court as he may direct. The President may by rule, however require that in such cases as may be specified in the rule, no person not already attached to the Court shall be appointed to any office connected with the Court except after consultation with the Union Public Service Commission.

Subject to the provisions of any law made by Parliament, the *conditions of service* of officers and servants of the Supreme Court shall be such as may be prescribed by rules made by the Chief Justice of India or by some other Judge or officer of the Court authorised by the Chief Justice of India to make rules for the purpose. The rules so made shall so far as they relate to salaries, allowances, leaves or pensions require the approval of the President.

The administrative expenses of the Supreme Court including all salaries, allowances and pensions payable to or in respect of the officers and servants of the Court shall be charged on the Consolidated Fund of India.

(3) Persons serving in the Indian Audit and Accounts Department

Conditions of service—Subject to the provisions of the Constitution and of any law made by Parliament, the conditions of service of persons serving in the Indian Audit and Accounts Department shall be such as may be prescribed by rules made by the President after consultation with the Comptroller and Auditor-General.

The salaries, allowances and pensions payable to or in respect of the persons serving in the office of the Comptroller and Auditor-General of India shall be charged upon the Consolidated Fund of India. Art. 148 (5) and (6)

(*b*) *States.*

(4) Secretariat of the State Legislature

Art 187 of the Constitution provides for a separate secretarial staff in respect of the House or each House of the Legislature of a State with power to create posts common to both the Houses.

The recruitment and conditions of persons appointed to such secretarial staff may be regulated by law made by the Legislature of a State and until provision is so made in that respect, by rules made by the Governor or Rajpramukh after consultation with the Speaker of the Legislative Assembly or the Chairman of the Legislative Council as the case may be. Such rules shall be subject to the provisions of any law so made.

(5) Officers & Servants of High Courts

Appointments of officers and servants of a High Court shall be made by the Chief Justice of the Court or any other Judge or officer of the Court as he may direct. The Governor or Rajpramukh of the State in which the High Court has its principal seat may, however, by rule require that such appointments to any office connected with the Court in specified cases to be made only after consultation with the State Public Service Commission.

Art. 229 (I)

Conditions of service—Subject to the provisions of any law made by the State Legislature, the conditions of service of officers and servants of a High Court shall be prescribed, by rules, made by the Chief Justice of the Court or by some other Judge or officer of the Court authorised by the Chief Justice to make rules for the purpose. The rules so far as they relate to salaries, allowances, leave or pensions shall, however, require the approval of the Governor or Rajpramukh.

The administrative expenses of a High Court including all salaries, allowances and pensions payable to or. in respect of the officers and servants of the Court shall be charged upon the Consolidated Fund of the State. Art. 229 (2)

(6) Application of Constitutional provisions and rules made thereunder in respect of persons belonging to Judicial Service to certain class of Magistrates

The provisions made in the Constitution in respect of perons appointed to the judicial service of the State and the rules respecting thereto can be made applicable to certain class or classes of magistrates by the Governor or Rajpramukh by public notification. Art. 237

(7) Provisions as to the Administration and Control of Scheduled Areas and Scheduled Tribes

(1) The Governor or Rajpramukh may make rules prescribing or regulating the number of members of the Tribes Advisory Council, the mode of their appointment, and the appointment of the Chairman of the Council and of the officers and servants thereof, and all other incidental matters.

Art. 244 (i) and Schedule 8, para. 4 (3)

(8) Provisions as to the Administration of Tribal Areas in Assam.

(1) The Governor shall by rule provide for the term of office of members and the appointment of officers and staff for the first constitution of District Councils and Regional Councils and after first constitution, such rule-making power will devolve on the Councils themselves.

Art. 244 (2) and Schedule VI, Para 2 (6) & (7)

(2) Para. 14 of the Sixth Schedule to the Constitution empowers the Governor of Assam to appoint a Commission to enquire into and report on the administration of autonomous districts and regions.

C. Appointments of Commissions, Councils, Committees, Authorities etc. under the Constitution.

The Constitution provides for the appointment of various Commissions, Councils, Committees, Authorities etc. to discharge certain functions and carrying out certain purposes mentioned therein. The details of such commissions etc. are given below:—

(1) *Finance Commission*

(2) *Public Service Commissions for the Union and for the States.* These have been dealt with under separate Chapters.

(3) *Election Commission* —

The superintendence, direction and control of election is to be vested in a commission known as Election Commission.

Art. 324 (1)

Election Commission consists of Chief Election Comnmissioner and such number of other Commissioners as may be fixed by the President.

The *appointment* of the Chief Election Commissioner and other Election Commissioners shall subject to the provisions of any law of Parliament, be made by the President. Art. 324 (2)

When any other Election Commissioner is appointed, the Chief Election Commissioner shall act as the Chairman of the Election Commission. Art. 324(3)

Conditions of service and tenure of office—The conditions of service and tenure of office of the Election Commissioners and Regional Commissioners shall be such as the President may by rule, determine.

The Chief Election Commissioner shall not be removed from his office except in like manner and on like grounds as a Judge of the Supreme Court and the conditions of service of the Chief Election Commissioner shall not be varied to his disadvantage after his appointment.

Any other Election Commissioner or a Regional Commissioner shall not be removed from office except on the recommendation of the Chief Election Commissioner. Art. 324 (5)

Staff—Necessary staff for the Election Commission or Regional Commissioner shall be made available by the President, Governor or Rajpramukh when so requested. Art. 324 (6)

(4) *Commission to report on the administration of the Scheduled Areas and the Welfare of the Scheduled Tribes in Parts A & B States*—

The appointment of such a commission at the expiration of 10 years from the commencement of the Constitution is obligatory. The President has also the power to appoint the Commission any time before this period. Art. 339 (1)

(5) *Commission to investigate the conditions of backward classes.* Art. 340

(6) *Commission of Parliament on official language.* Art. 344 (1)

(7) *Committee of Parliament on official language.* Art. 344 (4)

(8) *Inter-State Council*—In order to facilitate co-ordination between States, the Constitution provides for the establishment of an Inter-State Council charged with the duty of—

(*a*) enquiring into and advising upon disputes between States;

(*b*) investigating and discussing subjects in which some or all of the States or the Union and one or more of the States have a common interest;

or

(*c*) making recommendations, upon any such subject and in particular, recommendations for the better co-ordination of policy and action with respect to that subject.

The President may, by order, establish such a Council at any time, if it appears to him in the public interest, defining its nature of duties, organisation and procedure. — Art. 263.

(9) *Authority for carrying out the purposes of Art. 301 to 304 viz. "Freedom of trade, commerce and intercourse and restrictions thereon"* — Art. 307

(10) *Special officer for Scheduled Castes and Scheduled Tribes.* — Art. 338

PENALITY, VALUATION, PRESENTS, GRANTS, FEES ETC.

A. Penalty prescribed in the Constitution.

A sum of rupees five hundred has been prescribed in Arts. 104 and 193 as penalty to be recovered as a debt due to the Union State in respect of each day, when a person sits or votes as a member of either House of Parliament or State Legislature before making oath or affirmation or when not qualified or when disqualified or when prohibited by any law from so doing.

B. Valuation to determine appellate jurisdiction of the Supreme Court.

If the valuation of a civil suit is not less than Rs. 20,000 or such other sum as may be specified by Parliament by law, an appeal lies to the Supreme Court.

C. Present, emolument or office from or under Foreign State.

Art. 18 (4) of the Constitution provides that no person holding any office of profit or trust under *the State* shall, without the consent of the President, accept any present, emolument or office of any kind from or under any foreign State.

Note —Unless the context otherwise requires, *"the State"* includes the Government and Parliament of India and the Government and the Legislature of each of the States and all local or other authorities within the territory of India and under the control of the Government of India.

D. Maximum Limit of Taxes on Professions, Trades, Callings and Employments.

Under Art. 276 (2), the maximum amount payable in respect

of any one person to the State or to any one municipality, district board, local board or other local authority in the State by way of taxes on professions, trades, callings and employments is Rs. 250/- per annum. The amount in force immediately preceding the commencement of the Constitution is, however, to continue until altered.

E. Provision for Educational Grants for the benefit of Anglo-Indian Community.

Educational institutions in which at least 40% of the annual admissions are made available to non-Anglo-Indian communities are entitled, under the provisions of Art. 337, to receive grants as follows:—

(*a*) During first three financial years from the commencement of the Constitution.	— Same as were made in year 1947-48.
(*b*) During every succeeding period of three years.	— 10% less than the grants made for the immediatley preceding period of 3 years.
(*c*) At the end of 10 years	—Such grants shall cease.

F. Legislation relating to Fees

An extract of items relating to Fees from the three Legislative Lists *viz,* Union, State and Concurrent, is given below. While the Parliament and State Legislatures have exclusive powers of legislation in respect of items enumerated in the Union and State List respectively, the items in the Concurrent List are shared by both of them, for the purposes of Legislation. *Extracts*

Union List	**State List**	**Concurrent List**
1	**2**	**3**
Entry 76. Fees taken in Supreme Court.	Entry 3. Fees taken in all courts except the Supreme Court.	
Entry 96. Fees taken	**Entry 66.** Fees in	**Entry 47.** Fees in

1	2	3
in respect of any of the matters in the Union List but not including fees taken in any Court.	respect of any of the matters in the State List but not including fees taken in any Court.	respect of any of the matters in the Concurrent List but not including fees taken in any Court.

G. Fees to be allowed to the Sheriff and Clerks etc. of a Court

The High Court has the power to settle the tables of fees with the approval of the Governor or Rajpramukh to be allowed to the sheriff and all clerks and officers of the Courts in relation to which it exercises jurisdiction and to attorneys, advocates and pleaders practising therein. Art. 227 (3).

20

ADMINISTRATIVE EVOLUTION IN KARNATAKA

Anyone who takes up the study of the administration system of Karnataka must at the outset understand the guiding principles of administration which were firmly believed in and adhered to almost all over India. Administration, like all other activities of group effort, was based on Dharma, a concept which has not been properly understood by many thinkers. It is not necessary to explain the full connotation of that word here. Suffice to say that according to that guiding principle, rulers, though vested with absolute powers over their subjects, had to conform to certain definite lines of conduct and policy in administration, the moral consequences of the their violation being a matter which they feared. Thus, moral values prescribed the lines of policy and conduct in ruling the country; the king might be regarded as having the sanctity of God, but that sanctity disappeared as soon as he failed to conform to the ideal of his kingly duties. A Kannda classic says, "Jagadolagarasingam prajeye daivam". Its implication is that the king should think of his subjects as his God and devote himself to the promoting of their safety and welfare. Thus tradition and scriptural authority prescribed reciprocal duties and obligations between the rulers and the ruled, and moral ideas guided those relationships. The aim of every Government, whether under a king or in a reapublic was punishment of the wicked and protection of the loyal, conforming to what Virgil prescribed as the duties of a king, "to spare those who were cast down and to subdue those who have set themselves up".

Buddhism and Jainism, with their insistence on kindness, non-violence and charity in human affairs, served to mitigate the severities in administration, and the happy touch of humanism which Asoka imparted to his rule spread into Karnataka also, since a large part of Karnataka was included in his empire. Because administration was carried on in conformity with time-honoured values and principles of social justice and welfare, whoever might have been the ruler or minister, one can find an unbroken continuity in administration, behind all the variety in form. It can safely be said that there was an evolution in administration in Karnataka.

During the rule of Asoka the northern parts of Karnataka were ruled by an Ayapute or prince of the royal family with the assistance of Dharmamatras in charge of religious and moral duties of citizens and Mahamatras in Charge of the different departments of governments. The emperor exercised vigilant supervision over the conduct of the local governor and ministers. When Karnataka came under the rule of the Sathavahanas in the first and second centuries of the Christian era, Rajjukas were appointed to conduct a thorough measurement of lands and to assess the revenue. The Kadambas and the Gangas, who next ruled over Karnataka in succession, divided the country into *Nadus*, each *nadu* being subdivided into groups of villages ostensibly to make the collection of revenue easy. There was a marked decentralisation, since the Mahajanas who were in charge of village administration looked after the affairs of the villages in their charge without any interference from the provincial or imperial officers, except for an over-all supervision. This decentralisation was more pronounced under the Cholas who ruled the southern parts of Karnataka. Under their rule there were district assemblies and village assemblies, and committees whose members were required to be men of learning and property, carried on the administration including justice.

During the time of the Rashtrakutas and later Chalakyas in the eleventh and twelfth centuries, there was a further development in the system of administration. It was in this period that the kings turned their eyes north ward and sought to establish their superiority over the other kings of India by undertaking *digvijayas*. Dhruva and Govinda III of the Rashtrakuta dynasty, and Someswara Ahavamalla and Vikramaditya among the Chalukyas of Kalyani, led repeated expeditions into north India. On account of their continued absence from the capital they had to delegate a large part of their authority to their chief ministers or Mahamathyas, and to their viceroys, most of whom were princes of royal blood, in the outlying provinces. The ministers came to be called Karunas; under these Karunas were Nalgavundas in charge of large divisions, while Urgavundas administered the smaller units. These local officers were vested with considerable powers, since they had to be responsible for the maintenance of law and order, and were required to supply troops in times of emergency. The Karunas of the Chalukyan period came to be called Karanams under the Kalachuryas and Hoysalas. It was imperative for the Governors to tour all over the province and maintain a strict supervision over their offices.

The Hoysalas continued the system of administration which had been built up under the earlier dynasties, but the nature and objects of administrative authority came to be more clearly defined. It was the duty of the king to rule the country according to the time-honoured principles of Dharma and his success was measured by the welfare of his people. He had to follow traditional laws of the state, and the Panchapradhans or the council of ministers who assisted him was an effective check on his arbitrary powers. There was also the fear of opposition from the provincial governors or Samantas who enjoyed autonomous powers. An important feature of the administration which prevented the growth of fissiparous tendencies was the conception of the state as a secular body and the absence of religious intolerance; indeed, a study of the administrative system under the different dynasties of Karnataka reveals the refreshing fact that the rulers never tried to make their country a theocratic state.

The existence of checks and balances, preventing the king from usurping absolute powers, was thus a characteristic feature of Hoysala administration. And another feature, equally remarkable, needs mention. The control and management of the finances and the treasure were vested in two ministers of the council of Panchapradhans, the Hiriya Bhandari and Srikarana

Sarvadhikari. While the Hiriya Bhandari controlled the revenue collections and all treasures, the Srikarna Sarvadhikari was in charge of all accounts of income and expenditure. Such a clear demarcation helped to prevent misuse of funds and led to a healthy growth of integrity in financial administration. This excellent system prevailed in the government of the provinces also. The political achievements and administrative traditions of Karnataka are noteworthy. From the begining of the Christian era Karnataka produced mighty rules and statesmen. Distinguished administrators like Pulikeshi II of Badami, Krishna Devaraya of Vijayanagar, Sivappa Naik of Keladi, Hyder Ali of Mysore are Karnataka's gifts to India. These and many other rulers and statesmen fostered high administrative traditions. Pulikeshi who defeated Harshavardhana, bringing nearly two-thirds of the Indian continent under his empire, is ranked among the greatest administrators of India. His military genius capacity for organization, courage and administrative skill are remarkable and ought to serve as a source of inspiration to succeeding generations.

The administrative practices of Vijayanagar and Keladi rulers were based on the principles of Dharma and are reminiscent of the glory of Pulikesh's administration. Vijayanagar not only successfully defended freedom and culture against incursions from the North but also maintained administrative policies worthy to be emulated by any civilized people. The political ideals and administrative practices of Vijayanagar inspired Sivaji. Keladi rulers continued the high tradition of Vijayanagar and sought as promote the all-round progress of their subjects. Sivappa Naik of Keladi was a reputed and skilful administrative. He reformed the land revenue system and won universal admiration. He tried his best to achieve the welfare of his subjects. He respected all religions and languages. During his time trade contact between the West Coast and the Arabs increased. He expelled the Portuguese from Homvara and other places. He gave shelter to the Konkan speaking people who migrated from Goa into his territory. His political sagacity, broad outlook and benevolent rule are remembered even today.

One of the remarkable features of Karnataka is the notable role played by innumerable women in state affairs. As administrators they left a great legacy behind them. Gangambika of Vijayanagar accompanied her husband to the battle-field and composed a sanskrit work describing the millitary exploits of her husband. She is regarded as the first historian of South India. Keladi Principality produced two queens; of these Rani Channamma ruled for 15 years. It is this queen that gave shelter to Rajaram and successfully fought the forces of Aurangzeb. Her words of advice to her adopted son illustrate her qualities of statesmanship "......Always fulfil your promises. Do not disclose your mind to others. Abandon the unworthy path and engage in noble deeds. Be kind to all and protect those who seek protection. Exercise self-restraint". Karnataka can boast of many patriotic and spirited queens and gallant women. Idawadi Mallamma's stiff fight evoked the admiration of Sivaji himself. The name of Kittur Rani has become a source of inspiration to all. She was the first Indian woman warrior to fight the British. Her just and impartial rule evoked the spontaneous affection of her subjects for her.

The people of Karnataka were virtuous, brave and honest Administration in the past became an easy job in Karnataka because of the honesty of the people. Describing the qualities of the people the Chinesse pilgrim Hieun Tsang who sojourned in India from A.D. 629 to 645 as observed follows: "....... .The natives are tall, and lengthy and superstitious in character; whoever does them a service may count on their gratitude but he that offends them will not escape their revenge". Speaking of the people of the mountainous parts of Karnataka Stokes wrote in 1838 "I have nowhere in India seen so much honest and veracity as among the country people of Nagara, and their superiority in this respect greatly facilitated successive police and judicial investigations".

The above account, however sketchy, will give some idea about the glorious heritage of Karnataka. The ruler of Mysore like many other kings of Karnataka contributed to this administrative heritage. Chikkadevaraja Wodiar and Hyder Ali were Mysore's outstanding administration. Hyder built a vast empire by virtue of his superior diplomacy and statesmanship. His was the first concerned example of national exertion against the British. His catholicity of outlook, organising ability, political shrewdness and discretion made him the foremost statesman of the time in India. No contemporary Indian excepting Phadnavis can be compared with Hyder Ali in respect of vision, decision-making and action-mindedness. Hyder Ali was magnanimous and polite, and he protected his subjects without discrimination. This was the reason why he was popular among all sections of people. Before he advised Tippoo Sultan in these words. "My son leave you an Empire which I have not received from my ancestors.......... I do not leave you any enemies among my subjects".

IMPACT OF THE WEST

Tippu Sultan was no doubt courageous but he could succeed in fulfilling his father's last wishes. He fell fighting in the battlefield, desperately trying to stem the advance of the British army into his capital. His territories were divided among those who helped in the conquest of Mysore. The territory south of the Tungabhadra river was parcelled out to the Mysore king who was expected to be a puppet in their hands. The rest of the territory north of this was handed over to their allies.

As in other parts of India the government in ancient Karnataka was monarchical in character, but the monarchs did not conduct themselves as arbitrary rulers. They were deeply conscious of their duties towards their subjects. The motto behind their administration was justice. This outlook of the Karnataka governments is reflected in the passages taken from the Badami inscription of 7th century AD. "Friendly to the good, gentle to the gentle, formidable to the enemy, to the inflictors of cruelty the very embodiment of cruelty; indeed he was God". These political ideas of Chalukyas guided the political conduct of Karnataka rulers down the ages. The administrative machinery was inspired and guided by a sense of duty and devotion to work.

The following passage by Someswar, a famous Kannada poet of 4th century, clearly brings out the administrative ideas of the Kannada people. "The king, who neglecting his legitimate duty towards the land and people, spends his time in a life of dissipation and pleasure is comparable to an intoxicated bison" (One of the ferocious forest of the Karnatak jungle). An ideal minister, according to the poet, must be serious, generous, courageous and truthful. An Officer who enriches himself with malpractices without regard to the welfare of the people is compared to a bandicoot. The conception of good government is indicated in the poetic utterances of a celebrated Kannada poet. In an ideal state people are blessed with noble ministers. People attain material prosperity; the country is secure; the treasury is full and there is universal abundance. Such lofty principles and high ideals guided the people and rulers of the Kannada country. Although the administration in Karnataka was carried on under the guidance to benevolent monarchs, village autonomy and corporate life were the common features of the various administration of the Karnatak country. Karnatak witnessed the rise of many big empires. But small autonomus kingdoms were the real strength behind the mighty empires, and they managed the affairs of their principalities on efficient lines. The administration in the small kingdoms was characterised by religious tolerance, harmony, justice and welfare activities.

With the advent of the British and the conquest of the North Karnatak country, excepting for a few small states, the so-called "Southern Maratha" country became British territory. In 1818 after the annexation of the Peshwa territory a Madras civil servant by name Chaplin was appointed the principal collector of the "Maratha country", south of the Krishna. The intention of the British government at the time was that the newly conquered country south of river Krishna should eventually form part of the Madras presidency. But it was finally decided by the Court of Directors that it should be part of Bombay Presidency. With the defeat of the Peshwa in 1818, the British, ignoring the erstwhile alliance and forgetting past pledges, engaged themselves unscrupulously in consolidating their territory. The policy of non-interference was abandoned, and a new policy of ruthless annexation was followed. They reduced many parts of Karnatak to servility. They partitioned the country into political divisions in order to rule the country in peace. As a result of their cruel conquest people became demoralised. The British suppressed many risings in Karnataka and consolidated their administration.

In spite of their shady activities in the early days, British administrators in the post-1857 period inaugurated many ameliorative measures. They established administrative departments, opened schools etc. with the result that the British impact on India became formidable. More than 80% of the present day administrative structure in India is the creation of the British. India and Karnatak was an exception to this rule. A short survey of the administrative history of Karnatak during the British period will demostrate the above point.

The people of Karnatak not only came under the British influence but also under the influence of Tamils in the South and Maharastrians in the North. Many Tamalians Telugus flocked to Bangalore and other places in search of employment and settled down. Similarly many Marathi speaking families which served the British administration settled down in cities and towns of north Karnatka. The natives of Karnatak being self-contented people and also being blessed with fertile lands did not go in search of jobs and did not come forward to join government service.

This partly accounts for their inadequate representation in government service in the initial stages. Moreover for educationally forward Marathis in Karnatak did no view with favour the entry of the Kannada people into educational institutions and government service. The Kannadigas were not very enterprising and united, and therefore they remained a minority in administration. But with the expansion of educational opportunities and their entry into government service, administration gradually came into the hands of Kannadigas.

The history of Modern Mysore may be divided into three periods; namely (i) 1799-1831, (2) 1831-1881, (3) 1881-1956. Between 1799 and 1810 Dewan Poorniah tried his best to restore law and order. But after him Regency administration became corrupt and officials began to harass the people. The farmers of Malnad raised a revolt against the corrupt and unscrupulous officials. The British had to interfere and quel the popular revolts. A committee was appointed to enquire into the causes of the insurrection. The British took over the administration of Mysore. Ever since the annexation of Bidnur by Hyder the territory was neglected by the government. Moreover those that were in charge of administration were not familiar with the problems of Malnad. As Stokes observed in 1834 "by 1830 the condition of the Nagara province had been reduced to a melancholy who contrast of the former prosperity". The farmers who had been oppressed by the unscrupulous and corrupt officers had no other alternative except revolting against the authorities. This period, when Mysore was under the British Commission, (1831—1881) must be regarded as a formative one. It was during this period the foundations of modern Mysore were truely laid. New Departments such as the P. W. D. were started. Extensive surveys were undertaken. If one reads the Report of Stokes on Nagaro Division one cannot but admire the work done by the Commissioners for Mysore. Mysore was handed over again to the Mysore ruler in 1881. This Rendition marked the beginning of the welfare administration in Mysore. Mysore under the inspiring guidance of benevolent kings and the personal supervision of able Dewans achieved rapid development. The late Shri Krishnaraja Wodeyer IV was a noble monarch under whose reign (1901-1940) Mysore achieved all-round progress. His love for his subjects and devotion to public welfare provided an impetus to officials. Mysore was served by a hand of able Dewans from the beginning. Of these special mention should be made of C. Rangacharlu, K. Seshadri lyer, Sir M. Visweswariah, and Sir Mirza Ismail. These are the makers of modern Mysore. Seshadri lyer innagurated the Hydro-electric scheme. Sir M. Visweswaryya modernised Mysore through his planned activities. He founded the University of Mysore, started several industries. He laid the foundation of industrial Mysore. Sir Mirza Ismail continued the work of his predecessors. He strove to make Mysore a progressive State.

Mysore witnessed many political changes during the region of Shri Jaya Chamaraja Wodeyer who succeeded Uncle Shri Krishnaraja Wodeyer in 1940. It was during his time that Mysore attained democratic government and acceded to the Indian Union.

Another event of historic importance during his reign was the reorganisation of the Kannada-speaking areas under one administration. On November 1, 1956, the new Mysore State was born. Most of the Kannada areas were reconstituted into one State. Whether other areas merged with Mysore or Mysore merged with other areas the result was the same, namely integration of Karnataka territories. Although the new State was reorganised on linguistic basis such factors as administrative convenience, geographical compulsions etc. also influenced the re-organisation of the State. Karnatak has always given shelter to many outside religions and liuguistic groups, who have settled down on Karnatak soil. The spirit of tolerance shown by Kannada people deserves to be emulated by others.

— G.S. Halappa

INDEX

❑❑❑

ENCYCLOPAEDIA OF
ADMINISTRATIVE LAW

ENCYCLOPAEDIA OF ADMINISTRATIVE LAW

Vol. 5

American Administrative Law

Edited by

S.R. Sharma

ANMOL PUBLICATIONS PVT. LTD.

NEW DELHI - 110 002 (INDIA)

ANMOL PUBLICATIONS PVT. LTD.
4374/4B, Ansari Road, Daryaganj
New Delhi - 110 002
Ph.: 23261597, 23278000
Visit us at: www.anmolpublications.com

Encyclopaedia of Administrative Law

First Edition, 2003

ISBN 81-261-1478-9 (Set)

PRINTED IN INDIA

Published by J.L. Kumar for Anmol Publications Pvt. Ltd., New Delhi - 110 002 and Printed at Mehra Offset Press, Delhi.

Contents

Preface

In the modern political era administrative law has taken on a preeminent role in regulating relations between the machinery of government and the individual citizen. At its core is the control of power specifically the review by the judiciary of the way in which executive power has been used. Consequently the subject embraces a huge range of issues, some of them highly politicized. In recent years these have included the legality of a ban on blood sports, whether the courts can order a minister to suspend the operation of a primary Act of Parliament, whether a minister can ban certain types of interview from being broadcast, the powers of local authorities to spend public money, or to refuse to do so, the scope of the discretion vested in the police officers to determine policing policy, the scope of the powers vested in the Home Secretary regarding parole for prisoners convicted of murder, whether the courts could declare invalid an exercise of prerogative power, and the availability of damages in respect of unlawful action by public bodies. It will be seen that it is largely the product of judicial activity, although its existence is increasingly recognised in statutory provisions.

The growth in administrative law has to a large extent mirrored the increase in the level of state involvement in many aspects of every day life during the twentieth century, generating the need for a coherent and effective body of rules to govern relations between individuals and the state. Students of constitutional law will readily recognise that administrative law is in reality an out growth of the doctrine of the separation of powers. It is evidence of the judiciary acting as a check on the powers of the executive, and perhaps even the legislature, in some respects. It should not be assumed, however, that any such coherent and effective body of rules actually exists yet. Administrative law is a constantly evolving subject.

In view of the above consideration in mind about the administrative law, that a comprehensive encyclopaedia has been prepared which focuses on the comparative dimensions of administrative law.

The editor is extremely grateful to the British Council Library in New Delhi, the American Information Centre, New Delhi, and the Central Secretariat Library, New Delhi for their valuable assistance in preparing the encyclopaedia. The editor is equally beholden to Shri J.L. Kumar, Managing Director, Anmol Publications Pvt. Ltd., New Delhi for publishing the encyclopaedia in a very short time.

—Dr. S.R. Sharma

I

Administrative Law in the United States of America

Aside from the intrinsic importance of the inquiry, an examination of the juristic nature of the American Federal Union is of value to the analytical jurist because of the excellent opportunity it offers him to apply and test the value of the abstract doctrines he has deductively obtained.

The States' Rights Theory. In the controversies, which have been waged as to the nature of the American Union, the so-called States Rights School advanced a single and logical theory. According to this theory the constitution was declared to have been a compact to which the original States, acting as severally sovereign political bodies, were the contracting parties, and that it was not intended by these States, by the agreement into which they entered, to create a political entity that would be legally superior to themselves, and, therefore, in derogation of their own several sovereignties. Starting from this premise, this school deduced from it the essentially confederate nature of the Union and the denial that secession from it by any State at any time would be an illegal act.

This juristic interpretation of the nature of the union entered into in 1789 was explicitly put forth as early as 1798 in the "Resolutions" of the legislature of the State of Kentucky which asserted : "That the several States comprising the United States of America are not united on the principles of unlimited submission to their General Government for special purposes. That to this compact each State acceded as a State and as an integral party, its co-States forming, as to itself, the other party." In the Resolutions adopted by the Virginia legislature the same year it was declared : "That this Assembly doth explicitly and peremptorily declare that it views the powers of the Federal Government as resulting from the compact to which the States arc partics."

This doctrine was still more explicitly stated in 1803 by the first commentator upon the new Constitution, St. George Tucker.[1] He said : "The Constitution of the United States in an original, written, federal and social compact, freely, voluntarily and solemnly entered in by the several States and ratified by the people thereof respectively. It is a federal compact; several sovereign and independent States may unite themselves together by a perpetual confederacy, without each ceasing to be a perfect State. The Union is, in fact, as well as in theory, an association of States, or a Confederacy."

In another place he said : "The Federal Government, then appears to be the organ through which the United Republics communicate with foreign nations, and with each other. Their submission to its operation is voluntary; its councils, its engagements, its authority, are theirs, modified and united. Its sovereignty is an emanation from theirs, not a flame in which they have been consumed, nor a vortex in which they are swallowed up. Each is still a perfect State, still sovereign, still independent, and still capable, should the occasion require, of assuming the exercise of its functions, as such, to the most unlimited extent."

Calhoun. States' Rights assertions of a similar tenor continued from time to time to be made but the theory did not receive its final elaboration until John C. Calhoun took up the argument in behalf of the State of South Carolina in the controversy which had arisen between that State and the Federal Government with reference to a protective federal tariff.

Nationalistic Theories. Those who have asserted the legal supremacy of the United States as a single sovereign State have advanced a number of theories, not always concordant with one another, and have put forward varying interpretations of the circumstances attending the historical birth of the Union. The Chief of these theories and statements of alleged fact will be discussed.

The Constituent States Sovereign in 1789. By some it was declared that the original thirteen States never were severally sovereign bodies-politic, and that therefore the General Government, created in 1789, could not have been the product of their compacting sovereign wills. This statement of fact, it is now generally agreed, cannot be substantiated. There has, of course, been no difficulty on the part of those who have asserted the theory in showing that the independence of the original

States from the dominion of Great Britain was, and could have been, obtained only by co-operative and associated action, but there is practically no evidence to show that a single sovereignty was created or intended to be created. The most that can be claimed is that common governmental agencies were established for the convenient and effective execution of the several but identical aims of the original thirteen bodies-politic which had been brought into being when the single legal bond which had previously united them (common subordination to British dominion) was removed. Furthermore, all jurists are agreed that, whatever may have been the legal situation prior to 1781, the Articles of Confederation, which were adopted in 1781 and which remained in force until replaced by the present constitution of the United States made provision for a Confederacy and not a sovereign federally organized State. In other words, that the thirteen States were then severally sovereign.[2]

Their Sovereignty Not Usurped. Some writers have attempted to overcome this conclusion as to the sovereignty of the individual States during the years immediately prior to the adoption of the present Constitution, by asserting that, during those years, the States had "usurped" the attributes of sovereignty that rightfully belonged to that single national sovereignty which, they have declared, came into existence as a result of the American Revolution. Thus, Pomeroy, in his treatise on "*United States Constitutional Law,*" declare: "However much the States may have exercised usurped attributes of sovereignty during the unhappy Confederation; however much the conception of one people acting as a unit may have been forgotten or abandoned amid the jealousies and destructive rivalries of the commonwealths claiming substantial independence, the people had now [with the adoption of the Constitution in 1789] arisen, reasserted the original idea, repudiated the assumption of local supremacy, and uttered their organic will in terms which we hope will have a meaning and power to the end of time." Van Holst, speaking of the establishment of the Confederation under the Articles, says that the Continental Congress "exhorted the legislatures, by an act of public usurpation against the legal consequences of historical facts, to transform the Union into a league of States, and the legislatures recklessly responded to this demand."[3]

Little argument is required to show the futility of such as attempt as is indicated in these quotations to escape from the juristic consequences of the facts which their authors were constrained to admit. Whatever may have been the wisdom or propriety of entering into an association under which the States were to be severally sovereign, and whatever effect this may have had upon a previously existing national sovereignty—granting, *arguendo*, that such a sovereignty had come into being—the juristic fact that the States were severally sovereign in 1789 at the time the new Union was entered into would not be disturbed.

Views of Burgess Examined. Most unsatisfactory is the reasoning of Burgess. In his *Political Science and Comparative Constitutional Law*, published in 1891, he asserts that a true National State was created at the time of the establishment of the first Continental Congress in 1774, that is, even before the colonies had declared their intention to obtain legal separation from Great Britain. "From the first moment of its existence," he declares, "there was something more upon this side of the Atlantic than thirteen local governments. There was a sovereignty, a State, not in idea simple, or upon paper, but in fact and organization." "The first paper constitution enacted by the American State," he continues, "was that of November, 1777, called the 'Articles of Confederation'. The one fatal and disastrous defect of this organization was that it provided no continuing organization of the State. It created only a central government, and that, too, of the weakest character. When, therefore, the continental Congress, the revolutionary organization of the American State and its revolutionary central government gave way, in March of 1781, to the central government created by this constitution, the American State ceased to exist in objective organization. It returned to its subjective condition merely, as 'idea in the consciousness of the people'. From the standpoint of political science, what existed now, as objective institutions, was a central government and thirteen local governments. From the standpoint of public law, on the other hand, what existed, as objective institutions was thirteen States, thirteen local governments, and one Central Government. This was a perfectly unbearable condition of things in theory, and was bound to become so in fact."[4]

The sense of the phrase "unbearable condition of things in theory," is difficult to discover. A given theory explaining a given institution may be valid or invalid according to whether or not its premises are correctly assumed and its deductions logical. But, as a theory, it is a mere matter of reasoning, and as such, how can it properly be spoken of as unbearable? The facts which lead to the theory may be unbearable, but not the theory which explain them. Probably, however, what Professor Burgess had in mind was that, viewed in the light of what we know generally regarding the requirements of political order and development, the condition of the

American States during the period when the Articles of Confederation were in force was bound to lead to unsatisfactory reason. Also the distinction which Professor Burgess makes in this connection between the viewpoint of public law and the viewpoint of political science is not clear. Apparently he holds that during these eight years there existed in theory no sovereign power whatever. If this be so, then, logically, he would have to hold that there existed neither laws nor governments, for, without a sovereign to declare and support them, there could have been no laws, without a State to recognize and endow them with power there could have been no governments having a legally valid claim to existence. If Professor Burgess had said that, during this period, there existed in the minds of the Americans a certain amount of national feeling and demand for national unity, and that thus was furnished the psychological and moral basis upon which a national State might be, and was to be, founded, he would have been correct. But the existence of this sentiment which had not yet to a realization of the desires which it prompted, even with the admitted necessity for a better form of union than that supplied by the Articles, cannot be said to have indicated the actual absence of sovereignty in both the Central Government and the individual States. For, if this be a valid conclusion, when is one safe in affirming, from the viewpoint of political science, the existence anywhere of sovereignty? In no State in the world are political conditions completely satisfactory, and, this being so, what definite criteria does Professor Burgess furnish for determining when political inefficiency is sufficient to warrant one in denying the existence of sovereignty over a given territory and people? Would he hold that at the present time there is not a State in Russia, or in the Chinese Republic, or in the considerable parts of Central and South America? If he would affirm this, then the ordinarily accepted definition of a State must be radically modified. Yet this relation of political efficiency to sovereignty Professor Burgess certainly holds, for he does not deny sovereignty to the thirteen States during the years from 1781 to 1789 because of the possession of sovereignty by the central power; instead, he declares that they were not States because the thirteen local units were not able to secure certain desirable results.

In truth it may be pointed out that Professor Burgess' assumption that there existed at this time a national State in a "subjective condition," as "idea in the consciousness of the people," may be denied. The allegation of the existence at a given time in the minds of a group of persons, now all dead, of a certain idea or sentiment is, of course, one incapable either of absolute proof or absolute disproof, but certainly there cannot, with confidence, be claimed to have existed in the minds of the Americans of the period a desire for national unity of a sufficient intensity to warrant one in declaring that there then existed, subjectively, a national sovereignty, when, in fact, during those years the several sovereignties of the thirteen States were recognized and obeyed by those very people without a single suggestion upon their part, so far as we now know, that the authorities thus recognized and obeyed were not entitled to their allegiance; and when, upon the contrary, it is known that it was only after strenuous exertions upon the part of their leaders that they were finally led to establish a central sovereignty which, more or less to their surprise, they were later to find resulted in the destruction of the sovereignties of the thirteen commonwealths.

It may be said, however, that Professor Burgess admits that, from the viewpoint of public law, there did then exit, as objective institutions, thirteen States as well as one central and thirteen local governments. But it would seem that he means that this was true only in a formal and not an essential sense,—only on paper and not in fact, for the real basis upon which the thirteen States founded their several sovereignties he declares to have been destroyed by the existence of this predicated national sovereignty, which, however, had not yet obtained for itself an organ through which it might be expressed and executed.

Turning to the question of the source whence the Constitution derived, and was at the time conceived by the American people to have derived, its force as fundamental law, Professor Burgess that the adoption of the Constitution was a purely national act. Furthermore, according to his view, the Constitution derived its validity, not, as its own terms assert, from the ratifications of the necessary number of the States conventions, but from the authority of the federal constitutional convention; in other words, that the Convention not only drafted the instrument, but breathed into it its legal life. He writes: "I have endeavored to show that the real organization of the United States as the sovereign, the State, in our present system, was in the constitutional convention. This, like the Continental Congress, was a single body, representing the whole people of the United States and passing its resolves by simple majority. The people of the United States were behind this body, and gave it the power to ignore practically the Confederate Congress and the legislatures of the commonwealths, and, while formally submitting its work to ratification by the immediate representatives of the people in that commonwealths, chosen by the people for that special purpose, to really ordain the Constitution."[5]

It is difficult to have patience with such a position, contradicted as it is by the very terms of the instrument itself, by the unambiguous acts of the convention, and unsupported by a single recorded expression of contemporaneous opinion.[6]

Theory That the Adoption of the Constitution Was a National Act. A second group of nationalistic publicists or politicians have said that, even if it be admitted that the States were severally sovereign prior to 1789, and that the Constitution then adopted was a product of their compacting wills, nevertheless, by that act, they created a truly sovereign national State to which they surrendered up their own several sovereignties. The juristic impossibility of such an act we have already seen, and, in fact, after the logic of Calhoun's reasoning had made this plain, the Nationalist School, in general, fell back upon a third theory, which was the one that Webster relied upon in his famous debates in the Senate. This theory was that, though the States existed in 1789 as thirteen severally sovereign bodies politic, and though the Constitution was formally ratified by conventions convened for that purpose in and by each of such States, the act of adopting the Constitution was, in essence, not the act of the several States but of the whole American people united into a single political body by that subjective feeling of, or desire for, political unity which is the ultimate factual foundation of every sovereign State. In other words, this theory asserted that, prior to 1789, a National State existed subjectively in the minds of thepeople, and wasw made objectively manifest by the creation of a National Government, and that the existing political machineries of the then thirteen States were used merely as convenient means for realizing this end. This view, it will be seen, admitted that the States were sovereign in 1789 and, therefore, by necessary implication, conceded that, as to them, the establishment of the new National State was an illegal or revolutionary act.

Regarding this theory the point especially to be observed is that it put the controversy upon a plane where absolute demonstration, either for or against, was rendered impossible. The allegation that, though the Constitution which had been drafted by the Convention of 1787 was ratified by conventions assembled in the several States, the peoples of those States believed themselves to be acting, and intended to act, as a single national body, is an assertion that can be proved or disproved only by determining the state of mind of the participants as evidenced in the historical records that have been preserved. Unfortunately, however, the statesmen of those times were neither skilled in juristic distinctions nor gifted with a foresight that would lead them to render perfectly explicit what they conceived to be the essential character of the constitutional transaction upon which they were engaged. Whatever the reasons may have been, the fact remains that neither the records of what was said at the time, nor the language of the Constitution itself, furnishes conclusive evidence as to what were the beliefs and intentions of the Statesmen of the time as to the juristic relation the newly established Union was to bear to the individual States.

Though, from the nature of the case, it is impossible to demonstrate the invalidity of this nationalistic interpretation of the nature of the constitutive act of 1789 is the conclusive manner in which an alleged mathematical or other purely logical proposition may be exposed, it may be pointed out that the burden of proof would seem to rest upon those who assert that he adoption of the Constitution, though in form that of thirteen bodies-politic was, in reality, that of a single national unit. There is, however, no record of a declaration, contemporaneously made, that the peoples of the thirteen States felt or believed that they were acting otherwise than as distinct bodies-politic. Upon the contrary, there were repeated contemporaneous statements of the view that the Constitution was a compact between the States. In fact, that instrument itself declares that its ratification by conventions of nine States would be sufficient for its establishment as "between the States so ratifying the same."[7] Furthermore, as has been already pointed out, this compact doctrine was explicitly asserted in 1798 and 1799 by the legislatures of the States of Virginia and Kentucky. It is true that the other States of the Union which replied to these Resolutions did not agree with the deductions which the Resolutions drew with regard to the action that the States of the Union might rightfully take with regard to national measures deemed by them unwarranted by the Constitution, but none of those replying States, with the possible exception of Vermont, expressed any dissent from the premise that the Union resulted from a compact between its constituent members.[8]

A National State Intended. Even if it be accepted that the preponderant historical evidence is in favor of the view that, in 1789, the American people believed that the new Constitution resulted from, and was, in essential character, a compact between the thirteen severally sovereign peoples of the original States, it does not follow that they believed that they were creating only a league or confederacy in which the States were to remain severally sovereign, and by which no national sovereignty was to be brought into being. Upon the contrary, there is considerable and perhaps preponderant historical evidence to show that the statesmen of that time intended to establish, and believed that they were establishing, not simply a central governmental organization that was to act as the common agent of the States for the attainment of certain common ends, but a true National State, withdrawal from which by a State would be an illegal act. To be sure, as is now generally agreed by jurists, these two views that the Union was a product of the compacting wills of severally sovereign States, and that a National State was thereby created, were logically inconsistent with each other, but this does not argue against the historical fact that both views were held.

Influence of the Social Compact Theory. It is well known that the political and juristic thought of that time was saturated with, largely dominated by, doctrines of natural rights, and by the theory that political authority is legitimized by mutual agreements between the governed, or between them and their rulers. If, then, it was generally held that a public will could be created by a union of private wills, and that public could be based upon a surrender of rights by individuals originally and severally sovereign, it was but natural and logically consistent that it should also have been believed that a national sovereignty could be created by a mutual agreement between a number of severally sovereign bodies-politic. The reasoning which supported the the one view would equally support other.

There were, this theory admitted, certain practical considerations which made those who favored the adoption of the Constitution provide that it should be ratified by conventions specially assembled in the several States, rather than by legislatures of those States, but it, was argued, the decisive reason why this mode of ratification was decided upon was because of the general conviction that though the existing governments of the States might be constitutionally competent to create a league or confederation of the respective States which they represented, only the citizen bodies of those States, acting in their original sovereign capacities could, as a matter of inherent political right, create a genuine National State; for, according to then prevailing political thought, this sovereignty, which the peoples of the States were conceived to possess as an original right, could be exercised by them only directly, or through conventions specially assembled for the express purpose.

In the Constitutional Convention of 1789 Madison said that "he considered the difference between a system founded on the legislature only, and one founded on the people, to be the true difference between a league or treaty, and a constitution". Rufus King declared that a proper ratification was the surest way of dispelling "all doubts and disputes concerning the legitimacy of the new Constitution".[9] As Chief Justice Marshall later said in his opinion in the case of *McCulloch* v. *Maryland*,[10] "To the formation of a league such as was the Confederacy, the State sovereignties were clearly competent. But when, in order to form a more perfect union "it was deemed necessary to change this alliance into an effective government, possessing great and sovereign powers and acting directly on the people, the necessity of referring it to the people, and of deriving its powers directly from them, was felt and acknowledged by all".

Secession. Whether or not the view was held at the time of the adoption of the Constitution that the States, having once entered the Union, would be legally able to escape from it by secession, will always remain a matter for discussion. It is, however, worthy of remark that there is no record that such a right was explicitly declared, although several of the States, in their resolutions of ratification, did assume a moral and revolutionary right upon their part to reassume the powers they were parting with should they be used by the National Government to injure or oppress the governed. Furthermore, there are recorded statements in which a legal right of secession upon the part of the States was expressed and explicitly denied. A conspicuous instance of this was in the reply which Madison made to the inquiry of Hamilton as to the propriety of giving to the States, for a limited time, the right to withdraw from the Union should certain suggested amendments to the Constitution as drafted by the Convention be not adopted. Madison said: "The Constitution requires an adoption *in toto* and for ever. It has been so adopted by the other States. An adoption for a limited time would be as ineffective as an adoption of some of the articles only; in short, any condition whatever must vitiate the ratification." This letter was read to the New York Convention prior to its ratification of the Constitution, and its contents were well known to the peoples of the other States who, so far as is known, did not deny the doctrine it declared.

A Divided Sovereignty Intended. One further fact regarding this theory as to the nature of the constitutive act of 1789 is to be observed. Though the people of that time almost indubitably intended to create, and believed that they were creating, a true National State, it is reasonably certain that they thought that they were establishing a political entity that would not possess supreme or sovereign authority over all possible matters of legal regulation. The doctrines that sovereignty necessarily denotes unlimited legal competence, and that it is a quality or power not susceptible of division, were not then held. Instead, there is abundant evidence that, influenced by the theories of Locke, the American people believed that individuals, when creating a State by their common agreement, might exempt certain interests from its sphere of legitimate legal control, with the result that the regulation of these interests were to be regarded as reserved to the individual citizens. Thus, when the thirteen States were conceived of as creating, by their joint agreement, a National State, it was but natural that they would deem it possible to exempt from national control the exercise of certain legal rights of regulation, and to reserve these powers to the compacting States or to their respective citizen`bodies. Thus, in the ninth and tenth Articles of Amendment to the Constitution which, at the time of the adoption it was understood would be added to that instrument, it was provided that the enumeration of certain rights in the Constitution was not to be construed to deny or disparage others retained by the people, and that "the powers not delegated to the United States by the Constitution, nor prohibited by it to the States, are reserved to the States respectively, or to the people". It was this reasoning which, as we shall presently see, made possible the holding of a theory of divided sovereignty which, after the adoption of the Constitution, played such a conspicuous and detrimental part in the constitutional history of the United States.

Space will not permit the presentation of all the historical evidence that might be advanced to show that the doctrines which have been described were the ones generally held by the statesmen of the period under discussion. A few illustrative examples may, however, be given.

Pelatish Webster, in his *Dissertation on the Political Union and Constitution of the United States*, published in 1783, and in which he urged the calling of a convention to frame a new Constitution, declared : "A number of sovereign States uniting into one Commonwealth and appointing a supreme power to manage the affairs of the Union, do necessarily and unavoidably part with and transfer to such supreme power so much of their own sovereignty as is necessary to render the ends of the Union effectual.... In like manner, every member of civil society parts with many of his natural rights that he may enjoy the rest in greater security under the protection of society."

James Wilson, in the Constitutional Convention, declared that "Federal Liberty is to the States what civil liberty is to private individuals; and States are not more unwilling to purchase it, by the necessary concession of their political sovereignty, than the savage is to purchase civil liberty by the surrender of the personal sovereignty which he enjoys in a state of nature."[11]

Washington, writing to the Congress of the Confederation, said: "It is...impracticable in the federal government of these States, to assure all its rights of independent sovereignty to each, and yet provide for the interest and safety of all. Individuals entering into society must give up a share of liberty to secure the rest."[12]

In the very ratification of the Constitution the compact theory was stated by some of the States. Thus Massachusetts, when giving her assent, spoke of the States as entering into an "explicit and solemn compact with each other," by assenting to and "ratifying the new Constitution". To the same effect spoke New Hampshire.

Conclusion. In result, then, it seems reasonably certain that, so far as the intentions and beliefs of those who framed and adopted the Constitution are concerned, the view was held that a true National State was created, but that it was to be sovereign only as to the powers expressly or by necessary implication granted to it. All other powers were deemed to be reserved by the States or by their peoples.[13]

Constitutional Fathers Left Indeterminate the Situs of Sovereignty. It is not reasonable to believe that it wholly escaped the thought of the constitutional fathers that, ultimately, there must be, in every civil society, some single final source of political authority. But it would appear that they deemed this logical necessity sufficiently satisfied by the premise that all right to exercise political authority is drawn from the consent of the governed and remains subject to their will. It further appears that they did not foresee the disputes that were later to arise as to whether this ultimate basis of right for the National States was to be found in the general will of the governed conceived of as a single national body, or as grouped into thirteen or more distinct bodies-politic. Thus both the Union and the State were regarded as agencies for the exercise of sovereignty rather than as possessors of sovereignty. Instead of giving a real answer to the question of the ultimate location of sovereignty in the United States, men of the time merely pushed the problem one step further back and left it still undetermined. Because they did not appreciate this, they did not take the care that they otherwise might have done so to do word the Constitution itself, or their acts of ratification of it, as to place beyond all possible controversy the constitutional status that the member States were to have in the Union, and the legal action that they might take in case they should deem that the National State was attempting to exercise powers not constitutionally vested in it.[14]

By adopting the explanation which has been given of the political doctrines and intentions of those who established the American Union in 1789, we seem to be put in the peculiar position of holding that the statesmen of that time intended to obtain, and thought that they were obtaining, a result which we now know to have been a logical impossibility, and which, in fact, as events soon showed, was one which it was in practice impossible to maintain. If, then, we are asked to decide, from the strictly juristic point of view, what was the character of the Union at the time it was entered into, we can only answer that it is impossible to say. This, however, is not a surprising confession, for, as we have earlier learned, the existence of sovereignty is a fact which, by its very nature, is one that cannot be determined by the historical processes that have brought a political organization into being. The existence of sovereignty, in other words, is a fact that is made manifest by the legal competence that is effectively asserted by a political organization, and especially, whether this is claimed as originating in itself and not by way of delegation from any other political authority. This being so, it may easily happen that, when several governmental organizations are in close association with one another, uncertainty may exist as to which of them is or are sovereign. Indeed, as has already been pointed out in the discussion of the distinction between governments *de facto* and governments *de jure*, the political entities that lie back of these governments may or may not be considered as sovereign political persons, according to the point of view of the persons regarding them. So, similarly, with respect to such a federal form of political organization as that exhibited in the United States after 1789, it was possible that a portion of the people should regard the National Government as nothing more than a common agent of the severally sovereign States, and, therefore, that these States might, without legal wrong upon their part, either refuse obedience to federal commands of which they disapproved, or refuse longer to co-operate with the other States of the Union. At the same time, another portion of the people could regard the National Government as the agent of a true National State, possessing sovereignty it its own right, and in this respect, superior to the member States of the Union. Still a third portion of the people could regard the National State and the individual States, as having the same juristic status, co-ordinate in authority, and each possessing supreme legal authority within their respective spheres as marked out by the Constitution. This condition of affairs could, and did, exist in the United States until the necessities of practical political life made it imperative that a choice should be made between these views; that is, until political action had to be taken which could be legally justified only by assuming one of these views rather than the others to be the correct one.

The Manifestation of National Sovereignty. The necessity for taking action that indicated, if it did not conclusively determine, which of these views was to be the one in accordance with which the constitutional life of the American people was to be conducted, arose very soon after the establishment of the Union. The view thus selected and acted upon was that there existed a national authority which was legally superior to that of the individual States. For years, however, lip service continued to be given to the doctrine of a sovereignty divided between the Union and its constituent States, although, whenever an issue arose between the two, the legal supremacy of the former was vindicated.

A liberal construction of national power by the National Congress and by the federal Executive was at once shown by the provision of the Judiciary Act of 1789, which provided for a final determination by the federal Supreme Court of all cases in which state Courts might render decisions adverse to claims by litigants of federal rights, privileges or immunities,[15] and by the establishment, in 1791, of a National Bank.

In 1793 the federal Supreme Court asserted its jurisdiction to give judgment in suit brought by a citizen of one State of the Union against another State of the Union, despite the claim by the defendant State that such a proceeding was practically a denial of the sovereignty which it claimed to possess.[16]

The next year resistance to a federal tax law upon the part of the people of the State of Pennsylvania was overcome by a display of military force, summoned to the field by the Federal Government.

In 1798-1799 occurred the vehement protest of the States of Virginia and Kentucky against certain acts of the federal Congress which they declared unwarranted by the federal Constitution. The resolutions, in which these protests were made, were submitted to the other States for their approval, but the conclusions which they declared, involving as they did a threat of refusal of obedience to the laws in question, were repudiated by the other States.

The year 1803 witnessed the acquisition by the United States of the vast Louisiana Territory and the passage by Congress of the Cumberland Road Act, both of which measures required, in order to sustain their legality, a very liberal interpretation of federal powers as defined by the Constitution.

In 1803 came also the decision of the Federal Supreme Court in the famous case of *Marbury* v. *Madison*[17] in which, for the first time, an act of Congress was declared void because not warranted by the federal Constitution. The significance of this case, as regards the matter of the location of sovereignty in the American Union, was that it pointed to the federal court as the proper tribunal for the final and authoritative construction of the provisions of the federal Constitution.

A few years later the State of Pennsylvania attempted to prevent the enforcement of a decree of a federal court, and, in fact, by an act of its legislature denied the authority of the federal court in the premises and directed the executive of the State to prevent, by force of arms if necessary, the execution of the federal decree that had been rendered. A writ having been asked of the federal Supreme Court to compel the lower federal court to proceed with the enforcement of its decree, the Supreme Court, in 1809, declared that the act of the Pennsylvania legislature was a legal nullity; that the State possessed no constitutional right to resist the legal process of a federal court; and that a peremptory mandamus should issue.[18] In obedience to this order the lower federal court issued a writ of attachment, the service of which was at first sought to be prevented by state troops which had been called out by the Governor of the State. However, a comitatus of two thousand men having been summoned by the federal marshal, and the President of the United States having been appealed to in vain by the State Governor, the Pennsylvania authorities ceased their resistance which they saw would be futile, and the supremacy of the federal authority was thus fully vindicated.

In 1810, in the case of *Fletcher* v. *Peck*,[19] the federal Supreme Court again asserted and exercised the right to as treat as void an act of a State legislature which the Supreme Court deemed unwarranted by the federal Constitution.

In 1819, was decided the case of *McCulloch* v. *Maryland*[20] in which it was held that a State of the Union could not, even in the exercise of such an important power as that of taxation, interfere in any way with the efficient operation of any agency of the Federal Government, even though the existence of that agency might not be an essential part of the federal machinery of government, and, indeed might be one which the United States could be conceded the right to maintain only by a very liberal definition of the so-called implied powers provided for in Clause 18 of Section 8 of Article I of the Constitution.[21]

This holding of the federal Supreme Court squarely declared the doctrine that the individual States and the United States were not to be regarded as upon a plane of constitutional equality, for, as has been said, it was held that when the powers of the Union came into conflict with those of the States, the exercise of the latter would have to be foregone.

In 1816, in *Martin* v. *Hunter's Lessee*[22], and again, in 1921, in *Cohens* v. *Virginia*[23] the federal Supreme Court upheld the constitutionality of that provision of the Judiciary Act of 1789, which has been earlier referred to, according to which the Supreme Court was given the right to decide, upon writ of error, whether state Courts have denied to litigants federal rights, privileges or immunities which they had rightfully claimed. This assertion that, as to such claims, the States were not to have the final decision, even in cases arising in their own courts, was a crucial matter. Calhoun saw clearly the decisive character of this assertion of federal right. "The effect of this is," he wrote, "to make the Government of the United States the sole judge, in the last resort, as to the extent of its powers, and to place the States and their separate Governments and institutions at its mercy". "It would be a waste of time," he continued "to undertake to show that an assumption that would destroy the relation of co-ordinates between the Government of the United States and those of the several States—which would enable the former, at pleasure, to absorb the reserved powers and to destroy the institutions, social and political, which the Constitution was ordained to establish and protect—is wholly inconsistent with the federal theory of government, though in perfect accordance with the national theory. Indeed, I might go further and assert that it is, of itself, all sufficient to convert it into a national, consolidated government".[24]

In the years next following the federal Supreme Court repeatedly exercised the right to hold invalid laws of the States which it deemed not warranted by the federal Constitution.[25]

In 1832 the question as to where rested the real sovereignty in the American Union was put to a still more decisive test. In 1828 Congress had enacted a tariff law which was very objectionable to the State of South Carolina, and which contained features which that State declared were not warranted by the federal Constitution. Its legislature thereupon adopted an "exposition," drawn up by Calhoun, which explicitly asserted the legal right of a State of the Union to refuse obedience, and to direct its citizens to refuse obedience, to national acts which the States should deem unconstitutional. This assertion of the right of "Nullification" led, in 1830, to the famous debate in the United States between Webster and Hayne. In 1832 the people of South Carolina assembled in convention and issued "an ordinance to nullify certain acts of the Congress of the United

States purporting to be laws". This ordinance went on to declare that "it shall not be lawful for any of the constitutional authorities, whether of this State or of the United States, to enforce the payment of duties imposed by the said acts within the limits of this State"; and concluded with the statement that any attempt upon the part of the National Government to enforce the law within the limits of South Carolina will be "inconsistent with the longer continuance of South Carolina in the Union; and that the people of South Carolina will henceforth hold themselves absolved from all further obligation to maintain or preserve their political connection with the peoples of the other States, and will forthwith proceed to organize a separate government, and do all other acts and things which sovereign and independent States may of right do".

In pursuance of this ordinance the legislature of the State enacted laws which, as was said at the time, legislated the Federal Government out of the State.

South Carolina sent the proclamation of her ordinance to the other States. Without exception those which answered it condemned the doctrines it enunciated. This was true no less of the Southern than of the Northern States. Furthermore, Andrew Jackson, then President of the United States, in unmistakable terms declared his intention to enforce the federal law, whatever might be the attempted resistance of South Carolina. In result, that State was obliged to abandon any attempt to make good the threats it had made.

Reviewing the events that have been summarized, it would seem that proof had been piled upon proof that the claim that the States of the Union had a legal status co-ordinate in authority with that of the United States was not consistent with the actual facts of the case. History brought it about, however, that those who were still unwilling to admit the juristic conclusion that logically followed from these successive events, should subject the controversy to the final physical test of war. Claiming that, whatever constitutional concessions the States might have made in the past, they still had reserved to themselves a legal right of secession from the Union, eleven of the States, constituting a compact body in the South, and exercising what they claimed to be a right belonging to them as severally sovereign bodies-politic, seceded from the Union in 1861, and for four years by force of arms resisted the efforts of the National Government to enforce its law and authority within their limits.

The result of this Civil War is well-known. Federal authority was finally re-established, and, since that time, there has been no serious claim from any quarter that the United States is not a sovereign State and that the individual States of the Union have any other political status than that of non-sovereign bodies-politic within the Union and subject to its superior authority.

Tests of Sovereignty. If it be asked by what tests at the present time it can be determined that sovereignty inheres in the United States as a single national State, and not in the individual States of the Union, the following facts of Juristic significance may be pointed to.

Under the amending power, by a vote of three-fourths of the States acting through their legislatures or specially convened conventions, according as the one or the other method is proposed by Congress, it is possible to take away from any given State, against its will, and by a perfectly legal process, any or all of the powers which it now possesses, and from this result the objecting State has no legal means of escape by secession from the Union or otherwise. Also, there is no legal process by means of which a State, solely through its own legal will and legal competence can draw to itself any of the powers not now constitutionally possessed by it. Furthermore, no State can in any way, or upon any pretext, offer legal resistance to the operation within its limits of a national law.

As regards the rights of a federal government, such as the United States is now conceded to be, to enforce its laws within the States and against any opposition that may be raised against them, we may quote the following striking language of the federal Supreme Court, in the so-called Debs Case:[26] "The entire strength of the Nation may be used to enforce in any part of the land the full and free exercise of all national powers and the security of all rights intrusted by the Constitution to its care... If the emergency arises, the army of the Nation and all its militia are at the service of the Nation to compel obedience to its laws."

It is therefore plain that the constituent States have no sovereignty of their own, and that such autonomous powers as they now possess are had and exercised by the express will or by the constitutional forbearance of the national sovereignty. The Supreme Court of the United States has held that, even when selecting members for the national legislature, or electing the President, or ratifying proposed amendments to the federal Constitution, the States act, *ad hoc*, as agents of the National Government.

Putting the matter in affirmative terms, the sovereignty of the United States is fixed by the fact that it determines, through its own tribunals, the extent of its constitutional powers, and has the legal power to enforce its will without regard to the will or judgment of the States as to the constitutionality or wisdom of its acts. And, through the process provided for amending the federal Constitution, it has the legal right to vest in its own Government any power now entrusted for exercise to the State governments, or reserved to the people. In connection with the Nineteenth Amendment to the federal Constitution, ratified in 1920, the argument was put forward that there are inherent limitations upon the amending power—that there are some matters which cannot be legally justified even by a constitutional amendment, but this view has been emphatically rejected by the federal Supreme Court.[27]

The foregoing facts are sufficient to fix the juristic character of the American Union and to determine the subordinate status of its individual State members. Of further significance, however, is the fact that the United States has not only the exclusive and unlimited power to determine the territorial extent of its authority, but also to declare what persons shall be deemed its own citizens, as well as the citizens of the States. The Fourteenth Amendment made this no longer debatable by the provision that "all persons born or naturalized in the United States, and subject to the jurisdiction thereof, are citizens of the United States and of the States wherein they reside".[28]

That the right of permitting the naturalization or expatriation of citizens is an exclusive federal right has been judicially determined, as has also been the doctrine that a State has not the constitutional right (except perhaps as a police measure with reference, for example, to persons with infectious diseases) to prevent persons obtaining residence within its limits. Thus, in result, the States are not able to determine who shall be their own citizens; whereas the United States, through its own Constitution and statutes, has complete discretion in the matter.

This is the situation at the present time. The sovereignty of the United States and the non-sovereign status of the individual States is no longer contested. Thus, even though it be admitted, as it must be admitted, that there are grounds for holding that, originally, the United States was a confederacy of sovereign States united only by a treaty or compact, it nevertheless is a fair juristic reference from the events that occurred soon after the Union was established, that the confederate conception of the Union was no longer in consonance with the facts, and that the opposing nationalistic conception had been impliedly accepted by the American people when they acquiesced in the powers which the National Government had asserted and exercised. Certainly this establishment of a national sovereignty had been made sufficiently manifest before 1861 by the events that have been referred to. It would seem, therefore that the supporters of, the National sovereignty had good reason for saying that the leaders of the secessionist movement in 1861 were fairly estopped, at that late time, from claiming, on behalf of the States, a juristic status of sovereign bodies-politic.

This much, however may be said for the States' rights position. If it be admitted that the Union was originally a league or confederacy of several sovereign States, the establishment of the national sovereignty, however peaceably brought about or clothed in apparent legal form, was, as to those States, an essentially illegal or revolutionary act. As regards the victory of the National Government in the Civil War of 1861-1865, it can be said that its result determined the fact that henceforth there was to be no dispute as to the sovereignty of the United States; but it is not correct to say that that result operated to render legally valid the exercise by the National Government of powers that otherwise might have been regarded as illegal. No physical force of coercion, however overwhelmingly applied, can possibly transmute a legal wrong into a legal right. The quality of legality is so distinct, *in genere*, from that of physical might, that the two can have no effect upon each other. All that physical force advocated by those who claim a legal right to exercise it, is able to do is to overcome the physical force of those who deny this legal right, and possibly, to convince them of the practical futility or inexpediency of further attempting to urge the correctness of their own view of what are their legal rights. The real result, then, of the American Civil War was to produce this conviction in the minds of those who had previously believed that the States of the Union were sovereign bodies-politic and could, without legal wrong upon their part, withdraw at will from the union.

References

1. In an appendix to his edition of Blackstone's *Commentaries.*
2. For example, such a staunch Nationalist as Chief Justice Manhill felt constrained to admit this. In *Gibbons* v. *Ogden* (9 Wh. 1), Speaking for the whole Supreme Court, he said, "It has been said that they [the States] were sovereign, were completely independent, and were connected with each other by a league. This is true."
3. *Constitutional Law of the United States*, p. 9. See also Vol. I, Chap. I, of his *Constitutional History of the United States.*
4. *Op. cit.*, I, p. 101.
5. *Op. cit.*, I, p. 143.

6. Professor Burgess does not attempt to adduce historical evidence is its support.
7. Article VII.
8. Vermont declared: "the old Confederation, it is true, was formed by the State legislatures, but the present Constitution was derived from a higher authority. The people of the United States formed the federal Constitution, and not the States, or their legislatures." But even this assertion probably meant nothing more than that the new Constitution rested upon the assent of the sovereign peoples of the States and not merely upon the sanctions of the Governments of those States.
9. The Articles of the Existing Confederation provided that they might be amended only by a unanimous vote of the States. The proposed new Constitution provided that it should go into effect when ratified by nine States, as between the States so ratifying.
10. 4 Wheaton 316.
11. *Madison Papers,* Vol. II, p. 824.
12. *Elliot's Debates*, Vol. I, p. 305. For reference to other statements showing the application of the social compact theory to the formulation of a federal State, see the scholarly article by Professor McLaughlin in the *American Historical Review* for April, 1900, entitled "Social Compact and Constitutional Construction."
13. As to the general acceptance of this doctrine of divided sovereignty see Merriam, *History of American Political Theories*, Chap. VII.
14. Some few writers have asserted that the men of the time perceived that they had left this matter undetermined, but that, for reasons of practical expediency, they deliberately left it in that condition. This is the view, for example, of A. H. Small, in his monograph. *The Beginnings of American Nationality*, published in the Johns Hopkins University *Studies in Historical and Political Science* (Vol. VIII); and of Francis A. Walker in his article "*The Growth of American Nationality,*" published in 1895. There is no historical evidence to support this opinion, and it seems to the writer almost inconceivable that, if this had been a policy deliberately pursued, there would not have come down to us, in the notes or writings of the men of that time, some record of it.
15. The crucial importance of this assertion of federal right of determination will presently be discussed.
16. *Chisholm* v. *Georgia*, 2 Dall. 419.
17. 1. Cr. 137.
18. *United States* v. *Peters*, 5 Cr. 115.
19. 5 Cr. 87.
20. Wh. 316.
21. Congress shall have power to make all laws which shall be necessary and proper for carrying into execution the foregoing specifically powers and

all other powers vested by this Constitution in the Government of the United States, or in any department or office thereof.

22. 1 Wh. 304.
23. 6 Wh. 264.
24. *Discourse on the Constitution and Government of the United States.* Works of Calhoun, Vol. I, p. 338.
25. See for example *Osborn* v. *Bank of the United States* (9 Wh. 738), *Weston* v. *Charleston* (2 Pet. 449), *Gibbons* v. *Ogden* (9 Wh. 1); *Green* v. *Biddle* (8 Wh. 1); and *Craig* v. *Missouri* (4 Pet. 410)..
26. *In re Debs,* 158 U. S. Reports, 564.
27. Article V of the federal Constitution, which relates to amendments, provides that "no State, without its consent, shall be deprived of its equal suffrage in the Senate." It has been suggested that even this limitation upon the amending power can be overcome by first amending Article V so as to delete this limitation.
28. In the *United States* v. *Wong Kim Ark,* 169 U. S. 649, the Supreme Court said that the real object of the words "and subject to the jurisdiction thereof" was to exclude by the fewest and fittest words possible, members of Indian tribes, children born of alien enemies in hostile occupation, and children born of diplomatic representatives of foreign powers—persons generally recognized by American as well as by foreign law as exceptions to the fundamental *jus soli* rule of citizenship.

II

The Basis of Limited Constitutional Government

The Natural Law and Constitutional Law

Ancient Chinese philosophers were wont to distinguish the passive and active elements of Being, called respectively *yin* and *yang*. If I may be permitted to employ this locution for a moment, the "yang" element of American constitutional law is judicial review, the power and corresponding duty of a court to pass upon the validity of legislative acts in relation to a higher law which is regarded as being binding on both the legislature and the court. By the same token the "yin" element is the aforesaid higher law. Today this role is ordinarily filled by a constitutional document, the Constitution of the United States being the supreme example; but earlier, natural law or some derivative concept took the part of "yin". Hence the purpose of this discourse – which is to demonstrate how very large a part of its content American constitutional law has always owed, and still owes, to its natural law genesis. As the matrix of American constitutional law, the documentary Constitution is still, in important measure, natural law under the skin.

Of natural law there is no end of definitions, as a casual examination of Sir Thomas Erskine Holland's *Elements of Jurisprudence* suffices to show. I venture to quote a few passages from the 13th edition:

Aristotle fully recognizes the existence of a natural as well as of a legal Justice. He mentions as an ordinary device of rhetoric the distinction which may be drawn between the written law, and "the common law" which is in accordance with Nature and immutable.

The Stoics were in the habit of identifying Nature with Law in the higher sense, and of opposing both of these terms to Law which is such by mere human appointment. "Justice," they say, "is by Nature and not by imposition". "It proceeds from Zeus and the common Nature."

The same view finds expression in the Roman lawyers. "Law," says Cicero, "is the highest reason, implanted in Nature, which commands those things which ought to be done and prohibits the reverse". "The highest law was born in all the ages before any law was written or State was formed.... " "We are by Nature inclined to love mankind, which is the foundation of law.... "

S. Thomas Aquinas: "Participatio legis aeternae in rationali creatura lex naturalis dicitur."

Grotius: "Jus naturale est dictatum rectae rationis.... "[1]

For our purposes it is not essential to choose nicely among these definitions of what Cicero and St. Thomas call *lex naturalis* and Grotius terms *jus naturale*. We are concerned only with certain juristic connotations of the concept: first, that natural law is entitled by its intrinsic excellence to prevail over any law which rests solely on human authority; second, that natural law may be appealed to by human beings against injustices sanctioned by human authority.

I. Natural Law into Natural Rights

In a famous passage in the *Rhetoric*, Aristotle advised advocates that when they had "no case according to the law of the land," they should "appeal to the law of nature," and, quoting from *Antigone* of Sophocles, argue that "an unjust law is not a law".[2] While this advice scarcely reveals any deep devotion on Aristotle's part to the natural law concept, it does evidence the short step, which even at that date existed in men's minds, between the concept and the idea of a *juridical* recourse to it. Three hundred years later we find Cicero in his *De Legibus* contrasting *summa lex* and *lex scripta; summum, jus* and *jus civile; universum jus* and *jus civile*; and on one occasion appealing in the Senate to *recta ratio* against the *lex scripta.* [3]

It was during the Middle Ages, however, that the conception of natural law as a code of human rights first took on real substance and importance. This was so even on the Continent,[4] albeit institutions were lacking there through which such ideas could be rendered effective practically. In England, on the other hand, this lack was supplied by the royal courts, administering the common law. The impregnation of the common law with higher law concepts proceeded rapidly in the fourteenth century under Edward III. Of the thirty-two royal confirmations of the Charter noted by Sir Edward Coke, fifteen occurred in this reign; and near the end of it, in 1368, to the normal form of confirmation the declaration was added by statute that any statute passed contrary to Magna Carta "soit tenuz p'nul," words which seem clearly to have been addressed to the royal officials, including the judges.[5]

Here, to be sure, Magna Carta fills the role of natural law, but it is a Magna Carta already infused with natural law content, as is shown by Bracton's earlier designation of Chapter 29 as *constitutio libertatis*; and in the fifteenth century the *lex naturae* has completely replaced Magna Carta in the juristic equation. This is notably so, for example, in the pages of Fortescue's famous *In Praise of the Law of England (De Laudibus Legum Angliae),* which was but one of many similar encomia. As Father Figgis has written of this period:

The Common Law is pictured invested with a halo of dignity peculiar to the embodiment of the deepest principles and to the highest expression of human reason and of the law of nature implanted by God in the heart of man. As yet men are not clear that an Act of Parliament can do more than declare the Common Law. It is the Common Law which men set up as an object of worship. The Common Law is the perfect ideal of law; for it is natural reason developed and expounded by a collective wisdom of many generations. ... Based on long usage and almost supernatural wisdom, its authority is above, rather than below that of Acts of Parliament or royal ordinances, which owe their fleeting existence to the caprice of the King or to the pleasure of councillors, which have a merely material sanction and may be repealed at any moment.[6]

Thus the common law becomes higher law, without at all losing its quality as positive law, the law of the King's courts and of the rising Inns of Court. Nor does Fortescue fail to stress its dual character. Asserting the identity of "perfect justice" with "legal justice," and the subordination of the King to the law, i.e., the law courts, he proceeds to counsel his Prince as follows:

... There will be no occasion for you to search into the arcana of our laws with such tedious application and study.... It will not be convenient by severe study, or at the expense of the best of your time, to pry into nice points of law : such matters may be left to your judges;... furthermore, you will pronounce judgment in the courts by others than in person, it being not customary for the Kings of England to sit in courts or pronounce judgment themselves *(proprio ore nullus regum Angilae judicium profere uses est).* I know very well the quickness of your apprehension and the forwardness of your parts; but for that expertness in the laws which is requisite for judges the studies of twenty years *(viginti annorum lucubrationes)* barely suffice.[7]

In short, natural law has become a craft mystery – the mystery of Bench and Bar – what it has remained, now in greater, now in lesser measure ever since.

A century and a half later we find Lord Coke, Chief Justice of the Common Pleas, describing a scene[8] which reads like a re-enactment of that imagined by Fortescue. But to his predecessor's work of edification, Coke adds official recognition that judicial custodianship of the common law signifies the power and duty of the law courts to apply its measure both to the royal prerogative and to the power of Parliament. The latter claim appears in his famous "dictum," so-called, in Dr. Bonham's case,[9] which reads:

And it appears in our books, that in many cases, the common law will controul Acts of Parliament, and sometimes adjudge them to be utterly void: for when an Act of Parliament is against common right and reason, or repugnant, or impossible to be performed, the common law will controul it and adjudge such Act to be void.... [10]

And this was said, it should be noted, at the end of a century in which the thesis of Parliament's absolute power to alter and abrogate any and all laws had been asserted again and again;[11] and not only asserted but demonstrated by its part in the Tudor ecclesiastical and religious revolution.

Eighty years after Dr. Bonham's case, "the great Mr. Locke" produced his second *Treatise on Civil Government,* in which the dissolution of natural law into the natural rights of the individual – the rights of "life, liberty and estate" – is completed through the agency of the social compact. Of judicial review, to be sure, Locke appears to have no inkling. He relied for the protection of the individual's inherent and inalienable rights on: first, Parliament; second, the right of revolution. Even so, Locke's contribution to both the doctrinal justification of judicial review and to the theory of its proper scope is first and last a very considerable one.

Coke and Locke are the two great names in the common Anglo-American higher law tradition, and the contribution of each is enhanced by that of the other. Locke's version of natural law not only rescues Coke's version of the English Constitution from a localized patois, restating it in the universal tongue of the eighteenth century, it also supplements it in important respects. Coke's endeavor was to put forward the historical *procedures* of the common law as a permanent restraint on power, and especially on the power of the English crown. Locke, in the limitations which he imposes on legislative power, is looking rather to the security of the *substantive* rights of the individual – those rights which are implied in the basic arrangements of society at all times and in all places. While Coke extricated the notion of fundamental law from what must sooner or later have proved a fatal nebulosity, he did so at the expense of archaism. Locke, on the other hand, in cutting loose in great measure from the historical method of reasoning, opened the way to the larger issues with which American constitutional law has been called upon to grapple in its latest maturity.[12]

II. Natural Law and Judicial Review

The *fons et origo* of both the doctrine and the practice of judicial review in the United States is Coke's invocation in Dr. Bonham's Case of "common right and reason," which as explained by the sixteenth-century author of *Doctor and Student*, was the term used "by them that be learned in the laws of England" in place of the term "law and nature".[13] Commended by two Lord Chief Justices, Hobart and Holt, the dictum had won repeated recognition in various legal abridgements and digests before the outbreak of the American Revolution.[14] In the early 1700's, it was relied on by a British colonial law officer as affixing the stigma of invalidity to an act of the Barbadoes assembly creating paper money.[15] In 1759, we encounter a casual reference by Governor Cadwallader Colden of the Province of New York to "a judicial power of declaring them [laws] void".[16]

But just as Coke had forged his celebrated dictum as a possible weapon for the struggle which he already foresaw against the divine rights pretensions of James I, so its definitive reception in this country was motivated by the rising agitation against the mother country. The creative first step was taken by James Otis in February,1761, in his argument for the Boston merchants against an application by a British customs official for a general warrant authorizing him to search their cellars and warehouses for smuggled goods. An act of Parliament "against natural Equity," Otis asserted, was void. "If an Act of Parliament," he continued, "should be made in the very Words of this Petition, it would be void," and it would be the duty of the executive courts to pass it "into disuse".[17] Four years later, according to Governor Hutchinson of Massachusetts, the prevailing argument against the Stamp Act was that it was "against Magna Charta and the natural rights of Englishmen, and therefore, according to Lord

Coke, null and void," testimony which is borne out by a contemporaneous decision of a Virginia county court.[18] On the very eve of the Declaration of Independence, Judge William Cushing, later to become one of Washington's appointees to the original bench of the Supreme Court, charged a Massachusetts jury to ignore certain acts of Parliament as "void and inoperative" and was congratulated by John Adams for doing so.[19]

And meantime, in 1772, George Mason had developed a similar argument against an act of the Virginia assembly of 1682, under which certain Indian women had been sold into slavery. The act in question, he asserted, "was originally void of itself, because contrary to natural right".[20] And, he continued:

If natural right, independence, defect of representation, and disavowal of protection, are not sufficient to keep them from the coercion of our laws, on what other principles can we justify our opposition to some late acts of power exercised over us by the British legislature? Yet they only pretended to impose on us a paltry tax in money; we on our free neighbours, the yoke of perpetual slavery. Now all acts of legislature apparently contrary to natural right and justice, are, in our laws, and must be in the nature of things, considered as void. The laws of nature are the laws of God; whose authority can be superseded by no power on earth... All human constitutions which contradict his laws, we are in conscience bound to disobey. Such have been the adjudications of our courts of justice.[21]

Mason concluded by citing Coke and Hobart. The court adjudged the act of 1682 repealed.[22]

Nor did the establishment of the first American constitutions cause this course of reasoning to be abandoned. To the contrary, the most eminent judges of the first period of American constitutional law, which comes to an end approximately with the death of Marshall in 1835, appealed freely to natural rights and the social compact as limiting legislative power, and based decisions on this ground, and the same doctrine was urged by the greatest lawyers of the period without reproach. Typical in this connection is the case of Wilkinson *v.* Leland, which was decided by the Supreme Court in 1829.[23] Attorney for the defendants in error was Daniel Webeter. "If," said he, "at this period there is not a general restraint on Legislatures in favor of private rights, there is an end to private property. Though there may be no prohibition in the Constitution, the Legislature is restrained ... from acts subverting the great principles of republican liberty and of the social compact.... "[24] To this contention his opponent William Wirt responded thus: "Who is the sovereign?... Is it not the Legislature of the State, and are not its acts effectual... unless they come in contact with the great principles of the social compact?"[25] The act of the Rhode Island legislature under review was upheld, but said Justice Story speaking for the Court: "That government can scarcely be deemed to be free where the rights of property are left solely dependent upon the will of a legislative body without any restraint. The fundamental maxims of a free government seem to require that the rights of personal liberty and private property should be held sacred."[26] Indeed, fourteen years before this the same court had unanimously held void, on the basis of these same principles, an act of the Virginia legislature which purported to revoke a grant of land.[27]

In short, *judicial review initially had nothing to do with a written constitution.* In point of fact, the first appearance of the idea of judicial review in this country antedated the first written constitution by at least two decades. Judicial review continued, moreover, in a relationship of semi-independence of the written constitution on the basis of "common right and reason," natural law, natural rights, and kindred postulates throughout the first third of the nineteenth century. But meantime, a competing conception of judicial review as something anchored to the *written constitution* had been in the process of formulation in answer to Blackstone's doctrine that in every State there is a *supreme, absolute power*, and that this power is vested in the *legislature*. From this angle judicial review based on "common right and reason," or on natural law ideas, was an impertinence, as Blackstone took pains to point out in his *Commentaries*.[28] But suppose that the supreme will in the State was not embodied in the *legislature* and its *acts*, but in the *people at large* and their *constitution* – what conclusions would follow from this premise? In *the Federalist* No. 78, Hamilton suggested an answer to this question, and in 1803, in Marbury *v.* Madison,[29] Chief Justice Marshall elaborated the answer: it is the duty of courts when confronted with a conflict between an act (i.e., a *statute)* of "the mere agents of the people" (that is, of the ordinary legislature) and the act of the people themselves (to wit, the Constitution) to prefer the latter.

The inevitable clash between the two conceptions of judicial review was first unfolded in the case of Calder *v.* Bull, decided by the Supreme Court in 1798.[30] There it was held that the "ex post facto" clause of Article 1, section 10 of the Constitution applied only to penal legislation and hence did not protect rights of property and contract from interference by a state legislature; but Justice Samuel Chase endeavoured to soften this blow to proprietarian interests by citing the power of the state courts to enforce extra-constitutional limitations on legislative power, such as many of them were in fact already doing. Said he:

I cannot subscribe to the *omnipotence of a state Legislature*, or that it is *absolute and without control*; although its authority should not be *expressly* restrained by the *constitution,* or *fundamental law,* of the state.... There are certain *vital* principles in our *free Republican governments,* which will determine and overrule an *apparent and flagrant* abuse of *legislative* power.... The *genius,* the *nature,* and the *spirit* of our state governments, amount to a prohibition of *such acts of legislation;* and the *general principles of law and reason* forbid them.[31]

To hold otherwise, it was stated, would be "political heresy, altogether inadmissible."[32]

Chase belonged to the older generation of American lawyers and had been brought up on Coke-Littleton, having received much of his legal education in London in the Inns of Court. Alongside him on the Supreme Bench, however, sat a very different type of lawyer, one of "that brood of young lawyers," characterized by Jefferson as "ephemeral insects of the law," who had imbibed their law from Blackstone's *Commentaries.* This was James Iredell of North Carolina, who demurred strongly to Chase's natural rights doctrine. "True," said he, "some speculative jurists" had held "that a legislative act against natural justice must, in itself, be void; but the correct view, he stated, was that:

If ... a government, composed of legislative, executive and judicial departments, were established, by a Constitution, which imposed no limits on the legislative power, ... whatever the legislative power chose to enact, would be lawfully enacted, and the judicial power, could never interpose to pronounce it void.... Sir William Blackstone, having put the strong case of an act of parliament, which should authorize a man to try his own cause, explicitly adds, that even in that case, "there is no court that has power to defeat the intent of the legislature when couched in such evident ... words ...."[33]

The debate thus begun was frequently renewed in other jurisdictions; and long before the Civil War, Iredell had won the fight – but as we shall see, more in *appearance* than in *reality.* In 1868, Judge Cooley, in considering the circumstances in which a legislative enactment may be declared unconstitutional, wrote:

The rule of law upon this subject appears to be, that, except where the constitution has imposed limits upon the legislative power, it must be considered as practically absolute, whether it operate according to natural justice or not in any particular case. The courts are not the guardians of the rights of the people of the State, except as those rights are secured by some constitutional provision which comes within the judicial cognizance.[34]

Yet, six years later we find the Supreme Court of the United States pronouncing a statute of the state of Kansas void on the very grounds that had been laid down in Chase's dictum. Speaking for an all but unanimous Court, Justice Miller said:

It must be conceded that there are … rights in every free government beyond the control of the State. A government which recognized no such rights, which held the lives, the liberty, and the property of its citizens subject at all times to the absolute disposition and unlimited control of even the most democratic depository of power, is after all but a despotism. It is true it is a despotism of the many, of the majority, if you choose to call it so, but it is nonetheless a despotism. It may well be doubted if a man is to hold all that he is accustomed to call his own, all in which he has placed his happiness, and the security of which is essential to that happiness, under the unlimited dominion of others, whether it is not wiser that this power should be exercised by one man than by many.[35]

One Justice dissented, asserting that such views tended to "convert the government into a judicial despotism".[36]

But vastly more important is the fact that in the very process of discarding the doctrine of natural rights and adherent doctrines as the basis of judicial review, the courts have contrived to throw about those rights, which originally owed their protection to these doctrines, the folds of the documentary constitution. In short, things are not always what they seem to be, even when they seem so most.[37] The indebtedness of the institution of judicial review and of the rights protected by it to natural law ideas is by no means sufficiently summed up in the glib statement that nowadays judicial review is confined to the four corners of the written constitution.

III. How Natural Law Doctrines Were Used to Fill a Gap in the Written Constitution

It is a commonplace that the doctrine of natural rights was conveyed into the American written Constitution by bills of rights, the earliest example of which was the Virginia Declaration of Rights of June 12, 1776. This commonplace is, however, only a half of the truth, and indeed the lesser half. As has been indicated, the type of judicial review which stemmed from Coke's dictum supplied a second avenue for natural rights concepts into the constitutional document. In this section I shall first illustrate this proposition with the doctrine of vested rights.

Not all the early state constitutions were accompanied by bills of rights. Moreover, the availability of such bills of rights as existed as a basis for judicial inquiry into the validity of legislative measures was sharply challenged at times. Even more important was the fact that, as it came early to be appreciated, bills of rights or no bills of rights, the early state constitutions left proprietarian interests in a very exposed position vis-à-vis the new popular assemblies, for which the prerogatives of the British Parliament itself were sometimes claimed.[38]

The formidable character of legislative power in these early instruments of government as regards the property interest was exhibited in more ways than one. In the first place, in the prevailing absence of courts of equity, legislative assemblies interfered almost at will with judicial decisions, and particularly those involving disputes over property. The case of Calder v. Bull, mentioned earlier, affords an example of this sort of thing.[39] The Connecticut courts, having refused to probate a certain will, were to all intents and purposes ordered to revise their decision, which they did, with the result that the heirs at law to an estate were ousted, after a year and a half of possession, by the beneficiaries of the will. A second and highly impressive proof of early state legislative power is afforded by the ferocious catalogue of legislation directed against the Tories, embracing acts of confiscation, bills of pains and penalties, even acts of attainder. One sample of such legislation came under the scrutiny of the United States Supreme Court in 1800, in the case of Cooper *v.* Telfair.[40] Said Justice Washington: "The presumption, indeed, must always be in favor of the validity of laws, if the contrary is not clearly demonstrated."[41] On this ground and one or two others, the Georgia act was sustained, although Justice Chase opined that with the federal Constitution now in effect such an act would be clearly void; but this act was passed during the Revolution. Thirdly, with the general collapse of values early in 1780, every state legislature became a scene of vehement agitation on the part of the widespread farmer-debtor class in favor of paper money laws and other measures of like intent. For the first time, the property interest was confronted with "the power of numbers," and, in the majority of cases, the power of numbers triumphed.

Could the state bills of rights withstand the flood? It soon transpired that they were an utterly ineffective bulwark of private rights against state legislative power. And so the movement was launched which led to the Philadelphia Convention of 1787. That abuse by the state legislatures of their powers had been the most important single cause leading to the Convention was asserted by Madison early in the course of its deliberations, and others agreed.[42] So far as we are concerned, the most important expression of the Convention's anxiety to clip the wings of the high-flying local sovereignties is to be found in the opening paragraph of Section10 of Article I, which reads:

No State shall enter into any Treaty, Alliance, or Confederation; grant Letters of Marque and Reprisal; coin Money, emit Bills of Credit; make any Thing but gold and silver Coin a Tender in Payment of Debts; pass any Bill of Attainder, *ex post facto* Law or Law impairing the Obligation of Contracts, or grant any Title of Nobility.

The provision which here claims attention is the prohibition of *ex post facto* laws. What did those who urged their insertion in the Constitution think these words meant? Some of them, we know, thought the clause would rule out *all* "retrospective" legislation, meaning thereby legislation which operated detrimentally upon existing property rights.[43] But as we have seen in Calder *v.* Bull, the clause was confined to penal legislation, to statutes making criminal an act which was innocent when done. That the Court was thoroughly aware of the breach it was thus creating in the Constitution, the opinions of all the Justices, except that of the Blackstonian Iredell, make amply apparent; and going beyond apology, Chase sought to show how the gap could be stopped by the local judiciaries by recourse to extra-constitutional limitations, "the spirit of our free republican governments," "the social compact," considerations of "natural justice," and the like. The local judiciaries responded to the suggestion with varying degrees of alacrity, and the sum total of their efforts was one of the most fertile doctrines of American constitutional law, the doctrine of vested rights, the practical purport of which was that the effect of legislation on existing property rights was a *primary* test of its validity, and that by this test legislation must stop short of curtailing existing rights of ownership, at least unduly or unreasonably.[44]

But in fact, Chase's dictum only stimulated a movement already begun. Three years prior to Calder *v.* Bull, we find Justice Paterson charging a federal jury in a case involving vested rights in these words:

... The right of acquiring and possessing property and having it protected, is one of the natural, inherent and unalienable rights of man. Men have a sense of property: Property is necessary to their subsistence, and correspondent to their natural wants and desires; its security was one of the objects, that induced them to unite in society ... The preservation of property... is a primary object of the social compact, and, by the late constitution of Pennsylvania, was made a fundamental law.[45]

Indeed, a majority of the cases of judicial review after the Cokian model, referred to in Section II of this paper, involved property rights. Nor should the great name of Chancellor Kent be overlooked in this connection. First as judge, then as Chancellor in his home state, and finally as author of the famed *Commentaries*, Kent developed the doctrine's fullest possibilities and spread its influence fastest and farthest.

Yet even as Kent was vaunting private property as an instrument of God for realizing his plans for the advancement of the race, it was becoming less and less practicable to urge such considerations on American judges. The old-type Cokian judge had about disappeared – Blackstone was in the saddle in the law offices and in the Court houses. What is more, with the accession of Jackson to the Presidency there took place an immense resurgence of the doctrine of popular sovereignty. Of the numerous corollaries into which the doctrine proliferated, two are relevant to our interest: first, the Constitution was an ordinance of the people, and its supremacy sprang from the fact that it embodied their will; second, of the three departments of state government, the legislature stood nearest the people. It followed that the courts had better go slow in holding state legislative acts invalid; and that on no account must they do so except for a plain violation of the Constitution, i.e., of the people's will as there expressed.

Bench and Bar were confronted with a dilemma: either they must cast the doctrine of vested rights to the wolves or they must bring it within the sheepfold of the written Constitution. The second alternative was adopted in due course. Ultimately the doctrine found a home within the "due process" clause, "no person shall be deprived of life, liberty, or property without due process of law". The original significance of the clause was purely procedural – nobody should be punished without a trial by jury or "writ original of the Common Law". In the revamped clause the term "due process of law" simply fades out and the clause comes to read, in effect, "no person shall be deprived of property, period". Thus was the narrow interpretation which was planted on the ex post facto clause in Calder *v.* Bull revenged in kind.[46]

This achievement was consummated in the famous case of Wynehamer *v.* People, in which, in 1856, the New York Court of Appeals set aside a state-wide prohibition law as comprising, with regard to liquors in existence at the time of its going into effect, an act of destruction of property not within the power of government to perform "even by the forms of due process of law".[47] An interesting feature of Judge Comstock's opinion in the case is his repudiation of all arguments against the statute sounding in natural law concepts, like "fundamental principles of liberty," "common reason and natural rights," and so forth. Such theories said he – squinting, one suspects, at the anti-slavery agitation – were subversive of the necessary powers of government. Furthermore, there was "no process of reasoning by which it could be demonstrated that the 'Act for the Prevention of Intemperance, Pauperism and Crime' is void, upon principles and theories outside the Constitution, which will not also, and by an easier induction, bring it in direct conflict with the Constitution itself."[48]

The expansion of the "obligation of contracts" clause of Article I, section 10, by resort to natural law concepts follows a similar, though briefer course. The master craftsman was Chief Justice Marshall, and this time the infusion of the constitutional clause with natural law concepts was direct. The great leading case was Fletcher *v.* Peck,[49] in which in 1810, Marshall, speaking for the Court, held that a state legislature was forbidden "either by general principles, which are common to our free institutions, or by the particular provisions of the constitution of the United States" [50] to rescind a previous land grant; while Justice Johnson based his concurring opinion altogether "on the reason and nature of things; a principle which will impose laws even on the Deity."[51] It is true that when, in 1819, the doctrine of Fletcher *v.* Peck was extended to the charters of eleemosynary corporations, the Court contented itself with invoking only the obligations clause.[52] The dependence, however, of the holding on natural law premises still remains. The constitutional clause presupposes a *pre-existent* obligation to be protected. Whence, if not from natural law, can such an obligation descend upon a public grant?

Of the four great doctrines of American constitutional law which the American judiciary developed prior to the Civil War, three (the doctrine of judicial review, the substantive doctrine of due process of law, and the doctrine that the obligation of contracts clause protects public contracts) are products of the infusion of the documentary Constitution with natural law, natural rights concepts. The fourth doctrine, that of dual federalism, was the creation of the Supreme Court at Washington under the presidency and guidance of Chief Justice Taney. It, of course, rests on different, highly political considerations. Yet even in this case, natural law may claim some credit if, as Thomas Hill Green argues in his *Principles of*

Political Obligation, the notion of sovereignty is also, in final analysis, rooted in the doctrine of natural law.[53] Green, of course, was thinking of "sovereignty" as it is known to Western political thought, not the kind of sovereignty that is the offspring of Byzantine absolutism married to Marxian materialism.

IV. The Bench and Bar Present Us with an Up-to-Date Doctrine of Natural Law

In 1868, the Fourteenth Amendment was added to the Constitution. The first section of it reads as follows:

All persons born or naturalized in the United States, and subject to the jurisdiction thereof, are citizens of the United States and of the State wherein they reside. No State shall make or enforce any law which shall abridge the privileges or immunities of citizens of the United States; nor shall any State deprive any person of life, liberty or property, without due process of law; nor deny to any person within its jurisdiction the equal protection of the laws.

The fifth and final section gave Congress the power "to enforce, by appropriate legislation, the provision of this Article".

In the understanding of most people at the time, the intended beneficiaries of the amendment were the recently emancipated freedmen, but in the very first cases to reach the Supreme Court under it, the famous Slaughter House cases of 1873,[54] this assumption was sharply challenged by counsel, John Archibald Campbell of New Orleans, a former Justice of the Court. No doubt, Campbell argued, the freedmen would and should derive benefit from the amendment, but their doing so would only be incidental to the realization of its much broader purpose, that of giving legal embodiment to the principle of "laissez-faire individualism which had been held by the colonists ever since they came to this soil".[55] "What," he asked, "did the colonists and their posterity seek for and obtain by their settlement of this continent?... *Freedom, free action, free enterprise, free competition.* It was in freedom they expected to find the best auspices for every kind of human success."[56]

Campbell lost his suit, by the narrow margin of five Justices to four; but he had sown an idea which, in the course of the next thirty years, imparted to judicial review a new and revolutionary extension. In 1878, the American Bar Association was founded from the elite of the American bar. Organized as it was in the wake of the "barbarous" decision – as one member termed it – in Munn *v.* Illinois,[57] in which the Supreme Court had held that states were entitled by virtue of their police power to prescribe the charges of "business affected with a public interest," the association, through its more eminent members, became the mouthpiece of a new constitutional philosophy which was compounded in about equal parts from the teachings of the British Manchester School of Political Economy and Herbert Spencer's highly sentimentalized version of the doctrine of evolution, just then becoming the intellectual vogue; plus a "booster" – in the chemical sense – from Sir Henry Maine's *Ancient Law,* first published in 1861. I refer to Maine's famous dictum that "the movement of the progressive societies has hitherto been a movement *from Status to Contract"*.[58] If hitherto, why not henceforth?

In short, the American people were presented *a new doctrine of natural law,* the content and purport of which appear – to take a specific example – in Professor William Graham Summer's *What Social Classes Owe to Each Other,* which was published in 1883. I quote a passage or two:

A society based on contract is a society of free and independent men, who form ties without favor or obligation, and co-operate without cringing or intrigues. A society based on contract, gives the utmost room and chance for individual development, and for all the self-reliance and dignity of a free man.... It follows that one man, in a free state, cannot claim help from, and cannot be charged to give help to, another.

And again:

All institutions are to be tested by the degree to which they guarantee liberty. It is not to be admitted for a moment that liberty is a means to social ends, and that it may be impaired for major considerations. Any one who so argues has lost the bearing and relations of all the facts and factors in a free state. He is a centre of powers to work, and of capacities to suffer. What his powers may be – whether they can carry him far or not; what his fortune may be, whether to suffer much or little – are questions of his personal destiny which he must work out and endure as he can; but for all that concerns the bearing of the society and its institutions upon that man, and upon the sum of happiness to which he can attain during his life on earth, the product of all history and all philosophy up to this time is summed up in the doctrine, that he should be left free to do the most for himself that he can, and should be guaranteed the exclusive enjoyment of all that he does.... Social improvement is not to be won by direct effort. It is secondary and results from physical or economic improvement.... An improvement in surgical instruments or in anesthetics really does more for those who are not well off than all the declamations of the orators and pious wishes of the reformers.... The yearning after equality is the offspring of envy and covetousness, and there is no possible plan for satisfying that yearning which can do aught else than rob A to give to B; consequently all such plans nourish some of the meanest vices of human nature, waste capital, and overthrow civilization...[59]

It is interesting to compare this new type of natural law, and its tremendous exaltation of individual effort, with the ancient type, which was set forth in the texts quoted in Section I of this paper. There are two differences, the first of which approximates that between a *moral* code, addressed to the reason, and natural law in the sense in which that term is employed by the natural sciences. The former operates *through* men; the latter *upon* men, and altogether independently of their attitude toward it, or even of their awareness of its existence. The results of its operation would therefore be of no moral significance, except for one circumstance, the assumption, to wit, that *compliance with* it – *whether conscious or unconscious – forwarded Progress.* Thus, according to Maine, it was *the progressive societies* which had heretofore moved from *status* to *contract;* while with Spencer *progressive societies* were destined to "evolve" from the *military state* into the *industrial society* – a process not yet completed, however, or the State would have vanished. In short, the laissez-faire version of natural law contrived, in the end, to combine the *moral* prestige of the older concept with the *scientific* prestige of the newer.[60]

The second difference can be put more briefly, although it is perhaps the more important one. The natural law of Cicero, of St. Thomas, Grotius – even of Locke – always conceives of man as *in* society. The natural law of Spencer, Sumner, et al., sets man, the supreme product of a highly competitive struggle for existence, *above* society – an impossible station in both logic and fact.

The chief constitutional law precipitate from the new natural law, the doctrine of freedom of contract, confirms and illustrates this fatal characteristic of it. By this doctrine, persons *sui juris* engaged in the ordinary employments were entitled to contract regarding their services without interferences from government; as reciprocally were those who sought their services. Endorsed by such writers as Cooley, Tiedemann, James Coolidge Carter, J. F. Dillon, and by a growing procession of state high courts headed by those of New York, Pennsylvania, Massachusetts, and Illinois, the doctrine attained culminating expression in 1905 in the famous Bakeshop case.[61] There a New York statute which limited the hours of labor in bakeries to ten hours a day and sixty hours a week was set aside five Justices to four as not "a fair, reasonable and appropriate exercise of the police power of the state" but "an unreasonable, unnecessary and arbitrary interference with the right of the individual to his personal liberty...".[62]

How was this result reached? Very simply: it was the automatic result of the conception of an area of individual action *any* interference with which by the state put upon it a burden of justification not required in other cases. On this basis the Court came to operate a kind of "automatic" judicial review, the product of which was labeled by its critics "mechanical jurisprudence". Nor is this type of jurisprudence extinct today, as I shall now point out. Its application has merely been transferred to a different set of values and interests.

V. Natural Law and Constitutional Law Today

In 1925, in the now famous Gitlow case,[63] which involved a conviction under the New York Anti-Syndicalist Act, the Supreme Court adopted tentatively the thesis, which it had rejected earlier, that the word "liberty" in the Fourteenth Amendment adopts and makes effective against state legislatures the limitations which the First Amendment imposes upon Congress in favor of "freedom of speech and press". Then in 1940 in the Cantwell case,[64] the Court upset a conviction under Connecticut law of two Jehovah's Witnesses for breach of the peace on the ground that the proselyting activities of the said Witnesses did not under the circumstances constitute a "clear and present danger" to public order; and since then a majority of the Court has gone to the verge, at least, of making the "clear and present danger" formula a direct test of legislation, although in the Gitlow case it had rejected the rule as spurious.

And what has all this to do with natural law? The answer is discovered when we note the rule by which the Court professes to be guided when interpreting the word "liberty" in the Fourteenth Amendment in the light of the Bill of Rights. Not all the provisions of the latter are regarded as having been converted by the Fourteenth Amendment into restrictions on the states, but only those that are protective of the "immutable principles of justice which inhere in the very idea of free government"; of the "fundamental principles of liberty and justice which lie at the base of all our civil and political institutions"; of the "immunities... implicit in the concept of ordered liberty"; of principles of justice "rooted in the traditions and conscience of our people"; principles, the violation of which would be "repugnant to the conscience of mankind".[65]

This is entirely in line with the natural law tradition. But does it suffice to elevate the rights it deals with into a *super-constitution,* so that any law touching them is *ipso facto* "infected with presumptive invalidity"? As we have seen, this is precisely what happened in the case of "liberty of contract"; and today, "liberty of contract" thus distended "is all," as they say in Pennsylvania; and may not a like fate overtake freedom of speech, press, and religion in time if the same slide-rule methods are applied to legislation touching them? I am thinking especially of such decisions as those in Saia *v.* New York,[66] McCollum v. Board of Education,[67] and Terminiello *v.* City of Chicago.[68] These were very ill-considered decisions to my way of thinking, and in fact the first of these has already been repudiated by the Court,[69] at least four of the five Justices who were responsible for it lugubriously so assert. I contend, in short, that any patent formula or device which relieves the Justices from considering relevant, however recalcitrant facts, or which exonerates them of the characteristic judicial duty of adjusting the universal and eternal to the local and contingent, the here and the now, is to be deplored. I contend further that the "clear and present danger" rule is just such a patent formula.

How are we to assess the importance of the natural law concept in the development of American constitutional law? What it all simmers down to is essentially this: while that distinctive American institution, judicial review, is regarded today as stemming from the principle of popular sovereignty, it sprang in the first instance from "common right and reason," the equivalent with men of law in the sixteenth-century England of natural law. What is more, popular sovereignty in the last analysis is itself a derivative from the natural law postulate, being neither more nor less than a sort of *ad hoc* consolidation of the natural right of human beings to choose their own governing institutions.

And the indebtedness of American constitutional law to natural law, natural rights concepts for its content in the field of private rights is vital and well-nigh all-comprehensive. It is, of course, true that not all of the corollaries that the courts have endeavored to attach to their premises have survived; and few have survived without modification. Yet it is a striking fact that while hundreds of constitutional provisions have been adopted since judicial review was established, not one has ever proposed its abolition and only very few its modification. And meantime the American states have continued to incorporate in their successive constitutions, virtually without comment, the constitutional clauses – the due process clause, for example – that today incorporate the principal judicial doctrines which I have traced to natural law bases. It is true, as I just remarked, that some of these doctrines have become extinct and others have been qualified; but invariably these results have been achieved by judicial massage, as it were – sometimes a rather rugged massage – and not by legislative or constitutional surgery.

Not that the doctrine of natural law itself has escaped disturbing comment at times, even from American jurists. Frequently citied in this connection is the late Justice Holmes' discourse on "Natural Law". "It is not enough," said Justice Holmes in a characteristic passage, "for the knight of romance that you agree that his lady is a very nice girl,– if you do not admit that she is the best that God ever made, you must fight"; and the same demand, he opines, "is at the bottom of the jurist's search for criteria of absolute validity."[70]

We can readily concede that such criteria may never be established in this far from perfect, and always changing world. Yet that admission does not necessarily discredit the search; perhaps, indeed, it makes it more necessary, as an alternative to despair. Holmes, in fact, exposes himself when he goes on to advance as an argument against natural law that the right to life "is sacrificed without a scruple whenever the interest of society, that is, of the predominant power of the community, is thought to demand it".[71] But the answer is plain: the right to life is more than the right to live – it is also the right to spend life for worthwhile ends; and so long as one is guaranteed a free man's part in determining what these ends are, natural law has *pro tanto* received institutional recognition and embodiment. But, of course, it is essential to this argument that the free man's part be kept a really vital one.

Our present interest, however, has been in natural law as a challenge to the notion of unlimited human authority. American constitutional law is the record of an attempt to implement that challenge. The record is a somewhat mixed one, but it is clear that in the judgment of the American people it has been on the whole a record of successes. May it continue to be!

WILSON AND "PRECEDENTS FOR PRESIDENTIAL DICTATORSHIP"

War, the Constitution Moulder

The concentration of power and responsibility demanded by war is apt to give a system grounded on the rigid maxims of republicanism a somewhat violent wrench. Fortunately the framers of the Constitution were not wholly unaware of the difficulty, which they proceeded to meet by conferring on the President as Commander-in-Chief of the army and navy all the prerogatives of monarchy in connection with war-making except only the power to declare war and the power to create armed forces. The clause of the Constitution which makes the President Commander-in-Chief may accordingly be described as the elastic block in the closed circle of constitutionalism; in the heat of war the powers it confers are capable of expanding tremendously, but upon the restoration of normal conditions they shrink with equal rapidity. The true nature of the presidential prerogative in war time was comprehended by Lincoln perfectly, who, when he was confronted with the argument that some of his measures were likely to constitute precedents injurious to liberty, answered the objection in his characteristic strain: "Nor," said he, "am I able to appreciate the danger apprehended that the American people will, by means of military arrests during the rebellion lose the right of public discussion, the liberty of speech and the press, the laws of evidence, trial by jury, and habeas corpus, throughout the indefinite peaceful future which I trust lies before them, any more than I am able to believe that a man could contract so strong an appetite for emetics during a temporary illness as to persist in feeding upon them during the remainder of his healthful life". History has amply vindicated Lincoln's judgment in this matter, for the direct effect of the Civil War in the way of enlarging national power or of altering the relations of the different branches of the national government to one another was comparatively slight.

Will those of us who survive be able to say the same of the present war fifty years hence? Probably not, at any rate if the war is prolonged. For it requires no inordinate insight to recognize already the beginnings of what may well prove to be revolutionary developments in our system.

Despite much that has been said implying the contrary, it is extremely unlikely that our participation in the present war will exact of us sacrifices at all approaching those with which our forefathers met the war for the Union. But our participation will be for the most part, it seems probable, of a different order and so will produce different results. The Civil War was *war* in the most elementary sense of the term; our assistance to the Allies, even though we eventually send a considerable army abroad, must still be primarily financial and industrial. And this means the regimentation of industry and commerce on a national scale. It means, if Congress follows the President in this matter, lodging in the hands of the national executive the power to direct transportation, to control exports, to prevent – in the

President's own words – "all unwarranted hoarding of every kind and the control of food stuffs by persons who are not in any legitimate sense producers, dealers, or traders," the power to requisition food supplies to meet public need, and the equipment necessary to handle them, the power to prohibit unnecessary and wasteful use of foods, and finally the power to fix maximum and minimum prices. No doubt, many of the measures suggested in the President's statement of Saturday, May 19, which I have just paraphrased, will be of a purely emergency character, and so will pass out of existence with the war. Yet it is clear that for some of them, and for others of a similar nature, the way had already been paved both by industrial development and political agitation long before our entrance into the war had been thought of Measures of this description look toward the permanent reshaping of both our governmental and our industrial systems, and the power upon which they rest will be relaxed only in part, if at all, with the return of peace.

This, however, is but the beginning of the changes which the war promises to engraft upon our constitutional arrangements. For the new faculties with which the national government will find itself endowed new channels must be provided or else existing channels must be enlarged. The latter is the more economical course, and already it is being resorted to. Moreover, we again perceive the stress of the immediate exigency striking hands with developments which were originally launched much earlier. In this connection it is interesting to refer to a paragraph in Mr. Wilson's own work, *The State,* in which he comments upon the administrative powers of the French executive in the following manner: "The Executive is expected to shape the laws to the cases that arise, and to supplement them where they lack completeness. The laws are, accordingly, for the most part themselves without detailed provisions. They give the officers of state, who are to execute them a principle by which to go rather than a body of minute instructions". He also makes it clear that this way of legislating presents a distinct contrast to the English-American method.

But these words were written nearly thirty years ago. Since then Congress, influenced partly by a growing appreciation of its own inability to provide wisely for the multiple phases of the complex matters that today frequently fall within its regulating power, and partly by the rising reputation of the "scientific expert," has fallen more and more into the French way of proceeding. Thus it has authorized the Commerce Commission to fix "reasonable" maximum rates for interstate transportation;

it has authorized the Secretary of the Treasury to say what varieties of tea are fit for importation; it has authorized the Secretary of Agriculture to prescribe regulations for governing the use of the public grazing lands; it has invested the Federal Reserve Board, the Federal Trade Commission, and the Shipping Board with the broadest kind of discretion within their several fields; and illustrations of the same character might be multiplied almost indefinitely. Such legislation plainly derogates from the principle of the separation of powers and the corollary doctrine that the legislature cannot delegate its powers. It had therefore, at first, a rather difficult gauntlet to run with the courts. But today the federal Supreme Court at least has definitely yielded its scruples on these points, and will sustain such legislation simply on the score of necessity. (See Buttfield *v.* Stranahan, 192 U.S., and Grimaud *v.* U.S., 220 U.S.) Necessity, however, is at best a vague concept, and it is especially so in wartime. One of the most conspicuous features, accordingly, of the legislation at present pending in Congress is the extent to which it relies upon executive discretion to supplement its provisions.

An even more striking possibility in the way of constitutional development than those just referred to is foreshadowed by section 6 of the Conscription Act. This section authorizes the President "to utilize the services" not only of all officers and agents of the United States and territories, but of the several states as well, and it further provides that any person "who in any manner shall fail or neglect fully to perform any duty required of him in the execution of this act, shall, if not subject to military law, be guilty of a misdemeanor and, upon conviction in the District Court of the United States having jurisdiction thereof, be punished by imprisonment for not more than one year". Students of constitutional law will at once appreciate how radically these provisions transgress the principle of dual sovereignty which has hitherto underlain our federal system, a corollary of which is that the national government can impose legal duties upon state officers only with the consent of and upon the terms imposed by the states themselves. It was upon this principle that the first Fugitive Slave Act was pronounced partially void in 1842 in the famous case of Prigg **v.** Pennsylvania, 16 Pet., while a few years afterward the Court held, on the same ground, that the "duty" with which the governor of a state is charged by the act of 1793 in connection with the rendition of fugitives from justice is not a legally enforcible one (Ky. *v.* Dennison, 24 How.). The Conscription Act is, however, vindicated to some degree by certain later utterances of the Court (see especially *Ex parte* Siebold, 100 U.S.), and at any rate it is clearly harmonious with the original intention of the Constitution. The younger Pinckney, speaking in this reference on the floor of the Philadelphia Convention, said: "They [the states] are the instruments upon which the Union must frequently depend for the support and execution of its powers." Then the Constitution itself requires an oath of fidelity from all state officers, commenting upon which fact, Hamilton wrote in *The Federalist* as follows: "Thus the legislatures, courts, and magistrates of the respective members will be incorporated into the operations of the national government as far as its just and constitutional authority extends, and will be rendered auxiliary to the enforcement of its laws." An interesting possibility is thus suggested: that, as the states diminish in importance in the legislative field, through the extension of congressional power, they may be afforded an opportunity to justify their continued existence in the capacity of administrative agents of the national government, and so our dual system would be gradually replaced by a federal system approximating to the German and Swiss type.

The general bearing of some other developments of the moment is not so easily perceived. What, for instance, will be the ultimate fate of such unofficial bodies as the Council of National Defense – are they merely "sports" which the body politic has put forth under an extraordinary stimulus and destined therefore to wither away when this stimulus is removed, or are they true species, the beginnings of valuable institutions? Again, what will be the permanent outcome of the President's notable efforts these days at "common counsel" with the congressional leaders – will they be likely to pave the way for the gradual displacement of the Cabinet in the American sense with a Cabinet in the British sense? Yet again, there is the ever-present question of budgetary reform. Must not the government's increasing resort to those forms of taxation which are most directly burdensome to the taxpayer bring this problem evermore to the front? And will not the recent reform of the Senate's rules, forced from the White House, have a similar tendency? To be sure, the practice of doing business by unanimous consent sometimes thwarted the congressional logrollers, as where an individual Senator or two held up a rivers and harbors bill at the end of the session; but ordinarily it promoted it, by giving disgruntled seekers after "pork" in the House a second chance to force their demands through friends in the upper chamber. Now, however, this opportunity for blackmail is at an end, together with the special defense that has hitherto existed against the worst scandals of logrolling. In both ways the case for executive budget-making will be considerably strengthened with Congress itself.

Thus war has overtaken us at a peculiarly favorable moment for effecting lasting constitutional changes. For several years forces have been accumulating behind the barriers of the old Constitution, straining and weakening them at many points, yet without finding adequate enlargement. Where the stress of war falls coincident with such forces we may expect it to thrust aside accepted principles, not for the time only, but permanently. Certainly if the war is considerably prolonged, we may expect our system to emerge from it substantially altered in numerous ways, with the result, however, it may be, of postponing more radical alterations many years.

Wilson and the Senate

The issue between the President and the Senate over the ratification of the (League of Nations) Covenant is developing a struggle for power between parties and between two branches of the national government that is of really historic dimensions. It is true that thus far both sides to the controversy have deprecated the charge of "partisanism" as explanatory of their respective attitudes, but there is no good reason why they should do so; and still less is there reason for the senatorial opponents of the league to fight shy of the other charge which has been leveled against them, that they are waging war upon the President's program in order to vindicate "the dignity and prerogatives of the Senate". The maintenance of the constitutional prerogatives and dignity of an important branch of the government is itself a matter of moment; and that must be exigent issue indeed which is capable of relegating it to a secondary or incidental role.

In a striking passage of his *Promise of American Life,* Mr. Herbert Croly passes estimate upon the outcome of the protracted struggle which took place in Jackson's time between the President and the Senate. It resulted, he says – I quote from recollection – in a victory for the President "because the people decided for him," "as they must always do" when the occupant of the presidential chair is a man "no worse than Andrew Jackson" and his antagonist a man "no better than Henry Clay". Is this interesting verdict applicable to the contest which today impends? That is to say, Woodrow Wilson being no worse than he is and Henry Cabot Lodge being no better than *he* is, which way ought popular sympathy to incline in a struggle for power between the institutions represented by these two men?

There is no quarreling with Mr. Croly's complacency over Jackson's triumph, for had not the presidency been aggrandized at the moment when John Marshall was sinking into his grave and the powers of Congress were being brought more and more under the surveillance of a jealous particularism, of which the Senate itself was the very citadel, the cause of the Union would have had in 1861 no rallying-point. But the situation has altered since then, and today the question is not the preservation of the Union, it is the preservation of constitutional government in face of an almost world-wide tendency towards one man power. Confronted with such a situation, the Senate may be very well warranted in feeling that it ought to insist somewhat upon "its dignity and prerogatives".

In his lectures on "Constitutional Government in the United States," which were published in the spring of 1908, Mr. Wilson discovers three seats of authority in the national government to wit, the Presidency, the Senate, and the Speakership of the House of Representatives. Since then the Speakership has been put in commission in great part, so that today, if the President is to be effectively checked, it is the Senate which must do the business. Nor has any writer presented the claims of the Senate to popular confidence more appealingly than Mr. Wilson himself, in the volume just cited. The Senate, he declares, "represents the country, as distinct from the accumulated populations of the country much more fully and much more truly than the House of Representatives does". It is a place too "of individual voices," and "the suppression of a single voice would radically change its constitutional character".(There is no thought here, it will be noted, of stigmatizing the "willfulness" of "little groups".) Again, the men who make up the Senate are "men much above the average in ability and in personal force," and if they are not always wise counselors, still their "experience of affairs is much mellower than the President's can be," for "the continuity of the Government lies in the keeping of the Senate more than in the keeping of the executive, even in respect of matters which are of the especial prerogative of the presidential office".

Turning then to the subject of the relations of the President and the Senate in the control of appointments to office and treaty-making, Mr. Wilson writes:

There can be little doubt in the mind of any one who has carefully studied the plans and opinions of the Constitutional Convention of 1787 that the relations of the President and Senate were intended to be very much more intimate and confidential than they have been; that it was expected that the Senate would give the President its advice and consent in respect of appointments and treaties in the spirit of an Executive Council associated with him upon terms of confidential co-operation rather than in the spirit of an independent branch of the Government, jealous lest he should in the least particular attempt to govern its judgment or infringe upon its prerogatives.

Unfortunately this idea has not in general prevailed, and the relations between the two branches have fallen too often under the control of a spirit of distrust, mitigated to some extent by a sort of "customary *modus vivendi,* as of rival powers. The Senate is expected in most instances to accept the President's appointments to office, and the President is expected to be very tolerant of the Senate's rejection of treaties, proposing but by no means disposing even in this chief field of his power." However, there have been "one or two Presidents of unusual sagacity" who have recurred to something like the earlier practice, as any President is free to do:

He may himself be less stiff and offish, may himself act in the true spirit of the Constitution and establish intimate relations with the Senate on his own initiative, not carrying his plans to completion and then laying them in final form before the Senate to be accepted or rejected, but keeping himself in confidential communication with the leaders of the Senate while his plans are in course – in order that there may be veritable counsel and a real accommodation of views instead of a final challenge and contrast. The policy which has made rivals of the President and Senate has shown itself in the President as often as in the Senate, and if the Constitution did indeed that the Senate should in such matters be an Executive Council it is not only the privilege of the President to treat it as such, it is also his best policy and his plain duty.

Could a more telling indictment be penned of President Wilson's entire course in connection with the League of Nations Covenant? Here is a proposal of vital interest to every section of the country, a proposal not needing to be elaborated in secret, certainly not after the first draft of it was published some months ago, a proposal furthermore for the final perfection of which the utmost allowance of time is even yet available, since it is now the announced intention of the Allies to act for some months to come in carrying out the peace treaty through the Council of Five. Yet not only has the President never consulted with the Senate as a body about this proposal, nor with any of its leaders except in the most cursory fashion, but he has expended the greatest ingenuity in an endeavor to deprive the Senate of all freedom of action with reference to the proposal when this shall finally come before it. Writers on our political system with a bias in favor of executive authority are prone to criticize the legislative "rider," a device whereby a measure of minor importance is put safely past the danger of veto on the back of a more important or more urgent measure. It is safe to say, however, that concocters of "riders" now have a new record in audacity set them. And in this connection it is pertinent to recall the announcement which was first given out from Paris regarding the proposed guaranty treaty with France. The President, we were told, had not positively committed himself to the arrangement but had promised to refer it to the Senate, presumably for advice. Yet, as compared with the covenant, the guaranty treaty would mark a relatively slight departure from our national traditions. Little wonder that the President has subsequently abandoned his scruples about the lesser compact – the discrepancy in procedure would have been too glaring. Yet even as matters stand, the Senate is to be allowed a free hand with the guaranty treaty.

There are certain other facts which cast additional light upon the constitutional significance of the impending struggle over the covenant that may be set down more or less at random. On the debit side of the ledger for the President appear such facts as the Ishii agreement, which was never referred to the Senate; also the understanding between the United States and Great Britain, which was testified to by General March the other day before the Senate Military Committee, that both these powers shall maintain a military establishment four times larger than before the war (we know now, perhaps, why President Wilson appealed to the country last autumn for a Democratic Congress); again, such facts as the numerous instances during the present Administration of wars waged without congressional sanction, indeed, without congressional knowledge; and the still more numerous instances of diplomatic appointments without reference to the Senate. Meantime, the demand for "open diplomacy," at least for democratic control of diplomacy, has been rising higher and higher throughout the world, while by the Seventeenth Amendment the Senate has been rendered a democratic body as never before.

Finally, it requires no extraordinary insight to perceive that if the League of Nations Covenant is ratified, the opportunity – indeed, the necessity – for independent presidential action in the diplomatic field will be much augmented. This is not of itself a conclusive argument against ratifying the covenant were it otherwise satisfactory, but it is a very powerful argument against the Senate's consenting to any unnecessary abdication of its participation in the shaping of our diplomatic policies.

Woodrow Wilson and the Presidency

When Thomas W. Wilson, Princeton '79, found it essential to select a theme for his senior essay – the institution goes back that far, apparently

– he chose "Cabinet Government in the United States". The choice was dictated by two circumstances: first, by the fact that he had been reading, especially in Bagehot's misnamed *English Constitution.*[72] about the British cabinet system and had come to admire it; secondly, by the scars which as a Southerner he bore vicariously from the enormities of Congressional Reconstruction.

It can hardly be claimed that young Wilson's essay was a literary masterpiece. The style is turgid, spasmodic, and the work abounds in repetition. For all that, it was, for so young a man, a notable production, in that it marked an effort to assess government under the Constitution *functionally*, in contrast to the customary legalistic approach. How good a government are we really getting under the Constitution was the question presented.

What Wilson found was, in effect, that Congress was a tyrant, indeed, a faceless, voiceless tyrant, all of its powers being at the disposal of a proliferation of committees, whose proceedings and decisions, when they reached the American public at all, did so haphazardly, sporadically. Above all, Congress lacked a central guiding leadership.

What then was the remedy? In *Cabinet Government* young Wilson goes back a half century to Story's *Commentaries* and takes from it the suggestion that heads of departments be allowed, like territorial delegates, seats in the House of Representatives, "where they might freely debate without a title to vote".[73] But then he broaches a much bolder suggestion. "The highest order of responsible government," he writes, "could … be established in the United States only by laying upon the President the necessity of selecting his Cabinet from among the number of representatives already chosen by the people, or by the legislatures of the States"[74] – in other words, from the House of Representatives and the Senate – in brief, by setting up a cabinet after the British model. Only thus, he argued, could governmental policy attain coherency; only thus could talent be drawn into the government. He continued:

> Responsible ministers must secure from the House and Senate an intelligent, thorough, and practical treatment of their affairs; must vindicate their principles in open battle on the floor of Congress. The public is thus enabled to exercise a direct scrutiny over the workings of the Executive departments, to keep all their operations under a constant stream of daylight. Ministers could do nothing under the shadow of darkness; committees do all in the dark.[75]

Apparently Wilson's instructor was well pleased with the young man's performance. *Cabinet Government in the United States* was published in the August, 1879, issue of *International Review*, the editor of which was one Henry Cabot Lodge!

In *Congressional Government,*[76] which was his Hopkins doctoral thesis, and which issued from the press in 1885, Wilson renewed and extended the argument of *Cabinet Government.* I quote some characteristic passages:

The noble charter of fundamental law given us by the Convention of 1787 is still our Constitution; but it is now out *form of government* rather in name than in reality, the form of the Constitution being one of nicely adjusted, ideal balances, whilst the actual form of our present government is simply a scheme of congressional supremacy.[77]

It is said that there is no single or central force in our federal scheme ... but only a balance of powers and a nice adjustment of interactive checks, as all the books say. How is it, however, in the practical conduct of the federal government? In that, unquestionably, the predominant and controlling force, the center and source of all motive and of all regulative power, is Congress....[78]

Congress [is] the dominant, nay, the irresistible, power of the federal system, relegating some of the chief balances of the Constitution to an insignificant role in the "literary theory" of our institutions.[79]

And again:

Congress is fast becoming the governing body of the nation, and yet the only power which it possesses in perfection is the power which is but a part of government, the power of legislation.[80]

With this, contrast the position which Wilson assigns the President of that period:

Except in-so-far as his power of veto constitutes him a part of the legislature, the President might, not inconveniently, be a permanent officer; the first official of a carefully-graded and impartially regulated civil service system, through whose sure series of merit-promotions the youngest clerk might rise even to the chief magistracy. He is a part of the official rather than of the political machinery of the government, and his duties call rather for training than for constructive genius. If there can be found in the official systems of the States a lower grade of service in which men may be advantageously drilled for Presidential functions, so much the better. The States will have better governors, the Union better presidents, and there will have been supplied one of the most serious needs left unsupplied by the Constitution – the need for a proper school in which to rear federal administrators.[81]

And the consequence of the low estate of the President was that "no office [was] set apart for the great party leadership in our government. ...[T] he presidency is ... too little like a premiership and too much like a superintendency."[82]

In short, the Presidency was written off as a bad job. But a decade later, in consequence of the Spanish-American War, Wilson indicates a disposition to revise his estimate of the potentialities of the office, at least in some measure. Thus in his preface to the 15th impression of *Congressional Government* written August 15, 1900, he says:

Much the most important change to be noticed [i.e., since 1885] is the result of the war with Spain upon the lodgment and exercise of power within our federal system: the greatly increased power and opportunity for constructive statesmanship given the President, by the plunge into international politics and into the administration of distant dependencies, which has been that war's most striking and momentous consequences. When foreign affairs play a prominent part in the politics and policy of a nation, its Executive must of necessity be its guide: must utter every initial judgment, take every first step of action, supply the information upon which it is to act, suggest and in large measure control its conduct. The President of the United States is now, as of course, at the front of affairs, as no president, except Lincoln, has been since the first quarter of the nineteenth century, when the foreign relations of the new nation had first to be adjusted. There is no trouble now about getting the President's speeches printed and read, every word. Upon his choice, his character, his experience hang some of the most weighty issues of the future. The government of dependencies must be largely in his hands. Interesting things may come out of the singular change.[83]

The real herald of the twentieth-century Presidency, however, its John the Baptist, was not Woodrow Wilson: it was a Pittsburgh editor named Henry Jones Ford, whose brilliant volume *The Rise and Growth of American Politics* spotlights the Presidency in the tradition of its successes, not of its failures.[84] In these discerning pages we read:

The agency of the presidential office has been such a master force in shaping public policy that to give a detailed account of it would be equivalent to writing the political history of the United States. From Jackson's time to the present day it may be said that political issues have been decided by executive policy.[85]

The rise of presidential authority cannot be accounted for by the intention of presidents: it is the product of political conditions which dominate all the departments of government, so that Congress itself shows an unconscious disposition to aggrandize the presidential office.[86]

The truth is that in the presidential office, as it has been constituted since Jackson's time, American democracy has revived the oldest political institution of the race, the elective kingship. It is all there: the precognition of the notables and the tumultuous choice of the freemen, only conformed to modern conditions. That the people have been able to accomplish this with such defective apparatus, and have been able to make good a principle which no other people have been able to reconcile with the safety of the state, indicates the highest degree of constitutional morality yet attained by any race.[87]

There is, to be sure, considerable exaggeration here. It is quite untrue that after Jackson's day political issues had been settled by executive policy. The issue of slavery in the territories first arose in Congress and was settled – temporarily to be sure – by the Supreme Court, eventually by war; and the issue of Reconstruction, as well as that of the tariff, was settled in Congress. But Ford's notable volume was really oriented toward the future, and the future came to its rescue.

The first exponent of the new Presidency was Theodore Roosevelt. Assessing his performance in the illumination sparked by Ford's volume and the Spanish-American War, Woodrow Wilson wrote in his Blumenthal Lectures given at Columbia University in 1907[88]:

He cannot escape being the leader of his party except by incapacity and lack of personal force, because he is at once the choice of the party and of the nation.... He can dominate his party by being spokesman for the real sentiment and purpose of the country, by giving direction to opinion, by giving the country at once the information and the statements of policy which will enable it to form its judgments alike of parties and of men.... His is the only national voice in affairs. Let him once win the admiration and confidence of the country, and no other single force can withstand him, no combination of forces will easily overpower him. His position takes the imagination of the country. He is the representative of no constituency, but the whole people.... He may be both the leader of his party and the leader of the nation, or he may be one or the other. If he lead the nation, his party can hardly resist him. His office is anything he has the sagacity and force to make it.

Some of our Presidents have deliberately held themselves off from using the full power they might legitimately have used, because of conscientious scruples, because they were more theorists than statesmen.... The President is at liberty, both in law and conscience, to be as big a man as he can.[89]

The following year the lectures were published under the title *Constitutional Government in the United States.* The same year Wilson, as president of Princeton University, offered its author {Wilson} a professorship in politics, which the latter in due course accepted. His indebtedness to Roosevelt Mr.Wilson was less prompt to acknowledge. In the index to *Constitutional Government* T.R.'s name appears just once, and the reference is of no significance. Indeed, without mentioning Roosevelt, who had just emerged victorious from a hard fought battle with the Senate over certain pending legislation – the famed Hepburn Act – Wilson contrives to read him a lecture on how Presidents ought to treat that august body. "If," he writes, "he [the President, has] character, modesty, devotion and insight as well as force, he can bring the contending elements into a great and efficient body of common counsel".[90] Little did he foresee that ten years later he would be describing the Senate as "the only legislative body in the world which cannot act when its majority is ready for action. A little group of wilful men, representing no opinion but their own, have rendered the great Government of the United States helpless and contemptible"![91]

Woodrow Wilson abandoned academic and entered public life in 1910. Was it *contingency* or *predestination* that determined this, the most momentous choice in his career? The question is the more intriguing for the reason that, as a sound Calvinist, Mr. Wilson undoubtedly believed in predestination, and identified with it his own destiny. Still that there was at the outset an element of contingency in his decision cannot be gainsaid, inasmuch as it was in the first place the consequence of his defeat in his controversy with Dean West over the location of the Graduate College. Was the college to be located on the Princeton campus or on the Princeton golf course? President Wilson wanted the former; Dean West the latter.

Early in 1910 William Cooper Procter, of Ivory Soap fame, offered Princeton $500,000 to be expended in furtherance of Dean West's plan, but when Mr. Wilson demanded that the condition be rescinded, Mr. Procter withdrew the gift. So far the President enjoyed the support of his Trustees, albeit by a precarious margin. In June, however, the news broke upon the world that a person named Wyman, of Marblehead, Massachusetts, had died leaving Princeton substantially his entire estate, which was variously estimated as falling "somewhere between three and thirty millions of dollars". The condition on which the bequest hinged was that it should be used to forward Dean West's design. Confronted with this turn of affairs, Mr. Wilson remarked with adequate decision, "The size of the gift alters the perspective." and the following October resigned as president of the university, whereupon he was quickly snatched up by expectant politicians and run for Governor of New Jersey.

For all that, I am quite convinced that Mr. Wilson would have resigned his academic post sooner or later to run for public office – and sooner rather than later – Wyman or no Wyman. Not only was there that hovering brood of politicians, which was headed in New Jersey by "Jim Smith Junior," there was also the redoubtable George Harvey, editor of the *North American Review* and *Harper's Weekly,* who had been for some years carrying Mr. Wilson's name at the mastheads of his publications as just the man needed to spike T.R.'s Square Deal. I also place reliance on the testimony of Mr. Talcott Williams, distinguished Philadelphia editor, who came to Princeton in 1906 or thereabouts to give a lecture. Following the talk, he and Mr. Wilson repaired to "Prospect," where they had a long conversation in the course of which Mr. Wilson told about certain reading he had been recently doing, including, mayhap, Mr. Ford's book. Mr. Williams listened with increasing intentness, and at the conclusion of Mr. Wilson's remarks charged the latter with harboring political ambitions, and Mr. Wilson admitted the soft imperchment {impeachment?}.

The real reason why Woodrow Wilson finally decided to enter public life was a two-fold one. On the one hand, he had learned that in the potentialities of the Presidency public life in the United States did, after all, afford ample field for talent. On the other hand, his defeat in his battle against the club system and his impending defeat – which he no doubt clearly foresaw – in the battle over the location of the Graduate College, had revealed a mission to him. What this mission was he clearly expressed in his famous Pittsburgh Speech of April 16, 1910. Referring to the question of the location of the Graduate College, Mr. Wilson asked:

What does the country expect of Princeton? It expects of Princeton what it expects of every other college, the accommodation of its life to the life of the country.

The colleges of this country are in exactly the same danger that the churches are in. I believe that the churches of this country, at any rate the Protestant churches, have dissociated themselves from the people of this country. They are serving the classes and they are not serving the masses. They serve certain strata, certain uplifted strata, but they are not serving the men whose need is dire. The churches have more regard to their pew-rents than to the souls of men, and in proportion as they look to the respectability of their congregations to lift them in esteem they are depressing the whole level of Christian endeavor.

Where does the strength of the nation come from? From the conspicuous classes? Not at all. It comes from the great mass of the unknown, of the unrecognized men, whose powers are being developed by struggle, who will form their opinions as they progress in that struggle, and who will emerge with opinions which will rule.

What we cry out against is that a handful of conspicuous men have thrust cruel hands among the heartstrings of the masses of men upon whose blood and energy they are subsisting.

The universities would make men forget their common origins, forget their universal sympathies, and join a class – and no class ever can serve America.

The great voice of America does not come from seats of learning. It comes in a murmur from the hills and woods and the farms and factories and the mills, rolling on and gaining volume until it comes to us from the homes of common men. Do these murmurs echo in the corridors of universities? I have not heard them.[92]

Thus was "the New Freedom" born which first spread its healing wings over New Jersey, then over the nation, then, bereft, to be sure, of some of its plumage, over "abroad".

In 1911 Mr. Wilson informed Editor Harvey that he wished the latter to discontinue his attentions, that they had become "embarrassing". In short, Mr. Wilson was not questing for Lotus Club votes. When Harvey next adopted a candidate for the Presidency, the beneficiary was one Warren G. Harding!

I turn now to evaluate Mr. Wilson's exercise of the office of President of the United States. What was his impact on the office; and first of all, by what procedures did he convert the Presidency into an instrument of social reform? The answer is, by making the President an active participant in the national legislative process far beyond any of his predecessors, even T.R.; by converting it, in other words, into a species of prime ministership. Mr. Wilson had dismissed his early idea of superseding the Presidency with a cabinet government after the British model. He now substituted for that idea an amalgamation, as it were, of the British prime ministership and the Presidency.

A document of first importance in this connection is the letter which Mr. Wilson wrote a short time before his inauguration to his future

Attorney General, A. Mitchell Palmer. The letter was in answer to one from Palmer urging the President elect to endorse a plank in the Democratic platform favoring a single term Presidency. Mr. Wilson sharply demurred:

[The President] is expected by the nation to be the leader of his party as well as the chief executive officer of the Government and the country will take no excuses from him. He must play the part and play it successfully or lose the country's confidence. He must be Prime Minister, as much concerned with the guidance of legislation as with just and orderly execution of law; and he is the spokesman of the nation in everything, even the most momentous and most delicate dealings of the Government in foreign affairs.[93]

To deny the President the possibility of re-election was out of the question. To be sure:

Sooner or later it would seem he must be made answerable to opinion in a somewhat more informal and intimate fashion, answerable, it may be, to the Houses whom he seeks to lead, either personally or through a cabinet, as well as to the people for whom they speak. But that is a matter to be worked out – as it will inevitably be in some natural American way which we cannot yet even predict.[94]

In fact, Mr. Wilson himself worked "the matter out" for one contingency. He planned that if Mr. Hughes was elected in 1916, he would ask Marshall to resign from the Vice-Presidency and then appoint Mr. Hughes Secretary of State so that, under the Succession Act of 1886, the latter could assume the office of President at once, as the logic of the prime minister concept undoubtedly required.

Mr. Wilson took office on March 4, 1913. His first official act after taking the oath was to summon Congress to met in special session on April 7. The following day he electrified the country by going up to Capitol Hill to present his first message in person, thereby returning to a practice which his great predecessor Jefferson had discarded 112 years earlier. "Gentlemen of the Congress" were his opening words, a locution which toppled an equally venerable precedent. For while the original Constitution does say "The Congress," the first amendment says "Congress," and I find no instance in which Washington, Jefferson, Lincoln, or John Marshall, not to mention sundry others, used the older form save when they were quoting directly from the Constitution.

But Wilson's greatest innovation is to be seen in the form and content of his message. The old State of the Union message which had become established custom on similar occasions, had grown to inordinate length. Some of T.R.'s ran to thirty thousand words and over. Sent up to Capitol

Hill by a messenger, they were handed over to a sleepy clerk who droned along for two or three hours, while the members drowsed.

Naturally, no President would care to submit himself in person to such an ordeal. Wilson's message was brief and was devoted to a single topic, tariff reduction; and his later messages followed this same model. They dealt crisply with banking and currency reform, with antitrust legislation, and so on. They asserted for the President his legislative leadership in the achievement of specific reforms. As Professor Small remarks:

Whereas Roosevelt confused both Congress and the public by attempting to enlist its attention immediately to his entire legislative program, as expounded in a vague message or two, Wilson, by proceeding in this more methodical fashion, enabled his legislative associates to direct their undivided attention to single items of his platform, and accordingly escaped many of the delays produced by congested calendars, Wilson's method also helped him in crystallizing and mobilizing public opinion in support of his proposals.[95]

One can readily imagine the chagrin of T.R. when he read in the morning papers of April 9, 1913, what Woodrow Wilson had been up to the day before. Why had he never thought that one up!

I also cite Dr. Small for his estimate of Wilson's achievement in the legislative field. He accords it an easy primacy, with the possible exception of that of Jefferson, whose methods were, however, vastly different, being conditioned by Jefferson's professed deference to the principle of the separation of powers. In these circumstances, while Jefferson's guidance of Congress was constant and unremitting, it was often secret and always disavowed.

Another facet of Wilson's legislative activities emerged in 1916. World War I had now broken; a presidential campaign was looming; and the Republican Party was split. To be sure, The Democrats had what many of them reckoned was a winning shibboleth, "He kept us out of war" – a slogan which Mr. Wilson himself endorsed in his Shadow Lawn speech early in September, when he warned the country, "If you elect my opponent [Mr. Hughes], you elect a war." But was this enough? Many Democrats doubted it. What the doubting Thomases demanded was that a definite effort be made to capture "Progressive" (Roosevelt) votes – but how? Looking to this end, Democratic leaders urged the passage of an anti-child labor bill. But could Mr. Wilson endorse it? Hardly, if he still adhered to the views he had expressed in his Blumenthal Lectures anent an earlier proposal of the same sort. There he wrote:

The proposed federal legislation with regard to the regulation of child labor affords a striking example [of the devitalization of the federal principle]. If the power to regulate commerce between the States can be stretched to include the regulation of labor in mills and factories, it can be made to embrace every particular of the industrial organization and action of the country. The only limitations Congress would observe, should the Supreme Court assent to such obviously absurd extravagancies of interpretation, would be the limitations of opinions and of circumstances.[96]

A bill after the pattern of the measure which Mr. Wilson had stigmatized as "absurd" passed the House of Representatives early in February, 1916, but got stalled in the Senate. On July 17, the President was warned by certain of his followers in that body that passage of the measure was "necessary," and the following day the President went to the Capitol to plead with the Democratic command of that body to permit the measure to come to a vote. The bill was finally passed on August 8 and was signed by the President on September 1, "with real emotion," he said. In point of fact, the bill had already become law several days earlier owing to the President's failure to disapprove it within the required "ten Days (Sunday excepted)". His belated signing of it was nevertheless valuable politically; it may even have turned the trick in closely-contested California.

Twenty-two months later the act was held void in a five-to-four decision of the Supreme Court,[97] which rested substantially on the grounds urged by Mr. Wilson in *Constitutional Government*, to wit, its damaging effect on the federal system. Fortunately, the decision was not retroactive as to the election of 1916. Mr. Wilson continued to be President till the end of his term on March 4, 1921. Not till 1941 did the Supreme Court accept – in a unanimous judgment – the principle underlying the measure, the simple principle, to wit, of national supremacy within the realm of national powers.[98]

I now turn to Mr. Wilson's exercise of the Presidency in the field of foreign relations. Here, too, at the outset his past caught up with him. Japan was demanding a treaty from Washington which would give its subjects the right to own land in the United States. Confronted with the choice of fighting Japan or "The Sons of the Golden West," the Administration elected to pursue a middle course. By what in effect was a *modus vivendi,* Japan abandoned her attempt to get the treaty and the Administration admitted her special rights in China. Thus early was Yalta foreshadowed.

For the rest, history was on Mr. Wilson's side, history that stemmed from the time of Washington. "The transaction of business with foreign nations," Jefferson proclaimed, was "Executive altogether,"[99] doctrine which was reiterated by Jefferson's little-loved cousin, John Marshall, on the floor of Congress: "The President is the sole organ of the nation in its external relations and its some representative with foreign nations";[100] and four years later, Marshall expounded even broader doctrine from the bench: "By the Constitution, the President is invested with certain important political powers, in the exercise of which he is to use his own discretion, and is accountable only to his country in his political character, and to his conscience" – is, in brief, autonomous.[101]

This autonomy Wilson labored constantly and successfully to maintain, bringing at times his Prime Minister conception of the office into operation in its support. Thus he repeatedly asked Congress during the war for what was in effect a "vote of confidence". Two items from the *New York Times* illustrate the point:

Washington, July 23, 1917. -- A virtual threat to veto the Administration Food Bill if the conferees retain the Senate amendment creating a joint committee to supervise war expenditures is contained in a letter sent tonight by President Wilson to Chairman Lever of the House Committee on Agriculture. The letter says the President would interpret "the final adoption of Section 23 as arising from a lack of confidence in myself".[102]

Washington, May 15, 1918. – Three moves of prime importance were made today in connection with the aircraft controversy:

President Wilson in a letter to Senator Martin, the Democratic floor leader, vehemently opposed the Chamberlain resolution for an investigation of the conduct of the war by the Committee on Military Affairs of the Senate. He said passage of the resolution would be "a direct vote of want of confidence in the Administration," and would constitute "nothing less than an attempt to take over the conduct of the war". The President called upon supporters of the Administration in the Senate to rally in his support".[103]

Mr. Wilson also contemplated resignation had he been defeated on the Panama tolls issue and in his opposition to the McLemore Resolution of March, 1916, warning American citizens to refrain from travelling in armed belligerent vessels. He got his way in all four instances. Mr. Wilson's famous appeal to the country of October 24, 1918, in behalf of the Treaty of Versailles and the League smacks also of the same general idea of prime ministership. It read, in part, as follows:

My fellow-Countrymen, the Congressional elections are at hand. They occur in the most critical period our country has ever faced or is likely to face in our time. If you have approved of my leadership and wish me to continue to be your unembarrassed spokesman in affairs at home and abroad, I earnestly beg that you will express yourselves unmistakably to that effect by returning a Democratic majority to both the Senate and the House of Representatives.

I have no thought of suggesting that any political party is paramount in matters of patriotism. I feel too deeply the sacrifices which have been made in this war by all our citizens, irrespective of party affiliations, to harbor such an idea. I mean only that the difficulties and delicacies of our present task are of a sort that makes it imperatively necessary that the nation should give its undivided support to the Government under a unified leadership, and that a Republican Congress would divide the leadership.[104]

Although this time he failed, he neglected to resign – an omission which some of his critics condemned as at least illogical.

The truth of the matter is that Mr. Wilson had always two strings to his official bow – the Prime Minister concept and the historic traditions of the American Presidency – and he retained to the end complete liberty of choice between them. Thus, when that "little group of wilful men" in the Senate foiled him in his effort early in 1917 to obtain congressional authorization to arm American merchantmen plying in the war zone, backed by high legal authority, he went ahead and did it anyway; and one of his last acts as President, following his partial recovery from his collapse in October, 1919, was to refuse to carry out a provision of the Jones Shipping Act of 1920, which ordered him to denounce certain treaties which other provisions of the measure overrode. The requirement, he asserted, invaded his prerogative in the field of foreign relations. His partisan enemies assailed his action as "unconstitutional" and "presumptuous". One of these same critics was Mr. W. G. Harding, one of whose first official acts on becoming President was to adopt his predecessor's position.

In asserting his monopoly of the right to determine the foreign relations of the United States, Mr. Wilson was fighting, as it were, a defensive action, the constitutional basis of which was the "executive power" clause as it had been interpreted by presidential spokesmen from the time of Washington. His direction of the domestic phases of our war with Germany was based, in important part, on that clause of Article II which makes the President "Commander-in-Chief of the Army and Navy of the United States, and of the Militia of the several States when called into the actual service of the United States...." But in this case the historical record was somewhat more complicated.

Expounding the "Commander-in-Chief" clause in *The Federalist* No. 69 Hamilton had asserted that it would be altogether erroneous to compare this power with the superficially similar prerogative of the British monarch. The President was top admiral and top general, and nobodssy could issue him a military command; but that was all. And in 1850, in a case growing out of the Mexican War, the Supreme Court, speaking by Chief Justice Taney, substantially repeated Hamilton's Language.[105] The "Commander-in-Chief" clause remained the forgotten clause of the Constitution until the day when Sumter fell, April 14, 1861. Then came the great breakthrough.

First calling Congress to assemble on July 4, then more than ten weeks away, Lincoln proceeded forthwith to take certain measures of his own, based on the idea that in the circumstances "the war power" was his; and on this premise proclaimed a blockade of the Southern ports, summoned an army of three hundred thousand volunteers, increased the regular army and navy, took over the rail and telegraph lines between Washington and Baltimore, and eventually as far as Boston, and suspended the writ of habeas corpus along these lines. Congress and/or the Supreme Court sustained all these measures as within the President's powers as Commander-in-Chief in a rebellion which had attained the dimensions of public war. Secretary Seward summed up the business more compactly in conversation with Russell. Washington correspondent of the *London Times:* "We elect a king for four years, and give him absolute power within certain limits, which after all he can interpret for himself."

Between the Civil War and World War I two profound contrasts appear in retrospect. In the first place, most of the fighting in World War I took place three thousand miles from our shores. There was, consequently, no question at any time of treating the country at large as a "theatre of military operations" in the conventional sense of that term. In the second place, however, the vast development between the two wars of the technological aspects of warfare had created in this greatest of industrial nations an industrial theatre of war of immense proportions. Great industry in the United States had, in brief, become part and parcel of the fighting forces not only of the United States but of its allies as well, and as such it had to be subjected to detailed regimentation by the government of the United States. To meet this requirement Congress was compelled to develop a new technique in legislative practice, one capable of meeting the fluctuating demands of a fluid war situation. This it did by delegating the President at his insistence vast unchannelled powers to be exercised by him through men of his own choosing. John Locke's ban upon delegated legislation simply went by the board, nor has it since been revived so far as concerns powers which are shared by the two departments. As to these "cognate" powers, as it terms them, the Court will not attempt nowadays to plot nicely, or at all, the delimiting line. More than that, however, President Wilson took upon himself, without consulting Congress, both the government of labor relations and the screening of information regarding the war, the former function being performed by the War Industries Board, under Mr. Baruch; the latter by the Committee of Public Information, headed by Mr. Creel. Both agencies were created out of hand by the President, as was also the later War Labor Board under the joint chairmanship of ex-President Taft and Frank P. Walsh.

But his hand-made solution of the problem of "agencies" soon gave rise to another, inasmuch as the powers and duties entrusted to these bodies were frequently unknown to any statute, with the result that if their orders – or rather, "advice," as the Court termed it – was ignored by those to whom it was addressed, the latter could not be brought to book for having committed an "offense against the United States". How were such recalcitrants to be dealt with?

Another Wilsonian contrivance speedily supplied the answer. I refer to what came to be variously known as "sanctions," "administrative sanctions," or "indirect sanctions". An illustration of the way in which "sanctions" were applied is afforded by an episode involving the Remington Arms Company of Bridgeport, Connecticut, in the autumn of 1918. I am following the narrative of a member of Mr. Wilson's War Labor Board. After a protracted strike and the rendering of a decision by the board, the strikers still refused to return to work, whereupon Mr. Wilson took his pen in hand in the board's behalf. He pointed out that an appeal from that body should be made through the regular channels and not by strike, and informed the strikers that if they did not return to work at once, they would be barred from any work in Bridgeport for a year; that the United States Employment Service would not obtain jobs for them elsewhere; and that the government would no longer consider their exemptions from the draft to be justified on the theory that they were useful in war production. The narrative concludes: "That ended the strike."[106]

Mr. Wilson's performance was important for its immediate effect; it was even more so for laying the groundwork for F.D.R.'s course in World War II. World War II is World War I writ large; and F.D.R's conduct of it is Mr. Wilson's conduct of World War I writ large; besides which F.D.R. did not wait for war to break; he went to meet it – "looked the brink in the face," as it were.

In 1942, I wrote the Executive Office of the President and asked it to give me a list of all the war agencies and to specify to me the supposed legal warrant by which they had been brought into existence. I got back a detailed answer which listed forty-three executive agencies, of which thirty-five were admitted to be of purely executive provenience. F.D.R's also governed labor relations, at times indeed with a high hand, albeit without statutory authorization prior to the enactment of the War Labor Disputes Act of June 25, 1943. His principal technique was to seize plants in which strikes were going on, and some plants he seized for other reasons. For example, he ordered Montgomery Ward to adopt a maintenance of membership rule. Ward's at first agreed, but after Mr. Sewell Avery got to thinking the matter over he decided that the President entirely lacked authority to issue such an order, and so reneged. A morning or two later, when he got down to his office, he found that the seventy persons whom the Chicago post office was accustomed to send Ward's each day to look after their parcel post orders had not shown up. He thereupon capitulated, but not until after the touching episode in which, looking "the knight of the rueful countenance," he was carried out of his office on the joined hands of Sergeant Lepak and Private Dies. Eventually a case dealing with the episode reached the Supreme Court, which declined jurisdiction, saying that the matter had become "moot".[107]

I come now to my final topic: How did Mr. Wilson's quest for international peace affect the Presidency; and how did it affect his own standing in history? I answer as follows: it added a vast new dimension to the Presidency; and despite its tragic failure, due to Mr. Wilson's own tragic errors, it adds immeasurably to the stature of the Woodrow Wilson of history.

Mr. Wilson came early to believe that the United States must take a hand in the making of the peace that would end the war, and in the possibility of doing so beneficially. In an address to The League to Enforce Peace on May 27, 1916, he said:

We are participants, whether we would or not, in the life of the world. The interests of all nations are our own also. We are partners with the rest. What affects mankind is inevitably our affair as well as the affair of Europe and of Asia.[108]

And again on May 30, 1916, he spoke of uniting "the people of the world to preserve the peace of the world upon a basis of common right and justice";[109] and on January 22, 1917, ten weeks before he asked for a declaration of war on the Teutonic powers, he urged before the Senate that no lasting peace could ensue from a "peace forced upon the loser". The peace must be one of which "the very principle is equality and a common participation in a common benefit." "[It must be a] peace without victory".[110]

Two immense difficulties confronted Mr. Wilson from the outset of his quest for "peace without victory". The first was the commitment of our "associates" to certain secret treaties comprising mutual promises of spoliation of the common enemy when and if they defeated him. Of these Mr. Wilson had been fully apprised when we entered the war, although he later made an ineffectual effort to obscure the fact. In the second place, the President had to win the support of an isolationist Senate.

The President announced his Fourteen Points in an address to Congress on January 18, 1918. Then taking a leaf from McKinley's book, who in 1898 had incorporated in the protocol leading to the Peace of Paris all the material provisions of that peace, the President set to work to get the Fourteen Points incorporated in an armistice bringing the war with Germany to an end. On October 24, as we have seen, he appealed to the people of the United States to give him a majority in the approaching November election "for the sake of the Nation itself, in order that its inward duty of purpose may be evident to the world itself".[111]

A fortnight later, on November 5, to be exact, two events took place, both of ominous significance for Mr. Wilson's program of "peace without victory". First, the Allies consented to embody the Fourteen Points in the Armistice which was offered the Teutonic Allies six days later, but with "reservations" touching "Freedom of the Seas" and with the stipulation that Germany must pay reparations for the damage she had wrought in the course of the war she had herself begun. In the second place, on this same day, November 5, the American people returned the Republican opposition to power in Congress. In the Senator to be sure, the Republican majority was a very narrow one, but counting Mr. Truman Newberry of Michigan, who was under indictment for violating the Federal Corrupt Practices Act, it was sufficient to enable the opposition to reorganize the all-important Foreign Relations Committee under the chairmanship of Senat or Lodge. As Mr. Wilson caustically remarked, "the Republican majority is out on bail". In fairness, however, it should be added, that when Newberry came to trial, the measure he was convicted under was pronounced void by the Supreme Court in a six to three decision which is no longer good law.[112]

On December 4, 1918, Mr. Wilson sailed for Europe to attend the Peace Conference. The rest is familiar history. The conference opened in Paris January 18, 1919. The treaty was signed at Versailles June 26. Mr. Wilson submitted it to the Senate July 10, and straightway began a speaking tour in its behalf. Unfortunately his own following was divided, the malcontents alleging that, while he had got his League of Nations, he had got it at the expense of "peace without victory". On September 26, the President was stricken in Colorado en route to Kansas, and brought back to Washington, where on October 3 he suffered a second stroke which paralyzed his left side, and insulated him from the world for several weeks, in the course of which twenty-eight bills became laws without his signature. Later he partially recovered and was urged by his supporters in the Senate to accept a modified version of the Lodge Reservations. He repelled the suggestion, and on March 19, 1920, the treaty was finally rejected by a vote of forty-nine for the treaty with reservations and thirty-five against it. The League of Nations was established; the United States was not a member of it.

Ought Wilson have accepted the league even with the Lodge Reservations added? It is certainly arguable in the light of subsequent events that great advantage might have ensued from his doing so. Had the United States been a member of the league, even with the Lodge Reservations to hamper its performance thereunder, Japan might well have hesitated to invade China in 1931; Mussolini might well have hesitated to invade Abyssinia in overt defiance of the League in 1935; and Hitler might well have hesitated to invade the Rhineland, to remilitarize Germany, and to seize Austria in the years 1934 to 1938, all in arrant defiance of the Treaty of Versailles. In a word, the league would have been in position to offset the imbecilities of British foreign policy which culminated in the Munich Pact and which, instead of giving us "peace in our time," led directly to World War II.

"Wisdom after the event," you may say. Yes; but not after events that could by no chance be foreseen or the league would never have been proposed in the first instance. For the rest, I find very persuasive the following passage from a recent defense by Henry Cabot Lodge, Jr., of his grandfather's course in 1920:

The Senate majority, 1919 and 1920, wanted to change the covenant in three major ways: (a) So that United States military actions to preserve the territorial integrity of a nation under Article X would first be approved by Congress; (b) so that the United States would be the sole judge of whether a matter involving its interests was or was not a domestic question;

and (c) so that the United States would not have merely equal power with the small nations. These are all implicit in the United Nations Charter today. No one even debates them any more.s[113]

In short, President Wilson demanded of the American people things they still would not concede even a quarter of a century later; or indeed, even today.

What was the motivation of Wilson's fight for the league; and how did the fight affect the Presidency? In his brilliant volume, W*oodrow Wilson and the People,* Professor Bell stresses the religious quality of Wilson's crusade.[114] From the first, and even before our own entrance into the war, Wilson, as I have noted, advanced the idea that it must eventuate in a peace embracing all men; and, as Professor Bell shows, his language is tinged not infrequently with an apocalyptic quality. Even so, I regard Mr. Wilson's quest for peace to be of essentially the same stamp as his quest for social justice; to have been governed by the same compassionate concern for the common lot. He was fighting the battle, as he thought, of the common man, always the helpless, hopeless victim of war and its outrages.

On the other hand, while Mr. Wilson was indeed a deeply religious man, I am constrained to add there were times when his Calvinistic faith hindered rather than assisted his last great fight, by stiffening his own stubborn nature. It compelled him to reject any accomodation with the infidel – with those, to wit, who disagreed with him.

"The office of President," Mr. Wilson remarked on one occasion, "is so much greater than any man could honestly imagine himself to be that the most he can do is to look grave enough and self-possessed enough to seem to fill it".s[115] And that is just what he himself was able to do. In this connection, I quote, with a few emendations, some words which I penned at the request of a friend at the time of Mr. Wilson's death:

The event of main interest this week has been Wilson's death. Though the University administration is largely in the hands of those who were in the opposition in his closing days here, everything in recognition of the occasion is being done which the demise of Princeton's most illustrious son properly calls for. Thus while individuals pass on, institutions remain, and recruit strength from the fame even of those whom in their lifetime they did not always support or even repudiated. My own opinion is that the elements of greatness were so intermingled in Wilson with cramping limitations that his fame, like that of Jefferson before the New Deal came to his rescue, will be slow to emerge from the folds of controversy. Wilson was a finished speaker, and this with his personal dignity made him a splendid figure on great occasions. But it also exposed him to the danger of self-deception, and to the temptation to substitute words for facts. A pure amateur when he entered politics, he soon displayed a finesse, an imperturbability, and a strategic skill that have been rarely equalled in American political annals. But, owing to his long residence in the shades of Academia, he was accessible much more readily to intellectual currents–or to intellectualized currents–than to the spontaneous reactions of the people, wherein he contrasted with his robustious Rival Roosevelt. For problems that demanded an intellectual approach he was masterly, but his emotional appeals did not always ring true, as in his unfortunate "too proud to fight" speech. When indeed was he ever too proud to fight?

Wilson's critics were wont to charge that he was more concerned with the appearance of achievement than in the solid reality, since the former most affected his fortune and fame at the moment, but certainly he did not sin more grievously in this respect than most public men do, and are constrained to do, in a democracy. It is perhaps as a judge of men that Mr. Wilson shone least in his day-to-day conduct of affairs, being prone to evaluate them for their attitude toward himself, rather than their ability or their competence for the assigned task. Partly this was egotism, but partly again it was political expediency. Woodrow Wilson was no snob, he was devoid of social ambitions, and unquestionably sympathized with the common lot. But the core of his being was a flaming ambition, which his religion fanned rather than quenched, by presenting it with successive programs of reform. And along with ambition went an impatient craving for immediate domination which was kept reasonably in curb by his own good sense until health deserted him. His career ended in defeat when he refused to accept much of the substance of what he was fighting for because the offer was not accompanied by tokens from his opponents of their discomfiture and surrender.[116]

Then, as to his impact on the Presidency – he not only filled it; he added dimensions to it, in three respects. In the first place, he made the President the leader of the legislative process. He made of the office what, in the words of Walter Lippmann, it ought always to be, "the active… the asking and the proposing power [of the State]".[117] Secondly, he established the precedents for presidential dictatorship in time of war or of grave international crisis – condition of affairs that is likely to remain a factor of our daily lives for many years to come. Finally, he converted the Presidency into an international, a global institution – into an office with a world-wide, non-voting constituency. To be sure, in this respect his performance was outstripped by that of the second Roosevelt. He, nevertheless, set the pattern; he created the precedents, he took that indispensable first step.

References

1. Holland, *Elements of Jurisprudence* 32-34 (13th ed. 1924).
2. *Id.* at 32 n.4.
3. *Id.* at 33 n.6; see also the present writer's book, Corwin, *Liberty Against Government* 15-17 (1948) and accompanying notes.
4. See Gierke, *Political Theories of the Middle Ages* 80-81 (Maitland's trans. 1927).
5. The preceding sentence is taken from Corwin, *Liberty Against Government* 26.
6. As quoted in *id.* at 28.
7. *Id.* at 30.
8. 12 Rep. 63-65, 77 Eng. Rep. 1341-43 (1609).
9. 8 Rep. 113b, 77 Eng. Rep. 646 (1610).
10. *Id.*, 8 Rep. at 118a; see also Proclamations, 12 Rep. 74, 77 Eng. Rep. 1352 (1611).
11. See Corwin, *Liberty Against Government* 32-33 and notes.
12. Parts of the above paragraph are taken from *id.* at 50-51.
13. See *id.* at 35, 35 n. 40.
14. *Id.* at 39 n. 43.
15. See 2 Chalmers, *Opinions of Eminent Lawyers* 27-38 (1814).
16. 2 New York Historical Society Collections 204; see also Chalmers, *Political Annals*, in 1 New York Historical Society Collections 81 (1868).
17. Adams' report of Otis argument in Paxton's case, Quincy (App. 1) 474 (Mass. 1761).
18. Quincy (App. 1) 519 n.18 (Mass.1761).
19. 5 McMaster, *History of the People of the United States* 395 (1905).
20. Robin *v.* Hardaway, Jeff. 109 (Va . 1772).
21. *Id.* at 114.
22. *Id.* at 114, 123.
23. 2 Pet. 627, 7 L. Ed. 542 (1829).
24. *Id.*, 2 Pet. at 646.
25. *Id.*, 2 Pet. at 652.
26. *Id.*, 2 Pet. at 657.
27. Terrett *v.* Taylor, 9 Cranch 43, 3 L. Ed. 650 (1815).
28. 1 *Blackstone Commentaries* 46, 91.
29. 1 Cranch 137, 2 L. Ed. 60 (1803).

30. 3 Dall. 386, 1 L. Ed. 648 (1798).
31. *Id.*, 3 Dall. at 387-89.
32. *Id.*
33. *Id.*, 3 Dall. at 398-99.
34. Cooley, *Constitutional Limitations* 168 (3d ed. 1874).
35. Citizen's Savings & Loan Ass'n *v.* Topeka, 20 Wall. 655, 662, 22 L. Ed. 455 (1874).
36. *Id.*, 20 Wall. at 669.
37. See e.g. Cooley, *Constitutional Limitations* 174-76, where the principle of the separation of powers is made to do duty for natural law concepts.
38. See Coxe, *An Essay on Judicial Power and Unconstitutional Legislation 223 et seq.* (1893); 5 *Hamilton's Works* 116 (Lodge ed. 1904); 7 *id.* at 198.
39. Note 30.
40. 4 Dall. 14, 1 L. Ed. 721 (1800).
41. *Id.*, 4 Dall. at 18.
42. See 1 Farrand, *The Records of the Federal Convention* 48, 133-34, 255, 424, 525, 533; *2 id.* at 285 (1937).
43. On this point see Corwin, *Liberty Against Government* 60-61 n. 4.
44. *Id.* at 72 *et seq.*
45. Van Horne's Lessee *v.* Dorrance, 2 Dall. 304, 310, 1 L. Ed. 391 (1795).
46. See Corwin, *Liberty Against Government* 84-115.
47. 13 N.Y. (3 Kern) 378 (1856).
48. *Id.* at 392.
49. 6 Cranch 87, 3 L. Ed. 162 (1810).
50. *Id.*, 6 Cranch at 139.
51. *Id.*, 6 Cranch at 143.
52. Dartmouth College *v.* Woodward, 4 Wheat. 518, 4 L. Ed. 629 (1819).
53. Green, *Principles of Political Obligation* (1901).
54. 16 Wall. 36, 21 L. Ed. 394 (1873).
55. These words are from Twiss, *Lawyers and the Constitution* 53 (1942).
56. *Id.* at 54, quoting Campbell's brief, pp. 42-44. Emphasis supplied.
57. 94 U.S. 113, 24 L. Ed. 77 (1876).
58. Maine, *Ancient Law* 165 (3d Amer. ed. 1873).
59. Extracted from Mason, *Free Government in the Making* 607-8 (1949).
60. Parts of this paragraph are taken from Corwin, *Liberty Against Government* 198.
61. Lochner *v.* New York. 198 U.S. 45, 25 S. Ct. 539, 49 L. Ed. 937 (1905).
62. *Id.*, 198 U.S. 56.
63. Gitlow *v.* NewYork, 268 U.S. 652, 45 S. Ct. 625, 69 L. Ed. 1138 (1925).
4. Cantwell *v.* Connecticut, 310 U.S. 296, 60 S. Ct. 900, 84 L. Ed. 1213 (1940).

65. Louisiana *v.* Resweber, 329 U.S. 459, 470-72, 67 S. Ct. 374, 91 L. Ed. 422 (1947), quoting from Holden *v.* Hardy, 169 U.S. 366, 389, 18 S. Ct. 383, 42 L. Ed. 780 (1898); Hebert *v.* Louisiana, 272 U.S. 312, 316, 47 S. Ct. 103, 71 L. Ed. 270 (1926); Palko *v.* Connecticut, 302 U.S. 319, 325, 58 S. Ct. 149, 82 L. Ed. 288(1937); Snyder *v.* Massachusetts, 291 U.S. 97, 105, 54 S. Ct. 330, 78 L. Ed. 674 (1934).
66. 334 U.S. 558, 68 S. Ct. 1148, 92 L. Ed. 1574 (1948).
67. 333 U.S. 203, 68 S. Ct. 461, 92 L. Ed. 649 (1948).
68. {337} U.S. {1}, 69 S. Ct. 894 (1949).
69. The reference is to Kovacs *v.* Cooper, 336 U.S. 17, 69 S. Ct. 448 (1949).
70. Holmes, *Collected Legal Papers* 310 (Laski ed. 1920).
71. *Id.* at 314.
72. Bagehot, *The English Constitution* (1901).
73. Wilson, *Cabinet Government in the United States* 8 (1947).
74. *Id.* at 11.
75. *Id.* at 23.
76. Wilson, *Congressional Government:* A *Study in American Politics* (1900).
77. *Id.* at 6.
78. *Id.* at 11.
79. *Id.* at 23.
80. *Id.* at 301.
81. *Id.* at 254.
82. *Id.* at 203-4.
83. *Id.* at xi-xii.
84. Ford, *The Rise and Growth of American Politics* (1914).
85. *Id.* at 279.
86. *Id.* at 284.
87. *Id.* at 293.
88. Wilson, *Constitutional Government in the United States* (1927).
89. *Id.* at 67-70.
90. *Id.* at 141.
91. II *The Public Papers of Woodrow Wilson,* Vol. 2, 435 (Baker and Dodd ed. 1927).
92. Speech by Woodrow Wilson, Princeton alumni meeting at Pittsburgh, April 16, 1910. Copy on file at the University of Virgina Law Library.
93. Binkley, *President and Congress* 206 ((1947).
94. *Id.*
95. Small, *Some Presidential Interpretations of the Presidency* 175 (1932).
96. Wison, *Constitutional Government* 179.
97. Hammer v. Dagenhart, 247 U.S. 251 (1918).
98. United States *v.* Darby, 312 U.S. 100 (1941).

99. Padover, *The Complete Jefferson* 138 (1943).
100. 2 Beveridge, *The Life of John Marshall* 470-71 (1919).
101. Marbury *v.* Madison, 5 U.S. (1 Cranch) 137, 164 (1803).
102. *New York Times*, July 24, 1917, p.1, col. 1.
103. *New York Times,* May 16, 1918, p.1, col. 3.
104. 56 Cong. Rec. 11494 (1918); Farmer, *The Wilson Reader 191*(1956).
105. Fleming *v.* Page, 50 U.S. (9 How.) 603 (1850).
106. See Corwin, *The President: Office and Powers* 490 (3rd ed., 1948).
107. Montgomery Ward & Company *v.* United States, 326 U.S. 690 (1945).
108. *Public Papers of Wilson* 185.
109. *Id.* at 195.
110. 54 Cong. Rec. 1742 (1917); Farmer, *Wilson Reader* 157.
111. III *Public Papers of Wilson,* Vol. 1, 287.
112. Cf. Newberry *v.* United States, 256 U.S. 232 (1921); Burroughts *v.* United States, 290 U.S. 534 (1934).
113. *New York Times Magazine,* January 22, 1956, p. 72, col. 3.
114. Bell, *Woodrow Wilson and the People* (1945).
115. Rossiter, *The American Presidency* 137 (1956).
116. See Myers, *Some Princeton Memories* 34-35 (1946).
117. Lippmann, *The Public Philosophy* 30 (1955).

III

Roosevelt and Constitutional Revolution

Some Probable Repercussions of "Nira" on Our Constitutional System

The notable feature of the President's message addressed to Congress the other day was undoubtedly his announcement that he considered the National Industrial Recovery Act a permanent part of the American arrangement of things. This announcement seems to have shocked some people. As Will Rogers said in the *Times* the other day, "Mr. Roosevelt proposed in his speech that the NRA and a lot of these other Government-regulated business ethics should be made permanent. Well, that was a terrible blow to some businessmen. They figured that they would only be required by the Government to be honest until the emergency was over."

I think, however, that those who have reflected on this subject must have come to the conclusion, prior to the President's announcement, that the "Nira," if not itself permanent, would undoubtedly lead to something permanent. The Nira was originally enacted as an emergency measure, to be sure, but the emergency was of a particular character. It was an emergency in the sense of a distressful condition that needed remedying, but it was not an emergency in the sense of being the extraordinary result of extraordinary causes. It was the normal result of normal cause operating in an environment to which those causes had become ill-adapted, and causes which could be counted on to resume their operation if the control represented by Nira, or by something equivalent, were once withdrawn.

It may be doubted, in fact, whether the Nira has been a great success as an emergency measure – whether it has accelerated rather than retarded recovery. I do not think that is the test to be applied. The real test is rather whether the Nira can so *guide* recovery as to prevent the kind of recovery that would lead again to collapse. In short, the Nira is regarded as a *reform* measure more accurately than as a *recovery* measure. And so regarding it, we see that it was good statesmanship to impose it while business was still down; because if business had been up, it would have been impossible to impose such a reform. "Don't interfere with business" would have become altogether too powerful a shibboleth to be resisted successfully.

Now, the permanency of Nira or something equivalent being taken for granted, it becomes interesting to inquire into the possible effects of this measure upon our constitutional system, and that is the subject on which I am going to address you briefly.

Constitutional Basis of Nira

The Nira may be regarded as a sort of declaratory statute; as declaratory, that is, of certain legal principles which it is hoped will prove to be adapted to the present economic situation of the United States. What, then, are the constitutional principles which this declaratory statute imports? If you turned to the Constitution of the United States, you would course be able to obtain very little enlightenment on the question of the power of the government to enact such a statute. There probably are about twenty words out of the thirty-five hundred words in the Constitution, that have any bearing whatsoever upon the subject. The problem is one rather of constitutional law and theory.

In the first place was we encounter the theory that the national government has only such powers as are quite clearly delegated to it. What clause, therefore, of the Constitution of the United States furnishes the generative source of the Nira? There is only one possible clause, that which gives Congress the power to regulate "commerce among the States". But commerce among the States is not the sum total of business, while Nira attempts to regulate the whole business structure. So at the very outset we encounter the theory upon which the National Industrial Recovery Act rests, and that is the *solidarity of American business*. Congress has the power to regulate commerce among the States, and hence has the power to protect that commerce. The theory of the Nira is that the health of commerce among the States depends upon the health of business in general, and that if commerce among the States cannot be restored except by measures which are conducive to the restoration of business in general, Congress has the power to take such measures.

Extent of Congressional powers

The power of Congress over interstate commerce is not and never has been confined to the regulation of acts of commerce among the States. Thus, from whatever source a detriment to interstate commerce proceeds, it falls under the controlling power of Congress by virtue of Congress power to protect interstate commerce. For example, Congress has the power to require that cars which are hauling goods from one point to another within a state shall be equipped with certain safety appliances, because such cars may link up with cars which are carrying goods from one state to another and so may become a source of danger to the latter. To repeat, Congress' power extends to matters which are not commerce among the States at all, simply by virtue of the fact that its power to *regulate* commerce includes the power to *safeguard* commerce.

A few years ago the United States Supreme Court was confronted with a case in which a man named Ferger was charged under a federal law with having issued a fraudulent bill of lading. He challenged the right of Congress to penalize such an act. He said that the issuance of a fraudulent bill of lading was not interstate commerce, in fact was not commerce of any kind, but was merely a violation of the law against fraud of the state where the act occurred. The Supreme Court nevertheless sustained Ferger's conviction under the act of Congress, Chief Justice White speaking as follows:

> This argument mistakenly assumes that the power to Congress is to be necessarily tested by the intrinsic existence of commerce in the particular subject dealt with instead of by relation of that subject to commerce and its effect upon it. We say mistakenly assumes, because we think it clear if the proposition were sustained it would destroy the power of Congress to regulate, as obviously that power, if it is to exist, must include the authority to deal with obstructions to interstate commerce and with a host of other acts which because of their relation to and influence upon interstate commerce come within the power of Congress to regulate, although they are not interstate commerce in and of themselves.

But it may be objected (and it is a natural objection to make) that production, which is a great part of industry, is *local*. The Supreme Court has said that many times. It has even been said that production is "inherently" local. But the fact is that production is not local in any sense that is relevant to our present problem, and this for the reason that *the vast proportion of production is for the interstate or the national market.* For example, what proportion of the fruit of California does California consume? What proportion of the automobiles that it manufactures does the state of Michigan purchase and use? Where does the raw material out of which automobiles are made in the state of Michigan come from?

Production, in short, is a function, as is interstate commerce a function, *of the interstate or national market*, and expands and contracts as the interstate market expands and contracts. So it is upon this proposition of the solidarity of business, on the idea that business involves interstate commerce and vice versa, and that the health of interstate commerce depends upon the health of the entity of which it is a part – it is upon this proposition that the constitutionality of Nira rests.

Obsolescent State Power

At this point, however, we encounter a most formidable objection, namely, that this line of reasoning tends to destroy the federal system, inasmuch as it expels the States very largely from the field of business relations, while even such power as it leaves them it necessarily subordinates to the supreme power of Congress. Well, that has to be admitted; but I think the answer is that in the field of business relations state power has long been moribund, so that the Nira simply recognizes and gives effect to a constitutional theory which is the counterpart of a condition already long established in the facts of our everyday economic life.

In this connection I wish to quote from an address made by Professor Gulick at the Chicago Fair last summer.

The American state is finished. I do not predict that the States will go, but affirm that they have gone. And why have they gone? Because they were unable to deal even inefficiently with the imperative, the life and death tasks of the new national economy. Where were the States when the banks went under?... Where were the States when all the railroads were on the verge of passing into the hands of the bondholders and suspending operations? Where were the States in the regulation of power and control of utilities? Where are the States now in regulating insurance companies with their fake balance sheets and high salaries? Where were the States in controlling blue sky securities? Where were the States in preventing destructive business competition and protecting labor and the public? Where were the States in the development of security through social insurance? In none of these fields affecting economic life was it possible for any state to do anything decisive without driving business out of its jurisdiction into areas where there was no regulation and no control.

So Professor Gulick draws this conclusion: "*Nothing effective can be done in the stabilization of economic affairs unless the area of planning and control has the same boundaries as the economic structure.*"

Some of that may appear to be couched in the language of exaggeration. But as a matter of fact Professor Gulick understates his case, because he confines his arrangement of the states to their regulation of of business relations; while the inefficiency of the States even in the field of the criminal law is being displayed to us daily, as well as their growing dependence upon federal assistance in this, the most primitive field of state power. So, granting the premise of the solidarity of business, the Nira becomes a measure well within the power of Congress to foster and protect interstate commerce, and the federal system, the federal balance, will have to take its chances in the resulting situation, which was one of fact long before it became one of law.

Effect on Judicial Review

That brings me to another point, the probable effect of the Nira on the most distinctive feature of our constitutional system, judicial review. One of the great purposes of judicial review, which is to say, of the power of the courts to pass on the constitutionality of laws, has been of course to maintain the federal balance; but if the federal balance is at an end, then naturally judicial review loses much of its reason for being.

I am not predicting, of course, that the Supreme Court will be deprived outright of its power of judicial review, nor even that the power of judicial review will *overtly* come to an end in the near future. What I do say is that we are to look forward to the gradual diminution in the years to come of the role of the Supreme Court in the determination of national policies. It will be something like the demise of the veto power of the English King. That took place very unobtrusively, so much so that when Blackstone wrote his *Commentaries* in 1765 he still regarded the royal veto as a factor of the British Constitution, and when De Lolme wrote his book on the British Constitution ten years later, he still reckoned the veto power of the King as an essential part of that Constitution. But in fact the veto had not been exercised since the year 1707.

The Supreme Court will still have, of course, a great role in our system, as exemplified in the recent Scottsboro case. That is the sort of thing it seems to me that the Court ought to be doing – intervening in behalf of the helpless and the oppressed against local injustice and prejudice, rather than intervening in the assertion of out-of-date economic theories, as it has done too often since 1890.

Delegation of Power

Another feature of the Nira is, obviously, the tremendous role which it recognizes the President as occupying in our system. The Nira was not drawn in Congress; it was drawn in the executive offices of the United States, and it delegates vast powers to the executive. We have a maxim of constitutional law that the legislature may not delegate its powers. Although there is nothing in the Constitution to this effect, this maxim, which was stated by John Locke as far back as 1690, has received more or less lip service from our courts and from our political scientists for many generations.

Actually, however, the Supreme Court of the United States has never pronounced any act of Congress void on the ground that it unconstitutionally delegated legislative power. And in recent years the Courts has developed this very interesting formula, that Congress may not delegate its power unless it becomes necessary to delegate it in order to exercise it effectively and conveniently. In other words, the maxim amounts simply to this, that Congress may not abdicate its power and so may not bind its successors. Of course, if all governmental power had to be exercised in the first instance in the form of detailed legislation, it really could not be exercised at all in a complex and rapidly changing society. It is only to a period of simple and slowly changing conditions that the maxim can be successfully applied with literal force.

So the Nira simply underscores this result of our constitutional law to date. What will be the effect of its doing so upon legislative processes under the Constitution? I rather think it will be beneficial. It seems to me that debate in Congress may become mush more vital when it is confined to questions of large, general principle and policy rather than to statutory details. And if this general idea of delegating legislative power is extended into the field of tariff making, as President Hoover was anxious that it should be, and as President Roosevelt apparently is also, then at last our Congress may be rescued form the stigma which Burke visited upon the House of Commons of his day when he called it “a bustle of local agencies”. The Congress of the United States has lost power by trying to exercise too much power. It has lost its due influence in our national system by trying to act as a legislature for local interests.

Problems Created by Nira

The Nira is bound to make such a change in our constitutional system that it will have to be followed up, no doubt, by that sort of operation which in the war was called "mopping up". It is going to make such a vast change, particularly in the relationship of the national government to the States, that the question of what role the States are henceforth to occupy in our system is going to become a vital problem in the next few years, without doubt.

The question also arises, of course, as to the institutionalization of those procedures by which, for example, General Johnson and his associates have been enacting their codes. Subordinate legislation, delegated legislation, it is obvious, is going to become a very important feature of government. Are the methods that have been applied in the drawing up of these codes entirely satisfactory, however? This is a question which will have to be met sooner or later.

Then the further question comes up, whether or not the President's Cabinet is exactly the most satisfactory type of advisory board for the President in the new situation. The President, of course, has absolute freedom in the choice of his Cabinet, which is a body not known to the Constitution of the United States; it is an "extra-constitutional" body. The President is free, for example, to choose his Cabinet from the chairmen of the committees of Congress, in which case we might gradually approximate the cabinet system of government. The President is also free to choose as his advisers, as President Roosevelt certainly has chosen some of his most important advisers, not from the heads of his administrative departments but from men who are subordinate officials in those departments. Very possibly, therefore, there will be gradually built up a rather different type of Cabinet.

The question may even come up whether the taboo on the third term is a desirable thing in a new system in which so much depends on continuity of policy, and where governmental policy and business policy are so interlocked and interwoven with each other.

Generally speaking, I should say that the leitmotif of the new constitutional system that the Nira adumbrates is the idea of fusion of powers and co-operation, in contrast to those ideas of separation, of tension, of competition, on which our system was originally based. Mr. Roosevelt had frequently and justifiably spoken of the success of the efforts of the Administration as depending upon the co-operation of business and government. It depends also on the co-operation of the national government and the state governments, and on the cooperation within the national government, of the executive and the legislative – in the words of Mr. Roosevelt, on "the firm and permanent union" of these bodies.

Flexibility of the Constitution

So to sum the whole thing up, I say that the Nira to some indefinite extent imports a constitutional revolution, but that this revolution corresponds to one of which we have not been sufficiently aware but which had already taken place in our economic life, in the facts of our everyday living. In this connection permit me to quote the words of James Madison in *The Federalist* No. 41. Discussing there the objection of certain opponents of the Constitution, that the relative importance of manufacturing and of agriculture was bound greatly to change in the years to come, to the disadvantage of the states, Madison concluded an argument of reassuring tenor with these words: "A system of government meant for duration ought to contemplate these revolutions and be able to accommodate itself to them".

I think the Constitution of the United States can accommodate itself to the revolution which the Nira undoubtedly does spell. I think further that this means a change in the character of the Constitution itself. The Constitution will accommodate itself to the revolution, will be absorbed into it more or less, and our attitude toward it will consequently become less legalistic and more political. We shall value it for the aid it lends to considered social purpose, not as a lawyers' document.

A historical parallel is suggested by the position of Magna Carta in the English Constitution. In the year 1400, Magna Carta *was* the English Constitution in great part; in the year 1700, Magna Carta had been absorbed into a vast complexus of environing institutions. And so it may be with the Constitution of the United States. It does not seem to me that there is anything very terrifying about this; it is one of the results of living politically in an age which lives adventurously in other respects.

6. President and Court: A Crucial Issue

Although the President's recommendation that the Supreme Court be enlarged to fifteen members is part and parcel of a general plan for the reform of the federal judiciary, and is cogently supported by his message as a measure for dealing with superannuation on the bench, it has already drawn fire as an "adroit" way of "packing the Court" with a membership favorable to the New Deal.

Indeed, the President himself says, at the close of his message, that if the measures which he recommends "achieve their aim, we may be relieved of the necessity of considering any fundamental changes in the powers of the courts or the Constitution of our government," words that are fairly interpretable as admitting the purpose which the critics of the proposal assert to be its controlling one.

Furthermore, the recommended enlargement of the Court appears as a logical – though not inevitable – outcome of the President's message of January 6, where, reporting on the state of the Union, he said:

Mean must be found to adapt our legal forms and our judicial interpretation to the actual present national needs of the largest progressive democracy in the modern world.... The judicial branch also is asked by the people to do its part in making democracy successful. We do not ask the courts to call nonexistent powers into being, but we have a right to expect that conceded powers of those legitimately implied shall be made effective instruments for the common good. The processes of our democracy must not be imperiled by the denial of essential power of free government.

But why should not the President's supporters frankly defend the proposal that the Court be enlarged, a measure necessary in the present situation to readjust the balance between the departments and to effect an application of the Constitution which is demanded by conditions and which has been sanctioned by the people?

One thing can be said at the outset, that this would not be the first time the Court has been "packed". There is still, for instance a tenth federal circuit for which there once existed, but no longer exists, a corresponding member of the Court. This anomaly is a memento of President Lincoln's well-warranted fear that the Court over which Roger Taney presided might upset important war measures. Nor did Lincoln act without precedent, for twenty-five years earlier the Court had been enlarged from seven to nine justices in order – among other things, perhaps – to water down the remnant of the old Marshall bench.

Also, we now know that when President Grant sent to the Senate the names of two new appointees to the Court, Messrs. Bradley and Strong, the same day that the decision in Hepburn *v*. Griswold was handed down, he did so in the fullest confidence that these gentlemen would do just what in fact they did do some time later, turn to and bring about a reversal of Hepburn *v*. Griswold. [On February 7, 1870, the Supreme Court held in the Hepburn-Griswold case that the legal tender act of February 25, 1862, making "greenbacks" legal tender, was unconstitutional].

In the words of Secretary Fish's diary, the President explained – this was some years later—

That at the time he felt it important that the constitutionality of the law should be sustained, and while he would do nothing to exact anything like a pledge or expression of opinion from the parties he might appoint to the bench, he had desired that the constitutionality should be sustained by the Supreme Court; that he believed such had been the opinion of all his Cabinet at the time.

The principal justification, however, for the President's recommendation must be found, if at all, not in the past but in the here and now. The question which it raises is really that of the soundness of the assumption which underlies the passages above quoted from his message of January 6. It is there assumed that the Court today enjoys great freedom of choice in interpreting the Constitution, that it can often give the Constitution a liberal or strict application as it elects, and that it is able therefore frequently to forward its own preferences without violating correct judicial decorum.

In other words, it is the President's evident belief that the Court has become a political body, not in the narrow partisan sense of the term, but in the immensely more important sense, of a determinator of public policies– a super-legislature, in brief.

This assumption, one may be sure, will be boldly contested. The evidence in support of it, nevertheless, is impressive. Thus, the President will be able to cite the present Chief Justice's statement, made many year ago and so before the Court's censorship of acts of Congress had taken on its present scope, that "the Constitution is what the judges say it is", also the late Mr. Root's admonition to the states in 1906 that if they did not exercise the powers theoretically belonging to them, interpretations would "be found" to enable the national government to take over those powers; likewise Justice Stone's statement in the AAA case that while unconstitutional exercise of power by the executive and legislative branches of the government is subject to judicial restraint, the only check upon our own exercise of power is our own sense of self-restraint.

Turning, moreover, from opinion to fact, what do we find? One thing is that the number of acts, whether state or national, which the Court has disallowed has increased enormously in recent years. Between 1789 and 1865 the Court pronounced void just two provisions of acts of Congress. Between 1920 and 1932, inclusive, it overturned twenty-two such provisions, while between 1934 and 1936, inclusive, it overturned thirteen such provisions.

These statistics standing by themselves are, to be sure, open to diverse interpretations. It is only when we look for the reason back of them that they take on their proper significance; but this too becomes evident on a little consideration.

The acts of Congress which the Court has set aside for transgressing clear, unmistakable words of the constitutional document are few indeed. Rather the basis of its decision has usually been some doctrine or theory which it has itself, not without popular approval necessarily, imported into the Constitution from the outside. Indeed, the New Deal legislation which has perished at the Court's hands has almost all fallen before just such doctrines or theories.

Thus the decision in the "Hot Oil" cases was based on the maxim which finds no mention in the Constitution, that "the Legislature may not delegate its powers"; and the Railway Retirement Act was set aside on the ground that it deprived the carriers of their property without "due process of law," although the conception of "due process" thus invoked was unknown to the Supreme Court prior to the Dred Scott case.

And when we turn to the decisions setting aside the NIRA and the Coal Conservation Act we encounter yet another significant feature of the Court's present power. Both of these acts were passed on the theory that conditions surrounding production often affect interstate commerce detrimentally. This theory the Court answered by saying that such effects, however extensive or inevitable, were "indirect" and hence beyond the power of Congress to govern.

But the Constitution itself says nothing about "indirect effects," and still less – if that were possible – does it say that Congress may not safeguard interstate commerce from them. Indeed, no further back than 1923, we find the Court saying through Chief Justice Taft:

This court will certainly not substitute its judgment for that of Congress in such a matter unless the relation of the subject to interstate commerce and its effect upon it are clearly nonexistent.

Thus, not only do the Court's most important decisions frequently rest on extremely vague grounds, on grounds which are open to a variety of interpretations, but they also rest on grounds the Court's own interpretation of which has varied from time to time. Especially is this true of its decisions in recent years concerning the crucial issue of state versus national power.

In the Shreveport case, which was decided in 1914, the Court, speaking by the present Chief Justice, held that Congress was entitled to regulate the local charges of interstate carriers when they discriminated against interstate commerce. Defending at the time this holding against the argument that it authorized Congress to intrude on the reserved powers of the States, Mr. Hughes said:

Within its sphere as recognized by the Constitution, the nation is supreme. The question is simply of the Federal power as granted; where there is authorized exercise of that power, there is no reserved power to nullify it – a principle obviously essential to our national integrity, yet continually calling for new applications.

In the face of which, we find the Court, in the NIRA, the AAA, and the Coal Act cases, treating the reserved powers of the State as if they comprised an independent limitation on national power.

But, it may be asked, does not the principle of *stare decisis* [the doctrine of following rules or principles laid down in previous judicial decisions] contradict the President's assumption that the Court has become a political body? Not, it would seem, to any serious extent.

In the words of Justice Brandeis, spoken a few years ago:

Stare decisis is not, like the rule of *res judicata* [a thing or matter finally decided on its merits], a universal, inexorable command. "The rule of *stare decisis*, though one tending to consistency and uniformity of decision, is not inflexible. Whether it shall be followed or departed from is a question entirely within the discretion of the court, which is again called upon to consider a question once decided."

It is true that these words occur in a dissenting opinion, but the opinions cited in support of them are not dissenting opinions. Furthermore, Justice Brandeis was able to fortify his statement with an impressive list of cases – between thirty and forty – which the court had, even at that date, overruled in whole or in part in the field of constitutional law.

Writing in 1932, Professor Thomas Reed Powell of Harvard summed up the position of the Court in relation to the Constitution in these words:

Nine men in Washington have a pretty arbitrary power to annul any statute or ordinance or administrative order that is properly brought before them. The power is an arbitrary power, even though it may not be arbitrarily exercised. It is arbitrary in the sense that in the last analysis it is exercised as five or more of the nine men think best.

The Supreme Court can hardly be said to be controlled by the Constitution because so seldom does the Constitution clearly dictate a decision. It is not controlled by its own precedents, for it feels free to overrule them. It feels even more free to make distinctions that no sensible person would think of making except to avoid confession that a precedent is being disregarded. All this remains true even though in most of the cases it is also true that applicable precedents are either followed or are not there to be invoked. The Supreme Court does what it prefers to do when it prefers to do as nearly as possible what it has done before.

Certainly nothing has happened since 1932 to cast doubt on the soundness of this verdict.

The origin of the Court's power of censorship over acts of Congress has been the subject of investigation again and again. It is a story not without support for the Cleopatra's nose view of history. One of the foremost problems confronting the Philadelphia Convention was that of providing a curb on the state legislatures, in the interest both of national power and of private rights.

The Virginia Plan, upon which the Constitution was largely elaborated, ignoring the idea of judicial review which had already appeared sporadically in three or four of the states, proposed a congressional veto. No sooner, however, did this proposal come up for discussion than the point was made that, on account of the bad condition of the roads, it must often be months before a state legislative act could be laid before Congress for its consideration. Must, it was asked, such acts be kept suspension until passed, or must they be permitted to operate during the interval – either alternative being undesirable? And must Congress remain in Continuous session in order to discharge its veto function?

Madison, principal author of the Virginia Plan, conceded the force of these objections, and as we know, the proposed congressional veto was ultimately tabled in favor of the idea, which is incorporated in the "supremacy" clause of the Constitution [Article VI, Section 2], of making the state courts – local bodies, in other words – a first line of defense of the constitutional powers of the new government. From this concession to the badness of transportation in 1787 sprang all the rest.

There is, to be sure, no necessary relation between the power which the state courts, and on appeal the Supreme Court, exercise when they censor state legislation in relation to the national Constitution. In such instances both judiciaries may logically be regarded as wielding the prerogative of a supreme government – a prerogative, moreover, for which a clear precedent existed from colonial days. When, on the other hand, the Supreme Court sets aside an act of Congress, it asserts the right, by virtue of judicial power alone, to censor the action of a constitutionally coordinate body – indeed, in the light both of British and colonial practice and theory, that of a superior body.

Nevertheless, the principle which today furnishes both branches of judicial review a common basis in constitutional theory was brought forward in the convention fairly early in the proceedings. Thus, in addition to the bad-roads argument, Sherman of Connecticut proffered the argument against the congressional veto that it involved "a wrong principle," to wit, that "acts contrary to the Articles of Union would be valid".

In other words, the Articles of Union would be law in the strict sense of being cognizable and applicable by courts in the decision of cases. The supremacy clause, to be sure, defines "the supreme law of the land" as comprising "this Constitution, the laws of the United States made in pursuance thereof and the treaties made under the authority of the United States". But at any rate, the Constitution is treated as law in the same sense as acts of Congress are; and who would question that of "the supreme law" it is supreme part?

And yet, did the members of the convention draw this conclusion which, obviously, is not inescapable? The answer seems to be that some did and some did not. Most of the discussion bearing on the question was evoked by another feature of the Virginia Plan, a proposal that a Council of Revision, to consist of the heads of the executive departments and "a convenient number of the national judiciary," should be vested with a veto power over national legislation.

The fact that the convention ultimately rejected this proposal also has given rise to the contention that it thereby indicated its disapproval of judicial review of acts of Congress. The conclusion is unwarranted. An argument against the Council of Revision was that, since the judges would have occasion to pass upon the constitutionality of the acts of Congress in the exercise of their judicial functions, it would be improper to associate them with the legislative process.

But, on the other hand, it would also be going too far to say that the defeat of the council proves that the convention accepted the thesis of judicial review. What the available records show is that judicial review was at the outset of the convention a still novel idea to those who had heard of it at all, that even its advocates had at first but the slightest provision of its possible uses as a check on legislative power; that as this began to appear somewhat more clearly, the discovery was not altogether favorable to judicial review – some, Dickinson for instance, and later Madison, beginning now to recoil from the idea of so great a power in judges; and finally, that after all very few members did directly express themselves on the merits of the question during the convention.

For all these reasons the statistics which various writers have complied to show a wide acceptance of the idea among the membership of the convention should be taken with a grain of salt. Not only do they depend far too much upon the argument from silence, but they also overlook the obvious fluctuation of opinion on the subject.

Nor is the verdict, which must be passed upon discussion of the subject while adoption of the Constitution was pending, substantially different. The great argument against the Constitution was, of course, that the new government would be dangerous to the rights of the states and the liberties of the people, and to this argument advocates of the Constitution occasionally found the idea of judicial review as a check on the national legislative power a very convenient answer. By far the most positive statement on the subject was that of Hamilton in one of the closing numbers of *The Federalist*, although he had overlooked the ideas in an earlier issue where it would have been pertinent to mention it. Without invoking any clause of the Constitution, Hamilton here asserts "the doctrine," as he terms it, that "the courts were designed to be an intermediate body between the people and the Legislature, in order to keep the latter within the limits assigned their authority".

Although the essay probably made converts, Madison was not among them. For a few months later we find him declaring with equal positiveness that judicial review made "the judiciary department paramount in fact to the legislative, which was never intended and can never be proper".

Though the question of the power of the Court to disallow acts of Congress on constitutional grounds was in form settled by Marshall's famous decision in Marbury *v*.ss Madison, it has taken many decades to unfold the full significance of this holding. Thus, as was pointed out earlier in this article, the grounds on which the Court can today over-turn an act of Congress are often vague and indefinite in the extreme, while frequently they appear in pairs of alternatives which vest the Court with uncontrolled freedom of choice.

Nor is this all, for the general trend of professional opinion has come to endow the Court's interpretation of the Constitution with the authority of the latter, until they have been changed by constitutional amendment or have been overturned by the Court itself as having been erroneous. As someone has put it, "the Constitution is the Supreme Court's last guess".

With the dogma of the "finality" of the Court's interpretations of the Constitution – their finality, that is to say, as respects everybody but the Court itself – we are brought back to the President's message of January

6 and his more recent recommendation that the Court be enlarged. What he is saying, in effect, is that, as between an attempt to amend the Constitution and trusting to the Court to correct its own errors, he prefers the latter method of bringing the Constitution, as it is applied through the judiciary, into harmony with the needs of the times.

As a matter of facts, the latter is the method on which we have generally relied in the past, so why not now?

Without a sympathetic Court to interpret them, even constitutional amendments must prove disappointing. Furthermore, the adoption of a needed amendment can be prevented by thirteen states which contain less than twentieth of the population of the country.

But there are those who say that the only "square and honest way" of bringing about constitutional change is by amendment. Such an attitude is specious. Certainly it is so unless its exponents are able to answer satisfactorily two questions: first, what course have they in mind in case an amendment which is desired by an unmistakable majority of the people is defeated? Second, would they support an amendment to make the amending process really democratic?

Besides, do they mean that the changes which the Court has in the past wrought in the Constitution were not "square and honest"? If not, what do they mean?

IV

The President as Administrative Chief

I

The President's primary duty, logically if not chronologically, is to create an administration and maintain one for the faithful execution of the laws. In this capacity he enjoys in relation to his official subordinates certain powers of appointment, supervision, and removal; and it is my purpose in the present essay to treat of these in some detail. The appointment power is, of course, shared by the Senate; but for the rest the principal limitations upon presidential authority in this field—as, in fact, in most others—arise from the impinging powers of Congress.

It was formerly, and within limits is still, an element of the royal prerogative in England to create offices as well as to appoint to them. At the outset indeed the two things were indistinguishable. Etymologically, an "office" is an *officium*, a duty; and an "officer" was simply one whom the King had charged with a duty. In the course of time certain frequently recurrent and naturally coherent duties came to be assigned more or less permanently, and so emerged the concept of "office" as an *institution* distinct from the person holding it and capable of persisting beyond his incumbency.

The Constitution, however, by the "necessary and proper" clause, assigns the power to *create* offices to Congress, while it deals with the *appointing power* in the following words of Article II, Section 2, paragraph 2 :

And he [the President] shall nominate, and by and with the advice and consent of the Senate, shall appoint ambassadors, other public ministers sand consuls, judges of the Supreme Court, and all other officers of the United States, whose appointments are not herein otherwise provided for, and which shall be established by law; but the Congress may by law vest the appointment of such inferior officers, as they think proper, in the President alone, in the courts of law, or in the heads of departments.

Appointment must therefore, be to an existing office. Furthermore, the choice of the appointing power to such an office may be severely limited. Thus the Constitution itself stipulates in paragraph 2 of Section 6 of Article I:

No Senator or Representative shall, during the time for which he was elected, be appointed to any civil office under the authority of the United States, whish shall have been created, or the emoluments whereof shall have been increased, during such time; and no person holding any office under the United States shall be a member of either House during his continuance in office.

Neither of these clauses has turned out in practice to be quite as potent a restraint on presidential power as it was, perhaps, originally intended to be. Thus members of Congress have been repeatedly designated by the President, at times with the consent of the Senate, to represent the United States on international commissions or at diplomatic conferences. Today, in fact, the practice has attained the dignity of usage, one which is reconcilable with the letter of the Constitution only on the theory that such assignments, being to fairly specific tasks and carrying with them no extra emolument, lack the essential tests of "office".

And a like explanation may vindicate the course of many Presidents since the time of Washington in sending abroad "personal" and "secret" agents on diplomatic or semi-diplomatic missions;[1] as well as of a practice resorted to by the first Roosevelt, of constituting "volunteer unpaid commissions" for the purpose of investigating certain factual situations and reporting their findings to the President.[2] Indeed, Mr. Roosevelt's enthusiasm for this method of informing himself concerning "the state of the nation" came eventually to be denounced in Congress as "unconstitutional," and an amendment to the Sundry Civil Act of 1909 undertook to forbid the practice.[3] Mr. Roosevelt signed the measure even while asserting his intention of ignoring the restriction. "Congress," he argued, "cannot prevent the President from seeking advice," nor disinterested men from giving their service to the people;[4] and that this eminently sensible view has won out would seem clear from the fact that

Mr. Hoover, when President, appointed literally dozens of fact-finding commissions, most of which were without statutory basis.[5] President Wilson's creation of the War Industries Board and the Committee on Public Information during the war with Germany, must on the other hand be set down, in view of the great powers which were exercised those bodies in the President's name, as illustrating the enlargement which presidential authority is apt to undergo in all directions in wartime.[6]

The opening clause of Article I, Section 7, paragraph 2, recently came under public scrutiny in connection with the appointment of Justice Hugo L. Black to the Supreme Court. This was because Congress had recently improved the financial position of Justices retiring at seventy, and the term for which Mr. Black had been elected to the Senate from Alabama in 1932 has still some time to run. The appointment was defended by the argument that inasmuch as Mr. Black was only fifty-one years old at the time and so would be ineligible for the "increased emolument" for nineteen years, it was not *as to him* an increased emolument.[7] Similarly, when in 1909 Senator Knox of Pennsylvania wished to become Secretary of State in President Taft's Cabinet, the salary of which office had been recently increased, Congress accommodatingly repealed the increase for the period which still remained of Mr. Knox's sensatorial term.[8] In other words, a Senator or Representative—but especially a Senator—may, "during the time for which he was elected, be appointed to any civil office under the authority of the United States,...the emoluments whereof shall have been increased during such time," *provided only* that the increase in emolument is not available to the appointee "during such time".

But the most serious limitations on the appointing power result from the fact that in creating an office, Congress may also stipulate the qualifications of appointees thereto. First and last, legislation of this character has laid down a great variety of qualifications, depending on citizenship, residence, professional attainments, occupational experience, age, race, property, sound habits, political, industrial or regional affiliations, and so on. It has even confined the President's selection to a small number of persons to be named by others.[9] Indeed, it has contrived at times, by particularly of description, to designate a definite eligible, thereby virtually usurping the appointing power.[10]

For the proposition is generally conceded that some choice, however small, must be left the appointing authority.[11] Thus the Civil Service Act of 1883 leaves the appointing officer the right to select from "*among* those graded highest as the result of" the competitive examinations for which the act provides,[12] and supplementary executive orders have customarily further restricted choice to the *three highest*. The Foreign Service Act of 1924 is notable in that it extended for the first time the principle of competitive examinations to certain offices appointment to which was formerly made with the advice and consent of the Senate.[13] But obviously there is no logical reason why this should not be done generally, there being no difference in the *nature* of the appointive power whether it is exercised by the President with the Senate, or by the President alone, or by a head of department.

Another power of Congress which must be distinguished from the appointing power is that of determining the powers and duties of officers of the United States. In the case of an existing office Congress may increase these to an indefinite extent without necessitating a reappointment to the office;[14] but it seems to be the Court's opinion and is certainly a very logical one, that new duties should be "germane" to the existing office, and especially that their assignment should not transgress the principle of the separation of powers.[15]

Another characteristic which usage has affixed to the President's power of appointment is that while the power connotes a choice among eligibles, it involves ordinarily no choice whether there shall be an appointment. Just as it is expected that a legally authorized appropriation will be spent, so it is expected that a legally authorized office will be filled. But what usage has created usage can also destroy, a fact which makes Mr. Roosevelt's success in keeping the office of Comptroller General unfilled for many months following Mr. McCarl's retirement of more than passing interest.

Except the President and Vice-President all members of the civil service of the national government are appointive and fall into one of three categories, those who are appointed by the President "by and with the advice and consent of the Senate"; "inferior" officers whose appointment Congress has vested by law "in the President alone, in the courts of law or in the heads of departments"; and "employees".

As it is here used the term "employee" bears a very special meaning. Ordinarily the term denotes one who stands in a contractual relationship to his "employer," but here it signifies all subordinate officials of the national government receiving appointment at the hands of officials who are not specifically recognized by the Constitution as capable of being vested by Congress with the appointing power.[16] The concept thus affords a way of circumventing the apparent purpose of the Constitution to continue the power to appoint "inferior" officers, by the authorization of Congress, to the President alone, the courts of law, and the heads of departments. As used in the statutes the term "officers" is frequently construed to cover "employees" in the above sense.

What are "inferior" officers in the sense of the Constitution has never been judicially determined, since, thanks to the jealous vigilance of the Senate. Congress has exercised its power in the vesting of appointments very sparingly. The term seems to suggest in this particular context officers intended to be subordinate to those in whom their appointment is vested, and at the same time to exclude the courts of law and heads of departments. If this is so, then it is at least doubtful whether the power may be lodged in a head of department to appoint members of an administrative commission which is intended to be independent of departmental direction; and even more questionable is such a proposal as one made in 1920 to vest in the Supreme Court the appointment of the Comptroller General, an officer whose functions lie entirely outside the judicial field.

The Constitution distinguishes three stages in appointments by the President with the advice and consent of the Senate. The first is the "nomination" of the candidate by the President alone; the second is the assent of the Senate to his "appointment"; and the third is the final appointment and commissioning of the appointee by the President. The first two stages are controlled to greater or less extent by a set of usages which go by the name of "senatorial courtesy". If the President, in nominating to an office within a state, fails to consult the preferences of the Senator or Senators of his own party from that state, he is very likely to see the appointment defeated upon an appeal to the Senate by the slighted member or members. Reciprocally, the Senate will ordinarily interpose no objection to the President's nominees for Cabinet posts. Any attempt to find a basis in the written Constitution for this interesting institution would be disappointing; it is the Senate, not individual Senators, whose advice and consent the Constitution requires.[17]

The only case in which the Supreme Court has had occasion to pass directly upon the participation of the Senate in the appointing power is the fairly recent one of Smith *v.* United States[18] which grew out of an attempt by the Senate early in 1931 to recall its consent to certain nominations by President Hoover to the Federal Power Commission. In support of its course, the Senate invoked a longstanding rule which permits a motion to reconsider a resolution of confirmation and to recall the notification thereof within "the next two days of actual executive session of the Senate". Inasmuch as the nominees involved had meantime taken the oath of office and entered upon the discharge of their duties, the President denied the request, which he stigmatized as an attempt "to encroach upon the executive function by removal of a duly appointed executive officers under the guise of reconsideration of his nomination".[19] The Senate thereupon voted to reconsider the nominations in question, again approving two of the nominees but rejecting the third, against whom by the Senate's order the district attorney of the District of Columbia forthwith instituted *quo warranto* proceedings on the ground that the Senate's rule as heretofore applied did not reach the case of an appointee who had already been installed in office on the faith of the Senate's initial consent and notification to the President.

Just how the Court became entitled to construe the Senate's rules, which it conceded were subject to change by the Senate without notice, does not appear from Justice Brandeis' opinion; but at any rate the expedient enabled the Court to evade the question whether the rule governing the reconsideration of nominations is valid once notification has gone forward to the President. Jefferson in his *Manual* asserts unqualifiedly that, "If, after the vote, the paper on which it [the Senate] passed has been parted with, there can be no reconsideration." Practice, however, has been far from supporting this sweeping assertion. Nor is its logic inescapable, for it may with equal logic be contended that the senatorial consent is only "a warrant of attorney, valid until revoked," or that it is akin to a proffer and hence may be withdrawn at any time before acceptance. In Smith's case the revocation or withdrawal—depending on the analogy adopted—clearly came too late.

Neither does the decision deal with the question whether the Senate may attach conditions to its approval of an appointment, as it frequently does to its approval of a treaty. The entire record of practice under the constitution, nevertheless, negatives the suggestion, as also does early opinion. Madison, Hamilton, Jefferson, and Story all expressed themselves to the effect that the Senate's role in relation to appointments is only that of rejecting or confirming nominations without condition.[20] Moreover, the conditions which the Senate would attempt to attach would be apt either to invade the powers of the office, which comes from the law, or to limit the officer's tenure, which also comes from the law or is subject to determination by the removal power. And in principle at least the Senate's pretensions would extend to judicial no less than to executive appointees.

Although the Constitution says that the President "*shall* commission all officers," etc., this, as applied in practice, does not appear to mean that he is under constitutional or legal obligation to commission those whose appointments have reached that stage, but merely that it is he and no one else who has the power to commission them.[21] The sealing and delivery of the commission is, on the other hand, in the case both of appointees by the President and Senate and by the President alone, a purely ministerial act which has been lodged by statute with the Secretary of State, and the performance of which may be compelled by mandamus unless the appointee has been in the meantime validity removed.[22]

A further element of the appointing power is contained in the following provision of Article II, Section 2, paragraph 3:

The president shall have power to fill up all vacancies that may happen during the recess of the Senate, by granting commissions which shall expire at the end of their next session.

The significant word is "happen". Setting out from the proposition that the very nature of the executive power requires that it shall always be "in capacity for action," Attorneys General came early to interpret this to mean "happen to exist," and long continued practice securely establishes this construction.[23] It follows that whenever a vacancy may have occurred in the first instance, or for whatever reason, if it still continues after the Senate has ceased to sit and hence cannot be consulted, the President may fill it in the way described. But a Senate "recess" does not include holiday or temporary adjournments,[24] while by an act of Congress, if the vacancy existed when the Senate was in session, the ad interim appointee may receive no salary until he has been confirmed by the Senate.[25] Also there is an informal understanding, although it is not always observed, that the President will not extend a recess appointment to a rejected nominee.[26]

To be distinguish from the power to make recess appointments is the power of the President to make temporary assignments of officials to the duties of other absent or incapacitated officials. Usually a situation of this nature is provided for in advance by a statute which designates the inferior officers who is to act in place of his immediate superior, but in the lack of such provision, theory and practice alike concede the President the power to make a designation.[27]

II

Unlike the British monarch, the President is under no constitutional necessity of acting through agents in order that his official acts may be judicially noticeable. On the contrary, there are many acts which to be done constitutionally must presumably have been done by him personally or in the exercise of his personal judgment. In the words of an opinion rendered by Attorney General Cushing in 1855:

It may be presumed that he, the *man* discharging the Presidential office, *and he alone*, grants reprieves and pardons for offenses against the United States.

And again:

No act of Congress, no act even of the President himself, can, by constitutional possibility authorize or create any military officer not subordinate to the President.[28]

May this type of obligation be enlarged by statute? Dealing with this question in a case before the Civil War, which grew out of a statutory provision expressly prohibiting the advancing of public money to the disbursing officers of the government except under "the special direction of the President," the Court, said:

The President's duty in general requires his superintendence of the administration; yet this duty cannot require of him to become the administrative officer to every department and bureau, or to perform in person the numerous details incident to services which, nevertheless, he is, in a correct sense, by the Constitution and laws required and expected to perform. This cannot be, 1st. Because, if it were practicable, it would be to absorb the duties and responsibilities of the various departments of the government in the personal action of one chief executive officer. It cannot be, for the stronger reason, that it is impracticable—nay, impossible.[29]

It is true that the Court once held that a certain decree of a court-martial was void because, although it had been confirmed by the Secretary of War, it was not specifically stated to have received the sanction of the President as required by the 65th Article of War;[30] but later decisions call this holding into question.[31] Such legislation is at any rate very exceptional. The general rule as stated by the Court is that when any duty is act by law upon the president, it may be exercised by him "through the head of the appropriate department," whose acts, if performed within the law, become the President's acts. In fact, as a matter of administrative practice, most orders and instructions emanating from the heads of the departments even when in pursuance of powers conferred by statute on the President do not refer to him.[32]

But suppose that the law casts a duty upon a subordinate executive agency *eo nomine,* does the President thereupon become entitled, by virtue of his "executive power" or of his duty to "take care that the laws be faithfully executed," to subsitute his own judgment for that of the agency regarding the discharge of such duty? An unqualified answer to this question would invite startling results. An affirmative answer would make all questions of law enforcement questions of discretion, and that the discretion of an independent and legally uncontrollable branch of the government. By the same token, it would render it impossible for Congress, notwithstanding its broad powers under the "necessary and proper" clause, to leave anything to the specially trained judgment of a subordinate executive official with any assurance that his discretion would not be perverted to political ends for the advantage of the administration in power. On the other hand, a flatly negative answer would hold out consequences equally unwelcome. It would, as Attorney General Cushing quaintly phrased it, leave it open to Congress so to divide and transfer "the executive power" by statute as to change the government "into a parliamentary despotism like that of Venezuela or Great Britain, with a *nominal* executive chief or president, who, however, would remain without a shred of actual power".[33] Or, in different words, it would leave it open to Congress to destroy unity of administration in the national government, as it has long since been destroy in the state governments.

Probably the earliest discussion of this highly important issue is the argument which was made by Madison in the first Congress in behalf of attributing the removal power to the President. It was "the intention of the Constitution," Madison contended, expressed especially in the "faithfully executed" clause, that the first magistrate should be responsible for the executive departments, and this responsibility, he urged, carried with it the power to "inspect and *control*" the conduct of all subordinate executive officers.[34]

Yet, when in the same year it organized the first executive departments, Congress itself adopted a radically different principle. The cats creating the Departments of State and of War specifically recognized the responsibility of the heads of those departments to the President; not so with the act organizing the Department of the Treasury. "The Secretary of the Treasury," this act read, and indeed still reads,

> shall from time to time... make report and give information to either branch of the legislature in person or in writing, as may be required, respecting all matters referred to him by the Senate or House of Representatives, or which shall appertain to his office; and generally shall perform all services relative to finances as he shall be directed to perform.[35]

directed, that is, by Congress. Nor is the reason underlying this difference far to seek. The State and War departments are principally, although not exclusively, organs of the President in the exercise of functions which are assigned him *by the Constitution*, while the Treasury Department is primarily an instrument for carrying into effect Congress' constitutional powers in the field of finance. For like reasons, when in 1794, the Post Office Department was established, it was not placed under the control of the President, nor was the Interior Department when it was formed in 1849; but the Navy Department, established in 1798, was so placed.[36]

And meantime, in Marbury *v.* Madison, Chief Justice Marshall had suggested a parallel distinction between the duties of the Secretary of State under the original act which had created a "Department of Foreign Affairs," and those which had been added by the later act changing the designation of the department to its present one. The former were, he pointed out, entirely in the "political field," and hence for their discharge the secretary was left responsible absolutely to the President. The latter, on the other hand, were exclusively of statutory origin and sprang from the powers of Congress. For these, therefore, the secretary was "an officer of the law" and "amenable to the law for his conduct".[37]

Nor is the doctrine which was advanced by Attorney General Wirt in 1823 of very different import when it is confined to the field of Congress' delegated powers, which is evidently what Wirt was thinking of. It is that the President's duty under the "faithfully executed" clause requires of him scarcely more than that he should bring a *criminally negligent* official to book for his derelictions, either by removing him or by setting in motion against him the processes of impeachment or of criminal prosecution,[38] an opinion which voiced the point of view of the "Virginia School" of Presidents, including the later Madison. And the obvious fact is that the President's power to direct his subordinates in the field of Congress powers can be magnified only at the expense of Congress own discretion in the exercise of these powers. The doctrine that Congress is unable to vest any subordinate executive agency even within the field of its own specifically delegated powers with any legal discretion which the President is not entitled to appropriate to himself, is, of course, the very hallmark of the Jacksonian conception of the Presidency. The groundwork for it, however, was prepared much earlier, first, by "the decision of 1789," which is treated in the following section, and secondly, by the rise of the President's Cabinet.

Like its British namesake, the American Cabinet is entirely extra-constitutional.[39] The President, the Constitution states, "may require the opinion, in writing, of the principal officer in each of the executive departments, upon any subject relating to the duties of their respective offices".[40] The consultative relationship thus suggested is an entirely one-sided affair, is to be conducted in writing, with the "principal officers" separately and individually, and is to relate only "to the duties of their respective offices." If an executive council was needed, it was the general idea in 1789 that the Senate would serve the purpose.

"Assembled consultation" of the Cabinet, as Miss Hinsdale points out in her excellent book, first became general practice during the diplomatic crisis of 1793. Two years later, as a result of the fight over the Jay Treaty and the equivocal attitude of Secretary of State Randolph on that occasion, Washington, who had thought at first to maintain recognized spokesmen of the leading political factions of the country in the departmental headships, reconstructed his Cabinet on the avowed basis of loyalty to his own policies, and in so doing created a precedent which, with negligible exceptions, has guided Presidents in their choice of departmental heads ever since. And meantime, by the "decision of 1789," the President had been endowed with an unqualified power of removal over the heads of the executive departments.

So from the first, the heads of these departments occupied, when exercising powers delegated them by statute, a dual role and were subject to a dual responsibility. The inevitable clash between these two roles came in 1833 as an incident of Jackson's "War on the Bank". Convincing himself by a characteristic process of self-hypnosis that the {national} bank was an unsafe depository for the national funds, Jackson ordered secretary of the Treasury Duane to transfer them, which Duane had power under the law to do. As it happened, however, the House of Representatives had recently expressed its confidence in the bank by formal resolution, and Duane's own instructed judgment was to the same effect. He accordingly refused to comply with Jackson's demand, was promptly removed, and his successor Taney at once gave the desired order.[41]

Although in commenting on this episode writers are apt to treat it as the outcome solely of the President's possession of the removal power,[42] this was far from Jackson's own theory of the matter. The latter, as state in his protest message to Congress, was "that the entire executive power is vested in the President"; that the power to remove "those officers who are to aid him in the execution of the laws" is an incident of that power; that the Secretary of the Treasury is such an officer; that "the custody of the public property and money is an executive function" exercised through the Secretary of the Treasury and his subordinates; that "in the performance of these duties he [the secretary] is subject to the supervision and control of the President"; and finally that the act establishing the bank "did not and could not change the relation between the President and Secretary—did not release the former from his obligation to see the law faithfully executed nor the latter from the president's supervision and control".[43]

In short, *the Constitution knows only one "executive power," that of the President, whose duty to "take care that the laws be faithfully executed" thus becomes the equivalent of the duty and power to execute them himself.* The removal of Duane was, therefore, the constitutionally ordained result of that officer's attempt to usurp the President's constitutional prerogative; or, in broader terms, the President's removal power, in this case unqualified, was *the sanction provided by the Constitution for his power and duty to control all his subordinates in all their official actions of public consequence.*

Five years later the case of Kendall v. United States[44] arose. The United States owed one Stokes money, and when Postmaster General Kendall, at Jackson's instigation, refused to pay it, Congress passed a special act ordering payment. Kendall, however, still proving non-compliant, Stokes sought and obtained a mandamus in the united States Circuit Court for the District of Columbia, and on appeal this decision was affirmed by the Supreme Court.

While Kendall *v.* United States, like Marbury *v.* Madison, involved the question of the responsibility of a head of department for the performance of a *ministerial* duty, the discussion by counsel before the Court and the Court's own opinion covered the entire subject of the relation of the President to his subordinates in the performance by them of statutory duties. The lower court had asserted that the duty of the President under the "faithfully executed" clause gave him "no other control over the officer than to see that he acts honestly, with proper motives," but "no power to construe the law and see that the executive action conforms to it".[45] Counsel for Kendall attacked this position vigorously, relying largely upon statements by Hamilton, Marshall, Wilson, and Story having to do with the President's power in the field of foreign relations.[46]

The Court rejected the latter argument with emphasis. "There are," it pointed out,

certain political duties imposed upon many officers in the executive departments, the discharge of which is under the direction of the President.

But it would be an alarming doctrine that Congress cannot impose upon any executive officer any duty they may think proper, which is not repugnant to any rights secured and protected by the Constitution; and in such cases, the duty and responsibility grow out of and are subject to the control of the law, and not to the direction of the President.[47]

In short, the Court recognized that the underlying question of the case was whether the President's "executive power," coupled with his duty to "take care that the laws be faithfully executed," made it constitutionally impossible for Congress ever to entrust the construction of its statutes to anybody but the President; and it answered this question with an emphatic "no".

How then does this exceedingly important issue stand today? It will aid clarity to distinguish at the outset two types of executive duty. As to the first, or "ministerial" type, the Court has held repeatedly that even a head of department may be compelled by mandamus to perform such a duty.[48] That is to say, not only is a head of department legally entitled to perform such a duty in defiance of the President, but he may be forced by judicial process to do so, and that notwithstanding the fact that he may be immediately removed by the President for compliance with the court's order.

All other executive duties, or powers—for the two terms are interchangeable in this connection—are "discretionary," in that the officer to whom they are entrusted is left a greater or less latitude of judgment respecting the occasion for their exercise, or the manner of it, or both. If such duties, or powers, have their origin in the constitutional prerogatives of the President, then the subordinate to whom they are entrusted is, of course, his mere instrument; and the same is true if they have been delegated by Congress to the President in the first instance.[49] But suppose they have been delegated by Congress, in the exercise of its own constitutional powers, to a subordinate executive officer or agency—then what power may the President constitutionally claim over their discharge? This, in precise terms, is the crucial question.

Again we encounter a dichotomy, inasmuch as discretionary powers may be of a "quasi-judicial" nature or otherwise, depending on whether or not they impinge upon private interests which are entitled to a hearing and other features of "due process of law" before the powers in question can be exercised. With regard to the former category, Presidents have been more than once informed by their own Attorneys General that they may not substitute themselves for the officer named by the statute, nor entertain appeals from such an officer, nor revise his findings; that in such situations their sole duty is to see that the proper officer acts *with proper diligence.*[50] Indeed it is with just such decisions in mind that Chief Justice Taft remarked in the Myers case that "there may be duties of a quasi-judicial character...the discharge of which the President cannot in a particular case properly influence or control".[51] Yet he straightway added that "even in such a case" the President might remove the responsible officer for rendering a decision not to liking, a paradox of which, as we shall see in a moment, the Court has subsequently tried to disburden itself, although with what degree of success is still a question.

Today, to be sure, the more important discretionary powers of a quasi-judicial character have been entrusted to administrative tribunals like the Interstate Commerce Commission, the Federal Trade Commission, the SEC, and so on, which are not connected with any department. But this is not always the case, for the same kind of duty may be and sometimes is entrusted to officials who are technically the subordinates of a head of a department, or even to heads of departments themselves. Thus the Commissioner of Patents is subordinate of the Secretary of the Interior, while the Secretaries of Agriculture and Commerce and the Attorney General constitute a commission for the enforcement of the Grain Futures Act of 1922, and so on.

Likewise, discretionary powers of a non-judicial type may be delegated to a head of department or subordinate thereof; or to an executive agency outside any department—TVA furnishing, as to most of its powers, an excellent example of the latter category. And it is this category which today furnishes the "no-man's land" between the Jeffersonian and the Jacksonian conception of presidential power and duty in the execution of the law. To state the issue in as concrete terms as possible—is the President entitled, as the law now stands, to construe the powers of the TVA for it, or is TVA entitled to construe the law of its creation for itself, subject of course to judicial review? I confess myself to be a Jeffersonian so far as this issue is concerned, and so take the position that the only power which the President can validly claim over TVA is the power—or rather duty—to see that TVA acts honestly and diligently. Were, however, TVA to be drawn into one of the great executive departments the answer to the above question would have to be framed, so it seems to me, along Jacksonian lines. For when Congress plants an executive agency within the domain of the member of the President's Cabinet, it must be deemed to have done so with its eyes open to the relationship which has developed between the President and his Cabinet— a relationship of unqualified domination on the one hand and of complete subordination on the other.

And it is from this angle that President Roosevelt's plan to reorganize the executive branch of the government should be in part evaluated, although not altogether. Within recent years many "independent agencies" have been set up by Congress outside the precincts of any of the great executive departments, and what the President now proposes is that they shall be brought within one of these departments or that their powers shall be transferred to some bureau or agency which is already there. Thus, if the reasoning of the foregoing paragraphs is correct, the discretionary powers of such agencies, when not of a quasi-judicial nature, would become *properly* subject through the heads of departments to ultimate direction and control by the President; and even those of a quasi-judicial nature would actually become so in time, on account of the inability of judicial power to cope effectively with the President's powers of appointment and removal.

Of course, the advocates of the President's plan strongly urge the claims of administrative *unity* and *efficiency*. But are the two things necessarily synonymous in the case of so vast an organization as the national government? It seems to me clearly not; but rather that efficient administration must in such a case always depend to an important extent upon the expert knowledge and pride in his job of the largely independent bureaucrat. In other words, administration in the sense of the daily task of carrying out the laws and performing the public services for which they provide is a *pluralistic*, not a *monistic* universe; and to imagine the President as a sort of boss of the works under whose all-seeing eye everything takes place, is merely to imagine something that does not exist and never will. To be sure, such considerations do not dispose entirely of the argument for the President's plan; and no one would care to deny that administrative set-up must be constantly tinkered to keep it at all efficient.[52]

We now turn to the President's removal power and the effort of the Court in recent years to equate this power with his supervisory powers; in other words, to stamp upon it the character of a sanctioning power in relation to these, and conversely to confine it to that scope.

III

Save for the provision which it makes for a power of impeachment of "civil officers to the United States,[53]" the Constitution contains no reference to a power to remove from office, a situation in which early resort to the judicial divining rod would seem on first consideration to have been highly likely and necessary. Actually, until its decision in Myers *v.* United States,[54] October 25, 1926, the Supreme Court had contrived to side-step every occasion for a decisive pronouncement regarding the removal power, its extent and location.

How explain this strange hesitancy on the Court's power to advance the cause of judicial review? Two reasons may be suggested. The first is the strong course taken by the first Congress under the Constitution in undertaking to settle the removal issue by legislation. Throughout the ensuing 140 years the initiative thus asserted, at first in favor of the power of the President and later against it, was respected by the Court.

But in the second place, it may be surmised, the Court has always been uneasily aware of its inability to intervene effectively in this field. So long as Congress chooses to permit it to do so, the Court is free to decree that an official who has been ousted contrary to its view of the constitutional proprieties shall be paid his salary, but it has no power to reinstate such an official, and ordinarily no power to invalidate his successor's official acts. Curiously enough, in the two principal cases which are reviewed below—the first being the Myers case—the ousted official died while his suit for salary was pending, and so the inadequacy of the Court's remedial power was conveniently obscured.

The point immediately at issue in the Myers case was the effectiveness of an order of the Postmaster General, acting by direction of the President, to remove from office a first-class postmaster, in view of the following provision of an act of Congress passed in 1876:

Post masters of the first, second and third classes shall be appointed and may be removed by the President with the advice and consent of the Senate, and shall hold their offices for four years unless sooner removed or suspended according to law.[55]

A divided Court, speaking through Chief Justice Taft, held the order of removal valid, and the statutory provision just quoted void. Standing by itself this disallowance does not necessarily imply more than that so long as Congress chooses to leave the appointment of an inferior officer with the President, acting with the advice and consent of the Senate, it may not make the officer's removal dependent also on such consent. With this comparatively narrow holding, however, the Court was not content, and in the Chief Justice's elaborate opinion the sweeping doctrine was advanced that the President is endowed by Article II with a power of removal which, so far as "executive officers of the United States appointed by him" are concerned, is not susceptible constitutionally of any restraints or limitation by Congress, and that all such officers are intended by the Constitution to be left removable at the President's will.[56]

The Chief Justice's main reliance was upon "the decision of 1789," previously alluded to. The incident may be described briefly.[57] On June 16 of that year the first House of Representatives under the Constitution went into committee of the whole to consider a bill proposed by Madison for establishing a Department of Foreign Affairs, the opening clause of which provided that the principal officer of the new department was "to be removable from office by the President of the United States". In the debate which ensued three fairly equal parties disclosed themselves: first, those who, headed by Madison, argued that the power of removal was an inherent element both of "executive power" and of the duty to "take care that the laws be faithfully executed"; secondly, those who, headed by Sherman—also a former member of the Philadelphia Convention—contended that the power of removal was conferred as an incident of the power of appointment jointly on the President and Senate; and thirdly, those who held that the Constitution had left it with Congress, by virtue of the "necessary and proper" clause, to locate the power of removal where it thought fit. A fourth party, comprising only three or four members, urged that unless removed for misbehavior in office by the power of impeachment, or by judicial process known to the common law, an officer had a vested right in his office for the term of his appointment as fixed by law.

The mode in which the theoretical issue that raised was disposed of is somewhat confusing. The objection having been raised to the clause "to be removable by the President" that it represented an attempt by Congress to confer power on the President which was not otherwise provided for in the Constitution, the clause was stricken out, and in its place were inserted the words "whenever the said principal officer shall be removed from office by the President of the United States," which were thought to infer that the President already had the power of removal, in certain cases at least, without grant from Congress. Subsequently the Senate ratified the action of the House by the casting vote of Vice-President Adams, and like action was later taken with regard to the Secretary of the Treasury and the Secretary of War.

Was the "decision of 1789" capable of sustaining the sweeping conclusions of the Chief Justice's opinion? The answer is, no. While the decision undoubtedly avoids the direct implication that the President owed the power of removal to a grant by Congress, yet this result was obtained by the indispensable support of those who throughout the debate had championed the doctrine that Congress could determine the question of the scope and location of the removal power in any way it saw fit. What is more, the question related, as was repeatedly emphasized in the debate by the champions of presidential power, to high political office, one which was to be the instrument of the President in the principal field of executive prerogative and whose tenure was, for this very reason, being left *indeterminate*. While, therefore, the decision may be fairly considered as ascribing to the President alone the power to remove executive officers appointed with the consent of the Senate whom Congress chooses to leave removable *by not fixing their terms*, it certainly did not established the proposition of the Myers case that Congress is without power to *fix the terms* of any executive officers whatever as against the President's power of removal.

Nor does the record of opinion respecting the power of removal under the Constitution, prior at least to the Civil War, generally support the results arrived at in the Myers case. In *The Federalist* Hamilton had stated explicitly that he Senate would be associated with the President in the removal of officers, although he seems later to have retracted this opinion.[58] Neither Marshall, Kent, Story, nor Webster regarded the decision of 1789 as reaching offices of determinate tenure; and all but Marshall were quite clearly of opinion that the correct reading of the Constitution located the power of removal in both the president and Senate in the case of officers appointed with the Senate's consent, although they were willing to concede the binding effect of the decision of 1789 as "a practical construction of the Constitution" till Congress should choose to reverse it.[59] And that the Supreme Court of the period shared these views is indicated by its opinion in *Ex parte* Hennen in 1839.[60]

The literary source of the Chief Justice's opinion is clearly Jackson's famous Message of Protest of April 15, 1834, which was dealt with in the previous section.[61] There all the essential elements of the Chief Justice's doctrine were assembled for the first time, and, it may be added, for the *last* time until the Myers case was decided. Other partial sources are certain opinions of Attorneys General although the real preponderance of opinion from this source by no means supports the sweeping propositions advanced by the Chief Justice. Still another source is the debate stirred by the Tenure of Office Act of 1867, while a fourth source is to be discovered in the arguments developed by President Johnson's counsel at the time of his impeachment trial. Yet even these gentlemen, it is worthnoting, generally contented themselves with asserting that Johnson, assuming that he had violated the Tenure of Office Act, had acted in good faith, not that he had beyond peradventure acted constitutionally.[62]

But apart from the verdict of past opinion, the Chief Justice also urged the theory that the power of removal was inherently "executive" on its own merits. His contention was based on the two grounds of history and of necessity; and in assertion of the former he instanced the power of "the British Crown" in the appointment and removal of officers. The argument proves too much. The power of the British Crown in the appointment and removal of officers, as we saw earlier, is an historical outgrowth of and is still intimately involved with a much wider prerogative in the creation of offices, while the only offices normally known to the Constitution of the United States are those "which shall be established by law".[63]

The ultimate basis, however, of the decision in the Myers case is to be sought far less in constitutional history and legal theory than in certain practical considerations which naturally loomed large in the mind of a Chief Justice who had once been President himself. That this is so is clearly indicated in the following salient passage of the opinion:

There is nothing in the Constitution which permits a distinction between the removal of the head of a department or a bureau, when he discharges a political duty of the President or exercises his discretion, and the removal of executive officers engaged in the discharge of their other normal duties. The imperative reasons requiring an unrestricted power to remove the most important of his subordinates in their most important duties must, therefore, control the interpretation of the Constitution as to all appointed by him.[64]

That the President ought to be able to remove at will all subordinates whose discretion he is entitled by the Constitution or by the laws of Congress to control, and for whose conduct he is hence responsible, must be granted, as we have seen. But the Chief Justice's conclusion that this fact "must control interpretation of the Constitution as to all appointed by him" was much too drastic and resulted in the paradox that, while the Constitution permitted Congress to vest duties in executive officers in the performance of which they were to exercise their own independent judgment, it at the same time permitted the President to guillotine such officers for exercising the very discretion which Congress had the right to require!

Nor was the menace of this paradox a merely theoretical one. For as was pointed out above, recent decades have witnessed the establishment of a number of "administrative tribunals" outside and independent of any department. The Interstate Commerce Commission was thus established in 1887, the Federal Trade Commission in 1914, the Federal Tariff Commission in 1916, the Federal Power Commission in 1920, the Federal Communications Commission (succeeding the Federal Radio Commission) in 1934, and the Securities and Exchange Commission, also in 1934. The members of all these bodies are appointed by the President and Senate *for fixed terms,* while the members of the first three are removable by the President for "inefficiency, neglect of duty or malfeasance in office"—a provision which is not repeated as to the last three, possibly because of the influence of the Myers case. Meantime, however, in the act of 1920 creating the Railroad Labor Board, Congress had taken a further step. In an endeavor to confer upon the members of this body a quasi-judicial status, it provided that they should be removable by the President "for neglect of duty or malfeasance in office, but for no other cause"; and a similar tenure was bestowed upon the members of the Board of General Appraisers and the Board of Tax Appeals by the acts of 1922 and 1924 respectively.[65]

Nor should the enactment in 1921 of the Budget and Accounting Act, whereby Congress inaugurated an almost revolutionary reform in methods of national financial legislation, be overlooked in this connection. The act pivots upon the office of Comptroller General of the United States, and the success of the reform unquestionably hinges upon the independence of this or some similar functionary from executive pressure. The act accordingly provides that the Comptroller General shall hold office for fifteen years, and save upon impeachment shall be removable only by joint resolution of Congress and then only after a hearing which shall establish to Congress' satisfaction his incapacity inefficiency, neglect of duty or malfeasance, or "conduct involving moral turpitude".[66]

There can be little doubt that all these measures, so far as they purported to restrict the President's power of removal, were, by the Chief Justice's opinion in the Myers case constitutionally in effective, and that the Court would have been compelled sooner or later, had it adhered to that opinion, either to set aside the restrictive provisions or to have interpreted them away. In point of fact, it has since recanted a good deal of the Taft opinion, though just how much may be a question. I refer to its decision in 1935 in Humphrey *v*. United States.[67]

The material facts of this case were as follows: Humphrey, a member of the Federal Trade Commission, was reappointed to his post by President Hoover, by and with the advice and consent of the Senate, on December

10, 1931, for a term of seven years. On July 25, 1933, and again on August 31, President Roosevelt wrote the commissioner requesting his resignation on the ground that the two entertained divergent views of public policy, but at the same time disclaiming any reflection on Mr. Humphrey personally or on his official conduct. Said the President:

> You will, I know, realize that I do not feel that your mind and my mind go along together on either the policies or the administering of the Federal Trade Commission, and, frankly, I think it is best for the people of this country that I should have a full confidence.

Humphrey having declined to resign, the President of October 7 notified him that he was from that date "removed" from office; and in due course Humphrey brought suit for salary.[68]

The principal basis of the Court's unanimous decision sustaining Humphrey's claim that he was wrongfully removed from office is indicated in the following paragraphs of Justice Sutherland's opinion. Distinguishing the Myers case, the Justice says:

> A postmaster is an executive officer restricted to the performance of executive functions. He is charged with no duty at all related to either the legislative or judicial power. The actual decision in the Myers Case finds support in the theory that such an office is merely one of the units in the executive department and hence inherently subject to the exclusive and illimitable power of removal by the chief executive, whose subordinate and aid he is....
>
> The Federal Trade Commission is an administrative body created by Congress to carry into effect legislative policies embodied in the statute. ...Its duties are performed without executive leave and in the contemplation of the statute must be free from executive control....
>
> We think it plain under the Constitution that illimitable power of removal is not possessed by the President in respect of officers of the character of those just named [the Interstate Commerce Commission, the Federal Trade Commission, the Court of Claims]. The authority of Congress, in creating quasi-legislative or quasi-judicial agencies, to require them to act in discharge of their duties independently of executive control, cannot well be doubted; and that authority includes, as an appropriate incident, power to fix the period during which they shall continue, and to forbid their removal except for cause in the meantime. For it is quite evident that one who holds his office only during the pleasure of another cannot be depended upon to maintain an attitude of independence against the latter's will.[69]

Elsewhere in his opinion Justice Sutherland takes pains to point out that "the decision of 1789" concerned an office which "was not only purely executive" but an officer "who was responsible to the President and to him alone, in a very definite sense".[70]

That this holding, considered in the light of this opinion, goes a long way toward scrapping the Myers case seems to me fairly clear. Not only does the opinion entirely ignore Chief Justice Taft's invocation of the opening clause of Article II, but it employs the "executive power" throughout in the narrow sense of non-discretionary powers. All other powers which grow out of and succeed to legislation by Congress within the field of its delegated powers are comprised, when they do not fall to the regular courts, under the captions of "quasi-legislative" and "quasi-judicial". It seems to follow that the President's unrestricted power of removal can reach only two classes of officials: (1) those whose statutory powers are ministerial merely; (2) those who exercise the President's own powers, whether of statutory or constitutional origin.[71]

At the same time, it should not be too hastily inferred that the President is entirely without a certain minimum power of removal of broader range, in which connection President Roosevelt's recent removal of Dr. A. E. Morgan from the chairmanship of TVA is of considerable interest. Dr. Morgan had made certain statements about his fellow directors which amounted to charges of gross malfeasance on their part, but when the President demanded that he produce evidence in support of these statements, Dr. Morgan refused to do so, and his dismissal thereupon followed.

The act of Congress creating the TVA contains two provisions regarding removal.[72] The first says that "any member of said board may be removed from office at any time by a concurrent resolution of the Senate and House of Representatives"; the other reads that "any member of said board who is found by the President of the United States to be guilty of a violation of this section [forbidding the application of political tests in the selection or promotion of the corporation's employees and officials] shall be removed from office by the President of the United States". The question raised by Dr. Morgan's dismissal is whether the latter provision should be given an exclusive construction. The answer is both yes and no. Inasmuch as it was the obvious intention of Congress that the board of directors of the TVA should be an independent body, the President has no right to construe their legal duties for them, and hence no right to remove them for a refusal on their part to permit him to do so.

But the President was not attempting to construe Dr. Morgan's legal duties for him. He was merely requiring his co-operation in attempting to clear up a charge which had called into question the honesty of the other directors and which had virtually brought the activities of the board to a standstill. To deny the President the power of removal in such a case would be to make it impossible for him to discharge his duty to "take care that the laws be faithfully executed" under the most modest interpretation of that duty.[73]

The provision of the TVA Act which purports to make the directors removable by a concurrent majority of the houses raises a rather different question. Nothing but a vote which the President has approved, or which has been passed over his veto, is recognized by the Constitution as capable of effecting a legal change. How then can a concurrent resolution remove from office one who has been appointed thereto by constitutional authority? Plainly, only on the theory that liability to removal in that way is one of the characteristics of the office as it was created by Congress. The question, despite its novelty, is not an entirely one-sided one. To deny Congress the power thus to qualify the tenure of an agent would be to force it to choose between relying solely on presidential control or leaving the agent uncontrolled. When private rights are not a stake the more flexible conception of constitutional arrangements is usually the more desirable one.[74]

And this brings us back to the case of the Comptroller General, which seems to be somewhat special one. Whether Congress may constitutionally restrict the President's removal power in his case depends on whether his power is to be deemed an extension of the legislative power over appropriations or of the executive power over expenditure. That the Constitution recognizes expenditure to be an executive function seems evident; and this too is the verdict of history (early appropriation acts were in the most general terms). But of course expenditure is conditional upon appropriation, and so the Comptroller's office may be regarded – and on historical grounds also – as a descendant of the British Comptroller and Auditor, "who holds his office during good behavior, with a salary paid by statute out of the Consolidated Fund and who considers himself in no sense a servant of the Treasury but an officer responsible to the House of Commons".[75] That Congress could protect the tenure of an Auditor General who would be vested merely with the function of post-audit, as is proposed in President Roosevelt's Reorganization Plan, seems even clearer, inasmuch as his powers would not commence until expenditure was past. [76]

To sum up: the Constitution refers specifically to only one kind of removal from office, that by the impeachment process. It early became accepted doctrine, however, that in the absence of constitutional or statutory provision to the contrary, all appointive officials are subject to removal by the appropriate authority, that there is "no estate in office". Previous to the Myers case the weight of opinion treated the removal power as an element of the power of appointment and on that ground attributed to the Senate a participation in the removal of officers appointed with its consent. At the same time, by the "decision of 1789" the first Congress Planted "a practical construction" upon the Constitution which ascribed the power to the President alone so far as "executive" officers were concerned; and by the decision in the Myers case this "practical construction" was converted temporarily into a rule of constitutional law which severely restricted Congress' power in the creation of offices to determine their tenure. But the pronouncement in the Myers case was from any point of view much too sweeping, and it has since been largely replaced by the doctrine of the Humphery case, that Congress is entitled in creating an administrative agency which it intends to vest with discretionary powers to qualify or restrict the removability of such agency. Conversely, the general principle which governs the President's power of removal is fairly clear too. *It is a function of his supervisory powers,* and where these are unlimited it also is unlimited. But in addition the President enjoys as do all non-judicial officers a minimum supervisory power and hence a minimum removal power which arises from his duty to "take care that the laws be faithfully executed," which is to say, that their legally designated enforces act *diligently and honestly;* yet even in this case Congress is probably entitled to prescribe a fair procedure for the determination of such questions.

In short, to a very great extent, the President's removal power is constitutionally subject to control by Congress. Actually it is very, very broad, partly because Congress has not chosen to fetter it; partly because, on the other hand, it has chosen so frequently to delegate the discretionary powers which its legislation has called into existence to the President himself. Furthermore, most of the heads of the great executive departments have at least some powers which have been delegated to them by the President. They, therefore, continue subject to the President's uncontrolled removal power, even though no account be taken of that course of history which, in Chief Justice Taft's words in the Myers case, renders them the President's "alter ego's".[77]

The War and the Constitution: President and Congress

The chief lesson of the war to date for constitutional interpretation is that the Constitution is an easily dispensable factor of our war effort – perhaps one might say an "expendable" factor. That the Constitution is not needed as a source of national power for war purposes has been stated by the Court itself. Speaking in 1936 for himself and brethren in United States *v.* Curtiss-Wright Export Corporation, Justice Sutherland said: "The investment of the Federal government with the powers of external sovereignty did not depend upon the affirmative grants of the Constitution. The powers to declare and *wage war* [my italics], to conclude peace, to make treaties, to maintain diplomatic relations with other sovereignties, if they had never been mentioned in the Constitution, would have been vested in the Federal government as necessary concomitants of nationality" (299 U.S. 304, 318).

From this it follows that silence of the Constitution is not a denial but an affirmance of power in the national government to adopt any measures that seem best calculated to bring a foreign war to a successful conclusion. Even, so, it may be contended that the Constitution is still of some importance in distributing the power which the above doctrine attributes to "the Federal government" as a whole. The suggestion is certainly a tenable one logically, but is hardly borne out by certain recent developments, of which the President's Labor Day address to Congress is an outstanding instance. Demanding on that occasion that Congress should repeal a provision of the Emergency Price Control Act of February 2, 1942, which prohibited ceilings on food products until farm prices had gone, on the average, sixteen per cent beyond "parity prices". Mr. Roosevelt said:

I ask the Congress to take this action by the first of October. Inaction on your part by that date will leave me with an inescapable responsibility to the people of this country to see to it that the war effort is no longer imperiled by threat of economic chaos.

In the event that the Congress should fail to act, and act adequately, I shall accept the responsibility, and I will act.

At the same time that farm prices are stabilized, wages can and will be stabilized also. This I will do.

The President has the power, under the Constitution and under Congressional acts, to take measures necessary to avert a disaster which would interfere with the winning of the war.

I have given the most thoughtful consideration to meeting this issue without further reference to the Congress. I have determined, however, on this vital matter to consult with the Congress....

The American people can be sure that I will use my powers with a full sense of my responsibility to the Constitution and to my country. The American people can also be sure that I shall not hesitate to use every power vested in me to accomplish the defeat of our enemies in any part of the world where our own safety demands such defeat.

When the war is won, the powers under which I act automatically revert to the people – to whom they belong.

I interpret these words as saying to Congress, in effect, "unless you repeal a certain statutory provision forthwith, I shall nevertheless treat it as repealed". On what grounds does Mr. Roosevelt rest his case for power in these premises? He makes a vague gesture toward "Congressional acts," and it is true that he and certain of his advisers have from time to time achieved some rather striking results in the name of statutory "interpretation" – the $25,000 limit on salaries, which purports to be based on the Anti-Inflation Act of October 2, being a notable example. Nevertheless, I opine, Mr. Roosevelt's principal reliance is on his "powers under... the Constitution". Now it is a fact that Presidents have before this on a few occasions announced that they did not consider themselves to be constitutionally obligated by something which Congress had enacted but which, they asserted, trenched on presidential prerogatives. But the position advanced by Mr. Roosevelt in the above quoted passage goes beyond this, for therein he claims the right and power to disregard a statutory provision which he does not deny, and indeed could not possibly deny, that Congress has full constitutional authority to enact, and which, therefore, he was under obligation by the Constitution to "take care" should be "faithfully executed". And yet to anyone who followed with care the controversy over the "fifty destroyer" deal, the course projected by the President in his Labor Day address can hardly appear surprising, inasmuch as he thrust aside on that occasion legislation which was undeniably enacted by Congress in the exercise of its constitutional powers.

Currently, moreover, the President has not hesitated either to add to or subtract from statutory provisions the enactment of which lay within the national legislative province beyond any possibility of challenge. One instance is afforded by his now famous order to Montgomery Ward and Company to accord CIO a maintenance of membership contract; and another is furnished by section 5 of his recent or on manpower, which declares that "no employer shall retain in his employ any worker whose services are more urgently needed in any establishment, plant, facility, occupation, or area designated as more essential by the chairman" of the War Manpower Commission. So far as I can discover, there is nothing in either of the War Powers acts, the Selective Service Act, or any other act, that remotely supports such a decree. And the vast proliferation of "defense agencies" embracing some forty "administrators," "agencies," "boards," "offices," "commissions," "committees," "authorities" – what have you? – have almost all (OPA is one exception) been summoned into existence by the magic wand of the President without reference to statutory authorization.

The President's main reliance, in fact, is upon his powers as "Commander-in-Chief of the Army and Navy" – or at times as "Commander-in-Chief in time of war". To the latter term it has been pertinently objected that the Constitution knows no such office. But whichever term is employed, the intention is generally the same, namely, to claim for the President the constitutional power and duty to take any steps which he may deem helpful in prosecuting the war, any act of Congress to the contrary notwithstanding. Indeed, in the final sentence of his Labor Day address, the President seems, to invoke for his measures an even higher sanction than the Constitution. He there says: "When the war is won, the powers under which I act automatically revert to the people – to whom they belong." This seems to suggest that the President derives his war powers *directly* from the people, and not *via* the Constitution, a doctrine closely akin to the Leadership principle which our armed forces are combating today in the four quarters of the globe. The sentence was unfortunate.

So much for what may be called the *civil* aspect of the President's power as Commander-in-Chief as that power is interpreted by Mr. Roosevelt. Let us now turn to its *martial* aspect. In this connection, two presidential acts are of outstanding importance to date: the order of February 19 last, directed primarily to the danger of Japanese sabotage on the West Coast, and the order of July 2 creating a military commission for the trial of the eight saboteurs. The essential paragraphs of the former document read as follows:

Whereas the successful prosecution of the war requires every possible protection against espionage and against sabotage to national-defense material, national-defense premises, and national-defense utilities....

Now, therefore, by virtue of the authority vested in me as President of the United States, and Commander-in-Chief of the Army and Navy, I hereby authorize and direct the Secretary of War, and the military commanders whom he may from time to time designate, whenever he or any designated commander deems such action necessary or desirable, to prescribe military areas in such places and of such extent as he or the appropriate military commander may determine, from which any or all persons may be excluded, and with respect to which, the right of any person to enter, remain in, or leave shall be subject to whatever restrictions the Secretary of War or the appropriate military commander may impose in his discretion.

The Secretary of War is hereby authorized to provide for residents of any such area who are excluded therefrom, such transportation, food, shelter, and other accommodations as may be necessary, in the judgment of the Secretary of War or the said military commander, and until other arrangements are made, to accomplish the purpose of this order....

I hereby further authorize and direct all executive departments, independent establishments and other Federal agencies, to assist the Secretary of War or the said military commanders in carrying out this Executive order, including the furnishing of medical aid, hospitalization, food clothing, transportation, use of land, shelter, and other supplies, equipment, utilities, facilities and services.

In pursuance of this order, about one hundred thousand Japanese residents of western states, the great majority of them native-born citizens of the United States, were in due course removed from their farms and homes and put in concentration camps, where many of them still are. In the entire history of the country, no comparable interference with the private security and private rights of citizens has been witnessed. How is it to be justified in terms of constitutional law?

By the tests imposed by the decisive opinion in the Milligan case, the President's order was totally unconstitutional, and even by the Chief Justice's concurring opinion for himself and three associates, it would have had to be authorized by Congress. Since the Milligan case, however, a new kind of martial law has been identified by the Court – "preventive" as against "punitive" – and in the leading case of Moyer *v.* Peabody [212 U.S. 78 (1909)] a situation roughly analogous to that which confronted the President was solved on the basis of this distinction. The facts, briefly, were these: Moyer, a labor leader, brought suit against Peabody, a former governor of Colorado, for ordering his imprisonment in the course of a strike which occurred during Peabody's incumbency. Speaking for the Court, Justice Holmes conceded that the state courts were open at the time; also, "as it must be, that the governor's declaration that a state of insurrection existed is convulsive on the Courts"; and, finally "that the governor, *without sufficient reason but in good faith* [my italics], in the course of putting the insurrection down, held the plaintiff until he thought he could safely release him". In the face of these admissions, the Court held that Moyer had no action. Conforming, therefore, the President's order of February 19 to the pattern furnished by the Moyer case, that order may be regarded as representing the President's judgment that the war situation on the West Coast threatened imminent violence that would be disastrous to our war effort. And the good faith of such a judgment being conceded, as it undoubtedly must be, the question of its reasonableness becomes, on the basis of the Moyer precedent, irrelevant. In short, the order of February 19 represents a qualified and limited declaration of marital law. *

The material facts in the case of the saboteurs [*Ex parte* Quirin, 317 U.S. 1 (1942)] are given sufficiently in the appended note.[78] The trial instituted under the President's order of July 2 began on July 8. While it was still going on, but after all the evidence was in, counsel for seven of the saboteurs petitioned both the Supreme Court and the United States District Court for the District of Columbia for leave to bring *habeas corpus* proceedings. Early in his opinion for the unanimous Court – Justice Murphy being absent – the Chief Justice makes it plain that the Court is not going to attempt to draw any line between the powers of Congress and those of the President in the premises of the case. "We are concerned only," he says, "with the question whether it is within the constitutional power of the national government to place petitioners upon trial before a military commission for the offenses with which they are charged". In arriving at an affirmative answer to this question, the opinion rebuts three principal contentions of the petitioners, the first of which was that "violation of the laws of war" – the first offense charged against the petitioners, and apparently the one which the Court regarded as best supported by the evidence – was not an offense known to the laws of the United States.

---

* Editor's Note: Corwin concludes here that the Japanese incarceration was "justified terms of consitutional law." But in 1951, again discussing the Japanese incarceration, he noted that under the act of March 21, 1942, "a military commander operating under the protection of the act would not be answerable to eth civil courts once war was over for his orders during its continuance. Could there be more conclusive proof of the triumph in wartime of personal rule, in which as Aristotle says there is always 'an element of the bestial,' over the rule of law?" ("The Impact of War on the Constitution," lecture at Emory University, 1951, Corwin Papers, Princeton University Library).

The Chief Justice admits that Congress has never attempted to codify violations of the laws of war, but holds that the reference in the 15th Article of War to "offenses that... by the laws of war are triable by a military commission" is sufficient to meet the objection, particularly when it is read in connection with the Rules of Land Warfare promulgated by the War Department and with the Hague Convention of 1907 (ratified by the Senate in 1909) by which is recogni; ˜d a class of "unlawful belligerents" not entitled to be treated as prisoners of war, among them being combatants not wearing fixed emblems. In short, petitioners' conduct fell within well-established legal categories which are addressed particularly to military tribunals.

Secondly, however, the petitioners urged that they were entitled by the Fifth and Sixth amendments to a civil trial, inasmuch as theirs was not a case "arising in the land or naval forces". The premise of this argument the Chief Justice concedes in effect. "We may assume, without deciding," he says, "that a trial prosecuted before a military commission created by military authority is not one 'arising in the land.... forces,' when the accused is not a member of or associated with these forces." But that concession, he immediately proceeded to add, did not affect petitioners' position, since "no exception is necessary to exclude from the operation of these provisions [of the Fifth and Sixth amendments] cases never deemed to be within their terms"; and petitioners' cases were of that kind. Nor was Haupt, although a citizen of the United States, in any different situation in this respect from the other petitioners, for all alike were enemy belligerents who by entering the country with hostile intent and in civilian garb had violated the usages of war. Nor did Milligan's case aid Haupt's cause, inasmuch as Milligan was found by the Court to be a non-belligerent, "not being a part of or associated with the armed forces of the enemy".

Lastly, the petitioners pointed out that the presidential order under which the trial was conducted departed sharply in certain respects from the requirements of the Articles of War. Thus, whereas the 43rd Article of War provides that "no person shall, be general court martial [no mention here of military commission] be convicted of an offense for which the death penalty is made mandatory by law, nor sentenced to death, except by the concurrence of all members of said court martial present at the time the vote is taken," the President's order expressly declared that the concurrence of only two-thirds of the members of the Commission should be necessary for conviction or sentence; and other material departures by the order from Articles 38, 46, 50½, and 70 were noted by counsel. Dealing with this argument, the Chief Justice says:

We need not inquire whether Congress may restrict the power of the Commander-in-Chief to deal with enemy belligerents. For the Court is unanimous in its conclusion that the Articles in question could not at any stage of the proceedings afford any basis for issuing the writ. But a majority of the full Court are not agreed on the appropriate grounds for decision. Some members of the Court are of opinion that Congress did not intend the Articles of War to govern a Presidential military commission convened for the determination of questions relating to admitted enemy invaders and that the context of the Articles makes clear that they should not be constructed to apply to that class of cases. Others are of the view that – even though this trial is subject to whatever provisions of the Articles of War Congress has in terms made applicable to "commissions" – the particular Articles in question, rightly construed, do not foreclose the procedure prescribed by the President or that shown to have been employed by the Commission, in a trial of offenses against the law of war and the 81st and 82nd Articles of War, by a military commission appointed by the President.

The main question which arises on the opinion as a whole is that of its necessity. In other words, was not the Court here performing a work of supererogation? The Chief Justice himself appears to have some such thought in mind when, in close proximity to the passage just quoted, he remarks: "Petitioners do not argue and we do not consider the question whether the President is compelled by the Articles of War to afford unlawful enemy belligerents a trial before subjecting them to disciplinary measures." And petitioners' reticence in this regard was, it seems to me, the better part of valor, although I do not think it should have precluded the Court from speaking on the point. These saboteurs were invaders, their penetration of the boundary of the country, projected from units of a hostile fleet, was essentially a military operation, their capture, followed by their surrender to the military arm of the government, was but a continuation of that operation. Punishment of the saboteurs was therefore within the President's power as Commander-in-Chief in the most elementary, the purely martial, sense of that power. Moreover, six of the petitioners were enemy aliens, and so, strictly speaking, without constitutional status. As to Haupt, the American citizen, the better course would possibly have been to try him in the civil courts as a traitor. It is certainly curious to compare the apparent hesitation of the President on this occasion to assert his indubitable authority as Commander-in-Chief with his lack of hesitation to appropriate the powers of Congress in his putative role of Commander-in-Chief in wartime".

Also, in view of a certain recent development, a glance should be paid the theory, so often voiced by writers (including the present one) that in its control of the purse-strings Congress possesses its most effective check on presidential power. At best, the promise of this rule is seriously impaired by war, inasmuch as legislative prying into presidential budgets at such a time always involves the danger of revealing military secrets. But when the President lays before Congress a budget which calls for appropriations amounting in the total to the national income, Congress' difficulties are multiplied indefinitely; and that is the situation which confronts Congress at this moment.

In an address which he gave early in World War I, the Honorable Charles Evans Hughes said: "While we are at war we are not in revolution. We are making war as Nation organized under the Constitution, from which the established national authorities derive all their powers either in war or in peace. The Constitution is as effective today [i.e., in the midst of war] as it ever was and the oath to support it is just as binding…."

I doubt if as circumspect a gentleman as Mr. Hughes would venture such a statement on the basis of the events of this war to date. The crucial matter is, of course, the question of the right of the President to invade the field of Congress and to set aside congressional legislation on his own finding that our war effort will be aided by his doing so. That this question should have been raised is, however, by no means the fault of the President alone – Congress, too, is to blame. Moreover, until recently it is the President rather than Congress that has enjoyed the support of dominant public opinion in this matter, a warning which Congress needs to take to heart. Unless Congress can, by improving its organization and reforming some of its procedures, render itself a more consistently useful public agency, it seems likely to be gradually reduced to the level of a badly tarnished pageant, and little more. And in this connection it should not escape attention that the operative Constitution of World War I has become since then, under the New Deal, the everyday Constitution of the country. There is always a tendency, even in democracies, for the emergency device to become the normal.

References

1. Below.
2. Roosevelt, *An Autobiography* 365–69 (1913). The original inventor of this practice, however, seems to have been President Tyler, who in 1841

appointed a non-statutory commission to conduct an investigation of the New York Customs House. His action led to a demand by the House of Representatives that he inform it under what authority the commission "was raised" Tyler answered by citing his duty to "take care that the laws be faithfully executed" (4 Richardson, *Messages and Papers of the Presidents* 99–100 [1903]).

3. 27 *Opinions of the Attorney General* 309-310 (1910).
4. Roosevelt, *An Autobiography* 416–17.
5. 34 *Current History* 491 (1931).
6. As to the vast powers actually exercised by these agencies in the name of the President, see Berdahl, *War Powers of the Executive of the United States* 197–200, 211–12 (1921).
7. On this and other constitutional questions raised by Justice Black's appointment, see McGovney, "Is Hugo L. Black a Supreme Court Justice De Jure?" 26 *California Law Review* 1–32 (1937).
8. 1 Willoughby, *Constitutional Law* 607.
9. On this point, examine the vast mass of data brought together in Justice Brandeis' dissenting opinion in Myers v. United States and accompanying notes. 272 U.S. 52, 264–74. Hundreds of statutory provisions are cited. "Thus," the opinion summarizes, "Congress has, from time to time, restricted the President's selection by the requirement of citizenship [some thirty distinct acts of Congress". It has limited the power of nomination by providing that the office may be held only by a resident of the United States [act of March 1, 1855, c. 133, dealing with ministers and their subordinates]; of a state [one act]; of a particular state [five acts]; of a particular district [two acts]; of a particular territory [three acts]; of the District of Columbia [act of May 3, 1802, and four other acts]; of a particular foreign country [one act]. It has limited the power of nomination further by prescribing professional attainments [some fifty-six acts and joint resolution], or occupational experience [eighteen acts and joint resolutions]. It has, in other cases, prescribed the test of examinations [seven acts, including the Civil Service Act of January 16, 1883, c. 27, Sec. 2, and the Foreign Service Act of May 24, 1924, c. 182, Sec. 5]. It has imposed the requirement of age [three acts]; of sex [two acts]; of race [one act]; of property [act of March 26, 1804, c. 38, Sec. 4, legislative council of Louisiana, to be selected from holders of realty]; and of habitual temperance in the use of intoxicating liquors [one act—obsolete, no doubt, under the Eighteenth Amendment]. Congress has imposed like restrictions on the power of nomination by requiring political representation [eighteen acts, including those organizing the interstate commerce and federal trade commissions]; or that the selection be made on a nonpartisan basis [twenty-three acts]. It has required, in some cases, that the representation be industrial [six acts]; in others that it be geographic [seventeen acts and

joint resolutions]. It has at time required that the President's nominees be taken from, or include representatives from, particular branches or departments of the government [twenty-six acts and joint resolutions]. By still other statutes, Congress has confined the president's selection to a small number of persons to be named by others [five acts, including act of February 23, 1920, c. 91, Sec. 304, requiring that the railroad labor board consist of three to be appointed from six nominees by employees, and three to be appointed from six nominees by carriers]."

Cf. an opinion by Attorney General Sargent advising against a similar feature of the McNary-Haugen Bill, *New York Times,* February 26, 1927; also a protest by President Harding against a proposal to require that one member of the Federal Reserve Board be "a farmer" (*id.,* February 6, 1922).

10. The following item from the *New York Times* of May 20, 1916, affords an illustration:

"Another joker in the Army Reorganization bill is very interesting to those who know of the circumstances connected with it. This joker, slipped into the bill behind the closed doors of the Conference Committee, as jokers frequently are, is contained in a paragraph providing for the appointment of Judge Advocates in the reorganized regular army. Probably there never was more peculiar language employed to frame a joker than that which reads this way: 'Provided further, that of the vacancies created in the Judge Advocate's Department by this act, one such vacancy, not below the rank of Major, shall be filled by the appointment of a person from civil life, not less than forty-five nor more than fifty years of age, who shall have been for ten years a Judge of the Supreme Court of the Philippine Islands, shall have served for two years as a Captain in the regular or volunteer army, and shall be proficient in the Spanish language and laws'.

"The one man in the world that this description seems to fit its Judge Adam C. Carson of the Supreme Court of the Philippines Islands, Judge Carson is now in the United States on leave of absence. His home is at Riverton, Va., in the Congressional district of Representatives James Hay, Chairman of the House Committee on Military Affairs, and Chairman of the House conferees on the Army Organization bill. Judge Carson went to Cuba after the Spanish war as an officer army which supplemented the work of the regular troops in suppressing the Aguinaldo insurrection. President Taft, while Governor General of the Philippines, appointed him a judge of the Court of First Instance and later he was appointed of judge of the Philippine Supreme Court."

The reader will be gratified to know that Judge Carson got the job. With this episode should be compared President Arthur's veto, July 2, 1884, of "an act for the relief of Fitz John Proter," the enacting clause of which reads as follows:

"That the President be, and he is hereby, authorized to nominate and, by and with the advice and consent of the Senate, to appoint Fitz John Porter, late a major-general of the United States Volunteers and a brevet brigadier-general colonel of the Army, to the position of colonel in the Army of the United States, of the same grade and rank held by him at the time of his dismissal from the Army by sentence of court-martial promulgated January 27, 1863…" (8 Richardson, *Message of the Presidents* 221).

To this the President objected:

"It is apparent that should this bill become a law it will create a new office which can be filled by the appointment of the particular individual whom it specifies, and cannot be filled otherwise; or it may be said with perhaps greater precision of statement that it will create a new office upon condition that the particular person designated shall be chosen to fill it. Such an act, as it seems to me, is either unnecessary and ineffective or it involves an encroachment by the legislative branch of the Government upon the authority of the Executive. As the Congress has no power under the Constitution to nominate or appoint an officer and cannot lawfully impose upon the President the duty of nominating or appointing to office any particular individual of its own selection, this bill, if it can fairly be construed as requiring the President to make the nomination and, by and with the advice and consent of the Senate, the appointment which it authorizes, is in manifest violation of the Constitution. If such be not its just interpretation, it must be regarded as a mere enactment of advice and counsel, which lacks in the very nature of things the force of a positive law and can serve no useful purpose upon the statute book." (*ibid.*).

The veto prevailed.

11. The above note; also 13 *Opinions of the Attorney General* 516 (1871).
12. U.S. Code, Tit. 5, Sec. 633 (2).
13. *Id.*, Tit. 22, Secs. 4, 5.
14. Shoemaker *v.* United States, 147 U.S. 283, 301 (1893).
15. *Id.;* United States *v.* Ferreira, 13 How. 40 (1851); *Ex parte* Siebold, 100 U.S. 371 (1879).
16. United States *v.* Germaine, 99 U.S. 508 (1878); United States *v.* Mouat, 124 U.S. 303 (1888).

The Court will, nevertheless, be astute to ascribe to a head of department an appointment made by an inferior of such head. Ekiu *v.* United States, 142 U.S. 651, 663 (1892). For the view that there is an intrinsic difference between a "public office" and a "public employment," see Mechem, *Law of Public Offices* 3–5.

17. In Marbury *v.* Madison Marshall concedes that in the case of officers appointed by the President with the consent of the Senate, appointment and Commissioning are practically indistinguishable, and the same is true

of course as to officers appointed by the President alone (1 Cranch 137, 156-57). In the case, on the other hand, of officers whose appointment is vested by act of Congress in the heads of departments, appointment and commissioning are distinct, since the latter has, by the requirement of the Constitution, to be by the President. Yet even such officers are covered by the legislative provision that their commissions shall not have the seal of the department affixed to them "before the same shall have been signed by the President of the United States" (U.S. Code, Tit. 5 Sec. 11), which seems to be designed to leave with the President the final say whether the appointment shall be consummated.

Senatorial courtesy is not quite automatic in the case of nominees to Cabinet posts. Taney was rejected for Secretary of the Treasury in 1834; three Tyler nominees were rejected in 1843 and 1844; and one Johnson nominee in 1868. The latest victim of senatorial wrath was Charles B. warren, whose nomination by President Coolidge to the attorney generalship was rejected in March, 1925.

A passing word should be paid the recent controversy between President Roosevelt and Senators Glass and Byrd of Virginia, growing out of the Senate's rejection of the President's nominee, Judge Floyd H. Roberts, for a federal judgeship in that State. The President charged the Senators, who invoked senatorial courtesy against Roberts, of "usurping" the presidential power of nominating to office. And finally it would seem that what happened—as in all such cases—was a temporary abdication by the *Senate* to one or two of its members of its participation in the appointing power. On the other hand, Senators Glass, in his answer to the President, was able to adduce facts which went some way to show that the President, in an effort to "purge" the Virginia Senators, had for the time being abdicated his nominating power to Governor Price and other political foes of Senators Glass and Byrd (*New York Times*, February 8 and 9, 1939).

18. 286 U.S. 6 (1932); Cf. United States *v.* LeBaron, 19 How. 73 (1856).
19. *New York Times*, January 11, 1931.
20. 9 *Writings of James Madison* 112–13 (Hunt ed. 1900-1910); *The Federalist* No. 76 at 493-94 (Earle ed.); 3 Adams, *Life and Works of John Adams*, 575–76 (1850–1856). "The Senate cannot originate an appointment. Its constitutional action is confined to the simple affirmation or rejection of the President's nominations, and such nominations fail when it rejects them. The Senate may suggest conditions and limitations to the President, but it cannot vary those submitted by him, for no appointment can be made except on his nomination, agreed to without qualification or alteration" (3 *Opinions of the Attorney General* 188-92 [1837]). The opinion cites two unsuccessful attempts by the Senate, one in the J. Q. Adams administrative, one in Jackson's, to reshape a nomination to a military grade to the advantage of the nominee.

21. Note 20.
22. U.S. Code, Tit. 4, Sec. 6; Marbury *v.* Madison, 1 Cranch 137 (1803).
23. 1 *Opinions of the Attorney General* 631 (1823); 2 *id.* at 222 (1830); 3 *id.* at 673 (1841); 4 *id.* at 523 (1846); 10 *id.* at 356 (1862); 11 *id.* at 179 (1865); 12 *id.* at 32 (1866) and 455 (1868); 14 *id.* at 563 (1875); 15 *id.* at 207 (1877); 16 *id.* at 523 (1880); 18 *id.* at 28 (1884); 19 *id.* at 261 (1889); 26 *id.* at 234 (1907); 30 *id.* at 314 (1914); 33 *id.* at 20 (1921).

    In 4 *id.* at 361, 363 (1845), the general doctrine was held not to apply to a yet unfilled office which was created during the previous session of Congress, but this distinction is rejected in 12 *id.* at 455 (1868); 18 *id.* at 28; and 19 *id.* at 261.

    In view of recent controversy it is interesting to note, on the authority of Mr. Krock, that there have been no fewer than twelve recess appointments to the Supreme Court, and that only one of the appointees, John Rutledge, whom Washington appointed as Chief Justice in 1975, was later rejected by the Senate (*New York Times,* July 29, 1937).
24. 23 *Opinions of the Attorney General* 599 (1901); 22 *id.* at 20 (1898).
25. U.S. Code, Tit. 5, Sec. 56.
26. The following extracts from a Washington press dispatch of December 18, 1914, tell how President Wilson once violated the understanding:

    "The Bloom case is unprecedented so far as Senators can recall. John H. Bloom was nominated for postmaster. Five hundred citizens of Devils Lake protested. The Charges against Bloom were serious and involved his personal character. The Senate Committee rejected it in August.

    "The President then sent to the Senate the nomination of Mrs. Marjorie Bloom, wife of the man whose nomination had been rejected. This nomination was in turn rejected. The President then conferred a recess nomination on Mrs. Bloom as soon as Congress adjourned and she took the office under a commission. Today her name was again sent to the Senate.

    "It is probable that when the Senate comes to deal with the case at Devils Lake it may go even further than a formal rejection and refer the nomination of Mrs. Bloom back to the President with a direction to the Secretary of the Senate to call his attention to the fact that the nomination was rejected by the Senate in October and citing the Constitution of the United States, which provides that such nominations shall be made 'by and with the advice and consent of the Senate's.

    What the final denouement of this episode was, I have not discovered.
27. 6 *Opinions of the Attorney General* 358 (1854); 12 *id.* at 41 (1866); 25 *id.* at 259 (1904); 28 *id.* at 95 (1909). Probably the most extreme case on record of the assignment of a person—and one apparently without official status at the time—to the duties of an absent official, occurred in Jefferson's second term. Henry Adams tells the story in his *History* as follows:

"When Congress met, Dec. 2, 1805, Breckinridge was attorney-general under a temporary commission, and Robert Smith who had ceased to be Secretary of the Navy on the confirmation of his successor, March 3, was acting as Secretary under no apparent authority. Dec 20, 1805, the President sent a message to the Senate making nominations for vacancies which had occurred during the recess, for which commissions had been granted 'to the persons herein respectively named'. One of these persons was John Breckinridge of Kentucky to be Attorney-General of the United States, and the nomination was duly confirmed. Breckinridge's permanent commission bore {the} date Jan. 17, 1806.

"These dates and facts are curious for the reason that Robert Smith, who had ceased to be Secretary of the Navy, March 3, 1805, ceased necessarily to be attorney-general on the confirmation of Breckinridge, and continued to act as Secretary of the Navy without authority of law. The President did not send his name to the Senate, or issue to him a new commission either permanent or temporary. On the official records of the Department of State, not Robert Smith, but Jacob Crowninshield, was Secretary of the Navy from March 3, 1805, till March 7, 1809, when his successor was appointed, although Jacob Crowninshiel died April 15, 1808, and Robert Smith never ceased to act as Secretary of the Navy from his appointment in 1801 to his appointment as Secretary of State in 1809. During the whole period of Jefferson's second administration, his Secretary of the Navy acted by no known authority except the verbal request or permission of the President" (3 *History of the United States* 11–12 [1893]).

For legislation governing this matter today, see U.S. Code, Tit. 5, Secs. 4-8.

Washington dispatches bearing the date of December 24, 1938, carry the statement that President Roosevelt has selected Colonel F. C. Harrington to succeed Mr. Harry L. Hopkins as WPA Administrator, but that Harrington's name will not be sent to the Senate, since he will remain on the army payroll and will be designated "acting Administrator". So far I have failed to find any basis in statute or precedent for this assignment of a military officer to a civilian post. The idea obviously has possibilities.

28. 7 *Opinions of the Attorney General* 453, 464–65 (1855).
29. Williams v. United States, 1 How. 290, 297 (8843). By the act of August 10, 1846 (9 Stat. 102), as amended, the President, Vice-President, the Chief Justice, and the heads of the executive departments are constituted the Smithsonian Institution, over whose meetings "the President, and in his absence the Vice-President, shall preside". U.S. Code, Tit. 20, secs. 41, 45. This is doubtless a personal duty, but not a very ardous one. Also by 2 Stat. 78, expenditures from the secret service fund had to be vouched for by the President personally, but this provision has dropped out of the statute book.

The *New York Times* of March 12, 1923, contained the following item:

"A little less than two years ago Judson C. Welliver, executive clerk at the White House, stepped across the corridor which separates his office from that of President Harding to place some papers on the President's desk. To his surprise, for it was but a few minutes after 8 o'clock in the morning, he found the President already seated and busily signing papers from a two-foot stack.

" 'Good morning, Mr. President,' Mr. Welliver said. 'I didn't know you had come to the office.'

" 'Yes, I came in just now,' the President replied. 'I had a lot of papers to sign, and thought I might as well get tem out of the way.'

" 'Anything important?'

' Yes and no,' said the President. 'I am beginning to find out something about being President and the amount of time it demands. You can hardly imagine what I am doing now. This stack of papers is just so much routine. They are the wills of Indians. The President has to countersign the will of every Indian with whom the Government has dealings. If the will is not so countersigned, it is null and void. And so I except to put in the next hour or so countersigning these wills.'

" 'But can't someone else sign them for you?' Mr. Welliver inquired.

" 'No; not under the law. There are only two—possibly three—persons in the United States authorized to sign the President's name. They are employees of the General Land Office and they sign the President's name, under certain safeguards and precautions, to the patents granted by that office. But there is no one else who may do so.'

" 'I am beginning to find out, 'Mr. Harding went on, 'that this job of being President is one that makes almost inordinate demands upon a man's time.'

I can find no justification in the U.S. Code for the statement that the President is required to sign the wills of Indians; that seems to be the duty of the Secretary of the Interior (Tit. 25, Sec. 373). The statement, however, that the President's name is affixed to land patents by authorized clerks of the General Land Office is correct (Tit. 43, Secs. 8, 9).

30. Runkle v. United States, 122 U.S. (1887). By the theory of the case the President was in this instance exercising a judicial, and hence non-delegable function; from which it followed that his approval of the decree "must be authenticated in a way to show" that it was "the result of his own judgment".

31. *In re* Chapman, 166 U.S. 661 (1897), and other cases there cited as establishing that "the presumptions in favor of official action...preclude collateral attack on the sentences of courts-martial". Confirmation by the President of sentences of courts-martial is still required in several instances (U.S. Code, Tit, 10, Sec. 1519). How this may be shown, however, still

remains a question, in view of the Chapman case.

32. Wilcox *v.* Jackson, 13 Pet. 498 (1839); United States v. Eliason, 16 Pet. 291 (1842); Williams v. United States, 1 How. 290 (1843); Confiscation Cases, 20 Wall. 92 (1874); Wolsey *v.* Chapman, 101 U.S. 755 (1879); etc.; 7 *Opinions of the Attorney General* 479 (1855).
33. 7 *Opinions of the Attorney General* 470.
34. 5 *Writings of James Madison* 392; also 398, 401-402, etc., where he insists upon the *unity* of the Executive Department; although in other passages (*id.* at 362, 364, 399-400), he seems to regard the power of removal as primarily a power to get rid of malfeasant subordinates.
35. Act of September 2, 1789, c. 12, sec. 2; U.S. Code, Tit. 5, Sec. 242.
36. Cf. U.S. Code, Tit. 5 Secs. 156, 190, 361, 412, 481, 485.
37. 1 Cranch 137, 165-66 (1803).
38. 1 *Opinions of the Attorney General* 624 (1828). Wirt continued: "To interpret this [the "faithfully executed"] clause so as to throw upon the President the duty of personal interference in every specific case of an alleged or defective execution of the laws, and to call upon him to perform such duties himself, would not only be to require him to perform an impossibility himself, but to take upon himself the responsibility of all the subordinate executive officers of the government—a construction too absurd to be seriously contended for." See also 4 *id.* At 515 (1846); 5 *id.* at 287 (1851) and 630 (1852); 11 *id.* at 109 (1864); etc. "The President has, under the Constitution and laws, certain duties to perform, among these being to take care that the laws be faithfully executed; that is, that the other executive and administrative officers of the government faithfully perform their duties; but the statutes regulate and prescribe these duties, and he has no more power to add to, or subtract from, the duties imposed upon subordinate executive and administrative officers by the law, than those officers have to add to or subtract form his duties" (19 *id.* at 686 [1890]).
39. See generally Hinsdale, *A History of the President's Cabinet* (1911); also the same writer's "Again the Cabinet," in 14 *Papers of the Michigan Academy of Science, Arts and letters* 515–23 (1930). Learned's *The President's Cabinet* (1912) is primarily a legislative history of the executive departments, rather than an account of the development of the Cabinet relationship.

    For first-hand Cabinet interiors see the *Memoirs of John Quincy Adams* (1874–1877); *Diary of James K. Polk during His Presidency* (1910); *Diary of Gideon Welles* (1911); and other similar works listed by Binkley in his *Powers of the President* 311–24 (1937).
40. Art. I, Sec. 2, para. 1. An "exclusive" construction of this language such as was applied in Marbury v. Madison to the opening clause of Art. III, Sec. 2, para. 1, defining the Supreme Court's original jurisdiction, would render the cabinet "unconstitutional".

41. For a reliable although rather caustic narrative of the episode, see Sumner's *Andrew Jackson* (American Statesman Series, Vol. 17) 339 ff. (1899).
42. Wyman, Willoughby, Fairlie, Finley, and Sanderson, all seem to take this general Position. Wyman's language is as follows; "This account of this event is worth a hundred cases from the law reports. The President, it appears, has the power in all matters whatsoever to enforce any officer whatsoever to do any act which the officer has the power to do. He can dictate in all matters because of his power of instant dismissal, without giving reasons therefore, and thereupon the rights to immediate appointment without limitation therein. …Might makes Right. *Whatever the Superior commands will be done by the inferior.* Because of this sanction, an administration which is centralized in its organization will always prove to be centralized in action" (Wyman, *Principles of the Administrative Law Governing the Relations of Public Officers* 233 [1903]).
43. 3 Richardson, *Message of the Presidents* 79–80. The date of the message was April 15, 1834.
44. 12 Pet. 524 (1838).
45. *Id.* at 539–40.
46. The following extraxt from the argument for the United States is worth quoting:

"The argument of the postmaster general, and of the attorney general, assumes that the post office department is an essential part of the executive department of the government; and from this position infers the want of the Jurisdiction claimed. The assumption has been shown to be inaccurate; but even if true, it is not easy to perceive the connection between the premises and the conclusion.

"We are referred to the debates in the convention, to show the anxiety of that body to preserve separate and distinct the three great departments. I will, in return, refer to the 47th and to the succeeding numbers of the Federalist, for a correct exposition of this maxim of political philosophy, and its practical adoption in our constitution.

"Starting from this basis, the constitution is appealed to; and by the aid of some interpolation and some extravagant interpretation, we are told substantially, if not in terms:

"1. That the clause in the constitution which provides that the executive power shall be vested in the President, actually confers upon him all that power which, in any age of the world and under any form of government, has been vested in the chief executive functionary; whether king or czar, emperor or dictator.

"2. That the clause which imposes upon the executive the duty of seeing that the laws are faithfully executed, contains another large grant of power.

"3. That, as a mean to the performance of this duty, he is invested with the power of appointment to and removal from office.

"4. That the power of appointment and removal carried with it the power to direct, instruct, and control every officer over whom it may be exercised, as to the manner in which he shall perform the duties of his office.

"My observations upon these points shall be few and brief:

"The first proposition was, perhaps, for the first time distinctly advanced by General Hamilton, in his Letters of Pacificus, No. 1, p. 535. A great and revered authority, but subject to occasional error. It was fully answered by Mr. Madison in the Letters of Helvidius, p. 594, etc., and has since remained dormant. The second is now for the first time broadly asserted. Its dangerous tendencies—its hostility to every principle of our institution, cannot be exaggerated. The true signification of this part of the constitution, I take to be simply this, that the President is authorized to employ those powers which are expressly entrusted to him to execute those laws which he is empowered to administer; or, in the language of the late Chief Justice, he is at liberty to employ any means which the constitution and laws place under his control. 2 Brockenb. 101.

"The third proposition is a palpable and unwarrantable interpolation of the constitution. The fourth, if the power claimed is derived from the power of appointment, would make the judges dependent upon executive dictation; if from that power and that of removal, conjointly, would make it the true theory of the English constitution, that the king might instruct, direct, and control the lord chancellor in the performance of his judicial duties. It would make him the keeper of the chancellor's conscience.

"The right to command, direct and control, involves the correlative duty of obedience. No officer can be criminally or civilly punished for obedience to the lawful command of a superior, which he is bound to abey. This doctrine, then, asserts the entire irresponsibility of all officers, except to this one superior.

"One of the practical inferences from these premises is, that the judiciary department cannot execute its own judgments; a proposition distinctly avowed by the postmaster general in his return, P. 127-9, and asserted, in terms equally distinct, by the attorney general, in p. 152" (*Id.* at 571-72).

47. *Id.* at 610. Further along the Court adds:

"It is urged at the bar, that the postmaster general was alone subject to the direction and control of the President, with respect to the execution of the duty imposed upon him by this law; and this right of the President is claimed, as growing out of the obligation imposed upon him by the constitution, to take care that the laws be faithfully executed. This is a doctrine that cannot receive the sanction of this court. It would be vesting in the President a dispensing power, which has no countenance for its support in any part of the constitution; and is asserting a principle, which, if carried out in its results, to all cases falling within it, would be clothing the President with a power entirely to control the legislation of Congress, and paralyze the administration of justice.

"To contend that the obligation imposed on the President to see the laws faithfully executed, implied a power to forbid their execution, is a novel construction of the constitution, and entirely inadmissible" (*Id.* at 612-13).

Although Stokes got his mandamus, it seems to have netted him little, and his later attempt to recover damages from Kendall was thrown out of Court on the ground that he had already exhausted his right to a remedy (Kendall v. Stokes et al., 3 How. 87 [1845]).

48. Notes 40 and 47; also United States *v.* Schurz, 102 U.S. 378 (1880); United States *v.* Black, 128 U.S. 40 (1888); etc.
49. Notes 35 and 40.
50. Most of the opinions of Attorneys General cited in Note 41 are to the point. The independence of subordinates in the discharge of quasi-judicial duties cast upon them by statute from a superior's direction is well illustrated in the case of the Commissioner of Patents. See Butterworth *v.* Hoe, 112 U.S. 50 (1884), and the United States *v.* Duell, 172 U.S. 376 (1899).
51. 272 U.S. 52, 135 (1926).
52. See further Dawson, *The Principle of Official Independence* (1922). It is true that the bureaucrat should not determine policies further than he has been commissioned to do so by the legislature—that is, Congress; but in this respect the President himself, when engaged in seeing to the execution of the laws, is a bureaucrat. Policy comes from the legislative power, and it is in his ability to guide the latter that the President exercises most of his influence upon domestic policy.
53. Art. II, Sec. 4.
54. 272 U.S. 52.
55. 19 Stat. 80, 91. To this day the Postmaster General and the Assistant Postmaster Generals are appointed and removable "by and with the advice and consent of the Senate" (U.S. Code, Tit. 5, Secs. 361, 363).
56. Much that I say below is taken from my *President's Removal Power Under the Constitution* (1927).
57. I *Annals of Congress* 368 ff., or 383 ff., according to the printing used.
58. *The Federalist* No. 77 at 497 (Earle ed.). "In the Federalist, he [Hamilton] had so explained the removal from office as to deny the power to the President. In an edition of the work at New York, there was a marginal note to the passage that 'Mr. Hamilton had changed his view of the Constitution on that point'" ("Madison to Rives, Jan. 10, 1829," 4 *Letters and Other Writings of James Madison* 5 [1865]).

59. My *Removal Power of the President* 26-31. Webster's Position, as set forth in his answer to Jackson's protest message, was as follows:

"The regulation of the tenure of office is a common exercise of legislative authority, and the power of congress in this particular is not at all restrained or limited by anything in the constitution, except in regard to judicial officers. All the rest is left to the ordinary discretion of the legislature. Congress may give to offices which it created (excepts those of judges) what duration it pleases. When the office is created and is to be filled, the President is to nominate the candidate to fill it; but when he comes into the office, he comes into it upon the conditions and restrictions which the law may have attached to it."

"If Congress," he continued, "were to declare by law that the Attorney General, or the Secretary of State should hold office during good behavior," its action might be unwise, but it would not be unconstitutional (7 *Writings and Speeches of Daniel Webster* 196-99 [National ed. 1903].

60. 13 Pet. 225, 230 (two cases). The argument of counsel on both sides affords an exposition of the common law theory of office. Jones, who appeared against Hennen's application for a mandamus, set forth theory adopted by the Court, as follows:

"The right to remove is an incident to the power of appointment. It is essential to the exercise of the power to appoint; and the power which is given by the law cannot exist without this incident.

"If the common law has any bearing on this question, it is very remote. The Constitution of the United States, and the laws made in conformity with the provisions of the Constitution, are essentially different from the common law, as to appointments to offices, and as to the tenure by which they are held. 2 Blackstone Commentaries 36, 37. The law of the tenure of office in England is regulated, not by any principles of ethics, or express provision, but by immemorial usage. Office is there an incorporeal hereditament, as a right of way. There is, under the common law, an estate in an office.

"But in the United States this is not so. There is in this country no estate in any office. No property in an office. Offices are held for the benefit of the community in which their functions are exercised. As to the tenure and nature of office in England: cited Coke Litt. 378a, 4 Institute 117; Coke Litt. 233b, 2 Institute 388.

"The position in England is, that unless the statute which creates the office limits its tenure, at the time of the creation; it is an office for life, as at the common law. But here no such principles prevail. The common law does not apply to offices, which are all created by the Constitution, or by express statute" (13 Pet. 253-54).

61. Pages above.

62. My *Removal Power of the President* 36-41.

63. Pages above.
64. 272 U.S. 134.
65. All these provisions can be easily traced through the index to the U.S. Code.
66. U.S. Code, Tit. 31, Sec. 43.
67. 295 U.S. 602 (also styled Rathbun *v.* U.S.).
68. These facts are given at the outset of Justice Sutherland's opinion for the Court. See also *New York Times*, October 8, 1933. The Federal Trade Commission at once recognized "the validity of said Executive order removing Mr. Humphrey"; and declined "to further recognize" him as a member of the Commission (*Id.,* October 10, 1933). Also, in due course, Comptroller General McCarl ruled that Humphrey was no longer entitled to the salary of the post from which he had been ousted (*Id.*, November 12, 1933). Both actions were doubtless based upon the decision in the Myers case.

Subsequently the case gave rise to a discussion in the Senate from which the following colloquy is extracted:

"MR. CLARK. We have referred several times today to the famous Humphrey case. I am one of those who are rather familiar with the record of the late Commissioner Humphrey. I do not think there is any question on earth that if the President of the United States had seen fit to comply with the law in the matter of removing Mr. Humphrey he would have been able to furnish adequate and complete grounds for removing him Mr. Humphrey had given out interviews which had been published in the public press.

"MR. WHEELER. And I was delighted when the President removed him.

"MR. CLARK. He sent out interviews which would undoubtedly have been held by any court of competent jurisdiction in this country as a ground for his removal. But the President of the United States did not see fit to follow what I would have regarded as the proper course. Instead of giving Mr. Humphrey a hearing, as required by law, and removing him for cause, he saw fit simply to remove him on the basis of a letter in which he stated that Mr. Humphrey's mind did not run along with him.

"This instance shows the danger which generally exists, although it did not exist in this particular case, because it so happened that the law was not complied with; but it is a danger that we might encounter were another President to come into office, no matter how upright he might be, or how fixed his mind as to his right to remove or not to remove individuals. As far as I am concerned, along with the Senator from Montana I was glad to see Mr. Humphrey removed, but I thought it should have been accomplished in line with the law rather than in the manner in which it was brought about."

What makes the above data interesting is the possibility which is foreshadowed in the concluding paragraph of Justice Sutherland's opinion:

"To the extent that, between the decision in the Myers case, which sustains the unrestrictable power of the President to remove purely executive officers, and our present decision that such power does not extend to an office such as that here involved, there shall remain a field of doubt, we leave such cases as may fall within it for future consideration and determination as they may arise."

Suppose such a doubtful case to arise, what attitude would the Trade Commission, or other similar body, and the Comptroller General be apt to take? Or suppose the Senate to have joined in a removal contrary to statute, would the Court itself interpose? Theoretically it ought to; but it would unquestionably be very astute to obviate such a situation. Cf. Blake *v.* U.S., 103 U.S. 227 (1880), and Wallace *v.* U.S., 257 U.S. 541 (1922).

69. 295 U.S. 627–29.

70. *Id.* at 631.

71. But this interpretation of the decision still leaves doubtful the constitutionality of the act of August 24, 1912, c. 389, 36, 37 Stat. 555, which provides that "no person in the classified civil service of the United States shall be removed therefrom except for such cause as will promote the efficiency of said service and for reason given in writing, and the person whose removal is sought shall have notice of the same and of any charges preferred against him, and be furnished with a copy of the same, and also be allowed a reasonable time for personally answering the same in writing; and affidavits in support thereof; but no examination of witnesses nor any trial or hearing shall be required except in the discretion of the officer making the removal..." (U.S. Code, Tit. 5, Sec. 652).

Even if this be considered as restrictive of the President's removal power, it seems to me to be entirely constitutional so far as it protects officers with merely ministerial duties vested in them by statute. The distinction in the Humphrey case between such an officer and those protected by that decision is not altogether logical. For there is no reason why Congress should not have power to protect against *arbitrary* removal even the humblest agents of its delegated powers, a conclusion to which Shurtleff *v.* United States, 189 U.S. 311, lends aid and comfort. On the other hand, once Congress designates any officer or agency of the government as an instrument of the President's constitutional or statutory powers, it thereby automatically renders such officers or agency, whatever may be its other powers or duties, removable by the President at will.

72. U.S. Code, Tit. 16, Secs. 831[c], c and e.

73. Or put the matter this way: if Dr. Morgan's charges were *untrue* he deserved to be removed for false and libellous statements damaging to *esprit de*

corps; while if they were *true*, his associates deserved removal, and he with them for hampering inquiry into their misconduct (83 Cong. Rec. 3896 [March 23, 1938]).

74. President Wilson, on June 4, 1920, vetoed the first Budget Bill, on account of the provision in it which made the Comptroller General and Assistant Comptroller General removable by a Concurrent resolution of the houses. He said:

"I am convinced that the Congress is without Constitutional powers to limit the appointing power and its incident power of removal derived from the Constitution.

"The section referred to not only forbids the Executive to remove these officers, but undertakes to empower the Congress by a concurrent resolution to remove an officer appointed by the President with the advice and consent of the Senate.

"I can find in the Constitution no warrant for the exercise of this power by the Congress. There is certainly no expressed authority conferred and I am unable to see that authority for the exercise of this power is implied in any expressed grant of power. On the contrary, I think its exercise is clearly negatived by Section 2 of Article II.

"That section, after providing that certain enumerated officers and all officers whose appointment are not otherwise provided for shall be appointed by the President with the advice and consent of the Senate provides that Congress may, by law, vest the appointment of such inferior officers as they think proper in the President alone, in the course of law, or in the heads of departments. It would have been within the constitutional power of the Congress, in creating these offices, to have vested the power of appointment in the President without the advice and consent of the Senate, or even in the head of a department. Regarding as I do the power of removal from office as an incident to the appointment power, I cannot escape the conclusion that the vesting of this power of removal in the Congress is unconstitutional and therefore I am unable to approve the bill."

So far as this argument depends upon theory of an illimitable power of removal, it is of course invalidated by the Humphrey decision. For another illustration, besides that afforded by the TVA act of legislation endowing the houses with power to act by concurrent resolution, see the act of June 16, 1933, c. 101, Sec. 1 (48 Stat. 291), whereby it is stipulated that "after June 16, 1933, no new investigations shall be initiated by the [Federal Trade] Commission as the result of a legislative resolution, except the same be by a concurrent resolution of the two Houses of Congress" (U.S. Code, Tit. 15, Sec. 46[a]). Prior to this, investigations were initiated on the request of either house.

75. 1 Lowell, *The Government of England* 289 (1908). For an excellent discussion of certain aspects of the Comptroller General's powers under

present legislation, see Mansfield, "Administrative Finality and Federal Expenditures," 47 *Yale Law Journal* 603–21 (1938).

76. President Coolidge attempted at least once, although unsuccessfully, to evade statutory restraints upon his removal power by demanding a blank resignation beforehand from the person whom he contemplated appointing. The story is told in the following memorandum of a conversation between the president and Hon. Wm. F. Culbertson, Vice Chairman of the Tariff Commission at the time, and a letter from Culbertson to the late Senator Costigan of Colorado:

"Contemporary memorandum of the interview with the President, Sept. 8, 1924:

"Shortly after I reached my office this morning, about 9:30, I received a request over the telephone to come to the White House to see the President. I went over immediately. The President was reasonably cordial. He began by saying that the subject of the interview was Mr. David J. Lewis's reappointment. Mr. Lewis's term as a member of the Tariff Commission expired yesterday. The President stated that he intended to reappoint Mr. Lewis, but that he desired that Mr. Lewis prepare and give to him a letter of resignation as a member of the Tariff Commission. At first I did not fully comprehend the nature of this request.

"I Spoke of Mr. Lewis's term having already expired. Then the President explained that he wanted Mr. Lewis's to submit his resignation under the new commission, to be effective in case he (the President) desired at any time in the future to accept it.

"The President at this point called in Mr. Forster, one of his secretaries, and instructed him to make out Mr. Lewis's commission of reappoint as a member of the Tariff Commission, effective today.

"The President then handed me a sheet of White House paper so that I could take down the tenor of the letter which is wished Mr. Lewis to write. I wrote down the following words: 'I hereby resign as a member of the Tariff Commission, to take effect upon your acceptance'.

"I raised the objection at this point that an unqualified resignation of this kind would imply on the record that Mr. Lewis did not desire to continue as a member of the Tariff Commission.

"The President replied that this was a matter for Mr. Lewis to decide. In explanation of his request, the President said he desired to be free after the election concerning the position filled by Mr. Lewis. He said that if he were not {re-} elected, the Democrats might undertake to hold up other appointments which he made during the next session of the Senate, and he implied that he desired to use the appointment of Mr. Lewis for trading purpose in case of necessity.

"I thereupon asked the President whether I could have his assurance that if he were re-elected Mr. Lewis could be continued as a member of the

Tariff Commission. He said that he could not at this time make any commitments.

"We then talked of other matters, and at the end the President asked me to and have Mr. Lewis see him during the afternoon, when he said he would give him his commission."

The letter, which bore the date of September 9, 1924, read as follows:

"My Dear Costigan: You will perhaps seen today in the press that Mr. Lewis was reappointed yesterday. I reached Washington Sunday evening and had not been in office very long Sunday morning before I was sent for by the President. The result of my interview is covered by a memorandum, a copy of which I enclose.

"When I returned to the office I took the President's suggestions up with Lewis, and later he reached the decision that he would not write the letter of resignation requested by the President. He, however, went to see the President during the afternoon and I presume he will you the details of what took place. In general this is what happened.

"He (Lewis) went into the President's office and the President had before him the commission. He took up his pen and signed it in Lewis's presence. He then turned to Lewis and asked him whether he had 'that letter'. Lewis then explained that he did not feel free to furnish the President with the letter which he requested. Lewis said that the President was visibly disturbed and said with a little heat that it did not make any difference any way, that the position would be held only at the pleasure of the President.

"Lewis then said to the President that only the two of them knew that the commission was signed, and he suggested that the President was at liberty to destroy the commission. The President, however, did not respond to this suggestion, and Lewis left the President's office with his commission. A little later he was sworn in.

"Thus ends another curious chapter in the Tariff Commission's history. It indicates clearly, I think that there is a line beyond which the President will not go in opposing the principle for which the three of us have stood in the development of the Tariff Commission.

"We miss your counsels very much, but I suggest that you stay in the Colorado climate until you are certain that your return here will not bring with it a return of your hay fever.

"Very cordially yours, Culbertson.

"Hon. Edward P. Costigan,

"Palmer Lake, Col."

New York Times, January 17, 1926. See also 68 Cong. Rec. 1952, 2187–89 (January 13 and 16, 1926). Of course, a really successful enterprise of this sort, in evasion of the laws, would not be apt to leak out.

77. Myers *v*. United States, 272 U.S. 52.

78. Only seven saboteurs were parties to the case, Dasch being the exception All except Haupt, an American citizen, were citizens of the Third Reich and hence enemy aliens. All of them following the outbreak of war between Germany and this country, being then in Germany, took a course of training in sabotage in a school near Berlin, their tutor being a member of the German High Command. Thereafter three of them, together with Dasch, boarded a German submarine at a French port and proceeded to Long Island; while the remaining four found their way in like fashion to the Florida coast. The courses pursued by the two groups on their arrival in this country were substantially identical. Coming ashore during hours of darkness on June 13 and June 17, respectively, they divested themselves of the German uniforms or parts of uniforms whish they had been wearing and buried them, along with a quantity of explosives, fuses, and timings devices in the sand. One party then went to New York City, the other to Jacksonville, Florida, all members being in civilian dress. In the course of the ensuing fortnight, all were picked up, either in New York or Chicago, by the FBI; and on July 2 the President appointed a military commission to try them for offenses against the laws of war and the 81st and 82nd Articles of War, which trial began on July 8. I ought to add that I prepared this article before I was aware of Professor Cushman's excellent review of the same case in the December issue of this *Review.*

V

Trueman and Presidential Prerogative

The Steel Seizure Case: A Judicial Brick Without Straw

President Truman's seizure of the steel industry without specific statutory warrant brings to a new pitch a developing reliance on the "executive power" which began almost at the inception of the federal government. True, this development has not always proceeded at the same pace; while at times it has seemed to be arrested, during the last fifty years its maturation has been virtually uninterrupted. Moreover, the forces, interests, and events which have energized the development are today more potent than ever.

The opening clause of Article II of the Constitution reads: "The executive Power shall be vested in a President of the United States of America." The records of the constitutional Convention make it clear that the purposes of this clause were simply to settle the question whether the executive branch should be plural or single and to give the executive a title. Yet, in the very first Congress to assemble under the Constitution, the opening clause of Article II was invoked by James Madison and others in order to endow the President with the power to remove officers whose appointments had been made with the advice and consent of the Senate. Madison's view prevailed, and was finally ratified by the Supreme Court in 1926. The same theory was invoked by Hamilton in support of President Washington's Proclamation of Neutrality upon the outbreak of war between France and Great Britain.[1] This time the Court's acquiescence was not long delayed. Even in the act of asserting the power of the Court to pass upon the constitutionality of acts of Congress, Chief Justice Marshall said: "By the Constitution of the United States the President is invested with certain important political powers, in the exercise of which he is to use his own discretion, and is accountable only to his country in his political character, and to his own conscience".[2] Even Thomas Jefferson, cousin and congenital enemy of Marshall, had said of the executive power in an official opinion as Secretary of State in 1790: " The Executive [branch of the government], possessing the rights of self-government from nature, cannot be controlled in the exercise of them but by a law, passed in the forms of the Constitution".[3]

Throughout the last half century the theory of presidential power has recruited strength from a succession of "strong" Presidents, from an economic crisis, from our participation in two world wars and a "cold" war, and finally from organization of the labor movement. Moreover, the constitutional basis of the doctrine has shifted somewhat since the early nineteenth century. It no longer relies exclusively, or even chiefly, on the opening clause of Article II. To the terminology of political disputation in the Jacksonian period it is indebted for such concepts as "residual," "resultant," and "inherent" powers. Thanks to Lincoln, it is able to invoke the President's duty to "take care that the laws," i.e., all the laws, "be faithfully executed," and his power as Commander-in-Chief of the armed forces. Of more recent origin is the quite baffling formula of an " aggregate of powers vested in the President by the Constitution and the laws".[4]

The chief constitutional value which overextension of presidential power threatens is, of course, the concept of a "government of laws and not of men"—the " rule of law" principle. In 1882 Justice Samuel Miller gave classical expression to this principle in the following words: "No man…is so high that he is above the law.... All officers of the government…are creatures of the law, and are bound to obey it".[5] Yet eight years later this same great judge queried whether the President's duty to "take care that the laws be faithfully executed is limited to the enforcement of the acts of Congress or treaties…[in] their *express terms*," or whether it embraces also "the rights, duties and obligations growing out of the Constitution itself… and all the protection implied by the nature of the government under the Constitution?" The answer assumed is evident.

In 1895 the Debs case, a landmark in the judicial history of Article II, was decided. Here the Court held that the United States has at all times the right to enter its courts to ask for an injunction to protect "matters which by the Constitution are entrusted to the care of the nation." The "United

States" here meant the President. The significance of the Court's choice of terminology is that it was not basing its holding on the duty of the President "to take care that the laws be faithfully executed," but on a broader principle – national interest.

The procession of "strong" Presidents was headed by Theodore Roosevelt, who asserts in his *Autobiography* that the principle which governed him in his exercise of the presidential office was that he had not only a right but a duty "to do anything that the needs of the Nation demanded unless such action was forbidden by the Constitution or by the laws." Although in his book, *Our Chief Magistrate and His Powers,* ex-President Taft warmly protested against the notion that the President has any constitutional warrant to attempt the role of a "Universal Providence," yet, as Chief Justice, he later relied on the opening clause of Article II as a grant of power. He also interpreted the Debs case as signifying that the national executive may seek an injunction in any case involving a widespread public interest.

As for the influence of the labor movement and the resultant consolidation of labor's political strength in a few great organizations subject to a highly autocratic leadership, it is sufficient to mention that, between the anthracite strike of 1902 and the bituminous coal strike of 1946, Presidents intervened in a purely personal or political capacity in no fewer than twenty-six strikes.[6] Indeed, President Truman's course of action in dealing with the bituminous coal situation in 1946 may be regarded as having both foreshadowed his conduct in the steel strike of 1952[7] and influenced judicial attitudes in some measure in the Youngstown (Steel Seizure) case.[8]

The Facts of the Youngstown Case

To avert a nationwide strike of steel workers which he believed would jeopardize the national defense, President Truman, on April 8, 1952, issued Executive Order 10340[9] directing the Secretary of Commerce to seize and operate most of the country's steel mills. The order cited no specific statutory authorization, but invoked generally the powers vested in the President by the Constitution and laws of the United States. Secretary Sawyer forthwith issued an order seizing the mills and directing their presidents to operate them as mangers for the United States in accordance with his regulations and directions. The President promptly reported these events to Congress,[10] conceding Congress' power to supersede his order; but Congress failed to take action either than or a fortnight later, when the

President again raised the problem in a special letter.[11] Of course, in the Defense Production Act of 1950,[12] the Labor Management Relations (Taft-Hartley) Act of 1947,[13] and the Selective Service Act of 1948,[14] Congress had in fact provided other procedures for dealing with such situations; and in the elaboration of these statutory schemes it had repeatedly declined to authorize governmental seizures of property to settle labor disputes. The steel companies sued the Secretary in a federal district court, praying for a declaratory judgment and injunctive relief. The district judge issued a preliminary injunction, which the court of appeals stayed. On certiorari to the court of appeals, the Supreme Court affirmed the district court's order by a vote of six to three. Justice Black delivered the opinion of the Court in which Justices Frankfurter, Douglas, Jackson, and Burton concurred; Justice Clark expressly limited his concurrence to the judgment of the Court. All these Justices presented what are termed "concurring" opinions. The Chief Justice, speaking for himself and Justices Reed and Minton, dissented.

The Doctrine of the Opinion of the Court

The chief point urged in Justice Black's opinion is that there was no statute which expressly or impliedly authorized the President to take possession of the steel mills. On the contrary, in its consideration of the Taft-Hartley Act in 1947, Congress refused to authorize governmental seizures of property as a method of preventing work stoppages and settling labor disputes. Authority to issue such an order in the circumstances of the case was not deducible from the aggregate of the executive powers under Article II of the Constitution; nor was the order maintainable as an exercise of the President's powers as Commander-in-Chief of the armed forces. The power sought to be exercised was the lawmaking power. Even if it were true that other presidents have taken possession of private business enterprises without congressional authority in order to settle labor disputes, Congress was not thereby divested of its exclusive constitutional authority to make the laws necessary and proper to carry out all powers vested by the Constitution "in the Government of the United States, or in any Department or Officer thereof".[15]

The pivotal proposition of the opinion is, in brief, that inasmuch as Congress could have ordered the seizure of the steel mills, there was a total absence of power in the President to do so without prior congressional authorization. To support this thesis no proof in the way of past opinion, practice, or adjudication is offered. Justice Black's attitude toward this matter of authority is, in fact, decidedly cavalier. The closing paragraph of his opinion reads:

The founders of this Nation entrusted the lawmaking power to the Congress alone in both good and bad times. It would do no good to recall the historical events, the fears of power and the hopes for freedom that lay behind their choice. Such a review would but confirm our holding that this seizure order cannot stand.[16]

The somewhat different truth of the matter is that the framers of the Constitution were compelled to defend their handiwork against the charge that it violated "the political maxim that the legislative, executive, and judicial departments ought to be separate and distinct".[17] To meet this charge Madison sought to show in *The Federalist* that the three departments ought not to be so far separated as to have no control over each other.[18] In his opinion for the court in *Ex parte* Grossman,[19] decided 137 years later, Chief Justice Taft adopted the same point of view: the fact that when two departments both operate upon the same subject matter the action of one may cancel that of the other *affords no criterion of the constitutional powers of either.* Rather the question is what does *the pertinent historical record* show with the regard to presidential action in the field of congressional power?

The Historical Record

Our history contains numerous instances in which, contrary to the pattern of departmental relationship assumed in the Black opinion, presidential action has occurred within a recognized field of congressional power and has, furthermore, fully maintained its tenancy until Congress adopted superseding legislation. And Congress' right to supersede was not contested. In brief, the mere existence in Congress of power to do something has not, of itself, excluded the President from the same field of power until Congress finally acted. But once this happened, its legislation was forthwith recognized as governing the subject and as controlling presidential action in the area.

An early example of this pattern of departmental relationship is afforded by the case of the *Flying fish,*[20] in which Chief Justice Marshall denied that the President had power to order the seizure of a vessel bound from a French port, *because* Congress had acted in the same field of power:

It is by no means clear that the president of the United States whose high duty it is to "take care that the laws be faithfully executed," and who is commander in chief of the armies and navies of the United States, might not, without any special authority for that purpose, in the then existing state of things, have empowered the officers commanding the armed vessels of the United States, to seize and sent into port for adjudication, American vessels which were forfeited by being engaged in this illicit commerce. But when it is observed that [an act of Congress] gives a special authority to seize on the high seas, and limits that authority to the seizure of vessels bound, or sailing to, a French port, the legislature seem to have prescribed that the manner in which this law shall be carried into execution, was to exclude a seizure of any vessel not bound to a French port.[21]

Another field which the President and Congress have occupied successively is extradition. In 1799 President Adams, in order to execute the extradition provisions of the Jay Treaty, issued a warrant for the arrest of one Jonathan Robbins. As Chief Justice Vinson recites in his opinion:

This action was challenged in Congress on the ground that no specific statute prescribed the method to be used in executing the treaty. John Marshall, then a member of the House of Representatives, in the course of his successful defense of the President's action, said: "Congress, unquestionably, may prescribe the mode, and Congress may devolve on others the whole execution of the contract; but, till this be done, it seems the duty of the Executive department to execute the contract by any means it possesses."[22]

Not until 1848 did Congress enact a statute governing extradition cases and conferring on the courts, both state and federal, the duty of handling them.[23]

The power of the President to act until Congress acts in the same field is also shown in these instances. The first Neutrality Proclamation, issued by President Washington in 1793, was also without congressional authorization.[24] The following year Congress enacted the first neutrality statute,[25] and subsequent proclamations of neutrality have been based on an act of Congress governing the matter. The President may, in the absence of legislation of Congress, control the landing of foreign cables in the United States and the passage of foreign troops through American territory, and has done so repeatedly.[26] Likewise, until Congress acts, he may govern conquered territory[27] and, 'in the absence of attempts by Congress to limit his power," may set up military commissions in territory occupied by the armed forces of the United States.[28] He may determine in a manner binding on the courts whether a treaty is still in force as law of the land, although again the final power in the field rests with Congress.[29]

One of the President's most ordinary powers and duties is that of ordering the prosecution of supposed offenders against the laws of the United States. Yet Congress may do the same thing under the "necessary and proper" clause.[30] On September 22, 1862, President Lincoln issued a proclamation suspending the privilege of the writ of *habeas corpus* throughout the Union in certain classes of cases. By an act passed March 3, 1863, Congress ratified his action and at the same time brought the whole subject of military arrests in the United States under statutory control.[31] Conversely, when President Wilson failed in March, 1917, to obtain Congress' consent to his arming American merchant vessels with defensive arms, he went ahead and did it anyway, "fortified not only by the known sentiments of the majority in Congress but also by the advice of his Secretary of State and Attorney General".[32]

To turn to the specific matter of property seizures, Justice Frankfurter's concurring opinion in the Youngstown case is accompanied by appendices containing a synoptic analysis of legislation authorizing seizures of industrial property and also a summary of seizures of industrial plants and facilities by Presidents without definite statutory warrant. Eighteen such statutes are listed, all but the first of which were enacted between 1916 and 1951. Of Presidential seizures unsupported by reference to specific statutory authorization he lists eight as occurring during World War I. One he fails to mention is the seizure of the Marconi Wireless Station at Siasconset in the late summer of 1914, as a result of the company's refusal to give assurance that it would comply with naval censorship regulation.[33] To justify these seizures it was deemed sufficient to refer to " the Constitution and laws" generally. For the World War II period he lists eleven seizures in justification of which no statutory authority was cited. The first of these was the seizure of North America Aviation, Inc., of Englewood, California. In support of this action Attorney General Jackson, as Chief Justice Vinson points out in his dissenting opinion, "vigorously proclaimed that the President had the moral duty to keep this Nation's defense effort a 'going concern'."[34] Said the then Attorney General:

For the faithful execution of... [the] laws the President has back of him not only each general law enforcement power conferred by the various acts of Congress but the aggregate of all such laws plus that wide discretion as to method vested in him by the Constitution for the purpose of executing the laws.[35]

In the War Labor Disputes Act of June 25, 1943,[36] all such seizures were put on a statutory basis. Congress having at last acted on the subject, its expressed will thereafter governed.

In United States *v.* Pewee Coal Co.,[37] the Court had before it the claim of a coal mine operator whose property was seized by the President without statutory authorization, "to avert a nation-wide strike of miners." The company brought an action in the Court of Claims to recover under the Fifth Amendment for the total operating losses sustained during the period in which this property was operated by the United States. The court awarded judgement for $2,241.46 and the Supreme Court sustained this judgment, a result which, by implying the validity of the seizure,[38] supported the government's position in the Youngstown case.[39]

The doctrine dictated by the above considerations as regards the exercise of executive power in the field of legislative power was well stated by Mr. John W. Davis, principal counsel on the present occasion for the steel companies, in a brief which he filed nearly forty years ago as Solicitor General. The brief defended the action of the President in withdrawing certain lands from public entry, although his doing so was at the time contrary to express statute. "Ours," the brief reads,

is a self-sufficient Government within its sphere. (*Ex parte Siebold*, 100 U.S. 371, 395; *in re Debs*, 158 U.S. 56, 564, 578.) "Its means are adequate to its ends" (*McCulloch* v. *Maryland*, 4 Wheat. 316, 424), and it is rational to assume that its active forces will be found equal in most things to the emergencies that confront it. While perfect flexibility is not to be expected in a Government of divided powers, and while division of power is one of the principal features of the Constitution, it is the plain duty of those who are called upon to draw the dividing lines to ascertain the essential, recognize the practical, and avoid a slavish formalism which can only serve to ossify the Government and reduce its efficiency without any compensating good. The function of making laws is peculiar to Congress, and the Executive can not exercise that function to any degree. But this is not to say that all of *subjects* concerning which laws might be made are perforce removed from the possibility of Executive influence. The Executive may act upon things and upon men in many relations which have not, though they might have, been actually regulated by Congress. In other words, just as there are fields which are peculiar to Congress and fields which are peculiar to the Executive, so there are fields which are common to both, in the sense that the Executive may move within them until they shall have been occupied by legislative action. These are not the fields of legislative prerogative, but fields within which the law-making power may enter and dominate whenever it chooses. This situation results from the fact that the President is the active agent, not of Congress, but of the Nation. As such he performs the duties which the Constitution lays upon him immediately, and as such, also, he executes the laws and regulations adopted by Congress. He is the agent of the people of the United States, deriving all his powers from the responsible directly to them. In no sense is he the agent of Congress. He obeys and executes the laws of Congress, not because Congress is enthroned in authority over him, but because the Constitution directs him to do so.

Therefore it follows that in ways short of making laws or disobeying them, the Executive may be under a grave constitutional duty to act for the national protection in situations not covered by the acts of the Congress, and in which, even, it may not be said that his action is the direct expression of any particular one of the independent powers which are granted to him specifically by the Constitution. Instances wherein the President has felt and fulfilled such a duty have not been rare in the history, though, being for the public benefit and approved by all, his acts have seldom been challenged in the courts.[40]

Some Logical Considerations

If the legislative power and executive power are not always mutually exclusive, neither, on the other hand, are the legislative and judicial powers. Replying to the contention in Wayman *v*. Southard that it was unconstitutional for Congress to delegate to the courts its power to regulate their practice,[41] Chief Justice Marshall answered that while Congress cannot delegate powers which are "strictly and exclusively legislative," the courts do have certain rule-making powers with respect, for example, to the returning of writs and processes and the filing of pleadings which Congress might have retained but which it had the right to confer on the judicial department.[42] Indeed, if the President was forbidden to seize the steel mills by virtue of the fact that Congress could have done so, the right of the Court to "invalidate" the seizure becomes highly questionable; and, as all admitted, Congress could have invalidated the seizure.

Actually the President was exercising the same *kind* of power that he would have exercised had the Taft-Hartley Act, for example, made provision for such a seizure "when necessary to avert a serious strike". The Court's opinion says, however:

The President's order does not direct that a congressional policy be executed in a manner prescribed by Congress—it directs that a presidential policy be executed in a manner prescribed by the President. The preamble of the order itself, like that of many statutes, sets out reasons why the President believes certain policies should be adopted, proclaims these policies as rules of conduct to be followed, and again, like a statute, authorizes a government official to promulgate additional rules and regulations consistent with the policy proclaimed and needed to carry that policy into execution.[43]

So what? The same thing can be said of orders of the Interstate Commerce Commission setting "reasonable rates," something which Congress can do directly any time it chooses to bypass or override the commission. Besides, the chief factors of the "national emergency" described in Executive Order 10340 put into operation "cognate powers" of President and Congress which may be merged indefinitely in the former at the option of Congress.[44]

The Concurring Opinions

Justice Frankfurter begins the material part of his opinion with the statement:

We must...put to one side consideration of what powers the President would have had if there had been no legislation whatever bearing on the authority asserted by the seizure, or if the seizure had been only for a short, explicitly temporary period, to be terminated automatically unless Congressional approval were given.[45]

He then enters upon a review of the proceedings of Congress which attended the enactment of the Taft-Hartley Act, and concludes that Congress expressed its intention to withhold the seizure power "as though it had said so in so many words".[46]

Justice Douglas' contribution consists in the argument that a necessary result of the condemnation provision of the Fifth Amendment is that the branch of government with "the power to pay compensation for a seizure is the only one able to authorize a seizure or make lawful one that the President has effected".[47] This contention overlooks such cases as Mitchell v. Harmony,[48] United States v. Russell,[49] Portsmouth Harbor Land & Hotel Co. *v.* United States[50] and United States *v.* Pewee Coal Co.[51] in all of which a right of compensation was recognized to exist in consequence of taking of property or damage to property which resulted from acts stemming ultimately from constitutional powers of the President. In United States *v.* Pink,[52] Justice Douglas quoted with approval the following words from *The Federalist:* "All constitutional acts of power, whether in the executive or in the judicial department, have as much... validity and obligation as if they proceeded from the legislature."[53] If this is so as to treaty obligations, then all the more must it be true of obligations which are based directly on the Constitution.[54]

Justice Jackson's rather desultory opinion contains little that is of direct pertinence to the constitutional issue. Important, however, is his contention, which seems to align him with Justice Frankfurter, that Congress has "not left seizure of private property an open field but has covered it by three statutory policies inconsistent with this seizure". From this he reasons that "we can sustain the president only by holding that seizure of such strike-bound industries is within his domain and beyond control by Congress".[55] The opinion concludes:

In view of the ease, expedition and safety with which Congress can grant and has granted large emergency powers, certainly ample to embrace this crisis, I am quite unimpressed with the argument that we should affirm possession of them without statute.... But I have no illusion that any decision by this Court can keep power in the hands of Congress if it is not wise and timely in meeting its problems. A crisis that challenges the President equally, or perhaps primarily, challenges Congress. If not good law, there was wordly wisdom in the maxim attributed to Napoleon that "The tools belong to the man who can use them." We may say that power to legislate for emergencies belongs in the hands of Congress, but only Congress itself can prevent power from slipping through its fingers.[56]

Justice Burton says that the Taft-Hartley Act, read in the light of its legislative history,[57] significantly fails to provide authority for seizures. He also agrees that "Congress authorized a procedure which the President declined to follow."[58] Justice Clark bases his position directly on Little v. Barreme.[59] The President must, he says, follow the procedures laid down in the Taft-Hartley, Selective Service and Defense Production acts.[60] At the same time he endorses the view, "taught me not only by the decision of Chief Justice Marshall in Little *v*. Barreme, but also by a score of other pronouncements of distinguished members of this bench," that "the Constitution does grant to the President extensive authority in times of grave and imperative national emergency".[61]

Dissenting Opinion

Chief Justice Vinson launched his dissent, for himself and Justices Reed and Minton, with a survey of the elements of the emergency which confronted the President: the Korean War, the obligations of the United States under the United Nations Charter and the Atlantic Pact, the appropriations acts by which Congress voted vast sums to be expended in our defense and that of our European allies, the fact that steel is a basic constituent of war material. He reproaches the Court for failing to give consideration to the President's finding of an emergency. According to the Court, he said, "the immediacy of the threatened disaster" is "irrelevant"; and the President, unable to use the executive power to avert the disaster, "must confine himself to sending a message to Congress". The opinion of the Chief Justice musters impressive evidence to show that the steel seizure, considering the emergency involved, fits into the picture of past presidential emergency action. And "plaintiffs admit that the emergency procedures of Taft-Hartley are not mandatory".[62]

Resume and Evaluation

Youngstown will probably go down in history as an outstanding example of the *sic volo, sic jubeo* frame of mind into which the Court is occasionally maneuvered by the public context of the case before it. The doctrine of the case, as stated in Justice Black's opinion of the Court, while purporting to stem from the principle of the separation of powers, is a purely arbitrary construct created out of hand for the purpose of disposing of this particular case, and is altogether devoid of historical verification. Nor do the concurring opinions contribute anything to the decision's claim to be regarded seriously as a doctrine of constitutional law. Their importance consists in the suggestion, cogently urged by Justice Frankfurter and endorsed by Justices Jackson, Burton, and Clark, that the President should have heeded the intention of the Taft-Hartley Act. Only Justice Clark, however, guided by Marshall's opinion in the early case of Little *v.* Barreme, had the courage to draw the appropriate conclusion: Congress having entered the field, its ascertainable intention supplied the law of the case. Justice Clark accordingly refused to concur in the opinion of the Court, while voting for its decision.

The Chief Justice's dissenting opinion is impressive for its delineation of the emergency and convincing in its summation of evidence regarding presidential emergency power. In view of the attitude of the concurring justices, however, his assertion as to the bearing of Taft-Hartley on the problem before the Court is deceptive. The statement that Taft-Hartley was "not mandatory" is equivocal. Granting that the act was not intended to require the President to resort to it in preference to permitting the situation to take an uncontrolled course, yet resort to it may very well have been intended as an indispensable preliminary to a seizure. This conclusion is borne out by the fact that when the procedures provided by the act fail, the President is required to submit a report and recommendations to Congress for action. In the opinion of the writer the case was rightly decided, but for wrong reasons. The line of reasoning suggested by Justices Frankfurter, Jackson, Burton, and Clark should have been pursued to its logical end, as by Justice Clark it was.[63]

The question remains whether the record of the case is of value for constitutional law and practice. It is. (1) That the President does possess "residual" or "resultant" powers over and above, or in consequence of, his specifically granted powers to take temporary alleviative action in the presence of serious emergency is a proposition to which all but Justices Black and Douglas would probably have assented in the absence of the complicating issue that was created by the president's refusal to follow the procedures laid down in the Taft-Hartley Act. (2) Such residual powers being conceded, it would follow logically that a seizure of property made by exercise of them would give rise to a constitutional obligation on the part of the United States to render "just compensation" in accordance with the requirements of the Fifth Amendment. (3) It is also fairly evident that the Court would never venture to traverse a presidential finding of "serious" emergency which was prima facie supported by judicially cognizable facts, but would wave aside a challenge to such a finding as raising a "political question". (4) The Court would unquestionably have assented to the proposition that in all emergency situations the last word lies with the Congress when it chooses to speak such last word. And the moral from all this is plain: namely, that escape must be sought from "presidential autocracy" by resort not to the judicial power, but to the legislative power – in other words, by resort to timely action by Congress and to procedures for the meeting of emergency situations so far as this can be intelligently anticipated.

And – not to give the thing too fine a point – what seems to be required at the present juncture is a new Labor Disputes Act which ordains procedures for the handling of industry-wide strike in terms so comprehensive and explicit that the most headstrong President cannot sidestep them without manifest attaint to the law, the Constitution, and his own oath of office. "Presidential autocracy," when it is justified, is an inrush of power to fill a power vacuum. Nature abhors a vacuum; so does an age of emergency. Let Congress see to it that no such vacuum occurs.

The President's Power

When in 1800 President Adams signed a deed conveying property to his "great and good friend" the Queen of Portugal for a legation in the

Federal City, he was informed by his Attorney General that only Congress had the constitutional power to dispose of public property. When, 140 years later, President Franklin Roosevelt handed over fifty naval units to Great Britain in return for leases of some West Atlantic naval bases, he was told by his Attorney General, now a member of the Supreme Court, that he was entirely within his rights, that his power to *dispose* the forces of the United States included the power to dispose *of* them. These two episodes stand at either end of a course of constitutional development, practical and polemical, which ascribes to the President a truly royal prerogative in the field of foreign relations, and does so without indicating any correlative legal or constitutional control to which he is answerable.

Indeed, our high-flying prerogative men appear to resent the very idea that the only possible source of such control, Congress to wit, has any effective power in the premises at all. Thus when Mr. Taft in his speech of January 5 asserted that President Truman "had no authority to commit American troops to Korea without consulting Congress and without Congressional approval," and that he "has no power to agree to send American troops to fight in Europe in a war between members of the Atlantic Pact and Soviet Russia," one of the aforesaid high prerogative spokesmen declared that "his [Taft's] statements are demonstrably irresponsible". The public "is entitled to know what provisions of the law or of the Constitution have been violated by President Truman in sending troops overseas. From the day that President Jefferson ordered Commodore Dale and two-thirds of the American Navy into the Mediterranean to repel the Barbary pirates, American Presidents have repeatedly committed American armed forces abroad without prior Congressional consultation or approval".[64]

The proffered demonstration is inconclusive at best. Jefferson, in reporting his action to Congress, explained that he had been careful to authorize only self-defensive measures on the part of our forces, and that when they had captured one of the pirate vessels they had, after disabling it for committing further hostilities, liberated it with its crew. He wished, he said, to have Congress, who "exclusively" had the power, to consider whether it would not be well to authorize measures of offense. Hamilton expressed great contempt for Jefferson's scruples, but that does not alter the record to which appeal has been made.

As to the cases in which "American Presidents have repeatedly committed armed forces abroad" without "Congressional consultation or approval," the vast majority involved fights with pirates, landings of small naval contingents on barbarous or semi-barbarous coasts, the dispatch of small bodies of troops to chase bandits or cattle rustlers across the Mexican border, and the like. Except for Polk's deliberate precipitation of war with Mexico in 1846 and a few cases occurring in the Caribbean area since 1902, they exhibit a uniform pattern of measures undertaken from the protection of American lives and property against impending or actual violence or for punishment of such violence. Such episodes are small compared with Truman's claim of power to put an indefinite number of troops in Europe for an indefinite time in anticipation of war, without consulting Congress.[65]

The power of Congress over the employment of the armed forces was repeatedly recognized in early legislation. The President's power to call forth the militia stems immediately from the act of February 28, 1795; and I should like to inform Professor Commager[66] that it was this act and not the Constitution which "the magisterial Story" was construing in the case of Martin v. Mott (12 Wheat. 19 [1827]); also, the President's power to employ the armed forces to suppress insurrections and enforce the law rests on the act of March 8, 1807. Formal declarations of war by Congress have always included a clause "authorizing" and "directing" the employment of the forces to support the declaration, and it may be remembered that the Conscription Act of September, 1940, specifically provided that the forces to be conscripted would not be sent abroad without the consent of Congress. When we were precipitated into the war by the Japanese attack on Pearl Harbor, this consent was given. It is also pertinent to recall that when President Wilson landed troops at Vera Cruz on April 21, 1914, he consulted Congress, which approved his action the following day; and President Franklin Roosevelt's "utmost sympathy" message to France, June 14, 1940, contained the caveat that "these statements carry no implication of military commitments. Only Congress can make such commitments".

Besides, the Constitution does not consist primarily of precedents but of principles with which precedents, to be valid, must be squared. The Administration's interpretation of the precedents which illustrate routine activities of the executive departments upsets the most fundamental principle of the Constitution, the balance between the departments. It distorts the Constitution.

The fact that a certain power is ascribable to the President does not prove that Congress possesses no power whereby Presidential employment of it may be brought under control and direction. This precise question was involved in the case of Little *v.* Barreme (2 Cranch 170, 177 [1804]). There Chief Justice Marshall, speaking with reference to the seizure of a vessel under the act of February 9, 1809, suspending intercourse with France, said:

It is by no means clear that the President of the United States whose high duty it is to "take care that the laws be faithfully executed," and who is Commander-in-Chief of the armies and navies of the United States, might not, without any special authority for that purpose, in the then existing state of things, have empowered the officers commanding the armed vessels of the United States, to seize and send into port for adjudication, American vessels which were forfeited by being engaged in this illicit commerce.

The court held, nevertheless, that since Congress had acted in the matter the President was bound to follow its directions and that the seizure had been illegal.

While the shadowy line that separates congressional power when raising an army and creating a navy or air force to specify the purposes for which they may be employed and the President's right to dispose the forces thus brought into existence has come to be drawn in the course of the years inside what was once deemed to be legislative domain, yet there are conceded to be other powers of Congress which are constitutionally unlimited and Congress' use of which is capable of upsetting the presidential applecart at any time. Congress can refuse to raise armies and navies at all, to borrow money, to levy taxes, to make appropriations. It can abrogate "so far as the people and authorities of the United States are concerned" any treaty to which the United States is a party, and has repealed a considerable number in whole or in part. (La Abro Silver Mining Co. *v.* United States, 175 U.S. 423, 460 [1899], citing cases.)

What then is the answer? Futile and embittered debate between the holders of powers that must be exercised in close co-operation if at all, or a decent consultation and accommodation of views between the two departments of government concerned? And surely, it is paradoxical in the extreme to reduce the legislative organ of government to the level of a mere rubber stamp of policies the professed purpose of which is the preservation of free institutions. Either the Brussels Agreement should be formally submitted to the Senate for approval by a constitutional two-thirds majority, or something akin to Coudert's resolution should be adopted. Our foreign policy has been elaborated in a political, and at times an intellectual, vacuum long enough.

References

1. Corwin, *President: Office and Powers* 217 *et seq*., 465, 474-75.
2. Marbury *v.* Madison, 1 Cranch 137, 166 (1803).
3. 5 *Writings of Jefferson* 209 (Ford ed. 1895).
4. 40 *Opinions of the Attorney General* 312, 319 (1944).
5. United States *v.* Lee, 106 U.S. 196, 220 (1882).
6. Corwin, *President: Office and Powers* 453-54 (figures compiled by Professor Dishman of Dartmouth College).
7. Corwin, *A Constitution of Powers in a Secular State* 76 n.20 (1951). See also *id.* at 62 n.8a.
8. Youngstown Sheet & Tube Co. *v.* Sawyer, 343 U.S. 579 (1952).
9. 17 l ed. Reg. 3139 (1952).
10. 98 Cong. Rec. 3962 (April 9, 1952).
11. 98 Cong. Rec. 4192 (April 21, 1952).
12. 64 Stat. 798 (1950), as amended, 50 U.S.C. App. sec. 2071 (Supp. 1952).
13. 61 Stat. 136 (1947), as amended, 29 U.S.C. secs. 141-97 (Supp. 1952).
14. 62 Stat. 604 (1948), 50 U.S.C. App. Secs. 451-62 (Supp.1952).
15. U.S. Constitution, Art. I, Sec. 8. See Youngstown Sheet & Tube Co. *v.* Sawyer, 343 U.S. 579, 660-61 (1952).
16. *Id.* at 589.
17. *The Federalist* No. 47 at 245 (Everyman's ed. 1929).
18. *The Federalist* No. 48 (Madison).
19. 267 U.S. 87 (1925). " The Federal Constitution nowhere expressly declares that the three branches of the Government shall be kept separate and independent. All legislative powers are vested in a Congress. The executive power is vested in a President. The judicial power is vested in one Supreme Court and in such inferior courts as Congress may from time to time establish. The Judges are given life tenure and a compensation that may not be diminished during their continuance in office, with the evident purpose of securing them and their courts an independence of Congress and the Executive,. Complete independence and separation between the three branches, however, are not attained, or intended, as other provisions of the Constitution and the normal operation of government under it easily demonstrate" (*id.* at 119-20).
20. Little *v.* Barreme, 2 Cranch 170 (1804).
21. Id. at 177-78, quoted in Youngstown Sheet & Tube Co. *v.* Sawyer, 343 U.S. 579, 660-61 (1952), Clark, J., concurring, Justice Clark added: "I know of no subsequent holding of this Court to the contrary" (*ibid.*).
22. Youngstown Sheet & Tube Co. *v.* Sawyer, 343 U.S. 579, 684 (1952), citing 10 *Annals of Congress* 619 (1948).

23. Rev. Stat. Secs. 5270-79 (1878), as amended, 18 U.S.C. Secs. 651-76 (1946).
24. For the controversy thereby precipitated between Hamilton (Pacificus) and Madison (Helvidius), see Corwin, *The President's Control of Foreign Relations* c. 1 (1917).
25. 1 Stat. 381 (1794). The act was the direct outcome of suggestions made by Washington in his message of December 3, 1793. See 1 Richardson, *Messages and Papers of the Presidents* 139 (1896).
26. 22 *Opinions of the Attorney General* 13 (1898); see Tucker *v.* Alexandroff, 183 U.S. 424, 434-35 (1902). An act was passed May 27, 1921, 42 Stat. 8 (1921), 47 U.S.C. Sec. 34 (1946) which requires presidential license for the landing and operation of cables connecting the United States with foreign countries. See Wright, *The Control of American Foreign Relations* 302 n.75 (1922).
27. Santiago *v.* Nagueras, 214 U.S. 260 (1909).
28. Madsen *v.* Kinsella, 343 U.S. 341 (1952).
29. Charlton *v.* Kelly, 229 U.S. 447 (1913). See also Botiller *v.* Dominguez, 130 U.S. 238 (1889).
30. See Sinclair *v.* United States, 279 U.S. 263, 289, 297 (1929).
31. 12 Stat. 755 (1863).
32. Berdahl, *War Powers of the Executive in the United States* 69 (1921).
33. Attorney General Gregory's justification of this action, 30 *Opinions of the Attorney General* 291 (1914), more or less set the style for similar future opinions.
34. Youngstown Sheet & Tube Co. v. Sawyer, 343 U.S. 579, 695 (1952).
35. 89 Cong. Rec. 3992 (1943).
36. 57 Stat. 163 (1943).
37. 341 U.S. 114 (1951).
38. Such suits are based on the Tucker Act, 24 Stat. 505 (1887), as amended, 28 U.S.C. Sec. 41 (20), 250 (1)(2), 287 (1946), and are founded upon the Constitution of the United States. " The constitutional prohibition against taking private property for public use without just compensation is directed against the Government, and not against individual or public officers proceeding without the authority of legislative enactment" (Hooe *v.* United States, 218 U.S. 322, 335-36 [1910]). See United States *v.* North American Co., 253 U.S. 330, 333 (1920). While the above quoted language is doubtless correct as an interpretation of the Tucker Act, it ignores the constitutional obligation of the United States to compensate for acts of "taking" which stem from the President's power, especially his power as Commander-in-Chief. See United States *v.* Causby, 328 U.S. 256, 267 (1946), and notes 58-61.
39. "The relatively new technique of temporary taking by eminent domain is a most useful administrative device: many properties, such as laundries, or

coal mines, or railroads, may be subjected to public operation for a short time to meet war or emergency needs, and can then be returned to their owners" (United States *v.* Pewee Coal Co., 341 U.S. 114, 119 [1951], Reed, J., concurring).

40. Brief for Appellant, pp. 75-77, United States *v.* Midwest Oil Co., 236 U.S. 459 (1915). Assistant Attorney General Knaebel's name was also on the brief.
41. 10 Wheat. 1 (1825).
42. See *id.* at 42-43.
43. Youngstown Sheet & Tube Co. *v.* Sawyer, 343 U.S. 579, 588 (1952).
44. United States *v.* Curtiss-Wright Corp., 299 U.S. 304, 319-29 (1936).
45. Youngstown Sheet & Tube Co. *v.* Sawyer, 343 U.S. 579, 597 (1952).
46. *Id.* at 602.
47. *Id.* at 631-32.
48. 13 How. 115 (1852).
49. 13 Wall. 623 (1871).
50. 260 U.S. 327 (1922).
51. 341 U.S. 114 (1951).
52. 315 U.S. 203, 230 (1942).
53. *The Federalist* No. 64 at 330 (Everyman's ed. 1929).
54. See 40 *Opinions of the Attorney General* 250, 253 (1942).
55. Youngstown Sheet & Tube Co. v. Sawyer, 343 U.S. 579, 639-40 (1952).
56. Id. at 653-54.
57. 93 Cong. Rec. 3835-36 (1947).
58. Youngstown Sheet & Tube Co. v. Sawyer, 343 U.S. 579, 659 (1952).
59. 2 Cranch 170 (1804).
60. Youngstown Sheet & Tube Co. v. Sawyer, 343 U.S. 579, 663-65 (1952).
61. *Id.* at 662.
62. *Id.* at 705.
63. The case for the President is not improved by Congress' adoption of the following provision as a part of the Defense Production Act amendments of 1952, Pub. L. No. 429, 82nd Cong., 2d sess., sec. 115 (June 30, 1952): "Section 503 of the Defense Production Act of 1950, as amended, is hereby amended by adding at the end thereof the following: 'It is the sense of the Congress that, by reason of the work stoppage now existing in the steel industry, the national safety is imperiled, and the Congress therefore requests the President to invoke immediately the national emergency provisions (sections 206 to 210, inclusive) of the Labor-Management Relations Act, 1947, for the purpose of terminating such work stoppage'."
64. Arthur Schlesinger, Jr., in the *New York Times*, January 9, 1951.
65. On this paragraph see Rogers, *World Policing and the Constitution* (1945).
66. See his article in the *New York Times Magazine*, January 14, 1951.

VI

After the Constitutional Revolution

The Dissolving Structure of Our Constitutional Law

There is a story that once upon a time a doctor, an engineer, and a politician were debating which of these callings was the most ancient. The doctors rested his case on the contention that the removal of the rib from Adam's side was obviously a surgical operation; to which the engineer rejoined that before Adam had even appeared on the scene the world itself had to be created out of chaos, and that this was clearly an engineering operation. "Very true," chimed in the politician, "but who do you think created chaos?"

Accepting the Clausewitz thesis that "war is only an extension of policy," we are free to say that the politicians have created chaos in these latter days in rather wholesale way. But that is another story. The world revolution is not my topic, but the comparatively limited revolution which we have been witnessing in our own country the last few years in consequence of the New Deal and more recently of the war. How has this revolution affected conceptions of governmental power in the United States; how is it to be evaluated in terms of American constitutional law? For constitutional law has always been the most distinctive feature of the American system of government, the result of a unique infusion of politics with jurisprudence, of current opinion with established principles. Today this remarkable product of American political genius appears to be undergoing a fundamental revision—even to be in the process of dissolution.[1]

What is constitutional law? As the term is employed in this country, it denotes a body of rules resulting from judicial interpretation of a written constitution, and particularly the interpretation of the Constitution of the United States by the Supreme Court at Washington. Its parental elements are, therefore, the constitutional document and the power of the Supreme Court to pass upon the validity of legislation both state and national in relation to that document—more briefly, judicial review. The latter is the active, generative element; the former is, *in theory*, the matrix, the receptive element.

Actually, when the subject is considered statistically, the theory that the constitutional document contained in embryo from the outset the entirely of constitutional law puts credulity to a quite impossible test. First and last the Supreme Court had handed down some fifteen or sixteen thousand opinions, occupying in the published *Reports* probably two hundred thousand pages, large octavo; and of this total, probably one-third comprises cases involving points of constitutional interpretation. But even more striking is the fact that by far the greater number of these have arisen out of four or five brief phrases of the constitutional document, "power to regulate commerce," "obligation of contracts," deprivation of "life, liberty or property without due process of law" (which phrase occurs both as a limitation on the national government and—since 1868—on the states), and out of three or four theories or doctrines which the Constitution is supposed to embody.

The latter are, in fact, the essence of the matter. That is to say, the effectiveness of constitutional law as a system of restraints on governmental power depends for the most part on the effectiveness of these doctrines as they are applied by the Court for that purpose. The doctrines to which I refer are (1) the doctrine or concept of dual federalism; (2) the doctrine of the separation of powers; (3) the doctrine and *practice* of judicial review; and finally, the substantive concept of due process of law, by which judicial review has been put beyond statable limits both as to subject matter and also as to the considerations determining its exercise. What I propose to do is to take up each of these four doctrines in turn, briefly sketch its origins, and then project against that background a short account of what has been happening to it in recent years.

Federalism in the United States embraces the following elements: (1) as in all federations, the union of several autonomous political entities, or states, for common purposes; (2) the division of legislative powers between a national government, on the one hand, and constituent states, on the other; (3) the direct operation for the most part of each of these centers of government, within its assigned sphere, upon all persons and property within its territorial limits; (4) the provision of each center with the complete apparatus of law enforcement, both executive and judicial; (5) the supremacy of the national government within its assigned sphere over any conflicting assertion of state power; (6) dual citizenship.

The third and fourth of the above-listed salient features of the American federal system are the ones which at the outset marked it off most sharply from all preceding systems, in which the member states generally agreed to obey the mandates of a common government for certain stipulated purposes, but retained to themselves the right of ordaining and enforcing the laws of the union. This, indeed, was the system provided in eth Articles of Confederation. The Convention of 1787 was well aware, of course, that if the inanities and futilities of the confederation were to be avoided in the new system the latter must incorporate "a coercive principle"; and as Ellsworth of Connecticut expressed it, the only question was whether it should be "a coercion of law, or a coercion of arms," that "coercion which acts only upon delinquent individuals" or that which is applicable to "sovereign bodies, states, in their political capacity". In judicial review the former principle was established, albeit without entirely discarding the latter, as the Civil War was to demonstrate.

The sheer fact of federalism comes within the purview of constitutional law, that is, becomes a judicial *concept*, in consequence of the conflicts which have at times arisen between the idea of state autonomy (state sovereignty) and the principle of national supremacy. Exaltation of the latter principle, as it is recognized in the supremacy clause (Article VI paragraph 2) of the Constitution, was the very keystone of Chief Justice Marshall's constitutional jurisprudence. It was his position that the supremacy clause should be applied literally, with the result that if an unforced reading of the terms in which legislative power was granted to Congress confirmed its right to enact a particular statute, the circumstance that the statute projected national power into an accustomed field of state power became a matter of complete indifference. State power, in short, was no ingredient of national power, and hence no independent limitation thereof.

Quite different was the outlook of the Court over which Marshall's successor, Chief Justice Taney, presided. That Court took as its point of departure the Tenth Amendment, which reads, "The powers not delegated to the United States by the Constitution, nor prohibited by it to the States, are reserved to the States respectively, or to the people." In construing this provision the States Right Court sometimes talked as if it regarded *all* the reserved powers of the states as limiting national power. At other times it talked as if it regarded certain "subjects" as reserved exclusively to the states, slavery being the outstanding instance.

But whether following the one line of reasoning or the other, the Court subtly transformed its function, and so that of judicial review, in relation to the federal system. Marshall viewed the Court as primarily an organ of the national government and of its supremacy. The Court under Taney regarded itself as standing outside of and above both the national government and the states, and as vested with a quasi-arbitral function between two centers of diverse but essentially equal, because "sovereign," powers. Thus in Ableman *v.* Booth,[2] which was decided on the eve of the Civil War, we find Taney himself using this arresting language:

This judicial power was justly regarded as indispensable, not merely to maintain the supremacy of the laws of the United States, but also to guard the States from any encroachments upon their reserved powers by the general government….So long…as thus Constitution shall endure, this tribunal must exist with it, deciding in the peaceful form of judicial proceeding, the angry and irritating controversies between sovereignties, which in other countries have been determined by the arbitrament of force.

Other justice of the period committed themselves even more unqualifiedly to the state sovereignty thesis.

It is the Taney Court, therefore, rather than the Marshall Court, which elaborated the concept of *dual federalism*. Marshall's federalism is more aptly termed *national* federalism; and turning to modern issues, we may say without exaggeration that the broad general constitutional issue between the Court and the New Deal in such case as Schechter Corp. *v.* U.S. and Carter v. Crater Coal *Co.*[3] was, whether dual federalism or national federalism should prevail. More narrowly, the issue in these cases was whether Congress' power to regulate commerce must stop short of regulating the employer-employee relationship in industrial production, that having been hitherto regulated by the states. We all know how this issue was finally determined. In the fair Labor Standards Act of 1938 Congress not only prohibits interstate commerce in goods produced by substandard labor, but it directly forbids, with penalties, the employment of labor in industrial production for interstate commerce on other than prescribed terms.[4] And in United States *v.* Darby[5] this act was sustained by the Court in all its sweeping provisions, on the basis of an opinion by Chief Justice Stone which purports to be based – and logically is based –

on Chief Justice Marshall's famous opinions in McCulloch *v.* Maryland[6] and Gibbons *v.* Ogden[7] of 120 years ago. In short, as a principle capable of limiting the national legislative power, the concept of dual federalism is today at an end, with consequent aggrandizement of national power.

This, however, is only a part of the story—perhaps even less than half of it. For in another respect even the great Marshall has been in effect overruled in support of enlarge views of national authority. Without essaying a vain task of "tithing mint, anise and cummin," it is fairly accurate to say that throughout the 100 years which lie between Marshall's death and the first New Deal cases, the conception of the federal relationship which on the whole prevailed with the Court was a *competitive conception*, one which pitted the national government and the states against each other. It is true that we occasionally get some striking statements of contrary tendency, as in Justice Bradley's opinion in 1880 for a divided Court in the Siebold case,[8] where is reflected recognition of certain results of the Civil War; or much later in a frequently quoted dictum by Justice McKenna, in Hoke *v.* United States,[9] in which the Mann White Slave Act was sustained in 1913:

> Our dual form of government has its perplexities, State and Nation having different spheres of jurisdiction…but it must be kept in mind that we are one people; and the powers reserved to the states and those conferred on the nation are adapted to be exercised, whether independently or concurrently, to promote the general welfare, material and moral.

The contrary outlook is nevertheless the one much more generally evident in the outstanding results for American constitutional law throughout three-quarters of its history. Consider, for example, the doctrine of tax exemption which converted federalism into a principle of private immunity from taxation, so that, for example, neither government could tax as income the official salaries paid by the other government. Consider, too, the paradox which is illustrated in the case of Hammer *v.* Dagenhart,[10] overruled in the Darby case, in which it was held that an attempt by Congress to exclude child-made goods from the channels of interstate commerce was not a regulation of commerce, but an invasion of the police powers of the states, although by other decisions then in good standing a similar attempt by a state would have been an invasion of Congress power to regulate commerce. Thus was a realm of no-power created—a veritable laissez-faire Utopia! And all such results sprang from a conception of the federal relationship which regards the national government and the states as rival governments bent on mutual frustration, and on a conception of the judicial role which made it the supreme duty of the Court to maintain the two centers of government in theoretical possession of their accustomed powers, however incapable either might be in fact of exercising them. Indeed, maintenance of the federal equilibrium became—the due process clause aside—the be-all and end-all of judicial review.

By the *co-operative* conception of the federal relationship, on the other hand, the states and the national government are regarded as mutually complementary parts of a *single* governmental mechanism all of whose powers are intended to realize the current purposes of government according to their applicability to the problem in hand. *This is the conception on which the New Deal rests.* It is, for example, the conception which the Court invokes throughout its decisions in sustaining the Social Security Act of 1935[11] and supplementary state legislation. It is also the conception which underlies congressional legislation of recent years making certain crimes against the states, like theft, racketeering, kidnapping, crimes also against the national government whenever the offender extends his activities beyond state boundary lines. The usually cited constitutional justification for such legislation is that which was established more than a quarter of a century ago in the Hoke case, from which I quoted just previously.

It has been argued, however, that the co-operative conception of the federal relationship, especially as it is realized in the policy of federal subventions to the states, tends to break down state initiative and to devitalize state policies. Actually, its effect has, to date, usually been just the contrary, and for the reason pointed out by Justice Cardozo in Helvering *v.* Davis,[12] also decided in 1937, namely that the states, competing as they do with one another to attract investors, have not been able to embark separately upon expensive programs of relief and social insurance. The other great objection to co-operative federalism is, however, much more difficult to meet. This is, that co-operative federalism spells further aggrandizement of national power. Unquestionably it does for when two co-operate it is the stronger member of the combination who calls the tunes. Resting as it does primarily on the superior fiscal resources of the national government, co-operative federalism has been, to date, a short expression for a constantly increasing concentration of power at Washington in the instigation and supervision of local policies.

The second great structural principle of American constitutional law is supplied by the doctrine of the separation of powers. How has this principle fared at the hands of recent tendencies, and more particularly, at the hands of New Deal?

The notion of three distinct functions of government approximating what we today term the legislative, the executive, and the judicial, is set forth in Aristotle's *Politics*, but it was "the celebrated Montesquieu" who by joining the idea to the notion of a "mixed constitution" of "checks and balances," in Book XI of his *Spirit of the Laws,* brought Aristotle's discovery to the service of the rising libertarianism of the eighteenth century. It was Montesquieu's fundamental contention that "men entrusted with power tend to abuse it." Hence it was desirable to divide the powers of government, first, in order to keep to a minimum the powers lodged in any single organ of government; secondly, in order to be able to oppose organ to organ. So vague a principle, nevertheless, was bound to take color from the institutional landscape against which it chanced to be projected. In England, where the principle formerly had currency in the "literary theory" of the British constitution, it early became subordinated to the doctrine of parliamentary sovereignty and to the cabinet system. On the other hand, while the principle was formerly thought to support the accountability of administrative officials to the ordinary courts—the so-called "rules of law"—in France it was invoked from the outset in behalf of the contrasted system of "droit administrative". Nor is the explanation of the difference far to seek. Whereas England was made a nation by her law courts and her Parliament, France was the creation primarily of the Capetian administrative system.

In the United States libertarian application of the principle was originally less embarrassed by inherited institutions. In its most dogmatic form the American conception of the separation of powers may be summed up in the following propositions: (1) there are three intrinsically distinct functions of government, the legislative, the executive, and the judicial; (2) these distinct functions ought to be exercised respectively by three separately manned departments of government; which, (3) should be constitutionally equal and mutually independent; and which, (4) taken together, cover the entire field of governmental power.

Even prior to the New Deal this entire colligation of ideas had been seriously impaired by three developments in national governmental practice: first, the growth of presidential initiative in legislation; secondly, the delegation by Congress of legislative powers to the President; thirdly, the delegation in many instances of like powers to so-called "independent agencies" or commissions, in which are merged "the three powers of government" of Montesquieu's postulate. The first two of these developments have been brought under the New Deal to a pitch not formerly approximated except temporarily during the war with Germany; the third development the Roosevelt Administration resisted and even attempted to nullify in the interest to further concentration of power in the hands of the President, and during the war succeeded more or less in doing so through the creation of such agencies as WPB, WMC, OWI, etc. I cannot, of course, go into detail; I can only indicate certain achieved results.

When people talk about "presidential autocracy" they are apt, especially under war conditions, to be thinking chiefly of those powers which the President gets directly from the Constitution. Actually, a vast proportion of the great powers which the President exercises even in wartime are the immediate donation of Congress. The reassurance afforded by this fact turns out on examination, nevertheless, to be rather meager. For the truth is that the practice of delegated legislation is inevitably and inextricably involved with the whole idea of governmental intervention in the economic field, where the condition to be regulated are of infinite complexity and are constantly undergoing change. In this situation it is simply out of the question to demand that Congress should attempt to impose upon the shifting and complex scene the relatively permanent molds of statutory provision, unqualified by a large degree of administrative discretion.

Nor again, can the presidential role in the formulation of legislation for congressional considerations be reasonably expected ever to become less than it is today. One of the major reasons urged for governmental intervention is furnished by the need for gearing the different parts of the industrial process with one another for a planned result. In wartime this need is freely conceded by all, but its need in peacetime is conceivably even greater, the results sought being so immeasurably more complex.

So, both in the interest of unity of design and of flexibility of detail, presidential power today takes increasing toll from both ends of the legislative process—both from the formulation of legislation and from its administration. In other words, the principle of the separation of powers as a barrier preventing the fusion of presidential and congressional power is today pretty shaky if it is not altogether defunct.

To sum up the argument to this point: the New Deal, and the doctrines of constitutional law on which it rests, and the conception of governmental function which it incorporates, have all tremendously strengthened forces which even earlier were making, slowly, to be sure, but with "the inevitability of gradualness," for the *concentration of governmental power in the United States, first in the hands of the national government; and, secondly, in the hands of the national executive.* In the constitutional law which the validation of the New Deal has brought into full being the two main structural elements of government in the United States in the past, the principle of dual federalism and the doctrine of the separation of powers, have undergone a radical and enfeebling transformation which the war has, naturally, carried still further.

We come now to judicial review. The matter of primary interest to us in connection with this unique institution is that it is not referable—as is, for example, the President's veto power—to a specific constitutional clause, but depends on a justifying *doctrine.* In brief, this doctrine claims for the courts the power to interpret with finality the standing law, of which the Constitution is a part—indeed, the supreme part. This is on the theory that when performed by a court in connection with the decision of a case, interpretation of the standing law is an act not of *will* or *power*, but of *knowledge*; and is hence preservative of the law, and so of the Constitution when that happens to be a part of the standing law which is applicable to the case under decision. As Chief Justice Marshall phrased the matter, "Judicial power, as contradistinguished from the power of the law, has no existence. Courts are the mere instruments of the law, and can will nothing."[13]

Now whether judicial interpretation of the Constitution does preserve—or on the contrary, does *not* preserve it—is frequently a question which lies outside the realm of verifiable phenomena, it being obviously impossible in this year of grace to know what *was* intended "by the Constitution," or by the framers or the ratifiers thereof, with regard to matters which did not exist in 1787. One is reminded of an old conundrum. Query: "Does your brother like cheese?" Answer: "I have no brother." Query: "But if you had a brother, would he like cheese?"

But the critics of judicial review have never been content with this agnostic position. The earliest of them, indeed, asserted that judicial reviews was itself a standing refutation of the proposition that it preserved the Constitution inasmuch as it was never intended by the framers of the Constitution—was, in other words, founded on usurpation. Although this thesis has produced a whole library either in reaffirmation or refutation thereof, it can be disposed of for our purposes fairly briefly.

The words of the Constitution itself make it amply clear that the framers intended that both state and national courts, and ultimately the Supreme Court, should be entrusted with the duty of maintaining the supremacy of the Constitution and of acts of Congress "made in pursuance thereof" against all conflicting State constitutional and legal provisions. Furthermore, there is evidence to show that many of the framers anticipated that the Supreme Court would be entitled, and hence obligated, to interpret and apply against acts of Congress direct prohibitions upon the national legislative power, as, for example, the provision against *ex post facto* laws.[14] But at this point anything approaching certainty ends, inasmuch as the experience of the framers in 1787 with judicial review was much too fragmentary to enable them to foresee the problems to which the institution would give rise, much less, to provide adequate and binding solutions for such problems.

Even so, to characterize judicial review, or to characterize Chief Justice Marshall's opinion on the leading case of Marbury *v*. Madison,[15] as "usurpation," is an altogether extravagant use of that term. Besides, a usurpation which still stands after 142 years must long since have outgrown its original taint.

Today's critics of judicial review delve much deeper, and bring to the surface more fundamental issues. They assert that interpretation – and hence the judicial function – is not seperable from the legislative, but is a continuation of it; that preservation of the law is a superstition, and a malignant one, in that the law must constantly change to meet social needs; and finally, that since it is the tendency of judicial review to hamper this process of change it is undesirable; while some add that it is incompatible with the underlying principle of democracy – that when the majority want change they are entitled to get it, and in short order.

The thesis of the total disinterestedness of the judicial process was first brought into the question by a critic whose own disinterestedness could not be challenged, in Oliver Wendell Holmes' *Common law*, published in 1881. On the opening page of this famous work one reads: "The law draws all its juices of life from considerations of what judges rarely mention, and always with apology, I mean considerations of what is expedient for the community concerned." A generation later, a friend of Justice Holmes, Professor John Chipman Gray of Harvard, enlarged upon the former's thesis in his *Law, Its Nature and Sources*. Gray, in fact, went to the extent of asserting that interpretation is *the* law-making functions par excellence, and he quoted repeatedly and with gusto the assertion of a certain Bishop Hoadly of the seventeenth century that "Whoever hath an absolute authority to interpret any written or spoken law, it is who is truly the law-giver…and not person who first wrote or spoke them."

Then a few years ago Mr. —now Judge—Jerome Frank brought out his *Law and the Modern Mind.* Here the notion of the stability of the law is attacked as an old wives' tale, belief in which has been kept up by "the father complex," the inclination, that is, of most people—or so Judge Frank alleges—when they leave the paternal roof to seek security from some other source. In the last analysis, Judge Frank, enlarging on Gray, as the latter had enlarged before on Holmes, denies that even the interpreters of the law give us *law*—they give us only decisions, he says. The Supreme Court of the United States is, therefore, one must conclude, only an enlarged version of the wise man of primitive communities who, to keep the communal peace, dispensed a ready-made justice by the wayside to settle neighborhood quarrels.

Frank's avowed anarchism fluttered the dove-cotes even of many self-proclaimed "legal pragmatists," but it must be admitted that he has been vindicated by subsequent events in two respects at least. The demand for *social* security has today reached a volume which is utterly dismaying both because of the expectation which it voices and because of the decline in what Frank himself calls "the spirit of adventure". The second way in which Frank has been vindicated is more immediately relevant to our theme; I mean, by the extent to which the Supreme Court has overruled earlier decisions in upholding the New Deal legislation. Many of these earlier decisions were, to my mind, erroneous and needed to be overturned. Nevertheless, the confession by the Court of having committed error on such a scale and involving constitutional interpretations of such magnitude, has presented the thesis of the Court's preservative function with the sharpest challenge it has ever met.

More than that, however, when this confession of error and the consequent acts of restitution by the Court are set against the background of the ideological motivation of the New Deal legislation, they force the conclusion that judicial review has today become, like dual federalism and like the principle of the separation of powers, a secondary and subordinate factor of national power, whether wielded by President or by Congress.

And this brings us to the fourth structural element of our Constitutional Law which has latterly undergone enfeeblement. I mean the doctrine of substantive due process of law.

The due process of law clause of the Fifth Amendment reads: "nor shall any person...be deprived [that is, by the national government] of life, liberty, or property, without due process of law". The clause derives, via a statute of Edward III's time, from the thirty-ninth chapter of Magna Carta (Chapter 29 of the issue of 1225). There the King promises that "no free man" shall be imprisoned or deprived of his estate, or otherwise despoiled except "in accordance with the judgment of his peers or the law of the land (*legem terrae*)". By the phrase *legem terrae* here was meant that mode of trial which eventually ripened into the grand jury—petit jury process of the common law; and there can be little doubt that it was the main concern of the men who were responsible for the Fifth Amendment to consecrate this process.

But the circumstances which render the due process clause a fundamental element of American constitutional law was the role it has played in articulating transcendental theories of private immunity with the constitutional document. Particularly did the framers subscribe to the notion that the property right, which they regarded as anterior to government, set a moral limit to the latter's powers. Yet could judicial review pretend to operate on a merely moral basis? Both the notion that the Constitution was an emanation from the *sovereignty* of the people, and the idea that judicial review was but a special aspect of normal judicial function, forbade the suggestion. It necessarily followed that unless judicial protection of the property right against legislative power was to be waived, it must be rested on some clause of the constitutional document; and, inasmuch as the due process clause, and the equivalent "law of the land" clause of certain of the early state constitutions, were the only constitutional provisions which specifically mentioned property, they were the ones selected for the purpose.

The absorptive power of the due process clause and the equivalent law of the land clause was foreshadowed as early as 1819 in a dictum by Justice William Johnson of the United States Supreme Court: "As to the words from *Magna Charta*...after volumes spoken and written with a view to their exposition, the good sense of mankind has at length settled down to this; that they were intended to secure the individual from the arbitrary exercise of the powers of government, unrestrained by the established principles of private rights and distributive justice."[16] Thirty-eight years later the prophecy of these words was realized in the famous Dred Scott case in which Section 8 of the Missouri Compromise, whereby slavery was excluded from the territories, was held void under the Fifth Amendment, not on the ground that the procedure for enforcing it was not due process of law, but because the Court regarded it as unjust to forbid people to take their slaves, or other property, into the territories, the common property of all the states.[17] Due process of law came, in short, to mean the Court's idea of what was just.

Then with the adoption of the Fourteenth Amendment in 1868 the Court found itself presented with a vast new jurisdiction by the clause which forbids any *state* to "deprive any person of life, liberty, or property, without due process of law". Although at first the Court manifested the greatest reluctance to enter upon its tempting heritage, when it finally did so, about 1895, it discovered that the clause had meantime acquired a new dimension in the conception of liberty as *freedom of contract.* The Court now became for more than a generation the ultimate guardian, in the name of the constitutional document, of the laissez-faire conception of the proper relation of government and private enterprise—a rather inconstant guardian, however, for its fluctuating membership tipped the scales now in favor of business, now in favor of government, that is, of "the power of numbers," as Justice Matthews once put it. And in the New Deal cases, the latter tendency appears to have won out definitely. Due process of law in those cases means Congress' view of what is just, without ordinarily any correction by the Court.

In short, the same dissolving tendency is seen to be operating today upon the due process clause as upon the separation of powers principle and the dual federalism principle, in favor of legislative power and in limitation of judicial review.

The fundamental elements of American constitutional law reduce, therefore, to a single element, judicial review, and this has gradually emancipated itself from all documentary and doctrinal restraints, and even from the restraint which was originally implicit in common law jurisdictions in the judicial functions as such—the principle of *stare decisis.* But now the result of this self-achieved emancipation has been to extend and at the same time to obliterate the frontier between constitutional law and policy; and without a definite boundary to defend, judicial review itself becomes an instrument of policy, and thereby exposes itself more and more to political criticism.

The consequence is that today American constitutional law appears to be in a highly deliquescent state. The old hard-and-fast distinctions are no more. As the final oracle of due process of law the Court is still able to defend certain values like fair trial and freedom of utterance against local prejudices and unfairness; but natural legislative power itself tends to become a due process of law which is coextensive with an already nationalized social and industrial life.

The question naturally arises whether these changes in the structure of our constitutional law are likely to persist. Considering their reach and scope, the answer would seem, on the face of things, to be yes; but there is an even more compelling reason for holding that they will endure and even be enlarged in the future. This is that they spring from a common underlying cause, one moreover which transcends juridical concepts and permeates popular outlook itself. I mean, of course, that altered conception of governmental function to which I have previously referred. American constitutional law came to maturity under, and received those characteristic features which I have been sketching, from the notion that government exists simply for the purpose of supplementing and reinforcing the non-political controls of society, and especially those which rest on social superiority and economic power. The theory to which our present-day constitutional law testifies increasingly is that government should correct these non-political controls from the point of view of the theory of the equality of man. Fusion of governmental functions translates to an increasing extent into a policy of social levelling.

Although the statement is subject to important correction at points—the case of the tariff furnishing the outstanding instance—yet it can be fairly said that from the fall of the Federalist Party in 1801 to the capture of the government at Washington by the New Deal 132 years later, the Jeffersonian, libertarian conception of governmental function generally prevailed in this country, the demand for equality meantime finding satisfying expression in purely political terms, more especially in the establishment of white manhood suffrage. Nor is the reason for this far to seek; it was stated indeed by the younger Pinckney in the Federal Convention in these words: "There is more equality of rank and fortune in America than in any other country under the sun, and this is likely to continue as long as the unappropriated western lands remain unsettled....I lay it therefore down as a settled principle that equality of condition is a leading axiom of our government."

So when the great panic of 1837 stimulated demands for governmental intervention, these demands met a confident rebuke from the shrewdest politician of the period. I quote from President Van Buren's message of September 4, 1837, dealing with the then burning issue of banks and currency:

> All communities are apt to look to government for too much. Even in our own country, where its powers and duties are so strictly limited, we are prone to do so, especially at periods of sudden embarrassment and distress. But this ought not to be. The framers of our excellent Constitution and the people who approved it with calm and sagacious deliberation acted at the time on a sounder principle. They wisely judged that the less government interferes with private pursuits the better for the general prosperity. It is not its legitimate object to make men rich or to repair by direct grants of money or legislation in favor of particular pursuits losses not incurred in the public service.

What, therefore, the government ought to do, Van Buren urged, was not to revive the defunct Bank of the United States, but get out of the banking business altogether—and this in due course is just what it did do.

What a contrast is this picture to what happened ninety-six years later! That the contrast is due to an important extent to difference in political leadership is no doubt true, but political leadership does not function in a vacuum. The fact is that the *New Deal came to power because it appealed to an altered outlook on the part of a large section of the American people toward the nature and purpose of government*, to an altered expectation on their part of what government can do if it only tries hard enough. Not did this change in outlook come in a day—it was in its inception a gradual development. Yet there can be no doubt that the collapse of 1929 and the succeeding depression strengthened and confirmed this change in outlook immensely. By the same token, the new outlook is likely to persist, as is shown for example in the confident talk about sixty million jobs and the commitments which many of our public men have assumed in this connection.

So again we must conclude that the changes in the structure of our constitutional law which this article traces will be on the whole permanent ones. In Thomas Wolfe's poignant words, "We can't go home again"—if indeed we should wish to.

Our Constitutional Revolution and How to Round It Out

The Constitution of the United States contains provisions of the following three types, among others: first, those which delineate the structure of the national government; second, those which define its powers; third, those which affirm certain rights of the individual as against the powers of the national government. In the course of the last thirty-one years the Constitution has been subjected to the impact of American participation in two world wars and to that of an economic crisis which was described by the late President as "a crisis greater than war". The effect of these impacts upon the formal structure of the national government has been slight, but its effect on the other two types of constitutional provision has been such as to convert what was originally deemed to be a *Constitution of Rights* into a *Constitution of Powers*. And it is this revolutionary reversal of constitutional values which furnishes the occasion for this discourse. I have in mind *two* purposes: first, to exhibit in detail just how this reversal has been brought about—the *modus operandi* of it; and secondly, to suggest that unless we are prepared to forego altogether the values of constitutionalism, we need to give some deliberate attention to that element of the Constitution which has remained comparatively unresponsive to crisis; I mean the structural element. The point is, that a structural arrangement which once served very well may have ceased to do so, just because it has not changed along with the rest of the Constitution with which it is integrated. Let me add that most of my examples of constitutional change are based on World War II, that being by far the greatest of the three crises as well as the one in which the effects of the other two were cumulative, so to speak.

What, then, do I mean by saying that the Constitution has been transformed from a *Constitution of Rights* into a *Constitution of Powers*? I certainly do not mean to suggest that the provisions of the Constitution which deal with either rights or powers have undergone visible, verbal change, for they have not. Rather, what I have in mind is the altered actual force of these provisions nowadays as compared with what it was forty years ago. But just how has this change come about—what has been the method of it? The change has been caused by the impact of certain crises, to be sure; but in just what terms precisely has this impact been translated into constitutional terms? The answer to this question is not recondite. It is discovered as soon as we turn to consider the effect of these crises, and particularly of World War II, upon certain principles or doctrines of constitutional interpretation which have always been held to apply to the *powers* of the national government. There are five of these, and I will now proceed to describe them briefly.

The first one is the doctrine that the national government, in contrast to the state governments, is one of *enumerated* powers only. Thus, as Cooley points out in his *Constitutional Limitations*, whereas the primary purpose of a state constitution is to impose limitations on otherwise plenary power, the primary purpose of the national constitution is to grant powers that would be otherwise non-existent. And especially does this contrast hold, Cooley adds, as to the provisions of the two types of Constitution which have to do with the legislative power.

The second principle of constitutional interpretation to which I refer is a corollary of the principle of the separation of powers. It is the doctrine that the legislature, i.e., Congress, may not delegate its powers. The source of this doctrine is John Locke's *Treatise on Civil Government*, where Locke is at great pains to emphasize the distinction between the prerogative of the King and the "legislative power" of Parliament. Of course what

Locke was thinking of was that if Parliament ever did delegate its powers to the King, the King could by virtue of his absolute veto always prevent the delegated power from being recovered.

The third doctrine above referred to is the doctrine that *this is a government of laws and not of men*. What is meant, more distinctively, is that everything that is done by an agent of government must be traced to some legal warrant; that is, the executive may not, for the most part, act except on the basis of a very definite delegation from the Constitution or on the basis of an act of Congress.

The fourth principle or doctrine is that *the powers of government are limited by certain outstanding rights of the individual*. Our forefathers were brought up in the belief that certain rights of the individual are anterior to government and that government was not endowed with power to transgress such rights. On the contrary, it was a trustee of them. Indeed, one of the main, if not the *principle*, reason for government was the protection it could affort such rights.

Fifth, and finally, we have what is not so much a doctrine as an *institution* or *practice,* the recognized right of the courts, and ultimately of the Supreme Court, to set their interpretation of the Constitution above even that of the legislature when they are asked to enforce its laws. And the consequence of the judiciary's acting after the legislature is that it is in a position to make its view of the Constitution prevail in particular cases, while that view will also be very influential in determining future readings of the Constitution by the other branches of the government as well as by the Court itself.

Let us now see what has happened to these different doctrines within late years and especially as the result of World War II. To begin with, war has itself undergone great development in recent times. The war power, as it was known to the framers of the Constitution, embraced, if we are to follow Hamilton's language in *The Federalist*, three relatively simple elements. In the first place, there was recruiting, which was on a voluntary basis for the most part. Secondly, there was the problem of supply, and in the main it would seem from Hamilton's language that this problem was expected to be met by purchases in the open market. Of course once war started, on the battlefield and in the war theater, there might be "requisitions," a subject which was discussed at great length in those days by writers on the law of nations. In the third place, there was the power to command the forces; that is, to dispose them. That, of course, belonged to the President of the United States, as Commander-in-Chief.

War today is a very different affair. In World War II the whole of our American society was regimented. Labor was regimented, industry and agriculture were regimented, even talent was regimented for use in propaganda work; and so on and so forth. War today is, in the functional sense, *total war*, in that it brings into operation all of the forces of the society that is involved. This functional totality is, in turn, the result of two things: conscription and technical progress. The first great conscript army was the *levée en masse,* which was proclaimed by the first French Republic in the fall of 1792 when the European powers began invading French territory. Prior to that time, forces were largely volunteer and mercenary. As to technical progress, I don't need to go into that subject further than to point to the culmination of it in the atomic bomb. But technical progress and the necessity of maintaining at the front the vast forces which are the product of conscription, those two facts simply mean that war while it is waging absorbs all the energies of society, which means in turn that a tremendous strain is placed on governmental powers and so on the Constitution itself.

What, then, has been the effect of war on the idea that this is a government of enumerated powers. In a word, the effect has been to water this idea down very decidedly. It is an interesting fact that while the Constitution says Congress has the power "to declare war," it doesn't say that anybody has the power to *wage* war. That no doubt was the result of the rather simple idea that people had of war in those days. As early, nevertheless, as 1795 a Philadelphia lawyer got up in the Supreme Court, which then sat in Philadelphia, and argued that the power to wage war did not come from the Constitution but stemmed from the fact that the United States is a nation. The power, he contended, was inherent in the American people as a community which possessed all the rights of any nation at international law, one of which was the right to wage war. One of the Justices accepted the argument, another one repudiated it, while the rest of the Court thought it unnecessary to pass on the question.

One hundred and forty-one years later, in 1936, the doctrine that the Court snubbed in 1795 was accepted by it *in toto*, and indeed with certain extensions and improvements. I quote Justice Sutherland's words for the Court on the occasion referred to:

> A political society [reads the passage referred to] cannot endure without a supreme will somewhere. Sovereignty is never held in suspense. When, therefore, the external sovereignty of Great Britain in respect of the colonies ceased, it immediately passed to the Union.

It results that the investment of the Federal government with the powers of external sovereignty did not depend upon the affirmative grants of the Constitution. The powers to declare and wage war, to conclude peace, to make treaties, to maintain diplomatic relations with other sovereignties, if they had never been mentioned in the Constitution, would have vested in the Federal government as necessary concomitants of nationality [299 U.S. 304, 317–18].

But, you may ask, what difference does it make whether ours is a government of *enumerated* power or a government of *plenary* powers in the waging of war? It makes just this difference, that under the doctrine of enumerated powers you must go to the Constitution to find a special warrant for the things that are necessary to be done, but that under the doctrine of a plenary *inherent* war power, you resort to the Constitution only to find out if there is definite language which *forbids* the things necessary to be done. The doctrine of inherent powers, in other words, *makes constitutionally available all of the resident forces of the United States as a national community in the waging of war.* It makes all of the resources of the nation constitutionally available.

We now turn to the proposition that the legislature cannot delegate its powers. That was cast overboard for purposes of war as early as World War I. The Congress of the United States was suddenly confronted with the problem of adapting legislative power to the exigencies of war, a vast new range of subject matter that had never before been brought within the national government's orbit, and at the same time to gives its legislation affecting this enlarged subject matter a form which would render it easily responsive to the ever-changing requirements of a naturally fluid war situation. How could that be done? There was only one way and that was to say to the President, you may do this, you may do that and the other thing, and to lay down only a minimum of restraints upon the exercise of these broad powers. Take, for example, the lend-Lease Act that preceded World War II. In this Act the Congress of the United States told the President that he could beg, borrow, steal, manufacture, or "otherwise procure" anything that he thought would be conducive to the waging of war and that he could lend, loan, grant, give away, or "otherwise dispose of" these things to anybody on the face of the earth whose possession and use of them might be deemed "to contribute to the defense of the United States."

But now, the precedents for the Lend-Lease Act and other legislation of the same kind in World War II were created in World War I. For example, there was the Food and Fuel Control Act which delegated to President

Wilson the power to deal in foods and fuels, power which he turned over to Mr. Garfield and Mr. Hoover, and there was very little language indeed used in the act which was of a restrictive character. Also there was the Trading with the Enemy Act, the Espionage Act, the Selective Service Act. All of these committed vast po wers to the President of the United States. It is interesting, I think, to note the fact that World War I was to a very great extent a rehearsal for World War II from the point of view of the solution of certain important problems of constitutional law.

We come now to our third doctrine; that this is a government of laws and not of men. It was the Civil War which brought about the demise of that doctrine so får as war is concerned. Under the Constitution the President is Commander-in-Chief of the army and navy and of the militia of the several states when in the service of the United States. This clause is expounded by Alexander Hamilton in *The Federalist* No. 69. I shall not brother to read the passage; what it boils down to is this: Hamilton points out there how very different the President's power as Commander-in-Chief is from the power of the King of Great Britain, that the President's power is merely that of top general and top admiral. Thus no officer can be created who can give orders to the President; no officer of the armed services can be created to whom the President may not give orders, but the integration of the power of Commander-in-Chief with that of President is not apparently regarded by Hamilton as being significant at all. There was, in other words, no particular reason from Hamilton's point of view why somebody other than the President might not be made top admiral and top general. For it was as purely military power that Hamilton found in the clause.

And as late as 1850 you find the United States Supreme Court, speaking by Chief Justice Taney, also contrasting the power of the President as Commander-in-Chief with the power of the King of England, in the following words:

His [the President's] duty and his power are purely military. As commander-in-Chief, he is authorized to direct the movements of the naval and military forces placed by law at his command, and to employ them in the manner he may deem most effectual to harass and conquer and subdue the enemy.

In the distribution of political power between the great departments of government, there is such a wide difference between the power conferred on the President of the United States, and the authority and sovereignty which belong to the English crown, that it would be altogether unsafe to reason from any supposed resemblance between them, either as regards conquest in war, or any other subject where the rights and powers of the executives arm of the government are brought into question [9 How. 603].

And the Commander-in-Chief clause remained "the forgotten clause" of the Constitution until April 14, 1861, when Fort Sumter surrendered, whereupon President Lincoln proceeded to take a series of measures of the most remarkable character. There was a period of more than ten weeks between the surrender of the Fort Sumter and the convening of Congress by the President's summons. During that period the President elected to handle the war situation entirely on his own without any assistance from Congress. As to why he did this there has always been a great deal of speculation. For one thing, he was by no means persuaded that Congress would agree with him as to the necessity of meeting the situation with force. And there were other reasons. But whatever they were, let me show you into what extraordinary courses Mr. Lincoln was driven in sustaining his policy.

During this period of ten weeks he enrolled the state militias in a huge volunteer army to serve for ninety days; created a volunteer army of forty thousand men to serve for three years; added twenty-three thousand men to the regular army; eighteen thousand men to the navy; paid out two million dollars from unappropriated funds in the Treasury; closed the Post Office to "treasonable correspondence"; subjected passengers to and from foreign countries to new passport regulations; suspended the writ of habeas corpus in certain localities; caused the arrest and military detention of persons who were "represented to him as being engaged in treasonable practices"–and all this, except for the call to the state militias, without any statutory authorization.

In his message of July 4, Lincoln informed Congress of most of the things he had done. He didn't tell them quite all. He didn't tell them about the two million dollars until after the thing was smoked out in May of the following year, when he had to admit he had done that too. But at any rate Congress promptly ratified everything the President had done with respect to the army and navy. The habeas corpus suspension, however, was not ratified, and the year following Lincoln effected a general suspension of the writ throughout the country. By the act of March 3, 1863, this more sweeping measure was ratified in language which seemed to indicate that Congress conceded the President's right to take it. In the meantime, in August, 1862, Lincoln had established a limited draft by presidential order, although the great Draft Act was not passed by Congress until July, 1863.

But to get to the point. Some of these things were ratified by Congress, some were not. Some of them, indeed, had their intended effect before Congress met. What conclusion is forced upon us? It is obvious that many of these acts assert for the President for the first time in our history *an initiative of indefinite scope in meeting the domestic aspects of a war emergency;* and in meeting them, by what was virtually an exercise of *legislative* power.

And, in World War I, Mr. Wilson imitated Lincoln to some, although not to a great extent. That war was far removed from the country and there was time for Congress to act. Even so, in some cases Mr. Wilson fell back upon his powers as Commander-in-Chief. Thus Mr. Creel's Committee on Public Information was a creation of the President, and the War Industries Board was another such creation. From early 1918, this latter agency, under Mr. Baruch's chairmanship, constituted a highly important segment of the government of the United States internally, and for as long as the war lasted.

In World War II you get a great expansion of this quasi-legislative power of the President, one that is simply amazing when you come to study it in detail. The precedent were there, to be sure, but these precedents were certainly blessed with a prolific progeny. What is more, Mr. Roosevelt took his first step of this nature some fifteen months *before* the outbreak of "shooting war". I mean his action in handing over fifty destroyers in September, 1940, to Great Britain in return for some leases of naval bases in British possessions in the West Atlantic. That measure gave rise to considerable controversy at the time and Mr. Jackson, then Attorney General, felt called upon to render an opinion in support of it. The Attorney General being the Administration's family lawyer, it is not his business to criticize what the family wants, but to show how well justified the family is in wanting it. So Mr. Jackson rendered an opinion on the "destroyer deal," and his argument boiled down to a neat little pun. First proving that the President had long been recognized as having the power to *dispose* the forces, he next inserted after the word "dispose," the word "of"!

But the most remarkable development of presidential legislative power is to be found in the creation of the so-called "war agencies". In April, 1942, I wrote the Executive Office of the President and asked them to give me a list of all these war agencies and to specify to me the warrant by which they had been brought into existence. I got back a very polite answer which listed forty-three executive agencies, of which thirty-five were admitted to be of purely executive provenience. Six of these raised no question because what they amounted to was an assignment by the

President of additional duties to already existing officers, and of officers whose appointment had been, in most cases, ratified by the Senate. For example, our participation in the Combined Chiefs of Staff was an additional duty, of course, of certain military and naval commanders, and the Combined Raw Materials Board was a like creation. Nobody was assigned to such duties who was not already in an office to which they were logically relevant. But take the Board of Economic Warfare, the National Housing Agency, the National War Labor Board, the Office of Censorship, the Office of Civilian Defense, the Office of Defense Transportation, the Office of Facts and Figures, the Office of War Information, the War Production Board, which superseded the earlier Office of Production Management, the War Manpower Commission, and later on the Economic Stabilization Board, all these and many others I could recite were created by the President simply by virtue of power which he claimed as Commander-in-Chief.

One result of the creation of these agencies was this: the President conferred upon them certain powers, some of which he had from statute, some of which he claimed as "Commander-in-Chief in wartime". But in either case the agencies themselves rested on no statutory foundation. And the result of this defect was curious enough. The question came up finally in the Court of Appeals of the District of Columbia whether an order issued by the War Labor Board was enjoinable and the court said, "No, it is not enjoinable because the law knows nothing about it. What we are asked to enjoin is only 'advice' to the President, the War Labor Board being only an 'advisory body'." That is, the court did not have before it a situation in which anybody was *doing* anything of which the court could take any notice. In short, the strictly legal status of these agencies was that of *advisory bodies merely*, although actually the President almost invariably followed their advice, that is, converted their advice into governing policy.

Oftentimes, moreover, even the powers concerning the exercise of which an agency "advised" the President were not to be traced to any statute, in which case violation of the orders of the President based on such "advice" was not an offense against the United States. What penalty was there, then? It is here that you encounter a very interesting phenomenon called *indirect sanctions*. When the President, for example, ordered Montgomery Ward to put a "maintenance clause" in their labor contracts, he had no statutory authority to do so, nor did the War Labor Board. Nevertheless, when Montgomery Ward refused to do as they were bid they speedily found that the seventy Post Office employees who had been handling their parcel post orders for years hadn't put in an appearance.

But ordinarily the indirect sanctions took this form: if the employers didn't follow the presidential line, they were informed they couldn't have priorities; and if the employees failed to comply with the orders, the director of the Selective Service was ordered to make a re-check of these gentlemen and the recalcitrants were confronted with the prospect of being put on the firing line.

An interesting illustration that occurred in World War I of indirect sanctions was furnished by the following episode involving the Remington Arms Company of Bridgeport, Connecticut, in the fall of 1918. The narrative is by a member of President Wilson's War Labor Board: "After a prolonged strike and the War Labor Board had rendered a decision, the strikers still refused to return to work. The President of the United States wrote the strikers upholding the board, pointing out that an appeal from it should be made through the regular channels and not by strike; and that if the strikers did not return to work, they would be barred from any work in Bridgeport for a year; that the United States Employment Service would not obtain positions for them elsewhere, and that the government would no longer consider their exemptions based on the theory that they were useful in war production. This ended the strike." Indirect sanctions *can* be very effective.

Nor did Mr. Roosevelt hesitate to state very early the theory on which he was operating. I refer to his famous address to Congress of September 7, 1942, when, in asking Congress to repeal certain provisions of the Emergency Price Control Act, he said:

I ask the Congress to take this action by the first of October. Inaction on your part by that data will leave me with an inescapable responsibility to the people of this country to see to it that the war effort is no longer imperiled by threat of economic chaos.

In the event that the Congress should fail to act, and act adequately, I shall accept the responsibility, and I will act.

At the same time that fair prices are stabilized, wages can and will be stabilized also. This I will do.

The President has the powers, under the Constitution and under Congressional acts, to take measures necessary to avert a disaster which would interfere with the winning of the war.

I have given the most thoughtful consideration to meeting this issue without further reference to the Congress. I have determined, however, on this vital matter to consult with Congress....

The American people can be sure that I will use my powers with a full sense of my responsibility to the Constitution and to my country. The American people can also be sure that I shall not hesitate to use every power vested in me to accomplish the defeat of our enemies in any part of the world where our own safety demands such defeat.

When the war is won, the powers under which I act automatically revert to the people—to whom they belong.

Here certainly is a very remarkable proposition. The President of the United States is claiming the right to repeal an act of Congress although he does not deny that Congress had the power to pass the act. To be sure, other Presidents have occasionally refused to enforce acts of Congress, though very rarely, and always on the ground that the acts in question were unconstitutional, and particularly that they constituted an invasion of the President's powers. That is what Andrew Johnson did in 1867, but nobody on the face of the earth can deny that Congress had the right to pass the Emergency Price Control Act, or that it was the only organ of government that did have that right; and yet the President is claiming the right to repeal the law. Undoubtedly that is a claim of power to suspend the Constitution and as to a very important feature of it, namely the division of power between the President and Congress. Any candid man must admit that a situation may arise in war in which it would be necessary to suspend the Constitution. Thus Abraham Lincoln admitted that he didn't know whether or not he had suspended the Constitution when he suspended to writ of habeas corpus; but said he, "Are all the laws to go unenforced in order that one law may be preserved?" But on the occasion when Mr. Roosevelt spoke, Congress was in session and it seems to me that if the situation is so desperate as to require suspension of the Constitution, the safe view to take is that Congress ought to be considered to be aware of the fact as well as the President, and so be joined in the enterprise.

I turn now to *the effect of war on private rights*. I think perhaps the best illustration of the effect of war on private rights is the growth of the use of military conscription. To begin with, when the Constitution was framed Congress was authorized to provide for the calling of the militia into the service of the United States to enforce the laws, to suppress insurrection and repel invasion. The clause of the Constitution bestowing this power reflects the old common law, and indeed legislation from the time of Edward III, when the King of England was conceded to have the power to call the militia out from the counties for the purpose of repelling invasion. Otherwise the militia could be required to serve only within the country's borders.

The first suggestion of conscription in this country for the raising of a national army was made by James Monroe when he was President Madison's Secretary of State during the War of 1812. Daniel Webster, then a member of the House of Representatives, made a most savage attack on the measure, calling it a "dance of blood" and a "gamble with death" and the House of Representatives failed to act till the end of the war made it unnecessary to do so. During the Civil War you get a draft to suppress "insurrection," that at least was the theory of the federal government. So you see the draft was still kept within the categories of repelling invasion, suppressing insurrection, and enforcement of the laws.

During World War I, of course, we had the Selective Service Act under which an army was raised to serve abroad. That circumstances gave rise to a very interesting case, in which Mr. Hannis Taylor made an attack on the constitutionally of the act with an interesting argument which was well buttressed with history. Chief Justice White, speaking for the Court, brushed the argument aside and sustained the draft. No doubt he necessarily must have done so, but he might have exhibited better manners.

Next we have in the act of September, 1940, the first *peacetime* draft, and there was assurance given that these men would not serve abroad, But when war came fifteen months later that clause of the act was quickly repealed. But the final step was Resident Roosevelt's surprise message of February 5, 1944, in which he asked for a conscription of labor, a suggestion which did not get to first base in Congress. This growth I have traced of the idea of conscription is an instructive illustration of the way in which previous privileges and immunities are eroded by the impact of war, or even by its imminence.

Finally, I wish to devote a moment or two to the subject of judicial review—the power of the Court to pass on the constitutionally of laws and other acts of public authority. The War Emergency Price Control Act of 1942 contained a clause to the effect that only the Emergency Court which the act created could enjoin an order of the OPA and that only in that court could the question of the validity of the act be raised. In the Yakus case, decided in 1944, the Supreme Court, after having avoided the issue as long as it could, finally found it necessary to consider the constitutional question this provoked. Yakus was convicted in a United States District Court of Violating an OPA order and sentenced to fine and imprisonment. He appealed to the United States Supreme Court on the ground that the District Court had not permitted him to plead the unconstitutionally of the act and of the order which he has charged with violating. The Supreme Court, however, sustained the sentence. In other words, Yakus was convicted without being permitted to plead his constitutional rights.

That is pretty serious business. Our lawyers and judges have always maintained that there is a fundamental distinction between *jurisdiction* and *judicial power*. A court has no jurisdiction except such as Congress has specifically given it. That is perfectly clear from the Constitution. On the other hand, once a court has jurisdiction of a case it is thereby put in possession of the power—the *judicial power*—to decide it in accordance with the law. Now, however, the Congress of the United States comes along and says, "Yes, you can decide cases under the Price Control Act in accordance with the law, except that you may not consider the Constitution, the Supreme Law, in this connection." Three of the Justices—one being former Justice Roberts—dissented along the line I have suggested, but unavailingly. For the country was engaged in *total war*, and the judicial power was regimented, like everything else.

But this, you will say, is simply the law of war. A great deal of it is *rather* the law of "emergency," a term which has come to have, nowadays, a very indefinite connotation. The first case ever decided by the United States Supreme Court in which an emergency was recognized that was not plainly war was the case of Wilson *v.* New, back in 1916. In the New Deal period, however, the justification of "emergency" was repeatedly invoked by the Court in support of legislation which by the older test of constitutional law were at least of doubtful validity. I have in mind the Minnesota Moratorium case, the Gold Clause cases, and some of the Social Security Act cases. Furthermore, it is a lesson of our constitutional history that a power claimed successfully on the justification of war emergency may come later to be assimilated to the normal peacetime powers of government. This happened in respect to the power of the national government to give its paper notes the legal tender quality; and I am not at all certain that some, if not most, of the measures put into operation over industry and labor by the government during World War II may not be justified under certain New Deal cases as regulations of commerce. It is, in short, impossible to say yet to what extent World War II has remade the Constitution not only for war, but for peace as well.

But I have dwelt too long on these details, I am afraid. I come now to my second main point. What you have here, in consequence of all these developments, is a tremendous increase in the powers of the national government. These additional powers of the *national government* are, moreover, all brought to focus and application upon the situations for which they were devised *by the President*—in other words, *the aggrandizement of the national government had meant the aggrandizement of the presidential office.*

Is there any change in the structural constitution indicated or demanded by this tremendous flow of power into the national government and through it into the hands of the President? That is the question to which I wish now to address myself briefly.

Of course, we want two things: an efficient government, a government that is capable of acting on serious matters before it is too late; we also, however, wish to preserve some of our constitutional liberties. What, then, can we do in the present situation?

In answering this question we need to look around and see what materials we have for constitutional reconstruction—for structural improvement, if such improvement is demanded. What materials have we got? I do not think that judicial review need be taken intro account. We can not rely upon judicial power in time of war or in time of great emergency; and, very naturally, since the Supreme Court is not going to take the risk of forbidding that things be done the failure to do which might turn out eventually to have been fatal to the country. No judiciary can assume such a risk. We still have, however, Congress, and Congress has one great power which, although it has sometimes been defied, sometimes circumvented, is yet a very great power, and the is *the power of the purse.*

Can we establish, then, a relationship between the President and Congress that will, on the one hand, *support* the President, and on the other hand *control* him? In 1940 I published a book called *The President Office and Powers*, and in that book I made a suggestion which some writers have taken up since, and which I myself still think is a good suggestion, and that was *that a new type of Cabinet be created.* The existing cabinet is not a success at all from the point of view of controlling the President, and not very much of a success from the point of view, even, of informing him. I have read Miss Perkins' book and I am now reading Mr. Hull's *Memoirs;* and each of them had said things which are not designed to strengthen one's admiration for the Cabinet as a body. The history of the Cabinet is to no small extent the history of a board the meetings of which are more or less ceremonial and casual. Meanwhile, the President gets his real counsel and advice from other quarters entirely.

Andrew Jackson had his "kitchen cabinet," President Roosevelt had his "brain trust," and other Presidents have had the equivalent of these. And in a recent article in the *American Political Science Review*, the authoritative writer, Mr. Don K. Price, expressed the opinion that the Cabinet was not a success, even from an administrative point of view, i.e., from the point of view of coordinating administration. The individual members of the Cabinet are doubtless very useful persons, often very well qualified persons, but the joint wisdom of the Cabinet is frequently very much less than the sum total of the wisdom of its individual members.

How, then, should this new Cabinet be made up? As I have said, we want a body which will support the President, and which, on the other hand, will be able to control him. We want a body which will facilitate action and which, on the other hand, will keep it within bounds. I think that a Cabinet made up in part of leading members of Congress would answer our prescription. Thus let us suppose the creation of a joint legislative council by the Senate and the House of Representatives, and let us suppose further a custom by which the President of the United States was required to consult that body regularly. He would then have to consult people who were not eating his salt, and who were under no obligation to him whatsoever, and yet who, on the other hand, by putting the stamp of their approval upon his proposals, would be able to facilitate their enactment into law. You would have a body, in other words, that would be both capable of controlling and, on the other hand, of supporting the President, of securing that the things needing to be done would be done on time; but, on the other hand, that the judgment that they needed to be done represented a wide consensus, a vastly wider consensus than the President can by himself supply.

The question may arise in your minds whether such an arrangement would be constitutional, inasmuch as office-holders cannot hold seats in Congress. But notice that I am not saying that there shouldn't be a Secretary of State, I am not saying that there shouldn't be a Secretary of the Treasury or an Attorney General. They are the chiefs of certain administrative departments. And then, of course, the Chairman of the Interstate Commerce Commission and the Chairman of the Federal Trade Commission, and so on and so forth, also are administrators, and are disqualified by the Constitution for election to Congress. But the answer is that membership in the Cabinet has no necessary connection with an administrative job. *Membership in the Cabinet is not an office*, it is simply a function which the Presidents of the United States have come automatically to fasten upon the chiefs of the great executive departments. But there is no reason in the world why the President of the United States should not make up a Cabinet consisting of the leaders of Congress—or, for that matter, of participants in this gathering.

Imagine the President of the United States desiring a Cabinet of the sort I have indicated. He would say to Mr. John Doe, "Now, I am making you Secretary of the Treasury, but So-and-So, the Chairman of the Houses Ways and Means Committee, is the man with whom I shall devise my fiscal policies, and you are expected to follow those out." And the same as to the Secretary of the State, "Now, I am going to make you Secretary of State, Mr. Roe, but I am going to settle my policy on foreign affairs in conference with Mr. So-and-So, the Chairman of the Foreign Relations Committee of the United States Senate, and you will take orders from him, or from me—take the orders that he and I agree are the ones that are desirable in the present situation."

I see no constitutional objection to this. Another objection, perhaps, is a little more difficult to meet, and that is that oftentimes, as is the case at present, the Congress of the United States represents one party and the President represents another party. What about that? I think that is really an argument *for* the proposal I am making. I think that the President of the United States has accumulated into his hands such vast powers—or, let us put it more justly—he has had such vast powers thrust into his hands, that it is high time that *the political significance* of the office be watered down a bit.

In time of emergency, the President and Congress co-operate, whether the President be of one party and Congress of another or otherwise. In time of war that happens; and in addition we have a maxim that partisanism should stop at the water's edge. In short, it is recognized that in very serious situations there ought not to be all this tugging and hauling between the President and Congress, this political competition between them. *But why should we reserve best methods for crises?* Why shouldn't we use best methods in times when there isn't a crisis, and when the use of best methods would perhaps prevent a crisis from arising? So I think that the argument which is urged on that ground, that the President might belong to one party and the Congress to another, really constitutes, in the last analysis, a good argument for the proposal.

Frankly, I think there is a great deal of nonsense to what I might describe as "the political racket". The attitude that should be taken toward government, to my mind, on the part of those who exercise its powers is that they are confronted with a job of housekeeping, and more and more is that the case as the government extends its guidance more and more to the normal activities of the people. To repeat, it seems to me that the attitude has to be taken toward *government*, that it *has become today a species of communal housekeeping*, and from that point of view the relationship between the President and Congress should not be one of political competition and bicker; it should be one of trying to arrive by compromise at those solutions which are, as the result of conference and consultation, agreed upon as being the best.

The President of the United States today occupies a very paradoxical position. Mr. Wilson says in his *Constitutional Government of the United States* that the President is "the leader of his party," and that he is "the leader of the nation". But the fact of the matter is that the two roles don't harmonize always. The President of the United States, as the leader of the party, will be tempted to do things that as leader of the nation he would not think of doing, and sometimes he will do them.

Take the situation in which Mr. Truman found himself in relation to the Taft-Hartley Act. I am not saying that the Taft-Hartley Act is a perfect law by any means; but it could have been made a better one if Mr. Truman and the people who were promoting the measure had gotten together and discussed matters with the purpose in mind of arriving at the best solution, that is to say, the solution that came nearest to meeting popular expectation. You would then have had a better act. Mr. Truman, however, sat back and saw the bill going through Congress with what he considered its objectionable features, and then when it was finally laid on his desk the proceeded to write a venomous veto message of it. Presently, however, the bill was passed over his veto; and the day following he came out with the statement, "I am still opposed to the law, but as the President of the United States I recognize that it is my duty to enforce it, and shall do so"—or words to that effect. Well, I think that there represents an ambivalent attitude toward the presidential office that is not wholesome, one for which, however, the present stereotyped relationship between President and Congress rather than Mr. Truman is to blame.

As a matter of fact, if I had my way I would go a considerable step farther. Thus I think those people in Congress who tinkered up the pending amendment to limit presidential tenure to ten years at the outside, simply missed a splendid opportunity, owing to the fact that they were so intent on showing how strongly they reprobated the late President Roosevelt's action in running for a fourth term. As somebody has said, having been unable to beat F.D.R. when he was alive, they decided that they could at least smear him in the grave. At any rate, the controlling motive was obviously political, and so the authors of the proposal did not give themselves the opportunity of discussing an amendment that would have been worth discussing. I mean an amendment which would disqualify the President of the United States from succeeding himself. The point is that *the President of the United States ought not have to think about his political future, because when he has to think about his political future his party demands that he do so* inasmuch as his political future is the party's. Relieved from that necessity, the President could be the kind of a President that George Washington was, or as close an approximation thereto as his character and abilities enabled him to be.

And in this connection the following passage from the famous Farewell Address is worthy of thoughtful consideration. The Spirit of party, it reads, "serves always to distract the public councils and enfeeble the public administration. It agitates the community with illfounded jealousies and false alarms, kindles the animosity of one party against the other, foments confusion, riot and insurrection. It opens the door to foreign influence and corruption, which find a facilitated access to the government itself through the channels of the party passion. Thus the policy and the will of one country is subjected to the policy and will of another. There is an opinion that parties in free countries are useful checks upon the government and serve to keep alive the spirit of liberty. This, within certain limits, is probably true, and in governments of monarchical character patriotism may look with indulgence, if not with favor, upon the spirit of party. But in those of a popular character, in governments purely elective, it is a spirit not to be encouraged. From their natural tendency it is certain there will always be enough of that spirit for every salutary purpose, and there being constant danger of excess, the effort ought to be by force of public opinion to mitigate and assuage it. A fire not to be quenched, it demands vigilance to prevent its bursting into a flame lest instead of warming it should consume."

I think there is a stupendous amount of good sense to that, good even, or indeed especially, for the present hour.

Well, now, ladies and gentlemen, I have laid my case before you. In a word, what I have said is that the Presidency of the United States needs reintegration, and the legislative power comprising the President and Congress needs reintegration. This end could be greatly furthered by a new types of Cabinet, but the achievement could be greatly reinforced by neutralizing the Presidency politically.

"I see no need to amend our constitution," said Louis Brandeis in 1915. "It has not lost its capacity for expansion to meet new conditions unless interpreted by rigid minds which have no such capacity. Instead of amending the Constitution, I would amend men's economic and social ideas. Law has always been a narrowing, conservatizing profession. What we must do in America is not to attack our judges, but to educate them."

When those words were spoken, they had a timely wisdom, a prophetic wisdom. Indeed, they might be fittingly termed the prologue of the New Deal revolution. But that revolution, plus two great wars, has raised new constitutional problems and especially the problem of *the sufficiency of the structural Constitution*, for its dual task of adequate action in crisis and the preservation of democratic values. I am not saying, mind you, that the Presidency has become a matrix of dictatorship. What could be more trite? But I am saying that the Presidency has reached a position of unhealthy dominance in the system, one which instead of expediting the formation of national policy stands often in the way of it.

How is this problem to be met? We certainly cannot rely on the judges to do it, we must needs rely on the political branches, so first of all upon popular understanding and demand. If given the opportunity to lay my case before this distinguished company I have made no contribution to that end, the fault is my own; the pleasure of the occasion is also mine.[18]

References

1. The writer is indebted to the Claremont Colleges, publishers of his *Constitutional Revolution, Ltd.* (1941), for the privilege of using some of the matter in that volume in the preparation of this paper.
2. 21 How. 406 (1859).
3. 265 U.S. 495 (1935); 298 U.S. 238 (1936).
4. 52 Stat. 1060, 29 U.S.C. Sec. 201 (1938).
5. 312 U.S. 100 (1941).
6. 4 Wheat. 316 (1819).
7. 9 Wheat. 1 (1824).
8. *Ex parte* Siebold, 100 U.S. 371 (1880).
9. 227 U.S. 328 (1913).
10. 247 U.S. 251 (1918).
11. 49 Stat. 620, 42 U.S.C. 7 (1935).
12. 301 U.S. 619 (1937).
13. Osborn *v.* The Bank, 9 Wheat. 738, at 866 (1824).
14. Art. I, Sec. 9, para. 3.

15. 1 Cranch 137 (1803).
16. The Bank of Columbia *v.* Okely, 4 Wheat. 235 (1819).
17. Scott *v.* Sanford, 19 How. 393 (1857).
18. In 1879, his senior year at Princeton, Woodrow Wilson published an article in the *International Review* entitled "Cabinet Government in the United States". In his Introductory Note to a reissue of this piece last year under the auspices of The Woodrow Wilson Foundation, Judge Finletter says, "The key suggestion... was to set up a Cabinet from among members of the House and Senate." But Wilson himself, putting the question, "What is the change Proposed?" answers thus: "Simply to give to the heads of the Executive departments—the members of the Cabinet—seats in Congress, with the privilege of the initiative in legislation and some part of the unbounded privilege now commanded by the Standing Committees," and he invokes the authority of "Chief-Justice [*sic*] Story" in support of a similar suggestion (see pp.8–9). Despite some rather confusing language at one point, it seems clear that Wilson did not contemplate putting members of Congress at the head of the executive departments, or on the other hand, making the latter members of Congress, otherwise he would have been obliged to discuss—certainly to indicate his awareness of—the constitutional ban on office-holders being members of congress. His proposal was apparently only an elaboration of the one which George H. Pendleton of Ohio had been agitating ever since the close of the Civil War and which in 1881 received the endorsement of a distinguished Senate committee. Congressman Kefauver of Tennessee has received it within recent years.

Additions to the Mason–Garvey Bibliography*

1. "The Pelatiah Webster Myth," 10 *Michigan Law Review* 619–26 (May, 1912).
2. "Tenure of Office and the Removal Power Under the Constitution," 27 *Columbia Law Review* 353–99 (April, 1927).
3. "Moratorium Over Minnesota," 82 *University of Pennsylvania Law Review* 311–16 (1934).
4. "The Schechter Case – Landmark, or What?" 13 *New York University Law Quarterly Review* 151–90 (January, 1936).
5. "The Constitution as Instrument and as Symbol," 30 *American Political Science Review* 1071–85 (December, 1936).
6. "Liberty and Juridical Restraint," in Anshen, ed., *Freedom: Its Meaning* 84–103 (1940).

*Alpheus Mason and Gerald Garvey, eds., *American Constitutional History: Essays by Edward S. Corwin* 216-29 (1964).

7. "Some Aspects of the Presidency," 218 *Annals of the American Academy of Political and Social Science* 122–31 (November, 1941).
8. "The Presidency in Prespective," 11 *Journal of Politics* 7–13 (1949).
9. "The Impact of the Idea of Evolution of the American Political and Constitutional Tradition," in Persons, ed., *Evolutionary Thought in America* 182–99 (1950).
10. "Of Presidential Prerogative," 47 *Whittier College Bulletin* 3–29 (September, 1954, first edition; revised July 1, 1955).
11. "Presidential 'Inability,'" *national Review* 9–10 (November 26, 1955).
12. "Franklin and the Constitution," 100 *Proceedings of the American Philosophical Society* 238–88 (August, 1956).

Table of Cases

VII

Drug Laws and Drug Use in Nineteenth-Century America

— *David T. Courtwright*

Consider a mystery. During the nineteenth-century, Americans' consumption of alcohol declines by more than two-thirds, from 6.6 gallons per person of drinking age per year to only a little more than 2 gallons. Most of the decline came before the Civil War; from 1870 onward consumption was stable and, by historical comparison, low. At the same time, beer, a more beneficent form of beverage alcohol, was gaining rapidly in popularity over hard spirits, the per capita consumption of which declined by one-half between 1870 and 1900. Yet a powerful and well-organized prohibition movement emerged during these same decades, a movement that by 1903 had thirty-five million Americans living under some form of prohibition regime.[1] The law was being applied in coercive fashion to a social and medical problem that seems to have been getting better rather than worse.

Consider a second mystery. The pattern of American drug consumption and abuse was in many respects the reverse of alcohol use during the nineteenth-century. Opiate addiction was a rarity in the early 1800s, and cocaine use of any sort was nonexistent. But after 1860 there was a major, sustained epidemic of opiate addiction, and after 1885, a national cocaine binge that peaked in the early 1900s. Yet the legal response to all of this was delayed, fragmentary, and generally ineffectual. Municipalities with substantial Chinese populations enacted ordinances against opium dens, but enforcement efforts were infrequent and of short duration. A correspondent who walked through San Francisco's Chinatown in 1887 saw hundreds of Chinese "smoking in full view of the street, and nothing is thought of it. The police disturb them not".[2] Festive opium smoking among New York City's Chinese residents was likewise quite open. If whites, particularly white women, were seen to be smoking with the Chinese, then there might be a temporary police crackdown, as happened in Denver in 1880. The real motives behind such actions were revulsion against miscegenation—the racial stereotype was of a fiendish, long-fingernailed Chinese man preying upon a wayward, narcotized young beauty—and the desire to protect whites from acquiring an alien vice. All that was achieved, however, was a measure of segregation; the dens themselves were soon back in business.[3] An opium-smoking subculture flourished well into the twentieth-century.

The control of medicine narcotics was even more lax. European doctors who came to the United States blamed much of the addiction epidemic on the ready availability of drugs like morphine. It was one of the disadvantages, a Danish physician tartly remarked, of being "the freest country in the world, [where] everybody can do as he pleases".[4] A 1903 report of the American Pharmaceutical Association conceded that in many drug stores customers could obtain cocaine and morphine as easily as Epsom salts.[5] The same was true of needles and hypodermic syringes. Until the New York Legislature finally enacted a law in 1911, addiction specialist Charles Towns recalled, "a boy of fifteen could buy a syringe as easily as he could buy a jack-knife".[6] Those who preferred discretion could make such purchases through mail-order catalogs.

Most states did not enact comprehensive drug control laws until well after 1900. These laws typically restricted the sale of opium and cocaine products (and, in some places, of cannabis and chloral hydrate) to those having a prescription written by a licensed practitioner. The pharmacists who sold the drugs had to make a permanent record of the transaction. Only patent or proprietary medicines having very small amounts of the regulated drugs were exempt from the prescription and record-keeping requirements. On paper, this represented a reasonably thorough system of control. In reality, state laws were passively and sporadically enforced. Drugs were mailed directly to users or sold by pharmacists who knew that their chances of being detected and prosecuted were nil. As late as 1915 the U.S. Public Health Service's resident expert on drug laws, Martin I. Wilbert, complained that direct state appropriation for the enforcement of antinarcotic legislation were practically nonexistent.[7]

The federal government failed to address the problem until 1906, the year of the passage of the Pure Food and Drug Act and the District of Columbia Pharmacy Act.[8] It was not until 1919 that the most important coercive aspect of federal policy—the denial of legal drugs to addicts—was firmly in place and upheld by a (narrow) majority of the Supreme Court. When the axe fell, it fell hard, but the puzzle is why there was such a long delay, in view of the vigor of the alcohol prohibition movement. Why was it that late nineteenth-century Americans did practically nothing in the midst of a drug epidemic, even as they used the law to attack an alcohol problem that was at a historically low level?

To begin to answer this question it is necessary to understand something of the origins and development of the widespread usage of opium and coca products and preparations in nineteenth-century America. Opium was above all a medicine, the one indispensable item in the armamentarium. It was unsurpassed as an analgesic and very effective in the treatment of diarrhea, a serious and potentially fatal disease of which our ancestors mush complained. Opium and its alkaloids were thus often used in medical preparations prescribed by physicians, purchased as nostrums, or concocted by the patients themselves. "Recipe for Cure of Cholera, Diarrhea, Dysentery, Cramp Cholic and Cholera Morbus," Confederate artilleryman Miles Bennet wrote confidently in his diary, "*Certain* cure—One pint of good Brandy, one ounce of Laudanum [tincture of opium], one ounce of gum Camphor, half ounce of Cayenne pepper. Mix well together and for dose take teaspoonful."[9]

The risks of medication with opiates were overdose and, if the treatment continued too long, addiction. What happened to "Mrs. B.," a thirty-four-year-old mother and widow who lived near Rochester, New York, was typical. She suffered from a uterine disorder that she palliated with laudanum, to which she became addicted. In the course of six years she consumed upward of an ounce of laudanum a day. She tried repeatedly to quit but always relapsed because she craved the drug and because of the stress of having to raise her young children alone.

Mrs. B.'s case appeared in the medical literature in 1871.[10] Over the next three decades she was joined in her misfortune by tens of thousands of other addicts—with one important difference. They generally became addicted through the injection of morphine rather than the ingestion of opium solutions. The 1870s and 1880s were the flush times of hypodermic medication. American doctors of this era were notorious for their willingness to inject patients with morphine, the principal active alkaloid of opium. Injection was a more immediate, powerful, and pleasure-producing experience, hence more likely to lead to addiction. Since patients could easily acquire drugs and syringes on their own, they could continue the injections even after the physician had ceased giving them. Those who suffered from a chronic, painful affliction or injury were particularly likely to do so. Numerous Civil War veterans became addicted, although they never made up the majority of addicts. We know this because several surveys published after 1878 showed that 60 to 80 per cent of those addicted to medicinal opiates were female.[11]

The hows and whys of narcotic addiction were much discussed. The condition was blamed on everything from defective heredity to nervous exhaustion to professional carelessness. What is striking is that this discussion was carried on mainly within the context of medicine rather than law or criminology. Chinese opium smokers may have been regarded with contempt, as were white criminals and prostitutes who became addicted to drugs, but the medical addicts, who were in the majority, were regarded more sympathetically. They were sick, or victims of unlabeled patent medicines, or they had been introduced to drugs under therapeutic auspices. Those whose addiction was of medical origin were not at all likely to behave violently or spread the habit to others. On the contrary, they were highly secretive. Mrs. B. went ten miles out of her way to purchase her laudanum so that her neighbors would not suspect her dependence on the drug. Post–Civil War Americans were unlikely to demand the rigorous exercise of the state or local police power, let alone the inchoate powers of the federal government, against persons who engendered no compelling threat to others. When, by contrast, the owners of rendering plants asserted their "private rights" to go on operating their fetid establishments, New York City's Metropolitan Board of Health did not hesitate to prosecute, for the noxious odors they released were feared as a potent source of deadly disease.[12]

The relatively sympathetic attitude toward medical opiate addicts also reflected the values of the larger culture. Then, as now, Americans were much concerned with blameworthiness. The poor, the incapacitated, and the homeless were afforded only the meanest of charity if they were held to be responsible for their own plight. Yet disabled servicemen and their families were given generous pensions, and victims of disasters like the 1871 Chicago fire received prompt financial help from all over the country.[13] The difference lay in the perception that they were not at fault.

This same preoccupation with blame and unworthy behavior helps to explain why prohibitionists were able to rapidly advance their cause.

Drunkards were drunkards not because they took alcohol as a medicine but because they frequented saloons and imbibed for pleasure. Their language was foul and their behavior obstreperous, just the opposite of the secretive, heavily tranquilized opiate addicts. Drunkards were also men, often of immigrant, Catholic, or lower-class backgrounds. Narcotic addicts were largely women, native-born, Protestant, and outwardly respectable. The prohibition movement had a pronounced nativist and middle-class bias. This is not to say that prohibition was simply a matter of prejudice; alcoholism was by any rational criterion a more serious problem than opiate addiction. The social costs it generated seemed to justify strong measures. Even reformers who balked at prohibition espoused the disfranchisement and incarceration of alcoholics in specially designed institutions where they might be forced to learn "useful habits" while recovering from the ravages of drink. A drunkard was a menace and a burden. An addict was someone's mother.

This situation changed, and as it did, the moral and emotional basis for stricter narcotic laws was laid. During the 1890s and early 1900s, medical journals, textbooks, and educators broadcast the dangers of the excessive administration of opium and morphine. At the same time new and safer therapies were popularized, such as the use of acetanilid for rheumatic and neuralgic disorders or naphthalene for diarrhea. Fewer narcotic prescriptions were written and fewer new medical addicts were created. Self-medication with patent medicines abated, thanks to the labeling provisions of the Pure Food and Drug Act and the efforts of muckraking journalists to alert the public to the dangers of their habit-forming ingredients, Opiate addicts began to decline in number—except in the underworld, where opium smoking persisted along with the use of morphine and, after 1910, heroin.

As the less blameworthy medical addicts diminished in number relative to the nonmedical addicts, perceptions of who drug users were and how they behaved inevitably began to alter. They were more often described as criminally inclined, psychopathic, and otherwise deranged men of the lower orders. They were like drunkards, though they had enslaved themselves to a different drug. The suggestion made in all seriousness by a Newark, Ohio, physician in 1889—that everyone would be far better off if alcoholics were converted into morphine addicts—would have struck middle-class Americans of thirty years later as risible. By 1919, drink and narcotic drugs were both firmly identified with dangerous and deviant behavior.

Attitudes toward cocaine use and addiction underwent a similar transformation, although within a more compressed span of time. Cocaine was the miracle drug of the 1880s. During that decade glowing articles testifying to cocaine's manifold usefulness appeared in European and American medical journals. Sigmund Freud's 1884 paper "Über Coca" recommended the drug for stomach upsets, tuberculosis, typhoid fever, asthma, the treatment of opiate addiction and alcoholism, and as a local anesthetic. On this last point his advice was sound: cocaine's anesthetizing properties were of great utility in eye, nose, and mouth surgery. The problem was that Freud and other enthusiasts touted cocaine in virtually panacean terms. They recommended it for too many conditions—everything from depression to hay fever—and without adequate attention to its potential for abuse and dependence. No less an authority than William Hammond, the former surgeon general, discounted the possibility of full-blown addiction to cocaine. It was, he said, more like the tea or coffee habit than addiction to opium or its derivatives.

The results of this may be readily guessed. There was a wave of iatrogenic (literally, "doctor-produced") cocaine addiction. By the early 1890s medical journals were publishing numerous case histories of men, women, and even children who had become "cocainists". Many of the men were doctors who had unwisely treated their own ailments with liberal applications of the miracle drug. There were also reports of cocaine overdose deaths, as in the case of an Arizona man who died from convulsions an hour after his dentist injected his gums with four grains of cocaine.

The early, cautionary articles about cocaine are of as mush interest for what they do not say as for what they do say about the dangers of misapplying the drug. No one proposed a crusade against cocaine, or anything like a prohibitionist stance. As with the opiates, the debate was initially conducted within a medical and scientific framework: doctors gave advice (sometimes sharply) to other doctors about whether, how, and with what precautions a new alkaloidal remedy should be used.

The tone soon changed. Articles appearing in the popular and medical press from the mid-1890s onward emphasized that while iatrogenic cocaine addiction was still a reality it was rapidly bring supplanted by a more sinister pattern of abuse. E. R. Waterhouse, a St. Louis physician, remarked that few people knew the true extent of the cocaine habit in the lower walks of city life. He described a local drug store that was in reality a "cocaine joint" where pulverized cocaine crystals were wrapped in paper and sold to prostitutes for ten cents apiece. Admitted through a portiere to a dimly lit back room, the prostitutes sniffed their purchases on the premises, ringing a bell when they wanted a clerk to bring them more. A woman reporter who managed to peck into the room spied a dozen lower-class prostitutes, black as well as white, seated on benches or sprawled across the floor. They were, Waterhouse commented, lost in a sort of dreamy intoxication, "not unlike the Chinaman 'hitting the pipe' in Dope Alley". Although the proprietor of the cocaine den was arrested under a statute regulating the sale of poisons, Waterhouse noted that the establishment was still going full blast, and hundreds of other people were buying the drug and sniffing it in the privacy of their own homes. "Some law," he concluded "should be made to reach this new state of affairs."

In using the expressions "joint" and "den" and "hitting the pipe," Waterhouse was drawing an explicit analogy between cocaine sniffing and opium smoking. That he did so is revealing, since opium smoking was virtually the only form of opiate use that was universally condemned and subject to prosecution. Morally, the cocaine sniffers he described were indistinguishable from the opium smokers: both groups used the drug as an intoxicant, were prone to vice and crime, and—no small matter in the St. Louis of 1896—were known to keep mixed racial company.

Waterhouse's allegation that cocaine use was fast becoming an indulgence of the vicious and criminally minded of both races and his belief that legislative action was needed to control its use were often repeated by doctors and public officials over the next several years. New details were added to the story. The declining price of cocaine, by 1897 a mere two dollars an ounce, had greatly increased its nonmedical use, especially among "the tramp and low criminal classes" of the cities. Many of cocaine's underworld devotees had used and become addicted to other drugs before discovering cocaine. When their funds were exhausted by their cocaine appetite, they resorted to petty theft and other crimes to obtain funds to purchase more of the drug.

The growing popularity of cocaine among blacks, who would purchase a nickel's worth of the drug and go on a "coke drunk," caused the greatest concern. Editorials in two leading professional journals, the *Journal of the American Medical Association* and the *American Druggist and Pharmaceutical Record*, pointed to increased cocaine use by blacks as a justification for restrictive legislation. "I am convinced," declared Colonel J. W. Watson of Georgia in 1903, "that if some stringent law is not enacted and enforced against [cocaine sniffing] the habit will grow and extend to such proportions that great injury will result; in fact, great and extend to injury has already resulted, for I am satisfied that many of the horrible crimes committed in the Southern States by the colored people can be traced directly to the cocaine habit".

Whether and to what extent there was a cocaine-inspired crime wave at the turn of the century has been much debated by historians. It is possible that the allegations of Watson and others were exaggerated as a disingenuous way of attacking prohibition, the idea being that voters might balk at banning liquor if they thought that drinkers would turn to cocaine instead. "I am not an advocate of whiskey," the colonel slyly observed, "but I am fully convinced that if a man feels he must have a stimulant, the best thing he can do is to get a bottle of liquor". Whatever the merits of this bold assertion (and they are dubious), it is striking that cocaine should be compared so unfavorably with alcohol. Only two decades earlier doctors had been urging the opposite course, that coca preparation could be successfully used in treating alcoholics.

In the end we are left with an excellent illustration of the principle, which Harold Hyman was wont to drill into his students, that legal history cannot be properly studied apart from social history. The presence or absence, the enforcement or nonenforcement, and the content and timing of antidrug laws are not fully comprehensible without an understanding of who was using drugs and why they had begun using them. One of the primary reasons that the bulk of legislation came after 1900 was the growing perception that opiate and cocaine use and addiction were moving from private misfortune to public threat, from the respectable province of medicine and middle-class ladies to the fallen masculine world of alleys and dives. This was not, to be sure, the only reason. Twentieth-century drug laws were something more than the inevitable, legally codified expression of prejudice against disliked or deviant groups. They were also configured by diplomatic, constitutional, and political pressures, particularly at the federal level. The worsening social characteristics of the drug-using population are best understood as a necessary, rather than a sufficient, cause for the emergence of a police-oriented system of narcotic control—a system that by the 1920s and for many decades thereafter was among the most punitive in the world.

References

1. Mark Edward Lender and James Kirby Martin, *Drinking in America: A History* (New York: Free Press, 1982), 87--132, 196.
2. Letter from "J. F. M.," reprinted in Samuel B. Collins, *Theriaki: A Treatise on the Habitual Use of Narcotic Poison: How the Habit Is Formed, Its Consequences and Cure* (Laporte, Ind.: n.p., 1887), 64.
3. "The Chinese New York: Idolatry in Baxter Street Feasting and Smoking Opium," *New York Times*, February 16, 1874, 5: Henry O. Whiteside, "The Drug Habit in Nineteenth-century Colorado," *Colorado Magazine* 55 (1978): 52–54. In Los Angeles the police left Chinese smokers alone; only white smokers were occasionally prosecuted. See C. W. Bonyge to Hamilton Wright, August 8, 1908, Records of the U.S. Delegation to the International Opium Commission and Conference, 1909–1913, Record Group 43, National Archives, Washington, D. C. A partial exception to this generalization is Chicago, where police raids in the 1880s were reportedly more successful in breaking up public opium dens. Rather than ceasing, however, opium smoking apparently shifted to private quarters. See Charles Warrington Earle, "Opium-Smoking in Chicago," *Chicago Medical Journal and Examiner* 52 (1886): 105–6.
4. C. Stensen, "Misbrug af Opium og Morfin i Amerika," *Ugeskrift for Laeger* 7 (1883): 165–67.
5. E. G. Eberle et al., "Report of Committee on the Acquirement of Drug Habits," *Proceedings of the American Pharmaceutical Association* 51 (1903): 476.
6. Charles B. Towns, "The Peril of the Drug Habit and the Need of Restrictive Legislation," *Century* 84 (1912): 582.
7. Martin I. Wilbert, "Efforts to Curb the Misuse of Narcotic Drugs: A Comparative Analysis of the Federal and State Laws Designed to Restrict or to Regulate the Distribution and Use of Opium, Coca, and Other Narcotic or Habit-Forming Drugs," *Public Health Reports* 30 (1915): 893-923 (comment on enforcement appropriations at 898).
8. A year earlier, in 1905, Congress passed a law gradually prohibiting the non-medical use of opium in the Philippines, but this did not affect the continental United States.
9. Miles S. Bennet diary, 71, Eugene C. Barker Research Center, University of Texas, Austin. Women often kept similar formulas in their recipe books; e.g., *Mrs. McKenney's Cook Book* (MS, n.d., probably 1830s–1860s), 77, 83, 88, 91-92, Daughters of the Republic of Texas History Research Library, San Antonio, Texas.
10. In Alonzo Calkins, *Opium and the Opium Appetite* (Philadelphia: J. B. Lippincott and Company, 1871), 152.

11. For more details on the nature and extent of medically related opiate addiction see chapters I and 2 of David Courtwright, *Dark Paradise: Opiate Addiction in America before 1940* (Cambridge, Mass.: Harvard University Press, 1982).
12. Details in the board's *Annual Report* (New York: Westcott, Union Printing House, 1866), 36–37. Harold M. Hyman, *A More Perfect Union: The Impact of the Civil War and Reconstruction on the Constitution* (Boston: Houghton Mifflin, 1975, 306 summarizes prevailing postwar attitudes toward state and federal power.
13. Robert H. Bremner, *The Public Good: Philanthropy and Welfare in the Civil War Era* (New York: Alfred A. Knopf, 1980), 150, 191.

VIII

Commitment Law, Family Stress and Legal Culture: The Case of Victorian Alabama

— *John S. Hughes*

As the Confederacy's founding fathers were meeting in Montgomery, Alabama, to launch their revolutionary regime, a far less dramatic and almost unheralded reform was commencing in the university town of Tuscaloosa in 1861. In April the Alabama Insane Hospital, the first and only such institution in the state's history, opened its doors and encouraged families to commit their disturbed members. Fittingly enough, the first inmate was a forty-eight-year-old Confederate recruit who suffered, perhaps understandably, from a madness brought on by the "political excitement".[1]

Unlike this inaugural inmate, most of the seven thousand Alabamians committed over the next forty years suffered from derangements that were more private and less connected with public affairs. Private grief and family distress more often eclipsed political turmoil in the lives of average folks. Even while the war was under way, the commitment dramas of Alabama's families only rarely reflected the political or economic circumstances. Private, even deliberately hidden, realities, it seems, contributed at least as mush to shaping the emerging Victorian legal culture of southerners as did the public and powerful forces of disunion, war, and Reconstruction.

Commitment provided a powerful and unprecedented process that expanded the legal options of average people.[2] In less than a generation

Alabamians came to accept commitment as a solution to many problems in their families' lives. In doing so, they subtly changed their legal culture—that is, the ideas and behaviors that gave vitality to their legal system. Moreover, this reliance on commitment came to alter their perceptions of where private and social problems diverged.

Victorian southerners had at their disposal few charitable institutions designed to alleviate either personal or social distress. Above the local level, which provided often haphazard church support and public poor relief, there was an absence of alternatives for families experiencing distress. Age-old problems caused by senile elders, deranged members, spouse abuse, drug use excessive drinking, embarrassing eccentricity, petty criminality, or the unwelcome dependence of unmarried adult daughters all created stress within Alabama's families. As genuine and deeply troubling to relatives and neighbors as these concerns often were, few would have considered them social problems. Legitimate and respected public institutions to meet these concerns were still lacking.

The opening of the Alabama Insane Hospital provided the institutional framework for translating family distress into recognizable social problems. Thereafter, when families proved unable to care for the disturbed, when they simply became exasperated, or when the person's conditions became a public nuisance, they could look to outsiders, in this case doctors and the courts, to help them vent their frustration. Physicians and the courts rather the family thus came officially to be recognized as the ultimate experts in what was best for the afflicted.

Alabama's history of commitment shows, however, that this translation of family distress into a social problem by no means left families powerless. In a wholly unexpected way the process actually empowered families. As we shall see, insanity was an amazingly vague category. Lay persons certainly had no precise meaning for the concept. Neither, it turns out, did the medical authorities. And, unlike in criminal proceedings, the courts offered no definition at all. But the lack of clarity in the diagnosis of insanity meant that a great many conditions—indeed, all those noted above—could be and on occasion were subsumed under the label. In an ironic way, then, the deference to authority required by this medical-legal process actually empowered Alabama's inexpert families to formulate their own conclusions about behavioral deviance. In doing so they exploited the new commitment process and thereby placed many kinds of domestic distress in a realm reachable by law.

Rapid Acceptance of the Hospital

Dr. Peter Bryce, the asylum's only superintendent until his death in 1892, promised the state's families that if they committed patients soon after the disease appeared, a cure was possible, even likely.[3] Within a short time Alabamians embraced his optimism. No matter how many new inmates Bryce received, there were always more families pleading for the admission of wayward members. According to an economy of insanity, as it were, the public's demand grew even more rapidly than the hospital's ability to supply space. In July 1862, only about a year after its opening, the asylum held but 31 inmates. By 1869, at the height of Reconstruction and amidst fiscal peril, the inmate population climbed to 191, in 1875 to 365, and by 1886 there were 733 inmates. In 1896 the then seriously over-crowded Insane Hospital housed 1,215 patients and was turning away as many applicants as it accepted. In 1900 Bryce's successors had managed to make room for 1,486 deranged Alabamians. No amount of expansion ever solved the problem of crowding .[4]

Architecturally, the asylum itself impressed its beholders as few buildings anywhere in the South.[5] By the 1890s it constituted the largest single structure anywhere in Alabama, and probably anywhere for hundreds of miles in all directions. No traveler on the busy Black Warrior River bordering the hospital on the north, or on the railroad that stopped at its front gate to the south, could easily forget the Insane Hospital or the images of authority and permanence it projected.

Even the many who never saw the asylum in person had heard of it. In his annual report for 1897 the superintendent boasted that the asylum was "by far the largest public charity in the State; there is hardly a hamlet or family that is not interested in us".[6] Even those who had not committed members acknowledged the hospital's place in their society when they offered distressed neighbors words of support and condolence, or when they whispered gossip about the hidden history of an acquaintance's lunacy. By the 1880s hundreds of former inmates had drifted back into the larger society, carrying tales of the asylum and providing constant reminders of the institution's presence.

In a single generation Alabama's residents passed from an age when the state lacked any respectable public, or even private, institution to care for the insane. Commitment to the hospital had become one of the most important and most familiar legal mechanisms for dealing with domestic distress. A century after Peter Bryce admitted his first patient, Alabama novelist Harper Lee observed casually in *To Kill a Mockingbird* that her silent and peculiar character Boo Radley might have profited from a "season in Tuscaloosa".[7] Few Alabamians would have failed to catch her meaning.

The Hospital as a Legal Institution

Though promoted exclusively as a medical establishment and viewed as such by the state's families, the Alabama Insane Hospital was fundamentally a legal institution. Few families probably gave much thought to the legal framework that supported the institution. They understandably cared little about the considerable extent to which medicine had become and adjunct to law. But statutory provisions for commitment—the people's link to the hospital—were essential because the institution held virtually all of its patients against their wishes. Almost every patient who passed through the asylum before 1900 came at the behest of others who acted in what they believed to be the best interests of the patient, the patient's family, and neighbors. As a house of incarceration, then, the hospital relied absolutely on the support of the free society's laws and courts. It was, in this narrow sense at least, not unlike a prison.

Historians, sociologists, and others have long made much of the similarities between asylums and penitentiaries; and in a great many respects the comparison is apt. In both, inmates ordinarily live highly regimented lives in carefully constructed, artificial environments designed by their keepers to amend deviant behavior. In antebellum America the founders of both kinds of institutions projected and optimism that through benevolent authoritarianism, the lives of the wayward could be salvaged, disciplined, and rendered productive. By the century's end most of this optimism had eroded, leaving behind only a residue of authoritarianism and discipline. Few of the keepers still preached a philosophy of cure; most focused instead on the onerous chore of maintaining the growing numbers of the state's wards.[8]

The literature comparing asylums and prisons has focused principally on the common aspects of daily life and the inmates' "careers". Less attention has been directed to the crucial process by which outsiders became transformed into inmates. In this regard, criminals and lunatics alike followed paths that passed through legal institutions and procedures that legitimated the loss of freedom and incarceration.

For the most part the similarity ended there. Legal procedure for accused criminals' cases was far more rigorous than for the allegedly insane. Prospective hospital inmates received none of the traditional guarantees accorded to accused criminals. Unlike criminals, supposed lunatics travelled their paths to confinement under no presumption of "innocence". In most states during the late nineteenth century families and friends could commit a person on the certificate of one or two respectable physicians (only one was required in Alabama). The majority of the insane were indigent, and in their cases the law also required papers from the county probate judge that were to be drawn after an investigation of the person's supposed insanity. In Alabama private patients (the minority whose families rather than the state paid for their maintenance) needed no order from the probate court. State law required only a certificate of insanity, advance payment, and a proper bond.

Civil proceedings for the indigent insane bore no resemblance to a criminal trial. With some important exceptions, few states during the nineteenth century required the presence of the supposed lunatic before the judge who officially sanctioned the confinement. Often the prospective patient received no notice at all of the legal proceeding. Some patients, in fact, learned of it only when they arrived at the asylum. Probate judges generally accommodated families in such matters of secrecy and took care to reduce any unnecessary exposure of private grief.

Commitment proceedings and criminal trials differed in another quite significant respect. In addition to formal notice and the opportunity to defend themselves, criminal defendants were accused of a violation of a law that was clearly spelled out. Whether it be larceny, assault, or murder, for example, all parties generally accepted the court's definition. And because crimes were offenses subject to definition, they likewise could be challenged through the presentation of evidence according to prescribed rules. Only clear and compelling evidence sufficed in criminal trials to warrant the taking of a person's freedom. The burden of proof lay with those seeking to take away liberty.

For prospective mental patients the legal journey to incarceration was more muddled. Insanity, unlike criminality, lacked anything approaching definitional precision. Legal, medical, and lay notions of insanity varied widely. Moreover, few procedural obstacles exited to prevent families from making expansive use of term. The general practitioners who supplied the certificates of insanity possessed no real expertise in mental disease. Even as late as the 1890s a great many of Alabama's doctors were only marginally trained. A few had graduated from respectable institutions, but most had attended haphazard proprietary medical schools known for their easy admission policies, ill-organized lectures, and high graduation rates. A good many older physicians at the turn of the century were only apprentice trained. But in a larger sense, the supposed quality of the doctors' training was beside the point. Even the best medical schools offered lectures on insanity only on an elective basis.

The incarceration of insane persons was acceptable to a society that otherwise jealously guarded the ideal of liberty because the insane person, unlike the criminal, engendered pity rather than contempt. Those responsible for the forced confinement of family members or friends—whether that person be a parent, child neighbor, family doctor, probate judge, or hospital superintendent—could rest assured that their act, trying and painful as it often was, could be defined as humane and altruistic, In support of the concept of insanity as a disease were the legitimating forces of the state's public policy, its medical elite, and the law.

Routine Commitment in Alabama: Law without Lawyers

As is true of many procedures that operate outside public scrutiny, the actual process of commitment in Victorian Alabama often lapsed into a ritual do informal as hardly to merit being called a proceeding. Under state law the probate judge could, if he chose, call a jury to determine whether the person under investigation was actually insane. Careful reading of the thousands of judge's orders in the hospital's records office reveals, however, that this practically never occurred. More often the judge, usually from a rural county, knew personally or by reputation some or all of the parties involved. In such cases the calling of a jury would have risked the suggestion that the judge, an elected official, suspected something dishonorable. Most judges acknowledged their own ignorance of insanity and showed considerable deference to families, who were often neighbors and were always constituents, and to the doctors who lent their prestige to the process.

Many probate judges had no legal training; none was required. In addition, families only rarely sought out counsel. As a result, this increasingly important process of law developed largely without the routine participation of lawyers. Institutional incentives to require procedural rigor were consequently limited. Just as there were no real experts in insanity to oversee this new and emerging process, neither were there experts in law.

Superintendent Bryce, however, stopped short of admitting everyone whom the nonexpert families and courts considered proper inmates. From its inception the hospital's statutes gave preference to persons suffering from acute mental disease (that is, from insanity of recent standing and thus presumably more curable). Bryce personally urged this policy, and with good reason. He realized that if he admitted large numbers of the chronically insane he would soon have no other kinds of patients populating his wards. The chronically insane seldom improved, and once admitted often occupied valuable bed space until they died.

Despite his unflagging efforts, Bryce could not keep out chronic cases entirely. Statutes forced him to accept them whenever he had space available and no acute case had presented itself. As a result, more and more incurables found their way into the asylum. Though Bryce and his successors tried hard to release many of the harmless incurables, they seldom succeeded. In most cases families either disappeared, abdicated all responsibility, or steadfastly refused to care again for these chronic unfortunates. Dr. James T. Searcy, who took over as superintendent after Bryce's death, complained to the trustees in 1897 that "many efforts are made to get into the Hospital persons who are simply dependent character, sick, or feeble objects of charity. We have necessarily to guard with great care this point in accepting patients. We have had to decline some even after they were brought to our door, because their applications grossly misrepresented them in this particular."

State law provided Bryce and Searcy with only one imperfect way to alleviate the problem of admitting these incurables. Before any commitment could proceed, someone at the place of commitment (usually a family member but sometimes the doctor or the judge) was required to respond to a printed questionnaire that solicited specific information about the length of the current attack, how the insanity was manifested, and whether the person was dangerous, clean or filthy, and so on. Given this information, the hospital's staff could screen unfit patients and give preference to acute over chronic patients. But those who responded to the questions generally had no previous experience with insanity. In addition, some general practitioners and judges acquired experience with these questionnaires and counseled families on what kinds of responses had succeeded in the past. As a result, the hospital always faced the growing problem that Searcy bemoaned in 1897: unfit applicant showing up at the door. And more often than not, the feeble and incurable were not turned away. Charity dictated that a place be made for them.

The hospital's questionnaire had another, more powerful, effect on the commitment process. According to the statutes governing commitment, judges submitted the answers to the superintendent before they took any other action. Only after the superintendent agreed to admit the patient was the judge authorized to investigate the person's sanity. "When informed that the patient can be received," the Alabama code of

1876 stated, "the judge must call one respectable physician and other credible witnesses and fully investigate the facts in the case". This assured that the probate judge's investigation would be only a formality, because everyone knew that the hospital's experts considered the facts sufficient to warrant confinement. In most cases the superintendent's willingness to accept the application created a clear presumption that the person involved was truly insane. It was indeed a rare probate judge who ruled at this point that the party was sane.

Contributing further to making the judicial process only a technical formality, the statutes did not require that the judge give the supposedly insane person any notice of the proceedings. Neither was the judge required to order the person to be presented in court. Many judges committed persons they had never seen. Ordinarily commitments, then, shared these features: the hospital approved the patient before any legal proceeding; and when that proceeding occurred, the person about to be committed received no notice, appeared before no magistrate, and marshalled no "defense".

A quarter of a century ago sociologist Erving Goffman offered a sort of sociology of commitment in his famous study of asylums as total institutions: "The society's official view is that inmates of mental hospitals are there primarily because they are suffering from mental illness. However, in the degree that the 'mentally ill' outside hospitals numerically approach or surpass those inside hospitals, we could say that mental patients distinctively suffer not from mental illnesses, but from contingencies." By "contingencies" Goffman meant largely the changing circumstances of the prospective patient's domestic situation. In discussing this same issue, Goffman's fellow sociologist Edwin M. Lemert said in 1946 that families committed certain of their members not so much for mental illness per se as for "deviations...from customary role expectations which increase [their] social visibility".

When it opened in 1861, the Alabama Insane Hospital offered a new remedy to families distressed by the deranged, eccentric, violent, or embarrassing behavior of their members. Moreover, by defining behavioral deviance (like alienation of affection, subtle threats, actual violence, delusions, and so on) as a disease curable at the Hospital. Alabama's families acquired a new and potent perspective on age-old problems. A lax legal process made the new medical intervention possible. Indeed, the legal system's uncritical acceptance of insanity as disease facilitated doctors' appropriation of the problem. But unlike other medical concerns such as tuberculosis or yellow fever, the object of the intervention lacked any clear definition. Consequently, when legal process opened this remedy to Alabama's lay families, it empowered them to reach a wide range of "contingencies".

Rationales for Commitment

While it is true that commitment served many ends, there exists little evidence to support the familiar melodramas of false imprisonment. Alabama seems to have been largely lacking in sinister and grasping relatives who lurked in its shadows and schemed to lock up innocent family members in order to exploit some hard-earned life savings. To be sure, not all who sought to confine family members operated from unalloyed altruism. Many acted from ulterior motives that mingles with and supported reasons more justifiable in humanitarian terms. But within the complexity of motivations one point seems fairly consistent: most who sought out the probate judge to commit a family member saw it as a burden and took up the heavy task out of distress, exasperation, and often love.

Most did not, however, act from medical necessity. Sociologist Goffman, Lemert and others were correct; the clinical classification of a person's behavior as a "mental disease" was largely irrelevant. Most of the persons responsible for committing others to the hospital understood nothing of insanity as a disease, except perhaps that medical and legal elites assured them that it was such. Ordinary people knew only of changed behavior in a loved one and of the domestic distress that the change had caused.

In most cases families tried to solve their problems at home and sought the help of the hospital only after more private remedies failed. In 1865, while the asylum was still quite small, Bryce admitted twenty-one patients. The average length of their present attack was over four years. These data, while inexact, offer some valuable insights. Bryce got his information on the duration of his patients' insanity through answer to the questionnaire filled out by family members or their doctors. Reports of insanity lasting for years, then, came not from physicians specializing in insanity as a clinical entity but from relatives measuring the duration of distress.

For patients admitted in 1870 the length of attacks remained high, at slightly over five years. A decade later, however, the average plummeted to only four months, reflecting Bryce's success in keeping away chronic cases. The figure also reveals that the hospital, which was quite crowded in 1880, had begun to turn away many cases of long standing. Bryce's success in restricting admissions to recent cases was short-lived. By 1890 the average length of attack had reached two and a half years.

In summary, Alabama's families generally sought out the probate judge after having coped for a protracted period with a member's insanity. Despite doctors' commonplace analogies to physical disease such as tuberculosis or typhoid, management of insanity followed a rather different course. Families only occasionally were reacting to something analogous to a medical emergency. More often, they were responding to problems that had eroded patience.

Marriages in Trouble

Commitment histories of this period frequently told stories of unhappy marriages. To modern eyes these nineteenth–century cases appear better suited to divorce court then to probate court. But divorce remained rare in Alabama throughout the period, even though it was becoming more common in the United States during the late nineteenth century. Residents could file for divorce in chancery courts, but only on narrow grounds: physical incapacity to consummate the marriage, adultery, desertion (for at least two years), imprisonment (for at least two years with in a term lasting at least seven), crimes "against nature," and, beginning in 1870, habitual drunkenness. Needless to say, a great many sources of matrimonial friction failed to make this rather scant list.

In any event, few Alabamians viewed legal divorce as a workable solution to an unhappy marriage. Some who faced exceptional problems relieved their distress by committing their spouses to the hospital in Tuscaloosa. Several factors made this a viable alternative. First, commitment statutes set out no grounds for inanity. Courts, in fact, left definition of the condition almost entirely up to others, mostly family members and their doctors. As we have seen, even lawyers were largely absent from the process. Statutes governing divorce, on the other hand, defined quite clearly the requisite grounds, regulated what evidence was admissible, and made the presence of an attorney practically essential. Commitment to the asylum could also be carried out quietly, even without the knowledge of the other spouse.

Second, divorce in Alabama's male-dominated society generally left former wives financially vulnerable. Cast by convention into a financially dependent status and generally debarred from a livelihood, women sought divorce only as a last resort in this era when alimony awards were small and rarely enforced. Civil commitment, however, could benefit a distressed wife by effecting a desired separation while keeping open her access to her husband's estate.

Finally, divorce and confinement carried different social stigmas. In divorce, the grounds generally amounted to some species of depravity in one of the marriage partners. Even aggrieved spouses often shrank from publicity labeling their partners as depraved. Commitment, although stigmatizing to the patient and perhaps the family, obviated this unpleasant need to discover evil. Since both legal and medical institutions encouraged Alabamians to view insanity as a disease, troubled spouses could formulate their plight in terms of the visitation of inescapable misfortune rather than in acts of willful wickedness. Friends and neighbors who viewed divorced persons with suspicion might well pity and support someone who found it necessary to commit a spouse to Tuscaloosa. In short, divorce required that one spouse or the other accept responsibility for being bad, whereas commitment enabled all concerned to locate the source of trouble outside the partners per se and in the mysterious workings of nature. In Alabama's emerging legal culture, commitment thus provided a bypass around the socially unacceptable divorce process.

During the 1890s the hospital's questionnaire included inquiries about relations between husbands and wives. As a result, many case histories from these years include mention of whether the inmate's marriage had been "happy," "unhappy," "jealous," and so on. For the year 1895, records for all 144 admissions of married persons were examined. Sixty-four case histories included clear references to the marriage (more often than not this space on the form was left blank). Thirty-eight marriages were regarded as happy, while twenty-six were characterized as unhappy. About 40 percent of the admissions for which there is information therefore suggest some marital unhappiness. Few histories clearly indicate whether the unhappiness predated the insanity or resulted from it. Still, a significant number of the hospital's inmates left behind troubled marriages.

True to their Victorian professionalism, physicians at the hospital seldom pried too deeply into the private reaches of their patients' lives. But their records do allow occasional glimpses of material discord and the insanity associated with it. On November 15, 1889, for example, staff physician W.G. Somerville admitted a thirty-seven-year-old private patient who had been married for only a year. Somerville reported that the man's "wife, without any assigned reason, would permit no approaches and refused to sleep in the room with her husband from the time they were married". At first, the patient had decided that his bride was excessively modest and "submitted to this treatment for several months". When the condition continued, he decided to get a divorce. As it came time to file, however, he changed his mind, "saying it would bring dishonor on his family". In time he became "gloomy and neglected his business, taking little interest in anything". Somerville added that although he was quiet, the patient insisted that he was sane and demanded his freedom. Only with "much difficulty" did the staff get him to remain.

Twenty years earlier, Bryce had admitted a similar case involving almost stereotypical Victorian repression. On March 24, 1869, he examined a man, twenty-nine years old, who five months earlier had married "a good woman" who was "said to be… fine looking". She allowed the patient "to remain two nights with her, and it is thought they had no intercourse." At that point she claimed illness and agreed to see only her mother and physician. Her groom, according to Bryce "is said to have been very affectionate, and greatly distressed about his wife's conditions. Finally [, he] became insane about three weeks ago". On admission, the young man displayed considerable anger and was hard to manage. Subsequently, the hospital released and then readmitted him twice. He died (still married) in the institution nineteen years later of what his doctors surmised to be "organic disease of the brain".

In another case a husband committed his wife privately in order to prevent her from securing a divorce. Superintendent Searcy admitted the woman in December 1895 after a telegraphed plea from Dr. B. L. Wyman, a former staff physician at the hospital who had entered private practice in Birmingham. According to the case history taken on her admission, the woman "had a stormy time with her husband, who is intemperate". As a result, she filed for divorce, perhaps on the grounds of habitual drunkenness. Incensed at her husband for confirming her, she claimed that he was seeking to prevent her divorce and gain control of her estate, which was considerable.

Clearly marked at the top of her case history appeared the following unorthodox instruction: "Note: —— [the patient] is not to write or receive letters from any persons except her husband and Col. [Sam Will] John [a prominent resident of Birmingham and later a hospital trustee] and her Aunt." Given these restrictions, there was no way that she could contact her lawyers. With the help of Searcy's staff the husband thus succeeded in preventing her from seeking a divorce.

Some inmates came to the hospital not because of a contemplated separation but because their spouses became abusive. In such a case

Bryce learned in 1892 of the real history of a woman he had admitted in 1885. He had written to her family, informing them that she was well enough to return home and was anxious to do so. Instead of agreeing to receive the woman, the family unexpectedly attempted to block her discharge. Her grown children quietly approached J.C. Kumpe, the probate judge, and asked him to intercede on their behalf. The judge wrote to Bryce unofficially in September 1892 to try and prevent her discharge, explaining that "it was his [the husband's] unkind treatment and neglect that contributed to place his wife where she is and...I join the family in the hopes that he will not be able to get control of her. It would be the most tr[y]ing [thing] that could happen [*sic*] for both of them and trust you can prevent him from taking her".

Kumpe, who had presided at the woman's commitment seven years earlier but had been silent on the matter of abuse at that time, pleaded with Bryce in 1892 not to divulge to the husband, who was then escorting another patient to the asylum, that he or the family had blocked his wife's discharge. Everyone had labored hard during the commitment proceedings to divert attention from the husband's "unkind treatment and neglect". Again, years later, the family preferred to work behind the scenes by manipulating the superintendent and misleading the husband in order to keep the woman incarcerated. Confronting the husband would have required coping directly with the tragic reality of abuse. As matters stood, the husband's mistreatment came thereby to be "solved" by the wife's insanity. The strategy worked; the women remained an inmate for another fourteen years until Searcy released her to her son's custody following her husband's death.

Kumpe's intercession and the hospital's reversal of its decision to discharge this patient point eloquently to the difficult position of the asylum as an outside agent for helping families in distress. On one hand, Bryce's staff made a professional decision to release the patient based on her mental condition and life within the hospital. On the other hand, for reasons beyond the control of the institution or the woman herself, the family refused to take her. As a result, the doctors retained her against her wishes in order to please her relatives and protect her from domestic abuse. It seemed to them the humane alternative; but it was a choice founded primarily on what Goffman called "contingencies," not on medical considerations. Moreover, it was a choice with a cost—the woman's freedom. There is no doubt that she wanted to leave the hospital. In 1892 she wrote to Kumpe, pleading for his help to arrange her return home.

Nor was it always the victim of spouse abuse who ended up in the hospital. Sometimes aggrieved spouses committed the abusive party. On August 6, 1886, a woman and her relatives confined her husband at the hospital because she claimed that he had assaulted her several times, once with a hatchet. In a letter to Bryce she expressed concern that despite these episodes of private criminality, her husband seemed outwardly rational. The admitting physician agreed. When he examined the fifty-five-year-old man, the doctor noted that except for excitement at being brought against his will, the new patient was otherwise rational. His wife reported that his "condition just at this time is not nearly so bad as it very often is". But she cautioned Bryce not to be disarmed: "he is so cunning and plausible that a good many people think there is nothing wrong with him".

Bryce accepted the wife's construction of the case and admitted the man despite his overt signs of rationality. After observing him for a day or two, however, the superintendent had still discerned no insanity and wrote the wife asking for more details. She responded that she "knew pretty well that…[her husband] would be so plausible at first that you might be misled a little—Still," she added, perhaps with a touch of pique, "I thought that a Physician of your experience and skill would soon find out where his failure of reason was". But because Bryce had proved unable to divine the nature of the problem, she consented to supply some of the gruesome particulars. Her husband, once "a good man[,] husband and Father," had gradually become "indescribably bad wicked profane". He made obscene threats to their impressionable daughters, and on one occasion had threatened her by holding a pocketknife to her throat. Besides the obscenity and violence, he stole small items from family members and inexplicably refused to eat the food prepared for him or to take his meals with others. The distressed wife concluded her letter with the following insight: "there is only two constructions to be put on his conduct—he is an insane man or he is a thief, a rascal is a brute in Human shape with the most complete powers of dissembling that God has ever give to the Devil power to put into a human being heart". She pleaded with Bryce that if he had any regard at all for her or their "innocent daughter," he would not release her husband before she could "enforce the civil law by a divorce". "I am affird of him," she repeated.

Despite this urgent plea for help, Bryce proved unable to solve her problem. Weeks later, he wrote to the woman, explaining again that her husband was sane and would have to be discharged. With sad resignation she wrote back and agreed that if her husband was truly sane, then release was only proper. Still, she had hoped that he was really insane:

I must confess that his very proper conduct and pleasant manners to you and others since he has been in the Asylum only goes to prove conclusively that he can behave himself genteelly when he sees he is compelled to do so, and therefore filthy and obscene insults to his helpless wife and daughters, was only the cowardly indulgence of a wicked and depraved mind toward those he knew were powerless to recent it.

She closed by refusing to send money for his transport home to Birmingham. He was, she said, debarred "from being received into our home again".

Between writing this note and her husband's release she lost her resolve. She neither sought a divorce not refused to take him in again. Within a month her son-in-law wrote to Bryce, appealing for help anew. On his release, the man had gone directly home and resumed his abusive habits. According to the son-in-law, there were rages in which he knocked down doors, delivered "kicks and blows" aimed at his wife and daughters, and uttered "terrible and indecent language". Worse, he "expos[ed] his person…shamefully before the female members of the family".

Perhaps recognizing the limits of his powers, Bryce refused to become involved again in this sad affair. But ten years later, in 1896, after Bryce had died and memories of this episode had faded, the man's wife committed him again, this time with the authority of a jury verdict declaring him insane. At the time of his trial the man sent two urgent notes to Superintendent Searcy (who had not worked at the hospital during the earlier confinement), pleading for someone to testify to his sanity. B.L. Wyman, the former staff physician who now practical in Birmingham, had testified that the man was sane and wrote to Searcy expressing this view. Searcy consented to admit the man anyway. Along with her husband, the wife sent a letter telling the superintendent of the man's abusiveness. As she had done years earlier with Bryce. She pleaded with Searcy not to release him. For "Auld lang synd [*sic*]," she urged him to take a personal interest in the case.

Searcy retained the distressed woman's husband, who, as during the earlier confinement, proved to be a model inmate. After four months the man tired again of hospital life and escaped to live with relatives in Lowndes County in the south-central part of the state. Searcy made no effort to retrieve the man; in fact, he packaged and mailed his belongings to him. Surprisingly, though, he neglected to inform the patient's wife in

Birmingham. She wrote him two months after the escape when she learned from others that her husband was at large. She expressed her outrage that the hospital had allowed the escape of an abusive man without contacting family members who claimed to be his victims. Like Bryce, Searcy simply let the matter drop. And on that unhappy note the institution ended its involvement in the family's problems.

Returning to Goffman's analytic framework, it seems that in these cases commitment operated as a device that vented distress in families and, by extension, the society they formed. It provided a legal remedy of last resort for troubled, often abusive, marriages that avoided the pitfalls of a divorce proceeding. Commitment also imparted a particular configuration to the region's legal system and the culture that gave it meaning. Perhaps Alabamians resorted to divorce less often than they otherwise might have. Certainly commitment reduced pressures to reform the rigidity of divorce litigation by accommodating at least some difficult cases.

The commitment process also reinforced a legal culture in which average people dealt with problems obliquely rather than directly. For example, Victorian Alabamians did not come to define abusive marriages as a social problem in need of legal remedy. The state's legal culture embraced the more encompassing, though less specific, problem of insanity. So even though citizens acquired an expanded legal system capable of translating private grief into social problems, their emerging legal culture addressed those new problems only circuitously.

Nonmarital Sources of Domestic Distress

Commitment ameliorated other sources of distress, also rather obliquely, that could have founded no resolution in divorce. Many Alabamians committed during this period experienced domestic trouble that was unrelated to marital turmoil. Some were defiant or abused children. Others were unmarried aunts or daughters. A large number were simply peculiar and eccentric people who embarrassed other family members. Others skirted the edge of criminality and were confined as sick to avoid the stigma of criminal proceedings. More than a few suffered with narcotic or alcohol addictions that alarmed their families.

In a particularly disturbing case of incest, the parents of a seventeen-year-old woman committed her to the hospital in March 1895. During the admitting physician's initial examination, in which he diagnosed her as suffering from acute melancholia, he also reported that "she states, and insists that her father has been criminally intimate with her, and she became pregnant four months ago". The patient added that "her mother produced an abortion upon her about a month ago, by introducing into her uterus 'a long rubber thing' (a catheter probably)". Ordinarily the hospital's doctors, like most people at this time, discounted such tales of sexual abuse, at most referring cryptically to "erotic delusions". But struck by the fact that this marginally literate young woman could so accurately describe an abortion, this doctor added an uncharacteristic comment to his notes classifying the story as "a coherent and circumstantial account" that "may be true".

Confinement failed to improve the young woman's mental condition. Over the next year she slipped periodically from her melancholia into what the staff described as a catatonic condition; she withdrew entirely and became unresponsive to outside stimuli. Sadly, her physical condition worsened as well. She contracted tuberculosis in the hospital. As a result, thirteen months after her admission, the doctors released her to be escorted home by the same parents whose abuse had placed her under their care. Commitment had thus temporarily transformed the parents' problem of abuse into the problem of their daughter's insanity, which in turn failed to succumb to the hospital's ministrations.

The hardest group of commitments to classify involved no such clear abuse or obvious mental illness. These were single women who had passed the age of a likely marriage. Blocked as they were from pursuing their own livelihood, they often became financially dependent on their families. More than others, these women fit Lemert's categorization of mental patient as those who deviated from "customary role expectations" and thereby increased their "social visibility". One case fitting this category was that of a forty-year-old woman who was committed by a married sister with whom she lived. A college-educated woman, the patient had grown temperamental and, according to Bryce, who interviewed her when she was admitted, had become obsessed with "erotic ideas". Bryce, however, saw no evidence of insanity. Her sister agreed, saying that she "cant [*sic*] control her affections, yet is too sensitive, and refined in her nature ever to act wrong". Like Bryce, the sister did not consider her insane. In fact, she tricked her sister into going to Tuscaloosa by telling her that she was to be employed in the hospital as a music teacher. To elicit support for the ruse, the sister said to Bryce, "I write to beg you not to put her with insane people but treat her as a boarder." She hoped that with Bryce's "skilful treatment she may be restored & be useful & happy in her old age".

This middle-aged single woman, peculiar and perhaps sexually curious, ended up a patient in the hospital and remained one most of the rest of her life. Neither the person who committed her nor the doctor who admitted her were convinced that she was insane. Yet both understood, albeit mutely, the domestic stress caused by a dependent, eccentric, and aging female member.

In other cases similar embarrassment to the family played a significant role in the commitment of peculiar or unorthodox women. In an example from October 1893, the hospital received a twenty-eight-year-old woman who, according to the admitting physician, seemed "perfectly rational, displaying no incoherence, dullness, delusions, nor emotional disturbance, beyond a natural depression of spirits". The patient claimed to have "been very unkindly used by her mother and sisters, who drove her from home on account of 'some trouble she got into with a young man'".

After a month of observation, evidence of insanity remained absent. When the hospital contacted the woman's widowed mother to inform her of this, she responded that her daughter was deceiving them. She must be insane, the mother insisted, because she "wanders into places I do not want her at". The mother told the doctors to keep her daughter at the hospital, "for I am satisfied now, and know she is protected". Without such "protection" she might continue to wander about unsupervised. Before being committed, "she was on her way to Florida when we caught her". In closing, the saddened widow added a note of exasperation: "God knows what I have gone through with her."

The doctors continued to find no evidence of insanity, repeatedly noting in the casebook that she was "quiet, rational, cheerful". After three months they decided that they had no choice but to release her, even through the mother refused to "permit her in the house". Here again is an example of contingencies. A widowed mother exasperated with an unmanageable daughter went through the process of committing her for the "protection" of the daughter's and her own reputation. She found in civil commitment a remedy, albeit a temporary one, for long-standing distress.

In June 1895 the hospital received another rebellious woman with a colorful, although more distressing, past. Ten year earlier, when she was twenty-seven, she had become engaged to marry the son of one of Alabama's senators. When the young suitor tried to "terminate his relations with her, she fired two or three shots at him in the streets of Selma..., wounding him slightly". The young man then retreated to Washington to assume a government position. She followed, securing employment as a stenographer and typist in government agencies. For unexplained reasons the romance reignited, only to end in another showdown in the streets hen he attempted "to end the matter again". Luckily, her marksmanship had deteriorated and the man escaped injury.

While in Washington she became, according to her own account, "nothing but a prostitute," as were "all the government women". She also commenced a morphine habit, which continued until her confinement in Tuscaloosa. This alarming behavior caused her family to commit her to St. Elizabeths, the federal government's asylum near Washington. Following her discharge in the late 1880s she returned to Alabama, where she resumed her adventurous social life. According to her case history, she soon filed suit against a leading citizen of Selma for breach of a promise of marriage. Another man reportedly "went West" to get away from her. To break this alarming cycle of what the admitting physician called a "checkered" career, her family committed her to the asylum, where she remained for more than two years, only to be readmitted several times thereafter. Evidently, she never managed to meet her family's expectations.

Another inmate, perhaps the most notorious to the hospital's doctors and nurses, embodied many sources of family distress, including the taint of criminality. A single woman, forty-one-years-old, had been committed in 1890 before her trial for arson on the intercession of her father, a prominent resident of Montgomery, and her brother, the probate judge of Marshall County. The patient, however, denied that she was guilty of the arson and insisted that her lover, with whom she had lived in Marshall County, was responsible. Her father deprived her of any opportunity to prove this, however. In defense of her and the family's honor, he shot and killed "her paramour…on account of the intimate relations existing between this man and his daughter".

This woman's career as an asylum inmate lasted for thirty years—until her death. From the outset she assertively defended her sanity, claiming that her family had committed her to avoid further shame and the prospect of a female member wasting away in the penitentiary. Because of her aggressive and intelligent self-defense and her unflagging hatred for the hospital and everyone associated with it, she became infamous to generations of doctors and nurses. During her years in Tuscaloosa she wrote hundreds of letters: to doctors and nurses inside the asylum as well as to numerous dignitaries on the outside. Every governor received at least one letter, and each was struck by her rationality and intelligence. As a sane and presumably criminal woman, she reasoned to these officials that she should be locked up at the penitentiary, not the asylum.

Her doctors at the hospital and her family placed another construction on her case. As one physician remarked in a case note from May 12, 1891, they considered her " to be a woman of considerable intellectual capacity, but devoid of moral stamina". Superintendent Searcy characterized her to one governor who had been troubled by her lucidity as "morally insane".

Regardless of her mental condition, family members accomplished their objective. They saved her (and themselves) from the stigma of a prison term. Moreover, her eccentric and supposedly immoral personality never again became a matter of public scrutiny to cause the family anguish. Indeed, it seems that she died nearly forgotten by all but her keepers. Her brother, for example, occasionally corresponded with the hospital in his capacity as probate judge, but he never inquired about his sister's welfare. For the family, though not for the patient, the problem of this troublesome daughter and sister thus found solution in a quiet legal process.

Problems of alcohol and drug addiction, like the distress of criminality and the failure to fill role expectations, supplied some families with the rationale for commitment. Bryce and the hospital's trustees, however, never looked favorably on admitting alcoholics and addicts. In October 1869 the board of trustees unanimously resolved that it was "impractible [*sic*] to admit inebriates and opium eaters into the Insane Hospital". Such patients usually resented their incarceration bitterly and retained the mental acuity to scheme and connive, thereby disrupting the rather rigid routine of asylum life.

Despite this policy, though, addicts often found their way into the hospital's wards. A typical case of alcoholism, from 1869, involved an irregular, largely unlearned physician who practiced medicine in Butler County when he was sufficiently sober to do so. After being confined for a few months at Tuscaloosa, he recovered enough to return to his family. Bryce wrote to L. M. Lane, the probate judge, inquiring about the advisability of sending the man home. Lane responded that the man's family would have no more to do with him: "They say, and I know it to be true, that they kept him here as long as the citizens wouid stand him." When drunk, it seems, the doctor had "a perfect mania for letting down his pants in the front yards of the best people". If he returned, even sane and sober, Lane feared that his neighbors would harm him. Besides, he concluded, a drunkard practicing medicine posed a danger to the unsuspecting. It was better for all that the man should stay where he was.

Records for drug addicts are most extensive than those for alcoholics. The hospital's doctors often classified "morphinism" or "narcomania" as a clinical entity like mania or melancholia, and thereby left a discernible trail through the records. In the twenty-five years between 1863 (when Bryce admitted the first addict) and 1898 (when, for some reason, record keeping became lax), at least sixty-six users of opium, morphine, or cocaine were admitted (thirty-five men and thirty-one women). Almost all of these (85 per cent) were admitted after 1885, many several times each. Typical of their era, all were white, most were from either the middle or upper class, and most were well educated. Many, especially the women, had become addicted as a result of medical treatment. The men were less likely to have started using drugs under a doctor's care and were more likely to have combined the use of narcotics with alcoholism.

A typical patient whose family committed her for opium use was a woman from Mount Meigs, first admitted in early 1887 and them again in 1888. This daughter of a physician had become addicted to morphine in 1880 as a result of medical treatment, and since then her father had tried unsuccessfully to break her of the habit. For many years she had been a source of friction in her rather large extended family. She, her husband, and their children lived in her father's home. When deprived of the drug, she reportedly berated every member of the large household.

Before the woman's second admission, her sister wrote to Bryce, outlining the domestic anguish that necessitated the commitment. In addition to her insatiable appetite for morphine, she had developed an intense dislike of her stepmother. Often, sister told Bryce, she begged from neighbors, saying that her father's wife refused to feed her. Worse, she "talks principally to Negroes, whose company she seems to prefer". To the grieving, exasperated sister it was "mortifying to state all these things," but she forced herself to do so in order to impress upon the doctor the need for confinement.

Another morphine addict was admitted and released six times between 1887 and 1898. Like many others she started using the drug to ease the pain of menstruation. Unlike others, though, she returned voluntarily to the hospital after her first release. In October 1890, for example, she wrote to Bryce, begging to be readmitted: "I want to come back before I have to be sent back publicly." She wanted to protect her young daughters, who would suffer if she continued her habit and had to be committed forcibly. In short, she acted to relieve her family's distress before it grew too great.

In June 1893, a month after returning to the hospital for the third time, she wrote a sad note to the supervisor of her ward, explaining that, as before, she had failed to please her family. "I am in the way here [in the hospital]," she told the nurse, "and my friends and relatives are afraid to trust me out of here". In her depression she begged the supervisor to "get me 25 cents worth of morphine," enough, she believed, to effect an overdose. The supervisor refused to co-operate, and in time the patient improved enough to return to her family yet again. But after several failed trails at home, she returned unescorted by any family members in July 1896. She had resumed taking morphine and told her doctor that she never wanted to leave again, that she was unwanted and useless.

Few drug addicted shared this woman's self-pity or resignation to asylum life. Most bitterly resented their incarceration. Typical of such rebellious patients was a forty-one-year-old, widowed lawyer who was related by marriage to a prominent official of the hospital and was himself a former officer of the asylum. Admitted on three occasions between 1890 and 1892, the man began taking opium in 1879 "as a cure for [the] whiskey habit". By 1890 he was drinking a pint of whiskey and ingesting ten grains of morphine daily, sometimes more. His family committed him each time he began to suffer convulsions and hallucinations. Within days or weeks of admission, however, he typically became lucid and intractable. On July 5, 1892, for example, he had been in the asylum for about a month. His doctor reported that his "headaches have disappeared and he is stringer and less tremulous". As a result, he was "determined to leave the Hospital as soon as possible, even if by habeas corpus if necessary". Two days later, the institution released the troubled lawyer as "improved".

Another recalcitrant patient, a single, forty-year-old school-teacher, was admitted twice in the 1890s fore a laudanum and morphine habit that she had maintained for a dozen years. Her family became alarmed as her physical health deteriorated and she began to be delusional, always smelling chloroform and hearing the voices of what she called "low negroes". She came willingly at first, stayed less than two months, and returned to her family. At home she immediately resumed her habit, causing her family to commit her again three weeks later. This time she resisted and was carried to Tuscaloosa forcibly.

Seven months later, in October 1892, her doctor reported that she had "written to a Huntsville lawyer regarding a writ of *habeas corpus*". Evidently, she kept up a stream of complaining letters to lawyers and others. Her brother, who was her legal guardian, wrote to Searcy in August 1894 to put a stop to his sister's epistles. The letters, he said, "only advertise her unfortunate condition, and [do] no good to either herself or family". He asked that she be allowed to post letters only to her immediate family.

The hospital granted these wishes, and in doing so helped to resolve the family's long-standing distress.

Summary and Conclusions

A consensus of sorts has emerged among historians that the profound social changes of the late nineteenth century placed significant pressure on the family. Robert Griswold, Elizabeth Pleck, and Michael Grossberg, among others, have shown that legal doctrine relating to the family (and, by extension, the family itself) experienced new challenges and underwent significant change. And Christopher Lasch has argued that there was, in fact, a "crisis of the family at the end of the nineteenth century". In support of such assertions historians have cited a fifteenfold increase in divorce nationally in the half-century after 1870 and a rising perception of emotional and physical cruelty in marriage.

This essay attempts to refine our understanding of the legal response to family distress during this period. Focusing on the consequences rather than the sources of distress, it shows that the legal system was considerably more pliant than an overview of doctrine alone suggests. Consider the area best understood by historians, marriage and divorce. Recent studies have shown that as Victorian America gave way to the Progressive Era, the allowable grounds for divorce expanded and the divorce rate increased significantly. Despite this liberalization, however, the grounds for divorce continued to be narrow, and divorce remained embedded in an adversarial process that made it public, confrontational, and morally charged. Commitment offered some spouses a more private and less adversarial means for solving problems that was clothed with the respectability of objective science. Moreover, the grounds for commitment were hardly precise and almost never articulated.

Thus, while other studies have enhanced our understanding of how the legal system changed and expanded the remedies for marital conflict, this essay suggests that the real expansion of legal remedies was even greater than the statutes and case law would indicate. Commitment offered an alternative course, albeit one that may have been seen as a last resort, for addressing a wide variety of domestic distress, including failed marriages.

The real (as opposed to the ideal) functioning of Alabama's commitment system also as important implications for understanding the relationship between elite reformers and social control. The founders and physicians of the Alabama Insane Hospital fit the definition of humanitarian social controllers so familiar in the historical literature: they hoped to provide a mechanism of reform, both individual and social, over which a small group of doctors, judges, and trustees maintained formal control. But in the half-century following the institution's opening something quite unanticipated occurred. Plain folks took the medical-scientific elite's doctrines of madness and the procedures of commitment and fashioned them to meet their own needs. By the century's end it was but no means clear who was controlling whom. The hospital's founders clearly had not anticipated the creative ways in which average families would seize upon insanity's definitional flexibility and the commitment procedure's informal qualities to solve problems of long standing—problems that might otherwise have ended up in divorce court, criminal court, or even beyond the reach of legal remedy of any kind.

Ironically, this expanding framework for defining new social concerns actually limited the potential sources of stress that could attain social visibility. While families did gain a valuable remedy for deranged members, that label's imprecise meaning allowed it to subsume other sources of concern that may not have been best served by its application. Troubled marriages, abusive spouses, addiction to drugs and alcohol, and the social anomaly of often strong-willed and aging single women who failed to meet their communities' role expectations were some of the causes of distress that occasionally came to be labeled insane. The recognized problem, however expanded beyond madness. Consequently, concerns about addiction as well as a host of what today are called women's issues never acquired the legal remedies or institutional arrangements that accommodated insanity. Alabama's legal system and the Victorian culture that supported it made no provision for conceptualizing these matters as ones requiring social action, and many years passed before more constructive solutions were sought.

References

1. Entry 1, Admissions Book, Staff Library, Bryce Hospital; file of patient 1, Medical-Records Office, Bryce Hospital. The Alabama Insane Hospital became the Alabama Bryce Insane Hospital following the death of Peter Bryce, its first superintendent, in 1892. Today it is simply called Bryce Hospital.
2. In a strict sense commitment was not unprecedented; common law had long provided for the confinement of those who posed a danger to themselves or to others. But in the absence of a place to send lunatics, such commitment

was of little value to distressed families. The opening of an avowedly curative institution changed all that. In this basic sense it was indeed a milestone.

3. Bryce's fullest early discussion of insanity's curability is found in his *Annual Report* (Tuscaloosa: John F. Warren, 1867), 9-10. Bryce claimed that 80 per cent of all cases treated within the first six months were curable.
4. "Superintendent's Report," July 1, 1862, in "Proceedings of the Board of Trustees," Trustees' Record Book 1, 9, Staff Library; "Superintendent's Report," July 1, 1864, Book 1, 17; "Superintendent's Report," October 1, 1869, Book 1, 43; *Annual Report, 1875* (Montgomery: W.W. Screws, 1875), 21; *Biennial Report, 1886* (Montgomery: Barrett and Company, 1886), 8; *Biennial Report, 1896* ([Tuscaloosa]: Hospital Print, 1896), 12; *Biennial Report, 1900* (Montgomery: Roemer Printing Co., 1900), 8.
5. The *Montgomery Advertiser* reported on August 23, 1907, for example, that "the State Hospital for the Insane [is] the largest single building in Alabama" (see p. 1, col. 1).
6. "Annual Report," 1897, unpublished typescript, p. 2, Documents of State Hospitals, Alabama Department of Archives and History, Montgomery.
7. *To Kill a Mockingbird* (1960; New York: Warner Books Edition, 1982), 15. Interestingly, Boo's father refused to allow his son to be carried to Tuscaloosa, believing that it would mark the family too visibly with a stigma.
8. See, for example, David J. Rothman, *The Discovery of the Asylum: Social Order and Disorder in the New Republic* (Boston: Little, Brown, 1971); and Erving Goffman, *Asylums: Essays on the Social Situation of Mental Patients and Other Inmates* (New York: Doubleday and Co., 1961).

Index

❑❑❑